General Information 1

LSI Devices 2

Application Reports 3

Mechanical Data 4

LSI Logic Data Book

Texas Instruments

IMPORTANT NOTICE

Texas Instruments (TI) reserves the right to make changes in the devices or the device specifications identified in this publication without notice. TI advises its customers to obtain the latest version of device specifications to verify, before placing orders, that the information being relied upon by the customer is current.

TI warrants performance of its semiconductor products, including SNJ and SMJ devices, to current specifications in accordance with TI's standard warranty. Testing and other quality control techniques are utilized to the extent TI deems such testing necessary to support this warranty. Unless mandated by government requirements, specific testing of all parameters of each device is not necessarily performed.

In the absence of written agreement to the contrary, TI assumes no liability for TI applications assistance, customer's product design, or infringement of patents or copyrights of third parties by or arising from use of semiconductor devices described herein. Nor does TI warrant or represent that any license, either express or implied, is granted under any patent right, copyright, or other intellectual property right of TI covering or relating to any combination, machine, or process in which such semiconductor devices might be or are used.

Specifications contained in this data book supersede all data for these products published by TI in the United States before November 1985.

ISBN 0-89512-197-2

INTRODUCTION

The LSI Logic Data Book presents pertinent technical information on Texas Instruments complex bipolar and CMOS LSI logic integrated circuits. The bipolar LSI products described in this volume include:

- The fastest TTL-compatible 8-bit processor slice chip set available. The chip set includes an 8-bit registered ALU, a 14-bit microsequencer, a 16- and 32-bit expandable barrel shifter, and a 16-word by 4-bit register file.
- The fastest stand-alone 32-bit error detection and correction circuit (EDAC)
- High-performance 16 × 4 and 16 × 5 ''zero-fall-through'' FIFOs (first in, first out) memory devices with 24-nanosecond fall-through times
- A high-speed ''flash'' 32-bit barrel shifter (SN74AS8838). The SN74AS8838 is the first member of the Texas Instruments 32-bit processor chip set.

Specifications on CMOS LSI products included in this volume describe the following:

- The THCT1010, which is the lowest power 16- × 16-bit multiplier and accumulator (MAC) available.
- Two 64K and 256K DRAM controllers with inputs that are TTL- and CMOS-voltage compatible.
- Two high-speed CMOS multilevel pipeline registers, which offer a reduction in power over previously available devices.

To assist you in the selection of complex MSI logic components to complement a system design, the LSI Logic Data Book contains specifications on high-performance bus transceivers, readback latches, comparators, and controllers.

Many Texas Instruments leadership bipolar LSI functions use our new advanced bipolar technology, IMPACT™ (IMPlanted Advanced Composed Technology). This unique innovation offers performance advantages in speed, power, and circuit density over preceding bipolar technologies. The process offers such features as:

- 2-μm feature size
- 7-μm metal pitch
- Walled emitters
- Ion implantation
- Oxide isolation
- Composed masks

This data book provides a functional index to all bipolar digital device types available or under development. Packaging dimensions given in the Mechanical Data section of this book are in metric measurement (and parenthetically in inches), which should simplify board layout for designers involved in metric conversion and new designs. The general information section includes an explanation of the function tables, parameter measurement information, and typical characteristics related to the products listed in this volume.

Complete technical data for any Texas Instruments semiconductor/component product is available from your nearest TI field sales office, local authorized TI distributor, or by writing direct to:

Texas Instruments Incorporated
P.O. Box 225012, MS 308
Dallas, Texas 75265

We sincerely believe that you will find the new LSI Logic Data Book a meaningful addition to your technical library.

NUMERICAL INDEX

General Information

INTRODUCTION

These symbols, terms, and definitions are in accordance with those currently agreed upon by the JEDEC Council of the Electronic Industries Association (EIA) for use in the USA and by the International Electrotechnical Commission (IEC) for international use.

PART I — OPERATING CONDITIONS AND CHARACTERISTICS (IN SEQUENCE BY LETTER SYMBOLS)

f_{max} **Maximum clock frequency**
The highest rate at which the clock input of a bistable circuit can be driven through its required sequence while maintaining stable transitions of logic level at the output with input conditions established that should cause changes of output logic level in accordance with the specification.

I_{CC} **Supply current**
The current into* the V_{CC} supply terminal of an integrated circuit.

I_{CCH} **Supply current, outputs high**
The current into* the V_{CC} supply terminal of an integrated circuit when all (or a specified number) of the outputs are at the high level.

I_{CCL} **Supply current, outputs low**
The current into* the V_{CC} supply terminal of an integrated circuit when all (or a specified number) of the outputs are at the low level.

I_{IH} **High-level input current**
The current into* an input when a high-level voltage is applied to that input.

I_{IL} **Low-level input current**
The current into* an input when a low-level voltage is applied to that input.

I_{OH} **High-level output current**
The current into* an output with input conditions applied that, according to the product specification, will establish a high level at the output.

I_{OL} **Low-level output current**
The current into* an output with input conditions applied that, according to the product specification, will establish a low level at the output.

I_{OS} **Short-circuit output current**
The current into* an output when that output is short-circuited to ground (or other specified potential) with input conditions applied to establish the output logic level farthest from ground potential (or other specified potential).

I_{OZH} **Off-state (high-impedance-state) output current (of a three-state output) with high-level voltage applied**
The current flowing into* an output having three-state capability with input conditions established that, according to the product specification, will establish the high-impedance state at the output and with a high-level voltage applied to the output.
NOTE: This parameter is measured with other input conditions established that would cause the output to be at a low level if it were enabled.

*Current out of a terminal is given as a negative value.

I_{OZL} **Off-state (high-impedance-state) output current (of a three-state output) with low-level voltage applied**
The current flowing into* an output having three-state capability with input conditions established that, according to the product specification, will establish the high-impedance state at the output and with a low-level voltage applied to the output.
NOTE: This parameter is measured with other input conditions established that would cause the output to be at a high level if it were enabled.

V_{IH} **High-level input voltage**
An input voltage within the more positive (less negative) of the two ranges of values used to represent the binary variables.
NOTE: A minimum is specified that is the least-positive value of high-level input voltage for which operation of the logic element within specification limits is guaranteed.

V_{IK} **Input clamp voltage**
An input voltage in a region of relatively low differential resistance that serves to limit the input voltage swing.

V_{IL} **Low-level input voltage**
An input voltage level within the less positive (more negative) of the two ranges of values used to represent the binary variables.
NOTE: A maximum is specified that is the most-positive value of low-level input voltage for which operation of the logic element within specification limits is guaranteed.

V_{OH} **High-level output voltage**
The voltage at an output terminal with input conditions applied that, according to the product specification, will establish a high level at the output.

V_{OL} **Low-level output voltage**
The voltage at an output terminal with input conditions applied that, according to the product specification, will establish a low level at the output.

t_a **Access time**
The time interval between the application of a specified input pulse and the availability of valid signals at an output.

t_{dis} **Disable time (of a three-state or open-collector output)**
The propagation time between the specified reference points on the input and output voltage waveforms with the output changing from either of the defined active levels (high or low) to a high-impedance (off) state.
NOTE: For 3-state outputs, $t_{dis} = t_{PHZ}$ or t_{PLZ}. Open-collector outputs will change only if they are low at the time of disabling so $t_{dis} = t_{PLH}$.

t_{en} **Enable time (of a three-state or open-collector output)**
The propagation time between the specified reference points on the input and output voltage waveforms with the output changing from a high-impedance (off) state to either of the defined active levels (high or low).
NOTE: In the case of memories, this is the access time from an enable input (e.g., $\overline{G}$). For 3-state outputs, $t_{en} = t_{PZH}$ or t_{PZL}. Open-collector outputs will change only if they are responding to data that would cause the output to go low so $t_{en} = t_{PHL}$.

*Current out of a terminal is given as a negative value.

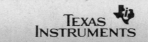

t_h **Hold time**

The time interval during which a signal is retained at a specified input terminal after an active transition occurs at another specified input terminal.

NOTES: 1. The hold time is the actual time interval between two signal events and is determined by the system in which the digital circuit operates. A minimum value is specified that is the shortest interval for which correct operation of the digital circuit is guaranteed.

2. The hold time may have a negative value in which case the minimum limit defines the longest interval (between the release of the signal and the active transition) for which correct operation of the digital circuit is guaranteed.

t_{pd} **Propagation delay time**

The time between the specified reference points on the input and output voltage waveforms with the output changing from one defined level (high or low) to the other defined level. (t_{pd} = t_{PHL} or t_{PLH}).

t_{PHL} **Propagation delay time, high-to-low-level output**

The time between the specified reference points on the input and output voltage waveforms with the output changing from the defined high level to the defined low level.

t_{PHZ} **Disable time (of a three-state output) from high level**

The time interval between the specified reference points on the input and output voltage waveforms with the three-state output changing from the defined high level to a high-impedance (off) state.

t_{PLH} **Propagation delay time, low-to-high-level output**

The time between the specified reference points on the input and output voltage waveforms with the output changing from the defined low level to the defined high level.

t_{PLZ} **Disable time (of a three-state output) from low level**

The time interval between the specified reference points on the input and output voltage waveforms with the three-state output changing from the defined low level to a high-impedance (off) state.

t_{PZH} **Enable time (of a three-state output) to high level**

The time interval between the specified reference points on the input and output voltage waveforms with the three-state output changing from a high-impedance (off) state to the defined high level.

t_{PZL} **Enable time (of a three-state output) to low level**

The time interval between the specified reference points on the input and output voltage waveforms with the three-state output changing from a high-impedance (off) state to the defined low level.

t_{sr} **Sense recovery time**

The time interval needed to switch a memory from a write mode to a read mode and to obtain valid data signals at the output.

t_{su} **Setup time**

The time interval between the application of a signal at a specified input terminal and a subsequent active transition at another specified input terminal.

NOTES: 1. The setup time is the actual time interval between two signal events and is determined by the system in which the digital circuit operates. A minimum value is specified that is the shortest interval for which correct operation of the digital circuit is guaranteed.

2. The setup time may have a negative value in which case the minimum limit defines the longest interval (between the active transition and the application of the other signal) for which correct operation of the digital circuit is guaranteed.

t_w **Pulse duration (width)**

The time interval between specified reference points on the leading and trailing edges of the pulse waveform.

PART II — CLASSIFICATION OF CIRCUIT COMPLEXITY

Gate Equivalent Circuit

A basic unit-of-measure of relative digital-circuit complexity. The number of gate equivalent circuits is that number of individual logic gates that would have to be interconnected to perform the same function.

Large-Scale Integration, LSI

A concept whereby a complete major subsystem or system function is fabricated as a single microcircuit. In this context a major subsystem or system, whether digital or linear, is considered to be one that contains 100 or more equivalent gates or circuitry of similar complexity.

Medium-Scale Integration, MSI

A concept whereby a complete subsystem or system function is fabricated as a single microcircuit. The subsystem or system is smaller than for LSI, but whether digital or linear, is considered to be one that contains 12 or more equivalent gates or circuitry of similar complexity.

Small-Scale Integration, SSI

Integrated circuits of less complexity than medium-scale integration (MSI).

Very-Large-Scale Integration, VLSI

The description of any IC technology that is much more complex than large-scale integration (LSI), and involves a much higher equivalent gate count. At this time an exact definition including a minimum gate count has not been standardized by JEDEC or the IEEE.

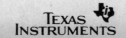

The following symbols are used in function tables on TI data sheets:

H	=	high level (steady state)
L	=	low level (steady state)
↑	=	transition from low to high level
↓	=	transition from high to low level
→	=	value/level or resulting value/level is routed to indicated destination
↶	=	value/level is re-entered
X	=	irrelevant (any input, including transitions)
Z	=	off (high-impedance) state of a 3-state-output
a . . h	=	the level of steady-state inputs at inputs A through H respectively
Q_0	=	level of Q before the indicated steady-state input conditions were established
$\overline{Q}_0$	=	complement of Q_0 or level of $\overline{Q}$ before the indicated steady-state input conditions were established
Q_n	=	level of Q before the most recent active transition indicated by ↓ or ↑
$\sqcap$	=	one high-level pulse
$\sqcup$	=	one low-level pulse
TOGGLE	=	each output changes to the complement of its previous level on each active transition indicated by ↓ or ↑.

If, in the input columns, a row contains only the symbols H, L, and/or X, this means the indicated output is valid whenever the input configuration is achieved and regardless of the sequence in which it is achieved. The output persists so long as the input configuration is maintained.

If, in the input columns, a row contains H, L, and/or X together with ↑ and/or ↓, this means the output is valid whenever the input configuration is achieved but the transition(s) must occur following the achievement of the steady-state levels. If the output is shown as a level (H, L, Q_0, or $\overline{Q}_0$), it persists so long as the steady-state input levels and the levels that terminate indicated transitions are maintained. Unless otherwise indicated, input transitions in the opposite direction to those shown have no effect at the output. (If the output is shown as a pulse, $\sqcap$ or $\sqcup$, the pulse follows the indicated input transition and persists for an interval dependent on the circuit.)

EXPLANATION OF FUNCTION TABLES

Among the most complex function tables in this book are those of the shift registers. These embody most of the symbols used in any of the function tables, plus more. Below is the function table of a 4-bit bidirectional universal shift register, e.g., type SN74194.

FUNCTION TABLE

INPUTS										OUTPUTS			
CLEAR	MODE		CLOCK	SERIAL		PARALLEL				Q_A	Q_B	Q_C	Q_D
	S1	S0		LEFT	RIGHT	A	B	C	D				
L	X	X	X	X	X	X	X	X	X	L	L	L	L
H	X	X	L	X	X	X	X	X	X	Q_{A0}	Q_{B0}	Q_{C0}	Q_{D0}
H	H	H	↑	X	X	a	b	c	d	a	b	c	d
H	L	H	↑	X	H	X	X	X	X	H	Q_{An}	Q_{Bn}	Q_{Cn}
H	L	H	↑	X	L	X	X	X	X	L	Q_{An}	Q_{Bn}	Q_{Cn}
H	H	L	↑	H	X	X	X	X	X	Q_{Bn}	Q_{Cn}	Q_{Dn}	H
H	H	L	↑	L	X	X	X	X	X	Q_{Bn}	Q_{Cn}	Q_{Dn}	L
H	L	L	X	X	X	X	X	X	X	Q_{A0}	Q_{B0}	Q_{C0}	Q_{D0}

The first line of the table represents a synchronous clearing of the register and says that if clear is low, all four outputs will be reset low regardless of the other inputs. In the following lines, clear is inactive (high) and so has no effect.

The second line shows that so long as the clock input remains low (while clear is high), no other input has any effect and the outputs maintain the levels they assumed before the steady-state combination of clear high and clock low was established. Since on other lines of the table only the rising transition of the clock is shown to be active, the second line implicitly shows that no further change in the outputs will occur while the clock remains high or on the high-to-low transition of the clock.

The third line of the table represents synchronous parallel loading of the register and says that if S1 and S0 are both high then, without regard to the serial input, the data entered at A will be at output Q_A, data entered at B will be at Q_B, and so forth, following a low-to-high clock transition.

The fourth and fifth lines represent the loading of high- and low-level data, respectively, from the shift-right serial input and the shifting of previously entered data one bit; data previously at Q_A is now at Q_B, the previous levels of Q_B and Q_C are now at Q_C and Q_D respectively, and the data previously at Q_D is no longer in the register. This entry of serial data and shift takes place on the low-to-high transition of the clock when S1 is low and S0 is high and the levels at inputs A through D have no effect.

The sixth and seventh lines represent the loading of high- and low-level data, respectively, from the shift-left serial input and the shifting of previously entered data one bit; data previously at Q_B is now at Q_A, the previous levels of Q_C and Q_D are now at Q_B and Q_C, respectively, and the data previously at Q_A is no longer in the register. This entry of serial data and shift takes place on the low-to-high transition of the clock when S1 is high and S0 is low and the levels at inputs A through D have no effect.

The last line shows that as long as both mode inputs are low, no other input has any effect and, as in the second line, the outputs maintain the levels they assumed before the steady-state combination of clear high and both mode inputs low was established.

PARAMETER MEASUREMENT INFORMATION

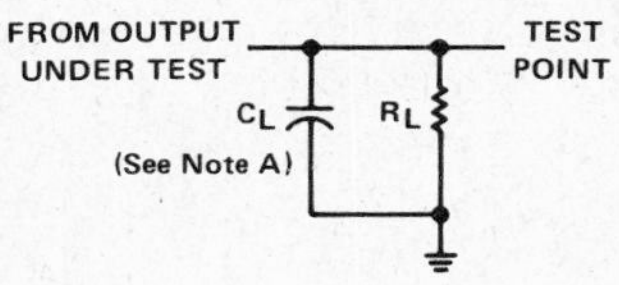
FROM OUTPUT
UNDER TEST
TEST
POINT
C_L
R_L
(See Note A)

LOAD CIRCUIT FOR
BI-STATE
TOTEM-POLE OUTPUTS

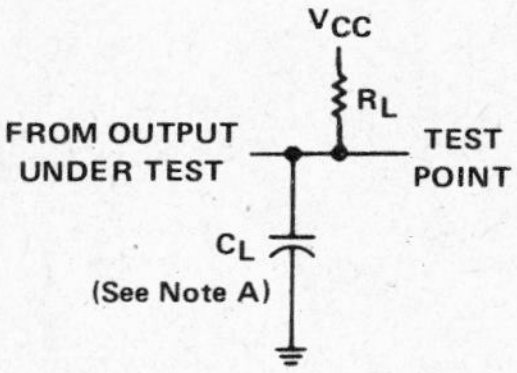
V_{CC}
R_L
FROM OUTPUT
UNDER TEST
TEST
POINT
C_L
(See Note A)

LOAD CIRCUIT FOR
OPEN-COLLECTOR OUTPUTS

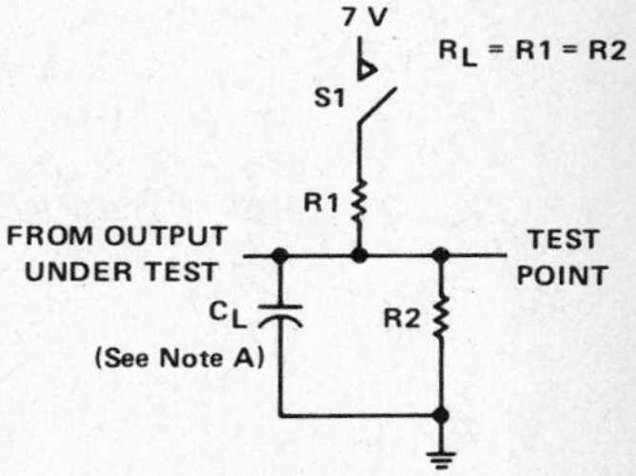
7 V
R_L = R1 = R2
S1
R1
FROM OUTPUT
UNDER TEST
TEST
POINT
C_L
R2
(See Note A)

LOAD CIRCUIT FOR
THREE-STATE OUTPUTS

NOTE A: C_L includes probe and jig capacitance.

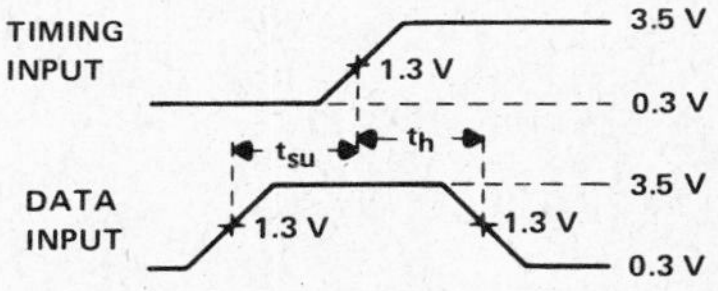
TIMING
INPUT
3.5 V
1.3 V
0.3 V
t_{su}
t_h
DATA
INPUT
3.5 V
1.3 V
1.3 V
0.3 V

VOLTAGE WAVEFORMS
SETUP AND HOLD TIMES

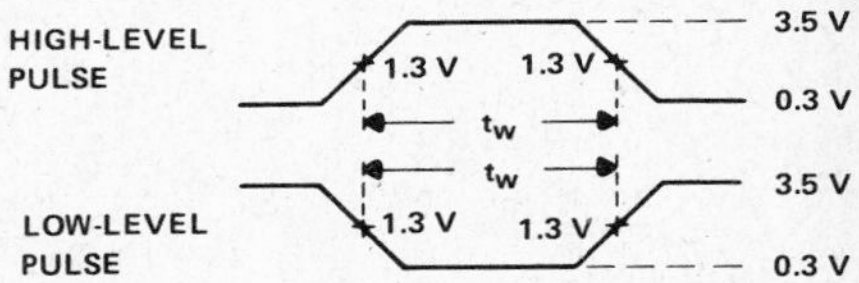
HIGH-LEVEL
PULSE
3.5 V
1.3 V
1.3 V
0.3 V
t_w
t_w
3.5 V
LOW-LEVEL
PULSE
1.3 V
1.3 V
0.3 V

VOLTAGE WAVEFORMS
PULSE WIDTHS

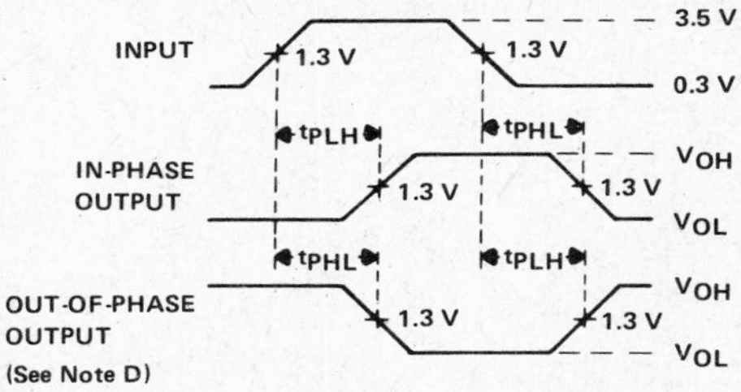
INPUT
3.5 V
1.3 V
1.3 V
0.3 V
t_{PLH}
t_{PHL}
IN-PHASE
OUTPUT
V_{OH}
1.3 V
1.3 V
V_{OL}
t_{PHL}
t_{PLH}
OUT-OF-PHASE
OUTPUT
(See Note D)
V_{OH}
1.3 V
1.3 V
V_{OL}

VOLTAGE WAVEFORMS
PROPAGATION DELAY TIMES

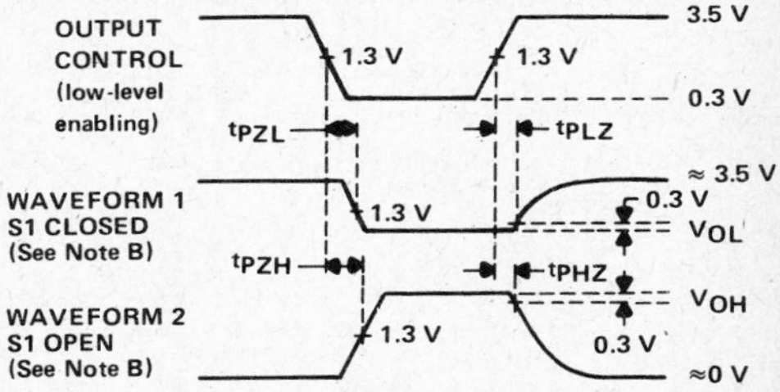
OUTPUT
CONTROL
(low-level
enabling)
3.5 V
1.3 V
1.3 V
0.3 V
t_{PZL}
t_{PLZ}
≈ 3.5 V
WAVEFORM 1
S1 CLOSED
(See Note B)
1.3 V
0.3 V
V_{OL}
t_{PZH}
t_{PHZ}
V_{OH}
WAVEFORM 2
S1 OPEN
(See Note B)
1.3 V
0.3 V
≈0 V

VOLTAGE WAVEFORMS
ENABLE AND DISABLE TIMES, THREE-STATE OUTPUTS

NOTES: B. Waveform 1 is for an output with internal conditions such that the output is low except when disabled by the output control. Waveform 2 is for an output with internal conditions such that the output is high except when disabled by the output control.
C. All input pulses have the following characteristics: PRR ≤ 1 MHz, $t_r = t_f$ = 2 ns, duty cycle = 50%.
D. When measuring propagation delay times of 3-state outputs, switch S1 is closed.

GATES AND INVERTERS

POSITIVE-NAND GATES AND INVERTERS

DESCRIPTION	TYPE	TECHNOLOGY STD TTL	ALS	AS	H	L	LS	S	VOLUME
Hex 2-Input Gates	'804		A	B					3
Hex Inverters	'04	●			●	●	●	●	2
			A	●					3
	'1004		●	●					
Quadruple 2-Input Gates	'00	●			●	●	●	●	2
			A	●					3
	'1000		A	A					
Triple 3-Input Gates	'10	●			●	●	●	●	2
			A	●					3
	'1010		A						3
Dual 4-Input Gates	'20	●			●	●	●	●	2
			A	●					3
	'1020		A						
8-Input Gates	'30	●			●	●	●	●	2
			A	●					3
13-Input Gates	'133							●	2
			●						3
Dual 2-Input Gates	'8003		●						

POSITIVE-NAND GATES AND INVERTERS WITH OPEN-COLLECTOR OUTPUTS

DESCRIPTION	TYPE	TECHNOLOGY STD TTL	ALS	AS	H	L	LS	S	VOLUME
Hex Inverters	'05	●			●		●	●	2
			A						3
	'1005		●						
Quadruple 2-Input Gates	'01	●			●		●		2
			●						3
	'03	●				●	●	●	2
			B						3
	'1003		A						
Triple 3-Input Gates	'12	●					●		2
			A						3
Dual 4-Input Gates	'22	●			●		●	●	2
			B						3

POSITIVE-AND GATES

DESCRIPTION	TYPE	TECHNOLOGY STD TTL	ALS	AS	H	LS	S	VOLUME
Hex 2-Input Gates	'808		A	B				3
Quadruple 2-Input Gates	'08	●				●	●	2
			●	●				3
	'1008		A	●				
Triple 3-Input Gates	'11				●	●	●	2
			A	●				3
	'1011		A					3
Dual 4-Input Gates	'21				●	●		2
			●	●				3
Triple 4-Input AND/NAND	'800			▲				

POSITIVE-AND GATES WITH OPEN-COLLECTOR OUTPUTS

DESCRIPTION	TYPE	TECHNOLOGY STD TTL	ALS	AS	H	LS	S	VOLUME
Quadruple 2-Input Gates	'09	●				●	●	2
			●					3
Triple 3-Input Gates	'15				●	●	●	2
			A					3

POSITIVE-OR GATES

DESCRIPTION	TYPE	TECHNOLOGY STD TTL	ALS	AS	LS	S	VOLUME
Hex 2-Input Gates	'832		A	B			3
Quadruple 2-Input Gates	'32	●			●	●	2
			●	●			3
	'1032		A	●			
Triple 4-Input OR/NOR	'802			▲			

POSITIVE-NOR GATES

DESCRIPTION	TYPE	TECHNOLOGY STD TTL	ALS	AS	L	LS	S	VOLUME
Hex 2-Input Gates	'805		A	B				3
Quadruple 2-Input Gates	'02	●			●	●	●	2
			●	●				3
	'1002		A					
Triple 3-Input Gates	'27	●				●		2
			●	●				3
Dual 4-Input Gates with Strobe	'25	●						2
Dual 5-Input Gates	'260						●	

SCHMITT-TRIGGER POSITIVE-NAND GATES AND INVERTERS

DESCRIPTION	TYPE	TECHNOLOGY STD TTL	ALS	AS	LS	S	VOLUME
Hex Inverters	'14	●			●		2
	'19				●		
Octal Inverters	'619				●		
Dual 4-Input Positive-NAND	'13	●			●		
	'18				●		
Triple 4-Input Positive-NAND	'618				●		
Quadruple 2-Input Positive-NAND	'24				●		
	'132	●			●	●	

CURRENT-SENSING GATES

DESCRIPTION	TYPE	TECHNOLOGY ALS	AS	LS	VOLUME
Hex	'63			●	2

DELAY ELEMENTS

DESCRIPTION	TYP	TECHNOLOGY ALS	AS	LS	VOLUME
Inverting and Noninverting Elements, 2-Input NAND Buffers	'31			●	2

● Denotes available technology.
▲ Denotes planned new products.
A Denotes "A" suffix version available in the technology indicated.
B Denotes "B" suffix version available in the technology indicated.

GATES, EXPANDERS, BUFFERS, DRIVERS, AND TRANSCEIVERS

AND-OR-INVERT GATES

DESCRIPTION	TYPE	TECHNOLOGY							VOLUME
		STD TTL	ALS	AS	H	L	LS	S	
2-Wide 4-Input	'55				●	●	●		2
4-Wide 4-2-3-2 Input	'64							●	
4-Wide 2-2-3-2 Input	'54				●				
4-Wide 2-Input	'54	●							
4-Wide 2-3-3-2 Input	'54					●	●		
Dual 2-Wide 2-Input	'51	●			●	●	●	●	

AND-OR-INVERT GATES WITH OPEN-COLLECTOR OUTPUTS

DESCRIPTION	TYPE	TECHNOLOGY				VOLUME
		STD TTL	ALS	AS	S	
4-Wide 4-2-3-2 Input	'65				●	2

EXPANDABLE GATES

DESCRIPTION	TYPE	TECHNOLOGY						VOLUME
		STD TTL	ALS	AS	H	L	LS	
Dual 4-Input Positive-NOR with Strobe	'23	●						2
4-Wide AND-OR	'52				●			
4-Wide AND-OR-INVERT	'53	●			●			
2-Wide AND-OR-INVERT	'55				●	●	●	
Dual 2-Wide AND-OR-INVERT	'50	●			●			

EXPANDERS

DESCRIPTION	TYPE	TECHNOLOGY				VOLUME
		STD TTL	ALS	AS	H	
Dual 4-Input	'60	●			●	2
Triple 3-Input	'61				●	
3-2-2-3 Input AND-OR	'62				●	

BUFFER AND INTERFACE GATES WITH OPEN-COLLECTOR OUTPUTS

DESCRIPTION	TYPE	TECHNOLOGY					VOLUME
		STD TTL	ALS	AS	LS	S	
Hex	'07	●					2
	'17	●					
	'35		●				3
	'1035		●				3
Hex Inverter	'06	●					2
	'16	●					
	'1005		●				3
Quad 2-Input Positive-NAND	'26	●			●		2
	'38	●			●	●	
			A				3
	'39	●					2
	'1003		A				3
Quad 2-Input Positive-NOR	'33	●			●		2
			A				3

BUFFERS, DRIVERS, AND BUS TRANSCEIVERS WITH OPEN-COLLECTOR OUTPUTS

DESCRIPTION	TYPE	TECHNOLOGY					VOLUME
		STD TTL	ALS	AS	LS	S	
Noninverting Octal Buffers/Drivers	'743		▲				3
	'757		●	●			
	'760			●			
Inverting Octal Buffers/Drivers	'742		▲				
	'756			●			
	'763		●	●			
Inverting and Noninverting Octal Buffers/Drivers	'762		●	●			
Noninverting Quad Transceivers	'759			●			
Inverting Quad Transceivers	'758			●			

● Denotes available technology.

▲ Denotes planned new products.

A Denotes "A" suffix version available in the technology indicated.

GATES, EXPANDERS, BUFFERS, DRIVERS, AND TRANSCEIVERS

GATES, BUFFERS, DRIVERS, AND BUS TRANSCEIVERS WITH 3-STATE OUTPUTS

DESCRIPTION	TYPE	TECHNOLOGY STD TTL	ALS	AS	LS	S	VOLUME
Noninverting 10-Bit Buffers/Drivers	'29827		▲				LSI
Inverting 10-Bit Buffers/Drivers	'29828		▲				
Noninverting 10-Bit Transceivers	'29861		▲				
Inverting 10-Bit Transceivers	'29862		▲				
Noninverting 9-Bit Transceivers	'29863		▲				
Inverting 9-Bit Transceivers	'29864		▲				
Noninverting Octal Buffers/Drivers	'241				●	●	2
			A	●			3
	'244				●	●	2
			A	●			3
	'465				●		2
			A				3
	'467				●		2
			A				3
	'541				●		2
			●				3
	'1241¶		▲				
	'1244¶		A				
Inverting Octal Buffers/Drivers	'231		●	●			
	'240				●	●	2
			A	●			3
	'466				●		2
			A				3
	'468				●		2
			A				3
	'540				●		2
			●				3
	'1240¶		●				3
Inverting and Noninverting Octal Buffers/Drivers	'230			●			
Octal Transceivers	'245				●		2
			A	●			3
	'1245		A				
Noninverting Hex Buffers/Drivers	'365	A			A		2
			●				3
	'367	A			A		2
			●				3
Inverting Hex Buffers/Drivers	'366	A			A		2
			▲				3
	'368	A			A		2
			▲				3
Quad Buffers/Drivers with Independent Output Controls	'125	●			A		2
	'126	●			A		
	'425	●					
	'426	●					
Noninverting Quad Transceivers	'243				●		3
			A	●			
	'1243¶		▲				
Inverting Quad Transceivers	'242				●		2
			A	●			3
	'1242¶		●				
Quad Transceivers with Storage	'226					●	2
12-Input NAND Gate	'134					●	

50-OHM/75-OHM LINE DRIVERS

DESCRIPTION	TYPE	TECHNOLOGY STD TTL	ALS	AS	S	VOLUME
Hex 2-Input Positive-NAND	'804		A	B		3
Hex 2-Input Positive-NOR	'805		A	B		
Hex 2-Input Positive-AND	'808		A	B		
Hex 2-Input Positive-OR	'832		A	B		
Quad 2-Input Positive-NOR	'128	●				2
Dual 4-Input Positive-NAND	'140				●	

1

General Information

● Denotes available technology.
▲ Denotes planned new products.
¶ Denotes very low power.
A Denotes "A" suffix version available in the technology indicated.
B Denotes "B" suffix version available in the technology indicated.

BUFFERS, DRIVERS, TRANSCEIVERS, AND CLOCK GENERATORS

BUFFERS, CLOCK/MEMORY DRIVERS

DESCRIPTION	TYPE	STD TTL	ALS	AS	H	LS	S	VOLUME
		TECHNOLOGY						
Hex 2-Input Positive-NAND	'804		A	B				3
Hex 2-Input Positive-NOR	'805		A	B				
Hex 2-Input Positive-AND	'808		A	B				
Hex 2-Input Positive-OR	'832		A	B				
Hex Inverter	'1004		●	●				
Hex Buffer	'34		●	●				
	'1034		●	A				
Quad 2-Input Positive-NAND	'37	●				●	●	2
			A					3
	'1000		A	●				
Quad 2-Input Positive-NOR	'28	●				●		2
			A					3
	'1002		A					
	'1036			A				
Quad 2-Input Positive-AND	'1008		A	●				
Quad 2-Input Positive-OR	'1032		A	●				
Triple 3-Input Positive-NAND	'1010		A					
Triple 3-Input Positive-AND	'1011		A					
Triple 4-Input AND-NAND	'800			▲				
Triple 4-Input OR-NOR	'802			▲				
Dual 4-Input Positive-NAND	'40	●			●	●	●	2
			A					3
	'1020		A					
Line Driver/Memory Driver with Series Damping Resistor	'436						●	2
Line Driver/Memory Driver	'437						●	

BI-/TRI-DIRECTIONAL BUS TRANSCEIVERS AND DRIVERS

DESCRIPTION	TYPE OF OUTPUT	TYPE	ALS	AS	LS	S	VOLUME
			TECHNOLOGY				
Quad with Bit Direction Controls	3-State	'446			●		2
	3-State	'449			●		
Quad Tridirection	OC	'440			●		
	OC	'441			●		
	3-State	'442			●		
	3-State	'443			●		
	3-State	'444			●		
	OC	'448			●		
4-Bit with Storage	3-State	'226				●	

OCTAL BUS TRANSCEIVERS/MOS DRIVERS

DESCRIPTION	TYPE	STD TTL	ALS	AS	LS	S	VOLUME
		TECHNOLOGY					
Inverting Outputs, 3-State	'2620			●			3
	'2640			●			
True Outputs, 3-State	'2623			●			
	'2645			●			

OCTAL BUFFERS AND LINE DRIVERS WITH INPUT/OUTPUT RESISTORS

DESCRIPTION		TYPE	STD TTL	ALS	AS	LS	S	VOLUME
			TECHNOLOGY					
Input Resistors	Inverting Outputs	'746		●				3
	Noninverting Outputs	'747		●				
Output Resistors	Inverting Outputs	'2540		●				
	Noninverting Outputs	'2541		●				

OCTAL BI-/TRI-DIRECTIONAL BUS TRANSCEIVERS

DESCRIPTION		TYPE OF OUTPUT	TYPE	ALS	AS	LS	VOLUME
				TECHNOLOGY			
12 mA/24 mA/48 mA/64 mA Sink, True Outputs	Low Power	3-State	'245	A	●		3
						●	2
		OC	'621	A	●		3
						●	2
		3-State	'623	A	●		3
						●	2
		OC, 3-State	'639	A	●		3
						●	2
		3-State	'652	●	●		3 & LSI
						●	2
		OC, 3-State	'654	▲			3
						●	2
	Very Low Power	OC	'1621	▲			3
		3-State	'1623	▲			
		OC, 3-State	'1639	▲			
12 mA/24 mA/48 mA/64 mA Sink, Inverting Outputs	Low Power	3-State	'620	A	●		3
						●	2
		OC	'622	A	●		3
						●	2
		OC, 3-State	'638	A	●		3
						●	2
		3-State	'651	●	●		3 & LSI
						●	2
		OC, 3-State	'653	▲			3
						●	2
	Very Low Power	3-State	'1620	▲			3
		OC	'1622	▲			
		OC, 3-State	'1638	▲			
12 mA/24 mA/48 mA/64 mA Sink, True Outputs	Low Power	OC	'641	A	●		
						●	2
		3-State	'645	A	●		3
						●	2
	Very Low Power	OC	'1641	▲			3
		3-State	'1645	A			
12 mA/24 mA/48 mA/64 mA Sink, Inverting Outputs	Low Power	3-State	'640	A	●		
						●	2
		OC	'642	A	●		3
						●	2
	Very Low Power	3-State	'1640	A			3
		OC	'1642	▲			
12 mA/24 mA/48 mA/64 mA Sink, True and Inverting Outputs	Low Power	3-State	'643	A	●		
						●	2
		OC	'644	A	●		3
						●	2
	Very Low Power	3-State	'1643	▲			3
		OC	'1644	▲			
Registered with Multiplex 12 mA/24 mA/48 mA/64 mA True Outputs		3-State	'646	●	●		3 & LSI
						●	2
		OC	'647	●			3
						●	2
Registered with Multiplexed 12 mA/24 mA/48 mA/64 mA Inverting Outputs		3-State	'648	●	●		3 & LSI
						●	2
		OC	'649	●			3 & LSI
						●	2
Universal Transceiver/ Port Controllers		3-State	'877		●		3 & LSI
			'852		●		
			'856		●		

● Denotes available technology.
▲ Denotes planned new products.
A Denotes "A" suffix version available in the technology indicated.
B Denotes "B" suffix version available in the technology indicated.

FLIP-FLOPS

DUAL AND SINGLE FLIP-FLOPS

DESCRIPTION	TYPE	TECHNOLOGY: STD TTL	ALS	AS	H	L	LS	S	VOLUME
Dual J-K Edge-Triggered	'73	●			●	●	A		2
	'76						A		
	'78				●	●	A		
	'103				●				
	'106				●				
	'107	●					A		
	'108				●				
	'109	●					A		
			A	●					3
	'112						A	●	2
			A	▲					3
	'113						A	●	2
			A	▲					3
	'114						A	●	2
			A	▲					3
Single J-K Edge-Triggered	'70	●							2
	'101				●				
	'102				●				
Dual Pulse-Triggered	'73	●			●	●			
	'76	●			●				
	'78				●	●			
	'107	●							
Single Pulse-Triggered	'71				●	●			
	'72	●			●	●			
	'104	●							
	'105	●							
Dual J-K with Data Lockout	'111	●							
Single J-K with Data Lockout	'110	●							
Dual D-Type	'74	●			●	●	A	●	
			A	●					3

QUAD AND HEX FLIP-FLOPS

DESCRIPTION	NO. OF FFs	OUTPUTS	TYPE	TECHNOLOGY: STD TTL	ALS	AS	LS	S	VOLUME
D Type	6	Q	'174	●			●	●	2
					●	●			3
			'378				●		
	4	Q, $\overline{Q}$	'171				●		2
			'175	●			●	●	
					●	●			3
			'379				●		
J-K	4	Q	'276	●					2
			'376	●					

OCTAL, 9-BIT, AND 10-BIT D-TYPE FLIP-FLOPS

DESCRIPTION	NO. OF BITS	OUTPUT	TYPE	TECHNOLOGY: STD TTL	ALS	AS	LS	S	VOLUME
True Data	Octal	3-State	'374		●	●			3
							●	●	2
		3-State	'574		B	●			3
True Data with Clear	Octal	2-State	'273		●				
				●			●		2
		3-State	'575		●	●			3
		3-State	'874		●	●			
		3-State	'878		●	●			
True with Enable	Octal	2-State	'377				●		2
Inverting	Octal	3-State	'534		●	●			3
		3-State	'564		A				
		3-State	'576		A	●			
Inverting with Clear	Octal	3-State	'577		A	●			
		3-State	'879		A	●			
Inverting with Preset	Octal	3-State	'876		A	●			
True	Octal	3-State	'825			●			3 & LSI
Inverting	Octal	3-State	'826			●			
True	9-Bit	3-State	'823			●			
Inverting	9-Bit	3-State	'824			●			
True	10-Bit	3-State	'821			●			
Inverting	10-Bit	3-State	'822			●			
True	Octal	3-State	'29825		▲				
Inverting	Octal	3-State	'29826		▲				
True	9-Bit	3-State	'29823		▲				
Inverting	9-Bit	3-State	'29824		▲				
True	10-Bit	3-State	'29821		▲				
Inverting	10-Bit	3-State	'29822		▲				

● Denotes available technology.
▲ Denotes planned new products.
A Denotes "A" suffix version available in the technology indicated.
B Denotes "B" suffix version available in the technology indicated.

LATCHES AND MULTIVIBRATORS

QUAD LATCHES

DESCRIPTION	OUTPUT	TYPE	TECHNOLOGY					VOLUME
			STD TTL	ALS	AS	L	LS	
Dual 2-Bit Transparent	2-State	'75	●			●	●	2
	2-State	'77	●			●	●	
	2-State	'375					●	
S-R	2-State	'279	●				A	

RETRIGGERABLE MONOSTABLE MULTIVIBRATORS

DESCRIPTION	TYPE	TECHNOLOGY					VOLUME
		STD TTL	ALS	AS	LS	L	
Single	'122	●			●	●	2
	'130	●					
	'422				●		
Dual	'123	●			●	●	
	'423				●		

D-TYPE OCTAL, 9-BIT, AND 10-BIT READ-BACK LATCHES

DESCRIPTION	NO. OF BITS	TYPE	TECHNOLOGY					VOLUME
			STD TTL	ALS	AS	LS	S	
Edge-Triggered Inverting and Noninverting	Octal	'996		▲				3 & LSI
Transparent True	Octal	'990		●				
	9-Bit	'992		●				
	10-Bit	'994		●				
Transparent Noninverting	Octal	'991		●				
	9-Bit	'992		●				
	10-Bit	'994		●				
Transparent with Clear True Outputs	Octal	'666		●				
Transparent with Clear Inverting Outputs	Octal	'667		●				

OCTAL, 9-BIT, AND 10-BIT LATCHES

DESCRIPTION	NO. OF BITS	OUTPUT	TYPE	TECHNOLOGY					VOLUME
				STD TTL	ALS	AS	LS	S	
Transparent	Octal	3-State	'268					●	2
			'373				●	●	
					●	●			3
		3-State	'573		●	●			
Dual 4-Bit Transparent	Octal	2-State	'100	●					2
		2-State	'116	●					
		3-State	'873		B	●			3
Inverting Transparent	Octal	3-State	'533		●	●			
		3-State	'563		A				
		3-State	'580		A	●			
Dual 4-Bit Inverting Transparent	Octal	3-State	'880		A	●			
2-Input Multiplexed	Octal	3-State	'604				●		2
		OC	'605				●		
		3-State	'606				●		
		OC	'607				●		
Addressable	Octal	2-State	'259	●			●		
					●				3
Multi-Mode Buffered	Octal	3-State	'412					●	2
True	Octal	3-State	'845		●	●			3 & LSI
Inverting	Octal	3-State	'846		▲	●			
True	9-Bit	3-State	'843		●	●			
Inverting	9-Bit	3-State	'844		●	●			
True	10-Bit	3-State	'841		●	●			
Inverting	10-Bit	3-State	'842		●	●			

MONOSTABLE MULTIVIBRATORS WITH SCHMITT-TRIGGER INPUTS

DESCRIPTION	TYPE	TECHNOLOGY						VOLUME
		STD TTL	ALS	AS	LS	S	L	
Single	'121	●					●	2
Dual	'221	●			●			

● Denotes available technology.
▲ Denotes planned new products.
A Denotes "A" suffix version available in the technology indicated.
B Denotes "B" suffix version available in the technology indicated.

REGISTERS

SHIFT REGISTERS

DESCRIPTION	NO. OF BITS	MODES S-R	S-L	LOAD	HOLD	TYPE	TECHNOLOGY STD TTL	ALS	AS	L	LS	S	VOLUME
Sign-Protected		X		X	X	'322					A		
Parallel-In, Parallel-Out, Bidirectional	8	X	X	X	X	'198	●						2
		X	X	X	X	'299					●	●	
								●	▲				3
		X	X	X	X	'323					●		2
								●	▲				3
	4	X	X	X	X	'194	●				A	●	2
									▲				3
Parallel-In, Parallel-Out, Registered Outputs	4	X	X	X	X	'671					●		2
		X	X	X	X	'672					●		
Parallel-In, Parallel-Out	8	X		X	X	'199	●						
	5	X		X		'96	●			●	●		
	4	X		X		'95	A			●	B		2
									●				3
		X		X		'99				●			2
		X		X	X	'178	●						
		X		X	X	'179	●						
		X		X		'195	●				A	●	2
									▲				3
		X		X		'295					B		2
		X		X		'395					A		2
									▲				3
Serial-In Parallel-Out	16	X		X	X	'673					●		2
	8	X				'164	●			●	●		
								▲					3
Parallel-In, Serial-Out	16	X		X	X	'674					●		2
	8	X		X	X	'165	●				A		
								▲					3
		X		X	X	'166	●				A		2
								▲					3
Serial-In, Serial-Out	8	X				'91	A			●	●		2
	4	X		X		'94	●						

SHIFT REGISTERS WITH LATCHES

DESCRIPTION	NO. OF BITS	OUTPUTS	TYPE	TECHNOLOGY ALS	AS	LS	VOLUME
Parallel-In, Parallel-Out with Output Latches	4	3-State	'671			●	2
		3-State	'672			●	
Serial-In, Parallel-Out with Output Latches	16	2-State	'673			●	
	8	Buffered	'594			●	
		3-State	'595			●	
		OC	'596			●	
		OC	'599			●	
Parallel-In, Serial-Out, with Input Latches	8	2-State	'597			●	
		3-State	'589			●	
Parallel I/O Ports with Input Latches, Multiplexed Serial Inputs	8	3-State	'598			●	

SIGN-PROTECTED REGISTERS

DESCRIPTION	NO. OF BITS	MODES S-R	S-L	LOAD	HOLD	TYPE	TECHNOLOGY ALS	AS	LS	VOLUME
Sign-Protected Register	8	X		X	X	'322			A	2

REGISTER FILES

DESCRIPTION	OUTPUT	TYPE	TECHNOLOGY STD TTL	ALS	AS	LS	VOLUME
8 Words × 2 Bits	3-State	'172	●				2
4 Words × 4 Bits	OC	'170	●			●	
	3-State	'670				●	
Dual 16 Words × 4 Bits	3-State	'870			●		3 & LSI
	3-State	'871			●		
64 Words × 40 Bits	3-State	'8834			▲		LSI

OTHER REGISTERS

DESCRIPTION	TYPE	TECHNOLOGY STD TTL	ALS	AS	L	LS	S	VOLUME
Quadruple Multiplexers with Storage	'98				●			2
	'298	●				●		
				●				3
	'398				●			2
	'399				●			
8-Bit Universal Shift Registers	'299					●	●	
			●	▲				3
Quadruple Bus-Buffer Registers	'173	●				A		2
Octal Storage Register	'396					●		
Dual-Rank 8-Bit Shift Registers	'963		▲					3 & LSI
	'964		▲					
8-Bit Diagnostics/ Pipeline Registers	'29818		▲					
	'29819		▲					

● Denotes available technology.
▲ Denotes planned new products.
A Denotes "A" suffix version available in the technology indicated.
B Denotes "B" suffix version available in the technology indicated.

COUNTERS

SYNCHRONOUS COUNTERS — POSITIVE-EDGE TRIGGERED

DESCRIPTION	PARALLEL LOAD	TYPE	STD TTL	ALS	AS	L	LS	S	VOLUME
Decade	Sync	'160	•				A		2
				B	•				3
	Sync	'162	•				A	•	2
				B	•				3
	Sync	'560		A					
	Sync	'668					•		
	Sync	'690					•		2
	Sync	'692					•		
Decade Up/Down	Sync	'168					B	•	
				B	•				3
	Async	'190	•				•		2
				•					3
	Async	'192	•			•	•		2
				•					3
	Sync	'568		A					
	Sync	'696					•		
	Sync	'698					•		
Decade Rate Multipler, 1/N10	Async Set-to-9	'167	•						2
4-Bit Binary	Sync	'161	•				A		
				B	•				3
	Sync	'163	•				A	•	2
				B	•				3
	Sync	'561		A					
	Sync	'669					•		
	Sync	'691					•		2
	Sync	'693					•		
4-Bit Binary Up/Down	Sync	'169					B	•	
				B	•				3
	Async	'191	•				•		2
				•					3
	Async	'193	•			•	•		2
				•					3
	Sync	'569		A					
	Sync	'697					•		
	Sync	'699					•		2
6-Bit Binary Rate Multipler, 1/N2		'97	•						
8-Bit Up/Down	Async CLR	'867			•				3 & LSI
	Sync CLR	'869			•				

ASYNCHRONOUS COUNTERS (RIPPLE CLOCK) — NEGATIVE-EDGE TRIGGERED

DESCRIPTION	PARALLEL LOAD	TYPE	STD TTL	ALS	AS	L	LS	S	VOLUME
Decade	Set-to-9	'90	A			•	•		2
		'68					•		
	Yes	'176	•						
	Yes	'196	•				•	•	
	Set-to-9	'290	•				•		
4-Bit Binary	None	'93	A			•	•		
		'69					•		
	Yes	'177	•						
	Yes	'197	•				•	•	
	None	'293	•				•		
Divide-by-12	None	'92	A				•		
Dual Decade	None	'390	•				•		
	Set-to-9	'490	•				•		
Dual 4-Bit Binary	None	'393	•				•		

8-BIT BINARY COUNTERS WITH REGISTERS

DESCRIPTION	TYPE OF OUTPUT	TYPE	ALS	AS	LS	VOLUME
Parallel Register	3-State	'590			•	2
Outputs	OC	'591			•	
Parallel Register Inputs	2-State	'592			•	
Parallel I/O	3-State	'593			•	

FREQUENCY DIVIDERS, RATE MULTIPLIERS

DESCRIPTION	TYPE	STD TTL	ALS	AS	LS	VOLUME
50-to-1 Frequency Divider	'56				•	2
60-to-1 Frequency Divider	'57				•	
60-Bit Binary Rate Multiplier	'97	•				
Decade Rate Multiplier	'167	•				

• Denotes available technology.
A Denotes "A" suffix version available in the technology indicated.
B Denotes "B" suffix version available in the technology indicated.

TEXAS INSTRUMENTS
POST OFFICE BOX 225012 • DALLAS, TEXAS 75265

DECODERS, ENCODERS, DATA SELECTORS/MULTIPLEXERS AND SHIFTERS

DATA SELECTORS/MULTIPLEXERS

DESCRIPTION	TYPE OF OUTPUT	TYPE	TECHNOLOGY STD TTL	ALS	AS	L	LS	S	VOLUME
16-to-1	2-State	'150	●						2
	3-State	'250			●				
	3-State	'850			●				3 & LSI
	3-State	'851			●				
Dual 8-to-1	3-State	'351	●						2
8-to-1	2-State	'151	A				●	●	
				●	●				3
	2-State	'152	A				●		2
	3-State	'251	●				●	●	2
				●	▲				3
	3-State	'354					●		
	2-State	'355					●		
	3-State	'356					●		2
	OC	'357					●		
Dual 4-to-1	2-State	'153	●			●	●	●	
				●	●				3
	3-State	'253					●	●	2
				●	●				3
	2-State	'352					●		2
				●	●				3
	3-State	'353					●		2
				●	●				3
Octal 2-to-1 with Storage	3-State	'604					●		
	OC	'605					●		
	3-State	'606					●		2
	OC	'607					●		
Quad 2-to-1 with Storage	2-State	'98				●			
	2-State	'298	●				●		2
					●				3
	2-State	'398					●		
	2-State	'399					●		2
Quad 2-to-1	2-State	'157	●			●	●	●	
				●	●				3
	2-State	'158					●	●	2
				●	●				3
	3-State	'257					B	●	2
				A	●				3
	3-State	'258					B	●	2
				A	●				3
6-to-1 Universal Multiplexer	3-State	'857		●	●				3

DECODERS/DEMULTIPLEXERS

DESCRIPTION	TYPE OF OUTPUT	TYPE	TECHNOLOGY STD TTL	ALS	AS	L	LS	S	VOLUME
4-to-16	3-State	'154	●			●			
	OC	'159	●						
4-to-10 BCD-to-Decimal	2-State	'42	A			●	●		
4-to-10 Excess 3-to-Decimal	2-State	'43	A			●			2
4-to-10 Excess 3-Gray-to-Decimal	2-State	'44	A			●			
3-to-8 with Address Latches		'131		●	▲				3
	2-State	'137		●	▲				
							●		2
3-to-8	2-State	'138		●	▲				3
							●	●	2
	3-State	'538		▲					3
Dual 2-to-4	2-State	'139		▲	●				
							A	●	
	2-State	'155	●				A		2
	OC	'156	●				●		
Dual 1-to-4 Decoders	3-State	'539		▲					3

CODE CONVERTERS

DESCRIPTION	TYPE	TECHNOLOGY STD TTL	S	VOLUME
6-Line-BCD to 6-Line Binary, or 4-Line to 4-Line BCD 9's/BCD 10's Converters	'184	●		2
6-Bit-Binary to 6-Bit BCD Converters	'185	A		
BCD-to-Binary Converters	'484		A	4
Binary-to-BCD Converters	'485		A	

PRIORITY ENCODERS/REGISTERS

DESCRIPTION	TYPE	TECHNOLOGY STD TTL	ALS	AS	LS	VOLUME
Full BCD	'147	●			●	
Cascadable Octal	'148	●			●	2
Cascadable Octal with 3-State Outputs	'348				●	
4-Bit Cascadable with Registers	'278	●				

SHIFTERS

DESCRIPTION	OUTPUT	TYPE	TECHNOLOGY STD TTL	ALS	AS	L	LS	S	VOLUME
4-Bit Shifter	3-State	'350						●	2
Parallel 16-Bit Multi-Mode Barrel Shifter	3-State	'897			●				LSI
32-Bit Barrel Shifter	3-State	'8838			▲				

● Denotes available technology.
▲ Denotes planned new products.
A Denotes "A" suffix version available in the technology indicated.
B Denotes "B" suffix version available in the technology indicated.

DISPLAY DECODERS/DRIVERS, MEMORY/MICROPROCESSOR CONTROLLERS, AND VOLTAGE-CONTROLLED OSCILLATORS

OPEN-COLLECTOR DISPLAY DECODERS/DRIVERS

DESCRIPTION	OFF-STATE OUTPUT VOLTAGE	TYPE	TECHNOLOGY: STD TTL	ALS	AS	L	LS	VOLUME
BCD-to-Decimal	30 V	'45	●					2
	60 V	'141	●					
	15 V	'145	●				●	
	7 V	'445					●	
BCD-to-Seven-Segment	30 V	'46	A			●		
	15 V	'47	A			●	●	
	5.5 V	'48	●				●	
	5.5 V	'49	●				●	
	30 V	'246	●					
	15 V	'247	●				●	
	7 V	'347					●	
	7 V	'447					●	
	5.5 V	'248	●				●	
	5.5 V	'249	●				●	

OPEN COLLECTOR DISPLAY DECODERS/DRIVERS WITH COUNTERS/LATCH

DESCRIPTION	TYPE	TECHNOLOGY: STD TTL	ALS	AS	VOLUME
BCD Counter/4-Bit Latch/BCD-to-Decimal Decoder/Driver	'142	●			2
BCD Counter/4-Bit Latch/BCD-to-Seven-Segment Decoder/LED Driver	'143	●			
BCD Counter/4-Bit Latch/BCD-to-Seven-Segment Decoder/Lamp Driver	'144	●			

VOLTAGE-CONTROLLED OSCILLATORS

DESCRIPTION: No. VCOs	COMP'L Z_{OUT}	ENABLE	RANGE INPUT	R_{ext}	f_{max} MHz	TYPE	TECHNOLOGY: LS	S	VOLUME
Single	Yes	Yes	Yes	No	20	'624	●		2
Single	Yes	Yes	Yes	Yes	20	'628	●		
Dual	No	Yes	Yes	No	60	'124		●	
Dual	Yes	Yes	No	No	20	'626	●		
Dual	No	No	No	No	20	'627	●		
Dual	No	Yes	Yes	No	20	'629	●		

MEMORY/MICROPROCESSOR CONTROLLERS

DESCRIPTION			TYPE	TECHNOLOGY: ALS	AS	LS	S	VOLUME
System Controllers (Universal or for '888)			'890		●			LSI
Memory Refresh Controllers	Transparent, Burst Modes	4K, 16K	'600			A		2
		64K	'601			A		
	Cycle Steal, Burst Modes	4K, 16K	'602			A		
		64K	'603			A		
Memory Cycle Controller			'608			●		
Memory Mappers		3-State	'612			●		LSI
		OC	'613			●		
Memory Mappers with Output Latches		3-State	'610			●		
		OC	'611			●		
Multi-Mode Latches (8080A Applications)			'412				●	2
Dynamic Memory Controllers		16K, 64K, 256K	2967	▲				LSI
			'2968	▲				
		16K, 64K	'6301	▲				
		256K, 1 MEG	'6302	▲				

CLOCK GENERATOR CIRCUITS

DESCRIPTION	TYPE	TECHNOLOGY: STD TTL	ALS	AS	LS	S	VOLUME
Quadruple Complementary-Output Logic Elements	'265	●					2
Dual Pulse Synchronizers/Drivers	'120	●					
Crystal-Controlled Oscillators	'320				●		
	'321				●		
Digital Phase-Lock Loop	'297				●		
Programmable Frequency Dividers/Digital Timers	'292				●		
	'294				●		
Triple 4-Input AND/NAND Drivers	'800			▲			3
Triple 4-Input OR/NOR Drivers	'802			▲			
Dual VCO	'124					●	2

RESULTANT DISPLAYS USING '46A, '47A, '48, '49, 'L46, 'L47, 'LS47, 'LS48, 'LS49, 'LS347

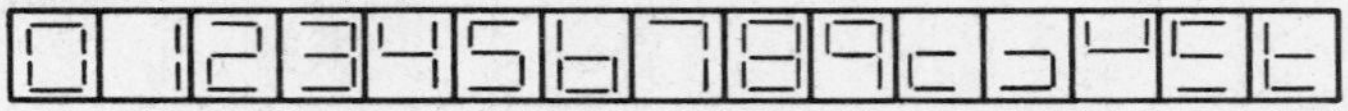
0 1 2 3 4 5 6 7 8 9 10 11 12 13 14

RESULTANT DISPLAYS USING '246, '247, '248, '249, 'LS247, 'LS248, 'LS249, 'LS447

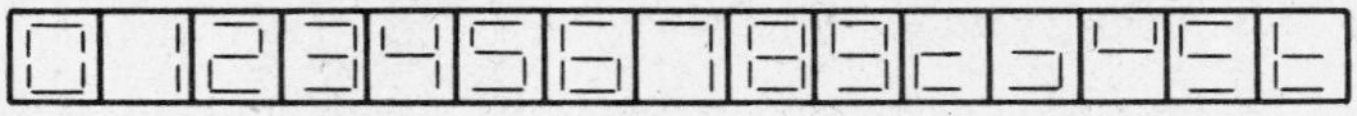
0 1 2 3 4 5 6 7 8 9 10 11 12 13 14

RESULTANT DISPLAYS USING '143, '144

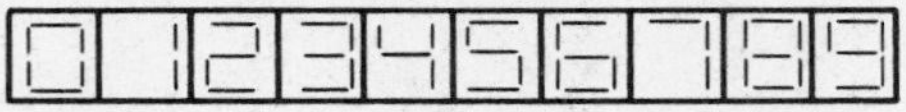
0 1 2 3 4 5 6 7 8 9

● Denotes available technology.
▲ Denotes planned new products.
A Denotes "A" suffix version available in the technology indicated.

COMPARATORS AND ERROR DETECTION CIRCUITS

4-BIT COMPARATORS

DESCRIPTION					TYPE	TECHNOLOGY						VOLUME
P=Q	P>Q	P<Q	OUTPUT	OUTPUT ENABLE		STD TTL	ALS	AS	L	LS	S	
Yes	Yes	No	2-State	No	'85	●			●	●	●	2

8-BIT COMPARATORS

DESCRIPTION								TYPE	TECHNOLOGY			VOLUME
INPUTS	P=Q	$\overline{P=Q}$	P>Q	$\overline{P>Q}$	P<Q	OUTPUT	OUTPUT ENABLE		ALS	AS	LS	
20-kΩ Pull-Up	Yes	No	No	No	No	OC	Yes	'518	●			3
	No	Yes	No	No	No	2-S	Yes	'520	●			
	No	Yes	No	No	No	OC	Yes	'522	●			
	No	Yes	No	Yes	No	2-S	No	'682			●	2
	No	Yes	No	Yes	No	OC	No	'683			●	
Standard	Yes	No	No	No	No	OC	Yes	'519	●			3
	No	Yes	No	No	No	2-S	Yes	'521	●			
	No	Yes	No	Yes	No	2-S	No	'684			●	2
	No	Yes	No	Yes	No	OC	No	'685			●	
	No	Yes	No	Yes	No	2-S	Yes	'686			●	
	No	Yes	No	Yes	No	OC	Yes	'687			●	
	No	Yes	No	No	No	2-S	Yes	'688	●			3
											●	2
	No	Yes	No	No	No	OC	Yes	'689	●			3
											●	2
Latched P Logic & Arith	No	No	Yes	No	Yes	2-S	Yes	'885		●		3 & LSI
Latched P&Q Logic & Arith	Yes	No	Yes	No	Yes	Latched	Yes	'866		●		3

ADDRESS COMPARATORS

DESCRIPTION	OUTPUT ENABLE	LATCHED OUTPUT	TYPE	TECHNOLOGY		VOLUME
				ALS	AS	
16-Bit to 4-Bit	Yes		'677	●		3
		Yes	'678	●		
12-Bit to 4-Bit	Yes		'679	●		
		Yes	'680	●		

PARITY GENERATORS/CHECKERS, ERROR DETECTION AND CORRECTION CIRCUITS

DESCRIPTION		NO. OF BITS	TYPE	TECHNOLOGY					VOLUME
				STD TTL	ALS	AS	LS	S	
Odd/Even Parity Generators/Checkers		8	'180	●					2
		9	'280				●	●	
					●	●			3 & LSI
		9	'286			●			
Parallel Error Detection/Correction Circuits	3-State	8	'636				●		2
	OC	8	'637				●		
	3-State	16	'616		●				3 & LSI
	OC	16	'617		▲				
	3-State	16	'630				●		2
	OC	16	'631				●		
	3-State	16	'8400		▲				LSI
	3-State	32	'632		A	▲			3 & LSI
	OC	32	'633		●	▲			
	3-State	32	'634		▲	▲			
	OC	32	'635		▲	▲			

FUSE-PROGRAMMABLE COMPARATORS

DESCRIPTION	TYPE	TECHNOLOGY					VOLUME
		STD TTL	ALS	AS	LS	S	
16-Bit Identity Comparator	'526		●				3
12-Bit identity Comparator	'528		●				
8-Bit Identity Comparator and 4-Bit Comparator	'527		●				

● Denotes available technology.
▲ Denotes planned new products.
A Denotes "A" suffix version available in the technology indicated.

ARITHMETIC CIRCUITS AND PROCESSOR ELEMENTS

PARALLEL BINARY ADDERS

DESCRIPTION	TYPE	TECHNOLOGY						VOLUME
		STD TTL	ALS	AS	H	LS	S	
1-Bit Gated	'80	●						2
2-Bit	'82	●						
4-Bit	'83	A				A		
	'283	●				●	●	
Dual 1-Bit Carry-Save	'183				●	●		

ACCUMULATORS, ARITHMETIC LOGIC UNITS, LOOK-AHEAD CARRY GENERATORS

DESCRIPTION		TYPE	TECHNOLOGY					VOLUME
			STD TTL	ALS	AS	LS	S	
4-Bit Parallel Binary Accumulators		'281					●	2
		'681				●		
4-Bit Arithmetic Logic Units/ Function Generators		'181	●			●	●	
					A			3 & LSI
		'1181			●			
		'381				A		2
							●	
		'881			A			3 & LSI
4-Bit Arithmetic Logic Unit with Ripple Carry		'382				●		2
Look-Ahead Carry Generators	16-Bit	'182	●				●	2
					▲			3
		'282			▲			
	32-Bit	'882			A			3 & LSI
Quad Serial Adder/Subtractor		'385				●		2

MULTIPLIERS

DESCRIPTION	TYPE	TECHNOLOGY					VOLUME
		STD TTL	ALS	AS	LS	S	
2-Bit-by-4-Bit Parallel Binary Multipliers	'261				●		2
4-Bit-by-4-Bit Parallel Binary Multipliers	'284	●					
	'285	●					
25-MHz 6-Bit Binary Rate Multipliers	'97	●					
25-MHz Decade Rate Multipliers	'167	●					
8-Bit × 1-Bit 2's Complement Multipliers	'384				●		

OTHER ARITHMETIC OPERATORS

DESCRIPTION	TYPE	TECHNOLOGY							VOLUME
		STD TTL	ALS	AS	H	L	LS	S	
Quad 2-Input Exclusive-OR Gates with Totem-Pole Outputs	'86	●				●	A	●	2
			●						3
	'386						A		2
Quad 2-Input Exclusive-OR Gates with Open-Collector Outputs	'136	●						●	
			●						3
Quad 2-Input Exclusive-NOR Gates	'266						●		2
	'810		●	▲					3
Quad 2-Input Exclusive-NOR Gates with Open-Collector Outputs	'811		●	▲					3
Quad Exclusive OR/NOR Gates	'135							●	2
4-Bit True/Complement Element	'87				●				

BIPOLAR BIT-SLICE PROCESSOR ELEMENTS

DESCRIPTION	CASCADABLE TO N-BITS	TYPE	TECHNOLOGY				VOLUME
			ALS	AS	LS	S	
8-Bit Slice	No	'887		●			LSI
	Yes	'888		●			
	Yes	'895		▲			

●Denotes available technology.
▲Denotes planned new products.
A Denotes "A" suffix version available in the technology indicated.

TEXAS INSTRUMENTS
POST OFFICE BOX 225012 ● DALLAS, TEXAS 75265

D2661, DECEMBER 1982—REVISED AUGUST 1985

- Package Options Include the 'AS181A in Compact 300-mil or Standard 600-mil DIPs. The 'AS881A is Offered in 300-mil DIPS. Both Devices are Available in Both Plastic and Ceramic Chip Carriers
- Full Look-Ahead for High-Speed Operations on Long Words
- Arithmetic Operating Modes:
  - Addition
  - Subtraction
  - Shift Operand A One Position
  - Magnitude Comparison
  - Plus Twelve Other Arithmetic Operations
- Logic Function Modes
  - Exclusive-OR
  - Comparator
  - AND, NAND, OR, NOR
  - 'AS881A Provides Status Register Checks
  - Plus Ten Other Logic Operations
- Dependable Texas Instruments Quality and Reliability

SN54AS181A . . . JT OR JW PACKAGE
SN54AS881A . . . JT PACKAGE
SN74AS181A . . . NT OR NW PACKAGE
SN74AS881A . . . NT PACKAGE
(TOP VIEW)

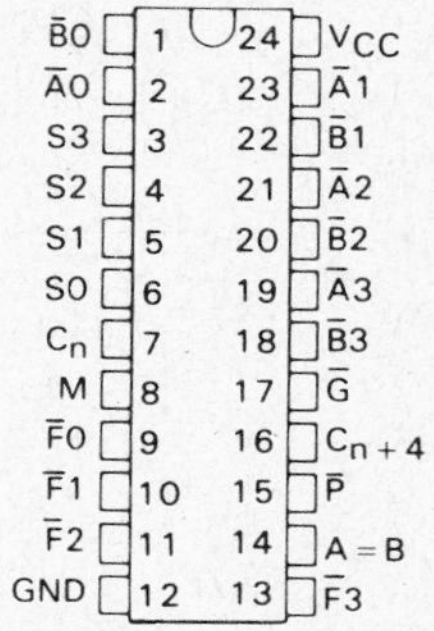
B̄0 1
Ā0 2
S3 3
S2 4
S1 5
S0 6
Cn 7
M 8
F̄0 9
F̄1 10
F̄2 11
GND 12
13 F̄3
14 A = B
15 P̄
16 Cn + 4
17 Ḡ
18 B̄3
19 Ā3
20 B̄2
21 Ā2
22 B̄1
23 Ā1
24 VCC

SN54AS181A, SN54AS881A . . . FK PACKAGE
SN74AS181A, SN74AS881A . . . FN PACKAGE
(TOP VIEW)

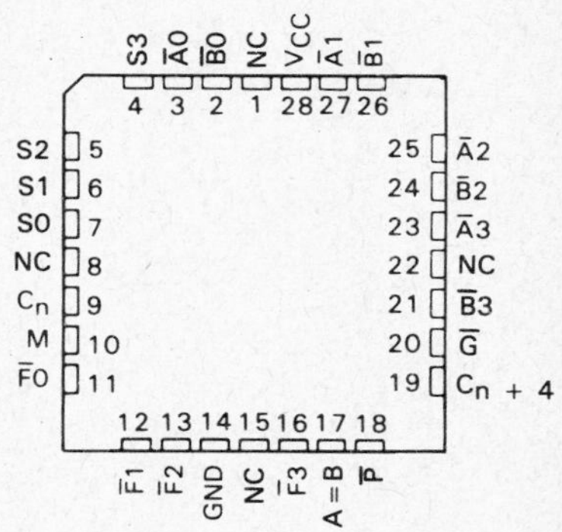
S3 Ā0 B̄0 NC VCC Ā1 B̄1
4 3 2 1 28 27 26
S2 5
S1 6
S0 7
NC 8
Cn 9
M 10
F̄0 11
25 Ā2
24 B̄2
23 Ā3
22 NC
21 B̄3
20 Ḡ
19 Cn + 4
12 13 14 15 16 17 18
F̄1 F̄2 GND NC F̄3 A = B P̄

NC—No internal connection

logic symbol

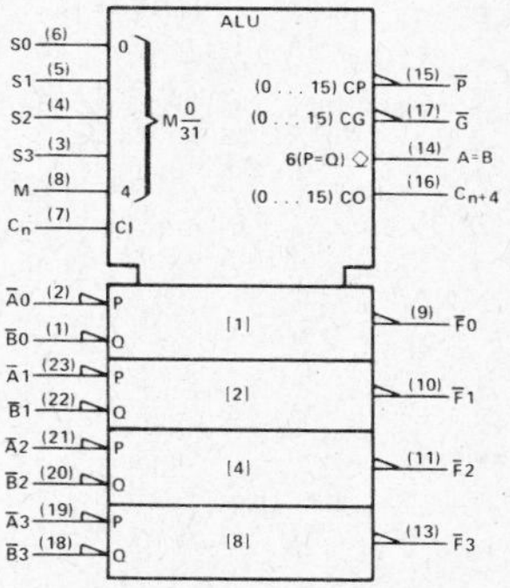
ALU
S0 (6)
S1 (5)
S2 (4)
S3 (3)
M (8)
Cn (7)
0
M 0/31
4
CI
(0 . . . 15) CP
(0 . . . 15) CG
6(P=Q)
(0 . . . 15) CO
(15) P̄
(17) Ḡ
(14) A=B
(16) Cn+4
Ā0 (2) P
B̄0 (1) Q
[1]
(9) F̄0
Ā1 (23) P
B̄1 (22) Q
[2]
(10) F̄1
Ā2 (21) P
B̄2 (20) Q
[4]
(11) F̄2
Ā3 (19) P
B̄3 (18) Q
[8]
(13) F̄3

Pin numbers shown are JT, JW, NT, and NW packages.

TYPICAL ADDITION TIMES (C_L = 15 pF, R_L = 280 Ω, T_A = 25°C)

NUMBER OF BITS	ADDITION TIMES			PACKAGE COUNT		CARRY METHOD BETWEEN ALUs
	USING 'AS881A AND 'AS882	USING 'AS181A AND 'AS882	USING 'S181 AND 'S182	ARITHMETIC LOGIC UNITS	LOOK-AHEAD CARRY GENERATORS	
1 to 4	5 ns	5 ns	11 ns	1		NONE
5 to 8	10 ns	10 ns	18 ns	2		RIPPLE
9 to 16	14 ns	14 ns	19 ns	3 or 4	1	FULL LOOK-AHEAD
17 to 64	19 ns	19 ns	28 ns	5 to 16	2 to 5	FULL LOOK-AHEAD

TEXAS INSTRUMENTS
POST OFFICE BOX 225012 • DALLAS, TEXAS 75265

description

The 'AS181A and 'AS881A are arithmetic logic units (ALU)/function generators that have a complexity of 75 and 77 equivalent gates, respectively, on a monolithic chip. These circuits perform 16 binary arithmetic operations on two 4-bit words as shown in Tables 1 and 2. These operations are selected by the four function-select lines (S0, S1, S2, S3) and include addition, subtraction, decrement, and straight transfer. When performing arithmetic manipulations, the internal carries must be enabled by applying a low-level voltage to the mode control input (M). A full carry look-ahead scheme is made available in these devices for fast, simultaneous carry generation by means of two cascade-outputs (pins 15 and 17) for the four bits in the package. When used in conjunction with the SN54AS882 or SN74AS882 full carry look-ahead circuits, high-speed arithmetic operations can be performed. The typical addition times shown previously illustrate the little additional time required for addition of longer words when full carry look-ahead is employed. The method of cascading 'AS882 circuits with these ALUs to provide multilevel full carry look-ahead is illustrated under signal designations.

If high speed is not of importance, a ripple-carry input (C_n) and a ripple-carry output (C_{n+4}) are available. However, the ripple-carry delay has also been minimized so that arithmetic manipulations for small word lengths can be performed without external circuitry.

The 'AS181A and 'AS881A will accommodate active-high or active-low data if the pin designations are interpreted as follows:

PIN NUMBER	2	1	23	22	21	20	19	18	9	10	11	13	7	16	15	17
Active-low data (Table 1)	$\overline{A0}$	$\overline{B0}$	$\overline{A1}$	$\overline{B1}$	$\overline{A2}$	$\overline{B2}$	$\overline{A3}$	$\overline{B3}$	$\overline{F0}$	$\overline{F1}$	$\overline{F2}$	$\overline{F3}$	C_n	C_{n+4}	$\overline{P}$	$\overline{G}$
Active-high data (Table 2)	A0	B0	A1	B1	A2	B2	A3	B3	F0	F1	F2	F3	$\overline{C}_n$	$\overline{C}_{n+4}$	X	Y

Subtraction is accomplished by 1's complement addition where the 1's complement of the subtrahend is generated internally. The resultant output is A−B−1, which requires an end-around or forced carry to provide A−B.

The 'AS181A and 'AS881A can also be utilized as a comparator. The A = B output is internally decoded from the function outputs (F0, F1, F2, F3) so that when two words of equal magnitude are applied at the A and B inputs, it will assume a high level to indicate equality (A = B). The ALU must be in the subtract mode with C_n = H when performing this comparison. The A = B output is open-collector so that it can be wire-AND connected to give a comparison for more than four bits. The carry output (C_{n+4}) can also be used to supply relative magnitude information. Again, the ALU must be placed in the subtract mode by placing the function select input S3, S2, S1, S0 at L, H, H, L, respectively.

INPUT C_n	OUTPUT C_{n+4}	ACTIVE-LOW DATA (FIGURE 1)	ACTIVE-HIGH DATA (FIGURE 2)
H	H	$A \geq B$	$A \leq B$
H	L	$A < B$	$A > B$
L	H	$A > B$	$A < B$
L	L	$A \leq B$	$A \geq B$

These circuits have been designed to not only incorporate all of the designer's requirements for arithmetic operations, but also to provide 16 possible functions of two Boolean variables without the use of external circuitry. These logic functions are selected by use of the four function-select inputs (S0, S1, S2, S3) with the mode-control input (M) at a high level to disable the internal carry. The 16 logic functions are detailed in Tables 1 and 2 and include exclusive-OR, NAND, AND, NOR, and OR functions.

description (continued)

The 'AS881A has the same pinout and same functionality as the 'AS181A except for the $\overline{P}$, $\overline{G}$, and C_{n+4} outputs when the device is in the logic mode (M = H).

In the logic mode the 'AS881A provides the user with a status check on the input words A and B, and the ouput word F. While in the logic mode the $\overline{P}$, $\overline{G}$, and C_{n+4} outputs supply status information based upon the following logical combinations:

$\overline{P} = F0 + F1 + F2 + F3$
$\overline{G} = H$
$C_{n+4} = PC_n$

FUNCTION TABLE FOR INPUT BITS EQUAL/NOT EQUAL

S0 = S3 = H, S1 = S2 = L, and M = H

C_n	DATA INPUTS				OUTPUTS		
					$\overline{G}$	$\overline{P}$	C_{n+4}
H	$\overline{A0} = \overline{B0}$	$\overline{A1} = \overline{B1}$	$\overline{A2} = \overline{B2}$	$\overline{A3} = \overline{B3}$	H	L	H
L	$\overline{A0} = \overline{B0}$	$\overline{A1} = \overline{B1}$	$\overline{A2} = \overline{B2}$	$\overline{A3} = \overline{B3}$	H	L	L
X	$\overline{A0} \neq \overline{B0}$	X	X	X	H	H	L
X	X	$\overline{A1} \neq \overline{B1}$	X	X	H	H	L
X	X	X	$\overline{A2} \neq \overline{B2}$	X	H	H	L
X	X	X	X	$\overline{A3} \neq \overline{B3}$	H	H	L

FUNCTION TABLE FOR INPUT PAIRS HIGH/NOT HIGH

S0 = S1 = S3 = L, S2 = H, and M = H

C_n	DATA INPUTS				OUTPUTS		
					$\overline{G}$	$\overline{P}$	C_{n+4}
H	$\overline{A0}$ or $\overline{B0}$ = L	$\overline{A1}$ or $\overline{B1}$ = L	$\overline{A2}$ or $\overline{B2}$ = L	$\overline{A3}$ or $\overline{B3}$ = L	H	L	H
L	$\overline{A0}$ or $\overline{B0}$ = L	$\overline{A1}$ or $\overline{B1}$ = L	$\overline{A2}$ or $\overline{B2}$ = L	$\overline{A3}$ or $\overline{B3}$ = L	H	L	L
X	$\overline{A0} = \overline{B0} = H$	X	X	X	H	H	L
X	X	$\overline{A1} = \overline{B1} = H$	X	X	H	H	L
X	X	X	$\overline{A2} = \overline{B2} = H$	X	H	H	L
X	X	X	X	$\overline{A3} = \overline{B3} = H$	H	H	L

The combination of signals on the S3 through S0 control lines determine the operation performed on the data words to generate the output bits $\overline{F}i$. By monitoring the $\overline{P}$ and C_{n+4} outputs, the user can determine if all pairs of input bits are equal (see table above) or if any pair of inputs are both high (see table above). The 'AS881A has the unique feature of providing an A = B status while the exclusive-OR($\oplus$) function is being utilized. When the control inputs (S3, S2, S1, S0) equal H, L, L, H; a status check is generated to determine whether all pairs ($\overline{A}i$, $\overline{B}i$) are equal in the following manner: $\overline{P} = (A0 \oplus B0) + (A1 \oplus B1) + (A2 \oplus B2) + (A3 \oplus B3)$. This unique bit-by-bit comparison of the data words, which is available on the totem-pole $\overline{P}$ output, is particularly useful when cascading 'AS881s. As the A = B condition is sensed in the first stage, the signal is propagated through the same ports used for carry generation in the arithmetic mode ($\overline{P}$ and $\overline{G}$). Thus the A = B status is transmitted to the second stage more quickly without the need for external multiplexing logic. The A = B open-collector output allows the user to check the validity of the bit-by-bit result by comparing the two signals for parity.

If the user wishes to check for any pair of data inputs ($\overline{A}i$, $\overline{B}i$) being high, it is necessary to set the control lines (S3,S2,S1,S0) to L, H, L, L. The data pairs will then be ANDed together and the results ORed in the following manner: $\overline{P} = \overline{A0}\overline{B0} + \overline{A1}\overline{B1} + \overline{A2}\overline{B2} + \overline{A3}\overline{B3}$.

S3	S2	S1	S0	M	$\overline{P} = F0 + F1 + F2 + F3$
L	H	L	L	H	$\overline{A0}\overline{B0} + \overline{A1}\overline{B1} + \overline{A2}\overline{B2} + \overline{A3}\overline{B3}$
H	L	L	H	H	$(A0 \oplus B0) + (A1 \oplus B1) + (A2 \oplus B2) + (A3 \oplus B3)$

signal designations

In both Figures 1 and 2, the polarity indicators (⊾) indicate that the associated input or output is active-low with respect to the function shown inside the symbol and the symbols are the same in both figures. The signal designations in Figure 1 agree with the indicated internal functions based on active-low data, and are for use with the logic functions and arithmetic operations shown in Table 1. The signal designations have been changed in Figure 2 to accommodate the logic functions and arithmetic operations for the active-high data given in Table 2. The 'AS181A and 'AS881A together with 'AS882 and 'S182 can be used with the signal designation of either Figure 1 or Figure 2.

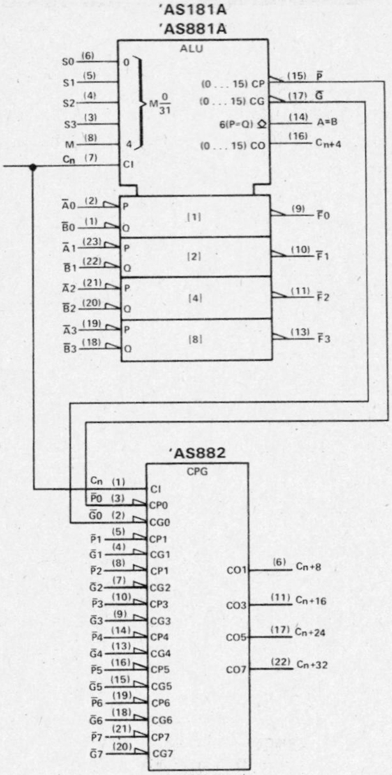

'AS181A
'AS881A
ALU
S0 (6)
S1 (5)
S2 (4)
S3 (3)
M (8)
Cn (7)
CI
(0 . . . 15) CP (15) P̄
(0 . . . 15) CG (17) Ḡ
6(P=Q) (14) A=B
(0 . . . 15) CO (16) Cn+4
Ā0 (2)
B̄0 (1)
Ā1 (23)
B̄1 (22)
Ā2 (21)
B̄2 (20)
Ā3 (19)
B̄3 (18)
(9) F̄0
(10) F̄1
(11) F̄2
(13) F̄3
'AS882
CPG
Cn (1) CI
P̄0 (3) CP0
Ḡ0 (2) CG0
CO1 (6) Cn+8
CO3 (11) Cn+16
CO5 (17) Cn+24
CO7 (22) Cn+32

FIGURE 1
(USE WITH TABLE 1)

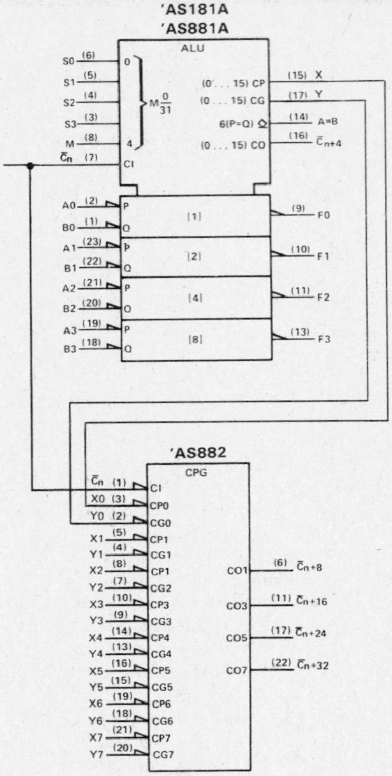

'AS181A
'AS881A
ALU
S0 (6)
S1 (5)
S2 (4)
S3 (3)
M (8)
C̄n (7)
CI
(0 . . . 15) CP (15) X
(0 . . . 15) CG (17) Y
6(P=Q) (14) A=B
(0 . . . 15) CO (16) C̄n+4
A0 (2)
B0 (1)
A1 (23)
B1 (22)
A2 (21)
B2 (20)
A3 (19)
B3 (18)
(9) F0
(10) F1
(11) F2
(13) F3
'AS882
CPG
C̄n (1) CI
X0 (3) CP0
Y0 (2) CG0
CO1 (6) C̄n+8
CO3 (11) C̄n+16
CO5 (17) C̄n+24
CO7 (22) C̄n+32

FIGURE 2
(USE WITH TABLE 2)

TABLE 1

SELECTION				ACTIVE-LOW DATA		
				M = H	M = L; ARITHMETIC OPERATIONS	
S3	S2	S1	S0	LOGIC FUNCTIONS	C_n = L (no carry)	C_n = H (with carry)
L	L	L	L	F = $\overline{A}$	F = A MINUS 1	F = A
L	L	L	H	F = $\overline{AB}$	F = AB MINUS 1	F = AB
L	L	H	L	F = $\overline{A}$ + B	F = A$\overline{B}$ MINUS 1	F = A$\overline{B}$
L	L	H	H	F = 1	F = MINUS 1 (2's COMP)	F = ZERO
L	H	L	L	F = $\overline{A + B}$	F = A PLUS (A + $\overline{B}$)	F = A PLUS (A + $\overline{B}$) PLUS 1
L	H	L	H	F = $\overline{B}$	F = AB PLUS (A + $\overline{B}$)	F = AB PLUS (A + $\overline{B}$) PLUS 1
L	H	H	L	F = $\overline{A \oplus B}$	F = A MINUS B MINUS 1	F = A MINUS B
L	H	H	H	F = A + $\overline{B}$	F = A + $\overline{B}$	F = (A + $\overline{B}$) PLUS 1
H	L	L	L	F = $\overline{A}$B	F = A PLUS (A + B)	F = A PLUS (A + B) PLUS 1
H	L	L	H	F = A $\oplus$ B	F = A PLUS B	F = A PLUS B PLUS 1
H	L	H	L	F = B	F = A$\overline{B}$ PLUS (A + B)	F = A$\overline{B}$ PLUS (A + B) PLUS 1
H	L	H	H	F = A + B	F = (A + B)	F = (A + B) PLUS 1
H	H	L	L	F = 0	F = A PLUS A†	F = A PLUS A PLUS 1
H	H	L	H	F = A$\overline{B}$	F = AB PLUS A	F = AB PLUS A PLUS 1
H	H	H	L	F = AB	F = A$\overline{B}$ PLUS A	F = A$\overline{B}$ PLUS A PLUS 1
H	H	H	H	F = A	F = A	F = A PLUS 1

†Each bit is shifted to the next more significant position.

TABLE 2

SELECTION				ACTIVE-HIGH DATA		
				M = H	M = L; ARITHMETIC OPERATIONS	
S3	S2	S1	S0	LOGIC FUNCTIONS	$\overline{C}_n$ = H (no carry)	$\overline{C}_n$ = L (with carry)
L	L	L	L	F = $\overline{A}$	F = A	F = A PLUS 1
L	L	L	H	F = $\overline{A + B}$	F = A + B	F = (A + B) PLUS 1
L	L	H	L	F = $\overline{A}$B	F = A + $\overline{B}$	F = (A + $\overline{B}$) PLUS 1
L	L	H	H	F = 0	F = MINUS 1 (2's COMPL)	F = ZERO
L	H	L	L	F = $\overline{AB}$	F = A PLUS A$\overline{B}$	F = A PLUS A$\overline{B}$ PLUS 1
L	H	L	H	F = $\overline{B}$	F = (A + B) PLUS A$\overline{B}$	F = (A + B) PLUS A$\overline{B}$ PLUS 1
L	H	H	L	F = A $\oplus$ B	F = A MINUS B MINUS 1	F = A MINUS B
L	H	H	H	F = A$\overline{B}$	F = A$\overline{B}$ MINUS 1	F = A$\overline{B}$
H	L	L	L	F = $\overline{A}$ + B	F = A PLUS AB	F = A PLUS AB PLUS 1
H	L	L	H	F = $\overline{A \oplus B}$	F = A PLUS B	F = A PLUS B PLUS 1
H	L	H	L	F = B	F = (A + $\overline{B}$) PLUS AB	F = (A + $\overline{B}$) PLUS AB PLUS 1
H	L	H	H	F = AB	F = AB MINUS 1	F = AB
H	H	L	L	F = 1	F = A PLUS A†	F = A PLUS A PLUS 1
H	H	L	H	F = A + $\overline{B}$	F = (A + B) PLUS A	F = (A + B) PLUS A PLUS 1
H	H	H	L	F = A + B	F = (A + $\overline{B}$) PLUS A	F = (A + $\overline{B}$) PLUS A PLUS 1
H	H	H	H	F = A	F = A MINUS 1	F = A

logic diagram (positive logic)

'AS181A

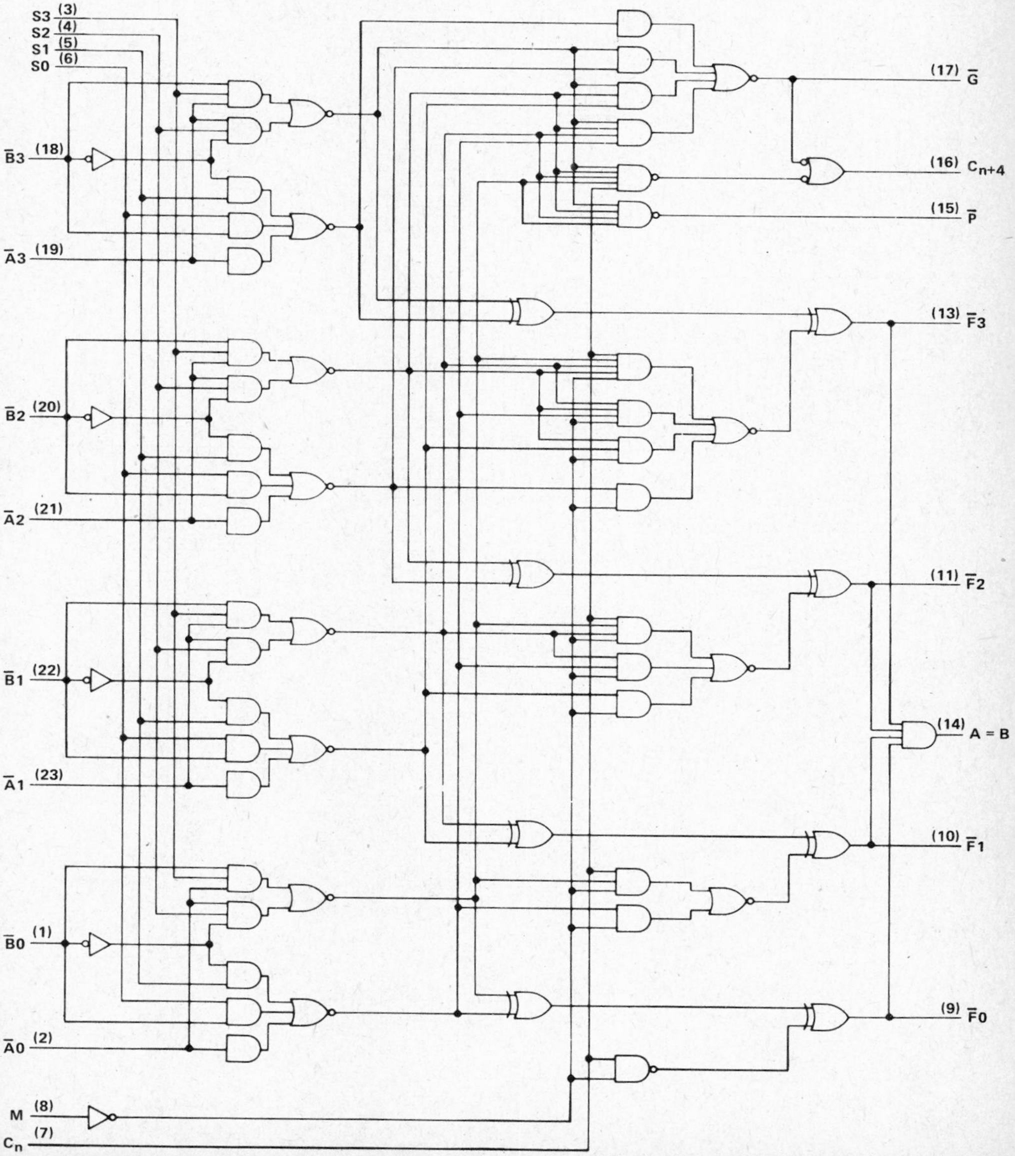
S3 (3)
S2 (4)
S1 (5)
S0 (6)
B̄3 (18)
Ā3 (19)
B̄2 (20)
Ā2 (21)
B̄1 (22)
Ā1 (23)
B̄0 (1)
Ā0 (2)
M (8)
Cn (7)
(17) Ḡ
(16) Cn+4
(15) P̄
(13) F̄3
(11) F̄2
(14) A = B
(10) F̄1
(9) F̄0

logic diagram (positive logic)

'AS881A

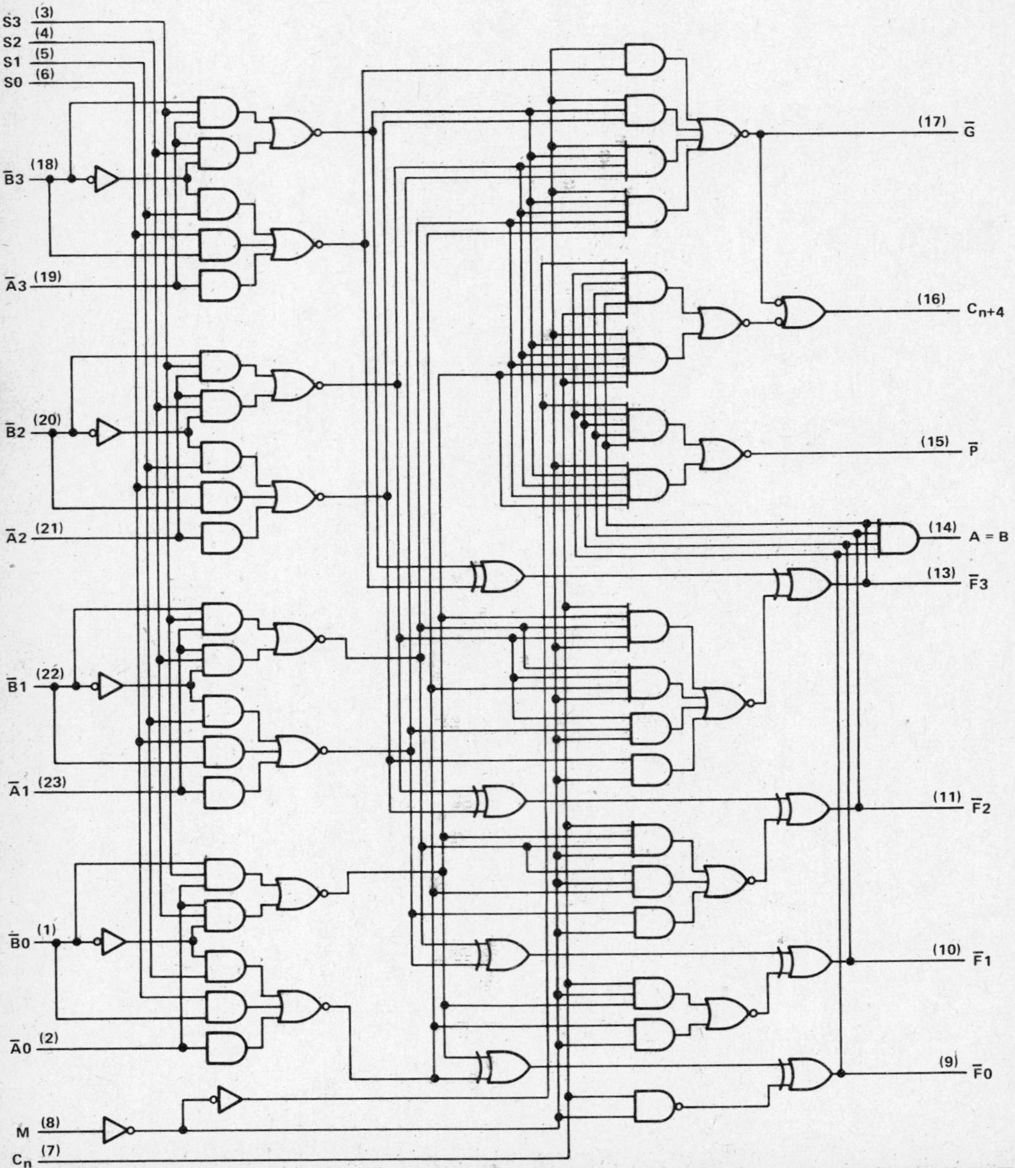
S3 (3)
S2 (4)
S1 (5)
S0 (6)
B̄3 (18)
Ā3 (19)
B̄2 (20)
Ā2 (21)
B̄1 (22)
Ā1 (23)
B̄0 (1)
Ā0 (2)
M (8)
Cn (7)
(17) Ḡ
(16) Cn+4
(15) P̄
(14) A = B
(13) F̄3
(11) F̄2
(10) F̄1
(9) F̄0

TEXAS INSTRUMENTS
POST OFFICE BOX 225012 • DALLAS, TEXAS 75265

absolute maximum ratings over operating free-air temperature range (unless otherwise noted)

Supply voltage, V_{CC} . . . . 7 V
Input voltage . . . . 7 V
Off-state output voltage (A = B output only) . . . . 7 V
Operating free-air temperature range: SN54AS181A, SN54AS881A . . . . −55°C to 125°C
SN74AS181A, SN74AS881A . . . . 0°C to 70°C
Storage temperature range . . . . −65°C to 150°C

recommended operating conditions

			SN54AS'			SN74AS'			UNIT
			MIN	NOM	MAX	MIN	NOM	MAX	
V_{CC}	Supply voltage		4.5	5	5.5	4.5	5	5.5	V
V_{IH}	High-level input voltage		2			2			V
V_{IL}	Low-level input voltage				0.8			0.8	V
V_{OH}	High-level output voltage	A = B output only			5.5			5.5	V
I_{OH}	High-level output current	All outputs except A = B and $\overline{G}$			−2			−2	mA
		$\overline{G}$			−3			−3	mA
I_{OL}	Low-level output current	All outputs except $\overline{G}$			20			20	mA
		$\overline{G}$			48			48	mA
T_A	Operating free-air temperature		−55		125	0		70	°C

2

LSI Devices

electrical characteristics over recommended operating free-air temperature range (unless otherwise noted)

PARAMETER		TEST CONDITIONS		SN54AS' MIN	SN54AS' TYP†	SN54AS' MAX	SN74AS' MIN	SN74AS' TYP†	SN74AS' MAX	UNIT
V_{IK}		V_{CC} = 4.5 V,	I_I = −18 mA			−1.2			−1.2	V
V_{OH}	Any output except A = B	V_{CC} = 4.5 V to 5.5 V,	I_{OH} = −2 mA	V_{CC}−2			V_{CC}−2			V
	$\overline{G}$	V_{CC} = 4.5 V,	I_{OH} = −3 mA	2.4	3.4		2.4	3.4		V
I_{OH}	A = B	V_{CC} = 4.5 V,	V_{OH} = 5.5 V			0.1			0.1	mA
V_{OL}	Any output except $\overline{G}$	V_{CC} = 4.5 V,	I_{OL} = 20 mA		0.3	0.5		0.3	0.5	V
	$\overline{G}$	V_{CC} = 4.5 V,	I_{OL} = 48 mA		0.4	0.5		0.4	0.5	V
I_I	M input	V_{CC} = 5.5 V,	V_I = 7 V			0.1			0.1	mA
	Any A or B input					0.3			0.3	
	Any S input					0.4			0.4	
	Carry input					0.6			0.6	
I_{IH}	M input	V_{CC} = 5.5 V,	V_I = 2.7 V			20			20	μA
	Any A or B input					60			60	
	Any S input					80			80	
	Carry input					120			120	
I_{IL}	M input	V_{CC} = 5.5 V,	V_I = 0.4 V			−2			−2	mA
	Any A or B input					−6			−6	
	Any S input					−8			−8	
	Carry input					−12			−12	
I_O‡	All outputs except A = B and $\overline{G}$	V_{CC} = 5.5 V,	V_O = 2.25 V	−30	−45	−112	−30	−45	−112	mA
	$\overline{G}$				−165			−165		
I_{CC}		V_{CC} = 5.5 V	'AS181A		135	200		135	200	mA
			'AS881A		135	210		135	210	

†All typical values are at V_{CC} = 5 V, T_A = 25°C.
‡The output conditions have been chosen to produce a current that closely approximates one-half of the true short-circuit current, I_{OS}.

TEXAS INSTRUMENTS
POST OFFICE BOX 225012 • DALLAS, TEXAS 75265

switching characteristics (see Note 1)

PARAMETER	FROM (INPUT)	TO (OUTPUT)	TEST CONDITIONS	V_{CC} = 5 V, C_L = 15 pF, R_L = 500 Ω (280 Ω for A = B), T_A = 25 °C			V_{CC} = 4.5 V to 5.5 V, C_L = 50 pF (15 pF for A = B), R_L = 500 Ω (280 Ω for A = B), T_A = MIN to MAX						UNIT
				'AS181A 'AS881A			SN54AS181A SN54AS881A			SN74AS181A SN74AS881A			
				MIN	TYP†	MAX	MIN	TYP†	MAX	MIN	TYP†	MAX	
t_{pd}	C_n	C_{n+4}			5		2	7	11	2	7	9	ns
t_{pd}	Any $\overline{A}$ or $\overline{B}$	C_{n+4}	M = 0 V, S1 = S2 = 0 V, S0 = S3 = 4.5 V ($\overline{\text{SUM}}$ mode)		6		2	8	14	2	8	12	ns
t_{pd}	Any $\overline{A}$ or $\overline{B}$	C_{n+4}	M = 0 V, S0 = S3 = 0 V, S1 = S2 = 4.5 V ($\overline{\text{DIFF}}$ mode)		7		2	8	20	2	8	16	ns
t_{pd}	C_n	Any $\overline{F}$	M = 0 V ($\overline{\text{SUM}}$ or $\overline{\text{DIFF}}$ mode)		5		3	6	11	3	6	9	ns
t_{pd}	Any $\overline{A}$ or $\overline{B}$	$\overline{G}$	M = 0 V, S1 = S2 = 0 V, S0 = S3 = 4.5 V ($\overline{\text{SUM}}$ mode)		4		2	5	9	2	5	7	ns
t_{pd}	Any $\overline{A}$ or $\overline{B}$	$\overline{G}$	M = 0 V, S0 = S3 = 0 V, S1 = S2 = 4.5 V ($\overline{\text{DIFF}}$ mode)		5		2	6	12	2	6	9	ns
t_{pd}	Any $\overline{A}$ or $\overline{B}$	$\overline{P}$	M = 0 V, S1 = S2 = 0 V, S0 = S3 = 4.5 V ($\overline{\text{SUM}}$ mode)		5		2	6	11	2	6	8	ns
t_{pd}	Any $\overline{A}$ or $\overline{B}$	$\overline{P}$	M = 0 V, S0 = S3 = 0 V, S1 = S2 = 4.5 V ($\overline{\text{DIFF}}$ mode)		5		2	6	13	2	6	10	ns
t_{pd}	$\overline{A}i$ or $\overline{B}i$	$\overline{F}i$	M = 0 V, S1 = S2 = 0 V, S0 = S3 = 4.5 V ($\overline{\text{SUM}}$ mode)		5		2	5	11	2	5	8	ns
t_{pd}	$\overline{A}i$ or $\overline{B}i$	$\overline{F}i$	M = 0 V, S0 = S1 = 0 V, S1 = S2 = 4.5 V ($\overline{\text{DIFF}}$ mode)		5		2	6	12	2	6	10	ns
t_{pd}	$\overline{A}i$ or $\overline{B}i$	$\overline{F}i$	M = 4.5 V (LOGIC mode)		6		2	6	16	2	6	11	ns
t_{pd}	Any $\overline{A}$ or $\overline{B}$	A = B	M = 0 V, S0 = S3 = 0 V, S1 = S2 = 4.5 V ($\overline{\text{DIFF}}$ mode)		12		4	14	26	4	14	21	ns

additional 'AS881A switching characteristics involving status checks (see Note 1)

PARAMETER	FROM (INPUT)	TO (OUTPUT)	TEST CONDITIONS	V_{CC} = 5 V, C_L = 15 pF, R_L = 500 Ω, T_A = 25 °C			V_{CC} = 4.5 V to 5.5 V, C_L = 50 pF, R_L = 500 Ω, T_A = MIN to MAX						UNIT
				'AS881A			SN54AS881A			SN74AS881A			
				MIN	TYP†	MAX	MIN	TYP†	MAX	MIN	TYP†	MAX	
t_{pd}	Any $\overline{A}$ or $\overline{B}$	$\overline{P}$	C_n = 4.5V, M = 4.5 V, S0 = S3 = 4.5 V, S1 = S2 = 0 V, Equality ($\overline{A}i = \overline{B}i$ or $\overline{A}i \neq \overline{B}i$)		8		2	10	19	2	10	15	ns
t_{pd}	Any $\overline{A}$ or $\overline{B}$	C_{n+4}	C_n = 4.5 V, M = 4.5 V, S0 = S3 = 4.5 V, S1 = S2 = 0 V, Equality ($\overline{A}i = \overline{B}i$ or $\overline{A}i \neq \overline{B}i$)		10		2	12	24	2	12	18	ns
t_{pd}	Any $\overline{A}$ or $\overline{B}$	$\overline{P}$	C_n = 4.5 V, M = 4.5 V, S2 = 4.5 V, S0 = S1 = S3 = 0 V, ($\overline{A}i = \overline{B}i$ = H or $\overline{A}i$ or $\overline{B}i$ = L)		8		2	10	19	2	10	15	ns
t_{pd}	Any $\overline{A}$ or $\overline{B}$	C_{n+4}	C_n = 4.5 V, M = 4.5 V, S2 = 4.5 V, S0 = S1 = S3 = 0 V, ($\overline{A}i = \overline{B}i$ = H or $\overline{A}i$ or $\overline{B}i$ = L)		11		2	13	25	2	13	19	ns

t_{pd} = t_{PHL} or t_{PLH}

†All typical values are at V_{CC} = 5 V, T_A = 25 °C.

NOTE 1: Load circuit and voltage waveforms are shown in Section 1.

2

LSI Devices

PARAMETER MEASUREMENT INFORMATION

$\overline{\text{SUM}}$ MODE TEST TABLE

FUNCTION INPUTS: S0 = S3 = 4.5 V, S1 = S2 = M = 0 V

PARAMETER	INPUT UNDER TEST	OTHER INPUT SAME BIT		OTHER DATA INPUTS		OUTPUT UNDER TEST	OUTPUT WAVEFORM (SEE NOTE 1)
		APPLY 4.5 V	APPLY GND	APPLY 4.5 V	APPLY GND		
t_{PLH} t_{PHL}	$\overline{A}i$	$\overline{B}i$	None	Remaining $\overline{A}$ and $\overline{B}$	C_n	$\overline{F}i$	In-Phase
t_{PLH} t_{PHL}	$\overline{B}i$	$\overline{A}i$	None	Remaining $\overline{A}$ and $\overline{B}$	C_n	$\overline{F}i$	In-Phase
t_{PLH} t_{PHL}	$\overline{A}i$	$\overline{B}i$	None	None	Remaining $\overline{A}$ and $\overline{B}$, C_n	$\overline{P}$	In-Phase
t_{PLH} t_{PHL}	$\overline{B}i$	$\overline{A}i$	None	None	Remaining $\overline{A}$ and $\overline{B}$, C_n	$\overline{P}$	In-Phase
t_{PLH} t_{PHL}	$\overline{A}i$	None	$\overline{B}i$	Remaining $\overline{B}$	Remaining $\overline{A}$, C_n	$\overline{G}$	In-Phase
t_{PLH} t_{PHL}	$\overline{B}i$	None	$\overline{A}i$	Remaining $\overline{B}$	Remaining $\overline{A}$, C_n	$\overline{G}$	In-Phase
t_{PLH} t_{PHL}	C_n	None	None	All $\overline{A}$	All $\overline{B}$	Any $\overline{F}$ or C_{n+4}	In-Phase
t_{PLH} t_{PHL}	$\overline{A}i$	None	$\overline{B}i$	Remaining $\overline{B}$	Remaining $\overline{A}$, C_n	C_{n+4}	Out-of-Phase
t_{PLH} t_{PHL}	$\overline{B}i$	None	$\overline{A}i$	Remaining $\overline{B}$	Remaining $\overline{A}$, C_n	C_{n+4}	Out-of-Phase

$\overline{\text{DIFF}}$ MODE TEST TABLE

FUNCTION INPUTS: S1 = S2 = 4.5 V, S0 = S3 = M = 0 V

PARAMETER	INPUT UNDER TEST	OTHER INPUT SAME BIT		OTHER DATA INPUTS		OUTPUT UNDER TEST	OUTPUT WAVEFORM (SEE NOTE 1)
		APPLY 4.5 V	APPLY GND	APPLY 4.5 V	APPLY GND		
t_{PLH} t_{PHL}	$\overline{A}i$	None	$\overline{B}i$	Remaining $\overline{A}$	Remaining B, C_n	$\overline{F}i$	In-Phase
t_{PLH} t_{PHL}	$\overline{B}i$	$\overline{A}i$	None	Remaining $\overline{A}$	Remaining B, C_n	$\overline{F}i$	Out-of-Phase
t_{PLH} t_{PHL}	$\overline{A}i$	None	$\overline{B}i$	None	Remaining $\overline{A}$ and $\overline{B}$, C_n	$\overline{P}$	In-Phase
t_{PLH} t_{PHL}	$\overline{B}i$	$\overline{A}i$	None	None	Remaining $\overline{A}$ and $\overline{B}$, C_n	$\overline{P}$	Out-of-Phase
t_{PLH} t_{PHL}	$\overline{A}i$	$\overline{B}i$	None	None	Remaining $\overline{A}$ and $\overline{B}$, C_n	$\overline{G}$	In-Phase
t_{PLH} t_{PHL}	$\overline{B}i$	None	$\overline{A}i$	None	Remaining $\overline{A}$ and $\overline{B}$, C_n	$\overline{G}$	Out-of-Phase
t_{PLH} t_{PHL}	$\overline{A}i$	None	$\overline{B}i$	Remaining $\overline{A}$	remaining $\overline{B}$, C_n	A = B	In-Phase
t_{PLH} t_{PHL}	$\overline{B}i$	$\overline{A}i$	None	Remaining $\overline{A}$	Remaining $\overline{B}$, C_n	A = B	Out-of-Phase
t_{PLH} t_{PHL}	C_n	None	None	All $\overline{A}$ and $\overline{B}$	None	C_{n+4} or any $\overline{F}$	In-Phase
t_{PLH} t_{PHL}	$\overline{A}i$	$\overline{B}i$	None	None	Remaining $\overline{A}$, $\overline{B}$, C_n	C_{n+4}	Out-of-Phase
t_{PLH} t_{PHL}	$\overline{B}i$	None	$\overline{A}i$	None	Remaining $\overline{A}$, $\overline{B}$, C_n	C_{n+4}	In-Phase

NOTE 1: Load circuit and voltage waveforms are shown in Section 1.

TEXAS INSTRUMENTS
POST OFFICE BOX 225012 • DALLAS, TEXAS 75265

SN54LS222, SN54LS224, SN54LS227, SN54LS228
SN74LS222, SN74LS224, SN74LS227, SN74LS228
16 X 4 SYNCHRONOUS FIRST-IN FIRST-OUT MEMORIES

JANUARY 1981 – REVISED MARCH 1985

- **Independent Synchonous Inputs and Outputs**
- **16 Words of 4 Bits Each**
- **3-State Outputs Drive Bus Lines Directly**
- **Data Rates from 0 to 10 MHz**
- **Fall-Through Time . . . 50 ns Typ**
- **Data Terminals Arranged for Optimum PC Board Layout**
- **Expandable Using External Gating**

SN54LS222, SN54LS227 . . . J PACKAGE
SN74LS222, SN74LS227 . . . J OR N PACKAGE
(TOP VIEW)

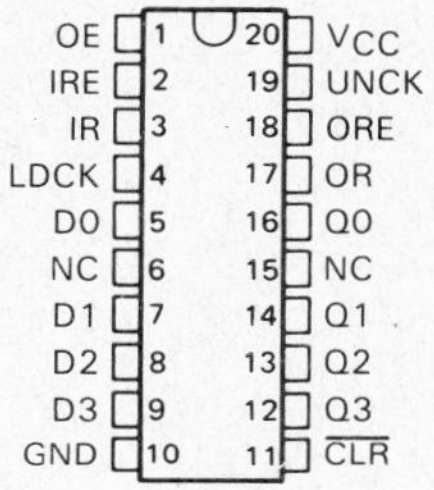
OE 1
IRE 2
IR 3
LDCK 4
D0 5
NC 6
D1 7
D2 8
D3 9
GND 10
20 VCC
19 UNCK
18 ORE
17 OR
16 Q0
15 NC
14 Q1
13 Q2
12 Q3
11 CLR

SN54LS224, SN54LS228 . . . J PACKAGE
SN74LS224, SN74LS228 . . . J OR N PACKAGE
(TOP VIEW)

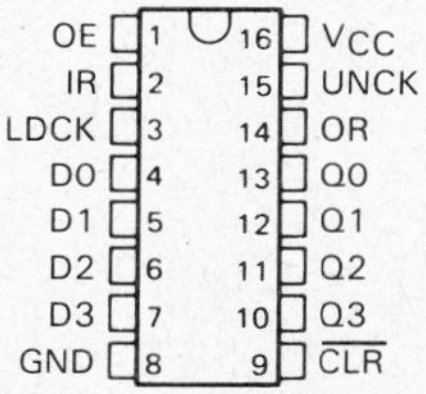
OE 1
IR 2
LDCK 3
D0 4
D1 5
D2 6
D3 7
GND 8
16 VCC
15 UNCK
14 OR
13 Q0
12 Q1
11 Q2
10 Q3
9 CLR

NC – No internal connection

For chip carrier information contact the factory.

description

These 64-bit memories are Low-Power Schottky memory arrays organized as 16 words of 4 bits each. They can be expanded in multiples of 15m + 1 words or 4n bits, or both, (where n is the number of packages in the vertical array and m is the number of packages in the horizontal array) however some external gating is required (see Figure 1). For longer words using the 'LS224 or 'LS228, the IR signals of the first-rank packages and OR signals of the last-rank packages must be ANDed for proper synchronization.

TYPE	INPUT-READY ENABLE AND OUTPUT-READY ENABLE	OUTPUT
'LS222	Yes	3-State
'LS224	No	3-State
'LS227	Yes	Open-collector
'LS228	No	Open-collector

operation

A FIFO memory is a storage device that allows data to be written into and read from its array at independent data rates. These FIFOs are designed to process data at rates from 0 to 10 MHz in a bit-parallel format, word by word. Data is written into the memory on a high-to-low transition at the load clock input (LDCK) and read out on a low-to-high transition at the unload clock input (UNCK).

The memory is full when the number of words clocked in exceeds the number of words clocked out by 16. When the memory is full, LDCK signals have no effect. When the memory is empty, UNCK signals have no effect.

Status of the FIFO memory (see timing diagram) is monitored by the input ready (IR) and output ready (OR) flags that indicate "not full" and "not empty" conditions. The IR output will be high only when the memory is not full and the LDCK input is low. The OR output will be high only when the memory is not empty and UNCK is high.

A low level at the clear ($\overline{CLR}$) input resets the internal stack control counters and also sets IR high and OR low to indicate that old data remaining at the data outputs is invalid. Data outputs are noninverting with respect to the data inputs and are at high impedance when output enable (OE) is low. OE does not affect the IR and OR outputs.

TEXAS INSTRUMENTS
POST OFFICE BOX 225012 • DALLAS, TEXAS 75265

functional block diagram (positive logic)

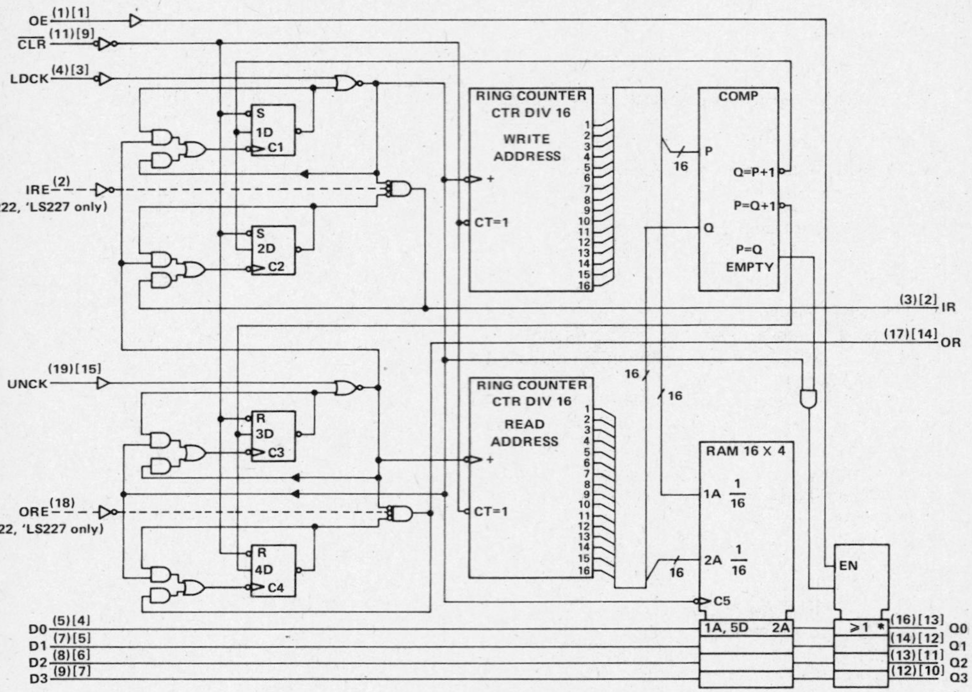
OE (1)[1]
CLR (11)[9]
LDCK (4)[3]
IRE (2)
('LS222, 'LS227 only)
UNCK (19)[15]
ORE (18)
('LS222, 'LS227 only)
RING COUNTER
CTR DIV 16
WRITE
ADDRESS
CT=1
READ
ADDRESS
COMP
P
Q
Q=P+1
P=Q+1
P=Q
EMPTY
RAM 16 X 4
1A
2A
C5
1A, 5D
EN
(3)[2] IR
(17)[14] OR
D0 (5)[4]
D1 (7)[5]
D2 (8)[6]
D3 (9)[7]
(16)[13] Q0
(14)[12] Q1
(13)[11] Q2
(12)[10] Q3

*'LS222 and 'LS224 have 3-state (▽)outputs.
'LS227 and 'LS228 have open-collector (◇) outputs.

('LS222 and 'LS227 pin numbers)
['LS224 and 'LS228 pin numbers]

timing diagram

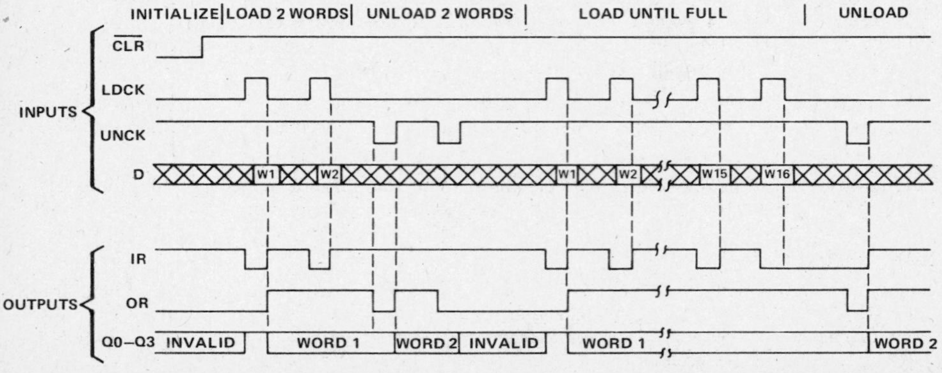
INITIALIZE
LOAD 2 WORDS
UNLOAD 2 WORDS
LOAD UNTIL FULL
UNLOAD
INPUTS
CLR
LDCK
UNCK
D
W1
W2
W15
W16
OUTPUTS
IR
OR
Q0–Q3
INVALID
WORD 1
WORD 2

TEXAS INSTRUMENTS
POST OFFICE BOX 225012 • DALLAS, TEXAS 75265

logic symbols†

'LS222

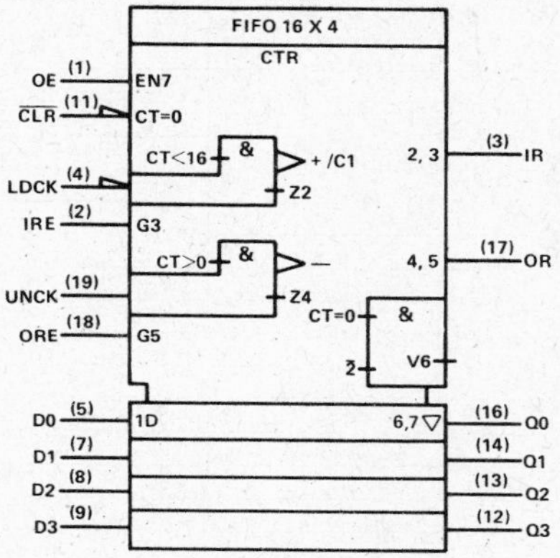
FIFO 16 X 4
CTR
OE (1) EN7
CLR (11) CT=0
CT<16 & +/C1
Z2
2, 3 (3) IR
LDCK (4)
IRE (2) G3
CT>0 & —
Z4
4, 5 (17) OR
UNCK (19)
CT=0 &
ORE (18) G5
2 V6
D0 (5) 1D
6,7 (16) Q0
D1 (7)
(14) Q1
D2 (8)
(13) Q2
D3 (9)
(12) Q3

'LS224

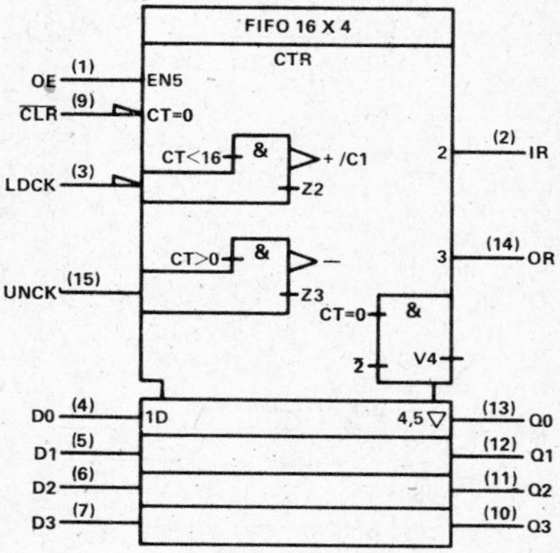
FIFO 16 X 4
CTR
OE (1) EN5
CLR (9) CT=0
CT<16 & +/C1
Z2
2 (2) IR
LDCK (3)
CT>0 & —
3 (14) OR
UNCK (15)
Z3
CT=0 &
2 V4
D0 (4) 1D
4,5 (13) Q0
D1 (5)
(12) Q1
D2 (6)
(11) Q2
D3 (7)
(10) Q3

'LS227

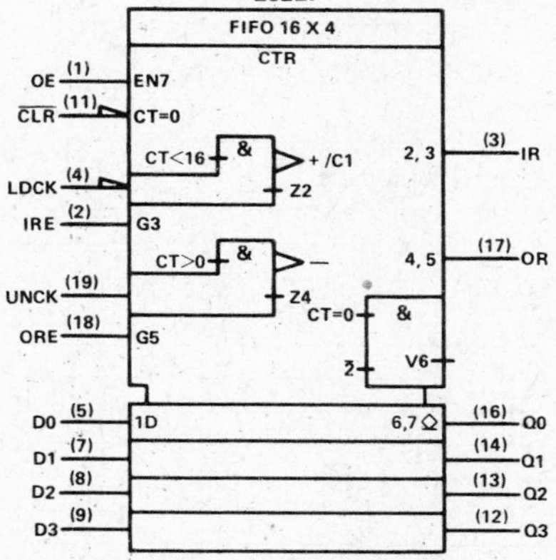
FIFO 16 X 4
CTR
OE (1) EN7
CLR (11) CT=0
CT<16 & +/C1
Z2
2, 3 (3) IR
LDCK (4)
IRE (2) G3
CT>0 & —
4, 5 (17) OR
UNCK (19)
Z4
CT=0 &
ORE (18) G5
2 V6
D0 (5) 1D
6,7 (16) Q0
D1 (7)
(14) Q1
D2 (8)
(13) Q2
D3 (9)
(12) Q3

'LS228

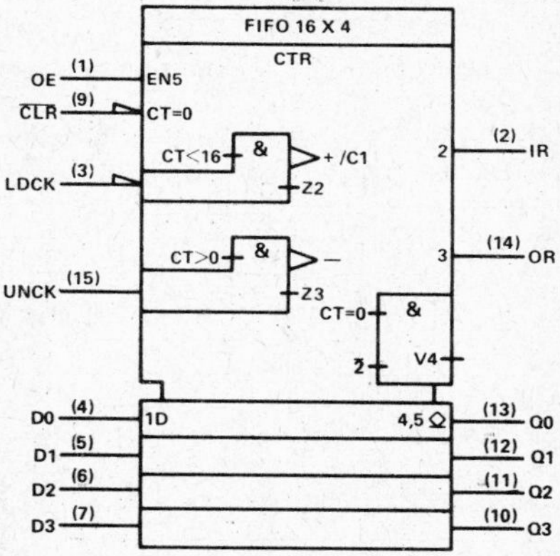
FIFO 16 X 4
CTR
OE (1) EN5
CLR (9) CT=0
CT<16 & +/C1
Z2
2 (2) IR
LDCK (3)
CT>0 & —
3 (14) OR
UNCK (15)
Z3
CT=0 &
2 V4
D0 (4) 1D
4,5 (13) Q0
D1 (5)
(12) Q1
D2 (6)
(11) Q2
D3 (7)
(10) Q3

† These symbols are in accordance with ANSI/IEEE Std 91-1984 and IEC Publication 617-12.
These symbols are functionally accurate but do not show the details of implementation; for these, see the functional block diagram. The symbol represents the memory as if it were controlled by a single counter whose content is the number of words stored at that time. Output data is invalid when the counter content is 0.

absolute maximum ratings over operating free-air temperature range (unless otherwise noted)

Supply voltage, V_{CC} (See Note 1)	7 V
Input voltage	7 V
Off-state output voltage	5.5 V
Operating free-air temperature range:	
SN54LS222, SN54LS224, SN54LS227, SN54LS228	−55°C to 125°C
SN74LS222, SN74LS224, SN74LS227, SN74LS228	0°C to 70°C
Storage temperature range	−65°C to 150°C

NOTE 1: Voltage values are with respect to network ground terminal.

2

LSI Devices

recommended operating conditions

			SN54LS'			SN74LS'			UNIT
			MIN	NOM	MAX	MIN	NOM	MAX	
V_{CC}	Supply voltage		4.5	5	5.5	4.75	5	5.25	V
V_{IH}	High-level input voltage		2			2			V
V_{IL}	Low-level input voltage				0.7			0.8	V
I_{OH}	High-level output current	Q			−1			−2.6	mA
		IR, OR			−0.4			−0.4	
I_{OL}	Low-level output current	Q			12			24	mA
		IR, OR			4			8	
t_w	Pulse duration	LDCK high	60			60			ns
		LDCK low	15			15			
		UNCK low	30			30			
		UNCK high	30			30			
		$\overline{CLR}$ low	20			20			
t_{su}	Setup time	D to LDCK↓	50			50			ns
		LDCK↓ before UNCK↓	50			50			
		UNCK↑ before LDCK↑	50			50			
t_h	Hold time	D from LDCK↓	0			0			ns
T_A	Operating free-air temperature		−55		125	0		70	°C

electrical characteristics over recommended operating free-air temperature range (unless otherwise noted)

PARAMETER		TEST CONDITIONS†		SN54LS' MIN	SN54LS' TYP‡	SN54LS' MAX	SN74LS' MIN	SN74LS' TYP‡	SN74LS' MAX	UNIT
V_{IK}		V_{CC} = MIN,	I_I = −18 mA			−1.5			−1.5	V
V_{OH}	Q	V_{CC} = MIN,	I_{OH} = MAX	2.4	3.3		2.4	3.4		V
	IR, OR	V_{CC} = MIN,	I_{OH} = −0.4 mA	2.5	3.4		2.7	3.4		
V_{OL}	Q	V_{CC} = MIN,	I_{OL} = 12 mA		0.25	0.4		0.25	0.4	V
		V_{CC} = MIN,	I_{OL} = 24 mA					0.35	0.5	
	IR, OR	V_{CC} = MIN,	I_{OL} = 4 mA		0.25	0.4		0.25	0.4	
		V_{CC} = MIN,	I_{OL} = 8 mA					0.35	0.5	
I_{OZH}	Q	V_{CC} = MAX,	V_O = 2.7 V			20			20	μA
I_{OZL}	Q	V_{CC} = MAX,	V_O = 0.4 V			−20			−20	μA
I_I		V_{CC} = MAX,	V_I = 7 V			0.1			0.1	mA
I_{IH}		V_{CC} = MAX,	V_I = 2.7 V			20			20	μA
I_{IL}		V_{CC} = MAX,	V_I = 0.4 V			−0.4			−0.4	mA
I_{OS}§	Q	V_{CC} = MAX,		−30		−130	−30		−130	mA
	IR, OR			−20		−100	−20		−100	
I_{CC}		V_{CC} = MAX,	Outputs high		84	135		84	135	mA
			Outputs low		87	155		87	155	
			Outputs disabled		89	155		89	155	

†For conditions shown as MIN or MAX, use the appropriate value specified under recommended operating conditions.
‡All typical values are at V_{CC} = 5 V, T_A = 25°C.
§Not more than one output should be shorted at a time, and duration of the short-circuit should not exceed one second.

switching characteristics, V_{CC} = 5 V, T_A = 25°C

PARAMETER	FROM	TO	TEST CONDITIONS	'LS222			'LS224			UNIT
				MIN	TYP	MAX	MIN	TYP	MAX	
t_{PLH}	IRE↑	IR	R_L = 2 kΩ, C_L = 15 pF, See Note 2		23	35				ns
t_{PHL}	IRE↓	IR			9	15				ns
t_{PLH}	ORE↑	OR			22	35				ns
t_{PHL}	ORE↓	OR			9	15				ns
t_{PLH}	LDCK↓	IR			25	40		25	40	ns
t_{PHL}	LDCK↑	IR			36	50		36	50	ns
t_{PLH}	LDCK↓	OR			48	70		48	70	ns
t_{PLH}	UNCK↑	OR			29	45		29	45	ns
t_{PHL}	UNCK↓	OR			28	45		28	45	ns
t_{PLH}	UNCK↑	IR			49	70		49	70	ns
t_{PLH}	$\overline{CLR}$↓	IR			36	55		36	55	ns
t_{PHL}	$\overline{CLR}$↓	OR			25	40		25	40	ns
t_{PHL}	LDCK↓	Q	R_L = 667 Ω, C_L = 45 pF, See Note 2		34	50		34	50	ns
t_{PLH}	UNCK↑	Q			54	80		54	80	ns
t_{PHL}	UNCK↑	Q			45	70		45	70	ns
t_{PZL}	OE↑	Q			22	35		22	35	ns
t_{PZH}	OE↑	Q			21	35		21	35	ns
t_{PLZ}	OE↓	Q	R_L = 667 Ω, C_L = 5 pF, See Note 2		16	30		16	30	ns
t_{PHZ}	OE↓	Q			18	30		18	30	ns

NOTE 2: Load circuits and voltage waveforms are shown in Section 1.

schematics of inputs and outputs

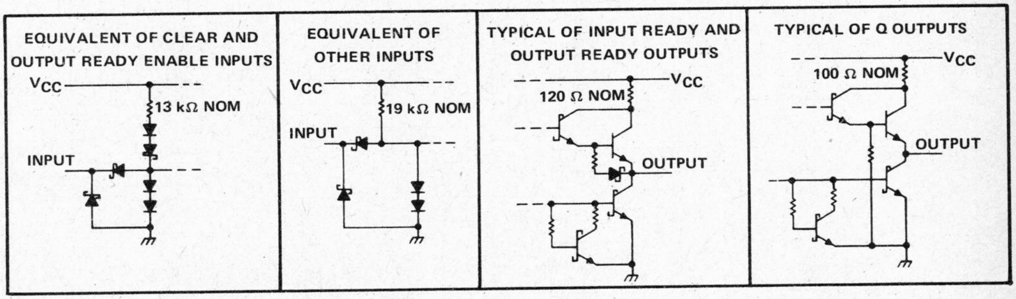
EQUIVALENT OF CLEAR AND OUTPUT READY ENABLE INPUTS
VCC
13 kΩ NOM
INPUT
EQUIVALENT OF OTHER INPUTS
VCC
19 kΩ NOM
INPUT
TYPICAL OF INPUT READY AND OUTPUT READY OUTPUTS
VCC
120 Ω NOM
OUTPUT
TYPICAL OF Q OUTPUTS
VCC
100 Ω NOM
OUTPUT

2

LSI Devices

recommended operating conditions

			SN54LS'			SN74LS'			UNIT
			MIN	NOM	MAX	MIN	NOM	MAX	
V_{CC}	Supply voltage		4.5	5	5.5	4.75	5	5.25	V
V_{IH}	High-level input voltage		2			2			V
V_{IL}	Low-level input voltage				0.7			0.8	V
V_{OH}	High-level output voltage	Q			5.5			5.5	V
I_{OH}	High-level output current	IR, OR			−0.4			−0.4	mA
I_{OL}	Low-level output current	Q			12			24	mA
		IR, OR			4			8	mA
t_w	Pulse duration	LDCK high	60			60			ns
		LDCK low	15			15			ns
		UNCK low	30			30			ns
		UNCK high	30			30			ns
		$\overline{CLR}$ low	20			20			ns
t_{su}	Setup time	D to LDCK↓	50			50			ns
		LDCK↓ before UNCK↓	50			50			ns
		UNCK↑ before LDCK↑	50			50			ns
t_h	Hold time	D from LDCK↓	0			0			ns
T_A	Operating free-air temperature		−55		125	0		70	°C

electrical characteristics over recommended operating free-air temperature range (unless otherwise noted)

PARAMETER		TEST CONDITIONS†		SN54LS'			SN74LS'			UNIT
				MIN	TYP‡	MAX	MIN	TYP‡	MAX	
V_{IK}		V_{CC} = MIN,	I_I = −18 mA			−1.5			−1.5	V
I_{OH}	Q	V_{CC} = MIN,	V_{OH} = 5.5 V			0.1			0.1	mA
V_{OH}	IR, OR	V_{CC} = MIN,	I_{OH} = −0.4 mA	2.5	3.4		2.7	3.4		V
V_{OL}	Q	V_{CC} = MIN,	I_{OL} = 12 mA		0.25	0.4		0.25	0.4	V
	Q	V_{CC} = MIN,	I_{OL} = 24 mA					0.35	0.5	V
	IR, OR	V_{CC} = MIN,	I_{OL} = 4 mA		0.25	0.4		0.25	0.4	V
	IR, OR	V_{CC} = MIN,	I_{OL} = 8 mA					0.35	0.5	V
I_{OZH}	Q	V_{CC} = MAX,	V_O = 2.7 V			20			20	μA
I_{OZL}	Q	V_{CC} = MAX,	V_O = 0.4 V			−20			−20	μA
I_I		V_{CC} = MAX,	V_I = 7 V			0.1			0.1	mA
I_{IH}		V_{CC} = MAX,	V_I = 2.7 V			20			20	μA
I_{IL}		V_{CC} = MAX,	V_I = 0.4 V			−0.4			−0.4	mA
I_{OS}§	IR, OR	V_{CC} = MAX		−20		−100	−20		−100	mA
I_{CC}		V_{CC} = MAX	Outputs high		84	135		84	135	mA
			Outputs low		87	155		87	155	mA
			Outputs disabled		89	155		89	155	mA

†For conditions shown as MIN or MAX, use the appropriate value specified under recommended operating conditions.
‡All typical values are at V_{CC} = 5 V, T_A = 25°C.
§Not more than one output should be shorted at a time, and duration of the short-circuit should not exceed one second.

switching characteristics, V_{CC} = 5 V, T_A = 25°C

PARAMETER	FROM	TO	TEST CONDITIONS	'LS227 MIN	'LS227 TYP	'LS227 MAX	'LS228 MIN	'LS228 TYP	'LS228 MAX	UNIT
t_{PLH}	IRE↑	IR	R_L = 2 kΩ, C_L = 15 pF, See Note 2		23	35				ns
t_{PHL}	IRE↓	IR			9	15				ns
t_{PLH}	ORE↑	OR			22	35				ns
t_{PHL}	ORE↓	OR			9	15				ns
t_{PLH}	LDCK↓	IR			25	40		25	40	ns
t_{PHL}	LDCK↑	IR			36	50		36	50	ns
t_{PLH}	LDCK↓	OR			48	70		48	70	ns
t_{PLH}	UNCK↑	OR			29	45		29	45	ns
t_{PHL}	UNCK↓	OR			28	45		28	45	ns
t_{PLH}	UNCK↑	IR			49	70		49	70	ns
t_{PLH}	CLR↓	IR			36	55		36	55	ns
t_{PHL}	CLR↓	OR			25	40		25	40	ns
t_{PHL}	LDCK↓	Q	R_L = 667 Ω, C_L = 45 pF, See Note 2		34	50		34	50	ns
t_{PLH}	UNCK↑	Q			54	80		54	80	ns
t_{PHL}	UNCK↑	Q			45	70		45	70	ns
t_{PLH}	OE↓	Q			21	30		21	30	ns
t_{PHL}	OE↑	Q			20	35		20	35	ns

NOTE 2: Load circuits and voltage waveforms are shown in Section 1.

schematics of inputs and outputs

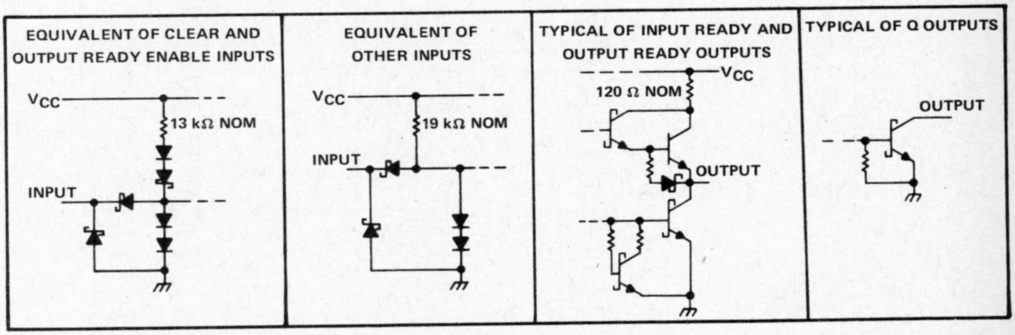
EQUIVALENT OF CLEAR AND
OUTPUT READY ENABLE INPUTS
VCC
13 kΩ NOM
INPUT
EQUIVALENT OF
OTHER INPUTS
VCC
19 kΩ NOM
INPUT
TYPICAL OF INPUT READY AND
OUTPUT READY OUTPUTS
VCC
120 Ω NOM
OUTPUT
TYPICAL OF Q OUTPUTS
OUTPUT

TYPICAL APPLICATIONS INFORMATION

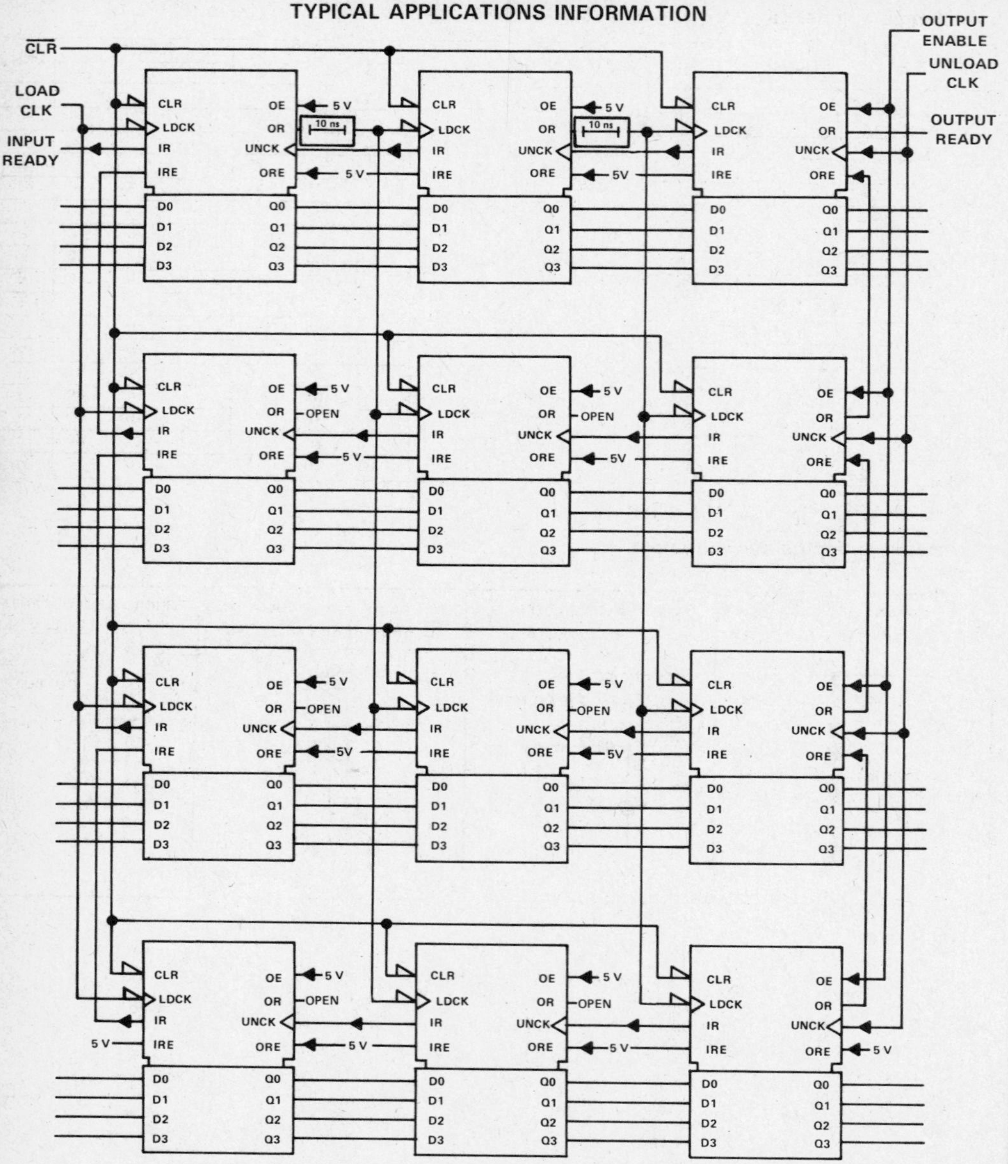
CLR
LOAD CLK
INPUT READY
OUTPUT ENABLE
UNLOAD CLK
OUTPUT READY
CLR
LDCK
IR
IRE
OE
OR
UNCK
ORE
D0
D1
D2
D3
Q0
Q1
Q2
Q3
5 V
OPEN
10 ns

FIGURE 1. 46-WORD BY 16-BIT EXPANSION USING 'LS222

[10 ns] ≡ Noninverting delay ≥ 10 ns (e.g., 2 stages of 'LS04), 2 places.

TEXAS INSTRUMENTS
POST OFFICE BOX 225012 • DALLAS, TEXAS 75265

16 × 5 ASYNCHRONOUS FIRST-IN FIRST-OUT MEMORY

D1733, SEPTEMBER 1976—REVISED SEPTEMBER 1985

- **Independent Asynchronous Inputs and Outputs**
- **Organized as 16-Words of 5 Bits**
- **DC to 10-MHz Data Rate**
- **3-State Data Outputs**
- **20-Pin, 300-mil, High-Density Package**

SN74S225 . . . J OR N PACKAGE
(TOP VIEW)

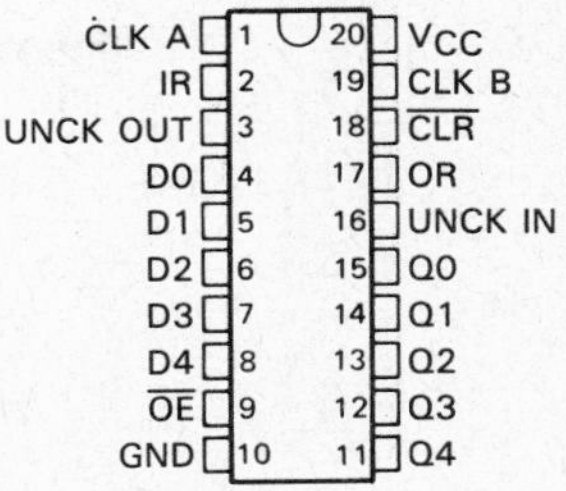
CLK A 1
IR 2
UNCK OUT 3
D0 4
D1 5
D2 6
D3 7
D4 8
OE 9
GND 10
20 VCC
19 CLK B
18 CLR
17 OR
16 UNCK IN
15 Q0
14 Q1
13 Q2
12 Q3
11 Q4

description

This 80-bit active-element memory is a monolithic Schottky-clamped transistor-transistor logic (STTL) array organized as 16 words of five-bits each. A memory system using the SN74S225 can easily be expanded in multiples of 16 words or of 5 bits as shown in Figure 2. The three-state outputs controlled by a single enable, $\overline{OE}$, makes bus connection and multiplexing easy.

operation

A FIFO is a memory storage device that allows data to be written into and/or read from its array at independent data rates. The 'S225 FIFO will process data at any desired clock rate from DC to 10 MHz. The data is processed in a parallel format, word by word.

Reading or writing is done independently utilizing separate asynchronous data clocks. Data may be written into the array on the low-to-high transition of either load clock input. Data may be read out of the array on the low-to-high transition of the unload clock input (normally high). Writing data into the FIFO may be accomplished in one of two manners: 1) In applications not requiring a gated clock control, best results will be achieved by applying the clock input to one of the clocks while tying the other clock input high. 2) In applications needing a gated clock, the load clock (gate control) must be high in order for the FIFO to load on the next clock pulse. The clock A and B inputs can be used interchangeably for either clock gate control or clock input.

Status of the 'S225 is provided by three outputs. Input ready monitors the status of the last word location and signifies when the memory is full. This output is high whenever the memory is available to accept any data. The unload clock output also monitors the last word location. This output generates a low-logic-level pulse (synchronized to the internal clock pulse) when the location is vacant. The third status output, output ready, is high when the first word location contains valid data and unload clock input is high. When unload clock input goes low, output ready will go low and stay low until new valid data is in the first word position. The first word location is defined as the location from which data is provided to the outputs.

The data outputs are noninverted with respect to the data inputs and are three-state with a common control input, output enable. When output enable is low, the data outputs are enabled to function as totem-pole outputs. A high-logic-level forces each data output to a high-impedance state while all other inputs and outputs remain active.

The clear input invalidates all data stored in the memory array by clearing the control logic and setting output ready to a low-logic-level on the high-to-low transition of a low-active pulse.

FUNCTION TABLES

TABLE 1 INPUT FUNCTIONS

Input	Pin	Description
CLK A	1	Load Clock A
D0-D4	4-8	Data Inputs
$\overline{OE}$	9	Output Enable
UNCK IN	16	Unload Clock
$\overline{CLR}$	18	Clear
CLK B	19	Load Clock B
GND	10	Ground pin
V_{CC}	20	Supply Voltage

TABLE 2 OUTPUT FUNCTIONS

Output	Pin	Description
IR	2	Input Ready
UNCK OUT	3	Unload Clock
Q4-D0	11-15	Data Outputs
OR	17	Output Ready

schematics of inputs and outputs

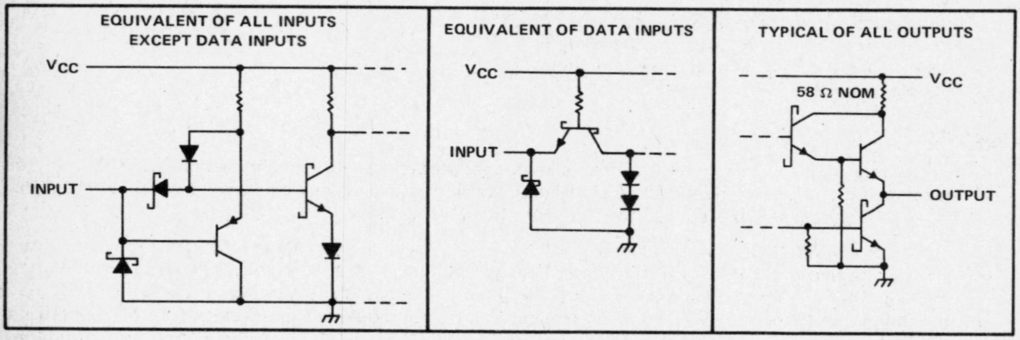
EQUIVALENT OF ALL INPUTS EXCEPT DATA INPUTS
VCC
INPUT
EQUIVALENT OF DATA INPUTS
VCC
INPUT
TYPICAL OF ALL OUTPUTS
VCC
58 Ω NOM
OUTPUT

logic symbol†

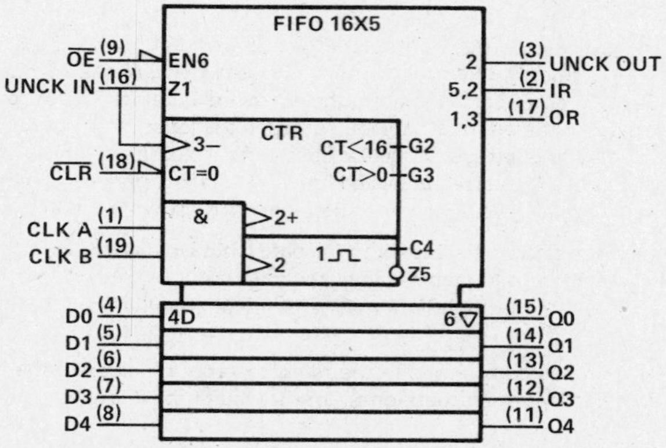
FIFO 16X5
OE (9) EN6
UNCK IN (16) Z1
CTR
3–
CLR (18) CT=0
CT<16 G2
CT>0 G3
CLK A (1)
CLK B (19)
&
2+
2
1
C4
Z5
2 (3) UNCK OUT
5,2 (2) IR
1,3 (17) OR
D0 (4) 4D
D1 (5)
D2 (6)
D3 (7)
D4 (8)
6▽ (15) Q0
(14) Q1
(13) Q2
(12) Q3
(11) Q4

† This symbol is in accordance with ANSI/IEEE Std 91-1984 and IEC Publication 617-12.

functional block diagram

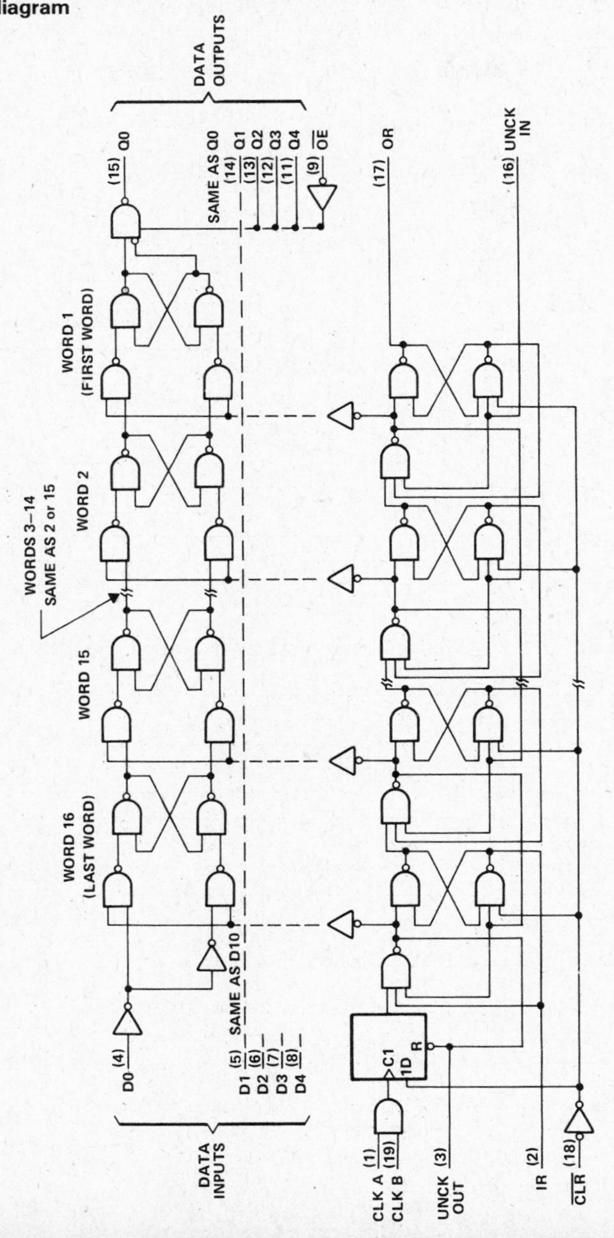
DATA OUTPUTS
(15) Q0
SAME AS Q0 (14) Q1
(13) Q2
(12) Q3
(11) Q4
(9) OE
(17) OR
(16) UNCK IN
WORD 1 (FIRST WORD)
WORD 2
WORDS 3–14 SAME AS 2 or 15
WORD 15
WORD 16 (LAST WORD)
D0 (4)
D1 (5)
D2 (6)
D3 (7)
D4 (8)
SAME AS D10
DATA INPUTS
CLK A (1)
CLK B (19)
C1
1D
R
UNCK OUT (3)
IR (2)
CLR (18)

absolute maximum ratings over operating free-air temperature range (unless otherwise noted)

Supply voltage, V_{CC} (see Note 1) . . . 7 V
Input voltage . . . 5.5 V
Off-state output voltage . . . 5.5 V
Operating free-air temperature range . . . 0 °C to 70 °C
Storage temperature range . . . −65 °C to 150 °C

NOTE 1: All voltage values are with respect to network ground terminal.

recommended operating conditions

			MIN	NOM	MAX	UNIT
V_{CC}	Supply voltage		4.75	5	5.25	V
V_{IH}	High-level input voltage		2			V
V_{IL}	Low-level input voltage				0.8	V
I_{OH}	High-level output current	Q outputs			−6.5	mA
		All other outputs			−3.2	mA
I_{OL}	Low-level output current	Q outputs			16	mA
		All other outputs			8	mA
t_w	Pulse duration	CLK A or CLK B (high)	25			ns
		$\overline{\text{UNCK IN}}$ (low)	7			ns
		$\overline{\text{CLR}}$ (low)	40			ns
t_{su}	Setup time before CLK A↑ or CLK B↑	Data (See Note 2)	−20			ns
		$\overline{\text{CLR}}$ inactive	25			ns
t_h	Hold time after CLK A↑ or CLK B↑		70			ns
T_A	Operating free-air temperature		0		70	°C

NOTE 2: Data must be setup within 20 ns after the load clock positive transition.

electrical characteristics over recommended operating free-air temperature range (unless otherwise noted)

PARAMETER		TEST CONDITIONS	MIN	TYP†	MAX	UNIT
V_{IK}		V_{CC} = 4.75 V, I_I = −18 mA			−1.2	V
V_{OH}	Q	V_{CC} = 4.75 V, I_{OH} = −6.5 mA	2.4	2.9		V
	All others	V_{CC} = 4.75 V, I_{OH} = −3.2 mA	2.4	2.9		V
V_{OL}	Q	V_{CC} = 4.75 V, I_{OL} = 16 mA		0.35	0.5	V
	All others	V_{CC} = 4.75 V, I_{OL} = 8 mA		0.35	0.5	V
I_{OZH}		V_{CC} = 5.25 V, V_O = 2.4 V			50	μA
I_{OZL}		V_{CC} = 5.25 V, V_O = 0.5 V			−50	μA
I_I		V_{CC} = 5.25 V, V_I = 5.5 V			1	mA
I_{IH}	Data	V_{CC} = 5.25 V, V_I = 2.7 V			40	μA
	All others				25	μA
I_{IL}	Data	V_{CC} = 5.25 V, V_I = 0.5 V			−1	mA
	All others				−0.25	mA
I_{OS}‡		V_{CC} = 5.25 V, V_O = 0 V	−30		−100	mA
I_{CC}		V_{CC} = 5.25 V, (See Note 3)		80	120	mA

†All typical values are at V_{CC} = 5 V, T_A = 25 °C.
‡Duration of the short circuit should not exceed one second.
NOTE 3: I_{CC} is measured with all inputs grounded and the output open.

switching characteristics over recommended operating ranges of T_A and V_{CC} (unless otherwise noted)

PARAMETERS†	FROM	TO	TEST CONDITIONS	MIN	TYP‡	MAX	UNIT
f_{max}	CLK A		C_L = 30 pF, See Note 4	10	20		MHZ
f_{max}	CLK B			10	20		MHz
f_{max}	UNCK IN			10	20		MHz
t_w	UNCK OUT			7	14		ns
t_{dis}	$\overline{OE}$	Any Q	C_L = 5 pF		10	25	ns
t_{en}			C_L = 30 pF, See Note 4		25	40	
t_{PLH}	UNCK IN	Any Q			50	75	ns
t_{PHL}					50	75	
t_{PLH}	CLK A or CLK B	OR			190	300	ns
t_{PLH}	UNCK IN	OR			40	60	ns
t_{PHL}					30	45	
t_{PHL}	$\overline{CLR}$	OR			35	60	ns
t_{PHL}	CLK A or CLK B	UNCK OUT			25	45	ns
t_{PHL}	UNCK IN	UNCK OUT			270	400	ns
t_{PHL}	CLK A or CLK B	IR			55	75	ns
t_{PLH}	UNCK IN	IR			255	400	ns
t_{PLH}	$\overline{CLR}$	IR			16	35	ns
t_{PLH}	OR↑	Any Q			10	20	ns

†f_{max} ≡ maximum clock frequency
t_w ≡ pulse width (output)
↑↓ ≡ The arrow indicates that the low-to-high (↑) or high-to-low (↓) transition of the output ready (OR) output is used for reference.
t_{PLH} ≡ propagation delay time, low-to-high-level output.
t_{PHL} ≡ propagation delay time, high-to-low-level output.
‡All typical values are at V_{CC} = 5 V, T_A = 25°C.
NOTE 4: Load circuit and voltage waveforms are shown in Section 1.

2

LSI Devices

TYPICAL WAVEFORMS FOR A 16-WORD FIFO

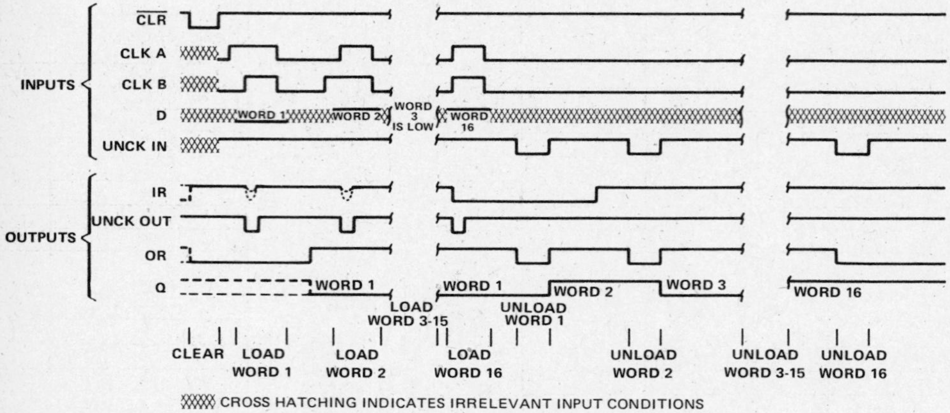
CLR
CLK A
CLK B
D
UNCK IN
INPUTS
WORD 1
WORD 2
WORD 3 IS LOW
WORD 16
IR
UNCK OUT
OR
Q
OUTPUTS
WORD 1
WORD 2
WORD 3
WORD 16
LOAD WORD 3-15
UNLOAD WORD 1
CLEAR
LOAD WORD 1
LOAD WORD 2
LOAD WORD 16
UNLOAD WORD 2
UNLOAD WORD 3-15
UNLOAD WORD 16
CROSS HATCHING INDICATES IRRELEVANT INPUT CONDITIONS

FIGURE 1. TYPICAL WAVEFORMS FOR A 16-WORD FIFO

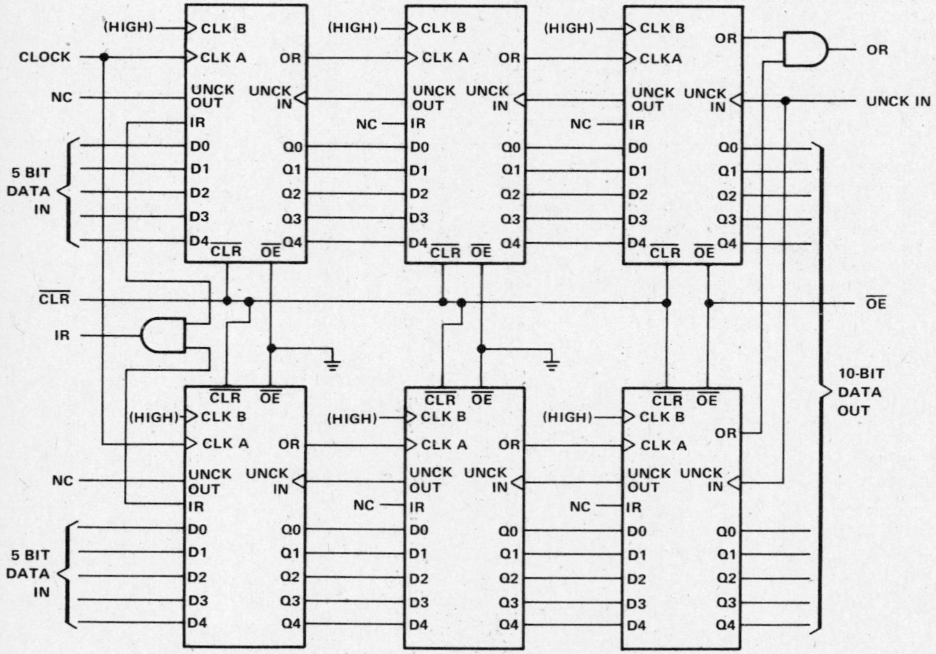
(HIGH)
CLK B
CLOCK
CLK A
OR
NC
UNCK OUT
UNCK IN
IR
5 BIT DATA IN
D0
D1
D2
D3
D4
Q0
Q1
Q2
Q3
Q4
CLR
OE
UNCK IN
10-BIT DATA OUT

FIGURE 2. EXPANDING THE 'S225 FIFO (48 WORDS OF 10 BITS SHOWN)

D2876, MARCH 1986—REVISED APRIL 1986

- **Independent Asychronous Inputs and Outputs**
- **16 Words by 5 Bits Each**
- **Data Rates from 0 to 30 MHz**
- **Fall-Through Time . . . 24 ns Typ**
- **3-State Outputs**

SN54ALS229A . . . J PACKAGE
SN74ALS229A . . . DW OR N PACKAGE
(TOP VIEW)

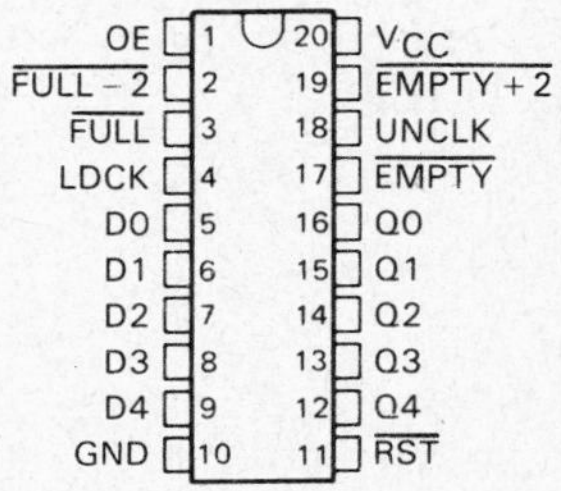
OE 1
$\overline{FULL-2}$ 2
$\overline{FULL}$ 3
LDCK 4
D0 5
D1 6
D2 7
D3 8
D4 9
GND 10
20 V_{CC}
19 $\overline{EMPTY+2}$
18 UNCLK
17 $\overline{EMPTY}$
16 Q0
15 Q1
14 Q2
13 Q3
12 Q4
11 $\overline{RST}$

SN54ALS229A . . . FK PACKAGE
SN74ALS229A . . . FN PACKAGE
(TOP VIEW)

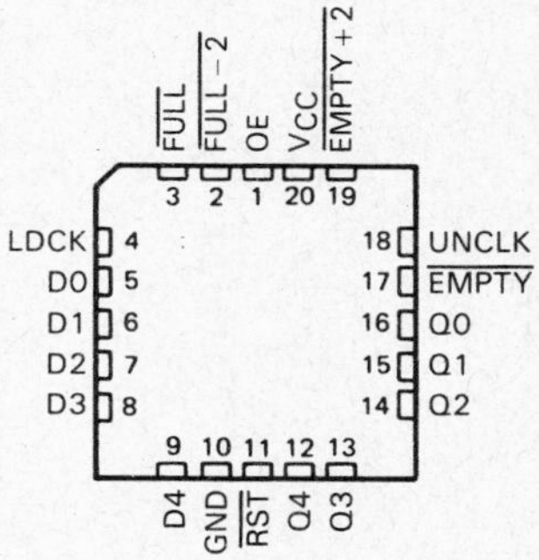
$\overline{FULL}$
$\overline{FULL-2}$
OE
V_{CC}
$\overline{EMPTY+2}$
3 2 1 20 19
LDCK 4
D0 5
D1 6
D2 7
D3 8
18 UNCLK
17 $\overline{EMPTY}$
16 Q0
15 Q1
14 Q2
9 10 11 12 13
D4
GND
$\overline{RST}$
Q4
Q3

description

These 80-bit memories utilize Advanced Low-Power Schottky technology and feature high speed and fast fall-through times. They are organized as 16 words by 5 bits each.

A FIFO memory is a storage device that allows data to be written into and read from its array at independent data rates. These FIFOs are designed to process data at rates from 0 to 25 megahertz in a bit-parallel format, word by word.

Data is written into memory on a low-to-high transition at the load clock input (LDCK) and is read out on a low-to-high transition at the unload clock input (UNCK). The memory is full when the number of words clocked in exceeds by 16 the number of words clocked out. When the memory is full, LDCK signals will have no effect. When the memory is empty, UNCK signals have no effect.

Status of the FIFO memory is monitored by the $\overline{FULL}$, $\overline{EMPTY}$, $\overline{FULL-2}$, and $\overline{EMPTY+2}$ output flags. The $\overline{FULL}$ output will be low whenever the memory is full, and high whenever not full. The $\overline{FULL-2}$ output will be low whenever the memory contains 14 data words. The $\overline{EMPTY}$ output will be low whenever the memory is empty, and high whenever it is not empty. The $\overline{EMPTY+2}$ output will be low whenever 2 words remain in memory.

A low level on the reset input ($\overline{RST}$) resets the internal stack control pointers and also sets $\overline{EMPTY}$ low and sets $\overline{FULL}$, $\overline{FULL-2}$, and $\overline{EMPTY+2}$ high. The Q outputs are not reset to any specific logic level. The first low-to-high transition on LDCK, after either a $\overline{RST}$ pulse or from an empty condition, will cause $\overline{EMPTY}$ to go high and the data to appear on the Q outputs. It is important to note that the first word does not have to be unloaded. Data outputs are noninverting with respect to the data inputs and are at high impedance when the output enable input (OE) is low. OE does not affect the output flags. Cascading is easily accomplished in the word-width direction, but is not possible in the word-depth direction.

logic symbol†

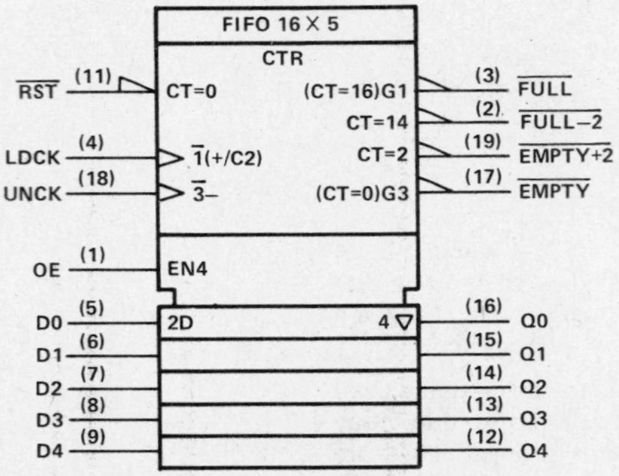
FIFO 16 X 5
CTR
RST (11) CT=0
LDCK (4) 1̄(+/C2)
UNCK (18) 3̄–
OE (1) EN4
D0 (5) 2D
D1 (6)
D2 (7)
D3 (8)
D4 (9)
(CT=16)G1 (3) FULL
CT=14 (2) FULL–2
CT=2 (19) EMPTY+2
(CT=0)G3 (17) EMPTY
4 ▽ (16) Q0
(15) Q1
(14) Q2
(13) Q3
(12) Q4

† This symbol is in accordance with ANSI/IEEE Standard 91-1984 and IEC Publication 617-12. The symbol is functionally accurate but does not show the details of implementation; for these, see the logic diagram. The symbol represents the memory as if it were controlled by a single counter whose content is the number of words stored at the time. Output data is invalid when the counter content (CT) is 0.

TEXAS INSTRUMENTS
POST OFFICE BOX 225012 • DALLAS, TEXAS 75265

logic diagram (positive logic)

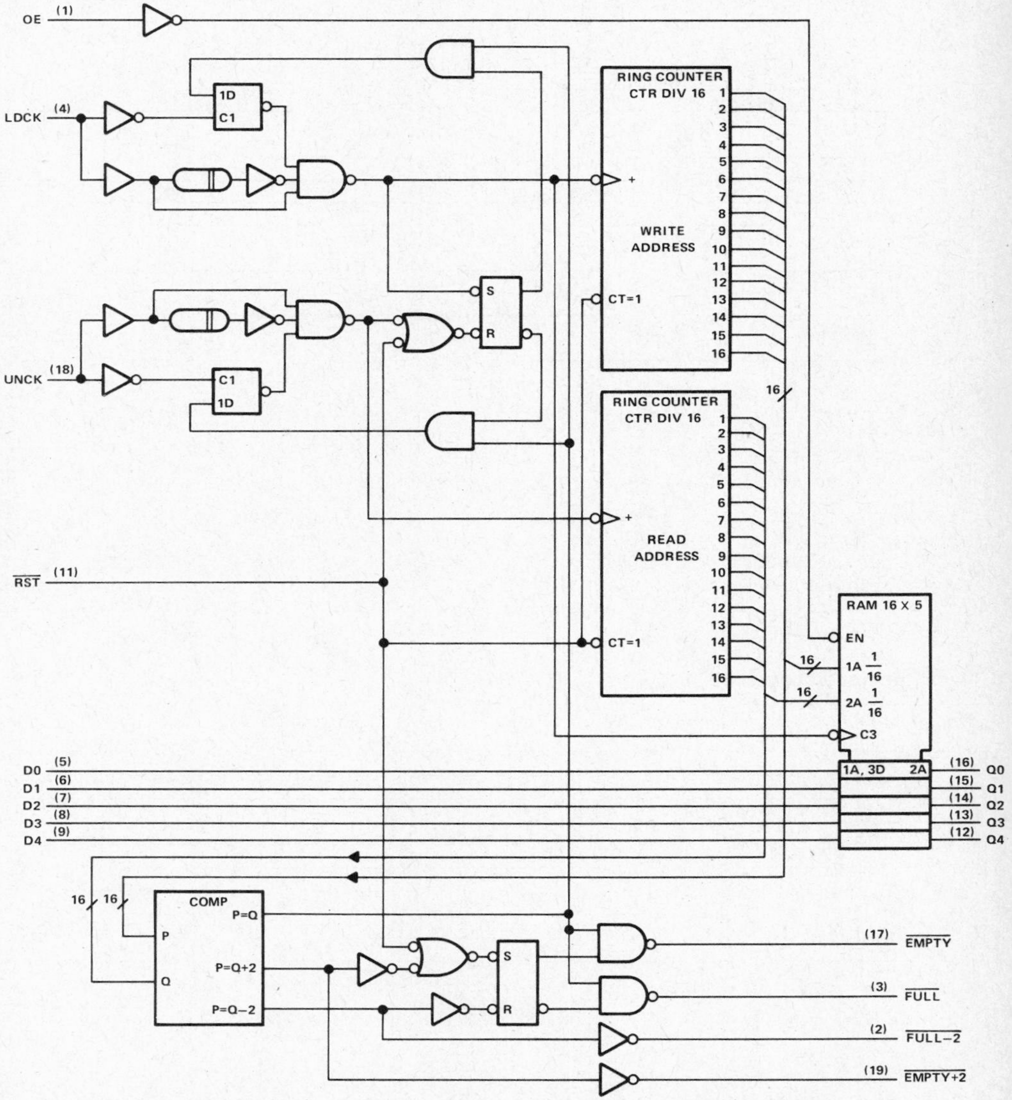
OE (1)
LDCK (4)
1D
C1
RING COUNTER
CTR DIV 16
WRITE
ADDRESS
CT=1
S
R
UNCK (18)
C1
1D
RING COUNTER
CTR DIV 16
READ
ADDRESS
CT=1
RST (11)
RAM 16 X 5
EN
1A 1/16
2A 1/16
C3
1A, 3D
2A
D0 (5)
D1 (6)
D2 (7)
D3 (8)
D4 (9)
(16) Q0
(15) Q1
(14) Q2
(13) Q3
(12) Q4
COMP
P=Q
P
P=Q+2
Q
P=Q−2
S
R
(17) EMPTY
(3) FULL
(2) FULL−2
(19) EMPTY+2

timing diagram

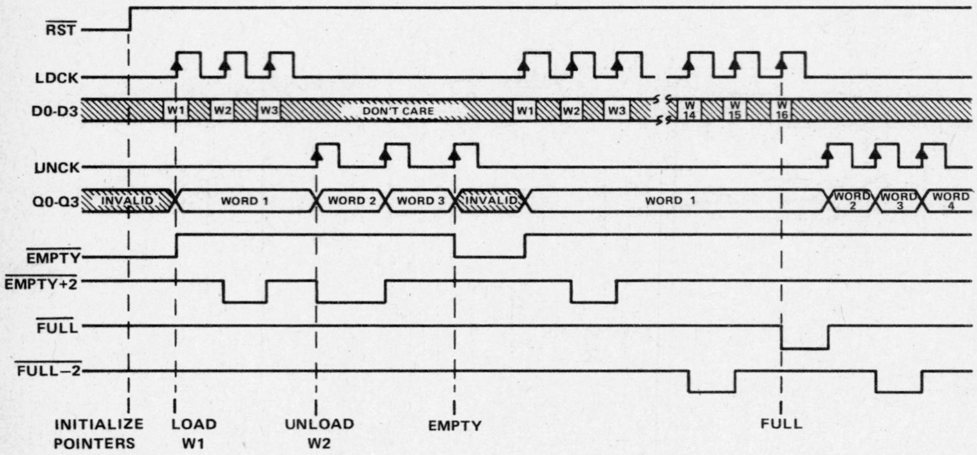
RST
LDCK
D0-D3
W1
W2
W3
DON'T CARE
W1
W2
W3
W 14
W 15
W 16
UNCK
Q0-Q3
INVALID
WORD 1
WORD 2
WORD 3
INVALID
WORD 1
WORD 2
WORD 3
WORD 4
EMPTY
EMPTY+2
FULL
FULL−2
INITIALIZE POINTERS
LOAD W1
UNLOAD W2
EMPTY
FULL

absolute maximum ratings over operating free-air temperature range (unless otherwise noted)

Supply voltage, V_{CC} . . . . 7 V
Input voltage . . . . 7 V
Voltage applied to a disabled 3-state output . . . . 5.5 V
Operating free-air temperature range: SN54ALS229A . . . . −55°C to 125°C
SN74ALS229A . . . . 0°C to 70°C
Storage temperature range . . . . −65°C to 150°C

recommended operating conditions

			SN54ALS229A MIN	SN54ALS229A NOM	SN54ALS229A MAX	SN74ALS229A MIN	SN74ALS229A NOM	SN74ALS229A MAX	UNIT
V_{CC}	Supply voltage		4.5	5	5.5	4.5	5	5.5	V
V_{IH}	High-level input voltage		2			2			V
V_{IL}	Low-level input voltage				0.8			0.8	V
I_{OH}	High-level output current	Q outputs			−1.0			−1.6	mA
		Status flags			−0.4			−0.4	
I_{OL}	Low-level output current	Q outputs			12			24	mA
		Status flags			4			8	
f_{clock}	Clock frequency	LDCK	0		25	0		30	MHz
		UNCK	0		25	0		30	
t_w	Pulse duration	$\overline{RST}$ low	20			15			ns
		LDCK low	15			10			
		LDCK high	25			20			
		UNCK low	15			10			
		UNCK high	25			20			
t_{su}	Setup time	Data before LDCK↑	10			10			ns
		$\overline{RST}$ (inactive) before LDCK↑	5			5			
t_h	Hold time	Data after LDCK↑	5			5			ns
T_A	Operating free-air temperature		−55		125	0		70	°C

electrical characteristics over recommended operating free-air temperature range (unless otherwise noted)

PARAMETER		TEST CONDITIONS		SN54ALS229A MIN	SN54ALS229A TYP†	SN54ALS229A MAX	SN74ALS229A MIN	SN74ALS229A TYP†	SN74ALS229A MAX	UNIT
V_{IK}		V_{CC} = 4.5 V,	I_I = −18 mA			−1.2			−1.2	V
V_{OH}	Status flags	V_{CC} = 4.5 V to 5.5 V,	I_{OH} = −0.4 mA	$V_{CC}-2$			$V_{CC}-2$			V
	Q outputs	V_{CC} = 4.5 V,	I_{OH} = −1 mA	2.4	3.3					
		V_{CC} = 4.5 V,	I_{OH} = −2.6 mA				2.4	3.2		
V_{OL}	Q outputs	V_{CC} = 4.5 V,	I_{OL} = 12 mA		0.25	0.4		0.25	0.4	V
		V_{CC} = 4.5 V,	I_{OL} = 24 mA					0.35	0.5	
	Status flags	V_{CC} = 4.5 V,	I_{OL} = 4 mA		0.25	0.4		0.25	0.4	
		V_{CC} = 4.5 V,	I_{OL} = 8 mA					0.35	0.5	
I_{OZH}		V_{CC} = 5.5 V,	V_O = 2.7 V			20			20	μA
I_{OZL}		V_{CC} = 5.5 V,	V_O = 0.4 V			−20			−20	μA
I_I		V_{CC} = 5.5 V,	V_I = 7 V			0.1			0.1	mA
I_{IH}		V_{CC} = 5.5 V,	V_I = 2.7 V			20			20	μA
I_{IL}		V_{CC} = 5.5 V,	V_I = 0.4 V			−0.2			−0.2	mA
I_O‡		V_{CC} = 5.5 V,	V_O = 2.25 V	−30		−112	−30		−112	mA
I_{CC}		V_{CC} = 5.5 V			95	150		95	140	mA

† All typical values are at V_{CC} = 5 V, T_A = 25 °C.
‡ The output conditions have been chosen to produce a current that closely approximates one half of the true short-circuit output current, I_{OS}.

switching characteristics (see Note 1)

PARAMETER	FROM (INPUT)	TO (OUTPUT)	V_{CC} = 5 V, C_L = 50 pF, R1 = 500 Ω, R2 = 500 Ω, T_A = 25 °C 'ALS229A MIN	TYP	MAX	V_{CC} = 4.5 V to 5.5 V, C_L = 50 pF, R1 = 500 Ω, R2 = 500 Ω, T_A = MIN to MAX SN54ALS229A MIN	MAX	SN74ALS229A MIN	MAX	UNIT
f_{max}	LDCK					25		30		MHz
	UNCK					25		30		
t_{pd}	LDCK↑	Any Q		24	47	7	54	7	50	ns
t_{pd}	UNCK↑	Any Q		19	29	9	35	9	33	ns
t_{PLH}	LDCK↑	$\overline{EMPTY}$		18	26	9	32	9	30	ns
t_{PHL}	UNCK↑	$\overline{EMPTY}$		18	25	9	32	9	29	ns
t_{PHL}	$\overline{RST}$↓	$\overline{EMPTY}$		15	21	6	26	6	24	ns
t_{pd}	LDCK↑	$\overline{EMPTY+2}$		23	33	10	40	10	38	ns
t_{pd}	UNCK↑	$\overline{EMPTY+2}$		20	29	9	38	9	35	ns
t_{PLH}	$\overline{RST}$↓	$\overline{EMPTY+2}$		20	28	9	35	9	33	ns
t_{pd}	LDCK↑	$\overline{FULL-2}$		23	33	10	40	10	38	ns
t_{pd}	UNCK↑	$\overline{FULL-2}$		20	29	9	38	9	35	ns
t_{PLH}	$\overline{RST}$↓	$\overline{FULL-2}$		20	28	9	35	9	33	ns
t_{PHL}	LDCK↑	$\overline{FULL}$		21	28	10	35	10	33	ns
t_{PLH}	UNCK↑	$\overline{FULL}$		17	23	8	29	8	27	ns
t_{PLH}	$\overline{RST}$↓	$\overline{FULL}$		18	27	8	33	8	31	ns
t_{en}	OE↑	Q		8	13	1	16	2	15	ns
t_{dis}	OE↓	Q		8	14	2	20	2	17	ns

NOTE 1: Load circuit and voltage waveforms are shown in Section 1.

2

LSI Devices

2

LSI Devices

D2876, OCTOBER 1985—REVISED APRIL 1986

- **Independent Asynchronous Inputs and Outputs**
- **16 Words by 4 Bits Each**
- **Data Rates From 0 to 30 MHz**
- **Fall-Through Time . . . 24 ns Typ**
- **3-State Outputs**

SN54ALS232A . . . J PACKAGE
SN74ALS232A . . . D OR N PACKAGE
(TOP VIEW)

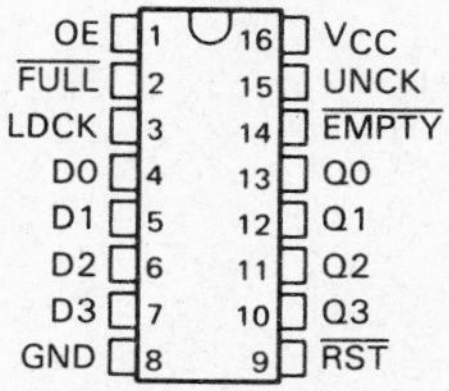
OE 1
$\overline{\text{FULL}}$ 2
LDCK 3
D0 4
D1 5
D2 6
D3 7
GND 8
16 V_{CC}
15 UNCK
14 $\overline{\text{EMPTY}}$
13 Q0
12 Q1
11 Q2
10 Q3
9 $\overline{\text{RST}}$

SN54ALS232A . . . FK PACKAGE
SN74ALS232A . . . FN PACKAGE
(TOP VIEW)

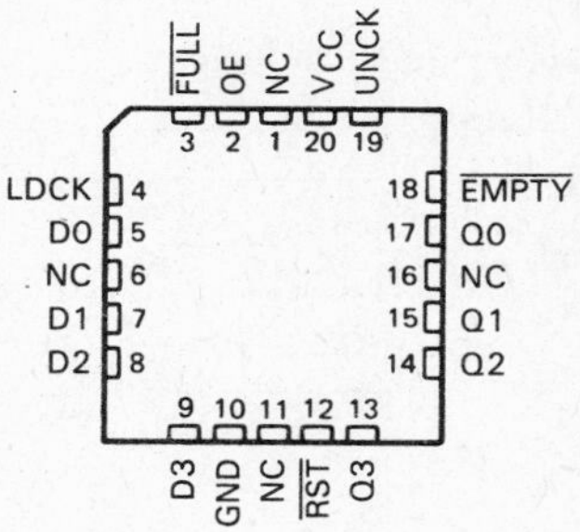
$\overline{\text{FULL}}$
OE
NC
VCC
UNCK
3 2 1 20 19
LDCK 4
D0 5
NC 6
D1 7
D2 8
18 $\overline{\text{EMPTY}}$
17 Q0
16 NC
15 Q1
14 Q2
9 10 11 12 13
D3
GND
NC
$\overline{\text{RST}}$
Q3

NC—No internal connection.

description

These 64-bit memories use Advanced Low-Power Schottky technology and feature high speed and fast fall-through times. They are organized as 16 words by 4 bits each.

A FIFO memory is a storage device that allows data to be written into and read from its array at independent data rates. These FIFOs are designed to process data at rates from 0 to 25 megahertz in a bit-parallel format, word by word.

Data is written into memory on a low-to-high transition at the load clock input (LDCK) and is read out on a low-to-high transition at the unload clock input (UNCK). The memory is full when the number of words clocked in exceeds by 16 the number of words clocked out. When the memory is full, LDCK signals have no effect on the data residing in memory. When the memory is empty, UNCK signals have no effect.

Status of the FIFO memory is monitored by the $\overline{\text{FULL}}$ and $\overline{\text{EMPTY}}$ output flags. The $\overline{\text{FULL}}$ output will be low when the memory is full, and high when the memory is not full. The $\overline{\text{EMPTY}}$ output will be low when the memory is empty, and high when it is not empty.

A low level on the reset input ($\overline{\text{RST}}$) resets the internal stack control pointers and also sets $\overline{\text{EMPTY}}$ low and sets $\overline{\text{FULL}}$ high. The outputs are not reset to any specific logic levels. The first low-to-high transition on LDCK, either after a $\overline{\text{RST}}$ pulse or from an empty condition, will cause $\overline{\text{EMPTY}}$ to go high and the data to appear on the Q outputs. It is important to note that the first word does not have to be unloaded. Data outputs are noninverting with respect to the data inputs and are at high impedance when the output-enable input (OE) is low. OE does not affect either the $\overline{\text{FULL}}$ or $\overline{\text{EMPTY}}$ output flags. Cascading is easily accomplished in the word-width direction, but is not possible in the word-depth direction.

TEXAS INSTRUMENTS
POST OFFICE BOX 225012 • DALLAS, TEXAS 75265

logic symbol†

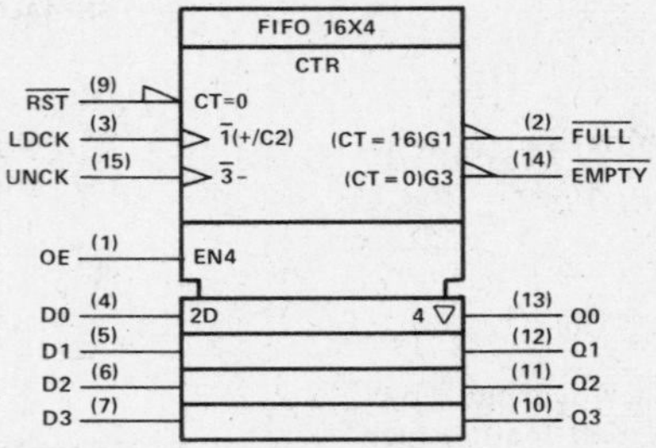
FIFO 16X4
CTR
RST (9) CT=0
LDCK (3) 1(+/C2)
UNCK (15) 3-
(CT=16)G1 (2) FULL
(CT=0)G3 (14) EMPTY
OE (1) EN4
D0 (4) 2D
D1 (5)
D2 (6)
D3 (7)
4
(13) Q0
(12) Q1
(11) Q2
(10) Q3

†This symbol is in accordance with ANSI/IEEE Standard 91-1984 and IEC Publication 617-12. The symbol is functionally accurate but does not show the details of implementation; for these, see the logic diagram. The symbol represents the memory as if it were controlled by a single counter whose content is the number of words stored at the time. Output data is invalid when the counter content (CT) is 0.

logic diagram (positive logic)

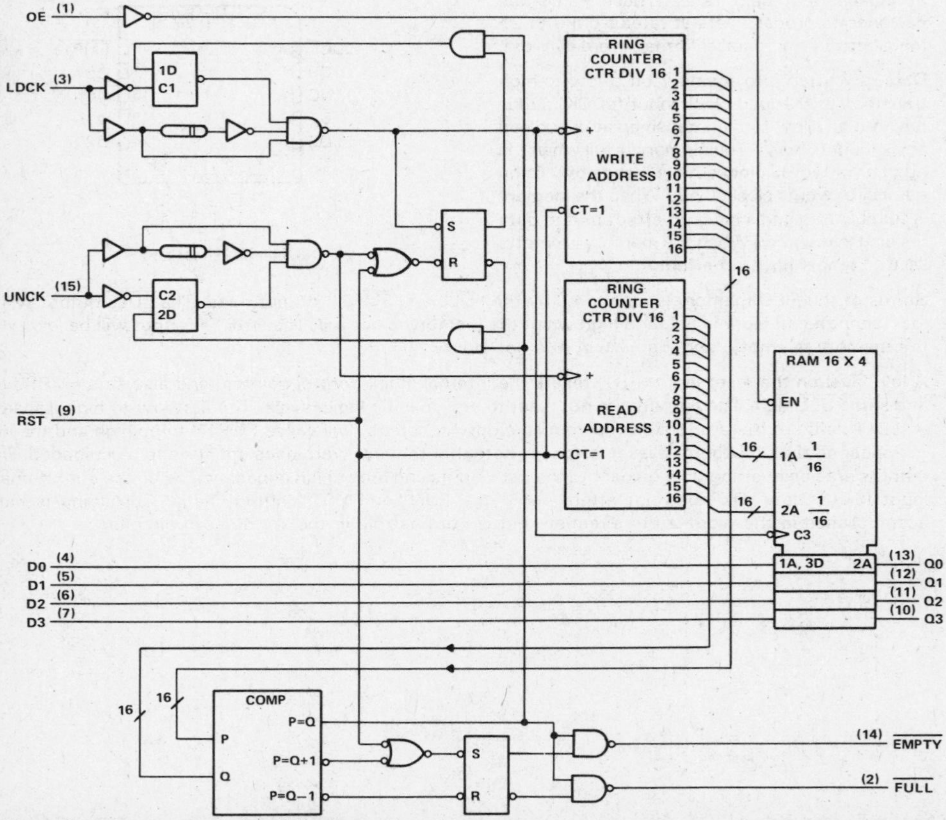
OE (1)
LDCK (3)
1D
C1
UNCK (15)
C2
2D
S
R
RING COUNTER CTR DIV 16
WRITE ADDRESS
CT=1
RING COUNTER CTR DIV 16
READ ADDRESS
CT=1
RAM 16 X 4
EN
1A
2A
C3
1A, 3D
RST (9)
D0 (4)
D1 (5)
D2 (6)
D3 (7)
(13) Q0
(12) Q1
(11) Q2
(10) Q3
COMP
P=Q
P
P=Q+1
Q
P=Q−1
(14) EMPTY
(2) FULL

Pin numbers shown are for D, J, and N packages.

timing diagram

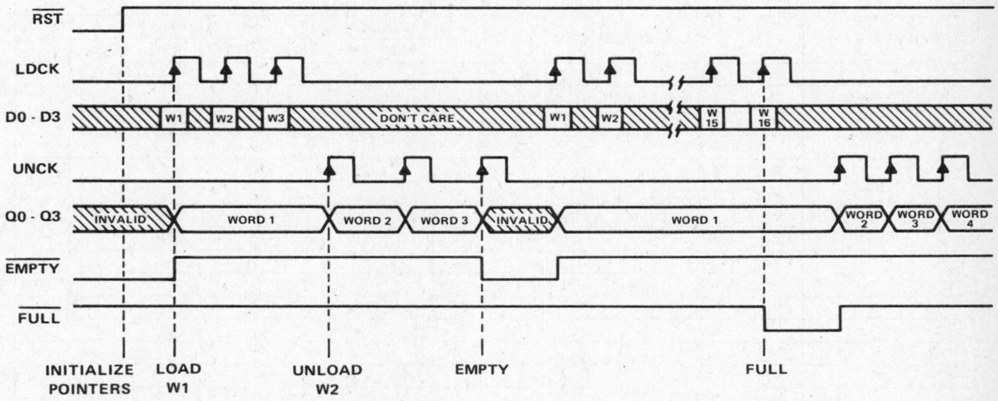
$\overline{RST}$
LDCK
D0 - D3
W1
W2
W3
DON'T CARE
W1
W2
W 15
W 16
UNCK
Q0 - Q3
INVALID
WORD 1
WORD 2
WORD 3
INVALID
WORD 1
WORD 2
WORD 3
WORD 4
$\overline{EMPTY}$
$\overline{FULL}$
INITIALIZE POINTERS
LOAD W1
UNLOAD W2
EMPTY
FULL

absolute maximum ratings over operating free-air temperature (unless otherwise noted)

Supply voltage, V_{CC} . . . . 7 V
Input voltage . . . . 7 V
Voltage applied to a disabled 3-state output . . . . 5.5 V
Operating free-air temperature range: SN54ALS232A . . . . −55°C to 125°C
SN74ALS232A . . . . 0°C to 70°C
Storage temperature range . . . . −65°C to 150°C

recommended operating conditions

			SN54ALS232A			SN74ALS232A			UNIT
			MIN	NOM	MAX	MIN	NOM	MAX	
V_{CC}	Supply voltage		4.5	5	5.5	4.5	5	5.5	V
V_{IH}	High-level input voltage		2			2			V
V_{IL}	Low-level input voltage				0.8			0.8	V
I_{OH}	High-level output current	Q outputs			−1			−1.6	mA
		$\overline{FULL}$, $\overline{EMPTY}$			−0.4			−0.4	
I_{OL}	Low-level output current	Q outputs			12			24	mA
		$\overline{FULL}$, $\overline{EMPTY}$			4			8	
f_{clock}	Clock frequency	LDCK	0		25	0		30	MHz
		UNCK	0		25	0		30	
t_w	Pulse duration	$\overline{RST}$ low	20			15			ns
		LDCK low	15			10			
		LDCK high	25			20			
		UNCK low	15			10			
		UNCK high	25			20			
t_{su}	Setup time	Data before LDCK↑	10			10			ns
		$\overline{RST}$ (inactive) before LDCK↑	5			5			
t_h	Hold time	Data after LDCK↑	5			5			ns
T_A	Operating free-air temperature		−55		125	0		70	°C

electrical characteristics over recommended operating free-air temperature range (unless otherwise noted)

PARAMETER		TEST CONDITIONS		SN54ALS232A MIN	SN54ALS232A TYP†	SN54ALS232A MAX	SN74ALS232A MIN	SN74ALS232A TYP†	SN74ALS232A MAX	UNIT
V_{IK}		V_{CC} = 4.5 V,	I_I = −18 mA			−1.2			−1.2	V
V_{OH}	$\overline{FULL}$, EMPTY	V_{CC} = 4.5 V to 5.5 V,	I_{OH} = −0.4 mA	V_{CC}−2			V_{CC}−2			V
	Q outputs	V_{CC} = 4.5 V,	I_{OH} = −1 mA	2.4	3.3					
		V_{CC} = 4.5 V,	I_{OH} = −2.6 mA				2.4	3.2		
V_{OL}	Q outputs	V_{CC} = 4.5 V,	I_{OL} = 12 mA		0.25	0.4		0.25	0.4	V
		V_{CC} = 4.5 V,	I_{OL} = 24 mA					0.35	0.5	
	$\overline{FULL}$, $\overline{EMPTY}$	V_{CC} = 4.5 V,	I_{OH} = 4 mA		0.25	0.4		0.25	0.4	
		V_{CC} = 4.5 V,	I_{OL} = 8 mA					0.35	0.5	
I_{OZH}		V_{CC} = 5.5 V,	V_O = 2.7 V			20			20	μA
I_{OZL}		V_{CC} = 5.5 V,	V_O = 0.4 V			−20			−20	μA
I_I		V_{CC} = 5.5 V,	V_I = 7 V			0.1			0.1	mA
I_{IH}		V_{CC} = 5.5 V,	V_I = 2.7 V			20			20	μA
I_{IL}		V_{CC} = 5.5 V,	V_I = 0.4 V			−0.2			−0.2	mA
I_O‡		V_{CC} = 5.5 V,	V_O = 2.25 V	−30		−112	−30		−112	mA
I_{CC}		V_{CC} = 5.5 V			75	125		75	125	mA

† All typical values are at V_{CC} = 5 V, T_A = 25°C.
‡ The output conditions have been chosen to produce a current that closely approximates one half of the true short-circuit output current, I_{OS}.

switching characteristics (see Note 1)

PARAMETER	FROM (INPUT)	TO (OUTPUT)	V_{CC} = 5 V, C_L = 50 pF, R1 = 500 Ω, R2 = 500 Ω, T_A = 25°C			V_{CC} = 4.5 V to 5.5 V, C_L = 50 pF, R1 = 500 Ω, R2 = 500 Ω, T_A = MIN to MAX				UNIT
			'ALS232A			SN54ALS232A		SN74ALS232A		
			MIN	TYP	MAX	MIN	MAX	MIN	MAX	
f_{max}	LDCK			40		25		30		MHz
	UNCK			40		25		30		
t_{pd}	LDCK↑	Any Q		30	40	4	50	4	46	ns
t_{pd}	UNCK↑	Any Q		20	27	7	35	7	31	ns
t_{PLH}	LDCK↑	$\overline{EMPTY}$		17	23	8	29	8	26	ns
t_{PHL}	UNCK↑	$\overline{EMPTY}$		19	24	10	36	10	29	ns
t_{PHL}	$\overline{RST}$↓	$\overline{EMPTY}$		13	18	5	23	5	20	ns
t_{PHL}	LDCK↑	$\overline{FULL}$		21	26	10	35	10	31	ns
t_{PLH}	UNCK↑	$\overline{FULL}$		17	23	8	28	8	25	ns
t_{PLH}	$\overline{RST}$↓	$\overline{FULL}$		18	24	8	31	8	28	ns
t_{en}	OE↑	Q		7	12	1	16	1	14	ns
t_{dis}	OE↓	Q		10	16	2	23	2	21	ns

NOTE 1: Load circuit and voltage waveforms are shown in Section 1.

2 LSI Devices

D2876, JANUARY 1986—REVISED APRIL 1986

- **Independent Asychronous Inputs and Outputs**
- **16 Words by 5 Bits Each**
- **Data Rates from 0 to 30 MHz**
- **Fall-Through Time . . . 24 ns Typ**
- **3-State Outputs**

SN54ALS233A . . . J PACKAGE
SN74ALS233A . . . DW OR N PACKAGE
(TOP VIEW)

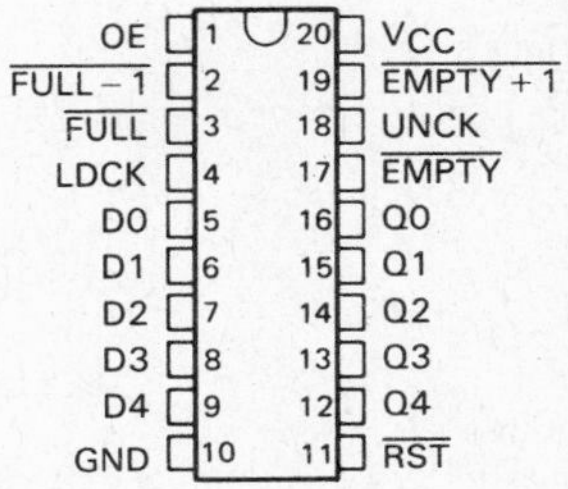
OE 1
FULL – 1 2
FULL 3
LDCK 4
D0 5
D1 6
D2 7
D3 8
D4 9
GND 10
20 VCC
19 EMPTY + 1
18 UNCK
17 EMPTY
16 Q0
15 Q1
14 Q2
13 Q3
12 Q4
11 RST

SN54ALS233A . . . FK PACKAGE
SN74ALS233A . . . FN PACKAGE
(TOP VIEW)

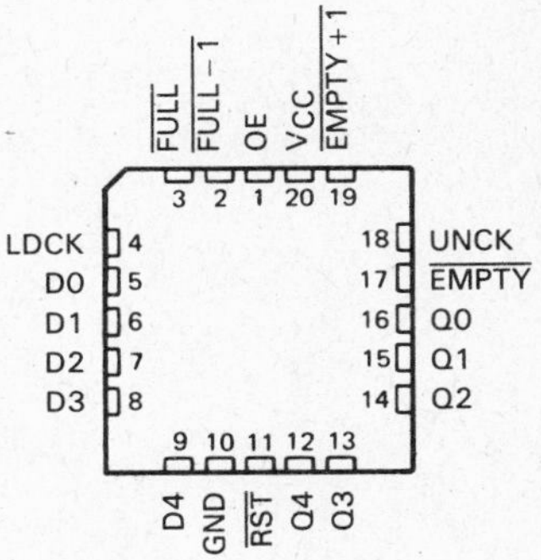
FULL
FULL – 1
OE
VCC
EMPTY + 1
3 2 1 20 19
LDCK 4
D0 5
D1 6
D2 7
D3 8
18 UNCK
17 EMPTY
16 Q0
15 Q1
14 Q2
9 10 11 12 13
D4
GND
RST
Q4
Q3

description

These 80-bit memories utilize Advanced Low-Power Schottky technology and feature high speed and fast fall-through times. They are organized as 16 words by 5 bits each.

A FIFO memory is a storage device that allows data to be written into and read from its array at independent data rates. These FIFOs are designed to process data at rates from 0 to 25 megahertz in a bit-parallel format, word by word.

Data is written into memory on a low-to-high transition at the load clock input (LDCK) and is read out on a low-to-high transition at the unload clock input (UNCK). The memory is full when the number of words clocked in exceeds by 16 the number of words clocked out. When the memory is full, LDCK signals will have no effect. When the memory is empty, UNCK signals have no effect.

Status of the FIFO memory is monitored by the FULL, EMPTY, FULL – 1, and EMPTY + 1 output flags. The FULL output will be low whenever the memory is full, and high whenever not full. The FULL – 1 output will be low whenever the memory contains 15 data words. The EMPTY output will be low whenever the memory is empty, and high whenever it is not empty. The EMPTY + 1 output will be low whenever one word remains in memory.

A low level on the reset input (RST) resets the internal stack control pointers and also sets EMPTY low and sets FULL, FULL – 1, and EMPTY + 1 high. The Q outputs are not reset to any specific logic level. The first low-to-high transition on LDCK, after either a RST pulse or from an empty condition, will cause EMPTY to go high and the data to appear on the Q outputs. It is important to note that the first word does not have to be unloaded. Data outputs are noninverting with respect to the data inputs and are at high impedance when the output enable input (OE) is low. OE does not affect the output flags. Cascading is easily accomplished in the word-width direction, but is not possible in the word-depth direction.

logic symbol†

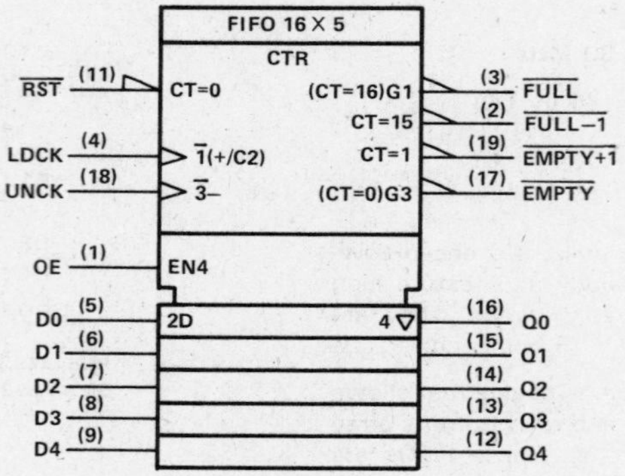
FIFO 16 X 5
CTR
RST
(11)
CT=0
(CT=16)G1
(3)
FULL
CT=15
(2)
FULL−1
LDCK
(4)
1(+/C2)
CT=1
(19)
EMPTY+1
UNCK
(18)
3−
(CT=0)G3
(17)
EMPTY
OE
(1)
EN4
D0
(5)
2D
4
(16)
Q0
D1
(6)
(15)
Q1
D2
(7)
(14)
Q2
D3
(8)
(13)
Q3
D4
(9)
(12)
Q4

† This symbol is in accordance with ANSI/IEEE Standard 91-1984 and IEC Publication 617-12. The symbol is functionally accurate but does not show the details of implementation; for these, see the logic diagram. The symbol represents the memory as if it were controlled by a single counter whose content is the number of words stored at the time. Output data is invalid when the counter content (CT) is 0.

TEXAS INSTRUMENTS
POST OFFICE BOX 225012 • DALLAS, TEXAS 75265

logic diagram (positive logic)

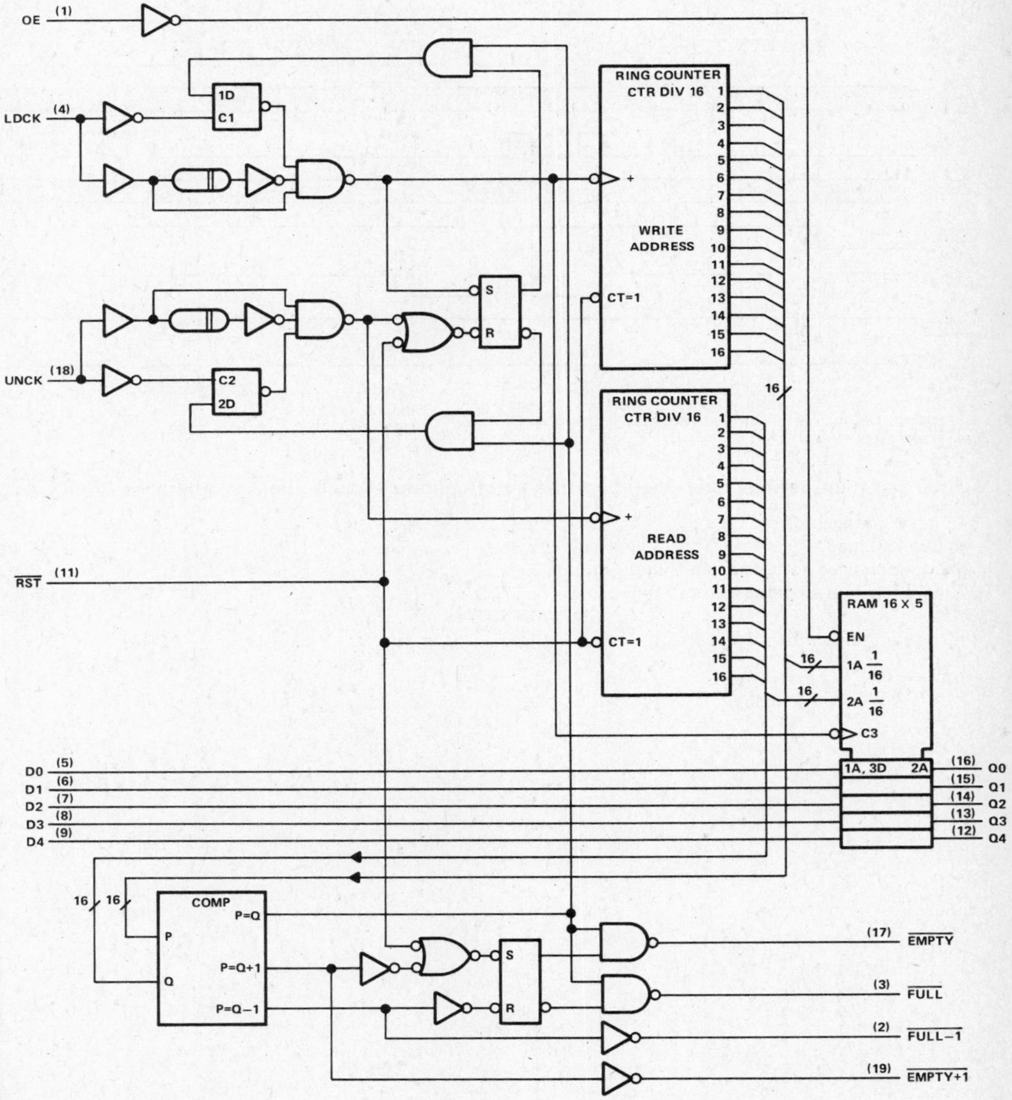
OE (1)
LDCK (4)
1D
C1
RING COUNTER
CTR DIV 16
WRITE
ADDRESS
CT=1
S
R
UNCK (18)
C2
2D
RING COUNTER
CTR DIV 16
READ
ADDRESS
CT=1
RST (11)
RAM 16 × 5
EN
1A 1/16
2A 1/16
C3
1A, 3D
2A
D0 (5)
D1 (6)
D2 (7)
D3 (8)
D4 (9)
(16) Q0
(15) Q1
(14) Q2
(13) Q3
(12) Q4
COMP
P=Q
P
P=Q+1
Q
P=Q−1
(17) EMPTY
(3) FULL
(2) FULL−1
(19) EMPTY+1

timing diagram

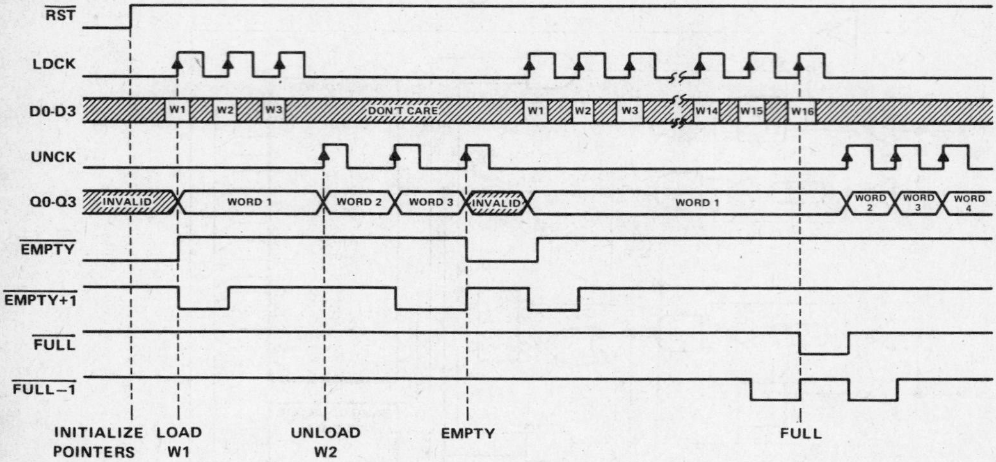
RST
LDCK
D0-D3
W1
W2
W3
DON'T CARE
W14
W15
W16
UNCK
Q0-Q3
INVALID
WORD 1
WORD 2
WORD 3
WORD 4
EMPTY
EMPTY+1
FULL
FULL−1
INITIALIZE POINTERS
LOAD W1
UNLOAD W2
EMPTY
FULL

absolute maximum ratings over operating free-air temperature range (unless otherwise noted)

Supply voltage, V_{CC}		7 V
Input voltage		7 V
Voltage applied to a disabled 3-state output		5.5 V
Operating free-air temperature range:	SN54ALS233A	−55°C to 125°C
	SN74ALS233A	0°C to 70°C
Storage temperature range		−65°C to 150°C

TEXAS INSTRUMENTS
POST OFFICE BOX 225012 • DALLAS, TEXAS 75265

recommended operating conditions

			SN54ALS233A			SN74ALS233A			UNIT
			MIN	NOM	MAX	MIN	NOM	MAX	
V_{CC}	Supply voltage		4.5	5	5.5	4.5	5	5.5	V
V_{IH}	High-level input voltage		2			2			V
V_{IL}	Low-level input voltage				0.8			0.8	V
I_{OH}	High-level output current	Q outputs			−1			−1.6	mA
		Status flags			−0.4			−0.4	
I_{OL}	Low-level output current	Q outputs			12			24	mA
		Status flags			4			8	
f_{clock}	Clock frequency	LDCK	0		25	0		30	MHz
		UNCK	0		25	0		30	
t_w	Pulse duration	$\overline{RST}$ low	20			15			ns
		LDCK low	15			10			
		LDCK high	25			20			
		UNCK low	15			10			
		UNCK high	25			20			
t_{su}	Setup time	Data before LDCK↑	10			10			ns
		$\overline{RST}$ inactive before LDCK↑	5			5			
t_h	Hold time	Data after LDCK↑	5			5			ns
T_A	Operating free-air temperature		−55		125	0		70	°C

electrical characteristics over recommended operating free-air temperature range (unless otherwise noted)

PARAMETER		TEST CONDITIONS		SN54ALS233A			SN74ALS233A			UNIT
				MIN	TYP†	MAX	MIN	TYP†	MAX	
V_{IK}		V_{CC} = 4.5 V,	I_I = −18 mA			−1.2			−1.2	V
V_{OH}	Status flags	V_{CC} = 4.5 V to 5.5 V,	I_{OH} = −0.4 mA	V_{CC}−2			V_{CC}−2			V
	Q outputs	V_{CC} = 4.5 V,	I_{OH} = −1 mA	2.4	3.3					
		V_{CC} = 4.5 V,	I_{OH} = −2.6 mA				2.4	3.2		
V_{OL}	Q outputs	V_{CC} = 4.5 V,	I_{OL} = 12 mA		0.25	0.4		0.25	0.4	V
		V_{CC} = 4.5 V,	I_{OL} = 24 mA					0.35	0.5	
	Status flags	V_{CC} = 4.5 V,	I_{OL} = 4 mA		0.25	0.4		0.25	0.4	
		V_{CC} = 4.5 V,	I_{OL} = 8 mA					0.35	0.5	
I_{OZH}		V_{CC} = 5.5 V,	V_O = 2.7 V			20			20	μA
I_{OZL}		V_{CC} = 5.5 V,	V_O = 0.4 V			−20			−20	μA
I_I		V_{CC} = 5.5 V,	V_I = 7 V			0.1			0.1	mA
I_{IH}		V_{CC} = 5.5 V,	V_I = 2.7 V			20			20	μA
I_{IL}		V_{CC} = 5.5 V,	V_I = 0.4 V			−0.2			−0.2	mA
I_O‡		V_{CC} = 5.5 V,	V_O = 2.25 V	−30		−112	−30		−112	mA
I_{CC}		V_{CC} = 5.5 V			88	143		88	133	mA

† All typical values are at V_{CC} = 5 V, T_A = 25 °C.
‡ The output conditions have been chosen to produce a current that closely approximates one half of the true short-circuit output current, I_{OS}.

switching characteristics (see Note 1)

PARAMETER	FROM (INPUT)	TO (OUTPUT)	V_{CC} = 5 V, C_L = 50 pF, R1 = 500 Ω, R2 = 500 Ω, T_A = 25°C			V_{CC} = 4.5 V to 5.5 V, C_L = 50 pF, R1 = 500 Ω, R2 = 500 Ω, T_A = – MIN to MAX				UNIT
			'ALS233A			SN54ALS233A		SN74ALS233A		
			MIN	TYP	MAX	MIN	MAX	MIN	MAX	
f_{max}	LDCK			40		25		30		MHz
	UNCK			40		25		30		MHz
t_{pd}	LDCK↑	Any Q		24	44	7	52	7	48	ns
t_{pd}	UNCK↑	Any Q		19	29	9	35	9	33	ns
t_{PLH}	LDCK↑	$\overline{\text{EMPTY}}$		18	25	9	30	9	28	ns
t_{PHL}	UNCK↑	$\overline{\text{EMPTY}}$		18	25	9	33	10	30	ns
t_{PHL}	$\overline{\text{RST}}$↓	$\overline{\text{EMPTY}}$		13	19	6	24	6	22	ns
t_{pd}	LDCK↑	$\overline{\text{EMPTY+1}}$		22	31	10	40	10	37	ns
t_{pd}	UNCK↑	$\overline{\text{EMPTY+1}}$		22	31	9	40	10	37	ns
t_{PLH}	$\overline{\text{RST}}$↓	$\overline{\text{EMPTY+1}}$		19	27	8	32	8	31	ns
t_{pd}	LDCK↑	$\overline{\text{FULL}-1}$		23	32	11	38	12	36	ns
t_{pd}	UNCK↑	$\overline{\text{FULL}-1}$		23	32	11	39	12	36	ns
t_{PLH}	$\overline{\text{RST}}$↓	$\overline{\text{FULL}-1}$		20	28	10	34	11	32	ns
t_{PHL}	LDCK↑	$\overline{\text{FULL}}$		21	28	10	35	12	33	ns
t_{PLH}	UNCK↑	$\overline{\text{FULL}}$		17	24	8	29	9	27	ns
t_{PLH}	$\overline{\text{RST}}$↓	$\overline{\text{FULL}}$		18	27	8	32	9	30	ns
t_{en}	OE↑	Q		8	13	1	16	2	15	ns
t_{dis}	OE↓	Q		8	12	2	20	2	17	ns

NOTE 1: Load circuit and voltage waveforms are shown in Section 1.

TEXAS INSTRUMENTS
POST OFFICE BOX 225012 • DALLAS, TEXAS 75265

1-OF-16 DATA GENERATORS/MULTIPLEXERS WITH 3-STATE OUTPUTS

D2910, DECEMBER 1983—REVISED JANUARY 1986

- 4-Line to 1-Line Multiplexer that can Select 1 and 16 Data Inputs
- Applications:
  - Boolean Function Generator
  - Parallel-to-Serial Converter
  - Data Source Selector
- Buffered 3-State Bus Driver Inputs Permit Multiplexing from N Lines to One Line
- Dependable Texas Instruments Quality and Reliability

description

The 'AS250 provides full binary decoding to select one of sixteen data sources with an inverting $\overline{W}$ output. The selected sources are buffered with symmetrical propagation delay times. This reduces the possibility of transients occurring at the output.

A buffered enable output ($\overline{G}$) may be used for n-line-to-one-line cascading. Taking the $\overline{G}$ high will place the output in a high-impedance state. In the high-impedance state, the output neither loads nor drives the bus lines significantly.

The enable ($\overline{G}$) does not affect the internal operations of the data selector/multiplexer. New data can be set up while the outputs are disabled.

The SN74AS250 is characterized for operation from 0°C to 70°C.

SN74AS250 . . . DW OR NT PACKAGE

(TOP VIEW)

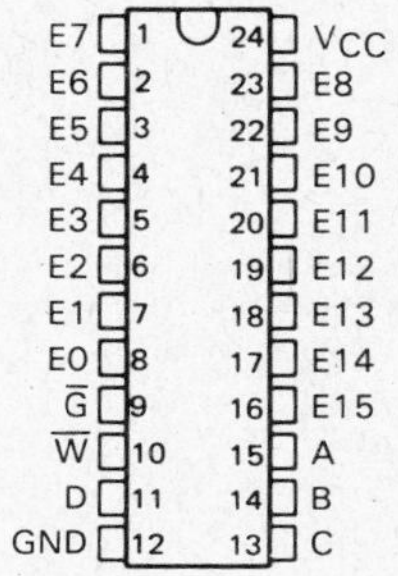
E7 1
E6 2
E5 3
E4 4
E3 5
E2 6
E1 7
E0 8
G 9
W 10
D 11
GND 12
24 VCC
23 E8
22 E9
21 E10
20 E11
19 E12
18 E13
17 E14
16 E15
15 A
14 B
13 C

SN74AS250 . . . FN PACKAGE

(TOP VIEW)

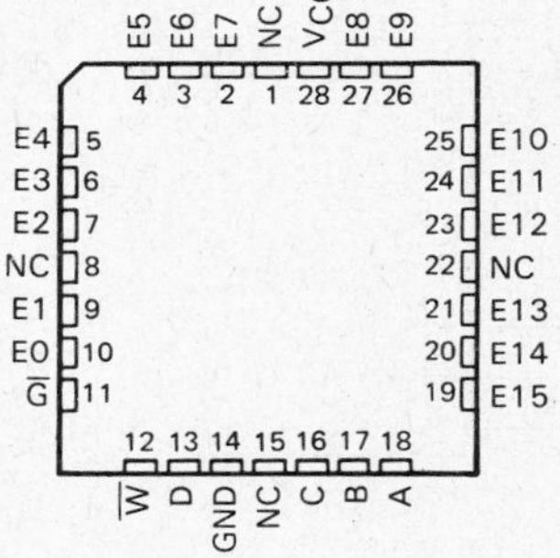
E5 E6 E7 NC VCC E8 E9
4 3 2 1 28 27 26
E4 5
E3 6
E2 7
NC 8
E1 9
E0 10
G 11
25 E10
24 E11
23 E12
22 NC
21 E13
20 E14
19 E15
12 13 14 15 16 17 18
W D GND NC C B A

NC—No internal connection

TEXAS INSTRUMENTS
POST OFFICE BOX 225012 • DALLAS, TEXAS 75265

logic symbol†

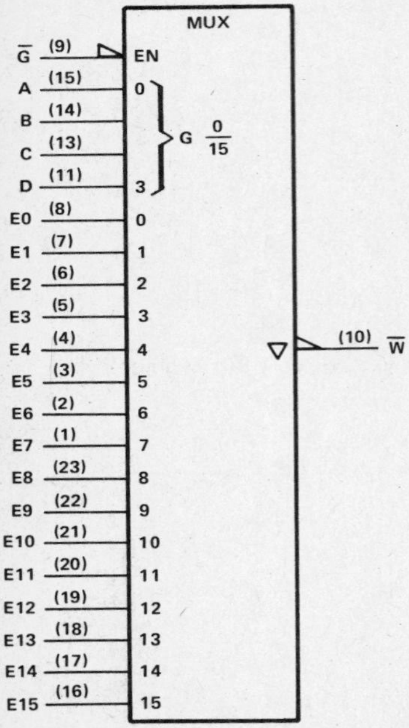
MUX
G̅ (9) EN
A (15) 0
B (14)
C (13)
D (11) 3
G 0/15
E0 (8) 0
E1 (7) 1
E2 (6) 2
E3 (5) 3
E4 (4) 4
E5 (3) 5
E6 (2) 6
E7 (1) 7
E8 (23) 8
E9 (22) 9
E10 (21) 10
E11 (20) 11
E12 (19) 12
E13 (18) 13
E14 (17) 14
E15 (16) 15
(10) W̅

†This symbol is in accordance with ANSI/IEEE Std 91-1984 and IEC Publicatin 617-12.

Pin numbers shown are for DW or NT packages.

logic diagram (positive logic)

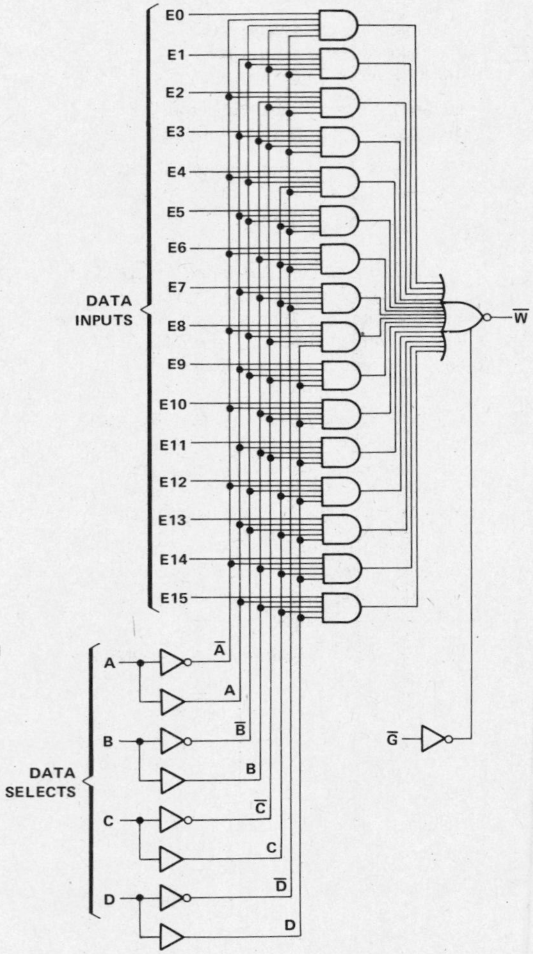
DATA INPUTS
E0
E1
E2
E3
E4
E5
E6
E7
E8
E9
E10
E11
E12
E13
E14
E15
W̅
DATA SELECTS
A
A̅
A
B
B̅
B
C
C̅
C
D
D̅
D
G̅

FUNCTION TABLE

INPUT						OUTPUT
$\overline{G}$	A	B	C	D	Ei	$\overline{W}$
L	L	L	L	L	E0	E0
L	H	L	L	L	E1	E1
L	L	H	L	L	E2	E2
L	H	H	L	L	E3	E3
L	L	L	H	L	E4	E4
L	H	L	H	L	E5	E5
L	L	H	H	L	E6	E6
L	H	H	H	L	E7	E7
L	L	L	L	H	E8	E8
L	H	L	L	H	E9	E9
L	L	H	L	H	E10	E10
L	H	H	L	H	E11	E11
L	L	L	H	H	E12	E12
L	H	L	H	H	E13	E13
L	L	H	H	H	E14	E14
L	H	H	H	H	E15	E15
H	X	X	X	X	X	Z

absolute maximum ratings over operating free-air temperature range (unless otherwise noted)

Supply voltage, V_{CC} . . . . 7 V
Input voltage . . . . 7 V
Operating free-air temperature range . . . . 0 °C to 70 °C
Storage temperature range . . . . −65 °C to 150 °C

recommended operating conditions

		MIN	NOM	MAX	UNIT
V_{CC}	Supply voltage	4.5	5	5.5	V
V_{IH}	High-level input voltage	2			V
V_{IL}	Low-level input voltage			0.8	V
I_{OH}	High-level output current			−15	mA
I_{OL}	Low-level output current			48	mA
T_A	Operating free-air temperature	0		70	°C

electrical characteristics over recommended operating free-air temperature range (unless otherwise noted)

PARAMETER	TEST CONDITIONS		MIN	TYP†	MAX	UNIT
V_{IK}	V_{CC} = 4.5 V,	I_I = −18 mA			−1.2	V
V_{OH}	V_{CC} = 4.5 V to 5.5 V,	I_{OH} = −2 mA	$V_{CC}-2$			V
	V_{CC} = 4.5 V,	I_{OH} = −15 mA	2.4	3.3		
V_{OL}	V_{CC} = 4.5 V,	I_{OL} = 48 mA		0.35	0.5	V
I_{OZH}	V_{CC} = 5.5 V,	V_O = 2.7 V			50	μA
I_{OZL}	V_{CC} = 5.5 V,	V_O = 0.4 V			−50	μA
I_I	V_{CC} = 5.5 V,	V_I = 7 V			0.1	mA
I_{IH}	V_{CC} = 5.5 V,	V_I = 2.7 V			20	μA
I_{IL}	V_{CC} = 5.5 V,	V_I = 0.4 V			−0.5	mA
I_O‡	V_{CC} = 5.5 V,	V_O = 2.25 V	−30		−112	mA
I_{CC}	V_{CC} = 5.5 V	Outputs high		26	42	mA
		Outputs low		31	50	
		Outputs disabled		30	48	

†All typical values are at V_{CC} = 5 V, T_A = 25°C.
‡The output conditions have been chosen to produce a current that closely approximates one half of the true short-circuit output current, I_{OS}.

switching characteristics (see Note 1)

PARAMETER	FROM (INPUT)	TO (OUTPUT)	V_{CC} = 4.5 V to 5.5 V, C_L = 50 pF, R1 = 500 Ω, R2 = 500 Ω, T_A = 0°C to 70°C			UNIT
			MIN	TYP†	MAX	
t_{PLH}	DATA	$\overline{W}$	3		8	ns
t_{PHL}			2		6	
t_{PLH}	SELECT	$\overline{W}$	4		13	ns
t_{PHL}			4		10	
t_{PZH}	$\overline{G}$	$\overline{W}$	2		7	ns
t_{PZL}			4		20	
t_{PHZ}	$\overline{G}$	$\overline{W}$	2		6	ns
t_{PLZ}			2		6	

†All typical values are at V_{CC} = 5 V, T_A = 25°C.
NOTE 1: Load circuit and voltage waveforms are shown in Section 1.

D2661, DECEMBER 1982—REVISED AUGUST 1985

- **Generates Either Odd or Even Parity for Nine Data Lines**
- **Cascadable for n-Bits Parity**
- **Can Be Used to Upgrade Existing Systems Using MSI Parity Circuits**
- **Package Options Include Both Plastic and Ceramic Chip Carriers in Addition to Plastic and Ceramic DIPs**
- **Dependable Texas Instruments Quality and Reliability**

SN54ALS280, SN54AS280 . . . J PACKAGE
SN74ALS280, SN74AS280 . . . D OR N PACKAGE
(TOP VIEW)

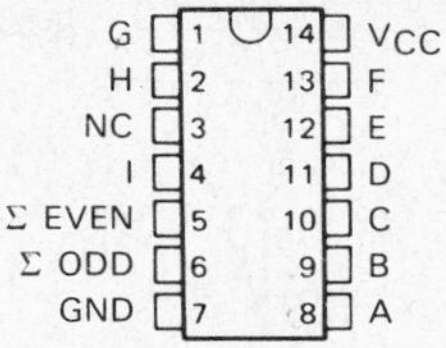
G 1
H 2
NC 3
I 4
Σ EVEN 5
Σ ODD 6
GND 7
14 VCC
13 F
12 E
11 D
10 C
9 B
8 A

SN54ALS280, SN54AS280 . . . FK PACKAGE
SN74ALS280, SN74AS280 . . . FN PACKAGE
(TOP VIEW)

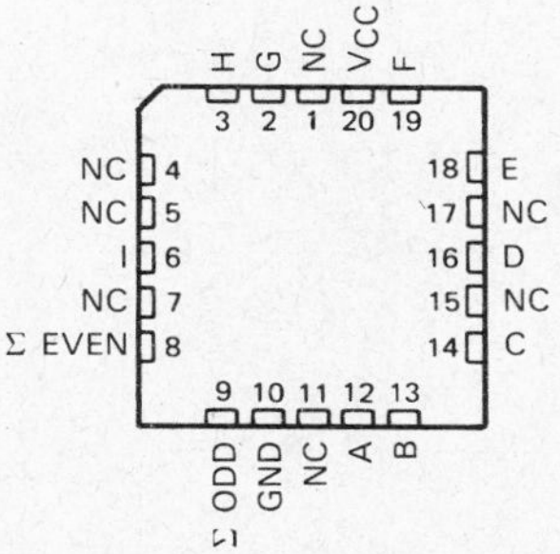
H G NC VCC F
3 2 1 20 19
NC 4
NC 5
I 6
NC 7
Σ EVEN 8
18 E
17 NC
16 D
15 NC
14 C
9 10 11 12 13
Σ ODD GND NC A B

NC—No internal connection

description

These universal, monolithic, nine-bit parity generators/checkers utilize Advanced Schottky high-performance circuitry and feature odd and even outputs to facilitate operation of either odd or even parity application. The word-length capability is easily expanded by cascading.

These devices can be used to upgrade the performance of most systems utilizing the '180 parity generator/checker. Although the 'ALS280 and 'AS280 are implemented without expander inputs, the corresponding function is provided by the availability of an input at pin 4 and the absence of any internal connection at pin 3. This permits the 'ALS280 and 'AS280 to be substituted for the '180 in existing designs to produce an identical function even if the devices are mixed with existing '180's.

All 'AS280 inputs are buffered to lower the drive requirements.

The SN54' family is characterized for operation over the full military temperature range of −55°C to 125°C. The SN74' family is characterized for operation from 0°C to 70°C.

FUNCTION TABLE

NUMBER OF INPUTS A THRU I THAT ARE HIGH	OUTPUTS	
	Σ EVEN	Σ ODD
0,2,4,6,8	H	L
1,3,5,7,9	L	H

logic symbol†

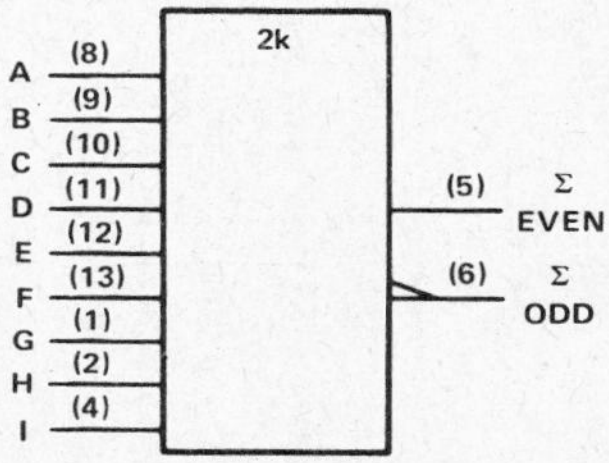
2k
A (8)
B (9)
C (10)
D (11)
E (12)
F (13)
G (1)
H (2)
I (4)
(5) Σ EVEN
(6) Σ ODD

†This symbol is in accordance with ANSI/IEEE Std 91-1984 and IEC Publication 617-12.
Pin numbers shown are for D, J, and N packages.

logic diagram

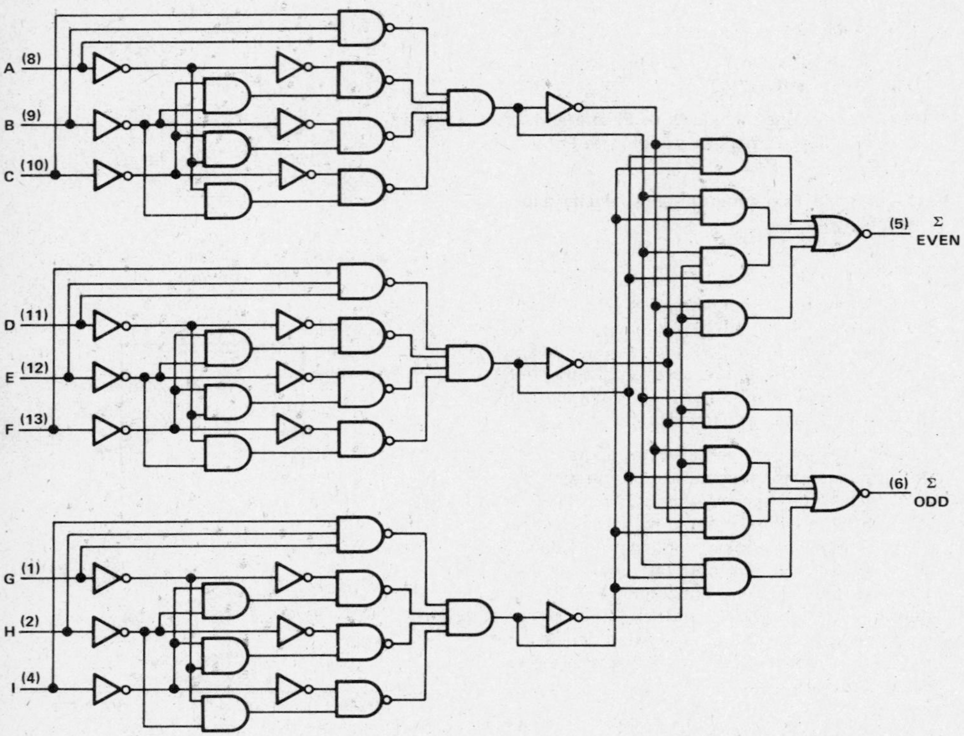
A (8)
B (9)
C (10)
D (11)
E (12)
F (13)
G (1)
H (2)
I (4)
(5) Σ EVEN
(6) Σ ODD

absolute maximum ratings over operating free-air temperature range (unless otherwise noted)

Supply voltage, V_{CC} . . . . . 7 V
Input voltage . . . . . 7 V
Operating free-air temperature range: SN54ALS280 . . . . . −55 °C to 125 °C
SN74ALS280 . . . . . 0 °C to 70 °C
Storage temperature range . . . . . −65 °C to 150 °C

recommended operating conditions

		SN54ALS280			SN74ALS280			UNIT
		MIN	NOM	MAX	MIN	NOM	MAX	
V_{CC}	Supply voltage	4.5	5	5.5	4.5	5	5.5	V
V_{IH}	High-level input voltage	2			2			V
V_{IL}	Low-level input voltage			0.8			0.8	V
I_{OH}	High-level output current			−1			−2.6	mA
I_{OL}	Low-level output current			12			24	mA
T_A	Operating free-air temperature	−55		125	0		70	°C

electrical characteristics over recommended operating free-air temperature range (unless otherwise noted)

PARAMETER	TEST CONDITIONS		SN54ALS280 MIN	SN54ALS280 TYP†	SN54ALS280 MAX	SN74ALS280 MIN	SN74ALS280 TYP†	SN74ALS280 MAX	UNIT
V_{IK}	V_{CC} = 4.5 V,	I_I = −18 mA			−1.2			−1.2	V
V_{OH}	V_{CC} = 4.5 V to 5.5 V,	I_{OH} = −0.4 mA	$V_{CC}-2$			$V_{CC}-2$			V
	V_{CC} = 4.5 V,	I_{OH} = −1 mA	2.4	3.3					
	V_{CC} = 4.5 V,	I_{OH} = −2.6 mA				2.4	3.2		
V_{OL}	V_{CC} = 4.5 V,	I_{OL} = 12 mA		0.25	0.4		0.25	0.4	V
	V_{CC} = 4.5 V,	I_{OL} = 24 mA					0.35	0.5	
I_I	V_{CC} = 5.5 V,	V_I = 7 V			0.1			0.1	mA
I_{IH}	V_{CC} = 5.5 V,	V_I = 2.7 V			20			20	μA
I_{IL}	V_{CC} = 5.5 V,	V_I = 0.4 V			−0.1			−0.1	mA
I_O‡	V_{CC} = 5.5 V,	V_O = 2.25 V	−30		−112	−30		−112	mA
I_{CC}	V_{CC} = 5.5 V			10	16		10	16	mA

†All typical values are at V_{CC} = 5 V, T_A = 25°C.
‡The output conditions have been chosen to produce a current that closely approximates one half of the true short-circuit output current, I_{OS}.

switching characteristics (see Note 1)

PARAMETER	FROM (INPUT)	TO (OUTPUT)	V_{CC} = 5 V, C_L = 50 pF, R_L = 500 Ω, T_A = 25°C 'ALS280 MIN	TYP	MAX	V_{CC} = 4.5 V to 5.5 V, C_L = 50 pF, R_L = 500 Ω, T_A = MIN to MAX SN54ALS280 MIN	SN54ALS280 MAX	SN74ALS280 MIN	SN74ALS280 MAX	UNIT
t_{PLH}	Any	Σ Even		12	16	3	24	3	20	ns
t_{PHL}				12	17	3	24	3	20	
t_{PLH}	Any	Σ Odd		12	16	3	24	3	20	ns
t_{PHL}				13	18	4	26	4	22	

NOTE 1: Load circuit and voltage waveforms are shown in Section 1.

logic diagram

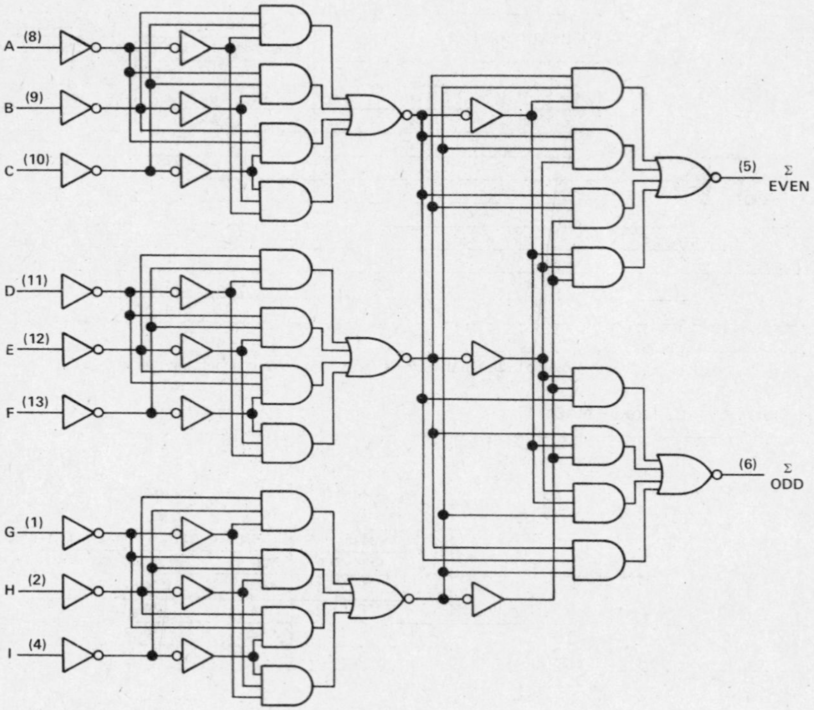
A (8)
B (9)
C (10)
D (11)
E (12)
F (13)
G (1)
H (2)
I (4)
(5) Σ EVEN
(6) Σ ODD

absolute maximum ratings over operating free-air temperature range (unless otherwise noted)

Supply voltage, V_{CC} . . . 7 V
Input voltage . . . 7 V
Operating free-air temperature range: SN54AS280 . . . −55 °C to 125 °C
SN74AS280 . . . 0 °C to 70 °C
Storage temperature range . . . −65 °C to 150 °C

recommended operating conditions

		SN54AS280			SN74AS280			UNIT
		MIN	NOM	MAX	MIN	NOM	MAX	
V_{CC}	Supply voltage	4.5	5	5.5	4.5	5	5.5	V
V_{IH}	High-level input voltage	2			2			V
V_{IL}	Low-level input voltage			0.8			0.8	V
I_{OH}	High-level output current			−2			−2	mA
I_{OL}	Low-level output current			20			20	mA
T_A	Operating free-air temperature	−55		125	0		70	°C

electrical characteristics over recommended operating free-air temperature range (unless otherwise noted)

PARAMETER	TEST CONDITIONS		SN54AS280			SN74AS280			UNIT
			MIN	TYP†	MAX	MIN	TYP†	MAX	
V_{IK}	V_{CC} = 4.5 V,	I_I = −18 mA			−1.2			−1.2	V
V_{OH}	V_{CC} = 4.5 V to 5.5 V,	I_{OH} = −2 mA	$V_{CC}-2$			$V_{CC}-2$			V
V_{OL}	V_{CC} = 4.5 V,	I_{OL} = 20 mA		0.35	0.5		0.35	0.5	V
I_I	V_{CC} = 5.5 V,	V_I = 7 V			0.1			0.1	mA
I_{IH}	V_{CC} = 5.5 V,	V_I = 2.7 V			20			20	μA
I_{IL}	V_{CC} = 5.5 V,	V_I = 0.4 V			−0.5			−0.5	mA
I_O‡	V_{CC} = 5.5 V,	V_O = 2.25 V	−30		−112	−30		−112	mA
I_{CC}	V_{CC} = 5.5 V			25	40		25	35	mA

† All typical values are at V_{CC} = 5 V, T_A = 25°C.
‡ The output conditions have been chosen to produce a current that closely approximates one half of the true short-circuit output current, I_{OS}.

switching characteristics (see Note 1)

PARAMETER	FROM (INPUT)	TO (OUTPUT)	V_{CC} = 4.5 V to 5.5 V, C_L = 50 pF, R_L = 500 Ω, T_A = MIN to MAX				UNIT
			SN54AS280		SN74AS280		
			MIN	MAX	MIN	MAX	
t_{PLH}	Any	Σ Even	3	13	3	12	ns
t_{PHL}			3	12.5	3	11	
t_{PLH}	Any	Σ Odd	3	13	3	12	ns
t_{PHL}			3	12.5	3	11.5	

NOTE 1: Load circuit and voltage waveforms are shown in Section 1.

2
LSI Devices

TYPICAL APPLICATION DATA

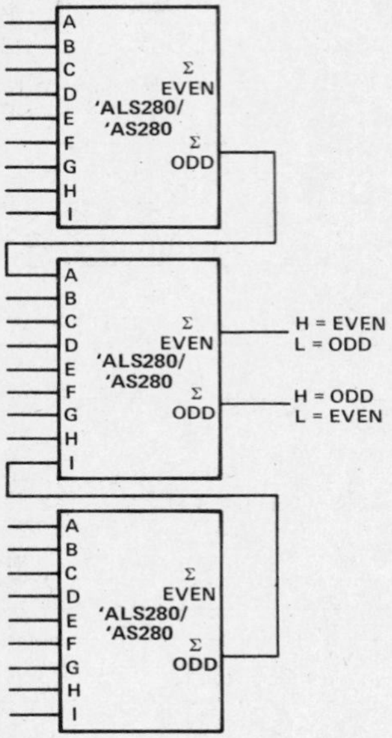
25-LINE PARITY/GENERATOR CHECKER
A
B
C
D
E
F
G
H
I
Σ EVEN
'ALS280/ 'AS280
Σ ODD
H = EVEN
L = ODD
H = ODD
L = EVEN

Three 'ALS280/'AS280 can be used to implement a 25-line parity generator/checker.

As an alternative, the Σ ODD outputs of two or three parity generators/checkers can be decoded with a 2-input ('S86 or 'LS86) or 3-input ('S135) exclusive-OR gate for 18- or 27-line parity applications.

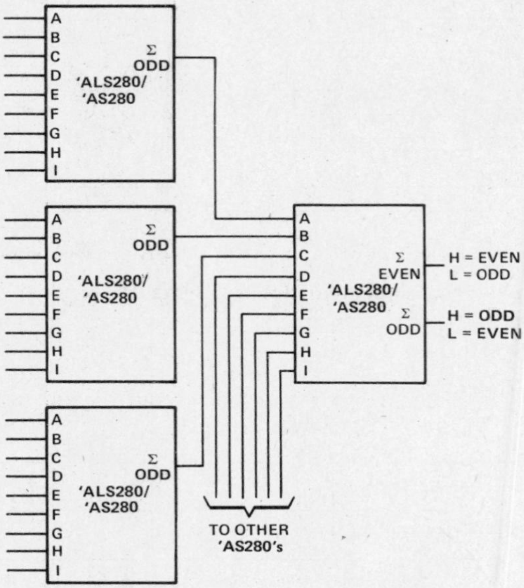
81-LINE PARITY/GENERATOR CHECKER
A
B
C
D
E
F
G
H
I
Σ ODD
'ALS280/ 'AS280
Σ EVEN
H = EVEN
L = ODD
H = ODD
L = EVEN
TO OTHER 'AS280's

Longer word lengths can be implemented by cascading 'ALS280/'AS280. As shown here, parity can be generated for word lengths up to 81 bits.

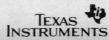

TEXAS INSTRUMENTS
POST OFFICE BOX 225012 • DALLAS, TEXAS 75265

9-BIT PARITY GENERATORS/CHECKER WITH BUS DRIVER PARITY I/O PORT

D2809, DECEMBER 1983—REVISED AUGUST 1985

- **Generates Either Odd or Even Parity for Nine Data Lines**
- **Cascadable for n-Bits Parity**
- **Direct Bus Connection for Parity Generation or for Checking by Using the Parity I/O Port**
- **Glitch-Free Bus During Power Up/Down**
- **Package Options Include both Plastic and Ceramic Carriers in Addition to Plastic and Ceramic DIPs**
- **Dependable Texas Instruments Quality and Reliability**

SN54AS286 . . . J PACKAGE
SN74AS286 . . . D OR N PACKAGE
(TOP VIEW)

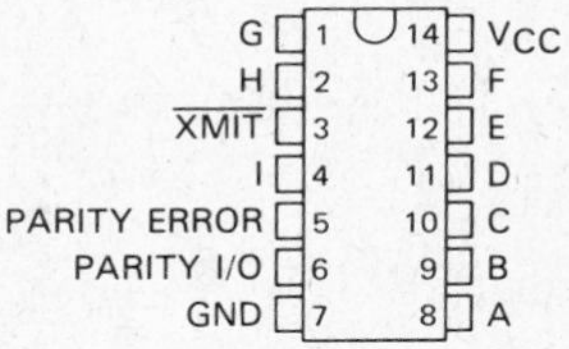
G 1
H 2
XMIT 3
I 4
PARITY ERROR 5
PARITY I/O 6
GND 7
14 VCC
13 F
12 E
11 D
10 C
9 B
8 A

SN54AS286 . . . FK PACKAGE
SN74AS286 . . . FN PACKAGE
(TOP VIEW)

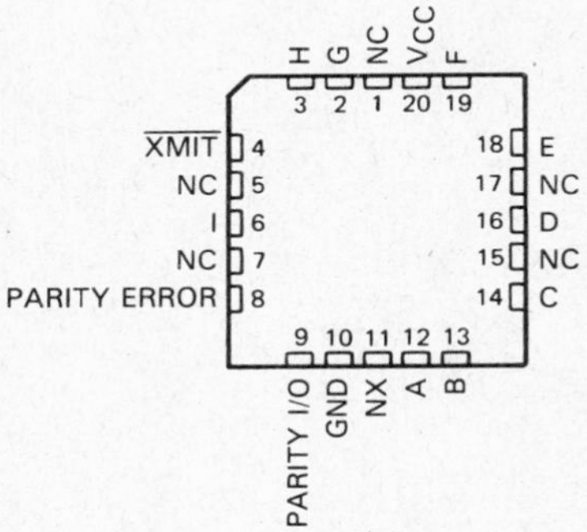
H G NC VCC F
3 2 1 20 19
XMIT 4
NC 5
I 6
NC 7
PARITY ERROR 8
18 E
17 NC
16 D
15 NC
14 C
9 10 11 12 13
PARITY I/O GND NX A B

NC—No internal connection

description

The SN54AS286 and SN74AS286 universal nine-bit parity generators/checkers feature a local output for parity checking and a 48-milliampere bus-driving parity I/O port for parity generation/checking. The word-length capability is easily expanded by cascading.

The $\overline{\text{XMIT}}$ control input is implemented specifically to accommodate cascading. When $\overline{\text{XMIT}}$ is low the parity tree is disabled and PE will remain at a high logic level regardless of the input levels. When $\overline{\text{XMIT}}$ is high the parity tree is enabled. The Parity Error output will indicate a parity error when either an even number of inputs (A through I) are high and Parity I/O is forced to a low logic level, or when an odd number of inputs are high and Parity I/O is forced to a high logic level.

The I/O control circuitry was designed so that the I/O port will remain in the high-impedance state during power-up or power-down to prevent bus glitches.

The SN54AS286 is characterized for operation over the full military range of $-55\,^{\circ}C$ to $125\,^{\circ}C$. The SN74AS286 is characterized for operation from $0\,^{\circ}C$ to $70\,^{\circ}C$.

FUNCTION TABLE

NUMBER OF INPUTS (A THRU I) THAT ARE HIGH	$\overline{XMIT}$	PARITY I/O	PARITY ERROR
0, 2, 4, 6, 8	l	H	H
1, 3, 5, 7, 9	l	L	H
0, 2, 4, 6, 8	h	h	H
	h	l	L
1, 3, 5, 7, 9	h	h	L
	h	l	H

h — high input level   l — low input level
H — high output level   L — low output level

logic symbol†

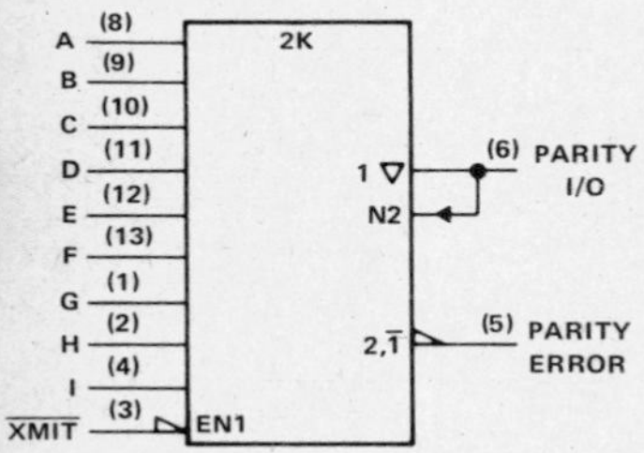
2K
A (8)
B (9)
C (10)
D (11)
E (12)
F (13)
G (1)
H (2)
I (4)
XMIT (3)
EN1
1 ▽
N2
(6) PARITY I/O
2,1̄
(5) PARITY ERROR

logic diagram (positive logic)

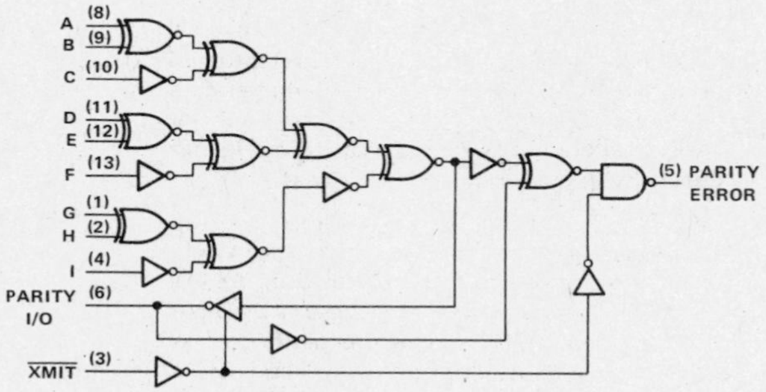
A (8)
B (9)
C (10)
D (11)
E (12)
F (13)
G (1)
H (2)
I (4)
PARITY I/O (6)
XMIT (3)
(5) PARITY ERROR

†This symbol is in accordance with ANSI/IEEE Std 91-1984 and IEC Publication 617-12.
Pin numbers shown are for D, J, and N packages.

absolute maximum ratings over operating free-air temperature range

Supply voltage, V_{CC} . . . . 7 V
Input voltage . . . . 7 V
Voltage applied to a disabled 3-state output . . . . 5.5 V
Operating free-air temperature range: SN54AS286 . . . . −55°C to 125°C
SN74AS286 . . . . 0°C to 70°C
Storage temperature . . . . −65°C to 140°C

recommended operating conditions

			SN54AS286 MIN	SN54AS286 NOM	SN54AS286 MAX	SN74AS286 MIN	SN74AS286 NOM	SN74AS286 MAX	UNIT
V_{CC}	Supply voltage		4.5	5	5.5	4.5	5	5.5	V
V_{IH}	High-level input voltage		2			2			V
V_{IL}	Low-level input voltage				0.8			0.8	V
I_{OH}	High-level output current	Parity error			−2			−2	mA
		Parity I/O			−12			−15	
I_{OL}	Low-level output current	Parity error			20			20	mA
		Parity I/O			32			48	
T_A	Operating free-air temperature		−55		125	0		70	°C

TEXAS INSTRUMENTS
POST OFFICE BOX 225012 • DALLAS, TEXAS 75265

electrical characteristics over recommended free-air temperature range (unless otherwise noted)

PARAMETER		TEST CONDITIONS		SN54AS286			SN74AS286			UNIT
				MIN	TYP†	MAX	MIN	TYP†	MAX	
V_{IK}		V_{CC} = 4.5 V,	I_I = −18 mA			−1.2			−1.2	V
V_{OH}	All outputs	V_{CC} = 4.5 V to 5.5 V,	I_{OH} = −2 mA	V_{CC}−2			V_{CC}−2			V
	Parity I/O	V_{CC} = 4.5 V,	I_{OH} = −3 mA	2.4	2.9		2.4	3		
		V_{CC} = 4.5 V,	I_{OH} = −12 mA	2.4						
		V_{CC} = 4.5 V,	I_{OH} = −15 mA				2.5			
V_{OL}	Parity error	V_{CC} = 4.5 V,	I_{OL} = 20 mA		0.35	0.5		0.35	0.5	V
	Parity I/O	V_{CC} = 4.5 V,	I_{OL} = 32 mA			0.5				
		V_{CC} = 4.5 V,	I_{OL} = 48 mA						0.5	
I_I	Parity I/O	V_{CC} = 5.5 V,	V_I = 5.5 V			0.1			0.1	mA
	All other inputs	V_{CC} = 5.5 V,	V_I = 7 V			0.1			0.1	
I_{IH}	Parity I/O‡	V_{CC} = 5.5 V,	V_I = 2.7 V			50			50	μA
	All other inputs					20			20	
I_{IL}	Parity I/O‡	V_{CC} = 5.5 V,	V_I = 0.4 V			0.5			-0.5	mA
	All other inputs					0.5			-0.5	
I_O§		V_{CC} = 5.5 V,	V_O = 2.25 V	−30		−112	−30		−112	mA
I_{CC}	Transmit	V_{CC} = 5.5 V			30	43		30	43	mA
	Receive				35	50		35	50	

†All typical values are at V_{CC} = 5 V, T_A = 25°C.
‡For I/O ports, the parameters I_{IH} and I_{IL} include the off-state current.
§The output conditions have been chosen to produce a current that closely approximates one half of the true short-circuit output current, I_{OS}.

switching characteristics (see Note 1)

PARAMETER	FROM (INPUT)	TO (OUTPUT)	V_{CC} = 4.5 V to 5.5 V, C_L = 50 pF, R1 = 500 Ω, R2 = 500 Ω, T_A = MIN to MAX				UNIT
			SN54AS286		SN74AS286		
			MIN	MAX	MIN	MAX	
t_{PLH}	Any A thru I	Parity I/O	3	17	3	15	ns
t_{PHL}			3	15	3	14	
t_{PLH}	Any A thru I	Parity error	3	20	3	16.5	ns
t_{PHL}			3	18	3	16.5	
t_{PLH}	Parity I/O	Parity error	3	10	3	9	ns
t_{PHL}			3	10	3	9	
t_{PZH}	$\overline{XMIT}$	Parity I/O	3	14	3	13	ns
t_{PZL}			3	17	3	16	
t_{PHZ}			3	13	3	11.5	
t_{PLZ}			3	11	3	10	

NOTE 1: Load circuit and voltage waveforms ar shown in Section 1.

TYPICAL APPLICATION DATA

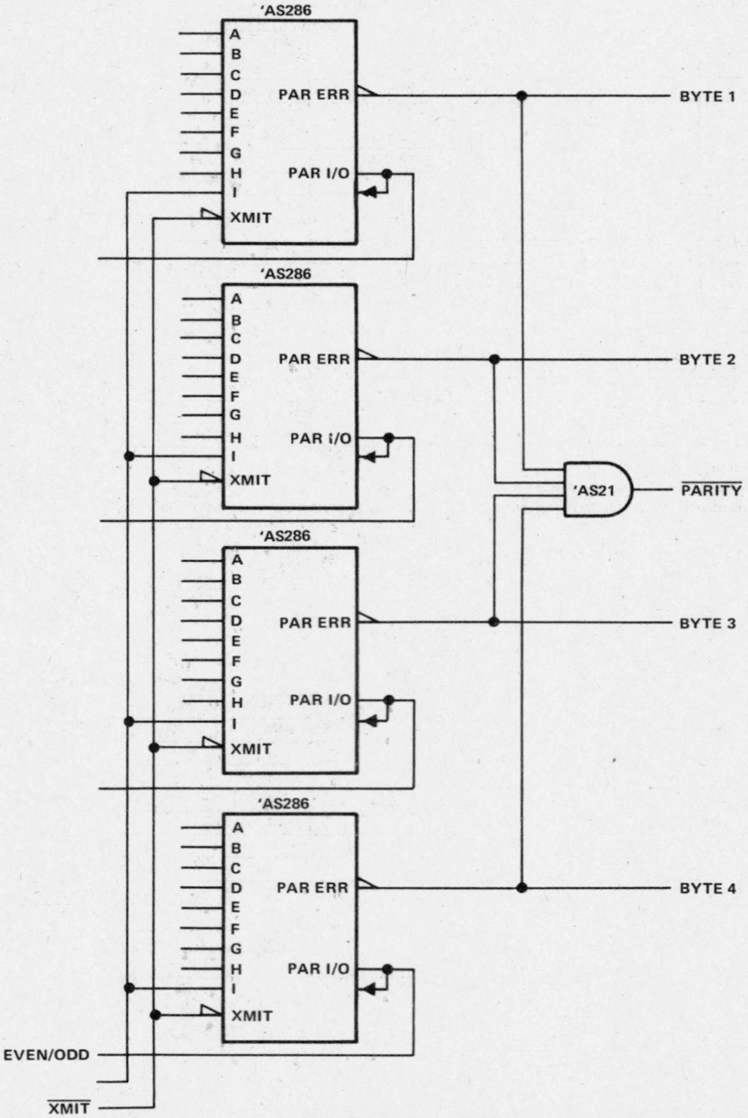
'AS286
A
B
C
D
E
F
G
H
I
PAR ERR
PAR I/O
XMIT
BYTE 1
BYTE 2
BYTE 3
BYTE 4
'AS21
PARITY
EVEN/ODD
XMIT

FIGURE 1. 32-BIT PARITY GENERATOR/CHECKER

Figure 1 shows a 32-bit parity generator/checker with output polarity-switching, parity error detection, and parity on every byte.

TYPICAL APPLICATION DATA

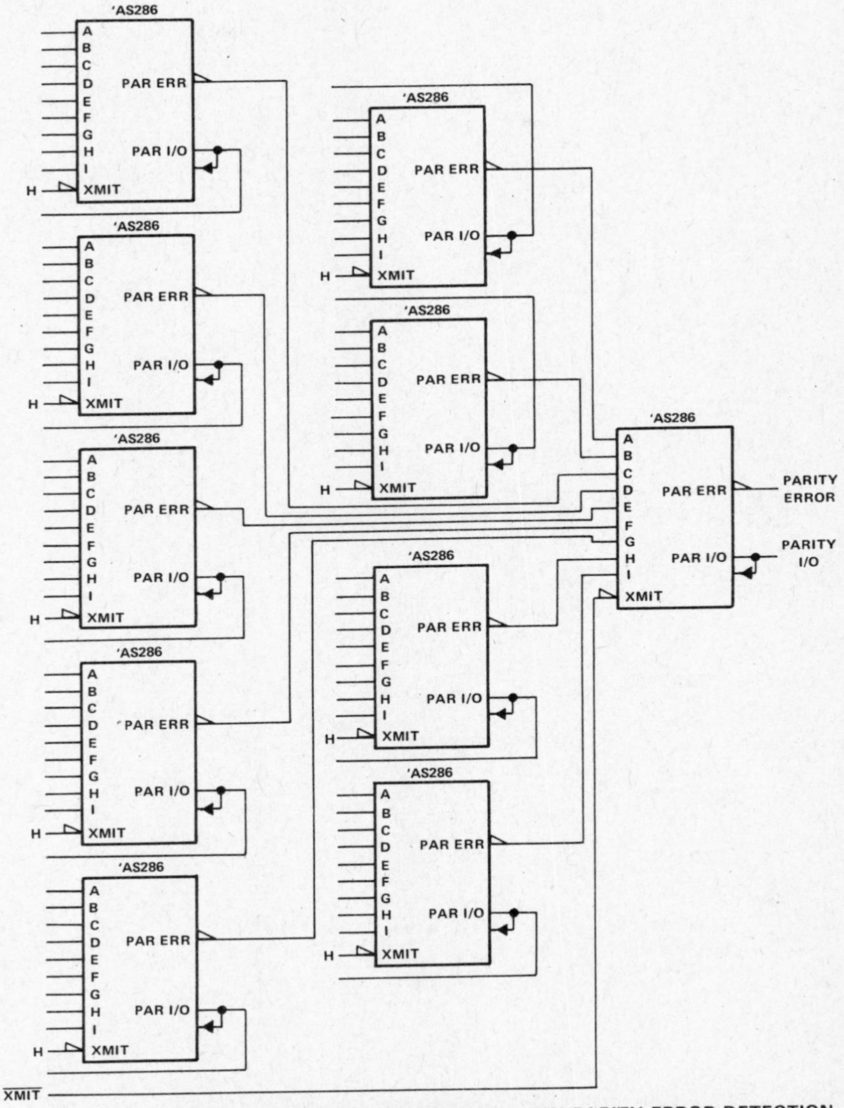
'AS286
A
B
C
D
E
F
G
H
I
PAR ERR
PAR I/O
XMIT
H
PARITY ERROR
PARITY I/O
XMIT

FIGURE 2. 90-BIT PARITY GENERATOR/CHECKER WITH PARITY ERROR DETECTION

In Figure 2, a 90-bit parity generator/checker with the $\overline{\text{XMIT}}$ on the last stage is available for use with parity detection.

2
LSI Devices

D2549, JANUARY 1981—REVISED DECEMBER 1985

- **Expands 4 Address Lines to 12 Address Lines**
- **Designed for Paged Memory Mapping**
- **Output Latches Provided on 'LS610 and 'LS611**
- **Choice of 3-State or Open-Collector Map Outputs**
- **Compatible with TMS9900 and Other Microprocessors**

DEVICE	OUTPUTS LATCHED	MAP OUTPUT TYPE
'LS610	Yes	3-State
'LS611	Yes	Open-Collector
'LS612	No	3-State
'LS613	No	Open-Collector

SN54LS' . . . JD PACKAGE
SN74LS' . . . JD OR N PACKAGE
(TOP VIEW)

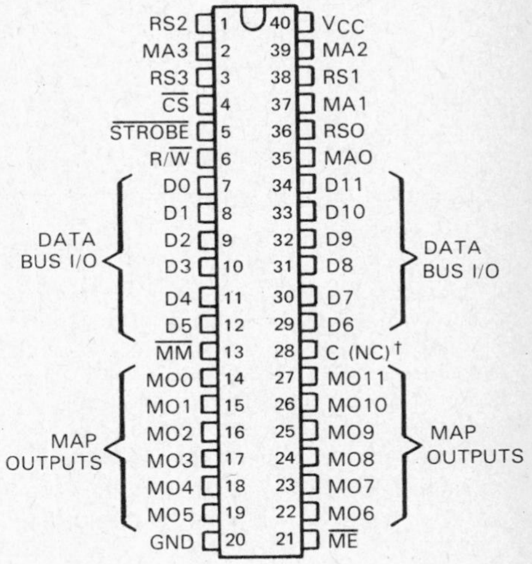
RS2 1 40 VCC
MA3 2 39 MA2
RS3 3 38 RS1
CS 4 37 MA1
STROBE 5 36 RSO
R/W 6 35 MAO
D0 7 34 D11
D1 8 33 D10
D2 9 32 D9
D3 10 31 D8
D4 11 30 D7
D5 12 29 D6
MM 13 28 C (NC)†
MO0 14 27 MO11
MO1 15 26 MO10
MO2 16 25 MO9
MO3 17 24 MO8
MO4 18 23 MO7
MO5 19 22 MO6
GND 20 21 ME
DATA BUS I/O
MAP OUTPUTS

SN54LS' . . . FK PACKAGE
SN74LS' . . . FN PACKAGE
(TOP VIEW)

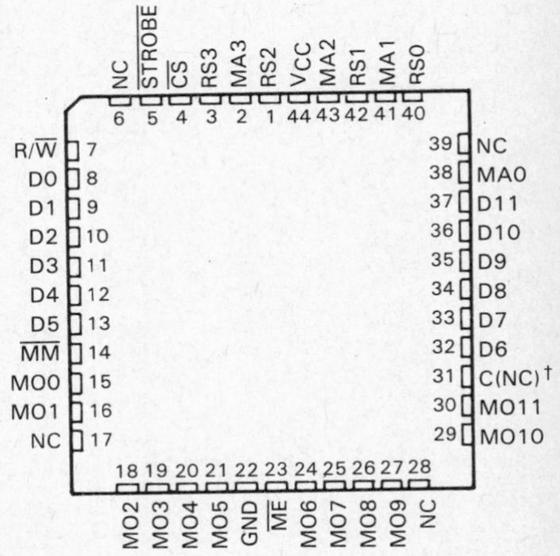
NC 6, STROBE 5, CS 4, RS3 3, MA3 2, RS2 1, VCC 44, MA2 43, RS1 42, MA1 41, RSO 40
R/W 7, D0 8, D1 9, D2 10, D3 11, D4 12, D5 13, MM 14, MO0 15, MO1 16, NC 17
39 NC, 38 MAO, 37 D11, 36 D10, 35 D9, 34 D8, 33 D7, 32 D6, 31 C(NC)†, 30 MO11, 29 MO10
MO2 18, MO3 19, MO4 20, MO5 21, GND 22, ME 23, MO6 24, MO7 25, MO8 26, MO9 27, NC 28

† This pin has no internal connection on 'LS612 and 'LS613
NC—No internal connection

description

Each 'LS610 through 'LS613 memory-mapper integrated circuit contains a 4-line to 16-line decoder, a 16-word by 12-bit RAM, 16 channels of 2-line to 1-line multiplexers, and other miscellaneous circuitry on a monolithic chip. Each 'LS610 and 'LS611 also contains 12 latches with an enable control.

The memory mappers are designed to expand a microprocessor's memory address capability by eight bits. Four bits of the memory address bus (see System Block Diagram) can be used to select one of 16 map registers that contain 12 bits each. These 12 bits are presented to the system memory address bus through the map output buffers along with the unused memory address bits from the CPU. However, addressable memory space without reloading the map registers is the same as would be available with the memory mapper left out. The addressable memory space is increased only by periodically reloading the map registers from the data bus. This configuration lends itself to memory utilization of 16 pages of $2^{(n-4)}$ registers each without reloading (n = number of address bits available from CPU).

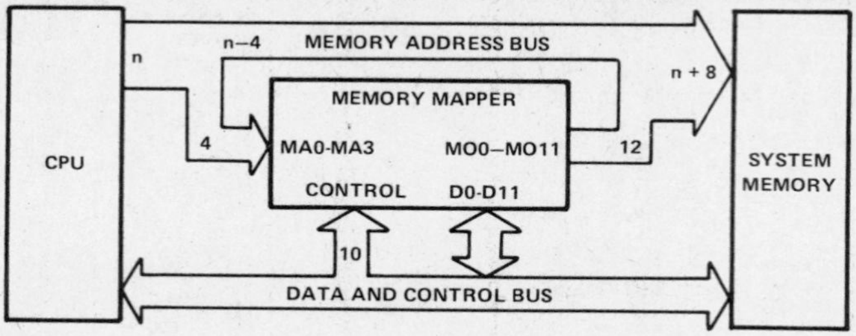
MEMORY ADDRESS BUS
n−4
n
n + 8
MEMORY MAPPER
4
MA0-MA3
MO0–MO11
12
CPU
CONTROL
D0-D11
SYSTEM MEMORY
10
DATA AND CONTROL BUS

SYSTEM BLOCK DIAGRAM

These devices have four modes of operation: read, write, map, and pass. Data may be read from or loaded into the map register selected by the register select inputs (RS0 thru RS3) under control of R/$\overline{W}$ whenever chip select ($\overline{CS}$) is low. The data I/O takes place on the data bus D0 thru D7. The map operation will output the contents of the map register selected by the map address inputs (MA0 thru MA3) when $\overline{CS}$ is high and $\overline{MM}$ (map mode control) is low. The 'LS612 and 'LS613 output stages are transparent in this mode, while the 'LS610 and 'LS611 outputs may be transparent or latched. When $\overline{CS}$ and $\overline{MM}$ are both high (pass mode), the address bits on MA0 thru MA3 appear at MO8-MO11, respectively, (assuming appropriate latch control) with low levels in the other bit positions on the map outputs.

logic diagram (positive logic)

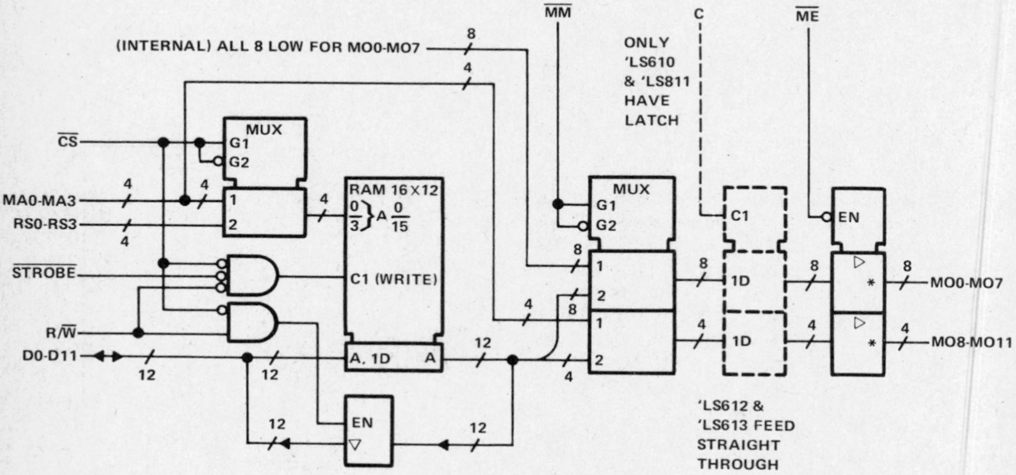
(INTERNAL) ALL 8 LOW FOR MO0-MO7
MM
C
ME
ONLY 'LS610 & 'LS811 HAVE LATCH
CS
MUX
G1
G2
MA0-MA3
RS0-RS3
RAM 16×12
C1 (WRITE)
STROBE
R/W
D0-D11
A, 1D
A
EN
C1
1D
MO0-MO7
MO8-MO11
'LS612 & 'LS613 FEED STRAIGHT THROUGH

*'LS610 and 'LS612 have 3-state (▽) map outputs.
'LS611 and 'LS613 have open-collector (◇) map outputs.

2

LSI Devices

PIN		DESCRIPTION
NO.	NAME	
7-12 29-34	D0 thru D11	I/O connections to data and control bus used for reading from and writing to the map register selected by RS0-RS3 when $\overline{CS}$ is low. Mode controlled by R/$\overline{W}$.
36, 38, 1, 3	RS0 thru RS3	Register select inputs for I/O operations.
6	R/$\overline{W}$	Read or write control used in I/O operations to select the condition of the data bus. When high, the data bus outputs are active for reading the map register. When low, the data bus is used to write into the register.
5	$\overline{STROBE}$	Strobe input used to enter data into the selected map register during I/O operations.
4	$\overline{CS}$	Chip select input. A low input level selects the memory mapper (assuming more than one used) for an I/O operation.
35, 37, 39, 2	MA0 thru MA3	Map address inputs to select one of 16 map registers when in map mode ($\overline{MM}$ low and $\overline{CS}$ high).
14-19, 22-27	MO0 thru MO11	Map outputs. Present the map register contents to the system memory address bus in the map mode. In the pass mode, these outputs provide the map address data on MO8-MO11 and low levels on MO0-MO7.
13	$\overline{MM}$	Map mode input. When low, 12 bits of data are transferred from the selected map register to the map outputs. When high (pass mode), the 4 bits present on the map address inputs MA0-MA3 are passed to the map outputs MO8-MO11, respectively, while MO0-MO7 are set low.
21	$\overline{ME}$	Map enable for the map outputs. A low level allows the outputs to be active while a high input level puts the outputs at high impedance.
28	C	Latch enable input for the 'LS610 and 'LS611 (no internal connection for 'LS612 and 'LS613). A high level will transparently pass data to the map outputs. A low level will latch the outputs.
40, 20	V_{CC}, GND	5 V power supply and network ground (substrate) pins.

schematics of inputs and outputs

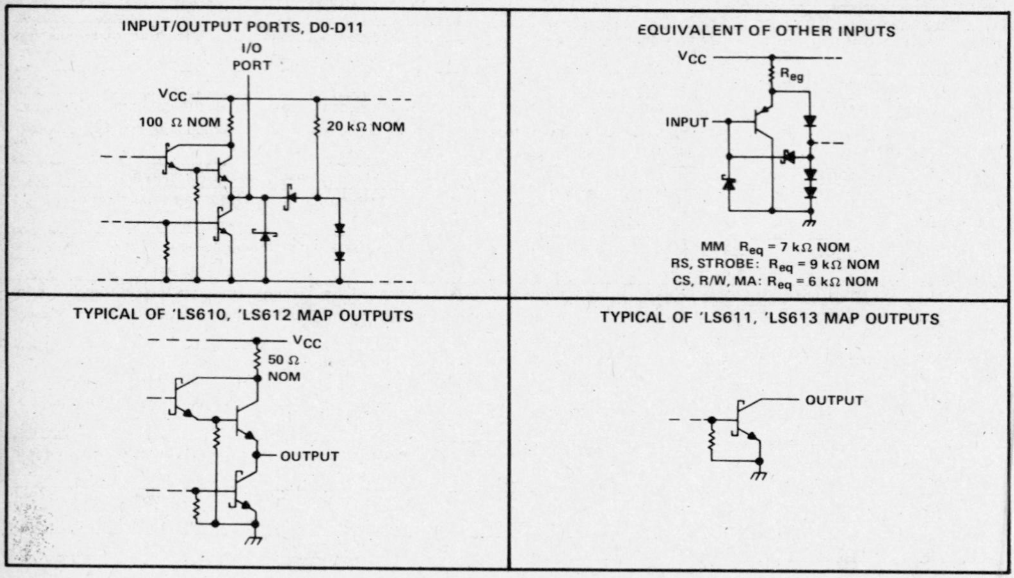
INPUT/OUTPUT PORTS, D0-D11
I/O PORT
V_{CC}
100 Ω NOM
20 kΩ NOM
EQUIVALENT OF OTHER INPUTS
V_{CC}
R_{eq}
INPUT
MM R_{eq} = 7 kΩ NOM
RS, STROBE: R_{eq} = 9 kΩ NOM
CS, R/W, MA: R_{eq} = 6 kΩ NOM
TYPICAL OF 'LS610, 'LS612 MAP OUTPUTS
V_{CC}
50 Ω NOM
OUTPUT
TYPICAL OF 'LS611, 'LS613 MAP OUTPUTS
OUTPUT

absolute maximum ratings over operating free-air temperature (unless otherwise noted)

Supply voltage, V_{CC} (see Note 1)		7 V
Input voltage:	Data Bus I/O	5.5 V
	All other inputs	7 V
Operating free-air temperature range:	SN54LS610 through SN54LS613	−55°C to 125°C
	SN74LS610 through SN74LS613	0°C to 70°C
Storage temperature range		−65°C to 150°C

NOTE 1: Voltage values are with respect to network ground terminal.

TEXAS INSTRUMENTS
POST OFFICE BOX 225012 • DALLAS, TEXAS 75265

recommended operating conditions

				SN54LS610 SN54LS612			SN74LS610 SN74LS612			UNIT
				MIN	NOM	MAX	MIN	NOM	MAX	
V_{CC}	Supply voltage			4.5	5	5.5	4.75	5	5.25	V
V_{IH}	High-level input voltage			2			2			V
V_{IL}	Low-level input voltage					0.7			0.8	V
I_{OH}	High-level output current		MO			−12			−15	mA
			D			−1			−2.6	
I_{OL}	Low-level output current		MO			12			24	mA
			D			4			8	
t_{AVCL}	Address setup time (AV before C low)	'LS610 only	See Figure 2	30			30			ns
t_{SLSH}	Duration of strobe input pulse		See Figure 1	75			75			ns
t_{CSLSL}	$\overline{CS}$ setup time ($\overline{CS}$ low to strobe low)			20			20			ns
t_{WLSL}	R/$\overline{W}$ setup time (R/$\overline{W}$ low to strobe low)			20			20			ns
t_{RVSL}	RS setup time (RS valid to strobe low)			20			20			ns
t_{DVSH}	Data setup time (D0-D11 valid to strobe high)			75			75			ns
t_{SHCSH}	$\overline{CS}$ hold time (Strobe high to $\overline{CS}$ high)			20			20			ns
t_{SHWH}	R/$\overline{W}$ hold time (Strobe high to R/$\overline{W}$ high)			20			20			ns
t_{SHRX}	RS hold time (Strobe high to RS invalid)			20			20			ns
t_{SHDX}	Data hold time (Strobe high to D0-D11 invalid)			20			20			ns
T_A	Operating free-air temperature			−55		125	0		70	°C

electrical characteristics over recommended operating free-air temperature range (unless otherwise noted)

PARAMETER		TEST CONDITIONS†		SN54LS610 SN54LS612			SN74LS610 SN74LS612			UNIT
				MIN	TYP‡	MAX	MIN	TYP‡	MAX	
V_{IK}		V_{CC} = MIN, I_I = −18 mA				−1.5			−1.5	V
V_{OH}	MO	V_{CC} = MIN, V_{IH} = 2 V, V_{IL} = MAX	I_{OH} = −3 mA	2.4			2.4			V
			I_{OH} = MAX	2			2			
	D		I_{OH} = MAX	2.4			2.4			
V_{OL}	MO	V_{CC} = MIN, V_{IH} = 2 V, V_{IL} = MAX	I_{OL} = 12 mA		0.25	0.4		0.25	0.4	V
			I_{OL} = 24 mA					0.35	0.5	
	D		I_{OL} = 4 mA		0.25	0.4		0.25	0.4	
			I_{OL} = 8 mA					0.35	0.5	
I_{OZH}		V_{CC} = MAX, V_{IH} = 2 V, V_{IL} = MAX, V_O = 2.7 V				20			20	μA
I_{OZL}	MO	V_{CC} = MAX, V_{IH} = 2 V, V_{IL} = MAX, V_O = 0.4 V				−20			−20	μA
	D					−400			−400	
I_I	D	V_{CC} = MAX	V_I = 5.5 V			0.1			0.1	mA
	All others		V_I = 7 V			0.1			0.1	
I_{IH}		V_{CC} = MAX, V_I = 2.7 V				20			20	μA
I_{IL}		V_{CC} = MAX, V_I = 0.4 V				−0.4			−0.4	mA
I_{OS}§	MO	V_{CC} = MAX		−40		−225	−40		−225	mA
	D			−30		−130	−30		−130	
I_{CC}		V_{CC} = MAX	Outputs high		112	180		112	180	mA
			Outputs low		112	180		112	180	
			Outputs disabled		150	230		180	230	

†For conditions shown as MIN or MAX, use the appropriate value specified under recommended operating conditions.
‡All typical values are at V_{CC} = 5 V, T_A = 25°C.
§Not more than one output should be shorted at a time, and duration of the short-circuit should not exceed one second.

switching characteristics, V_{CC} = 5 V, T_A = 25°C, C_L = 45 pF to GND

PARAMETER		FROM (INPUT)	TO (OUTPUT)	TEST CONDITIONS	'LS610			'LS612			UNIT
					MIN	TYP	MAX	MIN	TYP	MAX	
t_{CSLDV}	Access (enable) time	$\overline{CS}$↓	D0-11	R_L = 2 kΩ, See Figure 1, See Notes 2 and 3		28	50		26	50	ns
t_{WHDV}	Access (enable) time	R/$\overline{W}$↑	D0-11			20	35		20	35	ns
t_{RVDV}	Access time	RS	D0-11			49	75		39	75	ns
t_{WLDZ}	Disable time	R/$\overline{W}$↓	D0-11			32	50		30	50	ns
t_{CSHDZ}	Disable time	$\overline{CS}$↑	D0-11			42	65		38	65	ns
t_{ELQV}	Access (enable) time	$\overline{ME}$↓	MO0-11	R_L = 667 Ω, See Figure 2, See Notes 2 and 3		19	30		17	30	ns
t_{CSHQV}	Access time	$\overline{CS}$↑	MO0-11			56	85		48	85	ns
t_{MLQV}	Access time	$\overline{MM}$↓	MO0-11			25	40		22	40	ns
t_{CHQV}	Access time	C↑	MO0-11			24	40				ns
t_{AVQV1}	Access time ($\overline{MM}$ low)	MA	MO0-11			46	70		39	70	ns
t_{MHQV}	Access time	$\overline{MM}$↑	MO0-11			24	40		22	40	ns
t_{AVQV2}	Propagation time ($\overline{MM}$ high)	MA	MO8-11			19	30		13	30	ns
t_{EHQZ}	Disable time	$\overline{ME}$↑	MO0-11			14	25		14	25	ns

NOTES: 2. Access times are tested as t_{PLH} and t_{PHL} or t_{PZH} or t_{PZL}. Disable times are tested as t_{PHZ} and t_{PLZ}.
3. Load circuits and voltage waveforms are shown in Section 1.

TEXAS INSTRUMENTS
POST OFFICE BOX 225012 • DALLAS, TEXAS 75265

recommended operating conditions

				SN54LS611 SN54LS613 MIN	NOM	MAX	SN74LS611 SN74LS613 MIN	NOM	MAX	UNIT
V_{CC}	Supply voltage			4.5	5	5.5	4.75	5	5.25	V
V_{IH}	High-level input voltage			2			2			V
V_{IL}	Low-level input voltage					0.7			0.8	V
V_{OH}	High-level output voltage		MO			5.5			5.5	V
I_{OH}	High-level output current		D			−1			−2.6	mA
I_{OL}	Low-level output current		MO			12			24	mA
			D			4			8	
t_{AVCL}	Address setup time (AV before C low)	'LS611 only	See Figure 2	30			30			ns
t_{SLSH}	Duration of strobe input pulse		See Figure 1	75			75			ns
t_{CSLSL}	$\overline{CS}$ setup time ($\overline{CS}$ low to strobe low)			20			20			ns
t_{WLSL}	R/$\overline{W}$ setup time (R/$\overline{W}$ low to strobe low)			20			20			ns
t_{RVSL}	RS setup time (RS valid to strobe low)			20			20			ns
t_{DVSH}	Data setup time (D0-D11 valid to strobe high)			75			75			ns
t_{SHCSH}	$\overline{CS}$ hold time (Strobe high to $\overline{CS}$ high)			20			20			ns
t_{SHWH}	R/$\overline{W}$ hold time (Strobe high to R/$\overline{W}$ high)			20			20			ns
t_{SHRX}	RS hold time (Strobe high to RS invalid)			20			20			ns
t_{SHDX}	Data hold time (Strobe high to D0-D11 invalid)			20			20			ns
T_A	Operating free-air temperature			−55		125	0		70	°C

electrical characteristics over recommended operating free-air temperature range (unless otherwise noted)

PARAMETER		TEST CONDITIONS†		SN54LS611 SN54LS613 MIN	TYP‡	MAX	SN74LS611 SN74LS613 MIN	TYP‡	MAX	UNIT
V_{IK}		V_{CC} = MIN, I_I = −18 mA				−1.5			−1.5	V
V_{OH}	D	V_{CC} = MIN, V_{IH} = 2 V, V_{IL} = MAX, I_{OH} = MAX		2.4			2.4			V
I_{OH}	MO	V_{CC} = MIN, V_{IH} = 2 V, V_{OH} = 5.5 V				0.1			0.1	mA
V_{OL}	MO	V_{CC} = MIN, V_{IH} = 2 V, V_{IL} = MAX	I_{OL} = 12 mA		0.25	0.4		0.25	0.4	V
			I_{OL} = 24 mA					0.35	0.5	
	D		I_{OL} = 4 mA		0.25	0.4		0.25	0.4	
			I_{OL} = 8 mA					0.35	0.5	
I_{OZH}	D	V_{CC} = MAX, V_{IH} = 2 V, V_{IL} = MAX, V_O = 2.7 V				20			20	μA
I_{OZL}	D	V_{CC} = MAX, V_{IH} = 2 V, V_O = 0.4 V				−0.4			−0.4	mA
I_I	D	V_{CC} = MAX	V_I = 5.5 V			0.1			0.1	mA
	All others		V_I = 7 V			0.1			0.1	
I_{IH}		V_{CC} = MAX, V_I = 2.7 V				20			20	μA
I_{IL}		V_{CC} = MAX, V_I = 0.4 V				−0.4			−0.4	mA
I_{OS}§	D	V_{CC} = MAX		−30		−130	−30		−130	mA
I_{CC}		V_{CC} = MAX	Outputs high		100	170		100	170	mA
			Outputs low		100	170		100	170	
			Outputs disabled		110	200		110	200	

†For conditions shown as MIN or MAX, use the appropriate value specified under recommended operating conditions.
‡All typical values are at V_{CC} = 5 V, T_A = 25°C.
§Not more than one output should be shorted at a time, and duration of the short-circuit should not exceed one second.

switching characteristics, V_{CC} = 5 V, T_A = 25°C, C_L = 45 pF to GND

PARAMETER		FROM (INPUT)	TO (OUTPUT)	TEST CONDITIONS	'LS611 MIN	TYP	MAX	'LS613 MIN	TYP	MAX	UNIT
t_{CSLDV}	Access (enable) time	$\overline{CS}$↓	D0-11	R_L = 2 kΩ, See Figure 1, See Notes 2 and 3		31	50		28	50	ns
t_{WHDV}	Access (enable) time	R/$\overline{W}$↑	D0-11			23	35		21	35	ns
t_{RVDV}	Access time	RS	D0-11			51	75		47	75	ns
t_{WLDZ}	Disable time	R/$\overline{W}$↓	D0-11			32	50		31	50	ns
t_{CSHDZ}	Disable time	$\overline{CS}$↑	D0-11			41	65		40	65	ns
t_{ELQV}	Access (enable) time	$\overline{ME}$↓	MO0-11	R_L = 667 Ω, See Figure 2, See Notes 2 and 3		21	30		19	30	ns
t_{CSHQV}	Access time	$\overline{CS}$↑	MO0-11			57	90		53	90	ns
t_{MLQV}	Access time	MM↓	MO0-11			25	40		25	40	ns
t_{CHQV}	Access time	C↑	MO0-11			30	45				ns
t_{AVQV1}	Access time ($\overline{MM}$ low)	MA	MO0-11			47	70		44	70	ns
t_{MHQV}	Access time	MM↑	MO0-11			31	50		31	50	ns
t_{AVQV2}	Propagation time ($\overline{MM}$ high)	MA	MO8-11			21	30		20	30	ns
t_{EHQZ}	Disable time	ME↑	MO0-11			15	25		15	25	ns

NOTES: 2. Access times are tested as t_{PLH} and t_{PHL} or t_{PZH} or t_{PZL}. Disable times are tested as t_{PHZ} and t_{PLZ}.
3. Load circuits and voltage waveforms are shown in Section 1.

TEXAS INSTRUMENTS
POST OFFICE BOX 225012 • DALLAS, TEXAS 75265

explanation of letter symbols

This data sheet uses a new type of letter symbol based on JEDEC Standard 100 to describe time intervals. The format is:

$$t_{AB\text{-}CD}$$

where: subscripts A and C indicate the names of the signals for which changes of state or level or establishment of state or level constitute signal events assumed to occur first and last, respectively, that is, at the beginning and end of the time interval.

Subscripts B and D indicate the direction of the transitions and/or the final states or levels of the signals represented by A and C, respectively. One or two of the following is used:

H = high or transition to high
L = low or transition to low
V = a valid steady-state level
X = unknown, changing, or ''don't care'' level
Z = high-impedance (off) state.

The hyphen between the B and C subscripts is omitted when no confusion is likely to occur. For these letter symbols on this data sheet, the signal names are further abbreviated as follows:

SIGNAL NAME	A AND C SUBSCRIPT	SIGNAL NAME	A AND C SUBSCRIPT
C	C	$\overline{ME}$	E
$\overline{CS}$	CS	$\overline{MM}$	M
D0–11	D	R/$\overline{W}$	W
MA0–MA3	A	RS0–RS3	R
MO0–MO11	Q	$\overline{STROBE}$	S

TIMING DIAGRAMS

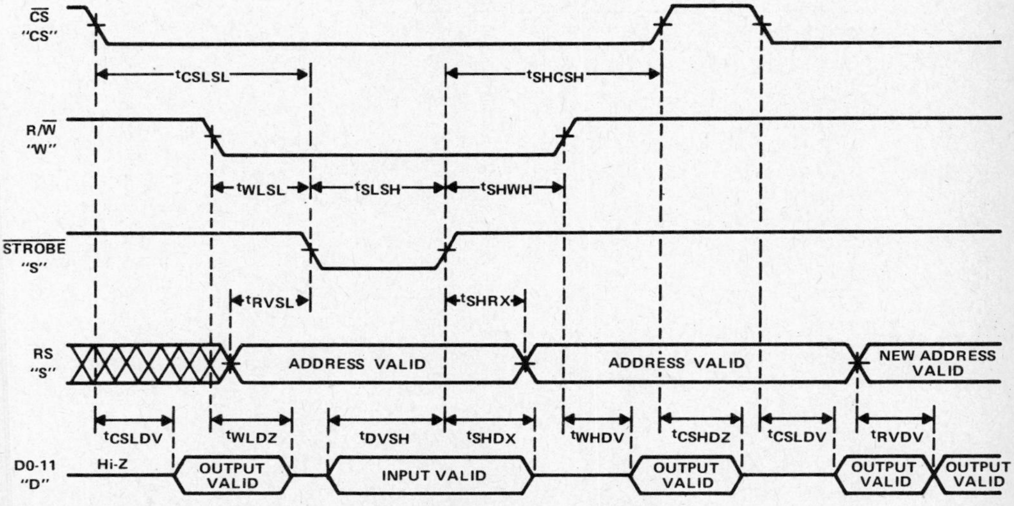
$\overline{CS}$
"CS"
tCSLSL
tSHCSH
R/$\overline{W}$
"W"
tWLSL
tSLSH
tSHWH
$\overline{STROBE}$
"S"
tRVSL
tSHRX
RS
"S"
ADDRESS VALID
ADDRESS VALID
NEW ADDRESS VALID
tCSLDV
tWLDZ
tDVSH
tSHDX
tWHDV
tCSHDZ
tCSLDV
tRVDV
D0-11
"D"
Hi-Z
OUTPUT VALID
INPUT VALID
OUTPUT VALID
OUTPUT VALID
OUTPUT VALID

FIGURE 1. WRITE AND READ MODES

TIMING DIAGRAMS

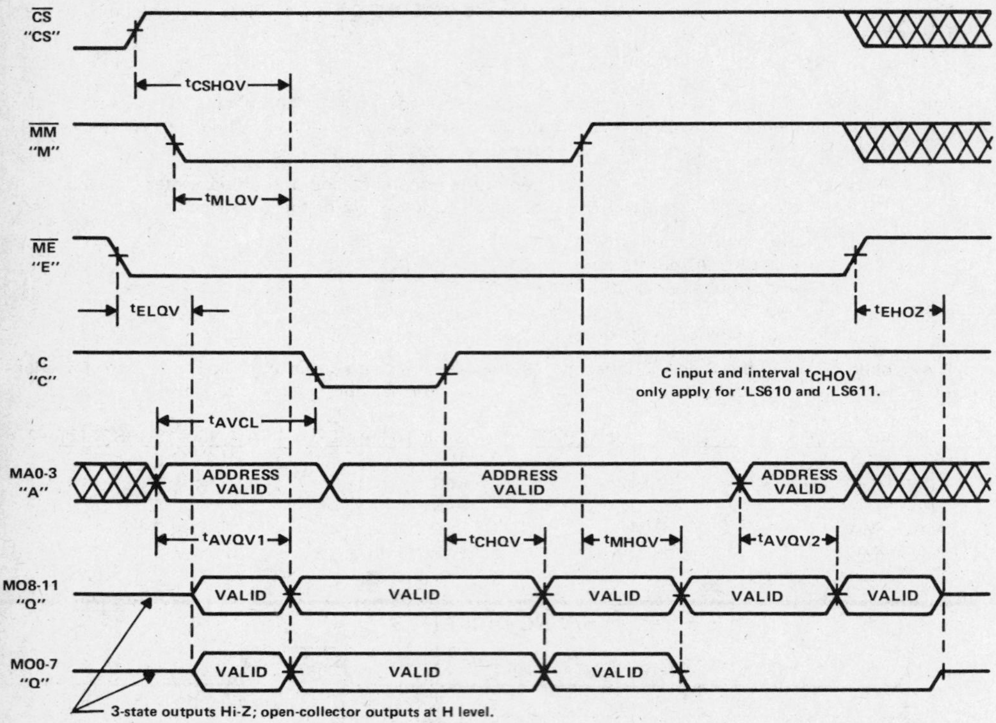
CS
"CS"
tCSHQV
MM
"M"
tMLQV
ME
"E"
tELQV
tEHOZ
C
"C"
C input and interval tCHOV only apply for 'LS610 and 'LS611.
tAVCL
MA0-3
"A"
ADDRESS VALID
ADDRESS VALID
ADDRESS VALID
tAVQV1
tCHQV
tMHQV
tAVQV2
MO8-11
"Q"
VALID
VALID
VALID
VALID
VALID
MO0-7
"Q"
VALID
VALID
VALID
3-state outputs Hi-Z; open-collector outputs at H level.

FIGURE 2. MAP AND PASS MODES

TEXAS INSTRUMENTS
POST OFFICE BOX 225012 • DALLAS, TEXAS 75265

D2840, APRIL 1984—REVISED SEPTEMBER 1985

- Detects and Corrects Single-Bit Errors
- Detects and Flags Dual-Bit Errors
- Built-In Diagnostic Capability
- Fast Write and Read Cycle Processing Times
- Byte-Write Capability
- Dependable Texas Instruments Quality and Reliability

DEVICE	OUTPUT
'ALS616	3-State
'ALS617	Open-Collector

SN54ALS616, SN54ALS617 . . . JD PACKAGE
SN74ALS616, SN74ALS617 . . . JD OR N PACKAGE
(TOP VIEW)

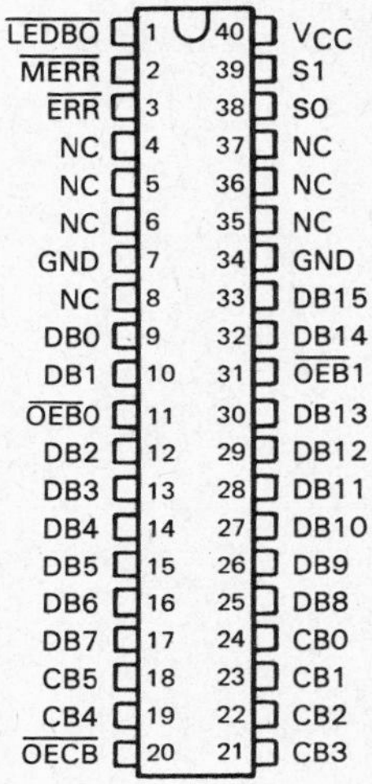
LEDBO 1 40 VCC
MERR 2 39 S1
ERR 3 38 S0
NC 4 37 NC
NC 5 36 NC
NC 6 35 NC
GND 7 34 GND
NC 8 33 DB15
DB0 9 32 DB14
DB1 10 31 OEB1
OEB0 11 30 DB13
DB2 12 29 DB12
DB3 13 28 DB11
DB4 14 27 DB10
DB5 15 26 DB9
DB6 16 25 DB8
DB7 17 24 CB0
CB5 18 23 CB1
CB4 19 22 CB2
OECB 20 21 CB3

SN74ALS616, SN74ALS617 . . . FN PACKAGE
(TOP VIEW)

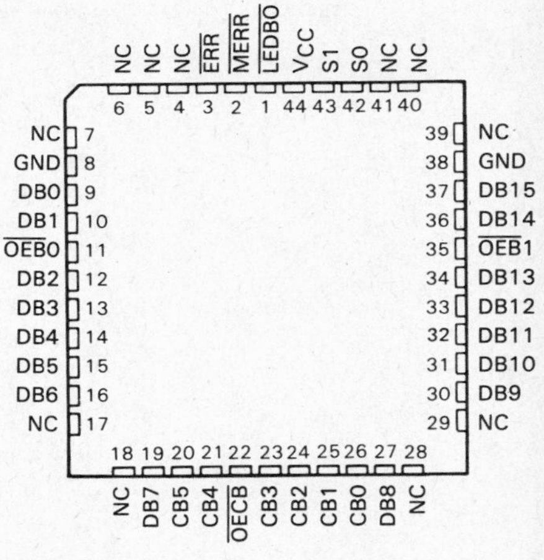
NC NC NC ERR MERR LEDBO VCC S1 S0 NC NC
6 5 4 3 2 1 44 43 42 41 40
NC 7
GND 8
DB0 9
DB1 10
OEB0 11
DB2 12
DB3 13
DB4 14
DB5 15
DB6 16
NC 17
39 NC
38 GND
37 DB15
36 DB14
35 OEB1
34 DB13
33 DB12
32 DB11
31 DB10
30 DB9
29 NC
18 19 20 21 22 23 24 25 26 27 28
NC DB7 CB5 CB4 OECB CB3 CB2 CB1 CB0 DB8 NC

NC—No internal connection

description

The 'ALS616 and 'ALS617 are 16-bit parallel error detection and correction circuits in 40-pin, 600-mil packages. The EDACs use a modified Hamming code to generate a 6-bit check word from a 16-bit data word. This check word is stored along with the data word during the memory write cycle. During memory read cycles, the 22-bit words from memory are processed by the EDACs to determine if errors have occurred in memory.

Single-bit errors in the 16-bit data word are flagged and corrected. Single-bit errors in the 6-bit check word are flagged, but the data word will remain unaltered. The 6-bit error syndrome code will pinpoint the error-generating location.

Dual-bit errors are flagged but not corrected. These errors may occur in any two bits of the 22-bit word from memory. The gross-error condition of all lows or all highs from memory will be detected. Otherwise, errors in three or more bits of the 22-bit word are beyond the capabilities of these devices to detect.

Read-modify-write (byte-control) operations can be performed with the 'ALS616 and 'ALS617 EDACs by using output latch enable, LEDBO, and individual OEB0 and OEB1 byte control pins.

Diagnostics are performed on the EDACs by controls and internal paths that allow the user to read the contents of the DB and CB input latches. These will determine if the failure occurred in memory or in the EDAC.

The SN54ALS616 and SN54ALS617 are characterized for operation over the full military temperature range of −55°C to 125°C. The SN74ALS616 and SN74ALS617 are characterized for operation from 0°C to 70°C.

2

LSI Devices

TABLE 1. WRITE CONTROL FUNCTION

MEMORY CYCLE	EDAC FUNCTION	CONTROL S1 S0	DATA I/O	DB CONTROL $\overline{OEB0}$ & $\overline{OEB1}$	DB OUTPUT LATCH $\overline{LEDBO}$	CHECK I/O	CB CONTROL $\overline{OECB}$	ERROR FLAGS $\overline{ERR}$ $\overline{MERR}$
Write	Generate check word	L L	Input	H	X	Output check bits†	L	H H

†See Table 2 for details on check bit generation.

memory write cycle details

During a memory write cycle, the check bits (CB0 thru CB5) are generated internally in the EDAC by six 8-input parity generators using the 16-bit data word as defined in Table 2. These six check bits are stored in memory along with the original 16-bit data word. This 22-bit word will later be used in the memory read cycle for error detection and correction.

TABLE 2. PARITY ALGORITHM

CHECK WORD	16-BIT DATA WORD															
BIT	15	14	13	12	11	10	9	8	7	6	5	4	3	2	1	0
CB0			X		X	X	X			X			X		X	X
CB1		X		X		X	X	X				X		X		X
CB2	X			X	X			X	X		X			X	X	
CB3	X	X	X				X	X			X	X	X			
CB4	X	X	X	X	X	X			X	X						
CB5									X	X	X	X	X	X	X	X

The six check bits are parity bits derived from the matrix of data bits as indicated by "X" for each bit.

error detection and correction details

During a memory read cycle, the 6-bit check word is retrieved along with the actual data. In order to be able to determine whether the data from memory is acceptable to use as presented to the bus, the error flags must be tested to determine if they are at the high level.

The first case in Table 3 represents the normal, no-error conditions. The EDAC presents highs on both flags. The next two cases of single-bit errors give a high on $\overline{MERR}$ and a low on $\overline{ERR}$, which is the signal for a correctable error, and the EDAC should be sent through the correction cycle. The last three cases of double-bit errors will cause the EDAC to signal lows on both $\overline{ERR}$ and $\overline{MERR}$, which is the interrupt indication for the CPU.

TABLE 3. ERROR FUNCTION

TOTAL NUMBER OF ERRORS		ERROR FLAGS		DATA CORRECTION
16-BIT DATA WORD	6-BIT CHECK WORD	$\overline{ERR}$	$\overline{MERR}$	
0	0	H	H	Not applicable
1	0	L	H	Correction
0	1	L	H	Correction
1	1	L	L	Interrupt
2	0	L	L	Interrupt
0	2	L	L	Interrupt

TABLE 4. READ, FLAG, AND CORRECT FUNCTION

MEMORY CYCLE	EDAC FUNCTION	CONTROL S1	CONTROL S0	DATA I/O	DB CONTROL $\overline{OEB0}$ & $\overline{OEB1}$	DB OUTPUT LATCH $\overline{LEDBO}$	CHECK I/O	CB CONTROL $\overline{OECB}$	ERROR FLAGS $\overline{ERR}$ $\overline{MERR}$
Read	Read & flag	H	L	Input	H	X	Input	H	Enabled†
Read	Latch input data & check bits	H	H	Latched input data	H	L	Latched input check word	H	Enabled†
Read	Output corrected data and syndrome bits	H	H	Output corrected data word	L	X	Output syndrome bits‡	L	Enabled†

†See Table 3 for error description.
‡See Table 5 for error location.

Error detection is accomplished as the 6-bit check word and the 16-bit data word from memory are applied to the internal parity generators/checkers. If the parity of all six groupings of data and check bits are correct, it is assumed that no error has occurred and both error flags will be high.

If the parity of one or more of the check groups is incorrect, an error has occurred and the proper error flag or flags will be set low. The two-bit error is not correctable since the parity tree can only identify single-bit errors. Both error flags are set low when any two-bit error is detected.

Three or more simultaneous bit errors can cause the EDAC to believe that no error, a correctable error, or an uncorrectable error has occurred and will produce erroneous results in all three cases. It should be noted that the gross-error conditions of all highs will be detected.

As the corrected word is made available on the data I/O port (DB0 thru DB15), the check word I/O port (CB0 thru CB5) presents a 6-bit syndrome error code. This syndrome code can be used to locate the bad memory chip. See Table 5 for syndrome decoding.

TABLE 5. SYNDROME DECODING

SYNDROME BITS						ERROR
5	4	3	2	1	0	
L	L	L	L	L	L	2-bit
L	L	L	L	L	H	unc
L	L	L	L	H	L	unc
L	L	L	L	H	H	2-bit
L	L	L	H	L	L	unc
L	L	L	H	L	H	2-bit
L	L	L	H	H	L	2-bit
L	L	L	H	H	H	unc
L	L	H	L	L	L	unc
L	L	H	L	L	H	2-bit
L	L	H	L	H	L	2-bit
L	L	H	L	H	H	DB7
L	L	H	H	L	L	2-bit
L	L	H	H	L	H	unc
L	L	H	H	H	L	DB6
L	L	H	H	H	H	2-bit

SYNDROME BITS						ERROR
5	4	3	2	1	0	
L	H	L	L	L	L	unc
L	H	L	L	L	H	2-bit
L	H	L	L	H	L	2-bit
L	H	L	L	H	H	DB5
L	H	L	H	L	L	2-bit
L	H	L	H	L	H	DB4
L	H	L	H	H	L	DB3
L	H	L	H	H	H	2-bit
L	H	H	L	L	L	2-bit
L	H	H	L	L	H	DB2
L	H	H	L	H	L	DB1
L	H	H	L	H	H	2-bit
L	H	H	H	L	L	DB0
L	H	H	H	L	H	2-bit
L	H	H	H	H	L	2-bit
L	H	H	H	H	H	CB5

SYNDROME BITS						ERROR
5	4	3	2	1	0	
H	L	L	L	L	L	unc
H	L	L	L	L	H	2-bit
H	L	L	L	H	L	2-bit
H	L	L	L	H	H	DB15
H	L	L	H	L	L	2-bit
H	L	L	H	L	H	DB14
H	L	L	H	H	L	DB13
H	L	L	H	H	H	2-bit
H	L	H	L	L	L	2-bit
H	L	H	L	L	H	DB12
H	L	H	L	H	L	DB11
H	L	H	L	H	H	2-bit
H	L	H	H	L	L	DB10
H	L	H	H	L	H	2-bit
H	L	H	H	H	L	2-bit
H	L	H	H	H	H	CB4

SYNDORME BITS						ERROR
5	4	3	2	1	0	
H	H	L	L	L	L	2-bit
H	H	L	L	L	H	DB8
H	H	L	L	H	L	unc
H	H	L	L	H	H	2-bit
H	H	L	H	L	L	DB9
H	H	L	H	L	H	2-bit
H	H	L	H	H	L	2-bit
H	H	L	H	H	H	CB3
H	H	H	L	L	L	unc
H	H	H	L	L	H	2-bit
H	H	H	L	H	L	2-bit
H	H	H	L	H	H	CB2
H	H	H	H	L	L	2-bit
H	H	H	H	L	H	CB1
H	H	H	H	H	L	CB0
H	H	H	H	H	H	none

CB X = error in check bit X
DB Y = error in data bit Y
2-bit = double-bit error
unc = uncorrectable multibit error

read-modify-write (byte control) operations

The 'ALS616 and 'ALS617 devices are capable of byte-write operations. The 22-bit word from memory must first be latched into the DB and CB input latches. This is easily accomplished by switching from the read and flag mode (S1 = H, S0 = L) to the latch input mode (S1 = H, S0 = H). The EDAC will then make any corrections, if necessary, to the data word and place it at the input of the output data latch. This data word must then be latched into the output data latch by taking $\overline{\text{LEDBO}}$ from a low to a high.

Byte control can now be employed on the data word through the $\overline{\text{OEB0}}$ or $\overline{\text{OEB1}}$ controls. $\overline{\text{OEB0}}$ controls DB0-DB7 (byte 0), $\overline{\text{OEB1}}$ controls DB8-DB15 (byte 1).

Placing a high on the byte control will disable the output and the user can modify the byte. If a low is placed on the byte control, then the original byte is allowed to pass onto the data bus unchanged. If the original data word is altered through byte control, a new check word must be generated before it is written back into memory. This is easily accomplished by taking control S1 and S0 low. Table 6 lists the read-modify-write functions.

TABLE 6. READ-MODIFY-WRITE FUNCTION

MEMORY CYCLE	EDAC FUNCTION	CONTROL S1 S0	BYTEn†	$\overline{\text{OEBn}}$†	DB OUTPUT LATCH $\overline{\text{LEDBO}}$	CHECK I/O	CB CONTROL	ERROR FLAG $\overline{\text{ERR}}$ $\overline{\text{MERR}}$
Read	Read & Flag	H L	Input	H	X	Input	H	Enabled
Read	Latch input data & check bits	H H	Latched Input data	H	L	Latched input check word	H	Enabled
Read	Latch corrected data word into output latch	H H	Latched output data word	H	H	Hi-Z Output Syndrome bits	H L	Enabled
Modify/ write	Modify appropriate byte or bytes & generate new check word	L L	Input modified BYTE0 Output unchanged BYTE0	H L	H	Output check word	L	H H

†$\overline{\text{OEB0}}$ controls DB0-DB7 (BYTE0), $\overline{\text{OEB1}}$ controls DB8-DB15 (BYTE1)

diagnostic operations

The 'ALS616 and 'ALS617 are capable of diagnostics that allow the user to determine whether the EDAC or the memory is failing. The diagnostic function tables will help the user to see the possibilities for diagnostic control.

In the diagnostic mode (S1 = L, S0 = H), the checkword is latched into the input latch while the data input latch remains transparent. This lets the user apply various data words against a fixed known checkword. If the user applies a diagnostic data word with an error in any bit location, the $\overline{\text{ERR}}$ flag should be low. If a diagnostic data word with two errors in any bit location is applied, the $\overline{\text{MERR}}$ flag should be low. After the checkword is latched into the input latch, it can be verified by taking $\overline{\text{OECB}}$ low. This outputs the latched checkword. The diagnostic data word can be latched into the output data latch and verified via the $\overline{\text{LEDBO}}$ control pin. By changing from the diagnostic mode (S1 = L, S0 = H), the user can verify that the EDAC will correct the diagnostic data word. Also, the syndrome bits can be produced to verify that the EDAC pinpoints the error location. Table 7 lists the diagnostic functions.

2

LSI Devices

TABLE 7. DIAGNOSTIC FUNCTION

EDAC FUNCTION	CONTROL S1	CONTROL S0	DATA I/O	DB BYTE CONTROL $\overline{OEBn}$	DB OUTPUT LATCH $\overline{LEDBO}$	CHECK I/O	CB CONTROL $\overline{OECB}$	ERROR FLAGS $\overline{ERR}$	ERROR FLAGS $\overline{MERR}$
Read & flag	H	L	Input correct data word	H	X	Input correct check bits	H	H	H
Latch input check word while data input latch remains transparent	L	H	Input diagnostic data word†	H	L	Latched input check bits	H	Enabled	
Latch diagnostic data word into output latch	L	H	Input diagnostic data word†	H	H	Output latched check bits Hi-Z	L H	Enabled	
Latch diagnostic data word into input latch	H	H	Latched input diagnostic data word	H	H	Output syndrome bits Hi-Z	L H	Enabled	
Output diagnostic data word & syndrome bits	H	H	Output diagnostic data word	L	H	Output syndrome bits Hi-Z	L H	Enabled	
Output corrected diagnostic data word & output syndrome bits	H	H	Output corrected diagnostic data word	L	L	Output syndrome bits Hi-Z	L H	Enabled	

†Diagnostic data is a data word with an error in one bit location except when testing the $\overline{MERR}$ error flag. In this case, the diagnostic data word will contain errors in two bit locations.

TEXAS INSTRUMENTS
POST OFFICE BOX 225012 • DALLAS, TEXAS 75265

logic diagram (positive logic)

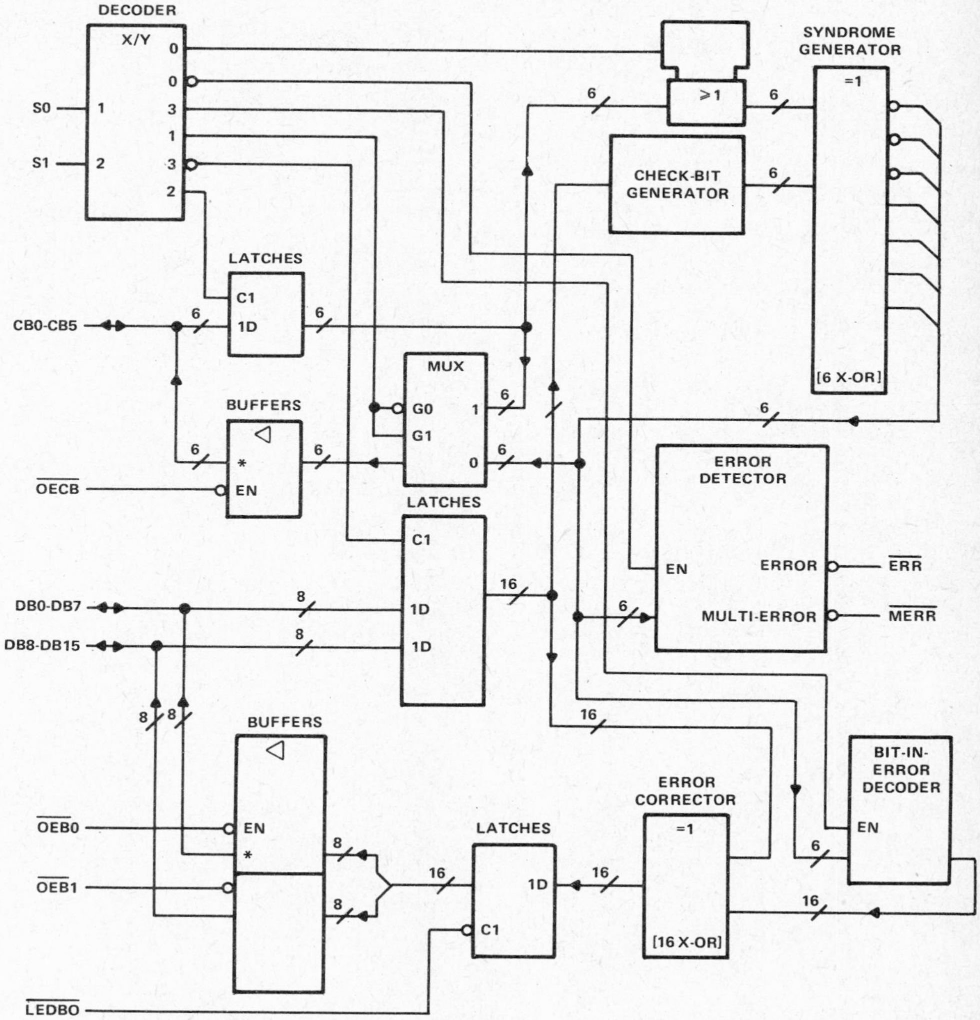
DECODER
X/Y
S0
S1
SYNDROME GENERATOR
=1
≥1
CHECK-BIT GENERATOR
[6 X-OR]
LATCHES
C1
1D
CB0-CB5
MUX
G0
G1
BUFFERS
OECB
EN
ERROR DETECTOR
ERROR
ERR
MULTI-ERROR
MERR
DB0-DB7
DB8-DB15
BIT-IN-ERROR DECODER
ERROR CORRECTOR
[16 X-OR]
OEB0
OEB1
LEDBO

*'ALS616 has 3-state (▽) check-bit and data outputs.
'ALS617 has open-collector(◇) check-bit and data outputs.

absolute maximum ratings over operating free-air temperature range (unless otherwise noted)

Supply voltage, V_{CC} (see Note 1) . . . . 7 V
Input voltage: CB and DB . . . . 5.5 V
All others . . . . 7 V
Operating case temperature range SN54ALS616, SN54ALS617, ... −55°C to 125°C
Operating free-air temperature range, SN74ALS616, SN74ALS617 . . . . 0°C to 70°C
Storage temperature range . . . . −65°C to 150°C

recommended operating conditions

			SN54ALS616 SN54ALS617			SN74ALS616 SN74ALS617			UNIT
			MIN	NOM	MAX	MIN	NOM	MAX	
V_{CC}	Supply voltage		4.5	5	5.5	4.5	5	5.5	V
V_{IH}	High-level input voltage		2			2			V
V_{IL}	Low-level input voltage				0.8			0.8	V
V_{OH}	High-level output voltage	DB or CB 'ALS617			5.5			5.5	V
I_{OH}	High-level output current	$\overline{ERR}$ or $\overline{MERR}$			−0.4			−0.4	mA
		DB or CB 'ALS616			−1			−2.6	
I_{OL}	Low-level output current	$\overline{ERR}$ or $\overline{MERR}$			4			8	mA
		DB or CB			12			24	
t_w	Pulse duration	$\overline{LEDBO}$ low	45			25			ns
t_{su}	Setup time	(1) Data and check word before S0↑ (S1 = H)	15			12			ns
		(2) S0 high before $\overline{LEDBO}$↑ (S1 = H)†	45			45			
		(3) $\overline{LEDBO}$ high before the earlier of S0↓ or S1↓†	0			0			
		(4) $\overline{LEDBO}$ high before S1↑ (S0 = H)	0			0			
		(5) Diagnostic data word before S1↑ (S0 = H)	28			12			
		(6) Diagnostic check word before the later of S1↓ or S0↑	15			12			
		(7) Diagnostic data word before $\overline{LEDBO}$↑ (S1 = L and S0 = H)†	35			20			
t_h	Hold time	(8) Read-mode, S0 low and S1 high	35			30			ns
		(9) Data and check word after S0↑ (S1 = H)	20			15			
		(10) Data word after S1↑ (S0 = H)	20			15			
		(11) Check word after the later of S1↓ or S0↑	20			15			
		(12) Diagnostic data word after $\overline{LEDBO}$↑ (S1 = L, S0 = H)‡	0			0			
t_{corr}	Correction time (see Figure 1)		70			65			ns
T_C	Operating case temperature		−55		125				°C
T_A	Operating free-air temperature					0		70	°C

†These times ensure that corrected data is saved in the output data latch.
‡These times ensure that the diagnostic data word is saved in the output data latch.

'ALS616 electrical characteristics over recommended operating temperature range (unless otherwise noted)

PARAMETER		TEST CONDITIONS		SN54ALS616 MIN	SN54ALS616 TYP†	SN54ALS616 MAX	SN74ALS616 MIN	SN74ALS616 TYP†	SN74ALS616 MAX	UNIT
V_{IK}		V_{CC} = 4.5 V,	I_I = −18 mA			−1.5			−1.5	V
V_{OH}	All outputs	V_{CC} = 4.5 V to 5.5 V,	I_{OH} = −0.4 mA	V_{CC}−2			V_{CC}−2			V
	DB or CB	V_{CC} = 4.5 V,	I_{OH} = −1 mA	2.4	3.3					
		V_{CC} = 4.5 V,	I_{OH} = −2.6 mA				2.4	3.2		
V_{OL}	$\overline{ERR}$ or $\overline{MERR}$	V_{CC} = 4.5 V,	I_{OH} = 4 mA		0.25	0.4		0.25	0.4	V
		V_{CC} = 4.5 V,	I_{OL} = 8 mA					0.35	0.5	
	DB or CB	V_{CC} = 4.5 V,	I_{OL} = 12 mA		0.25	0.4		0.25	0.4	
		V_{CC} = 4.5 V,	I_{OL} = 24 mA					0.35	0.5	
I_I	S0 or S1	V_{CC} = 5.5 V,	V_I = 7 V			0.1			0.1	mA
	DB or CB	V_{CC} = 5.5 V,	V_I = 5.5 V			0.1			0.1	
I_{IH}	S0 or S1	V_{CC} = 5.5 V,	V_I = 2.7 V			20			20	μA
	DB or CB‡					20			20	
I_{IL}	S0 or S1	V_{CC} = 5.5 V,	V_I = 0.4 V			−0.4			−0.4	mA
	DB or CB‡					−0.1			−0.1	
I_O§		V_{CC} = 5.5 V,	V_O = 2.25 V	−30		−112	−30		−112	mA
I_{CC}		V_{CC} = 5.5 V	See Note 1		110	190		110	170	mA

†All typical values are at V_{CC} = 5 V, T_A = 25°C.
‡For I/O ports, the parameters I_{IH} and I_{IL} include the off-state output current.
§The output conditions have been chosen to produce a current that closely approximates one half of the true short-circuit output current, I_{OS}.
NOTE 1: I_{CC} is measured with S0 and S1 at 4.5 V and all CB and DB pins grounded.

'ALS616 switching characteristics, V_{CC} = 4.5 V to 5.5 V, C_L = 50 pF, T_C = −55°C to 125°C for SN54ALS616, T_A = 0°C to 70°C for SN74ALS616

PARAMETER	FROM (INPUT)	TO (OUTPUT)	TEST CONDITIONS	SN54ALS616 MIN	SN54ALS616 MAX	SN74ALS616 MIN	SN74ALS616 MAX	UNIT
t_{pd}	DB and CB	$\overline{ERR}$	S1 = H, S0 = L, R_L = 500 Ω	10	43	10	40	ns
	DB	$\overline{ERR}$	S1 = L, S0 = H, R_L = 500 Ω	10	43	10	40	
t_{pd}	DB and CB	$\overline{MERR}$	S1 = H, S0 = L, R_L = 500 Ω	15	65	15	55	ns
	DB	$\overline{MERR}$	S1 = L, S0 = H, R_L = 500 Ω	15	65	15	55	
t_{pd}	S0↓ and S1↓	CB	R1 = R2 = 500 Ω	10	60	10	49	ns
t_{pd}	DB	CB	S1 = L, S0 = L, R1 = R2 = 500 Ω	10	60	10	49	ns
t_{pd}	$\overline{LEDBO}$↓	DB	S1 = X, S0 = H, R1 = R2 = 500 Ω	7	35	7	30	ns
t_{pd}	S1↑	CB	S0 = H, R1 = R2 = 500 Ω	10	50	10	50	ns
t_{en}	$\overline{OECB}$↓	CB	S0 = H, S1 = X, R1 = R2 = 500 Ω	2	30	2	27	ns
t_{dis}	$\overline{OECB}$↑	CB	S0 = H, S1 = X, R1 = R2 = 500 Ω	2	30	2	27	ns
t_{en}	$\overline{OEB0}$ and $\overline{OEB1}$↓	DB	S0 = H, S1 = X, R1 = R2 = 500 Ω	2	30	2	27	ns
t_{dis}	$\overline{OEB0}$ and $\overline{OEB1}$↑	DB	S0 = H, S1 = X, R1 = R2 = 500 Ω	2	30	2	27	ns

'ALS617 electrical characteristics over recommended operating temperature range (unless otherwise noted)

PARAMETER		TEST CONDITIONS		SN54ALS617			SN74ALS617			UNIT
				MIN	TYP†	MAX	MIN	TYP†	MAX	
V_{IK}		V_{CC} = 4.5 V,	I_I = −18 mA			−1.5			−1.5	V
V_{OH}	$\overline{ERR}$ or $\overline{MERR}$	V_{CC} = 4.5 V to 5.5 V,	I_{OH} = −0.4 mA	$V_{CC}-2$			$V_{CC}-2$			V
I_{OH}	DB or CB	V_{CC} = 4.5 V,	V_{OH} = 5.5 V			0.1			0.1	mA
V_{OL}	$\overline{ERR}$ or $\overline{MERR}$	V_{CC} = 4.5 V,	I_{OH} = 4 mA		0.25	0.4		0.25	0.4	V
		V_{CC} = 4.5 V,	I_{OL} = 8 mA					0.35	0.5	
	DB or CB	V_{CC} = 4.5 V,	I_{OL} = 12 mA		0.25	0.4		0.25	0.4	
		V_{CC} = 4.5 V,	I_{OL} = 24 mA					0.35	0.5	
I_I	S0 or S1	V_{CC} = 5.5 V,	V_I = 7 V			0.1			0.1	mA
	DB or CB	V_{CC} = 5.5 V,	V_I = 5.5 V			0.1			0.1	
I_{IH}	S0 or S1	V_{CC} = 5.5 V,	V_I = 2.7 V			20			20	μA
	DB or CB‡					20			20	
I_{IL}	S0 or S1	V_{CC} = 5.5 V,	V_I = 0.4 V			−0.4			−0.4	mA
	DB or CB‡					−0.1			−0.1	
I_O§	$\overline{ERR}$ or $\overline{MERR}$	V_{CC} = 5.5 V,	V_O = 2.25 V	−30		−112	−30		−112	mA
I_{CC}		V_{CC} = 5.5 V	See Note 1		110			110		mA

†All typical values are at V_{CC} = 5 V, T_A = 25°C.
‡For I/O ports, the parameters I_{IH} and I_{IL} include the off-state output current.
§The output conditions have been chosen to produce a current that closely approximates one half of the true short-circuit output current, I_{OS}.
NOTE 1: I_{CC} is measured with S0 and S1 at 4.5 V and all CB and DB pins grounded.

'ALS617 switching characteristics, V_{CC} = 4.5 V to 5.5 V, C_L = 50 pF, T_C = −55°C to 125°C for SN54ALS617, T_A = 0°C to 70°C for SN74ALS617

PARAMETER	FROM (INPUT)	TO (OUTPUT)	TEST CONDITIONS	SN54ALS617			SN74ALS617			UNIT
				MIN	TYP†	MAX	MIN	TYP†	MAX	
t_{pd}	DB and CB	$\overline{ERR}$	S1 = H, S0 = L, R_L = 500 Ω		26			26		ns
	DB	$\overline{ERR}$	S1 = L, S0 = H, R_L = 500 Ω		26			26		
t_{pd}	DB and CB	$\overline{MERR}$	S1 = H, S0 = L, R_L = 500 Ω		40			40		ns
			S1 = L, S0 = H, R_L = 500 Ω		40			40		
t_{pd}	S0↓ and S1↓	CB	R_L = 680 Ω		40			40		ns
t_{pd}	DB	CB	S1 = L, S0 = L, R_L = 680 Ω		40			40		ns
t_{pd}	$\overline{LEDBO}$↓	DB	S1 = X, S0 = H, R_L = 680 Ω		26			26		ns
t_{pd}	S1↑	CB	S0 = H, R_L = 680 Ω		40			40		ns
t_{PLH}	$\overline{OECB}$↑	CB	S1 = X, S0 = H, R_L = 680 Ω		24			24		ns
t_{PHL}	$\overline{OECB}$↓	CB	S1 = X, S0 = H, R_L = 680 Ω		24			24		ns
t_{PLH}	$\overline{OEB0}$ and $\overline{OEB1}$↑	DB	S1 = X, S0 = H, R_L = 680 Ω		24			24		ns
t_{PHL}	$\overline{OEB0}$ and $\overline{OEB1}$↓	DB	S1 = X, S0 = H, R_L = 680 Ω		24			24		ns

†All typical values are at V_{CC} = 5 V, T_A = 25°C.

Additional information on these products can be obtained from the factory as it becomes available.

TEXAS INSTRUMENTS
POST OFFICE BOX 225012 • DALLAS, TEXAS 75265

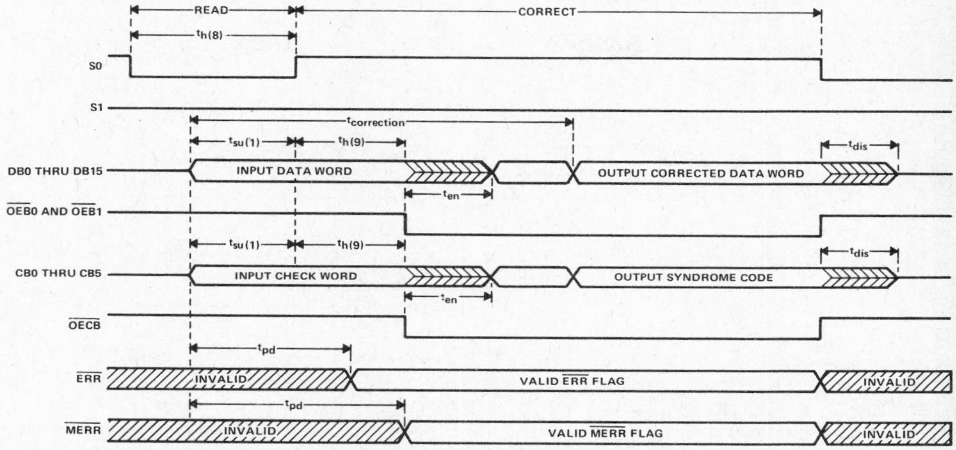
READ
CORRECT
$t_{h(8)}$
S0
S1
$t_{correction}$
$t_{su(1)}$
$t_{h(9)}$
t_{dis}
DB0 THRU DB15
INPUT DATA WORD
OUTPUT CORRECTED DATA WORD
t_{en}
OEB0 AND OEB1
CB0 THRU CB5
INPUT CHECK WORD
OUTPUT SYNDROME CODE
OECB
t_{pd}
ERR
INVALID
VALID ERR FLAG
MERR
VALID MERR FLAG

FIGURE 1. READ, FLAG, AND CORRECT MODE SWITCHING WAVEFORMS

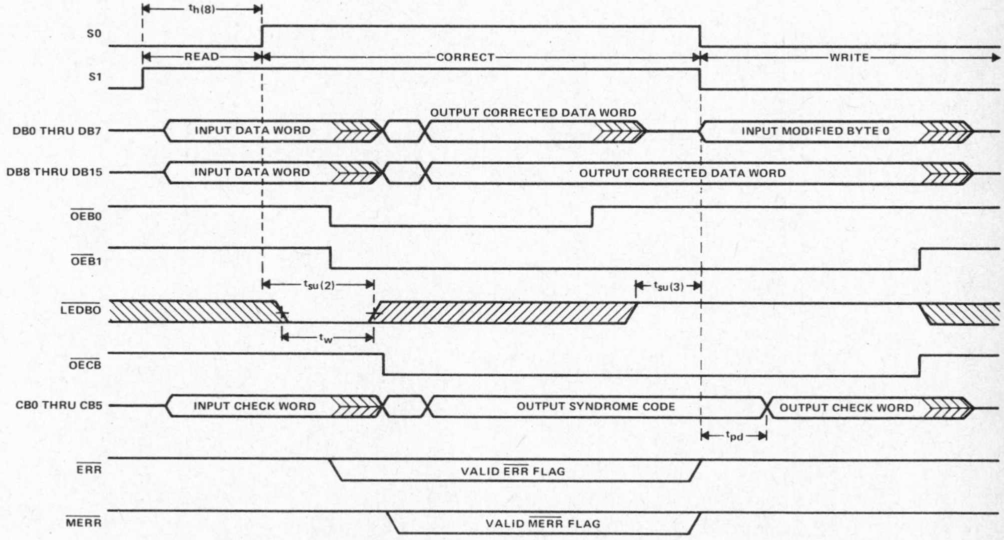
$t_{h(8)}$
S0
READ
CORRECT
WRITE
S1
OUTPUT CORRECTED DATA WORD
DB0 THRU DB7
INPUT DATA WORD
INPUT MODIFIED BYTE 0
DB8 THRU DB15
OEB0
OEB1
$t_{su(2)}$
$t_{su(3)}$
LEDBO
t_w
OECB
CB0 THRU CB5
INPUT CHECK WORD
OUTPUT SYNDROME CODE
OUTPUT CHECK WORD
t_{pd}
ERR
VALID ERR FLAG
MERR
VALID MERR FLAG

FIGURE 2. READ, CORRECT, MODIFY MODE SWITCHING WAVEFORMS

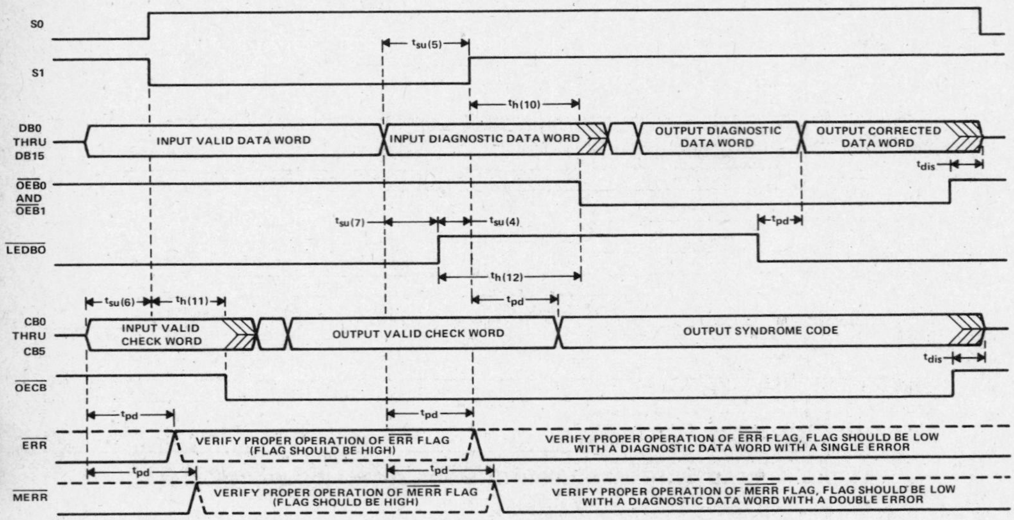
S0
S1
$t_{su(5)}$
$t_{h(10)}$
DB0 THRU DB15
INPUT VALID DATA WORD
INPUT DIAGNOSTIC DATA WORD
OUTPUT DIAGNOSTIC DATA WORD
OUTPUT CORRECTED DATA WORD
t_{dis}
OEB0 AND OEB1
$t_{su(7)}$
$t_{su(4)}$
t_{pd}
LEDBO
$t_{h(12)}$
$t_{su(6)}$
$t_{h(11)}$
CB0 THRU CB5
INPUT VALID CHECK WORD
OUTPUT VALID CHECK WORD
OUTPUT SYNDROME CODE
OECB
ERR
VERIFY PROPER OPERATION OF ERR FLAG (FLAG SHOULD BE HIGH)
VERIFY PROPER OPERATION OF ERR FLAG, FLAG SHOULD BE LOW WITH A DIAGNOSTIC DATA WORD WITH A SINGLE ERROR
MERR
VERIFY PROPER OPERATION OF MERR FLAG (FLAG SHOULD BE HIGH)
VERIFY PROPER OPERATION OF MERR FLAG, FLAG SHOULD BE LOW WITH A DIAGNOSTIC DATA WORD WITH A DOUBLE ERROR

FIGURE 3. DIAGNOSTIC MODE SWITCHING WAVEFORM

SN54ALS632A, SN54ALS633 THRU SN54ALS635
SN74ALS632A, SN74ALS633 THRU SN74ALS635
32-BIT PARALLEL ERROR DETECTION AND CORRECTION CIRCUITS

D2661, DECEMBER 1982—REVISED DECEMBER 1985

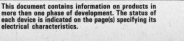

- **Detects and Corrects Single-Bit Errors**
- **Detects and Flags Dual-Bit Errors**
- **Built-In Diagnostic Capability**
- **Fast Write and Read Cycle Processing Times**
- **Byte-Write Capability . . . 'ALS632A and 'ALS633**
- **Dependable Texas Instruments Quality and Reliability**

DEVICE	PACKAGE	BYTE-WRITE	OUTPUT
'ALS632A	52-pin	yes	3-State
'ALS633	52-pin	yes	Open-Collector
'ALS634	48-pin	no	3-State
'ALS635	48-pin	no	Open-Collector

'ALS632A, 'ALS633 . . . JD PACKAGE

(TOP VIEW)

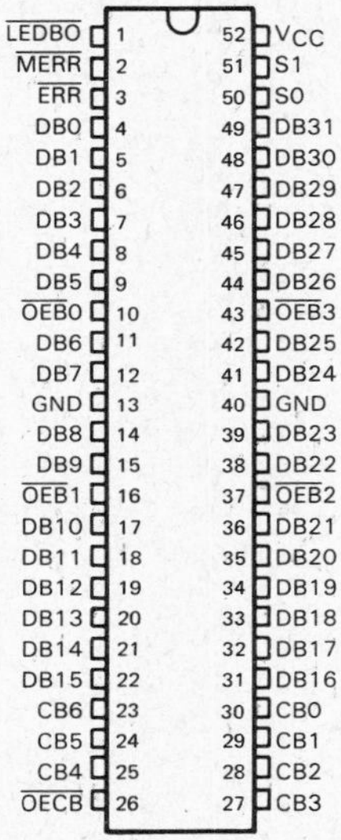

LEDBO 1
MERR 2
ERR 3
DB0 4
DB1 5
DB2 6
DB3 7
DB4 8
DB5 9
OEB0 10
DB6 11
DB7 12
GND 13
DB8 14
DB9 15
OEB1 16
DB10 17
DB11 18
DB12 19
DB13 20
DB14 21
DB15 22
CB6 23
CB5 24
CB4 25
OECB 26
52 VCC
51 S1
50 S0
49 DB31
48 DB30
47 DB29
46 DB28
45 DB27
44 DB26
43 OEB3
42 DB25
41 DB24
40 GND
39 DB23
38 DB22
37 OEB2
36 DB21
35 DB20
34 DB19
33 DB18
32 DB17
31 DB16
30 CB0
29 CB1
28 CB2
27 CB3

'ALS632A, 'ALS633 . . . FN PACKAGE

(TOP VIEW)

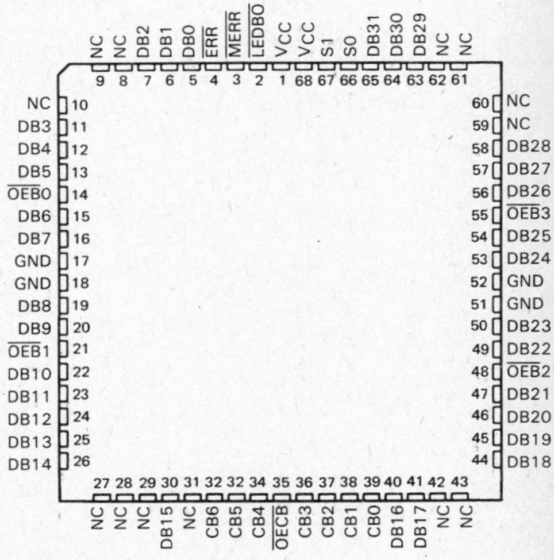

NC NC DB2 DB1 DB0 ERR MERR LEDBO VCC VCC S1 S0 DB31 DB30 DB29 NC NC
9 8 7 6 5 4 3 2 1 68 67 66 65 64 63 62 61
NC 10
DB3 11
DB4 12
DB5 13
OEB0 14
DB6 15
DB7 16
GND 17
GND 18
DB8 19
DB9 20
OEB1 21
DB10 22
DB11 23
DB12 24
DB13 25
DB14 26
60 NC
59 NC
58 DB28
57 DB27
56 DB26
55 OEB3
54 DB25
53 DB24
52 GND
51 GND
50 DB23
49 DB22
48 OEB2
47 DB21
46 DB20
45 DB19
44 DB18
27 28 29 30 31 32 32 34 35 36 37 38 39 40 41 42 43
NC NC NC DB15 NC CB6 CB5 CB4 OECB CB3 CB2 CB1 CB0 DB16 DB17 NC NC

NC—No internal connection

description

The 'ALS632A and 'ALS633 through 'ALS635 devices are 32-bit parallel error detection and correction circuits (EDACs) in 52-pin ('ALS632A and 'ALS633) or 48-pin ('ALS634 and 'ALS635) 600-mil packages. The EDACs use a modified Hamming code to generate a 7-bit check word from a 32-bit data word. This check word is stored along with the data word during the memory write cycle. During the memory read cycle, the 39-bit words from memory are processed by the EDACs to determine if errors have occurred in memory.

Single-bit errors in the 32-bit data word are flagged and corrected.

Single-bit errors in the 7-bit check word are flagged, and the CPU sends the EDAC through the correction cycle even though the 32-bit data word is not in error. The correction cycle will simply pass along the original 32-bit data word in this case and produce error syndrome bits to pinpoint the error-generating location.

Dual-bit errors are flagged but not corrected. These errors may occur in any two bits of the 39-bit data word from memory (two errors in the 32-bit data word, two errors in the 7-bit check word, or one error in each word). The gross-error condition of all lows or all highs from memory will be detected. Otherwise, errors in three or more bits of the 39-bit word are beyond the capabilities of these devices to detect.

This document contains information on products in more than one phase of development. The status of each device is indicated on the page(s) specifying its electrical characteristics.

Read-modify-write (byte-control) operations can be performed with the 'ALS632A and 'ALS633 EDACs by using output latch enable, $\overline{LEDBO}$, and the individual $\overline{OEB0}$ thru $\overline{OEB3}$ byte control pins.

Diagnostics are performed on the EDACs by controls and internal paths that allow the user to read the contents of the DB and CB input latches. These will determine if the failure occurred in memory or in the EDAC.

'ALS634, 'ALS635 . . . JD PACKAGE
(TOP VIEW)

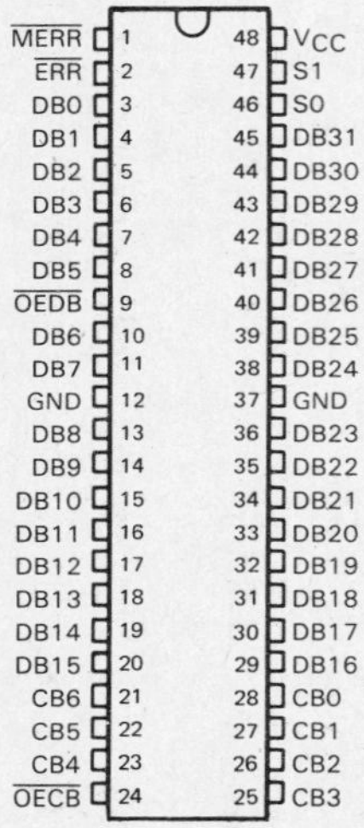
MERR 1
ERR 2
DB0 3
DB1 4
DB2 5
DB3 6
DB4 7
DB5 8
OEDB 9
DB6 10
DB7 11
GND 12
DB8 13
DB9 14
DB10 15
DB11 16
DB12 17
DB13 18
DB14 19
DB15 20
CB6 21
CB5 22
CB4 23
OECB 24
25 CB3
26 CB2
27 CB1
28 CB0
29 DB16
30 DB17
31 DB18
32 DB19
33 DB20
34 DB21
35 DB22
36 DB23
37 GND
38 DB24
39 DB25
40 DB26
41 DB27
42 DB28
43 DB29
44 DB30
45 DB31
46 S0
47 S1
48 VCC

'ALS634, 'ALS635 . . . FN PACKAGE
(TOP VIEW)

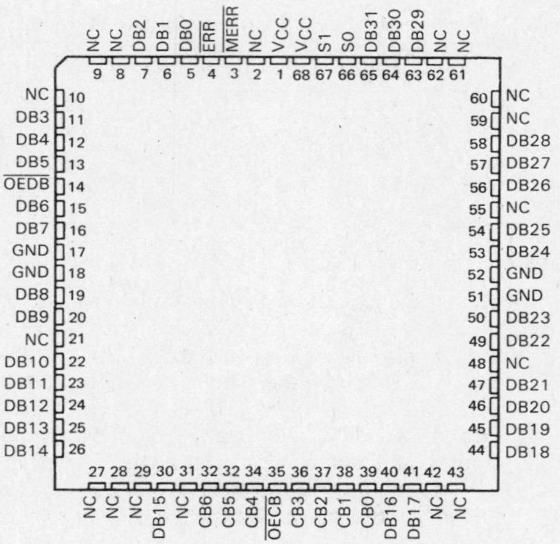
NC NC DB2 DB1 DB0 ERR MERR NC VCC VCC S1 S0 DB31 DB30 DB29 NC NC
9 8 7 6 5 4 3 2 1 68 67 66 65 64 63 62 61
NC 10
DB3 11
DB4 12
DB5 13
OEDB 14
DB6 15
DB7 16
GND 17
GND 18
DB8 19
DB9 20
NC 21
DB10 22
DB11 23
DB12 24
DB13 25
DB14 26
60 NC
59 NC
58 DB28
57 DB27
56 DB26
55 NC
54 DB25
53 DB24
52 GND
51 GND
50 DB23
49 DB22
48 NC
47 DB21
46 DB20
45 DB19
44 DB18
27 28 29 30 31 32 32 34 35 36 37 38 39 40 41 42 43
NC NC NC DB15 NC CB6 CB5 CB4 OECB CB3 CB2 CB1 CB0 DB16 DB17 NC NC

NC—No internal connection

TABLE 1. WRITE CONTROL FUNCTION

MEMORY CYCLE	EDAC FUNCTION	CONTROL S1	CONTROL S0	DATA I/O	DB CONTROL $\overline{OEBn}$ OR $\overline{OEDB}$	DB OUTPUT LATCH ('ALS632A, 'ALS633) $\overline{LEDBO}$	CHECK I/O	CB CONTROL $\overline{OECB}$	ERROR FLAGS $\overline{ERR}$	ERROR FLAGS $\overline{MERR}$
Write	Generate check word	L	L	Input	H	X	Output check bits†	L	H	H

†See Table 2 for details on check bit generation.

memory write cycle details

During a memory write cycle, the check bits (CB0 thru CB6) are generated internally in the EDAC by seven 16-input parity generators using the 32-bit data word as defined in Table 2. These seven check bits are stored in memory along with the original 32-bit data word. This 32-bit word will later be used in the memory read cycle for error detection and correction.

TABLE 2. PARITY ALGORITHM

CHECK WORD	32-BIT DATA WORD																														
BIT	31	30	29	28	27	26	25	24	23	22	21	20	19	18	17	16	15	14	13	12	11	10	9	8	7	6	5	4	3	2	1	0
CB0	X		X	X		X					X		X	X	X			X			X		X	X	X	X		X				X
CB1				X		X		X		X		X		X	X	X				X		X		X		X		X		X	X	X
CB2	X		X			X	X		X			X	X			X	X		X			X	X		X			X	X			X
CB3			X	X	X				X	X	X				X	X			X	X	X				X	X	X				X	X
CB4	X	X							X	X	X	X	X	X			X	X							X	X	X	X	X	X		
CB5	X	X	X	X	X	X	X	X									X	X	X	X	X	X	X	X								
CB6	X	X	X	X	X	X	X	X																	X	X	X	X	X	X	X	X

The seven check bits are parity bits derived from the matrix of data bits as indicated by "X" for each bit.

error detection and correction details

During a memory read cycle, the 7-bit check word is retrieved along with the actual data. In order to be able to determine whether the data from memory is acceptable to use as presented to the bus, the error flags must be tested to determine if they are at the high level.

The first case in Table 3 represents the normal, no-error conditions. The EDAC presents highs on both flags. The next two cases of single-bit errors give a high on $\overline{\text{MERR}}$ and a low on $\overline{\text{ERR}}$, which is the signal for a correctable error, and the EDAC should be sent through the correction cycle. The last three cases of double-bit errors will cause the EDAC to signal lows on both $\overline{\text{ERR}}$ and $\overline{\text{MERR}}$, which is the interrupt indication for the CPU.

TABLE 3. ERROR FUNCTION

TOTAL NUMBER OF ERRORS		ERROR FLAGS		DATA CORRECTION
32-BIT DATA WORD	7-BIT CHECK WORD	$\overline{\text{ERR}}$	$\overline{\text{MERR}}$	
0	0	H	H	Not applicable
1	0	L	H	Correction
0	1	L	H	Correction
1	1	L	L	Interrupt
2	0	L	L	Interrupt
0	2	L	L	Interrupt

Error detection is accomplished as the 7-bit check word and the 32-bit data word from memory are applied to internal parity generators/checkers. If the parity of all seven groupings of data and check bits are correct, it is assumed that no error has occurred and both error flags will be high.

If the parity of one or more of the check groups is incorrect, an error has occurred and the proper error flag or flags will be set low. Any single error in the 32-bit data word will change the state of either three or five bits of the 7-bit check word. Any single error in the 7-bit check word changes the state of only that one bit. In either case, the single error flag ($\overline{\text{ERR}}$) will be set low while the dual error flag ($\overline{\text{MERR}}$) will remain high.

Any two-bit error will change the state of an even number of check bits. The two-bit error is not correctable since the parity tree can only identify single-bit errors. Both error flags are set low when any two-bit error is detected.

Three or more simultaneous bit errors can cause the EDAC to believe that no error, a correctable error, or an uncorrectable error has occurred and will produce erroneous results in all three cases. It should be noted that the gross-error conditions of all lows and all highs will be detected.

TABLE 4. READ, FLAG, AND CORRECT FUNCTION

MEMORY CYCLE	EDAC FUNCTION	CONTROL S1	CONTROL S0	DATA I/O	DB CONTROL $\overline{OEBn}$ OR $\overline{OEDB}$	DB OUTPUT LATCH ('ALS632A, 'ALS633) $\overline{LEDBO}$	CHECK I/O	CB CONTROL $\overline{OECB}$	ERROR FLAGS $\overline{ERR}$ $\overline{MERR}$
Read	Read & flag	H	L	Input	H	X	Input	H	Enabled†
Read	Latch input data & check bits	H	H	Latched input data	H	L	Latched input check word	H	Enabled†
Read	Output corrected data & syndrome bits	H	H	Output corrected data word	L	X	Output syndrome bits‡	L	Enabled†

†See Table 3 for error description.
‡See Table 5 for error location.

As the corrected word is made available on the data I/O port (DB0 thru DB31), the check word I/O port (CB0 thru CB6) presents a 7-bit syndrome error code. This syndrome error code can be used to locate the bad memory chip. See Table 5 for syndrome decoding.

TEXAS INSTRUMENTS
POST OFFICE BOX 225012 • DALLAS, TEXAS 75265

TABLE 5. SYNDROME DECODING

SYNDROME BITS							ERROR
6	5	4	3	2	1	0	
L	L	L	L	L	L	L	unc
L	L	L	L	L	L	H	2-bit
L	L	L	L	L	H	L	2-bit
L	L	L	L	L	H	H	unc
L	L	L	L	H	L	L	2-bit
L	L	L	L	H	L	H	unc
L	L	L	L	H	H	L	unc
L	L	L	L	H	H	H	2-bit
L	L	L	H	L	L	L	2-bit
L	L	L	H	L	L	H	unc
L	L	L	H	L	H	L	DB31
L	L	L	H	L	H	H	2-bit
L	L	L	H	H	L	L	unc
L	L	L	H	H	L	H	2-bit
L	L	L	H	H	H	L	2-bit
L	L	L	H	H	H	H	DB30
L	L	H	L	L	L	L	2-bit
L	L	H	L	L	L	H	unc
L	L	H	L	L	H	L	DB29
L	L	H	L	L	H	H	2-bit
L	L	H	L	H	L	L	DB28
L	L	H	L	H	L	H	2-bit
L	L	H	L	H	H	L	2-bit
L	L	H	L	H	H	H	DB27
L	L	H	H	L	L	L	DB26
L	L	H	H	L	L	H	2-bit
L	L	H	H	L	H	L	2-bit
L	L	H	H	L	H	H	DB25
L	L	H	H	H	L	L	2-bit
L	L	H	H	H	L	H	DB24
L	L	H	H	H	H	L	unc
L	L	H	H	H	H	H	2-bit

SYNDROME BITS							ERROR
6	5	4	3	2	1	0	
L	H	L	L	L	L	L	2-bit
L	H	L	L	L	L	H	unc
L	H	L	L	L	H	L	DB7
L	H	L	L	L	H	H	2-bit
L	H	L	L	H	L	L	DB6
L	H	L	L	H	L	H	2-bit
L	H	L	L	H	H	L	2-bit
L	H	L	L	H	H	H	DB5
L	H	L	H	L	L	L	DB4
L	H	L	H	L	L	H	2-bit
L	H	L	H	L	H	L	2-bit
L	H	L	H	L	H	H	DB3
L	H	L	H	H	L	L	2-bit
L	H	L	H	H	L	H	DB2
L	H	L	H	H	H	L	unc
L	H	L	H	H	H	H	2-bit
L	H	H	L	L	L	L	DB0
L	H	H	L	L	L	H	2-bit
L	H	H	L	L	H	L	2-bit
L	H	H	L	L	H	H	unc
L	H	H	L	H	L	L	2-bit
L	H	H	L	H	L	H	DB1
L	H	H	L	H	H	L	unc
L	H	H	L	H	H	H	2-bit
L	H	H	H	L	L	L	2-bit
L	H	H	H	L	L	H	unc
L	H	H	H	L	H	L	unc
L	H	H	H	L	H	H	2-bit
L	H	H	H	H	L	L	unc
L	H	H	H	H	L	H	2-bit
L	H	H	H	H	H	L	2-bit
L	H	H	H	H	H	H	CB6

SYNDROME BITS							ERROR
6	5	4	3	2	1	0	
H	L	L	L	L	L	L	2-bit
H	L	L	L	L	L	H	unc
H	L	L	L	L	H	L	unc
H	L	L	L	L	H	H	2-bit
H	L	L	L	H	L	L	unc
H	L	L	L	H	L	H	2-bit
H	L	L	L	H	H	L	2-bit
H	L	L	L	H	H	H	unc
H	L	L	H	L	L	L	unc
H	L	L	H	L	L	H	2-bit
H	L	L	H	L	H	L	2-bit
H	L	L	H	L	H	H	DB15
H	L	L	H	H	L	L	2-bit
H	L	L	H	H	L	H	unc
H	L	L	H	H	H	L	DB14
H	L	L	H	H	H	H	2-bit
H	L	H	L	L	L	L	unc
H	L	H	L	L	L	H	2-bit
H	L	H	L	L	H	L	2-bit
H	L	H	L	L	H	H	DB13
H	L	H	L	H	L	L	2-bit
H	L	H	L	H	L	H	DB12
H	L	H	L	H	H	L	DB11
H	L	H	L	H	H	H	2-bit
H	L	H	H	L	L	L	2-bit
H	L	H	H	L	L	H	DB10
H	L	H	H	L	H	L	DB9
H	L	H	H	L	H	H	2-bit
H	L	H	H	H	L	L	DB8
H	L	H	H	H	L	H	2-bit
H	L	H	H	H	H	L	2-bit
H	L	H	H	H	H	H	CB5

SYNDROME BITS							ERROR
6	5	4	3	2	1	0	
H	H	L	L	L	L	L	unc
H	H	L	L	L	L	H	2-bit
H	H	L	L	L	H	L	2-bit
H	H	L	L	L	H	H	DB23
H	H	L	L	H	L	L	2-bit
H	H	L	L	H	L	H	DB22
H	H	L	L	H	H	L	DB21
H	H	L	L	H	H	H	2-bit
H	H	L	H	L	L	L	2-bit
H	H	L	H	L	L	H	DB20
H	H	L	H	L	H	L	DB19
H	H	L	H	L	H	H	2-bit
H	H	L	H	H	L	L	DB18
H	H	L	H	H	L	H	2-bit
H	H	L	H	H	H	L	2-bit
H	H	L	H	H	H	H	CB4
H	H	H	L	L	L	L	2-bit
H	H	H	L	L	L	H	DB16
H	H	H	L	L	H	L	unc
H	H	H	L	L	H	H	2-bit
H	H	H	L	H	L	L	DB17
H	H	H	L	H	L	H	2-bit
H	H	H	L	H	H	L	2-bit
H	H	H	L	H	H	H	CB3
H	H	H	H	L	L	L	unc
H	H	H	H	L	L	H	2-bit
H	H	H	H	L	H	L	2-bit
H	H	H	H	L	H	H	CB2
H	H	H	H	H	L	L	2-bit
H	H	H	H	H	L	H	CB1
H	H	H	H	H	H	L	CB0
H	H	H	H	H	H	H	none

CB X= error in check bit X
DB Y= error in data bit Y
2-bit = double-bit error
unc = uncorrectable multibit error

read-modify-write (byte control) operations

The 'ALS632A and 'ALS633 devices are capable of byte-write operations. The 39-bit word from memory must first be latched into the DB and CB input latches. This is easily accomplished by switching from the read and flag mode (S1 = H, S0 = L) to the latch input mode (S1 = H, S0 = H). The EDAC will then make any corrections, if necessary, to the data word and place it at the input of the output data latch. This data word must then be latched into the output data latch by taking $\overline{\text{LEDBO}}$ from a low to a high.

Byte control can now be employed on the data word through the $\overline{\text{OEB0}}$ through $\overline{\text{OEB3}}$ controls. $\overline{\text{OEB0}}$ controls DB0-DB7 (byte 0), $\overline{\text{OEB1}}$ controls DB8-DB15 (byte 1), $\overline{\text{OEB2}}$ controls DB16-DB23 (byte 2), and $\overline{\text{OEB3}}$ controls DB24-DB31 (byte 3). Placing a high on the byte control will disable the output and the user can modify the byte. If a low is placed on the byte control, then the original byte is allowed to pass onto the data bus unchanged. If the original data word is altered through byte control, a new check word must be generated before it is written back into memory. This is easily accomplished by taking control S1 and S0 low. Table 6 lists the read-modify-write functions.

TABLE 6. READ-MODIFY-WRITE FUNCTION

MEMORY CYCLE	EDAC FUNCTION	CONTROL S1 S0	BYTEn†	$\overline{\text{OEBn}}$†	DB OUTPUT LATCH $\overline{\text{LEDBO}}$	CHECK I/O	CB CONTROL	ERROR FLAG $\overline{\text{ERR}}$ $\overline{\text{MERR}}$
Read	Read & Flag	H L	Input	H	X	Input	H	Enabled
Read	Latch input data & check bits	H H	Latched Input data	H	L	Latched input check word	H	Enabled
Read	Latch corrected data word into output latch	H H	Latched output data word	H	H	Hi-Z Output Syndrome bits	H L	Enabled
Modify /write	Modify appropriate byte or bytes & generate new check word	L L	Input modified BYTE0 Output unchanged BYTE0	H L	H	Output check word	L	H H

†$\overline{\text{OEB0}}$ controls DB0-DB7 (BYTE0), $\overline{\text{OEB1}}$ controls DB8-DB15 (BYTE1), $\overline{\text{OEB3}}$ controls DB16-DB23 (BYTE2), $\overline{\text{OEB3}}$ controls DB24-DB31 (BYTE3).

diagnostic operations

The 'ALS632A and 'ALS633 thru 'ALS635 are capable of diagnostics that allow the user to determine whether the EDAC or the memory is failing. The diagnostic function tables will help the user to see the possibilities for diagnostic control.

In the diagnostic mode (S1 = L, S0 = H), the checkword is latched into the input latch while the data input latch remains transparent. This lets the user apply various data words against a fixed known checkword. If the user applies a diagnostic data word with an error in any bit location, the $\overline{\text{ERR}}$ flag should be low. If a diagnostic data word with two errors in any bit location is applied, the $\overline{\text{MERR}}$ flag should be low. After the checkword is latched into the input latch, it can be verified by taking $\overline{\text{OECB}}$ low. This outputs the latched checkword. With the 'ALS632A and 'ALS633, the diagnostic data word can be latched into the output data latch and verified. It should be noted that the 'ALS634 and 'ALS635 do not have this pass-through capability because they do not contain an output data latch. By changing from the diagnostic mode (S1 = L, S0 = H) to the correction mode (S1 = H, S0 = H), the user can verify that the EDAC will correct the diagnostic data word. Also, the syndrome bits can be produced to verify that the EDAC pinpoints the error location. Table 7 ('ALS632A and 'ALS633) and Table 8 ('ALS634 and 'ALS635) list the diagnostic functions.

TABLE 7. 'ALS632A, 'ALS633 DIAGNOSTIC FUNCTION

EDAC FUNCTION	CONTROL S1 S0	DATA I/O	DB BYTE CONTROL $\overline{OEBn}$	DB OUTPUT LATCH $\overline{LEDBO}$	CHECK I/O	CB CONTROL $\overline{OECB}$	ERROR FLAGS $\overline{ERR}$ $\overline{MERR}$
Read & flag	H L	Input correct data word	H	X	Input correct check bits	H	H H
Latch input check word while data input latch remains transparent	L H	Input diagnostic data word†	H	L	Latched input check bits	H	Enabled
Latch diagnostic data word into output latch	L H	Input diagnostic data word†	H	H	Output latched check bits Hi-Z	L H	Enabled
Latch diagnostic data word into input latch	H H	Latched input diagnostic data word	H	H	Output syndrome bits Hi-Z	L H	Enabled
Output diagnostic data word & syndrome bits	H H	Output diagnostic data word	L	H	Output syndrome bits Hi-Z	L H	Enabled
Output corrected diagnostic data word & output syndrome bits	H H	Output corrected diagnostic data word	L	L	Output syndrome bits Hi-Z	L H	Enabled

†Diagnostic data is a data word with an error in one bit location except when testing the $\overline{MERR}$ error flag. In this case, the diagnostic data word will contain errors in two bit locations.

TABLE 8. 'ALS634, 'ALS635 DIAGNOSTIC FUNCTION

EDAC FUNCTION	CONTROL S1 S0	DATA I/O	DB CONTROL $\overline{OEDB}$	CHECK I/O	DB CONTROL $\overline{OECB}$	ERROR FLAGS $\overline{ERR}$ $\overline{MERR}$
Read & flag	H L	Input correct data word	H	Input correct check bits	H	H H
Latch input check bits while data input latch remains transparent	L H	Input diagnostic data word†	H	Latched input check bits	H	Enabled
Output input check bits	L H	Input diagnostic data word†	H	Output input check bits	L	Enabled
Latch diagnostic data into input latch	H H	Latched input diagnostic data word	H	Output syndrome bits Hi-Z	L H	Enabled
Output corrected diagnostic data word	H H	Output corrected diagnostic data word	L	Output syndrome bits Hi-Z	L H	Enabled

†Diagnostic data is a data word with an error in one bit location except when testing the $\overline{MERR}$ error flag. In this case, the diagnostic data word will contain errors in two bit locations.

'ALS632A, 'ALS633 logic diagram (positive logic)

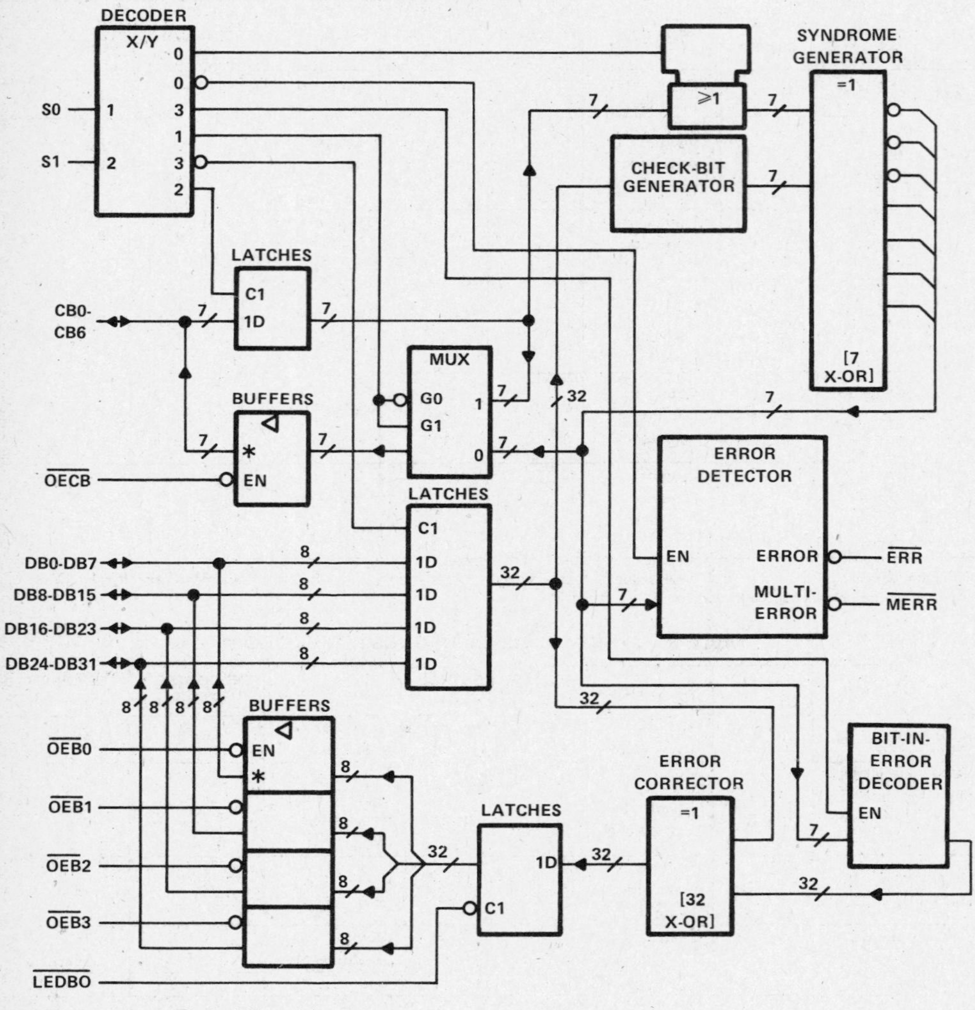
DECODER
X/Y
S0
S1
SYNDROME GENERATOR
=1
≥1
CHECK-BIT GENERATOR
[7 X-OR]
LATCHES
C1
1D
CB0-CB6
MUX
G0
G1
BUFFERS
EN
OECB
ERROR DETECTOR
ERROR
MULTI-ERROR
ERR
MERR
DB0-DB7
DB8-DB15
DB16-DB23
DB24-DB31
OEB0
OEB1
OEB2
OEB3
LEDBO
ERROR CORRECTOR
[32 X-OR]
BIT-IN-ERROR DECODER

*'ALS632A has 3-state (▽) check-bit and data outputs.
'ALS633 has open-collector (⬙) check-bit and data outputs.

TEXAS INSTRUMENTS
POST OFFICE BOX 225012 • DALLAS, TEXAS 75265

'ALS634, 'ALS635 logic diagram (positive logic)

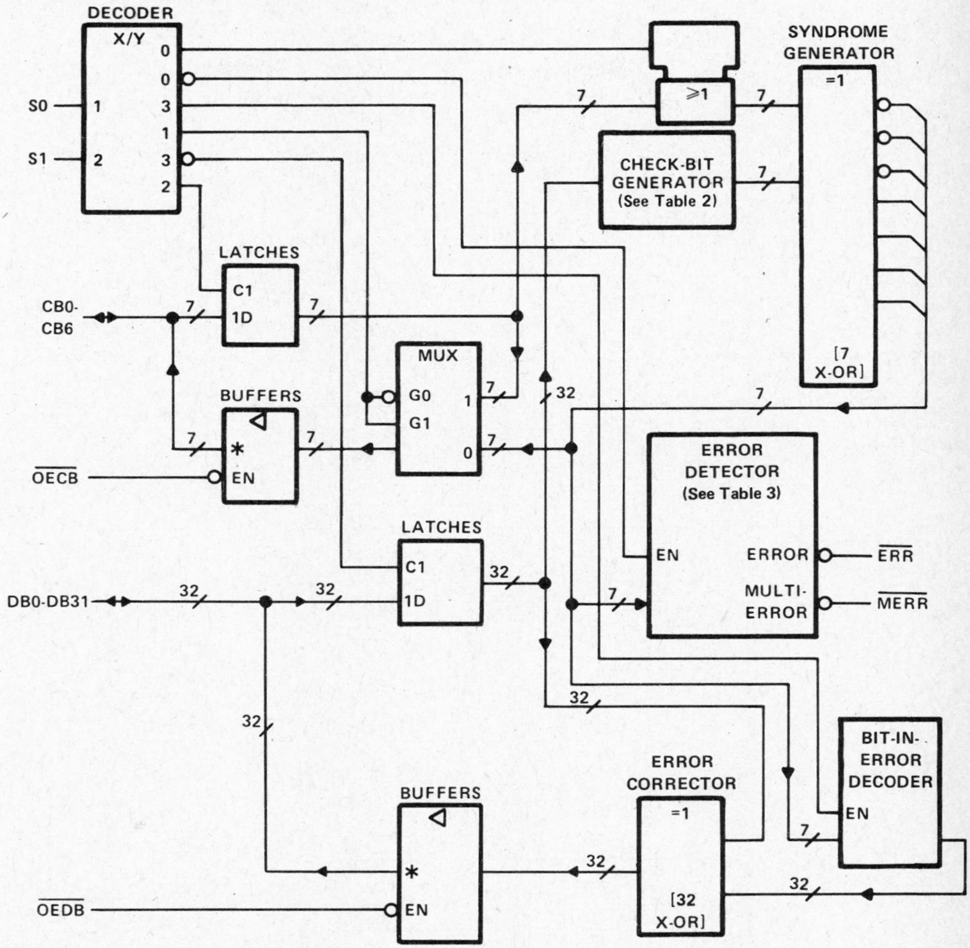
DECODER
X/Y
S0
S1
SYNDROME GENERATOR
=1
≥1
CHECK-BIT GENERATOR (See Table 2)
LATCHES
C1
1D
CB0-CB6
MUX
G0
G1
BUFFERS
OECB
EN
[7 X-OR]
ERROR DETECTOR (See Table 3)
ERROR
MULTI-ERROR
ERR
MERR
DB0-DB31
BIT-IN-ERROR DECODER
ERROR CORRECTOR
[32 X-OR]
OEDB

*'ALS634 has 3-state (▽) check-bit and data outputs.
'ALS635 has open-collector (⩡) check-bit and data outputs.

absolute maximum ratings over operating free-air temperature range (unless otherwise noted)

Supply voltage, V_{CC} (see Note 1) . . . . 7 V
Input voltage: CB and DB . . . . 5.5 V
All others . . . . 7 V
Operating free-air temperature range:
SN74ALS632A, SN74ALS633 thru SN74ALS635 . . . . 0°C to 70°C
Operating case temperature range:
SN54ALS632A, SN54ALS633 thru SN54ALS635 . . . . −55°C to 125°C
Storage temperature range . . . . −65°C to 150°C

recommended operating conditions

			SN54ALS632A SN54ALS633 THRU SN54ALS635			SN74ALS632A SN74ALS633 THRU SN74ALS635			UNIT
			MIN	NOM	MAX	MIN	NOM	MAX	
V_{CC}	Supply voltage		4.5	5	5.5	4.5	5	5.5	V
V_{IH}	High-level input voltage		2			2			V
V_{IL}	Low-level input voltage				0.8			0.8	V
I_{OH}	High-level output current	$\overline{ERR}$ or $\overline{MERR}$			−0.4			−0.4	mA
		DB or CB 'ALS632A, 'ALS634			−1			−2.6	
I_{OL}	Low-level output current	$\overline{ERR}$ or $\overline{MERR}$			4			8	mA
		DB or CB			12			24	
t_w	Pulse duration	$\overline{LEDBO}$ low	25			25			ns
t_{su}	Setup time	(1) Data and check word before $S0\uparrow$ (S1 = H)	15			10			ns
		(2) S0 high before $\overline{LEDBO}\uparrow$ (S1 = H)†	45			45			
		(3) $\overline{LEDBO}$ high before the earlier of $S0\downarrow$ or $S1\downarrow$†	0			0			
		(4) $\overline{LEDBO}$ high before $S1\uparrow$ (S0 = H)	0			0			
		(5) Diagnostic data word before $S1\uparrow$ (S0 = H)	15			10			
		(6) Diagnostic check word before the later of $S1\downarrow$ or $S0\uparrow$	15			10			
		(7) Diagnostic data word before $\overline{LEDBO}\uparrow$ (S1 = L and S0 = H)‡	25			20			
t_h	Hold time	(8) Read-mode, S0 low and S1 high	35			30			ns
		(9) Data and check word after $S0\uparrow$ (S1 = H)	20			15			
		(10) Data word after $S1\uparrow$ (S0 = H)	20			15			
		(11) Check word after the later of $S1\downarrow$ or $S0\uparrow$	20			15			
		(12) Diagnostic data word after $\overline{LEDBO}\uparrow$ (S1 = L, S0 = H)‡	0			0			
t_{corr}	Correction time (see Figure 1)		65			58			ns
T_C	Operating case temperature		−55		125				°C
T_A	Operating free-air temperature					0		70	°C

†These times ensure that corrected data is saved in the output data latch.
‡These times ensure that the diagnostic data word is saved in the output data latch.

2 LSI Devices

TEXAS INSTRUMENTS
POST OFFICE BOX 225012 • DALLAS, TEXAS 75265

'ALS632A, 'ALS634 electrical characteristics over recommended operating temperature range (unless otherwise noted)

PARAMETER		TEST CONDITIONS		SN54ALS632A SN54ALS634 MIN	TYP†	MAX	SN74ALS632A SN74ALS634 MIN	TYP†	MAX	UNIT
V_{IK}		V_{CC} = 4.5 V,	I_I = −18 mA			−1.5			−1.5	V
V_{OH}	All outputs	V_{CC} = 4.5 V to 5.5 V,	I_{OH} = −0.4 mA	V_{CC}−2			V_{CC}−2			V
	DB or CB	V_{CC} = 4.5 V,	I_{OH} = −1 mA	2.4	3.3					
		V_{CC} = 4.5 V,	I_{OH} = −2.6 mA				2.4	3.2		
V_{OL}	$\overline{ERR}$ or $\overline{MERR}$	V_{CC} = 4.5 V,	I_{OL} = 4 mA		0.25	0.4		0.25	0.4	V
		V_{CC} = 4.5 V,	I_{OL} = 8 mA					0.35	0.5	
	DB or CB	V_{CC} = 4.5 V,	I_{OL} = 12 mA		0.25	0.4		0.25	0.4	
		V_{CC} = 4.5 V,	I_{OL} = 24 mA					0.35	0.5	
I_I	S0 or S1	V_{CC} = 5.5 V,	V_I = 7 V			0.1			0.1	mA
	All others	V_{CC} = 5.5 V,	V_I = 5.5 V			0.1			0.1	
I_{IH}	S0 or S1	V_{CC} = 5.5 V,	V_I = 2.7 V			20			20	μA
	All others‡					20			20	
I_{IL}	S0 or S1	V_{CC} = 5.5 V,	V_I = 0.4 V			−0.4			−0.4	mA
	All others‡					−0.1			−0.1	
I_O§		V_{CC} = 5.5 V,	V_O = 2.25 V	−30		−112	−30		−112	mA
I_{CC}		V_{CC} = 5.5 V,	See Note 1		150	250		150	250	mA

† All typical values are at V_{CC} = 5 V, T_A = 25 °C.
‡ For I/O ports, the parameters I_{IH} and I_{IL} include the off-state output current.
§ The output conditions have been chosen to produce a current that closely approximates one half of the true short-circuit output current, I_{OS}.
NOTE 1: I_{CC} is measured with S0 and S1 at 4.5 V and all CB and DB pins grounded.

'ALS632A switching characteristics, V_{CC} = 4.5 V to 5.5 V, C_L = 50 pF, T_C = −55 °C to 125 °C for SN54ALS632A, T_A = 0 °C to 70 °C for SN74ALS632A

PARAMETER	FROM (INPUT)	TO (OUTPUT)	TEST CONDITIONS	SN54ALS632A MIN	MAX	SN74ALS632A MIN	MAX	UNIT
t_{pd}	DB and CB	$\overline{ERR}$	S1 = H, S0 = L, R_L = 500 Ω	10	43	10	40	ns
	DB	$\overline{ERR}$	S1 = L, S0 = H, R_L = 500 Ω	10	43	10	40	
t_{pd}	DB and CB	$\overline{MERR}$	S1 = H, S0 = L, R_L = 500 Ω	15	67	15	55	ns
	DB	$\overline{MERR}$	S1 = L, S0 = H, R_L = 500 Ω	15	67	15	55	
t_{pd}	S0↓ and S1↓	CB	R1 = R2 = 500 Ω	10	60	10	48	ns
t_{PLH}	S0↓ and S1↓	$\overline{ERR}$	R_L = 500 Ω	5	30	5	25	ns
t_{pd}	DB	CB	S1 = L, S0 = L, R1 = R2 = 500 Ω	10	60	10	48	ns
t_{pd}	$\overline{LEDBO}$↓	DB	S1 = X, S0 = H, R1 = R2 = 500 Ω	7	35	7	30	ns
t_{pd}	S1↑	CB	S0 = H, R1 = R2 = 500 Ω	10	60	10	50	ns
t_{en}	$\overline{OECB}$↓	CB	S0 = H, S1 = X, R1 = R2 = 500 Ω	2	30	2	25	ns
t_{dis}	$\overline{OECB}$↑	CB	S0 = H, S1 = X, R1 = R2 = 500 Ω	2	30	2	25	ns
t_{en}	$\overline{OEB0}$ thru $\overline{OEB3}$↓	DB	S0 = H, S1 = X, R1 = R2 = 500 Ω	2	30	2	25	ns
t_{dis}	$\overline{OEB0}$ thru $\overline{OEB3}$↑	DB	S0 = H, S1 = X, R1 = R2 = 500 Ω	2	30	2	25	ns

'ALS634 switching characteristics, V_{CC} = 4.5 V to 5.5 V, C_L = 50 pF, T_C = −55°C to 125°C for SN54ALS634, T_A = 0°C to 70°C for SN74ALS634

PARAMETER	FROM (INPUT)	TO (OUTPUT)	TEST CONDITIONS	SN54ALS634		SN74ALS634		UNIT
				MIN	MAX	MIN	MAX	
t_{pd}	DB and CB	$\overline{ERR}$	S1 = H, S0 = L, R_L = 500 Ω	10	43	10	40	ns
			S1 = L, S0 = H, R_L = 500 Ω	10	43	10	40	
t_{pd}	DB and CB	$\overline{MERR}$	S1 = H, S0 = L, R_L = 500 Ω	15	67	15	55	ns
			S1 = L, S0 = H, R_L = 500 Ω	15	67	15	55	
t_{pd}	S0↓ and S1↓	CB	R1 = R2 = 500 Ω	10	60	10	48	ns
t_{PLH}	S0↓ and S1↓	$\overline{ERR}$	R_L = 500 Ω	5	30	5	25	ns
t_{pd}	DB	CB	S1 = L, S0 = L, R1 = R2 = 500 Ω	10	60	10	48	ns
t_{pd}	S1↑	CB	S0 = H, R1 = R2 = 500 Ω	7	35	7	30	ns
t_{en}	$\overline{OECB}$↓	CB	S1 = X, S0 = H, R1 = R2 = 500 Ω	2	30	2	25	ns
t_{dis}	$\overline{OECB}$↑	CB	S1 = X, S0 = H, R1 = R2 = 500 Ω	2	30	2	25	ns
t_{en}	$\overline{OEDB}$↓	DB	S1 = X, S0 = H, R1 = R2 = 500 Ω	2	30	2	30	ns
t_{dis}	$\overline{OEDB}$↑	DB	S1 = X, S0 = H, R1 = R2 = 500 Ω	2	30	2	25	ns

TEXAS INSTRUMENTS
POST OFFICE BOX 225012 • DALLAS, TEXAS 75265

'ALS633 electrical characteristics over recommended operating temperature range (unless otherwise noted)

PARAMETER		TEST CONDITIONS		SN54ALS633			SN74ALS633			UNIT
				MIN	TYP†	MAX	MIN	TYP†	MAX	
V_{IK}		V_{CC} = 4.5 V,	I_I = −18 mA			−1.5			−1.5	V
V_{OH}	$\overline{ERR}$ or $\overline{MERR}$	V_{CC} = 4.5 V to 5.5 V,	I_{OH} = −0.4 mA	V_{CC}−2			V_{CC}−2			V
I_{OH}	DB or CB	V_{CC} = 4.5 V,	V_{OH} = 5.5 V			0.1			0.1	mA
V_{OL}	$\overline{ERR}$ or $\overline{MERR}$	V_{CC} = 4.5 V,	I_{OL} = 4 mA		0.25	0.4		0.25	0.4	V
		V_{CC} = 4.5 V,	I_{OL} = 8 mA					0.35	0.5	
	DB or CB	V_{CC} = 4.5 V,	I_{OL} = 12 mA		0.25	0.4		0.25	0.4	
		V_{CC} = 4.5 V,	I_{OL} = 24 mA					0.35	0.5	
I_I	S0 or S1	V_{CC} = 5.5 V,	V_I = 7 V			0.1			0.1	mA
	All others	V_{CC} = 5.5 V,	V_I = 5.5 V			0.1			0.1	
I_{IH}	S0 or S1	V_{CC} = 5.5 V,	V_I = 2.7 V			20			20	μA
	All others‡					20			20	
I_{IL}	S0 or S1	V_{CC} = 5.5 V,	V_I = 0.4 V			−0.4			−0.4	mA
	All others‡					−0.1			−0.1	
I_O§	$\overline{ERR}$ or $\overline{MERR}$	V_{CC} = 5.5 V,	V_O = 2.25 V	−30		−112	−30		−112	mA
I_{CC}		V_{CC} = 5.5 V,	See Note 1		150	250		150	250	mA

† All typical values are at V_{CC} = 5 V, T_A = 25°C.
‡ For I/O ports, the parameters I_{IH} and I_{IL} include the off-state output current.
§ The output conditions have been chosen to produce a current that closely approximates one half of the true short-circuit output current, I_{OS}.
NOTE 1: I_{CC} is measured with S0 and S1 at 4.5 V and all CB and DB pins grounded.

'ALS633 switching characteristics, V_{CC} = 4.5 V to 5.5 V, C_L = 50 pF, T_C = −55°C to 125°C for SN54ALS633, T_A = 0°C to 70°C for SN74ALS633

PARAMETER	FROM (INPUT)	TO (OUTPUT)	TEST CONDITIONS	SN54ALS633		SN74ALS633		UNIT
				MIN	MAX	MIN	MAX	
t_{pd}	DB and CB	$\overline{ERR}$	S1 = H, S0 = L, R_L = 500 Ω	10	43	10	40	ns
	DB	$\overline{ERR}$	S1 = L, S0 = H, R_L = 500 Ω	10	43	10	40	
t_{pd}	DB and CB	$\overline{MERR}$	S1 = H, S0 = L, R_L = 500 Ω	15	67	15	55	ns
			S1 = L, S0 = H, R_L = 500 Ω	15	67	15	55	
t_{pd}	S0↓ and S1↓	CB	R_L = 680 Ω	10	75	10	60	ns
t_{PLH}	S0↓ and S1↓	$\overline{ERR}$	R_L = 500 Ω	5	30	5	25	ns
t_{pd}	DB	CB	S1 = L, S0 = L, R_L = 680 Ω	10	70	10	60	ns
t_{pd}	$\overline{LEDBO}$↓	DB	S1 = X, S0 = H, R_L = 680 Ω	15	70	15	50	ns
t_{pd}	S1↑	CB	S0 = H, R_L = 680 Ω	10	60	10	45	ns
t_{PLH}	$\overline{OECB}$↑	CB	S1 = X, S0 = H, R_L = 680 Ω	2	35	2	30	ns
t_{PHL}	$\overline{OECB}$↓	CB	S1 = X, S0 = H, R_L = 680 Ω	2	35	2	30	ns
t_{PLH}	$\overline{OEB0}$ thru $\overline{OEB3}$↑	DB	S1 = X, S0 = H, R_L = 680 Ω	2	35	2	30	ns
t_{PHL}	$\overline{OEB0}$ thru $\overline{OEB3}$↓	DB	S1 = X, S0 = H, R_L = 680 Ω	2	35	2	30	ns

'ALS635 electrical characteristics over recommended operating temperature range (unless otherwise noted)

PARAMETER		TEST CONDITIONS		SN54ALS635			SN74ALS635			UNIT
				MIN	TYP†	MAX	MIN	TYP†	MAX	
V_{IK}		V_{CC} = 4.5 V,	I_I = −18 mA			−1.5			−1.5	V
V_{OH}	$\overline{ERR}$ or $\overline{MERR}$	V_{CC} = 4.5 V to 5.5 V,	I_{OH} = −0.4 mA	$V_{CC}-2$			$V_{CC}-2$			V
I_{OH}	DB or CB	V_{CC} = 4.5 V,	V_{OH} = 5.5 V			0.1			0.1	mA
V_{OL}	$\overline{ERR}$ or $\overline{MERR}$	V_{CC} = 4.5 V,	I_{OL} = 4 mA		0.25	0.4		0.25	0.4	V
		V_{CC} = 4.5 V,	I_{OL} = 8 mA					0.35	0.5	
	DB or CB	V_{CC} = 4.5 V,	I_{OL} = 12 mA		0.25	0.4		0.25	0.4	
		V_{CC} = 4.5 V,	I_{OL} = 24 mA					0.35	0.5	
I_I	S0 or S1	V_{CC} = 5.5 V,	V_I = 7 V							mA
	All others	V_{CC} = 5.5 V,	V_I = 5.5 V							
I_{IH}	S0 or S1	V_{CC} = 5.5 V,	V_I = 2.7 V							µA
	All others‡									
I_{IL}	S0 or S1	V_{CC} = 5.5 V,	V_I = 0.4 V							mA
	All others‡									
I_{OS}§	$\overline{ERR}$ or $\overline{MERR}$	V_{CC} = 5.5 V,	V_O = 2.25 V	−30		−112	−30		−112	mA
I_{CC}		V_{CC} = 5.5 V,	See Note 1		150			150		mA

† All typical values are at V_{CC} = 5 V, T_A = 25 °C.
‡ For I/O ports, the parameters I_{IH} and I_{IL} include the off-state output current.
§ The output conditions have been chosen to produce a current that closely approximates one half of the true short-circuit output current, I_{OS}.
NOTE 1: I_{CC} is measured with S0 and S1 at 4.5 V and all CB and DB pins grounded.

'ALS635 switching characteristics, V_{CC} = 4.5 V to 5.5 V, C_L = 50 pF, T_C = −55 °C to 125 °C for SN54ALS635, T_A = 0 °C to 70 °C for SN74ALS635

PARAMETER	FROM (INPUT)	TO (OUTPUT)	TEST CONDITIONS	SN54ALS635			SN74ALS635			UNIT
				MIN	TYP†	MAX	MIN	TYP†	MAX	
t_{pd}	DB and CB	$\overline{ERR}$	S1 = H, S0 = L, R_L = 500 Ω		26			26		ns
	DB	$\overline{ERR}$	S1 = L, S0 = H, R_L = 500 Ω		26			26		
t_{pd}	DB and CB	$\overline{MERR}$	S1 = H, S0 = L, R_L = 500 Ω		40			40		ns
			S1 = L, S0 = H, R_L = 500 Ω		40			40		
t_{pd}	S0↓ and S1↓	CB	R_L = 680 Ω		40			40		ns
t_{PLH}	S0↓ and S1↓	$\overline{ERR}$	R_L = 500 Ω		14			14		ns
t_{pd}	DB	CB	S1 = L, S0 = L, R_L = 680 Ω		40			40		ns
t_{pd}	S1↑	DB	S0 = H, R_L = 680 Ω		40			40		ns
t_{PLH}	$\overline{OECB}$↑	CB	S1 = X, S0 = H, R_L = 680 Ω		24			24		ns
t_{PHL}	$\overline{OECB}$↓	CB	S1 = X, S0 = H, R_L = 680 Ω		24			24		ns
t_{PLH}	$\overline{OEDB}$↑	DB	S1 = X, S0 = H, R_L = 680 Ω		24			24		ns
t_{PHL}	$\overline{OEDB}$↓	DB	S1 = X, S0 = H, R_L = 680 Ω		24			24		ns

† All typical values are at V_{CC} = 5 V, T_A = 25 °C.

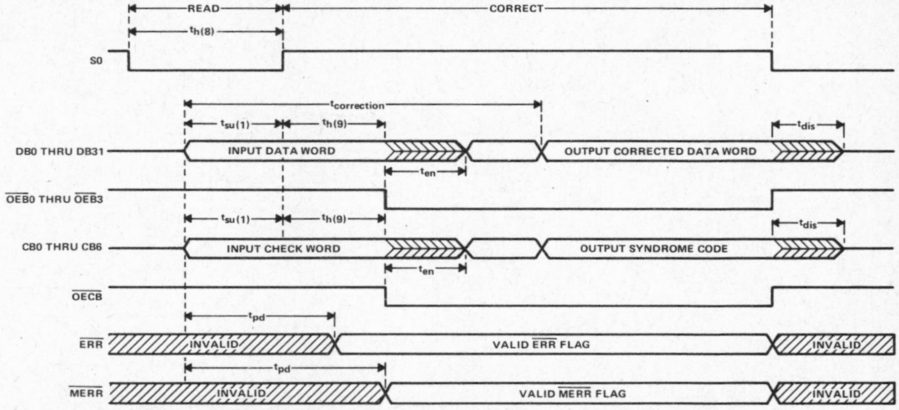
READ
CORRECT
th(8)
S0
tcorrection
tsu(1)
th(9)
tdis
DB0 THRU DB31
INPUT DATA WORD
OUTPUT CORRECTED DATA WORD
ten
OEB0 THRU OEB3
tsu(1)
th(9)
tdis
CB0 THRU CB6
INPUT CHECK WORD
OUTPUT SYNDROME CODE
ten
OECB
tpd
ERR
INVALID
VALID ERR FLAG
INVALID
tpd
MERR
INVALID
VALID MERR FLAG
INVALID

FIGURE 1. READ, FLAG, AND CORRECT MODE SWITCHING WAVEFORMS

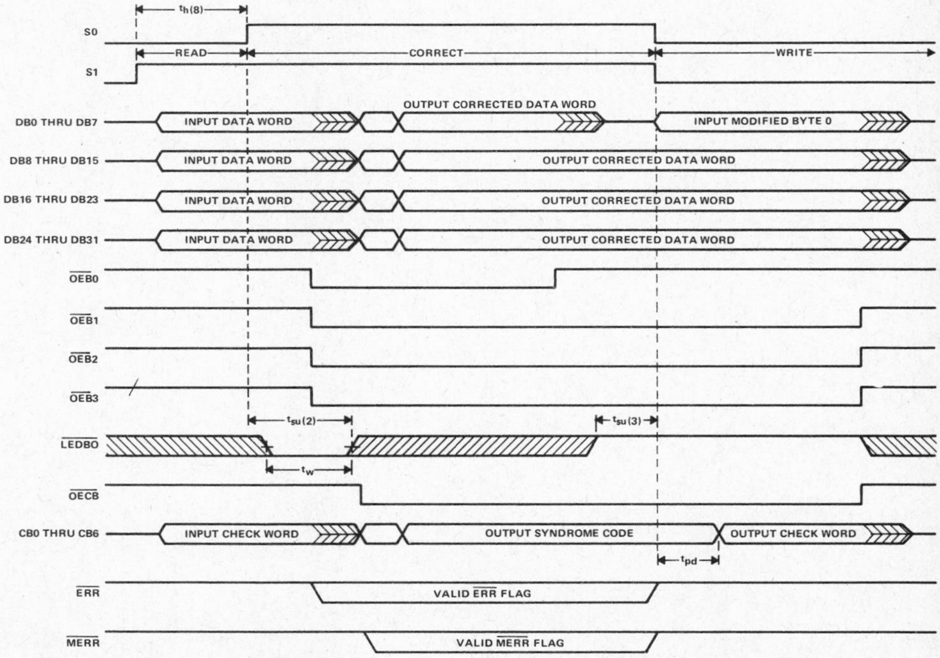
th(8)
S0
READ
CORRECT
WRITE
S1
OUTPUT CORRECTED DATA WORD
DB0 THRU DB7
INPUT DATA WORD
INPUT MODIFIED BYTE 0
DB8 THRU DB15
INPUT DATA WORD
OUTPUT CORRECTED DATA WORD
DB16 THRU DB23
INPUT DATA WORD
OUTPUT CORRECTED DATA WORD
DB24 THRU DB31
INPUT DATA WORD
OUTPUT CORRECTED DATA WORD
OEB0
OEB1
OEB2
OEB3
tsu(2)
tsu(3)
LEDBO
tw
OECB
CB0 THRU CB6
INPUT CHECK WORD
OUTPUT SYNDROME CODE
OUTPUT CHECK WORD
tpd
ERR
VALID ERR FLAG
MERR
VALID MERR FLAG

FIGURE 2. READ, CORRECT, MODIFY MODE SWITCHING WAVEFORMS

2

LSI Devices

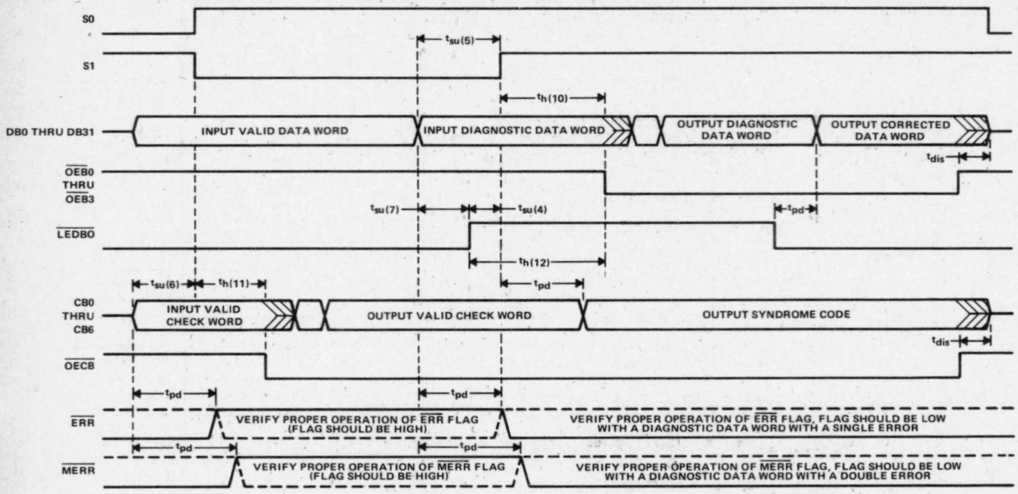
S0
S1
$t_{su(5)}$
$t_{h(10)}$
DB0 THRU DB31
INPUT VALID DATA WORD
INPUT DIAGNOSTIC DATA WORD
OUTPUT DIAGNOSTIC DATA WORD
OUTPUT CORRECTED DATA WORD
t_{dis}
OEB0 THRU OEB3
$t_{su(7)}$
$t_{su(4)}$
t_{pd}
LEDBO
$t_{h(12)}$
$t_{su(6)}$
$t_{h(11)}$
CB0 THRU CB6
INPUT VALID CHECK WORD
OUTPUT VALID CHECK WORD
OUTPUT SYNDROME CODE
OECB
ERR
VERIFY PROPER OPERATION OF ERR FLAG (FLAG SHOULD BE HIGH)
VERIFY PROPER OPERATION OF ERR FLAG, FLAG SHOULD BE LOW WITH A DIAGNOSTIC DATA WORD WITH A SINGLE ERROR
MERR
VERIFY PROPER OPERATION OF MERR FLAG (FLAG SHOULD BE HIGH)
VERIFY PROPER OPERATION OF MERR FLAG, FLAG SHOULD BE LOW WITH A DIAGNOSTIC DATA WORD WITH A DOUBLE ERROR

FIGURE 3. DIAGNOSTIC MODE SWITCHING WAVEFORM

TEXAS INSTRUMENTS
POST OFFICE BOX 225012 • DALLAS, TEXAS 75265

32-BIT PARALLEL ERROR DETECTION AND CORRECTION CIRCUITS

D2661, JANUARY 1986

- **Detects and Corrects Single-Bit Errors**
- **Detects and Flags Dual-Bit Errors**
- **Built-In Diagnostic Capability**
- **Fast Write and Read Cycle Processing Times**
- **Byte-Write Capability . . . 'AS632**
- **Dependable Texas Instruments Quality and Reliability**

DEVICE	PACKAGE	BYTE-WRITE	OUTPUT
'AS632	52-pin	yes	3-State
'AS634	48-pin	no	3-State

description

The 'AS632 and 'AS634 devices are 32-bit parallel error detection and correction circuits (EDACs) in 52-pin ('AS632) or 48-pin ('AS634) 600-mil packages. The EDACs use a modified Hamming code to generate a 7-bit check word from a 32-bit data word. This check word is stored along with the data word during the memory write cycle. During the memory read cycle, the 39-bit words from memory are processed by the EDACs to determine if errors have occurred in memory.

Single-bit errors in the 32-bit data word are flagged and corrected.

Single-bit errors in the 7-bit check word are flagged, and the CPU sends the EDAC through the correction cycle even though the 32-bit data word is not in error. The correction cycle will simply pass along the original 32-bit data word in this case and produce error syndrome bits to pinpoint the error-generating location.

Dual-bit errors are flagged but not corrected. These errors may occur in any two bits of the 39-bit data word from memory (two errors in the 32-bit data word, two errors in the 7-bit check word, or one error in each word). The gross-error condition of all lows or all highs from memory will be detected. Otherwise, errors in three or more bits of the 39-bit word are beyond the capabilities of these devices to detect.

'AS632 . . . JD PACKAGE
(TOP VIEW)

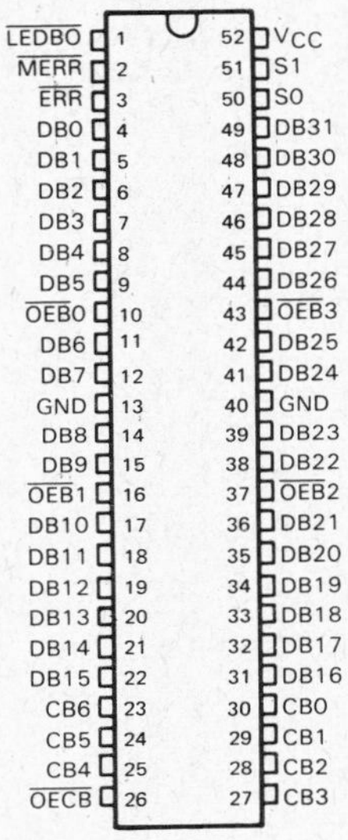
LEDBO 1
MERR 2
ERR 3
DB0 4
DB1 5
DB2 6
DB3 7
DB4 8
DB5 9
OEB0 10
DB6 11
DB7 12
GND 13
DB8 14
DB9 15
OEB1 16
DB10 17
DB11 18
DB12 19
DB13 20
DB14 21
DB15 22
CB6 23
CB5 24
CB4 25
OECB 26
52 VCC
51 S1
50 S0
49 DB31
48 DB30
47 DB29
46 DB28
45 DB27
44 DB26
43 OEB3
42 DB25
41 DB24
40 GND
39 DB23
38 DB22
37 OEB2
36 DB21
35 DB20
34 DB19
33 DB18
32 DB17
31 DB16
30 CB0
29 CB1
28 CB2
27 CB3

'AS632 . . . FN PACKAGE
(TOP VIEW)

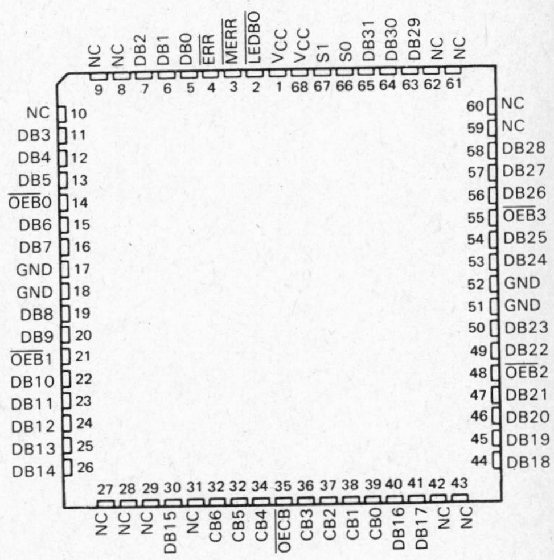
NC NC DB2 DB1 DB0 ERR MERR LEDBO VCC VCC S1 S0 DB31 DB30 DB29 NC NC
9 8 7 6 5 4 3 2 1 68 67 66 65 64 63 62 61
NC 10
DB3 11
DB4 12
DB5 13
OEB0 14
DB6 15
DB7 16
GND 17
GND 18
DB8 19
DB9 20
OEB1 21
DB10 22
DB11 23
DB12 24
DB13 25
DB14 26
60 NC
59 NC
58 DB28
57 DB27
56 DB26
55 OEB3
54 DB25
53 DB24
52 GND
51 GND
50 DB23
49 DB22
48 OEB2
47 DB21
46 DB20
45 DB19
44 DB18
27 28 29 30 31 32 33 34 35 36 37 38 39 40 41 42 43
NC NC NC DB15 NC CB6 CB5 CB4 OECB CB3 CB2 CB1 CB0 DB16 DB17 NC NC

NC—No internal connection

2

LSI Devices

Read-modify-write (byte-control) operations can be performed with the 'AS632 EDAC by using output latch enable, $\overline{\text{LEDBO}}$, and the individual $\overline{\text{OEB0}}$ thru $\overline{\text{OEB3}}$ byte control pins.

Diagnostics are performed on the EDACs by controls and internal paths that allow the user to read the contents of the DB and CB input latches. These will determine if the failure occurred in memory or in the EDAC.

'AS634 . . . JD PACKAGE
(TOP VIEW)

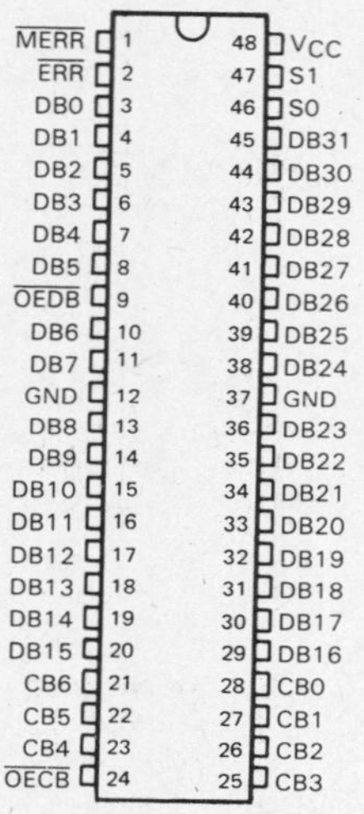
MERR 1
ERR 2
DB0 3
DB1 4
DB2 5
DB3 6
DB4 7
DB5 8
OEDB 9
DB6 10
DB7 11
GND 12
DB8 13
DB9 14
DB10 15
DB11 16
DB12 17
DB13 18
DB14 19
DB15 20
CB6 21
CB5 22
CB4 23
OECB 24
48 VCC
47 S1
46 S0
45 DB31
44 DB30
43 DB29
42 DB28
41 DB27
40 DB26
39 DB25
38 DB24
37 GND
36 DB23
35 DB22
34 DB21
33 DB20
32 DB19
31 DB18
30 DB17
29 DB16
28 CB0
27 CB1
26 CB2
25 CB3

'AS634 . . . FN PACKAGE
(TOP VIEW)

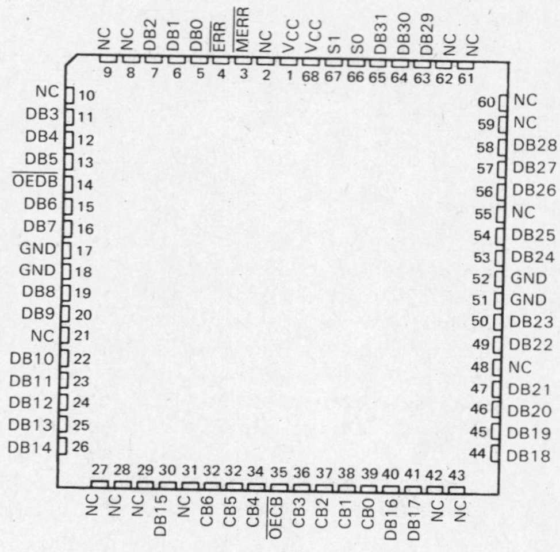
NC NC DB2 DB1 DB0 ERR MERR NC VCC VCC S1 S0 DB31 DB30 DB29 NC NC
9 8 7 6 5 4 3 2 1 68 67 66 65 64 63 62 61
NC 10
DB3 11
DB4 12
DB5 13
OEDB 14
DB6 15
DB7 16
GND 17
GND 18
DB8 19
DB9 20
NC 21
DB10 22
DB11 23
DB12 24
DB13 25
DB14 26
60 NC
59 NC
58 DB28
57 DB27
56 DB26
55 NC
54 DB25
53 DB24
52 GND
51 GND
50 DB23
49 DB22
48 NC
47 DB21
46 DB20
45 DB19
44 DB18
27 28 29 30 31 32 32 34 35 36 37 38 39 40 41 42 43
NC NC NC DB15 NC CB6 CB5 CB4 OECB CB3 CB2 CB1 CB0 DB16 DB17 NC NC

NC—No internal connection

TABLE 1. WRITE CONTROL FUNCTION

MEMORY CYCLE	EDAC FUNCTION	CONTROL S1	CONTROL S0	DATA I/O	DB CONTROL $\overline{\text{OEBn}}$ OR $\overline{\text{OEDB}}$	DB OUTPUT LATCH ('AS632) $\overline{\text{LEDBO}}$	CHECK I/O	CB CONTROL $\overline{\text{OECB}}$	ERROR FLAGS $\overline{\text{ERR}}$	ERROR FLAGS $\overline{\text{MERR}}$
Write	Generate check word	L	L	Input	H	X	Output check bits†	L	H	H

†See Table 2 for details on check bit generation.

memory write cycle details

During a memory write cycle, the check bits (CB0 thru CB6) are generated internally in the EDAC by seven 16-input parity generators using the 32-bit data word as defined in Table 2. These seven check bits are stored in memory along with the original 32-bit data word. This 32-bit word will later be used in the memory read cycle for error detection and correction.

TABLE 2. PARITY ALGORITHM

CHECK WORD	32-BIT DATA WORD																														
BIT	31	30	29	28	27	26	25	24	23	22	21	20	19	18	17	16	15	14	13	12	11	10	9	8	7	6	5	4	3	2	1	0
CB0	X		X	X		X					X		X	X	X			X			X		X	X	X	X		X				X
CB1				X		X		X		X		X		X	X	X				X		X		X		X		X		X	X	X
CB2	X		X			X	X		X			X	X			X	X		X			X	X		X			X	X			X
CB3			X	X	X				X	X	X				X	X			X	X	X				X	X	X				X	X
CB4	X	X							X	X	X	X	X	X			X	X							X	X	X	X	X	X		
CB5	X	X	X	X	X	X	X	X									X	X	X	X	X	X	X	X								
CB6	X	X	X	X	X	X	X	X																	X	X	X	X	X	X	X	X

The seven check bits are parity bits derived from the matrix of data bits as indicated by "X" for each bit.

error detection and correction details

During a memory read cycle, the 7-bit check word is retrieved along with the actual data. In order to be able to determine whether the data from memory is acceptable to use as presented to the bus, the error flags must be tested to determine if they are at the high level.

The first case in Table 3 represents the normal, no-error conditions. The EDAC presents highs on both flags. The next two cases of single-bit errors give a high on $\overline{\text{MERR}}$ and a low on $\overline{\text{ERR}}$, which is the signal for a correctable error, and the EDAC should be sent through the correction cycle. The last three cases of double-bit errors will cause the EDAC to signal lows on both $\overline{\text{ERR}}$ and $\overline{\text{MERR}}$, which is the interrupt indication for the CPU.

TABLE 3. ERROR FUNCTION

TOTAL NUMBER OF ERRORS		ERROR FLAGS		DATA CORRECTION
32-BIT DATA WORD	7-BIT CHECK WORD	$\overline{\text{ERR}}$	$\overline{\text{MERR}}$	
0	0	H	H	Not applicable
1	0	L	H	Correction
0	1	L	H	Correction
1	1	L	L	Interrupt
2	0	L	L	Interrupt
0	2	L	L	Interrupt

Error detection is accomplished as the 7-bit check word and the 32-bit data word from memory are applied to internal parity generators/checkers. If the parity of all seven groupings of data and check bits are correct, it is assumed that no error has occurred and both error flags will be high.

If the parity of one or more of the check groups is incorrect, an error has occurred and the proper error flag or flags will be set low. Any single error in the 32-bit data word will change the state of either three or five bits of the 7-bit check word. Any single error in the 7-bit check word changes the state of only that one bit. In either case, the single error flag ($\overline{\text{ERR}}$) will be set low while the dual error flag ($\overline{\text{MERR}}$) will remain high.

Any two-bit error will change the state of an even number of check bits. The two-bit error is not correctable since the parity tree can only identify single-bit errors. Both error flags are set low when any two-bit error is detected.

Three or more simultaneous bit errors can cause the EDAC to believe that no error, a correctable error, or an uncorrectable error has occurred and will produce erroneous results in all three cases. It should be noted that the gross-error conditions of all lows and all highs will be detected.

TABLE 4. READ, FLAG, AND CORRECT FUNCTION

MEMORY CYCLE	EDAC FUNCTION	CONTROL S1	CONTROL S0	DATA I/O	DB CONTROL $\overline{OEBn}$ OR $\overline{OEDB}$	DB OUTPUT LATCH ('AS632) $\overline{LEDBO}$	CHECK I/O	CB CONTROL $\overline{OECB}$	ERROR FLAGS $\overline{ERR}$ $\overline{MERR}$
Read	Read & flag	H	L	Input	H	X	Input	H	Enabled†
Read	Latch input data & check bits	H	H	Latched input data	H	L	Latched input check word	H	Enabled†
Read	Output corrected data & syndrome bits	H	H	Output corrected data word	L	X	Output syndrome bits‡	L	Enabled†

†See Table 3 for error description.
‡See Table 5 for error location.

As the corrected word is made available on the data I/O port (DB0 thru DB31), the check word I/O port (CB0 thru CB6) presents a 7-bit syndrome error code. This syndrome error code can be used to locate the bad memory chip. See Table 5 for syndrome decoding.

TABLE 5. SYNDROME DECODING

SYNDROME BITS 6	5	4	3	2	1	0	ERROR
L	L	L	L	L	L	L	unc
L	L	L	L	L	L	H	2-bit
L	L	L	L	L	H	L	2-bit
L	L	L	L	L	H	H	unc
L	L	L	L	H	L	L	2-bit
L	L	L	L	H	L	H	unc
L	L	L	L	H	H	L	unc
L	L	L	L	H	H	H	2-bit
L	L	L	H	L	L	L	2-bit
L	L	L	H	L	L	H	unc
L	L	L	H	L	H	L	DB31
L	L	L	H	L	H	H	2-bit
L	L	L	H	H	L	L	unc
L	L	L	H	H	L	H	2-bit
L	L	L	H	H	H	L	2-bit
L	L	L	H	H	H	H	DB30
L	L	H	L	L	L	L	2-bit
L	L	H	L	L	L	H	unc
L	L	H	L	L	H	L	DB29
L	L	H	L	L	H	H	2-bit
L	L	H	L	H	L	L	DB28
L	L	H	L	H	L	H	2-bit
L	L	H	L	H	H	L	2-bit
L	L	H	L	H	H	H	DB27
L	L	H	H	L	L	L	DB26
L	L	H	H	L	L	H	2-bit
L	L	H	H	L	H	L	2-bit
L	L	H	H	L	H	H	DB25
L	L	H	H	H	L	L	2-bit
L	L	H	H	H	L	H	DB24
L	L	H	H	H	H	L	unc
L	L	H	H	H	H	H	2-bit

SYNDROME BITS 6	5	4	3	2	1	0	ERROR
L	H	L	L	L	L	L	2-bit
L	H	L	L	L	L	H	unc
L	H	L	L	L	H	L	DB7
L	H	L	L	L	H	H	2-bit
L	H	L	L	H	L	L	DB6
L	H	L	L	H	L	H	2-bit
L	H	L	L	H	H	L	2-bit
L	H	L	L	H	H	H	DB5
L	H	L	H	L	L	L	DB4
L	H	L	H	L	L	H	2-bit
L	H	L	H	L	H	L	2-bit
L	H	L	H	L	H	H	DB3
L	H	L	H	H	L	L	2-bit
L	H	L	H	H	L	H	DB2
L	H	L	H	H	H	L	unc
L	H	L	H	H	H	H	2-bit
L	H	H	L	L	L	L	DB0
L	H	H	L	L	L	H	2-bit
L	H	H	L	L	H	L	2-bit
L	H	H	L	L	H	H	unc
L	H	H	L	H	L	L	2-bit
L	H	H	L	H	L	H	DB1
L	H	H	L	H	H	L	unc
L	H	H	L	H	H	H	2-bit
L	H	H	H	L	L	L	2-bit
L	H	H	H	L	L	H	unc
L	H	H	H	L	H	L	unc
L	H	H	H	L	H	H	2-bit
L	H	H	H	H	L	L	unc
L	H	H	H	H	L	H	2-bit
L	H	H	H	H	H	L	2-bit
L	H	H	H	H	H	H	CB6

SYNDROME BITS 6	5	4	3	2	1	0	ERROR
H	L	L	L	L	L	L	2-bit
H	L	L	L	L	L	H	unc
H	L	L	L	L	H	L	unc
H	L	L	L	L	H	H	2-bit
H	L	L	L	H	L	L	unc
H	L	L	L	H	L	H	2-bit
H	L	L	L	H	H	L	2-bit
H	L	L	L	H	H	H	unc
H	L	L	H	L	L	L	unc
H	L	L	H	L	L	H	2-bit
H	L	L	H	L	H	L	2-bit
H	L	L	H	L	H	H	DB15
H	L	L	H	H	L	L	2-bit
H	L	L	H	H	L	H	unc
H	L	L	H	H	H	L	DB14
H	L	L	H	H	H	H	2-bit
H	L	H	L	L	L	L	unc
H	L	H	L	L	L	H	2-bit
H	L	H	L	L	H	L	2-bit
H	L	H	L	L	H	H	DB13
H	L	H	L	H	L	L	2-bit
H	L	H	L	H	L	H	DB12
H	L	H	L	H	H	L	DB11
H	L	H	L	H	H	H	2-bit
H	L	H	H	L	L	L	2-bit
H	L	H	H	L	L	H	DB10
H	L	H	H	L	H	L	DB9
H	L	H	H	L	H	H	2-bit
H	L	H	H	H	L	L	DB8
H	L	H	H	H	L	H	2-bit
H	L	H	H	H	H	L	2-bit
H	L	H	H	H	H	H	CB5

SYNDROME BITS 6	5	4	3	2	1	0	ERROR
H	H	L	L	L	L	L	unc
H	H	L	L	L	L	H	2-bit
H	H	L	L	L	H	L	2-bit
H	H	L	L	L	H	H	DB23
H	H	L	L	H	L	L	2-bit
H	H	L	L	H	L	H	DB22
H	H	L	L	H	H	L	DB21
H	H	L	L	H	H	H	2-bit
H	H	L	H	L	L	L	2-bit
H	H	L	H	L	L	H	DB20
H	H	L	H	L	H	L	DB19
H	H	L	H	L	H	H	2-bit
H	H	L	H	H	L	L	DB18
H	H	L	H	H	L	H	2-bit
H	H	L	H	H	H	L	2-bit
H	H	L	H	H	H	H	CB4
H	H	H	L	L	L	L	2-bit
H	H	H	L	L	L	H	DB16
H	H	H	L	L	H	L	unc
H	H	H	L	L	H	H	2-bit
H	H	H	L	H	L	L	DB17
H	H	H	L	H	L	H	2-bit
H	H	H	L	H	H	L	2-bit
H	H	H	L	H	H	H	CB3
H	H	H	H	L	L	L	unc
H	H	H	H	L	L	H	2-bit
H	H	H	H	L	H	L	2-bit
H	H	H	H	L	H	H	CB2
H	H	H	H	H	L	L	2-bit
H	H	H	H	H	L	H	CB1
H	H	H	H	H	H	L	CB0
H	H	H	H	H	H	H	none

CB X= error in check bit X
DB Y= error in data bit Y
2-bit = double-bit error
unc = uncorrectable multibit error

read-modify-write (byte control) operations

The 'AS632 is capable of byte-write operations. The 39-bit word from memory must first be latched into the DB and CB input latches. This is easily accomplished by switching from the read and flag mode (S1 = H, S0 = L) to the latch input mode (S1 = H, S0 = H). The EDAC will then make any corrections, if necessary, to the data word and place it at the input of the output data latch. This data word must then be latched into the output data latch by taking $\overline{\text{LEDBO}}$ from a low to a high.

Byte control can now be employed on the data word through the $\overline{\text{OEB0}}$ through $\overline{\text{OEB3}}$ controls. $\overline{\text{OEB0}}$ controls DB0-DB7 (byte 0), $\overline{\text{OEB1}}$ controls DB8-DB15 (byte 1), $\overline{\text{OEB2}}$ controls DB16-DB23 (byte 2), and $\overline{\text{OEB3}}$ controls DB24-DB31 (byte 3). Placing a high on the byte control will disable the output and the user can modify the byte. If a low is placed on the byte control, then the original byte is allowed to pass onto the data bus unchanged. If the original data word is altered through byte control, a new check word must be generated before it is written back into memory. This is easily accomplished by taking control S1 and S0 low. Table 6 lists the read-modify-write functions.

TABLE 6. READ-MODIFY-WRITE FUNCTION

MEMORY CYCLE	EDAC FUNCTION	CONTROL S1	CONTROL S0	BYTEn†	$\overline{OEBn}$†	DB OUTPUT LATCH $\overline{LEDBO}$	CHECK I/O	CB CONTROL	ERROR FLAG $\overline{ERR}$	ERROR FLAG $\overline{MERR}$
Read	Read & Flag	H	L	Input	H	X	Input	H	Enabled	
Read	Latch input data & check bits	H	H	Latched Input data	H	L	Latched input check word	H	Enabled	
Read	Latch corrected data word into output latch	H	H	Latched output data word	H	H	Hi-Z	H	Enabled	
							Output Syndrome bits	L		
Modify /write	Modify appropriate byte or bytes & generate new check word	L	L	Input modified BYTE0	H	H	Output check word	L	H	H
				Output unchanged BYTE0	L					

†$\overline{OEB0}$ controls DB0-DB7 (BYTE0), $\overline{OEB1}$ controls DB8-DB15 (BYTE1), $\overline{OEB3}$ controls DB16-DB23 (BYTE2), $\overline{OEB3}$ controls DB24-DB31 (BYTE3).

diagnostic operations

The 'AS632 and 'AS634 are capable of diagnostics that allow the user to determine whether the EDAC or the memory is failing. The diagnostic function tables will help the user to see the possibilities for diagnostic control.

In the diagnostic mode (S1 = L, S0 = H), the checkword is latched into the input latch while the data input latch remains transparent. This lets the user apply various data words against a fixed known checkword. If the user applies a diagnostic data word with an error in any bit location, the $\overline{ERR}$ flag should be low. If a diagnostic data word with two errors in any bit location is applied, the $\overline{MERR}$ flag should be low. After the checkword is latched into the input latch, it can be verified by taking $\overline{OECB}$ low. This outputs the latched checkword. With the 'AS632, the diagnostic data word can be latched into the output data latch and verified. It should be noted that the 'AS634 does not have this pass-through capability because they do not contain an output data latch. By changing from the diagnostic mode (S1 = L, S0 = H) to the correction mode (S1 = H, S0 = H), the user can verify that the EDAC will correct the diagnostic data word. Also, the syndrome bits can be produced to verify that the EDAC pinpoints the error location. Table 7 ('AS632) and Table 8 ('AS634) list the diagnostic functions.

TABLE 7. 'AS632 DIAGNOSTIC FUNCTION

EDAC FUNCTION	CONTROL S1	CONTROL S0	DATA I/O	DB BYTE CONTROL $\overline{OEBn}$	DB OUTPUT LATCH $\overline{LEDBO}$	CHECK I/O	CB CONTROL $\overline{OECB}$	ERROR FLAGS $\overline{ERR}$	ERROR FLAGS $\overline{MERR}$
Read & flag	H	L	Input correct data word	H	X	Input correct check bits	H	H	H
Latch input check word while data input latch remains transparent	L	H	Input diagnostic data word†	H	L	Latched input check bits	H	Enabled	
Latch diagnostic data word into output latch	L	H	Input diagnostic data word†	H	H	Output latched check bits	L	Enabled	
						Hi-Z	H		
Latch diagnostic data word into input latch	H	H	Latched input diagnostic data word	H	H	Output syndrome bits	L	Enabled	
						Hi-Z	H		
Output diagnostic data word & syndrome bits	H	H	Output diagnostic data word	L	H	Output syndrome bits	L	Enabled	
						Hi-Z	H		
Output corrected diagnostic data word & output syndrome bits	H	H	Output corrected diagnostic data word	L	L	Output syndrome bits	L	Enabled	
						Hi-Z	H		

TABLE 8. 'AS634 DIAGNOSTIC FUNCTION

EDAC FUNCTION	CONTROL S1	CONTROL S0	DATA I/O	DB CONTROL $\overline{OEDB}$	CHECK I/O	DB CONTROL $\overline{OECB}$	ERROR FLAGS $\overline{ERR}$	ERROR FLAGS $\overline{MERR}$
Read & flag	H	L	Input correct data word	H	Input correct check bits	H	H	H
Latch input check bits while data input latch remains transparent	L	H	Input diagnostic data word†	H	Latched input check bits	H	Enabled	
Output input check bits	L	H	Input diagnostic data word†	H	Output input check bits	L	Enabled	
Latch diagnostic data into input latch	H	H	Latched input diagnostic data word	H	Output syndrome bits	L	Enabled	
					Hi-Z	H		
Output corrected diagnostic data word	H	H	Output corrected diagnostic data word	L	Output syndrome bits	L	Enabled	
					Hi-Z	H		

†Diagnostic data is a data word with an error in one bit location except when testing the $\overline{MERR}$ error flag. In this case, the diagnostic data word will contain errors in two bit locations.

2 LSI Devices

'AS632 logic diagram (positive logic)

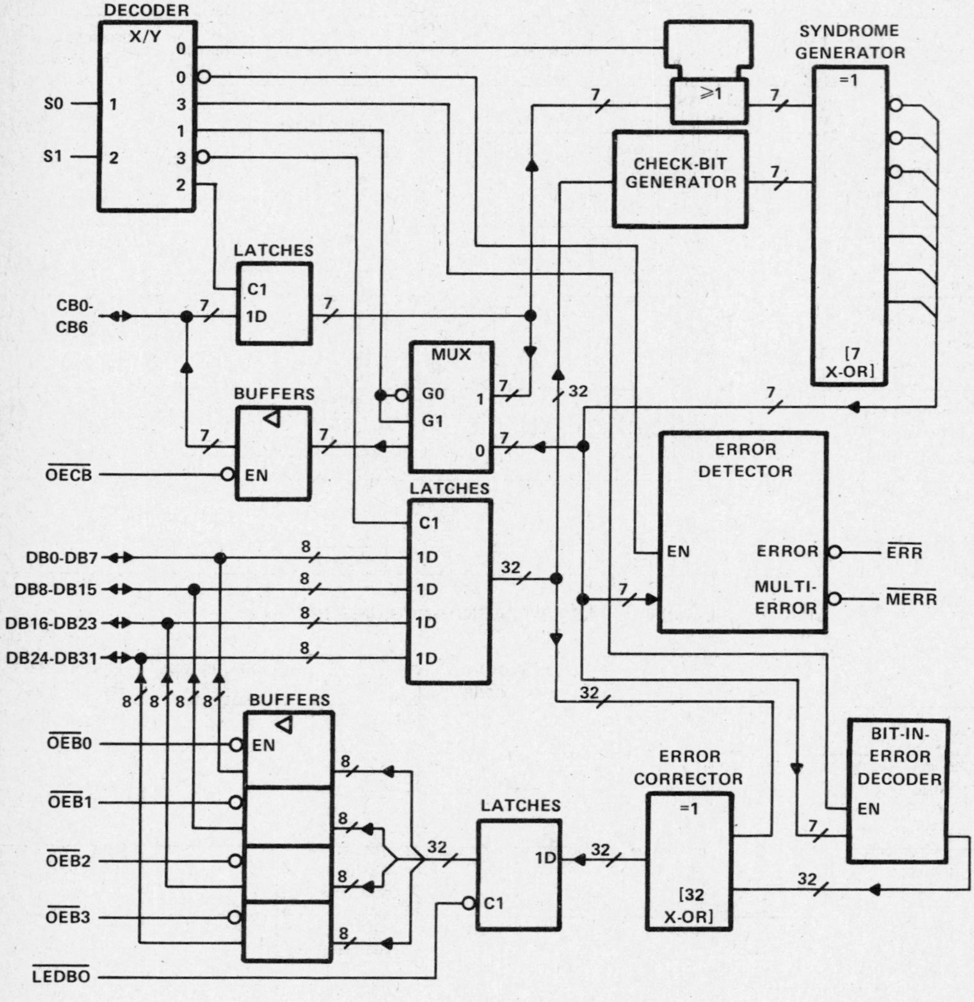
DECODER
X/Y
S0
S1
SYNDROME GENERATOR
=1
CHECK-BIT GENERATOR
[7 X-OR]
LATCHES
C1
1D
CB0-CB6
MUX
G0
G1
BUFFERS
EN
OECB
ERROR DETECTOR
ERROR
MULTI-ERROR
ERR
MERR
DB0-DB7
DB8-DB15
DB16-DB23
DB24-DB31
OEB0
OEB1
OEB2
OEB3
LEDBO
ERROR CORRECTOR
[32 X-OR]
BIT-IN-ERROR DECODER

TEXAS INSTRUMENTS
POST OFFICE BOX 225012 • DALLAS, TEXAS 75265

'AS634 logic diagram (positive logic)

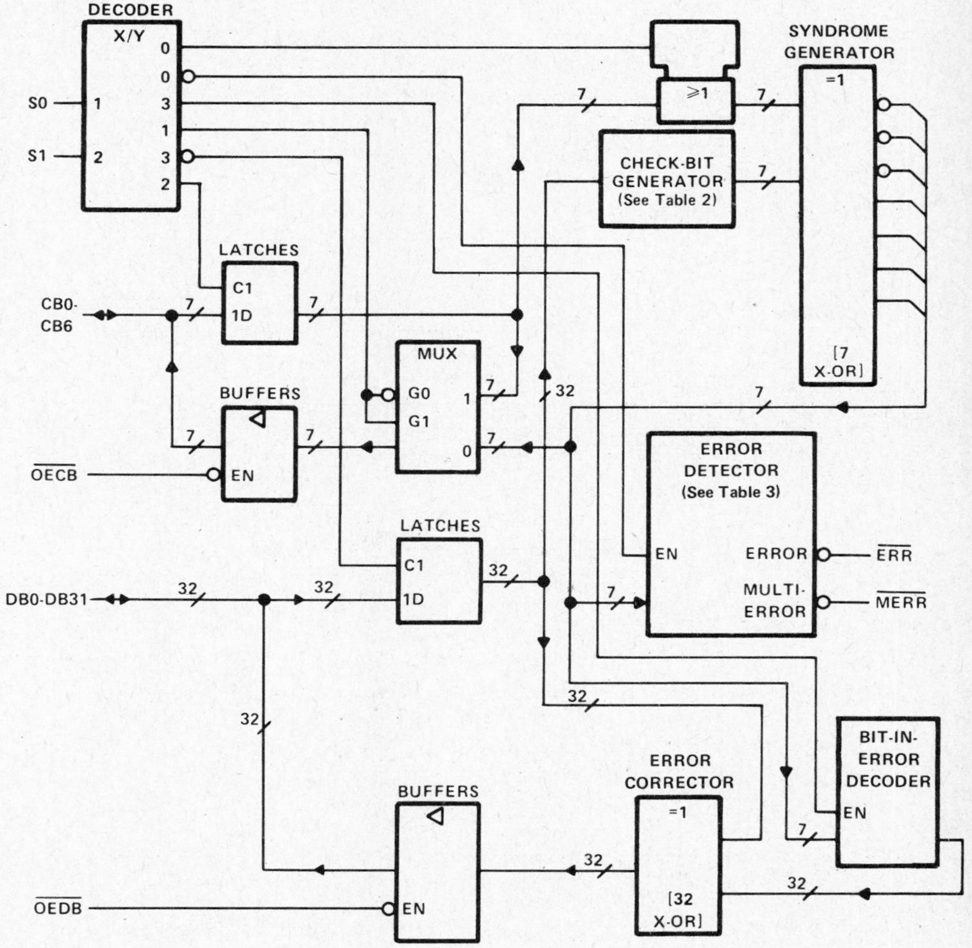
DECODER
X/Y
S0
S1
LATCHES
C1
1D
CB0-
CB6
BUFFERS
EN
OECB
MUX
G0
G1
SYNDROME
GENERATOR
=1
[7
X-OR]
≥1
CHECK-BIT
GENERATOR
(See Table 2)
ERROR
DETECTOR
(See Table 3)
ERROR
MULTI-
ERROR
ERR
MERR
LATCHES
DB0-DB31
BUFFERS
OEDB
ERROR
CORRECTOR
[32
X-OR]
BIT-IN-
ERROR
DECODER

absolute maximum ratings over operating free-air temperature range (unless otherwise noted)

Supply voltage, V_{CC} (see Note 1) . . . . 7 V
Input voltage: CB and DB . . . . 5.5 V
All others . . . . 7 V
Operating free-air temperature range:
SN74AS632, SN74AS634 . . . . 0°C to 70°C
Operating case temperature range:
SN54AS632, SN54AS634 . . . . −55°C to 125°C
Storage temperature range . . . . −65°C to 150°C

recommended operating conditions

			SN54AS632 SN54AS634			SN74AS632 SN74AS634			UNIT
			MIN	NOM	MAX	MIN	NOM	MAX	
V_{CC}	Supply voltage		4.5	5	5.5	4.5	5	5.5	V
V_{IH}	High-level input voltage		2			2			V
V_{IL}	Low-level input voltage				0.8			0.8	V
I_{OH}	High-level output current	$\overline{ERR}$ or $\overline{MERR}$			−0.4			−0.4	mA
		DB or CB			−1			−2.6	mA
I_{OL}	Low-level output current	$\overline{ERR}$ or $\overline{MERR}$			4			8	mA
		DB or CB			12			24	mA
t_w	Pulse duration	$\overline{LEDBO}$ low	25			25			ns
t_{su}	Setup time	(1) Data and check word before S0↑ (S1 = H)	15			10			ns
		(2) S0 high before $\overline{LEDBO}$↑ (S1 = H)†	45			45			ns
		(3) $\overline{LEDBO}$ high before the earlier of S0↓ or S1↓†	0			0			ns
		(4) $\overline{LEDBO}$ high before S1↑ (S0 = H)	0			0			ns
		(5) Diagnostic data word before S1↑ (S0 = H)	15			10			ns
		(6) Diagnostic check word before the later of S1↓ or S0↑	15			10			ns
		(7) Diagnostic data word before $\overline{LEDBO}$↑ (S1 = L and S0 = H)‡	25			20			ns
t_h	Hold time	(8) Read-mode, S0 low and S1 high	35			30			ns
		(9) Data and check word after S0↑ (S1 = H)	20			15			ns
		(10) Data word after S1↑ (S0 = H)	20			15			ns
		(11) Check word after the later of S1↓ or S0↑	20			15			ns
		(12) Diagnostic data word after $\overline{LEDBO}$↑ (S1 = L, S0 = H)‡	0			0			ns
t_{corr}	Correction time (see Figure 1)		65			58			ns
T_C	Operating case temperature		−55		125				°C
T_A	Operating free-air temperature					0		70	°C

† These times ensure that corrected data is saved in the output data latch.
‡ These times ensure that the diagnostic data word is saved in the output data latch.

'AS632, 'AS634 electrical characteristics over recommended operating temperature range (unless otherwise noted)

PARAMETER		TEST CONDITIONS		SN54AS632 SN54AS634 MIN	TYP†	MAX	SN74AS632 SN74AS634 MIN	TYP†	MAX	UNIT
V_{IK}		V_{CC} = 4.5 V,	I_I = −18 mA			−1.5			−1.5	V
V_{OH}	All outputs	V_{CC} = 4.5 V to 5.5 V,	I_{OH} = −0.4 mA	V_{CC}−2			V_{CC}−2			V
	DB or CB	V_{CC} = 4.5 V,	I_{OH} = −1 mA	2.4	3.3					
		V_{CC} = 4.5 V,	I_{OH} = −2.6 mA				2.4	3.2		
V_{OL}	$\overline{ERR}$ or $\overline{MERR}$	V_{CC} = 4.5 V,	I_{OH} = 4 mA		0.25	0.4		0.25	0.4	V
		V_{CC} = 4.5 V,	I_{OL} = 8 mA					0.35	0.5	
	DB or CB	V_{CC} = 4.5 V,	I_{OL} = 12 mA		0.25	0.4		0.25	0.4	
		V_{CC} = 4.5 V,	I_{OL} = 24 mA					0.35	0.5	
I_I	S0 or S1	V_{CC} = 5.5 V,	V_I = 7 V			0.1			0.1	mA
	All others	V_{CC} = 5.5 V,	V_I = 5.5 V			0.1			0.1	
I_{IH}	DB or CB‡	V_{CC} = 5.5 V,	V_I = 2.7 V			20			20	μA
	All others‡					20			20	
I_{IL}	S0 or S1	V_{CC} = 5.5 V,	V_I = 0.4 V			−0.4			−0.4	mA
	All others‡					−0.1			−0.1	
I_O§		V_{CC} = 5.5 V,	V_O = 2.25 V	−30		−112	−30		−112	mA
I_{CC}		V_{CC} = 5.5 V,	See Note 1		150			150		mA

NOTE 1: I_{CC} is measured with S0 and S1 at 4.5 V and all CB and DB pins grounded.

'AS632 switching characteristics, V_{CC} = 4.5 V to 5.5 V, C_L = 50 pF, T_C = −55°C to 125°C for SN54AS632, T_A = 0°C to 70°C for SN74AS632

PARAMETER	FROM (INPUT)	TO (OUTPUT)	TEST CONDITIONS	SN54AS632 MIN	TYP†	MAX	SN74AS632 MIN	TYP†	MAX	UNIT
t_{pd}	DB and CB	$\overline{ERR}$	S1 = H, S0 = L, R_L = 500 Ω		17			17		ns
	DB	$\overline{ERR}$	S1 = L, S0 = H, R_L = 500 Ω		17			17		
t_{pd}	DB and CB	$\overline{MERR}$	S1 = H, S0 = L, R_L = 500 Ω		26			26		ns
	DB	$\overline{MERR}$	S1 = L, S0 = H, R_L = 500 Ω		26			26		
t_{pd}	S0↓ and S1↓	CB	R1 = R2 = 500 Ω		26			26		ns
t_{PLH}	S0↓ and S1↓	$\overline{ERR}$	R_L = 500 Ω		9			9		ns
t_{pd}	DB	CB	S1 = L, S0 = L, R1 = R2 = 500 Ω		26			26		ns
t_{pd}	$\overline{LEDBO}$↓	DB	S1 = X, S0 = H, R1 = R2 = 500 Ω		17			17		ns
t_{pd}	S1↑	CB	S0 = H, R1 = R2 = 500 Ω		26			26		ns
t_{en}	$\overline{OECB}$↓	CB	S0 = H, S1 = X, R1 = R2 = 500 Ω		12			12		ns
t_{dis}	$\overline{OECB}$↑	CB	S0 = H, S1 = X, R1 = R2 = 500 Ω		12			12		ns
t_{en}	$\overline{OEB0}$ thru $\overline{OEB3}$↓	DB	S0 = H, S1 = X, R1 = R2 = 500 Ω		12			12		ns
t_{dis}	$\overline{OEB0}$ thru $\overline{OEB3}$↑	DB	S0 = H, S1 = X, R1 = R2 = 500 Ω		12			12		ns

† All typical values are at V_{CC} = 5 V, T_A = 25°C.
‡ For I/O ports, the parameters I_{IH} and I_{IL} include the off-state output current.
§ The output conditions have been chosen to produce a current that closely approximates one half of the true short-circuit output current, I_{OS}.

'AS634 switching characteristics, V_{CC} = 4.5 V to 5.5 V, C_L = 50 pF, T_C = −55°C to 125°C for SN54AS634, T_A = 0°C to 70°C for SN74AS634

PARAMETER	FROM (INPUT)	TO (OUTPUT)	TEST CONDITIONS	SN54AS634			SN74AS634			UNIT
				MIN	TYP†	MAX	MIN	TYP†	MAX	
t_{pd}	DB and CB	$\overline{ERR}$	S1 = H, S0 = L, R_L = 500 Ω		17			17		ns
			S1 = L, S0 = H, R_L = 500 Ω		17			17		
t_{pd}	DB and CB	$\overline{MERR}$	S1 = H, S0 = L, R_L = 500 Ω		26			26		ns
			S1 = L, S0 = H, R_L = 500 Ω		26			26		
t_{pd}	S0↓ and S1↓	CB	R1 = R2 = 500 Ω		23			23		ns
t_{PLH}	S0↓ and S1↓	$\overline{ERR}$	R_L = 500 Ω		9			9		ns
t_{pd}	DB	CB	S1 = L, S0 = L, R1 = R2 = 500 Ω		23			23		ns
t_{pd}	S1↑	CB	S0 = H, R1 = R2 = 500 Ω		23			23		ns
t_{en}	$\overline{OECB}$↓	CB	S1 = X, S0 = H, R1 = R2 = 500 Ω		12			12		ns
t_{dis}	$\overline{OECB}$↑	CB	S1 = X, S0 = H, R1 = R2 = 500 Ω		12			12		ns
t_{en}	$\overline{OEDB}$↓	DB	S1 = X, S0 = H, R1 = R2 = 500 Ω		12			12		ns
t_{dis}	$\overline{OEDB}$↑	DB	S1 = X, S0 = H, R1 = R2 = 500 Ω		12			12		ns

†All typical values are at V_{CC} = 5 V, T_A = 25°C.

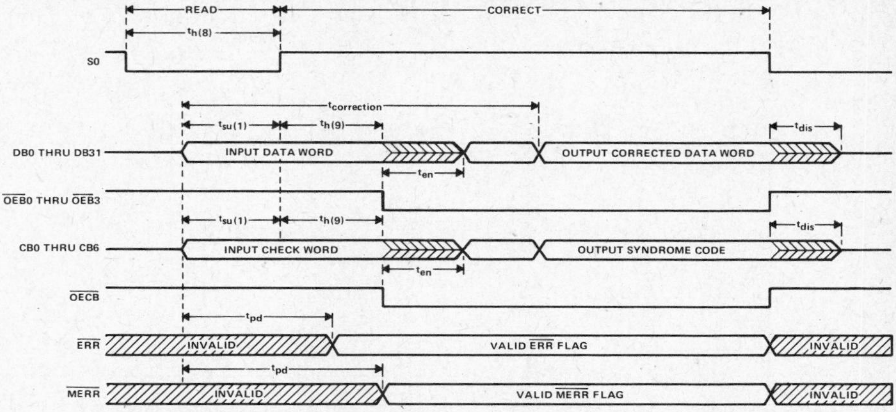
READ
CORRECT
S0
DB0 THRU DB31
INPUT DATA WORD
OUTPUT CORRECTED DATA WORD
OEB0 THRU OEB3
CB0 THRU CB6
INPUT CHECK WORD
OUTPUT SYNDROME CODE
OECB
ERR
INVALID
VALID ERR FLAG
MERR
VALID MERR FLAG

FIGURE 1. READ, FLAG, AND CORRECT MODE SWITCHING WAVEFORMS

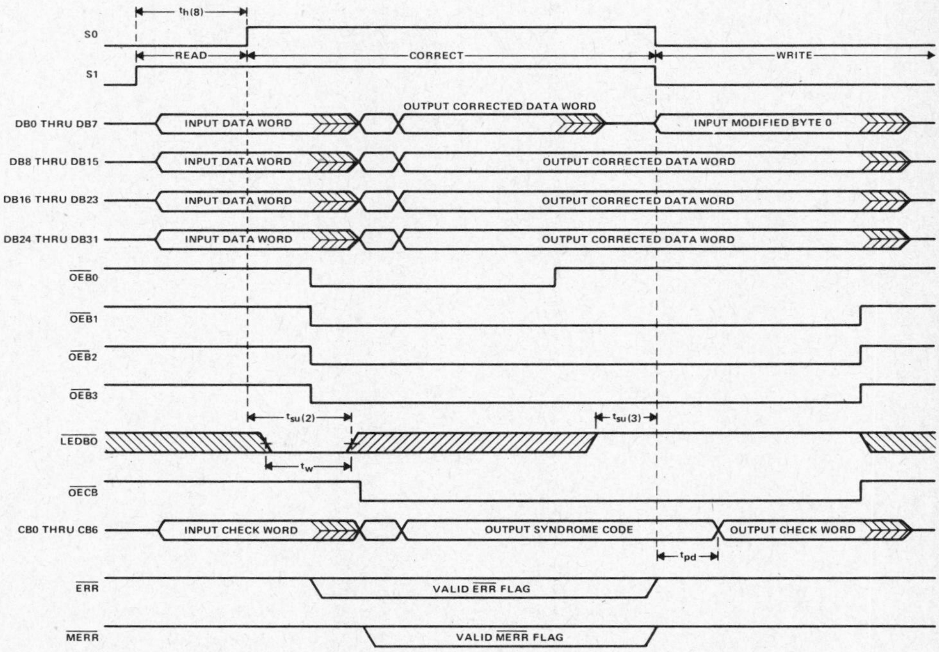
S0
S1
READ
CORRECT
WRITE
DB0 THRU DB7
DB8 THRU DB15
DB16 THRU DB23
DB24 THRU DB31
INPUT DATA WORD
OUTPUT CORRECTED DATA WORD
INPUT MODIFIED BYTE 0
OEB0
OEB1
OEB2
OEB3
LEDBO
OECB
CB0 THRU CB6
INPUT CHECK WORD
OUTPUT SYNDROME CODE
OUTPUT CHECK WORD
ERR
VALID ERR FLAG
MERR
VALID MERR FLAG

FIGURE 2. READ, CORRECT, MODIFY MODE SWITCHING WAVEFORMS

2

LSI Devices

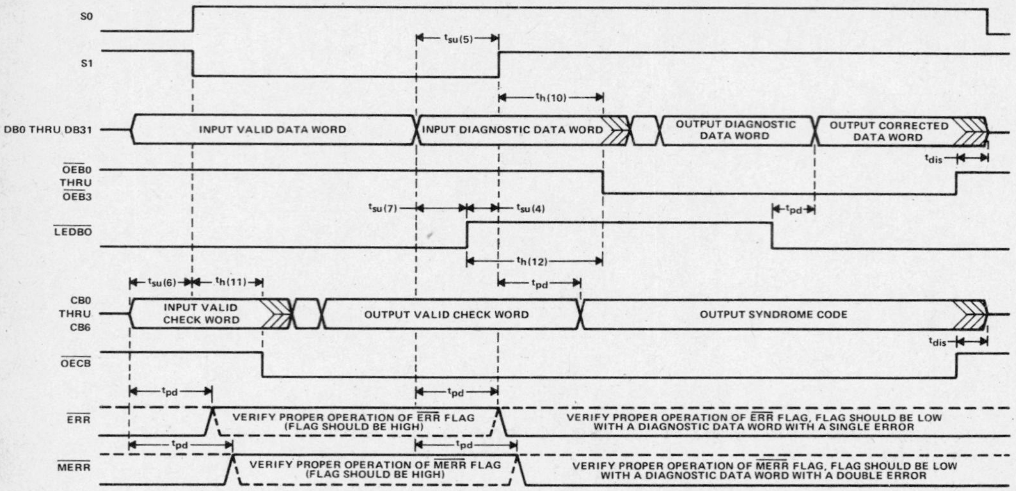
S0
S1
$t_{su(5)}$
$t_{h(10)}$
DB0 THRU DB31
INPUT VALID DATA WORD
INPUT DIAGNOSTIC DATA WORD
OUTPUT DIAGNOSTIC DATA WORD
OUTPUT CORRECTED DATA WORD
t_{dis}
OEB0 THRU OEB3
$t_{su(7)}$
$t_{su(4)}$
t_{pd}
LEDBO
$t_{h(12)}$
$t_{su(6)}$
$t_{h(11)}$
CB0 THRU CB6
INPUT VALID CHECK WORD
OUTPUT VALID CHECK WORD
OUTPUT SYNDROME CODE
OECB
ERR
VERIFY PROPER OPERATION OF ERR FLAG (FLAG SHOULD BE HIGH)
VERIFY PROPER OPERATION OF ERR FLAG, FLAG SHOULD BE LOW WITH A DIAGNOSTIC DATA WORD WITH A SINGLE ERROR
MERR
VERIFY PROPER OPERATION OF MERR FLAG (FLAG SHOULD BE HIGH)
VERIFY PROPER OPERATION OF MERR FLAG, FLAG SHOULD BE LOW WITH A DIAGNOSTIC DATA WORD WITH A DOUBLE ERROR

FIGURE 3. DIAGNOSTIC MODE SWITCHING WAVEFORM

TEXAS INSTRUMENTS
POST OFFICE BOX 225012 • DALLAS, TEXAS 75265

SN54ALS646 THRU SN54ALS649, SN54AS646, SN54AS648
SN74ALS646 THRU SN74ALS649, SN74AS646, SN74AS648
OCTAL BUS TRANSCEIVERS AND REGISTERS

D2661, DECEMBER 1983—NOVEMBER 1985

- Independent Registers for A and B Buses
- Multiplexed Real-Time and Stored Data
- Choice of True or Inverting Data Paths
- Choice of 3-State or Open-Collector Outputs
- Included Among the Package Options Are Compact 24-pin 300-mil Wide DIPs and Both 28-pin Plastic and Ceramic Chip Carriers
- Dependable Texas Instruments Quality and Reliability

DEVICE	OUTPUT	LOGIC
'ALS646, 'AS646	3-State	True
'ALS647	Open-Collector	True
'ALS648, 'AS648	3-State	Inverting
'ALS649	Open-Collector	Inverting

SN54ALS', SN54AS' . . . JT PACKAGE
SN74ALS', SN74AS' . . . DW OR NT PACKAGE
(TOP VIEW)

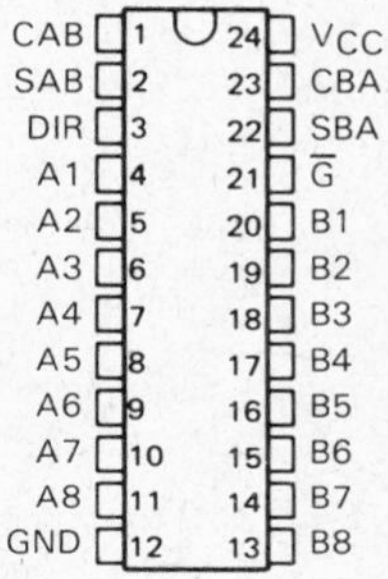
CAB 1
SAB 2
DIR 3
A1 4
A2 5
A3 6
A4 7
A5 8
A6 9
A7 10
A8 11
GND 12
24 VCC
23 CBA
22 SBA
21 G̅
20 B1
19 B2
18 B3
17 B4
16 B5
15 B6
14 B7
13 B8

SN54ALS', SN54AS' . . . FK PACKAGE
SN74ALS', SN74AS' . . . FN PACKAGE
(TOP VIEW)

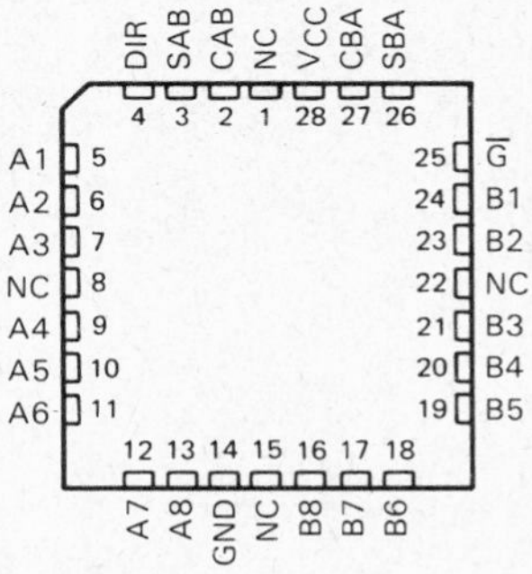
DIR SAB CAB NC VCC CBA SBA
4 3 2 1 28 27 26
A1 5
A2 6
A3 7
NC 8
A4 9
A5 10
A6 11
25 G̅
24 B1
23 B2
22 NC
21 B3
20 B4
19 B5
12 13 14 15 16 17 18
A7 A8 GND NC B8 B7 B6

NC—No internal connection

description

These devices consist of bus transceiver circuits, with 3-state or open-collector outputs, D-type flip-flops, and control circuitry arranged for multiplexed transmission of data directly from the data bus or from the internal storage registers. Data on the A or B bus will be clocked into the registers on the low-to-high transition of the appropriate clock pin (CAB or CBA). The following examples demonstrate the four fundamental bus-management functions that can be performed with the octal bus transceivers and registers.

Enable ($\overline{G}$) and direction (DIR) pins are provided to control the transceiver functions. In the transceiver mode, data present at the high-impedance port may be stored in either register or in both. The select controls (SAB and SBA) can multiplex stored and real-time (transparent mode) data. The circuitry used for select control will eliminate the typical decoding glitch which occurs in a multiplexer during the transition between stored and real-time data. The direction control determines which bus will receive data when enable $\overline{G}$ is active (low). In the isolation mode (control $\overline{G}$ high), A data may be stored in one register and/or B data may be stored in the other register.

When an output function is disabled, the input function is still enabled and may be used to store and transmit data. Only one of the two buses, A or B, may be driven at a time.

The -1 versions of the SN74ALS' parts are identical to the standard versions except that the recommended maximum I_{OL} is increased to 48 milliamperes. There are no -1 versions of the SN54ALS' parts.

The SN54' family is characterized for operation over the full military temperature range of −55°C to 125°C. The SN74' family is characterized for operation from 0°C to 70°C.

TEXAS INSTRUMENTS
POST OFFICE BOX 225012 • DALLAS, TEXAS 75265

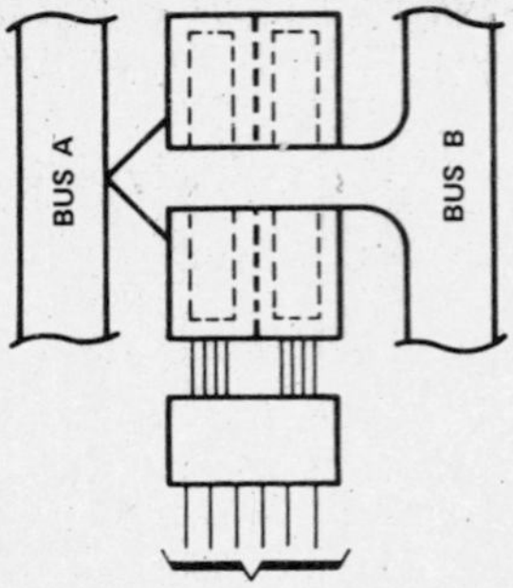
BUS A
BUS B

(21) G	(3) DIR	(1) CAB	(23) CBA	(2) SAB	(22) SBA
L	L	X	X	X	L

REAL-TIME TRANSFER
BUS B TO BUS A

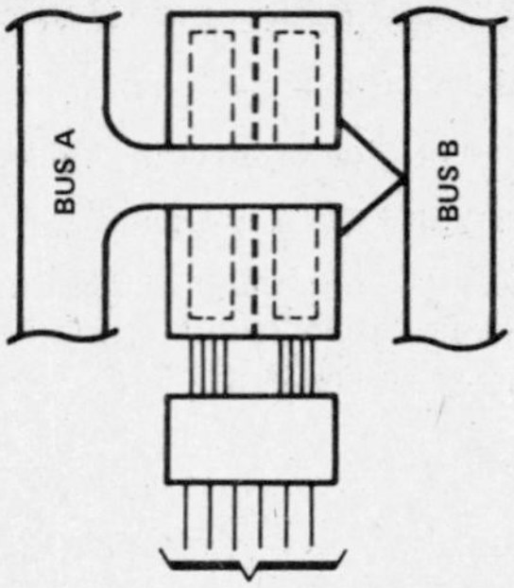
BUS A
BUS B

(21) G	(3) DIR	(1) CAB	(23) CBA	(2) SAB	(22) SBA
L	H	X	X	L	X

REAL-TIME TRANSFER
BUS A TO BUS B

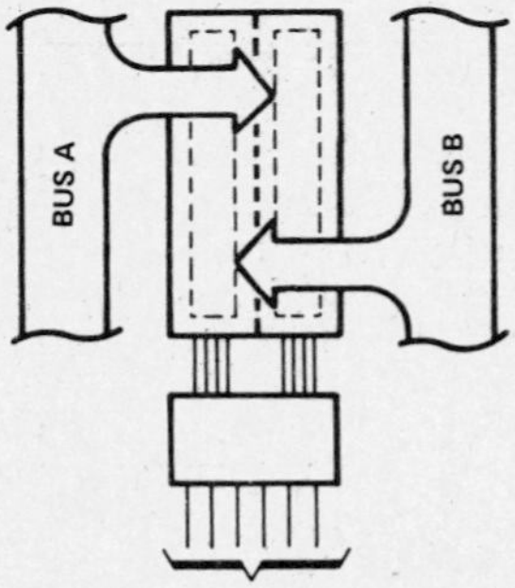
BUS A
BUS B

(21) G	(3) DIR	(1) CAB	(23) CBA	(2) SAB	(22) SBA
X	X	↑	X	X	X
X	X	X	↑	X	X
H	X	↑	↑	X	X

STORAGE FROM
A, B, OR A AND B

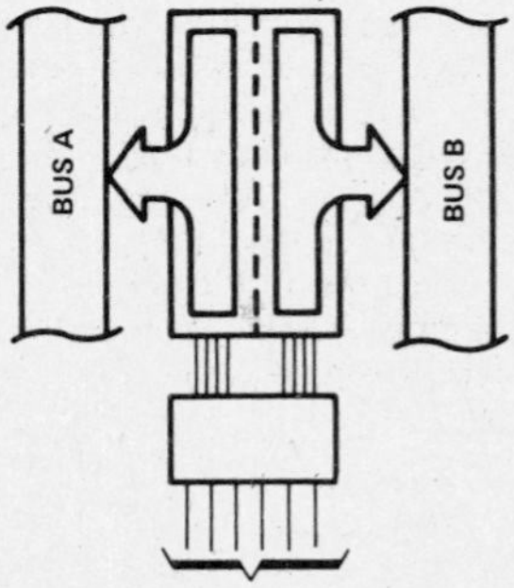
BUS A
BUS B

(21) G	(3) DIR	(1) CAB	(23) CBA	(2) SAB	(22) SBA
L	L	X	HorL	X	H
L	H	HorL	X	H	X

TRANSFER
STORED DATA
TO A OR B

FUNCTION TABLE

INPUTS						DATA I/O		OPERATION OR FUNCTION	
G	DIR	CAB	CBA	SAB	SBA	A1 THRU A8	B1 THRU B8	'ALS646, 'ALS647 'AS646	'ALS648, 'ALS649 'AS648
X	X	↑	X	X	X	Input	Unspecified†	Store A, B unspecified†	Store A, B unspecified†
X	X	X	↑	X	X	Unspecified†	Input	Store B, A unspecified†	Store B, A unspecified†
H	X	↑	↑	X	X	Input	Input	Store A and B Data	Store A and B Data
H	X	H or L	H or L	X	X			Isolation, hold storage	Isolation, hold storage
L	L	X	X	X	L	Output	Input	Real-Time B Data to A Bus	Real-Time $\overline{B}$ Data to A Bus
L	L	X	H or L	X	H			Stored B Data to A Bus	Stored $\overline{B}$ Data to A Bus
L	H	X	X	L	X	Input	Output	Real-Time A Data to B Bus	Real-Time $\overline{A}$ Data to B Bus
L	H	H or L	X	H	X			Stored A Data to B Bus	Store $\overline{A}$ Data to B Bus

†The data output functions may be enabled or disabled by various signals at the $\overline{G}$ and DIR inputs. Data input functions are always enabled, i.e., data at the bus pins will be stored on every low-to-high transition on the clock inputs.

functional block diagrams (positive logic)

'ALS646, 'AS646, 'ALS647

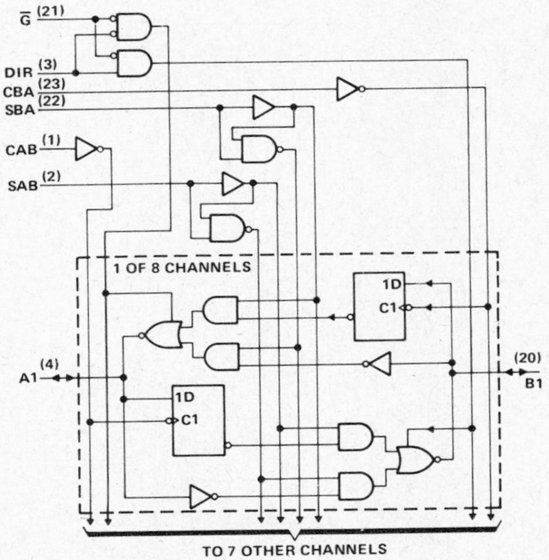
G (21)
DIR (3)
CBA (23)
SBA (22)
CAB (1)
SAB (2)
1 OF 8 CHANNELS
1D
C1
A1 (4)
(20)
B1
1D
C1
TO 7 OTHER CHANNELS

'ALS648, 'AS648, 'ALS649

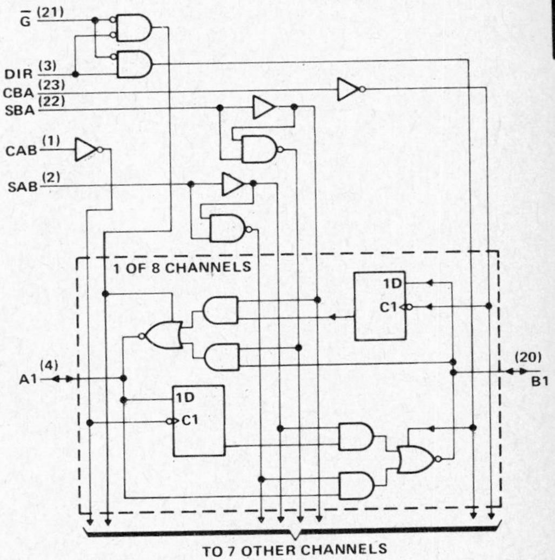
G (21)
DIR (3)
CBA (23)
SBA (22)
CAB (1)
SAB (2)
1 OF 8 CHANNELS
1D
C1
A1 (4)
(20)
B1
1D
C1
TO 7 OTHER CHANNELS

Pin numbers shown are for DW, JT, and NT packages.

logic symbols†

'ALS646, 'AS646

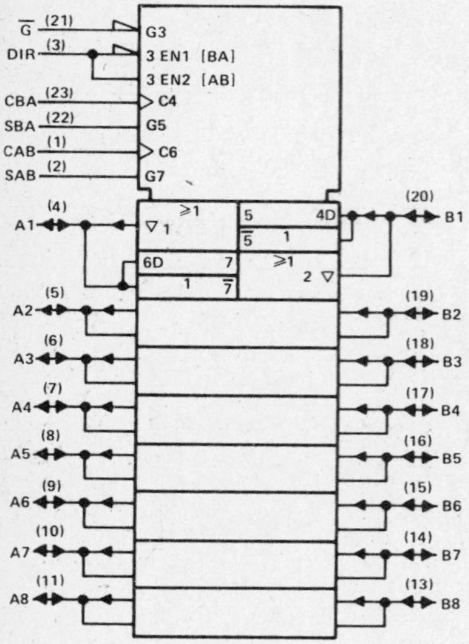
G (21)
DIR (3)
CBA (23)
SBA (22)
CAB (1)
SAB (2)
G3
3 EN1 [BA]
3 EN2 [AB]
C4
G5
C6
G7
≥1
▽ 1
5
4D
5̄
1
6D
7
7̄
≥1
2 ▽
A1 (4)
A2 (5)
A3 (6)
A4 (7)
A5 (8)
A6 (9)
A7 (10)
A8 (11)
(20) B1
(19) B2
(18) B3
(17) B4
(16) B5
(15) B6
(14) B7
(13) B8

'ALS647

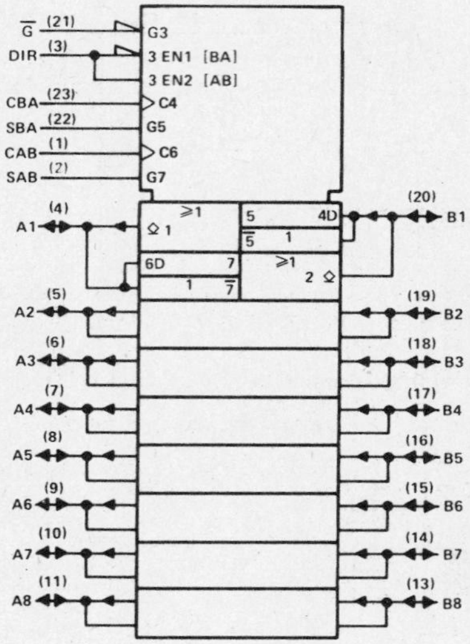
G (21)
DIR (3)
CBA (23)
SBA (22)
CAB (1)
SAB (2)
G3
3 EN1 [BA]
3 EN2 [AB]
C4
G5
C6
G7
≥1
1
5
4D
5̄
1
6D
7
7̄
≥1
2
A1 (4)
A2 (5)
A3 (6)
A4 (7)
A5 (8)
A6 (9)
A7 (10)
A8 (11)
(20) B1
(19) B2
(18) B3
(17) B4
(16) B5
(15) B6
(14) B7
(13) B8

'ALS648, 'AS648

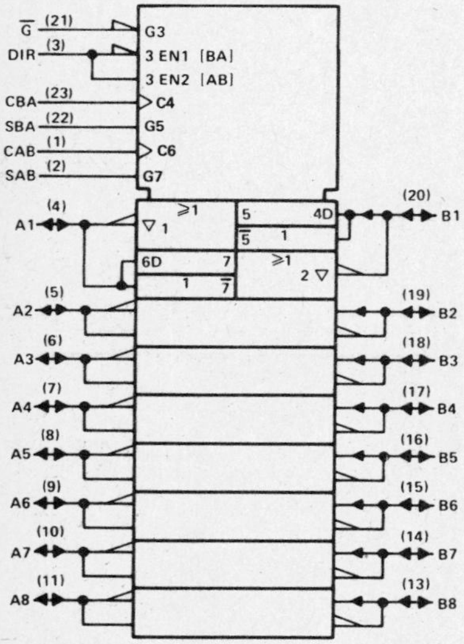
G (21)
DIR (3)
CBA (23)
SBA (22)
CAB (1)
SAB (2)
G3
3 EN1 [BA]
3 EN2 [AB]
C4
G5
C6
G7
≥1
▽ 1
5
4D
5̄
1
6D
7
7̄
≥1
2 ▽
A1 (4)
A2 (5)
A3 (6)
A4 (7)
A5 (8)
A6 (9)
A7 (10)
A8 (11)
(20) B1
(19) B2
(18) B3
(17) B4
(16) B5
(15) B6
(14) B7
(13) B8

'ALS649

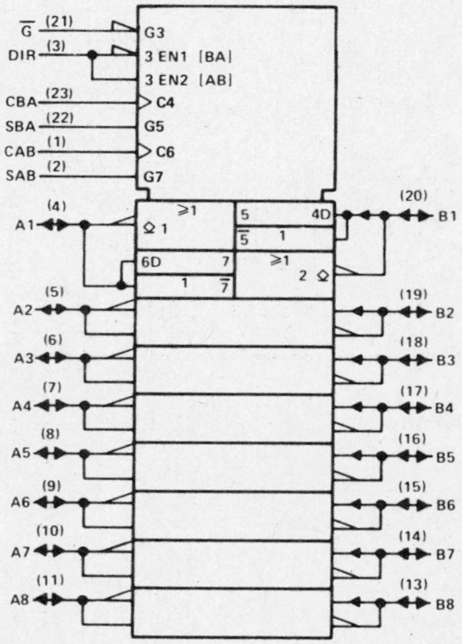
G (21)
DIR (3)
CBA (23)
SBA (22)
CAB (1)
SAB (2)
G3
3 EN1 [BA]
3 EN2 [AB]
C4
G5
C6
G7
≥1
1
5
4D
5̄
1
6D
7
7̄
≥1
2
A1 (4)
A2 (5)
A3 (6)
A4 (7)
A5 (8)
A6 (9)
A7 (10)
A8 (11)
(20) B1
(19) B2
(18) B3
(17) B4
(16) B5
(15) B6
(14) B7
(13) B8

†These symbols are in accordance with ANSI/IEEE Std 91-1984 and IEC Publication 617-12.
Pin numbers shown are for DW, JT, and NT packages.

TEXAS INSTRUMENTS
POST OFFICE BOX 225012 • DALLAS, TEXAS 75265

absolute maximum ratings over operating free-air temperature range (unless otherwise noted)

Supply voltage, V_{CC} . . . . . 7 V
Input voltage: Control inputs . . . . . 7 V
I/O ports . . . . . 5.5 V
Operating free-air temperature range: SN54ALS646 . . . . . −55°C to 125°C
SN74ALS646 . . . . . 0°C to 70°C
Storage temperature range . . . . . −65°C to 150°C

recommended operating conditions

		SN54ALS646			SN74ALS646			UNIT
		MIN	NOM	MAX	MIN	NOM	MAX	
V_{CC}	Supply voltage	4.5	5	5.5	4.5	5	5.5	V
V_{IH}	High-level input voltage	2			2			V
V_{IL}	Low-level input voltage			0.8			0.8	V
I_{OH}	High-level output current			−12			−15	mA
I_{OL}	Low-level output current			12			24	mA
							48†	
f_{clock}	Clock frequency	0		35	0		40	MHz
t_w	Pulse duration, clocks high or low	14.5			12.5			ns
t_{su}	Setup time, A before CAB↑ or B before CBA↑	15			10			ns
t_h	Hold time, A after CAB↑ or B after CBA↑	0			0			ns
T_A	Operating free-air temperature	−55		125	0		70	°C

†The extended condition applies if V_{CC} is maintained between 4.75 V and 5.25 V.
The 48-mA limit applies for the SN74ALS646-1 only.

electrical characteristics over recommended operating free-air temperature range (unless otherwise noted)

PARAMETER		TEST CONDITIONS		SN54ALS646			SN74ALS646			UNIT
				MIN	TYP‡	MAX	MIN	TYP‡	MAX	
V_{IK}		V_{CC} = 4.5 V,	I_I = −18 mA			−1.2			−1.2	V
V_{OH}		V_{CC} = 4.5 V to 5.5 V,	I_{OH} = −0.4 mA	$V_{CC}-2$			$V_{CC}-2$			V
		V_{CC} = 4.5 V,	I_{OH} = −3 mA	2.4	3.2		2.4	3.2		
		V_{CC} = 4.5 V,	I_{OH} = −12 mA	2						
		V_{CC} = 4.5 V,	I_{OH} = −15 mA				2			
V_{OL}		V_{CC} = 4.5 V,	I_{OL} = 12 mA		0.25	0.4		0.25	0.4	V
		V_{CC} = 4.5 V, (I_{OL} = 48 mA for −1 version)	I_{OL} = 24 mA					0.35	0.5	
I_I	Control inputs	V_{CC} = 5.5 V,	V_I = 7 V			0.1			0.1	mA
	A or B ports	V_{CC} = 5.5 V,	V_I = 5.5 V			0.1			0.1	
I_{IH}	Control inputs	V_{CC} = 5.5 V,	V_I = 2.7 V			20			20	μA
	A or B ports§					20			20	
I_{IL}	Control inputs	V_{CC} = 5.5 V,	V_I = 0.4 V			−0.2			−0.2	mA
	A or B ports§					−0.2			−0.2	
I_O¶		V_{CC} = 5.5 V,	V_O = 2.25 V	−30		−112	−30		−112	mA
I_{CC}		V_{CC} = 5.5 V	Outputs high		47	76		47	76	mA
			Outputs low		55	88		55	88	
			Outputs disabled		55	88		55	88	

‡All typical values are at V_{CC} = 5 V, T_A = 25°C
§For I/O ports, the parameters I_{IH} and I_{IL} include the off-state output current.
¶The output conditions have been chosen to produce a current that closely approximates one half of the true short-circuit output current, I_{OS}.

'ALS646 switching characteristics (see Note 1)

PARAMETER	FROM (INPUT)	TO (OUTPUT)	V_{CC} = 5 V, C_L = 50 pF, R1 = 500 Ω, R2 = 500 Ω, T_A = 25 °C			V_{CC} = 4.5 V to 5.5 V, C_L = 50 pF, R1 = 500 Ω, R2 = 500 Ω, T_A = MIN to MAX				UNIT
			'ALS646			SN54ALS646		SN74ALS646		
			MIN	TYP	MAX	MIN	MAX	MIN	MAX	
f_{max}				50		35		40		MHz
t_{PLH}	CBA or CAB	A or B		20	25	10	35	10	30	ns
t_{PHL}				11	15	5	20	5	17	
t_{PLH}	A or B	B or A		11	17	5	22	5	20	ns
t_{PHL}				7.5	10	3	15	3	12	
t_{PLH}	SBA or SAB† (with A or B high)	A or B		24	32	15	40	15	35	ns
t_{PHL}				13	17	5	23	5	20	
t_{PLH}	SBA or SAB† (with A or B low)	A or B		17	22	8	30	8	25	ns
t_{PHL}				13	17	5	24	5	20	
t_{PZH}	$\overline{G}$	A or B		10	15	3	20	3	17	ns
t_{PZL}				10	15	5	22	5	20	
t_{PHZ}	$\overline{G}$	A or B		6	8	1	12	1	10	ns
t_{PLZ}				10	13	2	20	2	16	
t_{PZH}	DIR	A or B		22	28	10	38	10	30	ns
t_{PZL}				14.5	20	5	30	5	25	
t_{PHZ}	DIR	A or B		6	8	1	12	1	10	ns
t_{PLZ}				10	13	2	21	2	16	

† These parameters are measured with the internal output state of the storage register opposite to that of the bus input.

NOTE 1: Load circuit and voltage waveforms are shown in Section 1.

absolute maximum ratings over operating free-air temperature range (unless otherwise noted)

Supply voltage, V_{CC} .... 7 V
Input voltage .... 7 V
Operating free-air temperature range: SN54ALS647 .... −55°C to 125°C
SN74ALS647 .... 0°C to 70°C
Storage temperature range .... −65°C to 150°C

recommended operating conditions

		SN54ALS647			SN74ALS647			UNIT
		MIN	NOM	MAX	MIN	NOM	MAX	
V_{CC}	Supply voltage	4.5	5	5.5	4.5	5	5.5	V
V_{IH}	High-level input voltage	2			2			V
V_{IL}	Low-level input voltage			0.8			0.8	V
V_{OH}	High-level output voltage			5.5			5.5	V
I_{OL}	Low-level output current			12			24	mA
							48†	mA
f_{clock}	Clock frequency	0		25	0		30	MHz
t_w	Pulse duration, clocks high or low	20			16.5			ns
t_{su}	Setup time, A before CAB↑ or B before CBA↑	15			10			ns
t_h	Hold time, A after CAB↑ or B after CBA↑	0			0			ns
T_A	Operating free-air temperature	−55		125	0		70	°C

†The extended condition applies if V_{CC} is maintained between 4.75 V and 5.25 V.
The 48-mA limit applies for the SN74ALS647-1 only.

electrical characteristics over recommended operating free-air temperature range (unless otherwise noted)

PARAMETER		TEST CONDITIONS			SN54ALS647			SN74ALS647			UNIT
					MIN	TYP‡	MAX	MIN	TYP‡	MAX	
V_{IK}		V_{CC} = 4.5 V,	I_I = −18 mA				−1.2			−1.2	V
I_{OH}		V_{CC} = 4.5 V,	V_{OH} = 5.5 V				0.1			0.1	mA
V_{OL}		V_{CC} = 4.5 V,	I_{OL} = 12 mA			0.25	0.4				V
V_{OL}		V_{CC} = 4.5 V, (I_{OL} = 48 mA for −1 versions)	I_{OL} = 24 mA						0.35	0.5	V
I_I	A or B ports	V_{CC} = 5.5 V,	V_I = 7 V				0.1			0.1	mA
I_I	Control inputs	V_{CC} = 5.5 V,	V_I = 7 V				0.1			0.1	mA
I_{IH}	A or ports§	V_{CC} = 5.5 V,	V_I = 2.7 V				20			20	μA
I_{IH}	Control inputs	V_{CC} = 5.5 V,	V_I = 2.7 V				20			20	μA
I_{IL}	Control inputs	V_{CC} = 5.5 V,	V_I = 0.4 V				−0.2			−0.2	mA
I_{IL}	A or B ports§	V_{CC} = 5.5 V,	V_I = 0.4 V				−0.2			−0.2	mA
I_{CC}		V_{CC} = 5.5 V		Outputs high		35	60		35	60	mA
I_{CC}		V_{CC} = 5.5 V		Outputs low		40	65		40	65	mA

‡All typical values are at V_{CC} = 5 V, T_A = 25°C
§For I/O ports, the parameters I_{IH} and I_{IL} include the off-state output current.

2
LSI Devices

'ALS647 switching characteristics (see Note 1)

PARAMETER	FROM (INPUT)	TO (OUTPUT)	V_{CC} = 5 V, C_L = 50 pF, R_L = 680 Ω, T_A = 25°C			V_{CC} = 4.5 V to 5.5 V, C_L = 50 pF, R_L = 680 Ω, T_A = MIN to MAX				UNIT
			'ALS647			SN54ALS647		SN74ALS647		
			MIN	TYP	MAX	MIN	MAX	MIN	MAX	
f_{max}				40		25		30		MHz
t_{PLH}	CBA or CAB	A or B		38	50	19	72	19	58	ns
t_{PHL}				12	20	6	24	6	22	
t_{PLH}	A or B	B or A		35	39	17	70	17	54	ns
t_{PHL}				10	13	4	19	4	16	
t_{PLH}	SBA or SAB† (with A or B high)	A or B		40	51	20	72	20	60	ns
t_{PHL}				12	17	6	26	6	22	
t_{PLH}	SBA or SAB† (with A or B low)	A or B		40	51	20	72	20	60	ns
t_{PHL}				12	17	6	26	6	22	
t_{PLH}	$\overline{G}$	A or B		20	27	10	37	10	31	ns
t_{PHL}				10	15	2	20	2	17	
t_{PLH}	DIR	A or B		20	25	9	34	9	29	ns
t_{PHL}				13	17	2	22	2	19	

†These parameters are measured with the internal output state of the storage register opposite to that of the bus input.

NOTE 1: For load circuit and voltage waveforms, see page 1-12 of *The TTL Data Book,* Volume 3, 1984.

absolute maximum ratings over operating free-air temperature range (unless otherwise noted)

Supply voltage, V_{CC} . . . . 7 V
Input voltage: Control inputs . . . . 7 V
I/O ports . . . . 5.5 V
Operating free-air temperature range: SN54ALS648 . . . . −55°C to 125°C
SN74ALS648 . . . . 0°C to 70°C
Storage temperature range . . . . −65°C to 150°C

recommended operating conditions

		SN54ALS648			SN74ALS648			UNIT
		MIN	NOM	MAX	MIN	NOM	MAX	
V_{CC}	Supply voltage	4.5	5	5.5	4.5	5	5.5	V
V_{IH}	High-level input voltage	2			2			V
V_{IL}	Low-level input voltage			0.8			0.8	V
I_{OH}	High-level output current			−12			−15	mA
I_{OL}	Low-level output current			12			24	mA
							48†	
f_{clock}	Clock frequency	0		35	0		40	MHz
t_w	Pulse duration, clocks high or low	14.5			12.5			ns
t_{su}	Setup time, A before CAB↑ or B before CBA↑	15			10			ns
t_h	Hold time, A after CAB↑ or B after CBA↑	0			0			ns
T_A	Operating free-air temperature	−55		125	0		70	°C

†The extended conditon applies if V_{CC} is maintained between 4.75 V and 5.25 V.
The 48-mA limit applies for the SN74ALS648-1 only.

electrical characteristics over recommended operating free-air temperature range (unless otherwise noted)

PARAMETER		TEST CONDITIONS		SN54ALS648			SN74ALS648			UNIT
				MIN	TYP‡	MAX	MIN	TYP‡	MAX	
V_{IK}		V_{CC} = 4.5 V,	I_I = −18 mA			−1.2			−1.2	V
V_{OH}		V_{CC} = 4.5 V to 5.5 V,	I_{OH} = −0.4 mA	V_{CC} − 2			V_{CC} − 2			V
		V_{CC} = 4.5 V,	I_{OH} = −3 mA	2.4	3.2		2.4	3.2		
		V_{CC} = 4.5 V,	I_{OH} = −12 mA	2						
		V_{CC} = 4.5 V,	I_{OH} = −15 mA				2			
V_{OL}		V_{CC} = 4.5 V,	I_{OL} = 12 mA		0.25	0.4		0.25	0.4	V
		V_{CC} = 4.5 V, (I_{OL} = 48 mA for −1 version)	I_{OL} = 24 mA					0.35	0.5	
I_I	Control inputs	V_{CC} = 5.5 V,	V_I = 7 V			0.1			0.1	mA
	A or B ports	V_{CC} = 5.5 V,	V_I = 5.5 V			0.1			0.1	
I_{IH}	Control inputs	V_{CC} = 5.5 V,	V_I = 2.7 V			20			20	μA
	A or B ports§					20			20	
I_{IL}	Control inputs	V_{CC} = 5.5 V,	V_I = 0.4 V			−0.2			−0.2	mA
	A or B ports§					−0.2			−0.2	
I_O¶		V_{CC} = 5.5 V,	V_O = 2.25 V	−30		−112	−30		−112	mA
I_{CC}		V_{CC} = 5.5 V	Outputs high		47	76		47	76	mA
			Outputs low		57	88		57	88	
			Outputs disabled		57	88		57	88	

‡All typical values are at V_{CC} = 5 V, T_A = 25°C
§For I/O ports, the parameters I_{IH} and I_{IL} include the off-state output current.
¶The output conditions have been chosen to produce a current that closely approximates one half of the true short-circuit output current, I_{OS}.

'ALS648 switching characteristics (see Note 1)

PARAMETER	FROM (INPUT)	TO (OUTPUT)	V_{CC} = 5 V, C_L = 50 pF, R1 = 500 Ω, R2 = 500 Ω, T_A = 25°C			V_{CC} = 4.5 V to 5.5 V, C_L = 50 pF, R1 = 500 Ω, R2 = 500 Ω, T_A = MIN to MAX				UNIT
			'ALS648			SN54ALS648		SN74ALS648		
			MIN	TYP	MAX	MIN	MAX	MIN	MAX	
f_{max}				50		35		40		MHz
t_{PLH}	CBA or CAB	A or B		21	29	8	39	8	33	ns
t_{PHL}				13	18	5	23	5	20	
t_{PLH}	A or B	B or A		10	15	3	20	3	17	ns
t_{PHL}				6	8	2	12	2	10	
t_{PLH}	SBA or SAB† (with A or B high)	A or B		24	32	5	44	5	39	ns
t_{PHL}				15	21	4	26	4	22	
t_{PLH}	SBA or SAB† (with A or B low)	A or B		16	22	6	30	6	25	ns
t_{PHL}				14	19	6	25	6	21	
t_{PLH}	$\overline{G}$	A or B		12	18	4	25	4	22	ns
t_{PHL}				12	18	4	25	4	22	
t_{PLH}	$\overline{G}$	A or B		5	8	1	12	1	10	ns
t_{PHL}				7	12	2	21	2	15	
t_{PZH}	DIR	A or B		14	22	4	35	4	27	ns
t_{PZL}				10	17	3	25	3	19	
t_{PHZ}	DIR	A or B		7	12	1	17	1	14	ns
t_{PLZ}				7	13	2	22	2	15	

† These parameters are measured with the internal output state of the storage register opposite to that of the bus input.
NOTE 1: Load circuit and voltage waveforms are shown in Section 1.

absolute maximum ratings over operating free-air temperature range (unless otherwise noted)

Supply voltage, V_{CC} .... 7 V
Input voltage .... 7 V
Operating free-air temperature range: SN54ALS649 .... −55°C to 125°C
SN74ALS649 .... 0°C to 70°C
Storage temperature range .... −65°C to 150°C

recommended operating conditions

		SN54ALS649			SN74ALS649			UNIT
		MIN	NOM	MAX	MIN	NOM	MAX	
V_{CC}	Supply voltage	4.5	5	5.5	4.5	5	5.5	V
V_{IH}	High-level input voltage	2			2			V
V_{IL}	Low-level input voltage			0.8			0.8	V
V_{OH}	High-level output voltage			5.5			5.5	V
I_{OL}	Low-level output current			12			24	mA
							48†	
f_{clock}	Clock frequency	0		25	0		30	MHz
t_w	Pulse duration, clocks high or low	20			16.5			ns
t_{su}	Setup time, A before CAB↑ or B before CBA↑	15			10			ns
t_h	Hold time, A after CAB↑ or B after CBA↑	0			0			ns
T_A	Operating free-air temperature	−55		125	0		70	°C

†The extended condition applies if V_{CC} is maintained between 4.75 V and 5.25 V. The 48-mA limit applies for the SN74ALS649-1 only.

electrical characteristics over recommended operating free-air temperature range (unless otherwise noted)

PARAMETER		TEST CONDITIONS		SN54ALS649			SN74ALS649			UNIT
				MIN	TYP‡	MAX	MIN	TYP‡	MAX	
V_{IK}		V_{CC} = 4.5 V,	I_I = −18 mA			−1.2			−1.2	V
I_{OH}		V_{CC} = 4.5 V,	V_{OH} = 5.5 V			0.1			0.1	mA
V_{OL}		V_{CC} = 4.5 V,	I_{OL} = 12 mA		0.25	0.4				V
		V_{CC} = 4.5 V, (I_{OL} = 48 mA for −1 versions)	I_{OL} = 24 mA					0.35	0.5	
I_I	A or B ports	V_{CC} = 5.5 V,	V_I = 7 V			0.1			0.1	mA
	Control inputs	V_{CC} = 5.5 V,	V_I = 7 V			0.1			0.1	
I_{IH}	A or ports§	V_{CC} = 5.5 V,	V_I = 2.7 V			20			20	μA
	Control inputs					20			20	
I_{IL}	Control inputs	V_{CC} = 5.5 V,	V_I = 0.4 V			−0.2			−0.2	mA
	A or B ports§					−0.2			−0.2	
I_{CC}		V_{CC} = 5.5 V	Outputs high		40	60		40	60	mA
			Outputs low		45	70		45	70	

‡All typical values are at V_{CC} = 5 V, T_A = 25°C
§For I/O ports, the parameters I_{IH} and I_{IL} include the off-state output current.

2

LSI Devices

'ALS649 switching characteristics (see Note 1)

PARAMETER	FROM (INPUT)	TO (OUTPUT)	V_{CC} = 5 V, C_L = 50 pF, R_L = 680 Ω, T_A = 25°C			V_{CC} = 4.5 V to 5.5 V, C_L = 50 pF, R_L = 680 Ω, T_A = MIN to MAX				UNIT
			'ALS649			SN54ALS649		SN74ALS649		
			MIN	TYP	MAX	MIN	MAX	MIN	MAX	
f_{max}				40		25		30		MHz
t_{PLH}	CBA or CAB	A or B		40	52	19	77	19	62	ns
t_{PHL}				12	18	6	22	6	20	
t_{PLH}	A or B	B or A		30	41	13	65	13	50	ns
t_{PHL}				6	9	2	11	2	10	
t_{PLH}	SBA or SAB† (with A or B high)	A or B		35	46	20	72	20	55	ns
t_{PHL}				15	21	6	26	6	22	
t_{PLH}	SBA or SAB† (with A or B low)	A or B		35	46	20	72	20	55	ns
t_{PHL}				15	21	6	26	6	22	
t_{PLH}	$\overline{G}$	A or B		16	22	8	28	8	25	ns
t_{PHL}				13	18	2	23	2	20	
t_{PLH}	DIR	A or B		16	22	8	28	8	25	ns
t_{PHL}				13	17	2	23	2	20	

† These parameters are measured with the internal output state of the storage register opposite to that of the bus input.

NOTE 1: Load circuit and voltage waveforms are shown in Section 1.

absolute maximum ratings over operating free-air temperature range (unless otherwise noted)

Supply voltage, V_{CC} . . . . 7 V
Input voltage: Control inputs . . . . 7 V
I/O ports . . . . 5.5 V
Operating free-air temperature range: SN54AS646, SN54AS648 . . . . −55°C to 125°C
SN74AS646, SN74AS648 . . . . 0°C to 70°C
Storage temperature range . . . . −65°C to 150°C

recommended operating conditions

			SN54AS646 SN54AS648			SN74AS646 SN74AS648			UNIT
			MIN	NOM	MAX	MIN	NOM	MAX	
V_{CC}	Supply voltage		4.5	5	5.5	4.5	5	5.5	V
V_{IH}	High-level input voltage		2			2			V
V_{IL}	Low-level input voltage				0.8			0.8	V
I_{OH}	High-level output current				−12			−15	mA
I_{OL}	Low-level output current				32			48	mA
f_{clock}	Clock frequency		0		75	0		90	MHz
t_w	Pulse duration	Clock high	6			5			ns
		Clock high	7			6			
t_{su}	Setup time, A before CAB↑ or B before CBA↑		7			6			ns
t_h	Hold time, A after CAB↑ or B after CBA↑		0			0			ns
T_A	Operating free-air temperature		−55		125	0		70	°C

electrical characteristics over recommended operating free-air temperature range (unless otherwise noted)

PARAMETER		TEST CONDITIONS		SN54AS646 SN54AS648			SN74AS646 SN74AS648			UNIT
				MIN	TYP†	MAX	MIN	TYP†	MAX	
V_{IK}		V_{CC} = 4.5 V,	I_I = −18 mA			−1.2			−1.2	V
V_{OH}		V_{CC} = 4.5 V to 5.5 V,	I_{OH} = −2 mA	$V_{CC}-2$			$V_{CC}-2$			V
		V_{CC} = 4.5 V,	I_{OH} = −3 mA	2.4	3.2		2.4	3.2		
		V_{CC} = 4.5 V,	I_{OH} = −12 mA	2						
		V_{CC} = 4.5 V,	I_{OH} = −15 mA				2			
V_{OL}		V_{CC} = 4.5 V,	I_{OL} = 32 mA		0.25	0.50				V
		V_{CC} = 4.5 V,	I_{OL} = 48 mA					0.35	0.50	
I_I	Control inputs	V_{CC} = 5.5 V,	V_I = 7 V			0.1			0.1	mA
	A or B ports	V_{CC} = 5.5 V,	V_I = 5.5 V			0.1			0.1	
I_{IH}	Control inputs	V_{CC} = 5.5 V,	V_I = 2.7 V			20			20	μA
	A or B ports‡					70			70	
I_{IL}	Control inputs	V_{CC} = 5.5 V,	V_I = 0.4 V			−0.5			−0.5	mA
	A or B ports§					−0.75			−0.75	
I_O§		V_{CC} = 5.5 V,	V_O = 2.25 V	−30		−112	−30		−112	mA
I_{CC}	'AS646	V_{CC} = 5.5 V	Outputs high		120	195		120	195	mA
			Outputs low		130	211		130	211	
			Outputs disabled		130	211		130	211	
	'AS648		Outputs high		110	185		110	185	
			Outputs low		120	195		120	195	
			Outputs disabled		120	195		120	195	

†All typical values are at V_{CC} = 5 V, T_A = 25°C
‡For I/O ports, the parameters I_{IH} and I_{IL} include the off-state output current.
§The output conditions have been chosen to produce a current that closely approximates one half of the true short-circuit output current, I_{OS}.

2
LSI Devices

'AS646 switching characteristics (see Note 1)

PARAMETER	FROM (INPUT)	TO (OUTPUT)	V_{CC} = 4.5 V to 5.5 V, C_L = 50 pF, R1 = 500 Ω, R2 = 500 Ω, T_A = MIN to MAX				UNIT
			SN54AS646		SN74AS646		
			MIN	MAX	MIN	MAX	
f_{max}			75		90		MHz
t_{PLH}	CBA or CAB	A or B	2	9.5	2	8.5	ns
t_{PHL}			2	10	2	9	
t_{PLH}	A or B	B or A	2	11	2	9	ns
t_{PHL}			1	8	1	7	
t_{PLH}	SBA or SAB†	A or B	2	12	2	11	ns
t_{PHL}			2	10	2	9	
t_{PZH}	$\overline{G}$	A or B	2	10	2	9	ns
t_{PZL}			3	15	3	14	
t_{PHZ}	$\overline{G}$	A or B	2	11	2	9	ns
t_{PLZ}			2	11	2	9	
t_{PZH}	DIR	A or B	3	19	3	16	ns
t_{PZL}			3	21	3	18	
t_{PHZ}	DIR	A or B	2	12	2	10	ns
t_{PLZ}			2	12	2	10	

'AS648 switching characteristics (see Note 1)

PARAMETER	FROM (INPUT)	TO (OUTPUT)	V_{CC} = 4.5 V to 5.5 V, C_L = 50 pF, R1 = 500 Ω, R2 = 500 Ω, T_A = MIN to MAX				UNIT
			SN54AS648		SN74AS648		
			MIN	MAX	MIN	MAX	
f_{max}			75		90		MHz
t_{PLH}	CBA or CAB	A or B	2	9.5	2	8.5	ns
t_{PHL}			2	10	2	9	
t_{PLH}	A or B	B or A	2	9	2	8	ns
t_{PHL}			1	8	1	7	
t_{PLH}	SBA or SAB†	A or B	2	12	2	11	ns
t_{PHL}			2	10	2	9	
t_{PZH}	$\overline{G}$	A or B	2	10	2	9	ns
t_{PZL}			3	18	3	15	
t_{PHZ}	$\overline{G}$	A or B	2	11	2	9	ns
t_{PLZ}			2	11	2	9	
t_{PZH}	DIR	A or B	3	19	3	16	ns
t_{PZL}			3	21	3	18	
t_{PHZ}	DIR	A or B	2	12	2	10	ns
t_{PLZ}			2	12	2	10	

† These parameters are measured with the internal output state of the storage register opposite to that of the bus input.
NOTE 1: Load circuit and voltage waveforms are shown in Section 1.

D2661, DECEMBER 1983—REVISED NOVEMBER 1985

- Bus Transceivers/Registers
- Independent Registers and Enables for A and B Buses
- Multiplexed Real-Time and Stored Data
- Choice of True and Inverting Data Paths
- Choice of 3-State or Open-Collector Outputs to A Bus
- Included Among the Package Options Are Compact 24-Pin 300-mil-Wide DIPs and Both 28-Pin Plastic and Ceramic Chip Carriers
- Dependable Texas Instruments Quality and Reliability

DEVICE	A OUTPUT	B OUTPUT	LOGIC
'ALS651, 'AS651	3-State	3-State	Inverting
'ALS652, 'AS652	3-State	3-State	True
'ALS653	Open-Collector	3-State	Inverting
'ALS654	Open-Collector	3-State	True

SN54ALS', SN54AS' . . . JT PACKAGE
SN74ALS', SN74AS' . . . DW OR NT PACKAGE
(TOP VIEW)

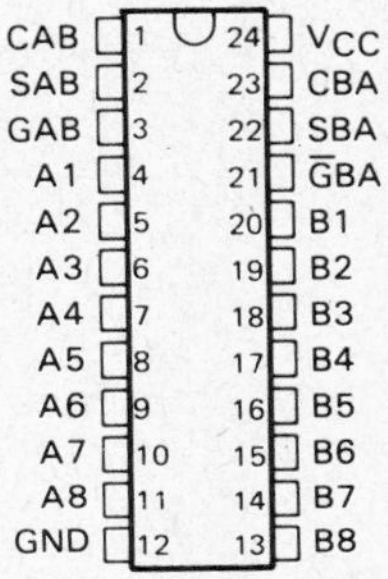
CAB 1
SAB 2
GAB 3
A1 4
A2 5
A3 6
A4 7
A5 8
A6 9
A7 10
A8 11
GND 12
24 VCC
23 CBA
22 SBA
21 GBA
20 B1
19 B2
18 B3
17 B4
16 B5
15 B6
14 B7
13 B8

SN54ALS', SN54AS' . . . FK PACKAGE
SN74ALS', SN74AS' . . . FN PACKAGE
(TOP VIEW)

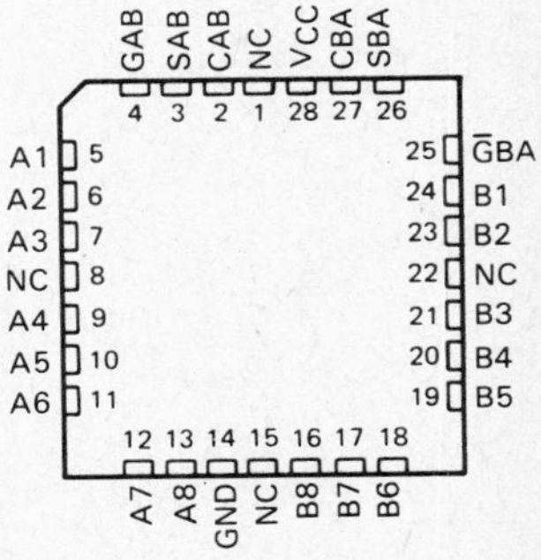
GAB SAB CAB NC VCC CBA SBA
4 3 2 1 28 27 26
A1 5
A2 6
A3 7
NC 8
A4 9
A5 10
A6 11
25 GBA
24 B1
23 B2
22 NC
21 B3
20 B4
19 B5
12 13 14 15 16 17 18
A7 A8 GND NC B8 B7 B6

NC — No internal connection

description

These devices consist of bus transceiver circuits, D-type flip-flops, and control circuitry arranged for multiplexed transmission of data directly from the data bus or from the internal storage registers. Enable GAB and $\overline{G}$BA are provided to control the transceiver functions. SAB and SBA control pins are provided to select whether real-time or stored data is transferred. The circuitry used for select control will eliminate the typical decoding glitch which occurs in a multiplexer during the transition between stored and real-time data. A low input level selects real-time data, and a high selects stored data. The following examples demonstrate the four fundamental bus-management functions that can be performed with the octal bus transceivers and registers.

Data on the A or B data bus, or both, can be stored in the internal D flip-flops by low-to-high transitions at the appropriate clock pins (CAB or CBA) regardless of the select or enable control pins. When SAB and SBA are in the real-time transfer mode, it is also possible to store data without using the internal D-type flip-flops by simultaneously enabling GAB and $\overline{G}$BA. In this configuration each output reinforces its input. Thus, when all other data sources to the two sets of bus lines are at high impedance, each set of bus lines will remain at its last state.

The -1 versions of the SN74ALS651 through SN74ALS654 are identical to the standard versions except that the recommended maximum I_{OL} is increased to 48 milliamperes. There are no -1 versions of the SN54ALS651 through SN54ALS654.

The SN54' family is characterized for operation over the full military temperature range of −55°C to 125°C. The SN74' family is characterized for operation from 0°C to 70°C.

This document contains information on products in more than one phase of development. The status of each device is indicated on the page(s) specifying its electrical characteristics.

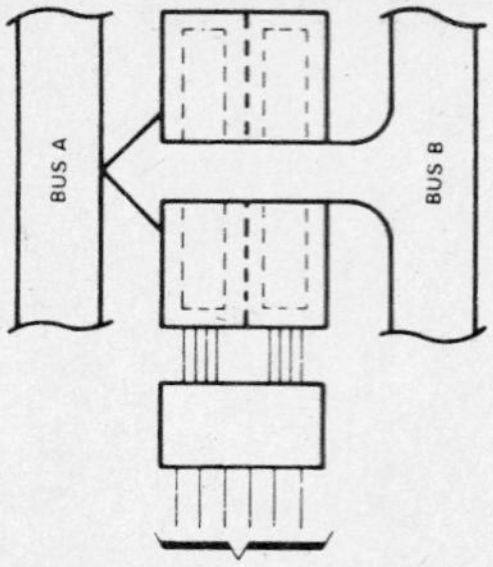
BUS A
BUS B

GAB	$\overline{G}BA$	CAB	CBA	SAB	SBA
L	L	X	X	X	L

REAL-TIME TRANSFER
BUS B TO BUS A

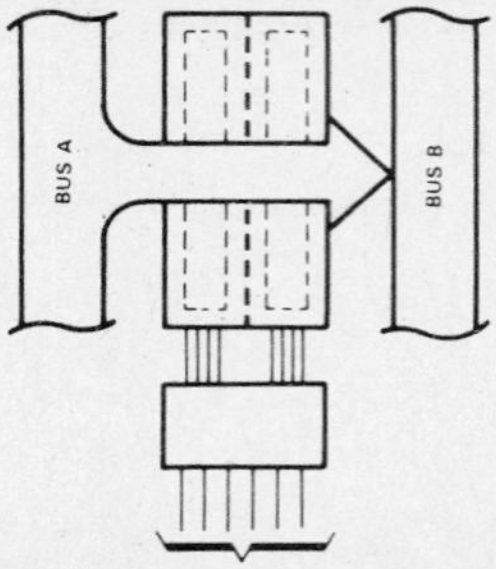
BUS A
BUS B

GAB	$\overline{G}BA$	CAB	CBA	SAB	SBA
H	H	X	X	L	X

REAL-TIME TRANSFER
BUS A TO BUS B

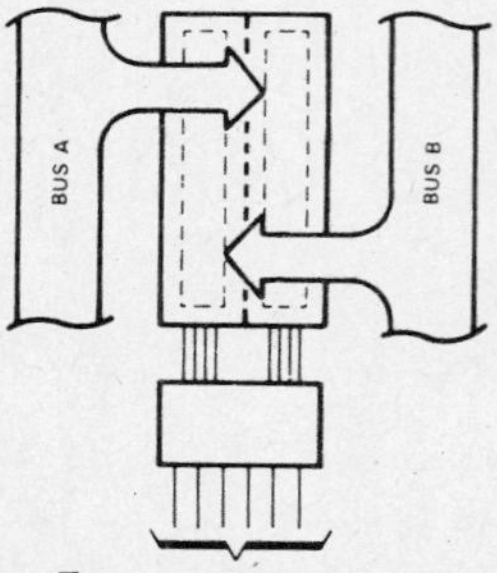
BUS A
BUS B

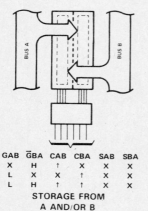

GAB	$\overline{G}BA$	CAB	CBA	SAB	SBA
X	H	↑	X	X	X
L	X	X	↑	X	X
L	H	↑	↑	X	X

STORAGE FROM
A AND/OR B

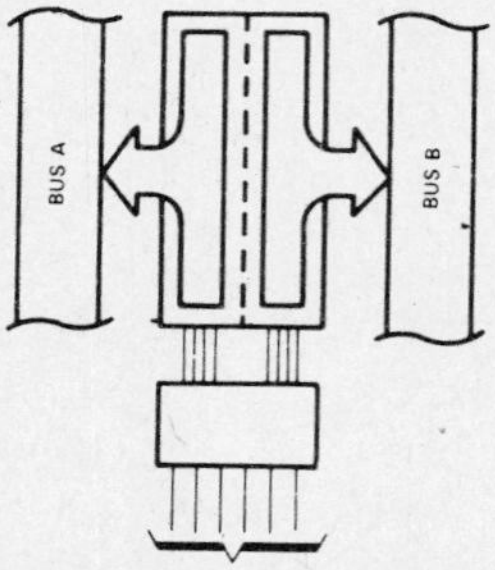
BUS A
BUS B

GAB	$\overline{G}BA$	CAB	CBA	SAB	SBA
H	L	H or L	H or L	H	H

TRANSFER
STORED DATA
TO A AND/OR B

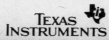

TEXAS INSTRUMENTS
POST OFFICE BOX 225012 • DALLAS, TEXAS 75265

FUNCTION TABLE

INPUTS						DATA I/O		OPERATION OR FUNCTION	
GAB	$\overline{GBA}$	CAB	CBA	SAB	SBA	A1 THRU A8	B1 THRU B8	'ALS651, 'ALS653 'AS651	'ALS652, 'ALS654 'AS652
L	H	H or L	H or L	X	X	Input	Input	Isolation	Isolation
L	H	↑	↑	X	X			Store A and B Data	Store A and B Data
X	H	↑	H or L	X	X	Input	Unspecified†	Store A, Hold B	Store A, Hold B
H	H	↑	↑	X‡	X	Input	Output	Store A in both registers	Store A in both registers
L	X	H or L	↑	X	X	Unspecified†	Input	Hold A, Store B	Hold A, Store B
L	L	↑	↑	X	X‡	Output	Input	Store B in both registers	Store B in both registers
L	L	X	X	X	L	Output	Input	Real-Time $\overline{B}$ Data to A Bus	Real-Time B Data to A Bus
L	L	X	H or L	X	H			Stored $\overline{B}$ Data to A Bus	Stored B Data to A Bus
H	H	X	X	L	X	Input	Output	Real-Time $\overline{A}$ Data to B Bus	Real-Time A Data to B Bus
H	H	H or L	X	H	X			Stored $\overline{A}$ Data to B Bus	Stored A Data to B Bus
H	L	H or L	H or L	H	H	Output	Output	Stored $\overline{A}$ Data to B Bus and Stored $\overline{B}$ Data to A Bus	Stored A Data to B Bus and Stored B Data to A Bus

†The data output functions may be enabled or disabled by various signals at the GAB or $\overline{GBA}$ inputs. Data input functions are always enabled, i.e., data at the bus pins will be stored on every low-to-high transition on the clock inputs.
‡Select control = L: clocks can occur simultaneously.
Select control = H: clocks must be staggered in order to load both registers.

logic diagrams (positive logic)

'ALS651, 'AS651, 'ALS653

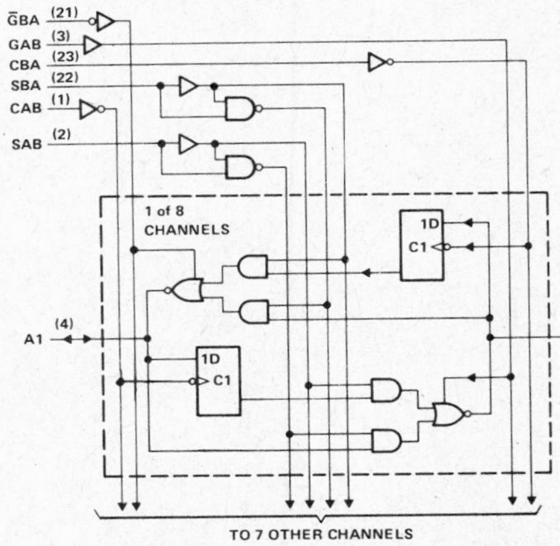
$\overline{GBA}$ (21)
GAB (3)
CBA (23)
SBA (22)
CAB (1)
SAB (2)
1 of 8 CHANNELS
1D
C1
A1 (4)
(20) B1
TO 7 OTHER CHANNELS

'ALS652, 'AS652, 'ALS654

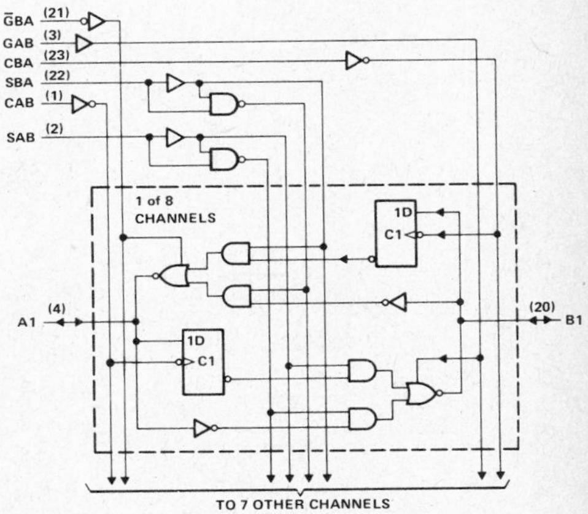
$\overline{GBA}$ (21)
GAB (3)
CBA (23)
SBA (22)
CAB (1)
SAB (2)
1 of 8 CHANNELS
1D
C1
A1 (4)
(20) B1
TO 7 OTHER CHANNELS

Pin numbers shown are for DW, JT, and NT packages.

2 LSI Devices

logic symbols†

'ALS651, 'AS651

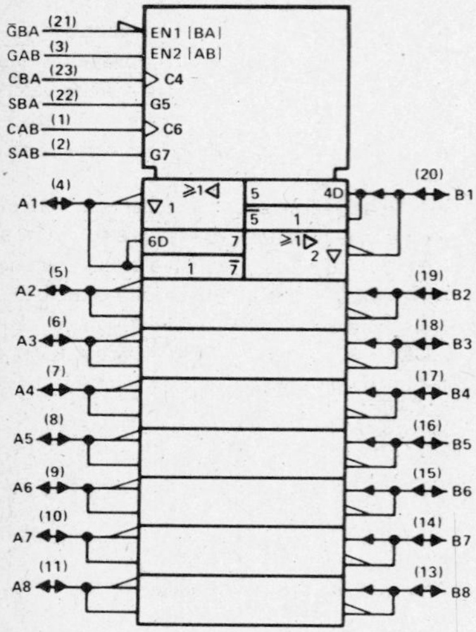
ḠBA (21)
GAB (3)
CBA (23)
SBA (22)
CAB (1)
SAB (2)
EN1 [BA]
EN2 [AB]
C4
G5
C6
G7
A1 (4)
A2 (5)
A3 (6)
A4 (7)
A5 (8)
A6 (9)
A7 (10)
A8 (11)
B1 (20)
B2 (19)
B3 (18)
B4 (17)
B5 (16)
B6 (15)
B7 (14)
B8 (13)
4D
6D

'ALS652, 'AS652

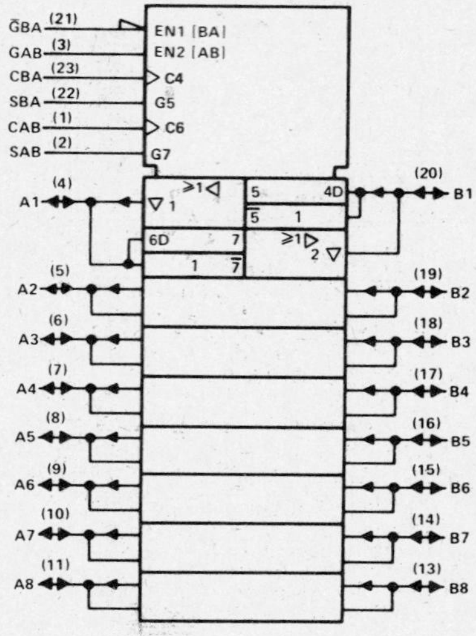
ḠBA (21)
GAB (3)
CBA (23)
SBA (22)
CAB (1)
SAB (2)
EN1 [BA]
EN2 [AB]
C4
G5
C6
G7
A1 (4)
A2 (5)
A3 (6)
A4 (7)
A5 (8)
A6 (9)
A7 (10)
A8 (11)
B1 (20)
B2 (19)
B3 (18)
B4 (17)
B5 (16)
B6 (15)
B7 (14)
B8 (13)
4D
6D

'ALS653

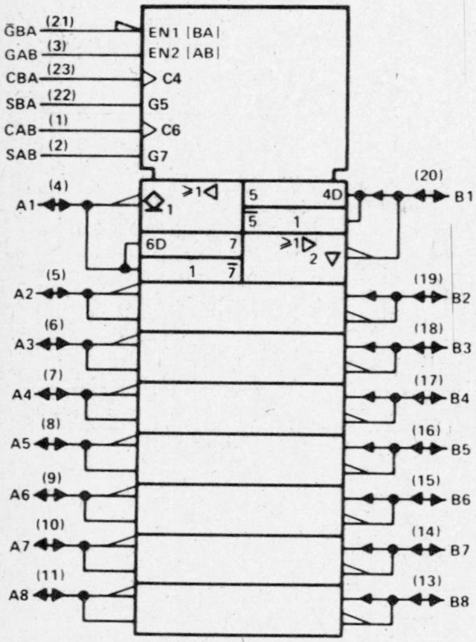
ḠBA (21)
GAB (3)
CBA (23)
SBA (22)
CAB (1)
SAB (2)
EN1 [BA]
EN2 [AB]
C4
G5
C6
G7
A1 (4)
A2 (5)
A3 (6)
A4 (7)
A5 (8)
A6 (9)
A7 (10)
A8 (11)
B1 (20)
B2 (19)
B3 (18)
B4 (17)
B5 (16)
B6 (15)
B7 (14)
B8 (13)
4D
6D

'ALS654

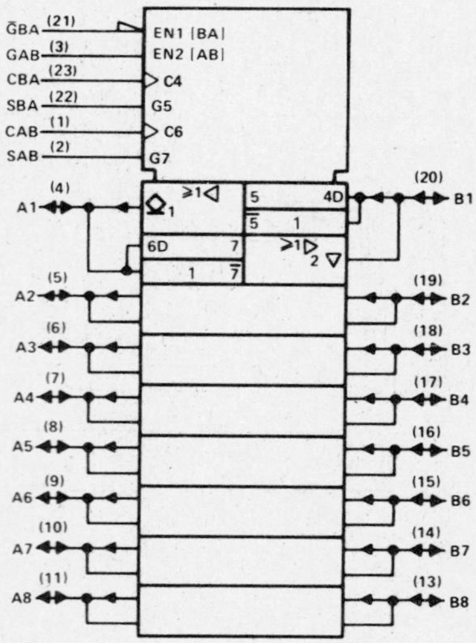
ḠBA (21)
GAB (3)
CBA (23)
SBA (22)
CAB (1)
SAB (2)
EN1 [BA]
EN2 [AB]
C4
G5
C6
G7
A1 (4)
A2 (5)
A3 (6)
A4 (7)
A5 (8)
A6 (9)
A7 (10)
A8 (11)
B1 (20)
B2 (19)
B3 (18)
B4 (17)
B5 (16)
B6 (15)
B7 (14)
B8 (13)
4D
6D

†These symbols are in accordance with ANSI/IEEE Std 91-1984 and IEC Publication 617-12.
Pin numbers shown are for DW, JT, and NT packages.

TEXAS INSTRUMENTS
POST OFFICE BOX 225012 • DALLAS, TEXAS 75265

absolute maximum ratings over operating free-air temperature range (unless otherwise noted)

Supply voltage, V_{CC} . . . . 7 V
Input voltage: Control inputs . . . . 7 V
I/O ports . . . . 5.5 V
Operating free-air temperature range: SN54ALS651, SN54ALS652 . . . . −55 °C to 125 °C
SN74ALS651, SN74ALS652 . . . . 0 °C to 70 °C
Storage temperature range . . . . −65 °C to 150 °C

recommended operating conditions

			SN54ALS651 SN54ALS652			SN74ALS651 SN74ALS652			UNIT
			MIN	NOM	MAX	MIN	NOM	MAX	
V_{CC}	Supply voltage		4.5	5	5.5	4.5	5	5.5	V
V_{IH}	High-level input voltage		2			2			V
V_{IL}	Low-level input voltage				0.8			0.8	V
I_{OH}	High-level output current				−12			−15	mA
I_{OL}	Low-level output current				12			24	mA
								48†	
f_{clock}	Clock frequency		0		35	0		40	MHz
t_w	Pulse duration	CBA or CAB high	14.5			12.5			ns
		CBA or CAB low	14.5			12.5			
t_{su}	Setup time before CAB↑ or CBA↑	A or B	15			10			ns
t_h	Hold time after CAB↑ or CBA↑	A or B	5			0			ns
T_A	Operating free-air temperature		−55		125	0		70	°C

† The extended condition applies if V_{CC} is maintained between 4.75 V and 5.25 V. The 48-mA limit applies for the SN74ALS651−1 and SN74ALS652−1 only.

electrical characteristics over recommended operating free-air temperature range (unless otherwise noted)

PARAMETER		TEST CONDITIONS		SN54ALS651 SN54ALS652			SN74ALS651 SN74ALS652			UNIT
				MIN	TYP‡	MAX	MIN	TYP‡	MAX	
V_{IK}		V_{CC} = 4.5 V,	I_I = −18 mA			−1.2			−1.2	V
V_{OH}		V_{CC} = 4.5 V to 5.5 V,	I_{OH} = −0.4 mA	V_{CC}−2			V_{CC}−2			V
		V_{CC} = 4.5 V,	I_{OH} = −3 mA	2.4	3.2		2.4	3.2		
		V_{CC} = 4.5 V,	I_{OH} = −12 mA	2						
		V_{CC} = 4.5 V,	I_{OH} = −15 mA				2			
V_{OL}		V_{CC} = 4.5 V,	I_{OL} = 12 mA		0.25	0.4		0.25	0.4	V
		V_{CC} = 4.5 V, (I_{OL} = 48 mA for −1 versions)	I_{OL} = 24 mA					0.35	0.5	
I_I	Control inputs	V_{CC} = 5.5 V,	V_I = 7 V			0.1			0.1	mA
	A or B ports	V_{CC} = 5.5 V,	V_I = 5.5 V			0.1			0.1	
I_{IH}	Control inputs	V_{CC} = 5.5 V,	V_I = 2.7 V			20			20	μA
	A or B ports§					20			20	
I_{IL}	Control inputs	V_{CC} = 5.5 V,	V_I = 0.4 V			−0.2			−0.2	mA
	A or B ports§					−0.2			−0.2	
I_O¶		V_{CC} = 5.5 V,	V_O = 2.25 V	−30		−112	−30		−112	mA
I_{CC}	'ALS651	V_{CC} = 5.5 V	Outputs high		42	68		42	68	mA
			Outputs low		52	82		52	82	
			Outputs disabled		52	82		52	82	
	'ALS652		Outputs high		47	76		47	76	
			Outputs low		55	88		55	88	
			Outputs disabled		55	88		55	88	

‡ All typical values are at V_{CC} = 5 V, T_A = 25 °C.
§ For I/O ports, the parameters I_{IH} and I_{IL} include the off-state output current.
¶ The output conditions have been chosen to produce a current that closely approximates one half of the true short-circuit output current, I_{OS}.

'ALS651 switching characteristics (see Note 1)

PARAMETER	FROM (INPUT)	TO (OUTPUT)	V_{CC} = 5 V, C_L = 50 pF, R1 = 500 Ω, R2 = 500 Ω, T_A = 25°C			V_{CC} = 4.5 V to 5.5 V, C_L = 50 pF, R1 = 500 Ω, R2 = 500 Ω, T_A = MIN to MAX				UNIT
			'ALS651			SN54ALS651		SN74ALS651		
			MIN	TYP	MAX	MIN	MAX	MIN	MAX	
f_{max}				50		35		40		MHz
t_{PLH}	CBA or CAB	A or B		20	27	10	38	10	32	ns
t_{PHL}				11	15	5	21	5	17	
t_{PLH}	A or B	B or A		9	13	4	20	4	18	ns
t_{PHL}				5	8	2	12	2	10	
t_{PLH}	SBA or SAB† (with A or B high)	A or B		24	31	13	45	13	38	ns
t_{PHL}				13	18	7	25	7	21	
t_{PLH}	SBA or SAB† (with A or B low)	A or B		15	20	8	30	8	25	ns
t_{PHL}				13	18	7	25	7	21	
t_{PZH}	$\overline{G}$BA	A		12	16	5	22	5	20	ns
t_{PZL}				11	15	5	21	5	18	
t_{PHZ}	$\overline{G}$BA	A		4	7	2	10	2	9	ns
t_{PLZ}				7	10	3	16	3	12	
t_{PZH}	GAB	B		14	19	7	25	7	22	ns
t_{PZL}				13	18	7	25	7	21	
t_{PHZ}	GAB	B		5	10	2	14	2	12	ns
t_{PLZ}				7	10	2	20	2	14	

'ALS652 switching characteristics (see Note 1)

PARAMETER	FROM (INPUT)	TO (OUTPUT)	V_{CC} = 5 V, C_L = 50 pF, R1 = 500 Ω, R2 = 500 Ω, T_A = 25°C			V_{CC} = 4.5 V to 5.5 V, C_L = 50 pF, R1 = 500 Ω, R2 = 500 Ω, T_A = MIN to MAX				UNIT
			'ALS652			SN54ALS652		SN74ALS652		
			MIN	TYP	MAX	MIN	MAX	MIN	MAX	
f_{max}				50		35		40		MHz
t_{PLH}	CBA or CAB	A or B		20	25	10	35	10	30	ns
t_{PHL}				11	15	5	20	5	17	
t_{PLH}	A or B	B or A		11	15	5	20	5	18	ns
t_{PHL}				8	10	3	15	3	12	
t_{PLH}	SBA or SAB† (with A or B high)	A or B		24	32	15	40	15	35	ns
t_{PHL}				13	17	6	23	6	20	
t_{PLH}	SBA or SAB† (with A or B low)	A or B		17	22	8	30	8	25	ns
t_{PHL}				13	17	5	24	5	20	
t_{PZH}	$\overline{G}$BA	A		10	15	3	20	3	17	ns
t_{PZL}				10	14	5	22	5	18	
t_{PHZ}	$\overline{G}$BA	A		6	8	1	12	1	10	ns
t_{PLZ}				10	13	2	20	2	16	
t_{PZH}	GAB	B		15	20	8	25	8	22	ns
t_{PZL}				12	16	6	21	6	18	
t_{PHZ}	GAB	B		6	8	1	12	1	10	ns
t_{PLZ}				10	13	2	21	2	16	

† These parameters are measured with the internal output state of the storage register opposite to that of the bus input.

NOTE 1: Load circuit and voltage waveforms are shown in Section 1.

2 LSI Devices

TEXAS INSTRUMENTS
POST OFFICE BOX 225012 • DALLAS, TEXAS 75265

absolute maximum ratings over operating free-air temperature range (unless otherwise noted)

Supply voltage, V_{CC} . . . . 7 V
Input voltage: All inputs and A I/O ports . . . . 7 V
B I/O ports . . . . 5.5 V
Operating free-air temperature range: SN54ALS653, SN54ALS654 . . . . −55 °C to 125 °C
SN74ALS653, SN74ALS654 . . . . 0 °C to 70 °C
Storage temperature range . . . . −65 °C to 150 °C

recommended operating conditions

			SN54ALS653 SN54ALS654			SN74ALS653 SN74ALS654			UNIT
			MIN	NOM	MAX	MIN	NOM	MAX	
V_{CC}	Supply voltage		4.5	5	5.5	4.5	5	5.5	V
V_{IH}	High-level input voltage		2			2			V
V_{IL}	Low-level input voltage				0.8			0.8	V
V_{OH}	High-level output voltage	A ports			5.5			5.5	V
I_{OH}	High-level output current	B ports			−12			−15	mA
I_{OL}	Low-level output current				12			24	mA
								48†	
f_{clock}	Clock frequency								MHz
t_w	Pulse duration	CBA or CAB high							ns
		CBA or CAB low							
t_{su}	Setup time before CAB↑ or CBA↑	A or B							ns
t_h	Hold time after CAB↑ or CBA↑	A or B							ns
T_A	Operating free-air temperature		−55		125	0		70	°C

† The extended condition applies if V_{CC} is maintained between 4.75 V and 5.25 V. The 48-mA limit applies for the SN74ALS653−1 and SN74ALS654−1 only.

2

LSI Devices

electrical characteristics over recommended operating free-air temperature range (unless otherwise noted)

PARAMETER		TEST CONDITIONS		SN54ALS653 SN54ALS654 MIN	TYP†	MAX	SN74ALS653 SN74ALS654 MIN	TYP†	MAX	UNIT
V_{IK}		V_{CC} = 4.5 V,	I_I = −18 mA			−1.5			−1.5	V
V_{OH}	B ports	V_{CC} = 4.5 V to 5.5 V,	I_{OH} = −0.4 mA	V_{CC}−2			V_{CC}−2			V
		V_{CC} = 4.5 V,	I_{OH} = −3 mA	2.4	3.2		2.4	3.2		
		V_{CC} = 4.5 V,	I_{OH} = −12 mA	2						
		V_{CC} = 4.5 V,	I_{OH} = −15 mA				2			
I_{OH}	A ports	V_{CC} = 4.5 V,	V_{OH} = 5.5 V			0.1			0.1	mA
V_{OL}		V_{CC} = 4.5 V,	I_{OL} = 12 mA		0.25	0.4		0.25	0.4	V
		V_{CC} = 4.75 V, (I_{OL} = 48 mA for −1 versions)	I_{OL} = 24 mA					0.35	0.5	
I_I	Control inputs	V_{CC} = 5.5 V,	V_I = 7 V			0.1			0.1	mA
	A or B ports	V_{CC} = 5.5 V,	V_I = 5.5 V			0.1			0.1	
I_{IH}	Control inputs	V_{CC} = 5.5 V,	V_I = 2.7 V			20			20	μA
	A or B ports‡					20			20	
I_{IL}	Control inputs	V_{CC} = 5.5 V,	V_I = 0.4 V			−0.1			−0.1	mA
	A or B ports‡					−0.2			−0.2	
I_O¶	B ports	V_{CC} = 5.5 V,	V_O = 2.25 V	−30		−112	−30		−112	mA
I_{CC}	'ALS653	V_{CC} = 5.5 V	Outputs high		52			52		mA
			Outputs low		57			57		
			Outputs disabled		58			58		
	'ALS654		Outputs high		60			60		
			Outputs low		68			68		
			Outputs disabled		68			68		

† All typical values are at V_{CC} = 5 V, T_A = 25°C.
‡ For I/P ports, the parameters I_{IH} and I_{IL} include the off-state output current.
§ The output conditions have been chosen to produce a current that closely approximates one half of the true short-circuit output current, I_{OS}.

2 LSI Devices

'ALS653 switching characteristics (see Note 1)

PARAMETER	FROM (INPUT)	TO (OUTPUT)	V_{CC} = 4.5 V to 5.5 V, C_L = 50 pF, R_L = 680 Ω, (A outputs) R1 = R2 = 500 Ω, (B outputs) T_A = MIN to MAX						UNIT
			SN54ALS653			SN74ALS653			
			MIN	TYP†	MAX	MIN	TYP†	MAX	
f_{max}									MHz
t_{PLH}	CBA	A		24			24		ns
t_{PHL}				15			15		
t_{PLH}	CAB	B		11			11		ns
t_{PHL}				13			13		
t_{PLH}	A	B		10			10		ns
t_{PHL}				12			12		
t_{PLH}	B	A		24			24		ns
t_{PHL}				10			10		
t_{PLH}	SBA‡ (with B high)	A		26			26		ns
t_{PHL}				15			15		
t_{PLH}	SBA‡ (with B low)	A		26			26		ns
t_{PHL}				15			15		
t_{PLH}	SAB‡ (with A high)	B		16			16		ns
t_{PHL}				16			16		
t_{PLH}	SAB‡ (with A low)	B		15			15		ns
t_{PHL}				15			15		
t_{PLH}	$\overline{G}$BA	A		24			24		ns
t_{PHL}				17			17		
t_{PZH}	GAB	B		19			19		ns
t_{PZL}				22			22		
t_{PHZ}	GAB	B		12			12		ns
t_{PLZ}				14			14		

† All typical values are at V_{CC} = 5 V, T_A = 25 °C.
‡ These parameters are measured with the internal output state of the storage register opposite to that of the bus input.
NOTE 1: Load circuit and voltage waveforms are shown in Section 1.

Additional information on these products can be obtained from the factory as it becomes available.

2
LSI Devices

'ALS654 switching characteristics (see Note 1)

PARAMETER	FROM (INPUT)	TO (OUTPUT)	V_{CC} = 4.5 V to 5.5 V, C_L = 50 pF, R_L = 680 Ω, (A outputs) R1 = R2 = 500 Ω, (B outputs) T_A = MIN to MAX						UNIT
			SN54ALS654			SN74ALS654			
			MIN	TYP†	MAX	MIN	TYP†	MAX	
f_{max}									MHz
t_{PLH}	CBA	A		24			24		ns
t_{PHL}				15			15		
t_{PLH}	CAB	B		11			11		ns
t_{PHL}				13			13		
t_{PLH}	A	B		8			8		ns
t_{PHL}				8			8		
t_{PLH}	B	A		24			24		ns
t_{PHL}				10			10		
t_{PLH}	SBA‡ (with B high)	A		26			26		ns
t_{PHL}				15			15		
t_{PLH}	SBA‡ (with B low)	A		26			26		ns
t_{PHL}				15			15		
t_{PLH}	SBA‡ (with A high)	B		16			16		ns
t_{PHL}				16			16		
t_{PLH}	SAB‡ (with A low)	B		15			15		ns
t_{PHL}				12			12		
t_{PLH}	$\overline{G}$BA	A		24			24		ns
t_{PHL}				17			17		
t_{PZH}	GAB	B		19			19		ns
t_{PZL}				22			22		
t_{PHZ}	GAB	B		12			12		ns
t_{PLZ}				14			14		

† All typical values are at V_{CC} = 5 V, T_A = 25 °C.
‡ These parameters are measured with the internal output state of the storage register opposite to that of the bus input.
NOTE 1: Load circuit and voltage waveforms are shown in Section 1.

Additional information on these products can be obtained from the factory as it becomes available.

TEXAS INSTRUMENTS
POST OFFICE BOX 225012 • DALLAS, TEXAS 75265

absolute maximum ratings over operating free-air temperature range (unless otherwise noted)

Supply voltage, V_{CC} . . . . 7 V
Input voltage: Control inputs . . . . 7 V
I/O ports . . . . 5.5 V
Operating free-air temperature range: SN54AS651, SN54AS652 . . . . −55 °C to 125 °C
SN74AS651, SN74AS652 . . . . 0 °C to 70 °C
Storage temperature range . . . . −65 °C to 150 °C

recommended operating conditions

			SN54AS651 SN54AS652			SN74AS651 SN74AS652			UNIT
			MIN	NOM	MAX	MIN	NOM	MAX	
V_{CC}	Supply voltage		4.5	5	5.5	4.5	5	5.5	V
V_{IH}	High-level input voltage		2			2			V
V_{IL}	Low-level input voltage				0.8			0.8	V
I_{OH}	High-level output current				−12			−15	mA
I_{OL}	Low-level output current				32			48	mA
f_{clock}			0		75	0		90	MHz
t_w	Pulse duration	CBA or CAB high	6			5			ns
		CBA or CAB low	7			6			
t_{su}	Setup time before CAB↑ or CBA↑	A or B	7			6			ns
t_h	Hold time after CAB↑ or CBA↑	A or B	0			0			ns
T_A	Operating free-air temperature		−55		125	0		70	°C

electrical characteristics over recommended operating free-air temperature range (unless otherwise noted)

PARAMETER		TEST CONDITIONS			SN54AS651 SN54AS652			SN74AS651 SN74AS652			UNIT
					MIN	TYP†	MAX	MIN	TYP†	MAX	
V_{IK}		V_{CC} = 4.5 V,	I_I = −18 mA				−1.2			−1.2	V
V_{OH}		V_{CC} = 4.5 V to 5.5 V,	I_{OH} = −2 mA		V_{CC}−2			V_{CC}−2			V
		V_{CC} = 4.5 V,	I_{OH} = −3 mA		2.4	3.2		2.4	3.2		
		V_{CC} = 4.5 V,	I_{OH} = −12 mA		2						
		V_{CC} = 4.5 V,	I_{OH} = −15 mA					2			
V_{OL}		V_{CC} = 4.5 V,	I_{OL} = 32 mA			0.25	0.50				V
		V_{CC} = 4.5 V,	I_{OL} = 48 mA						0.35	0.50	
I_I	Control inputs	V_{CC} = 5.5 V,	V_I = 7 V				0.1			0.1	mA
	A or B ports	V_{CC} = 5.5 V,	V_I = 5.5 V				0.1			0.1	
I_{IH}	Control inputs	V_{CC} = 5.5 V,	V_I = 2.7 V				20			20	μA
	A or B ports‡						70			70	
I_{IL}	Control inputs	V_{CC} = 5.5 V,	V_I = 0.4 V				−0.5			−0.5	mA
	A or B ports‡						−0.75			−0.75	
I_O§		V_{CC} = 5.5 V,	V_O = 2.25 V		−30		−112	−30		−112	mA
I_{CC}	'AS651	V_{CC} = 5.5 V		Outputs high		110	185		110	185	mA
				Outputs low		120	195		120	195	
				Outputs disabled		130	195		130	195	
	'AS652			Outputs high		120	195		120	195	
				Outputs low		130	211		130	211	
				Outputs disabled		130	211		130	211	

†All typical values are at V_{CC} = 5 V, T_A = 25°C.
‡For I/O ports, the parameters I_{IH} and I_{IL} include the off-state output current.
§The output conditions have been chosen to produce a current that closely approximates one half of the true short-circuit output current, I_{OS}

2

LSI Devices

'AS651 switching characteristics (see Note 1)

PARAMETER	FROM (INPUT)	TO (OUTPUT)	V_{CC} = 4.5 V to 5.5 V, C_L = 50 pF, R1 = 500 Ω, R2 = 500 Ω, T_A = MIN to MAX				UNIT
			SN54AS651		SN74AS651		
			MIN	MAX	MIN	MAX	
f_{max}			75		90		MHz
t_{PLH}	CBA or CAB	A or B	2	9.5	2	8.5	ns
t_{PHL}			2	10	2	9	
t_{PLH}	A or B	B or A	2	9	2	8	ns
t_{PHL}			1	8	1	7	
t_{PLH}	SBA or SAB†	A or B	2	12	2	11	ns
t_{PHL}			2	10	2	9	
t_{PZH}	$\overline{G}$BA	A	2	11	2	10	ns
t_{PZL}			3	18	3	16	
t_{PHZ}	$\overline{G}$BA	A	2	10	2	9	ns
t_{PLZ}			2	10	2	9	
t_{PZH}	GAB	B	3	12	3	11	ns
t_{PZL}			3	20	3	16	
t_{PHZ}	GAB	B	2	11	2	10	ns
t_{PLZ}			2	12	2	11	

'AS652 switching characteristics (see Note 1)

PARAMETER	FROM (INPUT)	TO (OUTPUT)	V_{CC} = 4.5 V to 5.5 V, C_L = 50 pF, R1 = 500 Ω, R2 = 500 Ω, T_A = MIN to MAX				UNIT
			SN54AS652		SN74AS652		
			MIN	MAX	MIN	MAX	
f_{max}			75		90		MHz
t_{PLH}	CBA or CAB	A or B	2	9.5	2	8.5	ns
t_{PHL}			2	10	2	9	
t_{PLH}	A or B	B or A	2	11	2	9	ns
t_{PHL}			1	8	1	7	
t_{PLH}	SBA or SAB†	A or B	2	12	2	11	ns
t_{PHL}			2	10	2	9	
t_{PZH}	$\overline{G}$BA	A	2	11	2	10	ns
t_{PZL}			3	18	3	16	
t_{PHZ}	$\overline{G}$BA	A	2	10	2	9	ns
t_{PLZ}			2	10	2	9	
t_{PZH}	GAB	B	3	12	3	11	ns
t_{PZL}			3	20	3	16	
t_{PHZ}	GAB	B	2	11	2	10	ns
t_{PLZ}			2	12	2	11	

† These parameters are measured with the internal output state of the storage register opposite to that of the bus input.

NOTE 1: Load circuit and voltage waveforms are shown in Section 1.

TEXAS INSTRUMENTS
POST OFFICE BOX 225012 • DALLAS, TEXAS 75265

8-BIT D-TYPE TRANSPARENT READ-BACK LATCHES WITH 3-STATE OUTPUTS

D2855, JUNE 1984—REVISED DECEMBER 1985

- **3-State I/O-Type Read-Back Inputs**
- **Bus-Structured Pinout**
- **Choice of True or Inverting Logic**
  'ALS666 . . . True Outputs
  'ALS667 . . . Inverting Outputs
- **Preset and Clear Inputs**
- **Package Options Include Both Plastic and Ceramic Chip Carriers in Addition to Plastic and Ceramics DIPs**
- **Dependable Texas Instruments Quality and Reliability**

SN54ALS666 . . . JT PACKAGE
SN74ALS666 . . . DW OR NT PACKAGE
(TOP VIEW)

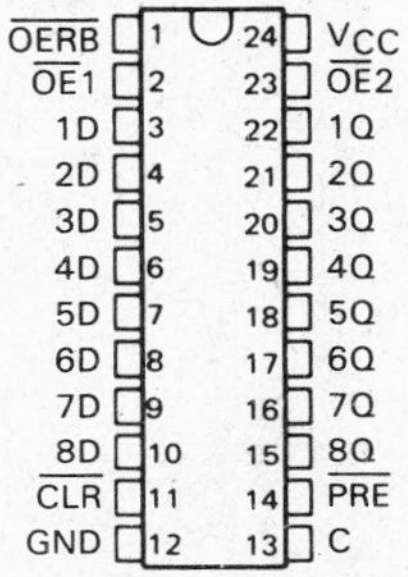
$\overline{OERB}$ 1
$\overline{OE}1$ 2
1D 3
2D 4
3D 5
4D 6
5D 7
6D 8
7D 9
8D 10
$\overline{CLR}$ 11
GND 12
24 V_{CC}
23 $\overline{OE}2$
22 1Q
21 2Q
20 3Q
19 4Q
18 5Q
17 6Q
16 7Q
15 8Q
14 $\overline{PRE}$
13 C

SN54ALS666 . . . FK PACKAGE
SN74ALS666 . . . FN PACKAGE
(TOP VIEW)

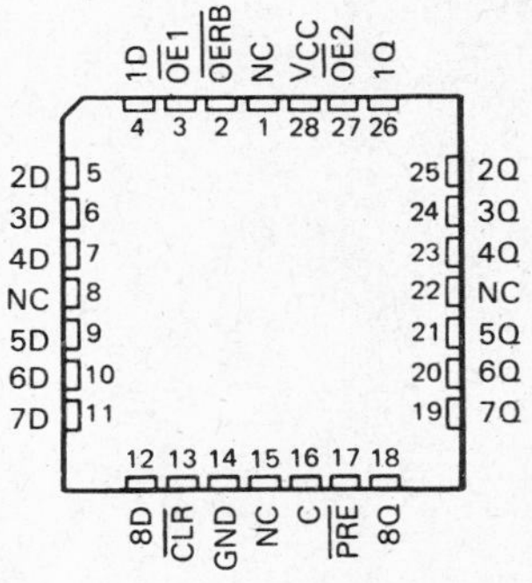
1D 4
$\overline{OE}1$ 3
$\overline{OERB}$ 2
NC 1
V_{CC} 28
$\overline{OE}2$ 27
1Q 26
2D 5
3D 6
4D 7
NC 8
5D 9
6D 10
7D 11
25 2Q
24 3Q
23 4Q
22 NC
21 5Q
20 6Q
19 7Q
12 8D
13 $\overline{CLR}$
14 GND
15 NC
16 C
17 $\overline{PRE}$
18 8Q

NC—No internal connection.

description

These 8-bit latches are designed specifically for storing the contents of the input data bus plus providing the capability of reading-back the stored data onto the input data bus. In addition, they provide a 3-state buffer type output and are easily utilized in bus-structured applications.

The eight latches of the 'ALS666 and 'ALS667 are transparent D-type. While the enable (C) is high, the Q outputs of the 'ALS666 will follow the data (D) inputs. On the 'ALS667, the $\overline{Q}$ outputs will provide the inverse of what is applied to its data (D) inputs. On both devices, the Q or $\overline{Q}$ output will be in the high-impedance state if either output control, $\overline{OE}1$ or $\overline{OE}2$, is at a high logic level.

Read-back is provided thru the read-back control input ($\overline{OERB}$). When $\overline{OERB}$ is taken low, the data present at the output of the data latches will be allowed to pass back onto the input data bus. When it is taken high, the output of the data latches will be isolated from the data (D) inputs. The read-back control does not affect the internal operation of the latches; however, caution should be exercised not to create a bus-conflict situation.

The SN54ALS666 and SN54ALS667 are characterized for operation over the full military temperature range of −55 °C to 125 °C. The SN74ALS666 and SN75ALS667 are characterized for operation from 0 °C to 70 °C.

SN54ALS667 . . . JT PACKAGE
SN74ALS667 . . . DW OR NT PACKAGE
(TOP VIEW)

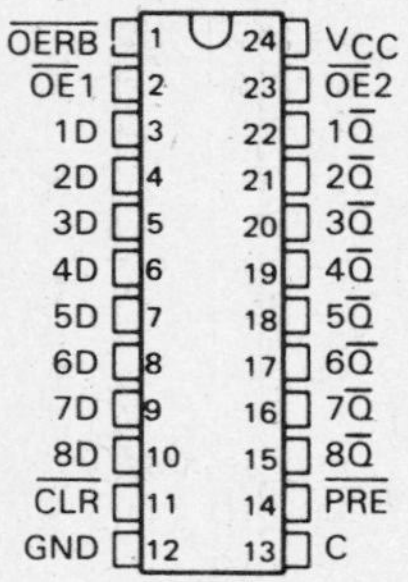
OERB 1 24 VCC
OE1 2 23 OE2
1D 3 22 1Q
2D 4 21 2Q
3D 5 20 3Q
4D 6 19 4Q
5D 7 18 5Q
6D 8 17 6Q
7D 9 16 7Q
8D 10 15 8Q
CLR 11 14 PRE
GND 12 13 C

SN54ALS667 . . . FK PACKAGE
SN74ALS667 . . . FN PACKAGE
(TOP VIEW)

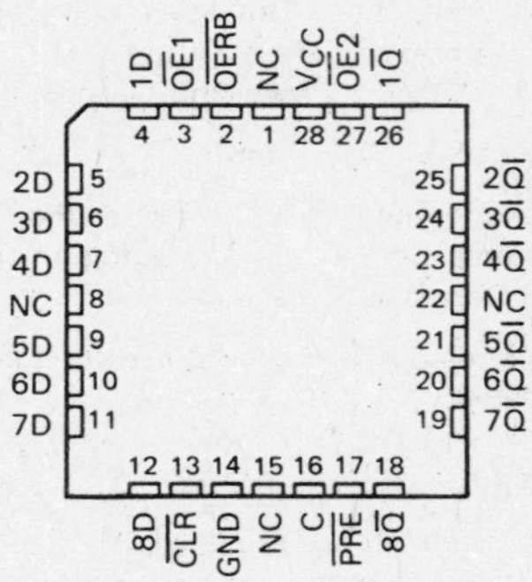
1D OE1 OERB NC VCC OE2 1Q
4 3 2 1 28 27 26
2D 5
3D 6
4D 7
NC 8
5D 9
6D 10
7D 11
25 2Q
24 3Q
23 4Q
22 NC
21 5Q
20 6Q
19 7Q
12 13 14 15 16 17 18
8D CLR GND NC C PRE 8Q

NC—No internal connection.

logic symbols†

'ALS666

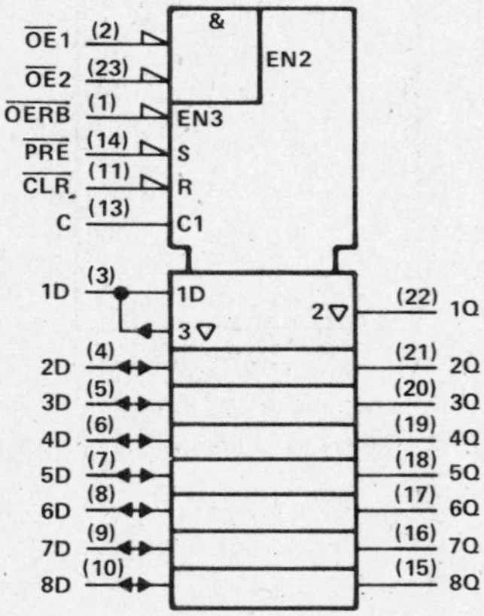
OE1 (2)
OE2 (23)
OERB (1)
PRE (14)
CLR (11)
C (13)
&
EN2
EN3
S
R
C1
1D (3) 1D 3▽ 2▽ (22) 1Q
2D (4) (21) 2Q
3D (5) (20) 3Q
4D (6) (19) 4Q
5D (7) (18) 5Q
6D (8) (17) 6Q
7D (9) (16) 7Q
8D (10) (15) 8Q

'ALS667

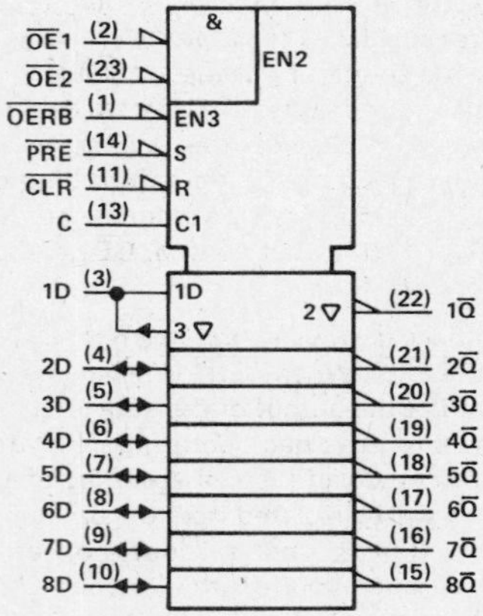
OE1 (2)
OE2 (23)
OERB (1)
PRE (14)
CLR (11)
C (13)
&
EN2
EN3
S
R
C1
1D (3) 1D 3▽ 2▽ (22) 1Q
2D (4) (21) 2Q
3D (5) (20) 3Q
4D (6) (19) 4Q
5D (7) (18) 5Q
6D (8) (17) 6Q
7D (9) (16) 7Q
8D (10) (15) 8Q

†These symbols are in accordance with ANSI/IEEE Std 91-1984 and IEC Publication 617-12.
Pin numbers shown are for DW, JT, and NT packages.

logic diagrams (positive logic)

'ALS666

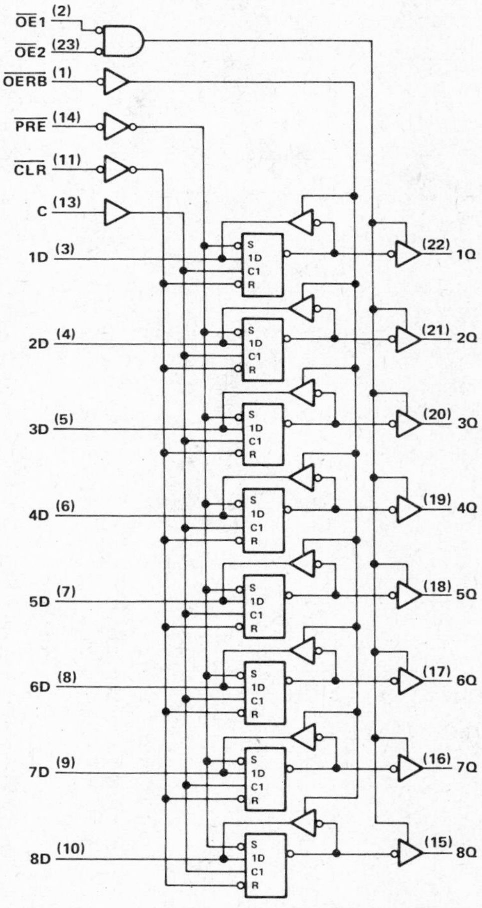
$\overline{\text{OE1}}$ (2)
$\overline{\text{OE2}}$ (23)
$\overline{\text{OERB}}$ (1)
$\overline{\text{PRE}}$ (14)
$\overline{\text{CLR}}$ (11)
C (13)
1D (3)
2D (4)
3D (5)
4D (6)
5D (7)
6D (8)
7D (9)
8D (10)
S
1D
C1
R
(22) 1Q
(21) 2Q
(20) 3Q
(19) 4Q
(18) 5Q
(17) 6Q
(16) 7Q
(15) 8Q

'ALS667

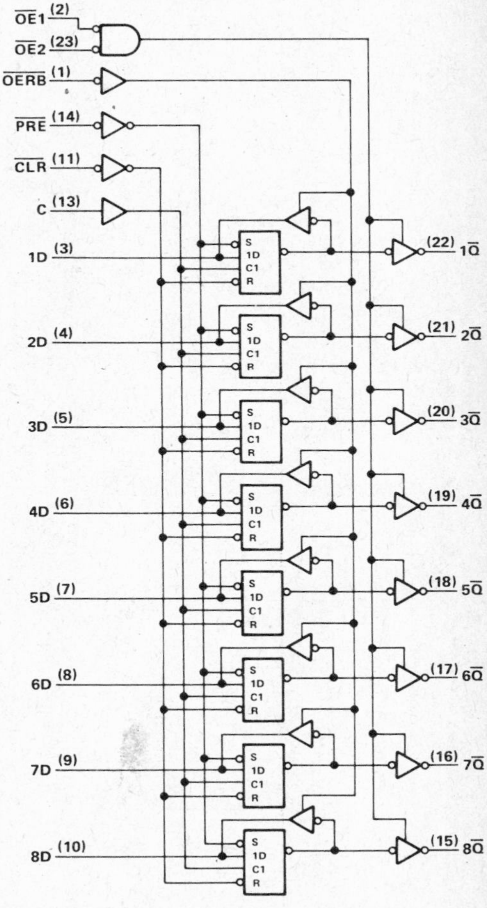
$\overline{\text{OE1}}$ (2)
$\overline{\text{OE2}}$ (23)
$\overline{\text{OERB}}$ (1)
$\overline{\text{PRE}}$ (14)
$\overline{\text{CLR}}$ (11)
C (13)
1D (3)
2D (4)
3D (5)
4D (6)
5D (7)
6D (8)
7D (9)
8D (10)
S
1D
C1
R
(22) $\overline{\text{1Q}}$
(21) $\overline{\text{2Q}}$
(20) $\overline{\text{3Q}}$
(19) $\overline{\text{4Q}}$
(18) $\overline{\text{5Q}}$
(17) $\overline{\text{6Q}}$
(16) $\overline{\text{7Q}}$
(15) $\overline{\text{8Q}}$

Pin numbers shown are for DW, JT, and NT packages.

timing diagram

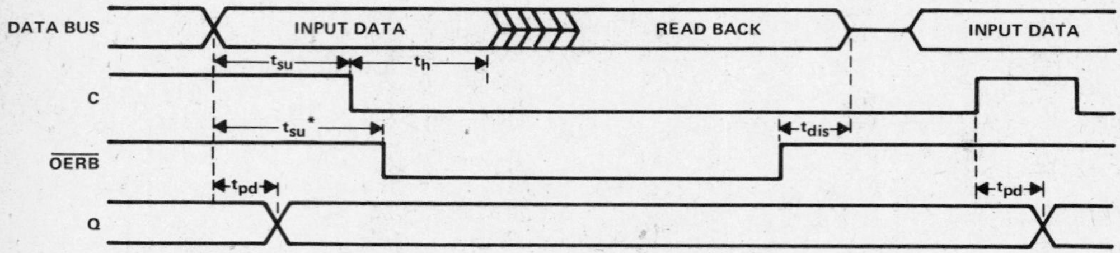
DATA BUS
INPUT DATA
READ BACK
INPUT DATA
t_{su}
t_h
C
t_{su}*
t_{dis}
OERB
t_{pd}
t_{pd}
Q

$\overline{CLR}$ = H, $\overline{PRE}$ = H, $\overline{OE1}$ = L, $\overline{OE2}$ = L

*This setup time ensures the readback circuit will not create a conflict on the input data bus.

absolute maximum ratings over operating free-air temperature range (unless otherwise noted)

Supply voltage, V_{CC} .... 7 V
Input voltage (all inputs except D input) .... 7 V
Voltage applied to D inputs and to disabled 3-state outputs .... 5.5 V
Operating free-air temperature range: SN54ALS666, SN54ALS667 .... −55°C to 125°C
SN74ALS666, SN74ALS667 .... 0°C to 70°C
Storage temperature range .... −65°C to 150°C

recommended operating conditions

			SN54ALS666 SN54ALS667 MIN	NOM	MAX	SN74ALS666 SN74ALS667 MIN	NOM	MAX	UNIT
V_{CC}	Supply voltage		4.5	5	5.5	4.5	5	5.5	V
V_{IH}	High-level input voltage		2			2			V
V_{IL}	Low-level input voltage				0.8			0.8	V
I_{OH}	High-level output current	Q			−1			−2.6	mA
		D			−0.4			−0.4	
I_{OL}	Load-level output current	Q			12			24	mA
		D			4			8	
t_w	Pulse duration	Enable C high	15			10			ns
		$\overline{CLR}$ low	10			10			
		$\overline{PRE}$ low	10			10			
t_{su}	Setup time	Data before C↓	15			10			ns
		Data before $\overline{OERB}$↓	15			10			
t_h	Hold time	Data after C↓	10			5			ns
T_A	Operating free-air temperature		−55		125	0		70	°C

2

LSI Devices

electrical characteristics over recommended operating free-air temperature range (unless otherwise noted)

PARAMETER		TEST CONDITIONS		SN54ALS666 SN54ALS667 MIN	TYP†	MAX	SN74ALS666 SN74ALS667 MIN	TYP†	MAX	UNIT
V_{IK}		V_{CC} = 4.5 V,	I_I = −18 mA			−1.2			−1.2	V
V_{OH}	All outputs	V_{CC} = 4.5 V to 5.5 V,	I_{OH} = −0.4 mA	$V_{CC}-2$			$V_{CC}-2$			V
	Q or $\overline{Q}$	V_{CC} = 4.5 V,	I_{OH} = −1 mA	2.4	3.3					
		V_{CC} = 4.5 V,	I_{OH} = −2.6 mA				2.4	3.2		
V_{OL}	D	V_{CC} = 4.5 V,	I_{OL} = 4 mA		0.25	0.4		0.25	0.4	V
		V_{CC} = 4.5 V,	I_{OL} = 8 mA					0.35	0.5	
	Q or $\overline{Q}$	V_{CC} = 4.5 V,	I_{OL} = 12 mA		0.25	0.4		0.25	0.4	
		V_{CC} = 4.5 V,	I_{OL} = 24 mA					0.35	0.5	
I_{OZH}	Q or $\overline{Q}$	V_{CC} = 5.5 V,	V_O = 2.7 V			20			20	μA
I_{OZL}		V_{CC} = 5.5 V,	V_O = 0.4 V			−20			−20	
I_I	D inputs	V_{CC} = 5.5 V,	V_I = 5.5 V			0.1			0.1	mA
	All others	V_{CC} = 5.5 V,	V = 7 V			0.1			0.1	
I_{IH}	D inputs‡	V_{CC} = 5.5 V,	V = 2.7 V			20			20	μA
	All others					20			20	
I_{IL}	D inputs‡	V_{CC} = 5.5 V,	V_I = 0.4 V			−0.1			−0.1	mA
	All others					−0.1			−0.1	
I_O§		V_{CC} = 5.5 V,	V_O = 2.25 V	−30		−112	−30		−112	mA
I_{CC}	'ALS666	V_{CC} = 5.5 V, $\overline{OERB}$ high	Q outputs high		25	50		25	50	mA
			Q outputs low		40	73		40	73	
			Q outputs disabled		30	55		30	55	
	'ALS667		$\overline{Q}$ outputs high		25	50		25	50	
			$\overline{Q}$ outputs low		45	79		45	79	
			$\overline{Q}$ outputs disabled		30	60		30	60	

† All typical values are at V_{CC} = 5 V, T_A = 25°C.
‡ For I/O ports, the parameters I_{IH} and I_{IL} include the off-state output current.
§ The output conditions have been chosen to produce a current that closely approximates one half the true short-circuit output currents, I_{OS}.

'ALS666 switching characteristics (see Figure 1)

PARAMETER	FROM (INPUT)	TO (OUTPUT)	V_{CC} = 5 V, C_L = 50 pF, T_A = 25°C			V_{CC} = 4.5 V to 5.5 V, C_L = 50 pF, T_A = MIN to MAX				UNIT
			'ALS666			SN54ALS666		SN74ALS666		
			MIN	TYP	MAX	MIN	MAX	MIN	MAX	
t_{PLH}	D	Q		7	10	3	18	3	14	ns
t_{PHL}				11	15	4	22	4	18	
t_{PLH}	C	Q		12	16	6	25	6	21	ns
t_{PHL}				16	21	8	32	8	27	
t_{PHL}	$\overline{CLR}$	Q		17	22	9	32	9	29	ns
t_{PHL}		D		17	24	11	36	11	32	
t_{PLH}	$\overline{PRE}$	Q		13	18	7	28	7	22	ns
t_{PHL}		D		17	22	9	35	9	28	
t_{en}	$\overline{OERB}$	D		11	17	4	25	4	21	ns
t_{dis}				6	11	1	18	1	14	
t_{en}	$\overline{OE}1$, $\overline{OE}2$	Q		11	17	4	25	4	21	ns
t_{dis}				6	11	1	18	1	14	

'ALS667 switching characteristics (see Figure 1)

PARAMETER	FROM (INPUT)	TO (OUTPUT)	V_{CC} = 5 V, C_L = 50 pF, T_A = 25°C			V_{CC} = 4.5 V to 5.5 V, C_L = 50 pF, T_A = MIN to MAX				UNIT
			'ALS667			SN54ALS667		SN74ALS667		
			MIN	TYP	MAX	MIN	MAX	MIN	MAX	
t_{PLH}	D	$\overline{Q}$		13	17	6	24	6	20	ns
t_{PHL}				9	13	4	18	4	15	
t_{PLH}	C	$\overline{Q}$		18	23	9	35	9	28	ns
t_{PHL}				14	19	7	27	7	22	
t_{PLH}	$\overline{CLR}$	$\overline{Q}$		14	19	7	28	7	24	ns
t_{PHL}		D		17	23	8	30	8	26	
t_{PHL}	$\overline{PRE}$	$\overline{Q}$		17	23	8	30	8	25	ns
t_{PLH}		D		18	25	9	35	9	28	
t_{en}	$\overline{OERB}$	D		11	17	4	25	4	21	ns
t_{dis}				6	11	1	20	1	14	
t_{en}	$\overline{OE}1$, $\overline{OE}2$	$\overline{Q}$		11	17	4	25	4	21	ns
t_{dis}				6	11	1	20	1	14	

t_{en} = t_{PZH} or t_{PZL}
t_{dis} = t_{PHZ} or t_{PLZ}

TEXAS INSTRUMENTS
POST OFFICE BOX 225012 • DALLAS, TEXAS 75265

PARAMETER MEASUREMENT INFORMATION

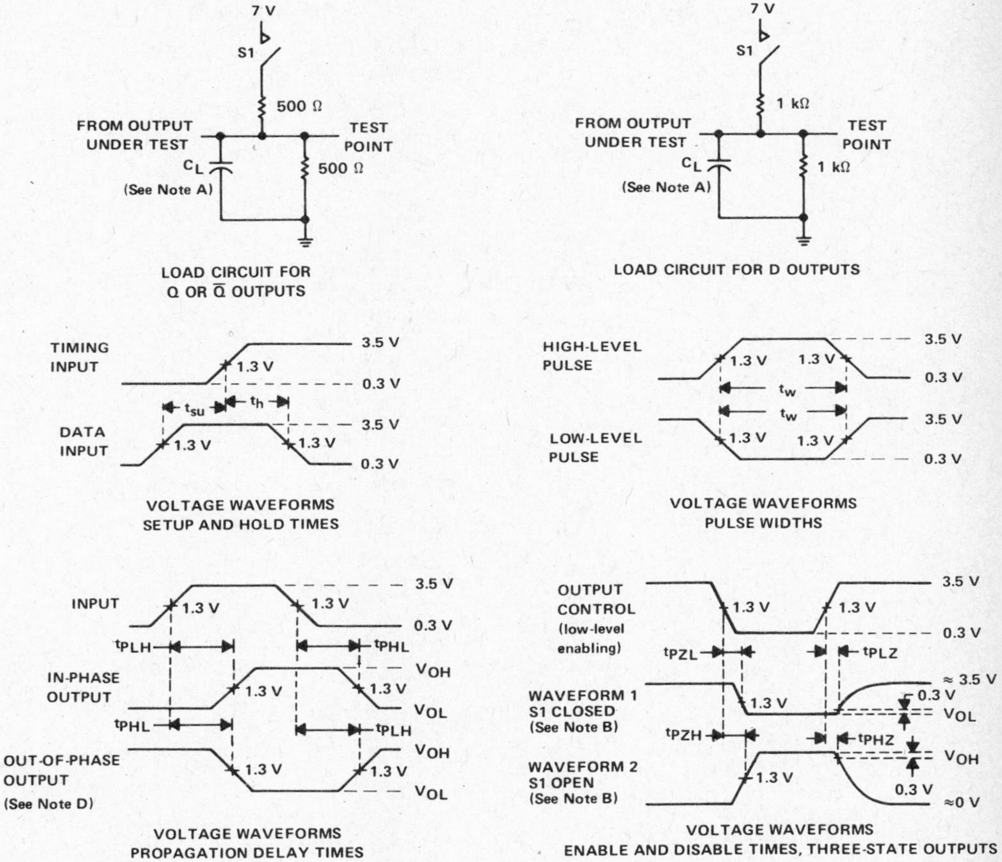
7 V
S1
500 Ω
FROM OUTPUT UNDER TEST
TEST POINT
CL (See Note A)
500 Ω
LOAD CIRCUIT FOR Q OR Q̄ OUTPUTS
7 V
S1
1 kΩ
FROM OUTPUT UNDER TEST
TEST POINT
CL (See Note A)
1 kΩ
LOAD CIRCUIT FOR D OUTPUTS
TIMING INPUT
DATA INPUT
3.5 V
0.3 V
1.3 V
tsu
th
VOLTAGE WAVEFORMS SETUP AND HOLD TIMES
HIGH-LEVEL PULSE
LOW-LEVEL PULSE
tw
VOLTAGE WAVEFORMS PULSE WIDTHS
INPUT
IN-PHASE OUTPUT
OUT-OF-PHASE OUTPUT (See Note D)
tPLH
tPHL
VOH
VOL
VOLTAGE WAVEFORMS PROPAGATION DELAY TIMES
OUTPUT CONTROL (low-level enabling)
WAVEFORM 1 S1 CLOSED (See Note B)
WAVEFORM 2 S1 OPEN (See Note B)
tPZL
tPLZ
tPZH
tPHZ
≈ 3.5 V
≈0 V
VOLTAGE WAVEFORMS ENABLE AND DISABLE TIMES, THREE-STATE OUTPUTS

NOTES: A. C_L includes probe and jig capacitance.

B. Waveform 1 is for an output with internal conditions such that the output is low except when disabled by the output control. Waveform 2 is for an output with internal conditions such that the output is high except when disabled by the output control.

C. All input pulses have the following characteristics: PRR $\leq$ 1 MHz, $t_r = t_f = 2$ ns, duty cycle = 50%.

D. When measuring propagation delay times of 3-state outputs, switch S1 is open.

FIGURE 1

D2825, DECEMBER 1983—REVISED JANUARY 1986

- **Functionally Equivalent to AMD's AM29821 and AM29822**
- **Provides Extra Data Width Necessary for Wider Address/Data Paths or Buses with Parity**
- **Outputs Have Undershoot Protection Circuitry**
- **Power-Up High-Impedance State**
- **Package Options Include Both Plastic and Ceramic Carriers in Addition to Plastic and Ceramic DIPs**
- **Buffered Control Inputs to Reduce DC Loading Effects**
- **Dependable Texas Instruments Quality and Reliability**

description

These 10-bit flip-flops feature three-state outputs designed specifically for driving highly-capacitive or relatively low-impedance loads. They are particularly suitable for implementing wider buffer registers, I/O ports, bidirectional bus drivers with parity, and working registers.

The ten flip-flops are edge-triggered D-type flip-flops. On the positive transition of the clock the Q outputs on the 'AS821 will be true, and on the 'AS822 will be complementary to the data input.

A buffered output-control input can be used to place the ten outputs in either a normal logic state (high or low levels) or a high-impedance state. In the high-impedance state the outputs neither load nor drive the bus lines significantly. The high-impedance state and increased drive provide the capability to drive the bus lines in a bus-organized system without need for interface or pull-up components. The output control ($\overline{OC}$) does not affect the internal operation of the flip-flops. Old data can be retained or new data can be entered while the outputs are in the high-impedance state.

The SN54AS' family is characterized for operation over the full military temperature range of −55 °C to 125 °C. The SN74AS' family is characterized for operation from 0 °C to 70 °C.

SN54AS821 . . . JT PACKAGE
SN74AS821 . . . DW OR NT PACKAGE
(TOP VIEW)

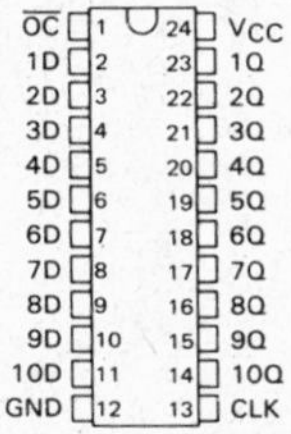
OC 1 24 VCC
1D 2 23 1Q
2D 3 22 2Q
3D 4 21 3Q
4D 5 20 4Q
5D 6 19 5Q
6D 7 18 6Q
7D 8 17 7Q
8D 9 16 8Q
9D 10 15 9Q
10D 11 14 10Q
GND 12 13 CLK

SN54AS821 . . . FK PACKAGE
SN74AS821 . . . FN PACKAGE
(TOP VIEW)

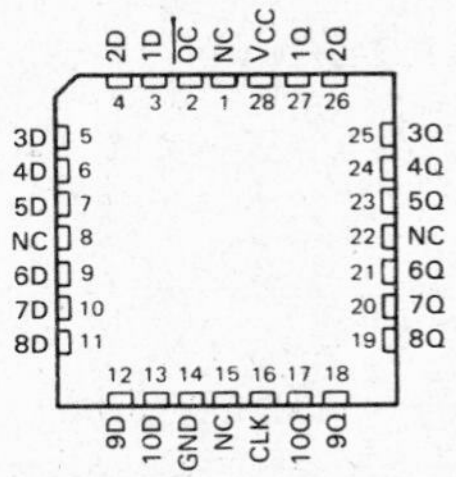
2D 1D OC NC VCC 1Q 2Q
4 3 2 1 28 27 26
3D 5
4D 6
5D 7
NC 8
6D 9
7D 10
8D 11
25 3Q
24 4Q
23 5Q
22 NC
21 6Q
20 7Q
19 8Q
12 13 14 15 16 17 18
9D 10D GND NC CLK 10Q 9Q

SN54AS822 . . . JT PACKAGE
SN74AS822 . . . DW OR NT PACKAGE
(TOP VIEW)

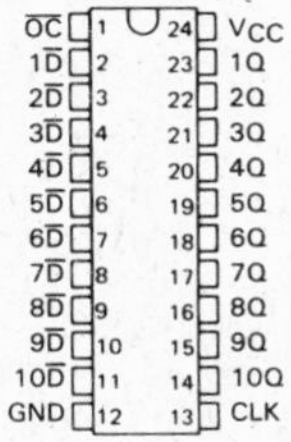
OC 1 24 VCC
1D 2 23 1Q
2D 3 22 2Q
3D 4 21 3Q
4D 5 20 4Q
5D 6 19 5Q
6D 7 18 6Q
7D 8 17 7Q
8D 9 16 8Q
9D 10 15 9Q
10D 11 14 10Q
GND 12 13 CLK

SN54AS822 . . . FK PACKAGE
SN74AS822 . . . FN PACKAGE
(TOP VIEW)

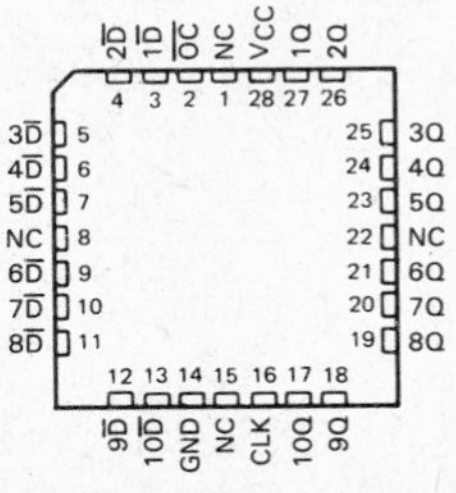
2D 1D OC NC VCC 1Q 2Q
4 3 2 1 28 27 26
3D 5
4D 6
5D 7
NC 8
6D 9
7D 10
8D 11
25 3Q
24 4Q
23 5Q
22 NC
21 6Q
20 7Q
19 8Q
12 13 14 15 16 17 18
9D 10D GND NC CLK 10Q 9Q

NC—No internal connection

'AS821 FUNCTION TABLE (EACH FLIP-FLOP)

INPUTS			OUTPUT
$\overline{OC}$	CLK	D	Q
L	↑	H	H
L	↑	L	L
L	L	X	Q_0
H	X	X	Z

'AS821 logic symbol†

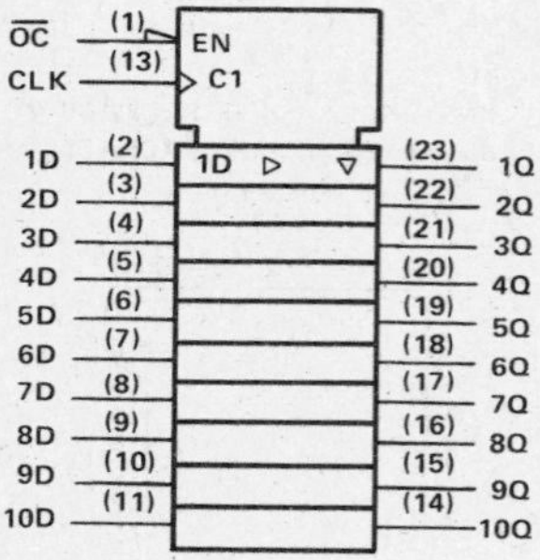
$\overline{OC}$
(1)
EN
CLK
(13)
C1
1D
(2)
1D
(23)
1Q
2D
(3)
(22)
2Q
3D
(4)
(21)
3Q
4D
(5)
(20)
4Q
5D
(6)
(19)
5Q
6D
(7)
(18)
6Q
7D
(8)
(17)
7Q
8D
(9)
(16)
8Q
9D
(10)
(15)
9Q
10D
(11)
(14)
10Q

†This symbol is in accordance with ANSI/IEEE Std 91-1984 and IEC Publication 617-12.

'AS821 logic diagram (positive logic)

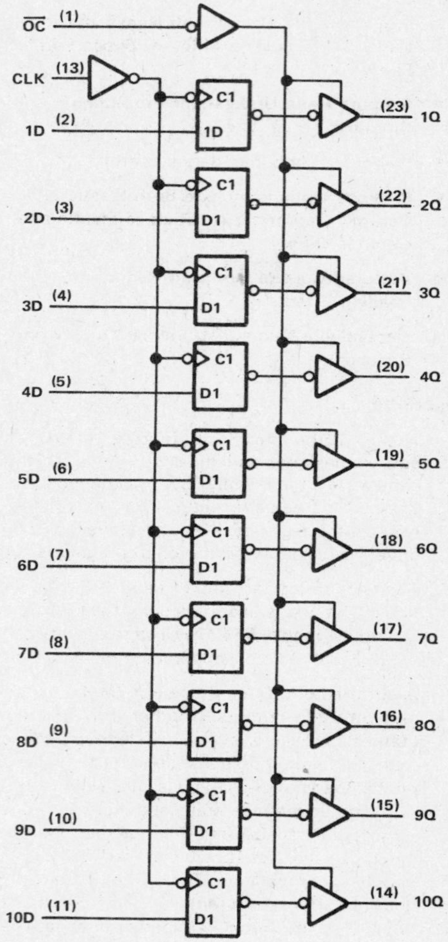
$\overline{OC}$ (1)
CLK (13)
1D (2)
C1
1D
(23) 1Q
2D (3)
D1
(22) 2Q
3D (4)
(21) 3Q
4D (5)
(20) 4Q
5D (6)
(19) 5Q
6D (7)
(18) 6Q
7D (8)
(17) 7Q
8D (9)
(16) 8Q
9D (10)
(15) 9Q
10D (11)
(14) 10Q

Pin numbers shown are for DW, JT, and NT packages.

'AS822 FUNCTION TABLE (EACH FLIP-FLOP)

INPUTS			OUTPUT
$\overline{OC}$	CLK	D	Q
L	↑	H	H
L	↑	L	L
L	L	X	Q_0
H	X	X	Z

'AS822 logic symbol†

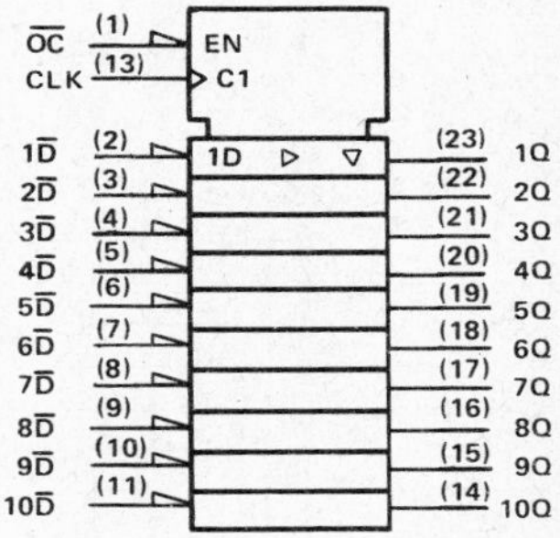

$\overline{OC}$ (1)
EN
CLK (13)
C1
1D̄ (2)
1D
(23) 1Q
2D̄ (3)
(22) 2Q
3D̄ (4)
(21) 3Q
4D̄ (5)
(20) 4Q
5D̄ (6)
(19) 5Q
6D̄ (7)
(18) 6Q
7D̄ (8)
(17) 7Q
8D̄ (9)
(16) 8Q
9D̄ (10)
(15) 9Q
10D̄ (11)
(14) 10Q

†This symbol is in accordance with ANSI/IEEE Std 91-1984 and IEC Publication 617-12.

'AS822 logic diagram (positive logic)

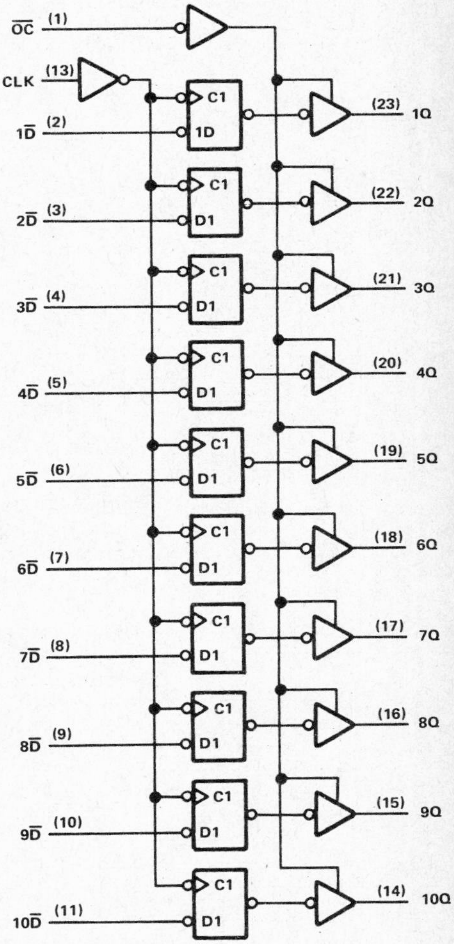

$\overline{OC}$ (1)
CLK (13)
C1
1D
D1
1D̄ (2)
(23) 1Q
2D̄ (3)
(22) 2Q
3D̄ (4)
(21) 3Q
4D̄ (5)
(20) 4Q
5D̄ (6)
(19) 5Q
6D̄ (7)
(18) 6Q
7D̄ (8)
(17) 7Q
8D̄ (9)
(16) 8Q
9D̄ (10)
(15) 9Q
10D̄ (11)
(14) 10Q

Pin numbers shown are for DW, JT, and NT packages.

2
LSI Devices

absolute maximum ratings over operating free-air temperature range (unless otherwise noted)

Supply voltage, V_{CC} . . . 7 V
Input voltage . . . 7 V
Voltage applied to a disabled 3-state output . . . 5.5 V
Operating free-air temperature range: SN54AS821, SN54AS822 . . . −55°C to 125°C
SN74AS821, SN74AS822 . . . 0°C to 70°C
Storage temperature range . . . −65°C to 150°C

recommended operating conditions

		SN54AS821 SN54AS822			SN74AS821 SN74AS822			UNIT
		MIN	NOM	MAX	MIN	NOM	MAX	
V_{CC}	Supply voltage	4.5	5	5.5	4.5	5	5.5	V
V_{IH}	High-level input voltage	2			2			V
V_{IL}	Low-level input voltage			0.8			0.8	V
I_{OH}	High-level output current			−24			−24	mA
I_{OL}	Low-level output currrent			32			48	mA
t_w	Pulse duration, CLK high or low	9			8			ns
t_{su}	Setup time, data before CLK↑	7			6			ns
t_h	Hold time, data after CLK↑	0			0			ns
T_A	Operating free-air temperature	−55		125	0		70	°C

electrical characteristics over recommended operating free-air temperature range (unless otherwise noted)

PARAMETER		TEST CONDITIONS		SN54AS821 SN54AS822			SN74AS821 SN74AS822			UNIT
				MIN	TYP†	MAX	MIN	TYP†	MAX	
V_{IK}		V_{CC} = 4.5 V,	I_I = −18 mA			−1.2			−1.2	V
V_{OH}		V_{CC} = 4.5 V to 5.5 V,	I_{OH} = −2 mA	V_{CC}−2			V_{CC}−2			V
		V_{CC} = 4.5 V,	I_{OH} = −15 mA	2.4	3.2		2.4	3.2		
		V_{CC} = 4.5 V,	I_{OH} = −24 mA	2			2			
V_{OL}		V_{CC} = 4.5 V,	I_{OL} = 32 mA		0.25	0.5				V
		V_{CC} = 4.5 V,	I_{OL} = 48 mA					0.35	0.5	
I_{OZH}		V_{CC} = 5.5 V,	V_O = 2.7 V			50			50	μA
I_{OZL}		V_{CC} = 5.5 V,	V_O = 0.4 V			−50			−50	μA
I_I		V_{CC} = 5.5 V,	V_I = 7 V			0.1			0.1	mA
I_{IH}		V_{CC} = 5.5 V,	V_I = 2.7 V			20			20	μA
I_{IL}		V_{CC} = 5.5 V,	V_I = 0.4 V			−0.5			−0.5	mA
I_O‡		V_{CC} = 5.5 V,	V_O = 2.25 V	−30		−112	−30		−112	mA
I_{CC}	'AS821	V_{CC} = 5.5 V	Outputs high		55	88		55	88	mA
			Outputs low		68	109		68	109	
			Outputs disabled		70	113		70	113	
	'AS822		Outputs high		55	88		55	88	
			Outputs low		68	109		68	109	
			Outputs disabled		70	113		70	113	

†All typical values are at V_{CC} = 5 V, T_A = 25°C.
‡The output conditions have been chosen to produce a current that closely approximates one half of the true short-circuit output current, I_{OS}.

switching characteristics (see Note 1)

PARAMETER	FROM (INPUT)	TO (OUTPUT)	V_{CC} = 4.5 V to 5.5 V, C_L = 50 pF, R1 = 500 Ω, R2 = 500 Ω, T_A = MIN to MAX				UNIT
			SN54AS821 SN54AS822		SN74AS821 SN74AS822		
			MIN	MAX	MIN	MAX	
t_{PLH}	CLK	Any Q	3.5	9	3.5	7.5	ns
t_{PHL}			3.5	11.5	3.5	10.5	
t_{PZH}	$\overline{OC}$	Any Q	4	12	4	11	ns
t_{PZL}			4	13	4	12	
t_{PHZ}	$\overline{OC}$	Any Q	2	10	2	8	ns
t_{PZL}			2	10	2	8	

NOTE 1: Load circuit and voltage waveforms are shown in Section 1.

2

LSI Devices

9-BIT BUS INTERFACE FLIP-FLOPS WITH 3-STATE OUTPUTS

D2825, JUNE 1984—REVISED JANUARY 1986

- **Functionally Equivalent to AMD's AM29823 and AM29824**
- **Provides Extra Data Width Necessary for Wider Address/Data Paths or Buses with Parity**
- **Outputs Have Undershoot Protection Circuitry**
- **Power-Up High-Impedance State**
- **Buffered Control Inputs to Reduce DC Loading Effects**
- **Package Options Include both Plastic and Ceramic Carriers in Addition to Plastic and Ceramic DIPs**
- **Dependable Texas Instruments Quality and Reliability**

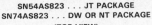

SN54AS823 . . . JT PACKAGE
SN74AS823 . . . DW OR NT PACKAGE
(TOP VIEW)

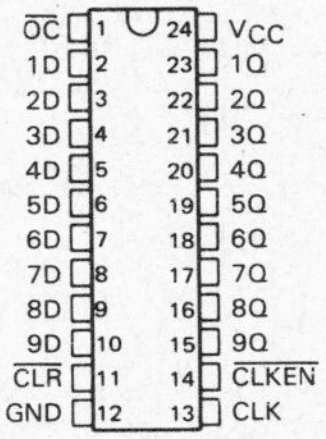
$\overline{OC}$ 1 24 VCC
1D 2 23 1Q
2D 3 22 2Q
3D 4 21 3Q
4D 5 20 4Q
5D 6 19 5Q
6D 7 18 6Q
7D 8 17 7Q
8D 9 16 8Q
9D 10 15 9Q
$\overline{CLR}$ 11 14 $\overline{CLKEN}$
GND 12 13 CLK

SN54AS823 . . . FK PACKAGE
SN74AS823 . . . FN PACKAGE
(TOP VIEW)

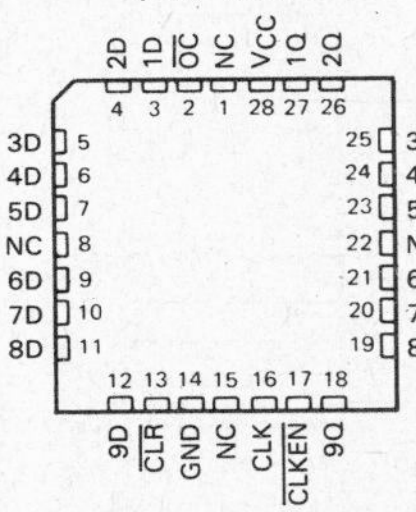
2D 1D $\overline{OC}$ NC VCC 1Q 2Q
4 3 2 1 28 27 26
3D 5
4D 6
5D 7
NC 8
6D 9
7D 10
8D 11
25 3Q
24 4Q
23 5Q
22 NC
21 6Q
20 7Q
19 8Q
12 13 14 15 16 17 18
9D $\overline{CLR}$ GND NC CLK $\overline{CLKEN}$ 9Q

SN54AS824 . . . JT PACKAGE
SN74AS824 . . . DW OR NT PACKAGE
(TOP VIEW)

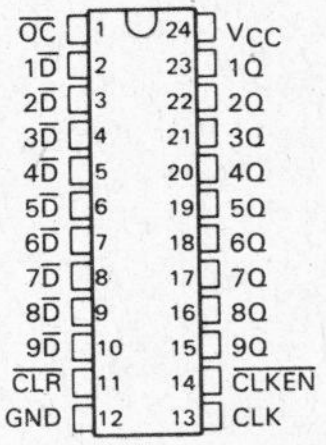
$\overline{OC}$ 1 24 VCC
$1\overline{D}$ 2 23 1Q
$2\overline{D}$ 3 22 2Q
$3\overline{D}$ 4 21 3Q
$4\overline{D}$ 5 20 4Q
$5\overline{D}$ 6 19 5Q
$6\overline{D}$ 7 18 6Q
$7\overline{D}$ 8 17 7Q
$8\overline{D}$ 9 16 8Q
$9\overline{D}$ 10 15 9Q
$\overline{CLR}$ 11 14 $\overline{CLKEN}$
GND 12 13 CLK

SN54AS824 . . . FK PACKAGE
SN74AS824 . . . FN PACKAGE
(TOP VIEW)

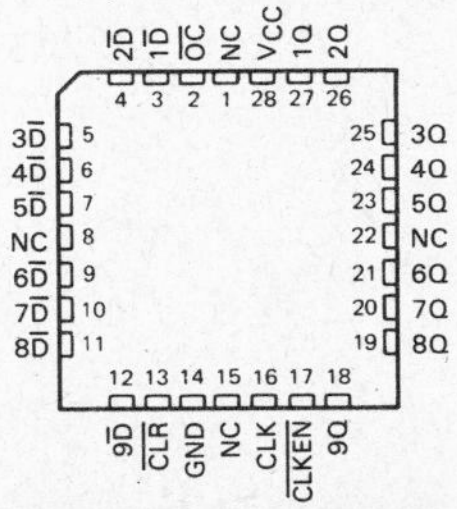
$2\overline{D}$ $1\overline{D}$ $\overline{OC}$ NC VCC 1Q 2Q
4 3 2 1 28 27 26
$3\overline{D}$ 5
$4\overline{D}$ 6
$5\overline{D}$ 7
NC 8
$6\overline{D}$ 9
$7\overline{D}$ 10
$8\overline{D}$ 11
25 3Q
24 4Q
23 5Q
22 NC
21 6Q
20 7Q
19 8Q
12 13 14 15 16 17 18
$9\overline{D}$ $\overline{CLR}$ GND NC CLK $\overline{CLKEN}$ 9Q

description

These 9-bit flip-flops feature three-state outputs designed specifically for driving highly capacitive or relatively low-impedance loads. They are particularly suitable for implementing wider buffer registers, I/O ports, bidirectional bus drivers, parity bus interfacing and working registers.

With the clock enable ($\overline{\text{CLKEN}}$) low, the nine D-type edge-triggered flip-flops enter data on the low-to-high transitions of the clock. Taking $\overline{\text{CLKEN}}$ high will disable the clock buffer, thus latching the outputs. The 'AS823 has noninverting D inputs and the 'AS824 has inverting D inputs. Taking the $\overline{\text{CLR}}$ input low causes the nine Q outputs to go low independently of the clock.

A buffered output-control input ($\overline{\text{OC}}$) can be used to place the nine outputs in either normal logic state (high or low level) or a high-impedance state. In the high-impedance state the outputs neither load nor drive the bus lines significantly. The high-impedance state and increased drive provide the capability to drive the bus lines in a bus-organized system without need for interface or pull-up components. The output control does not affect the internal operation of the flip-flops. Old data can be retained or new data can be entered while the outputs are in the high-impedance state.

The SN54AS' family is characterized for operation over the full military temperature range of −55°C to 125°C. The SN74AS' family is characterized for operation from 0°C to 70°C.

'AS823 FUNCTION TABLE

INPUTS					OUTPUT
$\overline{OC}$	$\overline{CLR}$	$\overline{CLKEN}$	CLK	D	Q
L	L	X	X	X	L
L	H	L	↑	H	H
L	H	L	↑	L	L
L	H	H	X	X	Q_0
H	X	X	X	X	Z

'AS823 logic symbol†

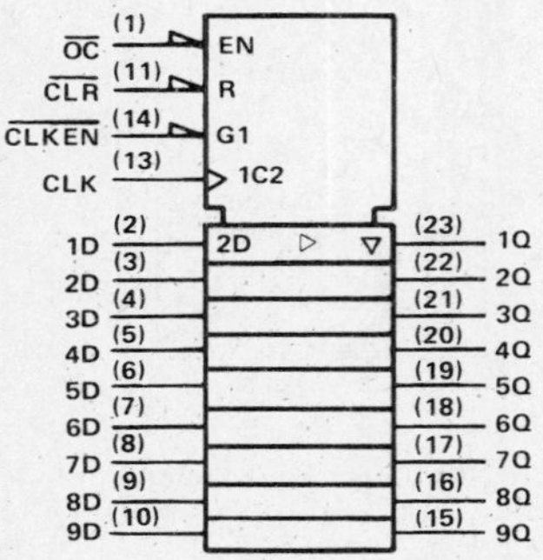
(1)
OC
EN
(11)
CLR
R
(14)
CLKEN
G1
(13)
CLK
1C2
2D
1D
2D
3D
4D
5D
6D
7D
8D
9D
(2)
(3)
(4)
(5)
(6)
(7)
(8)
(9)
(10)
(23)
(22)
(21)
(20)
(19)
(18)
(17)
(16)
(15)
1Q
2Q
3Q
4Q
5Q
6Q
7Q
8Q
9Q

† This symbol is in accordance with ANSI/IEEE Std 91-1984 and IEC Publication 617-12

'AS823 logic diagram (positive logic)

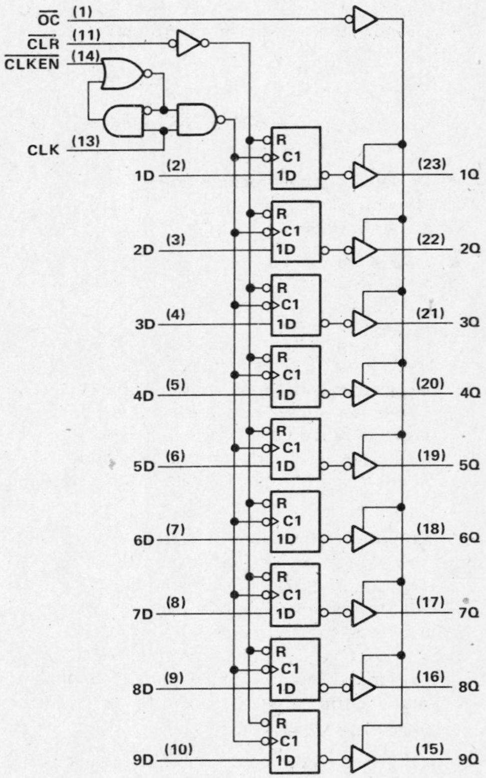
OC (1)
CLR (11)
CLKEN (14)
CLK (13)
R
C1
1D
1D (2)
2D (3)
3D (4)
4D (5)
5D (6)
6D (7)
7D (8)
8D (9)
9D (10)
(23) 1Q
(22) 2Q
(21) 3Q
(20) 4Q
(19) 5Q
(18) 6Q
(17) 7Q
(16) 8Q
(15) 9Q

Pin numbers shown are for DW, JT, and NT packages.

TEXAS INSTRUMENTS
POST OFFICE BOX 225012 • DALLAS, TEXAS 75265

'AS824 FUNCTION TABLE

INPUTS					OUTPUT
$\overline{OC}$	$\overline{CLR}$	$\overline{CLKEN}$	CLK	$\overline{D}$	Q
L	L	X	X	X	L
L	H	L	↑	H	L
L	H	L	↑	L	H
L	H	H	X	X	Q_0
H	X	X	X	X	Z

'AS824 logic symbol†

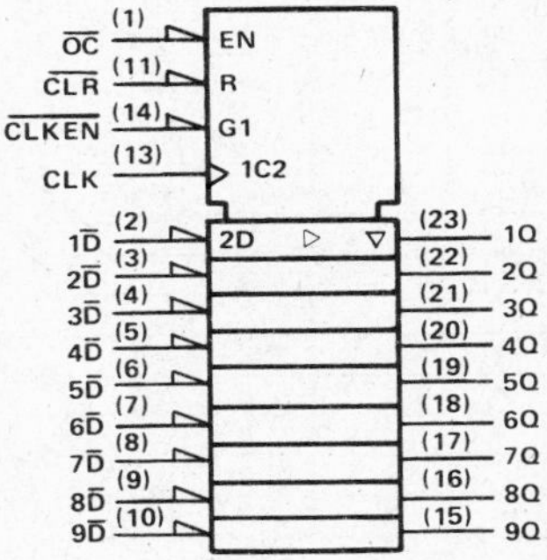
$\overline{OC}$ (1) EN
$\overline{CLR}$ (11) R
$\overline{CLKEN}$ (14) G1
CLK (13) 1C2
1$\overline{D}$ (2) 2D
(23) 1Q
2$\overline{D}$ (3) (22) 2Q
3$\overline{D}$ (4) (21) 3Q
4$\overline{D}$ (5) (20) 4Q
5$\overline{D}$ (6) (19) 5Q
6$\overline{D}$ (7) (18) 6Q
7$\overline{D}$ (8) (17) 7Q
8$\overline{D}$ (9) (16) 8Q
9$\overline{D}$ (10) (15) 9Q

† This symbol is in accordance with ANSI/IEEE Std 91-1984 and IEC Publication 617-12.

'AS824 logic diagram (positive logic)

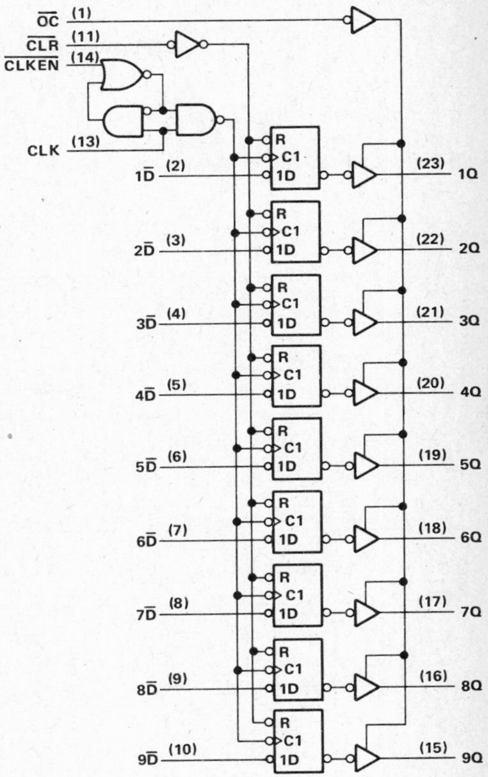
$\overline{OC}$ (1)
$\overline{CLR}$ (11)
$\overline{CLKEN}$ (14)
CLK (13)
R
C1
1D
1$\overline{D}$ (2) (23) 1Q
2$\overline{D}$ (3) (22) 2Q
3$\overline{D}$ (4) (21) 3Q
4$\overline{D}$ (5) (20) 4Q
5$\overline{D}$ (6) (19) 5Q
6$\overline{D}$ (7) (18) 6Q
7$\overline{D}$ (8) (17) 7Q
8$\overline{D}$ (9) (16) 8Q
9$\overline{D}$ (10) (15) 9Q

Pin numbers shown are for DW, JT, and NT packages.

absolute maximum ratings over operating free-air temperature range (unless otherwise noted)

Supply voltage, V_{CC} . . . . 7 V
Input voltage . . . . 7 V
Voltage applied to a disabled 3-state output . . . . 5.5 V
Operating free-air temperature range: SN54AS823, SN54AS824 . . . . −55°C to 125°C
SN74AS823, SN74AS824 . . . . 0°C to 70°C
Storage temperature range . . . . −65°C to 150°C

recommended operating conditions

			SN54AS823 SN54AS824			SN74AS823 SN74AS824			UNIT
			MIN	NOM	MAX	MIN	NOM	MAX	
V_{CC}	Supply voltage		4.5	5	5.5	4.5	5	5.5	V
V_{IH}	High-level input voltage		2			2			V
V_{IL}	Low-level input voltage				0.8			0.8	V
I_{OH}	High-level output current				−24			−24	mA
I_{OL}	Low-level output current				32			48	mA
t_w	Pulse duration	$\overline{CLR}$ low	5			4			ns
		CLK high or low	9			8			
t_{su}	Setup time before CLK↑	$\overline{CLR}$ inactive	8			8			ns
		Data	7			6			
		$\overline{CLKEN}$ high or low	7			6			
t_h	Hold time, $\overline{CLKEN}$ or data after CLK↑		0			0			ns
T_A	Operating free-air temperature		−55		125	0		70	°C

electrical characteristics over recommended operating free-air temperature range (unless otherwise noted)

PARAMETER		TEST CONDITIONS		SN54AS823 SN54AS824			SN74AS823 SN74AS824			UNIT
				MIN	TYP†	MAX	MIN	TYP†	MAX	
V_{IK}		V_{CC} = 4.5 V,	I_I = −18 mA			−1.2			−1.2	V
V_{OH}		V_{CC} = 4.5 V to 5.5 V,	I_{OH} = −2 mA	V_{CC}−2			V_{CC}−2			V
		V_{CC} = 4.5 V,	I_{OH} = −15 mA	2.4	3.2		2.4	3.2		
		V_{CC} = 4.5 V,	I_{OH} = −24 mA	2			2			
V_{OL}		V_{CC} = 4.5 V,	I_{OL} = 32 mA		0.3	0.5				V
		V_{CC} = 4.5 V,	I_{OL} = 48 mA					0.35	0.5	
I_{OZH}		V_{CC} = 5.5 V,	V_O = 2.7 V			50			50	μA
I_{OZL}		V_{CC} = 5.5 V,	V_O = 0.4 V			−50			−50	μA
I_I		V_{CC} = 5.5 V,	V_I = 7 V			0.1			0.1	mA
I_{IH}		V_{CC} = 5.5 V,	V_I = 2.7 V			20			20	μA
I_{IL}		V_{CC} = 5.5 V,	V_I = 0.4 V			−0.5			−0.5	mA
I_O‡		V_{CC} = 5.5 V,	V_O = 2.25 V	−30		−112	−30		−112	mA
I_{CC}	'AS823	V_{CC} = 5.5 V	Outputs high		49	80		49	80	mA
			Outputs low		61	100		61	100	
			Outputs disabled		64	103		64	103	
	'AS824	V_{CC} = 5.5 V	Outputs high		49	80		49	80	mA
			Outputs low		61	100		61	100	
			Outputs disabled		64	103		64	103	

†All typical values are at V_{CC} = 5 V, T_A = 25°C.
‡The output conditions have been chosen to produce a current that closely approximates one half of the true short-circuit output current, I_{OS}.

TEXAS INSTRUMENTS
POST OFFICE BOX 225012 • DALLAS, TEXAS 75265

switching characteristics (see Note 1)

PARAMETER	FROM (INPUT)	TO (OUTPUT)	V_{CC} = 4.5 V to 5.5 V, C_L = 50 pF, R1 = 500 Ω, R2 = 500 Ω, T_A = MIN to MAX				UNIT
			SN54AS823 SN54AS824		SN74AS823 SN74AS824		
			MIN	MAX	MIN	MAX	
t_{PLH}	CLK	Any Q	3.5	9	3.5	7.5	ns
t_{PHL}			3.5	12	3.5	11	
t_{PHL}	$\overline{CLR}$	Any Q	3.5	14	3.5	13	ns
t_{PZH}	$\overline{OC}$	Any Q	4	12	4	11	ns
t_{PZL}			4	13	4	12	
t_{PHZ}	$\overline{OC}$	Any Q	2	10	2	8	ns
t_{PLZ}			2	10	2	8	

NOTE 1: Load circuit and voltage waveforms are shown in Section 1.

D flip-flop signal conventions

It is normal TI practice to name the outputs and other inputs of a D-type flip-flop and to draw its logic symbol based on the assumption of true data (D) inputs. Then outputs that produce data in phase with the data inputs are called Q and those producing complementary data are called Q. An input that causes a Q output to go high or a Q output to go low is called Preset; an input that causes a Q output to go high or a Q output to go low is called Clear. Bars are used over these pin names (PRE and CLR) if they are active-low.

The devices on this data sheet are second-source designs and the pin-name convention used by the original manufacturer has been retained. That makes it necessary to designate the inputs and outputs of the inverting circuit D and Q. In some applications it may be advantageous to redesignate the inputs and outputs as D and Q. In that case, outputs should be renamed as shown below. Also shown are corresponding changes in the graphical symbol. Arbitrary pin numbers are shown in parentheses.

Notice that Q and Q exchange names, which causes Preset and Clear to do likewise. Also notice that the polarity indicators (⊳) on PRE and CLR remain since these inputs are still active-low, but that the presence or absence of the polarity changes at D, Q, and Q. Of course pin 5 (Q) is still in phase with the data input D, but now both are considered active high.

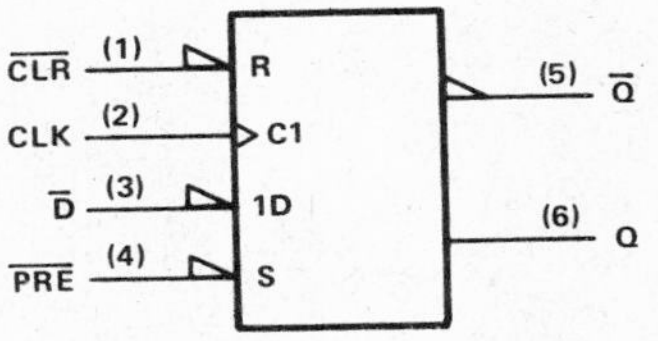
CLR
(1)
R
CLK
(2)
C1
D
(3)
1D
PRE
(4)
S
(5)
Q
(6)
Q

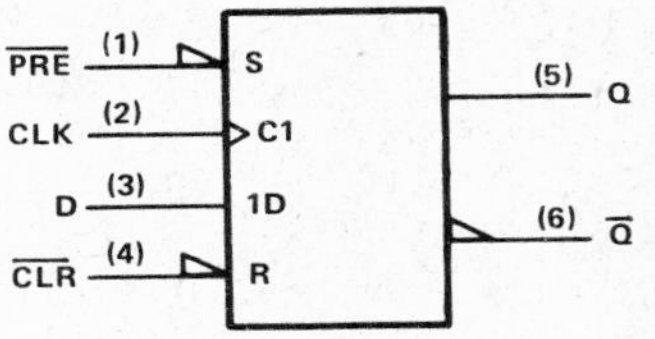
PRE
(1)
S
CLK
(2)
C1
D
(3)
1D
CLR
(4)
R
(5)
Q
(6)
Q

2

LSI Devices

8-BIT BUS INTERFACE FLIP-FLOPS WITH 3-STATE OUTPUTS

D2825, JUNE 1984—REVISED JANUARY 1986

- **Functionally Equivalent to AMD's AM29825 and AM29826**
- **Improved I_{OH} Specifications**
- **Multiple Output Enables Allow Multiuser Control of the Interface**
- **Outputs Have Undershoot Protection Circuitry**
- **Power-Up High-Impedance State**
- **Package Options Include Both Plastic and Ceramic Chip Carriers in Addition to Plastic and Ceramic DIPs**
- **Buffered Control Inputs to Reduce DC Loading Effect**
- **Dependable Texas Instruments Quality and Reliability**

description

These 8-bit flip-flops feature three-state outputs designed specifically for driving highly capacitive or relatively low-impedance loads. They are particularly suitable for implementing multiuser registers, I/O ports, bidirectional bus drivers, and working registers.

With the clock enable ($\overline{\text{CLKEN}}$) low, the eight D-type edge-triggered flip-flops enter data on the low-to-high transitions of the clock. Taking $\overline{\text{CLKEN}}$ high will disable the clock buffer, thus latching the outputs. The 'AS825 has non-inverting D inputs and the 'AS826 has inverting $\overline{\text{D}}$ inputs. Taking the $\overline{\text{CLR}}$ input low causes the eight Q outputs to go low independently of the clock.

Multiuser buffered output-control inputs ($\overline{\text{OC}}$1, $\overline{\text{OC}}$2, and $\overline{\text{OC}}$3) can be used to place the eight outputs in either a normal logic state (high or low level) or a high-impedance state. In the high-impedance state the outputs neither load nor drive the bus lines significantly. The high-impedance state and increased drive provide the capability to drive the bus lines in a bus-organized system without need for interface or pull-up components. The output controls do not affect the internal operation of the flip-flops. Old data can be retained or new data can be entered while the outputs are in the high-impedance state.

SN54AS825 . . . JT PACKAGE
SN74AS825 . . . DW OR NT PACKAGE
(TOP VIEW)

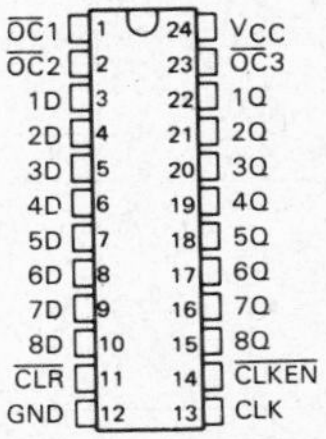
OC1 1 24 VCC
OC2 2 23 OC3
1D 3 22 1Q
2D 4 21 2Q
3D 5 20 3Q
4D 6 19 4Q
5D 7 18 5Q
6D 8 17 6Q
7D 9 16 7Q
8D 10 15 8Q
CLR 11 14 CLKEN
GND 12 13 CLK

SN54AS825 . . . FK PACKAGE
SN74AS825 . . . FN PACKAGE
(TOP VIEW)

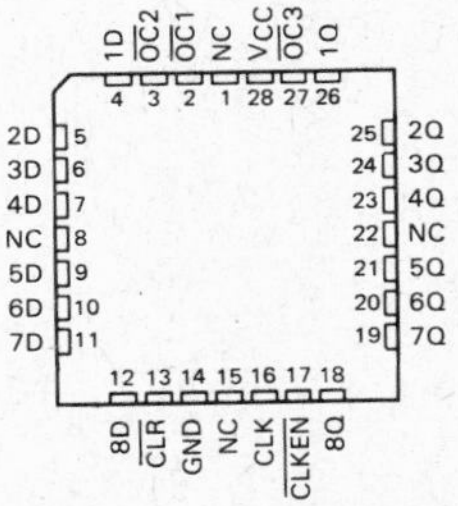
1D OC2 OC1 NC VCC OC3 1Q
4 3 2 1 28 27 26
2D 5
3D 6
4D 7
NC 8
5D 9
6D 10
7D 11
25 2Q
24 3Q
23 4Q
22 NC
21 5Q
20 6Q
19 7Q
12 13 14 15 16 17 18
8D CLR GND NC CLK CLKEN 8Q

SN54AS826 . . . JT PACKAGE
SN74AS826 . . . DW OR NT PACKAGE
(TOP VIEW)

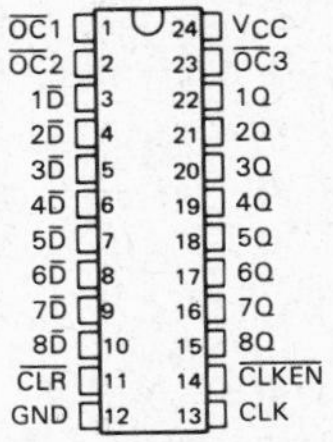
OC1 1 24 VCC
OC2 2 23 OC3
1D 3 22 1Q
2D 4 21 2Q
3D 5 20 3Q
4D 6 19 4Q
5D 7 18 5Q
6D 8 17 6Q
7D 9 16 7Q
8D 10 15 8Q
CLR 11 14 CLKEN
GND 12 13 CLK

SN54AS826 . . . FK PACKAGE
SN74AS826 . . . FN PACKAGE
(TOP VIEW)

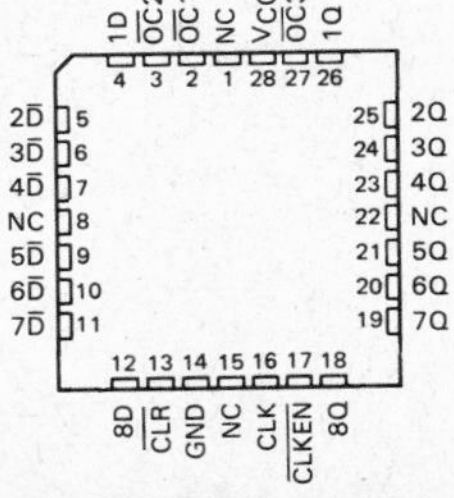
1D OC2 OC1 NC VCC OC3 1Q
4 3 2 1 28 27 26
2D 5
3D 6
4D 7
NC 8
5D 9
6D 10
7D 11
25 2Q
24 3Q
23 4Q
22 NC
21 5Q
20 6Q
19 7Q
12 13 14 15 16 17 18
8D CLR GND NC CLK CLKEN 8Q

NC—No internal connection

TEXAS INSTRUMENTS
POST OFFICE BOX 225012 • DALLAS, TEXAS 75265

The SN54AS' family is characterized for operation over the full military temperature range of −55°C to 125°C. The SN74AS' family is characterized for operation from 0°C to 70°C.

'AS825 FUNCTION TABLE

INPUTS					OUTPUT
$\overline{OC}$*	$\overline{CLR}$	$\overline{CLKEN}$	CLK	D	Q
L	L	X	X	X	L
L	H	L	↑	H	H
L	H	L	↑	L	L
L	H	H	X	X	Q_0
H	X	X	X	X	Z

$\overline{OC}$* = H if any of $\overline{OC}$1, $\overline{OC}$2, or $\overline{OC}$3 are high.
$\overline{OC}$* = L if all of $\overline{OC}$1, $\overline{OC}$2, and $\overline{OC}$3 are low.

'AS825 logic symbol†

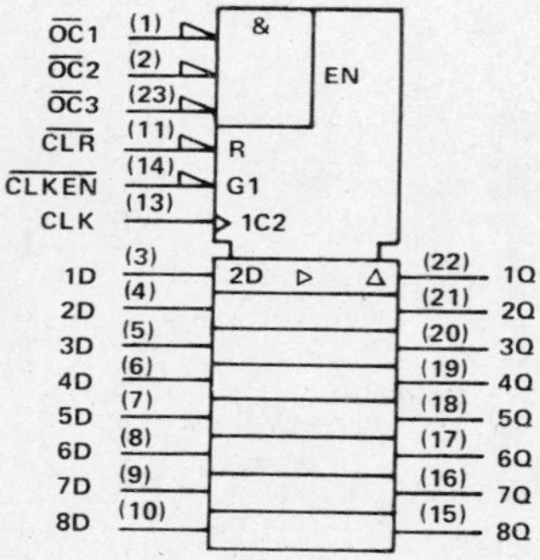
$\overline{OC1}$ (1)
$\overline{OC2}$ (2)
$\overline{OC3}$ (23)
$\overline{CLR}$ (11)
$\overline{CLKEN}$ (14)
CLK (13)
&
EN
R
G1
1C2
2D
1D (3)
2D (4)
3D (5)
4D (6)
5D (7)
6D (8)
7D (9)
8D (10)
(22) 1Q
(21) 2Q
(20) 3Q
(19) 4Q
(18) 5Q
(17) 6Q
(16) 7Q
(15) 8Q

† This symbol is in accordance with ANSI/IEEE Std 91-1984 and IEC Publication 617-12.

'AS825 logic diagram (positive logic)

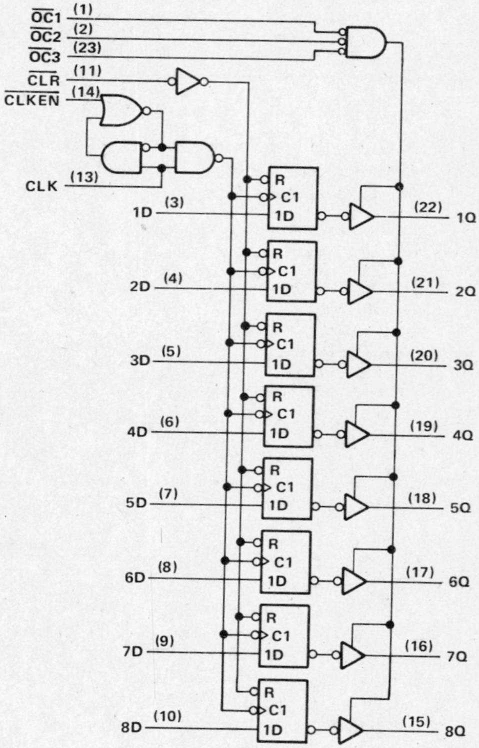
$\overline{OC1}$ (1)
$\overline{OC2}$ (2)
$\overline{OC3}$ (23)
$\overline{CLR}$ (11)
$\overline{CLKEN}$ (14)
CLK (13)
R
C1
1D
1D (3)
2D (4)
3D (5)
4D (6)
5D (7)
6D (8)
7D (9)
8D (10)
(22) 1Q
(21) 2Q
(20) 3Q
(19) 4Q
(18) 5Q
(17) 6Q
(16) 7Q
(15) 8Q

Pin numbers are for DW, JT, and NT packages.

'AS826 FUNCTION TABLE

INPUTS					OUTPUT
$\overline{OC}$*	$\overline{CLR}$	$\overline{CLKEN}$	CLK	$\overline{D}$	Q
L	L	X	X	X	L
L	H	L	↑	H	L
L	H	L	↑	L	H
L	H	H	X	X	Q_0
H	X	X	X	X	Z

$\overline{OC}$* = H if any of $\overline{OC}$1, $\overline{OC}$2, or $\overline{OC}$3 are high.
$\overline{OC}$* = L if all of $\overline{OC}$1, $\overline{OC}$2, and $\overline{OC}$3 are low.

'AS826 logic symbol†

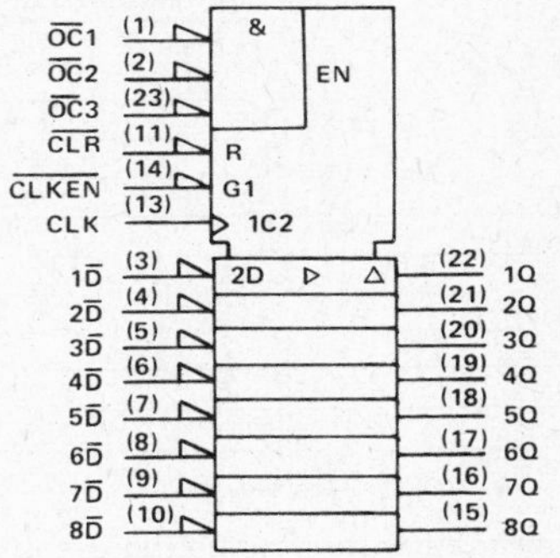
$\overline{OC1}$ (1)
$\overline{OC2}$ (2)
$\overline{OC3}$ (23)
$\overline{CLR}$ (11)
$\overline{CLKEN}$ (14)
CLK (13)
&
EN
R
G1
1C2
2D
1$\overline{D}$ (3)
2$\overline{D}$ (4)
3$\overline{D}$ (5)
4$\overline{D}$ (6)
5$\overline{D}$ (7)
6$\overline{D}$ (8)
7$\overline{D}$ (9)
8$\overline{D}$ (10)
(22) 1Q
(21) 2Q
(20) 3Q
(19) 4Q
(18) 5Q
(17) 6Q
(16) 7Q
(15) 8Q

† This symbol is in accordance with ANSI/IEEE Std 91-1984 and IEC Publication 617-12

'AS826 logic diagram (positive logic)

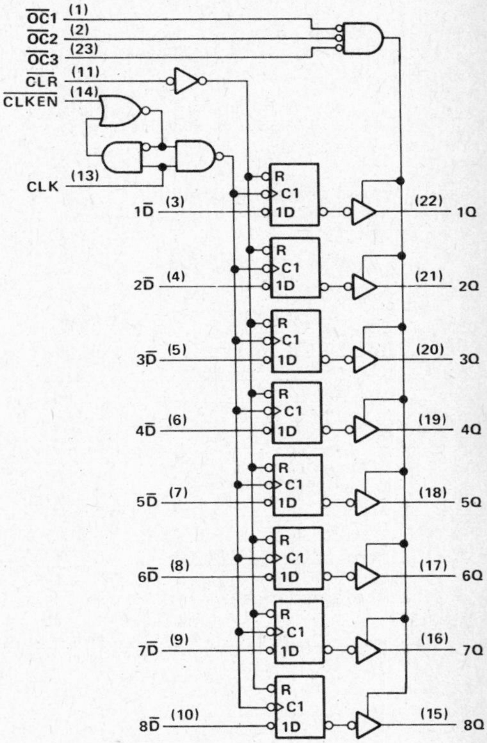
$\overline{OC1}$ (1)
$\overline{OC2}$ (2)
$\overline{OC3}$ (23)
$\overline{CLR}$ (11)
$\overline{CLKEN}$ (14)
CLK (13)
R
C1
1D
1$\overline{D}$ (3)
2$\overline{D}$ (4)
3$\overline{D}$ (5)
4$\overline{D}$ (6)
5$\overline{D}$ (7)
6$\overline{D}$ (8)
7$\overline{D}$ (9)
8$\overline{D}$ (10)
(22) 1Q
(21) 2Q
(20) 3Q
(19) 4Q
(18) 5Q
(17) 6Q
(16) 7Q
(15) 8Q

Pin numbers shown are for DW, JT, and NT packages.

absolute maximum ratings over operating free-air temperature range (unless otherwise noted)

Supply voltage, V_{CC} .... 7 V
Input voltage .... 7 V
Voltage applied to a disabled 3-state output .... 5.5 V
Operating free-air temperature range:
SN54AS825, SN54AS826 .... −55°C to 125°C
SN74AS825, SN74AS826 .... 0°C to 70°C
Storage temperature range .... −65 to 150°C

recommended operating conditions

			SN54AS825 SN54AS826			SN74AS825 SN74AS826			UNIT
			MIN	NOM	MAX	MIN	NOM	MAX	
V_{CC}	Supply voltage		4.5	5	5.5	4.5	5	5.5	V
V_{IH}	High-level input voltage		2			2			V
V_{IL}	Low-level input voltage				0.8			0.8	V
I_{OH}	High-level output current				−24			−24	mA
I_{OL}	Low-level output current				32			48	mA
t_w	Pulse duration	$\overline{CLR}$ low	5			4			ns
		CLK high or low	9			8			
t_{su}	Setup time before CLK↑	$\overline{CLR}$ inactive	8			8			ns
		Data	7			6			
		$\overline{CLKEN}$ high or low	7			6			
t_h	Hold time, $\overline{CLKEN}$ or data after CLK↑		0			0			ns
T_A	Operating free-air temperature		−55		125	0		70	°C

electrical characteristics over recommended operating free-air temperature range (unless otherwise noted)

PARAMETER		TEST CONDITIONS		SN54AS825 SN54AS826			SN74AS825 SN74AS826			UNIT
				MIN	TYP†	MAX	MIN	TYP†	MAX	
V_{IK}		V_{CC} = 4.5 V,	I_I = −18 mA			−1.2			−1.2	V
V_{OH}		V_{CC} = 4.5 V to 5.5 V,	I_{OH} = −2 mA	$V_{CC}-2$			$V_{CC}-2$			V
		V_{CC} = 4.5 V,	I_{OH} = −15 mA	2.4	3.2		2.4	3.2		
		V_{CC} = 4.5 V,	I_{OH} = −24 mA	2			2			
V_{OL}		V_{CC} = 4.5 V,	I_{OL} = 32 mA		0.3	0.5				V
		V_{CC} = 4.5 V,	I_{OL} = 48 mA					0.35	0.5	
I_{OZH}		V_{CC} = 5.5 V,	V_O = 2.7 V			50			50	μA
I_{OZL}		V_{CC} = 5.5 V,	V_O = 0.4 V			−50			−50	μA
I_I		V_{CC} = 5.5 V,	V_I = 7 V			0.1			0.1	mA
I_{IH}		V_{CC} = 5.5 V,	V_I = 2.7 V			20			20	μA
I_{IL}		V_{CC} = 5.5 V,	V_I = 0.4 V			−0.5			−0.5	mA
I_O‡		V_{CC} = 5.5 V,	V_O = 2.25 V	−30		−112	−30		−112	mA
I_{CC}	'AS825	V_{CC} = 5.5 V	Outputs high		45	73		45	73	mA
			Outputs low		56	90		56	90	
			Outputs disabled		59	95		59	95	
	'AS826	V_{CC} = 5.5 V	Outputs high		45	73		45	73	mA
			Outputs low		56	90		56	90	
			Outputs disabled		59	95		59	95	

† All typical values are at V_{CC} = 5 V, T_A = 25°C.
‡ The output conditions have been chosen to produce a current that closely approximates one half of the true short-circuit output current, I_{OS}.

TEXAS INSTRUMENTS
POST OFFICE BOX 225012 • DALLAS, TEXAS 75265

switching characteristics (see Note 1)

PARAMETER	FROM (INPUT)	TO (OUTPUT)	V_{CC} = 4.5 V to 5.5 V, C_L = 50 pF, R1 = 500 Ω, R2 = 500 Ω, T_A = MIN to MAX SN54AS825 SN54AS826		SN74AS825 SN74AS826		UNIT
			MIN	MAX	MIN	MAX	
t_{PLH}	CLK	Any Q	3.5	9	3.5	7.5	ns
t_{PHL}			3.5	11.5	3.5	11	
t_{PHL}	$\overline{CLR}$	Any Q	3.5	14	3.5	13	ns
t_{PZH}	$\overline{OC}$	Any Q	4	12	4	11	ns
t_{PZL}			4	13	4	12	
t_{PHZ}	$\overline{OC}$	Any Q	2	10	2	8	ns
t_{PLZ}			2	10	2	8	

NOTE 1: Load circuit and voltage waveforms are shown in Section 1.

D flip-flop signal conventions

It is normal TI practice to name the outputs and other inputs of a D-type flip-flop and to draw its logic symbol based on the assumption of true data (D) inputs. Then outputs that produce data in phase with the data inputs are called Q and those producing complementary data are called $\overline{Q}$. An input that causes a Q output to go high or a $\overline{Q}$ output to go low is called Preset; an input that causes a $\overline{Q}$ output to go high or a Q output to go low is called Clear. Bars are used over these pin names ($\overline{PRE}$ and $\overline{CLR}$) if they are active-low.

The devices on this data sheet are second-source designs and the pin-name convention used by the original manufacturer has been retained. That makes it necessary to designate the inputs and outputs of the inverting circuit $\overline{D}$ and Q. In some applications it may be advantageous to redesignate the inputs and outputs as D and $\overline{Q}$. In that case, outputs should be renamed as shown below. Also shown are corresponding changes in the graphical symbol. Arbitrary pin numbers are shown in parentheses.

Notice that Q and $\overline{Q}$ exchange names, which causes Preset and Clear to do likewise. Also notice that the polarity indicators (⊾) on $\overline{PRE}$ and $\overline{CLR}$ remain since these inputs are still active-low, but that the presence or absence of the polarity indicator changes at $\overline{D}$, Q, and $\overline{Q}$. Of course pin 5 (Q) is still in phase with the data input D, but now both are considered active high.

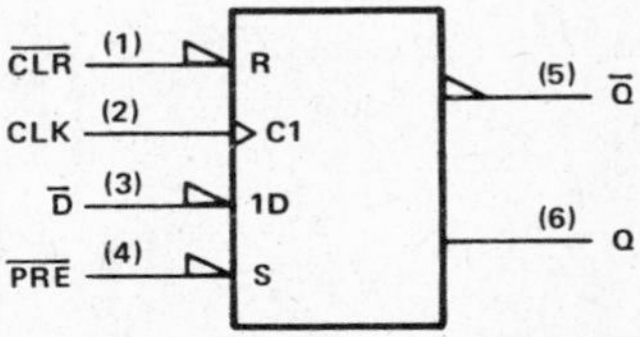
CLR (1) R
CLK (2) C1
D (3) 1D
PRE (4) S
(5) Q
(6) Q

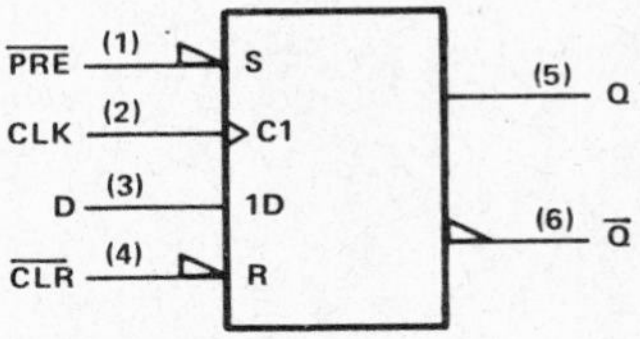
PRE (1) S
CLK (2) C1
D (3) 1D
CLR (4) R
(5) Q
(6) Q

SN54ALS841, SN54AS841, SN54ALS842, SN54AS842
SN74ALS841, SN74AS841, SN74ALS842, SN74AS842
10-BIT BUS INTERFACE D-TYPE LATCHES WITH 3-STATE OUTPUTS

D2910, DECEMBER 1983—REVISED OCTOBER 1985

- **3-State Buffer-Type Outputs Drive Bus-Lines Directly**
- **Bus-Structured Pinout**
- **Provide Extra Bus Driving Latches Necessary for Wider Address/Data Paths or Buses with Parity**
- **Buffered Control Inputs to Reduce DC Loading**
- **Power-Up High-Impedance State**
- **Package Options Include Both Plastic and Ceramic Chip Carriers in Addition to Plastic and Ceramic DIPs**
- **Dependable Texas Instruments Quality and Reliability**

SN54ALS841, SN54AS841 . . . JT PACKAGE
SN74ALS841, SN74AS841 . . . DW OR NT PACKAGE
(TOP VIEW)

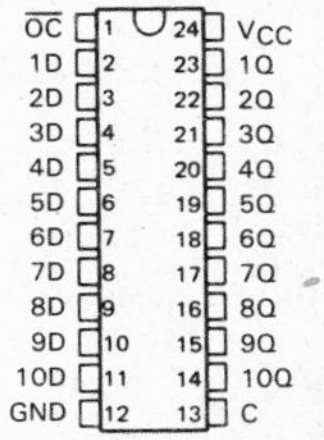
$\overline{OC}$ 1 24 V_{CC}
1D 2 23 1Q
2D 3 22 2Q
3D 4 21 3Q
4D 5 20 4Q
5D 6 19 5Q
6D 7 18 6Q
7D 8 17 7Q
8D 9 16 8Q
9D 10 15 9Q
10D 11 14 10Q
GND 12 13 C

SN54ALS841, SN54AS841 . . . FK PACKAGE
SN74ALS841, SN74AS841 . . . FN PACKAGE
(TOP VIEW)

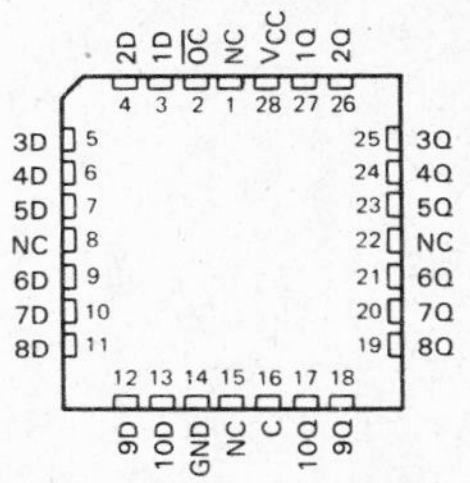
2D 1D $\overline{OC}$ NC V_{CC} 1Q 2Q
4 3 2 1 28 27 26
3D 5 25 3Q
4D 6 24 4Q
5D 7 23 5Q
NC 8 22 NC
6D 9 21 6Q
7D 10 20 7Q
8D 11 19 8Q
12 13 14 15 16 17 18
9D 10D GND NC C 10Q 9Q

SN54ALS842, SN54AS842 . . . JT PACKAGE
SN74ALS842, SN74AS842 . . . DW OR NT PACKAGE
(TOP VIEW)

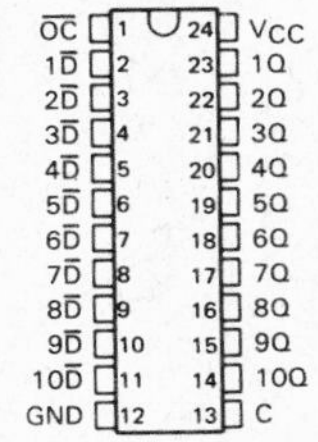
$\overline{OC}$ 1 24 V_{CC}
1$\overline{D}$ 2 23 1Q
2$\overline{D}$ 3 22 2Q
3$\overline{D}$ 4 21 3Q
4$\overline{D}$ 5 20 4Q
5$\overline{D}$ 6 19 5Q
6$\overline{D}$ 7 18 6Q
7$\overline{D}$ 8 17 7Q
8$\overline{D}$ 9 16 8Q
9$\overline{D}$ 10 15 9Q
10$\overline{D}$ 11 14 10Q
GND 12 13 C

SN54ALS842, SN54AS842 . . . FK PACKAGE
SN74ALS842, SN74AS842 . . . FN PACKAGE
(TOP VIEW)

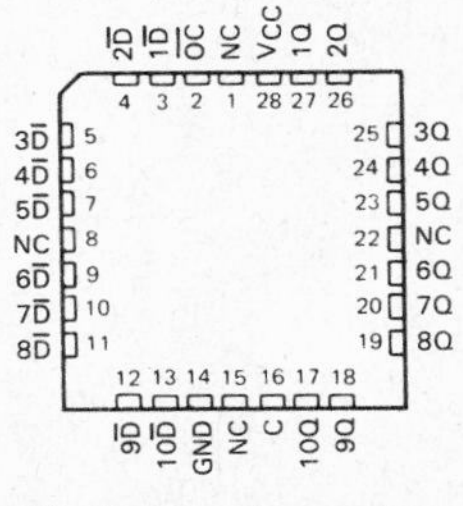
2$\overline{D}$ 1$\overline{D}$ $\overline{OC}$ NC V_{CC} 1Q 2Q
4 3 2 1 28 27 26
3$\overline{D}$ 5 25 3Q
4$\overline{D}$ 6 24 4Q
5$\overline{D}$ 7 23 5Q
NC 8 22 NC
6$\overline{D}$ 9 21 6Q
7$\overline{D}$ 10 20 7Q
8$\overline{D}$ 11 19 8Q
12 13 14 15 16 17 18
9$\overline{D}$ 10$\overline{D}$ GND NC C 10Q 9Q

NC—No internal connection

description

These 10-bit latches feature three-state outputs designed specifically for driving highly capacitive or relatively low-impedance loads. They are particularly suitable for implementing buffer registers, I/O ports, bidirectional bus drivers, and working registers.

The ten latches are transparent D-type. The 'ALS841 and 'AS841 have noninverting data (D) inputs. The 'ALS842 and 'AS842 have inverting $\overline{D}$ inputs.

A buffered output control ($\overline{OC}$) input can be used to place the ten outputs in either a normal logic state (high or low levels) or a high-impedance state. In the high-impedance state, the outputs neither load nor drive the bus lines significantly. The high-impedance state and increased drive provide the capability to drive the bus lines in a bus-organized system without need for interface or pull-up components.

The output control does not affect the internal operation of the latches. Old data can be retained or new data can be entered while the outputs are off.

The -1 versions of the SN74ALS841 and SN74ALS842 parts are identical to the standard versions except that the recommended maximum I_{OL} is increased to 48 milliamperes. There are no -1 versions of the SN54ALS841 and SN54ALS842.

The SN54ALS841, SN54AS841, SN54ALS842, and SN54AS842 are characterized for operation over the full military temperature range of −55°C to 125°C. The SN74ALS841, SN74AS841, SN74ALS842, and SN74AS842 are characterized for operation from 0°C to 70°C.

FUNCTION TABLES

'ALS841, 'AS841

INPUTS			OUTPUT
$\overline{OC}$	C	D	Q
L	H	H	H
L	H	L	L
L	L	X	Q_0
H	X	X	Z

'ALS842, 'AS842

INPUTS			OUTPUT
$\overline{OC}$	C	$\overline{D}$	Q
L	H	H	L
L	H	L	H
L	L	X	Q_0
H	X	X	Z

'ALS841, 'AS841 logic symbol†

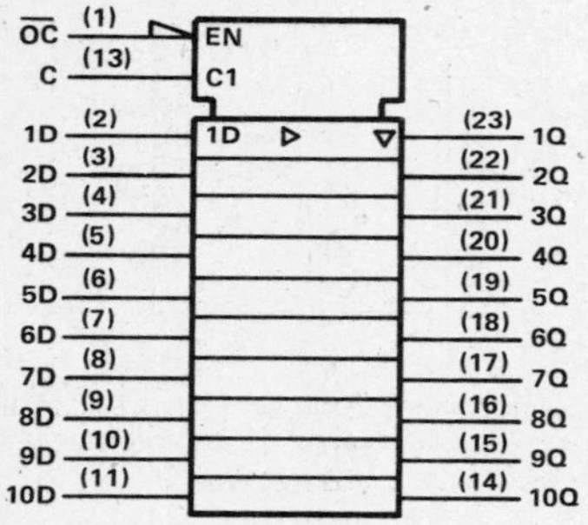
OC
C
EN
C1
1D
(1)
(13)
(2) (3) (4) (5) (6) (7) (8) (9) (10) (11)
1D 2D 3D 4D 5D 6D 7D 8D 9D 10D
(23) (22) (21) (20) (19) (18) (17) (16) (15) (14)
1Q 2Q 3Q 4Q 5Q 6Q 7Q 8Q 9Q 10Q

'ALS841, 'AS841 logic diagram (positive logic)

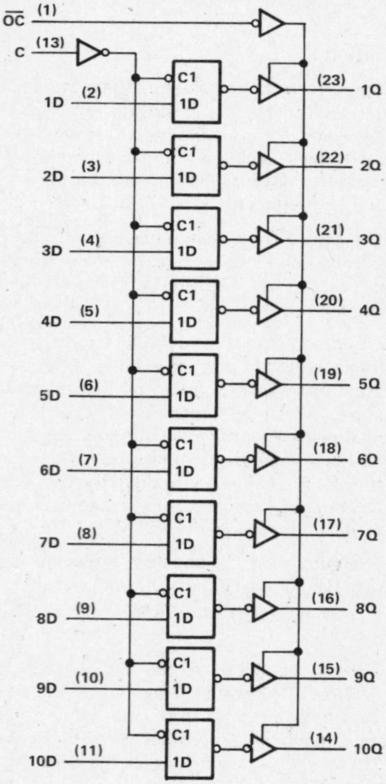
OC
C
(1)
(13)
C1
1D
(2) (3) (4) (5) (6) (7) (8) (9) (10) (11)
1D 2D 3D 4D 5D 6D 7D 8D 9D 10D
(23) (22) (21) (20) (19) (18) (17) (16) (15) (14)
1Q 2Q 3Q 4Q 5Q 6Q 7Q 8Q 9Q 10Q

† This symbol is in accordance with ANSI/IEEE Std 91-1984 and IEC Publication 617-12.

Pin numbers shown are for DW, JT, and NT packages.

TEXAS INSTRUMENTS
POST OFFICE BOX 225012 • DALLAS, TEXAS 75265

'ALS842, 'AS842 logic symbol†

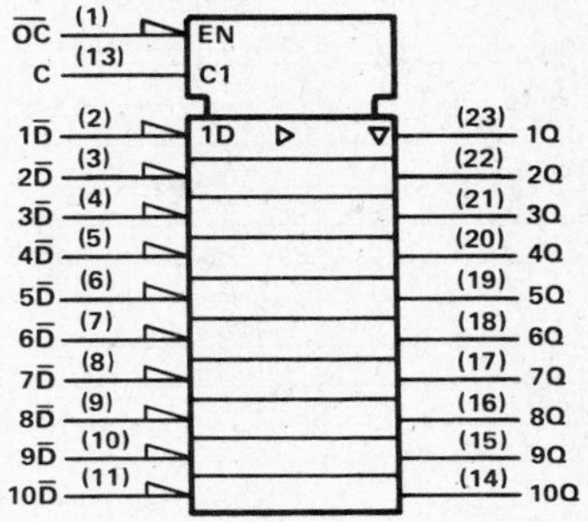
OC (1)
C (13)
EN
C1
1D (2)
2D (3)
3D (4)
4D (5)
5D (6)
6D (7)
7D (8)
8D (9)
9D (10)
10D (11)
1D
(23) 1Q
(22) 2Q
(21) 3Q
(20) 4Q
(19) 5Q
(18) 6Q
(17) 7Q
(16) 8Q
(15) 9Q
(14) 10Q

'ALS842, 'AS842 logic diagram (positive logic)

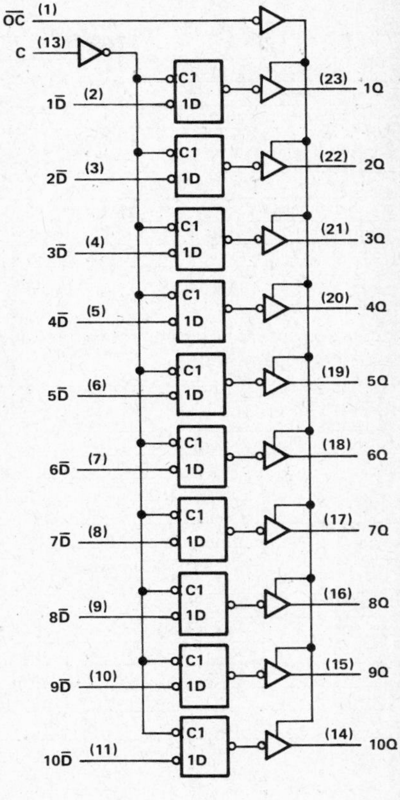
OC (1)
C (13)
1D (2)
2D (3)
3D (4)
4D (5)
5D (6)
6D (7)
7D (8)
8D (9)
9D (10)
10D (11)
C1
1D
(23) 1Q
(22) 2Q
(21) 3Q
(20) 4Q
(19) 5Q
(18) 6Q
(17) 7Q
(16) 8Q
(15) 9Q
(14) 10Q

† This symbol is in accordance with ANSI/IEEE Std 91-1984 and IEC Publication 617-12.
Pin numbers shown are for DW, JT, and NT packages.

absolute maximum ratings over operating free-air temperature range (unless otherwise noted)

Supply voltage, V_{CC}	7 V
Input voltage	7 V
Voltage applied to a disabled 3-state output	5.5 V
Operating free-air temperature range:	
SN54ALS841, SN54AS841, SN54ALS842, SN54AS842	−55°C to 125°C
SN74ALS841, SN74AS841, SN74ALS842, SN74AS842	0°C to 70°C
Storage temperature range	−65°C to 150°C

recommended operating conditions

		SN54ALS841			SN74ALS841			UNIT
		MIN	NOM	MAX	MIN	NOM	MAX	
V_{CC}	Supply voltage	4.5	5	5.5	4.5	5	5.5	V
V_{IH}	High-level input voltage	2			2			V
V_{IL}	Low-level input voltage			0.8			0.8	V
I_{OH}	High-level output current			−1			−2.6	mA
I_{OL}	Low-level output current			12			24	mA
							48†	mA
t_w	Pulse duration, enable C high	25			20			ns
t_{su}	Setup time, data before enable C↓	16			10			ns
t_h	Hold time, data after enable C↓	7			5			ns
T_A	Operating free-air temperature	−55		125	0		70	°C

† The extended limit applies only if V_{CC} is maintained between 4.75 V and 5.25 V. The 48 mA limit applies for SN74ALS841-1 only.

electrical characteristics over recommended operating free-air temperature range (unless otherwise noted)

PARAMETER	TEST CONDITIONS		SN54ALS841			SN74ALS841			UNIT
			MIN	TYP‡	MAX	MIN	TYP‡	MAX	
V_{IK}	V_{CC} = 4.5 V,	I_I = −18 mA			−1.2			−1.2	V
V_{OH}	V_{CC} = 4.5 V to 5.5 V,	I_{OH} = −0.4 mA	V_{CC}−2			V_{CC}−2			V
	V_{CC} = 4.5 V,	I_{OH} = −1 mA	2.4	3.3					
	V_{CC} = 4.5 V,	I_{OH} = −2.6 mA				2.4	3.2		
V_{OL}	V_{CC} = 4.5 V,	I_{OL} = 12 mA		0.25	0.4		0.25	0.4	V
	V_{CC} = 4.5 V, (I_{OL} = 48 mA for -1 versions)	I_{OL} = 24 mA					0.35	0.5	
I_{OZH}	V_{CC} = 5.5 V,	V_O = 2.7 V			20			20	μA
I_{OZL}	V_{CC} = 5.5 V,	V_O = 0.4			−20			−20	μA
I_I	V_{CC} = 5.5 V,	V_I = 7 V			0.1			0.1	mA
I_{IH}	V_{CC} = 5.5 V,	V_I = 2.7 V			20			20	μA
I_{IL}	V_{CC} = 5.5 V,	V_I = 0.4 V			−0.1			−0.1	mA
I_O§	V_{CC} = 5.5 V,	V_O = 2.25 V	−30		−112	−30		−112	mA
I_{CC}	V_{CC} = 5.5 V	Outputs high		19	30		19	30	mA
		Outputs low		38	62		38	62	
		Outputs disabled		23	40		23	40	

‡ All typical values are at V_{CC} = 5 V, T_A = 25°C.
§ The output conditions have been chosen to produce a current that closely approximates one half of the true short-circuit output current, I_{OS}.

TEXAS INSTRUMENTS
POST OFFICE BOX 225012 • DALLAS, TEXAS 75265

'ALS841 switching characteristics (see Note 1)

PARAMETER	FROM (INPUT)	TO (OUTPUT)	V_{CC} = 5 V, C_L = 50 pF, R1 = 500 Ω, R2 = 500 Ω, T_A = 25°C			V_{CC} = 4.5 V to 5.5 V, C_L = 50 pF, R1 = 500 Ω, R2 = 500 Ω, T_A = MIN to MAX						UNIT
			SN54/74ALS841			SN54ALS841			SN74ALS841			
			MIN	TYP	MAX	MIN	TYP	MAX	MIN	TYP	MAX	
t_{PLH}	D	Q		8.5	11	2		15	2		13	ns
t_{PHL}				8.5	11	2		15	2		13	
t_{PLH}	C	Q		14	18	7		25	7		21	ns
t_{PHL}				17	23	8		30	8		26	
t_{PZH}	$\overline{OC}$	Q		7.5	10	2		14	2		12	ns
t_{PZL}				7.5	10	2		14	2		12	
t_{PHZ}	$\overline{OC}$	Q		6	8	2		12	2		10	ns
t_{PLZ}				7	9	2		14	2		12	

NOTE 1: Load circuit and voltage waveforms are shown in Section 1.

recommended operating conditions

		SN54ALS842			SN74ALS842			UNIT
		MIN	NOM	MAX	MIN	NOM	MAX	
V_{CC}	Supply voltage	4.5	5	5.5	4.5	5	5.5	V
V_{IH}	High-level input voltage	2			2			V
V_{IL}	Low-level input voltage			0.8			0.8	V
I_{OH}	High-level output current			−1			−2.6	mA
I_{OL}	Low-level output current			12			24	mA
							48†	
t_w	Pulse duration, enable C high	25			20			ns
t_{su}	Setup time, data before enable C↓	16			10			ns
t_h	Hold time, data after enable C↓	7			5			ns
T_A	Operating free-air temperature	−55		125	0		70	°C

† The extended limit applies only if V_{CC} is maintained between 4.75 V and 5.25 V. The 48 mA limit applies for SN74ALS841-1 only.

electrical characteristics over recommended operating free-air temperature range (unless otherwise noted)

PARAMETER	TEST CONDITIONS		SN54ALS842			SN74ALS842			UNIT
			MIN	TYP‡	MAX	MIN	TYP‡	MAX	
V_{IK}	V_{CC} = 4.5 V,	I_I = −18 mA			−1.2			−1.2	V
V_{OH}	V_{CC} = 4.5 V to 5.5 V,	I_{OH} = −0.4 mA	$V_{CC}-2$			$V_{CC}-2$			V
	V_{CC} = 4.5 V,	I_{OH} = −1 mA	2.4	3.3					
	V_{CC} = 4.5 V,	I_{OH} = −2.6 mA				2.4	3.2		
V_{OL}	V_{CC} = 4.5 V,	I_{OL} = 12 mA		0.25	0.4		0.25	0.4	V
	V_{CC} = 4.5 V, (I_{OL} = 48 mA for -1 versions)	I_{OL} = 24 mA					0.35	0.5	
I_{OZH}	V_{CC} = 5.5 V,	V_O = 2.7 V			20			20	μA
I_{OZL}	V_{CC} = 5.5 V,	V_O = 0.4			−20			−20	μA
I_I	V_{CC} = 5.5 V,	V_I = 7 V			0.1			0.1	mA
I_{IH}	V_{CC} = 5.5 V,	V_I = 2.7 V			20			20	μA
I_{IL}	V_{CC} = 5.5 V,	V_I = 0.4 V			−0.1			−0.1	mA
I_O§	V_{CC} = 5.5 V,	V_O = 2.25 V	−30		−112	−30		−112	mA
I_{CC}	V_{CC} = 5.5 V	Outputs high		20	35		20	35	mA
		Outputs low		48	74		48	74	
		Outputs disabled		27	44		27	44	

‡ All typical values are at V_{CC} = 5 V, T_A = 25 °C.
§ The output conditions have been chosen to produce a current that closely approximates one half of the true short-circuit output current, I_{OS}.

'ALS842 switching characteristics (see Note 1)

PARAMETER	FROM (INPUT)	TO (OUTPUT)	V_{CC} = 5 V, C_L = 50 pF, R1 = 500 Ω, R2 = 500 Ω, T_A = 25°C			V_{CC} = 4.5 V to 5.5 V, C_L = 50 pF, R1 = 500 Ω, R2 = 500 Ω, T_A = MIN to MAX				UNIT
			'ALS842			SN54ALS842		SN74ALS842		
			MIN	TYP	MAX	MIN	MAX	MIN	MAX	
t_{PLH}	$\overline{D}$	Q		11	15	4	22	4	18	ns
t_{PHL}				8	11	3	17	3	13	
t_{PLH}	C	Q		17	23	8	31	8	27	ns
t_{PHL}				13	18	6	24	6	20	
t_{PZH}	$\overline{OC}$	Q		8	10	2	14	2	12	ns
t_{PZL}				8	11	2	14	2	12	
t_{PHZ}	$\overline{OC}$	Q		6	8	1	12	1	10	ns
t_{PLZ}				7	9	2	14	2	12	

NOTE 1: Load circuit and voltage waveforms are shown in Section 1.

recommended operating conditions

		SN54AS841 SN54AS842			SN74AS841 SN74AS842			UNIT
		MIN	NOM	MAX	MIN	NOM	MAX	
V_{CC}	Supply voltage	4.5	5	5.5	4.5	5	5.5	V
V_{IH}	High-level input voltage	2			2			V
V_{IL}	Low-level input voltage			0.8			0.8	V
I_{OH}	High-level output current			−24			−24	mA
I_{OL}	Low-level output current			32			48	mA
t_w	Pulse duration, enable C high	5			4			ns
t_{su}	Setup time, data before enable C↓	3.5			2.5			ns
t_h	Hold time, data after enable C↓	3.5			2.5			ns
T_A	Operating free-air temperature	−55		125	0		70	°C

electrical characteristics over recommended operating free-air temperature range (unless otherwise noted)

PARAMETER		TEST CONDITIONS		SN54AS841 SN54AS842			SN74AS841 SN74AS842			UNIT
				MIN	TYP†	MAX	MIN	TYP†	MAX	
V_{IK}		V_{CC} = 4.5 V,	I_I = −18 mA			−1.2			−1.2	V
V_{OH}		V_{CC} = 4.5 V to 5.5 V,	I_{OH} = −2 mA	$V_{CC}-2$			$V_{CC}-2$			V
		V_{CC} = 4.5 V,	I_{OH} = −15 mA	2.4	3.2		2.4	3.2		
		V_{CC} = 4.5 V,	I_{OH} = −24 mA	2			2			
V_{OL}		V_{CC} = 4.5 V,	I_{OL} = 32 mA		0.25	0.5				V
		V_{CC} = 4.5 V,	I_{OL} = 48 mA					0.35	0.5	
I_{OZH}		V_{CC} = 5.5 V,	V_O = 2.7 V			50			50	μA
I_{OZL}		V_{CC} = 5.5 V,	V_O = 0.4 V			−50			−50	μA
I_I		V_{CC} = 5.5 V,	V_I = 7 V			0.1			0.1	mA
I_{IH}		V_{CC} = 5.5 V,	V_I = 2.7 V			20			20	μA
I_{IL}		V_{CC} = 5.5 V,	V_I = 0.4 V			−0.5			−0.5	mA
I_O‡		V_{CC} = 5.5 V,	V_O = 2.25 V	−30		−112	−30		−112	mA
I_{CC}	'AS841	V_{CC} = 5.5 V	Outputs high		36	60		36	60	mA
			Outputs low		58	94		58	94	
			Outputs disabled		56	92		56	92	
	'AS842		Outputs high		38	62		38	62	
			Outputs low		60	97		60	97	
			Outputs disabled		58	95		58	95	

† All typical values are at V_{CC} = 5 V, T_A = 25°C.
‡ The output conditions have been chosen to produce a current that closely approximates one half of the true short-circuit output current, I_{OS}.

2 LSI Devices

'AS841 switching characteristics (see Note 1)

PARAMETER	FROM (INPUT)	TO (OUTPUT)	V_{CC} = 4.5 V to 5.5 V, C_L = 50 pF, R1 = 500 Ω, R2 = 500 Ω, T_A = MIN to MAX				UNIT
			SN54AS841		SN74AS841		
			MIN	MAX	MIN	MAX	
t_{PLH}	D	Q	1	8.5	1	6.5	ns
t_{PHL}			1	10	1	9	
t_{PLH}	C	Q	2	13	2	12	ns
t_{PHL}			2	13	2	12	
t_{PZH}	$\overline{OC}$	Q	2	13.5	2	10.5	ns
t_{PZL}			2	15	2	13.5	
t_{PHZ}	$\overline{OC}$	Q	1	10	1	8	ns
t_{PLZ}			1	10	1	8	

'AS842 switching characteristics (see Note 1)

PARAMETER	FROM (INPUT)	TO (OUTPUT)	V_{CC} = 4.5 V to 5.5 V, C_L = 50 pF, R1 = 500 Ω, R2 = 500 Ω, T_A = MIN to MAX				UNIT
			SN54AS842		SN74AS842		
			MIN	MAX	MIN	MAX	
t_{PLH}	$\overline{D}$	Q	1	11	1	8.5	ns
t_{PHL}			1	10	1	9	
t_{PLH}	C	Q	2	13	2	12	ns
t_{PHL}			2	13	2	12	
t_{PZH}	$\overline{OC}$	Q	2	14.5	2	12	ns
t_{PZL}			2	15	2	12.5	
t_{PHZ}	$\overline{OC}$	Q	1	10	1	8	ns
t_{PLZ}			1	10	1	8	

NOTE 1: Load circuit and voltage waveforms are shown in Section 1.

9-BIT BUS INTERFACE D-TYPE LATCHES WITH 3-STATE OUTPUTS

D2910, DECEMBER 1983—REVISED DECEMBER 1985

- **3-State Buffer-Type Outputs Drive Bus-Lines Directly**
- **Bus-Structured Pinout**
- **Provide Extra Bus Driving Latches Necessary for Wider Address/Data Paths or Buses with Parity**
- **Buffered Control Inputs to Reduce DC Loading**
- **Power-Up High Impedance**
- **Package Options Include Both Plastic and Ceramic Chip Carriers in Addition to Plastic and Ceramic DIPs**
- **Dependable Texas Instruments Quality and Reliability**

description

These 9-bit latches feature three-state outputs designed specifically for driving highly capacitive or relatively low-impedance loads. They are particularly suitable for implementing buffer registers, I/O ports, bidirectional bus drivers, and working registers.

The nine latches are transparent D-type. The 'ALS843 and 'AS843 have noninverting data (D) inputs. The 'ALS844 and 'AS844 have inverting D inputs.

A buffered output control ($\overline{OC}$) input can be used to place the nine outputs in either a normal logic state (high or low levels) or a high-impedance state. In the high-impedance state, the outputs neither load nor drive the bus lines significantly. The high-impedance state and increased drive provide the capability to drive the bus lines in a bus-organized system without need for interface or pull-up components.

The output control ($\overline{OC}$) does not affect the internal operation of the flip-flops. Old data can be retained or new data can be entered while the outputs are off.

The -1 versions of the SN74ALS843 and SN74ALS844 parts are identical to the standard versions except that the recommended maximum I_{OL} is increased to 48 milliamperes. There are no -1 versions of the SN54ALS843 and SN54ALS844.

SN54ALS843, SN54AS843 . . . JT PACKAGE
SN74ALS843, SN74AS843 . . . DW OR NT PACKAGE
(TOP VIEW)

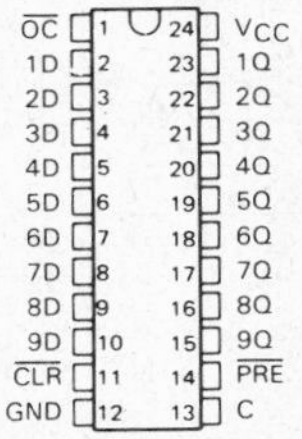
OC 1
1D 2
2D 3
3D 4
4D 5
5D 6
6D 7
7D 8
8D 9
9D 10
CLR 11
GND 12
24 VCC
23 1Q
22 2Q
21 3Q
20 4Q
19 5Q
18 6Q
17 7Q
16 8Q
15 9Q
14 PRE
13 C

SN54ALS843, SN54AS843. . . FK PACKAGE
SN74ALS843, SN74AS843 . . . FN PACKAGE
(TOP VIEW)

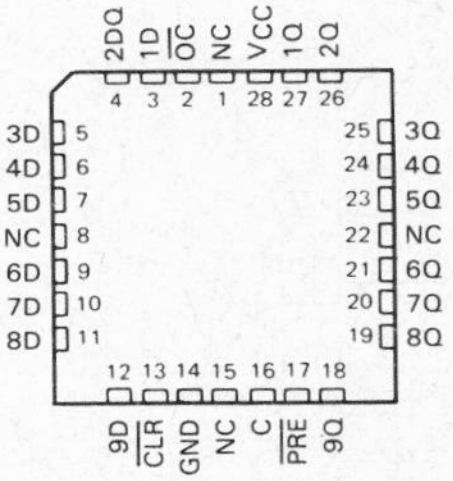
2D 1D OC NC VCC 1Q 2Q
4 3 2 1 28 27 26
3D 5
4D 6
5D 7
NC 8
6D 9
7D 10
8D 11
25 3Q
24 4Q
23 5Q
22 NC
21 6Q
20 7Q
19 8Q
12 13 14 15 16 17 18
9D CLR GND NC C PRE 9Q

SN54ALS844, SN54AS844 . . . JT PACKAGE
SN74ALS844, SN74AS844 . . . DW OR NT PACKAGE
(TOP VIEW)

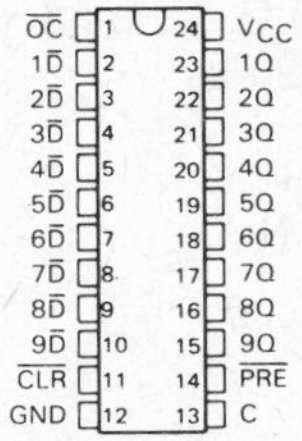
OC 1
1D 2
2D 3
3D 4
4D 5
5D 6
6D 7
7D 8
8D 9
9D 10
CLR 11
GND 12
24 VCC
23 1Q
22 2Q
21 3Q
20 4Q
19 5Q
18 6Q
17 7Q
16 8Q
15 9Q
14 PRE
13 C

SN54ALS844, SN54AS844 . . . FK PACKAGE
SN74ALS844, SN74AS844 .. . FN PACKAGE
(TOP VIEW)

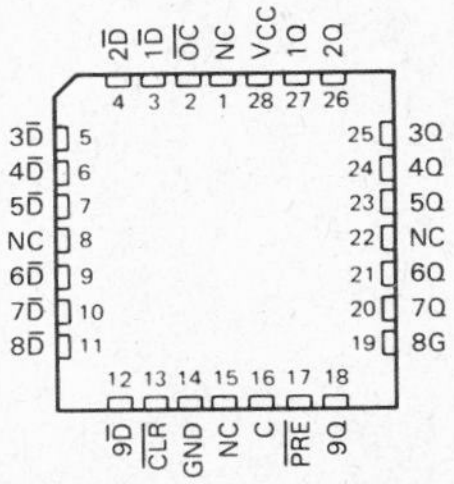
2D 1D OC NC VCC 1Q 2Q
4 3 2 1 28 27 26
3D 5
4D 6
5D 7
NC 8
6D 9
7D 10
8D 11
25 3Q
24 4Q
23 5Q
22 NC
21 6Q
20 7Q
19 8G
12 13 14 15 16 17 18
9D CLR GND NC C PRE 9Q

NC—No internal connection

The SN54ALS843, SN54AS843, SN54ALS844, and SN54AS844 are characterized for operation over the full military temperature range of −55°C to 125°C. The SN74ALS843, SN74AS843, SN74ALS844, and SN74AS844 are characterized for operation from 0°C to 70°C.

'ALS843, 'AS843 FUNCTION TABLE

INPUTS					OUTPUT
$\overline{PRE}$	$\overline{CLR}$	$\overline{OC}$	C	D	Q
L	X	L	X	X	H
H	L	L	X	X	L
H	H	L	H	L	L
H	H	L	H	H	H
H	H	L	L	X	Q_0
X	X	H	X	X	Z

'ALS843, 'AS843 logic symbol†

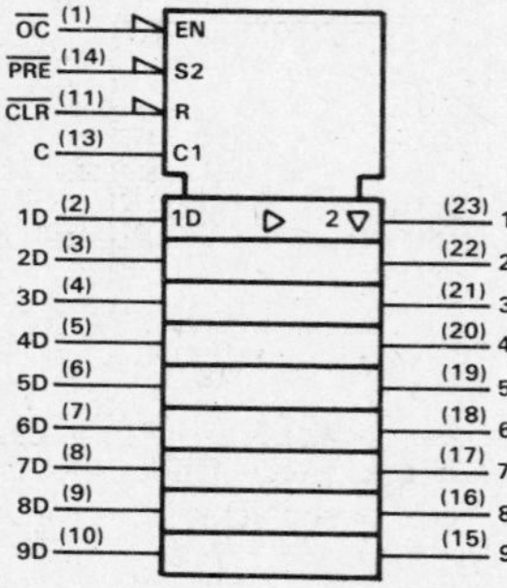
$\overline{OC}$ (1)
$\overline{PRE}$ (14)
$\overline{CLR}$ (11)
C (13)
EN
S2
R
C1
1D
2
1D (2)
2D (3)
3D (4)
4D (5)
5D (6)
6D (7)
7D (8)
8D (9)
9D (10)
(23) 1Q
(22) 2Q
(21) 3Q
(20) 4Q
(19) 5Q
(18) 6Q
(17) 7Q
(16) 8Q
(15) 9Q

† This symbol is in accordance with ANSI/IEEE Std 91-1984 and IEC Publication 617-12.

Pin numbers shown are for DW, JT, and NT packages.

'ALS843, 'AS843 logic diagram (positive logic)

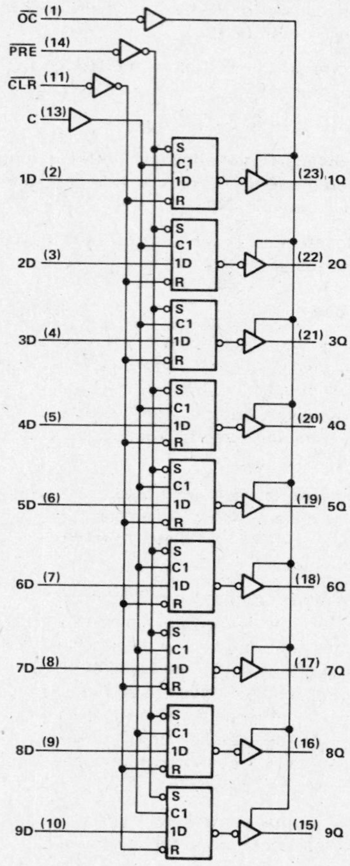
$\overline{OC}$ (1)
$\overline{PRE}$ (14)
$\overline{CLR}$ (11)
C (13)
S
C1
1D
R
1D (2)
2D (3)
3D (4)
4D (5)
5D (6)
6D (7)
7D (8)
8D (9)
9D (10)
(23) 1Q
(22) 2Q
(21) 3Q
(20) 4Q
(19) 5Q
(18) 6Q
(17) 7Q
(16) 8Q
(15) 9Q

TEXAS INSTRUMENTS
POST OFFICE BOX 225012 • DALLAS, TEXAS 75265

'ALS844, 'AS844 FUNCTION TABLE

INPUTS					OUTPUT
$\overline{PRE}$	$\overline{CLR}$	$\overline{OC}$	C	$\overline{D}$	Q
L	X	L	X	X	H
H	L	L	X	X	L
H	H	L	H	L	H
H	H	L	H	H	L
H	H	L	L	X	Q_0
X	X	H	X	X	Z

'ALS844, 'AS844 logic symbol†

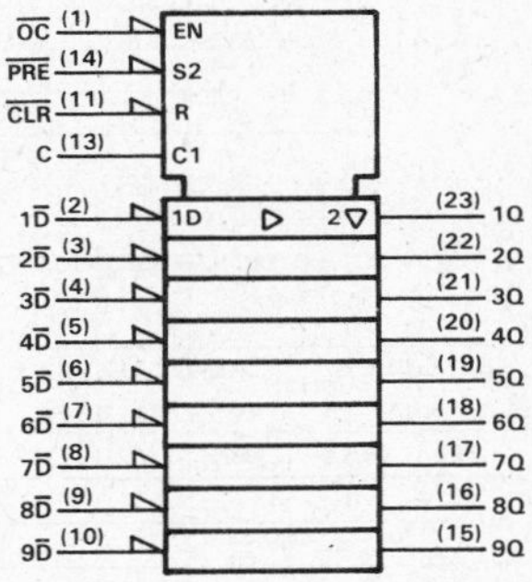
$\overline{OC}$ (1)
EN
$\overline{PRE}$ (14)
S2
$\overline{CLR}$ (11)
R
C (13)
C1
1D (2)
1D
2▽
(23) 1Q
2D (3)
(22) 2Q
3D (4)
(21) 3Q
4D (5)
(20) 4Q
5D (6)
(19) 5Q
6D (7)
(18) 6Q
7D (8)
(17) 7Q
8D (9)
(16) 8Q
9D (10)
(15) 9Q

† This symbol is in accordance with ANSI/IEEE Std 91-1984 and IEC Publication 617-12.

Pin numbers shown are for DW, JT, and NT packages.

'ALS844, 'AS844 logic diagram (positive logic)

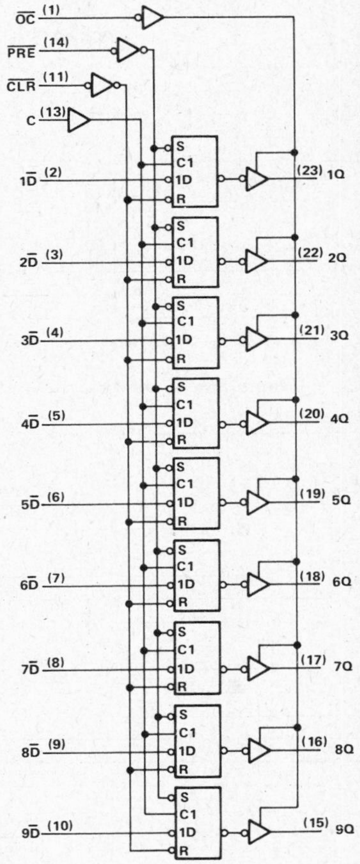
$\overline{OC}$ (1)
$\overline{PRE}$ (14)
$\overline{CLR}$ (11)
C (13)
S
C1
1D
R
1D (2)
(23) 1Q
2D (3)
(22) 2Q
3D (4)
(21) 3Q
4D (5)
(20) 4Q
5D (6)
(19) 5Q
6D (7)
(18) 6Q
7D (8)
(17) 7Q
8D (9)
(16) 8Q
9D (10)
(15) 9Q

2

LSI Devices

absolute maximum ratings over operating free-air temperature range (unless otherwise noted)

Supply voltage, V_{CC} . . . . 7 V
Input voltage . . . . 7 V
Voltage applied to a disabled 3-state output . . . . 5.5 V
Operating free-air temperature range: SN54ALS', SN54AS' . . . . −55°C to 125°C
SN74ALS', SN74AS' . . . . 0°C to 70°C
Storage temperature range . . . . −65°C to 150°C

recommended operating conditions

			SN54ALS843 SN54ALS844			SN74ALS843 SN74ALS844			UNIT
			MIN	NOM	MAX	MIN	NOM	MAX	
V_{CC}	Supply voltage		4.5	5	55	4.5	5	5.5	V
V_{IH}	High-level input voltage		2			2			V
V_{IL}	Low-level input voltage				0.8			0.8	V
I_{OH}	High-level output current				−1			−2.6	mA
I_{OL}	Low-level output current				12			24	mA
								48†	
t_w	Pulse duration	$\overline{CLR}$ or $\overline{PRE}$ low	40			35			ns
		C high	25			20			
t_{su}	Setup time, data before enable C↓		16			10			ns
t_h	Hold time, data after enable C↓		7			5			ns
T_A	Operating free-air temperature		−55		125	0		70	°C

† The 48-mA limit applies for SN74ALS843-1 and SN74ALS844-1 only and only if V_{CC} is maintained between 4.75 V and 5.25 V.

electrical characteristics over recommended operating free-air temperature range (unless otherwise noted)

PARAMETER		TEST CONDITIONS		SN54ALS843 SN54ALS844			SN74ALS843 SN74ALS844			UNIT
				MIN	TYP‡	MAX	MIN	TYP‡	MAX	
V_{IK}		V_{CC} = 4.5 V,	I_I = −18 mA			−1.2			−1.2	V
V_{OH}		V_{CC} = 4.5 V to 5.5 V,	I_{OH} = −0.4 mA	V_{CC}−2			V_{CC}−2			V
		V_{CC} = 4.5 V,	I_{OH} = −1 mA	2.4	3.3					
		V_{CC} = 4.5 V,	I_{OH} = −2.6 mA				2.4	3.2		
V_{OL}		V_{CC} = 4.5 V,	I_{OL} = 12 mA		0.25	0.4		0.25	0.4	V
		V_{CC} = 4.5 V, (I_{OL} = 48 mA for -1 versions)	I_{OL} = 24 mA					0.35	0.5	
I_{OZH}		V_{CC} = 5.5 V,	V_O = 2.7 V			20			20	μA
I_{OZL}		V_{CC} = 5.5 V,	V_O = 0.4 V			−20			−20	μA
I_I		V_{CC} = 5.5 V,	V_I = 7 V			0.1			0.1	mA
I_{IH}		V_{CC} = 5.5 V,	V_I = 2.7 V			20			20	μA
I_{IL}		V_{CC} = 5.5 V,	V_I = 0.4 V			−0.1			−0.1	mA
I_O§		V_{CC} = 5.5 V,	V_O = 2.25 V	−30		−112	−30		−112	mA
I_{CC}	'ALS843	V_{CC} = 5.5 V	Outputs high		21	36		21	36	mA
			Outputs low		41	67		41	67	
			Outputs disabled		25	42		25	42	
	'ALS844		Outputs high		21	36		21	36	
			Outputs low		41	72		41	72	
			Outputs disabled		28	48		28	48	

‡ All typical values are at V_{CC} = 5 V, T_A = 25°C.
§ The output conditions have been chosen to produce a current that closely approximates one half of the true short-circuit output current, I_{OS}.

2

LSI Devices

TEXAS INSTRUMENTS
POST OFFICE BOX 225012 • DALLAS, TEXAS 75265

'ALS843 switching characteristics (see Note 1)

PARAMETER	FROM (INPUT)	TO (OUTPUT)	V_{CC} = 5 V, C_L = 50 pF, R1 = 500 Ω, R2 = 500 Ω, T_A = 25°C			V_{CC} = 4.5 V to 5.5 V, C_L = 50 pF, R1 = 500 Ω, R2 = 500 Ω, T_A = MIN to MAX				UNIT
			'ALS843			SN54ALS843		SN74ALS843		
			MIN	TYP	MAX	MIN	MAX	MIN	MAX	
t_{PLH}	D	Q		7	11	2	15	2	13	ns
t_{PHL}				11	15	4	20	4	18	
t_{PLH}	C	Q		12	18	5	25	5	21	ns
t_{PHL}				16	23	8	30	8	26	
t_{PLH}	$\overline{PRE}$	Q		13	19	5	25	5	22	ns
t_{PHL}				19	26	4	35	6	30	
t_{PLH}	$\overline{CLR}$	Q		19	26	4	35	6	30	ns
t_{PHL}				14	21	6	27	6	23	
t_{PZH}	$\overline{OC}$	Q		7	10	2	14	2	12	ns
t_{PZL}				9	12	4	16	4	14	
t_{PHZ}	$\overline{OC}$	Q		6	9	2	12	2	10	ns
t_{PLZ}				7	10	2	14	2	12	

'ALS844 switching characteristics (see Note 1)

PARAMETER	FROM (INPUT)	TO (OUTPUT)	V_{CC} = 5 V, C_L = 50 pF, R1 = 500 Ω, R2 = 500 Ω, T_A = 25°C			V_{CC} = 4.5 V to 5.5 V, C_L = 50 pF, R1 = 500 Ω, R2 = 500 Ω, T_A = MIN to MAX				UNIT
			'ALS844			SN54ALS844		SN74ALS844		
			MIN	TYP	MAX	MIN	MAX	MIN	MAX	
t_{PLH}	$\overline{D}$	Q		11	16	4	22	4	20	ns
t_{PHL}				9	13	3	17	3	15	
t_{PLH}	C	Q		17	24	8	32	8	29	ns
t_{PHL}				14	19	6	26	6	22	
t_{PLH}	$\overline{PRE}$	Q		13	19	5	25	5	22	ns
t_{PHL}				19	26	4	35	6	30	
t_{PLH}	$\overline{CLR}$	Q		19	26	4	35	6	30	ns
t_{PHL}				16	23	8	29	8	25	
t_{PZH}	$\overline{OC}$	Q		10	15	2	19	4	17	ns
t_{PZL}				12	18	3	22	5	20	
t_{PHZ}	$\overline{OC}$	Q		7	10	1	12	1	11	ns
t_{PLZ}				5	9	1	14	1	12	

NOTE 1: Load circuit and voltage waveforms are shown in Section 1.

recommended operating conditions

			SN54AS843 SN54AS844			SN74AS843 SN74AS844			UNIT
			MIN	NOM	MAX	MIN	NOM	MAX	
V_{CC}	Supply voltage		4.5	5	55	4.5	5	5.5	V
V_{IH}	High-level input voltage		2			2			V
V_{IL}	Low-level input voltage				0.8			0.8	V
I_{OH}	High-level output current				−24			−24	mA
I_{OL}	Low-level output current				32			48	mA
t_w	Pulse duration, enable C high	$\overline{CLR}$ or $\overline{PRE}$ low	5			4			ns
		C high	5			4			ns
t_{su}	Setup time, data before enable C↓		3.5			2.5			ns
t_h	Hold time, data after enable C↓		3.5			2.5			ns
t_r	Recovery time	$\overline{PRE}$	17			15			ns
		$\overline{CLR}$	16			14			ns
T_A	Operating free-air temperature		−55		125	0		70	°C

electrical characteristics over recommended operating free-air temperature range (unless otherwise noted)

PARAMETER		TEST CONDITIONS		SN54AS843 SN54AS844			SN74AS843 SN74AS844			UNIT
				MIN	TYP†	MAX	MIN	TYP†	MAX	
V_{IK}		V_{CC} = 4.5 V,	I_I = −18 mA			−1.2			−1.2	V
V_{OH}		V_{CC} = 4.5 V,	I_{OH} = −2 mA	$V_{CC}-2$			$V_{CC}-2$			V
		V_{CC} = 4.5 V,	I_{OH} = −15 mA	2.4	3.2		2.4	3.2		V
		V_{CC} = 4.5 V,	I_{OH} = −24 mA	2			2			V
V_{OL}		V_{CC} = 4.5 V,	I_{OL} = 32 mA		0.25	0.5				V
		V_{CC} = 4.5 V,	I_{OL} = 48 mA					0.35	0.5	V
I_{OZH}		V_{CC} = 5.5 V,	V_O = 2.7 V			50			50	μA
I_{OZL}		V_{CC} = 5.5 V,	V_O = 0.4 V			−50			−50	μA
I_I		V_{CC} = 5.5 V,	V_I = 7 V			0.1			0.1	mA
I_{IH}		V_{CC} = 5.5 V,	V_I = 2.7 V			20			20	μA
I_{IL}		V_{CC} = 5.5 V,	V_I = 0.4 V			−0.5			−0.5	mA
I_O‡		V_{CC} = 5.5 V,	V_O = 2.25 V	−30		−112	−30		−112	mA
I_{CC}	'AS843	V_{CC} = 5.5 V,	Outputs high		37	62		37	62	mA
			Outputs low		56	92		56	92	mA
			Outputs disabled		56	92		56	92	mA
	'AS844		Outputs high		39	64		39	64	mA
			Outputs low		58	95		58	95	mA
			Outputs disabled		58	95		58	95	mA

†All typical values are at V_{CC} = 5 V, T_A = 25°C.
‡The output conditions have been chosen to produce a current that closely approximates one half of the true short-circuit output current, I_{OS}.

'AS843 switching characteristics (see Note 1)

PARAMETER	FROM (INPUT)	TO (OUTPUT)	V_{CC} = 4.5 V to 5.5 V, C_L = 50 pF, R1 = 500 Ω, R2 = 500 Ω, T_A = MIN to MAX				UNIT
			SN54AS843		SN74AS843		
			MIN	MAX	MIN	MAX	
t_{PLH}	D	Q	1	8.5	1	6.5	ns
t_{PHL}			1	10	1	9	
t_{PLH}	C	O	2	13	2	12	ns
t_{PHL}			2	13	2	12	
t_{PLH}	$\overline{PRE}$	Q	2	12	2	10	ns
t_{PHL}	$\overline{CLR}$	Q	2	14	2	13	ns
t_{PZH}	$\overline{OC}$	Q	2	13.5	2	10.5	ns
t_{PZL}			2	15	2	13.5	
t_{PHZ}	$\overline{OC}$	Q	1	10	1	8	ns
t_{PLZ}			1	10	1	8	

'AS844 switching characteristics (see Note 1)

PARAMETER	FROM (INPUT)	TO (OUTPUT)	V_{CC} = 4.5 V to 5.5 V, C_L = 50 pF, R1 = 500 Ω, R2 = 500 Ω, T_A = MIN to MAX				UNIT
			SN54AS844		SN74AS844		
			MIN	MAX	MIN	MAX	
t_{PLH}	D	Q	1	11	1	8.5	ns
t_{PHL}			1	11	1	10	
t_{PLH}	C	O	2	14	2	12.5	ns
t_{PHL}			2	14	2	13	
t_{PLH}	$\overline{PRE}$	Q	2	12	2	10	ns
t_{PHL}	$\overline{CLR}$	Q	2	14.5	2	13.5	ns
t_{PZH}	$\overline{OC}$	Q	2	14.5	2	12	ns
t_{PZL}			2	15	2	13.5	
t_{PHZ}	$\overline{OC}$	Q	1	10	1	8	ns
t_{PLZ}			1	10	1	8	

NOTE 1: Load circuit and voltage waveforms are shown in Section 1.

D latch signal conventions

It is normal TI practice to name the outputs and other inputs of a D-type latch and to draw its logic symbol based on the assumption of true data (D) inputs. Then outputs that produce data in phase with the data inputs are called Q and those producing complementary data are called $\overline{\text{Q}}$. An input that causes a Q output to go high or a $\overline{\text{Q}}$ output to go low is called Preset; an input that causes a $\overline{\text{Q}}$ output to go high or a Q output to go low is called Clear. Bars are used over these pin names ($\overline{\text{PRE}}$ and $\overline{\text{CLR}}$) if they are active low. The devices on this data sheet are second-source designs and the pin-name conventions used by the original manufacturer have been retained. That makes it necessary to designate the data inputs and outputs of the inverting circuit $\overline{\text{D}}$ and Q.

In some applications it may be advantageous to redesignate the inputs and outputs $\overline{\text{D}}$ and $\overline{\text{Q}}$ for the noninverting circuits or D and $\overline{\text{Q}}$ for the inverting circuits. In that case signal names should change as shown below. Also shown are corresponding changes in the logic symbols.

Notice that Q becoming $\overline{\text{Q}}$ causes $\overline{\text{PRE}}$ and $\overline{\text{CLR}}$ to exchange their names and their S and R function labels. The presence or absense of polarity indicators (⊳) changes at the data inputs and outputs, but not at $\overline{\text{PRE}}$, $\overline{\text{CLR}}$, and $\overline{\text{OC}}$ since these inputs are still active-low.

'ALS843, 'AS843

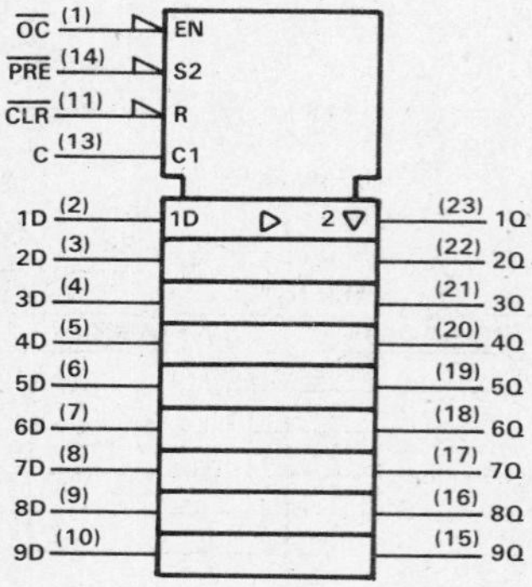
OC (1) EN
PRE (14) S2
CLR (11) R
C (13) C1
1D (2) 1D 2▽ (23) 1Q
2D (3) (22) 2Q
3D (4) (21) 3Q
4D (5) (20) 4Q
5D (6) (19) 5Q
6D (7) (18) 6Q
7D (8) (17) 7Q
8D (9) (16) 8Q
9D (10) (15) 9Q

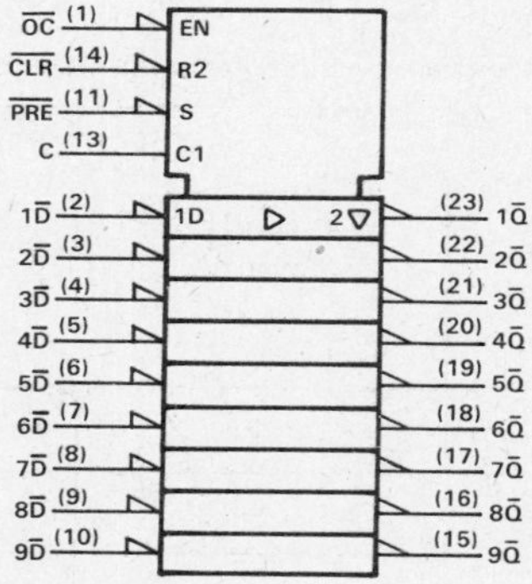
OC (1) EN
CLR (14) R2
PRE (11) S
C (13) C1
1D̄ (2) 1D 2▽ (23) 1Q̄
2D̄ (3) (22) 2Q̄
3D̄ (4) (21) 3Q̄
4D̄ (5) (20) 4Q̄
5D̄ (6) (19) 5Q̄
6D̄ (7) (18) 6Q̄
7D̄ (8) (17) 7Q̄
8D̄ (9) (16) 8Q̄
9D̄ (10) (15) 9Q̄

'ALS844, 'AS844

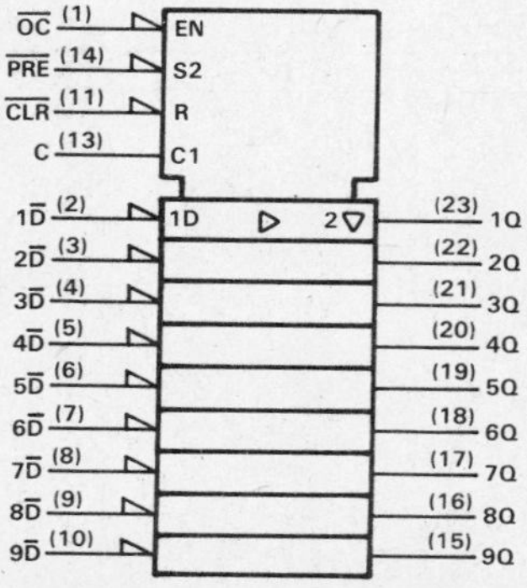
OC (1) EN
PRE (14) S2
CLR (11) R
C (13) C1
1D̄ (2) 1D 2▽ (23) 1Q
2D̄ (3) (22) 2Q
3D̄ (4) (21) 3Q
4D̄ (5) (20) 4Q
5D̄ (6) (19) 5Q
6D̄ (7) (18) 6Q
7D̄ (8) (17) 7Q
8D̄ (9) (16) 8Q
9D̄ (10) (15) 9Q

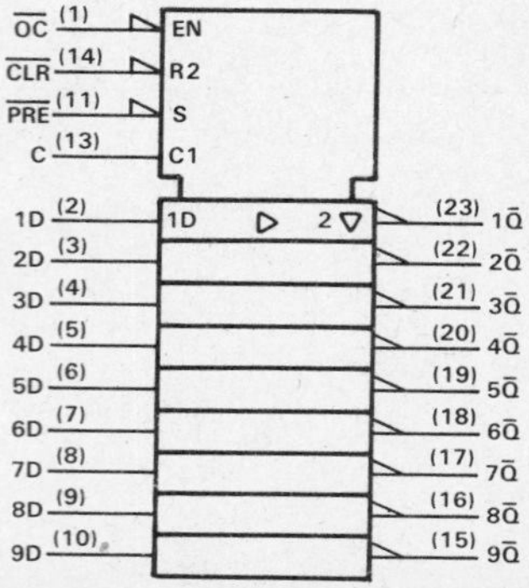
OC (1) EN
CLR (14) R2
PRE (11) S
C (13) C1
1D (2) 1D 2▽ (23) 1Q̄
2D (3) (22) 2Q̄
3D (4) (21) 3Q̄
4D (5) (20) 4Q̄
5D (6) (19) 5Q̄
6D (7) (18) 6Q̄
7D (8) (17) 7Q̄
8D (9) (16) 8Q̄
9D (10) (15) 9Q̄

TEXAS INSTRUMENTS
POST OFFICE BOX 225012 • DALLAS, TEXAS 75265

8-BIT BUS INTERFACE D-TYPE LATCHES WITH 3-STATE OUTPUTS

D2825, DECEMBER 1983—REVISED JANUARY 1986

- 3-State Buffer-Type Outputs Drive Bus-Lines Directly
- Bus-Structured Pinout
- Provides Extra Bus Driving Latches Necessary for Wider Address/Data Paths or Buses with Parity
- Buffered Control Inputs to Reduce DC Loading
- Power-Up High-Impedance State
- Package Options Include Both Plastic and Ceramic Chip Carriers in Addition to Plastic and Ceramic DIPs
- Dependable Texas Instruments Quality and Reliability

SN54ALS845, SN54AS845 . . . JT PACKAGE
SN74ALS845, SN74AS845 . . . DW OR NT PACKAGE
(TOP VIEW)

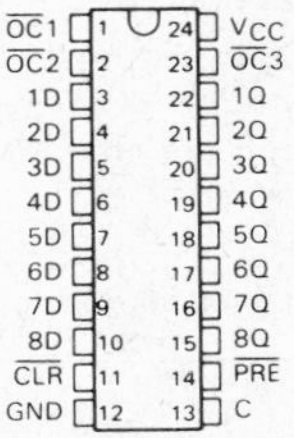
$\overline{OC}$1 1
$\overline{OC}$2 2
1D 3
2D 4
3D 5
4D 6
5D 7
6D 8
7D 9
8D 10
$\overline{CLR}$ 11
GND 12
24 V_{CC}
23 $\overline{OC}$3
22 1Q
21 2Q
20 3Q
19 4Q
18 5Q
17 6Q
16 7Q
15 8Q
14 $\overline{PRE}$
13 C

SN54ALS845, SN54AS845 . . . FK PACKAGE
SN74ALS845, SN74AS845 . . . FN PACKAGE
(TOP VIEW)

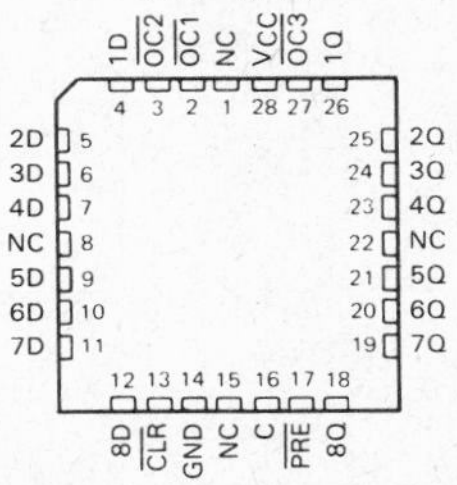
1D $\overline{OC}$2 $\overline{OC}$1 NC V_{CC} $\overline{OC}$3 1Q
4 3 2 1 28 27 26
2D 5
3D 6
4D 7
NC 8
5D 9
6D 10
7D 11
25 2Q
24 3Q
23 4Q
22 NC
21 5Q
20 6Q
19 7Q
12 13 14 15 16 17 18
8D $\overline{CLR}$ GND NC C $\overline{PRE}$ 8Q

SN54ALS846, SN54AS846 . . . JT PACKAGE
SN74ALS846, SN74AS846 . . . DW OR NT PACKAGE
(TOP VIEW)

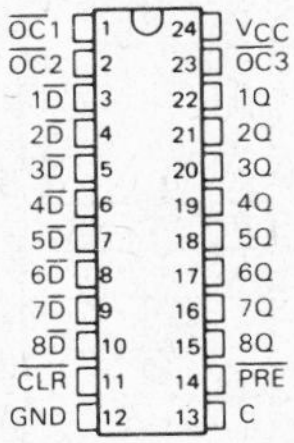
$\overline{OC}$1 1
$\overline{OC}$2 2
$\overline{1D}$ 3
$\overline{2D}$ 4
$\overline{3D}$ 5
$\overline{4D}$ 6
$\overline{5D}$ 7
$\overline{6D}$ 8
$\overline{7D}$ 9
$\overline{8D}$ 10
$\overline{CLR}$ 11
GND 12
24 V_{CC}
23 $\overline{OC}$3
22 1Q
21 2Q
20 3Q
19 4Q
18 5Q
17 6Q
16 7Q
15 8Q
14 $\overline{PRE}$
13 C

SN54ALS846, SN54AS846 . . . FK PACKAGE
SN74ALS846, SN74AS846 . . . FN PACKAGE
(TOP VIEW)

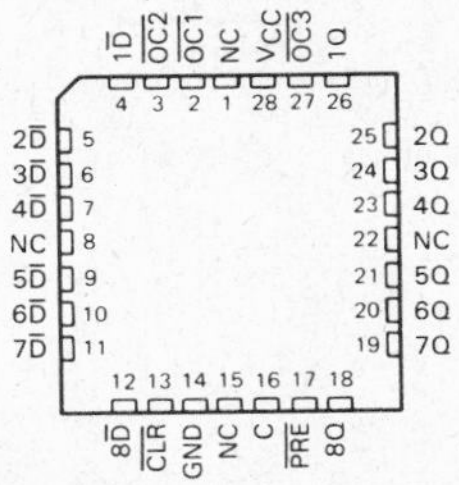
$\overline{1D}$ $\overline{OC}$2 $\overline{OC}$1 NC V_{CC} $\overline{OC}$3 1Q
4 3 2 1 28 27 26
$\overline{2D}$ 5
$\overline{3D}$ 6
$\overline{4D}$ 7
NC 8
$\overline{5D}$ 9
$\overline{6D}$ 10
$\overline{7D}$ 11
25 2Q
24 3Q
23 4Q
22 NC
21 5Q
20 6Q
19 7Q
12 13 14 15 16 17 18
$\overline{8D}$ $\overline{CLR}$ GND NC C $\overline{PRE}$ 8Q

NC—No internal connection

description

These 8-bit latches feature three-state outputs designed specifically for driving highly capacitive or relatively low-impedance loads. They are particularly suitable for implementing buffer registers, I/O ports, bidirectional bus drivers, and working registers.

The eight latches are transparent D-type. The 'ALS845 and 'AS845 have noninverting data (D) inputs. The 'ALS846 and 'AS846 have inverting $\overline{D}$ inputs. Since $\overline{CLR}$ and $\overline{PRE}$ are independent of the clock, taking the $\overline{CLR}$ input low will cause the eight Q outputs to go low. Taking the $\overline{PRE}$ input low will cause the eight Q outputs to go high. When both $\overline{PRE}$ and $\overline{CLR}$ are taken low, the outputs will follow the preset condition.

The buffered output control inputs ($\overline{OC}$1, $\overline{OC}$2, and $\overline{OC}$3) can be used to place the eight outputs in either a normal logic state (high or low levels) or a high-impedance state. In the high-impedance state, the outputs neither load nor drive the bus lines significantly. The high-impedance state and increased drive provide the capability to drive the bus lines in a bus-organized system without need for interface or pull-up components. The output controls do not affect the internal operation of the latches. Old data can be retained or new data can be entered while the outputs are in the high-impedance state.

2 LSI Devices

This document contains information on products in more than one phase of development. The status of each device is indicated on the page(s) specifying its electrical characteristics.

TEXAS INSTRUMENTS
POST OFFICE BOX 225012 • DALLAS, TEXAS 75265

The -1 versions of the SN74ALS845 and SN74ALS846 parts are identical to the standard versions except that the recommended maximum I_{OL} is increased to 48 milliamperes. There are no -1 versions of the SN54ALS845 and SN54ALS846.

The SN54ALS845, SN54AS845, SN54ALS846, and SN54AS846 are characterized for operation over the full military temperature range of −55 °C to 125 °C. The SN74ALS845, SN74AS845, SN74ALS846, and SN74AS846 are characterized for operation from 0 °C to 70 °C.

FUNCTION TABLES

'ALS845, 'AS845

INPUTS							OUTPUT
$\overline{PRE}$	$\overline{CLR}$	$\overline{OC1}$	$\overline{OC2}$	$\overline{OC3}$	C	D	Q
L	H	L	L	L	X	X	H
H	L	L	L	L	X	X	L
L	L	L	L	L	X	X	H
H	H	L	L	L	H	L	L
H	H	L	L	L	H	H	H
H	H	L	L	L	L	X	Q_0
X	X	X	X	H	X	X	Z
X	X	X	H	X	X	X	Z
X	X	H	X	X	X	X	Z

'ALS846, 'AS846

INPUTS							OUTPUT
$\overline{PRE}$	$\overline{CLR}$	$\overline{OC1}$	$\overline{OC2}$	$\overline{OC3}$	C	$\overline{D}$	Q
L	H	L	L	L	X	X	H
H	L	L	L	L	X	X	L
L	L	L	L	L	X	X	H
H	H	L	L	L	H	L	H
H	H	L	L	L	H	H	L
H	H	L	L	L	L	X	Q_0
X	X	X	X	H	X	X	Z
X	X	X	H	X	X	X	Z
X	X	H	X	X	X	X	Z

logic symbols†

'ALS845, 'AS845

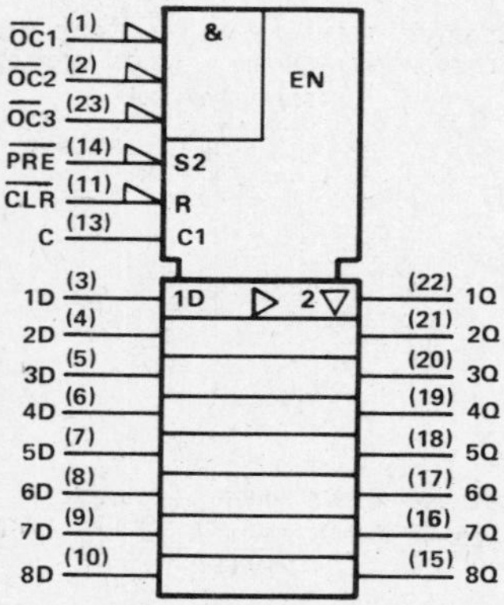
OC1 (1)
OC2 (2)
OC3 (23)
PRE (14)
CLR (11)
C (13)
&
EN
S2
R
C1
1D
2
1D (3)
2D (4)
3D (5)
4D (6)
5D (7)
6D (8)
7D (9)
8D (10)
(22) 1Q
(21) 2Q
(20) 3Q
(19) 4Q
(18) 5Q
(17) 6Q
(16) 7Q
(15) 8Q

'ALS846, 'AS846

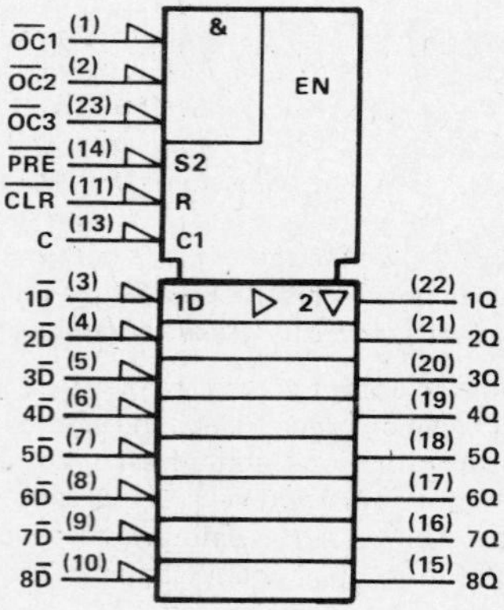
OC1 (1)
OC2 (2)
OC3 (23)
PRE (14)
CLR (11)
C (13)
&
EN
S2
R
C1
1D
2
1D (3)
2D (4)
3D (5)
4D (6)
5D (7)
6D (8)
7D (9)
8D (10)
(22) 1Q
(21) 2Q
(20) 3Q
(19) 4Q
(18) 5Q
(17) 6Q
(16) 7Q
(15) 8Q

† These symbols are in accordance with ANSI/IEEE Std 91-1984 and IEC Publication 617-12.

Pin numbers shown are for DW, JT, and NT packages.

TEXAS INSTRUMENTS
POST OFFICE BOX 225012 • DALLAS, TEXAS 75265

logic diagrams (positive logic)

'ALS845, 'AS845

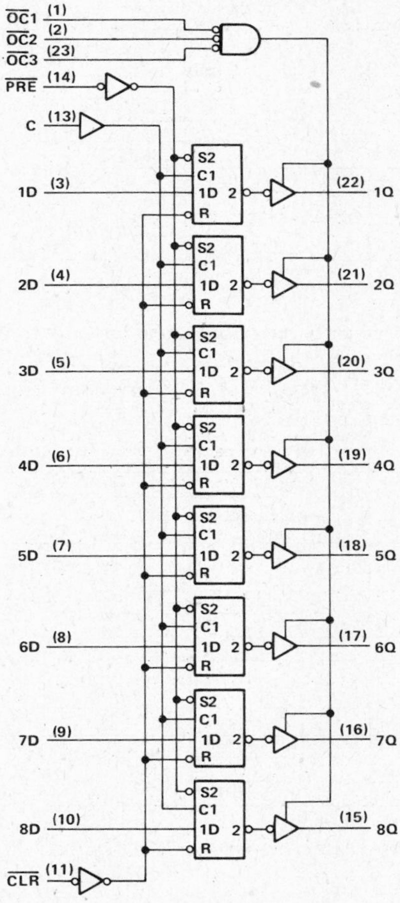
OC1 (1)
OC2 (2)
OC3 (23)
PRE (14)
C (13)
S2
C1
1D 2
R
1D (3)
(22) 1Q
2D (4)
(21) 2Q
3D (5)
(20) 3Q
4D (6)
(19) 4Q
5D (7)
(18) 5Q
6D (8)
(17) 6Q
7D (9)
(16) 7Q
8D (10)
(15) 8Q
CLR (11)

'ALS846, 'AS846

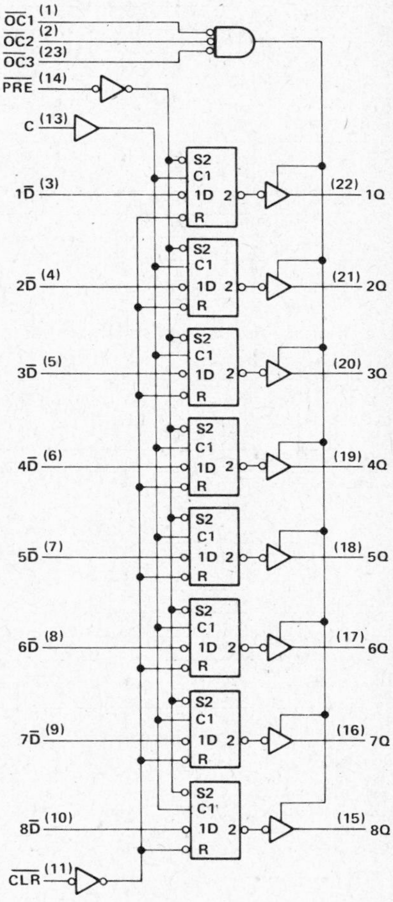
OC1 (1)
OC2 (2)
OC3 (23)
PRE (14)
C (13)
S2
C1
1D 2
R
1D̄ (3)
(22) 1Q
2D̄ (4)
(21) 2Q
3D̄ (5)
(20) 3Q
4D̄ (6)
(19) 4Q
5D̄ (7)
(18) 5Q
6D̄ (8)
(17) 6Q
7D̄ (9)
(16) 7Q
8D̄ (10)
(15) 8Q
CLR (11)

Pin numbers shown are for DW, JT, and NT packages.

absolute maximum ratings over operating free-air temperature range (unless otherwise noted)

Supply voltage, V_{CC} . . . . 7 V
Input voltage . . . . 7 V
Voltage applied to a disabled 3-state output . . . . 5.5 V
Operating free-air temperature range:
SN54ALS845, SN54AS845, SN54ALS846, SN54AS846 . . . . −55°C to 125°C
SN74ALS845, SN74AS845, SN74ALS846, SN74AS846 . . . . −0°C to 70°C
Storage temperature range . . . . −65°C to 150°C

recommended operating conditions

			SN54ALS845			SN74ALS845			UNIT
			MIN	NOM	MAX	MIN	NOM	MAX	
V_{CC}	Supply voltage		4.5	5	5.5	4.5	5	5.5	V
V_{IH}	High-level input voltage		2			2			V
V_{IL}	Low-level input voltage				0.8			0.8	V
I_{OH}	High-level output current				−1			−2.6	mA
I_{OL}	Low-level output current				12			24	mA
								48†	
t_w	Pulse duration	$\overline{CLR}$ or $\overline{PRE}$ low	40			35			ns
		C high	25			20			
t_{su}	Setup time, data before enable C↓		16			10			ns
t_h	Hold time, data after enable C↓		7			5			ns
T_A	Operating free-air temperature		−55		125	0		70	°C

†The extended limit applies only if V_{CC} is maintained between 4.75 V and 5.25 V. The 48 mA limit applies for SN74ALS845-1 only.

electrical characteristics over recommended operating free-air temperature range (unless otherwise noted)

PARAMETER	TEST CONDITIONS		SN54ALS845			SN74ALS845			UNIT
			MIN	TYP‡	MAX	MIN	TYP‡	MAX	
V_{IK}	V_{CC} = 4.5 V,	I_I = −18 mA			−1.2			−1.2	V
V_{OH}	V_{CC} = 4.5 V to 5.5 V,	I_{OH} = −0.4 mA	$V_{CC}-2$			$V_{CC}-2$			V
	V_{CC} = 4.5 V,	I_{OH} = −1 mA	2.4	3.3					
	V_{CC} = 4.5 V,	I_{OH} = −2.6 mA				2.4	3.2		
V_{OL}	V_{CC} = 4.5 V,	I_{OL} = 12 mA		0.25	0.4		0.25	0.4	V
	V_{CC} = 4.5 V, (I_{OL} = 48 mA for -1 versions)	I_{OL} = 24 mA					0.35	0.5	
I_{OZH}	V_{CC} = 5.5 V,	V_O = 2.7 V			20			20	μA
I_{OZL}	V_{CC} = 5.5 V,	V_O = 0.4 V			−20			−20	μA
I_I	V_{CC} = 5.5 V,	V_I = 7 V			0.1			0.1	mA
I_{IH}	V_{CC} = 5.5 V,	V_I = 2.7 V			20			20	μA
I_{IL}	V_{CC} = 5.5 V,	V_I = 0.4 V			−0.1			−0.1	mA
I_O§	V_{CC} = 5.5 V,	V_O = 2.25 V	−30		−112	−30		−112	mA
I_{CC}	V_{CC} = 5.5 V	Outputs high		21	36		21	36	mA
		Outputs low		41	67		41	67	
		Outputs disabled		25	42		25	42	

‡All typical values are at V_{CC} = 5 V, T_A = 25°C.

§The output conditions have been chosen to produce a current that closely approximates one half of the true short-circuit output current, I_{OS}.

switching characteristics (see Note 1)

PARAMETER	FROM (INPUT)	TO (OUTPUT)	V_{CC} = 5 V, C_L = 50 pF, R1 = 500 Ω, R2 = 500 Ω, T_A = 25°C			V_{CC} = 4.5 V to 5.5 V, C_L = 50 pF, R1 = 500 Ω, R2 = 500 Ω, T_A = MIN to MAX				UNIT
			'ALS845			SN54ALS845		SN74ALS845		
			MIN	TYP	MAX	MIN	MAX	MIN	MAX	
t_{PLH}	D	Q		7	11	2	15	2	13	ns
t_{PHL}				11	15	4	20	4	18	
t_{PLH}	C	Q		12	18	5	25	5	21	ns
t_{PHL}				16	23	8	30	8	26	
t_{PLH}	$\overline{PRE}$	Q		13	19	5	25	6	22	ns
t_{PHL}				19	26	4	35	6	30	ns
t_{PLH}	$\overline{CLR}$	Q		19	26	4	35	6	30	ns
t_{PHL}				16	22	6	28	6	24	ns
t_{PZH}	$\overline{OC}$	Q		9	14	2	18	3	16	ns
t_{PZL}				12	17	4	20	5	18	
t_{PHZ}	$\overline{OC}$	Q		4	9	1	12	1	11	ns
t_{PLZ}				6	11	2	14	2	12	

NOTE 1: Load circuit and voltage waveforms are shown in Section 1.

PRODUCT PREVIEW

recommended operating conditions

			SN54ALS846			SN74ALS846			UNIT
			MIN	NOM	MAX	MIN	NOM	MAX	
V_{CC}	Supply voltage		4.5	5	5.5	4.5	5	5.5	V
V_{IH}	High-level input voltage		2			2			V
V_{IL}	Low-level input voltage				0.8			0.8	V
I_{OH}	High-level output current				−1			−2.6	mA
I_{OL}	Low-level output current				12			24	mA
								48†	
t_w	Pulse duration	$\overline{CLR}$ or $\overline{PRE}$ low							ns
		C high							
t_{su}	Setup time, data before enable C↓								ns
t_h	Hold time, data after enable C↓								ns
T_A	Operating free-air temperature		−55		125	0		70	°C

† The extended limit applies only if V_{CC} is maintained between 4.75 V and 5.25 V. The 48 mA limit applies for SN74ALS846-1 only.

electrical characteristics over recommended operating free-air temperature range (unless otherwise noted)

PARAMETER	TEST CONDITIONS		SN54ALS846			SN74ALS846			UNIT
			MIN	TYP‡	MAX	MIN	TYP‡	MAX	
V_{IK}	V_{CC} = 4.5 V,	I_I = −18 mA			−1.2			−1.2	V
V_{OH}	V_{CC} = 4.5 V to 5.5 V,	I_{OH} = −0.4 mA	$V_{CC}-2$			$V_{CC}-2$			V
	V_{CC} = 4.5 V,	I_{OH} = −1 mA	2.4	3.3					
	V_{CC} = 4.5 V,	I_{OH} = −2.6 mA				2.4	3,2		
V_{OL}	V_{CC} = 4.5 V,	I_{OL} = 12 mA		0.25	0.4				V
	V_{CC} = 4.5 V, (I_{OL} = 48 mA for -1 versions)	I_{OL} = 24 mA					0.35	0.5	
I_{OZH}	V_{CC} = 5.5 V,	V_O = 2.7 V			20			20	μA
I_{OZL}	V_{CC} = 5.5 V,	V_O = 0.4 V			−20			−20	μA
I_I	V_{CC} = 5.5 V,	V_I = 7 V			0.1			0.1	mA
I_{IH}	V_{CC} = 5.5 V,	V_I = 2.7 V			20			20	μA
I_{IL}	V_{CC} = 5.5 V,	V_I = 0.4 V			−0.1			−0.1	mA
I_O§	V_{CC} = 5.5 V,	V_O = 2.25 V	−30		−112	−30		−112	mA
I_{CC}	V_{CC} = 5.5 V	Outputs high							mA
		Outputs low							
		Outputs disabled							

‡ All typical values are at V_{CC} = 5 V, T_A = 25°C.
§ The output conditions have been chosen to produce a current that closely approximates one half of the true short-circuit output current, I_{OS}.

Additional information on these products can be obtained from the factory as it becomes available.

switching characteristics (see Note 1)

PARAMETER	FROM (INPUT)	TO (OUTPUT)	V_{CC} = 5 V, C_L = 50 pF, R1 = 500 Ω, R2 = 500 Ω, T_A = 25°C			V_{CC} = 4.5 V to 5.5 V, C_L = 50 pF, R1 = 500 Ω, R2 = 500 Ω, T_A = MIN to MAX				UNIT
			'ALS846			SN54ALS846		SN74ALS846		
			MIN	TYP	MAX	MIN	MAX	MIN	MAX	
t_{PLH}	D	Q								ns
t_{PHL}										
t_{PLH}	C	Q								ns
t_{PHL}										
t_{PLH}	$\overline{PRE}$	Q								ns
t_{PHL}										ns
t_{PLH}	$\overline{CLR}$	Q								ns
t_{PHL}										ns
t_{PZH}	$\overline{OC}$	Q								ns
t_{PZL}										
t_{PHZ}	$\overline{OC}$	Q								ns
t_{PLZ}										

NOTE 1: Load circuit and voltage waveforms are shown in Section 1.

Additional information on these products can be obtained from the factory as it becomes available.

recommended operating conditions

			SN54AS845 SN54AS846			SN74AS845 SN74AS846			UNIT
			MIN	NOM	MAX	MIN	NOM	MAX	
V_{CC}	Supply voltage		4.5	5	5.5	4.5	5	5.5	V
V_{IH}	High-level input voltage		2			2			V
V_{IL}	Low-level input voltage				0.8			0.8	V
I_{OH}	High-level output current				−24			−24	mA
I_{OL}	Low-level output current				32			48	mA
t_w	Pulse duration	$\overline{CLR}$ or $\overline{PRE}$ low	5			4			ns
		C high	5			4			
t_{su}	Setup time, data before enable C↓		3.5			2.5			ns
t_h	Hold time, data after enable C↓		3.5			2.5			ns
t_r	Recovery time	$\overline{PRE}$	17			15			ns
		$\overline{CLR}$	16			14			
T_A	Operating free-air temperature		−55		125	0		70	°C

electrical characteristics over recommended operating free-air temperature range (unless otherwise noted)

PARAMETER		TEST CONDITIONS		SN54AS845 SN54AS846			SN74AS845 SN74AS846			UNIT
				MIN	TYP†	MAX	MIN	TYP†	MAX	
V_{IK}		V_{CC} = 4.5 V,	I_I = −18 mA			−1.2			−1.2	V
V_{OH}		V_{CC} = 4.5 V,	I_{OH} = −2 mA	$V_{CC}-2$			$V_{CC}-2$			V
		V_{CC} = 4.5 V,	I_{OH} = −15 mA	2.4	3.2		2.4	3.2		
		V_{CC} = 4.5 V,	I_{OH} = −24 mA	2			2			
V_{OL}		V_{CC} = 4.5 V,	I_{OL} = 32 mA		0.25	0.5				V
		V_{CC} = 4.5 V,	I_{OL} = 48 mA					0.35	0.5	
I_{OZH}		V_{CC} = 5.5 V,	V_O = 2.7 V			50			50	μA
I_{OZL}		V_{CC} = 5.5 V,	V_O = 0.4 V			−50			−50	μA
I_I		V_{CC} = 5.5 V,	V_I = 7 V			0.1			0.1	mA
I_{IH}		V_{CC} = 5.5 V,	V_I = 2.7 V			20			20	μA
I_{IL}		V_{CC} = 5.5 V,	V_I = 0.4 V			−0.5			−0.5	mA
I_O‡		V_{CC} = 5.5 V,	V_O = 2.25 V	−30		−112	−30		−112	mA
I_{CC}	'AS845	V_{CC} = 5.5 V	Outputs high		35	58		35	58	mA
			Outputs low		52	85		52	85	
			Outputs disabled		52	85		52	85	
	'AS846		Outputs high		36	59		36	59	
			Outputs low		53	87		53	87	
			Outputs disabled		53	87		53	87	

† All typical values are at V_{CC} = 5 V, T_A = 25°C.
‡ The output conditions have been chosen to produce a current that closely approximates one half of the true short-circuit output current, I_{OS}.

TEXAS INSTRUMENTS
POST OFFICE BOX 225012 • DALLAS, TEXAS 75265

'AS845 switching characteristics (see Note 1)

PARAMETER	FROM (INPUT)	TO (OUTPUT)	V_{CC} = 4.5 V to 5.5 V, C_L = 50 pF, R1 = 500 Ω, R2 = 500 Ω, T_A = MIN to MAX				UNIT
			SN54AS845		SN74AS845		
			MIN	MAX	MIN	MAX	
t_{PLH}	D	Q	1	8.5	1	6.5	ns
t_{PHL}			1	10	1	9	
t_{PLH}	C	Q	2	13	2	12	ns
t_{PHL}			2	13	2	12	
t_{PLH}	$\overline{PRE}$	Q	2	12	2	10	ns
t_{PHL}	$\overline{CLR}$	Q	2	14	2	13	ns
t_{PHL}	$\overline{OC}$	Q	2	13.5	2	10.5	ns
t_{PZL}			2	15	2	13.5	
t_{PHZ}	$\overline{OC}$	Q	1	10	1	8	ns
t_{PLZ}			1	10	1	8	

'AS846 switching characteristics (see Note 1)

PARAMETER	FROM (INPUT)	TO (OUTPUT)	V_{CC} = 4.5 V to 5.5 V, C_L = 50 pF, R1 = 500 Ω, R2 = 500 Ω, T_A = MIN to MAX				UNIT
			SN54AS846		SN74AS846		
			MIN	MAX	MIN	MAX	
t_{PLH}	D	Q	1	11	1	8.5	ns
t_{PHL}			1	11	1	10	
t_{PLH}	C	Q	2	14	2	12.5	ns
t_{PHL}			2	14	2	13	
t_{PLH}	$\overline{PRE}$	Q	2	12	2	10	ns
t_{PHL}	$\overline{CLR}$	Q	2	14.5	2	13.5	ns
t_{PHL}	$\overline{OC}$	Q	2	14.5	2	12	ns
t_{PZL}			2	15	2	13.5	
t_{PHZ}	$\overline{OC}$	Q	1	10	1	8	ns
t_{PLZ}			1	10	1	8	

NOTE 1: Load circuit and voltage waveforms are shown in Section 1.

D latch signal conventions

It is normal TI practice to name the outputs and other inputs of a D-type latch and to draw its logic symbol based on the assumption of true data (D) inputs. Then outputs that produce data in phase with the data inputs are called Q and those producing complementary data are called $\overline{Q}$. An input that causes a Q output to go high or a $\overline{Q}$ output to go low is called Preset; and input that causes a $\overline{Q}$ output to go high or a Q output to go low is called Clear. Bars are used over these pin names ($\overline{PRE}$ and $\overline{CLR}$) if they are active low. The devices on this data sheet are second-source designs and the pin-name conventions used by the original manufacturer have been retained. That makes it necessary to designate the data inputs and outputs of the inverting circuit $\overline{D}$ and Q.

In some applications it may be advantageous to redesignate the inputs and outputs $\overline{D}$ and $\overline{Q}$ for the noninverting circuits or D and $\overline{Q}$ for the inverting circuits. In that case signal names should change as shown below. Also shown are corresponding changes in the logic symbols.

Notice that Q becoming $\overline{Q}$ causes $\overline{PRE}$ and $\overline{CLR}$ to exchange their names and their S and R function labels. The presence or absence of polarity indicators (⊵) changes at the data inputs and outputs, but not at $\overline{CLR}$/$\overline{PRE}$, $\overline{OC}$1, $\overline{OC}$2, and $\overline{OC}$3 since these inputs are still active-low.

'ALS845, 'AS845

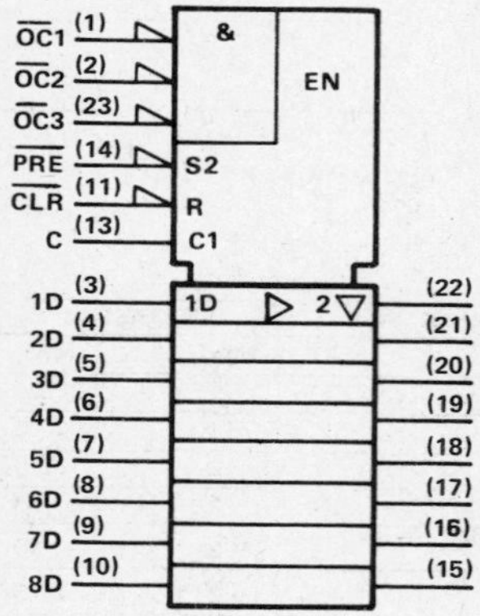
OC1 (1)
OC2 (2)
OC3 (23)
PRE (14)
CLR (11)
C (13)
&
EN
S2
R
C1
1D ▷ 2▽
1D (3) (22) 1Q
2D (4) (21) 2Q
3D (5) (20) 3Q
4D (6) (19) 4Q
5D (7) (18) 5Q
6D (8) (17) 6Q
7D (9) (16) 7Q
8D (10) (15) 8Q

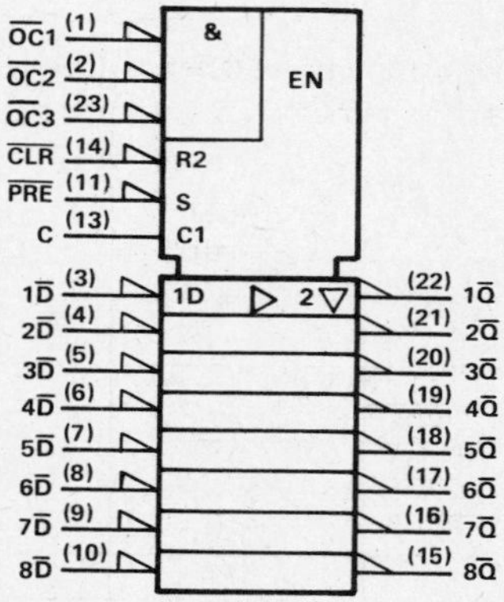
OC1 (1)
OC2 (2)
OC3 (23)
CLR (14)
PRE (11)
C (13)
&
EN
R2
S
C1
1D ▷ 2▽
1D̄ (3) (22) 1Q̄
2D̄ (4) (21) 2Q̄
3D̄ (5) (20) 3Q̄
4D̄ (6) (19) 4Q̄
5D̄ (7) (18) 5Q̄
6D̄ (8) (17) 6Q̄
7D̄ (9) (16) 7Q̄
8D̄ (10) (15) 8Q̄

'ALS846, 'AS846

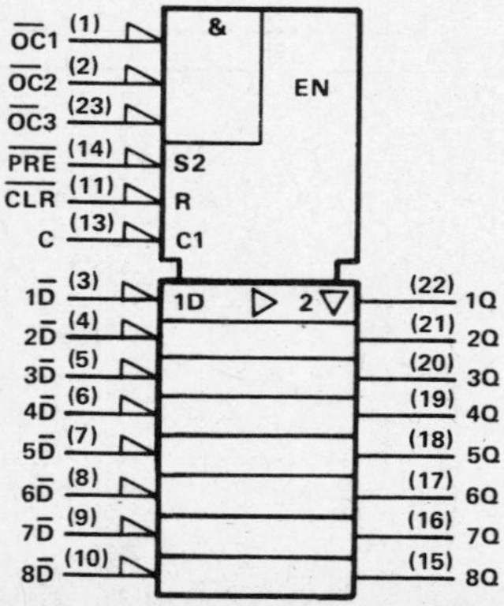
OC1 (1)
OC2 (2)
OC3 (23)
PRE (14)
CLR (11)
C (13)
&
EN
S2
R
C1
1D ▷ 2▽
1D̄ (3) (22) 1Q
2D̄ (4) (21) 2Q
3D̄ (5) (20) 3Q
4D̄ (6) (19) 4Q
5D̄ (7) (18) 5Q
6D̄ (8) (17) 6Q
7D̄ (9) (16) 7Q
8D̄ (10) (15) 8Q

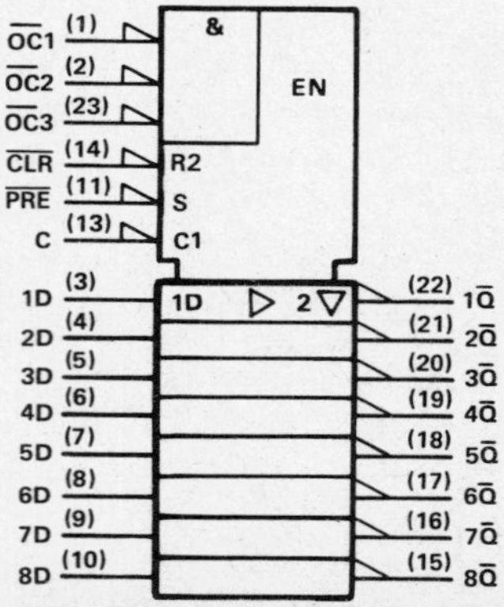
OC1 (1)
OC2 (2)
OC3 (23)
CLR (14)
PRE (11)
C (13)
&
EN
R2
S
C1
1D ▷ 2▽
1D (3) (22) 1Q̄
2D (4) (21) 2Q̄
3D (5) (20) 3Q̄
4D (6) (19) 4Q̄
5D (7) (18) 5Q̄
6D (8) (17) 6Q̄
7D (9) (16) 7Q̄
8D (10) (15) 8Q̄

D2822, DECEMBER 1983—REVISED JANUARY 1986

- **4-Line to 1-Line Data Selectors/Multiplexers That Can Select 1 of 16 Data Inputs. Typical Applications:**
  - **Boolean Function Generators**
  - **Parallel-to-Serial Converters**
  - **Data Source Selectors**
- **Cascadable to n-Bits**
- **3-State Bus Driver Outputs**
- **'AS850 Offers Clocked Selects; 'AS851 Offers Enable-Controlled Selects**
- **Has a Master Output Control ($\overline{G}$) for Cascading and Individual Output Controls ($\overline{GY}$, GW) for Each Output**
- **Package Options Include both Plastic and Ceramic Carriers in Addition to Plastic and Ceramic DIPs**
- **Dependable Texas Instruments Quality and Reliability**

SN74AS850, SN74AS851 . . . N PACKAGE
(TOP VIEW)

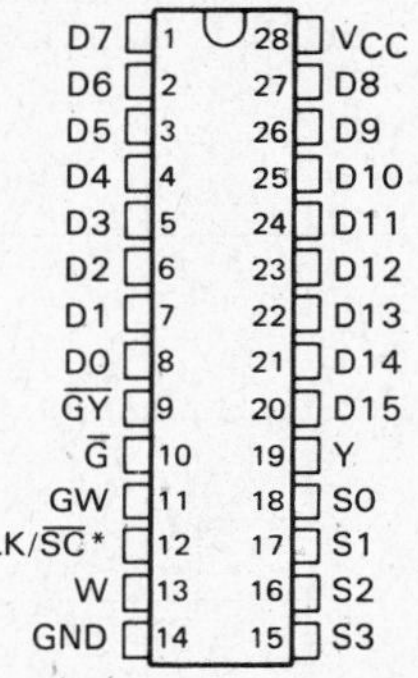
D7 1 28 VCC
D6 2 27 D8
D5 3 26 D9
D4 4 25 D10
D3 5 24 D11
D2 6 23 D12
D1 7 22 D13
D0 8 21 D14
GY 9 20 D15
G 10 19 Y
GW 11 18 S0
CLK/SC* 12 17 S1
W 13 16 S2
GND 14 15 S3

SN74AS850, SN74AS851 . . . FN PACKAGE
(TOP VIEW)

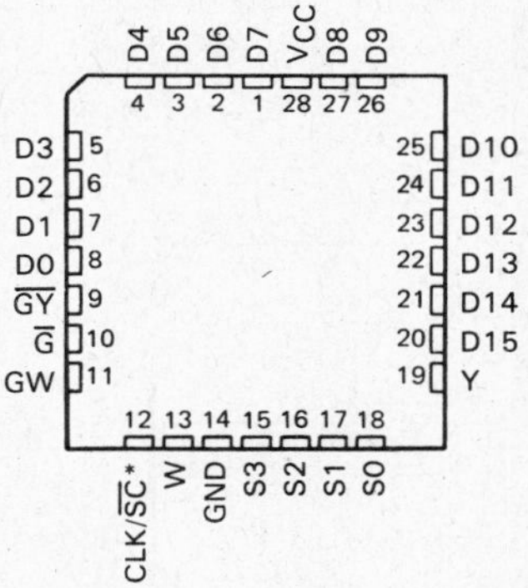
D4 D5 D6 D7 VCC D8 D9
4 3 2 1 28 27 26
D3 5
D2 6
D1 7
D0 8
GY 9
G 10
GW 11
25 D10
24 D11
23 D12
22 D13
21 D14
20 D15
19 Y
12 13 14 15 16 17 18
CLK/SC* W GND S3 S2 S1 S0

*CLK for 'AS850 or $\overline{SC}$ for 'AS851

description

These four-line to one-line data selectors/multiplexers provide full binary decoding to select one-of-sixteen data sources with complementary Y and W outputs. The 'AS850 has a clock-controlled select register allowing for a symmetrical presentation of the select inputs to the decoder while the 'AS851 has an enable-controlled select register allowing the user to select and hold one particular data line.

A buffered group of output controls ($\overline{G}$, $\overline{GY}$, GW) can be used to place the two-outputs in either a normal logic (high or low logic level) or a high-impedance state. In the high-impedance state the outputs neither load nor drive the bus lines significantly. The high-impedance third state and increased drive provide the capability to drive the bus lines in a bus-organized system without the need for interface or pull-up components.

The output controls do not affect the internal operations of the data selector/multiplexer. New data can be setup while the outputs are in the high-impedance state.

The SN74AS850 and SN74AS851 are characterized for operation from 0°C to 70°C.

INPUT SELECTION TABLE

SELECT INPUTS				'AS850	'AS851	INPUT
S3	S2	S1	S0	CLK	$\overline{SC}$	SELECTED
L	L	L	L	↑	L	D0
L	L	L	H	↑	L	D1
L	L	H	L	↑	L	D2
L	L	H	H	↑	L	D3
L	H	L	L	↑	L	D4
L	H	L	H	↑	L	D5
L	H	H	L	↑	L	D6
L	H	H	H	↑	L	D7
H	L	L	L	↑	L	D8
H	L	L	H	↑	L	D9
H	L	H	L	↑	L	D10
H	L	H	H	↑	L	D11
H	H	L	L	↑	L	D12
H	H	L	H	↑	L	D13
H	H	H	L	↑	L	D14
H	H	H	H	↑	L	D15
X	X	X	X	H or L	H	Dn

Dn = the input selected before the most-recent low-to-high transition of CLK or $\overline{SC}$.

OUTPUT FUNCTION TABLE

$\overline{G}$	$\overline{GY}$	GW	OUTPUTS	
			Y	W
H	X	X	Z	Z
L	H	L	Z	Z
L	L	L	D	Z
L	H	H	Z	$\overline{D}$
L	L	H	D	$\overline{D}$

D = level of selected input D0–D15

logic symbols†

'AS850

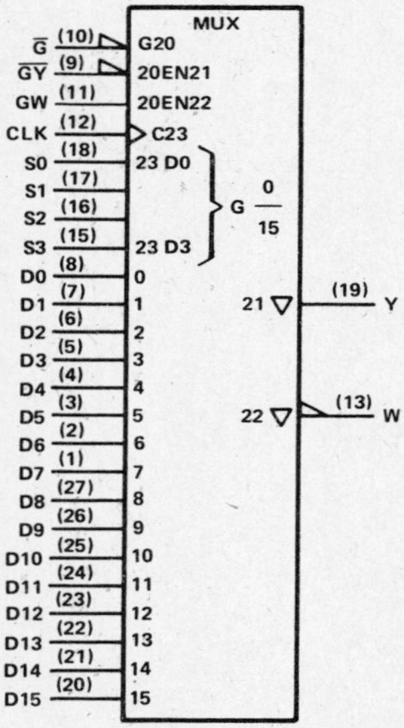
MUX
$\overline{G}$ (10) G20
$\overline{GY}$ (9) 20EN21
GW (11) 20EN22
CLK (12) C23
S0 (18) 23 D0
S1 (17)
S2 (16)
S3 (15) 23 D3
G 0/15
D0 (8) 0
D1 (7) 1
D2 (6) 2
D3 (5) 3
D4 (4) 4
D5 (3) 5
D6 (2) 6
D7 (1) 7
D8 (27) 8
D9 (26) 9
D10 (25) 10
D11 (24) 11
D12 (23) 12
D13 (22) 13
D14 (21) 14
D15 (20) 15
21 (19) Y
22 (13) W

'AS851

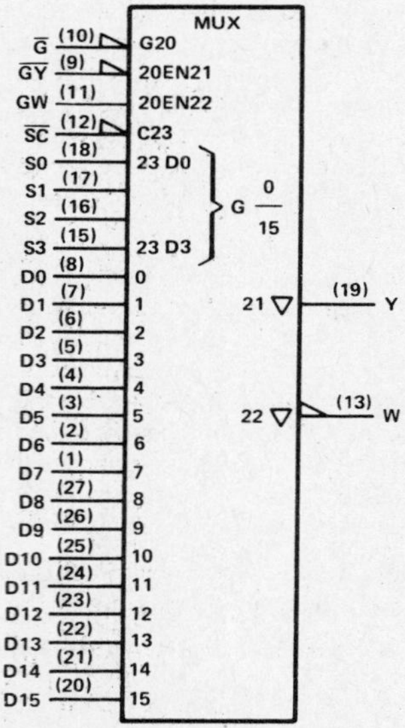
MUX
$\overline{G}$ (10) G20
$\overline{GY}$ (9) 20EN21
GW (11) 20EN22
$\overline{SC}$ (12) C23
S0 (18) 23 D0
S1 (17)
S2 (16)
S3 (15) 23 D3
G 0/15
D0 (8) 0
D1 (7) 1
D2 (6) 2
D3 (5) 3
D4 (4) 4
D5 (3) 5
D6 (2) 6
D7 (1) 7
D8 (27) 8
D9 (26) 9
D10 (25) 10
D11 (24) 11
D12 (23) 12
D13 (22) 13
D14 (21) 14
D15 (20) 15
21 (19) Y
22 (13) W

† These symbols are in accordance with ANSI/IEEE Std 91-1984 and IEC Publication 617-12.

TEXAS INSTRUMENTS
POST OFFICE BOX 225012 • DALLAS, TEXAS 75265

'AS850 logic diagrams (positive logic) (see inset for 'AS851)

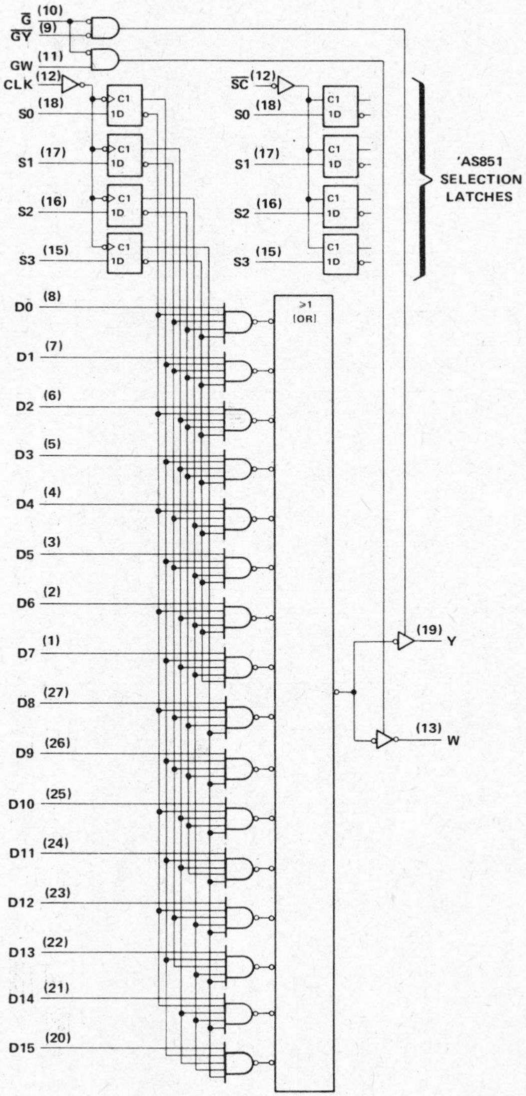
G (10)
GY (9)
GW (11)
CLK (12)
S0 (18)
S1 (17)
S2 (16)
S3 (15)
SC (12)
C1
1D
'AS851
SELECTION
LATCHES
D0 (8)
D1 (7)
D2 (6)
D3 (5)
D4 (4)
D5 (3)
D6 (2)
D7 (1)
D8 (27)
D9 (26)
D10 (25)
D11 (24)
D12 (23)
D13 (22)
D14 (21)
D15 (20)
≥1
[OR]
(19) Y
(13) W

absolute maximum ratings over operating free-air temperature range (unless otherwise noted)

Supply voltage, V_{CC} . . . . 7 V
Input voltage . . . . 7 V
Operating free-air temperature range . . . . 0°C to 70°C
Storage temperature range . . . . −65°C to 150°C

SN74AS850 recommended operating conditions

			MIN	NOM	MAX	UNIT
V_{CC}	Supply voltage		4.5	5	5.5	V
V_{IH}	High-level input voltage		2			V
V_{IL}	Low-level input voltage				0.8	V
I_{OH}	High-level output current				−15	mA
I_{OL}	Low-level output current				48	mA
f_{clock}	Clock frequency		0		60	MHz
t_w	Pulse duration	CLK high	8			ns
		CLK low	8			ns
t_{su}	Setup time, select inputs before CLK↑		10			ns
t_h	Hold time, select inputs after CLK↑		0			ns
T_A	Operating free-air temperature		0		70	°C

SN74AS850 electrical characteristics over recommended operating free-air temperature range (unless otherwise noted)

PARAMETER		TEST CONDITIONS		MIN	TYP†	MAX	UNIT
V_{IK}		V_{CC} = 4.5 V,	I_I = −18 mA			−1.2	V
V_{OH}		V_{CC} = 4.5 V to 5.5 V,	I_{OH} = −2 mA	$V_{CC}-2$			V
		V_{CC} = 4.5 V,	I_{OH} = −15 mA	2	3.3		V
V_{OL}		V_{CC} = 4.5 V,	I_{OL} = 48 mA		0.35	0.5	V
I_{OZH}		V_{CC} = 5.5 V,	V_O = 2.7 V			50	μA
I_{OZL}		V_{CC} = 5.5 V,	V_O = 0.4 V			−50	μA
I_I		V_{CC} = 5.5 V,	V_I = 7 V			0.1	mA
I_{IH}		V_{CC} = 5.5 V,	V_I = 2.7 V			20	μA
I_{IL}	D, $\overline{G}$	V_{CC} = 5.5 V,	V_I = 0.4 V			−1	mA
	All others					−0.5	mA
I_O‡		V_{CC} = 5.5 V,	V_O = 2.25 V	−30		−112	mA
I_{CC}		V_{CC} = 5.5 V	Outputs active		50	81	mA
			Outputs disabled		52	85	mA

† All typical values are at V_{CC} = 5 V, T_A = 25°C.
‡ The output conditions have been chosen to produce a current that closely approximates one-half of the true short-circuit current, I_{OS}.

SN74AS850 switching characteristics (see Note 1)

PARAMETER	FROM (INPUT)	TO (OUTPUT)	V_{CC} = 4.5 V to 5.5 V, C_L = 50 pF, R1 = 500 Ω, R2 = 500 Ω, T_A = 0°C to 70°C MIN	MAX	UNIT
f_{max}			60		MHz
t_{PLH}	Any D	Y	3	10.5	ns
t_{PHL}			3	11	
t_{PLH}	Any D	W	3	8	ns
t_{PHL}			1	6	
t_{PLH}	CLK	Y	3	14.5	ns
t_{PHL}			3	17.5	
t_{PLH}	CLK	W	3	15	ns
t_{PHL}			3.5	13	
t_{PZH}	$\overline{G}$	Y	2	8	ns
t_{PZL}			3	11	
t_{PHZ}	$\overline{G}$	Y	1	6	ns
t_{PLZ}			2	8	
t_{PZH}	$\overline{G}$	W	2	8	ns
t_{PZL}			3	21	
t_{PHZ}	$\overline{G}$	W	1	6	ns
t_{PLZ}			2	8	
t_{PZH}	$\overline{GY}$	Y	2	8	ns
t_{PZL}			3	11	
t_{PHZ}	$\overline{GY}$	Y	1	6	ns
t_{PLZ}			2	8	
t_{PZH}	GW	W	2	10	ns
t_{PZL}			3	25	
t_{PHZ}	GW	W	1	6	ns
t_{PLZ}			2	11	

NOTE 1: Load circuit and voltage waveforms are shown in Section 1.

SN74AS851 recommended operating conditions

		MIN	NOM	MAX	UNIT
V_{CC}	Supply voltage	4.5	5	5.5	V
V_{IH}	High-level input voltage	2			V
V_{IL}	Low-level input voltage			0.8	V
I_{OH}	High-level output current			−15	mA
I_{OL}	Low-level output current			48	mA
t_w	Pulse duration, $\overline{SC}$ low	10			ns
t_{su}	Setup time, select inputs before $\overline{SC}\uparrow$	4.5			ns
t_h	Hold time, select inputs after $\overline{SC}\uparrow$	0			ns
T_A	Operating free-air temperature	0		70	°C

SN74AS851 electrical characteristics over recommended operating free-air temperature range (unless otherwise noted)

PARAMETER		TEST CONDITIONS		MIN	TYP†	MAX	UNIT
V_{IK}		V_{CC} = 4.5 V,	I_I = −18 mA			−1.2	C
V_{OH}		V_{CC} = 4.5 V to 5.5 V,	I_{OH} = −2 mA	$V_{CC}-2$			V
		V_{CC} = 4.5 V,	I_{OH} = −15 mA	2	3.3		
V_{OL}		V_{CC} = 4.5 V,	I_{OL} = 48 mA		0.35	0.5	V
I_{OZH}		V_{CC} = 5.5 V,	V_O = 2.7 V			50	μA
I_{OZL}		V_{CC} = 5.5 V,	V_O = 0.4 V			−50	μA
I_I		V_{CC} = 5.5 V,	V_I = 7 V			0.1	mA
I_{IH}		V_{CC} = 5.5 V,	V_I = 2.7 V			20	μA
I_{IL}	D, $\overline{G}$	V_{CC} = 5.5 V,	V_I = 0.4 V			−1	mA
	All others					−0.5	
I_O‡		V_{CC} = 5.5 V,	V_O = 2.25 V	−30		−112	mA
I_{CC}		V_{CC} = 5.5 V	Outputs active		50	81	mA
			Outputs disabled		52	85	

† All typical values are at V_{CC} = 5 V, T_A = 25°C.
‡ The output conditions have been chosen to produce a current that closely approximates one-half of the true short-circuit current, I_{OS}.

TEXAS INSTRUMENTS
POST OFFICE BOX 225012 • DALLAS, TEXAS 75265

SN74AS851 switching characteristics (see Note 1)

PARAMETER	FROM (INPUT)	TO (OUTPUT)	V_{CC} = 4.5 V to 5.5 V, C_L = 50 pF, R1 = 500 Ω, R2 = 500 Ω, T_A = 0°C to 70°C MIN	MAX	UNIT
t_{PLH}	Any D	Y	3	10.5	ns
t_{PHL}			3	11	
t_{PLH}	Any D	W	3	8	ns
t_{PHL}			1	6	
t_{PLH}	S0, S1, S2, S3	Y	3	18	ns
t_{PHL}			3	19	
t_{PLH}	S0, S1, S2, S3	W	3	16	ns
t_{PHL}			3	15	
t_{PLH}	$\overline{SC}$	Y	3	18	ns
t_{PHL}			3	20	
t_{PLH}	$\overline{SC}$	W	3	16	ns
t_{PHL}			3	15	
t_{PZH}	$\overline{G}$	Y	2	8	ns
t_{PZL}			3	11	
t_{PHZ}	$\overline{G}$	Y	1	6	ns
t_{PLZ}			2	8	
t_{PZH}	$\overline{G}$	W	2	8	ns
t_{PZL}			3	21	
t_{PHZ}	$\overline{G}$	W	1	6	ns
t_{PLZ}			2	8	
t_{PZH}	$\overline{GY}$	Y	2	8	ns
t_{PZL}			3	11	
t_{PHZ}	$\overline{GY}$	Y	1	6	ns
t_{PLL}			2	8	
t_{PZH}	GW	W	2	10	ns
t_{PZL}			3	25	
t_{PHZ}	GW	W	1	6	ns
t_{PLZ}			2	11	

NOTE 1: Load circuit and voltage waveforms are shown in Section 1.

TYPICAL APPLICATION DATA

The 'AS850 or 'AS851 can be used as a 1-of-16 Boolean function generator. Figure 1 shows the 'AS850 in one example.

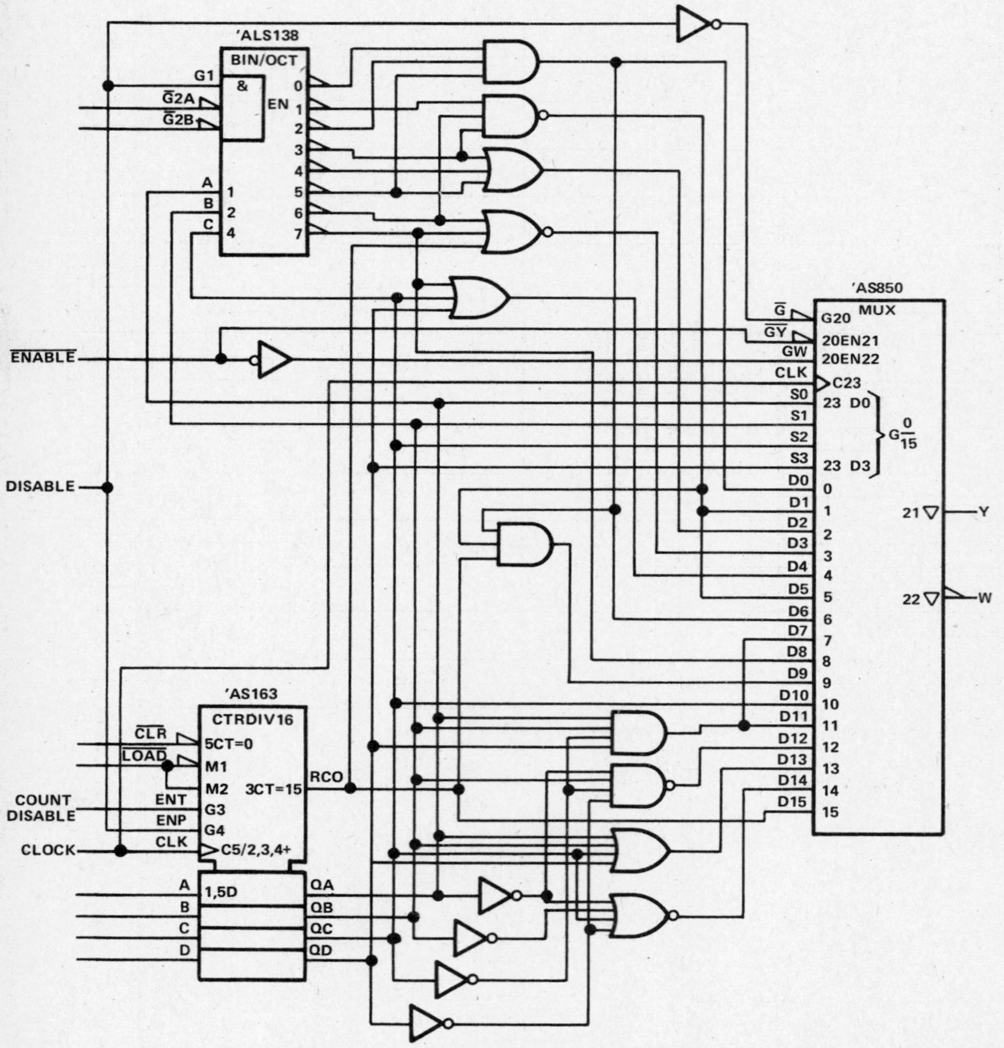
'ALS138
BIN/OCT
G1
&
G2A
G2B
EN
0
1
2
3
4
5
6
7
A
B
C
1
2
4
ENABLE
DISABLE
'AS850
MUX
G
GY
GW
CLK
S0
S1
S2
S3
D0
D1
D2
D3
D4
D5
D6
D7
D8
D9
D10
D11
D12
D13
D14
D15
G20
20EN21
20EN22
C23
23 D0
23 D3
G 0/15
0
1
2
3
4
5
6
7
8
9
10
11
12
13
14
15
21
Y
22
W
'AS163
CTRDIV16
CLR
LOAD
5CT=0
M1
M2
3CT=15
RCO
COUNT DISABLE
ENT
ENP
G3
G4
CLOCK
CLK
C5/2,3,4+
A
B
C
D
1,5D
QA
QB
QC
QD

FIGURE 1. 1-of-16 BOOLEAN FUNCTION GENERATOR

TEXAS INSTRUMENTS
POST OFFICE BOX 225012 • DALLAS, TEXAS 75265

TYPICAL APPLICATION DATA

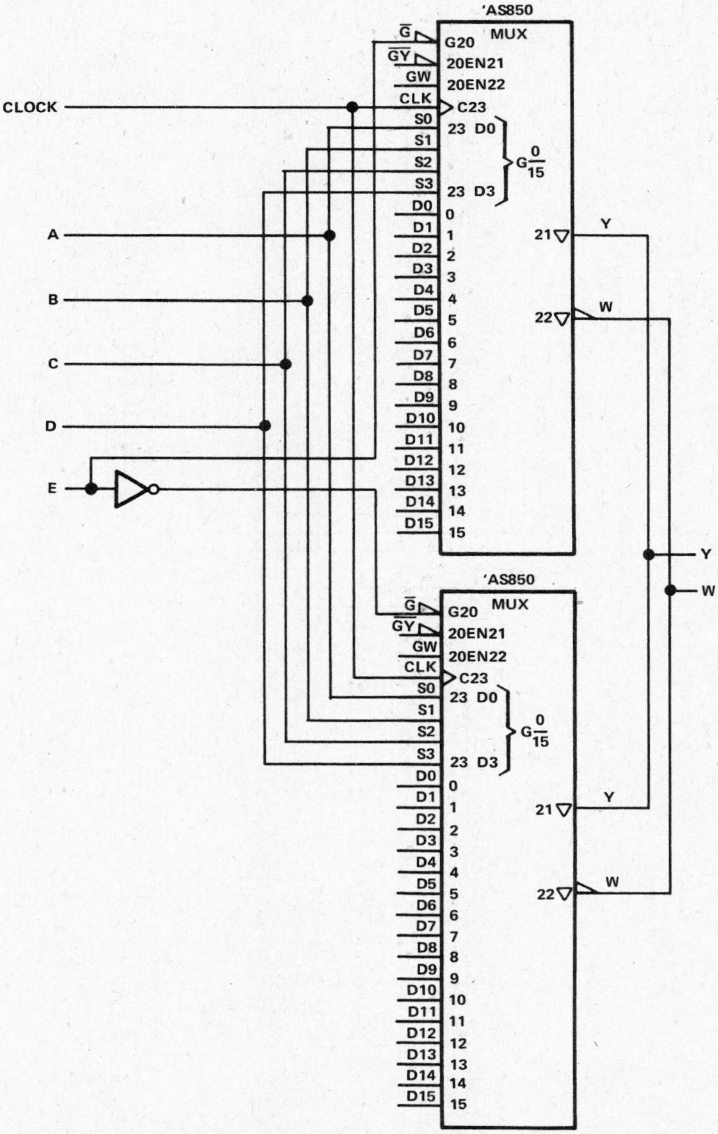
'AS850
MUX
G
GY
GW
CLK
S0
S1
S2
S3
G20
20EN21
20EN22
C23
23 D0
23 D3
CLOCK
A
B
C
D
E
21
22
Y
W
D0
D1
D2
D3
D4
D5
D6
D7
D8
D9
D10
D11
D12
D13
D14
D15

FIGURE 2. 1-of-32 DATA SELECTOR/MULTIPLEXER

TYPICAL APPLICATION DATA

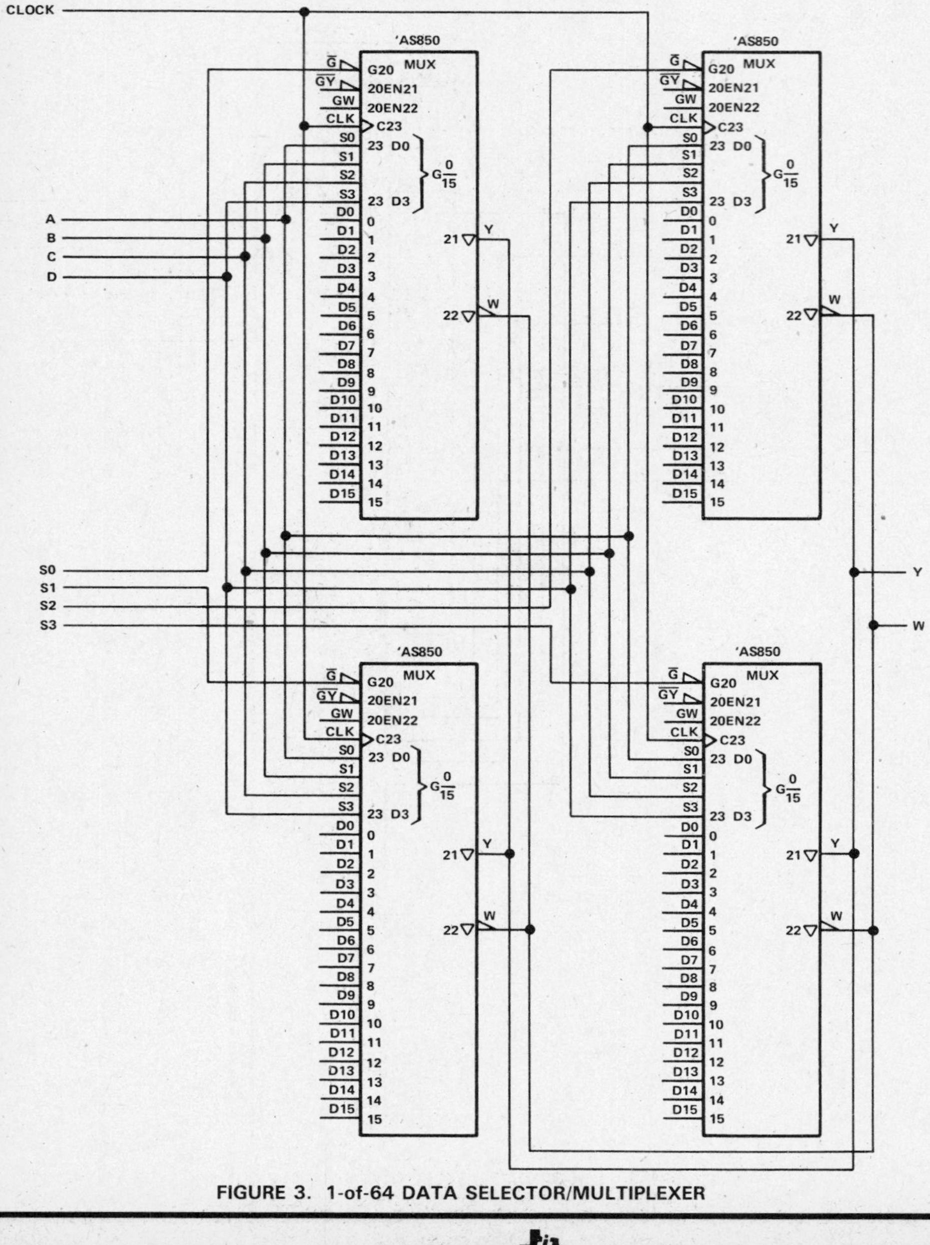
CLOCK
A
B
C
D
S0
S1
S2
S3
Y
W
'AS850
MUX
G
GY
GW
CLK
G20
20EN21
20EN22
C23
23 D0
23 D3
G 0/15
D0
D1
D2
D3
D4
D5
D6
D7
D8
D9
D10
D11
D12
D13
D14
D15
21
22

FIGURE 3. 1-of-64 DATA SELECTOR/MULTIPLEXER

D2810, JUNE 1984—REVISED JANUARY 1986

- **Included among the Package Options are Compact, 24-Pin, 300-mil-Wide DIPs and Both 28-Pin Plastic and Ceramic Chip Carriers**
- **Buffered 3-State Outputs Drive Bus Lines Directly**
- **Cascadable to n-Bits**
- **Eight Selectable Transceiver/Port Functions:**
  - **A to B or B to A**
  - **Register to A or B**
  - **Shifted to A from B or Shifted to B from A**
  - **Off-Line Shifts (A and B Ports Transceiving or in High-Impedance State)**
  - **Register Clear**
- **Particularly Suitable for Use in Diagnostics Circuitry**
- **Serial Register Provides:**
  - **— Parallel Storage of Either A or B Input Data**
  - **— Serial Transmission of Data from Either A or B Port**
- **Dependable Texas Instruments Quality and Reliability**

SN54AS852 . . . JT PACKAGE
SN74AS852 . . . DW or NT PACKAGE
(TOP VIEW)

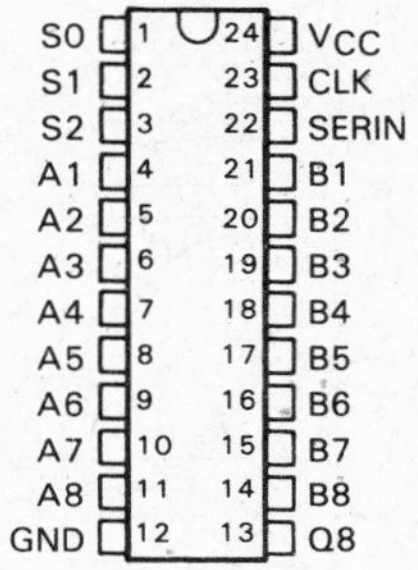
S0 1 24 VCC
S1 2 23 CLK
S2 3 22 SERIN
A1 4 21 B1
A2 5 20 B2
A3 6 19 B3
A4 7 18 B4
A5 8 17 B5
A6 9 16 B6
A7 10 15 B7
A8 11 14 B8
GND 12 13 Q8

SN54AS852 . . . FK PACKAGE
SN74AS852 . . . FN PACKAGE
(TOP VIEW)

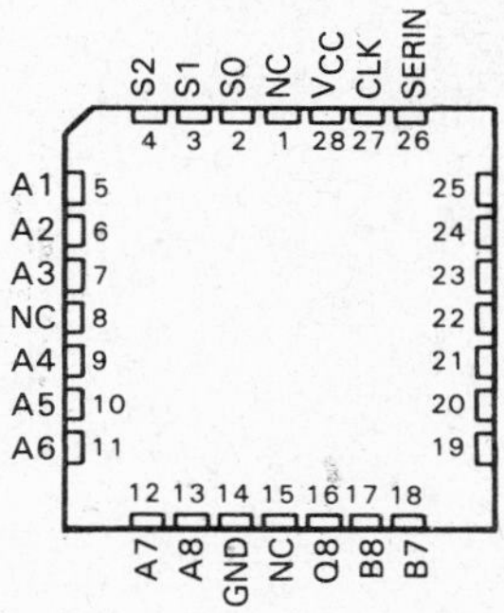
S2 S1 S0 NC VCC CLK SERIN
4 3 2 1 28 27 26
A1 5 25 B1
A2 6 24 B2
A3 7 23 B3
NC 8 22 NC
A4 9 21 B4
A5 10 20 B5
A6 11 19 B6
12 13 14 15 16 17 18
A7 A8 GND NC Q8 B8 B7

NC—No internal connection

description

The 'AS852 features two 8-bit I/O ports (A1-A8 and B1-B8), and 8-bit parallel-load, serial-in, parallel-out shift register, and control logic. With these features, this device is capable of performing eight selectable transceiver or port functions, depending on the state of the three select lines S0, S1, and S2. These functions include: transferring data from port A to port B or vice versa (i.e., the transceiver function), transferring data from the register to either port, serial shifting data to either port from the opposite port, performing off-line shifts (with A and B ports in high-impedance state), and clearing the register. The 'AS852 can simultaneously transfer data from A to B or B to A and perform an off-line serial shift of data in the register. Synchronous parallel loading of the internal register can be accomplished from either port on the positive transition of the clock while serially shifting data in via the SERIN input. The 'AS852 is ideally suited for applications implementing diagnostic circuitry to enhance system verification and/or fault analysis. All serial data is shifted right. All outputs are buffer-type outputs designed specifically to drive bus lines directly and all are 3-state except for Q8, which is a totem-pole output.

The SN54AS852 is characterized for operation over the full military temperature range of −55 °C to 125 °C. The SN74AS852 is characterized for operation from 0 °C to 70 °C.

logic diagram (positive logic)

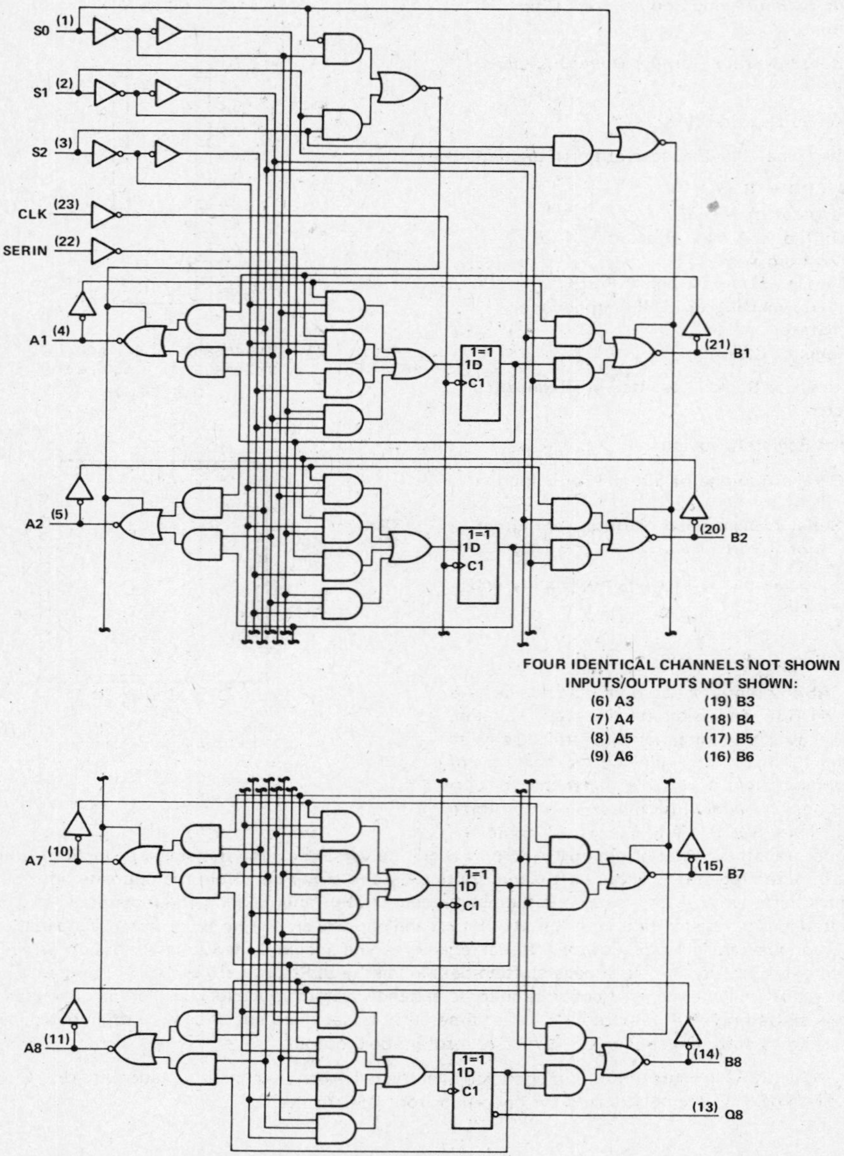
S0 (1)
S1 (2)
S2 (3)
CLK (23)
SERIN (22)
A1 (4)
(21) B1
1=1
1D
C1
A2 (5)
(20) B2
FOUR IDENTICAL CHANNELS NOT SHOWN
INPUTS/OUTPUTS NOT SHOWN:
(6) A3 (19) B3
(7) A4 (18) B4
(8) A5 (17) B5
(9) A6 (16) B6
A7 (10)
(15) B7
A8 (11)
(14) B8
(13) Q8

Pin numbers shown are for DW, JT, and NT packages.

TEXAS INSTRUMENTS
POST OFFICE BOX 225012 • DALLAS, TEXAS 75265

FUNCTION TABLE

MODE S2 S1 S0	CLOCK	SERIN	A1 Q1 B1	A2 Q2 B2	A3 Q3 B3	A4 Q4 B4	A5 Q5 B5	A6 Q6 B6	A7 Q7 B7	A8 Q8 B8	PORT FUNCTION
L L L	H or L	X	Z Q_n A1	Z Q_n A2	Z Q_n A3	Z Q_n A4	Z Q_n A5	Z Q_n A6	Z Q_n A7	Z Q_n A8	A TO B
L L L	↑	X	Z A1 A1	Z A2 A2	A A3 A3	Z A4 A4	Z A5 A5	Z A6 A6	Z A7 A7	Z A8 A8	
L L H	H or L	X	B1 Q_n Z	B2 Q_n Z	B3 Q_n Z	B4 Q_n Z	B5 Q_n Z	B6 Q_n Z	B7 Q_n Z	B8 Q_n Z	B TO A
L L H	↑	X	B1 B1 Z	B2 B2 Z	B3 B3 Z	B4 B4 Z	B5 B5 Z	B6 B6 Z	B7 B7 Z	B8 B8 Z	
L H L	H or L	X	X Q_n Q1	X Q_n Q2	X Q_n Q3	X Q_n Q4	X Q_n Q5	X Q_n Q6	X Q_n Q7	X Q_n Q8	Q_N TO B_N
L H L	↑	X	Z A1 A1	Z A2 A2	Z A3 A3	Z A4 A4	Z A5 A5	Z A6 A6	Z A7 A7	Z A8 A8	
L H H	H or L	X	Q1 Q_n X	Q2 Q_n X	Q3 Q_n X	Q4 Q_n X	Q5 Q_n X	Q6 Q_n X	Q7 Q_n X	Q8 Q_n X	Q_N TO A_N
L H H	↑	X	B1 B1 Z	B2 B2 Z	B3 B3 Z	B4 B4 Z	B5 B5 Z	B6 B6 Z	B7 B7 Z	B8 B8 Z	
H L L	H or L	X	Z Q_n A1	Z Q_n A2	Z Q_n A3	Z Q_n A4	Z Q_n A5	Z Q_n A6	Z Q_n A7	Z Q_n A8	SHIFT
H L L	↑	H	Z H A1	Z Q1 A2	Z Q2 A3	Z Q3 A4	Z Q4 A5	Z Q5 A6	Z Q6 A7	Z Q7 A8	AND
H L L	↑	L	Z L A1	Z Q1 A2	Z Q2 A3	Z Q3 A4	Z Q4 A5	Z Q5 A6	Z Q6 A7	Z Q7 A8	A TO B
H L H	H or L	X	B1 Q_n Z	B2 Q_n Z	B3 Q_n Z	B4 Q_n Z	B5 Q_n Z	B6 Q_n Z	B7 Q_n Z	B8 Q_n Z	SHIFT
H L H	↑	H	B1 H Z	B2 Q1 Z	B3 Q2 Z	B4 Q3 Z	B5 Q4 Z	B6 Q5 Z	B7 Q6 Z	B8 Q7 Z	AND
H L H	↑	L	B1 L Z	B2 Q1 Z	B3 Q2 Z	B4 Q3 Z	B5 Q4 Z	B6 Q5 Z	B7 Q6 Z	B8 Q7 Z	B TO A
H H L	H or L	X	Z Q_n Z	Z Q_n Z	Z Q_n Z	Z Q_n Z	Z Q_n Z	Z Q_n Z	Z Q_n Z	Z Q_n Z	
H H L	↑	H	Z H Z	Z Q1 Z	Z Q2 Z	Z Q3 Z	Z Q4 Z	Z Q5 Z	Z Q6 Z	Z Q7 Z	SHIFT
H H L	↑	L	Z L Z	Z Q1 Z	Z Q2 Z	Z Q3 Z	Z Q4 Z	Z Q5 Z	Z Q6 Z	Z Q7 Z	
H H H	H or L	X	Z Q_n Z	Z Q_n	Z Q_n Z	Z Q_n Z	Z Q_n Z	Z Q_n Z	Z Q_n Z	Z Q_n Z	CLEAR
H H H	↑	X	Z L Z	Z L Z	Z L Z	Z L Z	Z L Z	Z L Z	Z L Z	Z L Z	

n = level of Q_n(n = 1,2, . . . 8) established on the most recent ↑ transition of CLK. Q1 through Q8 are the shift register outputs; only Q8 is available externally. The double inversions that take place as data travels from port to port are ignored in this table.

logic symbol†

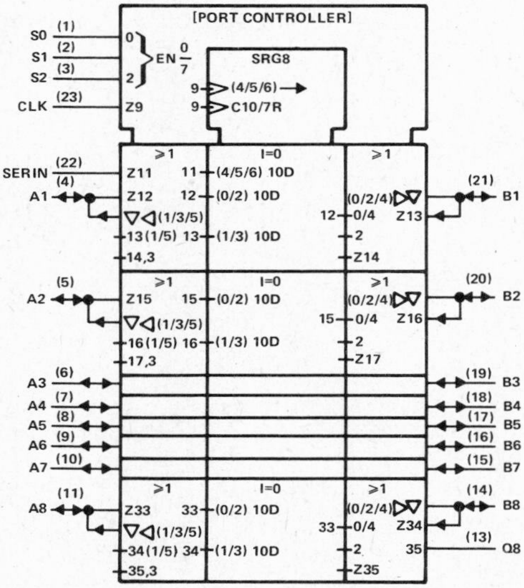
[PORT CONTROLLER]
S0
S1
S2
CLK
SERIN
A1
A2
A3
A4
A5
A6
A7
A8
B1
B2
B3
B4
B5
B6
B7
B8
Q8
EN 0/7
SRG8
Z9
9 (4/5/6)
9 C10/7R
Z11
Z12
11 (4/5/6) 10D
12 (0/2) 10D
(1/3/5)
13(1/5) 13 (1/3) 10D
14,3
(0/2/4)
12 0/4 Z13
2
Z14
Z15
15 (0/2) 10D
16(1/5) 16 (1/3) 10D
17,3
15 0/4 Z16
Z17
Z33
33 (0/2) 10D
34(1/5) 34 (1/3) 10D
35,3
33 0/4 Z34
35
Z35

†This symbol is in accordance with ANSI/IEEE Standard 91-1984 and IEC Publication 617-12.
Pin numbers shown are for DW, JT, and NT packages.

2 LSI Devices

absolute maximum ratings over free-air temperature range

- Supply voltage, V_{CC} .... 7 V
- Input voltage: All inputs .... 7 V
- I/O ports .... 5.5 V
- Voltage applied to a disabled 3-state output .... 5.5 V
- Operating free-air temperature range: SN54AS852 .... −55°C to 125°C
- SN74AS852 .... 0°C to 70°C
- Storage temperature range .... −65°C to 150°C

recommended operating conditions

			SN54AS852			SN74AS852			UNIT
			MIN	NOM	MAX	MIN	NOM	MAX	
V_{CC}	Supply voltage		4.5	5	5.5	4.5	5	5.5	V
V_{IH}	High-level input voltage		2			2			V
V_{IL}	Low-level input voltage				0.8			0.8	V
I_{OH}	High-level output current	A1-A8, B1-B8			−12			−15	mA
		Q8			−2			−2	
I_{OL}	Low-level output current	A1-A8, B1-B8			32			48	mA
		Q8			20			20	
f_{clock}	Clock frequency		0		45	0		50	MHz
t_w	Duration of clock pulse		11			10			ns
t_{su}	Setup time before CLK↑	A1-A8, B1-B8, SERIN	5.5			5.5			ns
		S0, S1, S2	5.5			5.5			
t_h	Hold-time, data after CLK↑	A1-A8, B1-B8, SERIN	0			0			ns
		S0, S1, S2	0			0			
T_A	Operating free-air temperture		−55		125	0		70	°C

electrical characteristics over recommended operating free-air temperature range (unless otherwise noted)

PARAMETER		TEST CONDITIONS		SN54AS852			SN74AS852			UNIT
				MIN	TYP†	MAX	MIN	TYP†	MAX	
V_{IK}		V_{CC} = 4.5 V,	I_I = −18 mA			−1.2			−1.2	V
V_{OH}	A1-A8, B1-B8	V_{CC} = 4.5 V,	I_{OH} = −12 mA	2.4	3.2					V
		V_{CC} = 4.5 V,	I_{OH} = −15 mA				2.4	3.3		
	All outputs	V_{CC} = 4.5 V to 5.5 V,	I_{OH} = −2 mA	$V_{CC}-2$			$V_{CC}-2$			
V_{OL}	All outputs except Q8	V_{CC} = 4.5 V,	I_{OL} = 32 mA		0.3	0.5				V
		V_{CC} = 4.5 V,	I_{OL} = 48 mA					0.35	0.5	
	Q8	V_{CC} = 4.5 V,	I_{OL} = 20 mA		0.25	0.5		0.25	0.5	
I_I	S0, S1, S2	V_{CC} = 5.5 V,	V_I = 7 V			0.3			0.3	mA
	CLK and SERIN					0.1			0.1	
	A1-A8, B1-B8	V_{CC} = 5.5 V,	V_I = 5.5 V			0.2			0.2	
I_{IH}	S0, S1, S2	V_{CC} = 5.5 V,	V_I = 2.7 V			60			60	μA
	CLK and SERIN					20			20	
	A1-A8, B1-B8‡					70			70	
I_{IL}	S0, S1, S2	V_{CC} = 5.5 V,	V_I = 0.4 V			−1			−1	mA
	CLK and SERIN					−0.5			−0.5	
	A1-A8, B1-B8‡					−0.5			−0.5	
I_O§	Except Q8	V_{CC} = 5.5 V,	V_O = 2.25 V	−30		−112	−30		−112	mA
	Q8			−20		−112	−20		−112	
I_{CC}		V_{CC} = 5.5 V			136	220		136	220	mA

†All typical values are at V_{CC} = 5 V, T_A = 25°C.
‡For I/O ports, the parameters I_{IH} and I_{IL} include the output currents I_{OZH} and I_{OZL}, respectively.
§The output conditions have been chosen to produce a current that closely approximates one half of the true short-circuit output current, I_{OS}.

switching characteristics (see Note 1)

PARAMETER	FROM (INPUT)	TO (OUTPUT)	R_L = 4.5 V to 5.5 V, C_L = 50 pF, R1 = 500 Ω, R2 = 500 Ω, T_A = MIN to MAX				UNIT
			SN54AS852		SN74AS852		
			MIN	MAX	MIN	MAX	
f_{max}			45		50		MHz
t_{PLH}	Any A port	Any B port	2	9	2	7.5	ns
t_{PHL}			3	12.5	3	11	
t_{PLH}	Any B port	Any A port	2	9	2	7.5	ns
t_{PHL}			3	12.5	3	11	
t_{PLH}	S0, S1, S2¶	Any A or B port	3	11.5	3	10	ns
t_{PHL}			3	12	3	10.5	
t_{PLH}	CLK	Any A or B port	2	11	2	9	ns
t_{PHL}			3	14	3	12.5	
t_{PLH}	CLK	Q8	2	10.5	2	8	ns
t_{PHL}			3	11.5	3	10	
t_{PHZ}	S0, S1, S2	Any A or B port	2	9	2	7	ns
t_{PLZ}			3	13	3	10.5	
t_{PZH}			2	9	2	7	ns
t_{PZL}			3	13	3	10.5	

NOTE 1: Load circuit and voltage waveforms are shown in Section 1.
¶ The positive transition of S1 control pin will cause low-level data on the A or B bus to be invalid for 17.5 ns.

2

LSI Devices

TYPICAL APPLICATION DATA

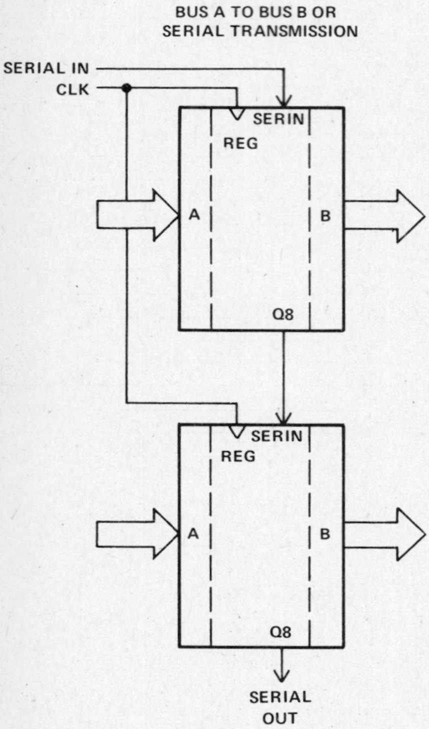
BUS A TO BUS B OR
SERIAL TRANSMISSION
SERIAL IN
CLK
SERIN
REG
A
B
Q8
SERIN
REG
A
B
Q8
SERIAL
OUT

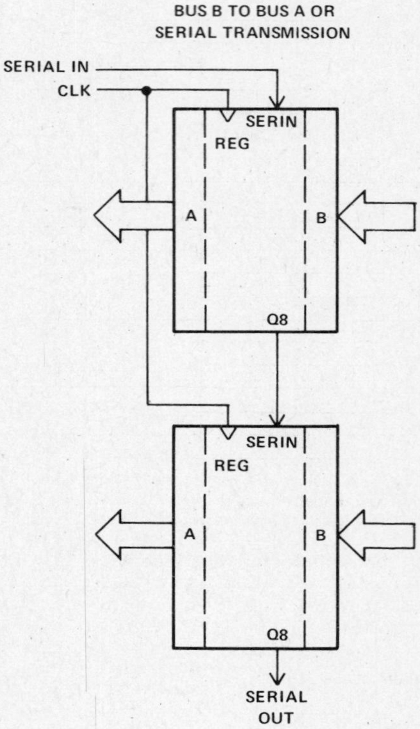
BUS B TO BUS A OR
SERIAL TRANSMISSION
SERIAL IN
CLK
SERIN
REG
A
B
Q8
SERIN
REG
A
B
Q8
SERIAL
OUT

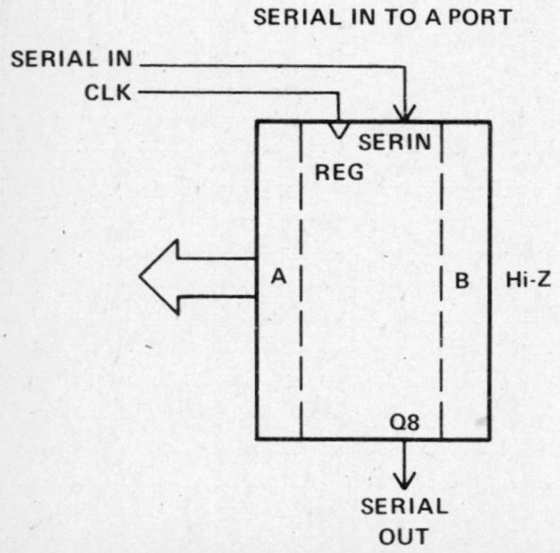
SERIAL IN TO A PORT
SERIAL IN
CLK
SERIN
REG
A
B
Hi-Z
Q8
SERIAL
OUT

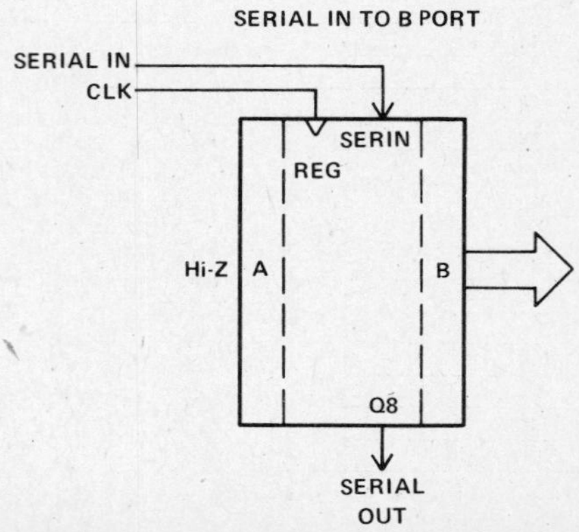
SERIAL IN TO B PORT
SERIAL IN
CLK
SERIN
REG
Hi-Z
A
B
Q8
SERIAL
OUT

TEXAS INSTRUMENTS
POST OFFICE BOX 225012 • DALLAS, TEXAS 75265

D2814, DECEMBER 1983—REVISED MARCH 1985

- **Included Among the Package Options are Compact, 24-Pin, 300-mil-Wide DIPs and Both 28-Pin Plastic and Ceramic Chip Carriers**
- **Buffered 3-State Outputs Drive Bus Lines Directly**
- **Cascadable to n-Bits**
- **Eight Selectable Transceiver/Port Functions:**
  - **B to A**
  - **Register to A and/or B**
  - **Off-Line Shifts (A and B Ports in High-Impedance State)**
  - **Shifted to A and/or B**
- **Particularly Suitable for Use in Diagnostics Analysis Circuitry**
- **Serial Register Provides:**
  - **Parallel Storage of Either A or B Input Data**
  - **Serial Transmission of Data from Either A or B Port**
  - **Readback Mode B to A**
- **Dependable Texas Instruments Quality and Reliability**

SN54AS856 . . . JT PACKAGE
SN74AS856 . . . DW or NT PACKAGE
(TOP VIEW)

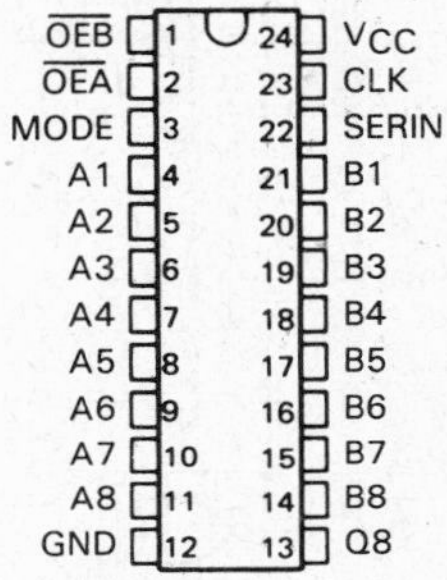
OEB 1
OEA 2
MODE 3
A1 4
A2 5
A3 6
A4 7
A5 8
A6 9
A7 10
A8 11
GND 12
24 VCC
23 CLK
22 SERIN
21 B1
20 B2
19 B3
18 B4
17 B5
16 B6
15 B7
14 B8
13 Q8

SN54AS856 . . . FK PACKAGE
SN74AS856 . . . FN PACKAGE
(TOP VIEW)

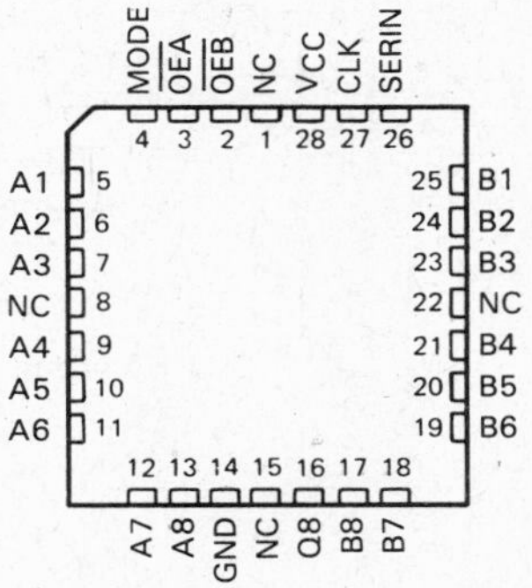
MODE OEA OEB NC VCC CLK SERIN
4 3 2 1 28 27 26
A1 5
A2 6
A3 7
NC 8
A4 9
A5 10
A6 11
25 B1
24 B2
23 B3
22 NC
21 B4
20 B5
19 B6
12 13 14 15 16 17 18
A7 A8 GND NC Q8 B8 B7

NC—No internal connection

description

The 'AS856 features two 8-bit I/O ports (A1-A8 and B1-B8), an 8-bit parallel-load, serial-in, parallel-out shift register, and control logic. With these features, this device is capable of performing eight selectable transceiver or port functions, depending on the state of the three control lines $\overline{\text{OEA}}$, $\overline{\text{OEB}}$, and MODE. These functions include: transferring data from port A to port B or vice versa (i.e., the transceiver function), serial shifting data to either or both ports, and performing off-line shifts (with A and B ports active as transceivers in a high-impedance state). Synchronous parallel loading of the internal register can be accomplished from either port on the positive transition of the clock while serially shifting data in via the SERIN input. The 'AS856 is ideally suited for applications needing signature-analysis circuitry to enhance system verification and/or fault analysis. All serial data is shifted right. All outputs are buffer-type outputs designed specifically to drive bus lines directly and all are 3-state except for Q8, which is a totem-pole output.

The SN54AS856 is characterized for operation over the full military temperaure range of −55°C to 125°C. The SN74AS856 is characterized for operation from 0°C to 70°C.

TEXAS INSTRUMENTS
POST OFFICE BOX 225012 • DALLAS, TEXAS 75265

logic diagram (positive logic)

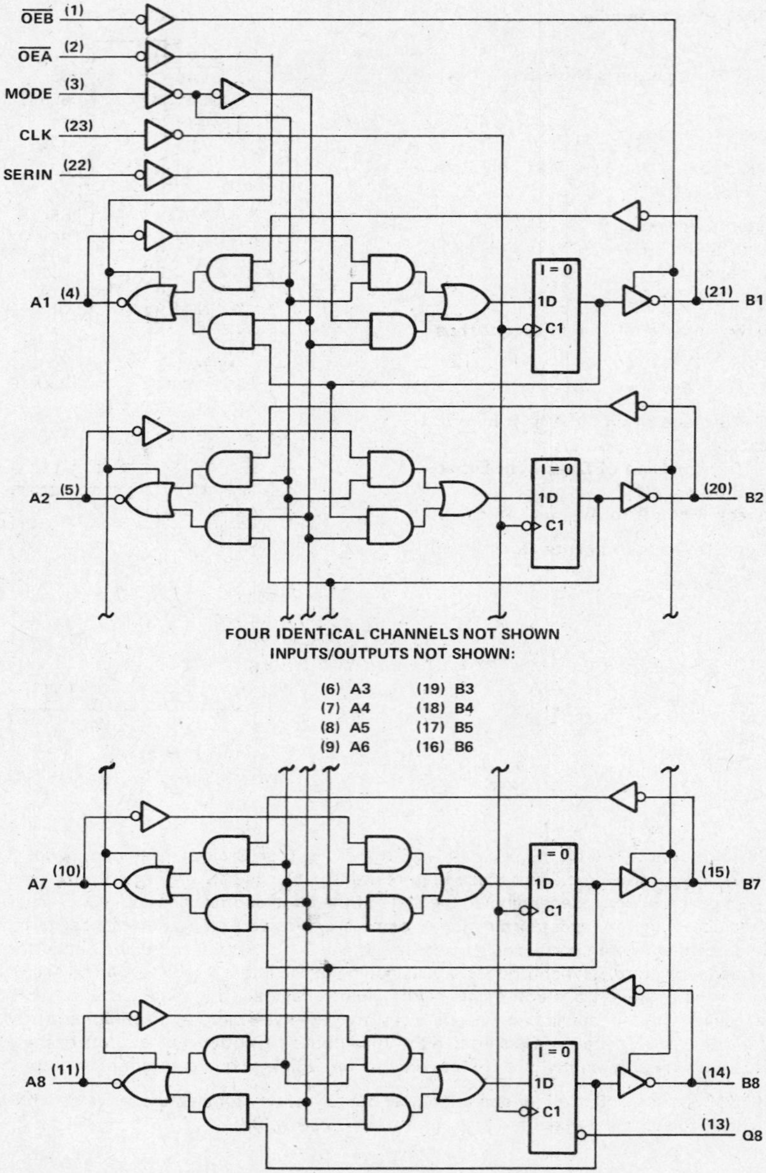
OEB (1)
OEA (2)
MODE (3)
CLK (23)
SERIN (22)
A1 (4)
(21) B1
I = 0
1D
C1
A2 (5)
(20) B2
A7 (10)
(15) B7
A8 (11)
(14) B8
(13) Q8

FOUR IDENTICAL CHANNELS NOT SHOWN
INPUTS/OUTPUTS NOT SHOWN:

(6) A3	(19) B3
(7) A4	(18) B4
(8) A5	(17) B5
(9) A6	(16) B6

FUNCTION TABLE

MODE: MODE	MODE: $\overline{OEA}$	MODE: $\overline{OEB}$	CLOCK	SERIN	A1 Q1 B1	A2 Q2 B2	A3 Q3 B3	A4 Q4 B4	A5 Q5 B5	A6 Q6 B6	A7 Q7 B7	A8 Q8 B8	FUNCTION
L	L	L	H or L	X	Q1 Q1 Q1	Q2 Q2 Q2	Q3 Q3 Q3	Q4 Q4 Q4	Q5 Q5 Q5	Q6 Q6 Q6	Q7 Q7 Q7	Q8 Q8 Q8	FEEDBACK
L	L	L	↑	X	Q1 Q1 Q1	Q2 Q2 Q2	Q3 Q3 Q3	Q4 Q4 Q4	Q5 Q5 Q5	Q6 Q6 Q6	Q7 Q7 Q7	Q8 Q8 Q8	
L	L	H	H or L	X	B1 Q1 Z	B2 Q2 Z	B3 Q3 Z	B4 Q4 Z	B5 Q5 Z	B6 Q6 Z	B7 Q7 Z	B8 Q8 Z	B to A
L	L	H	↑	X	B1 B1 Z	B2 B2 Z	B3 B3 Z	B4 B4 Z	B5 B5 Z	B6 B6 Z	B7 B7 Z	B8 B8 Z	A to Q
L	H	L	H or L	X	Z Q1 Q1	Z Q2 Q2	Z Q3 Q3	Z Q4 Q4	Z Q5 Q5	Z Q6 Q6	Z Q7 Q7	Z Q8 Q8	A to Q
L	H	L	↑	X	Z A1 A1	Z A2 A2	Z A3 A3	Z A4 A4	Z A5 A5	Z A6 A6	Z A7 A7	Z A8 A8	Q to B
L	H	H	H or L	X	Z Q1 Z	Z Q2 Z	Z Q3 Z	Z Q4 Z	Z Q5 Z	Z Q6 Z	Z Q7 Z	Z Q8 Z	A to Q
L	H	H	↑	X	Z A1 Z	Z A2 Z	Z A3 Z	Z A4 Z	Z A5 Z	Z A6 Z	Z A7 Z	Z A8 Z	
H	L	L	H or L	X	Q1 Q_n Q1	Q2 Q_n Q2	Q3 Q_n Q3	Q4 Q_n Q4	Q5 Q_n Q5	Q6 Q_n Q6	Q7 Q_n Q7	Q8 Q_n Q8	SHIFT
H	L	L	↑	H	H H H	Q1 Q1 Q1	Q2 Q2 Q2	Q3 Q3 Q3	Q4 Q4 Q4	Q5 Q5 Q5	Q6 Q6 Q6	Q7 Q7 Q7	TO
H	L	L	↑	L	L L L	Q1 Q1 Q1	Q2 Q2 Q2	Q3 Q3 Q3	Q4 Q4 Q4	Q5 Q5 Q5	Q6 Q6 Q6	Q7 Q7 Q7	A and B
H	L	H	H or L	X	Q1 Q_n Z	Q2 Q_n Z	Q3 Q_n Z	Q4 Q_n Z	Q5 Q_n Z	Q6 Q_n Z	Q7 Q_n Z	Q8 Q_n Z	SHIFT
H	L	H	↑	H	H H Z	Q1 Q1 Z	Q2 Q2 Z	Q3 Q3 Z	Q4 Q4 Z	Q5 Q5 Z	Q6 Q6 Z	Q7 Q7 Z	TO
H	L	H	↑	L	L L Z	Q1 Q1 Z	Q2 Q2 Z	Q3 Q3 Z	Q4 Q4 Z	Q5 Q5 Z	Q6 Q6 Z	Q7 Q7 Z	A
H	H	L	H or L	X	Z Q_n Q1	Z Q_n Q2	Z Q_n Q3	Z Q_n Q4	Z Q_n Q5	Z Q_n Q6	Z Q_n Q7	Z Q_n Q8	SHIFT
H	H	L	↑	H	Z H H	Z Q1 Q1	Z Q2 Q2	Z Q3 Q3	Z Q4 Q4	Z Q5 Q5	Z Q6 Q6	Z Q7 Q7	TO
H	H	L	↑	L	Z L L	Z Q1 Q1	Z Q2 Q2	Z Q3 Q3	Z Q4 Q4	Z Q5 Q5	Z Q6 Q6	Z Q7 Q7	B
H	H	H	H or L	X	Z Q_n Z	Z Q_n Z	Z Q_n Z	Z Q_n Z	Z Q_n Z	Z Q_n Z	Z Q_n Z	Z Q_n Z	SHIFT
H	H	H	↑	H	Z H Z	Z Q1 Z	Z Q2 Z	Z Q3 Z	Z Q4 Z	Z Q5 Z	Z Q6 Z	Z Q7 Z	
H	H	H	↑	L	Z L H	Z Q1 Z	Z Q2 Z	Z Q3 Z	Z Q4 Z	Z Q5 Z	Z Q6 Z	Z Q7 Z	

n = level of Q_n(n = 1, 2 . . . 8) established on most recent ↑ transition of CLK. Q1 through Q8 are the shift register outputs; only Q8 is available externally. The double inversions that take place as data travels from port to port are ignored in this table.

logic symbol†

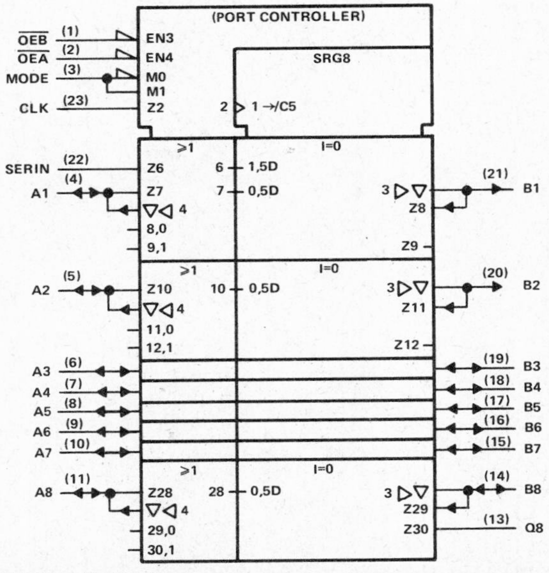
(PORT CONTROLLER)
OEB (1) EN3
OEA (2) EN4
MODE (3) M0
M1
CLK (23) Z2
SRG8
2 ▷ 1 →/C5
≥1
I=0
SERIN (22) Z6
6 1,5D
A1 (4) Z7
7 0,5D
▽◁ 4
8,0
9,1
3 ▷▽
Z8
Z9
(21) B1
A2 (5) Z10
10 0,5D
11,0
12,1
Z11
Z12
(20) B2
A3 (6)
A4 (7)
A5 (8)
A6 (9)
A7 (10)
(19) B3
(18) B4
(17) B5
(16) B6
(15) B7
A8 (11) Z28
28 0,5D
29,0
30,1
Z29
Z30
(14) B8
(13) Q8

Pin numbers shown are for DW, JT, and NT packages.

†This symbol is in accordance with ANSI/IEEE Std 91-1984 and IEC Publication 617-12.

2

LSI Devices

absolute maximum ratings over free-air temperature range

Supply voltage, V_{CC} . . . . . . 7 V
Input voltage: All inputs . . . . . . 7 V
I/O ports . . . . . . 5.5 V
Voltage applied to a disabled 3-state output . . . . . . 5.5 V
Operating free-air temperature range: SN54AS856 . . . . . . −55°C to 125°C
SN74AS856 . . . . . . 0°C to 70°C
Storage temperature range . . . . . . −65°C to 150°C

recommended operating conditions

			SN54AS856			SN74AS856			UNIT
			MIN	NOM	MAX	MIN	NOM	MAX	
V_{CC}	Supply voltage		4.5	5	5.5	4.5	5	5.5	V
V_{IH}	High-level input voltage		2			2			V
V_{IL}	Low-level input voltage				0.8			0.8	V
I_{OH}	High-level output current	A1-A8, B1-B8			−12			−15	mA
		Q8			−2			−2	
I_{OL}	Low-level output current	A1-A8, B1-B8			32			48	mA
		Q8			20			20	
f_{clock}	Clock frequency		0		45	0		50	MHz
t_w	Duration of clock pulse		11			10			ns
t_{su}	Setup time before CLK↑	A1-A8, B1-B8 SERIN	5.5			5.5			ns
		$\overline{OEB}$, $\overline{OEA}$, MODE	5.5			5.5			
t_h	Hold-time, data after CLK↑	A1-A8, B1-B8 SERIN	0			0			ns
		$\overline{OEB}$, $\overline{OEA}$, MODE	0			0			
T_A	Operating free-air temperature		−55		125	0		70	°C

LSI Devices

TEXAS INSTRUMENTS
POST OFFICE BOX 225012 • DALLAS, TEXAS 75265

electrical characteristics over recommended operating free-air temperature range (unless otherwise noted)

PARAMETER		TEST CONDITIONS		SN54AS856			SN74AS856			UNIT
				MIN	TYP†	MAX	MIN	TYP†	MAX	
V_{IK}		V_{CC} = 4.5 V,	I_I = −18 mA			−1.2			−1.2	V
V_{OH}	A1-A8	V_{CC} = 4.5 V,	I_{OH} = −12 mA	2	3.2					V
	B1-B8	V_{CC} = 4.5 V,	I_{OH} = −15 mA				2	3.3		
	All outputs	V_{CC} = 4.5 V to 5.5 V,	I_{OH} = −2 mA	V_{CC}−2			V_{CC}−2			
V_{OL}	All outputs except Q8	V_{CC} = 4.5 V,	I_{OL} = 32 mA		0.25	0.5				V
		V_{CC} = 4.5 V,	I_{OL} = 48 mA					0.35	0.5	
	Q8	V_{CC} = 4.5 V,	I_{OL} = 20 mA			0.5			0.5	
I_I	$\overline{OEB}$, $\overline{OEA}$, MODE	V_{CC} = 5.5 V,	V_I = 7 V			0.2			0.2	mA
	CLK and SERIN					0.1			0.1	
	A1-A8, B1-B8	V_{CC} = 5.5 V,	V_I = 5.5 V			0.2			0.2	
I_{IH}	$\overline{OEB}$, $\overline{OEA}$, MODE	V_{CC} = 5.5 V,	V_I = 2.7 V			40			40	μA
	CLK and SERIN					20			20	
	A1-A8, B1-B8‡					70			70	
I_{IL}	$\overline{OEB}$, $\overline{OEA}$, MODE	V_{CC} = 5.5 V,	V_I = 0.4 V			−1			−1	mA
	CLK and SERIN					−0.5			−0.5	
	A1-A8, B1-B8‡					−0.5			−0.5	
I_O§	Except Q8	V_{CC} = 5.5 V,	V_O = 2.25 V	−30		−112	−30		−112	mA
	Q8			−20		−112	−20		−112	
I_{CC}		V_{CC} = 5.5 V			118	200		118	200	mA

†All typical values are at V_{CC} = 5 V, T_A = 25 °C.
‡For I/O ports, the parameters I_{IH} and I_{IL} include the output currents I_{OZH} and I_{OZL}, respectively.
§The output conditions have been chosen to produce a current that closely approximates one half of the true short-circuit output current, I_{OS}.

switching characteristics (see Note 1)

PARAMETER	FROM (INPUT)	TO (OUTPUT)	V_{CC} = 4.5 V to 5.5 V, C_L = 50 pF, R1 = 500 Ω, R2 = 500 Ω, T_A = MIN to MAX				UNIT
			SN54AS856		SN74AS856		
			MIN	MAX	MIN	MAX	
f_{max}			45		50		MHz
t_{PLH}	Any B port	Any A port	2	8	2	7	ns
t_{PHL}			2	10.5	2	9.5	
t_{PLH}	↑MODE¶	Any A or B port	2	8.5	2	7.5	ns
t_{PHL}			5	20	5	19	
t_{PLH}	↓MODE	Any A or B port	2	8.5	2	7.5	ns
t_{PHL}			2	9.5	2	8	
t_{PLH}	CLK	Any A or B port	3	12	3	9	ns
t_{PHL}			3	12	3	11	
t_{PLH}	CLK	Q8	2	9	2	7.5	ns
t_{PHL}			2	10	2	9	
t_{PHZ}	$\overline{OEA}$ or $\overline{OEB}$	Any A or B port	2	9	2	7	ns
t_{PLZ}			2	12	2	9.5	
t_{PZH}			2	8	2	7	ns
t_{PZL}			2	11	2	10	

¶The positive transition of the MODE control will cause low-level data at the A output Bus or stored in Q to be invalid for 12 ns.
NOTE 1: Load circuit and voltage waveforms are shown in Section 1.

2
LSI Devices

D2661, DECEMBER 1982—AUGUST 1985

- Included among the Package Options are Compact, 24-Pin, 300-mil-Wide DIPs and 28-Pin Ceramic Chip Carriers
- Fully Programmable with Synchronous Counting and Loading
- 'AS867 Has Asynchronous Clear, 'AS869 Has Synchronous Clear
- Fully Independent Clock Circuit Simplifies Use
- Ripple Carry Output for n-Bit Cascading
- Improved Performance Compared to Schottky TTL:
  - Typical Power Reduced by 38%
  - Maximum Count Frequency is 25% Higher
- Dependable Texas Instruments Quality and Reliability

SN54AS867, SN54AS869 . . . . JT PACKAGE
SN74AS867, SN74AS869 . . . . DW OR NT PACKAGE
(TOP VIEW)

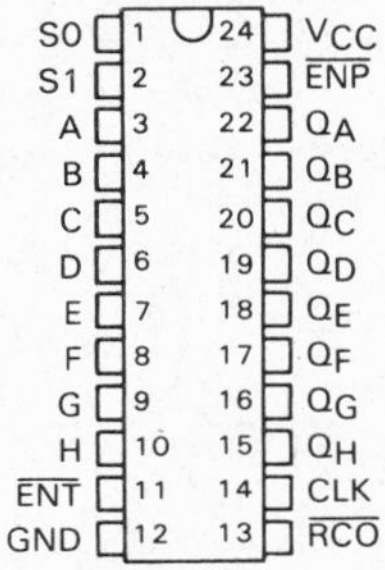
S0 1 24 VCC
S1 2 23 ENP
A 3 22 QA
B 4 21 QB
C 5 20 QC
D 6 19 QD
E 7 18 QE
F 8 17 QF
G 9 16 QG
H 10 15 QH
ENT 11 14 CLK
GND 12 13 RCO

SN54AS867, SN54AS869 . . . . FK PACKAGE
(TOP VIEW)

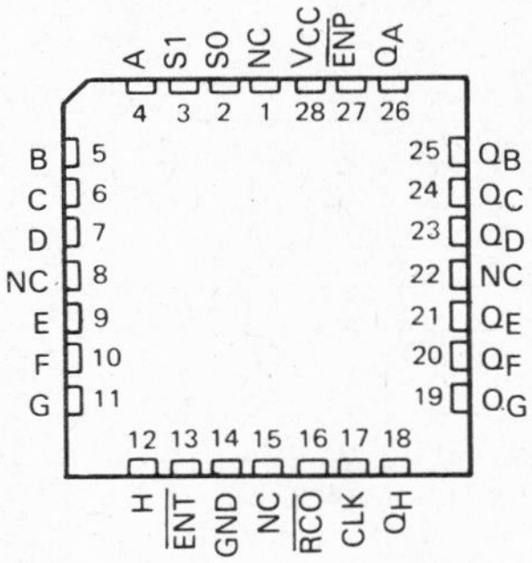
A S1 S0 NC VCC ENP QA
4 3 2 1 28 27 26
B 5
C 6
D 7
NC 8
E 9
F 10
G 11
25 QB
24 QC
23 QD
22 NC
21 QE
20 QF
19 QG
12 13 14 15 16 17 18
H ENT GND NC RCO CLK QH

NC—No internal connection

description

These synchronous presettable counters feature an internal carry look-ahead for cascading in high-speed counting applications. Synchronous operation is provided by having all flip-flops clocked simultaneously so that the outputs change coincident with each other when so instructed by the count-enable inputs and internal gating. This mode of operation helps eliminate the output counting spikes that are normally associated with asynchronous (ripple-clock) counters. A buffered clock input triggers the eight flip-flops on the rising (positive-going) edge of the clock waveform.

These counters are fully programmable; that is, the outputs may each be preset to either level. The load mode circuitry allows parallel loading of the cascaded counters. As loading is synchronous, selecting the load mode disables the counter and causes the outputs to agree with the data inputs after the next clock pulse.

The carry look-ahead circuitry provides for cascading counters for n-bit synchronous applications without additional gating. Instrumental in accomplishing this function are two count-enable inputs and a carry output. Both count enable inputs ($\overline{ENP}$ and $\overline{ENT}$) must be low to count. The direction of the count is determined by the levels of the select inputs (see Function Table). Input $\overline{ENT}$ is fed forward to enable the carry output. The ripple carry output thus enabled will produce a low-level pulse while the count is zero (all outputs low) counting down or 255 counting up (all outputs high). This low-level overflow carry pulse can be used to enable successive cascaded stages. Transitions at the enable $\overline{ENP}$ and $\overline{ENT}$ inputs are allowed regardless of the level of the clock input. All inputs are diode-clamped to minimize transmission-line effects, thereby simplifying system design.

TEXAS INSTRUMENTS
POST OFFICE BOX 225012 • DALLAS, TEXAS 75265

These counters feature a fully independent clock circuit. With the exception of the asynchronous clear on the 'AS867, changes at control inputs (S0, S1) that will modify the operating mode have no effect on the Q outputs until clocking occurs. Anytime the $\overline{\text{ENP}}$ and/or $\overline{\text{ENT}}$ is taken high, $\overline{\text{RCO}}$ will either go or remain high. The function of the counter (whether enabled, disabled, loading, or counting) will be dictated solely by the conditions meeting the stable setup and hold times.

The SN54AS867 and SN54AS869 are characterized for operation over the full military temperature range of −55°C to 125°C. The SN74AS867 and SN74AS869 are characterized for operation from 0°C to 70°C.

logic symbols†

'AS867

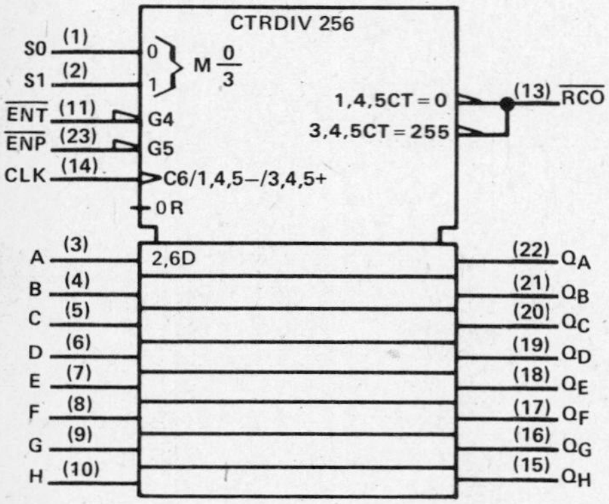
CTRDIV 256
S0 (1)
S1 (2)
M 0/3
ENT (11) G4
ENP (23) G5
CLK (14) C6/1,4,5−/3,4,5+
0R
1,4,5CT=0
3,4,5CT=255
(13) RCO
2,6D
A (3)
B (4)
C (5)
D (6)
E (7)
F (8)
G (9)
H (10)
(22) QA
(21) QB
(20) QC
(19) QD
(18) QE
(17) QF
(16) QG
(15) QH

'AS869

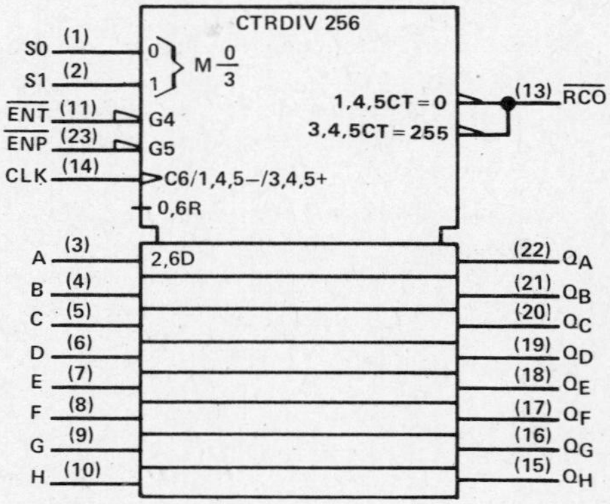
CTRDIV 256
S0 (1)
S1 (2)
M 0/3
ENT (11) G4
ENP (23) G5
CLK (14) C6/1,4,5−/3,4,5+
0,6R
1,4,5CT=0
3,4,5CT=255
(13) RCO
2,6D
A (3)
B (4)
C (5)
D (6)
E (7)
F (8)
G (9)
H (10)
(22) QA
(21) QB
(20) QC
(19) QD
(18) QE
(17) QF
(16) QG
(15) QH

†These symbols are in accordance with ANSI/IEEE Std 91-1984 and IEC Publication 617-12.
Pin numbers shown are for DW, JT, and NT packages.

FUNCTION TABLE

S1	S0	FUNCTION
L	L	Clear
L	H	Count down
H	L	Load
H	H	Count up

absolute maximum ratings over operating free-air temperature range (unless otherwise noted)

Supply voltage, V_{CC}		7 V
Input voltage		7 V
Operating free-air temperature range:	SN54AS867, SN54AS869	−55°C to 125°C
	SN74AS867, SN74AS869	0°C to 70°C
Storage temperature range		−65°C to 150°C

TEXAS INSTRUMENTS
POST OFFICE BOX 225012 • DALLAS, TEXAS 75265

logic diagram (positive logic)

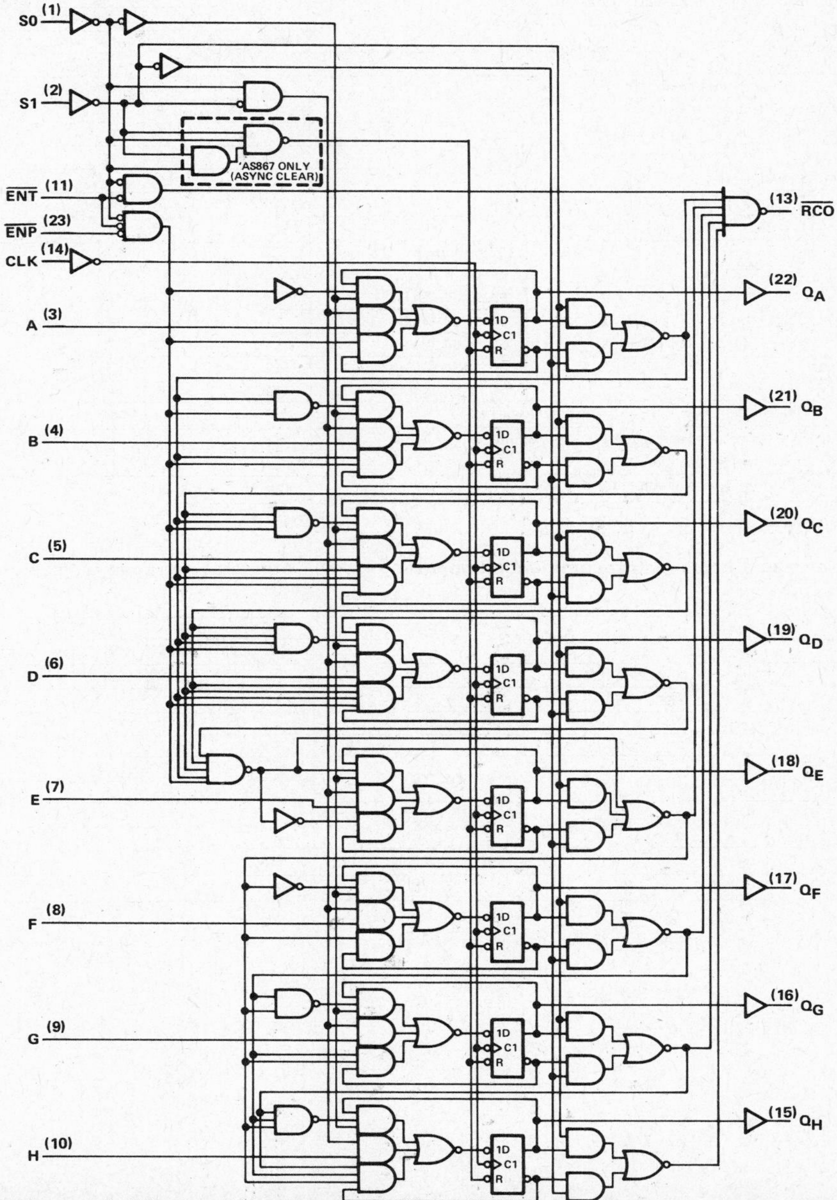
S0 (1)
S1 (2)
'AS867 ONLY (ASYNC CLEAR)
ENT (11)
ENP (23)
CLK (14)
A (3)
B (4)
C (5)
D (6)
E (7)
F (8)
G (9)
H (10)
1D
C1
R
(13) RCO
(22) QA
(21) QB
(20) QC
(19) QD
(18) QE
(17) QF
(16) QG
(15) QH

Pin numbers shown are for DW, JT, and NT packages.

recommended operating conditions

			SN54AS867			SN74AS867			UNIT
			MIN	NOM	MAX	MIN	NOM	MAX	
V_{CC}	Supply voltage		4.5	5	5.5	4.5	5	5.5	V
V_{IH}	High-level input voltage		2			2			V
V_{IL}	Low-level input voltage				0.8			0.8	V
I_{OH}	High-level output current				−2			−2	mA
I_{OL}	Low-level output current				20			20	mA
f_{clock}	Clock frequency		0		40	0		50	MHz
$t_{w(clock)}$	Duration		12.5			10			ns
$t_{w(clear)}$	Duration of clear pulse (S0 and S1 low)		12.5			10			ns
t_{su}	Setup time†	Data inputs A-H	5			4			ns
		Enable P ($\overline{ENP}$) or Enable T ($\overline{ENT}$)	9			8			ns
		S0 or S1 (load)	11			10			ns
		S0 or S1 (clear)	11			10			ns
		S0 or S1 (count down)	42			40			ns
		S0 or S1 (count up)	42			40			ns
t_h	Hold time at any input with respect to clock↑		0			0			ns
t_{skew}	Skew time between S0 and S1 (maximum to avoid inadvertent clear)		8			7			ns
T_A	Operating free-air temperature		−55		125	0		70	°C

†This setup time is required to ensure stable data.

electrical characteristics over recommended operating free-air temperature range (unless otherwise noted)

PARAMETER		TEST CONDITIONS		SN54AS867			SN74AS867			UNIT
				MIN	TYP†	MAX	MIN	TYP†	MAX	
V_{IK}		V_{CC} = 4.5 V,	I_I = 18 mA			−1.2			−1.2	V
V_{OH}		V_{CC} = 4.5 V to 5.5 V,	I_{OH} = −2 mA	$V_{CC}-2$			$V_{CC}-2$			V
V_{OL}		V_{CC} = 4.5 V,	I_{OL} = 20 mA		0.34	0.5		0.34	0.5	V
I_I		V_{CC} = 5.5 V,	V_I = 7 V			0.1			0.1	mA
I_{IH}	$\overline{ENT}$	V_{CC} = 5.5 V,	V_I = 2.7 V			40			40	μA
	Other inputs					20			20	
I_{IL}	$\overline{ENT}$	V_{CC} = 5.5 V,	V_I = 0.4 V			−4			−4	mA
	Other inputs					−2			−2	
I_O§		V_{CC} = 5.5 V,	V_O = 2.25 V	−30		−112	−30		−112	mA
I_{CC}		V_{CC} = 5.5 V			134	195		134	195	mA

†All typical values are at V_{CC} = 5 V, T_A = 25°C.
§The output conditions have been chosen to produce a current that closely approximates one half of the true short-circuit output current, I_{OS}.

recommended operating conditions

			SN54AS869			SN74AS869			UNIT
			MIN	NOM	MAX	MIN	NOM	MAX	
V_{CC}	Supply voltage		4.5	5	5.5	4.5	5	5.5	V
V_{IH}	High-level input voltage		2			2			V
V_{IL}	Low-level input voltage				0.8			0.8	V
I_{OH}	High-level output current				−2			−2	mA
I_{OL}	Low-level output current				20			20	mA
f_{clock}	Clock frequency		0		40	0		45	MHz
$t_{w(clock)}$	Duration		12.5			11			ns
t_{su}	Setup time†	Data inputs A-H	6			5			ns
		Enable P ($\overline{ENP}$) or Enable T ($\overline{ENT}$)	10			9			ns
		S0 or S1 (load)	13			11			ns
		S0 or S1 (clear)	13			11			ns
		S0 or S1 (count down)	52			50			ns
		S0 or S1 (count up)	52			50			ns
t_h	Hold time at any input with respect to clock†		0			0			ns
T_A	Operating free-air temperature		−55		125	0		70	°C

†This setup time is required to ensure stable data.

electrical characteristics over recommended operating free-air temperature range (unless otherwise noted)

PARAMETER		TEST CONDITIONS		SN54AS869			SN74AS869			UNIT
				MIN	TYP‡	MAX	MIN	TYP‡	MAX	
V_{IK}		V_{CC} = 4.5 V,	I_I = 18 mA			−1.2			−1.2	V
V_{OH}		V_{CC} = 4.5 V to 5.5 V,	I_{OH} = −2 mA	V_{CC} − 2			V_{CC} − 2			V
V_{OL}		V_{CC} = 4.5 V,	I_{OL} = 20 mA		0.34	0.5		0.34	0.5	V
I_I		V_{CC} = 5.5 V,	V_I = 7 V			0.1			0.1	mA
I_{IH}	$\overline{ENT}$	V_{CC} = 5.5 V,	V_I = 2.7 V			40			40	μA
	Other inputs					20			20	
I_{IL}	$\overline{ENT}$	V_{CC} = 5.5 V,	V_I = 0.4 V			−4			−4	mA
	Other inputs					−2			−2	
I_O§		V_{CC} = 5.5 V,	V_O = 2.25 V	−30		−112	−30		−112	mA
I_{CC}		V_{CC} = 5.5 V			125	180		125	180	mA

‡All typical values are at V_{CC} = 5 V, T_A = 25°C.
§The output conditions have been chosen to produce a current that closely approximates one half of the true short-circuit output current, I_{OS}.

'AS867 switching characteristics (see note 1)

PARAMETER	FROM (INPUT	TO OUTPUT	V_{CC} = 4.5 V to 5.5 V, C_L = 50 pF, R_L = 500 Ω, T_A = MIN to MAX				UNIT
			SN54AS867		SN74AS867		
			MIN	MAX	MIN	MAX	
f_{max}			40		50		MHz
t_{PLH}	CLK	$\overline{RCO}$	5	31	5	22	ns
t_{PHL}			6	19	6	16	
t_{PLH}	CLK	Any Q	3	12	3	11	ns
t_{PHL}			4	16	4	15	
t_{PLH}	$\overline{ENT}$	$\overline{RCO}$	3	19	3	10	ns
t_{PHL}			5	21	5	17	
t_{PLH}	$\overline{ENP}$	$\overline{RCO}$	5	14	5	14	ns
t_{PHL}			5	21	5	17	
t_{PHL}	Clear (S0, S1 low)	Any Q	7	23	7	21	ns

2

LSI Devices

'AS869 switching characteristics (see note 1)

PARAMETER	FROM (INPUT)	TO (OUTPUT)	V_{CC} = 4.5 V to 5.5 V, C_L = 50 pF, R_L = 500 Ω, T_A = MIN to MAX				UNIT
			SN54AS869		SN74AS869		
			MIN	MAX	MIN	MAX	
f_{max}			40		45		MHz
t_{PLH}	CLK	$\overline{RCO}$	6	35	6	35	ns
t_{PHL}			6	20	6	18	
t_{PLH}	CLK	Any Q	3	12	3	11	ns
t_{PHL}			4	16	4	15	
t_{PLH}	$\overline{ENT}$	$\overline{RCO}$	3	25	3	15	ns
t_{PHL}			6	21	6	17	
t_{PLH}	$\overline{ENP}$	$\overline{RCO}$	5	27	5	19	ns
t_{PHL}			6	21	6	18	

NOTE 1: Load circuit and voltage waveforms, are shown in Section 1.

TEXAS INSTRUMENTS
POST OFFICE BOX 225012 • DALLAS, TEXAS 75265

D2661, DECEMBER 1982—REVISED JANUARY 1986

- 'AS870 in 24-Pin Small Outline, 300-mil DIP and Both Plastic and Ceramic 28-Pin Chip Carriers
- 'AS871 in 28-Pin 600-mil DIP and Both Plastic and Ceramic Chip Carriers
- 3-State Buffer-Type Outputs Drive Bus Lines Directly
- Typical Access Time is 11 ns
- Each Register File Has Individual Write Enable Controls and Address Lines
- Designed Specifically for Multibus Architecture and Overlapping File Operations
- Prioritized B Input Port Prevents Write Conflicts During Dual Input Mode
- Dependable Texas Instruments Quality and Reliability

description

These devices feature two 16-word by 4-bit register files. Each register file has individual write-enable controls and address lines. The 'AS870 has two 4-bit data I/O ports (DQA1-DQA4 and DQB1-DQB4). The 'AS871 has one 4-bit data I/O port (DQB1-DQB4) with the other data port having individual data inputs (DA1-DA4) and data outputs (QA1-QA4). The data I/O ports can output to Bus A and Bus B, receive input from Bus A and Bus B, receive input from Bus A and output to Bus B, or output to Bus A and receive input from Bus B. To prevent writing conflicts in the dual-input mode, the B input port takes priority. Two select lines, S0 and S1, control which port has access to which register. S2 determines whether the A ports are in the input or the output modes and S3 does likewise for the B ports. The address lines (1A0-1A3 or 2A0-2A3) are decoded by an internal 1-of-16 decoder to select which register word is to be accessed. All outputs are 3-state buffer-type outputs designed specifically to drive bus lines directly.

The SN54AS870 and SN54AS871 are characterized for operation over the full military temperature range of −55°C to 125°C. The SN74AS870 and SN74AS871 are characterized for operation from 0°C to 70°C.

SN54AS870 . . . JT PACKAGE
SN74AS870 . . . DW OR NT PACKAGE
(TOP VIEW)

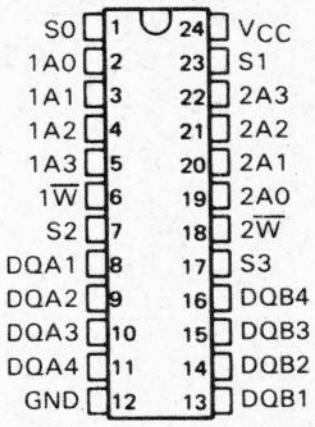
S0 1
1A0 2
1A1 3
1A2 4
1A3 5
1W̄ 6
S2 7
DQA1 8
DQA2 9
DQA3 10
DQA4 11
GND 12
24 VCC
23 S1
22 2A3
21 2A2
20 2A1
19 2A0
18 2W̄
17 S3
16 DQB4
15 DQB3
14 DQB2
13 DQB1

SN54AS871 . . . JD PACKAGE
SN74AS871 . . . N PACKAGE
(TOP VIEW)

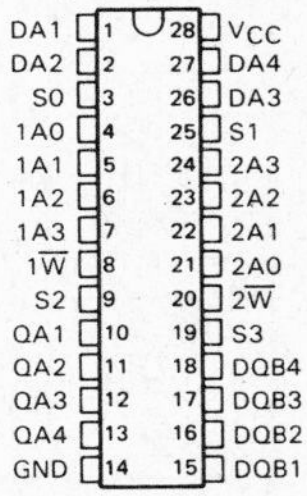
DA1 1
DA2 2
S0 3
1A0 4
1A1 5
1A2 6
1A3 7
1W̄ 8
S2 9
QA1 10
QA2 11
QA3 12
QA4 13
GND 14
28 VCC
27 DA4
26 DA3
25 S1
24 2A3
23 2A2
22 2A1
21 2A0
20 2W̄
19 S3
18 DQB4
17 DQB3
16 DQB2
15 DQB1

SN54AS870 . . . FK PACKAGE
SN74AS870 . . . FN PACKAGE
(TOP VIEW)

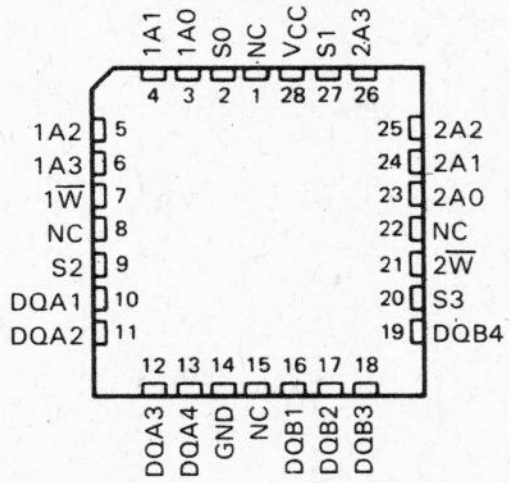
1A1 1A0 S0 NC VCC S1 2A3
4 3 2 1 28 27 26
1A2 5
1A3 6
1W̄ 7
NC 8
S2 9
DQA1 10
DQA2 11
25 2A2
24 2A1
23 2A0
22 NC
21 2W̄
20 S3
19 DQB4
12 13 14 15 16 17 18
DQA3 DQA4 GND NC DQB1 DQB2 DQB3

SN54AS871 . . . FK PACKAGE
SN74AS871 . . . FN PACKAGE
(TOP VIEW)

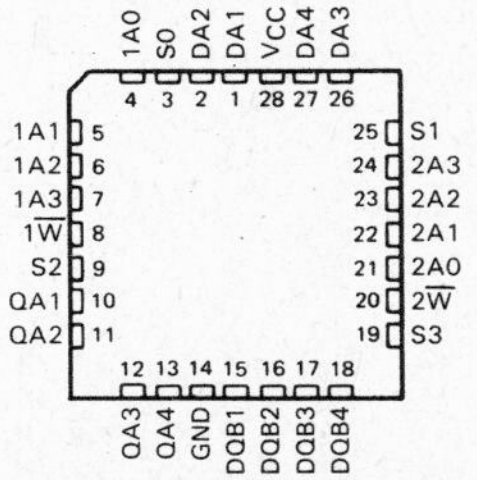
1A0 S0 DA2 DA1 VCC DA4 DA3
4 3 2 1 28 27 26
1A1 5
1A2 6
1A3 7
1W̄ 8
S2 9
QA1 10
QA2 11
25 S1
24 2A3
23 2A2
22 2A1
21 2A0
20 2W̄
19 S3
12 13 14 15 16 17 18
QA3 QA4 GND DQB1 DQB2 DQB3 DQB4

NC—No internal connection

logic symbols†

'AS870

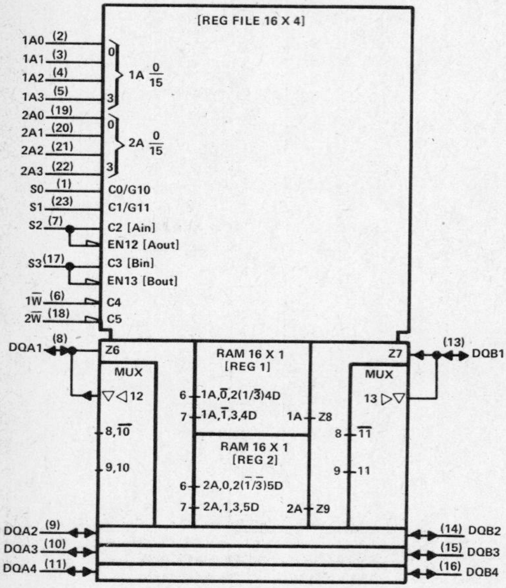
[REG FILE 16 X 4]
1A0 (2)
1A1 (3)
1A2 (4)
1A3 (5)
2A0 (19)
2A1 (20)
2A2 (21)
2A3 (22)
1A 0/15
2A 0/15
S0 (1)
S1 (23)
S2 (7)
S3 (17)
1W̄ (6)
2W̄ (18)
C0/G10
C1/G11
C2 [Ain]
EN12 [Aout]
C3 [Bin]
EN13 [Bout]
C4
C5
DQA1 (8)
Z6
MUX
12
8,1̄0̄
9,10
RAM 16 X 1
[REG 1]
6 1A,0̄,2(1/3̄)4D
7 1A,1̄,3,4D
1A Z8
RAM 16 X 1
[REG 2]
6 2A,0,2(1̄/3̄)5D
7 2A,1,3,5D
2A Z9
Z7
MUX
13
8 1̄1̄
9 11
(13) DQB1
DQA2 (9)
DQA3 (10)
DQA4 (11)
(14) DQB2
(15) DQB3
(16) DQB4

'AS871

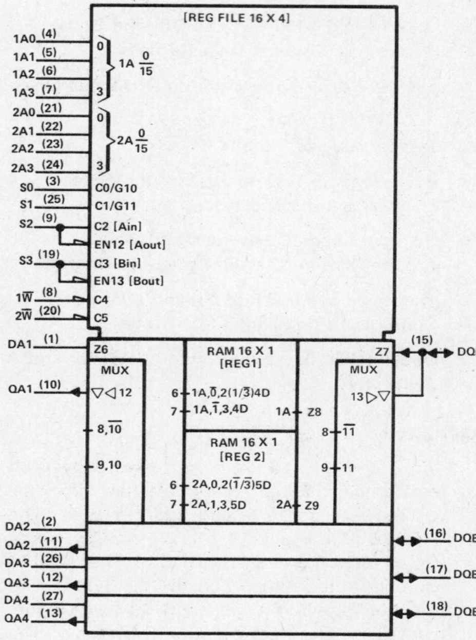
[REG FILE 16 X 4]
1A0 (4)
1A1 (5)
1A2 (6)
1A3 (7)
2A0 (21)
2A1 (22)
2A2 (23)
2A3 (24)
1A 0/15
2A 0/15
S0 (3)
S1 (25)
S2 (9)
S3 (19)
1W̄ (8)
2W̄ (20)
C0/G10
C1/G11
C2 [Ain]
EN12 [Aout]
C3 [Bin]
EN13 [Bout]
C4
C5
DA1 (1)
Z6
MUX
QA1 (10)
12
8,1̄0̄
9,10
RAM 16 X 1
[REG1]
6 1A,0̄,2(1/3̄)4D
7 1A,1̄,3,4D
1A Z8
RAM 16 X 1
[REG 2]
6 2A,0,2(1̄/3̄)5D
7 2A,1,3,5D
2A Z9
Z7
MUX
13
8 1̄1̄
9 11
(15) DQB1
DA2 (2)
QA2 (11)
DA3 (26)
QA3 (12)
DA4 (27)
QA4 (13)
(16) DQB2
(17) DQB3
(18) DQB4

† These symbols are in accordance with ANSI/IEEE Std 91-1984 and IEC Publication 617-12.

Pin numbers shown are for DW, JT, and NT packages.

logic diagram (positive logic)

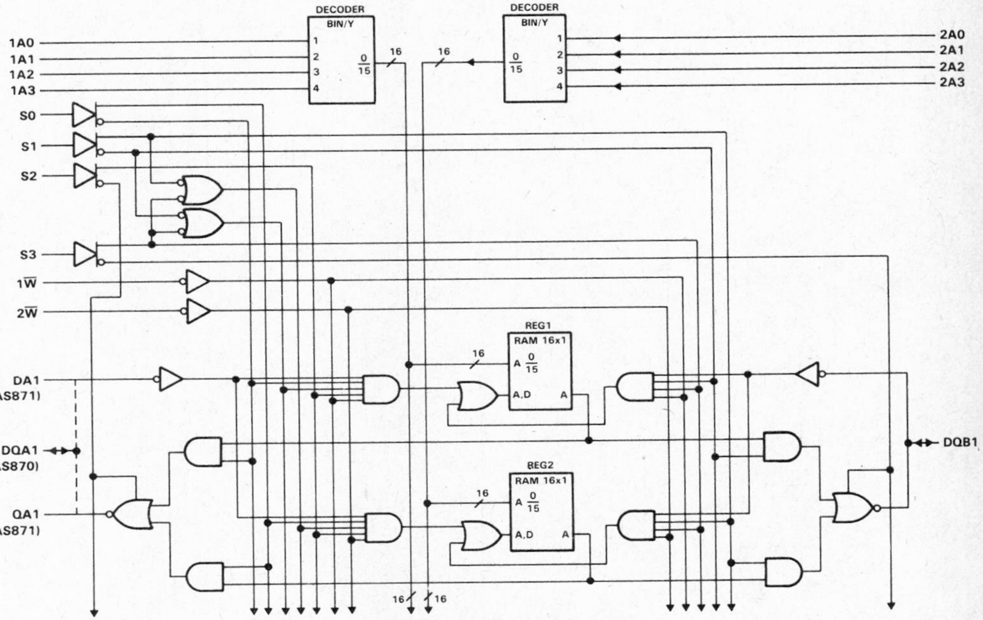
DECODER
BIN/Y
DECODER
BIN/Y
1A0
1A1
1A2
1A3
2A0
2A1
2A2
2A3
S0
S1
S2
S3
1W̄
2W̄
REG1
RAM 16x1
A,D
REG2
RAM 16x1
DA1
('AS871)
DQA1
('AS870)
QA1
('AS871)
DQB1
THREE IDENTICAL CHANNELS NOT SHOWN

FUNCTION TABLE

FILE SELECT			INPUT/OUTPUT		
S0	S1	FILE SEL	S2	S3	I/O SEL
L	L	1R TO A, 1R TO B	L	L	A OUT, B OUT
H	L	2R TO A, 1R TO B			
L	H	1R TO A, 2R TO B			
H	H	2R TO A, 2R TO B			
L	L	A TO 1R, 1R TO B	H	L	A IN, B OUT
H	L	A TO 2R, 1R TO B			
L	H	A TO 1R, 2R TO B			
H	H	A TO 2R, 2R TO B			
L	L	1R TO A, B TO 1R	L	H	A OUT, B IN
H	L	2R TO A, B TO 1R			
L	H	1R TO A, B TO 2R			
H	H	2R TO A, B TO 2R			
L	L	B TO 1R	H	H	A IN, B IN
H	L	A TO 2R, B TO 1R			
L	H	A TO 1R, B TO 2R			
H	H	B TO 2R			

absolute maximum ratings over operating free-air temperature range (unless otherwise noted)

Supply voltage, V_{CC} . . . . 7 V
Input voltage: All inputs . . . . 7 V
I/O ports . . . . 5.5 V
Voltage applied to a disabled 3-state output . . . . 5.5 V
Operating free-air temperature range: SN54AS870, SN54AS871 . . . . −55°C to 125°C
SN74AS870, SN74AS871 . . . . 0°C to 70°C
Storage temperature range . . . . −65°C to 150°C

recommended operating conditions

			SN54AS870 SN54AS871			SN74AS870 SN74AS871			UNIT
			MIN	NOM	MAX	MIN	NOM	MAX	
V_{CC}	Supply voltage		4.5	5	5.5	4.5	5	5.5	V
V_{IH}	High-level input voltage		2			2			V
V_{IL}	Low-level input voltage				0.8			0.8	V
I_{OH}	High-level output current				−12			−15	mA
I_{OL}	Low-level output current				32			48	mA
t_w	Duration of write pulse		12			12			ns
t_{su}	Setup times	Address before write↓	5			5			ns
		Data before write↑	15			15			
		Select before write↓	12			12			
t_h	Hold times	Address after write↑	0			0			ns
		Data after write↑	0			0			
		Select after write↑	12			12			
T_A	Operating free-air temperature		−55		125	0		70	°C

'AS870 electrical characteristics over recommended operating free-air temperature range (unless otherwise noted)

PARAMETER		TEST CONDITIONS		SN54AS870			SN74AS870			UNIT
				MIN	TYP†	MAX	MIN	TYP†	MAX	
V_{IK}		V_{CC} = 4.5 V,	I_I = −18 mA			−1.2			−1.2	V
V_{OH}		V_{CC} = 4.5 V to 5.5 V	I_{OH} = −2 mA	$V_{CC}-2$			$V_{CC}-2$			V
		V_{CC} = 4.5 V,	I_{OH} = −12 mA	2.4	3.2					
		V_{CC} = 4.5 V,	I_{OH} = −15 mA				2.4	3.2		
V_{OL}		V_{CC} = 4.5 V,	I_{OL} = 32 mA		0.25	0.5				V
		V_{CC} = 4.5 V,	I_{OL} = 48 mA					0.35	0.5	
I_I	Control inputs	V_{CC} = 5.5 V,	V_I = 7 V			0.1			0.1	mA
	DQA and DQB ports	V_{CC} = 5.5 V,	V_I = 5.5 V			0.2			0.2	
I_{IH}	$1\overline{W}$ and $2\overline{W}$	V_{CC} = 5.5 V,	V_I = 2.7 V			20			20	μA
	Other control inputs					40			40	
	DQA and DQB ports‡					50			50	
I_{IL}	Control inputs	V_{CC} = 5.5 V,	V_I = 0.4 V			−2			−2	mA
	DQA and DQB ports‡					−2			−2	
I_O§		V_{CC} = 5.5 V,	V_O = 2.25 V	−30		−112	−30		−112	mA
I_{CC}		V_{CC} = 5.5 V			120	190		120	190	mA

'AS871 electrical characteristics over recommended operating free-air temperature range (unless otherwise noted)

PARAMETER		TEST CONDITIONS		SN54AS871			SN74AS871			UNIT
				MIN	TYP†	MAX	MIN	TYP†	MAX	
V_{IK}		V_{CC} = 4.5 V,	I_I = −18 mA			−1.2			−1.2	V
V_{OH}		V_{CC} = 4.5 V to 5.5 V,	I_{OH} = −2 mA	$V_{CC}-2$			$V_{CC}-2$			V
		V_{CC} = 4.5 V,	I_{OH} = −12 mA	2.4	3.2					
		V_{CC} = 4.5 V,	I_{OH} = −15 mA				2.4	3.2		
V_{OL}		V_{CC} = 4.5 V,	I_{OL} = 32 mA		0.25	0.5				V
		V_{CC} = 4.5 V,	I_{OL} = 48 mA					0.35	0.5	
I_{OZH}	QA outputs	V_{CC} = 5.5 V,	V_O = 2.7 V			50			50	μA
I_{OZL}	QA outputs	V_{CC} = 5.5 V,	V_O = 0.4 V			−50			−50	μA
I_I	Control and DA inputs	V_{CC} = 5.5 V,	V_I = 7 V			0.1			0.1	mA
	DQB ports	V_{CC} = 5.5 V,	V_I = 5.5 V			0.2			0.2	
I_{IH}	$1\overline{W}$, $2\overline{W}$, and DA inputs	V_{CC} = 5.5 V,	V_I = 2.7 V			20			20	μA
	Other control inputs					40			40	
	DQB ports‡					50			50	
I_{IL}	Control and DA inputs	V_{CC} = 5.5 V,	V_I = 0.4 V			−2			−2	mA
	DQB ports‡					−2			−2	
I_O§		V_{CC} = 5.5 V,	V_O = 2.25 V	−30		−112	−30		−112	mA
I_{CC}		V_{CC} = 5.5 V			120	190		120	190	mA

†All typical values are at V_{CC} = 5 V, T_A = 25°C.
‡For I/O ports, the parameters I_{IH} and I_{IL} include the off-state output current.
§The output conditions have been chosen to produce a current that closely approximates one-half of the true short-circuit current, I_{OS}.

'AS870 switching characteristics (see Note 1)

PARAMETER	FROM (INPUT)	TO (OUTPUT)	V_{CC} = 4.5 V to 5.5 V, C_L = 50 pF, R_1 = 500 Ω, R2 = 500 Ω, T_A = MIN to MAX				UNIT
			SN54AS870		SN74AS870		
			MIN	MAX	MIN	MAX	
$t_{a(A)}$	Any A	Any DQ	5	20	5	15	ns
$t_{a(S)}$	S0	Any DQA	3	15	3	13	ns
	S1	Any DQB	3	15	3	13	
t_{dis}	S2	Any DQA	3	12	3	11	ns
	S3	Any DQB	3	12	3	11	
t_{en}	S2	Any DQA	3	15	3	12	ns
	S3	Any DQB	3	15	3	12	
t_{pd}	$\overline{W}$	Any DQ	5	23	5	19	ns
	DQA	DQB	5	25	5	22	
	DQB	DQA	5	25	5	22	

'AS871 switching characteristics (see Note 1)

PARAMETER	FROM (INPUT)	TO (OUTPUT)	V_{CC} = 4.5 V to 5.5 V, C_L = 50 pF, R_1 = 500 Ω, R2 = 500 Ω, T_A = MIN to MAX				UNIT
			SN54AS871		SN74AS871		
			MIN	MAX	MIN	MAX	
$t_{a(A)}$	Any A	Any QA or DQB	5	20	5	16	ns
$t_{a(S)}$	S0	Any QA	3	15	3	13	ns
	S1	Any DQB	3	15	3	13	
t_{dis}	S2	Any QA	3	12	3	11	ns
	S3	Any DQB	3	12	3	11	
t_{en}	S2	Any QA	3	15	3	12	ns
	S3	Any DQB	3	15	3	12	
t_{pd}	$\overline{W}$	Any QA or DQB	5	23	5	19	ns
	DA	DQB	5	26	5	23	
	DQB	QA	5	26	5	23	

NOTE 1: Load circuit and voltage waveforms are shown in Section 1.

D2661, DECEMBER 1982—REVISED AUGUST 1985

- **Included Among the Package Options are Compact, 24-Pin, 300-mil-Wide Dips and Both 28-Pin Plastic and Ceramic Chip Carriers**
- **Buffered 3-State Outputs Drive Bus Lines Directly**
- **Cascaded to n-Bits**
- **Eight Selectable Transceiver/Port Functions:**
  A to B or B to A
  Register to A or Register to B
  Shifted to A or Shifted to B
  Off-Line Shifts (A and B Ports in High-Impedance State)
  Register Clear
- **Particularly Suitable for Use in Signature-Analysis Circuitry**
- **Serial Register Provides:**
  Parallel Storage of Either A or B Input Data
  Serial Transmission of Data from Either A or B Port
- **Dependable Texas Instruments Quality and Reliability**

SN54AS877 . . . JT PACKAGE
SN74AS877 . . . DW OR NT PACKAGE
(TOP VIEW)

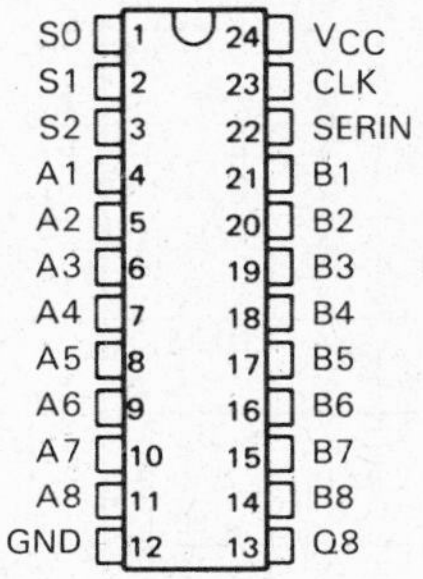
S0 1
S1 2
S2 3
A1 4
A2 5
A3 6
A4 7
A5 8
A6 9
A7 10
A8 11
GND 12
24 VCC
23 CLK
22 SERIN
21 B1
20 B2
19 B3
18 B4
17 B5
16 B6
15 B7
14 B8
13 Q8

SN54AS877....FK PACKAGE
SN74AS877....FN PACKAGE
(TOP VIEW)

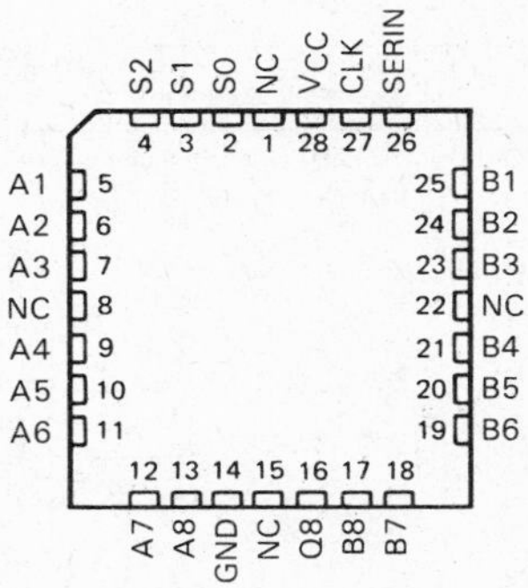
S2 S1 S0 NC VCC CLK SERIN
4 3 2 1 28 27 26
A1 5
A2 6
A3 7
NC 8
A4 9
A5 10
A6 11
25 B1
24 B2
23 B3
22 NC
21 B4
20 B5
19 B6
12 13 14 15 16 17 18
A7 A8 GND NC Q8 B8 B7

NC—No internal connection

description

The 'AS877 features two 8-bit I/O ports (A1-A8 and B1-B8), an 8-bit parallel-load, serial-in, parallel-out shift register, and control logic. With these features, this device is capable of performing eight selectable transceiver or port functions, depending on the state of the three select lines S0, S1, and S2. These functions include: transferring data from port A to port B or vice versa (i.e., the transceiver function), transferring data from the register to either port, serial shifting data to either port, performing off-line shifts (with A and B ports in high-impedance state), and clearing the register. Synchronous parallel loading of the internal register can be accomplished from either port on the positive transition of the clock while serially shifting data in via the SERIN input. The 'AS877 is ideally suited for applications needing signature-analysis circuitry to enhance system verification and/or fault analysis. All serial data is shifted right. All outputs are buffer-type outputs designed specifically to drive bus lines directly and all are 3-state except for Q8, which is a totem-pole output.

The SN54AS877 is characterized for operation over the full military temperature range of −55°C to 125°C. The SN74AS877 is characterized for operation from 0°C to 70°C.

TEXAS INSTRUMENTS
POST OFFICE BOX 225012 • DALLAS, TEXAS 75265

FUNCTION TABLE

MODE S2 S1 S0	CLOCK	SERIN	A1 Q1 B1	A2 Q2 B2	A3 Q3 B3	A4 Q4 B4	A5 Q5 B5	A6 Q6 B6	A7 Q7 B7	A8 Q8 B8	PORT FUNCTION
L L L	H or L	X	Z Q_n A1	Z Q_n A2	Z Q_n A3	Z Q_n A4	Z Q_n A5	Z Q_n A6	Z Q_n A7	Z Q_n A8	A TO B
L L L	↑	X	Z A1 A1	Z A2 A2	Z A3 A3	Z A4 A4	Z A5 A5	Z A6 A6	Z A7 A7	Z A8 A8	
L L H	H or L	X	B1 Q_n Z	B2 Q_n Z	B3 Q_n Z	B4 Q_n Z	B5 Q_n Z	B6 Q_n Z	B7 Q_n Z	B8 Q_n Z	B TO A
L L H	↑	X	B1 B1 Z	B2 B2 Z	B3 B3 Z	B4 B4 Z	B5 B5 Z	B6 B6 Z	B7 B7 Z	B8 B8 Z	
L H L	H or L	X	X Q_n Q1	X Q_n Q2	X Q_n Q3	X Q_n Q4	X Q_n Q5	X Q_n Q6	X Q_n Q7	X Q_n Q8	Q_N TO B_N
L H L	↑	X	Z A1 A1	Z A2 A2	Z A3 A3	Z A4 A4	Z A5 A5	Z A6 A6	Z A7 A7	Z A8 A8	
L H H	H or L	X	Q1 Q_n X	Q2 Q_n X	Q3 Q_n X	Q4 Q_n X	Q5 Q_n X	Q6 Q_n X	Q7 Q_n X	Q8 Q_n X	Q_N TO A_N
L H H	↑	X	B1 B1 Z	B2 B2 Z	B3 B3 Z	B4 B4 Z	B5 B5 Z	B6 B6 Z	B7 B7 Z	B8 B8 Z	
H L L	H or L	X	Z Q_n Q1	Z Q_n Q2	Z Q_n Q3	Z Q_n Q4	Z Q_n Q5	Z Q_n Q6	Z Q_n Q7	Z Q_n Q8	SHIFT
H L L	↑	H	Z H H	Z Q1 Q1	Z Q2 Q2	Z Q3 Q3	Z Q4 Q4	Z Q5 Q5	Z Q6 Q6	Z Q7 Q7	TO
H L L	↑	L	Z L L	Z Q1 Q1	Z Q2 Q2	Z Q3 Q3	Z Q4 Q4	Z Q5 Q5	Z Q6 Q6	Z Q7 Q7	B
H L H	H or L	X	Q1 Q_n Z	Q2 Q_n Z	Q3 Q_n Z	Q4 Q_n Z	Q5 Q_n Z	Q6 Q_n Z	Q7 Q_n Z	Q8 Q_n Z	SHIFT
H L H	↑	H	H H Z	Q1 Q1 Z	Q2 Q2 Z	Q3 Q3 Z	Q4 Q4 Z	Q5 Q5 Z	Q6 Q6 Z	Q7 Q7 Z	TO
H L H	↑	L	L L Z	Q1 Q1 Z	Q2 Q2 Z	Q3 Q3 Z	Q4 Q4 Z	Q5 Q5 Z	Q6 Q6 Z	Q7 Q7 Z	A
H H L	H or L	X	Z Q_n Z	Z Q_n Z	Z Q_n Z	Z Q_n Z	Z Q_n Z	Z Q_n Z	Z Q_n Z	Z Q_n Z	
H H L	↑	H	Z H Z	Z Q1 Z	Z Q2 Z	Z Q3 Z	Z Q4 Z	Z Q5 Z	Z Q6 Z	Z Q7 Z	SHIFT
H H L	↑	L	Z L Z	Z Q1 Z	Z Q2 Z	Z Q3 Z	Z Q4 Z	Z Q5 Z	Z Q6 Z	Z Q7 Z	
H H H	H or L	X	Z Q_n Z	Z Q_n Z	Z Q_n Z	Z Q_n Z	Z Q_n Z	Z Q_n Z	Z Q_n Z	Z Q_n Z	CLEAR
H H H	↑	X	Z L Z	Z L Z	Z L Z	Z L Z	Z L Z	Z L Z	Z L Z	Z L Z	

n = level of Q_n (n = 1, 2...8) established on most recent ↑ transition of CLK. Q1 thru Q8 are the shift register outputs; only Q8 is available externally. The double inversions that take place as data travels from port to port are ignored in this table.

logic symbol†

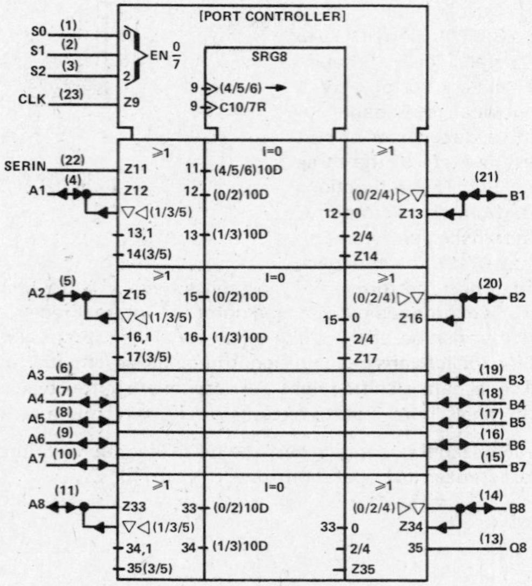
[PORT CONTROLLER]
SRG8
S0 (1)
S1 (2)
S2 (3)
EN 0/7
CLK (23)
Z9
9 ▷(4/5/6) →
9 ▷C10/7R
SERIN (22)
A1 (4)
Z11
Z12
≥1
I=0
11 (4/5/6)10D
12 (0/2)10D
13 (1/3)10D
13,1
14(3/5)
▽◁(1/3/5)
(0/2/4)▷▽
12 0
2/4
Z13
Z14
(21)
B1
A2 (5)
Z15
15 (0/2)10D
16 (1/3)10D
16,1
17(3/5)
15 0
Z16
Z17
(20)
B2
A3 (6)
A4 (7)
A5 (8)
A6 (9)
A7 (10)
(19) B3
(18) B4
(17) B5
(16) B6
(15) B7
A8 (11)
Z33
33 (0/2)10D
34 (1/3)10D
34,1
35(3/5)
33 0
Z34
35
Z35
(14) B8
(13) Q8

†This symbol is in accordance with ANSI/IEEE Std 91-1984 and IEC Publication 617-12.
Pin numbers shown are for DW, JT, and NT packages.

logic diagram (positive logic)

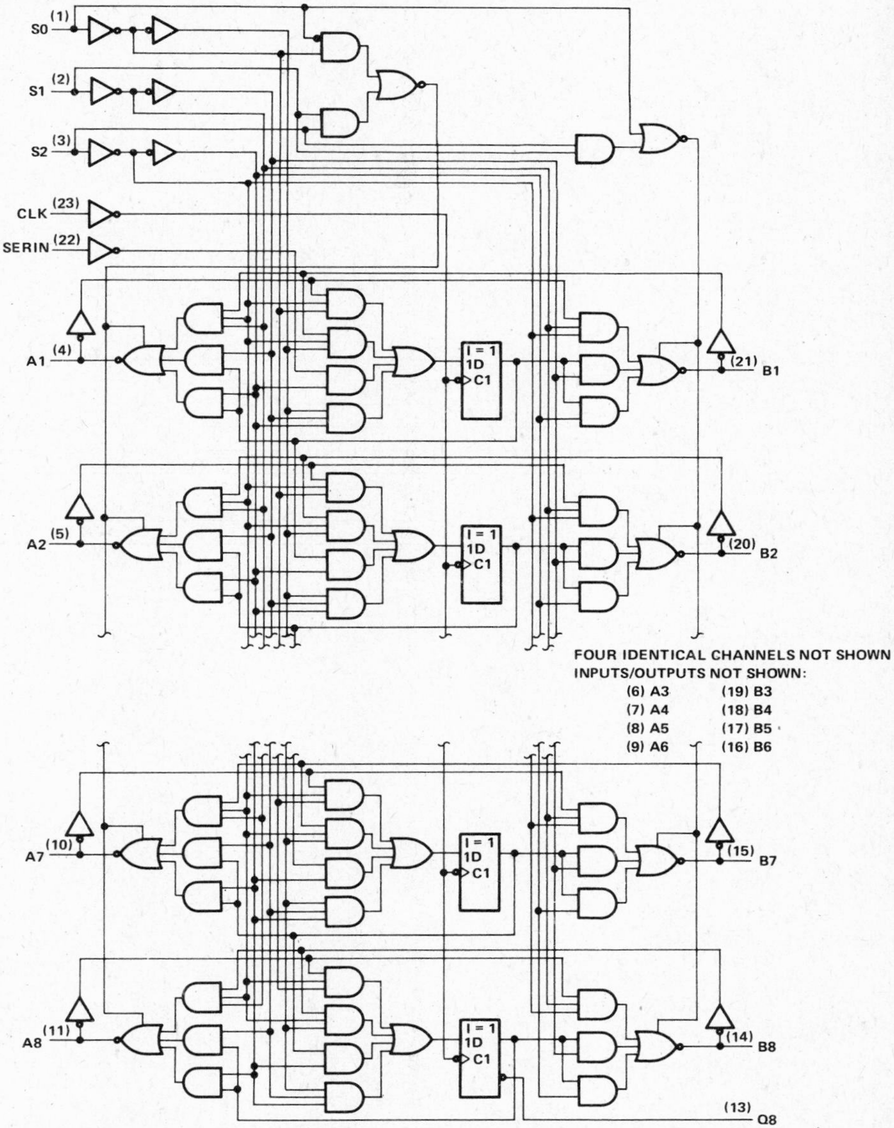
(1)
S0
(2)
S1
(3)
S2
(23)
CLK
(22)
SERIN
(4)
A1
(21)
B1
(5)
A2
(20)
B2
I = 1
1D
C1
FOUR IDENTICAL CHANNELS NOT SHOWN
INPUTS/OUTPUTS NOT SHOWN:
(6) A3 (19) B3
(7) A4 (18) B4
(8) A5 (17) B5
(9) A6 (16) B6
(10)
A7
(15)
B7
(11)
A8
(14)
B8
(13)
Q8

Pin numbers shown are for DW, JT, and NT packages.

absolute maximum ratings over free-air temperature range

Supply voltage, V_{CC} .... 7 V
Input voltage: All inputs .... 7 V
I/O ports .... 5.5 V
Voltage applied to a disabled 3-state output .... 5.5 V
Operating free-air temperature range: SN54AS877 .... −55°C to 125°C
SN74AS877 .... 0°C to 70°C
Storage temperature range .... −65°C to 150°C

recommended operating conditions

			SN54AS877			SN74AS877			UNIT
			MIN	NOM	MAX	MIN	NOM	MAX	
V_{CC}	Supply voltage		4.5	5	5.5	4.5	5	5.5	V
V_{IH}	High-level input voltage		2			2			V
V_{IL}	Low-level input voltage				0.8			0.8	V
I_{OH}	High-level output current	A1-A8, B1-B8			−12			−15	mA
		Q8			−2			−2	
I_{OL}	Low-level output current	A1-A8, B1-B8			32			48	mA
		Q8			20			20	
f_{clock}	Clock frequency		0		45	0		50	MHz
t_w	Duration of clock pulse		11			10			ns
t_{su}	Setup time before CLK↑	A1-A8, B1-B8 SERIN	5.5			5.5			ns
		S0, S1, S2	5.5			5.5			
t_h	Hold time, data after CLK↑	A1-A8, B1-B8 SERIN	0			0			ns
		S0, S1, S2	0			0			
T_A	Operating free-air temperature		−55		125	0		70	°C

electrical characteristics over recommended operating free-air temperature range (unless otherwise noted)

PARAMETER		TEST CONDITIONS		SN54AS877 MIN	SN54AS877 TYP†	SN54AS877 MAX	SN74AS877 MIN	SN74AS877 TYP†	SN74AS877 MAX	UNIT
V_{IK}		V_{CC} = 4.5 V,	I_I = −18 mA			−1.2			−1.2	V
V_{OH}	A1-A8	V_{CC} = 4.5 V,	I_{OH} = −12 mA	2	3.2					V
	B1-B8	V_{CC} = 4.5 V,	I_{OH} = −15 mA				2	3.3		
	All outputs	V_{CC} = 4.5 V to 5.5 V,	I_{OH} = −2 mA	$V_{CC}-2$			$V_{CC}-2$			
V_{OL}	All outputs except Q8	V_{CC} = 4.5 V,	I_{OL} = 32 mA		0.25	0.5				V
		V_{CC} = 4.5 V,	I_{OL} = 48 mA					0.35	0.5	
	Q8	V_{CC} = 4.5 V,	I_{OL} = 20 mA		0.25	0.5		0.25	0.5	
I_I	S0, S1, S2	V_{CC} = 5.5 V,	V_I = 7 V			0.3			0.3	mA
	CLK and SERIN					0.1			0.1	
	A1-A8, B1-B8	V_{CC} = 5.5 V,	V_I = 5.5 V			0.2			0.2	
I_{IH}	S0, S1, S2	V_{CC} = 5.5 V,	V_I = 2.7 V			60			60	μA
	CLK and SERIN					20			20	
	A1-A8, B1-B8‡					70			70	
I_{IL}	S0, S1, S2	V_{CC} = 5.5 V,	V_I = 0.4 V			−1			−1	mA
	CLK and SERIN					−0.5			−0.5	
	A1-A8, B1-B8‡					−0.75			−0.75	
I_O§	Except Q8	V_{CC} = 5.5 V,	V_O = 2.25 V	−30		−112	−30		−112	mA
	Q8			−20		−112	−20		−112	
I_{CC}		V_{CC} = 5.5 V			136	220		136	220	mA

†All typical values are at V_{CC} = 5 V, T_A = 25°C.
‡For I/O ports, the parameters I_{IH} and I_{IL} include the output currents I_{OZH} and I_{OZL}, respectively.
§The output conditions have been chosen to produce a current that closely approximates one half of the true short-circuit output current, I_{OS}.

switching characteristics (see Note 1)

PARAMETER	FROM (INPUT)	TO (OUTPUT)	V_{CC} = 4.5 V to 5.5 V, C_L = 50 pF, R1 = 500 Ω, R2 = 500 Ω, T_A = MIN to MAX				UNIT
			SN54AS877		SN74AS877		
			MIN	MAX	MIN	MAX	
f_{max}			45		50		MHz
t_{PLH}	Any A port	Any B port	2	8.5	2	7	ns
t_{PHL}			3	10.5	3	9	
t_{PLH}	Any B port	Any A port	2	9	2	7.5	ns
t_{PHL}			3	10.5	3	9	
t_{PLH}	S0, S1, S2¶	Any A or B port	3	11.5	3	10	ns
t_{PHL}			2	9.5	2	8	
t_{PLH}	CLK	Any A or B port	2	11	2	9	ns
t_{PHL}			3	13	3	11.5	
t_{PLH}	CLK	Q8	2	10.5	2	8	ns
t_{PHL}			3	10	3	8.5	
t_{PHZ}	S0, S1, S2	Any A or B port	2	7.5	2	6.5	ns
t_{PLZ}			3	13	3	10.5	
t_{PZH}			2	9	2	7	ns
t_{PZL}			3	11.5	3	9.5	

NOTE 1: Load circuit and voltage waveforms are shown in Section 1.
¶The positive transition of S2 will cause low-level data at the A output Bus or stored in the shift register to be invalid for 12 ns.

2

LSI Devices

TYPICAL APPLICATION DATA

BUS A TO BUS B OR
SERIAL TRANSMISSION

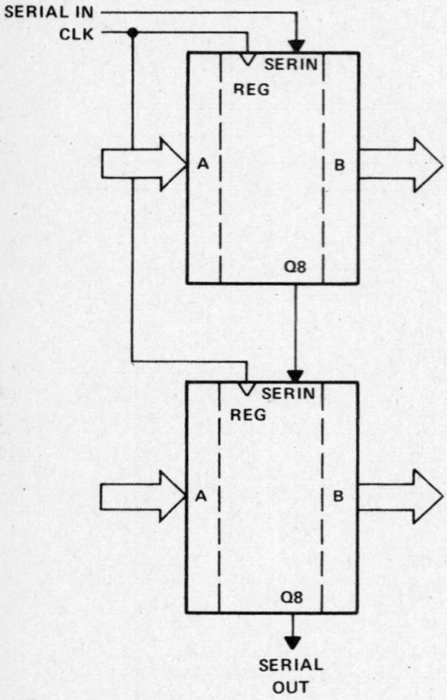
SERIAL IN
CLK
SERIN
REG
A
B
Q8
SERIN
REG
A
B
Q8
SERIAL
OUT

BUS B TO BUS A OR
SERIAL TRANSMISSION

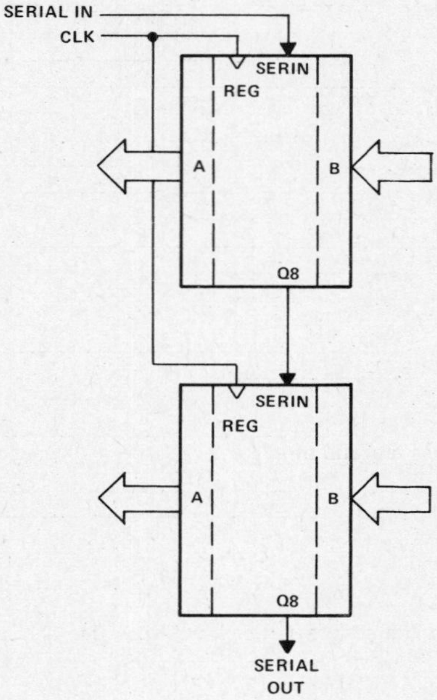
SERIAL IN
CLK
SERIN
REG
A
B
Q8
SERIN
REG
A
B
Q8
SERIAL
OUT

SERIAL IN TO A PORT

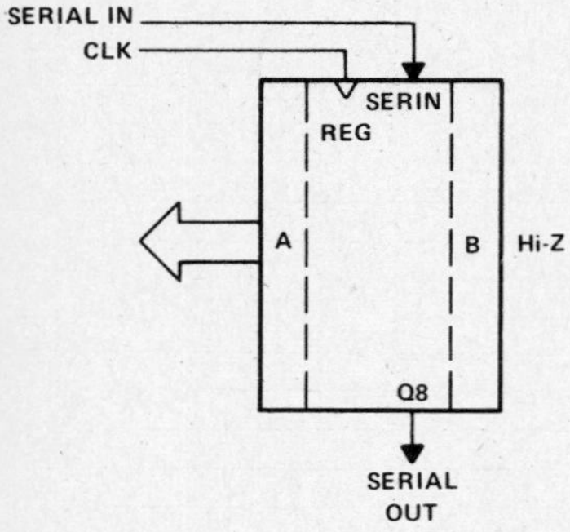
SERIAL IN
CLK
SERIN
REG
A
B
Hi-Z
Q8
SERIAL
OUT

SERIAL IN TO B PORT

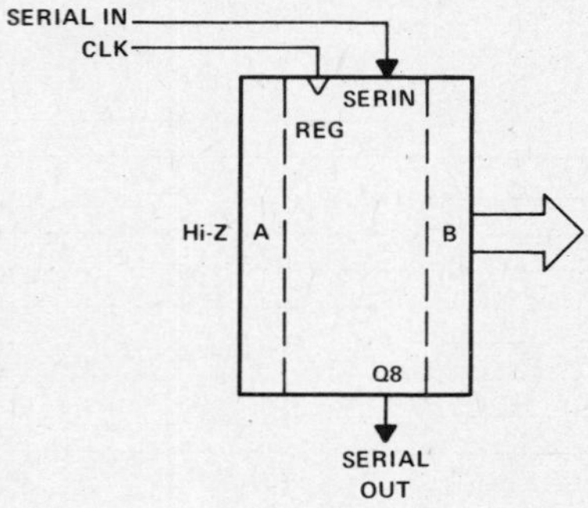
SERIAL IN
CLK
SERIN
REG
Hi-Z
A
B
Q8
SERIAL
OUT

D2661, DECEMBER 1982—REVISED NOVEMBER 1985

- **Directly Compatible with 'AS181B, 'AS1181, 'AS881B, and 'AS1881 ALUs**
- **Included among the Package Options are Compact, 24-Pin, 300-mil-Wide DIPs and Both 28-Pin Plastic and Ceramic Chip Carriers**
- **Capable of Anticipating the Carry Across a Group of Eight 4-Bit Binary Adders**
- **Cascadable to Perform Look-Ahead Across n-Bit Adders**
- **Typical Carry Time, C_n to Any C_{n+i}, is Less Than 6 ns**
- **Dependable Texas Instruments Quality and Reliability**

SN54AS882A . . . JT PACKAGE
SN74AS882A . . . DW OR NT PACKAGE
(TOP VIEW)

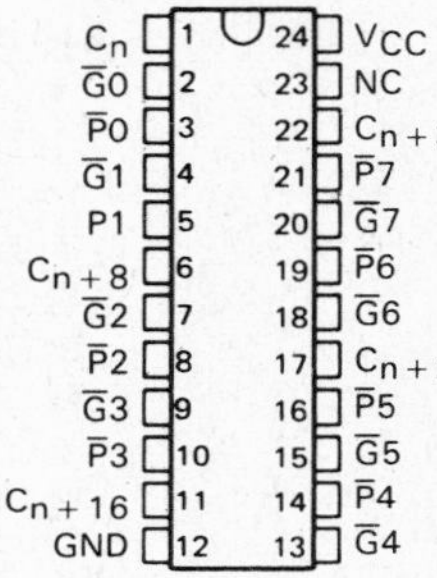
Cn 1
G̅0 2
P̅0 3
G̅1 4
P1 5
Cn+8 6
G̅2 7
P̅2 8
G̅3 9
P̅3 10
Cn+16 11
GND 12
24 VCC
23 NC
22 Cn+32
21 P̅7
20 G̅7
19 P̅6
18 G̅6
17 Cn+24
16 P̅5
15 G̅5
14 P̅4
13 G̅4

SN54AS882A . . . FK PACKAGE
SN74AS882A . . . FN PACKAGE
(TOP VIEW)

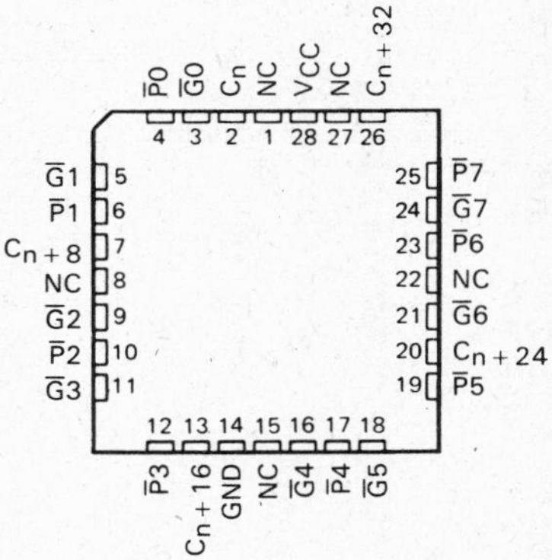
P̅0 G̅0 Cn NC VCC NC Cn+32
4 3 2 1 28 27 26
G̅1 5
P̅1 6
Cn+8 7
NC 8
G̅2 9
P̅2 10
G̅3 11
25 P̅7
24 G̅7
23 P̅6
22 NC
21 G̅6
20 Cn+24
19 P̅5
12 13 14 15 16 17 18
P̅3 Cn+16 GND NC G̅4 P̅4 G̅5

NC—No internal connection

description

The 'AS882A is a high-speed look-ahead carry generator capable of anticipating the carry across a group of eight 4-bit adders permitting the designer to implement look-ahead for a 32-bit ALU with a single package or, by cascading 'AS882A's, full look-ahead is possible across n-bit adders.

The SN54AS882A is characterized for operation over the full military temperature range of −55°C to 125°C. The SN74AS882A is characterized for operation from 0°C to 70°C.

'AS882A LOGIC EQUATIONS

$$C_{n+8} = G1 + P1G0 + P1P0C_n$$

$$C_{n+16} = G3 + P3G2 + P3P2G1 + P3P2P1G0 + P3P2P1P0C_n$$

$$C_{n+24} = G5 + P5G4 + P5P4G3 + P5P4P3G2 + P5P4P3P2G1 + P5P4P3P2P1G0 + P5P4P3P2P1P0C_n$$

$$C_{n+32} = G7 + P7G6 + P7P6G5 + P7P6P5G4 + P7P6P5P4G3 + P7P6P5P4P3G2 + P7P6P5P4P3P2G1 + P7P6P5P4P3P2P1G0 + P7P6P5P4P3P2P1P0C_n$$

logic symbol†

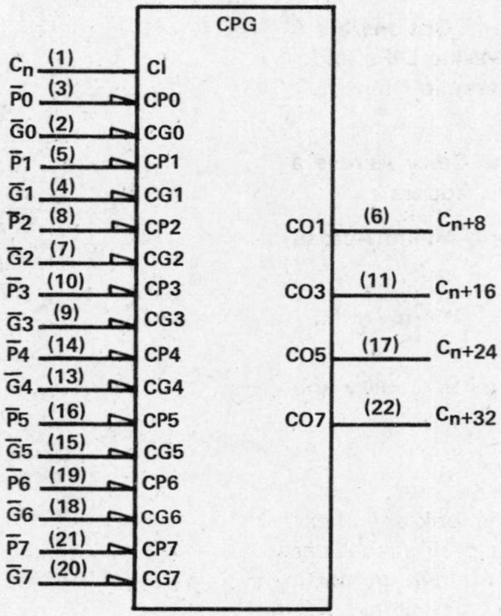
CPG
Cn (1) CI
P̄0 (3) CP0
Ḡ0 (2) CG0
P̄1 (5) CP1
Ḡ1 (4) CG1
P̄2 (8) CP2
Ḡ2 (7) CG2
P̄3 (10) CP3
Ḡ3 (9) CG3
P̄4 (14) CP4
Ḡ4 (13) CG4
P̄5 (16) CP5
Ḡ5 (15) CG5
P̄6 (19) CP6
Ḡ6 (18) CG6
P̄7 (21) CP7
Ḡ7 (20) CG7
CO1 (6) Cn+8
CO3 (11) Cn+16
CO5 (17) Cn+24
CO7 (22) Cn+32

†This symbol is in accordance with ANSI/IEEE Std 91-1984 and IEC Publication 617-12.
Pin numbers shown are for DW, JT, and NT packages.

FUNCTION TABLE
FOR C_{n+32} OUTPUT

INPUTS																	OUTPUT
$\overline{G7}$	$\overline{G6}$	$\overline{G5}$	$\overline{G4}$	$\overline{G3}$	$\overline{G2}$	$\overline{G1}$	$\overline{G0}$	$\overline{P7}$	$\overline{P6}$	$\overline{P5}$	$\overline{P4}$	$\overline{P3}$	$\overline{P2}$	$\overline{P1}$	$\overline{P0}$	C_n	C_{n+32}
L	X	X	X	X	X	X	X	X	X	X	X	X	X	X	X	X	H
X	L	X	X	X	X	X	X	L	X	X	X	X	X	X	X	X	H
X	X	L	X	X	X	X	X	L	L	X	X	X	X	X	X	X	H
X	X	X	L	X	X	X	X	L	L	L	X	X	X	X	X	X	H
X	X	X	X	L	X	X	X	L	L	L	L	X	X	X	X	X	H
X	X	X	X	X	L	X	X	L	L	L	L	L	X	X	X	X	H
X	X	X	X	X	X	L	X	L	L	L	L	L	L	X	X	X	H
X	X	X	X	X	X	X	L	L	L	L	L	L	L	L	X	X	H
X	X	X	X	X	X	X	X	L	L	L	L	L	L	L	L	H	H
All other combinations																	L

FUNCTION TABLE
FOR C_{n+24} OUTPUT

INPUTS													OUTPUT
$\overline{G5}$	$\overline{G4}$	$\overline{G3}$	$\overline{G2}$	$\overline{G1}$	$\overline{G0}$	$\overline{P5}$	$\overline{P4}$	$\overline{P3}$	$\overline{P2}$	$\overline{P1}$	$\overline{P0}$	C_n	C_{n+24}
L	X	X	X	X	X	X	X	X	X	X	X	X	H
X	L	X	X	X	X	L	X	X	X	X	X	X	H
X	X	L	X	X	X	L	L	X	X	X	X	X	H
X	X	X	L	X	X	L	L	L	X	X	X	X	H
X	X	X	X	L	X	L	L	L	L	X	X	X	H
X	X	X	X	X	L	L	L	L	L	L	X	X	H
X	X	X	X	X	X	L	L	L	L	L	L	H	H
All other combinations													L

FUNCTION TABLE
FOR C_{n+16} OUTPUT

INPUTS									OUTPUT
$\overline{G3}$	$\overline{G2}$	$\overline{G1}$	$\overline{G0}$	$\overline{P3}$	$\overline{P2}$	$\overline{P1}$	$\overline{P0}$	C_n	C_{n+16}
L	X	X	X	X	X	X	X	X	H
X	L	X	X	L	X	X	X	X	H
X	X	L	X	L	L	X	X	X	H
X	X	X	L	L	L	L	X	X	H
X	X	X	X	L	L	L	L	H	H
All other combinations									L

FUNCTION TABLE
FOR C_{n+8} OUTPUT

INPUTS					OUTPUT
$\overline{G1}$	$\overline{G0}$	$\overline{P1}$	$\overline{P0}$	C_n	C_{n+8}
L	X	X	X	X	H
X	L	L	X	X	H
X	X	L	L	H	H
All other combinations					L

Any inputs not shown in a given table are irrelevant with respect to that output.

logic diagram (positive logic)

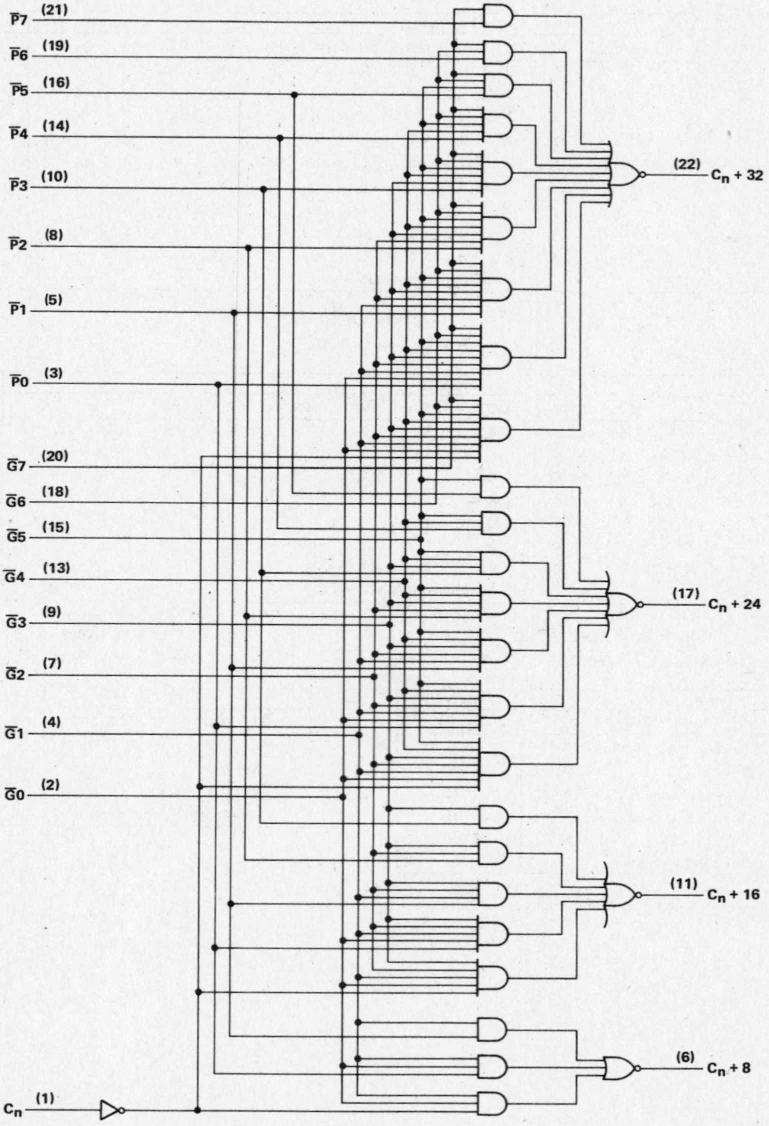
P̄7 (21)
P̄6 (19)
P̄5 (16)
P̄4 (14)
P̄3 (10)
P̄2 (8)
P̄1 (5)
P̄0 (3)
Ḡ7 (20)
Ḡ6 (18)
Ḡ5 (15)
Ḡ4 (13)
Ḡ3 (9)
Ḡ2 (7)
Ḡ1 (4)
Ḡ0 (2)
Cn (1)
(22) Cn + 32
(17) Cn + 24
(11) Cn + 16
(6) Cn + 8

Pin numbers shown are for DW, JT, and NT packages.

TEXAS INSTRUMENTS
POST OFFICE BOX 225012 • DALLAS, TEXAS 75265

absolute maximum ratings over operating free-air temperature range (unless otherwise noted)

Supply voltage, V_{CC} . . . . . 7 V
Input voltage . . . . . 7 V
Operating free-air temperature range: SN54AS882A . . . . . −55°C to 125°C
SN74AS822A . . . . . 0°C to 70°C
Storage temperature range . . . . . −65°C to 150°C

recommended operating conditions

		SN54AS882A			SN74AS882A			UNIT
		MIN	NOM	MAX	MIN	NOM	MAX	
V_{CC}	Supply voltage	4.5	5	5.5	4.5	5	5.5	V
V_{IH}	High-level input voltage	2			2			V
V_{IL}	Low-level input voltage			0.8			0.8	V
I_{OH}	High-level output current			−2			−2	mA
I_{OL}	Low-level output current			20			20	mA
T_A	Operating free-air temperature	−55		125	0		70	°C

2

LSI Devices

electrical characteristics over recommended operating free-air temperature range (unless otherwise noted)

PARAMETER		TEST CONDITIONS		SN54AS882A			SN74AS882A			UNIT
				MIN	TYP†	MAX	MIN	TYP†	MAX	
V_{IK}		V_{CC} = 4.5 V,	I_I = −18 mA			−1.2			−1.2	V
V_{OH}		V_{CC} = 4.5 V, to 5.5 V,	I_{OH} = −2 mA	$V_{CC}-2$			$V_{CC}-2$			V
V_{OL}		V_{CC} = 4.5 V,	I_{OL} = 20 mA		0.3	0.5		0.3	0.5	V
I_I	C_n, $\overline{P0}$, $\overline{P1}$	V_{CC} = 5.5 V,	V_I = 7 V			0.4			0.4	mA
	$\overline{G0}$, $\overline{G6}$					0.8			0.8	
	$\overline{G1}$, $\overline{G2}$, $\overline{G4}$					1.2			1.2	
	$\overline{G3}$, $\overline{G5}$					1.5			1.5	
	$\overline{G7}$					0.9			0.9	
	$\overline{P2}$, $\overline{P3}$					0.3			0.3	
	$\overline{P4}$, $\overline{P5}$					0.2			0.2	
	$\overline{P6}$, $\overline{P7}$					0.1			0.1	
I_{IH}	C_n, $\overline{P0}$, $\overline{P1}$	V_{CC} = 5.5 V,	V_I = 2.7 V			80			80	μA
	$\overline{G0}$, $\overline{G6}$					160			160	
	$\overline{G1}$, $\overline{G2}$, $\overline{G4}$					240			240	
	$\overline{G3}$, $\overline{G5}$					300			300	
	$\overline{G7}$					180			180	
	$\overline{P2}$, $\overline{P3}$					60			60	
	$\overline{P4}$, $\overline{P5}$					40			40	
	$\overline{P6}$, $\overline{P7}$					20			20	
I_{IL}	C_n, $\overline{P0}$, $\overline{P1}$	V_{CC} = 5.5 V,	V_I = 0.4 V			−2			−2	mA
	$\overline{G0}$, $\overline{G6}$					−4			−4	
	$\overline{G1}$, $\overline{G2}$, $\overline{G4}$					−6			−6	
	$\overline{G3}$, $\overline{G5}$					−7.5			−7.5	
	$\overline{G7}$					−4.5			−4.5	
	$\overline{P2}$, $\overline{P3}$					−1.5			−1.5	
	$\overline{P4}$, $\overline{P5}$					−1			−1	
	$\overline{P6}$, $\overline{P7}$					−0.5			−0.5	
I_O‡		V_{CC} = 5.5 V,	V_O = 2.25 V	−30		−130	−30		−130	mA
I_{CC}		V_{CC} = 5.5 V			44	70		44	70	mA

†All typical values are at V_{CC} = 5 V, T_A = 25°C.
‡The output conditions have been chosen to produce a current that closely approximates one half of the true short-circuit output current, I_{OS}.

2 LSI Devices

switching characteristics (see Note 1)

PARAMETER	FROM (INPUT)	TO (OUTPUT)	V_{CC} = 4.5 V to 5.5 V, C_L = 50 pF, R_L = 500 Ω, T_A = MIN to MAX				UNIT
			SN54AS822A		SN74AS882A		
			MIN	MAX	MIN	MAX	
t_{PLH}	C_n	Any output	2	10	2	9	ns
t_{PHL}			3	15	3	14	
t_{PLH}	$\overline{P}$ or $\overline{G}$	C_{n+8}	2	8	2	7	
t_{PHL}			2	8	2	7	
t_{PLH}	$\overline{P}$ or $\overline{G}$	C_{n+16}	2	8	2	7	
t_{PHL}			2	8	2	7	
t_{PLH}	$\overline{P}$ or $\overline{G}$	C_{n+24}	2	8	2	7	
t_{PHL}			2	11	2	10	
t_{PLH}	$\overline{P}$ or $\overline{G}$	C_{n+32}	1.5	9	2	8	
t_{PHL}			2	13	2	12	

NOTE 1: Load circuits and voltage waveforms are shown in Section 1.

TYPICAL APPLICATION DATA

The application given in Figure 1 illustrates how the 'AS882A can implement look-ahead carry for a 32-bit ALU (in this case, the popular 'AS881A) with a single package. Typical carry times shown are derived using the standard Advanced Schottky load circuit.

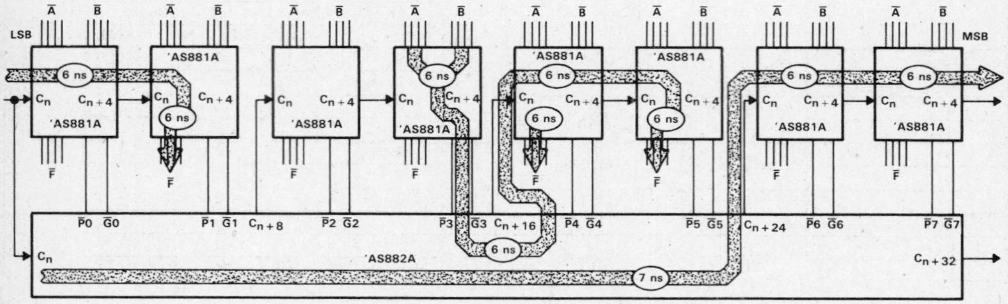
LSB
MSB
'AS881A
'AS882A
6 ns
7 ns
Cn+32

FIGURE 1

Likewise, Figure 2 illustrates the same 32-bit ALU using two 'AS882s. This shows the worst-case delay from LSB to MSB to be 19 ns as opposed to 25 ns in Figure 1.

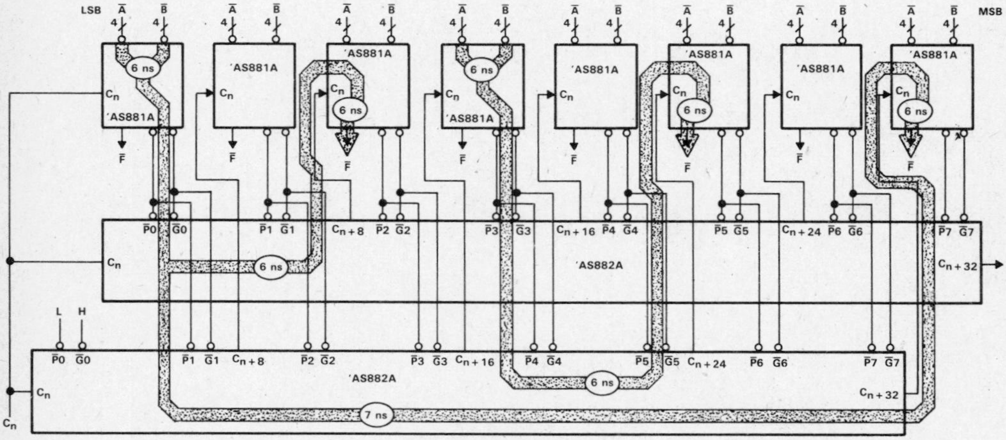
LSB
MSB
'AS881A
'AS882A
6 ns
7 ns
L
H
Cn+32

FIGURE 2

D2661, DECEMBER 1982—REVISED MARCH 1985

- Included among the Package Options Are Compact, 24-Pin, 300-mil DIPs and Both 28-Pin Ceramic and Plastic Chip Carriers
- Latchable P Input Ports with Power-Up Clear
- Choice of Logical or Arithmetic (2's Complement) Comparison
- Data and PLE Inputs Utilize P-N-P Input Transistors to Reduce DC Loading Effects
- Approximately 35% Improvement in AC Performance Over Schottky TTL while Performing More Functions
- Cascadable to n-Bits while Maintaining High Performance
- 10% Less Power than STTL for an 8-Bit Comparison
- Dependable Texas Instruments Quality and Reliability

SN54AS885 . . . . JT PACKAGE
SN74AS885 . . . . DW OR NT PACKAGE
(TOP VIEW)

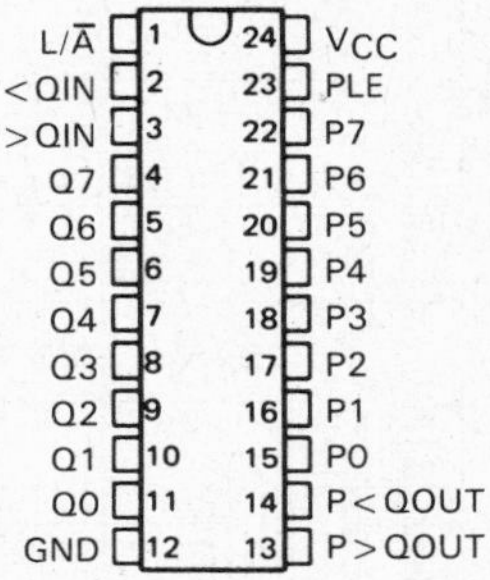
L/Ā 1
P<QIN 2
P>QIN 3
Q7 4
Q6 5
Q5 6
Q4 7
Q3 8
Q2 9
Q1 10
Q0 11
GND 12
24 VCC
23 PLE
22 P7
21 P6
20 P5
19 P4
18 P3
17 P2
16 P1
15 P0
14 P<QOUT
13 P>QOUT

SN54AS885 . . . . FK PACKAGE
SN74AS885 . . . . FN PACKAGE
(TOP VIEW)

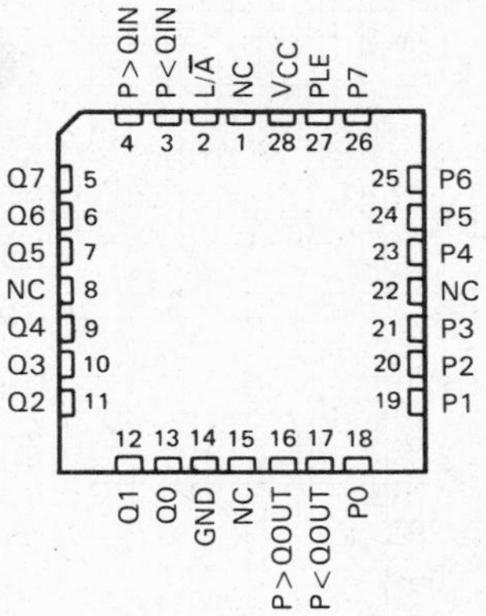
P>QIN P<QIN L/Ā NC VCC PLE P7
4 3 2 1 28 27 26
Q7 5
Q6 6
Q5 7
NC 8
Q4 9
Q3 10
Q2 11
25 P6
24 P5
23 P4
22 NC
21 P3
20 P2
19 P1
12 13 14 15 16 17 18
Q1 Q0 GND NC P>QOUT P<QOUT P0

description

These advanced Schottky devices are capable of performing high-speed arithmetic or logic comparisons on two 8-bit binary or two's complement words. Two fully decoded decisions about words P and Q are externally available at two outputs. These devices are fully expandable to any number of bits without external gates. The P > Q and P < Q outputs of a stage handling less-significant bits may be connected to the P > Q and P < Q inputs of the next stage handling more-significant bits to obtain comparisons of words of longer lengths. The cascading paths are implemented with only a two-gate-level delay to reduce overall comparison times for long words. Two alternative methods of cascading are shown in the typical application data.

The latch is transparent when P Latch Enable (PLE) is high; the P input port is latched when PLE is low. This provides the designer with temporary storage for the P data word. The enable circuitry is implemented with minimal delay times to enhance performance when cascaded for longer words. The PLE and P and Q data inputs utilize p-n-p input transistors to reduce the low-level current input requirement to typically −0.25 mA, which minimizes dc loading effects.

The SN54AS885 is characterized for operation over the full military temperature range of −55°C to 125°C. The SN74AS885 is characterized for operation from 0°C to 70°C.

TEXAS INSTRUMENTS
POST OFFICE BOX 225012 • DALLAS, TEXAS 75265

logic diagram (positive logic)

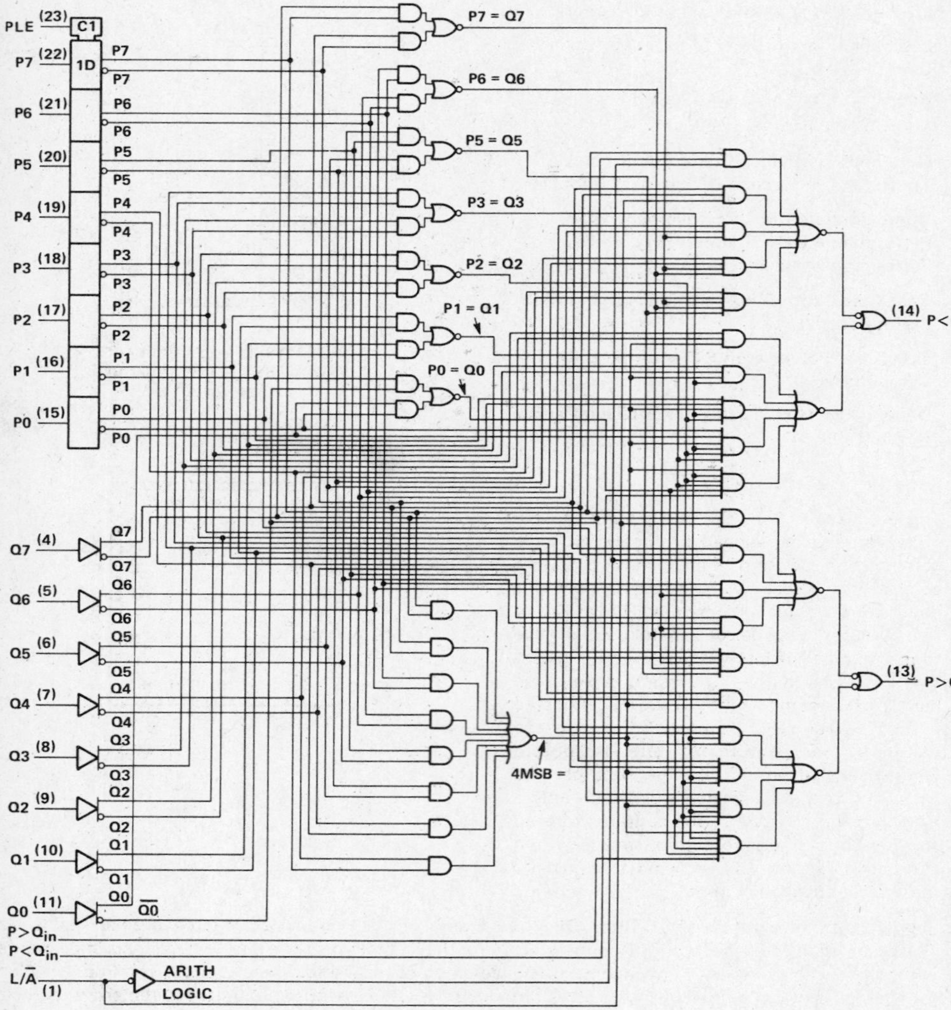
PLE (23)
C1
1D
P7 (22)
P6 (21)
P5 (20)
P4 (19)
P3 (18)
P2 (17)
P1 (16)
P0 (15)
P7
P6
P5
P4
P3
P2
P1
P0
P7 = Q7
P6 = Q6
P5 = Q5
P3 = Q3
P2 = Q2
P1 = Q1
P0 = Q0
Q7 (4)
Q6 (5)
Q5 (6)
Q4 (7)
Q3 (8)
Q2 (9)
Q1 (10)
Q0 (11)
Q7
Q6
Q5
Q4
Q3
Q2
Q1
Q0
$\overline{Q0}$
P>Q$_{in}$
P<Q$_{in}$
L/$\overline{A}$ (1)
ARITH
LOGIC
4MSB =
(14) P<Q
(13) P>Q

Pin numbers shown are for DW, JT, and NT packages.

logic symbol†

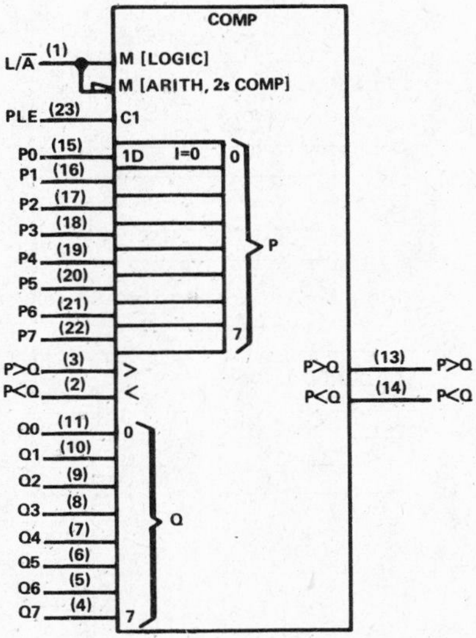
COMP
L/Ā (1)
M [LOGIC]
M [ARITH, 2s COMP]
PLE (23)
C1
P0 (15)
P1 (16)
P2 (17)
P3 (18)
P4 (19)
P5 (20)
P6 (21)
P7 (22)
1D
I=0
0
7
P
P>Q (3)
P<Q (2)
>
<
Q0 (11)
Q1 (10)
Q2 (9)
Q3 (8)
Q4 (7)
Q5 (6)
Q6 (5)
Q7 (4)
0
Q
7
P>Q (13) P>Q
P<Q (14) P<Q

†This symbol is in accordance with ANSI/IEEE Std 91-1984 and IEC Publication 617-12.
Pin numbers shown are for DW, JT, and NT packages.

FUNCTION TABLE

COMPARISON	L/Ā	DATA INPUTS P0-P7, Q0-Q7	INPUT P>Q	INPUT P<Q	OUTPUTS P>Q	OUTPUTS P<Q
LOGICAL	H	P>Q	X	X	H	L
LOGICAL	H	P<Q	X	X	L	H
LOGICAL‡	H	P=Q	H OR L	H OR L	H OR L	H OR L
ARITHMETIC	L	P AG Q	X	X	H	L
ARITHMETIC	L	Q AG P	X	X	L	H
ARITHMETIC‡	L	P=Q	H OR L	H OR L	H OR L	H OR L

‡In these cases the P>Q output will follow the P>Q input, and the P<Q output will follow the P<Q input.
AG — arithmetically greater than

absolute maximum ratings over operating free-air temperature range (unless otherwise noted)

Supply voltage, V_{CC} . . . . 7 V
Input voltage . . . . 7 V
Operating free-air temperature range: SN54AS885 . . . . −55°C to 125°C
SN74AS885 . . . . 0°C to 70°C
Storage temperature range . . . . −65°C to 150°C

recommended operating conditions

PARAMETER		SN54AS885 MIN	SN54AS885 NOM	SN54AS885 MAX	SN74AS885 MIN	SN74AS885 NOM	SN74AS885 MAX	UNIT
V_{CC}	Supply voltage	4.5	5	5.5	4.5	5	5.5	V
V_{IH}	High-level input voltage	2			2			V
V_{IL}	Low-level input voltage			0.8			0.8	V
I_{OH}	High-level output current			−2			−2	mA
I_{OL}	Low-level output current			20			20	mA
t_{su}	Setup time to PLE↓	2			2			ns
t_h	Hold time after PLE↓	4			4			ns
T_A	Operating free-air temperature	−55		125	0		70	°C

electrical characteristics over recommended operating free-air temperature range (unless otherwise noted)

PARAMETER		TEST CONDITIONS		SN54AS885 MIN	SN54AS885 TYP†	SN54AS885 MAX	SN74AS885 MIN	SN74AS885 TYP†	SN74AS885 MAX	UNIT
V_{IK}		V_{CC} = 4.5 V,	I_I = −18 mA			−1.2			−1.2	V
V_{OH}		V_{CC} = 4.5 to 5.5 V,	I_{OH} = −2 mA	$V_{CC}-2$			$V_{CC}-2$			V
V_{OL}		V_{CC} = 4.5 V,	I_{OL} = 20 mA		0.35	0.5		0.35	0.5	V
I_I		V_{CC} = 5.5 V,	V_I = 7 V			0.1			0.1	μA
I_{IH}	L/$\overline{A}$	V_{CC} = 5.5 V,	V_I = 2.7 V			40			40	μA
	Others					20			20	μA
I_{IL}	L/$\overline{A}$	V_{CC} = 5.5 V,	V_I = 0.4 V			−4			−4	mA
	P > Q_{in}, P < Q_{in}					−2			−2	mA
	P, Q, PLE					−1			−1	mA
I_O‡		V_{CC} = 5.5 V,	V_O = 2.25 V	−20		−112	−20		−112	mA
I_{CC}		V_{CC} = 5.5 V	See Note 1		130	210		130	210	mA

†All typical values are at V_{CC} = 5 V, T_A = 25°C.
‡The output conditions have been chosen to produce a current that closely approximates one half of the true short-circuit current, I_{OS}.
NOTE 1: I_{CC} is measured with all inputs high except L/$\overline{A}$, which is low.

switching characteristics (see Note 2)

V_{CC} = 4.5 V to 5.5 V, C_L = 50 pF, R_L = 500 Ω, T_A = MIN to MAX

PARAMETER	FROM (INPUT)	TO (OUTPUT)	SN54AS885 MIN	SN54AS885 TYP†	SN54AS885 MAX	SN74AS885 MIN	SN74AS885 TYP†	SN74AS885 MAX	UNIT
t_{PLH}	L/A	P < Q, P > Q		8.5	14		8.5	13	ns
t_{PHL}	L/A	P < Q, P > Q		7.5	14		7.5	13	ns
t_{PLH}	P < Q_{in}	P < Q, P > Q		5	10		5	8	ns
t_{PHL}	P > Q_{in}	P < Q, P > Q		5.5	10		5.5	8	ns
t_{PLH}	Any P or Q Data Input	P < Q, P > Q		13.5	21		13.5	17.5	ns
t_{PHL}	Any P or Q Data Input	P < Q, P > Q		10	17		10	15	ns

†All typical values are at V_{CC} = 5 V, T_A = 25°C.
NOTE 2: Load circuit and voltage waveforms are shown in Section 1.

TYPICAL APPLICATION DATA

The 'AS885 can be cascaded to compare words longer than 8-bits. Figure 1 shows the comparison of two 32-bit words; however, the design is expandable to n-bits. Figure 1 shows the optimum cascading arrangement for comparing words of 32 bits or greater. Typical delay times shown are at V_{CC} = 5 V, T_A = 25°C, and use the standard Advanced Schottky load of R_L = 500 Ω, C_L = 50 pF.

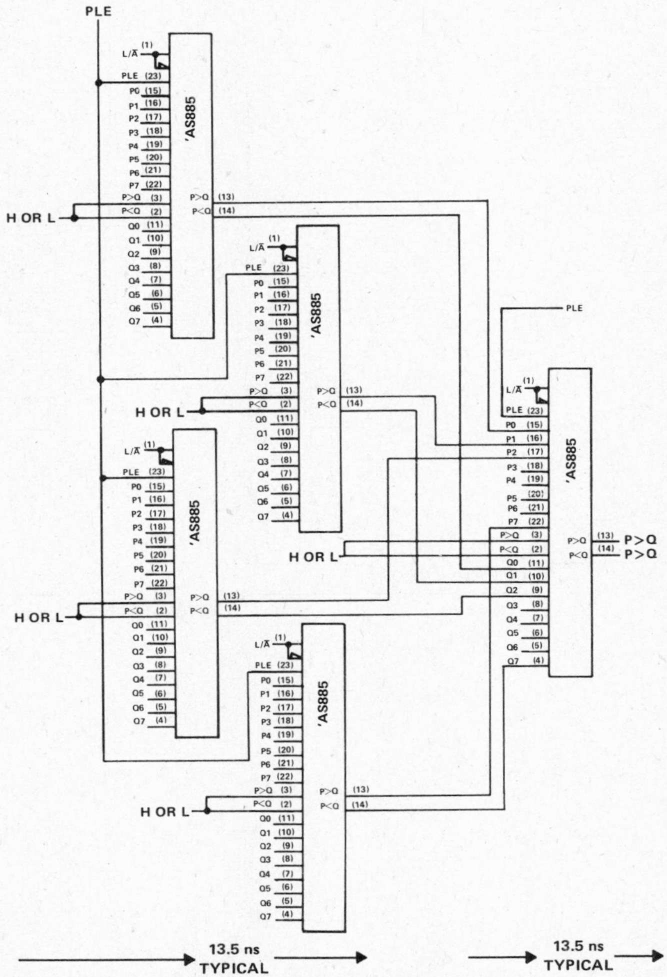
PLE
'AS885
L/Ā (1)
PLE (23)
P0 (15)
P1 (16)
P2 (17)
P3 (18)
P4 (19)
P5 (20)
P6 (21)
P7 (22)
P>Q (3)
P<Q (2)
Q0 (11)
Q1 (10)
Q2 (9)
Q3 (8)
Q4 (7)
Q5 (6)
Q6 (5)
Q7 (4)
P>Q (13)
P<Q (14)
H OR L
P>Q
P>Q
13.5 ns
TYPICAL
13.5 ns
TYPICAL

FIGURE 1. 32-BIT TO 72 (N)-BIT MAGNITUDE COMPARATOR

TYPICAL APPLICATION DATA

The method shown in Figure 2 is the fastest cascading arrangement for comparing 16-bit or 24-bit words. Typical delay times shown are at V_{CC} = 5 V, T_A = 25°C, and use the standard Advanced Schottky load of R_L = 500 Ω, C_L = 50 pF.

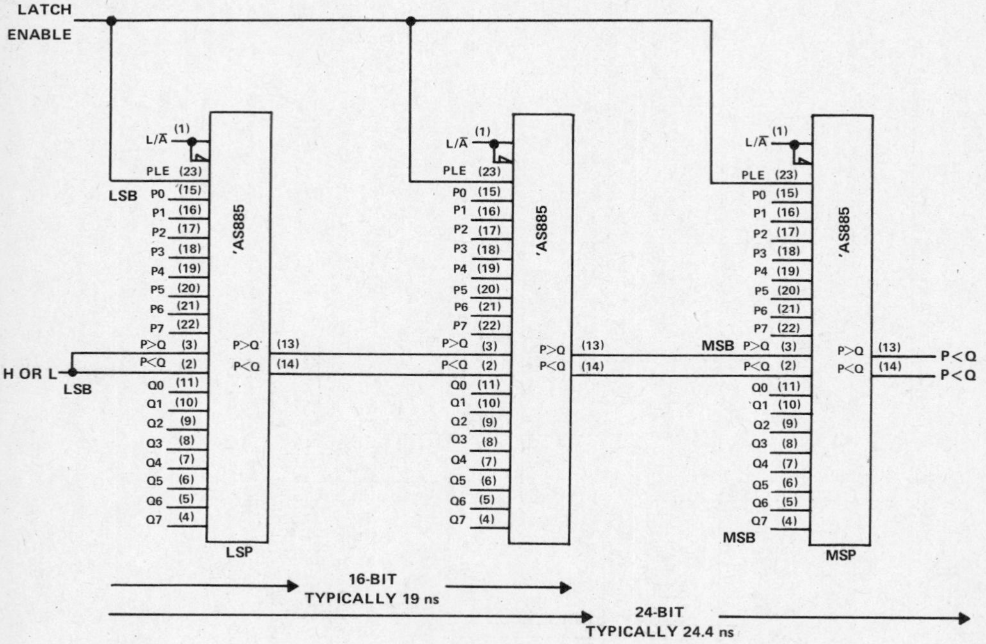
LATCH
ENABLE
L/Ā (1)
PLE (23)
LSB P0 (15)
P1 (16)
P2 (17)
P3 (18)
P4 (19)
P5 (20)
P6 (21)
P7 (22)
P>Q (3)
P<Q (2)
H OR L
LSB
Q0 (11)
Q1 (10)
Q2 (9)
Q3 (8)
Q4 (7)
Q5 (6)
Q6 (5)
Q7 (4)
'AS885
LSP
P>Q (13)
P<Q (14)
MSB
MSP
P<Q
P<Q
16-BIT
TYPICALLY 19 ns
24-BIT
TYPICALLY 24.4 ns

FIGURE 2

TEXAS INSTRUMENTS
POST OFFICE BOX 225012 • DALLAS, TEXAS 75265

FEBRUARY 1986

- STL-AS Technology
- Parallel 8-Bit ALU with Expansion Inputs and Outputs
- 13 Arithmetic and Logic Functions
- 8 Conditional Shifts (Single and Double Length)
- 4 Instructions that Manipulate Bits
- Add and Subtract Immediate Instructions
- Absolute Value Instruction
- Signed Magnitude to/from Two's Complement Conversion
- Single- and Double-Length Normalize
- Select Functions
- Signed and Unsigned Divides with Overflow Detection; Input does not Need to be Prescaled
- Signed, Mixed, and Unsigned Multiplies
- Three-Operand, 16-Word Register File
- Full Carry Look Ahead Support
- Sign, Carry Out, Overflow, and Zero-Detect Status Capabilities
- Excess-3 BCD Arithmetic
- Internal Shift Multiplexers that Eliminate the Need for External Shift Control Parts
- ALU Bypass Path to Increase Speeds of Multiply, Divide, and Normalize Instructions and to Provide New Instructions such as Bit Set, Bit Reset, and Bit Test
- 3-Operand Register Files to Allow an Operation and a Move Instruction to be Combined
- Bit Masks that are Shared with Register Address Fields to Minimize Control Store Word Width
- 3 Data Input/Output Paths to Maximize Data Throughput

description

These 8-bit Advanced Schottky TTL integrated circuits are designed to implement high performance digital computers or controllers. An architecture and instruction set has been chosen that supports a fast system clock, a narrow micro-code word width, and a high system throughput. The powerful instruction set allows high-speed system architecture to be implemented and also allows an existing system's performance to be upgraded while protecting software investments. These processors are non-cascadable versions of the 'AS888. They are designed for 8-bit applications only.

The SN54AS887 is characterized for operation over the full military temperature range of −55°C to 125°C. The SN74AS887 and SN74AS887-1 are characterized for operation from 0°C to 70°C.

Package options include both plastic and ceramic chip carriers in addition to a 68-pin grid array ceramic package.

SN54AS887, SN74AS887 . . . GB PACKAGE
(TOP VIEW)

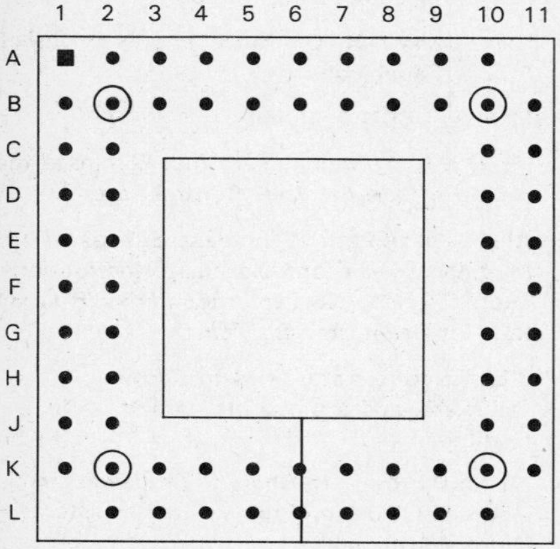
1 2 3 4 5 6 7 8 9 10 11
A B C D E F G H J K L

SN54AS887 . . . FK PACKAGE
SN74AS887 . . . FN PACKAGE
(TOP VIEW)

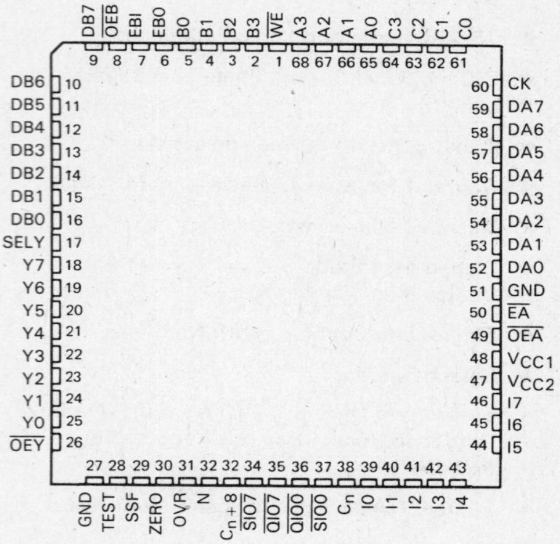
DB7 9
OEB 8
EBI 7
EB0 6
B0 5
B1 4
B2 3
B3 2
WE 1
A3 68
A2 67
A1 66
A0 65
C3 64
C2 63
C1 62
C0 61
DB6 10
DB5 11
DB4 12
DB3 13
DB2 14
DB1 15
DB0 16
SELY 17
Y7 18
Y6 19
Y5 20
Y4 21
Y3 22
Y2 23
Y1 24
Y0 25
OEY 26
60 CK
59 DA7
58 DA6
57 DA5
56 DA4
55 DA3
54 DA2
53 DA1
52 DA0
51 GND
50 EA
49 OEA
48 VCC1
47 VCC2
46 I7
45 I6
44 I5
27 GND
28 TEST
29 SSF
30 ZERO
31 OVR
32 N
32 Cn+8
34 SIO7
35 QIO7
36 QIO0
37 SIO0
38 Cn
39 I0
40 I1
41 I2
42 I3
43 I4

GB PACKAGE PIN ASSIGNMENTS

PIN	NAME	PIN	NAME	PIN	NAME	PIN	NAME
A-2	C_n	B-9	$\overline{\text{OEY}}$	F-10	Y3	K-4	C2
A-3	$\overline{\text{SIO0}}$	B-10	Y0	F-11	DB2	K-5	A0
A-4	$\overline{\text{QIO0}}$	B-11	Y1	G-1	DA2	K-6	A3
A-5	$\overline{\text{QIO7}}$	C-1	I5	G-2	DA0	K-7	$\overline{\text{WE}}$
A-6	C_{n+8}	C-2	V_{CC2}	G-10	DB0	K-8	DB7
A-7	N	C-10	Y4	G-11	DB3	K-9	$\overline{\text{OEB}}$
A-8	OVR	C-11	Y6	H-1	DA3	K-10	EB0
A-9	ZERO	D-1	I6	H-2	DA1	K-11	EB1
A-10	TEST	D-2	V_{CC1}	H-10	DB6	L-2	CK
B-1	I2	D-10	Y5	H-11	DB4	L-3	C1
B-2	I3	D-11	Y7	J-1	DA4	L-4	C3
B-3	I1	E-1	I7	J-2	DA5	L-5	A1
B-4	I0	E-2	$\overline{\text{OEA}}$	J-10	SELY	L-6	A2
B-5	I4	E-10	Y2	J-11	DB5	L-7	B3
B-6	$\overline{\text{SIO7}}$	E-11	DB1	K-1	DA6	L-8	B2
B-7	SSF	F-1	$\overline{\text{EA}}$	K-2	DA7	L-9	B1
B-8		F-2	GND	K-3	C0	L-10	B0

2

LSI Devices

PIN GRID ARRAY	CHIP CARRIER	NAME	I/O	DESCRIPTION
A-10	28	TEST	I	Test input pin. Connected to ground for normal operation.
B-7	29	SSF	I/O	Special shift function. Used to transfer required information between packages during special instruction execution.
A-9	30	ZERO	I/O	Device zero detection, open collector. Input during certain special instructions.
A-8	31	OVR	O	ALU overflow, low active.
A-7	32	N	O	ALU negative, low active.
A-6	33	C_{n+8}	O	ALU ripple carry output.
B-6	34	$\overline{SIO7}$	I/O	Bidirectional shift pin, low active.
A-5	35	$\overline{QIO7}$	I/O	
A-4	36	$\overline{QIO0}$	I/O	
A-3	37	$\overline{SIO0}$	I/O	
A-2	38	C_n	I	ALU carry input.
B-4	39	I0	I	Instruction input.
B-3	40	I1	I	
B-1	41	I2	I	
B-2	42	I3	I	
B-5	43	I4	I	
C-1	44	I5	I	
D-1	45	I6	I	
E-1	46	I7	I	
C-2	47	V_{CC2}		Low voltage power supply (2 V).
D-2	48	V_{CC1}		I/O interface supply voltage (5 V).
E-2	49	$\overline{OEA}$	I	DA bus enable, low active.
F-1	50	$\overline{EA}$	I	ALU input operand select. High state selects external DA bus and low state selects register file.
F-2	51	GND		Ground pin.
G-2	52	DA0	I/O	A port data bus. Outputs register file data ($\overline{EA}$ = 0) or inputs external data ($\overline{EA}$ = 1).
H-2	53	DA1	I/O	
G-1	54	DA2	I/O	
H-1	55	DA3	I/O	
J-1	56	DA4	I/O	
J-2	57	DA5	I/O	
K-1	58	DA6	I/O	
K-2	59	DA7	I/O	
L-2	60	CK	I	Clocks all synchronous registers on positive edge.
K-3	61	C0	I	Register file write address select.
L-3	62	C1	I	
K-4	63	C2	I	
L-4	64	C3	I	
K-5	65	A0	I	Register file A port read address select.
L-5	66	A1	I	
L-6	67	A2	I	
K-6	68	A3	I	

PIN GRID ARRAY	CHIP CARRIER	NAME	I/O	DESCRIPTION
K-7	1	$\overline{WE}$	I	Register file (RF) write enable. Data is written into RF when $\overline{WE}$ is low and a low-to-high clock transition occurs. RF write is inhibited when $\overline{WE}$ is high.
L-7	2	B3	I	Register file B port read address select. (0 = LSB).
L-8	3	B2	I	
L-9	4	B1	I	
L-10	5	B0	I	
K-10	6	EB0	I	ALU input operand select. EB0 and EB1 selects the source of data that the S multiplexer provides for the S bus. Independent control of the DB bus and data path selection allow the user to isolate the DB bus while the ALU continues to process data.
K-11	7	EB1	I	
K-9	8	$\overline{OEB}$	I	DB bus enable, low active.
K-8	9	DB7	I/O	B port data bus. Outputs register data ($\overline{OEB}$ = 0) or used to input external data ($\overline{OEB}$ = 1), (0 = LSB).
H-10	10	DB6	I/O	
J-11	11	DB5	I/O	
H-11	12	DB4	I/O	
G-11	13	DB3	I/O	
F-11	14	DB2	I/O	
E-11	15	DB1	I/O	
G-10	16	DB0	I/O	
J-10	17	SELY	I	Y bus select, high active.
D-11	18	Y7	I/O	Y port data bus. Outputs instruction results ($\overline{OEY}$ = 0) or used to put external data into register file ($\overline{OEY}$ = 1).
C-11	19	Y6	I/O	
D-10	20	Y5	I/O	
C-10	21	Y4	I/O	
F-10	22	Y3	I/O	
E-10	23	Y2	I/O	
B-11	24	Y1	I/O	
B-10	25	Y0	I/O	
B-9	26	$\overline{OEY}$	I	Y bus output enable, low active.
F-2	27	GND		Ground pin

functional block diagram

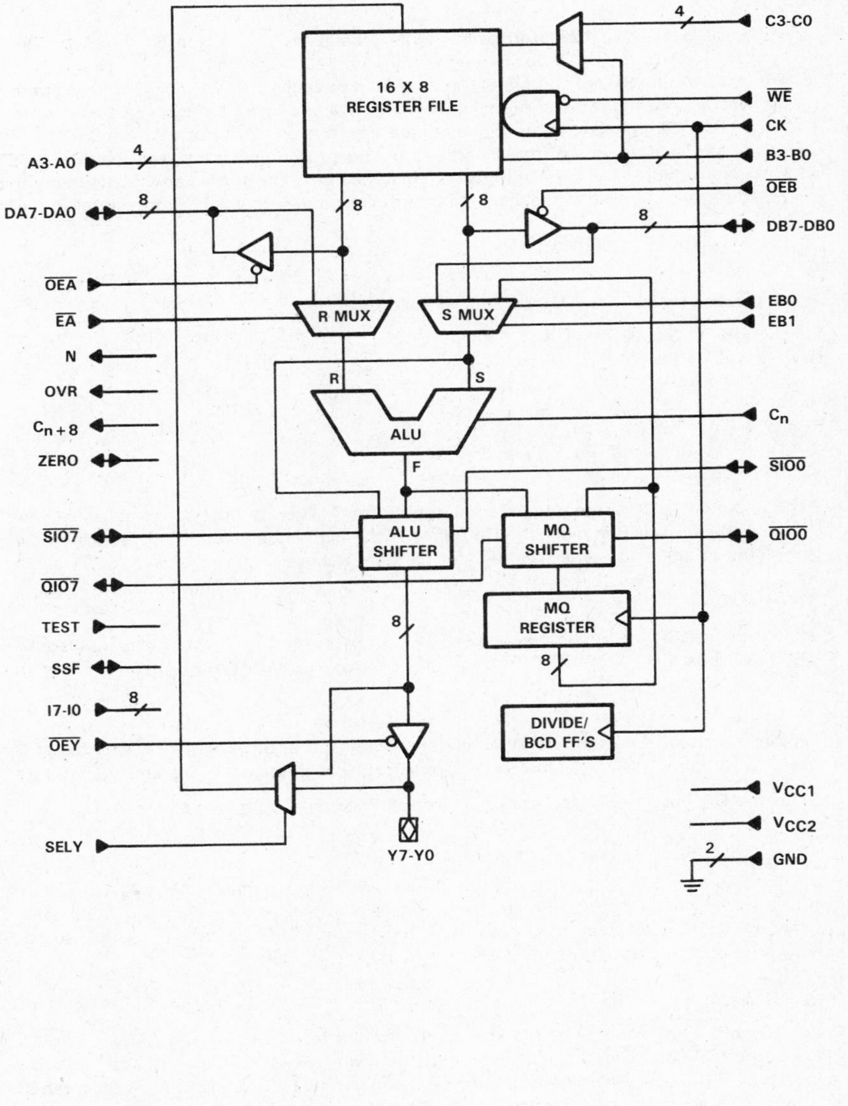
16 X 8
REGISTER FILE
C3-C0
WE
CK
B3-B0
OEB
DB7-DB0
A3-A0
DA7-DA0
OEA
EA
R MUX
S MUX
EB0
EB1
N
OVR
C_{n+8}
ZERO
R
S
ALU
C_n
F
SIO0
ALU
SHIFTER
MQ
SHIFTER
SIO7
QIO0
QIO7
MQ
REGISTER
TEST
SSF
I7-I0
OEY
DIVIDE/
BCD FF'S
SELY
Y7-Y0
V_{CC1}
V_{CC2}
GND

architectural elements

3-port register file

Working registers consist of 128 storage elements organized into sixteen 8-bit words. These storage elements appear to the user as 16 positive edge-triggered registers. The three port addresses, one write (C) and two reads (A and B), are completely independent of each other to implement a 3-operand register file. Data is written into the register file when $\overline{WE}$ is low and a low-to-high clock transition occurs. The ADD and SUBTRACT immediate instructions require only one source operand. The B address is used as the source address, and the bits of the A address are used to provide a constant field. The SET, RESET, and TEST BIT instructions use the B addressed register as both the source and destination register while the A and C addresses are used as masks. These instructions are explained in more detail in the instruction section.

S multiplexer

The S multiplexer selects the ALU operand, as follows:

EB1	EB0	S bus
Low	Low	RF data
Low	High	MQ data
High	Low	DB data
High	High	MQ data

DB port

The 8-bit bidirectional DB port inputs external data to the ALU or outputs the register file. If $\overline{OEB}$ is low, the DB bus is active; if $\overline{OEB}$ is high, the DB bus is in the high impedance state. Notice that the DB port may be isolated at the same time that register file data is passed to the ALU.

R multiplexer

The R multiplexer selects the other operand of the ALU. Except for those instructions that require constants or masks, the R bus will contain DA if $\overline{EA}$ is high or the RF data pointed to by A if $\overline{EA}$ is low.

DA port

The 8-bit bidirectional DA port inputs external data to the ALU or outputs the register file. If $\overline{OEA}$ is low, the DA bus is active; if $\overline{OEA}$ is high, the DA bus is in the high-impedance state.

Notice that the DA bus may be isolated while register file data is passed to the ALU.

ALU

The shift instructions are summarized in Table 4 and illustrated in Figure 2. The ALU can perform seven arithmetic and six logical instructions on two 8-bit operands. It also supports multiplication, division, normalization, bit set, reset, test, byte operations, and excess-3 BCD arithmetic. These source operands are the outputs of the S and R multiplexers.

ALU and MQ shifters

ALU and MQ shifters perform all of the shift, multiply, divide, and normalize functions. Table 4 shows the value of the $\overline{SIO7}$ and $\overline{QIO7}$ pins of the most significant package. The standard shifts may be made into conditional shifts and the serial data may be input or output with the aid of two three-state gates. These capabilities are discussed further in the arithmetic and logic section.

MQ register

The multiplier-quotient (MQ) register has specific functions in multiplication, division, and normalization. This register may also be used as a temporary storage register. The MQ register may be loaded if the instruction code on pins I7-I0 is E1-E7 or E9-EE (See Table 1).

Y bus

The Y bus contains the output of the ALU shifter if $\overline{OEY}$ is low and is a high impedance input if $\overline{OEY}$ is high. SELY must be low to pass the internal ALU shift bus and must be high to pass the external Y bus to the register file.

status

Four status pins are available on the most significant package, overflow (OVR), sign (N), carry out (C_{n+8}), and zero (ZERO). The C_{n+8} line signifies the ALU result while OVR, ZERO, and N refer the status after the ALU shift has occurred. Notice that the ZERO pin cannot be used to detect whether an input placed on a high impedance Y bus is zero.

divide BCD flip-flops

The multiply-divide flip-flops contain the status of the previous multiply or divide instruction. They are affected by the following instructions:

DIVIDE REMAINDER FIX
SIGNED DIVIDE QUOTIENT FIX
SIGNED MULTIPLY
SIGNED MULTIPLY TERMINATE
SIGNED DIVIDE INITIALIZE
SIGNED DIVIDE START
SIGNED DIVIDE ITERATE
UNSIGNED DIVIDE START
UNSIGNED DIVIDE ITERATE
UNSIGNED MULTIPLY
SIGNED DIVIDE TERMINATE
UNSIGNED DIVIDE TERMINATE

The excess-3 BCD flip-flops are affected by all instructions except NOP. The clear function clears these flip-flops. They preserve the carry from each nibble (4-bits) in excess-3/BCD operations.

test pin (test)

This pin should be connected to ground.

special shift function (SSF) pin

Conditional shifting algorithms may be implemented via control of the SSF pin. The applied voltage to this pin may be set as a function of a potential overflow condition (the two most significant bits are not equal) or any other condition (see Group 1 instructions).

instruction set

The 'AS887 bit-slice processor uses bits 17-I0 as instruction inputs. A combination of bits I3-I0 (Group 1 instructions) and bits I7-I4 (Group 2-5 instructions) are used to develop the 8-bit op code for a specific instruction. Group 1 and Group 2 instructions can be combined to perform arithmetic or logical functions plus a shift function in one instruction cycle. A summary of the instruction set is given in Table 1.

TABLE 1. INSTRUCTION SET

GROUP 1 INSTRUCTIONS

INSTRUCTION BITS (I3-I0) HEX CODE	MNEMONIC	FUNCTION
0		Accesses Group 4 instructions
1	ADD	$R+S+C_n$
2	SUBR	$\overline{R}+S+C_n$
3	SUBS	$R+\overline{S}+C_n$
4	INCS	$S+C_n$
5	INCNS	$\overline{S}+C_n$
6	INCR	$R+C_n$
7	INCNR	$\overline{R}+C_n$
8		Accesses Group 3 instructions
9	XOR	R XOR S
A	AND	R AND S
B	OR	R OR S
C	NAND	R NAND S
D	NOR	R NOR S
E	ANDNR	$\overline{R}$ AND S
F		Accesses Group 5 instructions

GROUP 2 INSTRUCTIONS

INSTRUCTION BITS (I7-I4) HEX CODE	MNEMONIC	FUNCTION
0	SRA	Arithmetic Right Single
1	SRAD	Arithmetic Right Double
2	SRL	Logical Right Single
3	SRLD	Logical Right Double
4	SLA	Arithmetic Left Single
5	SLAD	Arithmetic Left Double
6	SLC	Circular Left Single
7	SLCD	Circular Left Double
8	SRC	Circular Right Single
9	SRCD	Circular Right Double
A	MQSRA	Pass (F→Y) and Arithmetic Right MQ
B	MQSRL	Pass (F→Y) and Logical Right MQ
C	MQSLL	Pass (F→Y) and Logical Left MQ
D	MQSLC	Pass (F→Y) and Circular Left MQ
E	LOADMQ	Pass (F→Y) and Load MQ (F = MQ)
F	PASS	Pass (F→Y)

TEXAS INSTRUMENTS
POST OFFICE BOX 225012 • DALLAS, TEXAS 75265

TABLE 1. INSTRUCTION SET (Continued)

GROUP 3 INSTRUCTIONS

INSTRUCTION BITS (I7-I0) HEX CODE	MNEMONIC	FUNCTION
08	SET1	Set Bit
18	SET0	Reset Bit
28	TB1	Test Bit (One)
38	TB0	Test Bit (Zero)
48	ABS	Absolute Value
58	SMTC	Sign Magnitude/Two's Complement
68	ADDI	Add Immediate
78	SUBI	Subtract Immediate
88		Reserved
98		Reserved
A8		Reserved
B8		Reserved
C8		Reserved
D8		Reserved
E8		Reserved
F8		Reserved

GROUP 4 INSTRUCTIONS

INSTRUCTION BITS (I7-I0) HEX CODE	MNEMONIC	FUNCTION
00		Reserved
10	SEL	Select S/R
20	SNORM	Single Length Normalize
30	DNORM	Double Length Normalize
40	DIVRF	Divide Remainder Fix
50	SDIVQF	Signed Divide Quotient Fix
60	SMULI	Signed Multiply Iterate
70	SMULT	Signed Multiply Terminate
80	SDIVIN	Signed Divide Initialize
90	SDIVIS	Signed Divide Start
A0	SDIVI	Signed Divide Iterate
B0	UDIVIS	Unsigned Divide Start
C0	UDIVI	Unsigned Divide Iterate
D0	UMULI	Unsigned Multiply Iterate
E0	SDIVIT	Signed Divide Terminate
F0	UDIVIT	Unsigned Divide Terminate

TABLE 1. INSTRUCTION SET (Concluded)

GROUP 5 INSTRUCTIONS

INSTRUCTION BITS (I7-I0) HEX CODE	MNEMONIC	FUNCTION
0F	CLR	Clear
1F	CLR	Clear
2F	CLR	Clear
3F	CLR	Clear
4F	CLR	Clear
5F	CLR	Clear
6F	CLR	Clear
7F	BCDBIN	BCD to Binary
8F		Reserved
9F	EX3C	Excess-3 Word Correction
AF	SDIVO	Signed Divide Overflow Check
BF	CLR	Clear
CF	CLR	Clear
DF	BINEX3	Binary to Excess-3
EF	CLR	Clear
FF	NOP	No Operation

group 1 instructions

TABLE 2. GROUP 1 INSTRUCTIONS

INSTRUCTION BITS (I3-I0) HEX CODE	MNEMONIC	FUNCTION
0		Accesses Group 4 instructions
1	ADD	$R+S+C_n$
2	SUBR	$\overline{R}+S+C_n$
3	SUBS	$R+\overline{S}+C_n$
4	INCS	$S+C_n$
5	INCNS	$\overline{S}+C_n$
6	INCR	$R+C_n$
7	INCNR	$\overline{R}+C_n$
8		Accesses Group 3 instructions
9	XOR	R XOR S
A	AND	R AND S
B	OR	R OR S
C	NAND	R NAND S
D	NOR	R NOR S
E	ANDNR	$\overline{R}$ AND S
F		Accesses Group 5 instructions

TEXAS INSTRUMENTS
POST OFFICE BOX 225012 • DALLAS, TEXAS 75265

Group 1 instructions (excluding hex codes 0, 8, and F), shown in Table 2, may be used in conjunction with Group 2 shift instructions to perform arithmetic or logical functions plus a shift function† in one instruction cycle (hex codes 0, 8, and F are used to access Group 4, 3, and 5 instructions, respectively). Each shift may be made into a conditional shift by forcing the special shift function (SSF) pin into the proper state. If the SSF pin is high or floating, the shifted ALU output will be sent to the output buffers. If the SSF pin is pulled low externally, the ALU result will be passed directly to the output buffers. Conditional shifting is useful for scaling inputs in data arrays or in signal processing algorithms.

These instructions set the BCD flip-flop for the excess-3 correct instruction. The status is set with the following results (C_{n+8} is ALU carry out and is independent of shift operation; others are evaluated after shift operation).

†Double-precision shifts involve both the ALU and MQ register.

Status is set with the following results:

Arithmetic

N → MSB of result
OVR → Signed arithmetic overflow
C_{n+8} → Carry out equal one
Z → Result equal zero

Logic

N → MSB of result
OVR → None (force to zero)
C_{n+8} → None (force to zero)
Z → Result equal zero

group 2 instructions

TABLE 3. GROUP 2 INSTRUCTIONS

INSTRUCTION BITS (I7-I4) HEX CODE	MNEMONIC	FUNCTION
0	SRA	Arithmetic Right Single
1	SRAD	Arithmetic Right Double
2	SRL	Logical Right Single
3	SRLD	Logical Right Double
4	SLA	Arithmetic Left Single
5	SLAD	Arithmetic Left Double
6	SLC	Circular Left Single
7	SLCD	Circular Left Double
8	SRC	Circular Right Single
9	SRCD	Circular Right Double
A	MQSRA	Pass (F→Y) and Arithmetic Right MQ
B	MQSRL	Pass (F→Y) and Logical Right MQ
C	MQSLL	Pass (F→Y) and Logical Left MQ
D	MQSLC	Pass (F→Y) and Circular Left MQ
E	LOADMQ	Pass (F→Y) and Load MQ (F = MQ)
F	PASS	Pass (F→Y)

The processor's shift instructions are implemented using Group 2 instructions (Table 3). The connections are the same on all instructions including multiply, divide, and normalization functions.

The following external connections are required:

$\overline{SIO7}$ to $\overline{SIO0}$
$\overline{QIO7}$ to $\overline{QIO0}$

Single- and double-precision shifts are supported. Double-precision shifts assume the most significant half has come through the ALU and will be placed (if $\overline{WE}$ is low) into the register file on the rising edge of the clock and the least significant half lies in the MQ register. All Group 2 shifts may be made conditional. (see previous page)

The following definitions apply to Group 2 shift instructions:

Arithmetic right shifts copy the sign of the number if no overflow occurs from the ALU calculation; if overflow occurs, the sign bit is inverted.
Arithmetic left shifts do not retain the sign of the number if an overflow occurs. A zero is filled into the LSB if not forced externally.
Logical right shifts fill a zero in the MSB position if not forced externally.
Circular right shifts fill the LSB in the MSB position.
Circular left shifts fill the MSB in the LSB position.
Shifting left is defined as moving a bit position towards the MSB (doubling).
Shifting right is defined as moving a bit towards the LSB (halving).

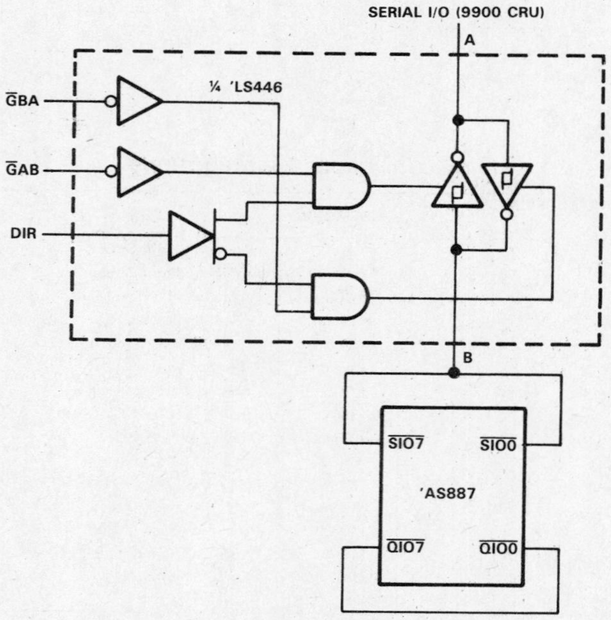
SERIAL I/O (9900 CRU)
A
¼ 'LS446
$\overline{G}$BA
$\overline{G}$AB
DIR
B
$\overline{SIO7}$
$\overline{SIO0}$
'AS887
$\overline{QIO7}$
$\overline{QIO0}$

FIGURE 1. SERIAL I/O

TEXAS INSTRUMENTS
POST OFFICE BOX 225012 • DALLAS, TEXAS 75265

Serial input may be performed using the circuitry shown in Figure 1. A single-/or double-precision arithmetic left or logical right shift fills the complement of the data on $\overline{SIO0}$ and $\overline{SIO7}$ into the LSB or MSB of the data word(s). Note that if $\overline{SIO0}$ and $\overline{SIO7}$ are floating (HI-Z), a zero will be filled as an end condition.

Serial output may be performed with circular instructions.

The shift instructions are summarized in Table 4 and illustrated in Figure 2. In Figure 2 and all succeeding figures that illustrate instruction execution, the following definitions apply:

QBT — End fill for signed divide.
MQF — End fill for unsigned divide.
SRF — End fill for signed multiply and the arithmetic right shifts.

TABLE 4. SHIFT INSTRUCTIONS

OP CODE†	SHIFT FUNCTION‡	$\overline{SIO7}$ · $\overline{SIO0}$ WIRED VALUE	$\overline{QIO7}$ · $\overline{QIO0}$ WIRED VALUE
0N	Arithmetic Right Single	ALU-LSB Output	—
1N	Arithmetic Right Double	MQ-LSB Output	ALU-LSB Output
2N	Logical Right Single	Input to ALU-MSB	ALU-LSB Output
3N	Logical Right Double	Input to ALU-MSB	ALU-LSB Output
4N	Arithmetic Left Single	Input to ALU-LSB	ALU-MSB Output
5N	Arithmetic Left Double	Input to MQ-LSB	MQ-MSB Output
6N	Circular Left Single	ALU-MSB Output	—
7N	Circular Left Double	ALU-MSB Output	MQ-MSB Output
8N	Circular Right Single	ALU-LSB Output	—
9N	Circular Right Double	MQ-LSB Output	ALU-LSB Output
AN	Arithmetic Right (MQ only)	MQ-LSB Output	MQ-LSB Output
BN	Logical Right (MQ only)	MQ-LSB Output	Input to MQ-MSB
CN	Logical Left (MQ only)	Input to MQ-LSB	MQ-MSB Output
DN	Circular Left (MQ only)	MQ-MSB Output	MQ-MSB Output

†Op Code N ≠ 0, 8, or F; these select special instruction Groups 4, 3, and 5 respectively.
‡Shift I/O pins are active low. Therefore, inputs and outputs must be inverted if true logical values are required.

Status is set with the following results:

Arithmetic

N → Result MSB equal one
OVR → Signed arithmetic overflow†
C_{n+8} → Carry out equal one
Z → Result equal zero

Logic

N → Result MSB equal one
OVR → Zero
C_{n+8} → Zero
Z → Result equal zero

† For the SLA and SLAD instructions, OVR is set if signed arithmetic overflow or if the ALU result MSB XOR MSB-1 equals one.

ARITHMETIC RIGHT SINGLE

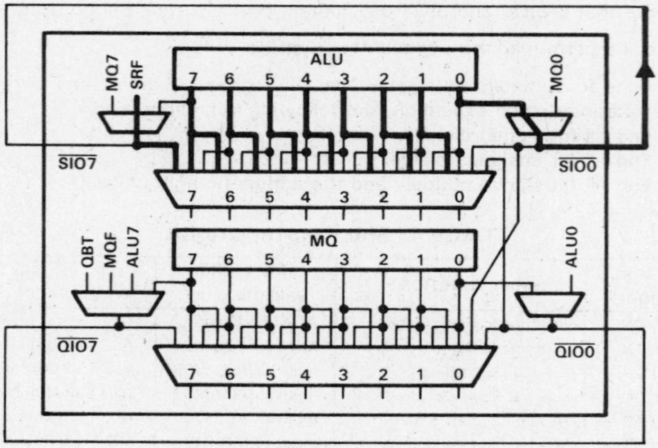
ALU
7 6 5 4 3 2 1 0
MQ7
SRF
MQ0
SIO7
SIO0
MQ
QBT
MQF
ALU7
ALU0
QIO7
QIO0

ARITHMETIC RIGHT DOUBLE

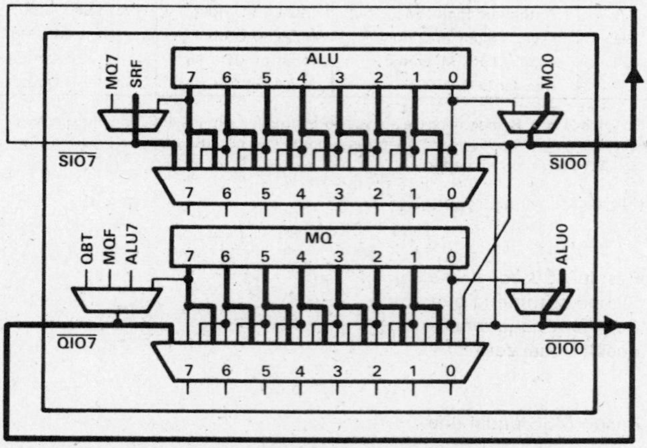
ALU
7 6 5 4 3 2 1 0
MQ7
SRF
MQ0
SIO7
SIO0
MQ
QBT
MQF
ALU7
ALU0
QIO7
QIO0

FIGURE 2. SHIFT INSTRUCTIONS

LOGICAL RIGHT SINGLE

FILLS ZERO IF NOT FORCED

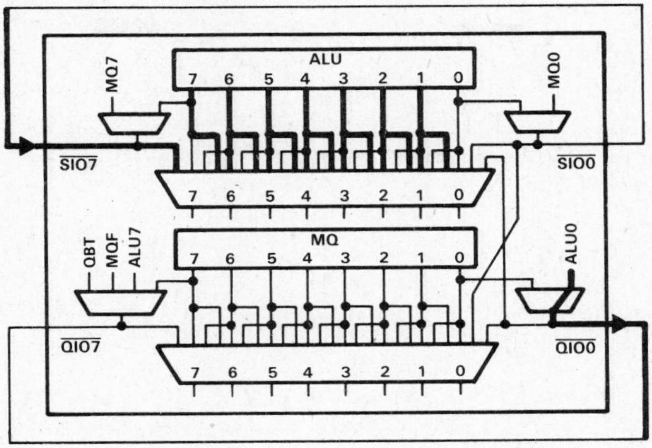
ALU
7 6 5 4 3 2 1 0
MQ7
MQ0
SIO7
SIO0
7 6 5 4 3 2 1 0
MQ
7 6 5 4 3 2 1 0
QBT
MQF
ALU7
ALU0
QIO7
QIO0
7 6 5 4 3 2 1 0

LOGICAL RIGHT DOUBLE

FILLS ZERO IF NOT FORCED

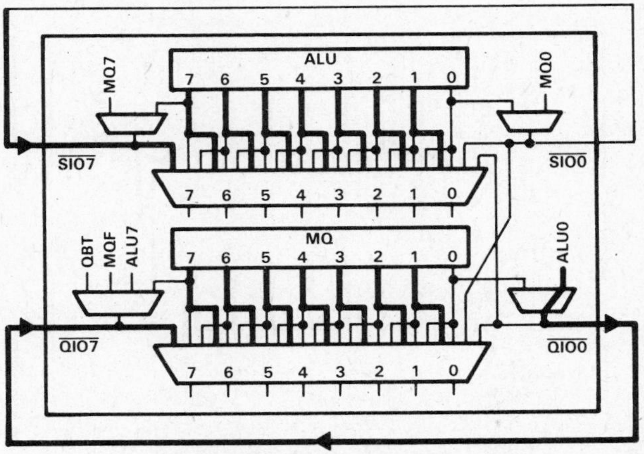
ALU
7 6 5 4 3 2 1 0
MQ7
MQ0
SIO7
SIO0
7 6 5 4 3 2 1 0
MQ
7 6 5 4 3 2 1 0
QBT
MQF
ALU7
ALU0
QIO7
QIO0
7 6 5 4 3 2 1 0

FIGURE 2. SHIFT INSTRUCTIONS (Continued)

ARITHMETIC LEFT SINGLE

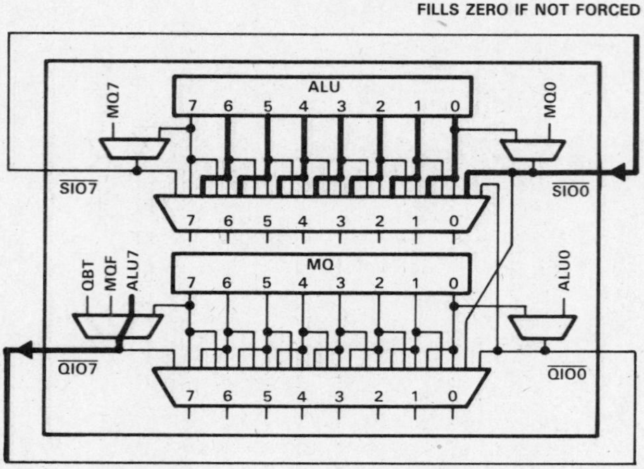
FILLS ZERO IF NOT FORCED
ALU
7 6 5 4 3 2 1 0
MQ7
MQ0
SIO7
SIO0
7 6 5 4 3 2 1 0
MQ
7 6 5 4 3 2 1 0
QBT
MQF
ALU7
ALU0
QIO7
QIO0
7 6 5 4 3 2 1 0

ARITHMETIC LEFT DOUBLE

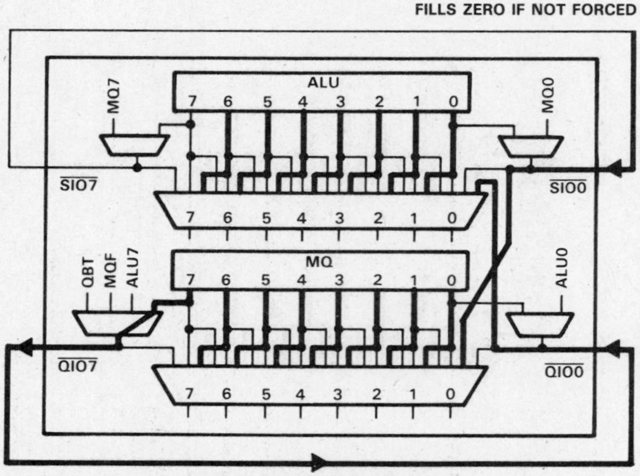
FILLS ZERO IF NOT FORCED
ALU
7 6 5 4 3 2 1 0
MQ7
MQ0
SIO7
SIO0
7 6 5 4 3 2 1 0
MQ
7 6 5 4 3 2 1 0
QBT
MQF
ALU7
ALU0
QIO7
QIO0
7 6 5 4 3 2 1 0

FIGURE 2. SHIFT INSTRUCTIONS (Continued)

CIRCULAR LEFT SINGLE

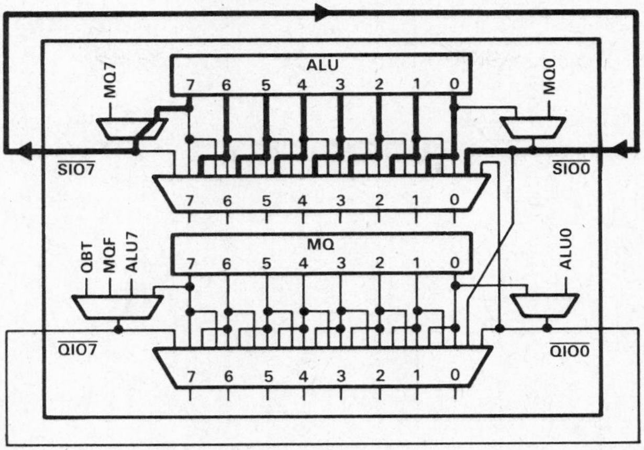
ALU
7 6 5 4 3 2 1 0
MQ7
MQ0
SIO7
SIO0
7 6 5 4 3 2 1 0
MQ
7 6 5 4 3 2 1 0
QBT
MQF
ALU7
ALU0
QIO7
QIO0
7 6 5 4 3 2 1 0

CIRCULAR LEFT DOUBLE

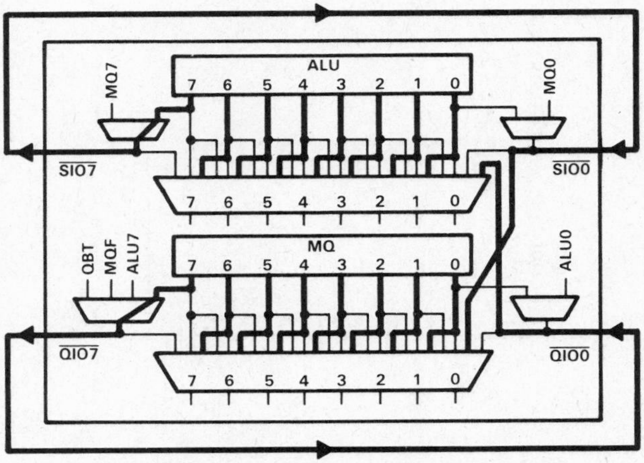
ALU
7 6 5 4 3 2 1 0
MQ7
MQ0
SIO7
SIO0
7 6 5 4 3 2 1 0
MQ
7 6 5 4 3 2 1 0
QBT
MQF
ALU7
ALU0
QIO7
QIO0
7 6 5 4 3 2 1 0

FIGURE 2. SHIFT INSTRUCTIONS (Continued)

2

LSI Devices

CIRCULAR RIGHT SINGLE

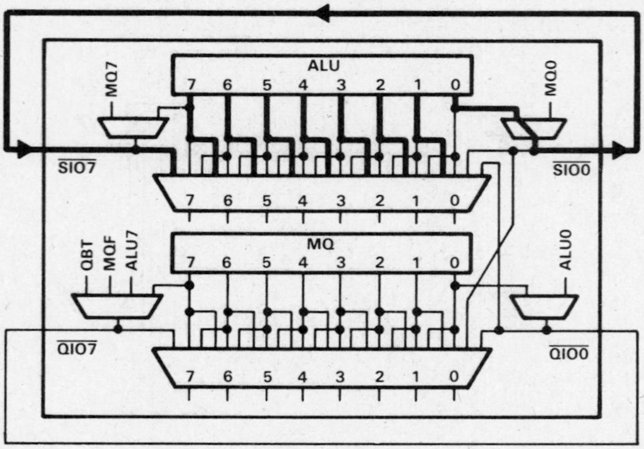
ALU
7 6 5 4 3 2 1 0
MQ7
MQ0
SIO7
SIO0
7 6 5 4 3 2 1 0
MQ
7 6 5 4 3 2 1 0
QBT
MQF
ALU7
ALU0
QIO7
QIO0
7 6 5 4 3 2 1 0

CIRCULAR RIGHT DOUBLE

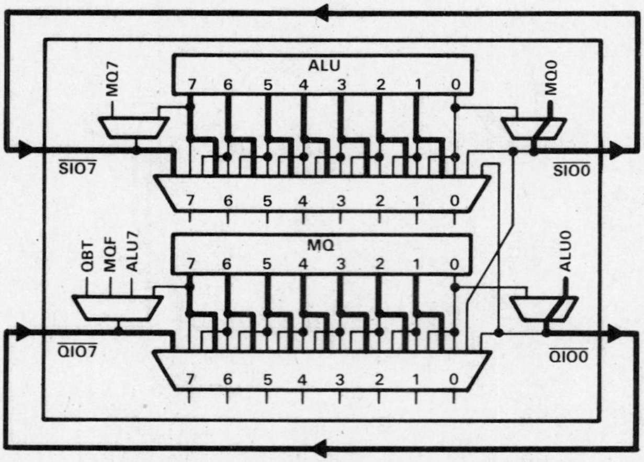
ALU
7 6 5 4 3 2 1 0
MQ7
MQ0
SIO7
SIO0
7 6 5 4 3 2 1 0
MQ
7 6 5 4 3 2 1 0
QBT
MQF
ALU7
ALU0
QIO7
QIO0
7 6 5 4 3 2 1 0

FIGURE 2. SHIFT INSTRUCTIONS (Continued)

TEXAS INSTRUMENTS
POST OFFICE BOX 225012 • DALLAS, TEXAS 75265

ARITHMETIC RIGHT (MQ ONLY)

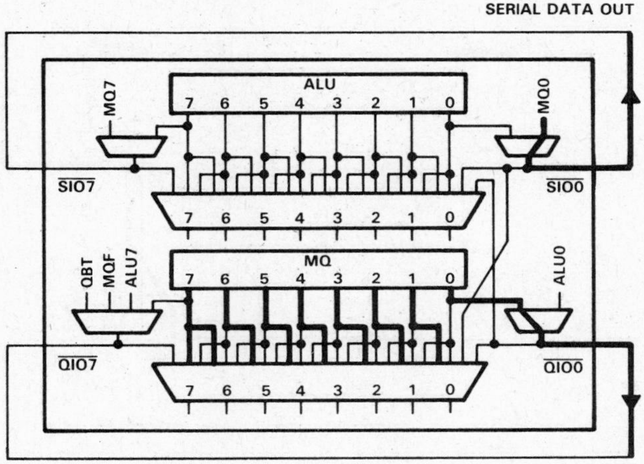
SERIAL DATA OUT
ALU
7 6 5 4 3 2 1 0
MQ7
MQ0
$\overline{SIO7}$
$\overline{SIO0}$
7 6 5 4 3 2 1 0
MQ
7 6 5 4 3 2 1 0
QBT
MQF
ALU7
ALU0
$\overline{QIO7}$
$\overline{QIO0}$
7 6 5 4 3 2 1 0

LOGICAL RIGHT (MQ ONLY)

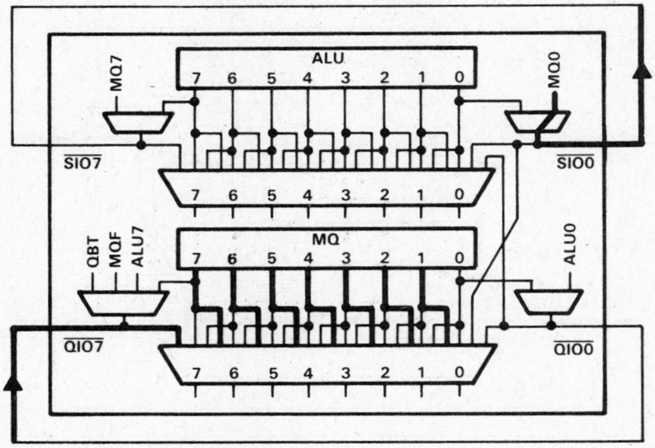
ALU
7 6 5 4 3 2 1 0
MQ7
MQ0
$\overline{SIO7}$
$\overline{SIO0}$
7 6 5 4 3 2 1 0
MQ
7 6 5 4 3 2 1 0
QBT
MQF
ALU7
ALU0
$\overline{QIO7}$
$\overline{QIO0}$
7 6 5 4 3 2 1 0
FILLS ZERO IF NOT FORCED

FIGURE 2. SHIFT INSTRUCTIONS (Continued)

LOGICAL LEFT (MQ ONLY)

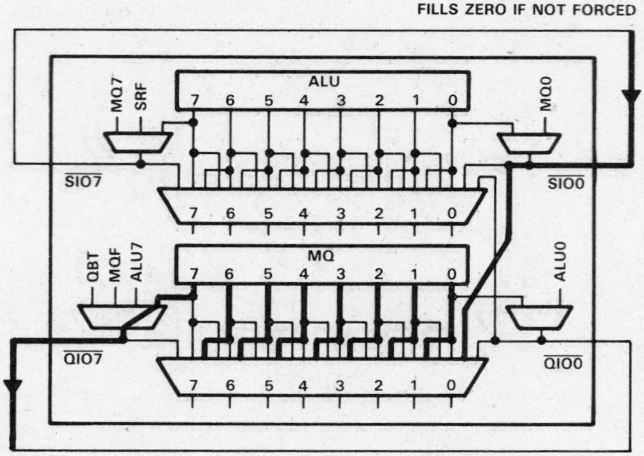
FILLS ZERO IF NOT FORCED
ALU
7 6 5 4 3 2 1 0
MQ7
SRF
MQ0
SIO7
SIO0
7 6 5 4 3 2 1 0
MQ
7 6 5 4 3 2 1 0
QBT
MQF
ALU7
ALU0
QIO7
QIO0
7 6 5 4 3 2 1 0

CIRCULAR LEFT (MQ ONLY)

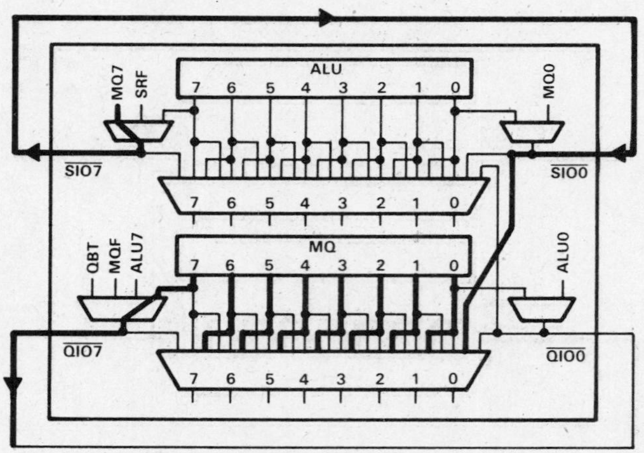
ALU
7 6 5 4 3 2 1 0
MQ7
SRF
MQ0
SIO7
SIO0
7 6 5 4 3 2 1 0
MQ
7 6 5 4 3 2 1 0
QBT
MQF
ALU7
ALU0
QIO7
QIO0
7 6 5 4 3 2 1 0

FIGURE 2. SHIFT INSTRUCTIONS (Concluded)

TEXAS INSTRUMENTS
POST OFFICE BOX 225012 • DALLAS, TEXAS 75265

group 3 instructions

Hex code 8 of Group 1 instructions is used to access Group 3 instructions. Group 3 instructions are summarized in Table 5.

TABLE 5. GROUP 3 INSTRUCTIONS

INSTRUCTION BITS (I7-I0) OP CODE (HEX)	MNEMONIC	FUNCTION
08	SET1	Set Bit
18	SET0	Reset Bit
28	TB1	Test Bit (One)
38	TB0	Test Bit (Zero)
48	ABS	Absolute Value
58	SMTC	Sign Magnitude/Two's Complement
68	ADDI	Add Immediate
78	SUBI	Subtract Immediate
88		Reserved
98		Reserved
A8		Reserved
B8		Reserved
C8		Reserved
D8		Reserved
E8		Reserved
F8		Reserved

set bit instruction (set1): I7-I0 = 08_{16}

This instruction (Figure 3) is used to force selected bits to one (any combination of zero to eight bits). The desired bits are specified by an 8-bit mask (C3-C0)::(A3-A0)† consisting of register file address ports that are not required to support this instruction. All bits that are in the same bit positions as ones in the mask are forced to a logical one. The B3-B0 address field is used for both source and destination of this instruction. The S bus is the source word for this instruction. $\overline{\text{SIO0}}$ must be forced low for proper operation. If $\overline{\text{SIO0}}$ is high, data on the S bus is passed unaltered. The status set by the set bit instruction is as follows:

N → None (force to zero)
OVR → None (force to zero)
C_{n+8} → None (force to zero)
Z → Result equal zero

† The symbol '::' is concatenation operator

reset bit instruction (set0): I7-I0 = 18_{16}

This instruction (Figure 3) is used to force selected bits to zero. The desired bits are specified by an 8-bit mask (C3-C0)::(A3-A0) consisting of register file address ports that are not required to support this instruction. All bits in the selected byte(s) that are in the same bit positions as ones in the mask are reset. The B3-B0 address field is used for both source and destination of this instruction. The S bus is the source word for this instruction. $\overline{\text{SIO0}}$ must be forced low for proper operation. If $\overline{\text{SIO0}}$ is high, data on the S bus is passed unaltered. The status set by the reset bit instruction is as follows:

N → None (force to zero)
OVR → None (force to zero)
C_{n+8} → None (force to zero)
Z → Result equal zero

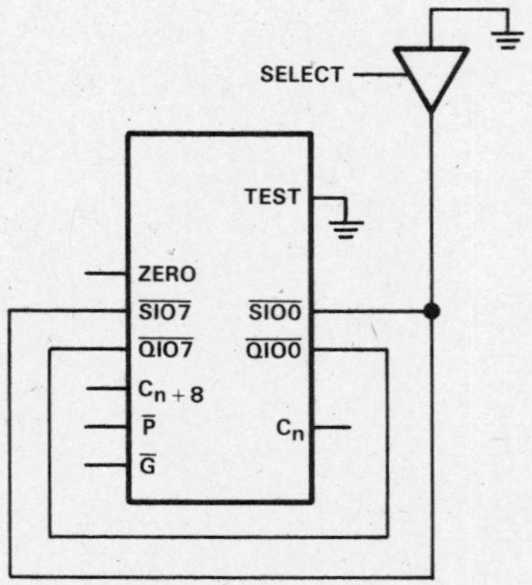
SELECT
TEST
ZERO
SIO7
SIO0
QIO7
QIO0
Cn+8
P
G
Cn

NOTES: 1. Force $\overline{\text{SIO0}}$ low for proper operation.
2. Bit mask (C3-C0)::(A3-A0) will set desired bits to one.

FIGURE 3. SET BIT (OR RESET BIT)

test bit (one) instruction (TB1): I7-I0 = 28_{16}

This instruction (Figure 4) is used to test selected bits for ones. Bits to be tested are specified by an 8-bit mask (C3-C0)::(A3-A0) consisting of register file address ports that are not required to support this instruction. Write Enable ($\overline{WE}$) is internally disabled during this instruction. The test will pass if the selected byte has ones at all bit locations specified by the ones of the mask (Figure 5). The S bus is the source word for this instruction. $\overline{SIO0}$ must be forced low for proper operation. The status set by the test bit (one) instruction is as follows:

N → None (force to zero)
OVR → None (force to zero)
C_{n+8} → None (force to zero)
Z → Pass

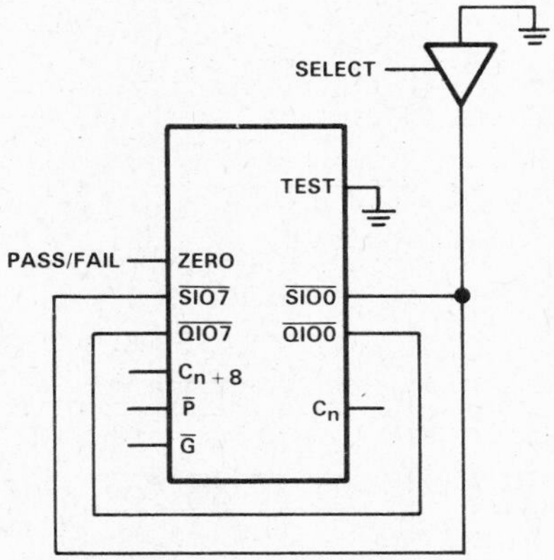
SELECT
TEST
PASS/FAIL
ZERO
SIO7
SIO0
QIO7
QIO0
Cn+8
P
G
Cn

NOTES: 1. Force $\overline{SIO0}$ low for proper operation.
2. Bit mask (C3-C0)::(A3-A0) will define bits for testing.
3. Pass/fail is indicated on Z output.

FIGURE 4. TEST BIT

test bit (zero) instruction (TB0): I7-I0 = 38_{16}

This instruction (Figure 4) is used to test selected bits for ones. Bits to be tested are specified by an 8-bit mask (C3-C0)::(A3-A0) consisting of register file address ports that are not required to support this instruction. Write Enable ($\overline{WE}$) is internally disabled during this instruction. The test will pass if the selected byte has zeros at all bit locations specified by the ones of the mask (Figure 6). The S bus is the source word for this instruction. $\overline{SIO0}$ must be forced low for proper operation. The status set by the test bit (zero) instruction is as follows:

N → None (force to zero)
OVR → None (force to zero)
C_{n+8} → None (force to zero)
Z → Pass

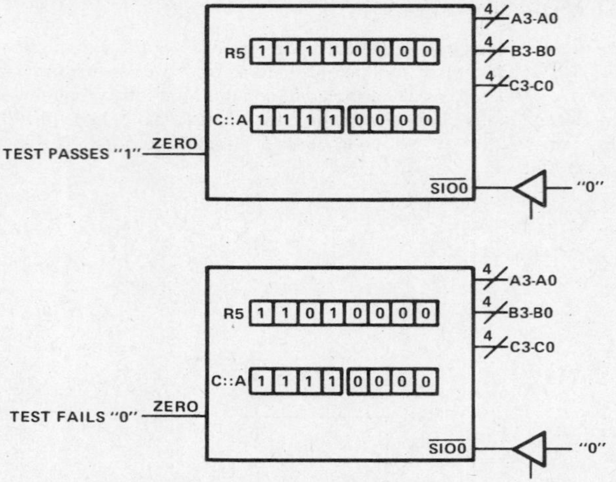
R5 1 1 1 1 0 0 0 0
C::A 1 1 1 1 0 0 0 0
TEST PASSES "1"
ZERO
SIO0
"0"
4 A3-A0
4 B3-B0
4 C3-C0
R5 1 1 0 1 0 0 0 0
C::A 1 1 1 1 0 0 0 0
TEST FAILS "0"
ZERO
SIO0
"0"
4 A3-A0
4 B3-B0
4 C3-C0

FIGURE 5. TEST BIT ONE EXAMPLES

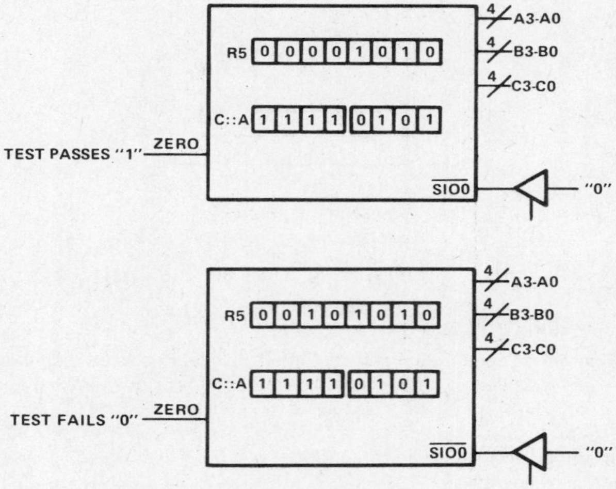
R5 0 0 0 0 1 0 1 0
C::A 1 1 1 1 0 1 0 1
TEST PASSES "1"
ZERO
SIO0
"0"
4 A3-A0
4 B3-B0
4 C3-C0
R5 0 0 1 0 1 0 1 0
C::A 1 1 1 1 0 1 0 1
TEST FAILS "0"
ZERO
SIO0
"0"
4 A3-A0
4 B3-B0
4 C3-C0

FIGURE 6. TEST BIT ZERO EXAMPLES

absolute value instruction (ABS): I7-I0 = 48_{16}

This instruction is used to convert two's complement numbers to their positive value. The operand placed on the S bus is the source for this instruction. The 'AS887 will test the sign of the S bus and force the SSF pin to the proper value. The status set by the absolute value instruction is as follows:

N → Input MSB equal one
OVR → Input equal 80 (hex)
C_{n+8} → S = 0
Z → Result equal zero

sign magnitude/two's complement instruction (SMTC): I7-I0 = 58_{16}

This instruction allows conversion from two's complement representation to sign magnitude representation, or vice-versa, in one clock cycle. The operand placed on the S bus is the source for this instruction.

When a negative zero (80 hex) is converted, the result is 00 with an overflow. If the input is in two's complement notation, the overflow indicates an illegal conversion. The status set by the sign magnitude/two's complement instruction is as follows:

N → Result MSB equal one
OVR → Input equal 80 (hex)
C_{n+8} → Input equal 00 (hex)
Z → Result equal zero

add immediate instruction (ADDI): I7-I0 = 68_{16}

This instruction is used to add a specified constant value to the operand placed on the S bus. The constant will be between the values of 0 and 15. The constant value is specified by the unused register file address (A port) not required to support this instruction. Forcing the carry input will add an additional one to the result. The status set by the add immediate instruction is as follows:

N → Result MSB equal one
OVR → Arithmetic signed overflow
C_{n+8} → Carry out equal one
Z → Result equal zero

subtract immediate instruction (SUBI): I7-I0 = 78_{16}

This instruction is used to subtract a specified constant value from the operand placed on the S bus. The constant value is specified by the unused register file address (A port) that is not required to support this instruction. The constant applied is the least significant four bits of a two's complement number. The device sign extends the constant over the entire word length. The status set by the subtract immediate instruction is as follows:

N → Result MSB equal one
OVR → Arithmetic signed overflow
C_{n+8} → Carry out equal one
Z → Result equal zero

2
LSI Devices

group 4 instructions

Hex code 0 of Group 1 instructions is used to access Group 4 instructions. Group 4 instructions are summarized in Table 6.

TABLE 6. GROUP 4 INSTRUCTIONS

INSTRUCTION BITS (I7-I0) OP CODE (HEX)	MNEMONIC	FUNCTION
00		Reserved
10	SEL	Select S/R
20	SNORM	Single Length Normalize
30	DNORM	Double Length Normalize
40	DIVRF	Divide Remainder Fix
50	SDIVQF	Signed Divide Quotient Fix
60	SMULI	Signed Multiply Iterate
70	SMULT	Signed Multiply Terminate
80	SDIVIN	Signed Divide Initialize
90	SDIVIS	Signed Divide Start
A0	SDIVI	Signed Divide Iterate
B0	UDIVIS	Unsigned Divide Start
C0	UDIVI	Unsigned Divide Iterate
D0	UMULI	Unsigned Multiply Iterate
E0	SDIVIT	Signed Divide Terminate
F0	UDIVIT	Unsigned Divide Terminate

select S/R instruction (SEL): I7-I0 = 10_{16}

This instruction is used to pass either the S bus or the R bus to the output depending on the state of the SSF input pin. Normally, the preceding instruction would test the two operands and the resulting status information would be used to force the SSF input pin. SSF = 0 will output the R bus and SSF = 1 will output the S bus. The status set by the select S/R instruction is as follows:

N → Result MSB equal one
OVR → None (force to zero)
C_{n+8} → None (force to zero)
Z → Result equal zero

single-length normalize instruction (SNORM): I7-I0 = 20_{16}

This instruction will cause the contents of the MQ register to shift toward the most significant bit. Zeros are shifted in via the $\overline{QIO0}$ input. The number of shifts performed can be counted and stored in one of the register files by forcing a high at the C_n input. When the two most significant bits are of opposite value, normalization is complete. This condition is indicated on the microcycle that completes the normalization at the OVR output.

The chip contains conditional logic that inhibits the shift function (and also inhibits the register file increment) if the number within the MQ register is already normalized at the beginning of the instruction (Figure 7). The status set by the single-length normalize instruction is as follows:

N → MSB of result
OVR → MSB XOR 2nd MSB
C_{n+8} → Carry out equal one
Z → Result equal zero

SINGLE-LENGTH NORMALIZE

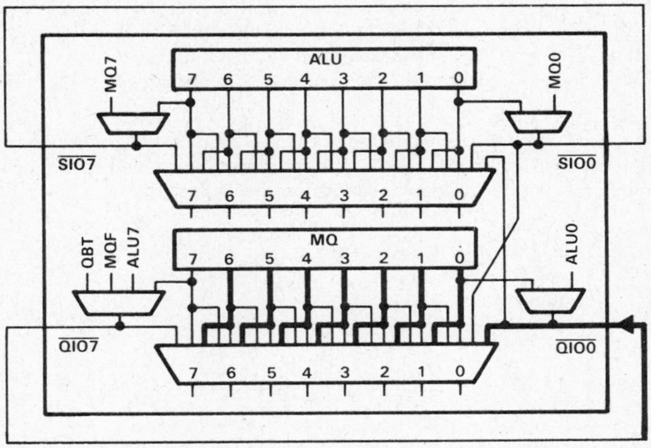
ALU
7 6 5 4 3 2 1 0
MQ7
MQ0
SIO7
SIO0
7 6 5 4 3 2 1 0
MQ
7 6 5 4 3 2 1 0
QBT
MQF
ALU7
ALU0
QIO7
QIO0
7 6 5 4 3 2 1 0

DOUBLE-LENGTH NORMALIZE

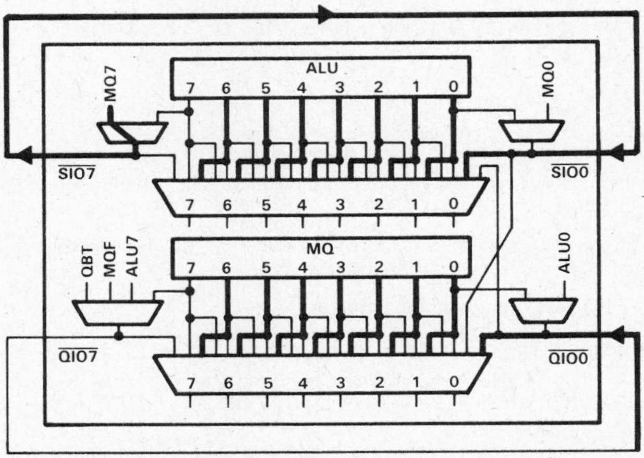
ALU
7 6 5 4 3 2 1 0
MQ7
MQ0
SIO7
SIO0
7 6 5 4 3 2 1 0
MQ
7 6 5 4 3 2 1 0
QBT
MQF
ALU7
ALU0
QIO7
QIO0
7 6 5 4 3 2 1 0

FIGURE 7. SINGLE- AND DOUBLE-LENGTH NORMALIZE

double-length normalize instruction (DNORM): I7-I0 = 30_{16}

This instruction will cause the contents of a double-length word (register file contains the most significant half and the MQ register contains the least significant half) to shift toward the most significant bit. Zeros are shifted in via the $\overline{QIO0}$ input. When the two most significant bits are of opposite value, normalization is complete. This condition is indicated on the microcycle that completes the normalization at the OVR output.

The chip contains conditional logic which inhibits the shift function if the number is already normalized at the beginning of the instruction (Figure 7). The most significant half of the operand must be placed on the S bus. The status set by the double-length normalize instruction is as follows:

N	→	MSB of result
OVR	→	MSB XOR 2nd MSB
C_{n+8}	→	None (force to zero)
Z	→	Result equal zero

multiply operations

The ALU performs three unique types of 8 by 8 multiplies each of which produces a 16-bit result (Figure 8). All three types of multiplication proceed via the following recursion:

$$P(J+1) = 2[P(J) + \text{Multiplicand} \times M(8\text{-}J)]$$

where

P(J) = partial product at iteration number J

P(J+1) = partial product at iteration number J+1

J varies from 0 to 8

M (8-J) = mode bit (unique to multiply type)

2 denotes some type of shift (unique to multiply)

Notice that by proper choice of mode terms and shifting operations, signed, unsigned, and mixed multiplies (signed times unsigned) may be performed.

All multiplies assume that the multiplier is stored in MQ before the operation begins (in the case of mixed multiply, the unsigned number must be the multiplier).

The processor has the following multiply instructions:

1. SIGNED MULTIPLY ITERATE (SMULI): I7-I0 = 60_{16}
2. SIGNED MULTIPLY TERMINATE (SMULT): I7-I0 = 70_{16}
3. UNSIGNED MULTIPLY ITERATE (UMULI): I7-I0 = $D0_{16}$

The signed multiply iterate (SMULI) instruction performs a signed times signed iteration. This instruction interprets M(8-J) as the 8-J bit of the multiplier. The shift is a double-precision right shift one bit. This instruction is repeated 7 times for a 8 × 8 signed multiply. This instruction will be used 7 consecutive times for a mixed multiplication.

The signed multiply terminate (SMULT) instruction provides correct (negative) weighting of the sign bit of a negative multiplier in signed multiplication. The instruction is identical to signed multiply iterate (SMULI) except that M(8-J) is interpreted as −1 if the sign bit of the multiplier is 1, and 0 if the sign bit of the multiplier is 0.

2 LSI Devices

SMULI, SMULT

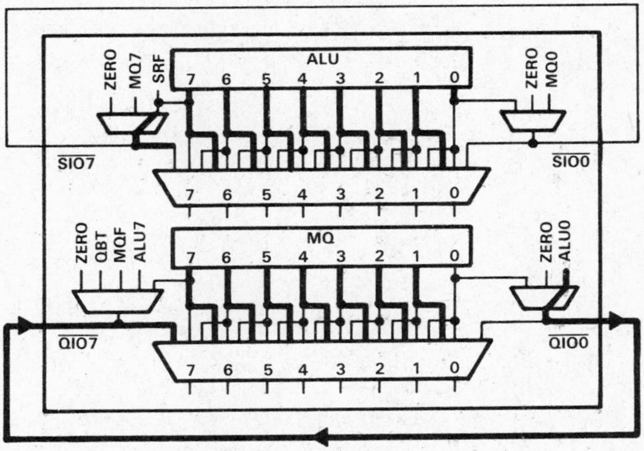
ALU
7 6 5 4 3 2 1 0
ZERO
MQ7
SRF
ZERO
MQ0
$\overline{SIO7}$
$\overline{SIO0}$
MQ
ZERO
QBT
MQF
ALU7
ZERO
ALU0
$\overline{QIO7}$
$\overline{QIO0}$

UMULI

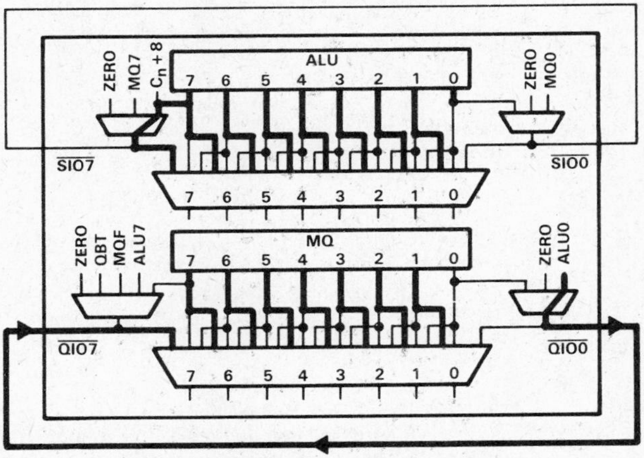
ALU
7 6 5 4 3 2 1 0
ZERO
MQ7
C_n+8
ZERO
MQ0
$\overline{SIO7}$
$\overline{SIO0}$
MQ
ZERO
QBT
MQF
ALU7
ZERO
ALU0
$\overline{QIO7}$
$\overline{QIO0}$

FIGURE 8. MULTIPLICATION OPERATIONS

The unsigned multiply iterate (UMULI) performs an unsigned multiplication iteration. This instruction interprets M(8-J) as the 8-J bit of the multiplier. The shift is a double-precision right shift with the carry out from the P(J) + Multiplicand × M(8-J) operation forced into bit 8 of P(J + 1). This instruction is used in unsigned and mixed multiplication.

signed multiplication

Signed multiplication performs a ten clock cycle, two's complement multiply. The instructions necessary to produce an algebraically correct result proceed in the following manner:

Zero register to be used for accumulator

Load MQ with multiplier

SMULI (repeat 7 times)	S port = Accumulator R port = Multiplicand F port = Iteration Result
SMULT	S port = Accumulator R port = Multiplicand F port = Product (MSH)

At completion, the accumulator will contain the 8 most significant bits and MQ will contain the 8 least significant bits of the product.

The status for the signed multiply iterate should not be used for any testing (overflow is not set by SMULI). The following status is set for the signed multiply terminate instruction:

N	→	Result MSB equal one
OVR	→	Forced to zero
C_{n+8}	→	Carry out equal to one
Z	→	Double precision result is zero

unsigned multiplication

Unsigned multiplication produces an unsigned times unsigned product in ten clocks. The instructions necessary to produce an algebraically correct result proceed in the following manner:

Zero register to be used for accumulator

Load MQ with multiplier

UMULI (8 times)	S port = Accumulator R port = Multiplicand F port = Iteration result (product MSH on final result)

Upon completion, the accumulator will contain the 8 most significant bits and MQ will contain the 8 least significant bits of the product.

TEXAS INSTRUMENTS
POST OFFICE BOX 225012 • DALLAS, TEXAS 75265

The status set by the unsigned multiply iteration is meaningless except on the final execution of the instruction. The status set by the unsigned multiply iteration instruction is as follows:

N	→	Result MSB equal one
OVR	→	Forced to zero
C_{n+8}	→	Carry out equal to one
Z	→	Double-precision result is zero

mixed multiplication

Mixed multiplication multiplies a signed multiplicand times an unsigned multiplier to produce a signed result in ten clocks. The steps are as follows:

Zero register used for accumulator

Load MQ with unsigned multipler

SMULI (8 times)	S port	=	Accumulator
	R port	=	Multiplicand
	F port	=	Iteration result

Upon completion, the accumulator will contain the 8 most significant bits and MQ will contain the 8 least significant bits of the product.

The following status is set by the last SMULI instruction:

N	→	Result MSB equal one
OVR	→	Forced to zero
C_{n+8}	→	Carry out equal to one
Z	→	Double-precision result is zero

divide operations

The divide uses a nonrestoring technique to perform both signed and unsigned division of a 16 bit integer dividend and an 8 bit integer divisor (Figure 9). It produces an 8 integer quotient and remainder.

The remainder and quotient will be such that the following equation is satisfied:

$$(\text{Quotient}) \times (\text{Divisor}) + \text{Remainder} = \text{Dividend}$$

The processor has the following divide instructions:

1. UNSIGNED DIVIDE START (UDIVIS): I7-I0 = $B0_{16}$
2. UNSIGNED DIVIDE ITERATE (UDIVI): I7-I0 = $C0_{16}$
3. UNSIGNED DIVIDE TERMINATE (UDIVIT): I7-I0 = $F0_{16}$
4. SIGNED DIVIDE INITIALIZE (SDIVIN): I7-I0 = 80_{16}
5. SIGNED DIVIDE OVERFLOW TEST (SDIVO): I7-I0 = AF_{16}
6. SIGNED DIVIDE START (SDIVIS): I7-I0 = 90_{16}
7. SIGNED DIVIDE ITERATE (SDIVI): I7-I0 = $A0_{16}$
8. SIGNED DIVIDE TERMINATE (SDIVIT): I7-I0 = $E0_{16}$
9. DIVIDE REMAINDER FIX (DIVRF): I7-I0 = 40_{16}
10. SIGNED DIVIDE QUOTIENT FIX (SDIVQF): I7-I0 = 50_{16}

2 LSI Devices

SDIVIN, SDIVS, SDIVI

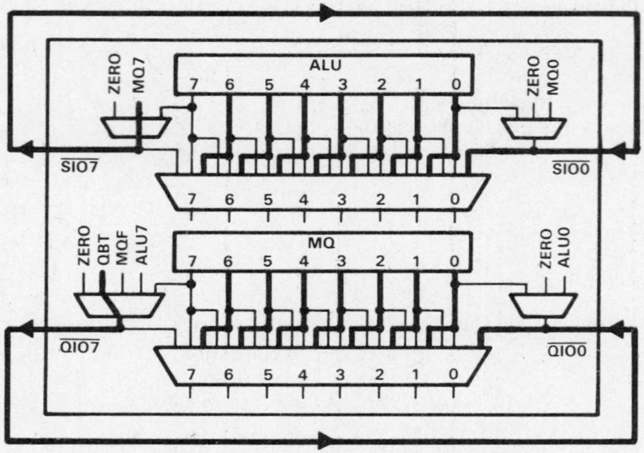
ALU
ZERO
MQ7
ZERO
MQ0
7 6 5 4 3 2 1 0
SIO7
SIO0
MQ
ZERO
QBT
MQF
ALU7
ZERO
ALU0
QIO7
QIO0

SDIVT

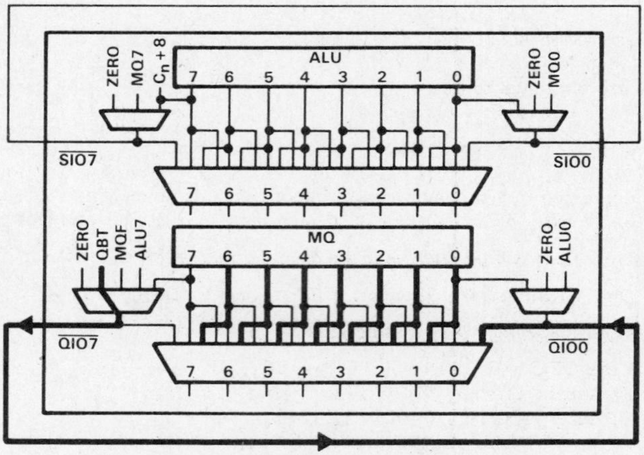
ALU
ZERO
MQ7
C_n+8
ZERO
MQ0
7 6 5 4 3 2 1 0
SIO7
SIO0
MQ
ZERO
QBT
MQF
ALU7
ZERO
ALU0
QIO7
QIO0

FIGURE 9. DIVIDE OPERATIONS

TEXAS INSTRUMENTS
POST OFFICE BOX 225012 • DALLAS, TEXAS 75265

UDIVS, UDIVI

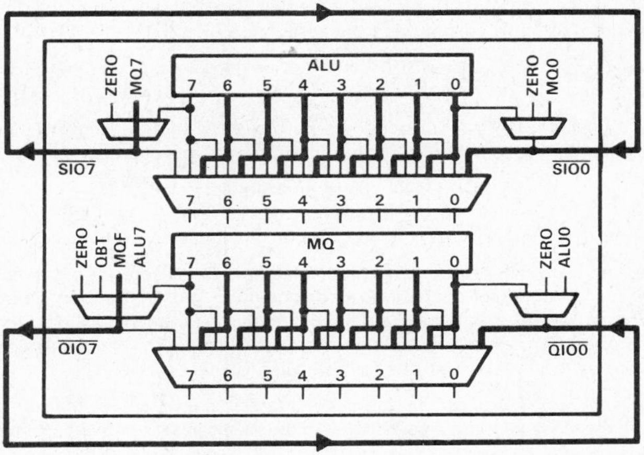
ALU
7 6 5 4 3 2 1 0
ZERO
MQ7
ZERO
MQ0
SIO7
SIO0
MQ
ZERO
QBT
MQF
ALU7
ZERO
ALU0
QIO7
QIO0

UDIVT

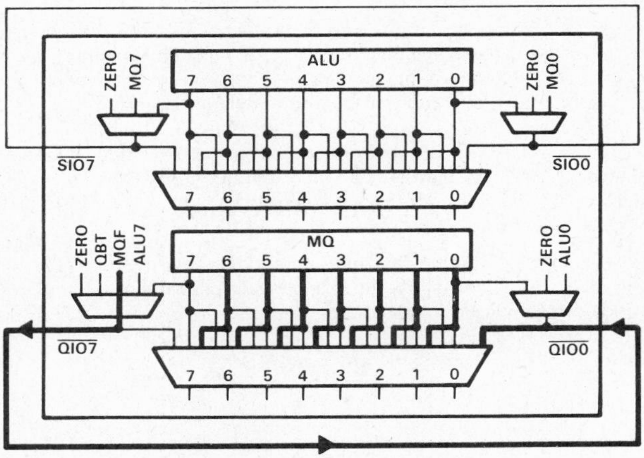
ALU
7 6 5 4 3 2 1 0
ZERO
MQ7
ZERO
MQ0
SIO7
SIO0
MQ
ZERO
QBT
MQF
ALU7
ZERO
ALU0
QIO7
QIO0

FIGURE 9. DIVIDE OPERATIONS (Continued)

The unsigned divide iterate start (UDIVIS) instruction begins the iterate procedure while testing for overflow. Overflow is reported when the first subtraction of the divisor from the MSH of the dividend produces carry out. The test detects quotient overflow and divide by zero.

The unsigned divide iterate terminate (UDIVIT) instruction completes the iterate procedure generating the last quotient bit.

The signed divide initialize (SDIVIN) instruction prepares for iteration by shifting the dividend and storing the sign of the dividend for use in the following instructions and overflow tests.

The signed divide overflow test (SDIVO) checks for overflow possibilities. This instruction may be deleted from the divide operation if the OVR pin is ignored. If it is removed some overflow conditions will go undetected. $\overline{WE}$ must be high (writing inhibited) when this instruction is used.

The signed divide iterate start (SDIVIS) instruction calculates the difference between the divisor and MSH of the dividend. Partial detection of overflow is also done during this instruction. Operations with like signs (positive quotient) and division by zero will overflow during this instruction (including zero divisor). Operations with unlike signs are tested for overflow during the signed divide quotient fix instruction (SDIVQF). Partial overflow results are saved and will be used during SDIVQF when overflow is reported.

The signed divide iterate (SDIVI) instruction forms the quotient and remainder through iterative subtract/add-shift operations of the divisor and dividend. One quotient bit is generated on each clock.

The signed divide iterate terminate (SDIVIT) instruction completes the iterate procedure, generating the last quotient bit. It also tests for a remainder equal to zero, which determines the action to be taken in the following correction (fix) instructions.

The divide remainder fix (DIVRF) instruction corrects the remainder. If a zero remainder was detected by the previous instructions, the remainder is forced to zero. For nonzero remainder cases where the remainder and dividend have the same sign, the remainder is correct. When the remainder and dividend have unlike signs, a correction add/subtract of the divisor to the remainder is performed.

The signed divide quotient fix (SDIVQF) instruction corrects the quotient if necessary. This correction requires adding one to the incorrect quotient. An incorrect quotient results if the signs of the divisor and dividend differ and the remainder is nonzero. An incorrect quotient also results if the sign of the divisor is negative and the remainder is zero.

Overflow detection is completed during this instruction. Overflow may be generated for differing signs of the dividend and divisor. The partial overflow test result performed during SDIVIS is ORed with this test result to produce a true overflow indication.

TEXAS INSTRUMENTS
POST OFFICE BOX 225012 • DALLAS, TEXAS 75265

signed divide usage

The instructions necessary to perform an algebraically correct division of signed numbers are as follows:

Load MQ with the least significant half of the dividend

SDIVIN	S port = MSH of dividend R port = Divisor F port = Intermediate result	
SDIVO	S port = Result of SDIVIN R port = Divisor F port = Test result ($\overline{WE}$ must be high)	
SDIVIS	S port = Result of SDIVIN R port = Divisor F port = Intermediate result	
SDIVI (8N-2 times)	S port = Result of SDIVIS (or SDIVI) R port = Divisor F port = Intermediate result	
SDIVIT	S port = Result of last SDIVI R port = Divisor F port = Intermediate result	
DIVRF	S port = Result of SDIVIT R port = Divisor F port = Remainder	
SDIVQF	S port = MQ register R port = Divisor F port = Quotient	

The status of all signed divide instructions except SDIVIN, DIVRF, and SDIVQF is as follows:

N → Forced to zero
OVR → Forced to zero
C_{n+8} → Carry out equal to one
Z → Intermediate result is zero

The status of the SDIVIN instruction is as follows:

N → Forced to zero
OVR → Forced to zero
C_{n+8} → Forced to zero
Z → Divisor is zero

The status of the DIVRF instruction is as follows:

N → Forced to zero
OVR → Forced to zero
C_{n+8} → Carry out equal to one
Z → Remainder is zero

2
LSI Devices

The status of the SDIVQF instruction is as follows:

N → Sign of quotient
OVR → Divide overflow
C_{n+8} → Carry out equal to one
Z → Quotient is zero

The quotient is stored in the MQ register and the remainder is stored in the register file location that originally held the most significant word of the dividend. If fractions are divided, the quotient must be shifted right one bit and the remainder right three bits to obtain the correct fractional representations.

The signed division algorithm is summarized in Table 7.

TABLE 7. SIGNED DIVISION ALGORITHM

OP CODE	MNEMONIC	CLOCK CYCLES	INPUT S PORT	INPUT R PORT	OUTPUT F PORT
E4	LOADMQ	1	Dividend (LSH)	—	Dividend (LSH)
80	SDIVIN	1	Dividend (MSH)	Divisor	Remainder
AF	SDIVO	1	Remainder	Divisor	Test Result
90	SDIVIS	1	Remainder	Divisor	Remainder
A0	SDIVI	7	Remainder	Divisor	Remainder
E0	SDIVIT	1	Remainder	Divisor	Remainder (Unfixed)
40	DIVRF	1	Remainder (Unfixed)	Divisor	Remainder
50	SDIVQF	1	MQ Register	Divisor	Quotient

unsigned divide usage

The instructions necessary to perform an algebraically correct division of unsigned numbers are as follows:

Load MQ with the least significant half of the dividend

UDIVIS
S port = MSH of dividend
R port = Divisor
F port = Intermediate result

UDIVI (8-1 times)
S port = Result of UDIVIS (OR UDIVI)
R port = Divisor
F port = Intermediate result

UDIVIT
S port = Result of last UDIVI
R port = Divisor
F port = Remainder (unfixed)

DIVRF
S port = Result of UDIVIT
R port = Divisor
F port = Remainder

The status of all unsigned divide instructions except UDIVIS is as follows:

N → Forced to zero
OVR → Forced to zero
C_{n+8} → Carry out equal to one
Z → Intermediate result is zero

The status of the UDIVIS instruction is as follows:

N → Forced to zero
OVR → Divide overflow
C_{n+8} → Carry out equal to one
Z → Intermediate result is zero

If fractions are divided, the remainder must be shifted right two bits to obtain the correct fractional representation. The quotient is correct as is. The quotient is stored in the MQ register at the completion of the divide.

The unsigned division algorithm is summarized in Table 8.

TABLE 8. UNSIGNED DIVISION ALGORITHM

OP CODE	MNEMONIC	CLOCK CYCLES	INPUT S PORT	INPUT R PORT	OUTPUT F PORT
E4	LOADMQ	1	Dividend (LSH)	—	Dividend (LSH)
B0	UDIVIS	1	Dividend (MSH)	Divisor	Remainder
C0	UDIVI	7	Remainder	Divisor	Remainder
F0	UDIVIT	1	Remainder	Divisor	Remainder (Unfixed)
40	DIVRF	1	Remainder (Unfixed)	Divisor	Remainder

group 5 instructions

Hex code F of Group 1 instructions is used to access Group 5 instructions. Group 5 instructions are summarized in Table 9.

TABLE 9. GROUP 5 INSTRUCTIONS

INSTRUCTION BITS (I7-I0) OP CODE (HEX)	MNEMONIC	FUNCTION
0F	CLR	Clear
1F	CLR	Clear
2F	CLR	Clear
3F	CLR	Clear
4F	CLR	Clear
5F	CLR	Clear
6F	CLR	Clear
7F	BCDBIN	BCD to Binary
8F		Reserved
9F	EX3C	Excess-3 Word Correction
AF	SDIVO	Signed Divide Overflow Check
BF	CLR	Clear
CF	CLR	Clear
DF	BINEX3	Binary to Excess-3
EF	CLR	Clear
FF	NOP	No Operation

clear instructions (CLR)

There are 11 clear instructions listed in Table 9. The instructions force the ALU output to be zero and the BCD flip-flops to be cleared. The status set by the clear instruction is as follows:

N → None (force to zero)
OVR → None (force to zero)
C_{n+8} → None (force to zero)
Z → Active (one)

no operation instruction (NOP): I7-I0 = FF_{16}

This instruction is identical to the clear instructions except that the BCD flip-flops retain their old value.

excess-3 correction instructions (EX3C): $9F_{16}$

This instruction corrects excess-3 additions (subtractions). For correct excess-3 arithmetic, this instruction must follow each add/subtract. The operand must be on the S port.

NOTE: The previous arithmetic overflow should be ignored.

The status set by the EX3C instruction is as follows:

N → MSB of result
OVR → Signed overflow
C_{n+8} → Carry out equal one
Z → None (force to one)

radix conversions

Conversions between decimal and binary number representations are performed with the aid of two special instructions: BINEX3 and BCDBIN.

BCD to binary instructions (BCDBIN): I7-I0 = $7F_{16}$

This instruction (Figure 10) allows the user to convert a 2-digit BCD number to an 8-bit binary number in 12 clocks. This function sums the R bus, the S bus, and the C_n bit, performs an arithmetic left shift on the ALU result, and simultaneously circular shifts the MQ left. The status set by the BCD to binary instruction is as follows:

N → MSB of result
OVR → Signed arithmetic overflow†
C_{n+8} → Carry out equal one
Z → Result equal zero

† Overflow may be the result of an ALU operation or the arithmetic left shift operation.

The following code illustrates the BCD to binary conversion technique.

Let ACC be an accumulator register
Let NUM be the register which contains the BCD number
Let MSK be a mask register

```
LOADMQ NUM                        ; LOAD MQ WITH BCD NUMBER
SUB ACC, ACC, SLCMQ               ; CLEAR ACC AND ALIGN MQ
SUB, MSK, MSK, SLCMQ              ; CLEAR MSK AND ALIGN MQ
SLCMQ                             ; ALIGN
SLCMQ                             ; ALIGN
ADDI ACC, MSK, 15(10)             ; MSK = 15(10)
AND MQ, MSK, R1, SLCMQ            ; EXTRACT ONE DIGIT
                                  ; ALIGN MQ
ADD, ACC, R1, R1, SLCMQ           ; ACC + DIGIT
                                  ; IS STORED IN R1
                                  ; ALIGN MQ
BCDBIN, R1, R1, ACC               ; 4 x (ACC + DIGIT)
                                  ; IS STORED IN ACC
                                  ; ALIGN MQ
BCDBIN, ACC, R1, ACC              ; 10 x (ACC + DIGIT)
                                  ; IS STORED IN ACC
                                  ; ALIGN MQ
AND MQ, MSK, R1                   ; FETCH LAST DIGIT
ACC+R1 → ACC                      ; ADD IN LAST DIGIT
```

The previous code generates a binary number by executing the standard conversion formula for a 2-digit BCD number.

$$AB = A \times 10 + B$$

Notice that the conversion begins with the most significant BCD digit and that the addition is performed in radix 2.

binary to excess-3 instructions (BINEX3): I7-I0 = DF_{16}

This instruction (Figure 11) allows the user to convert an 8-bit binary number to 2-digit excess-3 number representation in 19 clocks. The data on the R and S ports are summed with the MSB of the MQ register. The MQ register is simultaneously shifted left circularly. The status set by the binary to excess-3 instruction is as follows:

N	→	MSB of result
OVR	→	Signed arithmetic overflow
C_{n+8}	→	Carry out equal one
Z	→	Result equal zero

BCDBIN

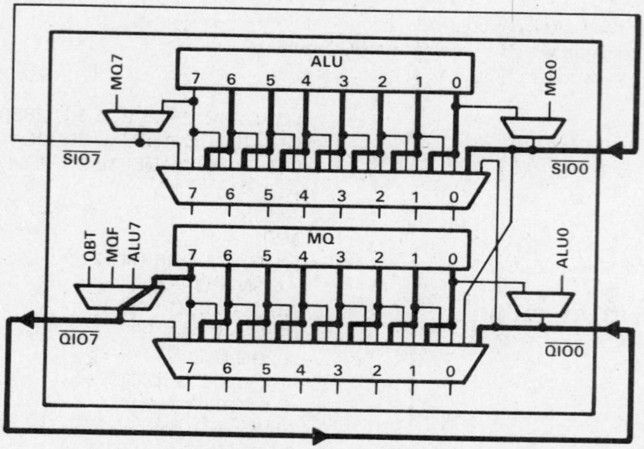
ALU
7 6 5 4 3 2 1 0
MQ7
MQ0
SIO7
SIO0
MQ
QBT
MQF
ALU7
ALU0
QIO7
QIO0

FIGURE 10. BCD TO BINARY

BINEX3

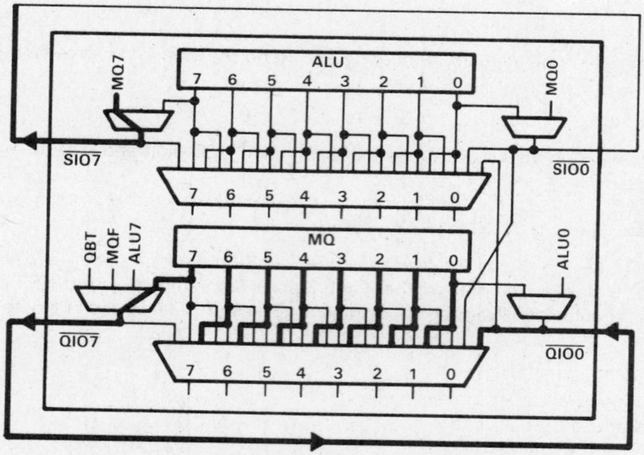
ALU
7 6 5 4 3 2 1 0
MQ7
MQ0
SIO7
SIO0
MQ
QBT
MQF
ALU7
ALU0
QIO7
QIO0

FIGURE 11. BINARY TO EXCESS-3

TEXAS INSTRUMENTS
POST OFFICE BOX 225012 • DALLAS, TEXAS 75265

The following illustrates the binary to excess-3 conversion technique.

Let NUM be a register containing an unsigned binary number
Let ACC be an accumulator

```
M1:     LOADMQ NUM              ; LOAD MQ WITH BINARY
                                ; NUMBER
M2:     CLEAR ACC               ; CLEAR ACC
M3:     SET1 ACC H/33/          ; ACC → HEX/3333 . . .
L1:     BINEX3 ACC, ACC, ACC    ; DOUBLE ACC AND ADD IN
                                ; MSB OF MQ
                                ; ALIGN MQ
L2:     EX3C ACC, ACC           ; EXCESS 3 CORRECT
                                ; REPEAT L1 AND L2
                                ; 7 TIMES
```

The previous code generates an excess-3 number by executing the standard conversion formula for a binary number.

$$a_n 2^n + a_{n-1} 2^{n-1} + a_{n-2} 2^{n-2} + \ldots a_0 2^0 = [(2a_n + a_{n-1})2 + a_{n-2}]2 + \ldots a_0$$

Notice that the conversion begins with the most significant binary bit and that the addition is performed in radix-10 (excess-3).

decimal arithmetic

Decimal numbers are represented in excess-3 code. Excess-3 code numbers may be generated by adding three to each digit of a Binary Coded Decimal (BCD) number. The hardware necessary to implement excess-3 arithmetic is only slightly different from binary arithmetic. Carries from one digit to another during addition in BCD occur when the sum of the two digits plus the carry-in is greater than or equal to ten. If both numbers are excess-3, the sum will be excess-6, which will produce the proper carries. Therefore, every addition or subtraction operation may use the binary adder. To convert the result from excess-6 to excess-3, one must consider two cases resulting from a BCD digit add: (1) where a carry-out is produced, and (2) where a carry-out is not produced. If a carry-out is not produced, three must be subtracted from the resulting digit. If a carry is produced, the digit is correct as a BCD number. For example, if BCD 5 is added to BCD 6, the excess-3 result would be $8 + 9 = 1$ (with a carry). A carry rolls the number through the illegal BCD representations into a correct BCD representation. Binary 3 must be added to digit positions that produce a carry-out to correct the result to an excess-3 representation. Every addition and subtraction instruction stores the carry generated from each 4-bit digit location for use by the excess-3 correction function. The correction instruction must be executed in the clock cycle immediately after the addition or subtraction operation.

absolute maximum rating over operating free-air temperature range (unless otherwise noted)

Supply voltage, V_{CC1} . . . . 7 V
Supply voltage, V_{CC2} . . . . 3 V
Input voltage . . . . 7 V
High-level voltage applied to 3-state outputs . . . . 5.5 V
Operating case temperature range: SN54AS887 . . . . −55°C to 125°C
Operating free-air temperature range: SN74AS887, SN74AS887-1 . . . . 0°C to 70°C
Storage temperature range . . . . −65°C to 150°C

recommended operating conditions

			SN54AS887			SN74AS887 SN74AS887-1			UNIT
			MIN	NOM	MAX	MIN	NOM	MAX	
V_{CC1}	I/O supply voltage		4.5	5	5.5	4.5	5	5.5	V
V_{CC2}	STL internal logic supply voltage		1.9	2	2.1	1.9	2	2.1	V
V_{IH}	High-level input voltage		2			2			V
V_{IL}	Low-level input voltage				0.8			0.8	V
I_{OH}	High-level output current				−1			−2.6	mA
I_{OL}	Low-level output current	All output except N and ZERO			8			8	mA
		N			16			16	
		ZERO			48			48	
T_C	Operating case temperature		−55		125				°C
T_A	Operating free-air temperature					0		70	

electrical characteristics over recommended operating free-air temperature range (unless otherwise noted)

PARAMETER		TEST CONDITIONS	SN54AS887			SN74AS887 SN74AS887-1			UNIT
			MIN	TYP†	MAX	MIN	TYP†	MAX	
V_{IK}		V_{CC1} = 4.5 V, I_I = −18 mA			−1.2			−1.2	V
V_{OH}	All outputs except ZERO	V_{CC1} = 4.5 V to 5.5 V, I_{OH} = −0.4 mA	V_{CC}−2			V_{CC}−2			V
		V_{CC1} = 4.5 V, I_{OH} = −1 mA	2.4						
		V_{CC1} = 4.5 V, I_{OH} = −2.6 mA				2.4			
I_{OH}	ZERO	V_{CC1} = 4.5 V, V_{OH} = 5.5 V			0.1			0.1	mA
V_{OL}	All outputs except N and ZERO	V_{CC1} = 4.5 V, I_{OL} = 8 mA			0.5			0.5	V
	N	V_{CC1} = 4.5 V, I_{OL} = 16 mA			0.5			0.5	
	ZERO	V_{CC1} = 4.5 V, I_{OL} = 48 mA			0.5			0.5	
I_I	I/O	V_{CC1} = 5.5 V, V_I = 5.5 V			0.1			0.1	mA
	All others	V_{CC1} = 5.5 V, V_I = 7 V			0.1			0.1	
I_{IH}‡		V_{CC1} = 5.5 V, V_I = 2.7 V			20			20	μA
I_{IL}‡		V_{CC1} = 5.5 V, V_I = 0.5 V			−0.4			−0.4	mA
I_O§		V_{CC1} = 5.5 V, V_O = 2.25 V	−30		−112	−30		−112	mA
I_{CC1}		V_{CC1} = 5.5 V			150			130	mA
I_{CC2}		V_{CC2} = 2.1 V			410			390	mA

†All typical values are at V_{CC} = 5 V, T_A = 25°C.
‡For I/O ports, the parameters I_{IH} and I_{IL} include the off-state current.
§The output conditions have been chosen to produce a current that closely approximates one-half the true short-circuit current, I_{OS}.

SN54AS887 maximum switching characteristics, V_{CC} = 4.5 V to 5.5 V, T_C = −55°C to 125°C (see Note 1)

PARAMETER	FROM (INPUT)	TO (OUTPUT)										UNIT
		Y	C_{n+8}	$\overline{G}$, $\overline{P}$	Z†	N	OVR	DA	DB	$\overline{QIO}$	$\overline{SIO}$	
t_{pd}	A3-A0 B3-B0	62	42	48	69	62	60	18	18	65	66	ns
	DA7-DA0, DB7-DB0	47	28	28	58	50	42	—	—	50	50	
	C_n	25	14	—	32	24	18	—	—	32	32	
	$\overline{EA}$	54	32	35	62	52	52	—	—	58	58	
	$\overline{EB}$	54	32	35	62	52	52	—	—	58	58	
	I7-I0	58	32	32	62	52	41	—	—	58	58	
	$\overline{OEB}$	—	—	—	—	—	—	—	14	—	—	
	$\overline{OEY}$	14	—	—	—	—	—	—	—	—	—	
	$\overline{QIO}$ (n) Shift	15	—	—	24	—	—	—	—	—	—	
	$\overline{SIO}$ (n) Shift	15	—	—	24	22	—	—	—	—	—	
	CK	68	60	56	62	50	68	38	38	70	70	
	$\overline{OEA}$	—	—	—	—	—	—	14	—	—	—	

†Load resistor R1 = 100 Ω.
NOTE 1: Load circuit and voltage waveforms are shown in Section 1.

SN74AS887 maximum switching characteristics, V_{CC} = 4.5 V to 5.5 V, T_A = 0°C to 70°C (see Note 1)

PARAMETER	FROM (INPUT)	TO (OUTPUT)										UNIT
		Y	C_{n+8}	$\overline{G}$, $\overline{P}$	Z†	N	OVR	DA	DB	$\overline{QIO}$	$\overline{SIO}$	
t_{pd}	A3-A0 B3-B0	54	36	42	60	52	50	18	18	58	58	ns
	DA7-DA0, DB7-DB0	44	26	26	52	46	38	—	—	44	44	
	C_n	25	8	—	32	24	18	—	—	31	31	
	$\overline{EA}$	49	29	29	58	49	47	—	—	54	54	
	$\overline{EB}$	49	29	29	58	49	47	—	—	54	54	
	I7-I0	55	30	30	60	49	39	—	—	54	54	
	$\overline{OEB}$	—	—	—	—	—	—	—	12	—	—	
	$\overline{OEY}$	12	—	—	—	—	—	—	—	—	—	
	$\overline{QIO}$ (n) Shift	15	—	—	24	—	—	—	—	—	—	
	$\overline{SIO}$ (n) Shift	15	—	—	24	19	—	—	—	—	—	
	CK	58	55	52	61	52	62	35	35	60	60	
	$\overline{OEA}$	—	—	—	—	—	—	12	—	—	—	

†Load resistor R1 = 100 Ω.
NOTE 1: Load circuit and voltage waveforms are shown in Section 1.

SN74AS887-1 maximum switching characteristics, V_{CC} = 4.5 V to 5.5 V, T_A = 0 °C to 70 °C (see Note 1)

PARAMETER	FROM (INPUT)	TO (OUTPUT)										UNIT
		Y	C_{n+8}	$\overline{G}$, $\overline{P}$	Z†	N	OVR	DA	DB	$\overline{QIO}$	$\overline{SIO}$	
t_{pd}	A3-A0 B3-B0	44	30	36	50	44	44	17	17	48	48	ns
	DA7-DA0, DB7-DB0	36	24	24	46	41	32	—	—	40	40	
	C_n	22	8	—	27	21	16	—	—	25	25	
	$\overline{EA}$	40	25	25	49	41	41	—	—	44	44	
	$\overline{EB}$	40	25	25	49	41	41	—	—	44	44	
	I7-I0	46	27	27	50	42	35	—	—	45	45	
	$\overline{OEB}$	—	—	—	—	—	—	—	12	—	—	
	$\overline{OEY}$	12	—	—	—	—	—	—	—	—	—	
	$\overline{QIO}$ (n) Shift	14	—	—	20	—	—	—	—	—	—	
	$\overline{SIO}$ (n) Shift	14	—	—	20	18	—	—	—	—	—	
	CK	50	46	46	50	50	50	30	30	50	50	
	$\overline{OEA}$	—	—	—	—	—	—	12	—	—	—	

† Load resistor R1 = 100 Ω.

NOTE 1: Load circuit and voltage waveforms are shown in Section 1.

register file write setup and hold times

PARAMETER		SN54AS887 MIN	SN54AS887 MAX	SN74AS887 MIN	SN74AS887 MAX	SN74AS887-1 MIN	SN74AS887-1 MAX	UNIT
t_{su}	C3-C0	8		7		6		ns
	DB§	14		12		11		
	I7-I4	16		14		13		
	I3-I0	24		22		21		
	$\overline{OEY}$	4		3		3		
	Y7-Y0	2		2		2		
	$\overline{WE}$	8		6		6		
	$\overline{QIO}$(n), $\overline{SIO}$(n)	6		5		5		
	SELY	8		6		6		
t_h	C3-C0	0		0		0		ns
	DB§	0		0		0		
	I7-I4	0		0		0		
	I3-I0	0		0		0		
	$\overline{OEY}$	6		5		5		
	Y7-Y0	10		10		10		
	$\overline{WE}$	3		2		2		
	$\overline{QIO}$(n), $\overline{SIO}$(n)	0		0		0		
	SELY	8		6		6		

§ DB (during select instruction) through Y port.

special instruction switching characteristics

The SSF pin is used internally during certain instructions. The following tables list the instructions which force the SSF pin during their execution. The propagation delay from various inputs is also shown. The parameter which limits normal system performance is indicated by a dagger.

SN54AS887 SSF PIN DELAYS AND SETUP TIMES

MNEMONIC	HEX CODE	INPUT → SSF (ns)				SSF SETUP TIME (ns)
		C_n	$I_{(n)}$	CK	$B_{(n)}$	
SNORM	20	—	29†	46	—	20
DNORM	30	—	29	55	40†	20
DIVRF	40	—	29†	46	—	20
SDIVQF	50	—	26†	—	—	18
SMULI	60	—	26†	43	—	0
SDIVIN	80	—	48	64	44†	0
SDIVIS	90	26†	51	64	55	0
SDIVI	A0	26†	51	64	55	0
UDIVIS	B0	18†	45	64	46	0
UDIVI	C0	18†	50	54	40	0
UMULI	D0	—	25†	48	—	0
SDIVIT	E0	26†	50	56	54	0
ABX	48	—	34	62	39†	20
SMTC	58	—	29	58	39†	20
BINEX3	DF	—	29†	58	—	18
LOADMQ (Arith)		23†	34	62	40	0
LOADMQ (Log)		—	33	62	40†	0

† This parameter limits normal system performance.

2

LSI Devices

SN74AS887 SSF PIN DELAYS AND SETUP TIMES

MNEMONIC	HEX CODE	INPUT → SSF (ns)				SSF SETUP TIME (ns)
		C_n	$I_{(n)}$	CK	$B_{(n)}$	
SNORM	20	–	26†	40	–	17
DNORM	30	–	26	52	37†	17
DIVRF	40	–	26†	40	–	17
SDIVQF	50	–	25†	–	–	17
SMULI	60	–	25†	40	–	0
SDIVIN	80	–	38	60	40†	0
SDIVIS	90	24†	48	60	52	0
SDIVI	A0	24†	48	60	52	0
UDIVIS	B0	17†	43	60	45	0
UDIVI	C0	17†	44	52	37	0
UMULI	D0	–	26†	40	–	0
SDIVIT	E0	25†	46	52	49	0
ABX	48	–	32	60	38	17
SMTC	58	–	26	52	38†	17
BINEX3	DF	–	26†	40	–	17
LOADMQ (Arith)		22†	32	50	38	0
LOADMQ (Log)		–	32	50	38†	0

† This parameter limits normal system performance.

SN74AS887-1 SSF PIN DELAYS AND SETUP TIMES

MNEMONIC	HEX CODE	INPUT → SSF (ns)				SSF SETUP TIME (ns)
		C_n	$I_{(n)}$	CK	$B_{(n)}$	
SNORM	20	–	23†	28	–	14
DNORM	30	–	23	40	34†	14
DIVRF	40	–	23†	27	–	14
SDIVQF	50	–	23†	–	–	14
SMULI	60	–	22†	27	–	0
SDIVIN	80	–	35	46	35†	0
SDIVIS	90	22†	42	48	42	0
SDIVI	A0	22†	42	46	42	0
UDIVIS	B0	16†	42	46	38	0
UDIVI	C0	16†	36	46	34	0
UMULI	D0	–	22†	27	–	0
SDIVIT	E0	21†	40	44	42	0
ABX	48	–	28	46	30†	14
SMTC	58	–	24	44	30†	14
BINEX3	DF	–	23†	27	–	14
LOADMQ (Arith)		19†	28	40	30	0
LOADMQ (Log)		–	28	35	30†	0

† This parameter limits normal system performance.

MARCH 1985—REVISED JANUARY 1986

- STL-AS Technology
- Parallel 8-Bit ALU with Expansion Inputs and Outputs
- 13 Arithmetic and Logic Functions
- 8 Conditional Shifts (Single and Double Length)
- 9 Instructions that Manipulate Bytes
- 4 Instructions that Manipulate Bits
- Add and Subtract Immediate Instructions
- Absolute Value Instruction
- Signed Magnitude to/from Two's Complement Conversion
- Single- and Double-Length Normalize
- Select Functions
- Signed and Unsigned Divides with Overflow Detection; Input does not Need to be Prescaled
- Signed, Mixed, and Unsigned Multiplies
- Three-Operand, 16-Word Register File
- Full Carry Look Ahead Support
- Sign, Carry Out, Overflow, and Zero-Detect Status Capabilities
- Excess-3 BCD Arithmetic
- Internal Shift Multiplexers that Eliminate the Need for External Shift Control Parts
- ALU Bypass Path to Increase Speeds of Multiply, Divide, and Normalize Instructions and to Provide New Instructions such as Bit Set, Bit Reset, Bit Test, Byte Subtract, Byte Add, and Byte Logical
- 3-Operand Register Files to Allow an Operation and a Move Instruction to be Combined
- Byte Select Controlled by External 3-State Buffers that may be Eliminated if Bit and Byte Manipulation are not Needed
- Bit and Byte Masks that are Shared with Register Address Fields to Minimize Control Store Word Width
- 3 Data Input/Output Paths to Maximize Data Throughput

description

These 8-bit Advanced Schottky TTL integrated circuits are designed to implement high performance digital computers or controllers. An architecture and instruction set has been chosen that supports a fast system clock, a narrow micro-code word width, and a high system throughput. The powerful instruction set allows high-speed system architecture to be implemented and also allows an existing system's performance to be upgraded while protecting software investments. These processors are designed to be cascadable to any word width 16 bits or greater.

The SN54AS888 is characterized for operation over the full military temperature range of −55 °C to 125 °C. The SN74AS888 and SN74AS888-1 are characterized for operation from 0 °C to 70 °C.

Package options include both plastic and ceramic chip carriers in addition to a 68-pin grid array ceramic package.

SN54AS888, SN74AS888 . . . GB PACKAGE

(TOP VIEW)

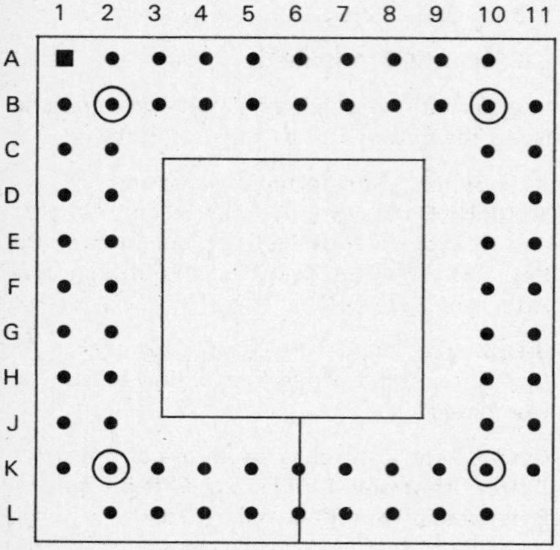
1 2 3 4 5 6 7 8 9 10 11
A
B
C
D
E
F
G
H
J
K
L

SN54AS888 . . . FK PACKAGE
SN74AS888 . . . FN PACKAGE

(TOP VIEW)

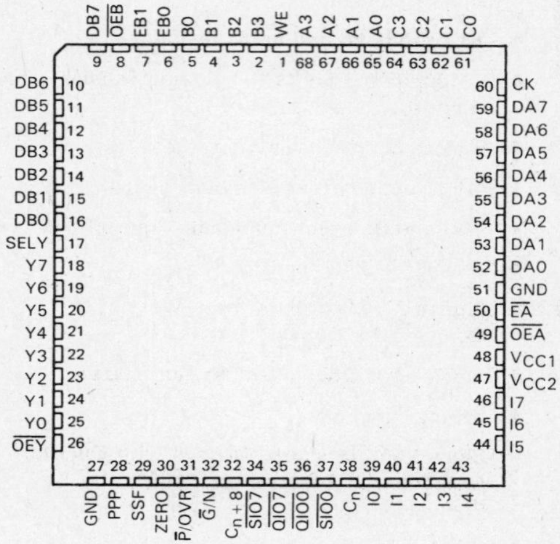
DB7 $\overline{OEB}$ EB1 EB0 B0 B1 B2 B3 WE A3 A2 A1 A0 C3 C2 C1 C0
9 8 7 6 5 4 3 2 1 68 67 66 65 64 63 62 61
DB6 10
DB5 11
DB4 12
DB3 13
DB2 14
DB1 15
DB0 16
SELY 17
Y7 18
Y6 19
Y5 20
Y4 21
Y3 22
Y2 23
Y1 24
Y0 25
$\overline{OEY}$ 26
60 CK
59 DA7
58 DA6
57 DA5
56 DA4
55 DA3
54 DA2
53 DA1
52 DA0
51 GND
50 $\overline{EA}$
49 $\overline{OEA}$
48 V_{CC1}
47 V_{CC2}
46 I7
45 I6
44 I5
27 28 29 30 31 32 32 34 35 36 37 38 39 40 41 42 43
GND PPP SSF ZERO $\overline{P}$/OVR $\overline{G}$/N C_{n+8} $\overline{SIO7}$ $\overline{QIO7}$ $\overline{QIO0}$ $\overline{SIO0}$ C_n I0 I1 I2 I3 I4

GB PACKAGE PIN ASSIGNMENTS

PIN	NAME	PIN	NAME	PIN	NAME	PIN	NAME
A-2	C_n	B-9	$\overline{OEY}$	F-10	Y3	K-4	C2
A-3	$\overline{SIO0}$	B-10	Y0	F-11	DB2	K-5	A0
A-4	$\overline{QIO0}$	B-11	Y1	G-1	DA2	K-6	A3
A-5	$\overline{QIO7}$	C-1	I5	G-2	DA0	K-7	$\overline{WE}$
A-6	C_{n+8}	C-2	V_{CC2}	G-10	DB0	K-8	DB7
A-7	$\overline{G}$/N	C-10	Y4	G-11	DB3	K-9	$\overline{OEB}$
A-8	$\overline{P}$/OVR	C-11	Y6	H-1	DA3	K-10	EB0
A-9	ZERO	D-1	I6	H-2	DA1	K-11	EB1
A-10	PPP	D-2	V_{CC1}	H-10	DB6	L-2	CK
B-1	I2	D-10	Y5	H-11	DB4	L-3	C1
B-2	I3	D-11	Y7	J-1	DA4	L-4	C3
B-3	I1	E-1	I7	J-2	DA5	L-5	A1
B-4	I0	E-2	$\overline{OEA}$	J-10	SELY	L-6	A2
B-5	I4	E-10	Y2	J-11	DB5	L-7	B3
B-6	$\overline{SIO7}$	E-11	DB1	K-1	DA6	L-8	B2
B-7	SSF	F-1	$\overline{EA}$	K-2	DA7	L-9	B1
B-8		F-2	GND	K-3	C0	L-10	B0

2

LSI Devices

PIN FUNCTIONAL DESCRIPTION

PIN GRID ARRAY	CHIP CARRIER	NAME	I/O	DESCRIPTION
A-10	28	PPP	I	Package position pin. Tri-level input used to define package significance during instruction execution. Leave open for intermediate positions, tie to V_{CC} for most significant package, and tie to GND for least significant package.
B-7	29	SSF	I/O	Special shift function. Used to transfer required information between packages during special instruction execution.
A-9	30	ZERO	I/O	Device zero detection, open collector. Input during certain special instructions.
A-8	31	$\overline{P}$/OVR	O	ALU propagate/instruction overflow for most significant package, low active.
A-7	32	$\overline{G}$/N	O	ALU generate/negative result for most significant package, low active.
A-6	33	C_{n+8}	O	ALU ripple carry output.
B-6	34	$\overline{SIO7}$	I/O	Bidirectional shift pin, low active.
A-5	35	$\overline{QIO7}$	I/O	
A-4	36	$\overline{QIO0}$	I/O	
A-3	37	$\overline{SIO0}$	I/O	
A-2	38	C_n	I	ALU carry input.
B-4	39	I0	I	Instruction input.
B-3	40	I1	I	
B-1	41	I2	I	
B-2	42	I3	I	
B-5	43	I4	I	
C-1	44	I5	I	
D-1	45	I6	I	
E-1	46	I7	I	
C-2	47	V_{CC2}		Low voltage power supply (2 V).
D-2	48	V_{CC1}		I/O interface supply voltage (5 V).
E-2	49	$\overline{OEA}$	I	DA bus enable, low active.
F-1	50	$\overline{EA}$	I	ALU input operand select. High state selects external DA bus and low state selects register file.
F-2	51	GND		Ground pin.
G-2	52	DA0	I/O	A port data bus. Outputs register file data ($\overline{EA}$ = 0) or inputs external data ($\overline{EA}$ = 1).
H-2	53	DA1	I/O	
G-1	54	DA2	I/O	
H-1	55	DA3	I/O	
J-1	56	DA4	I/O	
J-2	57	DA5	I/O	
K-1	58	DA6	I/O	
K-2	59	DA7	I/O	
L-2	60	CK	I	Clocks all synchronous registers on positive edge.
K-3	61	C0	I	Register file write address select.
L-3	62	C1	I	
K-4	63	C2	I	
L-4	64	C3	I	
K-5	65	A0	I	Register file A port read address select.
L-5	66	A1	I	
L-6	67	A2	I	
K-6	68	A3	I	

PIN FUNCTIONAL DESCRIPTION

PIN GRID ARRAY	CHIP CARRIER	NAME	I/O	DESCRIPTION
K-7	1	$\overline{WE}$	I	Register file (RF) write enable. Data is written into RF when $\overline{WE}$ is low and a low-to-high clock transition occurs. RF write is inhibited when $\overline{WE}$ is high.
L-7	2	B3	I	Register file B port read address select. (0 = LSB).
L-8	3	B2	I	
L-9	4	B1	I	
L-10	5	B0	I	
K-10	6	EB0	I	ALU input operand select. EB0 and EB1 selects the source of data that the S multiplexer provides for the S bus. Independent control of the DB bus and data path selection allow the user to isolate the DB bus while the ALU continues to process data.
K-11	7	EB1	1	
K-9	8	$\overline{OEB}$	I	DB bus enable, low active.
K-8	9	DB7	I/O	B port data bus. Outputs register data ($\overline{OEB}$ = 0) or used to input external data ($\overline{OEB}$ = 1), (0 = LSB).
H-10	10	DB6	I/O	
J-11	11	DB5	I/O	
H-11	12	DB4	I/O	
G-11	13	DB3	I/O	
F-11	14	DB2	I/O	
E-11	15	DB1	I/O	
G-10	16	DB0	I/O	
J-10	17	SELY	I	Y bus select, high active.
D-11	18	Y7	I/O	Y port data bus. Outputs instruction results ($\overline{OEY}$ = 0) or used to put external data into register file ($\overline{OEY}$ = 1).
C-11	19	Y6	I/O	
D-10	20	Y5	I/O	
C-10	21	Y4	I/O	
F-10	22	Y3	I/O	
E-10	23	Y2	I/O	
B-11	24	Y1	I/O	
B-10	25	Y0	I/O	
B-9	26	$\overline{OEY}$	I	Y bus output enable, low active.
F-2	27	GND		Ground pin

TEXAS INSTRUMENTS
POST OFFICE BOX 225012 • DALLAS, TEXAS 75265

functional block diagram

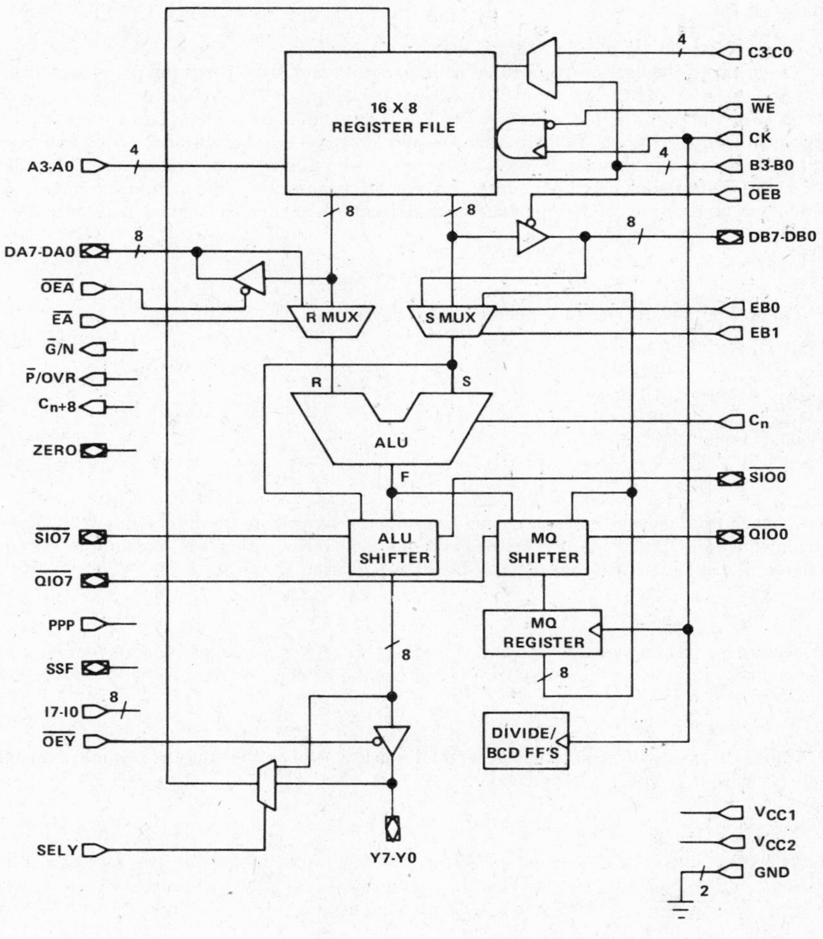
16 X 8
REGISTER FILE
C3-C0
WE
CK
B3-B0
OEB
DB7-DB0
A3-A0
DA7-DA0
OEA
EA
G/N
P/OVR
Cn+8
ZERO
R MUX
S MUX
EB0
EB1
R
S
ALU
Cn
F
SIO0
SIO7
ALU
SHIFTER
MQ
SHIFTER
QIO0
QIO7
MQ
REGISTER
PPP
SSF
I7-I0
OEY
DIVIDE/
BCD FF'S
SELY
Y7-Y0
VCC1
VCC2
GND

architectural elements

3-port register file

Working registers consist of 128 storage elements organized into sixteen 8-bit words. These storage elements appear to the user as 16 positive edge-triggered registers. The three port addresses, one write (C) and two reads (A and B), are completely independent of each other to implement a 3-operand register file. Data is written into the register file when $\overline{WE}$ is low and a low-to-high clock transition occurs. The ADD and SUBTRACT immediate instructions require only one source operand. The B address is used as the source address, and the bits of the A address are used to provide a constant field. The SET, RESET, and TEST BIT instructions use the B addressed register as both the source and destination register while the A and C addresses are used as masks. These instructions are explained in more detail in the instruction section.

S multiplexer

The S multiplexer selects the ALU operand, as follows:

EB1	EB0	S bus
Low	Low	RF data
Low	High	MQ data
High	Low	DB data
High	High	MQ data

DB port

Data is passed through the ALU or received from the register file on the 8-bit DB port. If $\overline{OEB}$ is low, the DB bus is active; if $\overline{OEB}$ is high, the DB bus is in the high impedance state. Notice that the DB port may be isolated at the same time that register file data is passed to the ALU.

R multiplexer

The R multiplexer selects the other operand of the ALU. Except for those instructions that require constants or masks, the R bus will contain DA if $\overline{EA}$ is high or the RF data pointed to by A if $\overline{EA}$ is low.

DA bus

The DA bus is active (with register file data) if $\overline{OEA}$ is low. Notice that the DA bus may be isolated while register file data is passed to the ALU.

ALU

The shift instructions are summarized in Table 4 and illustrated in Figure 2. The ALU can perform seven arithmetic and six logical instructions on two 8-bit operands. It also supports multiplication, division, normalization, bit set, reset, test, byte operations, and excess-3 BCD arithmetic. These source operands are the outputs of the S and R multiplexers.

ALU and MQ shifters

ALU and MQ shifters perform all of the shift, multiply, divide, and normalize functions. Table 4 shows the value of the $\overline{SIO7}$ and $\overline{QIO7}$ pins of the most significant package. The standard shifts may be made into conditional shifts and the serial data may be input or output with the aid of two three-state gates. These capabilities are discussed further in the arithmetic and logic section.

TEXAS INSTRUMENTS
POST OFFICE BOX 225012 • DALLAS, TEXAS 75265

MQ register

The multiplier-quotient (MQ) register has specific functions in multiplication, division, and normalization. This register may also be used as a temporary storage register. The MQ register may be loaded if the instruction code on pins I7-I0 is E1-E7 or E9-EE (See Table 1).

Y bus

The Y bus contains the output of the ALU shifter if $\overline{OEY}$ is low and is a high impedance input if $\overline{OEY}$ is high. SELY must be low to pass the internal ALU shift bus and must be high to pass the external Y bus to the register file.

status

Four status pins are available on the most significant package, overflow (OVR), sign (N), carry out (C_{n+8}), and zero (ZERO). The C_{n+8} line signifies the ALU result while OVR, ZERO, and N refer the status after the ALU shift has occurred. Notice that the ZERO pin cannot be used to detect whether an input placed on a high impedance Y bus is zero.

divide BCD flip-flops

The multiply-divide flip-flops contain the status of the previous multiply or divide instruction. They are affected by the following instructions:

- DIVIDE REMAINDER FIX
- SIGNED DIVIDE QUOTIENT FIX
- SIGNED MULTIPLY
- SIGNED MULTIPLY TERMINATE
- SIGNED DIVIDE INITIALIZE
- SIGNED DIVIDE START
- SIGNED DIVIDE ITERATE
- UNSIGNED DIVIDE START
- UNSIGNED DIVIDE ITERATE
- UNSIGNED MULTIPLY
- SIGNED DIVIDE TERMINATE
- UNSIGNED DIVIDE TERMINATE

The excess-3 BCD flip-flops are affected by all instructions except NOP. The clear function clears these flip-flops. They preserve the carry from each nibble (4-bits) in excess-3/BCD operations.

package position pin (PPP)

The position of the processor in the system is defined by the voltage level applied to the package position pin (PPP). Intermediate positions are selected by leaving the pin open. Tying the pin to V_{CC} makes the processor the most significant package and tying the pin to GND makes the processor the least significant package.

special shift function (SSF) pin

Conditional shifting algorithms may be implemented via control of the SSF pin. The applied voltage to this pin may be set as a function of a potential overflow condition (the two most significant bits are not equal) or any other condition (see Group 1 instructions).

instruction set

The 'AS888 bit-slice processor uses bits 17-I0 as instruction inputs. A combination of bits I3-I0 (Group 1 instructions) and bits I7-I4 (Group 2-5 instructions) are used to develop the 8-bit op code for a specific instruction. Group 1 and Group 2 instructions can be combined to perform arithmetic or logical functions plus a shift function in one instruction cycle. A summary of the instruction set is given in Table 1.

TABLE 1. INSTRUCTION SET

GROUP 1 INSTRUCTIONS

INSTRUCTION BITS (I3-I0) HEX CODE	MNEMONIC	FUNCTION
0		Accesses Group 4 instructions
1	ADD	$R+S+C_n$
2	SUBR	$\overline{R}+S+C_n$
3	SUBS	$R+\overline{S}+C_n$
4	INCS	$S+C_n$
5	INCNS	$\overline{S}+C_n$
6	INCR	$R+C_n$
7	INCNR	$\overline{R}+C_n$
8		Accesses Group 3 instructions
9	XOR	R XOR S
A	AND	R AND S
B	OR	R OR S
C	NAND	R NAND S
D	NOR	R NOR S
E	ANDNR	$\overline{R}$ AND S
F		Accesses Group 5 instructions

GROUP 2 INSTRUCTIONS

INSTRUCTION BITS (I7-I4) HEX CODE	MNEMONIC	FUNCTION
0	SRA	Arithmetic Right Single
1	SRAD	Arithmetic Right Double
2	SRL	Logical Right Single
3	SRLD	Logical Right Double
4	SLA	Arithmetic Left Single
5	SLAD	Arithmetic Left Double
6	SLC	Circular Left Single
7	SLCD	Circular Left Double
8	SRC	Circular Right Single
9	SRCD	Circular Right Double
A	MQSRA	Pass (F→Y) and Arithmetic Right MQ
B	MQSRL	Pass (F→Y) and Logical Right MQ
C	MQSLL	Pass (F→Y) and Logical Left MQ
D	MQSLC	Pass (F→Y) and Circular Left MQ
E	LOADMQ	Pass (F→Y) and Load MQ (F = MQ)
F	PASS	Pass (F→Y)

TEXAS INSTRUMENTS
POST OFFICE BOX 225012 • DALLAS, TEXAS 75265

TABLE 1. INSTRUCTION SET (Continued)

GROUP 3 INSTRUCTIONS

INSTRUCTION BITS (I7-I0) HEX CODE	MNEMONIC	FUNCTION
08	SET1	Set Bit
18	SET0	Reset Bit
28	TB1	Test Bit (One)
38	TB0	Test Bit (Zero)
48	ABS	Absolute Value
58	SMTC	Sign Magnitude/Two's Complement
68	ADDI	Add Immediate
78	SUBI	Subtract Immediate
88	BADD	Byte Add R to S
98	BSUBS	Byte Subtract S from R
A8	BSUBR	Byte Subtract R from S
B8	BINCS	Byte Increment S
C8	BINCNS	Byte Increment Negative S
D8	BXOR	Byte XOR R and S
E8	BAND	Byte AND R and S
F8	BOR	Byte OR R and S

GROUP 4 INSTRUCTIONS

INSTRUCTION BITS (I7-I0) HEX CODE	MNEMONIC	FUNCTION
00		Reserved
10	SEL	Select S/R
20	SNORM	Single Length Normalize
30	DNORM	Double Length Normalize
40	DIVRF	Divide Remainder Fix
50	SDIVQF	Signed Divide Quotient Fix
60	SMULI	Signed Multiply Iterate
70	SMULT	Signed Multiply Terminate
80	SDIVIN	Signed Divide Initialize
90	SDIVIS	Signed Divide Start
A0	SDIVI	Signed Divide Iterate
B0	UDIVIS	Unsigned Divide Start
C0	UDIVI	Unsigned Divide Iterate
D0	UMULI	Unsigned Multiply Iterate
E0	SDIVIT	Signed Divide Terminate
F0	UDIVIT	Unsigned Divide Terminate

2

LSI Devices

TABLE 1. INSTRUCTION SET (Concluded)

GROUP 5 INSTRUCTIONS

INSTRUCTION BITS (I7-I0) HEX CODE	MNEMONIC	FUNCTION
0F	CLR	Clear
1F	CLR	Clear
2F	CLR	Clear
3F	CLR	Clear
4F	CLR	Clear
5F	CLR	Clear
6F	CLR	Clear
7F	BCDBIN	BCD to Binary
8F	EX3BC	Excess-3 Byte Correction
9F	EX3C	Excess-3 Word Correction
AF	SDIVO	Signed Divide Overflow Check
BF	CLR	Clear
CF	CLR	Clear
DF	BINEX3	Binary to Excess-3
EF	CLR	Clear
FF	NOP	No Operation

group 1 instructions

TABLE 2. GROUP 1 INSTRUCTIONS

INSTRUCTION BITS (I3-I0) HEX CODE	MNEMONIC	FUNCTION
0		Accesses Group 4 instructions
1	ADD	$R + S + C_n$
2	SUBR	$\bar{R} + S + C_n$
3	SUBS	$R + \bar{S} + C_n$
4	INCS	$S + C_n$
5	INCNS	$\bar{S} + C_n$
6	INCR	$R + C_n$
7	INCNR	$\bar{R} + C_n$
8		Accesses Group 3 instructions
9	XOR	R XOR S
A	AND	R AND S
B	OR	R OR S
C	NAND	R NAND S
D	NOR	R NOR S
E	ANDNR	$\bar{R}$ AND S
F		Accesses Group 5 instructions

Group 1 instructions (excluding hex codes 0, 8, and F), shown in Table 2, may be used in conjunction with Group 2 shift instructions to perform arithmetic or logical functions plus a shift function† in one instruction cycle (hex codes 0, 8, and F are used to access Group 4, 3, and 5 instructions, respectively). Each shift may be made into a conditional shift by forcing the special shift function (SSF) pin into the proper state. If the SSF pin is high or floating, the shifted ALU output will be sent to the output buffers. If the SSF pin is pulled low externally, the ALU result will be passed directly to the output buffers. Conditional shifting is useful for scaling inputs in data arrays or in signal processing algorithms.

These instructions set the BCD flip-flop for the excess-3 correct instruction. The status is set with the following results (C_{n+8} is ALU carry out and is independent of shift operation; others are evaluated after shift operation).

†Double-precision shifts involve both the ALU and MQ register.

condition code

Arithmetic

- N — MSB of result
- OVR — Signed arithmetic overflow
- C_{n+8} — Carry out equal one
- Z — Result equal zero

Logic

- N — MSB of result
- OVR — None (force to zero)
- C_{n+8} — None (force to zero)
- Z — Result equal zero

group 2 instructions

TABLE 3. GROUP 2 INSTRUCTIONS

INSTRUCTION BITS (I7-I4) HEX CODE	MNEMONIC	FUNCTION
0	SRA	Arithmetic Right Single
1	SRAD	Arithmetic Right Double
2	SRL	Logical Right Single
3	SRLD	Logical Right Double
4	SLA	Arithmetic Left Single
5	SLAD	Arithmetic Left Double
6	SLC	Circular Left Single
7	SLCD	Circular Left Double
8	SRC	Circular Right Single
9	SRCD	Circular Right Double
A	MQSRA	Pass (F→Y) and Arithmetic Right MQ
B	MQSRL	Pass (F→Y) and Logical Right MQ
C	MQSLL	Pass (F→Y) and Logical Left MQ
D	MQSLC	Pass (F→Y) and Circular Left MQ
E	LOADMQ	Pass (F→Y) and Load MQ (F = MQ)
F	PASS	Pass (F→Y)

The processor's shift instructions are implemented by a combination of Group 2 instructions (Table 3) and certain wired connections on the packages used. The following external connections are required.

On intermediate packages:

- $\overline{\mathrm{SIO7}}$ is connected to $\overline{\mathrm{SIO0}}$ of the next most significant package
- $\overline{\mathrm{QIO7}}$ is connected to $\overline{\mathrm{QIO0}}$ of the next most significant package
- $\overline{\mathrm{SIO0}}$ is connected to $\overline{\mathrm{SIO7}}$ of the next least significant package
- $\overline{\mathrm{QIO0}}$ is connected to $\overline{\mathrm{QIO7}}$ of the next least significant package

On the two end packages:

- $\overline{\mathrm{SIO7}}$ on the most significant package is connected to $\overline{\mathrm{SIO0}}$ of the least significant package
- $\overline{\mathrm{QIO7}}$ on the most significant package is connected to $\overline{\mathrm{QIO0}}$ of the least significant package

The connections are the same on all instructions including multiply, divide, CRC, and normalization functions.

Single- and double-precision shifts are supported. Double-precision shifts assume the most significant half has come through the ALU and will be placed (if $\overline{\mathrm{WE}}$ is low) into the register file on the rising edge of the clock and the least significant half lies in the MQ register. All Group 2 shifts may be made conditional (see previous page).

The following definitions apply to Group 2 shift instructions:

- Arithmetic right shifts copy the sign of the number if no overflow occurs from the ALU calculation; if overflow occurs, the sign bit is inverted.
- Arithmetic left shifts do not retain the sign of the number if an overflow occurs. A zero is filled into the LSB if not forced externally.
- Logical right shifts fill a zero in the MSB position if not forced externally.
- Circular right shifts fill the LSB in the MSB position.
- Circular left shifts fill the MSB in the LSB position.
- Shifting left is defined as moving a bit position towards the MSB (doubling).
- Shifting right is defined as moving a bit towards the LSB (halving).

Serial input may be performed using the circuitry shown in Figure 1. A single-/or double-precision arithmetic left or logical right shift fills the complement of the data on $\overline{\mathrm{SIO0}}$ and $\overline{\mathrm{SIO7}}$ into the LSB or MSB of the data word(s). Note that if $\overline{\mathrm{SIO0}}$ and $\overline{\mathrm{SIO7}}$ are floating (HI-Z), a zero will be filled as an end condition.

Serial output may be performed with circular instructions.

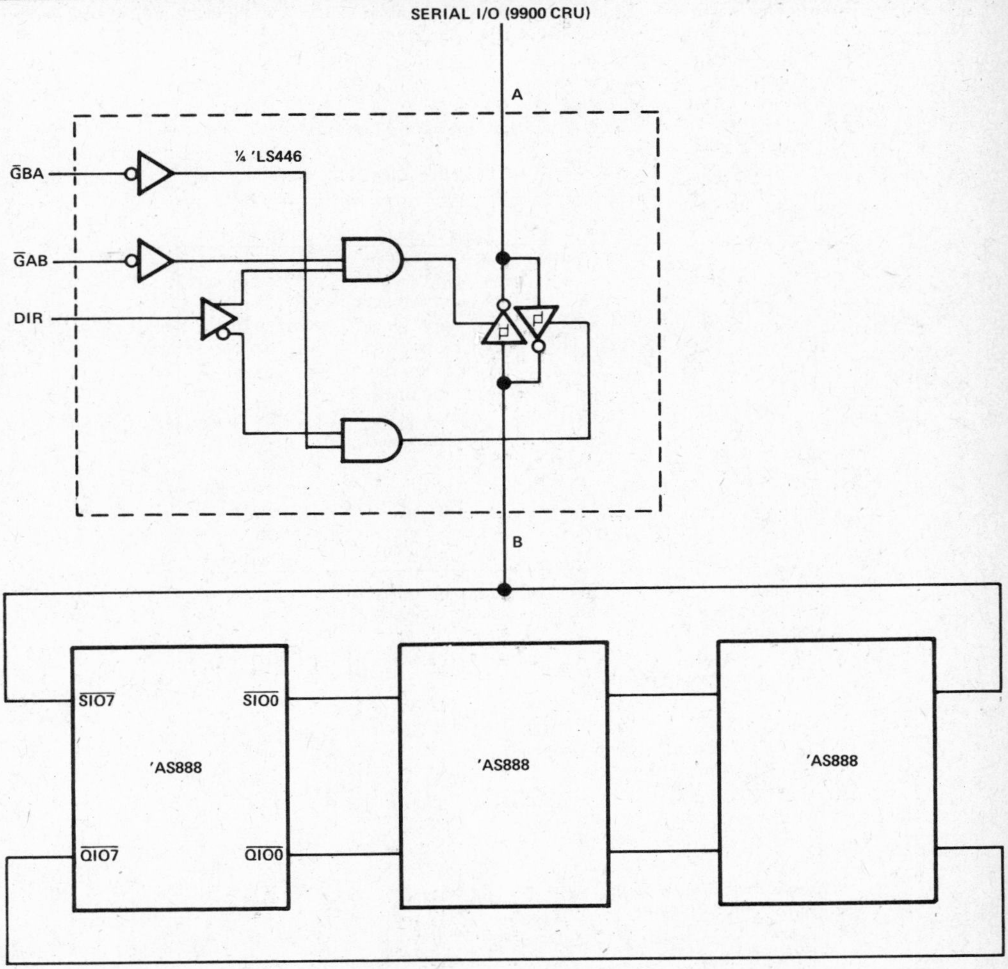
SERIAL I/O (9900 CRU)
A
¼ 'LS446
ḠBA
ḠAB
DIR
B
$\overline{SIO7}$
$\overline{SIO0}$
'AS888
$\overline{QIO7}$
$\overline{QIO0}$
'AS888
'AS888

FIGURE 1. SERIAL I/O

The shift instructions are summarized in Table 4 and illustrated in Figure 2. In Figure 2 and all succeeding figures that illustrate instruction execution, the following definitions apply:

CRF — CRC accumulator end fill.
QBT — End fill for signed divide.
MQF — End fill for unsigned divide.
SRF — End fill for signed multiply and the arithmetic right shifts.

TABLE 4. SHIFT INSTRUCTIONS

OP CODE†	SHIFT FUNCTION‡	$\overline{SIO7}$ · $\overline{SIO0}$ WIRED VALUE	$\overline{QIO7}$ · $\overline{QIO0}$ WIRED VALUE
0N	Arithmetic Right Single	ALU-LSB Output	—
1N	Arithmetic Right Double	MQ-LSB Output	ALU-LSB Output
2N	Logical Right Single	Input to ALU-MSB	ALU-LSB Output
3N	Logical Right Double	Input to ALU-MSB	ALU-LSB Output
4N	Arithmetic Left Single	Input to ALU-LSB	ALU-MSB Output
5N	Arithmetic Left Double	Input to MQ-LSB	MQ-MSB Output
6N	Circular Left Single	ALU-MSB Output	—
7N	Circular Left Double	ALU-MSB Output	MQ-MSB Output
8N	Circular Right Single	ALU-LSB Output	—
9N	Circular Right Double	MQ-LSB Output	ALU-LSB Output
AN	Arithmetic Right (MQ only)	MQ-LSB Output	MQ-LSB Output
BN	Logical Right (MQ only)	MQ-LSB Output	Input to MQ-MSB
CN	Logical Left (MQ only)	Input to MQ-LSB	MQ-MSB Output
DN	Circular Left (MQ only)	MQ-MSB Output	MQ-MSB Output

†Op Code N ≠ 0, 8, or F; these select special instruction Groups 4, 3, and 5 respectively.
‡Shift I/O pins are active low. Therefore, inputs and outputs must be inverted if true logical values are required.

Status is set with the following results:

Arithmetic

N → Result MSB equal one
OVR → Signed arithmetic overflow†
C_{n+8} → Carry out equal one
Z → Result equal zero

Logic

N → Result MSB equal one
OVR → Zero
C_{n+8} → Zero
Z → Result equal zero

† For the SLA and SLAD instructions, OVR is set if signed arithmetic overflow or if the ALU result MSB XOR MSB-1 equals one.

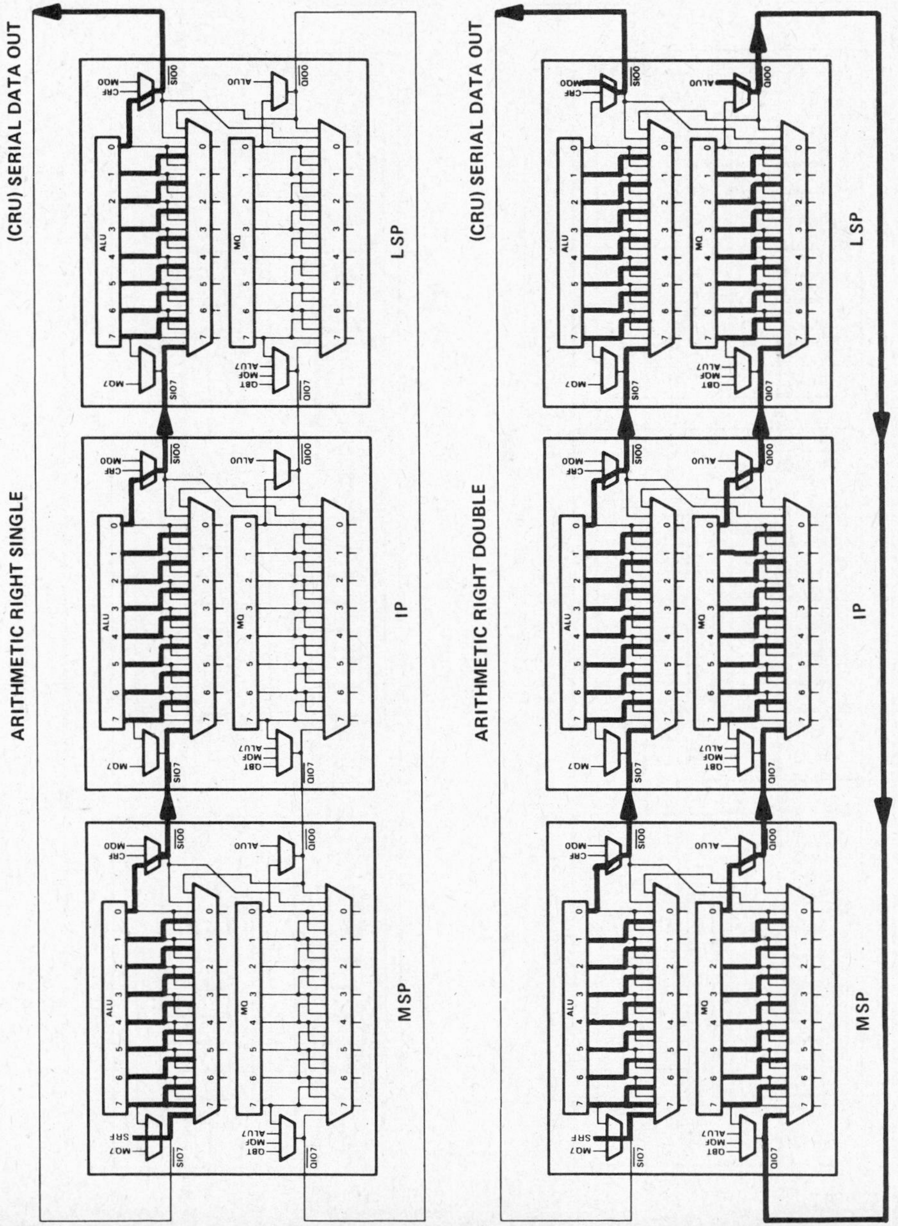
ARITHMETIC RIGHT SINGLE
(CRU) SERIAL DATA OUT
MSP
IP
LSP
ALU
MQ
ARITHMETIC RIGHT DOUBLE
(CRU) SERIAL DATA OUT
MSP
IP
LSP
ALU
MQ

FIGURE 2. SHIFT INSTRUCTIONS

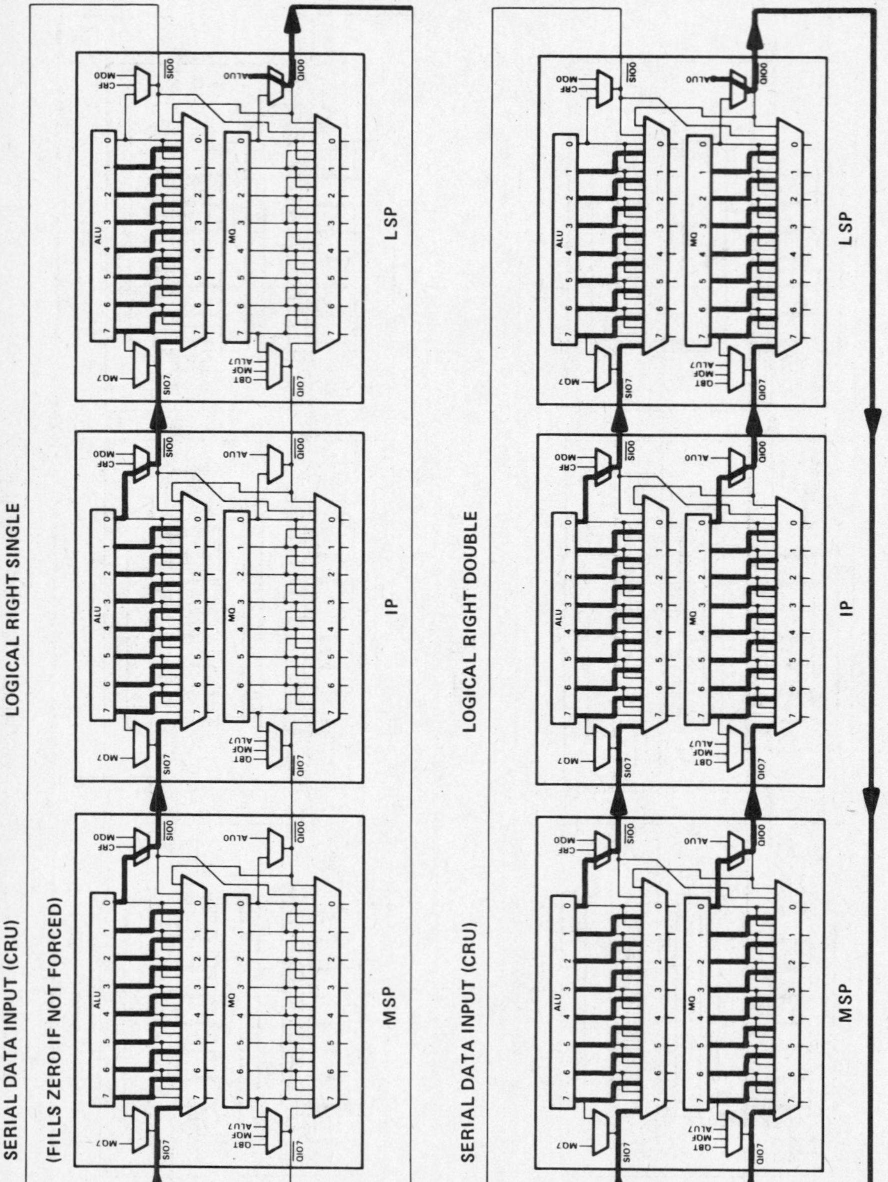
LOGICAL RIGHT SINGLE
SERIAL DATA INPUT (CRU)
(FILLS ZERO IF NOT FORCED)
LOGICAL RIGHT DOUBLE
SERIAL DATA INPUT (CRU)
LSP
IP
MSP
ALU
MQ
SIO7
QIO7
MQ7
QBT
MQF
ALU7
CRF
MQ0
ALU0
SIO0
QIO0

FIGURE 2. SHIFT INSTRUCTIONS (Continued)

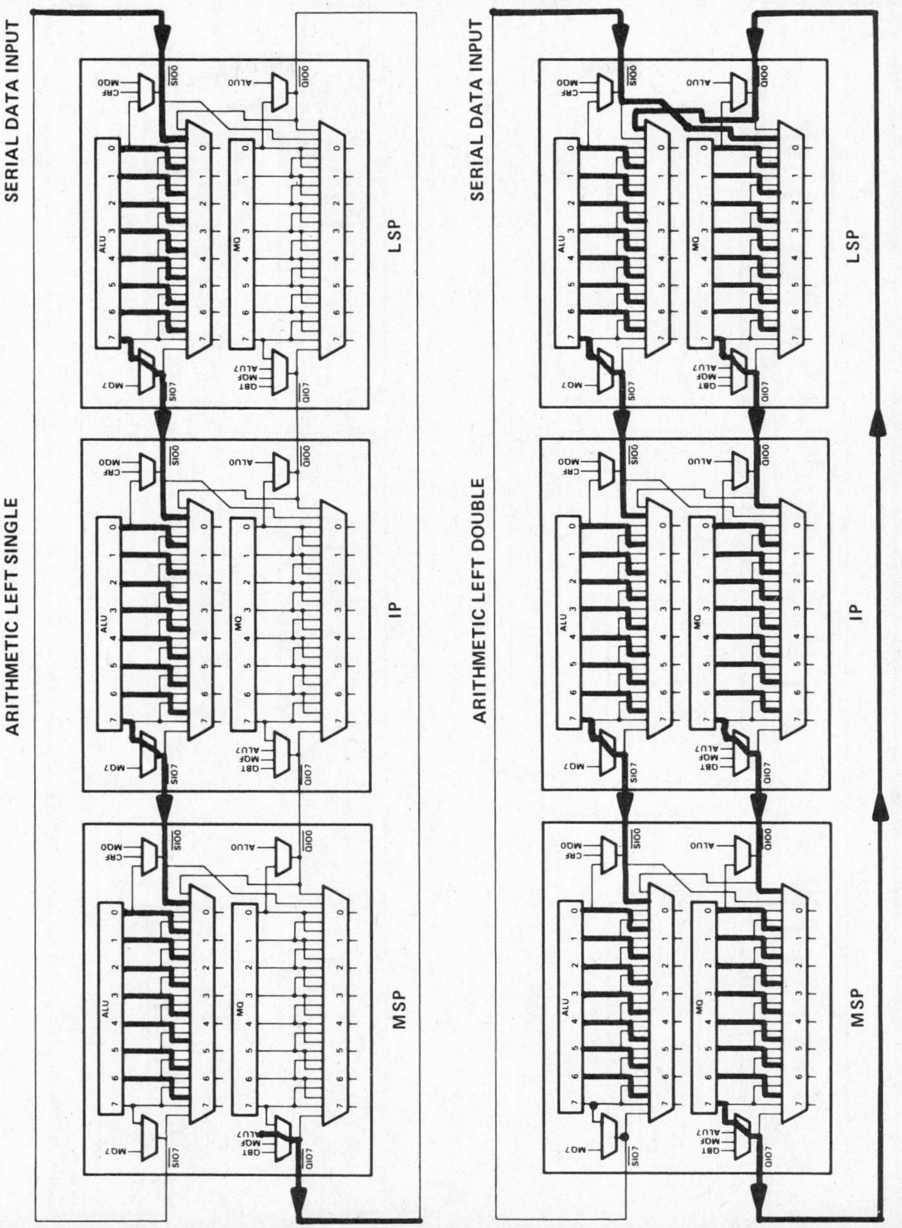
SERIAL DATA INPUT
ARITHMETIC LEFT SINGLE
SERIAL DATA INPUT
ARITHMETIC LEFT DOUBLE
LSP
IP
MSP
ALU
MQ
CRF
MQ0
ALU0
MQ7
QBT
MQF
ALU7
$\overline{SIO0}$
$\overline{QIO0}$
$\overline{SIO7}$
$\overline{QIO7}$

FIGURE 2. SHIFT INSTRUCTIONS (Continued)

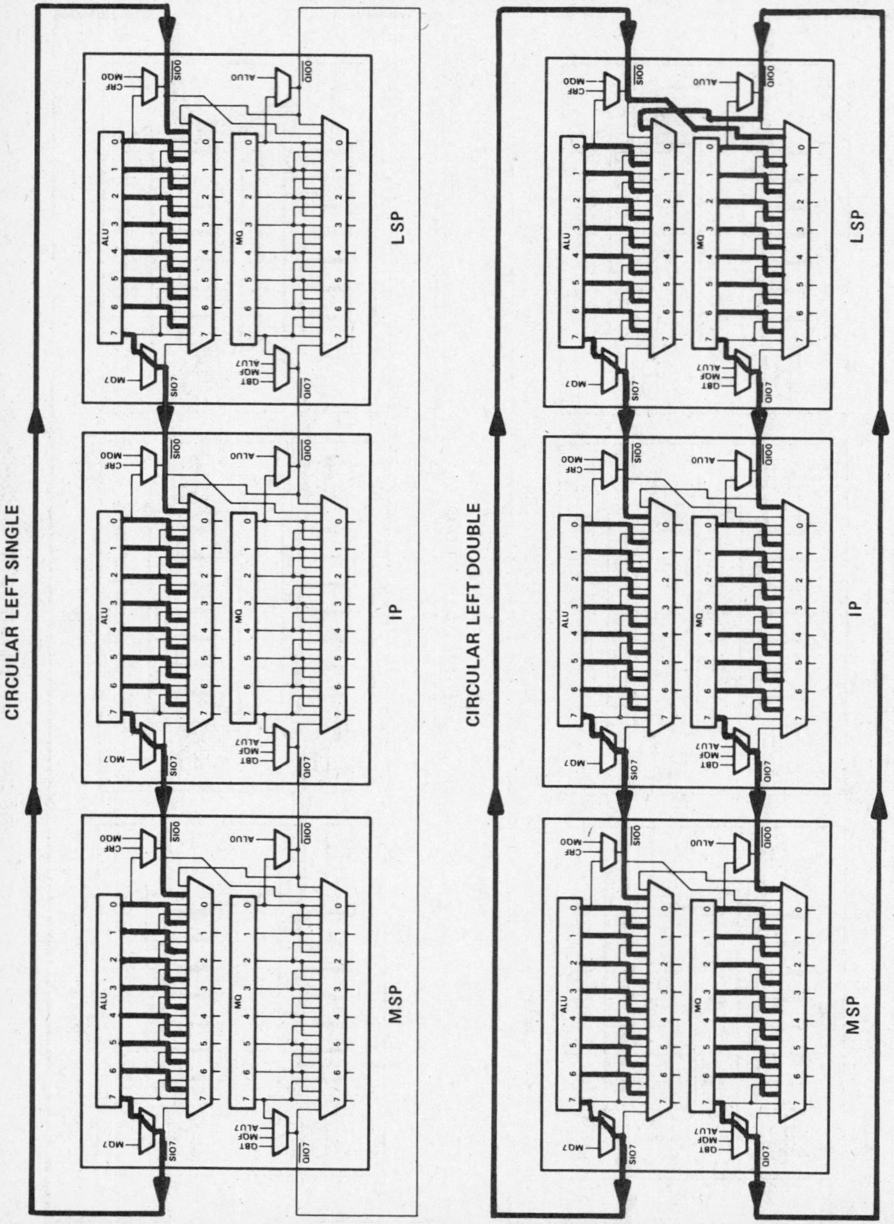
CIRCULAR LEFT SINGLE
CIRCULAR LEFT DOUBLE
LSP
IP
MSP
ALU
MQ
CRF
MQ0
ALU0
MQ7
QBT
MQF
ALU7
SIO0
SIO7
QIO0
QIO7

FIGURE 2. SHIFT INSTRUCTIONS (Continued)

TEXAS INSTRUMENTS
POST OFFICE BOX 225012 • DALLAS, TEXAS 75265

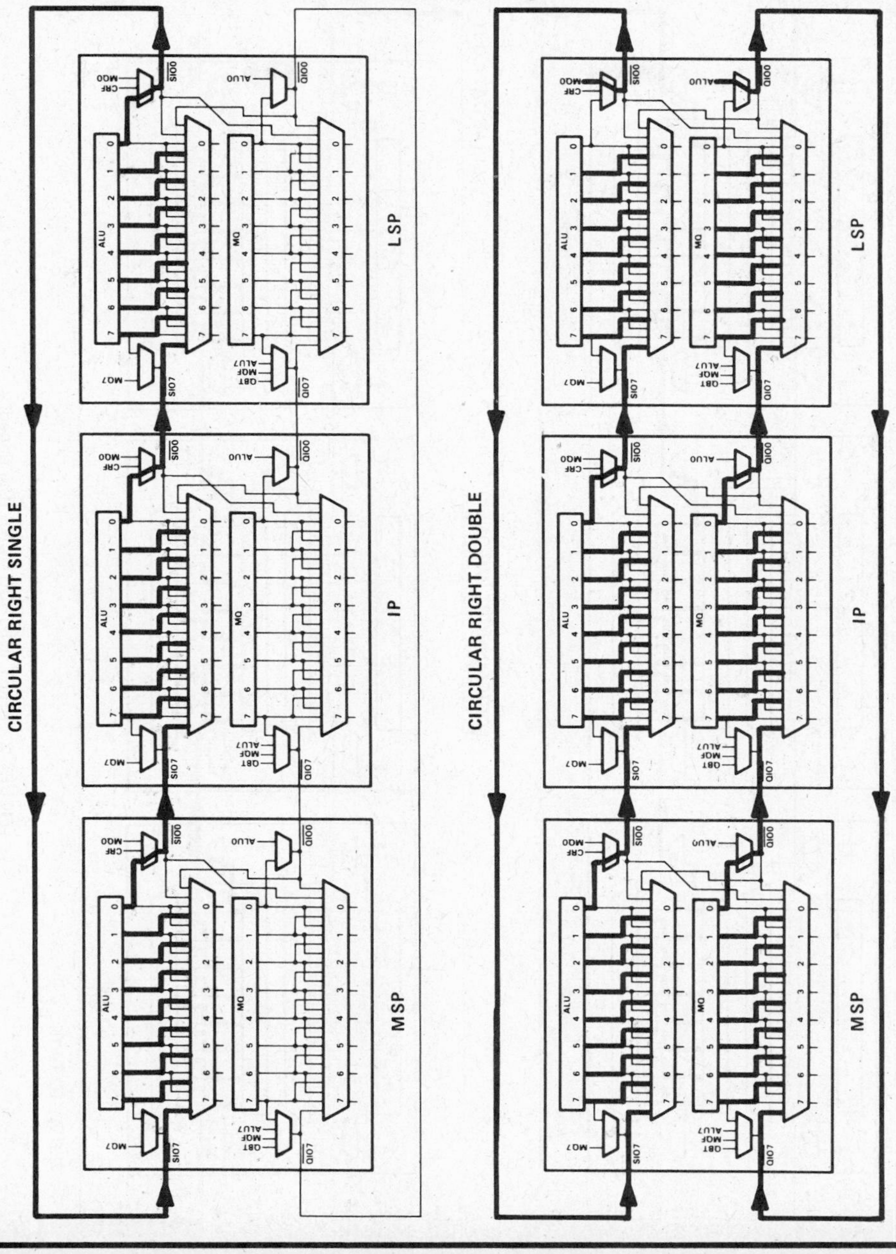
CIRCULAR RIGHT SINGLE
CIRCULAR RIGHT DOUBLE
MSP
IP
LSP
ALU
MQ
SIO0
SIO7
QIO0
QIO7
CRF
MQ0
MQ7
ALU0
ALU7
QBT
MQF

FIGURE 2. SHIFT INSTRUCTIONS (Continued)

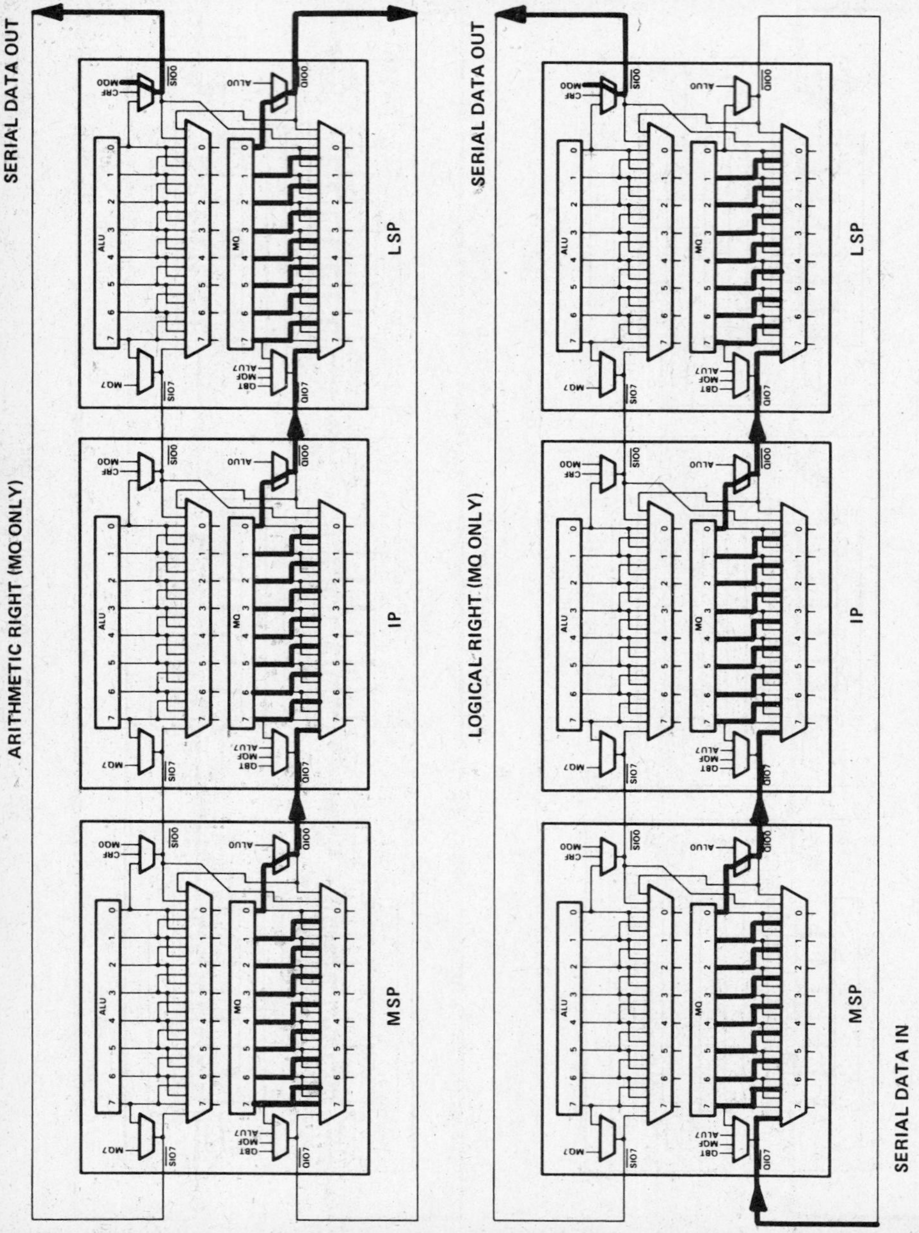
SERIAL DATA OUT
ARITHMETIC RIGHT (MQ ONLY)
LSP
IP
MSP
SERIAL DATA OUT
LOGICAL RIGHT (MQ ONLY)
LSP
IP
MSP
SERIAL DATA IN
ALU
MQ
CRF
MQ0
ALU0
MQ7
QBT
MQF
ALU7

FIGURE 2. SHIFT INSTRUCTIONS (Continued)

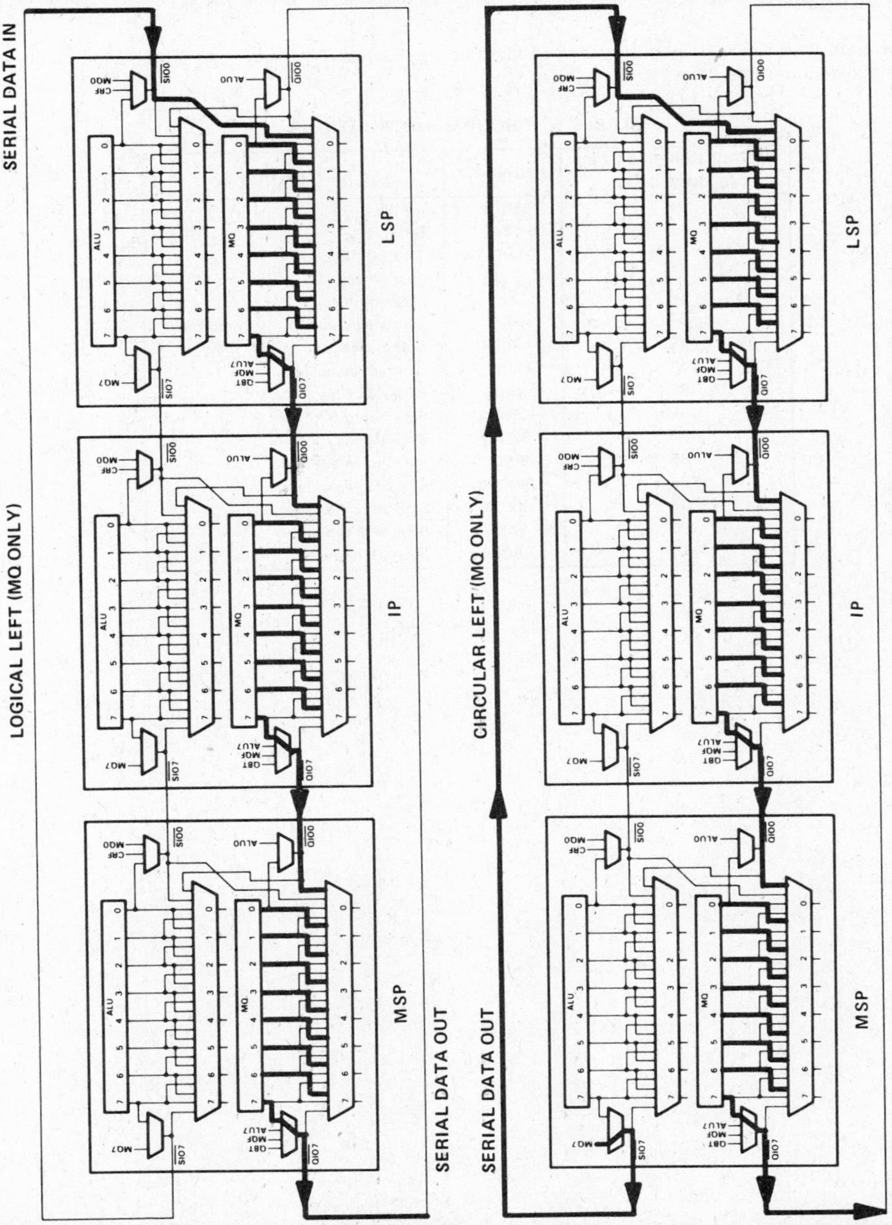
SERIAL DATA IN
LOGICAL LEFT (MQ ONLY)
SERIAL DATA OUT
CIRCULAR LEFT (MQ ONLY)
SERIAL DATA OUT
LSP
IP
MSP
ALU
MQ
CRF
MQ0
ALU0
SIO0
QIO0
MQ7
SIO7
QBT
MQF
ALU7
QIO7

FIGURE 2. SHIFT INSTRUCTIONS (Concluded)

group 3 instructions

Hex code 8 of Group 1 instructions is used to access Group 3 instructions. Group 3 instructions are summarized in Table 5.

TABLE 5. GROUP 3 INSTRUCTIONS

INSTRUCTION BITS (I7-I0) OP CODE (HEX)	MNEMONIC	FUNCTION
08	SET1	Set Bit
18	SET0	Reset Bit
28	TB1	Test Bit (One)
38	TB0	Test Bit (Zero)
48	ABS	Absolute Value
58	SMTC	Sign Magnitude/Two's Complement
68	ADDI	Add Immediate
78	SUBI	Subtract Immediate
88	BADD	Byte Add R to S
98	BSUBS	Byte Subtract S from R
A8	BSUBR	Byte Subtract R from S
B8	BINCS	Byte Increment S
C8	BINCNS	Byte Increment Negative S
D8	BXOR	Byte XOR R and S
E8	BAND	Byte AND R and S
F8	BOR	Byte OR R and S

set bit instruction (set1): I7-I0 = 08_{16}

This instruction (Figure 3) is used to force selected bits of a desired byte(s) to one (any combination of zero to eight bits). The desired bits are specified by an 8-bit mask (C3-C0)::(A3-A0)† consisting of register file address ports that are not required to support this instruction. All bits in the selected byte(s) that are in the same bit positions as ones in the mask are forced to a logical one. The B3-B0 address field is used for both source and destination of this instruction. The desired byte is specified by forcing $\overline{SIO0}$ to a low value. Nonselected packages pass the byte through unaltered. The S bus is the source word for this instruction. The status set by the set bit instruction is as follows:

N	→	None (force to zero)
OVR	→	None (force to zero)
C_{n+8}	→	None (force to zero)
Z	→	Result equal zero

† The symbol '::' is concatenation operator

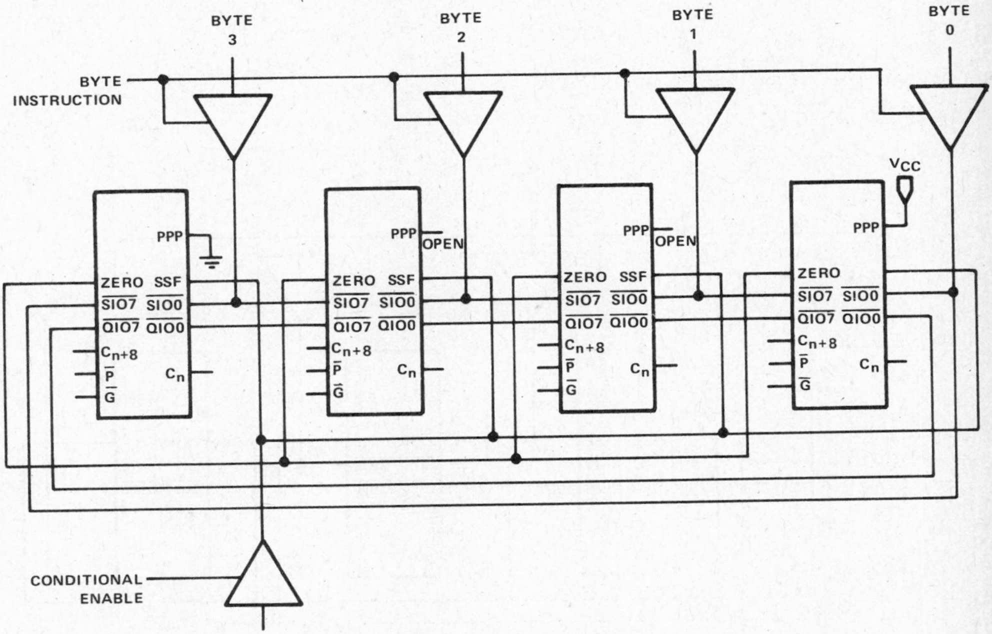
BYTE
3
BYTE
2
BYTE
1
BYTE
0
BYTE
INSTRUCTION
VCC
PPP
OPEN
ZERO SSF
SIO7 SIO0
QIO7 QIO0
Cn+8
P
G
Cn
ZERO
CONDITIONAL
ENABLE

FIGURE 3. SET BIT (OR RESET BIT)

NOTES: 1. Force $\overline{SIO0}$ low to select byte.
2. Bit mask (C3-C0)::(A3-A0) will set desired bits to one.

reset bit instruction (set0): I7-I0 = 18_{16}

This instruction (Figure 3) is used to force selected bits of a desired byte(s) to zero (any combination of one to eight bits). The desired bits are specified by an 8-bit mask (C3-C0)::(A3-A0) consisting of register file address ports that are not required to support this instruction. All bits in the selected byte(s) that are in the same bit positions as ones in the mask are reset. The B3-B0 address field is used for both source and destination of this instruction. The desired byte is specified by forcing $\overline{SIO0}$ to a low value. Nonselected packages pass the byte through unaltered. The S bus is the source word for this instruction. The status set by the reset bit instruction is as follows:

N → None (force to zero)
OVR → None (force to zero)
C_{n+8} → None (force to zero)
Z → Result equal zero

test bit (one) instruction (TB1): I7-I0 = 28_{16}

This instruction (Figure 4) is used to test selected bits of a desired byte(s)(any combination of one to eight bits). Bits to be tested are specified by an 8-bit mask (C3-C0)::(A3-A0) consisting of register file address ports that are not required to support this instruction. Write Enable ($\overline{WE}$) is internally disabled during this instruction. The desired byte is specified by forcing $\overline{SIO0}$ to a low value. The test will pass if the selected byte has ones at all bit locations specified by the ones of the mask (Figure 5). The S bus is the source word for this instruction. The status set by the test bit (one) instruction is as follows:

N → None (force to zero)
OVR → None (force to zero)
C_{n+8} → None (force to zero)
Z → Pass

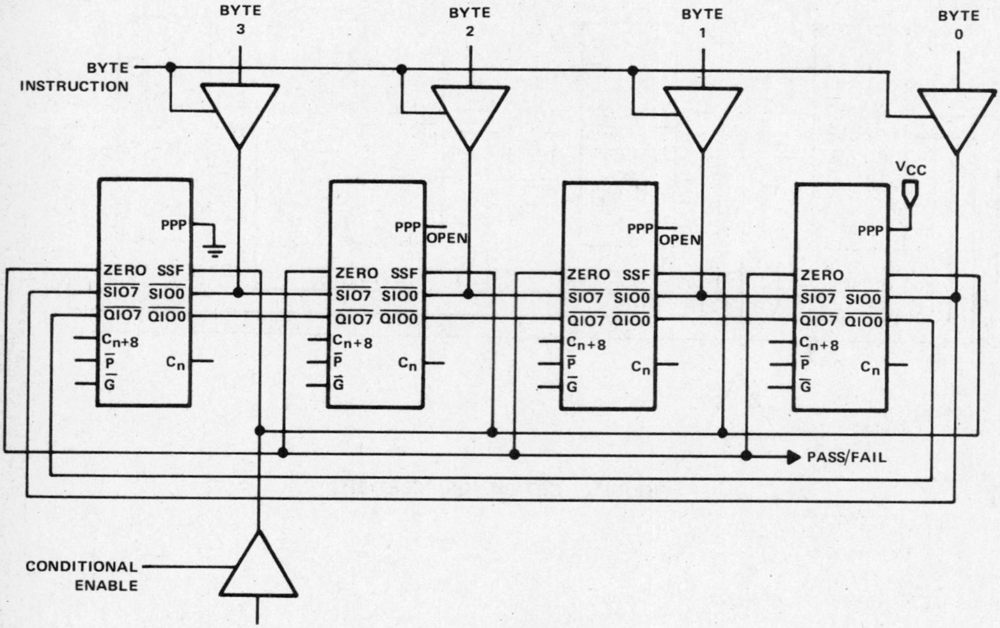
BYTE 3
BYTE 2
BYTE 1
BYTE 0
BYTE INSTRUCTION
VCC
PPP
OPEN
ZERO SSF
SIO7 SIO0
QIO7 QIO0
Cn+8
P
G
Cn
PASS/FAIL
CONDITIONAL ENABLE

FIGURE 4. TEST BIT

NOTES: 1. Force $\overline{SIO0}$ low to select byte.
2. Bit mask (C3-C0)::(A3-A0) will define bits for testing.
3. Pass/fail is indicated on Z output.

test bit (zero) instruction (TB0): I7-I0 = 38_{16}

This instruction (Figure 4) is used to test selected bits of a desired byte(s) (any combination of one to eight bits). Bits to be tested are specified by an 8-bit mask (C3-C0)::(A3-A0) consisting of register file address ports that are not required to support this instruction. Write Enable ($\overline{WE}$) is internally disabled during this instruction. The desired byte is specified by forcing $\overline{SIO0}$ to a low value. The test will pass if the selected byte has zeros at all bit locations specified by the ones of the mask (Figure 6). The S bus is the source word for this instruction. The status set by the test bit (zero) instruction is as follows:

N	→	None (force to zero)
OVR	→	None (force to zero)
C_{n+8}	→	None (force to zero)
Z	→	Pass

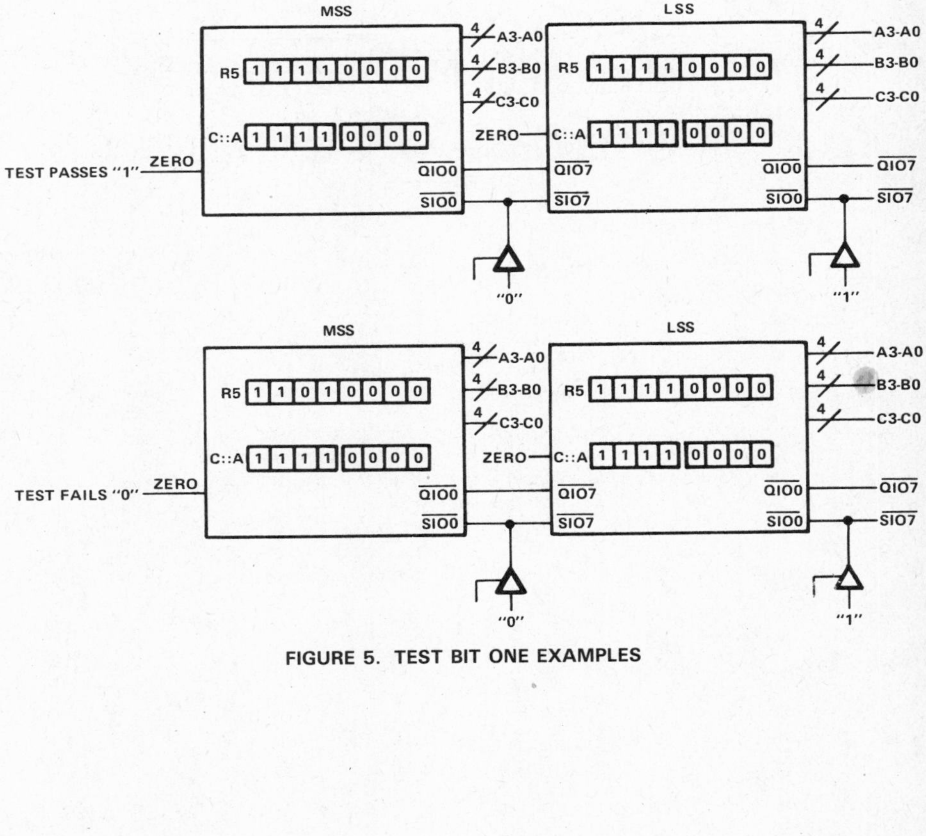
MSS
LSS
R5 1 1 1 1 0 0 0 0
C::A 1 1 1 1 0 0 0 0
A3-A0
B3-B0
C3-C0
ZERO
TEST PASSES "1"
QIO0
SIO0
QIO7
SIO7
"0"
"1"
R5 1 1 0 1 0 0 0 0
TEST FAILS "0"

FIGURE 5. TEST BIT ONE EXAMPLES

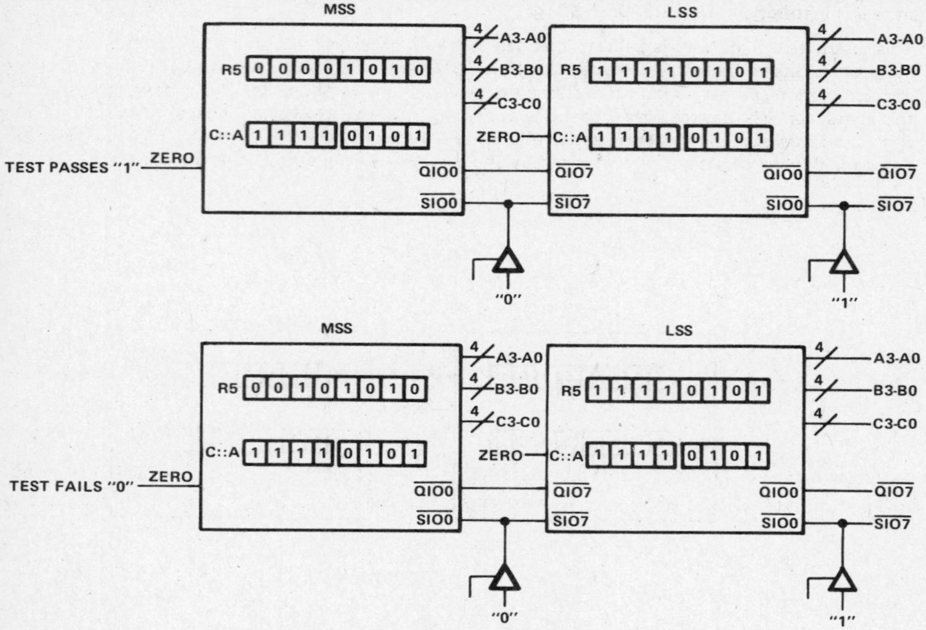
MSS
LSS
R5 0 0 0 0 1 0 1 0
C::A 1 1 1 1 0 1 0 1
R5 1 1 1 1 0 1 0 1
C::A 1 1 1 1 0 1 0 1
TEST PASSES "1"
ZERO
4
A3-A0
B3-B0
C3-C0
ZERO
QIO0
SIO0
QIO7
SIO7
"0"
"1"
MSS
LSS
R5 0 0 1 0 1 0 1 0
C::A 1 1 1 1 0 1 0 1
R5 1 1 1 1 0 1 0 1
C::A 1 1 1 1 0 1 0 1
TEST FAILS "0"
ZERO
"0"
"1"

FIGURE 6. TEST BIT ZERO EXAMPLES

absolute value instruction (ABS): I7-I0 = 48_{16}

This instruction is used to convert two's complement numbers to their positive value. The operand placed on the S bus is the source for this instruction. The MSP will test the sign of the S bus and force the SSF pin to the proper value. All other packages use the SSF pin as input to determine instruction execution. The status set by the absolute value instruction is as follows:

N	→	Input MSB equal one
OVR	→	Input equal 8000 (hex)
C_{n+8}	→	S = 0
Z	→	Result equal zero

sign magnitude/two's complement instruction (SMTC): I7-I0 = 58_{16}

This instruction allows conversion from two's complement representation to sign magnitude representation, or vice-versa, in one clock cycle. The operand placed on the S bus is the source for this instruction.

When a negative zero (8000 hex) is converted, the result is 0000 with an overflow. If the input is in two's complement notation, the overflow indicates an illegal conversion. The status set by the sign magnitude/two's complement instruction is as follows:

N	→	Result MSB equal one
OVR	→	Input equal 8000 (hex)
C_{n+8}	→	Input equal 0000 (hex)
Z	→	Result equal zero

add immediate instruction (ADDI): I7-I0 = 68_{16}

This instruction is used to add a specified constant value to the operand placed on the S bus. The constant will be between the values of 0 and 15. The constant value is specified by the unused register file address (A port) not required to support this instruction. Forcing the carry input will add an additional one to the result. The status set by the add immediate instruction is as follows:

N	→	Result MSB equal one
OVR	→	Arithmetic signed overflow
C_{n+8}	→	Carry out equal one
Z	→	Result equal zero

subtract immediate instruction (SUBI): I7-I0 = 78_{16}

This instruction is used to subtract a specified constant value from the operand placed on the S bus. The constant value is specified by the unused register file address (A port) that is not required to support this instruction. The constant applied is the least significant four bits of a two's complement number. The device sign extends the constant over the entire word length. The status set by the subtract immediate instruction is as follows:

N	→	Result MSB equal one
OVR	→	Arithmetic signed overflow
C_{n+8}	→	Carry out equal one
Z	→	Result equal zero

byte instructions

There are eight byte instructions in Group 3. These instructions modify selected bytes of the operand on the S bus. A byte is selected by forcing $\overline{SIO0}$ to a low value (same as SET1, SET0, TB1, and TB0 instructions). Multiple bytes may be selected only if they are adjacent to one another.

NOTE: At least one byte must be nonselected during these instructions.

The nonselected bytes are passed through unaltered. Byte status is forced through the most significant package except for the sign of the result (N), which is forced to zero (low). The status set by the byte instructions is as follows:

(Most Significant Package)

N	→	None (force to zero)
OVR	→	Byte signed overflow
C_{n+8}	→	Byte carry out equal one
Z	→	Byte result equal to zero

(Selected BYTES—other than MSP)

$\overline{G}$	→	Normal generate
$\overline{P}$	→	Normal propagate
C_{n+8}	→	Normal carry out
Z	→	Result equal to zero

(Nonselected BYTES—other than MSP)

$\overline{G}$	→	No generate (force to one)
$\overline{P}$	→	Propagate (force to zero)
C_{n+8}	→	C_n
Z	→	None (force to one)

2

LSI Devices

group 4 instructions

Hex code 0 of Group 1 instructions is used to access Group 4 instructions. Group 4 instructions are summarized in Table 6.

TABLE 6. GROUP 4 INSTRUCTIONS

INSTRUCTION BITS (I7-I0) OP CODE (HEX)	MNEMONIC	FUNCTION
00		Reserved
10	SEL	Select S/R
20	SNORM	Single Length Normalize
30	DNORM	Double Length Normalize
40	DIVRF	Divide Remainder Fix
50	SDIVQF	Signed Divide Quotient Fix
60	SMULI	Signed Multiply Iterate
70	SMULT	Signed Multiply Terminate
80	SDIVIN	Signed Divide Initialize
90	SDIVIS	Signed Divide Start
A0	SDIVI	Signed Divide Iterate
B0	UDIVIS	Unsigned Divide Start
C0	UDIVI	Unsigned Divide Iterate
D0	UMULI	Unsigned Multiply Iterate
E0	SDIVIT	Signed Divide Terminate
F0	UDIVIT	Unsigned Divide Terminate

select S/R instruction (SEL): I7-I0 = 10_{16}

This instruction is used to pass either the S bus or the R bus to the output depending on the state of the SSF input pin. Normally, the preceding instruction would test the two operands and the resulting status information would be used to force the SSF input pin. SSF = 0 will output the R bus and SSF = 1 will output the S bus. The status set by the select S/R instruction is as follows:

N → Result MSB equal one
OVR → None (force to zero)
C_{n+8} → None (force to zero)
Z → Result equal zero

single-length normalize instruction (SNORM): I7-I0 = 20_{16}

This instruction will cause the contents of the MQ register to shift toward the most significant bit. Zeros are shifted in via the $\overline{\text{QIO0}}$ input. The number of shifts performed can be counted and stored in one of the register files by forcing a high at the C_n input. When the two most significant bits are of opposite value, normalization is complete. This condition is indicated on the microcycle that completes the normalization at the OVR output.

The chip contains conditional logic that inhibits the shift function (and also inhibits the register file increment) if the number within the MQ register is already normalized at the beginning of the instruction (Figure 7). The status set by the single-length normalize instruction is as follows:

N → MSB of result
OVR → MSB XOR 2nd MSB
C_{n+8} → Carry out equal one
Z → Result equal zero

TEXAS INSTRUMENTS
POST OFFICE BOX 225012 • DALLAS, TEXAS 75265

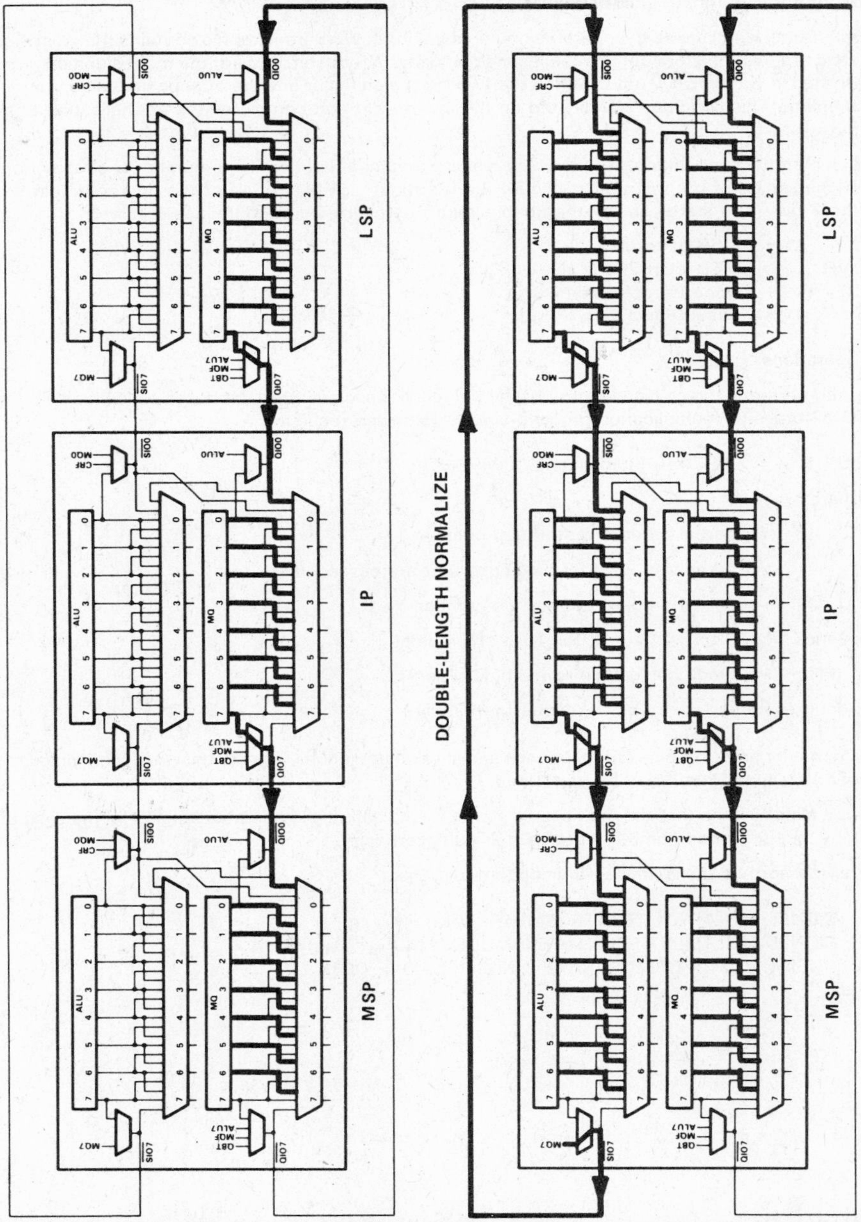
SINGLE-LENGTH NORMALIZE
DOUBLE-LENGTH NORMALIZE
LSP
IP
MSP
ALU
MQ
CRF
MQ0
ALU0
MQ7
QBT
MQF
ALU7
SIO0
QIO0
SIO7
QIO7

FIGURE 7. SINGLE- AND DOUBLE-LENGTH NORMALIZE

double-length normalize instruction (DNORM): I7-I0 = 30_{16}

This instruction will cause the contents of a double-length word (register file contains the most significant half and the MQ register contains the least significant half) to shift toward the most significant bit. Zeros are shifted in via the $\overline{QIO0}$ input. When the two most significant bits are of opposite value, normalization is complete. This condition is indicated on the microcycle that completes the normalization at the OVR output.

The chip contains conditional logic which inhibits the shift function if the number is already normalized at the beginning of the instruction (Figure 7). The most significant half of the operand must be placed on the S bus. The status set by the double-length normalize instruction is as follows:

N → MSB of result
OVR → MSB XOR 2nd MSB
C_{n+8} → None (force to zero)
Z → Result equal zero

multiply operations

The ALU performs three unique types of N by N multiplies each of which produces a 2N-bit result (Figure 8). All three types of multiplication proceed via the following recursion:

P(J+1) = 2[P(J) + Multiplicand × M (8N-J)]

where

P(J) = partial product at iteration number J

N = number of 'AS888 packages that are cascaded

P(J+1) = partial product at iteration number J+1

J varies from 0 to 8N [N = 2 for 16 × 16 multiply]

M (8N-J) = mode bit (unique to multiply type)

2 denotes some type of shift (unique to multiply)

Notice that by proper choice of mode terms and shifting operations, signed, unsigned, and mixed multiplies (signed times unsigned) may be performed.

All multiplies assume that the multiplier is stored in MQ before the operation begins (in the case of mixed multiply, the unsigned number must be the multiplier).

The processor has the following multiply instructions:

1. SIGNED MULTIPLY ITERATE (SMULI): I7-I0 = 60_{16}
2. SIGNED MULTIPLY TERMINATE (SMULT): I7-I0 = 70_{16}
3. UNSIGNED MULTIPLY ITERATE (UMULI): I7-I0 = $D0_{16}$

TEXAS INSTRUMENTS
POST OFFICE BOX 225012 • DALLAS, TEXAS 75265

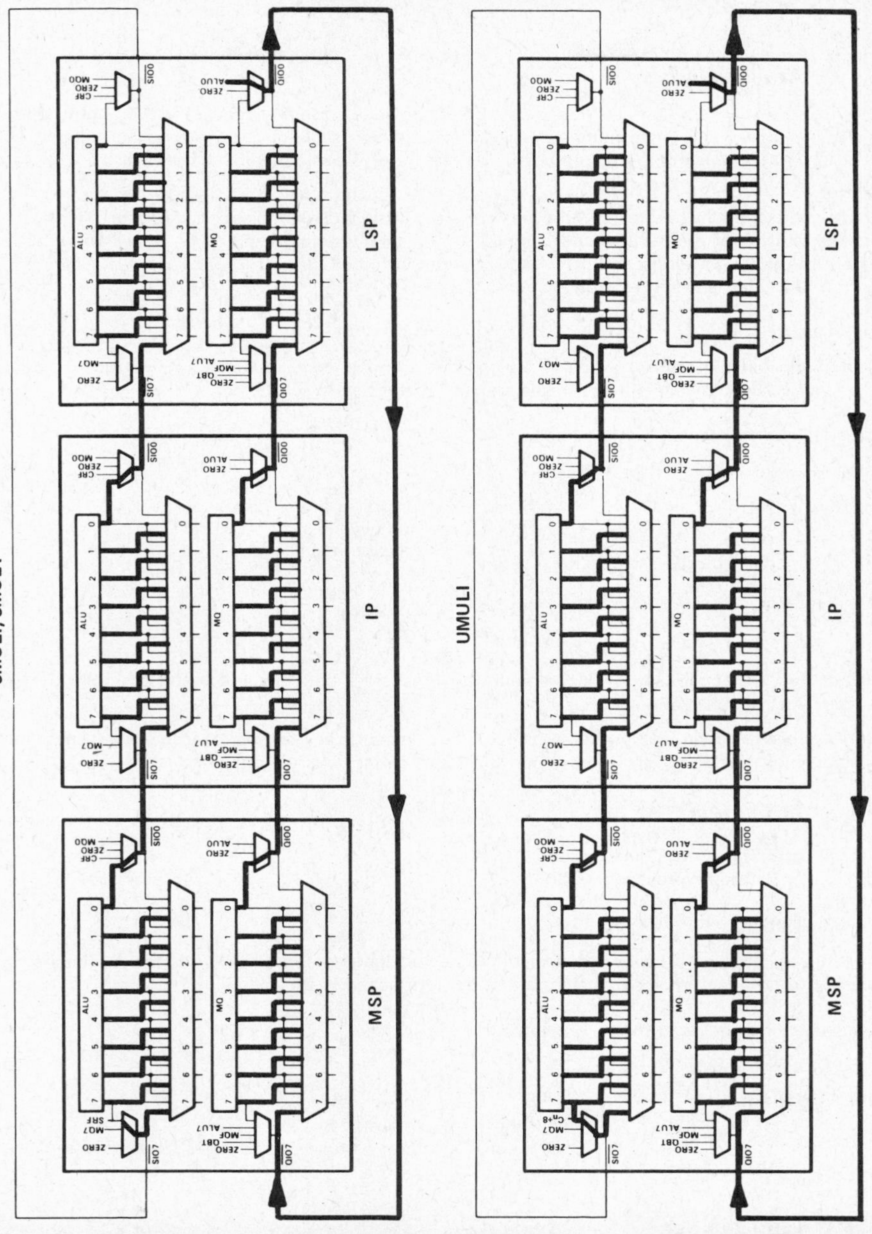

SMULI, SMULT
UMULI
LSP
IP
MSP
ALU
MQ

FIGURE 8. MULTIPLICATION OPERATIONS

The signed multiply iterate (SMULI) instruction performs a signed times signed iteration. This instruction interprets M(8N-J) as the 8N-J bit of the multiplier. The shift is a double-precision right shift one bit. This instruction is repeated 15 times for a 16 × 16 signed multiply. This instruction will be used 16 consecutive times for a mixed multiplication.

The signed multiply terminate (SMULT) instruction provides correct (negative) weighting of the sign bit of a negative multiplier in signed multiplication. The instruction is identical to signed multiply iterate (SMULI) except that M(8N-J) is interpreted as −1 if the sign bit of the multiplier is 1, and 0 if the sign bit of the multiplier is 0.

The unsigned multiply iterate (UMULI) performs an unsigned multiplication iteration. This instruction interprets M(8N-J) as the 8N-J bit of the multiplier. The shift is a double-precision right shift with the carry out from the P(J) + Multiplicand × M(8N-J) operation forced into bit 8N of P(J + 1). This instruction is used in unsigned and mixed multiplication.

signed multiplication

Signed multiplication performs an 8N + 2 clock two's complement multiply. The instructions necessary to produce an algebraically correct result proceed in the following manner:

Zero register to be used for accumulator

Load MQ with multiplier

SMULI (repeat 8N-1 times)	S port	=	Accumulator
	R port	=	Multiplicand
	F port	=	Iteration result
SMULT	S port	=	Accumulator
	R port	=	Multiplicand
	F port	=	Product (MSH)

At completion, the accumulator will contain the 8N most significant bits and the MQ contains the 8N least significant bits of the product.

The status for the signed multiply iterate should not be used for any testing (overflow is not set by SMULI). The following status is set for the signed multiply terminate instruction:

N	→	Result MSB equal one
OVR	→	Forced to zero
C_{n+8}	→	Carry out equal to one
Z	→	Double precision result is zero

unsigned multiplication

Unsigned multiplication produces an unsigned times unsigned product in 8N + 2 clocks. The instructions necessary to produce an algebraically correct result proceed in the following manner:

Zero register to be used for accumulator

Load MQ with multiplier

UMULI (8N times)	S port	=	Accumulator
	R port	=	Multiplicand
	F port	=	Iteration result (product MSH on final result)

Upon completion, the accumulator will contain the 8N most significant bits and the MQ contains the 8N least significant bits of the product.

The status set by the unsigned multiply iteration is meaningless except on the final execution of the instruction. The status set by the unsigned multiply iteration instruction is as follows:

N	→	Result MSB equal one
OVR	→	Forced to zero
C_{n+8}	→	Carry out equal to one
Z	→	Double-precision result is zero

mixed multiplication

Mixed multiplication multiplies a signed multiplicand times an unsigned multiplier to produce a signed result in 8N + 2 clocks. The steps are as follows:

Zero register used for accumulator

Load MQ with unsigned multipler

SMULI (8N times)	S port	=	Accumulator
	R port	=	Multiplicand
	F port	=	Iteration result

Upon completion, the accumulator will contain the 8N most significant bits and the MQ will contain the 8N least significant bits of the product.

The following status is set by the last SMULI instruction:

N	→	Result MSB equal one
OVR	→	Forced to zero
C_{n+8}	→	Carry out equal to one
Z	→	Double-precision result is zero

divide operations

The divide uses a nonrestoring technique to perform both signed and unsigned division of a 16N bit integer dividend and an 8N bit integer divisor (Figure 9). It produces an 8N integer quotient and remainder.

The remainder and quotient will be such that the following equation is satisfied:

$$(\text{Quotient}) \times (\text{Divisor}) + \text{Remainder} = \text{Dividend}$$

The processor has the following divide instructions:

1. UNSIGNED DIVIDE START (UDIVIS): I7-I0 = $B0_{16}$
2. UNSIGNED DIVIDE ITERATE (UDIVI): I7-I0 = $C0_{16}$
3. UNSIGNED DIVIDE TERMINATE (UDIVIT): I7-I0 = $F0_{16}$
4. SIGNED DIVIDE INITIALIZE (SDIVIN): I7-I0 = 80_{16}
5. SIGNED DIVIDE OVERFLOW TEST (SDIVO): I7-I0 = AF_{16}
6. SIGNED DIVIDE START (SDIVIS): I7-I0 = 90_{16}
7. SIGNED DIVIDE ITERATE (SDIVI): I7-I0 = $A0_{16}$
8. SIGNED DIVIDE TERMINATE (SDIVIT): I7-I0 = $E0_{16}$
9. DIVIDE REMAINDER FIX (DIVRF): I7-I0 = 40_{16}
10. SIGNED DIVIDE QUOTIENT FIX (SDIVQF): I7-I0 = 50_{16}

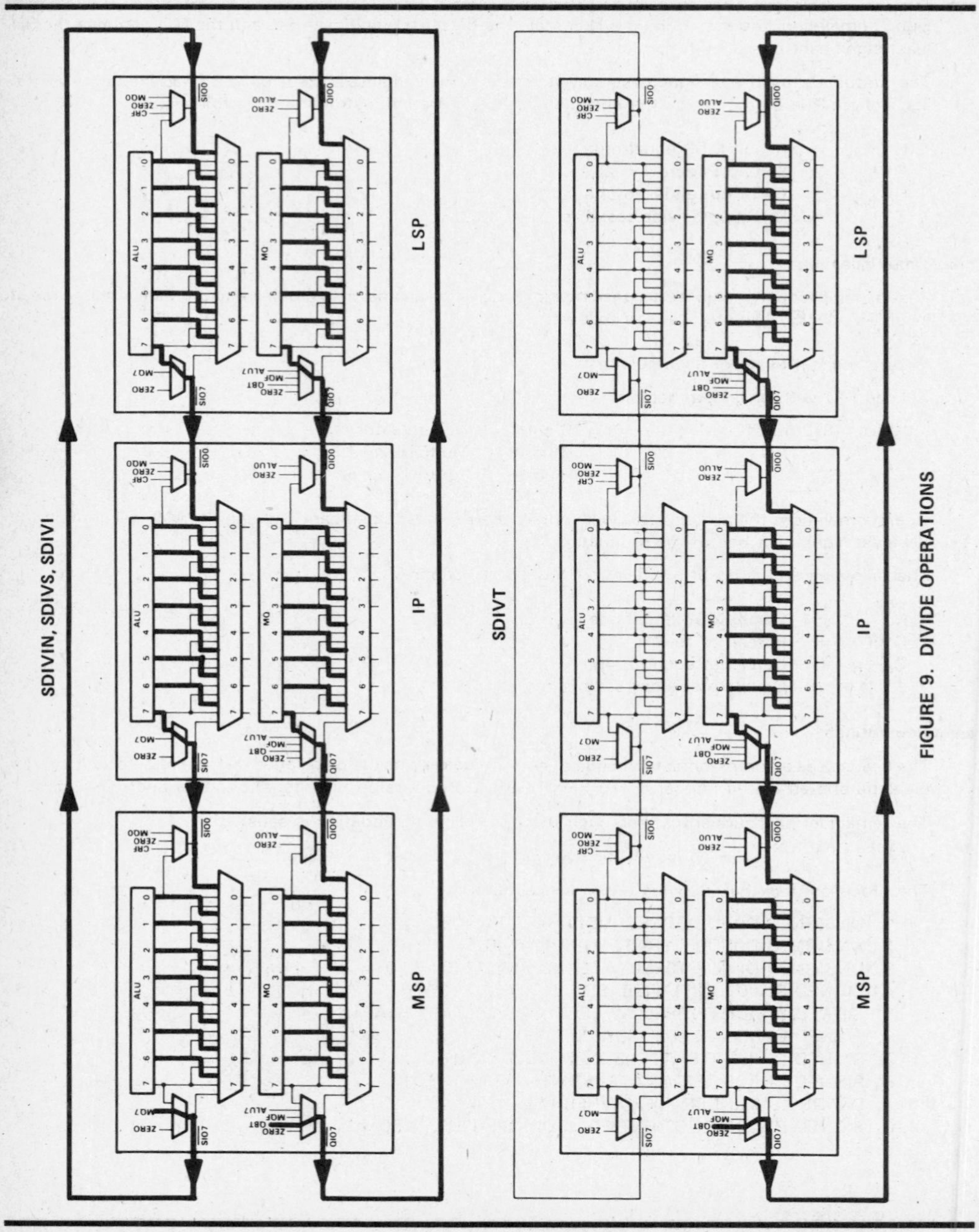
SDIVIN, SDIVS, SDIVI
SDIVT
LSP
IP
MSP
ALU
MQ
CRF
ZERO
MQ0
ALU0
MQ7
ALU7
MQF
QBT
SIO0
QIO0
SIO7
QIO7

FIGURE 9. DIVIDE OPERATIONS

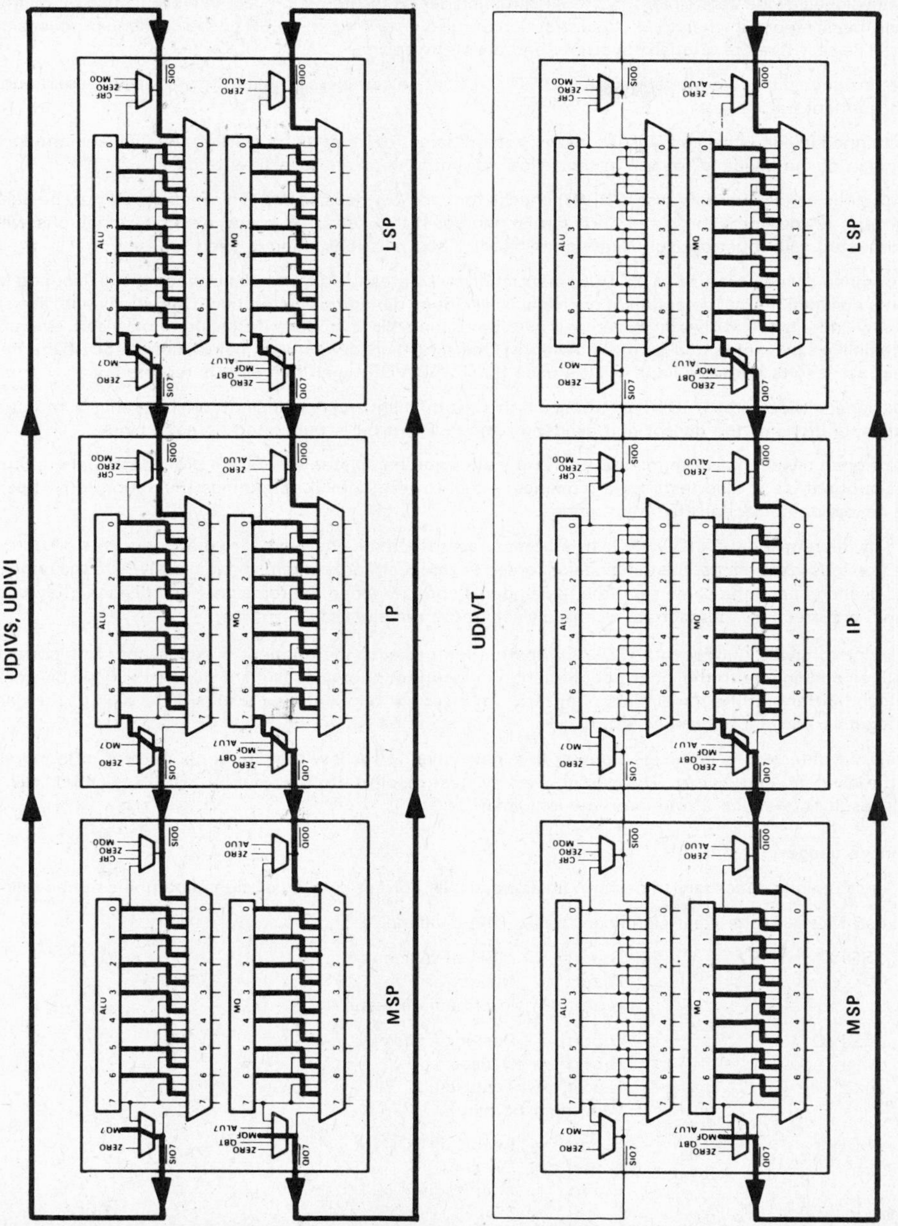
UDIVS, UDIVI
UDIVT
LSP
IP
MSP
ALU
MQ
CRF
ZERO
MQ0
ALU0
MQ7
ALU7
MQF
QBT
SIO0
QIO0
SIO7
QIO7

FIGURE 9. DIVIDE OPERATIONS (Continued)

The unsigned divide iterate start (UDIVIS) instruction begins the iterate procedure while testing for overflow. Overflow is reported when the first subtraction of the divisor from the MSH of the dividend produces carry out. The test detects quotient overflow and divide by zero.

The unsigned divide iterate terminate (UDIVIT) instruction completes the iterate procedure generating the last quotient bit.

The signed divide initialize (SDIVIN) instruction prepares for iteration by shifting the dividend and storing the sign of the dividend for use in the following instructions and overflow tests.

The signed divide overflow test (SDIVO) checks for overflow possibilities. This instruction may be deleted from the divide operation if the OVR pin is ignored. If it is removed some overflow conditions will go undetected. $\overline{\text{WE}}$ must be high (writing inhibited) when this instruction is used.

The signed divide iterate start (SDIVIS) instruction calculates the difference between the divisor and MSH of the dividend. Partial detection of overflow is also done during this instruction. Operations with like signs (positive quotient) and division by zero will overflow during this instruction (including zero divisor). Operations with unlike signs are tested for overflow during the signed divide quotient fix instruction (SDIVQF). Partial overflow results are saved and will be used during SDIVQF when overflow is reported.

The signed divide iterate (SDIVI) instruction forms the quotient and remainder through iterative subtract/add-shift operations of the divisor and dividend. One quotient bit is generated on each clock.

The signed divide iterate terminate (SDIVIT) instruction completes the iterate procedure, generating the last quotient bit. It also tests for a remainder equal to zero, which determines the action to be taken in the following correction (fix) instructions.

The divide remainder fix (DIVRF) instruction corrects the remainder. If a zero remainder was detected by the previous instructions, the remainder is forced to zero. For nonzero remainder cases where the remainder and dividend have the same sign, the remainder is correct. When the remainder and dividend have unlike signs, a correction add/subtract of the divisor to the remainder is performed.

The signed divide quotient fix (SDIVQF) instruction corrects the quotient if necessary. This correction requires adding one to the incorrect quotient. An incorrect quotient results if the signs of the divisor and dividend differ and the remainder is nonzero. An incorrect quotient also results if the sign of the divisor is negative and the remainder is zero.

Overflow detection is completed during this instruction. Overflow may be generated for differing signs of the dividend and divisor. The partial overflow test result performed during SDIVIS is ORed with this test result to produce a true overflow indication.

signed divide usage

The instructions necessary to perform an algebraically correct division of signed numbers are as follows:

Load MQ with the least significant half of the dividend

SDIVIN	S port	=	MSH of dividend
	R port	=	Divisor
	F port	=	Intermediate result
SDIVO	S port	=	Result of SDIVIN
	R port	=	Divisor
	F port	=	Test result
	($\overline{\text{WE}}$ must be high)		
SDIVIS	S port	=	Result of SDIVIN
	R port	=	Divisor
	F port	=	Intermediate result

SDIVI (8N-2 times)	S port	=	Result of SDIVIS (or SDIVI)
	R port	=	Divisor
	F port	=	Intermediate result
SDIVIT	S port	=	Result of last SDIVI
	R port	=	Divisor
	F port	=	Intermediate result
DIVRF	S port	=	Result of SDIVIT
	R port	=	Divisor
	F port	=	Remainder
SDIVQF	S port	=	MQ register
	R port	=	Divisor
	F port	=	Quotient

The status of all signed divide instructions except SDIVIN, DIVRF, and SDIVQF is as follows:

N	→	Forced to zero
OVR	→	Forced to zero
C_{n+8}	→	Carry out equal to one
Z	→	Intermediate result is zero

The status of the SDIVIN instruction is as follows:

N	→	Forced to zero
OVR	→	Forced to zero
C_{n+8}	→	Forced to zero
Z	→	Divisor is zero

The status of the DIVRF instruction is as follows:

N	→	Forced to zero
OVR	→	Forced to zero
C_{n+8}	→	Carry out equal to one
Z	→	Remainder is zero

The status of the SDIVQF instruction is as follows:

N	→	Sign of quotient
OVR	→	Divide overflow
C_{n+8}	→	Carry out equal to one
Z	→	Quotient is zero

The quotient is stored in the MQ register and the remainder is stored in the register file location that originally held the most significant word of the dividend. If fractions are divided, the quotient must be shifted right one bit and the remainder right three bits to obtain the correct fractional representations.

The signed division algorithm is summarized in Table 7.

TABLE 7. SIGNED DIVISION ALGORITHM

OP CODE	MNEMONIC	CLOCK CYCLES	INPUT S PORT	INPUT R PORT	OUTPUT F PORT
E4	LOADMQ	1	Dividend (LSH)	—	Dividend (LSH)
80	SDIVIN	1	Dividend (MSH)	Divisor	Remainder (N)
AF	SDIVO	1	Remainder (N)	Divisor	Test Result
90	SDIVIS	1	Remainder (N)	Divisor	Remainder (N)
A0	SDIVI	8N − 2†	Remainder (N)	Divisor	Remainder (N)
E0	SDIVIT	1	Remainder (N)	Divisor	Remainder (Unfixed)
40	DIVRF	1	Remainder (Unfixed)	Divisor	Remainder
50	SDIVQF	1	MQ Register	Divisor	Quotient

†N = Number of cascaded packages.

unsigned divide usage

The instructions necessary to perform an algebraically correct division of unsigned numbers are as follows:

Load MQ with the least significant half of the dividend

UDIVIS	S port =	MSH of dividend
	R port =	Divisor
	F port =	Intermediate result
UDIVI (8N-1 times)	S port =	Result of UDIVIS (OR UDIVI)
	R port =	Divisor
	F port =	Intermediate result
UDIVIT	S port =	Result of last UDIVI
	R port =	Divisor
	F port =	Remainder (unfixed)
DIVRF	S port =	Result of UDIVIT
	R port =	Divisor
	F port =	Remainder

The status of all unsigned divide instructions except UDIVIS is as follows:

- N → Forced to zero
- OVR → Forced to zero
- C_{n+8} → Carry out equal to one
- Z → Intermediate result is zero

The status of the UDIVIS instruction is as follows:

- N → Forced to zero
- OVR → Divide overflow
- C_{n+8} → Carry out equal to one
- Z → Intermediate result is zero

If fractions are divided, the remainder must be shifted right two bits to obtain the correct fractional representation. The quotient is correct as is. The quotient is stored in the MQ register at the completion of the divide.

The unsigned division algorithm is summarized in Table 8.

TEXAS INSTRUMENTS
POST OFFICE BOX 225012 • DALLAS, TEXAS 75265

TABLE 8. UNSIGNED DIVISION ALGORITHM

OP CODE	MNEMONIC	CLOCK CYCLES	INPUT S PORT	INPUT R PORT	OUTPUT F PORT
E4	LOADMQ	1	Dividend (LSH)	–	Dividend (LSH)
B0	UDIVIS	1	Dividend (MSH)	Divisor	Remainder (N)
C0	UDIVI	8N – 1†	Remainder (N)	Divisor	Remainder (N)
F0	UDIVIT	1	Remainder (N)	Divisor	Remainder (Unfixed)
40	DIVRF	1	Remainder (Unfixed)	Divisor	Remainder

† N = Number of cascaded packages.

group 5 instructions

Hex code F of Group 1 instructions is used to access Group 5 instructions. Group 5 instructions are summarized in Table 9.

TABLE 9. GROUP 5 INSTRUCTIONS

INSTRUCTION BITS (I7-I0) OP CODE (HEX)	MNEMONIC	FUNCTION
0F	CLR	Clear
1F	CLR	Clear
2F	CLR	Clear
3F	CLR	Clear
4F	CLR	Clear
5F	CLR	Clear
6F	CLR	Clear
7F	BCDBIN	BCD to Binary
8F	EX3BC	Excess-3 Byte Correction
9F	EX3C	Excess-3 Word Correction
AF	SDIVO	Signed Divide Overflow Check
BF	CLR	Clear
CF	CLR	Clear
DF	BINEX3	Binary to Excess-3
EF	CLR	Clear
FF	NOP	No Operation

clear instructions (CLR)

There are 11 clear instructions listed in Table 9. The instructions force the ALU output to be zero and the BCD flip-flops to be cleared. The status set by the clear instruction is as follows:

N → None (force to zero)
OVR → None (force to zero)
C_{n+8} → None (force to zero)
Z → Active (one)

no operation instruction (NOP): I7-I0 = FF_{16}

This instruction is identical to the clear instructions except that the BCD flip-flops retain their old value.

excess-3 correction instructions (EX3BC, EX3C)

Two excess-3 correction instructions are available:

1. Excess-3 byte correction (EX3BC): I7-I0 = $8F_{16}$
2. Excess-3 word correction (EX3C): I7-I0 = $9F_{16}$

One instruction supports the byte mode and the other supports the word mode. These instructions correct the excess-3 additions (subtractions) in either the byte or word mode. For correct excess-3 arithmetic, this instruction must follow each add/subtract. The operand must be on the S port.

NOTE: The previous arithmetic overflow should be ignored.

The status of the EX3C instruction is as follows:

N	→	MSB of result
OVR	→	Signed overflow
C_{n+8}	→	Carry out equal one
Z	→	None (force to one)

The status of the EX3BC instruction is as follows:

N	→	None (force to zero)
OVR	→	Byte signed overflow
C_{n+8}	→	Carry out equal one
Z	→	None (force to one)

radix conversions

Conversions between decimal and binary number representations are performed with the aid of two special instructions: BINEX3 and BCDBIN.

BCD to binary instructions (BCDBIN): I7-I0 = $7F_{16}$

This instruction (Figure 10) allows the user to convert an N-digit BCD number to a 4N-bit binary number in 4(N-1) plus 8 clocks. This function sums the R bus, the S bus, and the C_n bit, performs an arithmetic left shift on the ALU result, and simultaneously circular shifts the MQ left. The status set by the BCD to binary instruction is as follows:

N	→	MSB of result
OVR	→	Signed arithmetic overflow†
C_{n+8}	→	Carry out equal one
Z	→	Result equal zero

† Overflow may be the result of an ALU operation or the arithmetic left shift operation.

The following code illustrates the BCD to binary conversion technique.

Let ACC be an accumulator register
Let NUM be the register which contains the BCD number
Let MSK be a mask register

```
M1:    LOADMQ NUM                 ; LOAD MQ WITH BCD NUMBER
M2:    SUB ACC, ACC, SLCMQ        ; CLEAR ACC AND ALIGN MQ
M3:    SUB, MSK, MSK, SLCMQ       ; CLEAR MSK AND ALIGN MQ
M4:    SLCMQ                      ; ALIGN
M5:    SLCMQ                      ; ALIGN
M6:    ADDI ACC, MSK, 15₁₀        ; MSK = 15₁₀
                                  ; REPEAT L1 THRU L4
                                  ; N-1 TIMES (N = number of
                                  ; BCD digits)
L1:    AND MQ, MSK, R1, SLCMQ     ; EXTRACT ONE DIGIT
                                  ; ALIGN MQ
L2:    ADD, ACC, R1, R1, SLCMQ    ; ACC + DIGIT
                                  ; IS STORED IN R1
                                  ; ALIGN MQ
L3:    BCDBIN, R1, R1, ACC        ; 4 × (ACC + DIGIT)
                                  ; IS STORED IN ACC
                                  ; ALIGN MQ
L4:    BCDBIN, ACC, R1, ACC       ; 10 × (ACC + DIGIT)
                                  ; IS STORED IN ACC
                                  ; ALIGN MQ
M7:    AND MQ, MSK, R1            ; FETCH LAST DIGIT
M8:    ACC+R1 → ACC               ; ADD IN LAST DIGIT
```

The previous code generates a binary number by executing the standard conversion formula for a BCD number (shown for 32 bits).

$$ABCD = [(A \times 10 + B) \times 10 + C] \times 10 + D$$

Notice that the conversion begins with the most significant BCD digit and that the addition is performed in radix 2.

binary to excess-3 instructions (BINEX3): I7-I0 = DF_{16}

This instruction (Figure 11) allows the user to convert an N-bit binary number to an N/4-bit excess-3 number representation in 2N + 3 clocks. The data on the R and S ports are summed with the MSB of the MQ register. The MQ register is simultaneously shifted left circularly. The status set by the binary to excess-3 instruction is as follows:

N	→	MSB of result
OVR	→	Signed arithmetic overflow
C_{n+8}	→	Carry out equal one
Z	→	Result equal zero

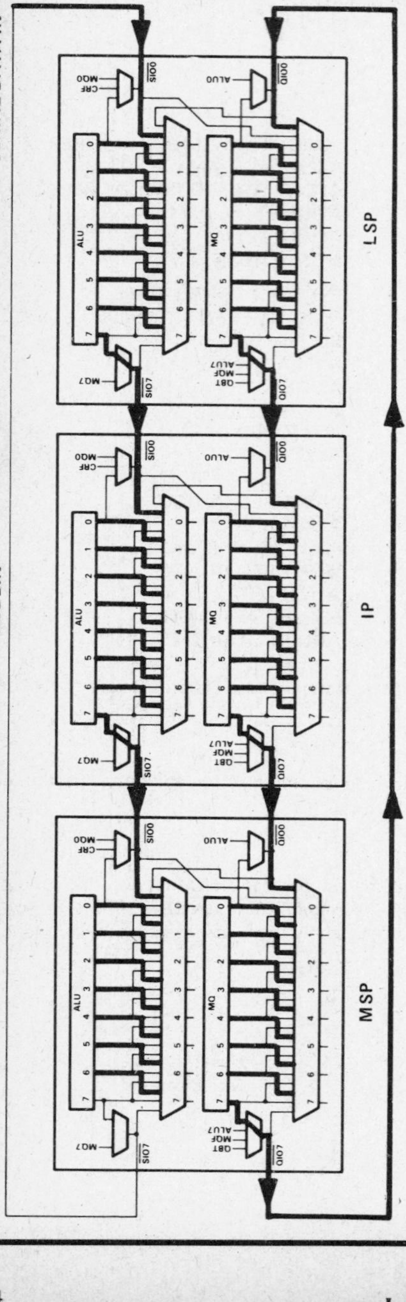
SERIAL DATA IN
BCDBIN
LSP
IP
MSP
ALU
MQ
CRF
MQ0
MQ7
ALU0
ALU7
QBT
MQF
SIO0
SIO7
QIO0
QIO7

FIGURE 10. BCD TO BINARY

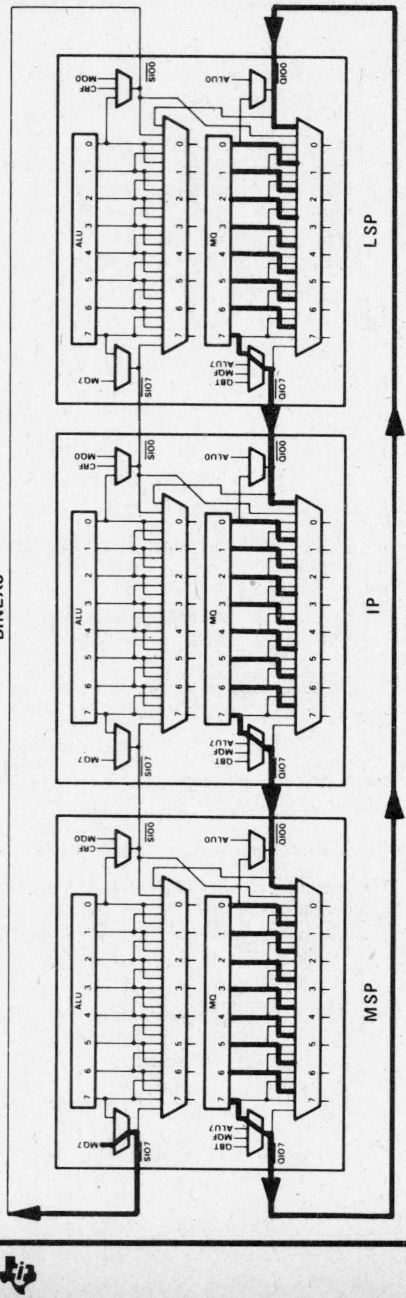
BINEX3
LSP
IP
MSP
ALU
MQ
CRF
MQ0
MQ7
ALU0
ALU7
QBT
MQF
SIO0
SIO7
QIO0
QIO7

FIGURE 11. BINARY TO EXCESS-3

The following illustrates the binary to excess-3 conversion technique.

Let NUM be a register containing an unsigned binary number
Let ACC be an accumulator

```
M1:    LOADMQ NUM              ; LOAD MQ WITH BINARY
                               ; NUMBER
M2:    CLEAR ACC               ; CLEAR ACC
M3:    SET1 ACC H/33/          ; ACC → HEX/3333 . . .
L1:    BINEX3 ACC, ACC, ACC    ; DOUBLE ACC AND ADD IN
                               ; MSB OF MQ
                               ; ALIGN MQ
L2:    EX3C ACC, ACC           ; EXCESS 3 CORRECT
                               ; REPEAT L1 AND L2
                               ; N-1 TIMES
```

The previous code generates an excess-3 number by executing the standard conversion formula for a binary number.

$$a_n 2^n + a_{n-1} 2^{n-1} + a_{n-2} 2^{n-2} + \ . \ . \ . \ a_0 2^0 = [(2a_n + a_{n-1})2 + a_{n-2}]2 \ + \ . \ . \ . \ a_0$$

Notice that the conversion begins with the most significant binary bit and that the addition is performed in radix-10 (excess-3).

decimal arithmetic

Decimal numbers are represented in excess-3 code. Excess-3 code numbers may be generated by adding three to each digit of a Binary Coded Decimal (BCD) number. The hardware necessary to implement excess-3 arithmetic is only slightly different from binary arithmetic. Carries from one digit to another during addition in BCD occur when the sum of the two digits plus the carry-in is greater than or equal to ten. If both numbers are excess-3, the sum will be excess-6, which will produce the proper carries. Therefore, every addition or subtraction operation may use the binary adder. To convert the result from excess-6 to excess-3, one must consider two cases resulting from a BCD digit add: (1) where a carry-out is produced, and (2) where a carry-out is not produced. If a carry-out is not produced, three must be subtracted from the resulting digit. If a carry is produced, the digit is correct as a BCD number. For example, if BCD 5 is added to BCD 6, the excess-3 result would be 8 + 9 = 1 (with a carry). A carry rolls the number through the illegal BCD representations into a correct BCD representation. Binary 3 must be added to digit positions that produce a carry-out to correct the result to an excess-3 representation. Every addition and subtraction instruction stores the carry generated from each 4-bit digit location for use by the excess-3 correction functions. These correction instructions (word or byte) must be executed in the clock cycle immediately after the addition or subtraction operation.

Signed numbers may be represented in ten's complement form by complementing the excess-3 number. As an example, add the decimal number −423 to the decimal number 24, which will be represented by 8AA and 357 in excess-3, respectively.

8AA	
357	
C01	Sum
011	Carry
934	Excess-3 correct
−6CC	Complement
−399	Excess-3 to decimal

Complements of excess-3 numbers may be generated by subtracting the excess-3 number from an excess-3 zero followed by an excess-3 correct.

2 LSI Devices

excess-3 to USASCII conversion

Input/output devices or files represent numbers differently than high-speed central processing units. I/O devices handle all alphanumeric data similarly. CPUs handle more numeric data than alphabetic data and store numeric data in packed form to minimize calculation throughout and reduce memory requirements. To represent the cost of a shirt that was $10.96, the I/O device would handle the six USASCII characters "$", "1","0",".","9","6", which would require 6 bytes of storage. In packed BCD, this number could be stored as 1096 in two bytes of data. The 'AS888 may be programmed to perform data format conversions such as converting excess-3 BCD to USASCII.

The code below converts a packed word of excess-3 BCD to two unpacked words of USASCII code. Instruction "MAIN1" reads the input word from memory into Register 0 (R0). For illustrative purposes, suppose this data was 43C9, which represents the $10.96 shirt in excess-3 code. "MAIN2" and "MAIN3" generate a constant of $2D2D_{16}$, which is an offset constant to convert excess-3 numbers to USASCII. "MAIN4" copies R0 into R2 to set up the subroutine parameters and calls the subroutine "UNPACK", UNPACK2" strips off the upper byte leaving 00C9 in R2. "UNPACK2" and "UNPACK3" together shift the contents of R2 one character position and places the result 0C90 into R3. "UNPACK4" performs a logical OR operation to produce 0CD9 in register 2. "UNPACK5" clears the most significant nibble in each byte to produce 0C09 in R2. "UNPACK6" adds the constant $2D2D_{16}$ to R2 to produce 3936 the USASCII representation of the numerals 96 and returns program control to "MAIN5". "MAIN5" through "MAIN9" align the two remaining characters and call UNPACK and the process repeats. Finally the USASCII representation of 1096 is stored into memory. (Note that no attempt was made to pack the "$" or "." characters.)

Unpacking Excess-3 to USASCII:

```
MAIN1:     READ, RFA(0)                                ; READ IN PACKED EXCESS-3
MAIN2:     XOR, RFA(4), RFB(4), RFC(4)                 ; CLEAR R4
MAIN3:     SET1, RFB(40), RDC(2), RFA(D),              ; GENERATE HEXADECIMAL
           MSH, LSH                                    ; 2D2D16
MAIN4:     MOVE, RFA(0), RFC(2), JSR(UNPACK)           ; COPY RFA(0) INTO RFA(2),
                                                       ; PROCEDURE CALL
MAIN5:     MOVE, RFA(2), RFC(1)                        ; TWO CHARACTERS IN R1
MAIN6:     ADDRS, RFB(0), RFA(0), RFC(0), SLC          ; R0 SHIFTED 2
MAIN7:     ADDRS, RFB(0), RFA(0), RFC(0), SLC          ; R0 SHIFTED 4
MAIN8:     ADDRS, RFB(0), RFA(0), RFC(0), SLC          ; R0 SHIFTED 6
MAIN9:     ADDRS, RFB(0), RFA(0), RFC(0), SLC          ; R0 SHIFTED 8
           JSR (UNPACK)
MAIN10:    STORE, RFA(1)                               ; STORE USASCII, TWO
                                                       ; CHARACTERS IN R2
MAIN11:    STORE, RFA(2)                               ; STORE USASCII
UNPACK1:   SET0, RFB(2), RFC(F), MSH                   ; CLEAR MSH
UNPACK2:   ADDRS, RFB(2), RFA(2), RFC(3), SLC          ; SHIFT R2 TWO PLACES
UNPACK3:   ADDRS, RFB(3), RFA(3), RFC(3), SLC          ; SHIFT R3 TWO PLACES
UNPACK4:   OR, RFB(2), RFA(3), RFC(2)                  ; OR R3 TO R2
UNPACK5:   SET0, RFB(2), RFC(F), RFA(0), LSH, MSH      ; CLEAR MOST SIGNIFICANT 4
                                                       ; BITS IN EACH BYTE
UNPACK6:   ADDRS, RFB(2), RFB(4), RFC(2), RTS          ; ADD HEX 2D, RETURN
```

2

LSI Devices

absolute maximum rating over operating free-air temperature range (unless otherwise noted)

Supply voltage, V_{CC1} .... 7 V
Supply voltage, V_{CC2} .... 3 V
Input voltage .... 7 V
High-level voltage applied to 3-state outputs .... 5.5 V
Operating case temperature range: SN54AS888 .... −55°C to 125°C
Operating free-air temperature range: SN74AS888, SN74AS888-1 .... 0°C to 70°C
Storage temperature range .... −65°C to 150°C

recommended operating conditions

			SN54AS888			SN74AS888 SN74AS888-1			UNIT
			MIN	NOM	MAX	MIN	NOM	MAX	
V_{CC1}	I/O supply voltage		4.5	5	5.5	4.5	5	5.5	V
V_{CC2}	STL internal logic supply voltage		1.9	2	2.1	1.9	2	2.1	V
V_{IH}	High-level input voltage		2			2			V
V_{IL}	Low-level input voltage				0.8			0.8	V
I_{OH}	High-level output current				−1			−2.6	mA
I_{OL}	Low-level output current	All output except $\overline{G}$ and ZERO			8			8	mA
		$\overline{G}$			16			16	
		ZERO			48			48	
T_C	Operating case temperature		−55		125				°C
T_A	Operating free-air temperature					0		70	

electrical characteristics over recommended operating free-air temperature range (unless otherwise noted)

PARAMETER		TEST CONDITIONS	SN54AS888			SN74AS888 SN74AS888-1			UNIT
			MIN	TYP†	MAX	MIN	TYP†	MAX	
V_{IK}		V_{CC1} = 4.5 V, I_I = −18 mA			−1.2			−1.2	V
V_{OH}	All outputs except ZERO	V_{CC1} = 4.5 V to 5.5 V, I_{OH} = −0.4 mA	V_{CC}−2			V_{CC}−2			V
		V_{CC1} = 4.5 V, I_{OH} = −1 mA	2.4						
		V_{CC1} = 4.5 V, I_{OH} = −2.6 mA				2.4			
I_{OH}	ZERO	V_{CC1} = 4.5 V, V_{OH} = 5.5 V			0.1			0.1	mA
V_{OL}	All outputs except $\overline{G}$ and ZERO	V_{CC1} = 4.5 V, I_{OL} = 8 mA			0.5			0.5	V
	$\overline{G}$	V_{CC1} = 4.5 V, I_{OL} = 16 mA			0.5			0.5	
	ZERO	V_{CC1} = 4.5 V, I_{OL} = 48 mA			0.5			0.5	
I_I	I/O	V_{CC1} = 5.5 V, V_I = 5.5 V			0.1			0.1	mA
	All others	V_{CC1} = 5.5 V, V_I = 7 V			0.1			0.1	
I_{IH}‡		V_{CC1} = 5.5 V, V_I = 2.7 V			20			20	μA
I_{IL}‡		V_{CC1} = 5.5 V, V_I = 0.5 V			−0.4			−0.4	mA
I_O§		V_{CC1} = 5.5 V, V_O = 2.25 V	−30		−112	−30		−112	mA
I_{CC1}		V_{CC1} = 5.5 V			150			130	mA
I_{CC2}		V_{CC2} = 2.1 V			410			390	mA

†All typical values are at V_{CC} = 5 V, T_A = 25°C.
‡For I/O ports, the parameters I_{IH} and I_{IL} include the off-state current.
§The output conditions have been chosen to produce a current that closely approximates one-half the true short-circuit current, I_{OS}.

SN54AS888 maximum switching characteristics, V_{CC} = 4.5 V to 5.5 V, T_C = −55 °C to 125 °C (see Note 1)

PARAMETER	FROM (INPUT)	TO (OUTPUT)										UNIT
		Y	C_{n+8}	$\overline{G}$, $\overline{P}$	Z†	N	OVR	DA	DB	$\overline{QIO}$	$\overline{SIO}$	
t_{pd}	A3-A0 B3-B0	62	42	48	69	62	60	18	18	65	66	ns
	DA7-DA0, DB7-DB0	47	28	28	58	50	42	—	—	50	50	
	C_n	25	14	—	32	24	18	—	—	32	32	
	$\overline{EA}$	54	32	35	62	52	52	—	—	58	58	
	$\overline{EB}$	54	32	35	62	52	52	—	—	58	58	
	I7-I0	58	32	32	62	52	41	—	—	58	58	
	$\overline{OEB}$	—	—	—	—	—	—	—	14	—	—	
	$\overline{OEY}$	14	—	—	—	—	—	—	—	—	—	
	$\overline{QIO}$ (n) Shift	15	—	—	24	—	—	—	—	—	—	
	$\overline{SIO}$ (n) Shift	15	—	—	24	22	—	—	—	—	—	
	CK	68	60	56	62	50	68	38	38	70	70	
	$\overline{OEA}$	—	—	—	—	—	—	14	—	—	—	
	SSF‡	—	—	—	—	—	14	—	—	—	—	

† Load resistor R1 = 100 Ω.
‡ For byte instructions only.
NOTE 1: Load circuit and voltage waveforms are shown in Section 1.

SN74AS888 maximum switching characteristics, V_{CC} = 4.5 V to 5.5 V, T_A = 0 °C to 70 °C (see Note 1)

PARAMETER	FROM (INPUT)	TO (OUTPUT)										UNIT
		Y	C_{n+8}	$\overline{G}$, $\overline{P}$	Z†	N	OVR	DA	DB	$\overline{QIO}$	$\overline{SIO}$	
t_{pd}	A3-A0 B3-B0	54	36	42	60	52	50	18	18	58	58	ns
	DA7-DA0, DB7-DB0	44	26	26	52	46	38	—	—	44	44	
	C_n	25	8	—	32	24	18	—	—	31	31	
	$\overline{EA}$	49	29	29	58	49	47	—	—	54	54	
	$\overline{EB}$	49	29	29	58	49	47	—	—	54	54	
	I7-I0	55	30	30	60	49	39	—	—	54	54	
	$\overline{OEB}$	—	—	—	—	—	—	—	12	—	—	
	$\overline{OEY}$	12	—	—	—	—	—	—	—	—	—	
	$\overline{QIO}$ (n) Shift	15	—	—	24	—	—	—	—	—	—	
	$\overline{SIO}$ (n) Shift	15	—	—	24	19	—	—	—	—	—	
	CK	58	55	52	61	52	62	35	35	60	60	
	$\overline{OEA}$	—	—	—	—	—	—	12	—	—	—	
	SSF‡	—	—	—	—	—	12	—	—	—	—	

† Load resistor R1 = 100 Ω.
‡ For byte instructions only.
NOTE 1: Load circuit and voltage waveforms are shown in Section 1.

TEXAS INSTRUMENTS
POST OFFICE BOX 225012 • DALLAS, TEXAS 75265

SN74AS888-1 maximum switching characteristics, V_{CC} = 4.5 V to 5.5 V, T_A = 0°C to 70°C (see Note 1)

PARAMETER	FROM (INPUT)	TO (OUTPUT) Y	C_{n+8}	$\overline{G}$, $\overline{P}$	Z†	N	OVR	DA	DB	$\overline{QIO}$	$\overline{SIO}$	UNIT
t_{pd}	A3-A0 B3-B0	44	30	36	50	44	44	17	17	48	48	ns
	DA7-DA0, DB7-DB0	36	24	24	46	41	32	–	–	40	40	
	C_n	22	8	–	27	21	16	–	–	25	25	
	$\overline{EA}$	40	25	25	49	41	41	–	–	44	44	
	$\overline{EB}$	40	25	25	49	41	41	–	–	44	44	
	I7-I0	46	27	27	50	42	35	–	–	45	45	
	$\overline{OEB}$	–	–	–	–	–	–	–	12	–	–	
	$\overline{OEY}$	12	–	–	–	–	–	–	–	–	–	
	$\overline{QIO}$ (n) Shift	14	–	–	20	–	–	–	–	–	–	
	$\overline{SIO}$ (n) Shift	14	–	–	20	18	–	–	–	–	–	
	CK	50	46	46	50	50	50	30	30	50	50	
	$\overline{OEA}$	–	–	–	–	–	–	12	–	–	–	
	SSF‡	–	–	–	–	–	12	–	–	–	–	

† Load resistor R1 = 100 Ω.
‡ For byte instructions only.
NOTE 1: Load circuit and voltage waveforms are shown in Section 1.

register file write setup and hold times

PARAMETER		SN54AS888 MIN	SN54AS888 MAX	SN74AS888 MIN	SN74AS888 MAX	SN74AS888-1 MIN	SN74AS888-1 MAX	UNIT
t_{su}	C3-C0	8		7		6		ns
	DB§	14		12		11		
	I7-I4	16		14		13		
	I3-I0	24		22		21		
	$\overline{OEY}$	4		3		3		
	Y7-Y0	2		2		2		
	$\overline{WE}$	8		6		6		
	$\overline{QIO}$(n), $\overline{SIO}$(n)	6		5		5		
	SELY	8		6		6		
t_h	C3-C0	0		0		0		ns
	DB§	0		0		0		
	I7-I4	0		0		0		
	I3-I0	0		0		0		
	$\overline{OEY}$	6		5		5		
	Y7-Y0	10		10		10		
	$\overline{WE}$	3		2		2		
	$\overline{QIO}$(n), $\overline{SIO}$(n)	0		0		0		
	SELY	8		6		6		

§ DB (during select instruction) through Y port.

special instruction switching characteristics

During various special instructions, the SSF pin is used to pass required information between the 'AS888 packages which make up a total system.

For instance, during the multiplication process, the LSB of the multiplier determines whether an ADD/SHIFT or SHIFT operation is performed. During multiplication, the SSF pin of the least significant package (LSP) becomes an output pin while all other packages become input pins.

Similarly, during normalization, the required operation depends on whether the two data MSBs are the same or different. Therefore, during normalization the SSF pin of the most significant package (MSP) becomes an output pin while all other packages become input pins.

Tables 10, 11, and 12 list the instructions which force the SSF pin during their execution. The propagation delay from various inputs is also shown. The parameter which limits normal system performance is indicated by a dagger.

TABLE 10. SN54AS888 SSF PIN DELAYS AND SETUP TIMES

MNEMONIC	HEX CODE	SSF SOURCE		INPUT → SSF (ns)				SSF SETUP TIME (ns)
		LSP	MSP	C_n	$I_{(n)}$	CK	$B_{(n)}$	
CRC	00	X		–	29	58	40†	20
SNORM	20		X	–	29†	46	–	20
DNORM	30		X	–	29	55	40†	20
DIVRF	40		X	–	29†	46	–	20
SDIVQF	50		X	–	26†	–	–	18
SMULI	60	X		–	26†	43	–	0
SDIVIN	80		X	–	48	64	44†	0
SDIVIS	90		X	26†	51	64	55	0
SDIVI	A0		X	26†	51	64	55	0
UDIVIS	B0		X	18†	45	64	46	0
UDIVI	C0		X	18†	50	54	40	0
UMULI	D0	X		–	25†	48	–	0
SDIVIT	E0		X	26†	50	56	54	0
ABX	48		X	–	34	62	39†	20
SMTC	58		X	–	29	58	39†	20
BINEX3	DF		X	–	29†	58	–	18
LOADMQ (Arith)		X		23†	34	62	40	0
LOADMQ (Log)		X		–	33	62	40†	0
BADD	88	↑ SOURCE IS MOST SIGNIFICANT BYTE SELECTED ↓		18†	58	62	49	–
BSUBS	98			18†	58	62	49	–
BSUBR	A8			18†	58	71	49	–
BINCS	B8			18†	58	60	49	–
BINCNS	C8			18†	58	71	49	–
BXOR	D8			–	58	–	–	–
BAND	E8			–	58	–	–	–
BOR	F8			–	58	–	–	–
EX3BC	8F			–	58	46	49†	–

† This parameter limits normal system performance.

TEXAS INSTRUMENTS
POST OFFICE BOX 225012 • DALLAS, TEXAS 75265

TABLE 11. SN74AS888 SSF PIN DELAYS AND SETUP TIMES

MNEMONIC	HEX CODE	SSF SOURCE LSP	SSF SOURCE MSP	INPUT → SSF (ns) C_n	INPUT → SSF (ns) $I_{(n)}$	INPUT → SSF (ns) CK	INPUT → SSF (ns) $B_{(n)}$	SSF SETUP TIME (ns)
CRC	00	X		–	26	52	37†	17
SNORM	20		X	–	26†	40	–	17
DNORM	30		X	–	26	52	37†	17
DIVRF	40		X	–	26†	40	–	17
SDIVQF	50		X	–	25†	–	–	17
SMULI	60	X		–	25†	40	–	0
SDIVIN	80		X	–	38	60	40†	0
SDIVIS	90		X	24†	48	60	52	0
SDIVI	A0		X	24†	48	60	52	0
UDIVIS	B0		X	17†	43	60	45	0
UDIVI	C0		X	17†	44	52	37	0
UMULI	D0	X		–	26†	40	–	0
SDIVIT	E0		X	25†	46	52	49	0
ABX	48		X	–	32	60	38	17
SMTC	58		X	–	26	52	38†	17
BINEX3	DF		X	–	26†	40	–	17
LOADMQ (Arith)		X		22†	32	50	38	0
LOADMQ (Log)		X		–	32	50	38†	0
BADD	88	↑ SOURCE IS MOST SIGNIFICANT BYTE SELECTED ↓		17†	52	55	46	–
BSUBS	98			17†	52	55	46	–
BSUBR	A8			17†	52	62	46	–
BINCS	B8			17†	52	55	46	–
BINCNS	C8			17†	52	62	46	–
BXOR	D8			–	52	–	–	–
BAND	E8			–	52	–	–	–
BOR	F8			–	52	–	–	–
EX3BC	8F			–	45	45	46†	–

† This parameter limits normal system performance.

TABLE 12. SN74AS888-1 SSF PIN DELAYS AND SETUP TIMES

MNEMONIC	HEX CODE	SSF SOURCE LSP	SSF SOURCE MSP	INPUT → SSF (ns) C_n	$I_{(n)}$	CK	$B_{(n)}$	SSF SETUP TIME (ns)
CRC	00	X		–	23	42	34†	14
SNORM	20		X	–	23†	28	–	14
DNORM	30		X	–	23	40	34†	14
DIVRF	40		X	–	23†	27	–	14
SDIVQF	50		X	–	23†	–	–	14
SMULI	60	X		–	22†	27	–	0
SDIVIN	80		X	–	35	46	35†	0
SDIVIS	90		X	22†	42	48	42	0
SDIVI	A0		X	22†	42	46	42	0
UDIVIS	B0		X	16†	42	46	38	0
UDIVI	C0		X	16†	36	46	34	0
UMULI	D0	X		–	22†	27	–	0
SDIVIT	E0		X	21†	40	44	42	0
ABX	48		X	–	28	46	30†	14
SMTC	58		X	–	24	44	30†	14
BINEX3	DF		X	–	23†	27	–	14
LOADMQ (Arith)		X		19†	28	40	30	0
LOADMQ (Log)		X		–	28	35	30†	0
BADD	88	↑ SOURCE IS MOST SIGNIFICANT BYTE SELECTED ↓		16†	42	42	40	–
BSUBS	98			16†	42	40	40	–
BSUBR	A8			16†	42	50	40	–
BINCS	B8			16†	42	46	40	–
BINCNS	C8			16†	42	54	42	–
BXOR	D8			–	42	–	–	–
BAND	E8			–	42	–	–	–
BOR	F8			–	42	–	–	–
EX3BC	8F			–	42	42	42†	–

† This parameter limits normal system performance.

D2662, NOVEMBER 1982—REVISED APRIL 1985

- 14 Bits Wide—Addresses up to 16,384 Words of Microcode with One Chip
- Selects Address from One of Eight Sources
- STL-AS Technology
- Independent Read Pointer for Aid in Microcode Diagnostics
- Supports Real-Time Interrupts
- Two Independent Loop Counters
- Supports 64 Powerful Instructions
- Dependable Texas Instruments Quality and Reliability

description

The 'AS890 is a powerful microsequencer that is the result of the implementation of TI's Advanced Schottky and Schottky Transistor Logic. Approximately 2400 Schottky gate equivalents are used to construct this high-performance sequencer. The 'AS890 can generate an address and provide register status in only 29 ns while typically requiring only 1.8 watts of power. All internal STL logic in these devices operates on a 2-volt power supply that must be supplied externally. The information generated by the internal STL logic is communicated in the rest of the system via 5-volt Advanced Schottky TTL-compatible I/O ports.

The microsequencers select a 14-bit microaddress from one of eight sources to provide the proper microinstruction sequence for bit-slice processor or other microcode based systems. These high-performance devices are capable of addressing 16,384 control store memory locations either sequentially or via conditional branching algorithms. This multiway branching capability, coupled with a nine-word deep FILO (first in, last out) stack, allows the microprogrammer to arrange his code in blocks so that microprograms may be structured in the same fashion as such high-level languages as ALGOL, Pascal, or Ada.

Both polled and real-time interrupt routines are supported by the 'AS890 to enhance system throughput capability. Vectored interrupts may occur during any instruction, including PUSHes and POPs.

SN74AS890 . . . GB PACKAGE
(TOP VIEW)

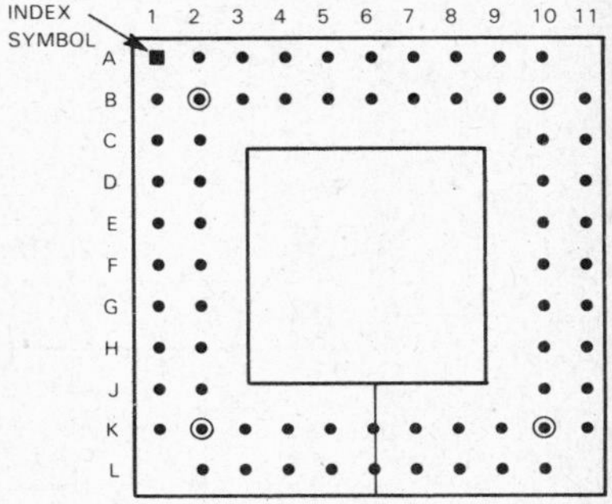
INDEX SYMBOL
1 2 3 4 5 6 7 8 9 10 11
A B C D E F G H J K L

AS890

PIN NO.	PIN NAME	PIN NO.	PIN NAME	PIN NO.	PIN NAME	PIN NO.	PIN NAME
A-2	DRB10	B-9	STKWRN/RER	F-10	V_{CC1}	K-4	DRA13
A-3	DRB9	B-10	ZERO	F-11	MUX2	K-5	DRA11
A-4	DRB8	B-11	CK	G-1	Y5	K-6	DRA8
A-5	DRB7	C-1	Y13	G-2	$\overline{YOE}$	K-7	DRA7
A-6	DRB6	C-2	Y10	G-10	RC1	K-8	DRA0
A-7	DRB5	C-10	$\overline{CC}$	G-11	MUX1	K-9	DRA1
A-8	DRB4	C-11	S1	H-1	Y4	K-10	DRA3
A-9	DRB3	D-1	Y12	H-2	Y6	K-11	DRA2
A-10	DRB1	D-2	Y9	H-10	B0	L-2	B2
B-1	DRB13	D10	S2	H-11	MUX0	L-3	INC
B-2	$\overline{INT}$	D-11	S0	J-1	Y3	L-4	DRA12
B-3	DRB12	E-1	Y11	J-2	Y2	L-5	DRA10
B-4	DRB11	E-2	Y8	J-10	RC2	L-6	DRA9
B-5	B3	E-10	V_{CC2}	J-11	OSEL	L-7	$\overline{RAOE}$
B-6	$\overline{RBOE}$	E-11	RC0	K-1	Y1	L-8	DRA6
B-7	DRB2	F-1	Y7	K-2	Y0	L-9	DRA5
B-8	DRB0	F-2	GND	K-3	B1	L-10	DRA4

SN54AS890 . . . FD PACKAGE
SN74AS890 . . . FN PACKAGE
(TOP VIEW)

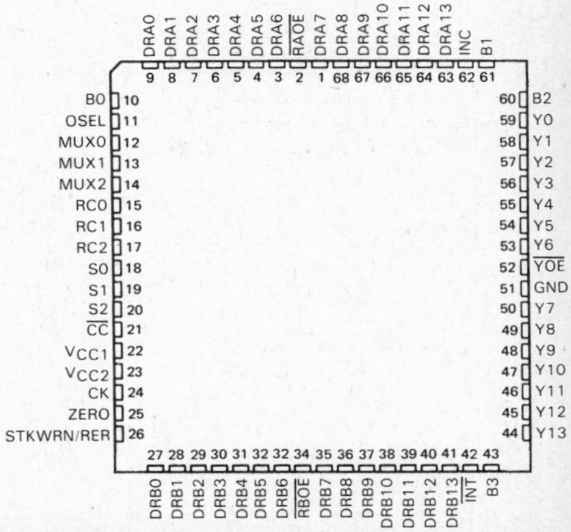
DRA0 DRA1 DRA2 DRA3 DRA4 DRA5 DRA6 $\overline{RAOE}$ DRA7 DRA8 DRA9 DRA10 DRA11 DRA12 DRA13 INC B1
9 8 7 6 5 4 3 2 1 68 67 66 65 64 63 62 61
B0 10
OSEL 11
MUX0 12
MUX1 13
MUX2 14
RC0 15
RC1 16
RC2 17
S0 18
S1 19
S2 20
$\overline{CC}$ 21
V_{CC1} 22
V_{CC2} 23
CK 24
ZERO 25
STKWRN/RER 26
60 B2
59 Y0
58 Y1
57 Y2
56 Y3
55 Y4
54 Y5
53 Y6
52 $\overline{YOE}$
51 GND
50 Y7
49 Y8
48 Y9
47 Y10
46 Y11
45 Y12
44 Y13
27 28 29 30 31 32 32 34 35 36 37 38 39 40 41 42 43
DRB0 DRB1 DRB2 DRB3 DRB4 DRB5 DRB6 $\overline{RBOE}$ DRB7 DRB8 DRB9 DRB10 DRB11 DRB12 DRB13 $\overline{INT}$ B3

2

LSI Devices

functional block diagram

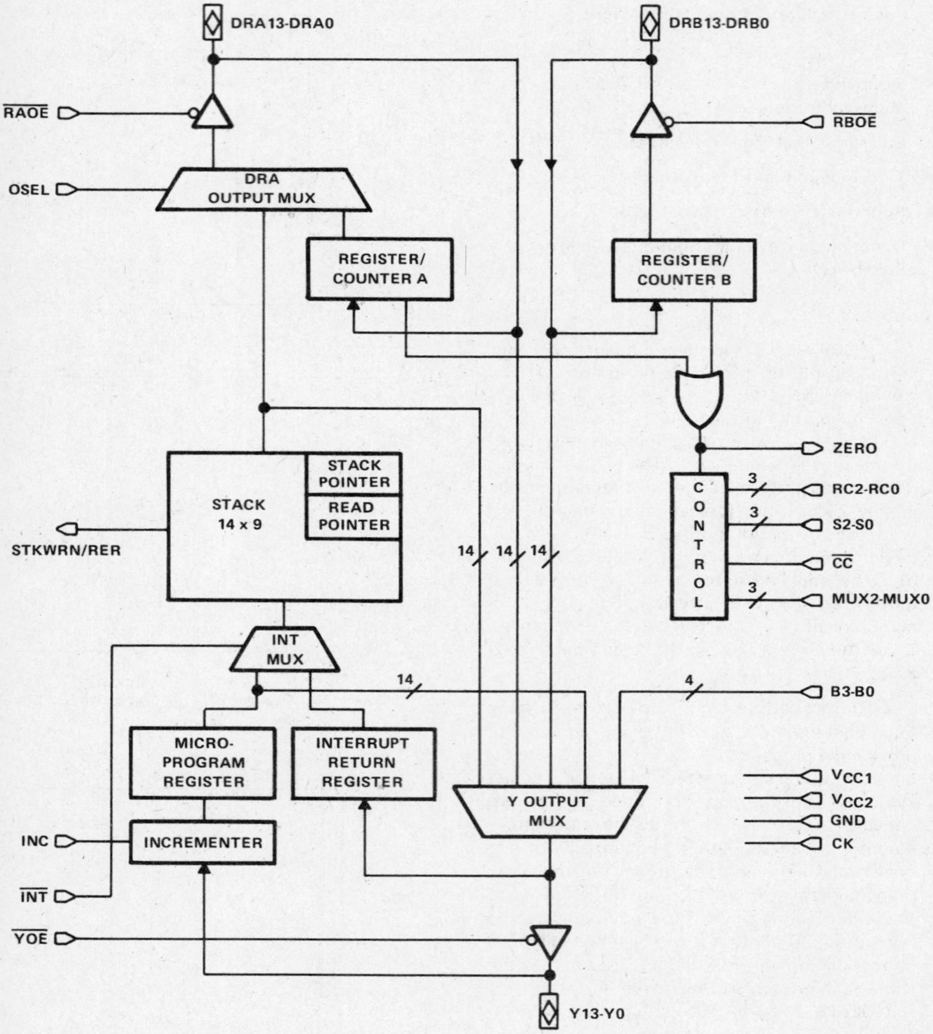
DRA13-DRA0
DRB13-DRB0
RAOE
RBOE
OSEL
DRA
OUTPUT MUX
REGISTER/
COUNTER A
REGISTER/
COUNTER B
ZERO
STACK
14 x 9
STACK
POINTER
READ
POINTER
STKWRN/RER
C O N T R O L
3
RC2-RC0
3
S2-S0
CC
3
MUX2-MUX0
14 14 14
INT
MUX
14
4
B3-B0
MICRO-
PROGRAM
REGISTER
INTERRUPT
RETURN
REGISTER
Y OUTPUT
MUX
VCC1
VCC2
GND
CK
INC
INCREMENTER
INT
YOE
Y13-Y0

TEXAS INSTRUMENTS
POST OFFICE BOX 225012 • DALLAS, TEXAS 75265

pin descriptions

PIN NAME	I/O	PIN FUNCTION
$\overline{RAOE}$	In	Enables DRA output, active low
DRA6-DRA0	In/Out	Seven LSBs of the A direct data I/O port
OSEL	In	MUX control for the source to DRA. Low selects RA, high selects stack.
MUX2-MUX0	In	MUX control for Y output bus (see Table 1)
RC2-RC0	In	Register/counter controls (see Table 3)
S2-S0	In	Stack control (see Table 2)
$\overline{CC}$	In	Condition code
V_{CC1}		5-volt supply for TTL compatible I/O
V_{CC2}		2-volt supply for internal STL
CK	In	Clock
ZERO	Out	Zero detect flag for register A and B
STKWRN/RER	Out	Stack overflow, underflow/read error flag
DRB6-DRB0	In/Out	Seven LSBs of the B direct data I/O port (0 = LSB)
$\overline{RBOE}$	In	Enables DRB output, active low
DRB13-DRB7	In/Out	Seven MSBs of the B direct data I/O port
$\overline{INT}$	In	Active low selects INT RT register to stack
Y13-Y8	In/Out	Six MSBs of bidirectional Y port
GND		Ground
Y7	In/Out	Seventh bit of bidirectional Y port
$\overline{YOE}$	In	Enables Y output bus, active low
Y6-Y0	In/Out	Seven LSBs of bidirectional Y port (0 = LSB)
INC	In	Incrementer control
DRA13-DRA7	In/Out	Seven MSBs of direct B data I/O port
B3-B0	In	16-way branch inputs on

description (continued)

Two 14-bit loadable registers/counters may be used for temporary storage of data or utilized as down counters for repetitive instructions such as multiplication and division or as loop counters when iterative routines are required.

An additional feature is a 24-bit port that appends four user-definable bits to the DRA or DRB address value for support of 16-way branches for the execution of relative branch addressing schemes.

Y output multiplexer

The Y output multiplexer of the 'AS890 is capable of selecting the next branch address from one of eight locations. Addresses may be sourced from:

1. The top of the 14-bit by 9-word address stack
2. An external input on the DRA port, potentially a pipeline register
3. An external input on the DRB port, potentially a pipeline register
4. Internal register/counter A
5. Internal register/counter B
6. An internal microprogram counter (MPC register)
7. An external input onto the bidirectional Y output port
8. A 16-way branch—4 bits appended to DRA, DRB, register/counter A or register/counter B.

The source of the next address is dependent upon the previous state of the microsequencer, the MUX controls (MUX2-MUX0), the condition code ($\overline{CC}$) input, and the state of an internal status flag (status externally available at the ZERO output) that indicates that one of the on-chip registers is being decremented to zero.

The entire instruction set may be made conditional by manipulation of the condition code ($\overline{CC}$) input. Allowing the $\overline{CC}$ value to vary as a result of data or status provides for state-dependent or data-dependent branching. Unconditional branches may be achieved by forcing $\overline{CC}$ high when selecting control store addresses. Holding this pin low will provide for conditional or unconditional branches as dictated by the state of the zero-detect flag. The required control signals for selection of the Y output source are listed in Table 1. Note that the dependence of the 'AS890 on two variables for conditional branches and jumps allows a conditional branch or conditional jump to subroutine in any clock cycle. Also note that all multiplexer inputs are overridden when all of the stack control inputs are pulled low. This instruction resets the stack and read pointers to zero and places all lines of the Y output bus at the low level.

TABLE 1. Y OUTPUT CONTROL

MUX CONTROL			RESET*	Y OUTPUT SOURCE		Y OUTPUT SOURCE
				$\overline{CC}$ = L		$\overline{CC}$ = H
MUX2	MUX1	MUX0		ZERO = L	ZERO = H	
X	X	X	YES	ALL LOW	ALL LOW	ALL LOW
L	L	L	NO	STK	MPC	DRA
L	L	H	NO	STK	MPC	DRB
L	H	L	NO	STK	DRA	MPC
L	H	H	NO	STK	DRB	MPC
H	L	L	NO	DRA	MPC	DRB
H	L	H	NO	DRA' (16-WAY BRANCH)	MPC	DRB' (16-WAY BRANCH)
H	H	L	NO	DRA	STK	MPC
H	H	H	NO	DRB	STK	MPC

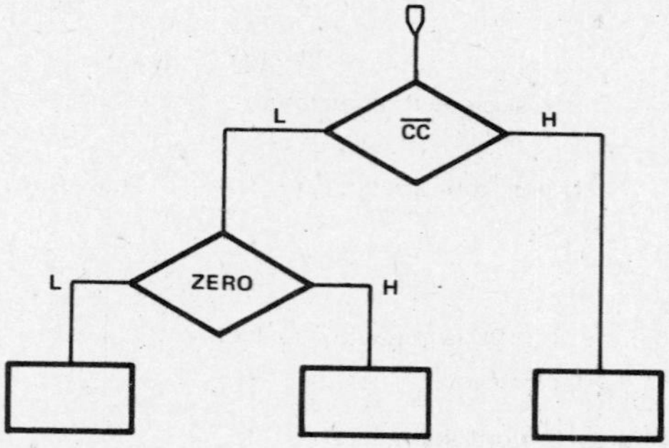
L
$\overline{CC}$
H
L
ZERO
H

H = high level, L = low level, X = irrelevant.
*Reset command is implemented by setting S2-S0 = LLL.

14-bit by 9-word address stack

The positive-edge-triggered 14-bit address stack supplies on-board storage of nine control store addresses that support up to nine nested levels of microsubroutine, looping, and real-time interrupt functions. The stack pointer (SP), which operates as an up-down counter, is updated after the execution of each PUSH operation and before each POP. In a PUSH operation, the address stored in the MPC register is loaded into the stack location addressed by the stack pointer, and the stack pointer is incremented. This address is available at the DRA port by enabling DRA ($\overline{\text{RAOE}}$ low and OSEL high).

A POP operation causes the stack pointer to be decremented on the first rising clock edge following the arrival of the POP instruction at the S2-S0 pins. The value that was indexed by the stack pointer is effectively removed from the top of the stack. All PUSH and POP instructions are conditionally dependent upon the stack control inputs (S2-S0), the condition code ($\overline{\text{CC}}$), the input value, and the zero-detect status. The desired option may be selected using the stack control inputs listed in Table 2.

TABLE 2. STACK CONTROL

STACK CONTROL				STACK OPERATION, $\overline{\text{CC}}$ = L		
S2	S1	S0	OSEL	ZERO = L	ZERO = H	$\overline{\text{CC}}$ = H
L	L	L	X	RESET/CLEAR	RESET/CLEAR	RESET/CLEAR
L	L	H	X	CLEAR SP, RP	HOLD	HOLD
L	H	L	X	HOLD	POP	POP
L	H	H	X	POP	HOLD	HOLD
H	L	L	X	HOLD	PUSH	PUSH
H	L	H	X	PUSH	HOLD	HOLD
H	H	L	X	PUSH	HOLD	PUSH
H	H	H	H	READ	READ	READ
H	H	H	L	HOLD	HOLD	HOLD

The read pointer (RP) is a useful tool in debugging microcoded systems. A microprogrammer now has the ability to perform a nondestructive, sequential read of the stack contents from the DRA port. This capability provides the user with a method of backtracking through the address sequence to determine the cause of overflow without affecting program flow, the status of the stack-pointer or the internal data of the stack. Placing a high value on all of the stack inputs (S2-S0) and OSEL places the 'AS890 into the read mode. At each low-to-high clock transition, the value pointed to by the read pointer is available at the DRA port and the read pointer is decremented. Microcode diagnostics are simplified by the ability of the 'AS890 to sequentially dump the contents of its stack. The bottom of the stack is detected by monitoring the STKWRN/RER (stack warning/read error) pin. A high will appear when the stack contains one word and a READ instruction is applied to the S2-S0 pins. This signifies that the last address has been read. The stack pointer and stack contents are uneffected by the READ operation. Under normal PUSH and POP operations the read pointer is updated with the stack pointer and contains identical information.

The STKWRN/RER pin alerts the system to a potential stack overflow or underflow condition. STKWRN/RER becomes active under two additional conditions. If seven of the nine stack locations (0-8) are full (the stack pointer is at 7) and a PUSH occurs, the STKWRN/RER pin will produce a high-level signal to warn that the stack is approaching its capacity, and will be full after one more PUSH. Knowledge that overflow potential exists allows bit-slice-based systems to continuously process real-time interrupt vectors. This signal will remain high, if HOLD, PUSH, or POP instructions occur, until the stack pointer is decremented to 7.

The user may be protected from attempting to POP an empty stack by monitoring STKWRN/RER before POP operations. A high level at this pin signifies that the last address has been removed from the stack (SP = 0). This condition remains until an address is pushed onto the stack and the stack pointer is incremented to one.

Clearing the stack and read pointer is accomplished by placing low levels onto the stack control lines (S2-S0). This function overrides all of the Y output MUX controls and places the Y bus into a low state.

LSI Devices 2

register/counters

Two loadable 14-bit registers extend the looping and branching capabilities. Addresses may be loaded directly into register/counter A (RA) and register/counter B (RB) through the direct data ports DRA13-DRA0 and DRB13-DRB0. The values stored in these registers may either be held, decremented, or read as a result of the register control inputs (RC2-RC0), $\overline{RAOE}$, and $\overline{RBOE}$. All combinations of these functions are supported with the exception of a simultaneous decrement of both registers. Generation of iteration routines may be accomplished by loading RA and/or RB and operating them as a down counter. Loop termination is acknowledged by the ZERO output going high to indicate that a register contains a binary one and that a decrement is about to take place. Because of this facility, a ''decrement and branch on loop'' termination may be executed in the same clock cycle.

The contents of RA are accessible to the DRA port when OSEL is low and the output bus is enabled by RAOE being low. Data from RB is available when DRB is enabled by $\overline{RBOE}$ being low. Note that control of the registers is maintained while an external value is active on the DRA and DRB ports. A value being directed from the DRA and DRB buses to the output will not inhibit the decrement operation.

Register/counter controls are listed in Table 3.

TABLE 3. REGISTER CONTROL

RC2	RC1	RC0	REG A	REG B
L	L	L	HOLD	HOLD
L	L	H	DEC	HOLD
L	H	L	LOAD	HOLD
L	H	H	DEC	LOAD
H	L	L	LOAD	LOAD
H	L	H	HOLD	DEC
H	H	L	HOLD	LOAD
H	H	H	LOAD	DEC

microprogram register and increment

The microprogram register (MPC) and the incrementer (INC) provide the means for generating the next microprogram address for sequential addressing operations. The MPC may be loaded with either the outgoing address on the Y bus or may receive an external address for processing interrupt vectors.

The current address on the Y bus is passed to the MPC at each rising clock edge, either unaltered (INC low) for repeating statements, or incremented by one (INC high) for addressing sequential control store locations.

The MPC may also be externally loaded for subroutine and interrupt functions. Taking $\overline{YOE}$ high and forcing the new address onto the bidirectional Y bus loads the MPC with the new address at the positive clock edge. This value may also be incremented prior to storage in the MPC for sequential addressing of subroutines or interrupt routines.

interrupts

Real-time vectored interrupt routines are supported for those applications where polling would impede system throughput. Any instruction, including PUSHes and POPs, may be interrupted. To process an interrupt, the following procedure should be followed:

1. The bidirectional Y bus is placed into the high-impedance state by forcing $\overline{YOE}$ high.
2. The interrupt entry point vector is then forced onto the Y bus and incremented to become the second microinstruction of the interrupt routine. This is accomplished by making INC high.

TEXAS INSTRUMENTS
POST OFFICE BOX 225012 • DALLAS, TEXAS 75265

3. At the following clock edge, the second microaddress is stored in the MPC and the interrupted address will be stored in the INT RT register which always contains the outgoing value on the Y bus. This edge also causes the processor to begin execution of the first instruction of the interrupt routine. This first instruction must PUSH the address stored in the INT RT register onto the stack so that the proper return linkage is maintained. This is accomplished by making $\overline{INT}$ low and performing a PUSH. If this instruction were to be interrupted, the process would be repeated and the proper return linkage preserved.

control inputs

A listing of the response of internal elements to various control inputs is given in Table 4.

TABLE 4. RESPONSE TO CONTROL INPUTS

PIN NAME	LOGIC LEVEL	
	HIGH	LOW
$\overline{RAOE}$	DRA output in high-Z state	DRA output is active
$\overline{RBOE}$	DRB output in high-Z state	DRB output is active
$\overline{YOE}$	Y output in high-Z state	Y output is active
$\overline{INT}$	MPC to stack	INT RT register to stack
OSEL	Stack to DRA buffer input	RA to DRA buffer input
INC	Adds one to Y output and stores in MPC	Passes Y output to MPC unaltered
MUX2-MUXO	Table 1	Table 1
S2-SO	Table 2	Table 2
RC2-RCO	Table 3	Table 3

instruction set

Sixty-four microsequencing instructions enable the 'AS890 to generate micro-addresses for up to 16,384 locations. Any instruction can be made conditional depending upon the value of the externally applied condition code ($\overline{CC}$) and the value stored in either of the internal register/counters.

The required signals for selection of the Y output source were listed in Table 1. Suggested methods for implementing a few commonly used instructions are given in Table 5 and flowcharts showing execution examples are illustrated in Figure 1.

It should be noted that the term jump refers to a subroutine call that must be accompanied by a return instruction. The term branch implies that a deviation from the program flow is accomplished but no return is required.

TABLE 5. SUGGESTED CODING FOR REPRESENTATIVE INSTRUCTIONS

FUNCTION	MNEMONIC	MUX2	MUX1	MUX0	S2	S1	S0	$\overline{CC}$	FIGURE
Continue	CONT	X	H	X	H	H	H	H	1(a)
Unconditional branch	BR	L	L	X	H	H	H	H	1(b)
Conditional branch	CBR	H	H	X	H	H	H	V	1(c)
Three-way branch	BR2W	H	L	L	H	H	H	V	1(d)
Conditional loop on stack	LOOPS	L	L	X	L	H	L	L	1(e)
Repeat	REPEAT	L	L	X	H	H	H	L	1(f)
Loop on stack with exit	LSWE	L	L	X	L	H	L	V	1(g)
Conditional jump to subroutine	CJSR	H	H	X	H	L	H	V	1(h)
Jump to subroutine	JSR	L	L	X	H	L	H	H	1(i)
Two-way jump to subroutine	JSR2W	H	L	L	H	H	L	V	1(j)
Repeat until	UNTIL	L	H	X	L	H	L	V	1(k)
Return from subroutine	RTS	L	H	X	L	H	H	L	1(l)
Conditional return from subroutine	CRTS	L	H	X	L	H	H	V	1(m)
Conditional return from subroutine or branch	CRTSB	L	H	X	L	H	H	V	1(n)
Conditional branch and PUSH	CBRP	H	H	X	H	L	H	V	1(o)
Conditional branch and POP	CBRPO	H	H	X	L	H	H	V	1(p)
PUSH and continue	PUSH	L	H	X	H	L	L	H	1(q)
POP and continue	POP	X	H	X	L	H	L	H	1(r)
Exit from loop	EXITLP	L	L	X	L	H	L	V	1(s)
Reset and clear stack/read pointer	RESET	X	X	X	L	L	L	X	1(t)
32-way branch	BR32W	H	L	H	H	H	H	V	1(u)
Execute n times	NEX	L	L	X	L	H	L	L	1(v)

H = high level, L = low level, X = irrelevant, V = varies (condition code value is dependent upon machine and data status and will vary accordingly).

LSI Devices

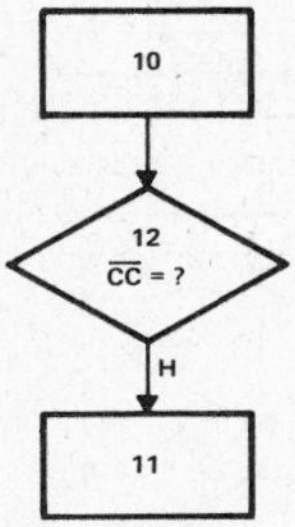
10
12
$\overline{CC}$ = ?
H
11

(a) CONTINUE
($\overline{CC}$ FORCED)

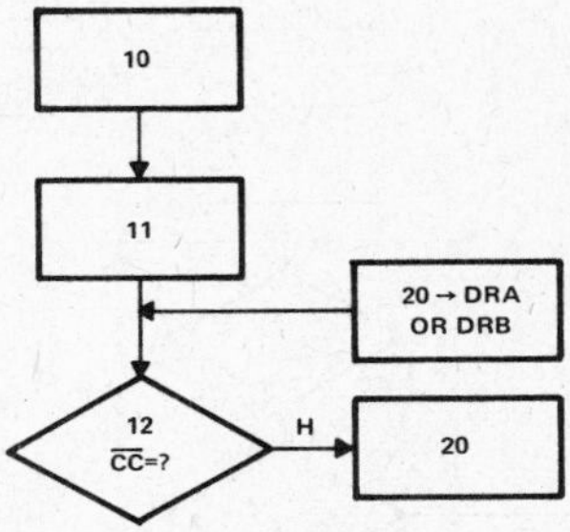
10
11
20 → DRA
OR DRB
12
$\overline{CC}$=?
H
20

(b) UNCONDITIONAL BRANCH
($\overline{CC}$ FORCED)

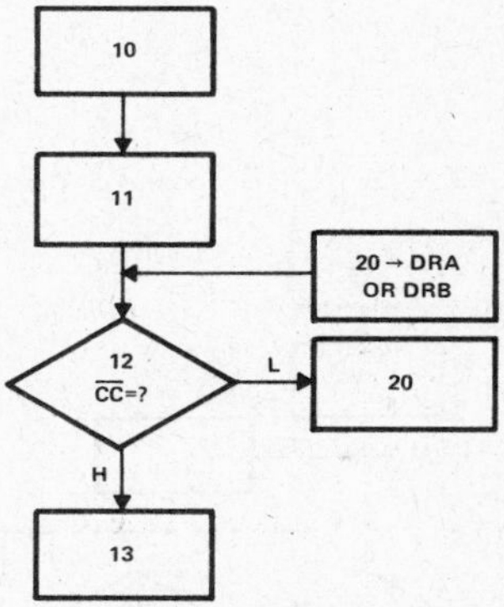
10
11
20 → DRA
OR DRB
12
$\overline{CC}$=?
L
20
H
13

(c) CONDITIONAL BRANCH
(DEC DISABLED)

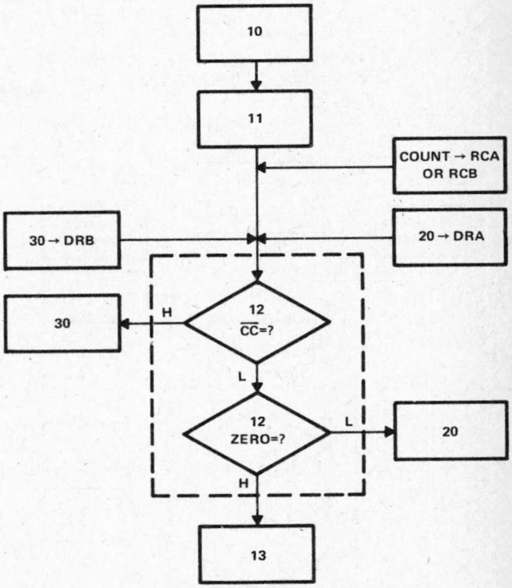
10
11
COUNT → RCA
OR RCB
30 → DRB
20 → DRA
30
H
12
$\overline{CC}$=?
L
12
ZERO=?
L
20
H
13

(d) THREE-WAY BRANCH (DEC ENABLED)[1]

NOTE 1: $\overline{CC}$ and ZERO are completed in the same clock cycle.

FIGURE 1. INSTRUCTION SET FLOWCHARTS

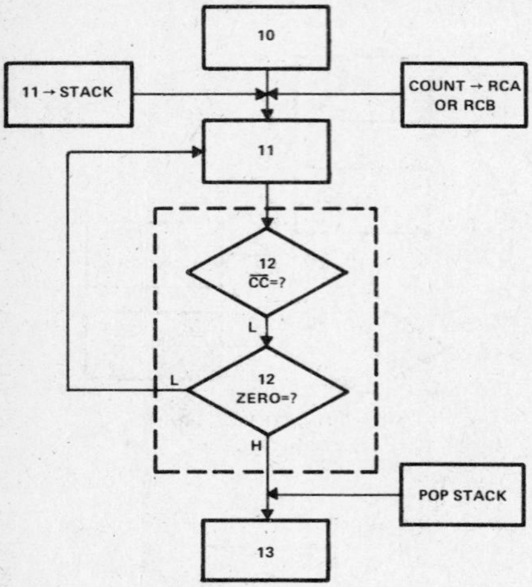
10
11 → STACK
COUNT → RCA OR RCB
11
12
$\overline{CC}$=?
L
12
ZERO=?
L
H
POP STACK
13

(e) CONDITIONAL LOOP ON STACK ($\overline{CC}$ FORCED, DEC ENABLED)[1]

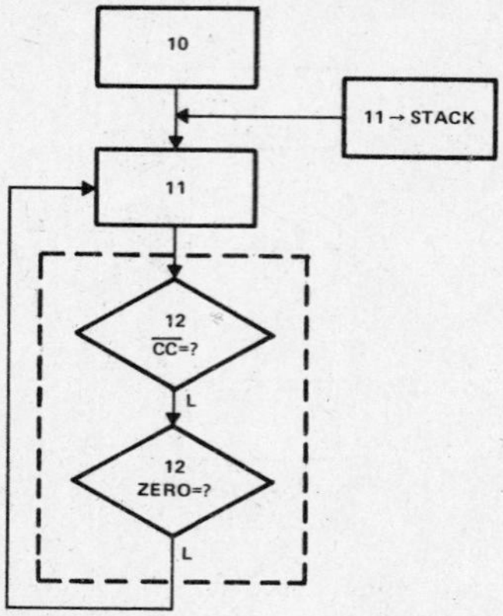
10
11 → STACK
11
12
$\overline{CC}$=?
L
12
ZERO=?
L

(f) REPEAT ($\overline{CC}$ FORCED, DEC DISABLED)[1]

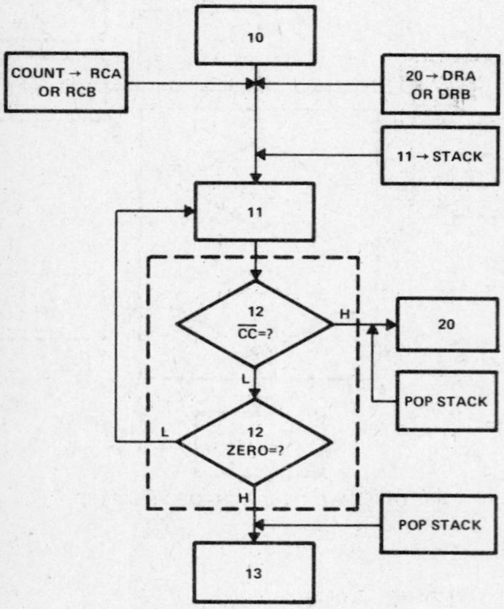
10
COUNT → RCA OR RCB
20 → DRA OR DRB
11 → STACK
11
12
$\overline{CC}$=?
H
20
L
POP STACK
L
12
ZERO=?
H
POP STACK
13

(g) CONDITIONAL LOOP ON STACK WITH EXIT (DEC ENABLED)[1]

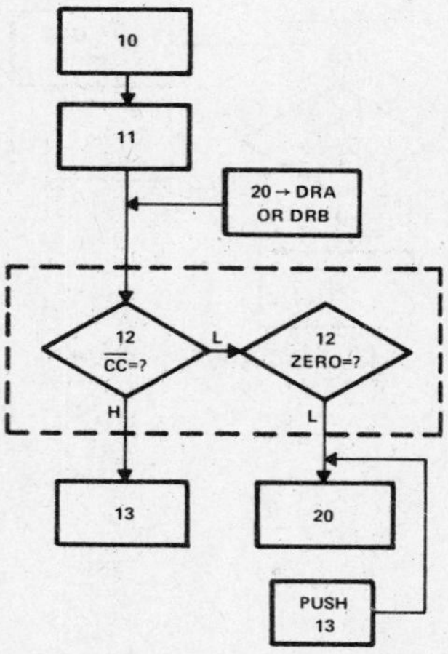
10
11
20 → DRA OR DRB
12
$\overline{CC}$=?
L
12
ZERO=?
H
L
13
20
PUSH 13

(h) CONDITIONAL JUMP TO SUBROUTINE (DEC DISABLED)[1]

NOTE 1: $\overline{CC}$ and ZERO are completed in the same clock cycle.

FIGURE 1. INSTRUCTION SET FLOWCHARTS (continued)

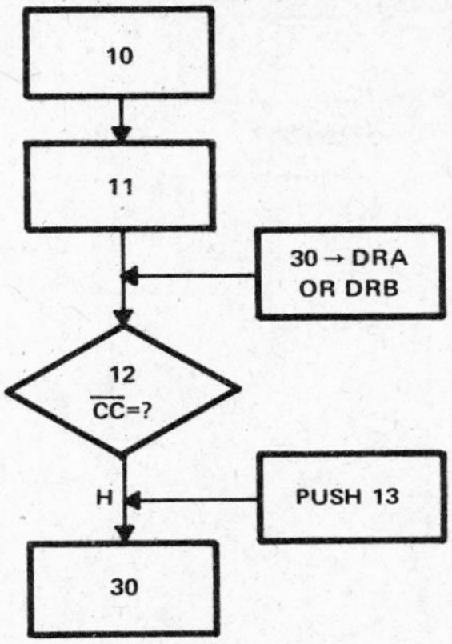
10
11
30 → DRA
OR DRB
12
$\overline{CC}$=?
H
PUSH 13
30

(i) JUMP TO SUBROUTINE
($\overline{CC}$ FORCED)

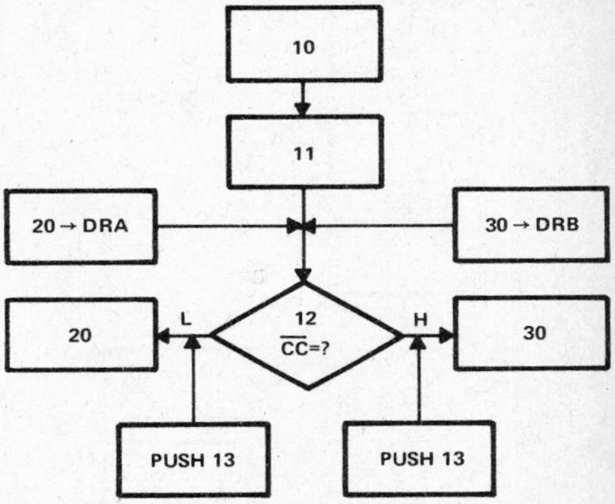
10
11
20 → DRA
30 → DRB
L
12
$\overline{CC}$=?
H
20
30
PUSH 13
PUSH 13

(j) TWO-WAY JUMP TO SUBROUTINE
(DEC DISABLED)

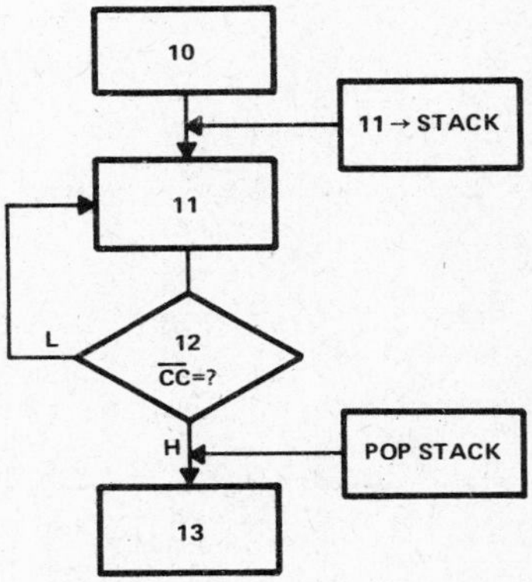
10
11 → STACK
11
L
12
$\overline{CC}$=?
H
POP STACK
13

(k) REPEAT UNTIL
(DEC DISABLED)

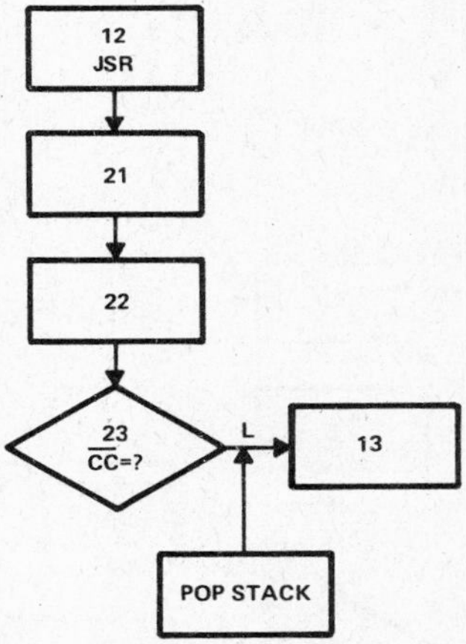
12
JSR
21
22
23
$\overline{CC}$=?
L
13
POP STACK

(l) RETURN FROM SUBROUTINE
($\overline{CC}$ FORCED, DEC DISABLED)

FIGURE 1. INSTRUCTION SET FLOWCHARTS (continued)

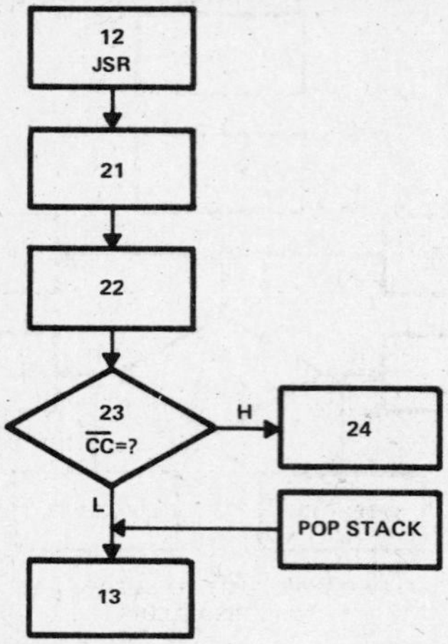
12
JSR
21
22
23
CC=?
H
24
L
POP STACK
13

(m) CONDITIONAL RETURN FROM SUBROUTINE (DEC DISABLED)

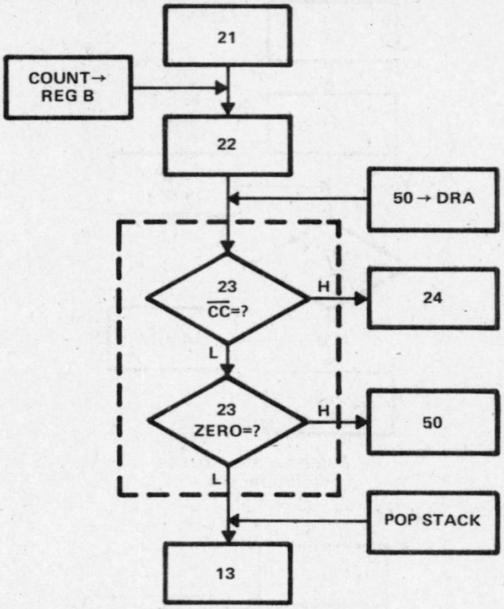
21
COUNT→
REG B
22
50 → DRA
23
CC=?
H
24
L
23
ZERO=?
H
50
L
POP STACK
13

(n) CONDITIONAL RETURN FROM SUBROUTINE OR BRANCH (DEC ENABLED)[1]

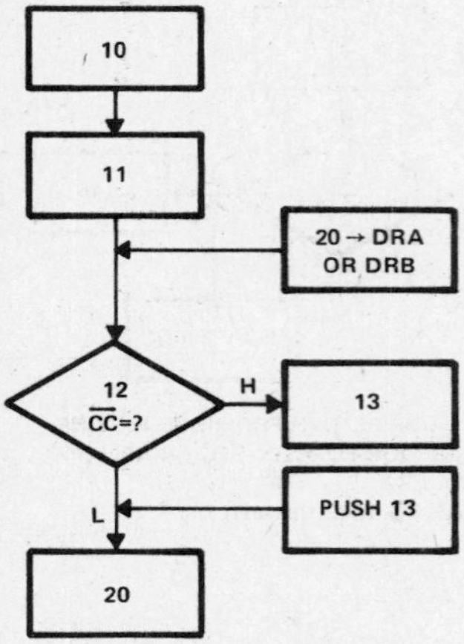
10
11
20 → DRA
OR DRB
12
CC=?
H
13
PUSH 13
L
20

(o) CONDITIONAL BRANCH AND PUSH (DEC DISABLED)

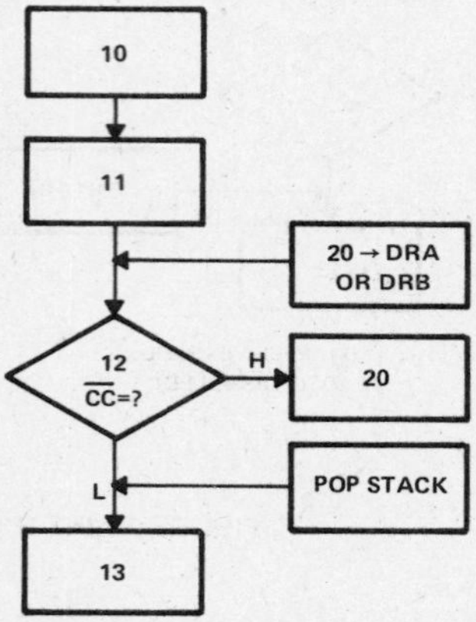
10
11
20 → DRA
OR DRB
12
CC=?
H
20
POP STACK
L
13

(p) CONDITIONAL BRANCH AND POP (DEC DISABLED)

NOTE 1: $\overline{CC}$ and ZERO are completed in the same clock cycle.

FIGURE 1. INSTRUCTION SET FLOWCHARTS (continued)

TEXAS INSTRUMENTS
POST OFFICE BOX 225012 • DALLAS, TEXAS 75265

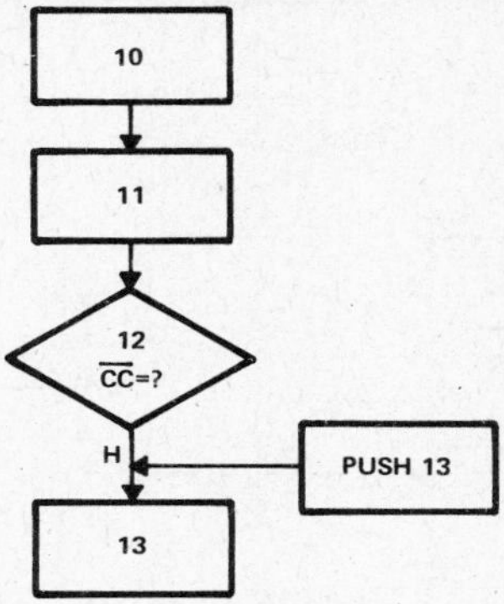
10
11
12
$\overline{CC}$=?
H
PUSH 13
13

(q) PUSH AND CONTINUE
($\overline{CC}$ FORCED)

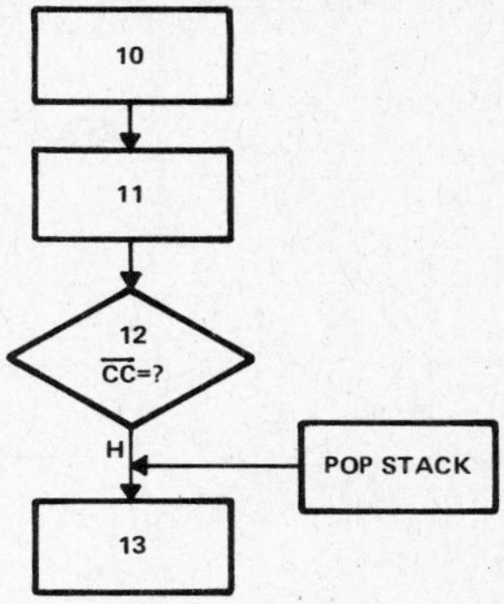
10
11
12
$\overline{CC}$=?
H
POP STACK
13

(r) POP AND CONTINUE
($\overline{CC}$ FORCED)

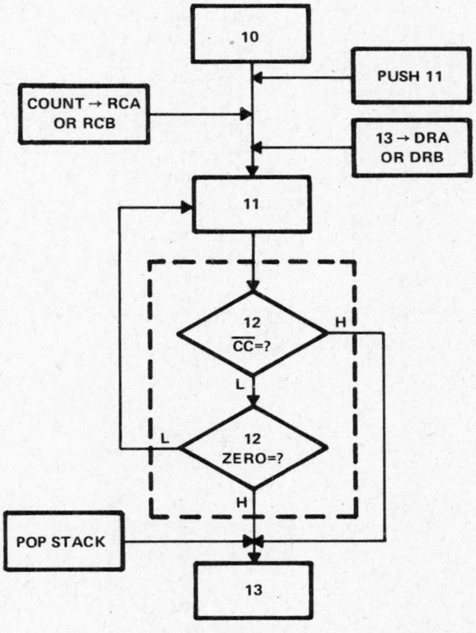
10
PUSH 11
COUNT → RCA OR RCB
13 → DRA OR DRB
11
12
$\overline{CC}$=?
H
L
12
ZERO=?
L
H
POP STACK
13

(s) EXIT FROM LOOP
(DEC ENABLED)[1]

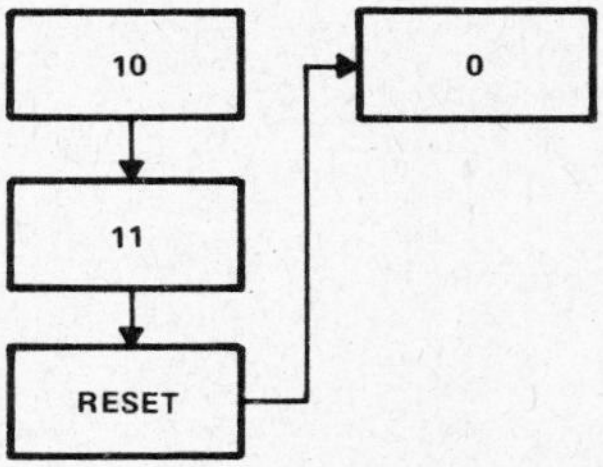
10
0
11
RESET

(t) RESET AND CLEAR

NOTE 1: $\overline{CC}$ and ZERO are completed in the same clock cycle.

FIGURE 1. INSTRUCTION SET FLOWCHARTS (continued)

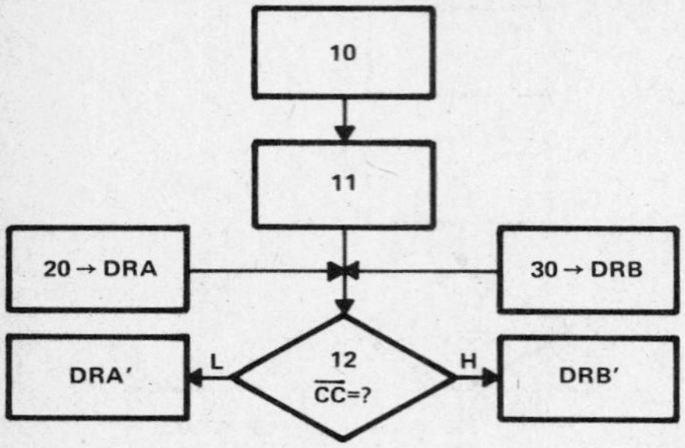
10
11
20 → DRA
30 → DRB
12
$\overline{CC}$=?
L
H
DRA'
DRB'

(u)32-WAY BRANCH
(DEC DISABLED)[2]

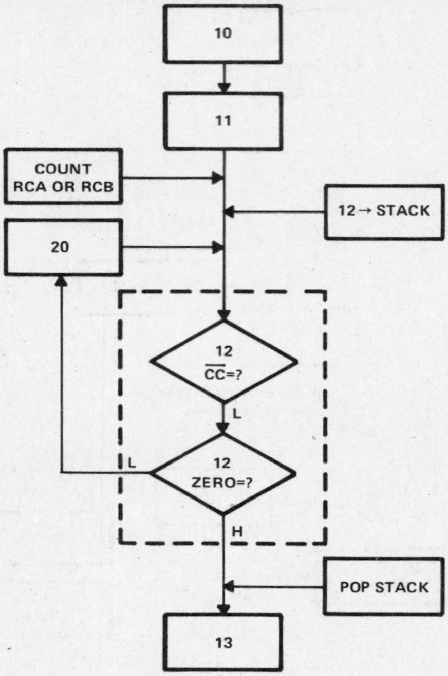
10
11
COUNT
RCA OR RCB
12 → STACK
20
12
$\overline{CC}$=?
L
L
12
ZERO=?
H
POP STACK
13

(v) EXECUTE N TIMES
($\overline{CC}$ FORCED, DEC ENABLED)[1]

NOTES: 1. $\overline{CC}$ and ZERO are completed in the same clock cycle.
2. The least significant four bits, DRA and DRB, will be stripped off and four new bits appended to them from the B3-B0 port.

FIGURE 1. INSTRUCTION SET FLOWCHARTS (concluded)

TEXAS INSTRUMENTS
POST OFFICE BOX 225012 • DALLAS, TEXAS 75265

absolute maximum ratings over operating temperature range (unless otherwise noted)

Supply voltage, V_{CC1} .... 7 V
Supply voltage, V_{CC2} .... 3 V
Input voltage: All inputs .... 7 V
I/O ports .... 5.5 V
Operating case temperature range, SN54AS890 .... −55 °C to 125 °C
Operating free-air temperature range, SN74AS890 .... 0 °C to 70 °C
Storage temperature range .... −65 °C to 150 °C

recommended operating conditions

			SN54AS890			SN74AS890			UNIT
			MIN	NOM	MAX	MIN	NOM	MAX	
V_{CC1}	I/O supply voltage		4.5	5	5.5	4.5	5	5.5	V
V_{CC2}	STL internal logic supply voltage		1.9	2	2.1	1.9	2	2.1	V
V_{IH}	High-level input voltage		2			2			V
V_{IL}	Low-level input voltge				0.8			0.8	V
I_{OH}	High-level output current				−1			−2.6	mA
I_{OL}	Low-level output current	All outputs except Y13-Y0			8			8	mA
		Y13-Y0			12			12	
T_C	Operating case temperature		−55		125				°C
T_A	Operating free air temperature					0		70	°C

electrical characteristics over recommended operating temperature range (unless otherwise noted)

PARAMETER		TEST CONDITIONS		SN54AS890			SN74AS890			UNIT
				MIN	TYP†	MAX	MIN	TYP†	MAX	
V_{IK}		V_{CC1} = 4.5 V,	I_I = −18 mA			−1.2			−1.2	V
V_{OH}		V_{CC1} = 4.5 V to 5.5 V,	I_{OH} = −0.4 mA	V_{CC}−2			V_{CC}−2			V
		V_{CC1} = 4.5 V,	I_{OH} = −1 mA	2.4	3.4					
		V_{CC1} = 4.5 V,	I_{OH} = −2.6 mA				2.4			
V_{OL}	All outputs except Y13-Y0	V_{CC1} = 4.5 V,	I_{OL} = 8 mA			0.5			0.5	V
	Y13-Y0	V_{CC1} = 4.5 V,	I_{OL} = 12 mA			0.5			0.5	
I_I	Inputs	V_{CC1} = 5.5 V,	V_I = 7 V			0.1			0.1	mA
	I/O ports	V_{CC1} = 5.5 V,	V_I = 5.5 V			0.1			0.1	
I_{IH}	Inputs	V_{CC1} = 5.5 V,	V_I = 2.7 V			20			20	μA
	I/O ports‡					40			40	
I_{IL}‡		V_{CC1} = 5.5 V,	V_I = 0.4 V			−0.4			−0.4	mA
I_O§		V_{CC1} = 5.5 V,	V_O = 2.25 V	−30		−112	−30		−112	mA
I_{CC1}		V_{CC1} = 5.5 V				185			178	mA
I_{CC2}		V_{CC2} = 2.1 V				420			400	mA

†All typical values are at V_{CC} = 5 V, T_A = 25 °C.
‡For I/O ports, the parameters I_{IH} and I_{IL} include output current I_{OZL} and I_{OZL}, respectively.
§The output conditions have been chosen to produce a current that closely approximates one-half of the true short-circuit current, I_{OS}.

SN54AS890 maximum switching characteristics: V_{CC1} = 4.5 V to 5.5 V, V_{CC2} = 1.9 V to 2.1 V, T_C = 55°C to 125°C (see Note 2)

PARAMETER	FROM (INPUT)	TO (OUTPUT) Y	ZERO	DRA	DRB	STKWRN	UNIT
t_{pd}	$\overline{CC}$	32					ns
	CK	32		30	30	30	
		53†	42†				
	DRA13-DRA0	16					
	DRB13-DRB0	16					
	MUX2-MUX0	36					
	RC2-RC0	32	14				
	S2-S0	32					
	B2-B0	22					
	OSEL			24			
t_{en}	$\overline{YOE}$	16					ns
	$\overline{RAOE}$			16			
	$\overline{RBOE}$				16		
t_{dis}	$\overline{YOE}$	16					ns
	$\overline{RAOE}$			16			
	$\overline{RBOE}$				16		

† Decrementing Register/Counter A or B and sensing a zero.

NOTE 2: Load circuit and voltage waveforms are shown in Section 1

SN54AS890 setup and hold times

PARAMETER	FROM	TO (DESTINATION)	MIN	MAX	UNIT
t_{su}	$\overline{CC}$	Stack	10		ns
	DRA13-DRA0	RCA, INT RT	5		
	DRB13-DRB0	RCB, INT RT	5		
	INC	MPC	10		
	$\overline{INT}$	Stack	10		
	RC2-RC0	Stack	16		
		RCA, RCB	10		
		INT RT	14		
	S2-S0	Stack	10		
		INT RT	10		
	MUX2-MUX0	INT RT	14		
	B3-B0	INT RT	14		
	Y13-Y0	MPC	12		
t_h	Any Input	Any Destination	2		

SN54AS890 minimum clock requirements (see Note 3)

PARAMETER		MIN	MAX	UNIT
$t_{wL(CK)}$	Pulse duration, clock low	10		ns
$t_{wH(CK)}$	Pulse duration, clock high	20		
$t_{c(CK)}$	Clock cycle time	55†		
		45		

†Decrementing Register/Counter A or B and sensing a zero.

NOTE 3: The total clock period of clock high and clock low must not be less than clock cycle time. The minimum pulse durations specified are only for clock high or clock low, but not for both simultaneously.

TEXAS INSTRUMENTS
POST OFFICE BOX 225012 • DALLAS, TEXAS 75265

SN74AS890 maximum switching characteristics: V_{CC1} = 4.5 V to 5.5 V, V_{CC2} = 1.9 V to 2.1 V, T_A = 0 °C to 70 °C (see Note 2)

PARAMETER	FROM (INPUT)	TO (OUTPUT) Y	ZERO	DRA	DRB	STKWRN	UNIT
t_{pd}	$\overline{CC}$	29					ns
	CK	29		29	29	29	
		50†	39†				
	DRA13-DRA0	15					
	DRB13-DRB0	15					
	MUX2-MUX0	35					
	RC2-RC0	30	13				
	S2-S0	28					
	B2-B0	20					
	OSEL			18			
t_{en}	$\overline{YOE}$	15					ns
	$\overline{RAOE}$			15			
	$\overline{RBOE}$				15		
t_{dis}	$\overline{YOE}$	16					ns
	$\overline{RAOE}$			16			
	$\overline{RBOE}$				16		

† Decrementing Register/Counter A or B and sensing a zero.
NOTE 2: Load circuit and voltage waveforms are shown in Section 1.

SN74AS890 setup and hold times

PARAMETER	FROM	TO (DESTINATION)	MIN	MAX	UNIT
t_{su}	$\overline{CC}$	Stack	10		ns
	DRA13-DRA0	RCA, INT RT	5		
	DRB13-DRB0	RCB, INT RT	5		
	INC	MPC	10		
	$\overline{INT}$	Stack	10		
	RC2-RC0	Stack	14		
		RCA, RCB	10		
		INT RT	12		
	S2-S0	Any Destination	10		
	MUX2-MUX0	INT RT	12		
	B3-B0	INT RT	14		
	Y13-Y0	MPC	10		
t_h	Any Input	Any Destination	2		

SN74AS890 minimum clock requirements (see Note 3)

PARAMETER		MIN	MAX	UNIT
$t_{wL(CK)}$	Pulse duration, clock low	10		ns
$t_{wH(CK)}$	Pulse duration, clock high	20		
$t_{c(CK)}$	Clock cycle time	50†		
		36		

†Decrementing Register/Counter A or B and sensing a zero.
NOTE 3: The total clock period of clock high and clock low must not be less than clock cycle time. The minimum pulse durations specified are only for clock high or clock low, but not for both simultaneously.

SN74AS890-1 maximum switching characteristics: V_{CC1} = 4.5 V to 5.5 V, V_{CC2} = 1.9 V to 2.1 V, T_A = 0°C to 70°C (see Note 2)

PARAMETER	FROM (INPUT)	TO (OUTPUT) Y	ZERO	DRA	DRB	STKWRN	UNIT
t_{pd}	$\overline{CC}$	25					ns
	CK	25		25	25	25	
		42†	34†				
	DRA13-DRA0	14					
	DRB13-DRB0	14					
	MUX2-MUX0	31					
	RC2-RC0	26	12				
	S2-S0	25					
	B2-B0	19					
	OSEL			17			
t_{en}	$\overline{YOE}$	15					ns
	$\overline{RAOE}$			15			
	$\overline{RBOE}$				15		
t_{dis}	$\overline{YOE}$	16					ns
	$\overline{RAOE}$			16			
	$\overline{RBOE}$				16		

† Decrementing Register/Counter A or B and sensing a zero.

NOTE 2: Load circuit and voltage waveforms are shown in Section 1.

SN74AS890-1 setup and hold times

PARAMETER	FROM	TO (DESTINATION)	MIN	MAX	UNIT
t_{su}	$\overline{CC}$	Stack	10		ns
	DRA13-DRA0	RCA, INT RT	5		
	DRB13-DRB0	RCB, INT RT	5		
	INC	MPC	10		
	$\overline{INT}$	Stack	10		
	RC2-RC0	Stack	14		
		RCA, RCB	10		
		INT RT	12		
	S2-S0	Any Destination	10		
	MUX2-MUX0	INT RT	12		
	B3-B0	INT RT	14		
	Y13-Y0	MPC	10		
t_h	Any Input	Any Destination	2		

SN74AS890-1 minimum clock requirements (see Note 3)

PARAMETER		MIN	MAX	UNIT
$t_{wL(CK)}$	Pulse duration, clock low	10		ns
$t_{wH(CK)}$	Pulse duration, clock high	20		
$t_{c(CK)}$	Clock cycle time	42†		
		34		

†Decrementing Register/Counter A or B and sensing a zero.

NOTE 3: The total clock period of clock high and clock low must not be less than clock cycle time. The minimum pulse durations specified are only for clock high or clock low, but not for both simultaneously.

NOVEMBER 1985—REVISED APRIL 1986

- STL-AS Technology
- Parallel 8-Bit ALU with Expansion Inputs and Outputs
- 13 Arithmetic and Logic Functions
- 8 Conditional Shifts (Single and Double Length)
- 9 Instructions that Manipulate Bytes
- 4 Instructions that Manipulate Bits
- Add and Subtract Immediate Instructions
- Absolute Value Instruction
- Signed Magnitude to/from Two's Complement Conversion
- Single- and Double-Length Normalize
- Select Functions
- Signed and Unsigned Divides with Overflow Detection; Input does not Need to be Prescaled
- Signed, Mixed, and Unsigned Multiplies
- Three-Operand, 16-Word Register File
- Full Carry Look Ahead Support
- Sign, Carry Out, Overflow, and Zero-Detect Status Capabilities
- Excess-3 BCD Arithmetic
- MQ Register is Externally Available through the DB Port
- Internal Shift Multiplexers that Eliminate the Need for External Shift Control Parts
- ALU Bypass Path to Increase Speeds of Multiply, Divide, and Normalize Instructions and to Provide New Instructions such as Bit Set, Bit Reset, Bit Test, Byte Subtract, Byte Add, and Byte Logical
- 3-Operand Register Files to Allow an Operation and a Move Instruction to be Combined
- Byte Select Controlled by External 3-State Buffers that may be Eliminated if Bit and Byte Manipulation are not Needed
- Bit and Byte Masks that are Shared with Register Address Fields to Minimize Control Store Word Width
- 3 Data Input/Output Paths to Maximize Data Throughput

description

These 8-bit Advanced Schottky TTL integrated circuits are designed to implement high performance digital computers or controllers. An architecture and instruction set has been chosen that supports a fast system clock, a narrow micro-code word width, and a high system throughput. The powerful instruction set allows high-speed system architecture to be implemented and also allows an existing system's performance to be upgraded while protecting software investments. These processors are designed to be cascadable to any word width 16 bits or greater.

The only difference between the 'AS888 Bit-Slice Processor and the 'AS895 Memory Address Generators is the function of the DB port. The 'AS888 DB port outputs the register file. The 'AS895 DB port can be used to read the MQ register result during the same clock cycle that the ALU result is available at the Y port.

The SN54AS895 is characterized for operation over the full military temperature range of −55 °C to 125 °C. The SN74AS895 and SN74AS895-1 are characterized for operation from 0 °C to 70 °C.

Package options include both plastic and ceramic chip carriers in addition to a 68-pin grid array ceramic package.

SN54AS895, SN74AS895 . . . GB PACKAGE
(TOP VIEW)

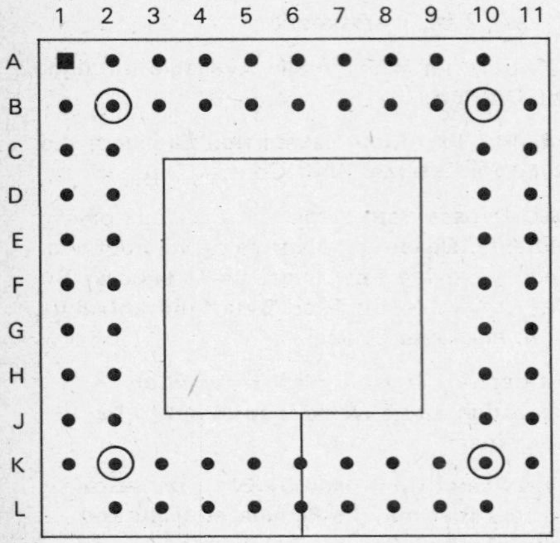
1 2 3 4 5 6 7 8 9 10 11
A
B
C
D
E
F
G
H
J
K
L

SN54AS895 . . . FK PACKAGE
SN74AS895 . . . FN PACKAGE
(TOP VIEW)

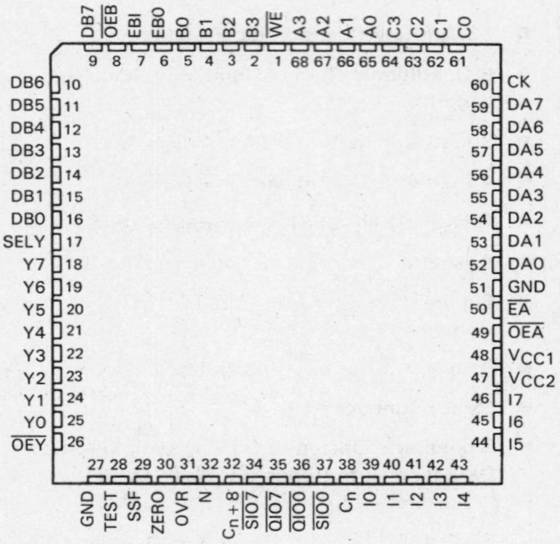
DB7 9
OEB 8
EBI 7
EB0 6
B0 5
B1 4
B2 3
B3 2
WE 1
A3 68
A2 67
A1 66
A0 65
C3 64
C2 63
C1 62
C0 61
DB6 10
DB5 11
DB4 12
DB3 13
DB2 14
DB1 15
DB0 16
SELY 17
Y7 18
Y6 19
Y5 20
Y4 21
Y3 22
Y2 23
Y1 24
Y0 25
OEY 26
60 CK
59 DA7
58 DA6
57 DA5
56 DA4
55 DA3
54 DA2
53 DA1
52 DA0
51 GND
50 EA
49 OEA
48 VCC1
47 VCC2
46 I7
45 I6
44 I5
27 GND
28 TEST
29 SSF
30 ZERO
31 OVR
32 N
32 Cn+8
34 SIO7
35 QIO7
36 QIO0
37 SIO0
38 Cn
39 I0
40 I1
41 I2
42 I3
43 I4

GB PACKAGE PIN ASSIGNMENTS

PIN	NAME	PIN	NAME	PIN	NAME	PIN	NAME
A-2	C_n	B-9	$\overline{OEY}$	F-10	Y3	K-4	C2
A-3	$\overline{SIO0}$	B-10	Y0	F-11	DB2	K-5	A0
A-4	$\overline{QIO0}$	B-11	Y1	G-1	DA2	K-6	A3
A-5	$\overline{QIO7}$	C-1	I5	G-2	DA0	K-7	$\overline{WE}$
A-6	C_{n+8}	C-2	V_{CC2}	G-10	DB0	K-8	DB7
A-7	$\overline{G}$/N	C-10	Y4	G-11	DB3	K-9	$\overline{OEB}$
A-8	$\overline{P}$/OVR	C-11	Y6	H-1	DA3	K-10	EB0
A-9	ZERO	D-1	I6	H-2	DA1	K-11	EB1
A-10	PPP	D-2	V_{CC1}	H-10	DB6	L-2	CK
B-1	I2	D-10	Y5	H-11	DB4	L-3	C1
B-2	I3	D-11	Y7	J-1	DA4	L-4	C3
B-3	I1	E-1	I7	J-2	DA5	L-5	A1
B-4	I0	E-2	$\overline{OEA}$	J-10	SELY	L-6	A2
B-5	I4	E-10	Y2	J-11	DB5	L-7	B3
B-6	$\overline{SIO7}$	E-11	DB1	K-1	DA6	L-8	B2
B-7	SSF	F-1	$\overline{EA}$	K-2	DA7	L-9	B1
B-8		F-2	GND	K-3	C0	L-10	B0

TEXAS INSTRUMENTS
POST OFFICE BOX 225012 • DALLAS, TEXAS 75265

PIN GRID ARRAY	CHIP CARRIER	NAME	I/O	DESCRIPTION
A-10	28	PPP	I	Package position pin. Tri-level input used to define package significance during instruction execution. Leave open for intermediate positions, tie to V_{CC} for most significant package, and tie to GND for least significant package.
B-7	29	SSF	I/O	Special shift function. Used to transfer required information between packages during special instruction execution.
A-9	30	ZERO	I/O	Device zero detection, open collector. Input during certain special instructions.
A-8	31	$\overline{P}$/OVR	O	ALU propagate/instruction overflow for most significant package, low active.
A-7	32	$\overline{G}$/N	O	ALU generate/negative result for most significant package, low active.
A-6	33	C_{n+8}	O	ALU ripple carry output.
B-6	34	$\overline{SIO7}$	I/O	Bidirectional shift pin, low active.
A-5	35	$\overline{QIO7}$	I/O	
A-4	36	$\overline{QIO0}$	I/O	
A-3	37	$\overline{SIO0}$	I/O	
A-2	38	C_n	I	ALU carry input.
B-4	39	I0	I	Instruction input.
B-3	40	I1	I	
B-1	41	I2	I	
B-2	42	I3	I	
B-5	43	I4	I	
C-1	44	I5	I	
D-1	45	I6	I	
E-1	46	I7	I	
C-2	47	V_{CC2}		Low voltage power supply (2 V).
D-2	48	V_{CC1}		I/O interface supply voltage (5 V).
E-2	49	$\overline{OEA}$	I	DA bus enable, low active.
F-1	50	$\overline{EA}$	I	ALU input operand select. High state selects external DA bus and low state selects register file.
F-2	51	GND		Ground pin.
G-2	52	DA0	I/O	A port data bus. Outputs register file data ($\overline{EA}$ = 0) or inputs external data ($\overline{EA}$ = 1).
H-2	53	DA1	I/O	
G-1	54	DA2	I/O	
H-1	55	DA3	I/O	
J-1	56	DA4	I/O	
J-2	57	DA5	I/O	
K-1	58	DA6	I/O	
K-2	59	DA7	I/O	
L-2	60	CK	I	Clocks all synchronous registers on positive edge.
K-3	61	C0	I	Register file write address select.
L-3	62	C1	I	
K-4	63	C2	I	
L-4	64	C3	I	
K-5	65	A0	I	Register file A port read address select.
L-5	66	A1	I	
L-6	67	A2	I	
K-6	68	A3	I	

PIN GRID ARRAY	CHIP CARRIER	NAME	I/O	DESCRIPTION
K-7	1	$\overline{WE}$	I	Register file (RF) write enable. Data is written into RF when $\overline{WE}$ is low and a low-to-high clock transition occurs. RF write is inhibited when $\overline{WE}$ is high.
L-7	2	B3	I	Register file B port read address select. (0 = LSB).
L-8	3	B2	I	
L-9	4	B1	I	
L-10	5	B0	I	
K-10	6	EB0	I	ALU input operand select. EB0 and EB1 selects the source of data that the S multiplexer provides for the S bus. Independent control of the DB bus and data path selection allow the user to isolate the DB bus while the ALU continues to process data.
K-11	7	EB1	I	
K-9	8	$\overline{OEB}$	I	DB bus enable, low active.
K-8	9	DB7	I/O	B port data bus. Outputs MQ register data ($\overline{OEB}$ = 0) or used to input external data ($\overline{OEB}$ = 1), (0 = LSB).
H-10	10	DB6	I/O	
J-11	11	DB5	I/O	
H-11	12	DB4	I/O	
G-11	13	DB3	I/O	
F-11	14	DB2	I/O	
E-11	15	DB1	I/O	
G-10	16	DB0	I/O	
J-10	17	SELY	I	Y bus select, high active.
D-11	18	Y7	I/O	Y port data bus. Outputs instruction results ($\overline{OEY}$ = 0) or used to put external data into register file ($\overline{OEY}$ = 1).
C-11	19	Y6	I/O	
D-10	20	Y5	I/O	
C-10	21	Y4	I/O	
F-10	22	Y3	I/O	
E-10	23	Y2	I/O	
B-11	24	Y1	I/O	
B-10	25	Y0	I/O	
B-9	26	$\overline{OEY}$	I	Y bus output enable, low active.
F-2	27	GND		Ground pin

functional block diagram

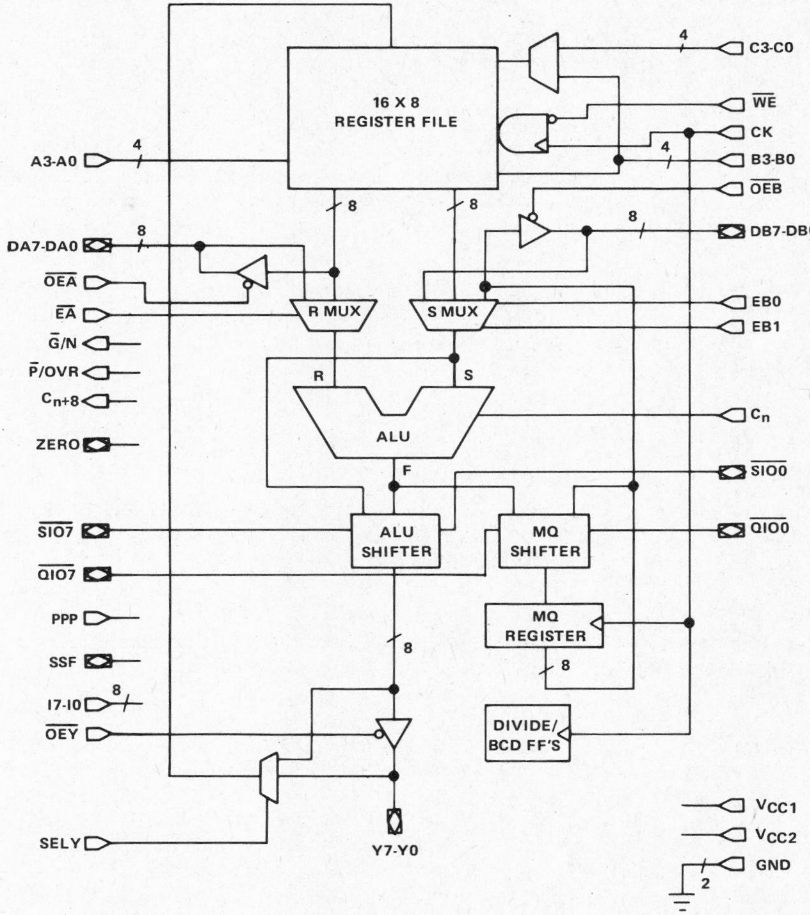
16 X 8
REGISTER FILE
A3-A0
4
C3-C0
WE
CK
B3-B0
OEB
DB7-DB0
8
DA7-DA0
OEA
EA
R MUX
S MUX
EB0
EB1
G/N
P/OVR
Cn+8
ZERO
R
S
ALU
Cn
F
SIO0
SIO7
ALU
SHIFTER
MQ
SHIFTER
QIO0
QIO7
PPP
MQ
REGISTER
SSF
I7-I0
OEY
DIVIDE/
BCD FF'S
SELY
Y7-Y0
VCC1
VCC2
GND
2

architectural elements

3-port register file

Working registers consist of 128 storage elements organized into sixteen 8-bit words. These storage elements appear to the user as 16 positive edge-triggered registers. The three port addresses, one write (C) and two reads (A and B), are completely independent of each other to implement a 3-operand register file. Data is written into the register file when $\overline{WE}$ is low and a low-to-high clock transition occurs. The ADD and SUBTRACT immediate instructions require only one source operand. The B address is used as the source address, and the bits of the A address are used to provide a constant field. The SET, RESET, and TEST BIT instructions use the B addressed register as both the source and destination register while the A and C addresses are used as masks. These instructions are explained in more detail in the instruction section.

S multiplexer

The S multiplexer selects the ALU operand, as follows:

EB1	EB0	S bus
Low	Low	RF data
Low	High	MQ data
High	Low	DB data
High	High	MQ data

DB port

The 8-bit bidirectional DB port inputs external data to the ALU or outputs the MQ register. If $\overline{OEB}$ is low, the DB bus is active; if $\overline{OEB}$ is high, the DB bus is in the high impedance state. Notice that the DB port may be isolated at the same time that MQ register data is passed to the ALU.

R multiplexer

The R multiplexer selects the other operand of the ALU. Except for those instructions that require constants or masks, the R bus will contain DA if $\overline{EA}$ is high or the RF data pointed to by A if $\overline{EA}$ is low.

DA port

The 8-bit bidirectional DA port inputs external data to the ALU or outputs the register file. If $\overline{OEA}$ is low, the DA bus is active; if $\overline{OEA}$ is high, the DA bus is in the high-impedance state. Notice that the DA bus may be isolated while register file data is passed to the ALU.

ALU

The shift instructions are summarized in Table 4 and illustrated in Figure 2. The ALU can perform seven arithmetic and six logical instructions on two 8-bit operands. It also supports multiplication, division, normalization, bit set, reset, test, byte operations, and excess-3 BCD arithmetic. These source operands are the outputs of the S and R multiplexers.

ALU and MQ shifters

ALU and MQ shifters perform all of the shift, multiply, divide, and normalize functions. Table 4 shows the value of the $\overline{SIO7}$ and $\overline{QIO7}$ pins of the most significant package. The standard shifts may be made into conditional shifts and the serial data may be input or output with the aid of two three-state gates. These capabilities are discussed further in the arithmetic and logic section.

TEXAS INSTRUMENTS
POST OFFICE BOX 225012 • DALLAS, TEXAS 75265

MQ register

The multiplier-quotient (MQ) register has specific functions in multiplication, division, and normalization. This register may also be used as a temporary storage register. The MQ register may be loaded if the instruction code on pins I7-I0 is E1-E7 or E9-EE (See Table 1).

Y bus

The Y bus contains the output of the ALU shifter if $\overline{OEY}$ is low and is a high impedance input if $\overline{OEY}$ is high. SELY must be low to pass the internal ALU shift bus and must be high to pass the external Y bus to the register file.

status

Four status pins are available on the most significant package, overflow (OVR), sign (N), carry out (C_{n+8}), and zero (ZERO). The C_{n+8} line signifies the ALU result while OVR, ZERO, and N refer the status after the ALU shift has occurred. Notice that the ZERO pin cannot be used to detect whether an input placed on a high impedance Y bus is zero.

divide BCD flip-flops

The multiply-divide flip-flops contain the status of the previous multiply or divide instruction. They are affected by the following instructions:

DIVIDE REMAINDER FIX
SIGNED DIVIDE QUOTIENT FIX
SIGNED MULTIPLY
SIGNED MULTIPLY TERMINATE
SIGNED DIVIDE INITIALIZE
SIGNED DIVIDE START
SIGNED DIVIDE ITERATE
UNSIGNED DIVIDE START
UNSIGNED DIVIDE ITERATE
UNSIGNED MULTIPLY
SIGNED DIVIDE TERMINATE
UNSIGNED DIVIDE TERMINATE

The excess-3 BCD flip-flops are affected by all instructions except NOP. The clear function clears these flip-flops. They preserve the carry from each nibble (4-bits) in excess-3/BCD operations.

package position pin (PPP)

The position of the processor in the system is defined by the voltage level applied to the package position pin (PPP). Intermediate positions are selected by leaving the pin open. Tying the pin to V_{CC} makes the processor the most significant package and tying the pin to GND makes the processor the least significant package.

special shift function (SSF) pin

Conditional shifting algorithms may be implemented via control of the SSF pin. The applied voltage to this pin may be set as a function of a potential overflow condition (the two most significant bits are not equal) or any other condition (see Group 1 instructions).

instruction set

The 'AS895 bit-slice processor uses bits I7-I0 as instruction inputs. A combination of bits I3-I0 (Group 1 instructions) and bits I7-I4 (Group 2-5 instructions) are used to develop the 8-bit op code for a specific instruction. Group 1 and Group 2 instructions can be combined to perform arithmetic or logical functions plus a shift function in one instruction cycle. A summary of the instruction set is given in Table 1.

TABLE 1. INSTRUCTION SET

GROUP 1 INSTRUCTIONS

INSTRUCTION BITS (I3-I0) HEX CODE	MNEMONIC	FUNCTION
0		Accesses Group 4 instructions
1	ADD	$R+S+C_n$
2	SUBR	$\overline{R}+S+C_n$
3	SUBS	$R+\overline{S}+C_n$
4	INCS	$S+C_n$
5	INCNS	$\overline{S}+C_n$
6	INCR	$R+C_n$
7	INCNR	$\overline{R}+C_n$
8		Accesses Group 3 instructions
9	XOR	R XOR S
A	AND	R AND S
B	OR	R OR S
C	NAND	R NAND S
D	NOR	R NOR S
E	ANDNR	$\overline{R}$ AND S
F		Accesses Group 5 instructions

GROUP 2 INSTRUCTIONS

INSTRUCTION BITS (I7-I4) HEX CODE	MNEMONIC	FUNCTION
0	SRA	Arithmetic Right Single
1	SRAD	Arithmetic Right Double
2	SRL	Logical Right Single
3	SRLD	Logical Right Double
4	SLA	Arithmetic Left Single
5	SLAD	Arithmetic Left Double
6	SLC	Circular Left Single
7	SLCD	Circular Left Double
8	SRC	Circular Right Single
9	SRCD	Circular Right Double
A	MQSRA	Pass (F→Y) and Arithmetic Right MQ
B	MQSRL	Pass (F→Y) and Logical Right MQ
C	MQSLL	Pass (F→Y) and Logical Left MQ
D	MQSLC	Pass (F→Y) and Circular Left MQ
E	LOADMQ	Pass (F→Y) and Load MQ (F=MQ)
F	PASS	Pass (F→Y)

TEXAS INSTRUMENTS
POST OFFICE BOX 225012 • DALLAS, TEXAS 75265

TABLE 1. INSTRUCTION SET (Continued)

GROUP 3 INSTRUCTIONS

INSTRUCTION BITS (I7-I0) HEX CODE	MNEMONIC	FUNCTION
08	SET1	Set Bit
18	SET0	Reset Bit
28	TB1	Test Bit (One)
38	TB0	Test Bit (Zero)
48	ABS	Absolute Value
58	SMTC	Sign Magnitude/Two's Complement
68	ADDI	Add Immediate
78	SUBI	Subtract Immediate
88	BADD	Byte Add R to S
98	BSUBS	Byte Subtract S from R
A8	BSUBR	Byte Subtract R from S
B8	BINCS	Byte Increment S
C8	BINCNS	Byte Increment Negative S
D8	BXOR	Byte XOR R and S
E8	BAND	Byte AND R and S
F8	BOR	Byte OR R and S

GROUP 4 INSTRUCTIONS

INSTRUCTION BITS (I7-I0) HEX CODE	MNEMONIC	FUNCTION
00		Reserved
10	SEL	Select S/R
20	SNORM	Single Length Normalize
30	DNORM	Double Length Normalize
40	DIVRF	Divide Remainder Fix
50	SDIVQF	Signed Divide Quotient Fix
60	SMULI	Signed Multiply Iterate
70	SMULT	Signed Multiply Terminate
80	SDIVIN	Signed Divide Initialize
90	SDIVIS	Signed Divide Start
A0	SDIVI	Signed Divide Iterate
B0	UDIVIS	Unsigned Divide Start
C0	UDIVI	Unsigned Divide Iterate
D0	UMULI	Unsigned Multiply Iterate
E0	SDIVIT	Signed Divide Terminate
F0	UDIVIT	Unsigned Divide Terminate

TABLE 1. INSTRUCTION SET (Concluded)

GROUP 5 INSTRUCTIONS

INSTRUCTION BITS (I7-I0) HEX CODE	MNEMONIC	FUNCTION
0F	CLR	Clear
1F	CLR	Clear
2F	CLR	Clear
3F	CLR	Clear
4F	CLR	Clear
5F	CLR	Clear
6F	CLR	Clear
7F	BCDBIN	BCD to Binary
8F	EX3BC	Excess-3 Byte Correction
9F	EX3C	Excess-3 Word Correction
AF	SDIVO	Signed Divide Overflow Check
BF	CLR	Clear
CF	CLR	Clear
DF	BINEX3	Binary to Excess-3
EF	CLR	Clear
FF	NOP	No Operation

group 1 instructions

TABLE 2. GROUP 1 INSTRUCTIONS

INSTRUCTION BITS (I3-I0) HEX CODE	MNEMONIC	FUNCTION
0		Accesses Group 4 instructions
1	ADD	$R+S+C_n$
2	SUBR	$\overline{R}+S+C_n$
3	SUBS	$R+\overline{S}+C_n$
4	INCS	$S+C_n$
5	INCNS	$\overline{S}+C_n$
6	INCR	$R+C_n$
7	INCNR	$\overline{R}+C_n$
8		Accesses Group 3 instructions
9	XOR	R XOR S
A	AND	R AND S
B	OR	R OR S
C	NAND	R NAND S
D	NOR	R NOR S
E	ANDNR	$\overline{R}$ AND S
F		Accesses Group 5 instructions

Group 1 instructions (excluding hex codes 0, 8, and F), shown in Table 2, may be used in conjunction with Group 2 shift instructions to perform arithmetic or logical functions plus a shift function† in one instruction cycle (hex codes 0, 8, and F are used to access Group 4, 3, and 5 instructions, respectively). Each shift may be made into a conditional shift by forcing the special shift function (SSF) pin into the proper state. If the SSF pin is high or floating, the shifted ALU output will be sent to the output buffers. If the SSF pin is pulled low externally, the ALU result will be passed directly to the output buffers. Conditional shifting is useful for scaling inputs in data arrays or in signal processing algorithms.

These instructions set the BCD flip-flop for the excess-3 correct instruction. The status is set with the following results (C_{n+8} is ALU carry out and is independent of shift operation; others are evaluated after shift operation).

†Double-precision shifts involve both the ALU and MQ register.

Status is set with the following results:

Arithmetic

N	→	MSB of result
OVR	→	Signed arithmetic overflow
C_{n+8}	→	Carry out equal one
Z	→	Result equal zero

Logic

N	→	MSB of result
OVR	→	None (force to zero)
C_{n+8}	→	None (force to zero)
Z	→	Result equal zero

group 2 instructions

TABLE 3. GROUP 2 INSTRUCTIONS

INSTRUCTION BITS (I7-I4) HEX CODE	MNEMONIC	FUNCTION
0	SRA	Arithmetic Right Single
1	SRAD	Arithmetic Right Double
2	SRL	Logical Right Single
3	SRLD	Logical Right Double
4	SLA	Arithmetic Left Single
5	SLAD	Arithmetic Left Double
6	SLC	Circular Left Single
7	SLCD	Circular Left Double
8	SRC	Circular Right Single
9	SRCD	Circular Right Double
A	MQSRA	Pass (F→Y) and Arithmetic Right MQ
B	MQSRL	Pass (F→Y) and Logical Right MQ
C	MQSLL	Pass (F→Y) and Logical Left MQ
D	MQSLC	Pass (F→Y) and Circular Left MQ
E	LOADMQ	Pass (F→Y) and Load MQ (F=MQ)
F	PASS	Pass (F→Y)

The processor's shift instructions are implemented by a combination of Group 2 instructions (Table 3) and certain wired connections on the packages used. The following external connections are required.

On intermediate packages:

$\overline{\text{SIO7}}$ is connected to $\overline{\text{SIO0}}$ of the next most significant package
$\overline{\text{QIO7}}$ is connected to $\overline{\text{QIO0}}$ of the next most significant package
$\overline{\text{SIO0}}$ is connected to $\overline{\text{SIO7}}$ of the next least significant package
$\overline{\text{QIO0}}$ is connected to $\overline{\text{QIO7}}$ of the next least significant package

On the two end packages:

$\overline{\text{SIO7}}$ on the most significant package is connected to $\overline{\text{SIO0}}$ of the least significant package
$\overline{\text{QIO7}}$ on the most significant package is connected to $\overline{\text{QIO0}}$ of the least significant package

The connections are the same on all instructions including multiply, divide, and normalization functions.

Single- and double-precision shifts are supported. Double-precision shifts assume the most significant half has come through the ALU and will be placed (if $\overline{\text{WE}}$ is low) into the register file on the rising edge of the clock and the least significant half lies in the MQ register. All Group 2 shifts may be made conditional (see previous page).

The following definitions apply to Group 2 shift instructions:

Arithmetic right shifts copy the sign of the number if no overflow occurs from the ALU calculation; if overflow occurs, the sign bit is inverted.
Arithmetic left shifts do not retain the sign of the number if an overflow occurs. A zero is filled into the LSB if not forced externally.
Logical right shifts fill a zero in the MSB position if not forced externally.
Logical left shifts fill a zero in the LSB position if not forced externally.
Circular right shifts fill the LSB in the MSB position.
Circular left shifts fill the MSB in the LSB position.
Shifting left is defined as moving a bit position towards the MSB (doubling).
Shifting right is defined as moving a bit towards the LSB (halving).

Serial input may be performed using the circuitry shown in Figure 1. A single-/or double-precision arithmetic left or logical right shift fills the complement of the data on $\overline{\text{SIO0}}$ and $\overline{\text{SIO7}}$ into the LSB or MSB of the data word(s). Note that if $\overline{\text{SIO0}}$ and $\overline{\text{SIO0}}$ are floating (HI-Z), a zero will be filled as an end condition.

Serial output may be performed with circular instructions.

TEXAS INSTRUMENTS
POST OFFICE BOX 225012 • DALLAS, TEXAS 75265

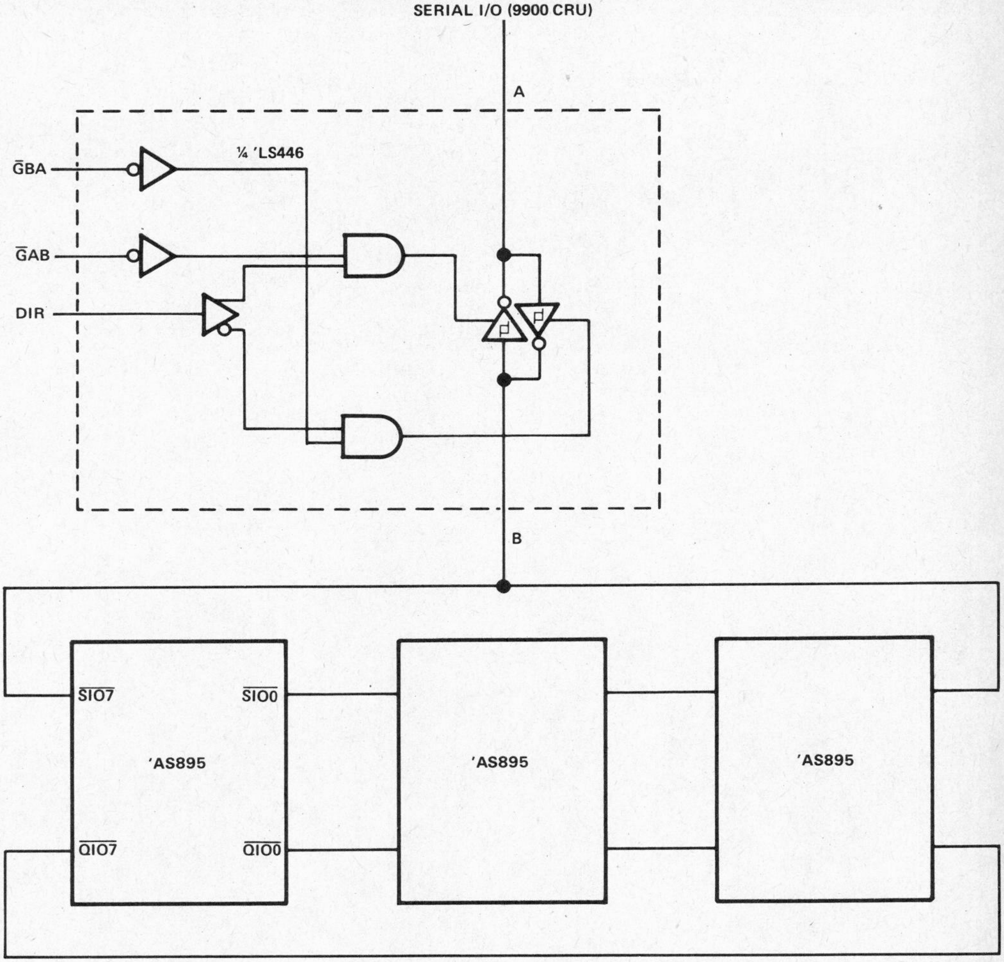
SERIAL I/O (9900 CRU)
A
¼ 'LS446
$\overline{G}$BA
$\overline{G}$AB
DIR
B
$\overline{SIO7}$
$\overline{SIO0}$
'AS895
$\overline{QIO7}$
$\overline{QIO0}$
'AS895
'AS895

FIGURE 1. SERIAL I/O

The shift instructions are summarized in Table 4 and illustrated in Figure 2. In Figure 2 and all succeeding figures that illustrate instruction execution, the following definitions apply:

QBT — End fill for signed divide.
MQF — End fill for unsigned divide.
SRF — End fill for signed multiply and the arithmetic right shifts.

TABLE 4. SHIFT INSTRUCTIONS

OP CODE†	SHIFT FUNCTION‡	SIO7 • SIO0 WIRED VALUE	QIO7 • QIO0 WIRED VALUE
0N	Arithmetic Right Single	ALU-LSB Output	—
1N	Arithmetic Right Double	MQ-LSB Output	ALU-LSB Output
2N	Logical Right Single	Input to ALU-MSB	ALU-LSB Output
3N	Logical Right Double	Input to ALU-MSB	ALU-LSB Output
4N	Arithmetic Left Single	Input to ALU-LSB	ALU-MSB Output
5N	Arithmetic Left Double	Input to MQ-LSB	MQ-MSB Output
6N	Circular Left Single	ALU-MSB Output	—
7N	Circular Left Double	ALU-MSB Output	MQ-MSB Output
8N	Circular Right Single	ALU-LSB Output	—
9N	Circular Right Double	MQ-LSB Output	ALU-LSB Output
AN	Arithmetic Right (MQ only)	MQ-LSB Output	MQ-LSB Output
BN	Logical Right (MQ only)	MQ-LSB Output	Input to MQ-MSB
CN	Logical Left (MQ only)	Input to MQ-LSB	MQ-MSB Output
DN	Circular Left (MQ only)	MQ-MSB Output	MQ-MSB Output

†Op Code N ≠ 0, 8, or F; these select special instruction Groups 4, 3, and 5 respectively.
‡Shift I/O pins are active low. Therefore, inputs and outputs must be inverted if true logical values are required.

Status is set with the following results:

Arithmetic

N → Result MSB equal one
OVR → Signed arithmetic overflow†
C_{n+8} → Carry out equal one
Z → Result equal zero

Logic

N → Result MSB equal one
OVR → Zero
C_{n+8} → Zero
Z → Result equal zero

† For the SLA and SLAD instructions, OVR is set if signed arithmetic overflow or if the ALU result MSB XOR MSB-1 equals one.

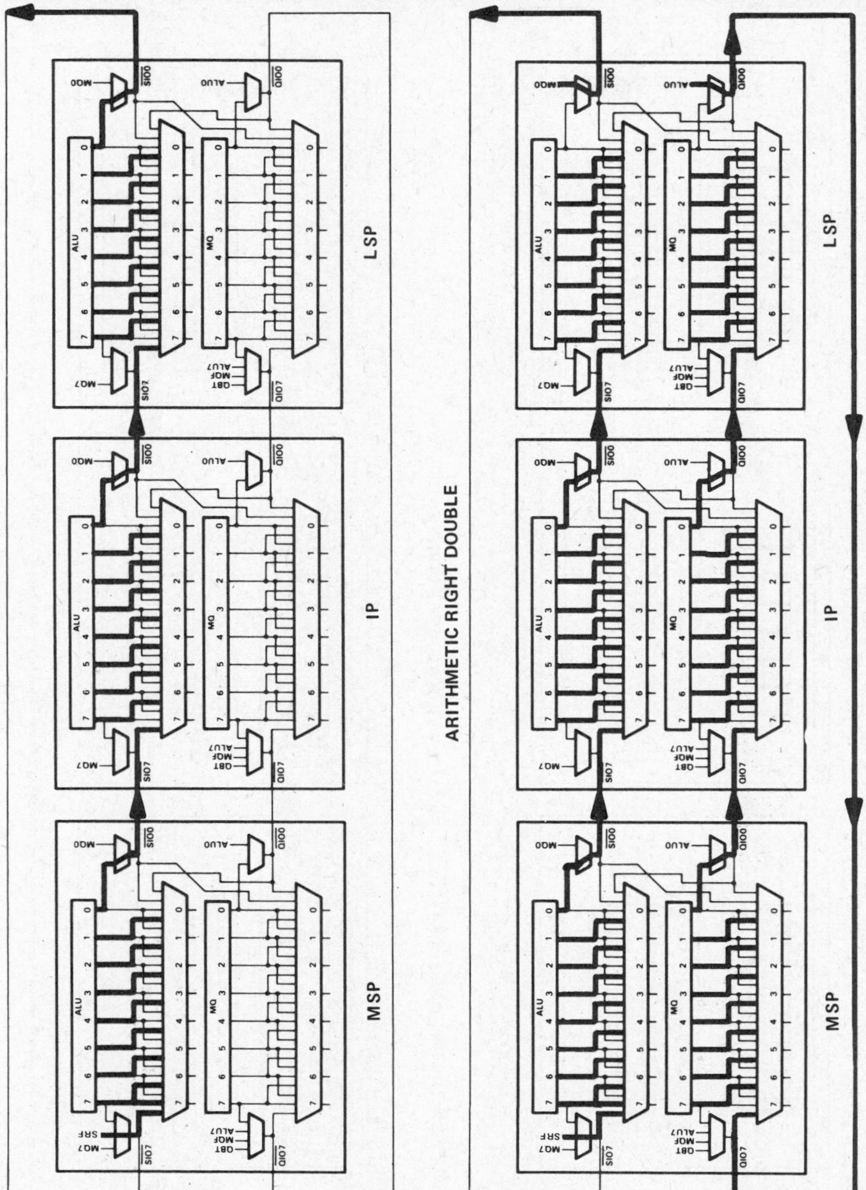
ARITHMETIC RIGHT SINGLE
ARITHMETIC RIGHT DOUBLE
LSP
IP
MSP
ALU
MQ
SIO0
SIO7
QIO0
QIO7
MQ0
MQ7
ALU0
ALU7
QBT
MQF
SRF

FIGURE 2. SHIFT INSTRUCTIONS

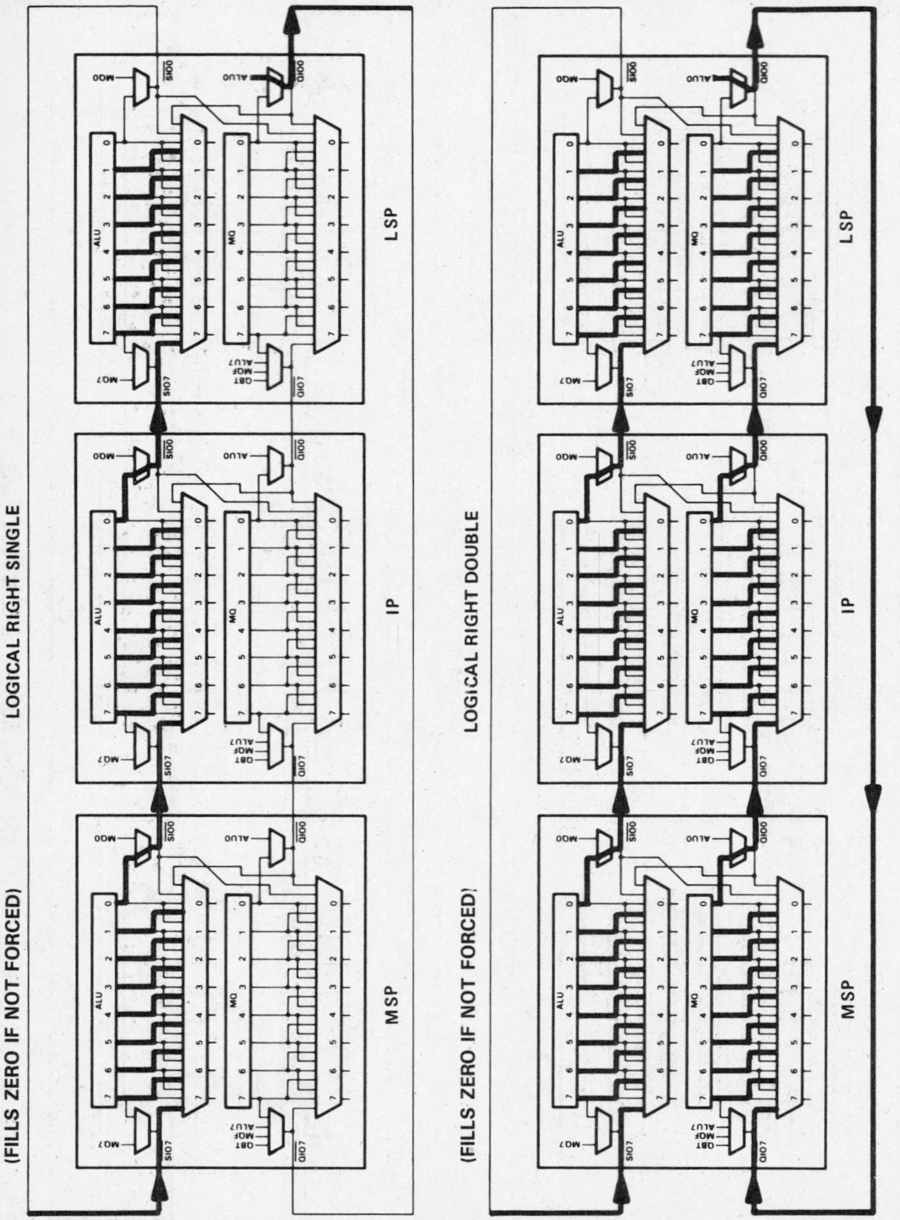
LOGICAL RIGHT SINGLE
(FILLS ZERO IF NOT FORCED)
LOGICAL RIGHT DOUBLE
(FILLS ZERO IF NOT FORCED)
LSP
IP
MSP
ALU
MQ
SIO7
SIO0
QIO7
QIO0
MQ0
MQ7
ALU0
QBT
MQF
ALU7

FIGURE 2. SHIFT INSTRUCTIONS (Continued)

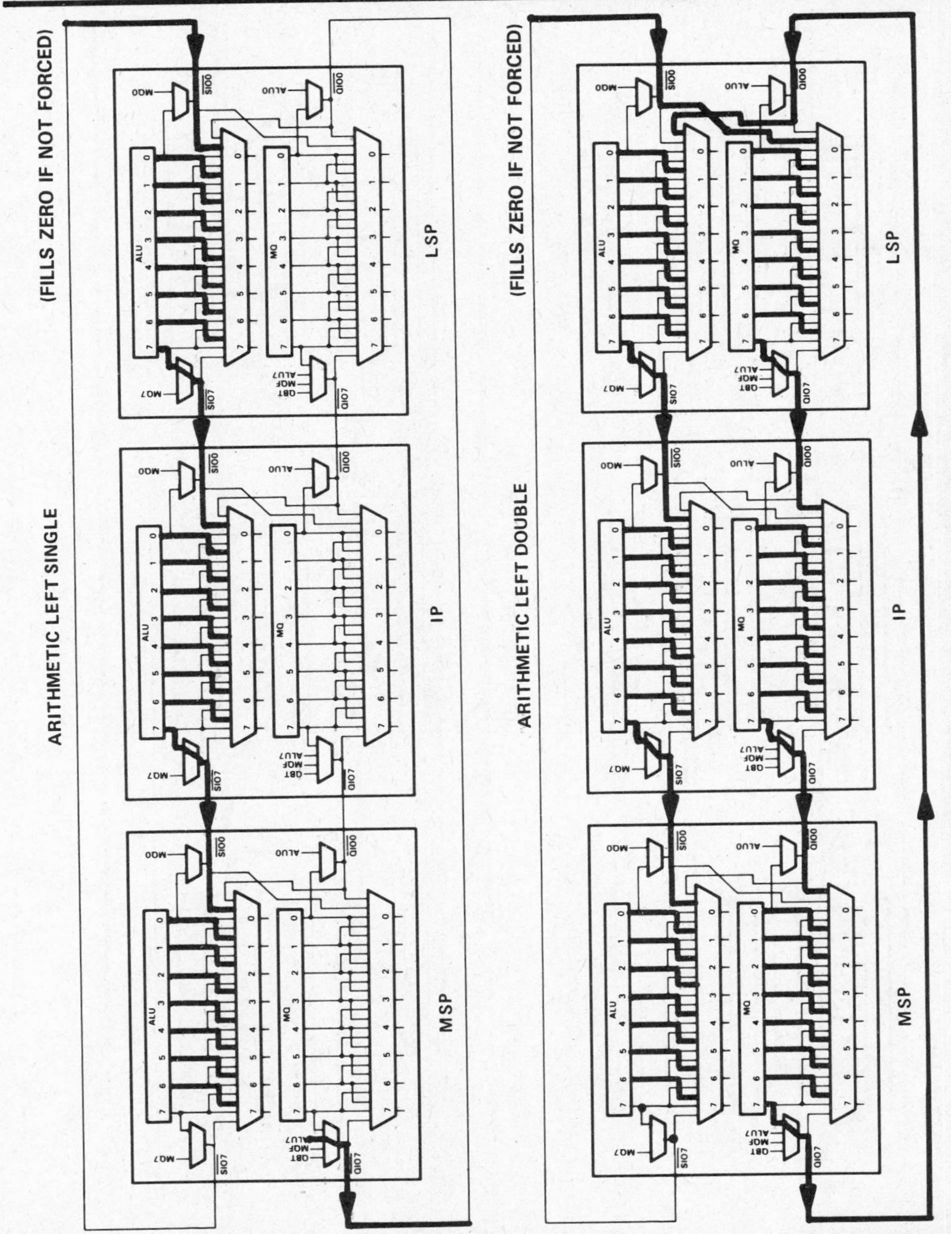
ARITHMETIC LEFT SINGLE
(FILLS ZERO IF NOT FORCED)
ARITHMETIC LEFT DOUBLE
(FILLS ZERO IF NOT FORCED)
LSP
IP
MSP
ALU
MQ
MQ0
ALU0
MQ7
QBT
MQF
ALU7
SIO0
QIO0
SIO7
QIO7

FIGURE 2. SHIFT INSTRUCTIONS (Continued)

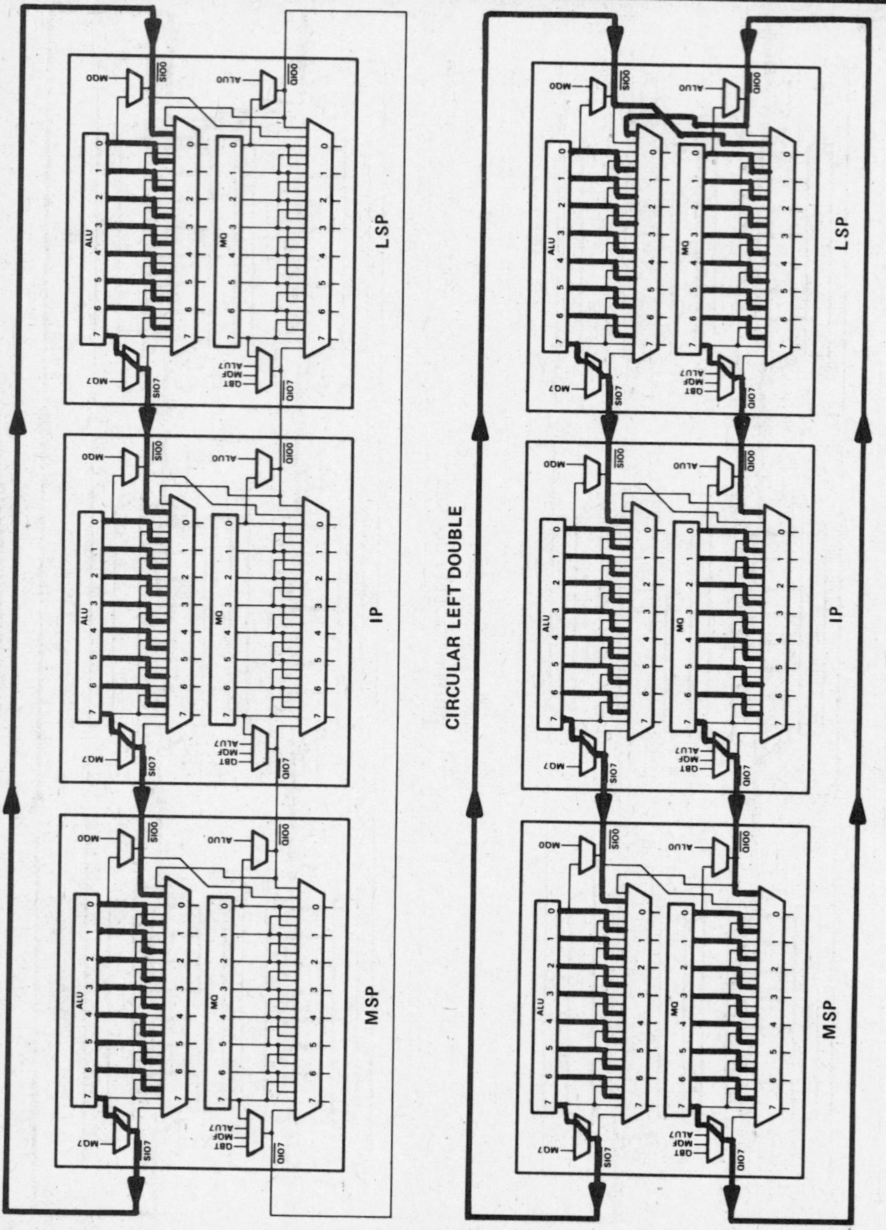
CIRCULAR LEFT SINGLE
CIRCULAR LEFT DOUBLE
LSP
IP
MSP
ALU
MQ
SIO0
SIO7
QIO0
QIO7
MQ0
MQ7
ALU0
ALU7
MQF
QBT

FIGURE 2. SHIFT INSTRUCTIONS (Continued)

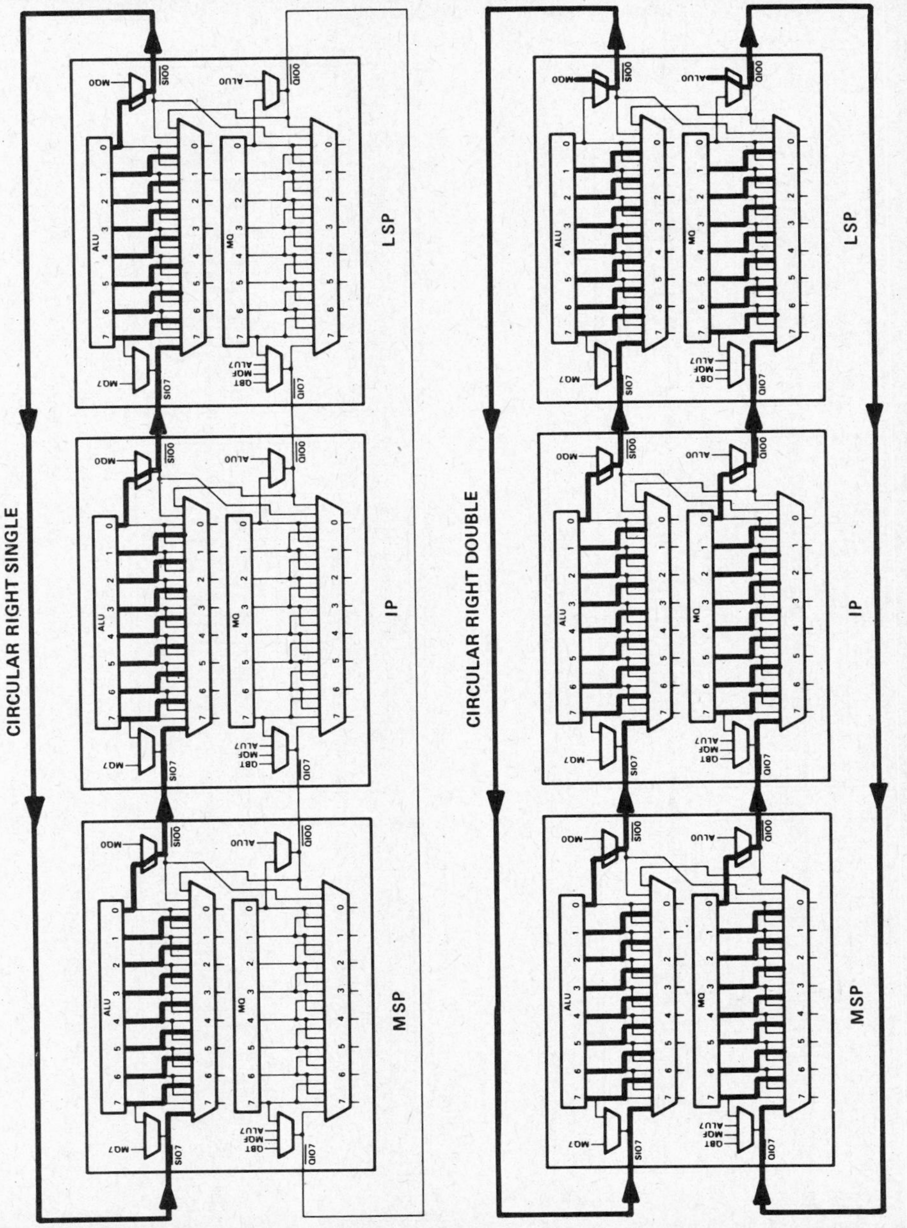
CIRCULAR RIGHT SINGLE
CIRCULAR RIGHT DOUBLE
LSP
IP
MSP
ALU
MQ
SIO0
SIO7
QIO0
QIO7
MQ0
MQ7
ALU0
QBT
MQF
ALU7

FIGURE 2. SHIFT INSTRUCTIONS (Continued)

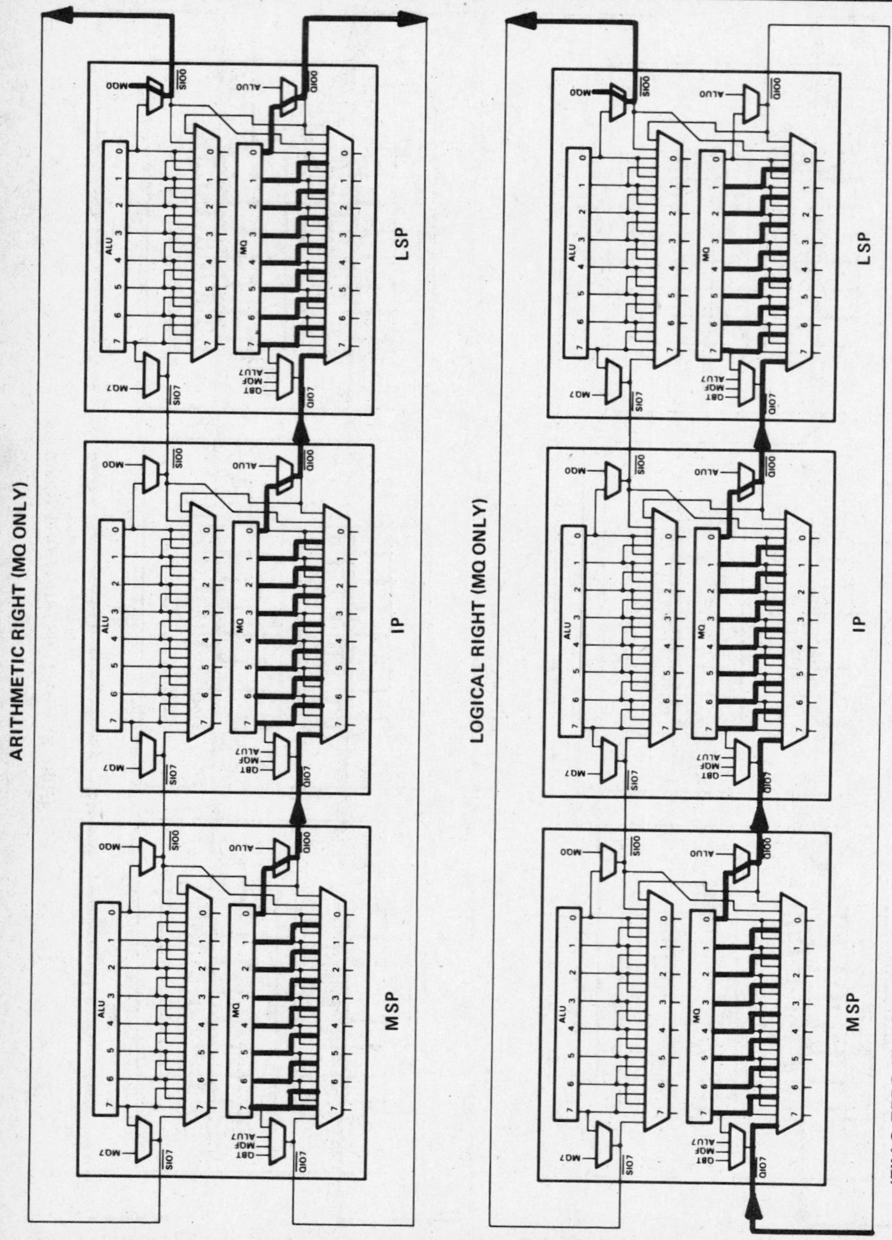
ARITHMETIC RIGHT (MQ ONLY)
LOGICAL RIGHT (MQ ONLY)
LSP
IP
MSP
ALU
MQ
MQ0
ALU0
MQ7
QBT
MQF
ALU7

(FILLS ZERO IF NOT FORCED)

FIGURE 2. SHIFT INSTRUCTIONS (Continued)

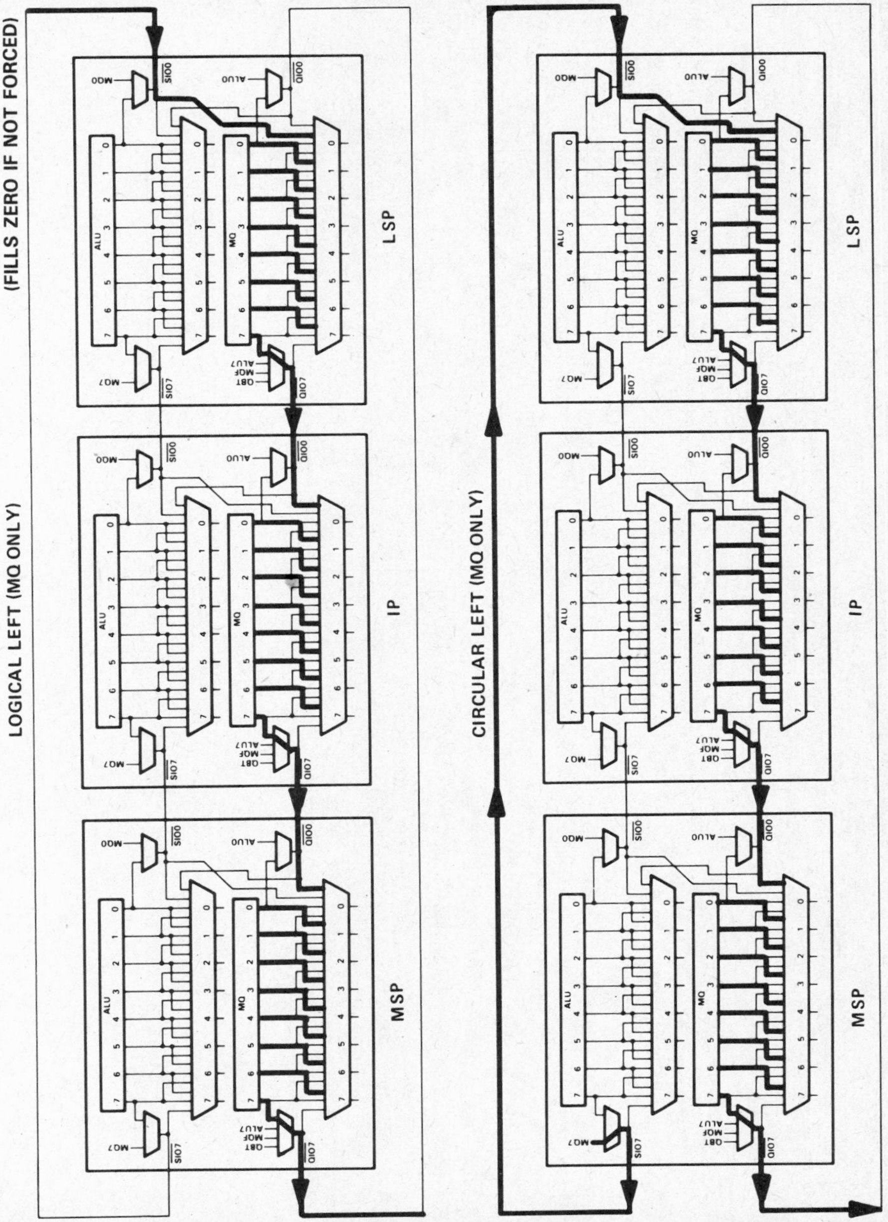
LOGICAL LEFT (MQ ONLY)
(FILLS ZERO IF NOT FORCED)
CIRCULAR LEFT (MQ ONLY)
ALU
MQ
MSP
IP
LSP
MQ0
MQ7
ALU0
ALU7
QBT
MQF
SIO0
SIO7
QIO0
QIO7

FIGURE 2. SHIFT INSTRUCTIONS (Concluded)

group 3 instructions

Hex code 8 of Group 1 instructions is used to access Group 3 instructions. Group 3 instructions are summarized in Table 5.

TABLE 5. GROUP 3 INSTRUCTIONS

INSTRUCTION BITS (I7-I0) OP CODE (HEX)	MNEMONIC	FUNCTION
08	SET1	Set Bit
18	SET0	Reset Bit
28	TB1	Test Bit (One)
38	TB0	Test Bit (Zero)
48	ABS	Absolute Value
58	SMTC	Sign Magnitude/Two's Complement
68	ADDI	Add Immediate
78	SUBI	Subtract Immediate
88	BADD	Byte Add R to S
98	BSUBS	Byte Subtract S from R
A8	BSUBR	Byte Subtract R from S
B8	BINCS	Byte Increment S
C8	BINCNS	Byte Increment Negative S
D8	BXOR	Byte XOR R and S
E8	BAND	Byte AND R and S
F8	BOR	Byte OR R and S

set bit instruction (set1): I7-I0 = 08_{16}

This instruction (Figure 3) is used to force selected bits of a desired byte(s) to one. The desired bits are specified by an 8-bit mask (C3-C0)::(A3-A0)† consisting of register file address ports that are not required to support this instruction. All bits in the selected byte(s) that are in the same bit positions as ones in the mask are forced to a logical one. The B3-B0 address field is used for both source and destination of this instruction. The desired byte is specified by forcing $\overline{SIO0}$ to a low value. Nonselected packages pass the byte through unaltered. The S bus is the source word for this instruction. The status set by the set bit instruction is as follows:

N	→	None (force to zero)
OVR	→	None (force to zero)
C_{n+8}	→	None (force to zero)
Z	→	Result equal zero

† The symbol '::' is concatenation operator

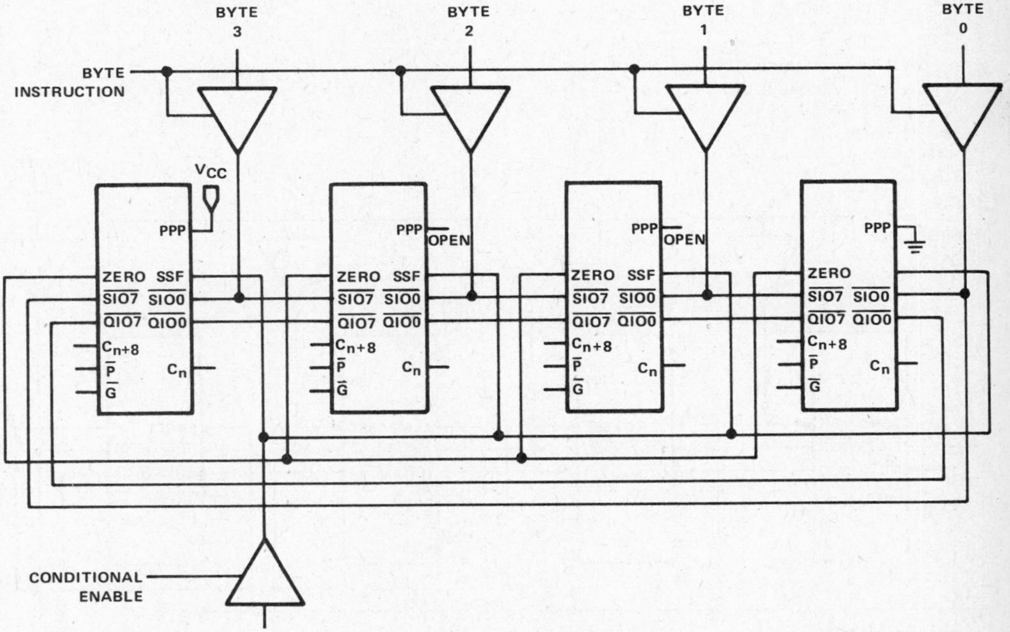
BYTE 3
BYTE 2
BYTE 1
BYTE 0
BYTE INSTRUCTION
VCC
PPP
PPP OPEN
PPP OPEN
PPP
ZERO SSF
SIO7 SIO0
QIO7 QIO0
Cn+8
P
G
Cn
CONDITIONAL ENABLE

FIGURE 3. SET BIT (OR RESET BIT)

NOTES: 1. Force $\overline{SIO0}$ = low to select byte.
2. Bit mast (C3-C0)::(A3-A0) will set desired bits to one.

reset bit instruction (set0): I7-I0 = 18_{16}

This instruction (Figure 3) is used to force selected bits of a desired byte(s) to zero. The desired bits are specified by an 8-bit mask (C3-C0)::(A3-A0) consisting of register file address ports that are not required to support this instruction. All bits in the selected byte(s) that are in the same bit positions as ones in the mask are reset. The B3-B0 address field is used for both source and destination of this instruction.

The desired byte is specified by forcing $\overline{SIO0}$ to a low value. Nonselected packages pass the byte through unaltered. The S bus is the source word for this instruction. The status set by the reset bit instruction is as follows:

N	→	None (force to zero)
OVR	→	None (force to zero)
C_{n+8}	→	None (force to zero)
Z	→	Result equal zero

test bit (one) instruction (TB1): I7-I0 = 28_{16}

This instruction (Figure 4) is used to test selected bits of a desired byte(s). Bits to be tested are specified by an 8-bit mask (C3-C0)::(A3-A0) consisting of register file address ports that are not required to support this instruction. Write Enable ($\overline{WE}$) is internally disabled during this instruction. The desired byte is specified by forcing $\overline{SIO0}$ to a low value. The test will pass if the selected byte has ones at all bit locations specified by the ones of the mask (Figure 5). The S bus is the source word for this instruction. The status set by the test bit (one) instruction is as follows:

N	→	None (force to zero)
OVR	→	None (force to zero)
C_{n+8}	→	None (force to zero)
Z	→	Pass

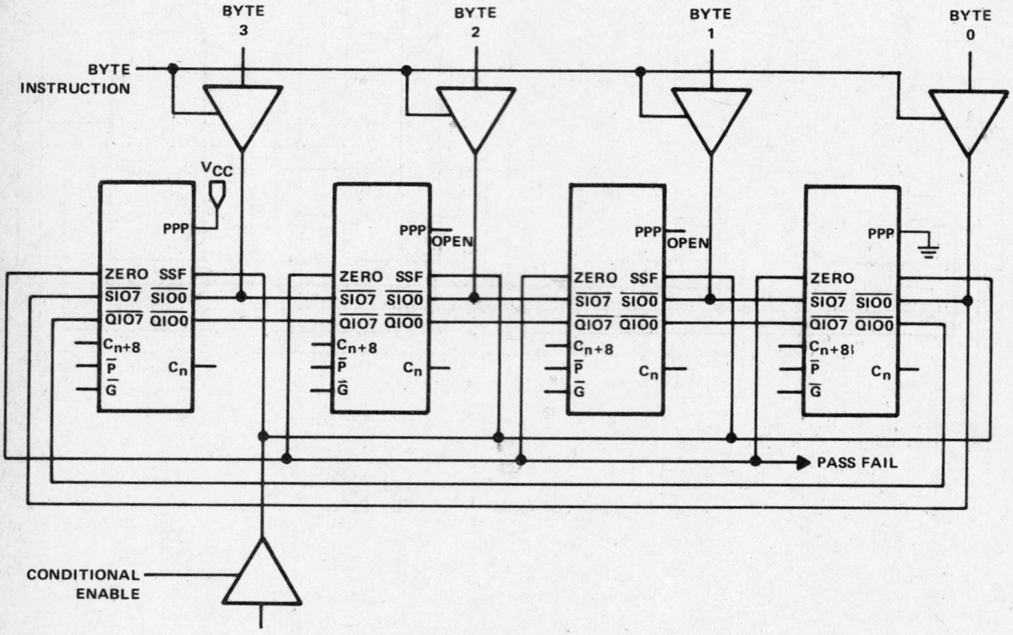
BYTE 3
BYTE 2
BYTE 1
BYTE 0
BYTE INSTRUCTION
VCC
PPP
OPEN
ZERO SSF
SIO7 SIO0
QIO7 QIO0
Cn+8
P
G
Cn
PASS FAIL
CONDITIONAL ENABLE

FIGURE 4. TEST BIT

NOTES: 1. Force $\overline{SIO0}$ = low to select byte.
2. Bit mask (C3-C0)::(A3-A0) will define bits for testing.
3. Pass/fail is indicated on Z output.

test bit (zero) instruction (TB0): I7-I0 = 38_{16}

This instruction (Figure 4) is used to test selected bits of a desired byte(s). Bits to be tested are specified by an 8-bit mask (C3-C0)::(A3-A0) consisting of register file address ports that are not required to support this instruction. Write Enable ($\overline{WE}$) is internally disabled during this instruction. The desired byte is specified by forcing $\overline{SIO0}$ to a low value. The test will pass if the selected byte has zeros at all bit locations specified by the ones of the mask (Figure 6). The S bus is the source word for this instruction. The status set by the test bit (zero) instruction is as follows:

N → None (force to zero)
OVR → None (force to zero)
C_{n+8} → None (force to zero)
Z → Pass

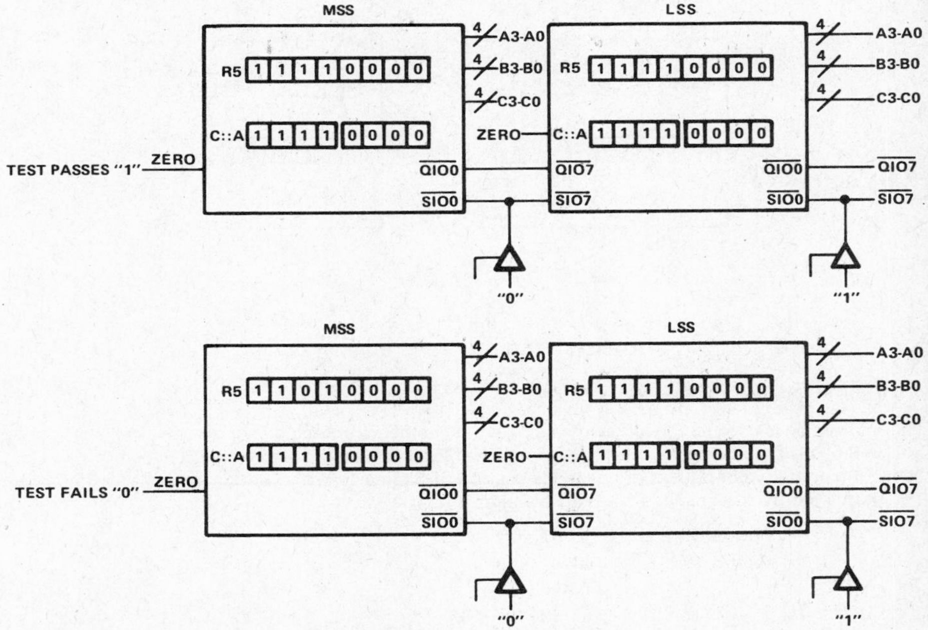
MSS
LSS
A3-A0
B3-B0
C3-C0
R5 1 1 1 1 0 0 0 0
C::A 1 1 1 1 0 0 0 0
ZERO
TEST PASSES "1"
QIO0
SIO0
QIO7
SIO7
"0"
"1"
MSS
LSS
R5 1 1 0 1 0 0 0 0
R5 1 1 1 1 0 0 0 0
C::A 1 1 1 1 0 0 0 0
TEST FAILS "0"

FIGURE 5. TEST BIT ONE EXAMPLES

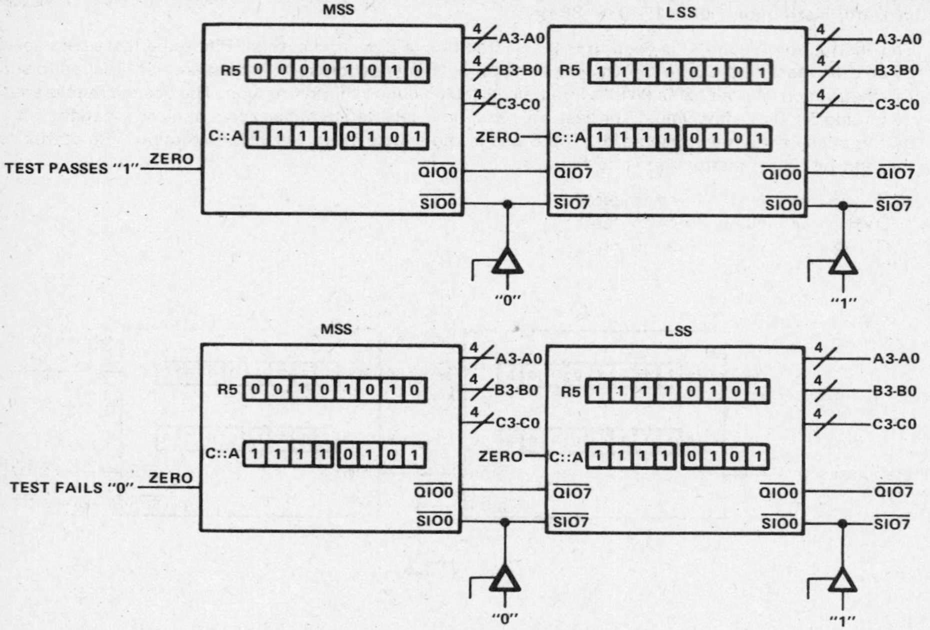
MSS
LSS
R5 0 0 0 0 1 0 1 0
R5 1 1 1 1 0 1 0 1
C::A 1 1 1 1 0 1 0 1
A3-A0
B3-B0
C3-C0
ZERO
TEST PASSES "1"
QIO0
QIO7
SIO0
SIO7
"0"
"1"
R5 0 0 1 0 1 0 1 0
TEST FAILS "0"

FIGURE 6. TEST BIT ZERO EXAMPLES

absolute value instruction (ABS): I7-I0 = 48_{16}

This instruction is used to convert two's complement numbers to their positive value. The operand placed on the S bus is the source for this instruction. The MSP will test the sign of the S bus and force the SSF pin to the proper value. All other packages use the SSF pin as input to determine instruction execution. The status set by the absolute value instruction is as follows:

N	→	Input MSB equal one
OVR	→	Input equal 8000 (hex)
C_{n+8}	→	S = 0
Z	→	Result equal zero

sign magnitude/two's complement instruction (SMTC): I7-I0 = 58_{16}

This instruction allows conversion from two's complement representation to sign magnitude representation, or vice-versa, in one clock cycle. The operand placed on the S bus is the source for this instruction.

When a negative zero (8000 hex) is converted, the result is 0000 with an overflow. If the input is in two's complement notation, the overflow indicates an illegal conversion. The status set by the sign magnitude/two's complement instruction is as follows:

N	→	Result MSB equal one
OVR	→	Input equal 8000 (hex)
C_{n+8}	→	Input equal 0000 (hex)
Z	→	Result equal zero

TEXAS INSTRUMENTS
POST OFFICE BOX 225012 • DALLAS, TEXAS 75265

add immediate instruction (ADDI): I7-I0 = 68_{16}

This instruction is used to add a specified constant value to the operand placed on the S bus. The constant will be between the values of 0 and 15. The constant value is specified by the unused register file address (A port) not required to support this instruction. Forcing the carry input will add an additional one to the result. The status set by the add immediate instruction is as follows:

N → Result MSB equal one
OVR → Arithmetic signed overflow
C_{n+8} → Carry out equal one
Z → Result equal zero

subtract immediate instruction (SUBI): I7-I0 = 78_{16}

This instruction is used to subtract a specified constant value from the operand placed on the S bus. The constant value is specified by the unused register file address (A port) that is not required to support this instruction. The constant applied is the least significant four bits of a two's complement number. The device sign extends the constant over the entire word length. The status set by the subtract immediate instruction is as follows:

N → Result MSB equal one
OVR → Arithmetic signed overflow
C_{n+8} → Carry out equal one
Z → Result equal zero

byte instructions

There are eight byte instructions in Group 3. These instructions modify selected bytes of the operand on the S bus. A byte is selected by forcing $\overline{SIO0}$ to a low value (same as SET1, SET0, TB1, and TB0 instructions). Multiple bytes may be selected only if they are adjacent to one another.

NOTE: At least one byte must be nonselected during these instructions.

The nonselected bytes are passed through unaltered. Byte status is forced through the most significant package except for the sign of the result (N), which is forced to zero (low). The status set by the byte instructions is as follows:

(Most Significant Package)

N → None (force to zero)
OVR → Byte signed overflow
C_{n+8} → Byte carry out equal one
Z → Byte result equal to zero

(Selected BYTES—other than MSP)

G → Normal generate
P → Normal propagate
C_{n+8} → Normal carry out
Z → Result equal to zero

(Nonselected BYTES—other than MSP)

G → No generate (force to one)
P → Propagate (force to zero)
C_{n+8} → C_n
Z → None (force to one)

group 4 instructions

Hex code 0 of Group 1 instructions is used to access Group 4 instructions. Group 4 instructions are summarized in Table 6.

TABLE 6. GROUP 4 INSTRUCTIONS

INSTRUCTION BITS (I7-I0) OP CODE (HEX)	MNEMONIC	FUNCTION
00		Reserved
10	SEL	Select S/R
20	SNORM	Single Length Normalize
30	DNORM	Double Length Normalize
40	DIVRF	Divide Remainder Fix
50	SDIVQF	Signed Divide Quotient Fix
60	SMULI	Signed Multiply Iterate
70	SMULT	Signed Multiply Terminate
80	SDIVIN	Signed Divide Initialize
90	SDIVIS	Signed Divide Start
A0	SDIVI	Signed Divide Iterate
B0	UDIVIS	Unsigned Divide Start
C0	UDIVI	Unsigned Divide Iterate
D0	UMULI	Unsigned Multiply Iterate
E0	SDIVIT	Signed Divide Terminate
F0	UDIVIT	Unsigned Divide Terminate

select S/R instruction (SEL): I7-I0 = 10_{16}

This instruction is used to pass either the S bus or the R bus to the output depending on the state of the SSF input pin. Normally, the preceding instruction would test the two operands and the resulting status information would be used to force the SSF input pin. SSF = 0 will output the R bus and SSF = 1 will output the S bus. The status set by the select S/R instruction is as follows:

N → Result MSB equal one
OVR → None (force to zero)
C_{n+8} → None (force to zero)
Z → Result equal zero

single-length normalize instruction (SNORM): I7-I0 = 20_{16}

This instruction will cause the contents of the MQ register to shift toward the most significant bit. Zeros are shifted in via the $\overline{\text{QIO0}}$ input. The number of shifts performed can be counted and stored in one of the register files by forcing a high at the C_n input. When the two most significant bits are of opposite value, normalization is complete. This condition is indicated on the microcycle that completes the normalization at the OVR output.

The chip contains conditional logic that inhibits the shift function (and also inhibits the register file increment) if the number within the MQ register is already normalized at the beginning of the instruction (Figure 7). The status set by the single-length normalize instruction is as follows:

N → MSB of result
OVR → MSB XOR 2nd MSB
C_{n+8} → Carry out equal one
Z → Result equal zero

TEXAS INSTRUMENTS
POST OFFICE BOX 225012 • DALLAS, TEXAS 75265

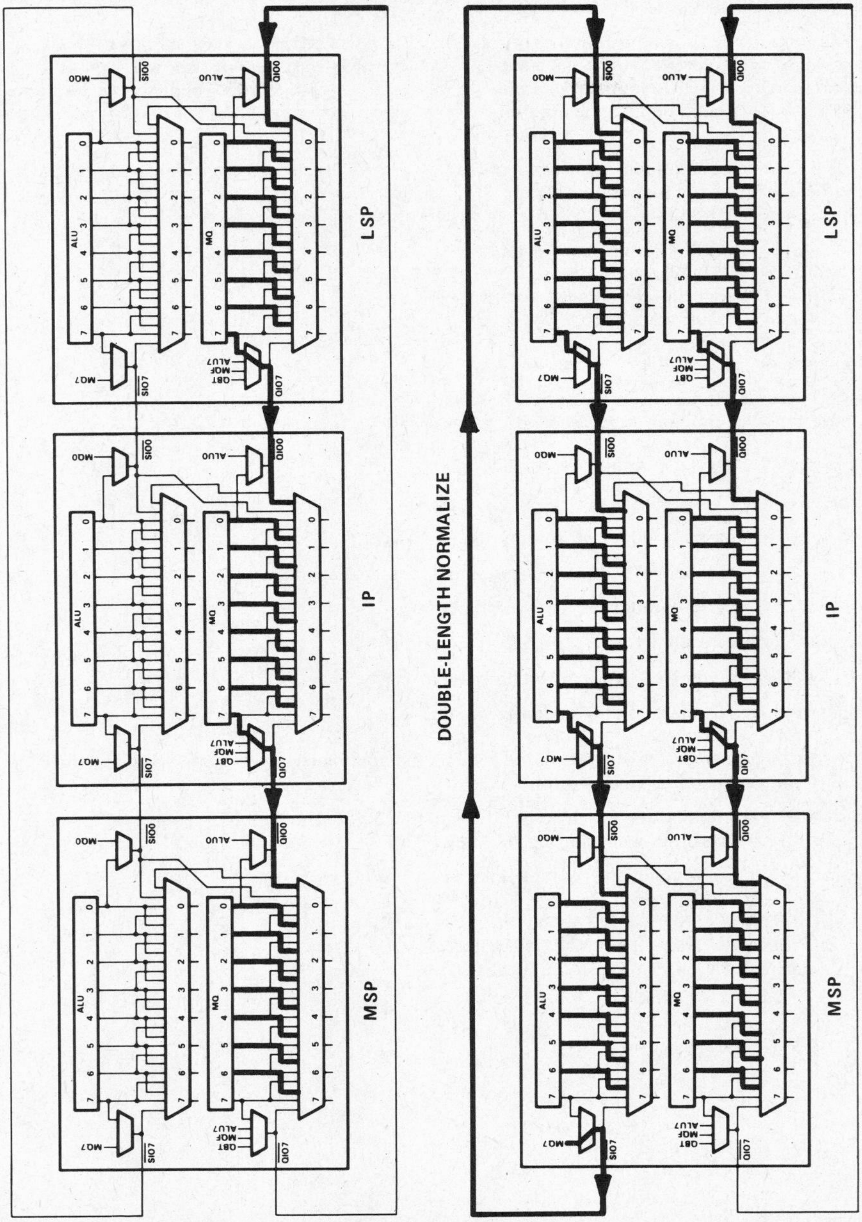
SINGLE-LENGTH NORMALIZE
DOUBLE-LENGTH NORMALIZE
LSP
IP
MSP
ALU
MQ
SIO0
QIO0
SIO7
QIO7
MQ0
ALU0
MQ7
QBT
MQF
ALU7

FIGURE 7. SINGLE-AND DOUBLE-LENGTH NORMALIZE

double-length normalize instruction (DNORM): I7-I0 = 30_{16}

This instruction will cause the contents of a double-length word (register file contains the most significant half and the MQ register contains the least significant half) to shift toward the most significant bit. Zeros are shifted in via the $\overline{QIO0}$ input. When the two most significant bits are of opposite value, normalization is complete. This condition is indicated on the microcycle that completes the normalization at the OVR output.

The chip contains conditional logic which inhibits the shift function if the number is already normalized at the beginning of the instruction (Figure 7). The most significant half of the operand must be placed on the S bus. The status set by the double-length normalize instruction is as follows:

N	→	MSB of result
OVR	→	MSB XOR 2nd MSB
C_{n+8}	→	None (force to zero)
Z	→	Result equal zero

multiply operations

The ALU performs three unique types of N by N multiplies each of which produces a 2N-bit result (Figure 8). All three types of multiplication proceed via the following recursion:

P(J+1) = 2[P(J) + Multiplicand × M (8N-J)]

where

P(J) = partial product at iteration number J

N = number of 'AS888 packages that are cascaded

P(J+1) = partial product at iteration number J+1

J varies from 0 to 8N [N = 2 for 16 × 16 multiply]

M (8N-J) = mode bit (unique to multiply type)

2 denotes some type of shift (unique to multiply)

Notice that by proper choice of mode terms and shifting operations, signed, unsigned, and mixed multiplies (signed times unsigned) may be performed.

All multiplies assume that the multiplier is stored in MQ before the operation begins (in the case of mixed multiply, the unsigned number must be the multiplier).

The processor has the following multiply instructions:

1. SIGNED MULTIPLY ITERATE (SMULI): I7-I0 = 60_{16}
2. SIGNED MULTIPLY TERMINATE (SMULT): I7-I0 = 70_{16}
3. UNSIGNED MULTIPLY ITERATE (UMULI): I7-I0 = $D0_{16}$

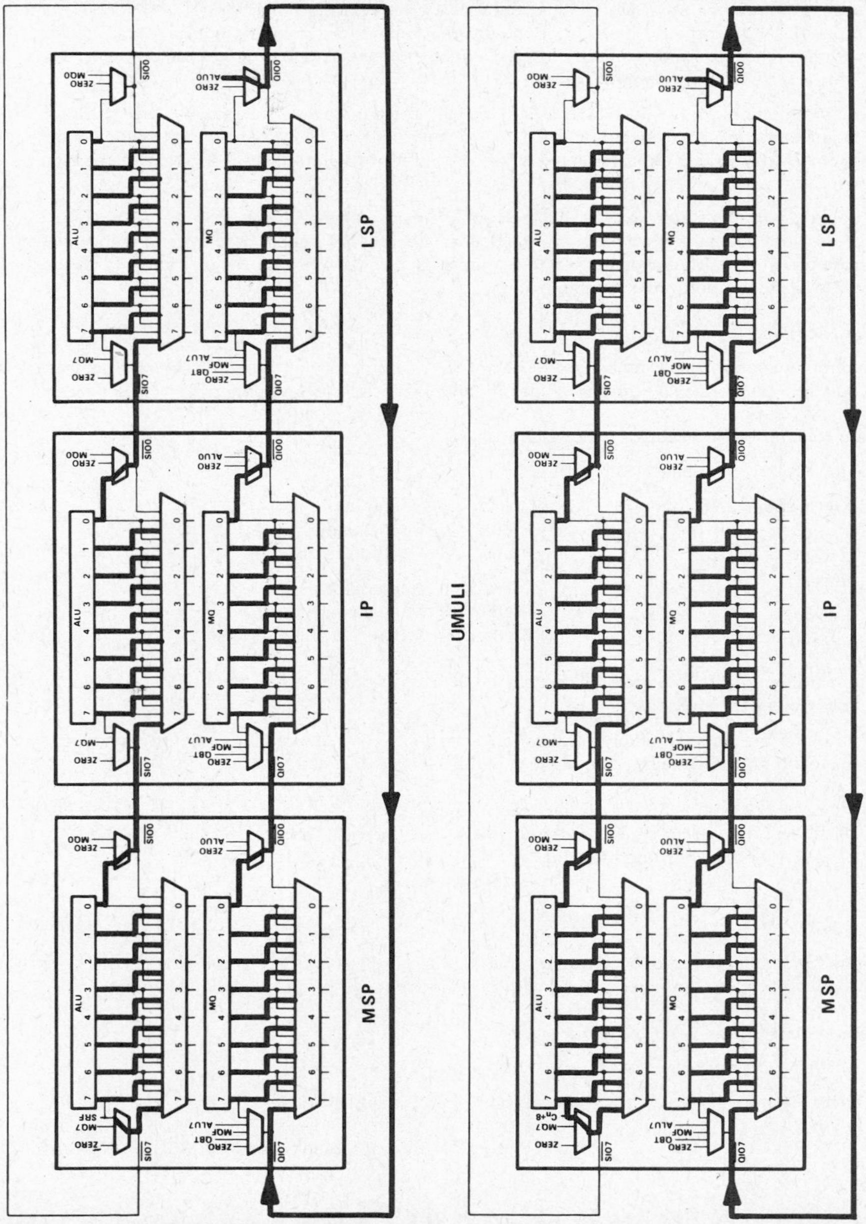
SMULI, SMULT
UMULI
LSP
IP
MSP
ALU
MQ
SIO0
SIO7
QIO0
QIO7
ZERO
MQ0
MQ7
ALU0
ALU7
QBT
MQF
SRF
Cn+8

FIGURE 8. MULTIPLICATION OPERATIONS

The signed multiply iterate (SMULI) instruction performs a signed times signed iteration. This instruction interprets M(8N-J) as the 8N-J bit of the multiplier. The shift is a double-precision right shift one bit. This instruction is repeated 15 times for a 16 × 16 signed multiply. This instruction will be used 16 consecutive times for a mixed multiplication.

The signed multiply terminate (SMULT) instruction provides correct (negative) weighting of the sign bit of a negative multiplier in signed multiplication. The instruction is identical to signed multiply iterate (SMULI) except that M(8N-J) is interpreted as −1 if the sign bit of the multiplier is 1, and 0 if the sign bit of the multiplier is 0.

The unsigned multiply iterate (UMULI) performs an unsigned multiplication iteration. This instruction interprets M(8N-J) as the 8N-J bit of the multiplier. The shift is a double-precision right shift with the carry out from the P(J) + Multiplicand × M(8N-J) operation forced into bit 8N of P(J + 1). This instruction is used in unsigned and mixed multiplication.

signed multiplication

Signed multiplication performs an 8N + 2 clock two's complement multiply. The instructions necessary to produce an algebraically correct result proceed in the following manner:

Zero register to be used for accumulator

Load MQ with multiplier

SMULI (repeat 8N-1 times)	S port = Accumulator R port = Multiplicand F port = Iteration result
SMULT	S port = Accumulator R port = Multiplicand F port = Product (MSH)

At completion, the accumulator will contain the 8N most significant bits and the MQ contains the 8N least significant bits of the product.

The status for the signed multiply iterate should not be used for any testing (overflow is not set by SMULI). The following status is set for the signed multiply terminate instruction:

N	→	Result MSB equal one
OVR	→	Forced to zero
C_{n+8}	→	Carry out equal to one
Z	→	Double precision result is zero

unsigned multiplication

Unsigned multiplication produces an unsigned times unsigned product in 8N + 2 clocks. The instructions necessary to produce an algebraically correct result proceed in the following manner:

Zero register to be used for accumulator

Load MQ with multiplier

UMULI (8N times)	S port = Accumulator R port = Multiplicand F port = Iteration result (product MSH on final result)

TEXAS INSTRUMENTS
POST OFFICE BOX 225012 • DALLAS, TEXAS 75265

Upon completion, the accumulator will contain the 8N most significant bits and the MQ contains the 8N least significant bits of the product.

The status set by the unsigned multiply iteration is meaningless except on the final execution of the instruction. The status set by the unsigned multiply iteration instruction is as follows:

N → Result MSB equal one
OVR → Forced to zero
C_{n+8} → Carry out equal to one
Z → Double-precision result is zero

mixed multiplication

Mixed multiplication multiplies a signed multiplicand times an unsigned multiplier to produce a signed result in 8N + 2 clocks. The steps are as follows:

Zero register used for accumulator

Load MQ with unsigned multipler

SMULI (8N times) S port = Accumulator
R port = Multiplicand
F port = Iteration result

Upon completion, the accumulator will contain the 8N most significant bits and the MQ will contain the 8N least significant bits of the product.

The following status is set by the last SMULI instruction:

N → Result MSB equal one
OVR → Forced to zero
C_{n+8} → Carry out equal to one
Z → Double-precision result is zero

divide operations

The divide uses a nonrestoring technique to perform both signed and unsigned division of a 16N bit integer dividend and an 8N bit integer divisor (Figure 9). It produces an 8N integer quotient and remainder.

The remainder and quotient will be such that the following equation is satisfied:

$$(\text{Quotient}) \times (\text{Divisor}) + \text{Remainder} = \text{Dividend}$$

The processor has the following divide instructions:

1. UNSIGNED DIVIDE START (UDIVIS): I7-I0 = $B0_{16}$
2. UNSIGNED DIVIDE ITERATE (UDIVI): I7-I0 = $C0_{16}$
3. UNSIGNED DIVIDE TERMINATE (UDIVIT): I7-I0 = $F0_{16}$
4. SIGNED DIVIDE INITIALIZE (SDIVIN): I7-I0 = 80_{16}
5. SIGNED DIVIDE OVERFLOW TEST (SDIVO): I7-I0 = AF_{16}
6. SIGNED DIVIDE START (SDIVIS): I7-I0 = 90_{16}
7. SIGNED DIVIDE ITERATE (SDIVI): I7-I0 = $A0_{16}$
8. SIGNED DIVIDE TERMINATE (SDIVIT): I7-I0 = $E0_{16}$
9. DIVIDE REMAINDER FIX (DIVRF): I7-I0 = 40_{16}
10. SIGNED DIVIDE QUOTIENT FIX (SDIVQF): I7-I0 = 50_{16}

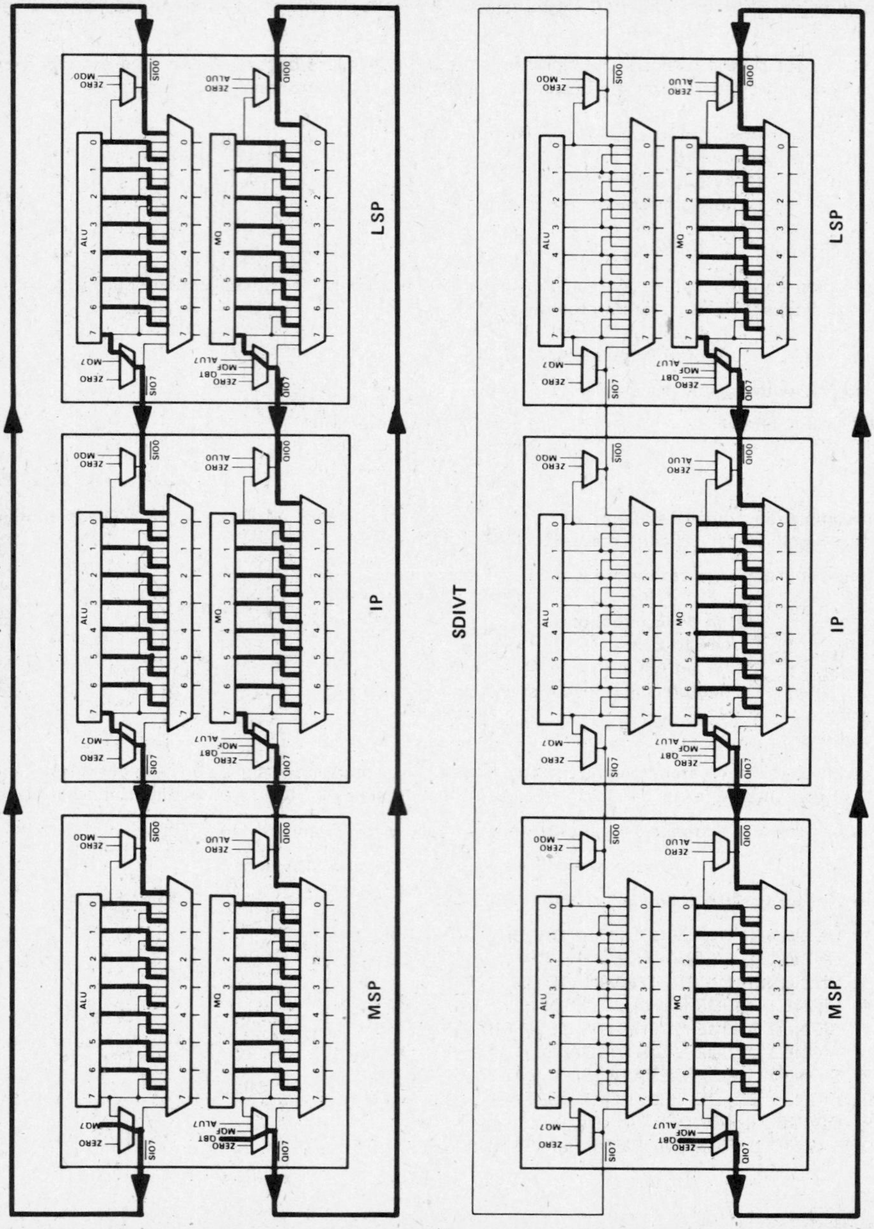
SDIVIN, SDIVS, SDIVI
SDIVT
LSP
IP
MSP
ALU
MQ
ZERO
MQ0
ALU0
MQ7
MQF
ALU7
QBT
SIO0
QIO0
SIO7
QIO7

FIGURE 9. DIVIDE OPERATIONS

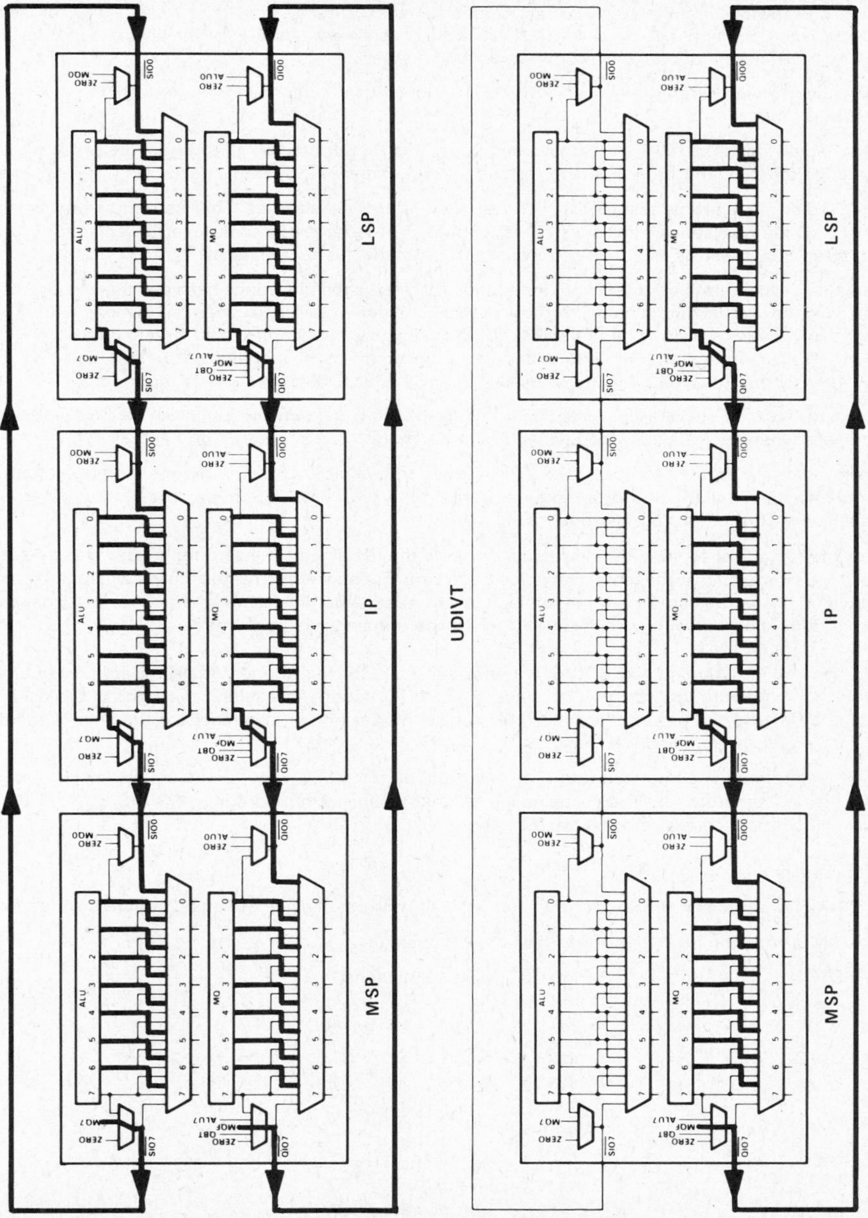
UDIVS, UDIVI
UDIVT
LSP
IP
MSP
ALU
MQ
ZERO
MQ0
ALU0
MQ7
ALU7
QBT
MQF
SIO0
QIO0
SIO7
QIO7

FIGURE 9. DIVIDE OPERATIONS (Continued)

The unsigned divide iterate start (UDIVIS) instruction begins the iterate procedure while testing for overflow. Overflow is reported when the first subtraction of the divisor from the MSH of the dividend produces carry out. The test detects quotient overflow and divide by zero.

The unsigned divide iterate terminate (UDIVIT) instruction completes the iterate procedure generating the last quotient bit.

The signed divide initialize (SDIVIN) instruction prepares for iteration by shifting the dividend and storing the sign of the dividend for use in the following instructions and overflow tests.

The signed divide overflow test (SDIVO) checks for overflow possibilities. This instruction may be deleted from the divide operation if the OVR pin is ignored. If it is removed some overflow conditions will go undetected. $\overline{WE}$ must be high (writing inhibited) when this instruction is used.

The signed divide iterate start (SDIVIS) instruction calculates the difference between the divisor and MSH of the dividend. Partial detection of overflow is also done during this instruction. Operations with like signs (positive quotient) and division by zero will overflow during this instruction (including zero divisor). Operations with unlike signs are tested for overflow during the signed divide quotient fix instruction (SDIVQF). Partial overflow results are saved and will be used during SDIVQF when overflow is reported.

The signed divide iterate (SDIVI) instruction forms the quotient and remainder through iterative subtract/add-shift operations of the divisor and dividend. One quotient bit is generated on each clock.

The signed divide iterate terminate (SDIVIT) instruction completes the iterate procedure, generating the last quotient bit. It also tests for a remainder equal to zero, which determines the action to be taken in the following correction (fix) instructions.

The divide remainder fix (DIVRF) instruction corrects the remainder. If a zero remainder was detected by the previous instructions, the remainder is forced to zero. For nonzero remainder cases where the remainder and dividend have the same sign, the remainder is correct. When the remainder and dividend have unlike signs, a correction add/subtract of the divisor to the remainder is performed.

The signed divide quotient fix (SDIVQF) instruction corrects the quotient if necessary. This correction requires adding one to the incorrect quotient. An incorrect quotient results if the signs of the divisor and dividend differ and the remainder is nonzero. An incorrect quotient also results if the sign of the divisor is negative and the remainder is zero.

Overflow detection is completed during this instruction. Overflow may be generated for differing signs of the dividend and divisor. The partial overflow test result performed during SDIVIS is ORed with this test result to produce a true overflow indication.

signed divide usage

The instructions necessary to perform an algebraically correct division of signed numbers are as follows:

Load MQ with the least significant half of the dividend

SDIVIN	S port	=	MSH of dividend
	R port	=	Divisor
	F port	=	Intermediate result
SDIVO	S port	=	Result of SDIVIN
	R port	=	Divisor
	F port	=	Test result
	($\overline{WE}$ must be high)		
SDIVIS	S port	=	Result of SDIVIN
	R port	=	Divisor
	F port	=	Intermediate result

SDIVI (8N-2 times)	S port	= Result of SDIVIS (or SDIVI)
	R port	= Divisor
	F port	= Intermediate result
SDIVIT	S port	= Result of last SDIVI
	R port	= Divisor
	F port	= Intermediate result
DIVRF	S port	= Result of SDIVIT
	R port	= Divisor
	F port	= Remainder
SDIVQF	S port	= MQ register
	R port	= Divisor
	F port	= Quotient

The status of all signed divide instructions except SDIVIN, DIVRF, and SDIVQF is as follows:

N	→	Forced to zero
OVR	→	Forced to zero
C_{n+8}	→	Carry out equal to one
Z	→	Intermediate result is zero

The status of the SDIVIN instruction is as follows:

N	→	Forced to zero
OVR	→	Forced to zero
C_{n+8}	→	Forced to zero
Z	→	Divisor is zero

The status of the DIVRF instruction is as follows:

N	→	Forced to zero
OVR	→	Forced to zero
C_{n+8}	→	Carry out equal to one
Z	→	Remainder is zero

The status of the SDIVQF instruction is as follows:

N	→	Sign of quotient
OVR	→	Divide overflow
C_{n+8}	→	Carry out equal to one
Z	→	Quotient is zero

The quotient is stored in the MQ register and the remainder is stored in the register file location that originally held the most significant word of the dividend. If fractions are divided, the quotient must be shifted right one bit and the remainder right three bits to obtain the correct fractional representations.

The signed division algorithm is summarized in Table 7.

TABLE 7. SIGNED DIVISION ALGORITHM

OP CODE	MNEMONIC	CLOCK CYCLES	INPUT S PORT	INPUT R PORT	OUTPUT F PORT
E4	LOADMQ	1	Dividend (LSH)	—	Dividend (LSH)
80	SDIVIN	1	Dividend (MSH)	Divisor	Remainder (N)
AF	SDIVO	1	Remainder (N)	Divisor	Test Result
90	SDIVIS	1	Remainder (N)	Divisor	Remainder (N)
A0	SDIVI	8N−2†	Remainder (N)	Divisor	Remainder (N)
E0	SDIVIT	1	Remainder (N)	Divisor	Remainder (Unfixed)
40	DIVRF	1	Remainder (Unfixed)	Divisor	Remainder
50	SDIVQF	1	MQ Register	Divisor	Quotient

†N = Number of cascaded packages.

unsigned divide usage

The instructions necessary to perform an algebraically correct division of unsigned numbers are as follows:

Load MQ with the least significant half of the dividend

UDIVIS	S port	=	MSH of dividend
	R port	=	Divisor
	F port	=	Intermediate result
UDIVI (8N-1 times)	S port	=	Result of UDIVIS (OR UDIVI)
	R port	=	Divisor
	F port	=	Intermediate result
UDIVIT	S port	=	Result of last UDIVI
	R port	=	Divisor
	F port	=	Remainder (unfixed)
DIVRF	S port	=	Result of UDIVIT
	R port	=	Divisor
	F port	=	Remainder

The status of all unsigned divide instructions except UDIVIS is as follows:

N → Forced to zero
OVR → Forced to zero
C_{n+8} → Carry out equal to one
Z → Intermediate result is zero

The status of the UDIVIS instruction is as follows:

N → Forced to zero
OVR → Divide overflow
C_{n+8} → Carry out equal to one
Z → Intermediate result is zero

If fractions are divided, the remainder must be shifted right two bits to obtain the correct fractional representation. The quotient is correct as is. The quotient is stored in the MQ register at the completion of the divide.

The unsigned division algorithm is summarized in Table 8.

TABLE 8. UNSIGNED DIVISION ALGORITHM

OP CODE	MNEMONIC	CLOCK CYCLES	INPUT S PORT	INPUT R PORT	OUTPUT F PORT
E4	LOADMQ	1	Dividend (LSH)	—	Dividend (LSH)
B0	UDIVIS	1	Dividend (MSH)	Divisor	Remainder (N)
C0	UDIVI	8N−1†	Remainder (N)	Divisor	Remainder (N)
F0	UDIVIT	1	Remainder (N)	Divisor	Remainder (Unfixed)
40	DIVRF	1	Remainder (Unfixed)	Divisor	Remainder

† N = Number of cascaded packages.

group 5 instructions

Hex code F of Group 1 instructions is used to access Group 5 instructions. Group 5 instructions are summarized in Table 9.

TABLE 9. GROUP 5 INSTRUCTIONS

INSTRUCTION BITS (I7-I0) OP CODE (HEX)	MNEMONIC	FUNCTION
0F	CLR	Clear
1F	CLR	Clear
2F	CLR	Clear
3F	CLR	Clear
4F	CLR	Clear
5F	CLR	Clear
6F	CLR	Clear
7F	BCDBIN	BCD to Binary
8F	EX3BC	Excess-3 Byte Correction
9F	EX3C	Excess-3 Word Correction
AF	SDIVO	Signed Divide Overflow Check
BF	CLR	Clear
CF	CLR	Clear
DF	BINEX3	Binary to Excess-3
EF	CLR	Clear
FF	NOP	No Operation

clear instructions (CLR)

There are 11 clear instructions listed in Table 9. The instructions force the ALU output to be zero and the BCD flip-flops to be cleared. The status set by the clear instruction is as follows:

N → None (force to zero)
OVR → None (force to zero)
C_{n+8} → None (force to zero)
Z → Active (one)

no operation instruction (NOP): I7-I0 = FF_{16}

This instruction is identical to the clear instructions except that the BCD flip-flops retain their old value.

excess-3 correction instructions (EX3BC, EX3C)

Two excess-3 correction instructions are available:

1. Excess-3 byte correction (EX3BC): I7-I0 = $8F_{16}$
2. Excess-3 word correction (EX3C): I7-I0 = $9F_{16}$

One instruction supports the byte mode and the other supports the word mode. These instructions correct the excess-3 additions (subtractions) in either the byte or word mode. For correct excess-3 arithmetic, this instruction must follow each add/subtract. The operand must be on the S port.

NOTE: The previous arithmetic overflow should be ignored.

The status of the EX3C instruction is as follows:

N → MSB of result
OVR → Signed overflow
C_{n+8} → Carry out equal one
Z → None (force to one)

The status of the EX3BC instruction is as follows:

N → None (force to zero)
OVR → Byte signed overflow
C_{n+8} → Carry out equal one
Z → None (force to one)

radix conversions

Conversions between decimal and binary number representations are performed with the aid of two special instructions: BINEX3 and BCDBIN. (Figure 10)

BCD to binary instructions (BCDBIN): I7-I0 = $7F_{16}$

This instruction (Figure 11) allows the user to convert an N-digit BCD number to a 4N-bit binary number in 4(N-1) plus 8 clocks. This function sums the R bus, the S bus, and the C_n bit, performs an arithmetic left shift on the ALU result, and simultaneously circular shifts the MQ left. The status set by the BCD to binary instruction is as follows:

N → MSB of result
OVR → Signed arithmetic overflow†
C_{n+8} → Carry out equal one
Z → Result equal zero

† Overflow may be the result of an ALU operation or the arithmetic left shift operation.

The following code illustrates the BCD to binary conversion technique.

Let ACC be an accumulator register
Let NUM be the register which contains the BCD number
Let MSK be a mask register

```
M1:     LOADMQ NUM                  ; LOAD MQ WITH BCD NUMBER
M2:     SUB ACC, ACC, SLCMQ         ; CLEAR ACC AND ALIGN MQ
M3:     SUB, MSK, MSK, SLCMQ        ; CLEAR MSK AND ALIGN MQ
M4:     SLCMQ                       ; ALIGN
M5:     SLCMQ                       ; ALIGN
M6:     ADDI ACC, MSK, 15₁₀         ; MSK = 15₁₀
                                    ; REPEAT L1 THRU L4
                                    ; N-1 TIMES (N = number of
                                    ; BCD digits)
L1:     AND MQ, MSK, R1, SLCMQ      ; EXTRACT ONE DIGIT
                                    ; ALIGN MQ
L2:     ADD, ACC, R1, R1, SLCMQ     ; ACC + DIGIT
                                    ; IS STORED IN R1
                                    ; ALIGN MQ
L3:     BCDBIN, R1, R1, ACC         ; 4 × (ACC + DIGIT)
                                    ; IS STORED IN ACC
                                    ; ALIGN MQ
L4:     BCDBIN, ACC, R1, ACC        ; 10 × (ACC + DIGIT)
                                    ; IS STORED IN ACC
                                    ; ALIGN MQ
M7:     AND MQ, MSK, R1             ; FETCH LAST DIGIT
M8:     ACC+R1 → ACC                ; ADD IN LAST DIGIT
```

The previous code generates a binary number by executing the standard conversion formula for a BCD number (shown for 32 bits).

$$ABCD = [(A \times 10 + B) \times 10 + C] \times 10 + D$$

Notice that the conversion begins with the most significant BCD digit and that the addition is performed in radix 2.

binary to excess-3 instructions (BINEX3): I7-I0 = DF_{16}

This instruction (Figure 12) allows the user to convert an N-bit binary number to an N/4-bit excess-3 number representation in 2N + 3 clocks. The data on the R and S ports are summed with the MSB of the MQ register. The MQ register is simultaneously shifted left circularly. The status set by the binary to excess-3 instruction is as follows:

N	→	MSB of result
OVR	→	Signed arithmetic overflow
C_{n+8}	→	Carry out equal one
Z	→	Result equal zero

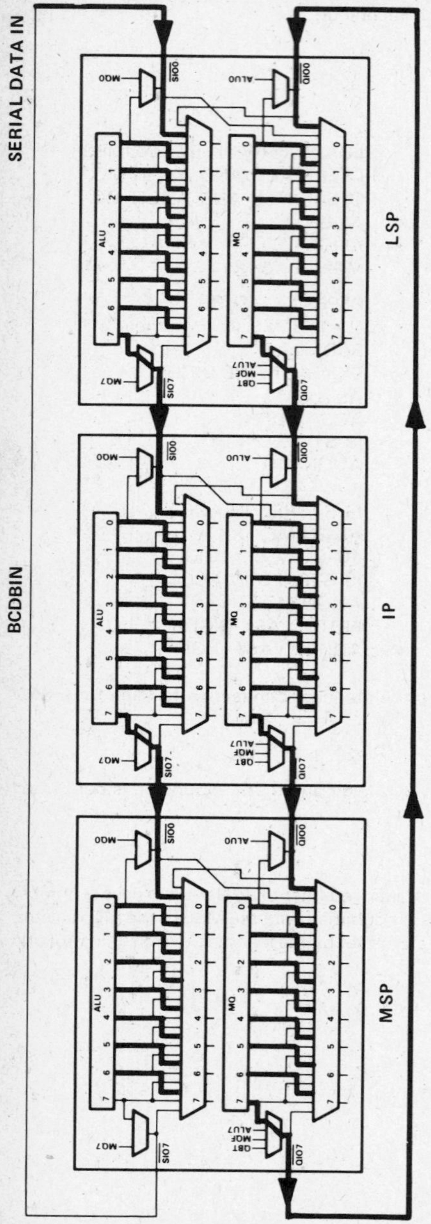
SERIAL DATA IN
BCDBIN
LSP
IP
MSP
ALU
MQ
SIO0
QIO0
MQ0
ALU0
MQ7
QBT
MQF
ALU7
SIO7
QIO7

FIGURE 10. BCD TO BINARY

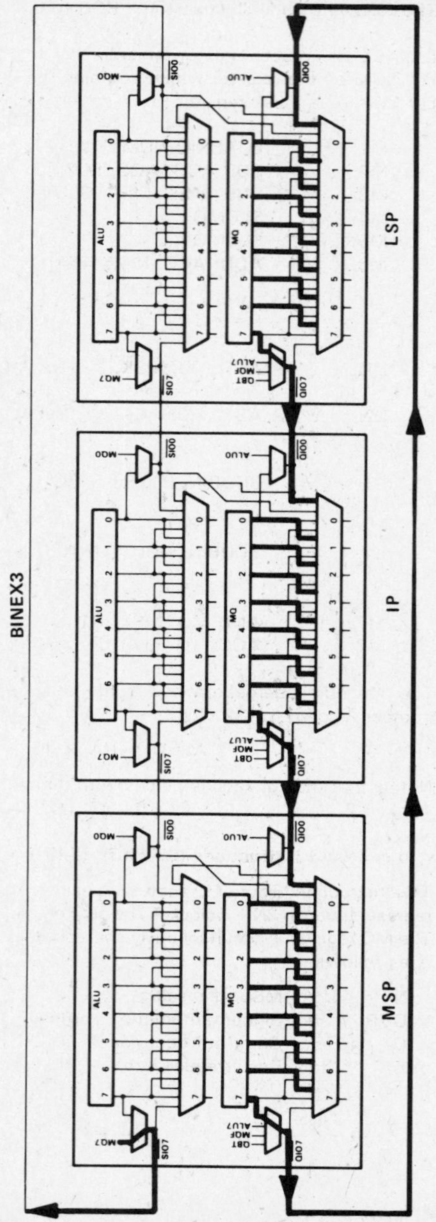
BINEX3
LSP
IP
MSP
ALU
MQ
SIO0
QIO0
MQ0
ALU0
MQ7
QBT
MQF
ALU7
SIO7
QIO7

FIGURE 11. BINARY TO EXCESS-3

The following illustrates the binary to excess-3 conversion technique.

Let NUM be a register containing an unsigned binary number
Let ACC be an accumulator

```
M1:    LOADMQ NUM               ; LOAD MQ WITH BINARY
                                ; NUMBER
M2:    CLEAR ACC                ; CLEAR ACC
M3:    SET1 ACC H/33/           ; ACC → HEX/3333 . . .
L1:    BINEX3 ACC, ACC, ACC     ; DOUBLE ACC AND ADD IN
                                ; MSB OF MQ
                                ; ALIGN MQ
L2:    EX3C ACC, ACC            ; EXCESS 3 CORRECT
                                ; REPEAT L1 AND L2
                                ; N-1 TIMES
```

The previous code generates an excess-3 number by executing the standard conversion formula for a binary number.

$$a_n 2^n + a_{n-1} 2^{n-1} + a_{n-2} 2^{n-2} + \ldots a_0 2^0 = [(2a_n + a_{n-1})2 + a_{n-2}]2 + \ldots a_0$$

Notice that the conversion begins with the most significant binary bit and that the addition is performed in radix-10 (excess-3).

decimal arithmetic

Decimal numbers are represented in excess-3 code. Excess-3 code numbers may be generated by adding three to each digit of a Binary Coded Decimal (BCD) number. The hardware necessary to implement excess-3 arithmetic is only slightly different from binary arithmetic. Carries from one digit to another during addition in BCD occur when the sum of the two digits plus the carry-in is greater than or equal to ten. If both numbers are excess-3, the sum will be excess-6, which will produce the proper carries. Therefore, every addition or subtraction operation may use the binary adder. To convert the result from excess-6 to excess-3, one must consider two cases resulting from a BCD digit add: (1) where a carry-out is produced, and (2) where a carry-out is not produced. If a carry-out is not produced, three must be subtracted from the resulting digit. If a carry is produced, the digit is correct as a BCD number. For example, if BCD 5 is added to BCD 6, the excess-3 result would be 8 + 9 = 1 (with a carry). A carry rolls the number through the illegal BCD representations into a correct BCD representation. Binary 3 must be added to digit positions that produce a carry-out to correct the result to an excess-3 representation. Every addition and subtraction instruction stores the carry generated from each 4-bit digit location for use by the excess-3 correction functions. These correction instructions (word or byte) must be executed in the clock cycle immediately after the addition or subtraction operation.

Signed numbers may be represented in ten's complement form by complementing the excess-3 number. As an example, add the decimal number −423 to the decimal number 24, which will be represented by 8AA and 357 in excess-3, respectively.

8AA	
357	
C01	Sum
011	Carry
934	Excess-3 correct
−6CC	Complement
−399	Excess-3 to decimal

Complements of excess-3 numbers may be generated by subtracting the excess-3 number from an excess-3 zero followed by an excess-3 correct.

2 LSI Devices

excess-3 to USASCII conversion

Input/output devices or files represent numbers differently than high-speed central processing units. I/O devices handle all alphanumeric data similarly. CPUs handle more numeric data than alphabetic data and store numeric data in packed form to minimize calculation throughout and reduce memory requirements. To represent the cost of a shirt that was $10.96, the I/O device would handle the six USASCII characters ''$'', ''1'',''0'',''.'',''9'',''6'', which would require 6 bytes of storage. In packed BCD, this number could be stored as 1096 in two bytes of data. The 'AS895 may be programmed to perform data format conversions such as converting excess-3 BCD to USASCII.

The code below converts a packed word of excess-3 BCD to two unpacked words of USASCII code. Instruction ''MAIN1'' reads the input word from memory into Register 0 (R0). For illustrative purposes, suppose this data was 43C9, which represents the $10.96 shirt in excess-3 code. ''MAIN2'' and ''MAIN3'' generate a constant of $2D2D_{16}$, which is an offset constant to convert excess-3 numbers to USASCII. ''MAIN4'' copies R0 into R2 to set up the subroutine parameters and calls the subroutine ''UNPACK'', UNPACK2'' strips off the upper byte leaving OOC9 in R2. ''UNPACK2'' and ''UNPACK3'' together shift the contents of R2 one character position and places the result 0C90 into R3. ''UNPACK4'' performs a logical OR operation to produce OCD9 in register 2. ''UNPACK5'' clears the most significant nibble in each byte to produce 0C09 in R2. ''UNPACK6'' adds the constant $2D2D_{16}$ to R2 to produce 3936 the USASCII representation of the numerals 96 and returns program control to ''MAIN5''. ''MAIN5'' through ''MAIN9'' align the two remaining characters and call UNPACK and the process repeats. Finally the USASCII representation of 1096 is stored into memory. (Note that no attempt was made to pack the ''$'' or ''.'' characters.)

Unpacking Excess-3 to USASCII:

```
MAIN1:     READ, RFA(0)                                ; READ IN PACKED EXCESS-3
MAIN2:     XOR, RFA(4), RFB(4), RFC(4)                 ; CLEAR R4
MAIN3:     SET1, RFB(40), RDC(2), RFA(D),              ; GENERATE HEXADECIMAL
           MSH, LSH                                    ; 2D2D16
MAIN4:     MOVE, RFA(0), RFC(2), JSR(UNPACK)           ; COPY RFA(0) INTO RFA(2),
                                                       ; PROCEDURE CALL
MAIN5:     MOVE, RFA(2), RFC(1)                        ; TWO CHARACTERS IN R1
MAIN6:     ADDRS, RFB(0), RFA(0), RFC(0), SLC          ; R0 SHIFTED 2
MAIN7:     ADDRS, RFB(0), RFA(0), RFC(0), SLC          ; R0 SHIFTED 4
MAIN8:     ADDRS, RFB(0), RFA(0), RFC(0), SLC          ; R0 SHIFTED 6
MAIN9:     ADDRS, RFB(0), RFA(0), RFC(0), SLC          ; R0 SHIFTED 8
           JSR (UNPACK)
MAIN10:    STORE, RFA(1)                               ; STORE USASCII, TWO
                                                       ; CHARACTERS IN R2
MAIN11:    STORE, RFA(2)                               ; STORE USASCII
UNPACK1:   SET0, RFB(2), RFC(F), MSH                   ; CLEAR MSH
UNPACK2:   ADDRS, RFB(2), RFA(2), RFC(3), SLC          ; SHIFT R2 TWO PLACES
UNPACK3:   ADDRS, RFB(3), RFA(3), RFC(3), SLC          ; SHIFT R3 TWO PLACES
UNPACK4:   OR, RFB(2), RFA(3), RFC(2)                  ; OR R3 TO R2
UNPACK5:   SET0, RFB(2), RFC(F), RFA(0), LSH, MSH      ; CLEAR MOST SIGNIFICANT 4
                                                       ; BITS IN EACH BYTE
UNPACK6:   ADDRS, RFB(2), RFB(4), RFC(2), RTS          ; ADD HEX 2D, RETURN
```


TEXAS INSTRUMENTS
POST OFFICE BOX 225012 • DALLAS, TEXAS 75265

absolute maximum rating over operating free-air temperature range (unless otherwise noted)

Supply voltage, V_{CC1} . . . . 7 V
Supply voltage, V_{CC2} . . . . 3 V
Input voltage . . . . 7 V
High-level voltage applied to 3-state outputs . . . . 5.5 V
Operating case temperature range: SN54AS895 . . . . −55°C to 125°C
Operating free-air temperature range: SN74AS895, SN74AS895-1 . . . . 0°C to 70°C
Storage temperature range . . . . −65°C to 150°C

recommended operating conditions

			SN54AS895			SN74AS895 SN74AS895-1			UNIT
			MIN	NOM	MAX	MIN	NOM	MAX	
V_{CC1}	I/O supply voltage		4.5	5	5.5	4.5	5	5.5	V
V_{CC2}	STL internal logic supply voltage		1.9	2	2.1	1.9	2	2.1	V
V_{IH}	High-level input voltage		2			2			V
V_{IL}	Low-level input voltage				0.8			0.8	V
I_{OH}	High-level output current				−1			−2.6	mA
I_{OL}	Low-level output current	All output except $\overline{G}$ and ZERO			8			8	mA
		$\overline{G}$			16			16	
		ZERO			48			48	
T_C	Operating case temperature		−55		125				°C
T_A	Operating free-air temperature					0		70	

electrical characteristics over recommended operating free-air temperature range (unless otherwise noted)

PARAMETER		TEST CONDITIONS	SN54AS895			SN74AS895 SN74AS895-1			UNIT
			MIN	TYP†	MAX	MIN	TYP†	MAX	
V_{IK}		V_{CC1} = 4.5 V, I_I = −18 mA			−1.2			−1.2	V
V_{OH}	All outputs except ZERO	V_{CC1} = 4.5 V to 5.5 V, I_{OH} = −0.4 mA	V_{CC}−2			V_{CC}−2			V
		V_{CC1} = 4.5 V, I_{OH} = −1 mA	2.4						
		V_{CC1} = 4.5 V, I_{OH} = −2.6 mA				2.4			
I_{OH}	ZERO	V_{CC1} = 4.5 V, V_{OH} = 5.5 V			0.1			0.1	mA
V_{OL}	All outputs except $\overline{G}$ and ZERO	V_{CC1} = 4.5 V, I_{OL} = 8 mA			0.5			0.5	V
	$\overline{G}$	V_{CC1} = 4.5 V, I_{OL} = 16 mA			0.5			0.5	
	ZERO	V_{CC1} = 4.5 V, I_{OL} = 48 mA			0.5			0.5	
I_I	I/O	V_{CC1} = 5.5 V, V_I = 5.5 V			0.1			0.1	mA
	All others	V_{CC1} = 5.5 V, V_I = 7 V			0.1			0.1	
I_{IH}‡		V_{CC1} = 5.5 V, V_I = 2.7 V			20			20	μA
I_{IL}‡		V_{CC1} = 5.5 V, V_I = 0.5 V			−0.4			−0.4	mA
I_O§		V_{CC1} = 5.5 V, V_O = 2.25 V	−30		−112	−30		−112	mA
I_{CC1}		V_{CC1} = 5.5 V			150			130	mA
I_{CC2}		V_{CC2} = 2.1 V			410			390	mA

†All typical values are at V_{CC} = 5 V, T_A = 25°C.
‡For I/O ports, the parameters I_{IH} and I_{IL} include the off-state current.
§The output conditions have been chosen to produce a current that closely approximates one-half the true short-circuit current, I_{OS}.

SN54AS895 maximum switching characteristics, V_{CC} = 4.5 V to 5.5 V, T_C = −55 °C to 125 °C (see Note 1)

PARAMETER	FROM (INPUT)	TO (OUTPUT) Y	C_{n+8}	$\overline{G}$, $\overline{P}$	Z†	N	OVR	DA	DB	$\overline{QIO}$	$\overline{SIO}$	UNIT
t_{pd}	A3-A0 B3-B0	62	42	48	69	62	60	18	—	65	66	ns
	DA7-DA0, DB7-DB0	47	28	28	58	50	42	—	—	50	50	
	C_n	25	14	—	32	24	18	—	—	32	32	
	$\overline{EA}$	54	32	35	62	52	52	—	—	58	58	
	$\overline{EB}$	54	32	35	62	52	52	—	—	58	58	
	I7-I0	58	32	32	62	52	41	—	—	58	58	
	$\overline{OEB}$	—	—	—	—	—	—	—	14	—	—	
	$\overline{OEY}$	14	—	—	—	—	—	—	—	—	—	
	$\overline{QIO}$ (n) Shift	15	—	—	24	—	—	—	—	—	—	
	$\overline{SIO}$ (n) Shift	15	—	—	24	22	—	—	—	—	—	
	CK	68	60	56	62	50	68	38	30	70	70	
	$\overline{OEA}$	—	—	—	—	—	—	14	—	—	—	
	SSF‡	—	—	—	—	—	14	—	—	—	—	

† Load resistor R1 = 100 Ω.
‡ For byte instructions only.
NOTE 1: Load circuit and voltage waveforms are shown in Section 1.

SN74AS895 maximum switching characteristics, V_{CC} = 4.5 V to 5.5 V, T_A = 0 °C to 70 °C (see Note 1)

PARAMETER	FROM (INPUT)	TO (OUTPUT) Y	C_{n+8}	$\overline{G}$, $\overline{P}$	Z†	N	OVR	DA	DB	$\overline{QIO}$	$\overline{SIO}$	UNIT
t_{pd}	A3-A0 B3-B0	54	36	42	60	52	50	—	—	58	58	ns
	DA7-DA0, DB7-DB0	44	26	26	52	46	38	—	—	44	44	
	C_n	25	9	—	32	24	18	—	—	31	31	
	$\overline{EA}$	49	29	29	58	49	47	—	—	54	54	
	$\overline{EB}$	49	29	29	58	49	47	—	—	54	54	
	I7-I0	55	30	30	60	49	39	—	—	54	54	
	$\overline{OEB}$	—	—	—	—	—	—	—	12	—	—	
	$\overline{OEY}$	12	—	—	—	—	—	—	—	—	—	
	$\overline{QIO}$ (n) Shift	15	—	—	24	—	—	—	—	—	—	
	$\overline{SIO}$ (n) Shift	15	—	—	24	19	—	—	—	—	—	
	CK	58	55	52	61	52	62	35	25	60	60	
	$\overline{OEA}$	—	—	—	—	—	—	12	—	—	—	
	SSF‡	—	—	—	—	—	12	—	—	—	—	

† Load resistor R1 = 100 Ω.
‡ For byte instructions only.
NOTE 1: Load circuit and voltage waveforms are shown in Section 1.

SN74AS895-1 maximum switching characteristics, V_{CC} = 4.5 V to 5.5 V, T_A = 0°C to 70°C (see Note 1)

PARAMETER	FROM (INPUT)	TO (OUTPUT)										UNIT
		Y	C_{n+8}	$\overline{G}$, $\overline{P}$	Z†	N	OVR	DA	DB	$\overline{QIO}$	$\overline{SIO}$	
t_{pd}	A3-A0 B3-B0	44	30	36	50	44	44	17	–	48	48	ns
	DA7-DA0, DB7-DB0	36	24	24	46	41	32	–	–	40	40	
	C_n	22	8	–	27	21	16	–	–	25	25	
	$\overline{EA}$	40	25	25	49	41	41	–	–	44	44	
	$\overline{EB}$	40	25	25	49	41	41	–	–	44	44	
	I7-I0	46	27	27	50	42	35	–	–	45	45	
	$\overline{OEB}$	–	–	–	–	–	–	–	12	–	–	
	$\overline{OEY}$	12	–	–	–	–	–	–	–	–	–	
	$\overline{QIO}$ (n) Shift	14	–	–	20	–	–	–	–	–	–	
	$\overline{SIO}$ (n) Shift	14	–	–	20	18	–	–	–	–	–	
	CK	50	46	46	50	50	50	30	22	50	50	
	$\overline{OEA}$	–	–	–	–	–	–	12	–	–	–	
	SSF‡	–	–	–	–	–	12	–	–	–	–	

† Load resistor R1 = 100 Ω.
‡ For byte instructions only.
NOTE 1: Load circuit and voltage waveforms are shown in Section 1.

register file write setup and hold times

PARAMETER		SN54AS895		SN74AS895		SN74AS895-1		UNIT
		MIN	MAX	MIN	MAX	MIN	MAX	
t_{su}	C3-C0	8		7		6		ns
	DB§	14		12		11		
	I7-I4	16		14		13		
	I3-I0	24		22		21		
	$\overline{OEY}$	4		3		3		
	Y7-Y0	2		2		2		
	$\overline{WE}$	8		6		6		
	$\overline{QIO}$(n), $\overline{SIO}$(n)	6		5		5		
	SELY	8		6		6		
t_h	C3-C0	0		0		0		ns
	DB§	0		0		0		
	I7-I4	0		0		0		
	I3-I0	0		0		0		
	$\overline{OEY}$	6		5		5		
	Y7-Y0	10		10		10		
	$\overline{WE}$	3		2		2		
	$\overline{QIO}$(n), $\overline{SIO}$(n)	0		0		0		
	SELY	8		6		6		

§DB (during select instruction) through Y port.

2
LSI Devices

special instruction switching characteristics

During various special instructions, the SSF pin is used to pass required information between the 'AS888 packages which make up a total system.

For instance, during the multiplication process, the LSB of the multiplier determines whether an ADD/SHIFT or SHIFT operation is performed. During multiplication, the SSF pin of the least significant package (LSP) becomes an output pin while all other packages become input pins.

Similarly, during normalization, the required operation depends on whether the two data MSBs are the same or different. Therefore, during normalization the SSF pin of the most significant package (MSP) becomes an output pin while all other packages become input pins.

Tables 10, 11, and 12 list the instructions which force the SSF pin during their execution. The propagation delay from various inputs is also shown. The parameter which limits normal system performance is indicated by a dagger.

TABLE 10. SN54AS895 SSF PIN DELAYS AND SETUP TIMES

MNEMONIC	HEX CODE	SSF SOURCE		INPUT → SSF (ns)				SSF SETUP TIME (ns)
		LSP	MSP	C_n	$I_{(n)}$	CK	$B_{(n)}$	
SNORM	20		X	—	29†	46	—	20
DNORM	30		X	—	29	55	40†	20
DIVRF	40		X	—	29†	46	—	20
SDIVQF	50		X	—	26†	—	—	18
SMULI	60	X		—	26†	43	—	0
SDIVIN	80		X	—	48	64	44†	0
SDIVIS	90		X	26†	51	64	55	0
SDIVI	A0		X	26†	51	64	55	0
UDIVIS	B0		X	18†	45	64	46	0
UDIVI	C0		X	18†	50	54	40	0
UMULI	D0	X		—	25†	48	—	0
SDIVIT	E0		X	26†	50	56	54	0
ABS	48		X	—	34	62	39†	20
SMTC	58		X	—	29	58	39†	20
BINEX3	DF		X	—	29†	58	—	18
LOADMQ (Arith)		X		23†	34	62	40	0
LOADMQ (Log)		X		—	33	62	40†	0
BADD	88	↑ SOURCE IS MOST SIGNIFICANT BYTE SELECTED ↓		18†	58	62	49	—
BSUBS	98			18†	58	62	49	—
BSUBR	A8			18†	58	71	49	—
BINCS	B8			18†	58	60	49	—
BINCNS	C8			18†	58	71	49	—
BXOR	D8			—	58	—	—	—
BAND	E8			—	58	—	—	—
BOR	F8			—	58	—	—	—
EX3BC	8F			—	58	46	49†	—

†This parameter limits normal system performance.

TABLE 11. SN74AS895 SSF PIN DELAYS AND SETUP TIMES

MNEMONIC	HEX CODE	SSF SOURCE		INPUT → SSF (ns)				SSF SETUP TIME (ns)
		LSP	MSP	C_n	$I_{(n)}$	CK	$B_{(n)}$	
SNORM	20		X	—	26†	40	—	17
DNORM	30		X	—	26	52	37†	17
DIVRF	40		X	—	26†	40	—	17
SDIVQF	50		X	—	25†	—	—	17
SMULI	60	X		—	25†	40	—	0
SDIVIN	80		X	—	38	60	40†	0
SDIVIS	90		X	24†	48	60	52	0
SDIVI	A0		X	24†	48	60	52	0
UDIVIS	B0		X	17†	43	60	45	0
UDIVI	C0		X	17†	44	52	37	0
UMULI	D0	X		—	26†	40	—	0
SDIVIT	E0		X	25†	46	52	49	0
ABS	48		X	—	32	60	38	17
SMTC	58		X	—	26	52	38†	17
BINEX3	DF		X	—	26†	40	—	17
LOADMQ (Arith)		X		22†	32	50	38	0
LOADMQ (Log)		X		—	32	50	38†	0
BADD	88	↑ SOURCE IS MOST SIGNIFICANT BYTE SELECTED ↓		17†	52	55	46	—
BSUBS	98			17†	52	55	46	—
BSUBR	A8			17†	52	62	46	—
BINCS	B8			17†	52	55	46	—
BINCNS	C8			17†	52	62	46	—
BXOR	D8			—	52	—	—	—
BAND	E8			—	52	—	—	—
BOR	F8			—	52	—	—	—
EX3BC	8F			—	45	45	46†	—

†This parameter limits normal system performance.

TABLE 12. SN74AS895-1 SSF PIN DELAYS AND SETUP TIMES

MNEMONIC	HEX CODE	SSF SOURCE		INPUT → SSF (ns)				SSF SETUP TIME (ns)
		LSP	MSP	C_n	$I_{(n)}$	CK	$B_{(n)}$	
SNORM	20		X	–	23†	28	–	14
DNORM	30		X	–	23	40	34†	14
DIVRF	40		X	–	23†	27	–	14
SDIVQF	50		X	–	23†	–	–	14
SMULI	60	X		–	22†	27	–	0
SDIVIN	80		X	–	35	46	35†	0
SDIVIS	90		X	22†	42	48	42	0
SDIVI	A0		X	22†	42	46	42	0
UDIVIS	B0		X	16†	42	46	38	0
UDIVI	C0		X	16†	36	46	34	0
UMULI	D0	X		–	22†	27	–	0
SDIVIT	E0		X	21†	40	44	42	0
ABS	48		X	–	28	46	30†	14
SMTC	58		X	–	24	44	30†	14
BINEX3	DF		X	–	23†	27	–	14
LOADMQ (Arith)		X		19†	28	40	30	0
LOADMQ (Log)		X		–	28	35	30†	0
BADD	88	↑ SOURCE IS MOST SIGNIFICANT BYTE SELECTED ↓		16†	42	42	40	–
BSUBS	98			16†	42	40	40	–
BSUBR	A8			16†	42	50	40	–
BINCS	B8			16†	42	46	40	–
BINCNS	C8			16†	42	54	42	–
BXOR	D8			–	42	–	–	–
BAND	E8			–	42	–	–	–
BOR	F8			–	42	–	–	–
EX3BC	8F			–	42	42	42†	–

†This parameter limits normal system performance.

2

LSI Devices

D2885, OCTOBER 1985—REVISED MARCH 1986

- High-Speed "Flash" Shift Operations
- Expandable to 32 Bits
- Hexadecimal and Binary Normalization with Leading Zero Detection
- Bit Reversal
- Merge Capabilities
- Texas Instruments Quality and Reliability

description

The SN54AS897A and SN74AS897A are multipurpose 16-bit barrel shifters in a 68-pin ceramic pin-grid-array package. The devices are capable of several different types of shift operations, as well as other more specialized functions such as hexadecimal and binary normalization, bit replacement, and leading-zero detection.

The unique feature of all barrel shifters is how the shift function is implemented. In conventional shift registers, shift operations are controlled by the number of input clock pulses applied. With barrel shifters, the desired number of positions to be shifted is determined by an input decoder. This form of implementation does not require an input clock and results in a shift operation that is restricted only by internal propagation delays. This delay is the same regardless of the number of positions to be shifted. The result is a high-speed "flash" type of shift.

The 'AS897A offers the system designer a much broader range of capabilities than previous conventional shift registers. Normalization of data in floating-point computations, bit-reversal when generating Fast Fourier Transform (FFT) addresses, and insertion of stop/start bits in asynchronous data communications are just a few of the applications that are possible with this device.

The 'AS897A can be operated as an 'AS897 by connecting the HEX/$\overline{\text{BIN}}$ pin (J1) to ground.

SN54AS897A, SN74AS897A
GB PIN-GRID ARRAY PACKAGE
(TOP VIEW)

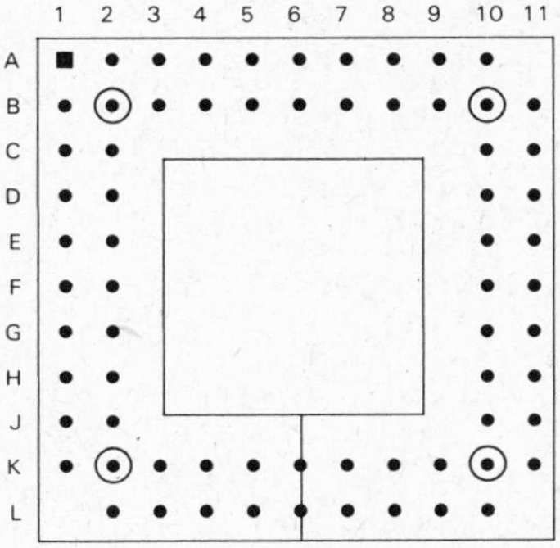
1 2 3 4 5 6 7 8 9 10 11
A
B
C
D
E
F
G
H
J
K
L

PIN ASSIGNMENT TABLE

PIN NO.	PIN NAME	PIN NO.	PIN NAME
A2	ZN1	F10	GND
A3	ZN2	F11	Y9
A4	ZN3	G1	D4
A5	GND	G2	GND
A6	$\overline{\text{NORM}}$	G10	Y11
A7	ZL	G11	Y8
A8	GND	H1	NC
A9	16B/$\overline{\text{32B}}$	H2	D5
A10	OP	H10	GND
B1	D14	H11	Y7
B2	D13	J1	HEX/$\overline{\text{BIN}}$
B3	D15	J2	D3
B4	ZN0	J10	GND
B5	V_{CC2}	J11	GND
B6	ZN4	K1	D2
B7	IP	K2	D1
B8	V_{CC1}	K3	V_{CC1}
B9	GND	K4	M1
B10	S	K5	GND
B11	Y15	K6	CLK
C1	D12	K7	GND
C2	D9	K8	V_{CC2}
C10	Y13	K9	Y6
C11	Y12	K10	Y4
D1	D11	K11	Y5
D2	D8	L2	D0
D10	NC	L3	M2
D11	GND	L4	M0
E1	D10	L5	TP
E2	D7	L6	$\overline{\text{OEY}}$
E10	Y14	L7	Y0
E11	Y10	L8	Y1
F1	GND	L9	Y2
F2	D6	L10	Y3

NC—No internal connection

Chip Carrier information available from factory upon request.

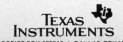

logic symbol†

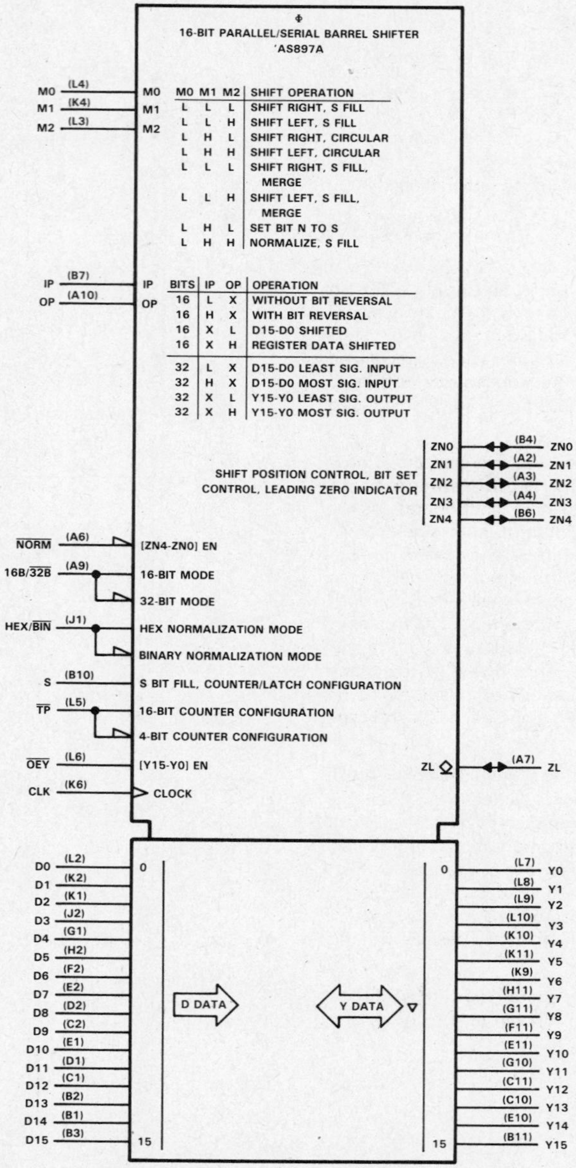
Φ
16-BIT PARALLEL/SERIAL BARREL SHIFTER
'AS897A
M0 (L4) M0
M1 (K4) M1
M2 (L3) M2
M0 M1 M2 SHIFT OPERATION
L L L SHIFT RIGHT, S FILL
L L H SHIFT LEFT, S FILL
L H L SHIFT RIGHT, CIRCULAR
L H H SHIFT LEFT, CIRCULAR
L L L SHIFT RIGHT, S FILL, MERGE
L L H SHIFT LEFT, S FILL, MERGE
L H L SET BIT N TO S
L H H NORMALIZE, S FILL
IP (B7) IP
OP (A10) OP
BITS IP OP OPERATION
16 L X WITHOUT BIT REVERSAL
16 H X WITH BIT REVERSAL
16 X L D15-D0 SHIFTED
16 X H REGISTER DATA SHIFTED
32 L X D15-D0 LEAST SIG. INPUT
32 H X D15-D0 MOST SIG. INPUT
32 X L Y15-Y0 LEAST SIG. OUTPUT
32 X H Y15-Y0 MOST SIG. OUTPUT
SHIFT POSITION CONTROL, BIT SET CONTROL, LEADING ZERO INDICATOR
ZN0 (B4) ZN0
ZN1 (A2) ZN1
ZN2 (A3) ZN2
ZN3 (A4) ZN3
ZN4 (B6) ZN4
NORM (A6) [ZN4-ZN0] EN
16B/32B (A9) 16-BIT MODE
32-BIT MODE
HEX/BIN (J1) HEX NORMALIZATION MODE
BINARY NORMALIZATION MODE
S (B10) S BIT FILL, COUNTER/LATCH CONFIGURATION
TP (L5) 16-BIT COUNTER CONFIGURATION
4-BIT COUNTER CONFIGURATION
OEY (L6) [Y15-Y0] EN
ZL (A7) ZL
CLK (K6) CLOCK
D0 (L2)
D1 (K2)
D2 (K1)
D3 (J2)
D4 (G1)
D5 (H2)
D6 (F2)
D7 (E2)
D8 (D2)
D9 (C2)
D10 (E1)
D11 (D1)
D12 (C1)
D13 (B2)
D14 (B1)
D15 (B3)
0
15
D DATA
Y DATA
0
15
(L7) Y0
(L8) Y1
(L9) Y2
(L10) Y3
(K10) Y4
(K11) Y5
(K9) Y6
(H11) Y7
(G11) Y8
(F11) Y9
(E11) Y10
(G10) Y11
(C11) Y12
(C10) Y13
(E10) Y14
(B11) Y15

† This symbol is in accordance with ANSI/IEEE Std 91-1984.

functional block diagram (positive logic)

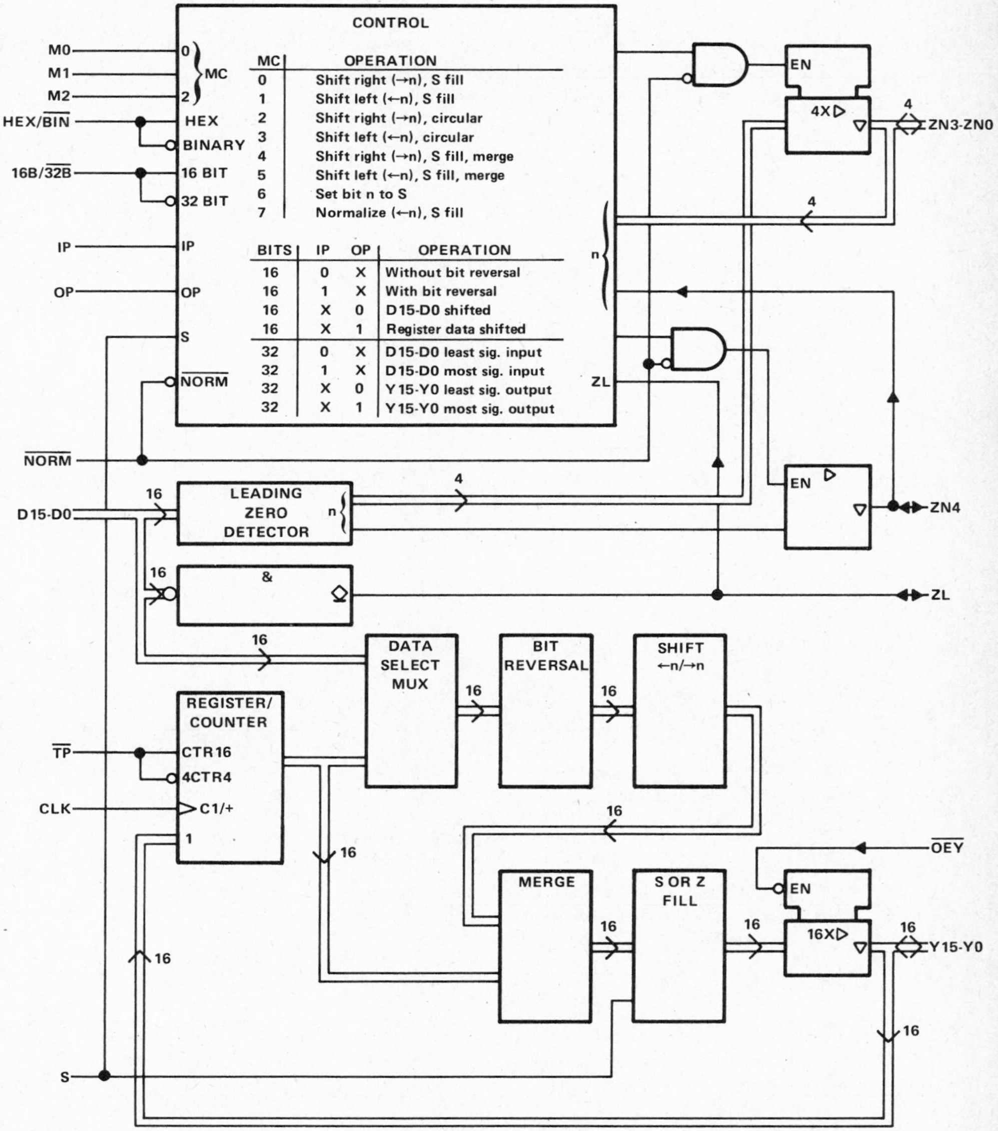
CONTROL
M0
M1
M2
MC
HEX/BIN
HEX
BINARY
16B/32B
16 BIT
32 BIT
IP
OP
S
NORM
MC | OPERATION
0 Shift right (→n), S fill
1 Shift left (←n), S fill
2 Shift right (→n), circular
3 Shift left (←n), circular
4 Shift right (→n), S fill, merge
5 Shift left (←n), S fill, merge
6 Set bit n to S
7 Normalize (←n), S fill
BITS | IP | OP | OPERATION
16 0 X Without bit reversal
16 1 X With bit reversal
16 X 0 D15-D0 shifted
16 X 1 Register data shifted
32 0 X D15-D0 least sig. input
32 1 X D15-D0 most sig. input
32 X 0 Y15-Y0 least sig. output
32 X 1 Y15-Y0 most sig. output
n
ZL
EN
4X
ZN3-ZN0
ZN4
D15-D0
LEADING ZERO DETECTOR
&
DATA SELECT MUX
BIT REVERSAL
SHIFT ←n/→n
REGISTER/ COUNTER
TP
CTR16
4CTR4
CLK
C1/+
MERGE
S OR Z FILL
OEY
16X
Y15-Y0
S

TEXAS INSTRUMENTS
POST OFFICE BOX 225012 • DALLAS, TEXAS 75265

PIN NAME	PIN NO.	I/O	DESCRIPTION
16B/$\overline{32B}$	A9	I	When high, 16-bit operation is selected. When low, 32-bit operation is selected.
CLK	K6	I	Clock input. Loads the internal register on the low-to-high transition. In 16-bit circular mode, acts as clock for the 16-bit/14-bit counter.
D0	L2	I	Input data bits 0 through 15
D1	K2	I	
D2	K1	I	
D3	J2	I	
D4	G1	I	
D5	H2	I	
D6	F2	I	
D7	E2	I	
D8	D2	I	
D9	C2	I	
D10	E1	I	
D11	D1	I	
D12	C1	I	
D13	B2	I	
D14	B1	I	
D15	B3	I	
GND	A5		Ground (All ground pins should be used)
GND	A8		
GND	B9		
GND	D11		
GND	F1		
GND	F10		
GND	G2		
GND	H10		
GND	J10		
GND	J11		
GND	K5		
GND	K7		
HEX/$\overline{BIN}$	J1	I	Controls mode of operation for leading zero detector. When low, causes the number of leading binary zeros to be counted. When high, causes the number of binary zeros in leading hexadecimal groups (binary 0000s) to be counted. When tied to ground, causes the 'AS897A to operate as an 'AS897.
IP	B7	I	In the 16-bit mode, controls the bit-reversal option. A high logic level causes data selected by OP to be bit-reversed before it is passed to the shifter. When IP is low, data is passed unaltered. In the 32-bit mode, defines the data input position. When IP is high, D15-D0 are in the most significant input position. When IP is low, D15-D0 are in the least significant position.
M0	L4	I	Shift instruction control. Determine the type of shift operation to be performed. See Table 1 for further information.
M1	K4	I	
M2	L3	I	
NC	D10		No internal connection
NC	H1		
$\overline{NORM}$	A6	I	A three-state control input for ZN4-ZN0 I/O ports used only in normalize instructions. When $\overline{NORM}$ is low, the number of leading zeros detected in the data present on D15-D0 is output on ZN4-ZN0. When $\overline{NORM}$ is high, ZN4-ZN0 act only as inputs.

PIN NAME	PIN NO.	I/O	DESCRIPTION
$\overline{OEY}$	L6	I	Control input for the Y15-Y0 I/O ports. When $\overline{OEY}$ is low, the Y outputs are enabled.
OP	A10	I	In the 16-bit mode, controls the source of input data. A logic high on this input selects data from the register/counter. A low selects data on the D15-D0 inputs. In the 32-bit mode, defines the package output positions. When OP is high, Y15-Y0 are in the most significant output position. When OP is low, Y15-Y0 are in the least significant output position.
S	B10	I	Specifies the logic level that will fill the bit position or positions vacated during all shift operations except 16-bit circular. In the 16-bit circular mode, when S is high, the data latch operates as a 16-bit binary counter. When S is low, the register functions as a data latch.
$\overline{TP}$	L5	I	Functional testing input. When low, transforms the 16-bit counter into four 4-bit counters. During normal operation, $\overline{TP}$ must be maintained at a high logic level.
V_{CC1} V_{CC1}	B8 K3		5-volt supply for TTL-compatible I/O
V_{CC2} V_{CC2}	B5 K8		2-volt supply for internal Schottky Transistor Logic (STL)
Y0 Y1 Y2 Y3 Y4 Y5 Y6 Y7 Y8 Y9 Y10 Y11 Y12 Y13 Y14 Y15	L7 L8 L9 L10 K10 K11 K9 H11 G11 F11 E11 G10 C11 C10 E10 B11	I/O I/O I/O I/O I/O I/O I/O I/O I/O I/O I/O I/O I/O I/O I/O I/O	Input/output bits 0-15. As an input, they load the data register. A an output, they present the shifted data.
ZL	A7	I/O	An input/open-collector output used primarily in 32-bit applications. When the input at D15-D0 is zero, the ZL output is high. The ZL outputs of cascaded packages are connected in a wired-AND configuration to detect if all inputs are zero. A recommended pull-up resistor of 200 to 680 Ω must be provided externally for proper operation in the 32-bit mode.
ZN0 ZN1 ZN2 ZN3	B4 A2 A3 A4	I/O I/O I/O I/O	A four-bit code that performs the following functions in the 16-bit mode: 1. As an input in shift instructions, specifies how many bit positions are to be shifted. 2. As an input in replace instructions, specifies position of the bit to be replaced. 3. As an input to the normalize instruction, specifies the number of left shifts to be performed. 4. As an output from the normalize instruction, when $\overline{NORM}$ = L, specifies the number of leading zeros in the data on D15-D0.
ZN4	B6	I/O	ZN4 is concatenated with ZN3-ZN0 for use in 32-bit shift operations as described above. In 16-bit normalization operations, ZN4 indicates when the input to the shifter is zero. In 16-bit left and right shifts and in shift and merge operations, a high on ZN4 causes all 16-bits to be filled with the logic level on the S input.

LSI Devices

description (continued)

control block

The control block decodes the M2-M0 instruction inputs, 16B/$\overline{32B}$ configuration select, IP and OP data select/bit reversal options, and other control inputs and transmits the resulting control signals to the rest of the internal logic.

instruction set

The 'AS897A can operate in any of the eight user-programmable shift modes shown in Table 1. Selection of these instructions is controlled by pins M2-M0.

TABLE 1. INSTRUCTION SET

M2	M1	M0	DESCRIPTION
L	L	L	Shift right the number of bit positions defined by ZN3-ZN0 (16-bit mode) or ZN4-ZN0 (32-bit mode). Fill vacated bit positions with logic level on S input. A high on ZN4 causes all bits in the 16-bit mode to be filled with the logic level on S.
L	L	H	Shift left the number of bit positions defined by ZN3-ZN0 (16-bit mode) or ZN4-ZN0 (32-bit mode). Fill vacated bit positions with logic level on S input. A high on ZN4 causes all bits in the 16-bit mode to be filled with the logic level on S.
L	H	L	Circular right shift the number or bit positions defined by ZN3-ZN0 (16-bit mode) or ZN4-ZN0 (32-bit mode).
L	H	H	Circular left shift the number of bit positions defined by ZN3-ZN0 (16-bit mode) or ZN4-ZN0 (32-bit mode).
H	L	L	Shift right the number of bit positions defined by ZN3-ZN0 (16-bit mode) or ZN4-ZN0 (32-bit mode). Fill vacated bit positions with logic level on S input. Merge result with data from the register/counter. A high on ZN4 causes all bits in the 16-bit mode to be filled with the logic level on S.
H	L	H	Shift left the number of bit positions defined by ZN3-ZN0 (16-bit mode) or ZN4-ZN0 (32-bit mode). Fill vacated bit positions with logic level on S input. Merge result with data from the register/counter. A high on ZN4 causes all bits in the 16-bit mode to be filled with the logic level on S.
H	H	L	Set the bit position defined by ZN3-ZN0 (16-bit mode) or ZN4-ZN0 (32-bit mode) to the logic level on the S input.
H	H	H	If $\overline{NORM}$ is low, shift data left the number of bit positions defined by the leading-zero detector. Fill vacated bit positions with logic level on S input. Output number of leading zeros in D15-D0 on ZN3-ZN0 (16-bit mode) or ZN4-ZN0 (32-bit mode). Note: If $\overline{NORM}$ is high, this instruction performs like the left shift described above for M2 = L, M1 = L, M0 = H.

mode configuration

The 'AS897A can be configured to operate on 16-bit or 32-bit words. Configuration is controlled by 16B/$\overline{32B}$. When 16B/$\overline{32B}$ is high, the 'AS897A operates in 16-bit mode.

Figure 1 illustrates the connection of four 'AS897As to provide a 32-bit barrel shifter that can perform all Table 1 shift instructions. For 32-bit mode operation, the 16B/$\overline{32B}$ inputs of all 'AS897A devices must be low and should be configured as shown in Figure 1.

TEXAS INSTRUMENTS
POST OFFICE BOX 225012 • DALLAS, TEXAS 75265

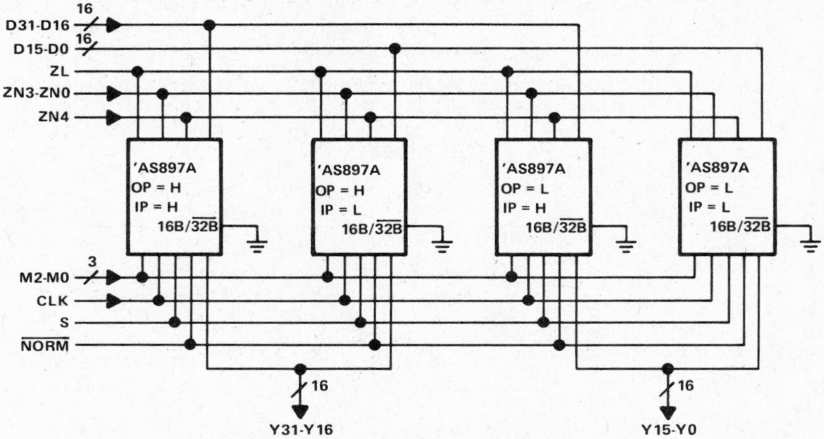
D31-D16
16
D15-D0
16
ZL
ZN3-ZN0
ZN4
'AS897A
OP = H
IP = H
16B/$\overline{32B}$
'AS897A
OP = H
IP = L
16B/$\overline{32B}$
'AS897A
OP = L
IP = H
16B/$\overline{32B}$
'AS897A
OP = L
IP = L
16B/$\overline{32B}$
M2-M0
3
CLK
S
$\overline{NORM}$
16
Y31-Y16
16
Y15-Y0

FIGURE 1. 32-BIT BARREL SHIFTER

data input/output

Data can be input to the chip from two ports: D15-D0, which passes data to the zero detector and to the shifter via the data select and bit-reversal multiplexers, and Y15-Y0, which passes data to the register/counter. Y15-Y0 is also used to output the shift result from the chip.

Data input and output positions in the 32-bit mode are defined by IP and OP (see Table 2). When IP is high, the D15-D0 port is the most significant input position; when IP is low, the D15-D0 input port is the least significant. If OP is high, the Y15-Y0 port is the most significant output position; if OP is low, the Y15-Y0 port is the least significant position.

TABLE 2. IP AND OP CONTROLS

SIGNAL	16-BIT OPERATION (16B/$\overline{32B}$ = H)	32-BIT OPERATION (16B/$\overline{32B}$ = L)
IP = L	Bit-reversal option off	D15-D0 is least significant input position
IP = H	Bit-reversal option on	D15-D0 is most significant input position
OP = L	D15-D0 is shifted	Y15-Y0 is least significant output position
OP = H	Register/counter data is shifted	Y15-Y0 is most significant output position

zero detector

The zero detector detects the number of leading zeros at the D15-D0 input port. If HEX/$\overline{BIN}$ is high, the zero detector counts only those binary zeros that are part of a leading hexadecimal zero group. For example, given the binary number 0000 0000 0001 0001, the leading-zero count will be decimal 11 if HEX/$\overline{BIN}$ is low and decimal 8 if HEX/$\overline{BIN}$ is high.

If all zeros are detected at the D port, the ZL output transistor will be turned off. If the ZL output pin is pulled up through the recommended pull-up resistor (see pin description table), the resulting signal will be high. If anything other than a zero is detected on the D15-D0 inputs, the output transistor will be turned on; this will pull the ZL signal low.

During data normalization (M2 = H, M1 = H, M0 = H), the zero-detector outputs the leading zero count to the ZN4-ZN0 I/O ports, provided $\overline{\text{NORM}}$ is low. When $\overline{\text{NORM}}$ is high, ZN4-ZN0 act only as inputs in this mode. For operations other than normalization, the state of $\overline{\text{NORM}}$ is irrelevant.

In the data-normalization mode, a high logic level will be output on the ZN4 pin when the D15-D0 bus contains all lows and $\overline{\text{NORM}}$ is low (see Table 3).

TABLE 3. ZN4 I/O PORT

SIGNAL	I/O	16-BIT CONFIGURATION (16B/$\overline{\text{32B}}$ = H)	32-BIT CONFIGURATION (16B/$\overline{\text{32B}}$ = L)
ZN4	I	In shift-left, shift-right, and shift-and-merge modes, a high fills all bits with the logic level on the S input. Inactive in other modes.	With ZN3-ZN0 indicates number of bits to be shifted in shift operations and position of bit to be replaced in replace-bit mode.
	O	In the normalization mode, when $\overline{\text{NORM}}$ = L, indicates when the input to the shifter is zero	In the normalization mode, when $\overline{\text{NORM}}$ = L, ZN4-ZN0 indicates number of leading zeros detected in D15-D0 and number of places to be shifted for normalization.

data selector multiplexer

The data selector multiplexer is used only in 16-bit operation (16B/$\overline{\text{32B}}$ = H). OP controls the mux and selects the data to be presented to the bit-reversal block. OP high selects the register/counter; OP low selects D15-D0 (see Table 2).

bit reversal

Bit reversal is also available only in the 16-bit mode (16B/$\overline{\text{32B}}$ = H) and is controlled by IP (see Table 2). When the bit-reversal option is selected (IP = H), data selected by OP is bit-reversed before it is passed to the shifter: the most significant bit becomes the least significant bit, the second most significant bit becomes the second least significant bit, and so forth. When the bit-reversal option is off (IP = L), the data presented to the shifter is not altered.

register/counter

During most instructions, the register/counter operates as a data latch. Data on the Y15-Y0 bus is latched into the register/counter on the rising edge of the clock. Data can be input to the register/counter from the shifter ($\overline{\text{OEY}}$ = L) or from the bidirectional Y port ($\overline{\text{OEY}}$ = H).

In the 16-bit circular-shift mode (16B/$\overline{\text{32B}}$ = H, M2 = L, M1 = H, M0 = X), the register counter will function as a 16-bit counter on the rising edge of the clock when S is high. Under these same conditions, the register/counter will function as four 4-bit counters when $\overline{\text{TP}}$ is low. In the 16-bit circular-shift mode, the register/counter functions as a register when S is low. The counter option is not available for other instructions in the 16-bit mode or for any instructions in the 32-bit mode.

shifter

The shifter performs the operations specified by the M2-M0 inputs (see Table 1). The number of bits to be shifted or the position of the bit to be replaced is specified by ZN3-ZN0 (16-bit operation) or ZN4-ZN0 (32-bit operation).

TEXAS INSTRUMENTS
POST OFFICE BOX 225012 • DALLAS, TEXAS 75265

merge

During the shift and merge instruction (M2 = H, M1 = L, M0 = X), the merge block ORs the shift result with data from the register/counter.

S or Z fill

During bit replacement (M2 = H, M1 = H, M0 = L) in the 16-bit mode, this block sets the bit specified on the ZN3-ZN0 inputs with the logic level on the S input. This option works identically in the 32-bit mode, except that the bit to be replaced is specified on the Z4-Z0 inputs. During all other instructions except circular shifts, the S input specifies the logic level that will fill the bit position or positions vacated during the shift.

Z fill is used in the 32-bit mode to selectively put the device outputs in a high-impedance state. This feature is necessary to properly select the correct bit locations that will combine to form the shifted output. An example of a 32-bit circular shift four positions to the right, which illustrates the Z-fill technique, is shown in Figure 2.

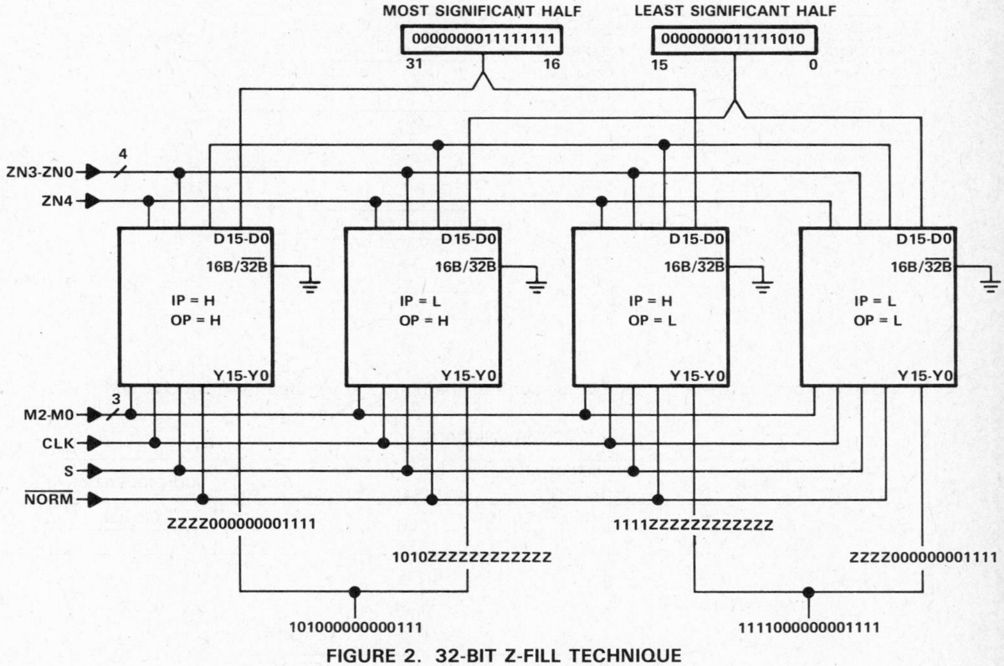
MOST SIGNIFICANT HALF
0000000011111111
31
16
LEAST SIGNIFICANT HALF
0000000011111010
15
0
ZN3-ZN0
4
ZN4
D15-D0
16B/32B
IP = H
OP = H
Y15-Y0
D15-D0
16B/32B
IP = L
OP = H
Y15-Y0
D15-D0
16B/32B
IP = H
OP = L
Y15-Y0
D15-D0
16B/32B
IP = L
OP = L
Y15-Y0
M2-M0
3
CLK
S
NORM
ZZZZ000000001111
1010ZZZZZZZZZZZZ
1111ZZZZZZZZZZZZ
ZZZZ000000001111
1010000000000111
1111000000001111

FIGURE 2. 32-BIT Z-FILL TECHNIQUE

SHIFT OPERATION EXAMPLES

Examples of 'AS897A shift instructions are provided in the following paragraphs. Unless otherwise specified, the examples assume a 16-bit configuration.

shift left or right (M2 = L, M1 = L, M0 = X)

When in the shift-right (M0 = L) or shift-left (M0 = H) modes, ZN3-ZN0 define the number of bit positions to be shifted. If, for example, ZN3-ZN0 is equal to a decimal 10, the data selected by OP will be shifted 10 bit positions. The positions vacated during the shift operation are filled with the logic level being applied to the S input. $\overline{\text{NORM}}$ is inactive in all shift modes except normalization and is therefore shown as a don't care. If IP is high, the data selected by OP will be bit-reversed before it is passed to the shifter.

Example

Shift a 16-bit word on the data bus ten positions to the left and fill the least significant bits with highs.

CONTROL SIGNALS

SHIFT INSTRUCTION	NORMALIZE	NUMBER OF BITS TO SHIFT	BIT REVERSAL	DATA SOURCE	BIT FILL	CONFIGURATION
M2-M0	$\overline{\text{NORM}}$	ZN4-ZN0	IP	OP	S	16B/$\overline{\text{32B}}$
001	X	01010	0	0	1	1

Assume D15-D0 contains hex AF50:

	D15-D0
Input Data	1010 1111 0101 0000
	Y15-Y0
Result	0100 0011 1111 1111

Example

Shift a 32-bit word on the data bus 20 positions to the right. Fill vacated bit positions with highs.

CONTROL SIGNALS

SHIFT INSTRUCTION	NORMALIZE	NUMBER OF BITS TO SHIFT	BIT REVERSAL	DATA SOURCE	BIT FILL	CONFIGURATION
M2-M0	$\overline{\text{NORM}}$	ZN4-ZN0	IP	OP	S	16B/$\overline{\text{32B}}$
000	X	10100	See Figure 1		1	1

Assume D15-D0 contains hex 75BB FCAE:

	D31-D16	D15-D0
Input Data	0111 0101 1011 1011	1111 1100 1010 1110
	Y31-Y16	Y15-Y0
Result	1111 1111 1111 1111	1111 0111 0101 1011

circular shift left or right (M2 = L, M1 = H, M0 = X)

In this mode, data selected by OP is circular shifted left (M0 = H) or right (M0 = L) the number of bit positions specified by ZN3-ZN0. If, for example, the device is in the circular-shift-right mode (M0 = L) and ZN3-ZN0 contains a decimal five, the data selected by OP will be shifted right five positions.

In all shift modes except 16-bit circular, the S input contains the bit used for end fill or bit replacement. In the 16-bit circular-shift mode, the S input controls whether the register/counter will operate as a 16-bit counter or as a data register. When S is high, the register/counter operates as a 16-bit binary counter; when S is low, the register/counter operates as a 16-bit data latch. Both functions are controlled on the positive edge of the CLK input. Data on Y15-Y0 will be latched into the register/counter on the rising edge of the clock when S is low.

Example

Circular shift a 16-bit word in the register/counter five positions to the right.

CONTROL SIGNALS

SHIFT INSTRUCTION	NORMALIZE	NUMBER OF BITS TO SHIFT	BIT REVERSAL	DATA SOURCE	LATCH OR COUNTER	CONFIGURATION
M2-M0	$\overline{NORM}$	ZN4-ZN0	IP	OP	S	16B/$\overline{32B}$
010	X	X0101	0	1	0	1

Assume the register/counter contains hex A016:

	Register/Counter
Input Data	1010 0000 0001 0110
	Y15-Y0
Result	1011 0101 0000 0000

shift and merge (M2 = H, M1 = L, M0 = X)

In the shift-and-merge mode, data selected by OP is shifted by OP is shifted left (M0 = H) or right (M0 = L) the number of positions specified by ZN3-ZN0, bit positions vacated by the shift are filled by the logic level on S, and the result is ORed with data in the register/counter.

Example

Shift data on the data bus six positions to the left, and fill vacated positions with zeros. Merge the shifted data with data from the data register.

CONTROL SIGNALS

SHIFT INSTRUCTION	NORMALIZE	NUMBER OF BITS TO SHIFT	BIT REVERSAL	DATA SOURCE	END FILL	CONFIGURATION
M2-M0	$\overline{NORM}$	ZN4-ZN0	IP	OP	S	16B/$\overline{32B}$
100	X	00110	0	0	0	1

2

LSI Devices

Assume D15-D0 contains hex 6174 and register/counter contains hex 320B:

	D15-D0
Input Data	0110 0001 0111 0100
	Shift Result
Intermediate Result	0101 1101 0000 0000
	Register/Counter
Input Data	0011 0010 0000 1011
	Y15-Y0
Result	0111 1111 0000 1011

bit replacement (M2 = H, M1 = H, M0 = L)

In the bit-replacement mode, data in the bit position specified by ZN3-ZN0 is replaced by the logic level on the S input. If, for example, ZN3-ZN0 contains a decimal seven and S contains a logic high, bit 7 of the data selected by OP will be set high regardless of its original state. In the following example, OP has been set high to select data from the register/counter. Because IP has been set high, the data will be bit-reversed before it enters the shifter.

Example

Bit-reverse the data in the register/counter and set bit 7 of the result to zero.

CONTROL SIGNALS

SHIFT INSTRUCTION	NORMALIZE	POSITION OF BIT TO BE INSERTED	BIT REVERSAL	DATA SOURCE	INSERT BIT	CONFIGURATION
M2-M0	$\overline{NORM}$	ZN4-ZN0	IP	OP	S	16B/$\overline{32B}$
110	X	X0111	1	1	0	1

	Register/Counter
Input Data	0110 0001 0011 0100
	Result after Bit-Reversal
Intermediate Result	0010 1100 1000 0110
	Y15-Y0
Result	0010 1100 0000 0110

data normalization (M2 = H, M1 = H, M0 = L)

The data-normalization mode shifts data on D15-D0 to the left until a high logic level appears in the most-significant-bit position of output Y15-Y0 if HEX/$\overline{BIN}$ is low. If HEX/$\overline{BIN}$ is high, only 4-digit groups containing leading zeros are shifted left. The number of positions shifted to accomplish this is determined by the leading-zero detector. This count will be output on ZN3-ZN0 when the $\overline{NORM}$ input is low.

Since the leading-zero detector counts leading zeros in the D15-D0 input, the normalization is designed to operate on data from the data bus rather than the register/counter. Therefore OP is set low in the following example. The S input is programmed low so that all bit positions vacated during the shift will be filled with zeros.

Example

Perform a hex normalization on a 16-bit data word from the data bus.

CONTROL SIGNALS

SHIFT INSTRUCTION	NORMALIZE	NUMBER OF BITS TO BE SHIFTED	LEADING-ZERO MODE	BIT REVERSAL	DATA SOURCE	INSERT BIT	CONFIGURATION
M2-M0	$\overline{NORM}$	ZN4-ZN0	HEX/$\overline{BIN}$	IP	OP	S	16B/$\overline{32B}$
111	0	Outputs leading zero count	1	0	0	0	1

Assume D15-D0 contains hex 002B:

	D15-D0
Input Data	0000 0000 0010 1011

	ZN3-ZN0
Leading-Zero Count	1000

	Y15-Y0
Result	1010 1011 0000 0000

Example

Perform a binary normalization on a 32-bit word from the data bus.

CONTROL SIGNALS

SHIFT INSTRUCTION	NORMALIZE	NUMBER OF BITS TO SHIFT	LEADING-ZERO MODE	BIT REVERSAL	DATA SOURCE	BIT FILL	CONFIGURATION
M2-M0	$\overline{NORM}$	ZN4-ZN0	HEX/$\overline{BIN}$	IP	OP	S	16B/$\overline{32B}$
111	0	Outputs leading zero count	0	See Figure 1		0	0

2

LSI Devices

Assume D31-D0 contains hex 0000 3D61:

	D31-D16	D15-D0
Input Data	0000 0000 0000 0000	0011 1101 0110 0001

	ZN4-ZN0
Leading-Zero Count	10010

	Y31-Y16	Y15-Y0
Result	1111 0101 1000 0100	0000 0000 0000 0000

IEEE floating-point normalization

Floating-point normalization is used to preserve number resolution after subtraction or some other floating-point algorithm that results in orders of magnitude reduction. Three 'AS897A devices can be configured to convert a 32-bit data word into the IEEE floating-point format shown in Figure 3.

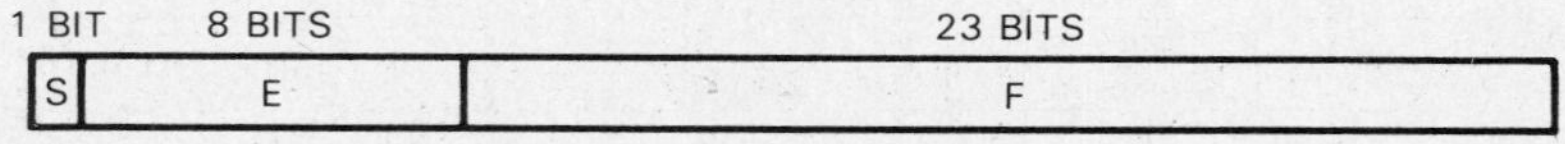
1 BIT
8 BITS
23 BITS
S
E
F

S — sign bit
E — 8-bit exponent
F — 23-bit fraction

FIGURE 3. IEEE FLOATING-POINT FORMAT

Figure 4 shows the three-device configuration. The limitation of this application is that only 23 bits of the 32 bits are used in the significand, and the sign bit must be set from hardware. As an alternate to the IEEE floating-point format, the same hardware configuration can be used to normalize a 32-bit data word resulting in a 32-bit significand and a five-bit exponent.

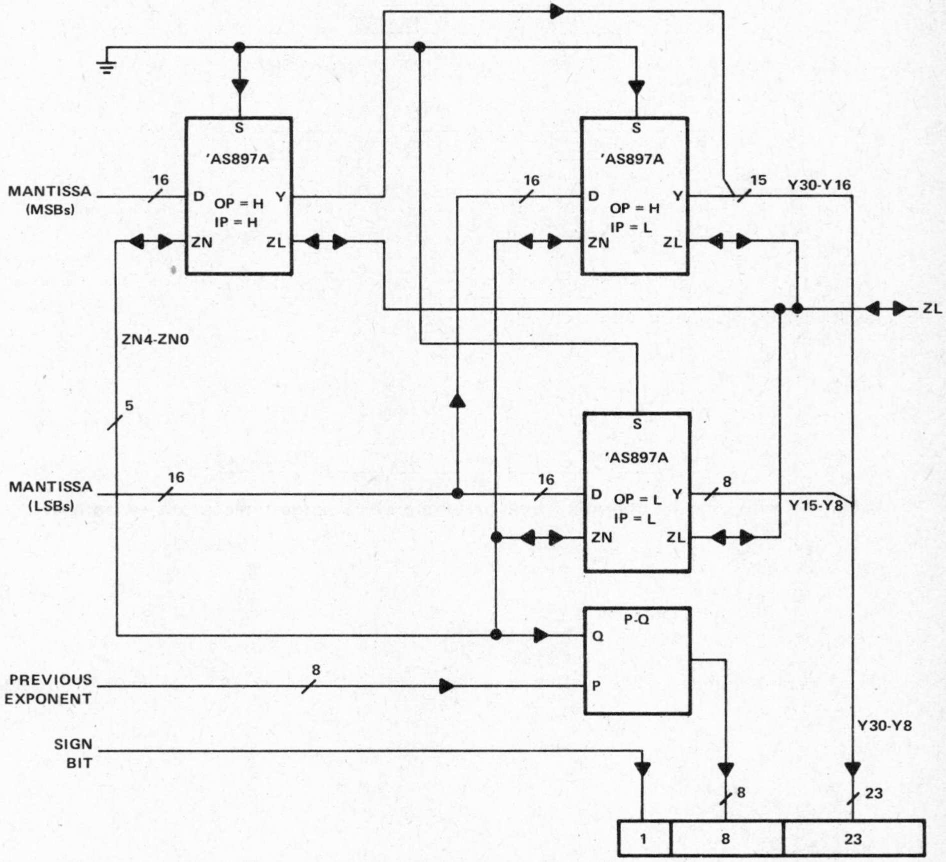
S
'AS897A
MANTISSA
(MSBs)
16
D
OP = H
IP = H
Y
ZN
ZL
S
'AS897A
16
D
OP = H
IP = L
Y
15
Y30-Y16
ZN
ZL
ZL
ZN4-ZN0
5
S
'AS897A
MANTISSA
(LSBs)
16
16
D
OP = L
IP = L
Y
8
Y15-Y8
ZN
ZL
P-Q
Q
PREVIOUS
EXPONENT
8
P
SIGN
BIT
Y30-Y8
8
23
1
8
23

FIGURE 4. THREE-DEVICE CONFIGURATION FOR IEEE FLOATING-POINT FORMAT

Example

Input data in IEEE floating point format

Sign Bit	Previous Exponent	Mantissa
1	0010 1001	000 1001 0001 0001 0001 0001

Input mantissa concatenated with: 0 0000 0000 to D31-D0 of the 'AS897As

D31-D16	D15-D0
0001 0010 0010 0010	0010 0010 0000 0000

Normalize mantissa and output the leading zero count on ZN4-ZN0.

D31-D16	D15-D0	ZN4-ZN0
1001 0001 0001 0001	0001 0000 0000 0000	00011

Pack result in IEEE floating point format
Note: Exponent = old exponent − ZN4-ZN0

Sign Bit	Exponent	Mantissa
1	0010 0110	001 0001 0001 0001 0001 0000

absolute maximum ratings over operating free-air temperature range (unless otherwise noted)

Supply voltage, V_{CC1}		7 V
Supply voltage, V_{CC2}		3 V
Input voltage:	I/O ports	5.5 V
	All other inputs	7 V
Operating case temperature range:	SN54AS897A	−55 °C to 125 °C
Operating free-air temperature range:	SN74AS897A	0 °C to 70 °C
Storage temperature range		−65 °C to 150 °C

TEXAS INSTRUMENTS
POST OFFICE BOX 225012 • DALLAS, TEXAS 75265

recommended operating conditions

			SN54AS897A			SN74AS897A			UNIT
			MIN	NOM	MAX	MIN	NOM	MAX	
V_{CC1}	Supply voltage		4.5	5	5.5	4.5	5	5.5	V
V_{CC2}	Supply voltage		1.9	2	2.1	1.9	2	2.1	V
V_{IH}	High-level input voltage		2			2			V
V_{IL}	Low-level input voltage				0.8			0.8	V
V_{OH}	High-level output voltage	ZL			5.5			5.5	V
I_{OH}	High-level output current	ZN4-ZN0			−0.4			−0.4	mA
		Y15-Y0			−1			−2.6	
I_{OL}	Low-level output current	ZN4-ZN0			4			8	mA
		ZL, Y15-Y0			12			24	
t_w	Pulse duration	CLK low	10			10			ns
		CLK high	10			10			
t_{su}	Setup time before CLK↑	Y15-Y0	10			10			ns
		S†	15			14			
		M0, M1, M2†	15			14			
		16B/$\overline{32B}$‡	20			18			
t_h	Hold time after CLK↑	Y15-Y0‡	2			2			ns
		S†	0			0			
		M0, M1, M2†	0			0			
		16B/$\overline{32B}$‡	8			8			
T_A	Operating free-air temperature		−55			0		70	°C
T_C	Operating case temperature				125				°C

† These parameters only apply in the circular mode and with 16B/$\overline{32B}$ high.
‡ These parameters only apply in the circular mode.

electrical characteristics over recommended operating temperature range (unless otherwise noted)

PARAMETER		TEST CONDITIONS		SN54AS897A			SN74AS897A			UNIT
				MIN	TYP†	MAX	MIN	TYP†	MAX	
V_{IK}		V_{CC} = 4.5 V,	I_I = 18 mA			−1.5			−1.5	V
I_{OH}	ZL	V_{CC} = 4.5 V,	V_{OH} = 5.5 V			0.1			0.1	mA
V_{OH}	All outputs	V_{CC} = 4.5 V to 5.5 V,	I_{OH} = −0.4 mA	V_{CC} −2			V_{CC} −2			V
	Y15-Y0	V_{CC} = 4.5 V,	I_{OH} = −1 mA	2.4	3.2					V
		V_{CC} = 4.5 V,	I_{OH} = −2.6 mA				2.4	3.2		
V_{OL}	ZN4-ZN0	V_{CC} = 4.5 V,	I_{OL} = 4 mA		0.25	0.4		0.25	0.4	V
		V_{CC} = 4.5 V,	I_{OL} = 8 mA					0.35	0.5	
	ZL, Y15-Y0	V_{CC} = 4.5 V,	I_{OL} = 12 mA		0.25	0.4		0.25	0.4	
		V_{CC} = 4.5 V,	I_{OL} = 24 mA					0.35	0.5	
I_I	I/O ports‡	V_{CC} = 5.5 V,	V_I = 5.5 V			0.1			0.1	mA
	All others	V_{CC} = 5.5 V,	V_I = 7 V			0.1			0.1	
I_{IH}	I/O ports‡	V_{CC} = 5.5 V,	V_I = 2.7 V			40			40	μmA
	All others					20			20	
I_{IL}	All inputs	V_{CC} = 5.5 V,	V_I = 0.4 V			−0.4			−0.4	mA
I_O§		V_{CC} = 5.5 V,	V_O = 2.25 V	−30		−112	−30		−112	mA
I_{CC1}		V_{CC} = 5.5 V,	See Note 1			100			90	mA
I_{CC2}		V_{CC} = 2.1 V,	See Note 1			180			170	mA

† All typical values are at V_{CC} = 5 V, T_A = 25°C.
‡ For I/O ports, the parameters I_{IH} and I_{IL} include the offstate output current.
§ The output conditions have been chosen to produce a current that closely approximates one half of the true short-circuit output current, I_{OS}.
NOTE 1: Supply currents I_{CC1} and I_{CC2} are measured with M0, M1, M2, IP, OP, S, ZN3-ZN0, D15-D0, and $\overline{OEY}$ low; 16B/$\overline{32B}$, $\overline{NORM}$, and CLK high; and Y15-Y0, ZL, and ZN4 open.

switching characteristics over recommended operating temperature range

PARAMETER	FROM (INPUT)	TO (OUTPUT)	V_{CC} = 4.5 V to 5.5 V, C_L = 50 pF, R1 = 500 Ω, R2 = 500 Ω SN54AS897A MIN	SN54AS897A MAX	SN74AS897A MIN	SN74AS897A MAX	UNIT
t_{pd}	D15-D0	Y15-Y0		37		33	ns
	S	Y15-Y0		20		17	
	ZN3-ZN0	Y15-Y0		24		22	
	IP	Y15-Y0		33		29	
	OP	Y15-Y0		33		29	
	M0, M1, M2	Y15-Y0		24		21	
	CLK†	Y15-Y0		47		42	
	D15-D0	ZL		28		27	
	D15-D0‡	ZN4-ZN0		28		26	
t_{en}	M0, M1, M2§	ZN4-ZN0		25		20	ns
	16B/$\overline{32B}$	Y15-Y0		29		26	
	$\overline{NORM}$‡	ZN3-ZN0		26		21	
	$\overline{OEY}$	Y15-Y0		22		19	
	ZN4, ZL	Y15-Y0		32		29	
t_{dis}	M0, M1, M2§	ZN4-ZN0		22		20	ns
	16B/$\overline{32B}$	Y15-Y0		31		27	
	$\overline{NORM}$‡	ZN3-ZN0		14		12	
	$\overline{OEY}$	Y15-Y0		10		9	
	ZN4, ZL	Y15-Y0		30		26	

† This parameter applies only to the circular mode with S high and OP high.
‡ These parameters apply only to the normalization mode.
§ These parameters apply only to the 32-bit mode (16B/$\overline{32B}$ = L).

2

LSI Devices

PRODUCT PREVIEW

SN54ALS963, SN54ALS964, SN74ALS963, SN74ALS964 DUAL-RANK 8-BIT SHIFT REGISTERS WITH 3-STATE OUTPUTS

D2881, NOVEMBER 1985

- **Serial-to-Parallel and Parallel-to-Serial Conversions**
- **Parallel I/O Registers**
- **Data Exchangeable Between I/O Register and Shift Register**
- **Choice of Synchronous and/or Asynchronous Clear**
- **Independent or Dual Register Clocking**
- **Functionally Similar to National Semiconductor DM74LS962**
- **Dependable Texas Instruments Quality and Reliability**

description

The 'ALS963 and 'ALS964 each contain an 8-bit shift register in parallel with an 8-bit I/O register. In addition to serial-to-parallel and parallel-to-serial conversions, these devices are capable of exchanging data between the shift and I/O registers. Control lines determine the mode of operation as shown in the function table.

The 'ALS963 features individual shift and I/O register clock inputs whereas the 'ALS964 features simultaneous register clocking through a single clock input. Clocking in both cases is achieved by positive transitions at the clock inputs.

The clear function for the 'ALS963 is synchronous (active high). The 'ALS964 features active-high synchronous and asynchronous clearing.

The SN54ALS963 and SN54ALS964 are characterized for operation over the full military of −55°C to 125°C. The SN74ALS963 and SN74ALS964 are characterized for operation from 0°C to 70°C.

SN54ALS963 . . . JT PACKAGE
SN74ALS963 . . . DW OR NT PACKAGE
(TOP VIEW)

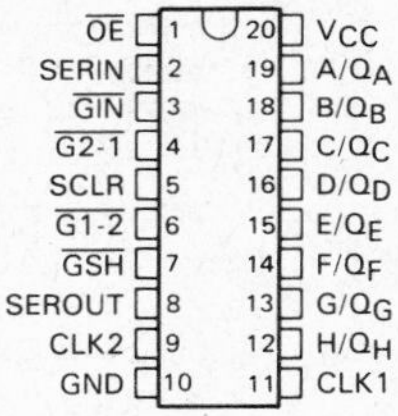
OE 1 20 VCC
SERIN 2 19 A/QA
GIN 3 18 B/QB
G2-1 4 17 C/QC
SCLR 5 16 D/QD
G1-2 6 15 E/QE
GSH 7 14 F/QF
SEROUT 8 13 G/QG
CLK2 9 12 H/QH
GND 10 11 CLK1

SN54ALS963 . . . FK PACKAGE
SN74ALS963 . . . FN PACKAGE
(TOP VIEW)

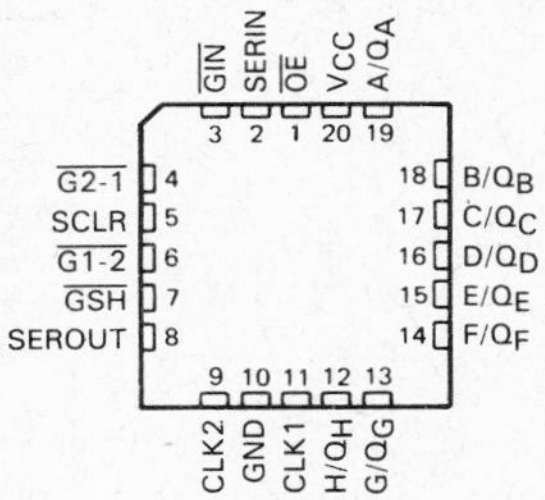
GIN SERIN OE VCC A/QA
3 2 1 20 19
G2-1 4
SCLR 5
G1-2 6
GSH 7
SEROUT 8
18 B/QB
17 C/QC
16 D/QD
15 E/QE
14 F/QF
9 10 11 12 13
CLK2 GND CLK1 H/QH G/QG

SN54ALS964 . . . JT PACKAGE
SN74ALS964 . . . DW OR NT PACKAGE
(TOP VIEW)

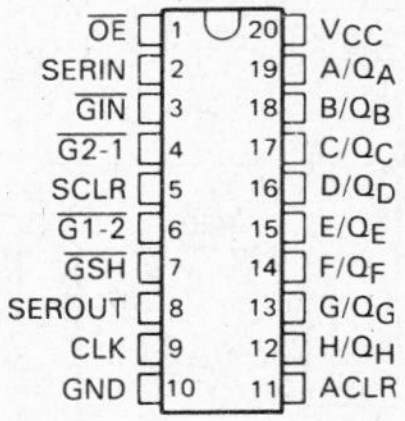
OE 1 20 VCC
SERIN 2 19 A/QA
GIN 3 18 B/QB
G2-1 4 17 C/QC
SCLR 5 16 D/QD
G1-2 6 15 E/QE
GSH 7 14 F/QF
SEROUT 8 13 G/QG
CLK 9 12 H/QH
GND 10 11 ACLR

SN54ALS964 . . . FK PACKAGE
SN74ALS964 . . . FN PACKAGE
(TOP VIEW)

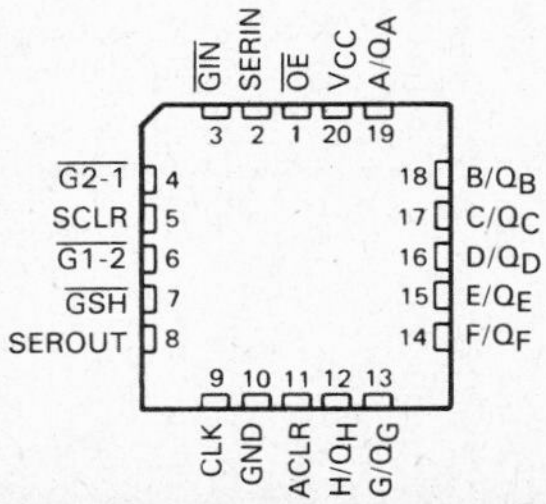
GIN SERIN OE VCC A/QA
3 2 1 20 19
G2-1 4
SCLR 5
G1-2 6
GSH 7
SEROUT 8
18 B/QB
17 C/QC
16 D/QD
15 E/QE
14 F/QF
9 10 11 12 13
CLK GND ACLR H/QH G/QG

TEXAS INSTRUMENTS

POST OFFICE BOX 225012 • DALLAS, TEXAS 75265

'ALS963 logic symbol†

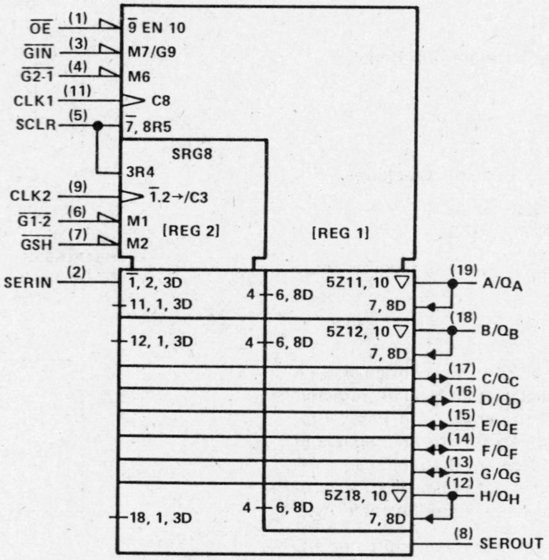
OE (1)
GIN (3)
G2·1 (4)
CLK1 (11)
SCLR (5)
9 EN 10
M7/G9
M6
C8
7, 8R5
SRG8
3R4
CLK2 (9)
G1·2 (6)
GSH (7)
1.2→/C3
M1
M2
[REG 2]
[REG 1]
SERIN (2)
1, 2, 3D
11, 1, 3D
12, 1, 3D
18, 1, 3D
4
6, 8D
5Z11, 10
7, 8D
5Z12, 10
5Z18, 10
(19) A/QA
(18) B/QB
(17) C/QC
(16) D/QD
(15) E/QE
(14) F/QF
(13) G/QG
(12) H/QH
(8) SEROUT

†This symbol is in accordance with ANSI/IEEE Std 91-1984 and IEC Publication 617-12.

'ALS963 register-level logic diagram

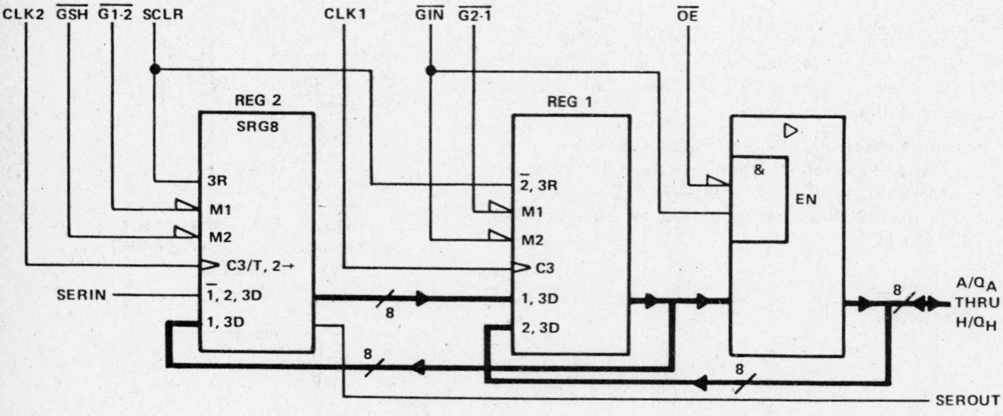
CLK2
GSH
G1·2
SCLR
CLK1
GIN
G2·1
OE
REG 2
SRG8
3R
M1
M2
C3/T, 2→
SERIN
1, 2, 3D
1, 3D
REG 1
2, 3R
M1
M2
C3
1, 3D
2, 3D
&
EN
8
A/QA
THRU
H/QH
SEROUT

TEXAS INSTRUMENTS
POST OFFICE BOX 225012 • DALLAS, TEXAS 75265

'ALS963 gate-level logic diagram (positive logic)

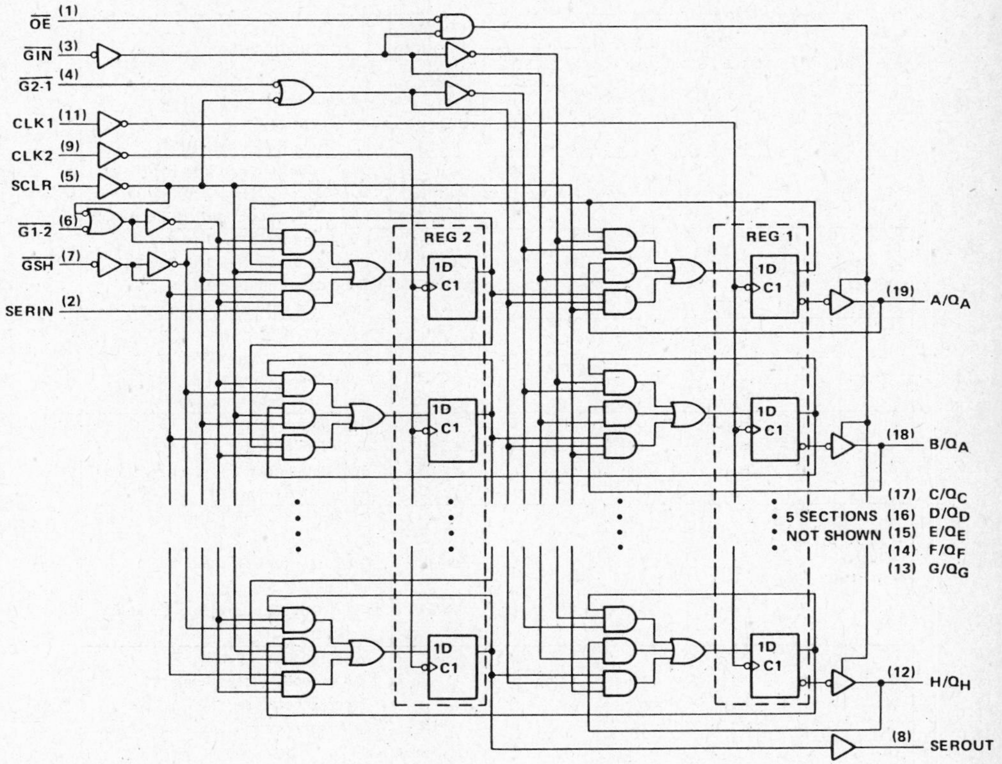
OE (1)
GIN (3)
G2-1 (4)
CLK1 (11)
CLK2 (9)
SCLR (5)
G1-2 (6)
GSH (7)
SERIN (2)
REG 2
REG 1
1D
C1
(19) A/QA
(18) B/QA
(17) C/QC
(16) D/QD
(15) E/QE
(14) F/QF
(13) G/QG
5 SECTIONS
NOT SHOWN
(12) H/QH
(8) SEROUT

'ALS963
FUNCTION TABLE

INPUTS								A/QA THROUGH H/QH	OPERATION OR FUNCTION
$\overline{OE}$	$\overline{GIN}$	$\overline{GE-1}$	$\overline{G1-2}$	$\overline{GSH}$	CLK1	CLK2	SCLR		
H	H	H	H	H	X	X	L	HI-Z	All data stable
L	H	H	H	H	X	X	L	OUTPUT	All data stable
X	L	H	H	H	↑	X	L	INPUT	Enter data from I/O into Reg 1
H	H	L	H	H	↑	X	L	HI-Z	Copy data from Reg 2 to Reg 1
L	H	L	H	H	↑	X	L	OUTPUT	Copy data from Reg 2 to Reg 1
X	L	L	H	H	↑	↑	L	INPUT	Reg 1 ORs data from Reg 2 and I/O
H	H	H	L	X	X	↑	L	HI-Z	Copy data from Reg 1 to Reg 2
L	H	H	L	X	X	↑	L	OUTPUT	Copy data from Reg 1 to Reg 2
X	L	H	L	X	↑	↑	L	INPUT	Copy data from Reg 1 to Reg 2, enter new data from I/O into Reg 1
H	H	L	L	X	↑	↑	L	HI-Z	Exchange data between registers
L	H	L	L	X	↑	↑	L	OUTPUT	Exchange data between registers
X	L	L	L	X	↑	↑	L	INPUT	Copy data from Reg 1 to Reg 2, Reg 1 ORs data from Reg 2 and I/O
H	H	H	H	L	X	↑	L	HI-Z	Shift data in Reg 2
L	H	H	H	L	X	↑	L	OUTPUT	Shift data in Reg 2
X	L	H	H	L	↑	↑	L	INPUT	Shift data in Reg 2, enter new data from I/O into Reg 1
H	H	L	H	L	↑	↑	L	HI-Z	Copy data from Reg 2 to Reg 1, shift data in Reg 2
L	H	L	H	L	↑	↑	L	OUTPUT	Copy data from Reg 2 to Reg 1, shift data in Reg 2
X	L	L	H	L	↑	↑	L	INPUT	Reg 1 ORs data from Reg 2 and I/O, shift data in Reg 2
X	H	X	X	X	↑	X	H		Synchronously clear Reg 1
X	X	X	X	X	X	↑	H		Synchronously clear Reg 2
X	H	X	X	X	↑	↑	H		Synchronously clear both registers
X	L	X	X	X	↑	↑	H	INPUT	Enter data from I/O into Reg 1 and synchronously clear Reg 2
X	L	X	X	X	↑	X	H	INPUT	Enter data from I/O into Reg 1

'ALS964 logic symbol†

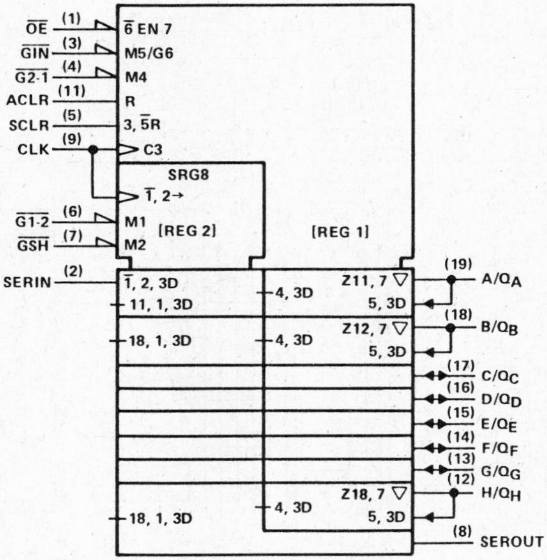
OE (1)
GIN (3)
G2-1 (4)
ACLR (11)
SCLR (5)
CLK (9)
G1-2 (6)
GSH (7)
SERIN (2)
6 EN 7
M5/G6
M4
R
3, 5R
C3
SRG8
1, 2→
M1
M2
[REG 2]
[REG 1]
1, 2, 3D
11, 1, 3D
18, 1, 3D
4, 3D
Z11, 7
5, 3D
Z12, 7
Z18, 7
(19) A/QA
(18) B/QB
(17) C/QC
(16) D/QD
(15) E/QE
(14) F/QF
(13) G/QG
(12) H/QH
(8) SEROUT

†This symbol is in accordance with ANSI/IEEE Std 91-1984 and IEC Publication 617-12.

'ALS964 register-level logic diagram

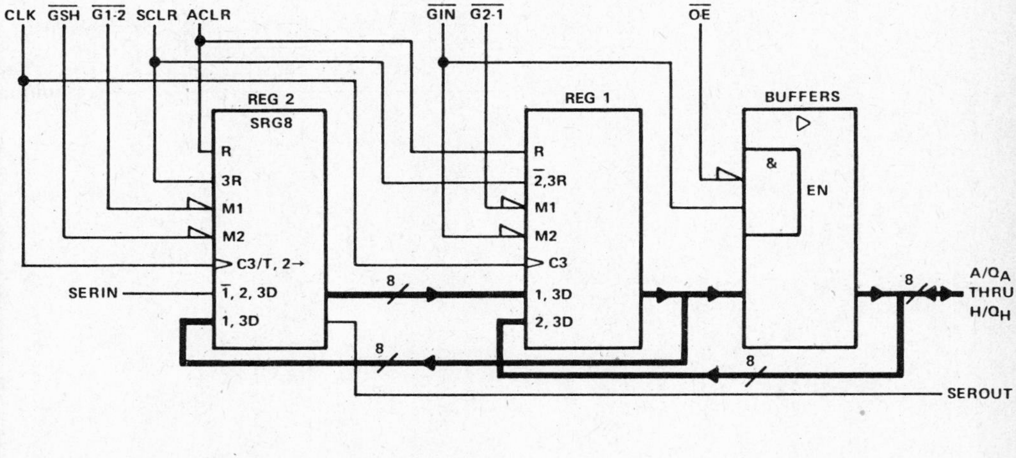
CLK
GSH
G1-2
SCLR
ACLR
GIN
G2-1
OE
REG 2
SRG8
R
3R
M1
M2
C3/T, 2→
1, 2, 3D
1, 3D
SERIN
REG 1
2,3R
C3
1, 3D
2, 3D
BUFFERS
&
EN
8
A/QA
THRU
H/QH
SEROUT

'ALS964 gate-level logic diagram (positive logic)

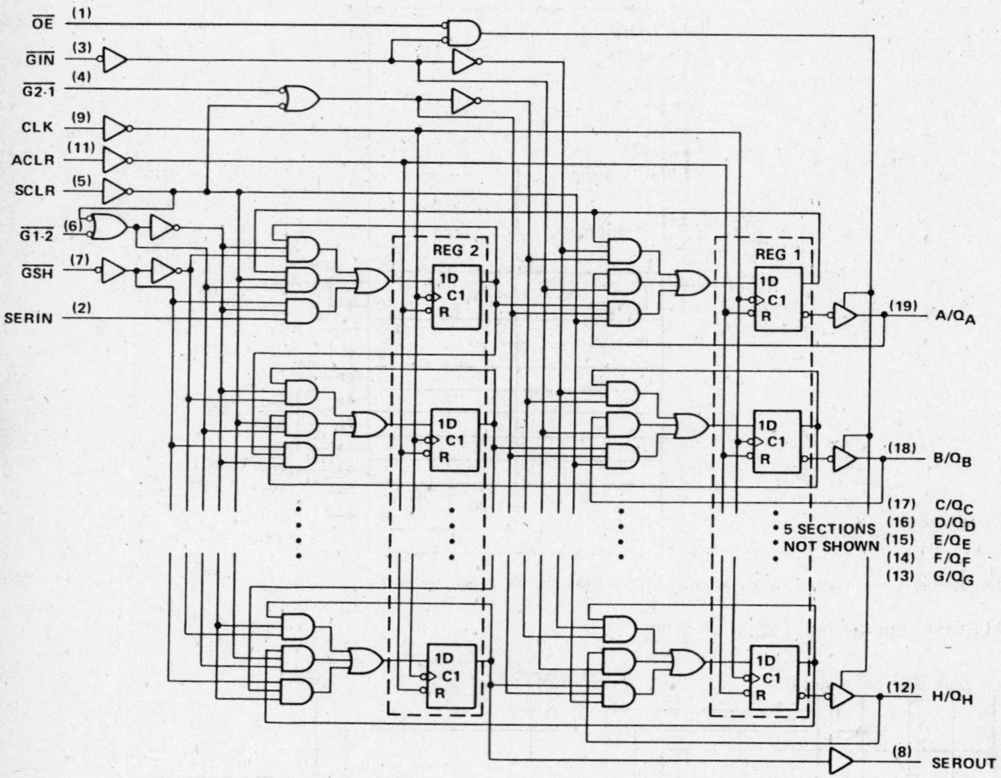
OE (1)
GIN (3)
G2-1 (4)
CLK (9)
ACLR (11)
SCLR (5)
G1-2 (6)
GSH (7)
SERIN (2)
REG 2
REG 1
1D
C1
R
(19) A/QA
(18) B/QB
(17) C/QC
(16) D/QD
(15) E/QE
(14) F/QF
(13) G/QG
5 SECTIONS
NOT SHOWN
(12) H/QH
(8) SEROUT

TEXAS INSTRUMENTS
POST OFFICE BOX 225012 • DALLAS, TEXAS 75265

'ALS964
FUNCTION TABLE

INPUTS								A/QA THROUGH H/QH	OPERATION OR FUNCTION
$\overline{OE}$	$\overline{GIN}$	$\overline{G2\text{-}1}$	$\overline{G1\text{-}2}$	$\overline{GSH}$	CLK	ACLR	SCLR		
H	H	H	H	H	X	L	L	HI-Z	All data stable
L	H	H	H	H	X	L	L	OUTPUT	All data stable
X	L	H	H	H	↑	L	L	INPUT	Enter data from I/O into Reg 1
H	H	L	H	H	↑	L	L	HI-Z	Copy data from Reg 2 to Reg 1
L	H	L	H	H	↑	L	L	OUTPUT	Copy data from Reg 2 to Reg 1
X	L	L	H	H	↑	L	L	INPUT	Reg 1 ORs data from Reg 2 and I/O
H	H	H	L	X	↑	L	L	HI-Z	Copy data from Reg 1 to Reg 2
L	H	H	L	X	↑	L	L	OUTPUT	Copy data from Reg 1 to Reg 2
X	L	H	L	X	↑	L	L	INPUT	Copy data from Reg 1 to Reg 2, enter new data from I/O into Reg 1
H	H	L	L	X	↑	L	L	HI-Z	Exchange data between registers
L	H	L	L	X	↑	L	L	OUTPUT	Exchange data between registers
X	L	L	L	X	↑	L	L	INPUT	Copy data from Reg 1 to Reg 2, Reg 1 ORs data from Reg 2 and I/O
H	H	H	H	L	↑	L	L	HI-Z	Shift data in Reg 2
L	H	H	H	L	↑	L	L	OUTPUT	Shift data in Reg 2
X	L	H	H	L	↑	L	L	INPUT	Shift data in Reg 2, enter new data from I/O into Reg 1
H	H	L	H	L	↑	L	L	HI-Z	Copy data from Reg 2 to Reg 1, shift data in Reg 2
L	H	L	H	L	↑	L	L	OUTPUT	Copy data from Reg 2 to Reg 1, shift data in Reg 2
X	L	L	H	L	↑	L	L	INPUT	Reg 1 ORs data from Reg 2 and I/O, shift data in Reg 2
X	H	X	X	X	↑	L	H		Synchronously clear Reg 1 and Reg 2
X	X	X	X	X	X	H	X		Asynchronously clear Reg 1 and Reg 2
X	L	X	X	X	↑	L	H	INPUT	Enter data from I/O into Reg 1 and synchronously clear Reg 2

'ALS963 typical sequence

Illustrated below is the following sequence:

1. Clear both registers to zero.
2. Input 0011 0011 in Reg 1.
3. Transfer 0011 0011 from Reg 1 to Reg 2.
4. Input 0111 0111 into Reg 1.
5. Shift contents of Reg 2, SERIN = 0
6. Shift contents of Reg 2, SERIN = 1
7. Exchange contents of Reg 1 with Reg 2.

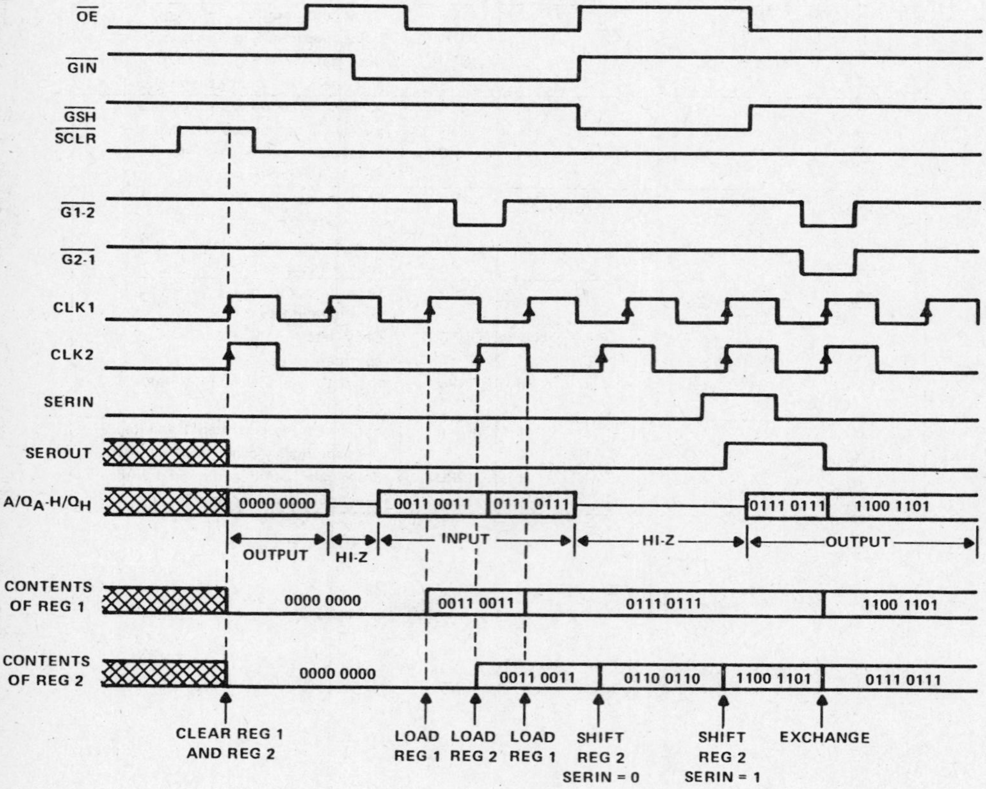
OE
GIN
GSH
SCLR
G1-2
G2-1
CLK1
CLK2
SERIN
SEROUT
A/QA-H/QH
0000 0000
0011 0011
0111 0111
0111 0111
1100 1101
OUTPUT
HI-Z
INPUT
HI-Z
OUTPUT
CONTENTS OF REG 1
0000 0000
0011 0011
0111 0111
1100 1101
CONTENTS OF REG 2
0000 0000
0011 0011
0110 0110
1100 1101
0111 0111
CLEAR REG 1 AND REG 2
LOAD REG 1
LOAD REG 2
LOAD REG 1
SHIFT REG 2 SERIN = 0
SHIFT REG 2 SERIN = 1
EXCHANGE

TEXAS INSTRUMENTS
POST OFFICE BOX 225012 • DALLAS, TEXAS 75265

'ALS964 typical sequence

Illustrated below is the following sequence:

1. Asynchronously clear Reg 1 and Reg 2 to zero, operate, then synchronously clear.
2. Input 0011 0011 into Reg 1.
3. Transfer 0011 0011 from Reg 1 to Reg 2 and input 0111 0111 into Reg 1.
4. Shift contents of Reg 2, SERIN = 0
5. Shift contents of Reg 2, SERIN = 1
6. Exchange contents of Reg 1 with Reg 2.

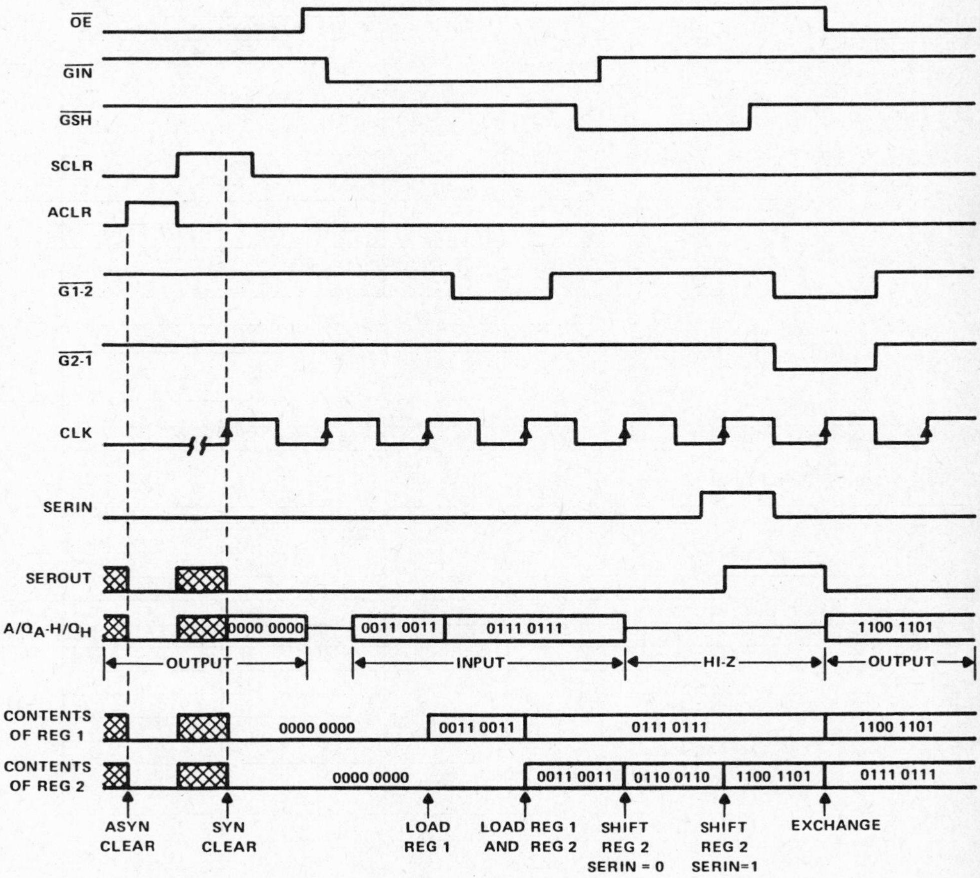
OE
GIN
GSH
SCLR
ACLR
G1-2
G2-1
CLK
SERIN
SEROUT
A/QA-H/QH
0000 0000
0011 0011
0111 0111
1100 1101
OUTPUT
INPUT
HI-Z
OUTPUT
CONTENTS OF REG 1
0000 0000
0011 0011
0111 0111
1100 1101
CONTENTS OF REG 2
0000 0000
0011 0011
0110 0110
1100 1101
0111 0111
ASYN CLEAR
SYN CLEAR
LOAD REG 1
LOAD REG 1 AND REG 2
SHIFT REG 2 SERIN = 0
SHIFT REG 2 SERIN=1
EXCHANGE

absolute maximum ratings over operating free-air temperature range (unless otherwise noted)

Supply voltage, V_{CC} . . . . 7 V
Input voltage: All inputs . . . . 7 V
I/O ports . . . . 5.5 V
Operating free-air temperature range: SN54ALS963, SN54ALS964 . . . . −55°C to 125°C
SN74ALS963, SN74ALS964 . . . . 0°C to 70°C
Storage temperature range . . . . −65°C to 150°C

'ALS963 recommended operating conditions

			SN54ALS963			SN74ALS963			UNIT
			MIN	NOM	MAX	MIN	NOM	MAX	
V_{CC}	Supply voltage		4.5	5	5.5	4.5	5	5.5	V
V_{IH}	High-level input voltage		2			2			V
V_{IL}	Low-level input voltage				0.8			0.8	V
I_{OH}	High-level output current				−1			−2.6	mA
I_{OL}	Low-level output current	SEROUT			8			16	mA
		Q_A thru Q_H			12			24	
f_{clock}	Clock frequency (at 50% duty cycle)		0		25	0		25	MHz
t_w	Pulse duration	CLK1 high or low	20			20			ns
		CLK2 high or low	20			20			
t_{su}	Setup time	Data before CLK1↑							ns
		$\overline{GIN}$ before CLK1↑							
		$\overline{G1\text{-}2}$ before CLK2↑							
		$\overline{G2\text{-}1}$ before CLK1↑							
		$\overline{GSH}$ before CLK2↑							
		SCLR before CLK1↑ or CLK2↑							
t_h	Hold time after CLK1↑ or CLK2↑								ns
T_A	Operating free-air temperature		−55		125	0		70	°C

'ALS964 recommended operating conditions

			SN54ALS964			SN74ALS964			UNIT
			MIN	NOM	MAX	MIN	NOM	MAX	
V_{CC}	Supply voltage		4.5	5	5.5	4.5	5	5.5	V
V_{IH}	High-level input voltage		2			2			V
V_{IL}	Low-level input voltage				0.8			0.8	V
I_{OH}	High-level output current				−1			−2.6	mA
I_{OL}	Low-level output current	SEROUT			8			16	mA
		Q_A thru Q_H			12			24	
f_{clock}	Clock frequency (at 50% duty cycle)		0		25	0		25	MHz
t_w	Pulse duration	CLK high or low	20			20			ns
		ACLR low							
t_{su}	Setup time	Data before CLK↑							ns
		$\overline{GIN}$ before CLK↑							
		$\overline{G1\text{-}2}$ before CLK↑							
		$\overline{G2\text{-}1}$ before CLK↑							
		$\overline{GSH}$ before CLK↑							
		SCLR before CLK↑							
t_h	Hold time after CLK↑								ns
T_A	Operating free-air temperature		−55		125	0		70	°C

electrical characteristics over recommended operating free-air temperature range (unless otherwise noted)

PARAMETER		TEST CONDITIONS		SN54ALS963 SN54ALS964 MIN	TYP†	MAX	SN74ALS963 SN74ALS964 MIN	TYP†	MAX	UNIT
V_{IK}		V_{CC} = 4.5 V,	I_I = −18 mA			−1.5			−1.5	V
V_{OH}		V_{CC} = 4.5 V to 5.5 V,	I_{OH} = −0.4 mA	$V_{CC}-2$			$V_{CC}-2$			V
		V_{CC} = 4.5 V,	I_{OH} = −1 mA	2.4	3.3					
		V_{CC} = 4.5 V,	I_{OH} = −2.6 mA				2.4	3.2		
V_{OL}	SEROUT	V_{CC} = 4.5 V,	I_{OL} = 8 mA		0.25	0.4		0.25	0.4	V
		V_{CC} = 4.5 V,	I_{OL} = 16 mA					0.35	0.5	
	Q_A thru Q_H	V_{CC} = 4.5 V,	I_{OL} = 12 mA		0.25	0.4		0.25	0.4	
		V_{CC} = 4.5 V,	I_{OL} = 24 mA					0.35	0.5	
I_I	A thru H	V_{CC} = 5.5 V,	V_I = 5.5 V			0.1			0.1	mA
	Any other	V_{CC} = 5.5 V,	V_I = 7 V			0.1			0.1	
I_{IH}‡		V_{CC} = 5.5 V,	V_I = 2.7 V			20			20	μA
I_{IL}‡		V_{CC} = 5.5 V,	V_I = 0.4 V			−0.1			−0.1	mA
I_O§		V_{CC} = 5.5 V,	V_O = 2.25 V	−30		−112	−30		−112	mA
I_{CC}	'ALS963	V_{CC} = 5.5 V	Outputs high							mA
			Outputs low							
			Outputs disabled							
	'ALS964	V_{CC} = 5.5 V	Outputs high							mA
			Outputs low							
			Outputs disabled							

†All typical values are at V_{CC} = 5 V, T_A = 25°C.
‡For I/O ports (Q_A throuh Q_H), the parameters I_{IH} and I_{IL} include the off-state output current.
§The output conditions have been chosen to produce a current that closely approximates one half of the true short-circuit output current, I_{OS}.

2 LSI Devices

'ALS963 switching characteristics (see Note 1)

PARAMETER	FROM (INPUT)	TO (OUTPUT)	V_{CC} = 4.5 V to 5.5 V, C_L = 50 pF, R1 = 500 Ω, R2 = 500 Ω, T_A = MIN to MAX						UNIT
			SN54ALS963			SN74ALS963			
			MIN	TYP	MAX	MIN	TYP	MAX	
f_{max}	CLK1 or CLK2	Any Q	25	30		25	30		MHz
t_{PLH}	CLK1	Any Q		10			10		ns
t_{PHL}				14			14		
t_{PLH}	CLK2	SEROUT		10			10		ns
t_{PHL}				14			14		
t_{PHZ}	$\overline{OE}$	Any Q		15			15		ns
t_{PLZ}				18			18		
t_{PZH}	$\overline{OE}$	Any Q		12			12		ns
t_{PZL}				12			12		

'ALS964 switching characteristics (see Note 1)

PARAMETER	FROM (INPUT)	TO (OUTPUT)	V_{CC} = 4.5 V to 5.5 V, C_L = 50 pF, R1 = 500 Ω, R2 = 500 Ω, T_A = MIN to MAX						UNIT
			SN54ALS964			SN74ALS964			
			MIN	TYP	MAX	MIN	TYP	MAX	
f_{max}	CLK	Any Q	25	30		25	30		MHz
t_{PLH}	CLK	Any Q		10			10		ns
t_{PHL}				14			14		
t_{PLH}	CLK	SEROUT		10			10		ns
t_{PHL}				14			14		
t_{PHZ}	ACLR	Any Q or SEROUT		14			14		ns
t_{PHZ}	$\overline{OE}$	Any Q		15			15		ns
t_{PLZ}				18			18		
t_{PZH}	$\overline{OE}$	Any Q		12			12		ns
t_{PZL}				12			12		

NOTE: Load circuit and voltage waveforms are shown in Section 1.

- 3-State I/O-Type Read-Back Inputs
- Bus-Structured Pinout
- Choice of True or Inverting Logic
  'ALS990 . . . True Outputs
  'ALS991 . . . Inverting Outputs
- Package Options Include Both Plastic and Ceramic Chip Carriers in Addition to Plastic and Ceramic DIPs
- Dependable Texas Instruments Quality and Reliability

description

These 8-bit latches are designed specifically for storing the contents of the input data bus plus providing the capability of reading-back the stored data onto the input data bus.

The eight latches of the 'ALS990 and 'ALS991 are transparent D-type. While the enable (C) is high, the Q outputs of the 'ALS990 will follow the data (D) inputs. For the 'ALS991, the Q outputs will provide the complement of what is applied to its data (D) inputs.

Read-back is provided through the read-back control input ($\overline{OERB}$). When the control is taken low, the data present at the output of the data latches will be allowed to pass back onto the input data bus. When it is taken high, the output of the data latches will be isolated from the data (D) inputs. The read-back control does not affect the internal operation of the latches; however, precautions should be taken not to create a bus-conflict situation.

The SN74ALS990 and SN74ALS991 are characterized for operation from 0°C to 70°C.

SN74ALS990 . . . DW OR N PACKAGE
(TOP VIEW)

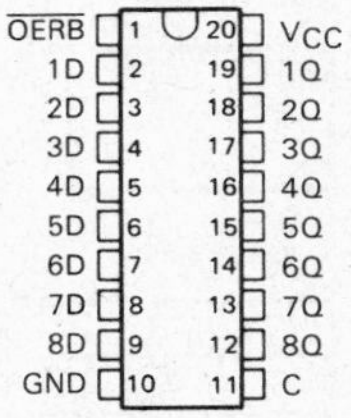
OERB 1 20 VCC
1D 2 19 1Q
2D 3 18 2Q
3D 4 17 3Q
4D 5 16 4Q
5D 6 15 5Q
6D 7 14 6Q
7D 8 13 7Q
8D 9 12 8Q
GND 10 11 C

SN74ALS990 . . . FN PACKAGE
(TOP VIEW)

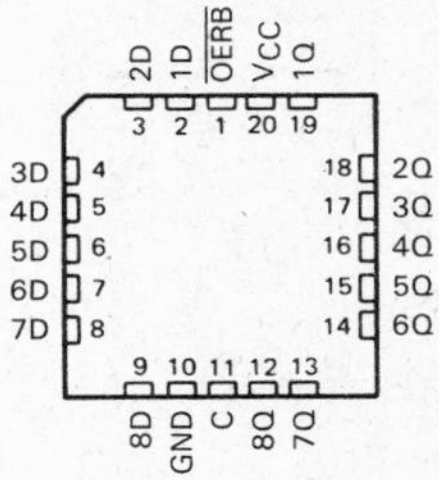
2D 1D OERB VCC 1Q
3 2 1 20 19
3D 4
4D 5
5D 6
6D 7
7D 8
18 2Q
17 3Q
16 4Q
15 5Q
14 6Q
9 10 11 12 13
8D GND C 8Q 7Q

SN74ALS991 . . . DW OR N PACKAGE
(TOP VIEW)

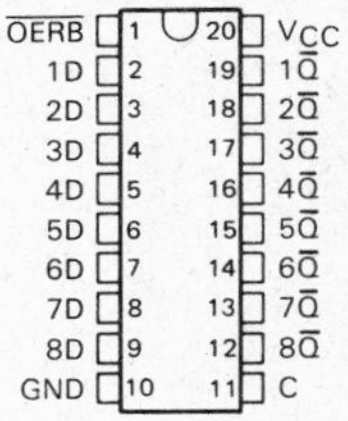
OERB 1 20 VCC
1D 2 19 1Q
2D 3 18 2Q
3D 4 17 3Q
4D 5 16 4Q
5D 6 15 5Q
6D 7 14 6Q
7D 8 13 7Q
8D 9 12 8Q
GND 10 11 C

SN74ALS991 . . . FN PACKAGE
(TOP VIEW)

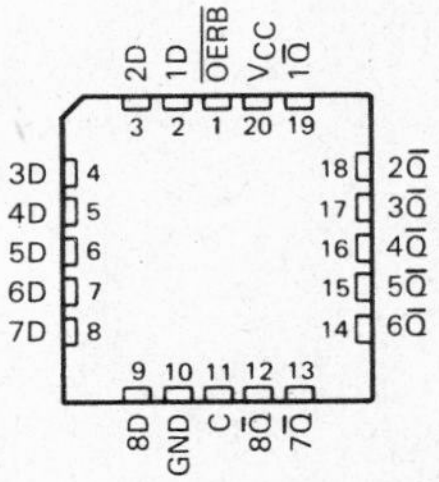
2D 1D OERB VCC 1Q
3 2 1 20 19
3D 4
4D 5
5D 6
6D 7
7D 8
18 2Q
17 3Q
16 4Q
15 5Q
14 6Q
9 10 11 12 13
8D GND C 8Q 7Q

logic symbols†

'ALS990

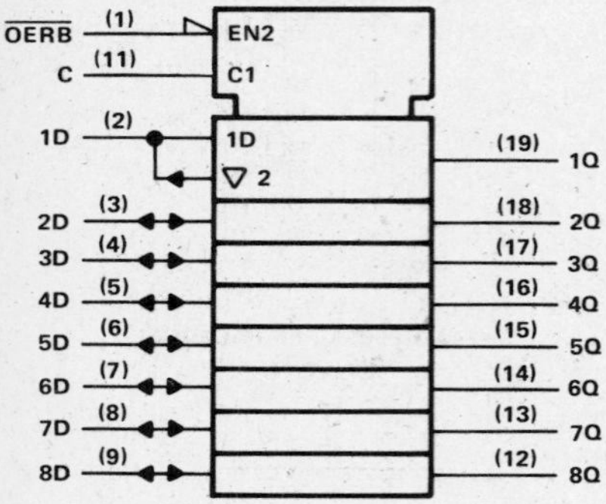
OERB
(1)
EN2
C
(11)
C1
1D
(2)
1D
▽ 2
(19)
1Q
2D (3)
(18) 2Q
3D (4)
(17) 3Q
4D (5)
(16) 4Q
5D (6)
(15) 5Q
6D (7)
(14) 6Q
7D (8)
(13) 7Q
8D (9)
(12) 8Q

'ALS991

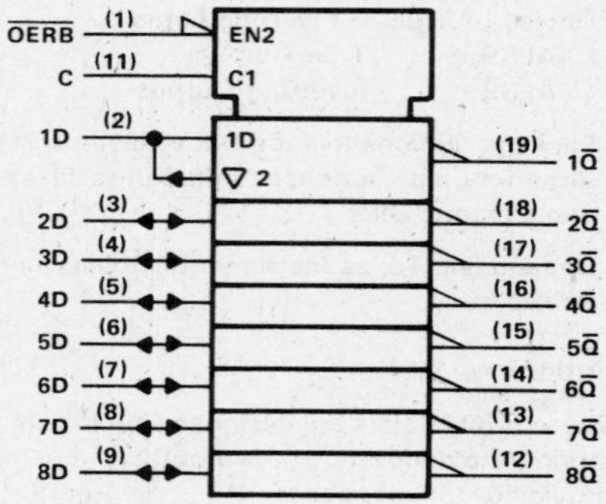
OERB
(1)
EN2
C
(11)
C1
1D
(2)
1D
▽ 2
(19)
1Q̄
2D (3)
(18) 2Q̄
3D (4)
(17) 3Q̄
4D (5)
(16) 4Q̄
5D (6)
(15) 5Q̄
6D (7)
(14) 6Q̄
7D (8)
(13) 7Q̄
8D (9)
(12) 8Q̄

†This symbol is in accordance with ANSI/IEEE Std 91-1984 and IEC Publication 617-12.

TEXAS INSTRUMENTS
POST OFFICE BOX 225012 • DALLAS, TEXAS 75265

logic diagrams (positive logic)

'ALS990

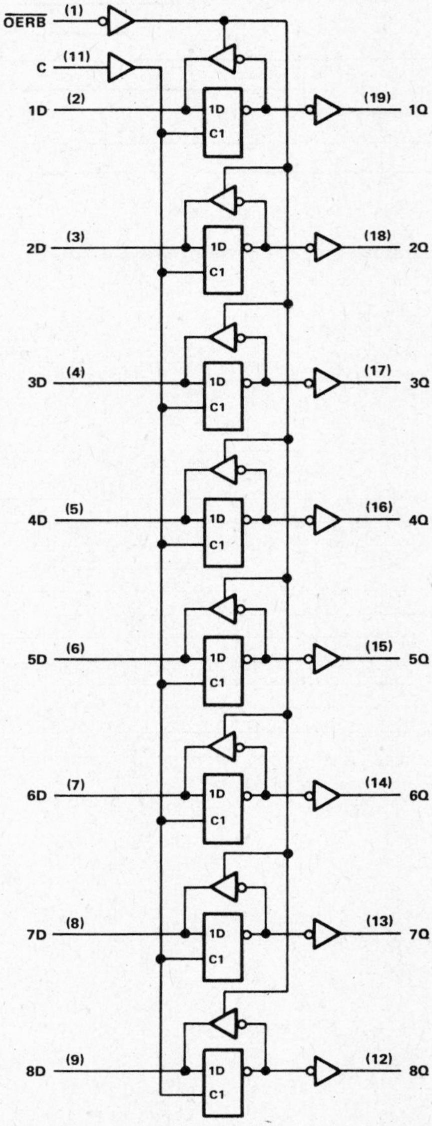
OERB
(1)
C
(11)
1D (2)
(19) 1Q
2D (3)
(18) 2Q
3D (4)
(17) 3Q
4D (5)
(16) 4Q
5D (6)
(15) 5Q
6D (7)
(14) 6Q
7D (8)
(13) 7Q
8D (9)
(12) 8Q
1D
C1

'ALS991

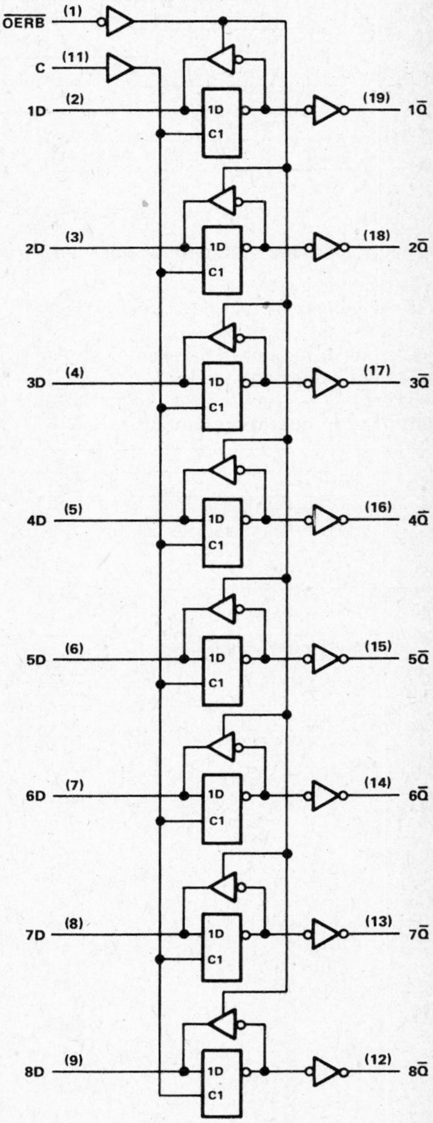
OERB
(1)
C
(11)
1D (2)
(19) 1Q̄
2D (3)
(18) 2Q̄
3D (4)
(17) 3Q̄
4D (5)
(16) 4Q̄
5D (6)
(15) 5Q̄
6D (7)
(14) 6Q̄
7D (8)
(13) 7Q̄
8D (9)
(12) 8Q̄
1D
C1

timing diagram

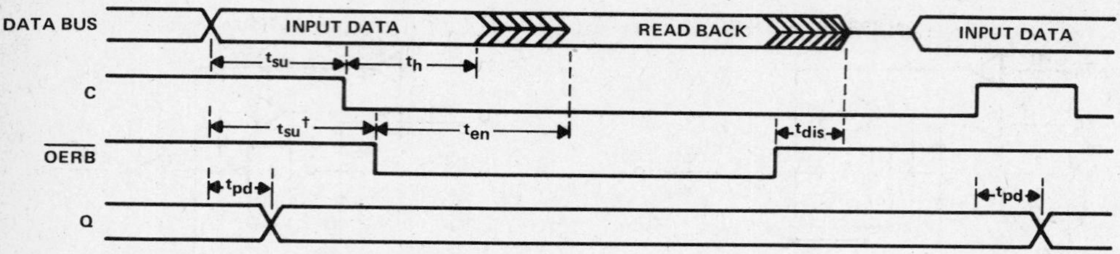
DATA BUS
INPUT DATA
READ BACK
INPUT DATA
t_{su}
t_h
C
t_{su}†
t_{en}
t_{dis}
OERB
t_{pd}
t_{pd}
Q

† This setup time ensures the readback circuit will not create a conflict on the input data bus.

absolute maximum ratings over operating free-air temperature range (unless otherwise noted)

Supply voltage, V_{CC} . . . . . 7 V
Input voltage, ($\overline{OERB}$ and C inputs) . . . . . 7 V
Voltage applied to D inputs . . . . . 5.5 V
Operating free-air temperature range SN74ALS990, SN74ALS991 . . . . . 0 °C to 70 °C
Storage temperature range . . . . . −65 °C to 150 °C

recommended operating conditions

			MIN	NOM	MAX	UNIT
V_{CC}	Supply voltage		4.5	5	5.5	V
V_{IH}	High-level input voltage		2			V
V_{IL}	Low-level input voltage				0.8	V
I_{OH}	High-level output current	Q			−2.6	mA
		D			−0.4	
I_{OL}	Low-level output current	Q			24	mA
		D			8	
t_w	Pulse duration, enable C high		10			ns
t_{su}	Setup time	Data before C↓	10			ns
		Data before $\overline{OERB}$↓	10			
t_h	Hold time	Data after C↓	5			ns
T_A	Operating free-air temperature		0		70	°C

TEXAS INSTRUMENTS
POST OFFICE BOX 225012 • DALLAS, TEXAS 75265

electrical characteristics over recommended operating free-air temperature range (unless otherwise noted)

PARAMETER		TEST CONDITIONS			MIN	TYP†	MAX	UNIT
V_{IK}		V_{CC} = 4.5 V,	I_I = −18 mA				−1.2	V
V_{OH}	All outputs	V_{CC} = 4.5 V to 5.5 V,	I_{OH} = −0.4 mA		$V_{CC}-2$			V
	Q or $\overline{Q}$	V_{CC} = 4.5 V,	I_{OH} = −2.6 mA		2.4	3.2		
V_{OL}	D	V_{CC} = 4.5 V,	I_{OL} = 4 mA			0.25	0.4	V
		V_{CC} = 4.5 V,	I_{OL} = 8 mA			0.35	0.5	
	Q or $\overline{Q}$	V_{CC} = 4.5 V,	I_{OL} = 12 mA			0.25	0.4	
		V_{CC} = 4.5 V,	I_{OL} = 24 mA			0.35	0.5	
I_I	$\overline{OERB}$, C	V_{CC} = 5.5 V,	V_I = 7 V				0.1	mA
	D inputs	V_{CC} = 5.5 V,	V_I = 5.5 V				0.1	
I_{IH}	$\overline{OERB}$, C	V_{CC} = 5.5 V,	V_I = 2.7 V				20	μA
	D inputs‡						20	
I_{IL}	$\overline{OERB}$, C	V_{CC} = 5.5 V,	V_I = 0.4 V				−0.1	mA
	D inputs‡						−0.1	
I_O§		V_{CC} = 5.5 V,	V_O = 2.25 V		−30		−112	mA
I_{CC}	'ALS990	V_{CC} = 5.5 V, $\overline{OERB}$ high		Q outputs high		27	50	mA
				Q outputs low		40	70	
	'ALS991			$\overline{Q}$ outputs high		25	45	
				$\overline{Q}$ outputs low		45	75	

†All typical values are at V_{CC} = 5 V, T_A = 25°C.
‡For I/O ports, the parameters I_{IH} and I_{IL} include the off-state output current.
§The output conditions have been chosen to produce a current that closely approximates one half the true short-circuit output current, I_{OS}.

'ALS990 switching characteristics

PARAMETER	FROM (INPUT)	TO (OUTPUT)	V_{CC} = 5 V, C_L = 50 pF, T_A = 25°C, See Figures 1 and 2			V_{CC} = 4.5 V to 5.5 V, C_L = 50 pF, T_A = 0°C to 70°C, See Figures 1 and 2		UNIT
			MIN	TYP	MAX	MIN	MAX	
t_{PLH}	D	Q		8	14	4	17	ns
t_{PHL}				11	22	5	24	
t_{PLH}	C	Q		13	22	6	26	ns
t_{PHL}				16	23	8	26	
t_{en}	$\overline{OERB}$	D		12	18	4	21	ns
t_{dis}				10	18	4	19	

$t_{en} = t_{PZL}$ or t_{PZH}
$t_{dis} = t_{PLZ}$ or t_{PHZ}

'ALS991 switching characteristics

PARAMETER	FROM (INPUT)	TO (OUTPUT)	V_{CC} = 5 V, C_L = 50 pF, T_A = 25°C, See Figures 1 and 2			V_{CC} = 4.5 V to 5.5 V, C_L = 50 pF, T_A = 0°C to 70°C, See Figures 1 and 2		UNIT
			MIN	TYP	MAX	MIN	MAX	
t_{PLH}	D	$\overline{Q}$		12	15	4	20	ns
t_{PHL}				9	12	4	15	
t_{PLH}	C	$\overline{Q}$		17	21	9	28	ns
t_{PHL}				14	18	7	23	
t_{en}	$\overline{OERB}$	D		12	17	4	22	ns
t_{dis}				8	12	4	17	

$t_{en} = t_{PZL}$ or t_{PZH}
$t_{dis} = t_{PLZ}$ or t_{PHZ}

PARAMETER MEASUREMENT INFORMATION

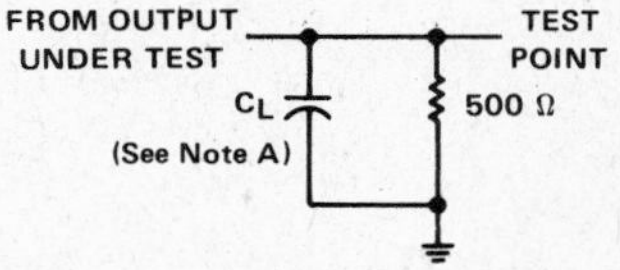
FROM OUTPUT
UNDER TEST
TEST
POINT
C_L
(See Note A)
500 Ω

LOAD CIRCUIT FOR
Q OR $\overline{Q}$ OUTPUTS

FIGURE 1

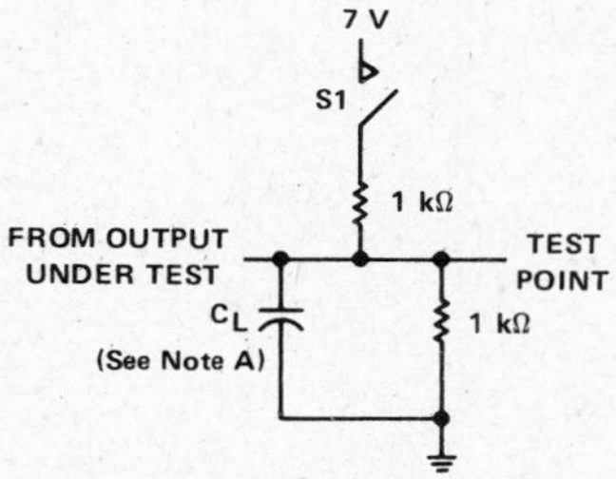
7 V
S1
1 kΩ
FROM OUTPUT
UNDER TEST
TEST
POINT
C_L
(See Note A)
1 kΩ

LOAD CIRCUIT FOR D OUTPUTS

FIGURE 2

NOTE A: C_L includes probe and jig capacitance.

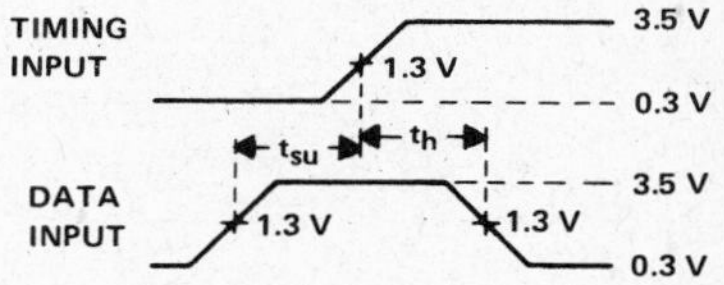
TIMING
INPUT
3.5 V
1.3 V
0.3 V
t_{su}
t_h
DATA
INPUT
3.5 V
1.3 V
1.3 V
0.3 V

VOLTAGE WAVEFORMS
SETUP AND HOLD TIMES

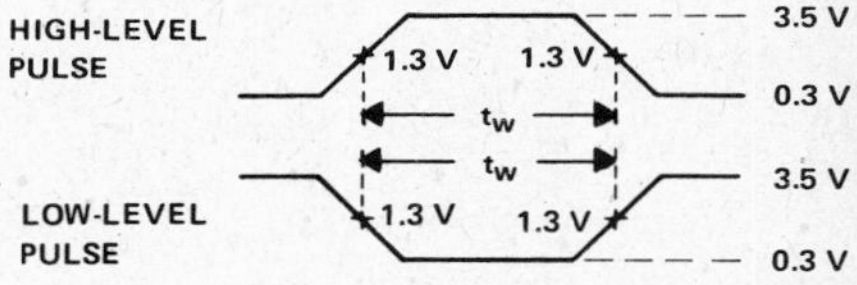
HIGH-LEVEL
PULSE
1.3 V
1.3 V
3.5 V
0.3 V
t_w
t_w
LOW-LEVEL
PULSE
1.3 V
1.3 V
3.5 V
0.3 V

VOLTAGE WAVEFORMS
PULSE WIDTHS

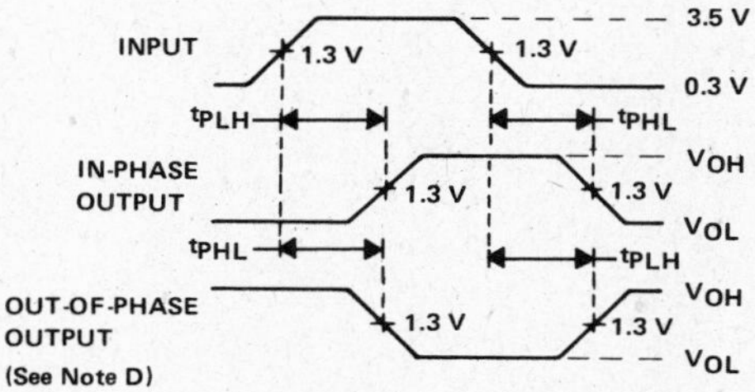
INPUT
1.3 V
1.3 V
3.5 V
0.3 V
t_{PLH}
t_{PHL}
IN-PHASE
OUTPUT
1.3 V
1.3 V
V_{OH}
V_{OL}
t_{PHL}
t_{PLH}
OUT-OF-PHASE
OUTPUT
(See Note D)
1.3 V
1.3 V
V_{OH}
V_{OL}

VOLTAGE WAVEFORMS
PROPAGATION DELAY TIMES

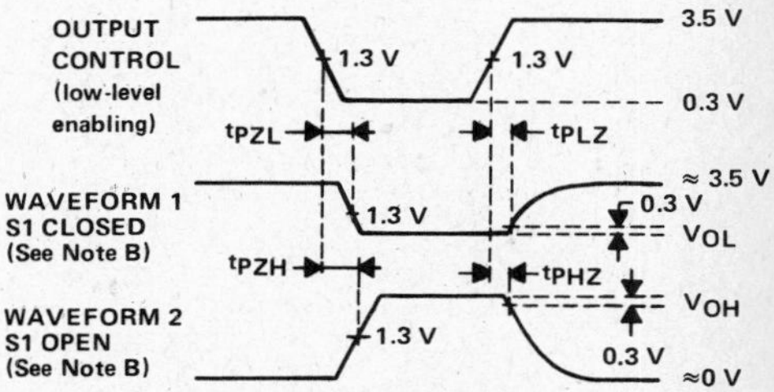
OUTPUT
CONTROL
(low-level
enabling)
1.3 V
1.3 V
3.5 V
0.3 V
t_{PZL}
t_{PLZ}
WAVEFORM 1
S1 CLOSED
(See Note B)
1.3 V
≈ 3.5 V
0.3 V
V_{OL}
t_{PZH}
t_{PHZ}
WAVEFORM 2
S1 OPEN
(See Note B)
1.3 V
V_{OH}
0.3 V
≈0 V

VOLTAGE WAVEFORMS
ENABLE AND DISABLE TIMES, THREE-STATE OUTPUTS

NOTES: B. Waveform 1 is for an output with internal conditions such that the output is low except when disabled by the output control. Waveform 2 is for an output with internal conditions such that the output is high except when disabled by the output control.
C. All input pulses have the following characteristics: PRR ≤ 1 MHz, $t_r = t_f = 2$ ns, duty cycle = 50%.
D. When measuring propagation delay times of 3-state outputs, switch S1 is open.

2
LSI Devices

9-BIT D-TYPE TRANSPARENT READ-BACK LATCHES WITH 3-STATE OUTPUTS

D2836, APRIL 1984—REVISED JANUARY 1986

- **3-State I/O-Type Read-Back Inputs**
- **Bus-Structured Pinout**
- **Choice of True or Inverting Logic**
  'ALS992 . . . True Outputs
  'ALS993 . . . Inverting Outputs
- **Designed with 9 Bits for Parity Applications**
- **Package Options Include Both Plastic and Ceramic Chip Carriers in Addition to Plastic and Ceramic DIPs**
- **Dependable Texas Instruments Quality and Reliability**

description

These 9-bit latches are designed specifically for storing the contents of the input data bus plus providing the capability of reading-back the stored data onto the input data bus. In addition, they provide a 3-state buffer-type output and are easily implemented in parity applications.

The nine latches of the 'ALS992 and 'ALS993 are transparent D-type. While the enable (C) is high, the Q outputs of the 'ALS992 will follow the data (D) inputs. For the 'ALS993, the $\overline{Q}$ outputs will provide the complement of what is applied to its data (D) inputs. On both devices, the Q or $\overline{Q}$ outputs will be in the 3-state condition when output enable $\overline{OEQ}$ is high.

Read-back is provided through the read-back control input ($\overline{OERB}$). When the control is taken low, the data present at the output of the data latches will be allowed to pass back onto the input data bus. When it is taken high, the output of the data latches will be isolated from the data (D) inputs. The read-back control does not affect the internal operation of the latches; however, precautions should be taken not to create a bus-conflict situation.

The SN74ALS992 and SN74ALS993 are characterized for operation from 0°C to 70°C.

SN74ALS992 . . . DW OR NT PACKAGE
(TOP VIEW)

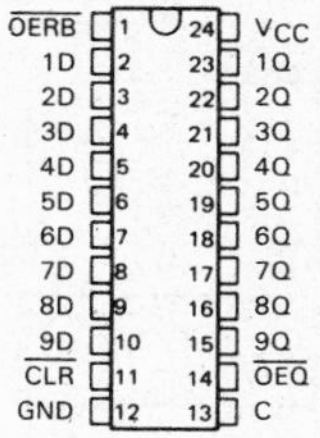
OERB 1 24 VCC
1D 2 23 1Q
2D 3 22 2Q
3D 4 21 3Q
4D 5 20 4Q
5D 6 19 5Q
6D 7 18 6Q
7D 8 17 7Q
8D 9 16 8Q
9D 10 15 9Q
CLR 11 14 OEQ
GND 12 13 C

SN74ALS992 . . . FN PACKAGE
(TOP VIEW)

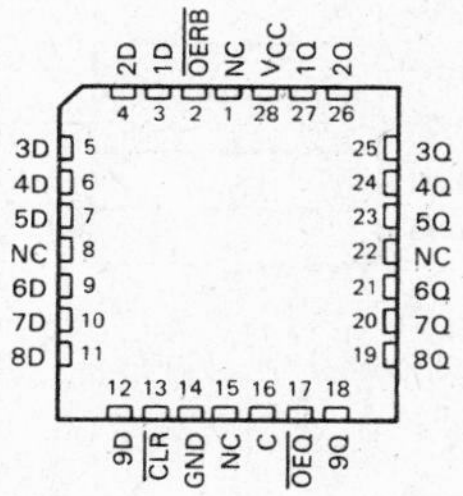
2D 1D OERB NC VCC 1Q 2Q
4 3 2 1 28 27 26
3D 5 25 3Q
4D 6 24 4Q
5D 7 23 5Q
NC 8 22 NC
6D 9 21 6Q
7D 10 20 7Q
8D 11 19 8Q
12 13 14 15 16 17 18
9D CLR GND NC C OEQ 9Q

SN74ALS993 . . . DW OR NT PACKAGE
(TOP VIEW)

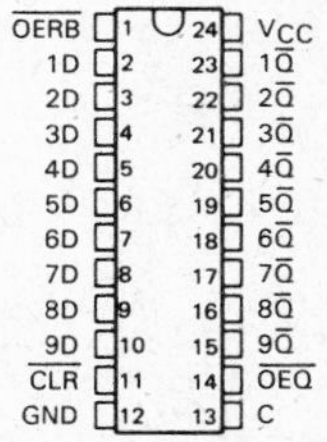
OERB 1 24 VCC
1D 2 23 1Q
2D 3 22 2Q
3D 4 21 3Q
4D 5 20 4Q
5D 6 19 5Q
6D 7 18 6Q
7D 8 17 7Q
8D 9 16 8Q
9D 10 15 9Q
CLR 11 14 OEQ
GND 12 13 C

SN74ALS993 . . . FN PACKAGE
(TOP VIEW)

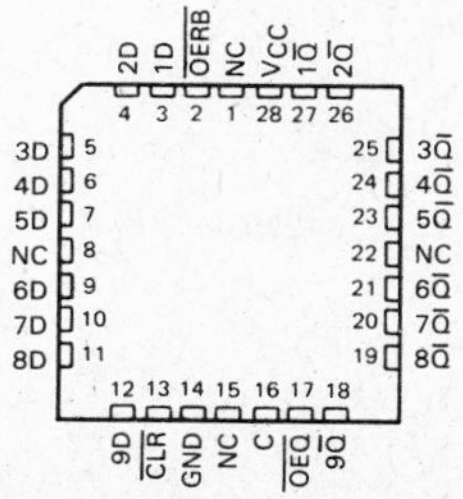
2D 1D OERB NC VCC 1Q 2Q
4 3 2 1 28 27 26
3D 5 25 3Q
4D 6 24 4Q
5D 7 23 5Q
NC 8 22 NC
6D 9 21 6Q
7D 10 20 7Q
8D 11 19 8Q
12 13 14 15 16 17 18
9D CLR GND NC C OEQ 9Q

NC—No internal connection

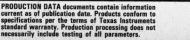

2
LSI Devices

TEXAS INSTRUMENTS
POST OFFICE BOX 225012 • DALLAS, TEXAS 75265

logic symbols†

'ALS992

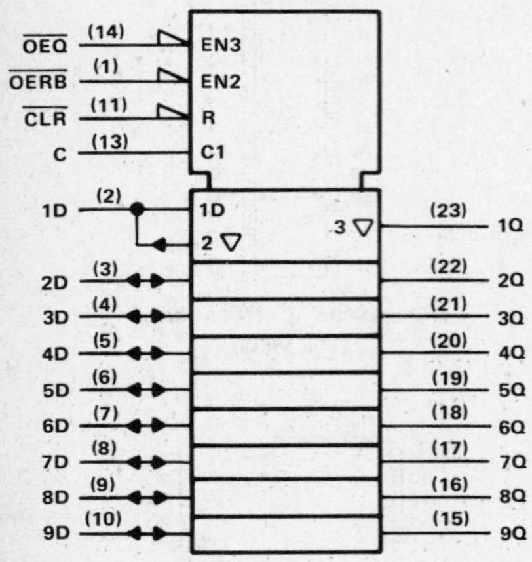
OEQ
(14)
EN3
OERB
(1)
EN2
CLR
(11)
R
C
(13)
C1
1D
(2)
1D
2
3
(23)
1Q
2D (3)
(22) 2Q
3D (4)
(21) 3Q
4D (5)
(20) 4Q
5D (6)
(19) 5Q
6D (7)
(18) 6Q
7D (8)
(17) 7Q
8D (9)
(16) 8Q
9D (10)
(15) 9Q

'ALS993

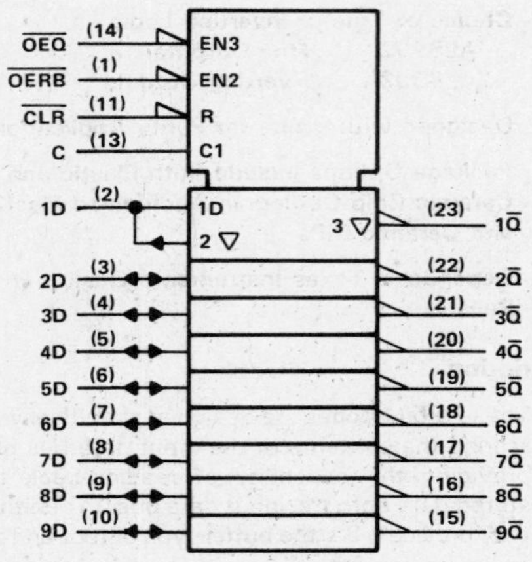
OEQ
(14)
EN3
OERB
(1)
EN2
CLR
(11)
R
C
(13)
C1
1D
(2)
1D
2
3
(23)
1Q̄
2D (3)
(22) 2Q̄
3D (4)
(21) 3Q̄
4D (5)
(20) 4Q̄
5D (6)
(19) 5Q̄
6D (7)
(18) 6Q̄
7D (8)
(17) 7Q̄
8D (9)
(16) 8Q̄
9D (10)
(15) 9Q̄

†These symbols are in accordance with ANSI/IEEE Std 91-1984 and IEC Publication 617-12.
Pin numbers are for DW and NT packages.

TEXAS INSTRUMENTS
POST OFFICE BOX 225012 • DALLAS, TEXAS 75265

logic diagrams (positive logic)

'ALS992

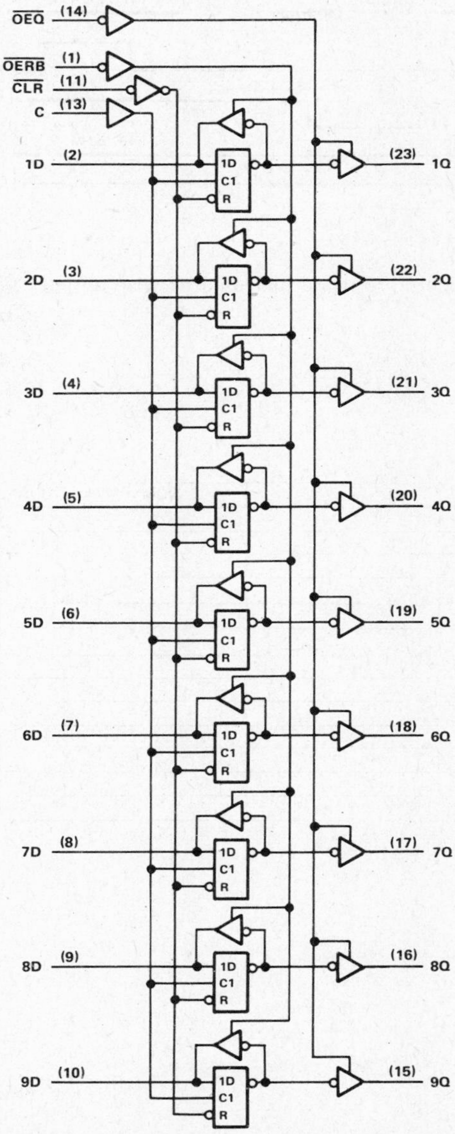
$\overline{OEQ}$ (14)
$\overline{OERB}$ (1)
$\overline{CLR}$ (11)
C (13)
1D (2)
2D (3)
3D (4)
4D (5)
5D (6)
6D (7)
7D (8)
8D (9)
9D (10)
1D
C1
R
(23) 1Q
(22) 2Q
(21) 3Q
(20) 4Q
(19) 5Q
(18) 6Q
(17) 7Q
(16) 8Q
(15) 9Q

'ALS993

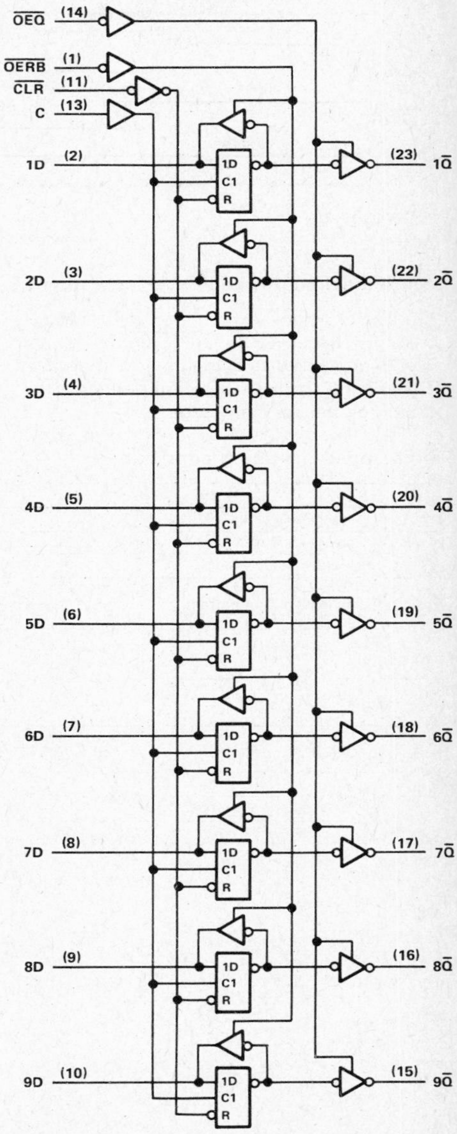
$\overline{OEQ}$ (14)
$\overline{OERB}$ (1)
$\overline{CLR}$ (11)
C (13)
1D (2)
2D (3)
3D (4)
4D (5)
5D (6)
6D (7)
7D (8)
8D (9)
9D (10)
1D
C1
R
(23) $1\overline{Q}$
(22) $2\overline{Q}$
(21) $3\overline{Q}$
(20) $4\overline{Q}$
(19) $5\overline{Q}$
(18) $6\overline{Q}$
(17) $7\overline{Q}$
(16) $8\overline{Q}$
(15) $9\overline{Q}$

Pin numbers are for DW and NT packages.

timing diagram

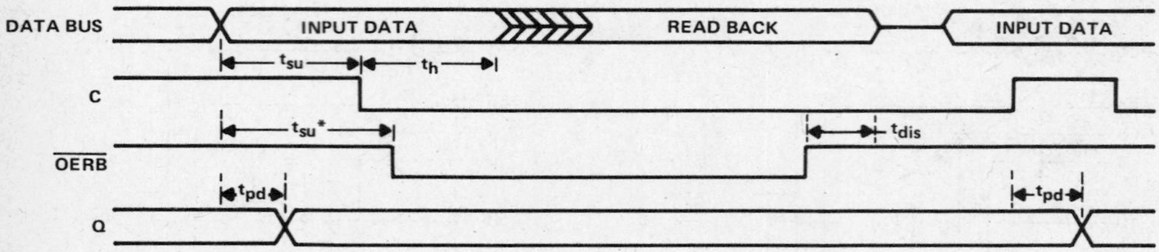
DATA BUS
INPUT DATA
READ BACK
INPUT DATA
t_{su}
t_h
C
t_{su}*
t_{dis}
$\overline{OERB}$
t_{pd}
t_{pd}
Q

$\overline{CLR}$ = H, $\overline{OEQ}$ = L

*This setup time ensures the readback circuit will not create a conflict on the input data bus.

absolute maximum ratings over operating free-air temperature range (unless otherwise noted)

Supply voltage, V_{CC}	7 V
Input voltage, ($\overline{OERB}$, $\overline{OE}$, $\overline{CLR}$, and C inputs)	7 V
Voltage applied to D inputs and to disabled 3-state outputs	5.5 V
Operating free-air temperature range	0°C to 70°C
Storage temperature range	−65°C to 150°C

recommended operating conditions

			MIN	NOM	MAX	UNIT
V_{CC}	Supply voltage		4.5	5	5.5	V
V_{IH}	High-level input voltage		2			V
V_{IL}	Low-level input voltage				0.8	V
I_{OH}	High-level output current	Q or $\overline{Q}$			−2.6	mA
		D			−0.4	
I_{OL}	Low-level output current	Q or $\overline{Q}$			24	mA
		D			8	
t_w	Pulse duration	Enable C high	10			ns
		$\overline{CLR}$ low	10			
t_{su}	Setup time	Data before C↓	10			ns
		Data before $\overline{OERB}$↓	10			
t_h	Hold time	Data after C↓	5			ns
T_A	Operating free-air temperature		0		70	°C

TEXAS INSTRUMENTS
POST OFFICE BOX 225012 • DALLAS, TEXAS 75265

electrical characteristics over recommended operating free-air temperature range (unless otherwise noted)

PARAMETER		TEST CONDITIONS		MIN	TYP†	MAX	UNIT
V_{IK}		V_{CC} = 4.5 V,	I_I = −18 mA			−1.2	V
V_{OH}	All outputs	V_{CC} = 4.5 V to 5.5 V,	I_{OH} = −0.4 mA	V_{CC}−2			V
	Q or Q	V_{CC} = 4.5 V,	I_{OH} = −2.6 mA	2.4	3.2		
V_{OL}	D	V_{CC} = 4.5 V,	I_{OL} = 4 mA		0.25	0.4	V
		V_{CC} = 4.5 V,	I_{OL} = 8 mA		0.35	0.5	
	Q or $\overline{Q}$	V_{CC} = 4.5 V,	I_{OL} = 12 mA		0.25	0.4	
		V_{CC} = 4.5 V,	I_{OL} = 24 mA		0.35	0.5	
I_{OZH}	Q or $\overline{Q}$	V_{CC} = 5.5 V,	V_O = 2.7 V			20	μA
I_{OZL}		V_{CC} = 5.5 V,	V_O = 0.4 V			−20	
I_I	D inputs	V_{CC} = 5.5 V,	V_I = 5.5 V			0.1	mA
	All other	V_{CC} = 5.5 V,	V_I = 7 V			0.1	
I_{IH}	D inputs‡	V_{CC} = 5.5 V,	V_I = 2.7 V			20	μA
	All other					20	
I_{IL}	D inputs‡	V_{CC} = 5.5 V,	V_I = 0.4 V			−0.1	mA
	All other					−0.1	
I_O§		V_{CC} = 5.5 V,	V_O = 2.25 V	−30		−112	mA
I_{CC}	'ALS992	V_{CC} = 5.5 V, $\overline{OERB}$ high	Q outputs high		30	50	mA
			Q outputs low		50	80	
			Q outputs disabled		35	55	
	'ALS993	V_{CC} = 5.5 V, $\overline{OERB}$ high	$\overline{Q}$ outputs high		30	50	mA
			$\overline{Q}$ outputs low		52	82	
			$\overline{Q}$outputs disabled		40	60	

† All typical values are at V_{CC} = 5 V, T_A = 25°C.
‡ For I/O ports, the parameters I_{IH} and I_{IL} include the off-state output current.
§ The output conditions have been chosen to produce a current that closely approximates one half the true short-circuit output current, I_{OS}.

'ALS992 switching characteristics (see Figure 1)

PARAMETER	FROM (INPUT)	TO (OUTPUT)	V_{CC} = 5 V, C_L = 50 pF, T_A = 25°C			V_{CC} = 4.5 V to 5.5 V, C_L = 50 pF, T_A = 0°C to 70°C		UNIT
			MIN	TYP	MAX	MIN	MAX	
t_{PLH}	D	Q		7	10	3	14	ns
t_{PHL}				9	13	4	16	
t_{PLH}	C	Q		12	15	6	20	ns
t_{PHL}				15	19	8	25	
t_{PHL}	$\overline{CLR}$	Q		12	16	6	20	ns
t_{PHL}		D		15	22	8	26	
t_{en}	$\overline{OERB}$	D		11	17	4	21	ns
t_{dis}				6	11	2	14	
t_{en}	$\overline{OEQ}$	Q		11	16	4	18	ns
t_{dis}				6	10	1	14	

'ALS993 switching characteristics (see Figure 1)

PARAMETER	FROM (INPUT)	TO (OUTPUT)	V_{CC} = 5 V, C_L = 50 pF, T_A = 25°C			V_{CC} = 4.5 V to 5.5 V, C_L = 50 pF, T_A = 0°C to 70°C		UNIT
			MIN	TYP	MAX	MIN	MAX	
t_{PLH}	D	$\overline{Q}$		11	14	6	20	ns
t_{PHL}				8	11	4	15	
t_{PLH}	C	$\overline{Q}$		16	20	9	28	ns
t_{PHL}				13	16	7	22	
t_{PLH}	$\overline{CLR}$	$\overline{Q}$		10	13	5	17	ns
t_{PLH}		D		15	22	8	26	
t_{en}	$\overline{OERB}$	D		11	17	4	21	ns
t_{dis}				6	11	2	14	
t_{en}	$\overline{OEQ}$	$\overline{Q}$		11	16	4	20	ns
t_{dis}				6	10	1	12	

t_{en} = t_{PZH} or t_{PZL}
t_{dis} = t_{PHZ} or t_{PLZ}

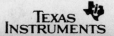

TEXAS INSTRUMENTS
POST OFFICE BOX 225012 • DALLAS, TEXAS 75265

PARAMETER MEASUREMENT INFORMATION

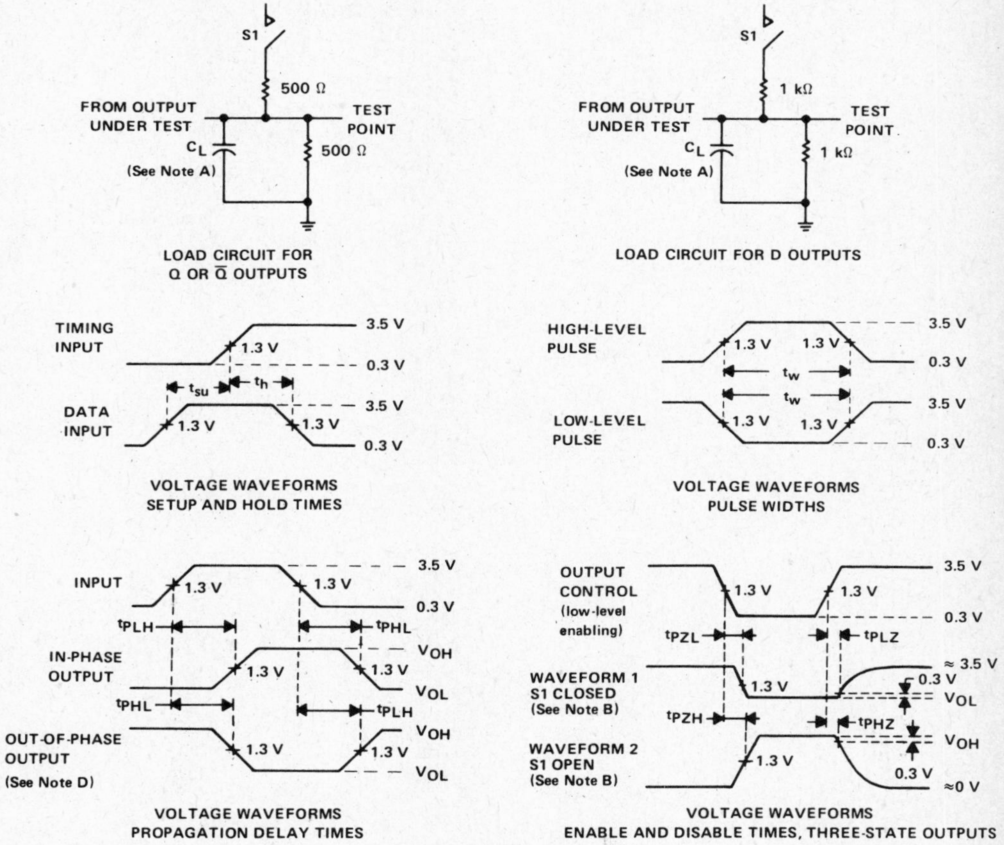
7 V
S1
500 Ω
FROM OUTPUT UNDER TEST
TEST POINT
C_L (See Note A)
500 Ω
LOAD CIRCUIT FOR Q OR Q̄ OUTPUTS
7 V
S1
1 kΩ
FROM OUTPUT UNDER TEST
TEST POINT
C_L (See Note A)
1 kΩ
LOAD CIRCUIT FOR D OUTPUTS
TIMING INPUT
DATA INPUT
1.3 V
3.5 V
0.3 V
t_su
t_h
VOLTAGE WAVEFORMS SETUP AND HOLD TIMES
HIGH-LEVEL PULSE
LOW-LEVEL PULSE
t_w
VOLTAGE WAVEFORMS PULSE WIDTHS
INPUT
IN-PHASE OUTPUT
OUT-OF-PHASE OUTPUT (See Note D)
t_PLH
t_PHL
V_OH
V_OL
VOLTAGE WAVEFORMS PROPAGATION DELAY TIMES
OUTPUT CONTROL (low-level enabling)
WAVEFORM 1 S1 CLOSED (See Note B)
WAVEFORM 2 S1 OPEN (See Note B)
t_PZL
t_PLZ
t_PZH
t_PHZ
≈ 3.5 V
≈0 V
VOLTAGE WAVEFORMS ENABLE AND DISABLE TIMES, THREE-STATE OUTPUTS

NOTES: A. C_L includes probe and jig capacitance.

B. Waveform 1 is for an output with internal conditions such that the output is low except when disabled by the output control. Waveform 2 is for an output with internal conditions such that the output is high except when disabled by the output control.

C. All input pulses have the following characteristics: PRR ≤ 1 MHz, $t_r = t_f = 2$ ns, duty cycle = 50%.

D. When measuring propagation delay times of 3-state outputs, switch S1 is open.

FIGURE 1

SN74ALS994, SN74ALS995
10-BIT D-TYPE TRANSPARENT READ-BACK LATCHES

D2856, OCTOBER 1984—REVISED JANUARY 1986

- **3-State I/O-Type Read-Back Inputs**
- **Bus-Structured Pinout**
- **Choice of True or Inverting Logic**
  'ALS994 . . . True Outputs
  'ALS995 . . . Inverting Outputs
- **Package Options Include Both Plastic and Ceramic Chip Carriers in Addition to Plastic and Ceramic DIPs**
- **Dependable Texas Instruments Quality and Reliability**

SN74ALS994 . . . DW OR NT PACKAGE
(TOP VIEW)

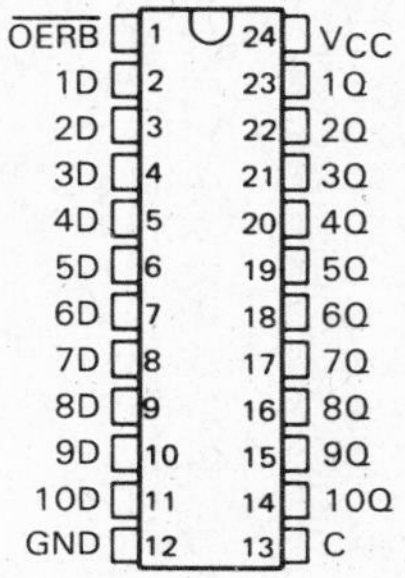
OERB 1
1D 2
2D 3
3D 4
4D 5
5D 6
6D 7
7D 8
8D 9
9D 10
10D 11
GND 12
24 VCC
23 1Q
22 2Q
21 3Q
20 4Q
19 5Q
18 6Q
17 7Q
16 8Q
15 9Q
14 10Q
13 C

SN74ALS994 . . . FN PACKAGE
(TOP VIEW)

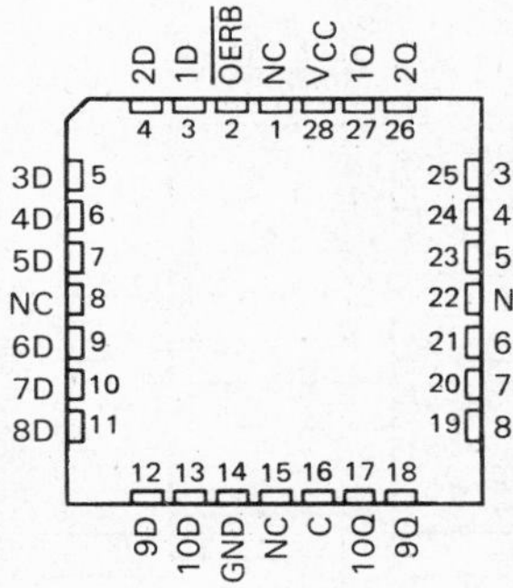
2D 1D OERB NC VCC 1Q 2Q
4 3 2 1 28 27 26
3D 5
4D 6
5D 7
NC 8
6D 9
7D 10
8D 11
25 3Q
24 4Q
23 5Q
22 NC
21 6Q
20 7Q
19 8Q
12 13 14 15 16 17 18
9D 10D GND NC C 10Q 9Q

NC—No internal connection.

description

These 10-bit latches are designed specifically for storing the contents of the input data bus plus providing the capability of reading-back the stored data onto the input data bus.

The ten latches of the 'ALS994 and 'ALS995 are transparent D-type. While the enable (C) is high, the Q outputs of the 'ALS994 will follow the data (D) inputs. For the 'ALS995, the Q outputs will provide the inverse of what is applied to its data (D) inputs.

Read-back is provided through the read-back control input ($\overline{\text{OERB}}$). When the control is taken low, the data present at the output of the data latches will be allowed to pass back onto the input data bus. When it is taken high, the output of the data latches will be isolated from the data (D) inputs. The read-back control does not affect the internal operation of the latches; however, precautions should be taken not to create a bus-conflict situation.

The SN74ALS994 and SN74ALS995 are characterized for operation from 0°C to 70°C.

SN74ALS995 . . . DW OR NT PACKAGE
(TOP VIEW)

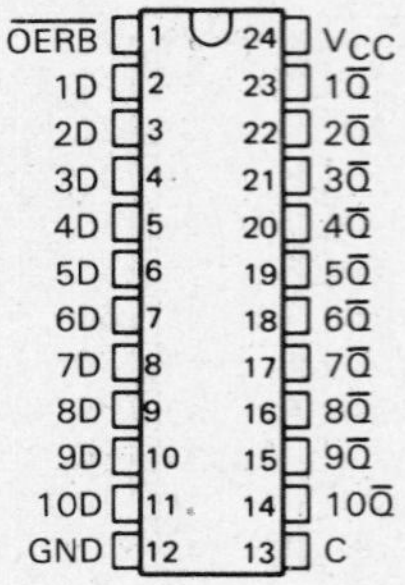
OERB 1
1D 2
2D 3
3D 4
4D 5
5D 6
6D 7
7D 8
8D 9
9D 10
10D 11
GND 12
24 VCC
23 1Q̄
22 2Q̄
21 3Q̄
20 4Q̄
19 5Q̄
18 6Q̄
17 7Q̄
16 8Q̄
15 9Q̄
14 10Q̄
13 C

NC—No internal connection

SN74ALS995 . . . FN PACKAGE
(TOP VIEW)

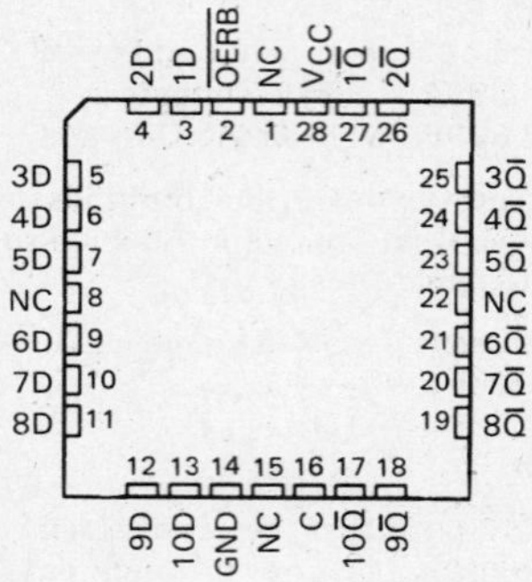
2D 4
1D 3
OERB 2
NC 1
VCC 28
1Q̄ 27
2Q̄ 26
3D 5
4D 6
5D 7
NC 8
6D 9
7D 10
8D 11
25 3Q̄
24 4Q̄
23 5Q̄
22 NC
21 6Q̄
20 7Q̄
19 8Q̄
12 9D
13 10D
14 GND
15 NC
16 C
17 10Q̄
18 9Q̄

logic symbols†

'ALS994

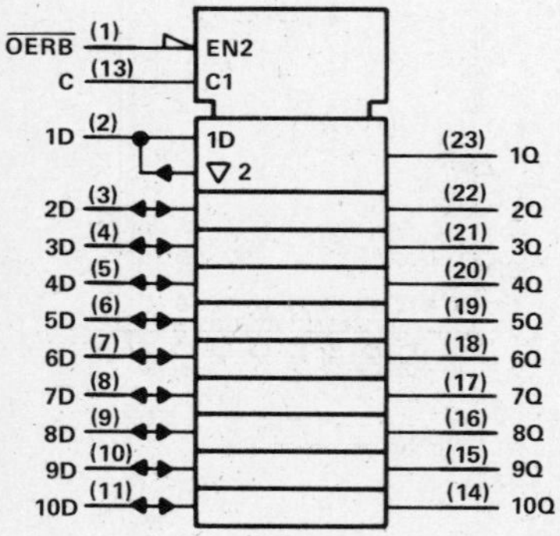
OERB (1) EN2
C (13) C1
1D (2) 1D
▽2
(23) 1Q
2D (3)
(22) 2Q
3D (4)
(21) 3Q
4D (5)
(20) 4Q
5D (6)
(19) 5Q
6D (7)
(18) 6Q
7D (8)
(17) 7Q
8D (9)
(16) 8Q
9D (10)
(15) 9Q
10D (11)
(14) 10Q

'ALS995

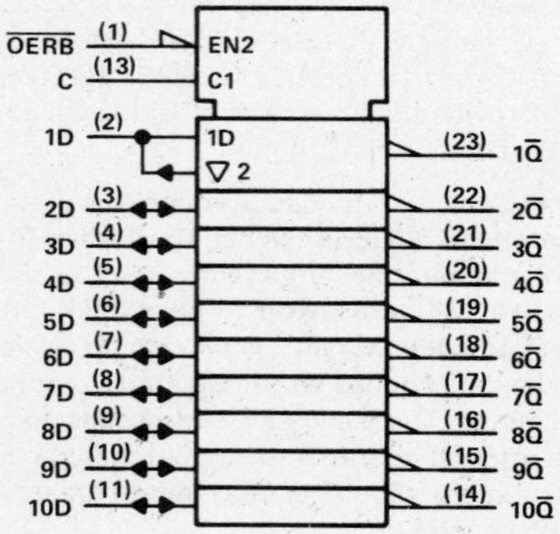
OERB (1) EN2
C (13) C1
1D (2) 1D
▽2
(23) 1Q̄
2D (3)
(22) 2Q̄
3D (4)
(21) 3Q̄
4D (5)
(20) 4Q̄
5D (6)
(19) 5Q̄
6D (7)
(18) 6Q̄
7D (8)
(17) 7Q̄
8D (9)
(16) 8Q̄
9D (10)
(15) 9Q̄
10D (11)
(14) 10Q̄

†These symbols are in accordance with ANSI/IEEE Std 91-1984 and IEC Publication 617-12.
Pin numbers shown are for DW and NT packages.

TEXAS INSTRUMENTS
POST OFFICE BOX 225012 • DALLAS, TEXAS 75265

logic diagrams (positive logic)

'ALS994

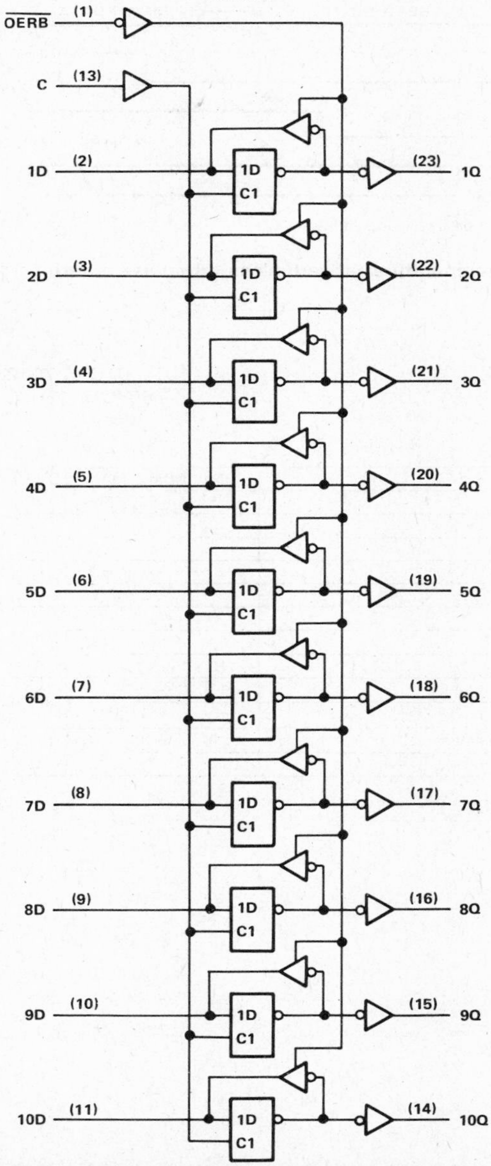
OERB
(1)
C
(13)
1D (2) 1D C1 (23) 1Q
2D (3) 1D C1 (22) 2Q
3D (4) 1D C1 (21) 3Q
4D (5) 1D C1 (20) 4Q
5D (6) 1D C1 (19) 5Q
6D (7) 1D C1 (18) 6Q
7D (8) 1D C1 (17) 7Q
8D (9) 1D C1 (16) 8Q
9D (10) 1D C1 (15) 9Q
10D (11) 1D C1 (14) 10Q

'ALS995

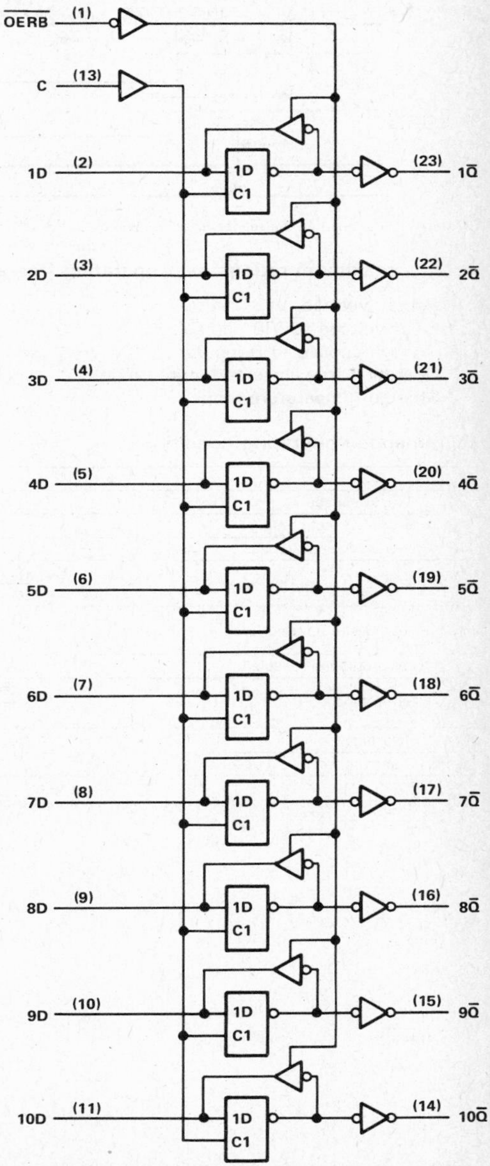
OERB
(1)
C
(13)
1D (2) 1D C1 (23) 1Q̄
2D (3) 1D C1 (22) 2Q̄
3D (4) 1D C1 (21) 3Q̄
4D (5) 1D C1 (20) 4Q̄
5D (6) 1D C1 (19) 5Q̄
6D (7) 1D C1 (18) 6Q̄
7D (8) 1D C1 (17) 7Q̄
8D (9) 1D C1 (16) 8Q̄
9D (10) 1D C1 (15) 9Q̄
10D (11) 1D C1 (14) 10Q̄

Pin numbers shown are for DW and NT packages.

2
LSI Devices

timing diagram

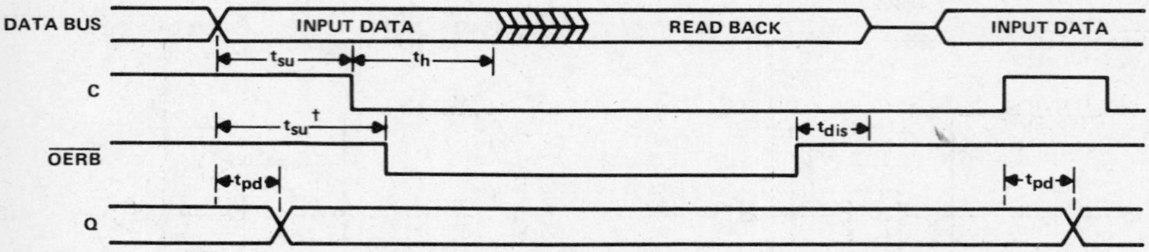
DATA BUS
INPUT DATA
READ BACK
INPUT DATA
C
OERB
Q
tsu
th
tsu†
tdis
tpd
tpd

†This setup time ensures the readback circuit will not create a conflict on the input data bus.

absolute maximum ratings over operating free-air temperature range (unless otherwise noted)

Supply voltage, V_{CC} .... 7 V
Input voltage ($\overline{OERB}$ and C) .... 7 V
Voltage applied to D inputs .... 5.5 V
Operating free-air temperature range .... 0°C to 70°C
Storage temperature range .... −65°C to 150°C

recommended operating conditions

			MIN	NOM	MAX	UNIT
V_{CC}	Supply voltage		4.5	5	5.5	V
V_{IH}	High-level input voltage		2			V
V_{IL}	Low-level input voltage				0.8	V
I_{OH}	High-level output current	Q or $\overline{Q}$			−2.6	mA
		D			−0.4	
I_{OL}	Low-level output current	Q or $\overline{Q}$			24	mA
		D			8	
t_w	Pulse duration, enable C high		10			ns
t_{su}	Setup time	Data before C↓	10			ns
		Data before $\overline{OERB}$↓†	10			
t_h	Hold time	Input data after C↓	5			ns
T_A	Operating free-air temperature		0		70	°C

† This setup time ensures the readback circuit will not create a conflict on the input data bus.

2
LSI Devices

electrical characteristics over recommended operating free-air temperature range (unless otherwise noted)

PARAMETER		TEST CONDITIONS			MIN	TYP†	MAX	UNIT
V_{IK}		V_{CC} = 4.5 V,	I_I = −18 mA				−1.2	V
V_{OH}	All outputs	V_{CC} = 4.5 V to 5 5 V,	I_{OH} = −0.4 mA		$V_{CC}-2$			V
	Q or $\overline{Q}$	V_{CC} = 4.5 V,	I_{OH} = −2.6 mA		2.4	3.2		
V_{OL}	D	V_{CC} = 4.5 V,	I_{OL} = 4 mA			0.25	0.4	V
		V_{CC} = 4.5 V,	I_{OL} = 8 mA			0.35	0.5	
	Q or $\overline{Q}$	V_{CC} = 4.5 V,	I_{OL} = 12 mA			0.25	0.4	
		V_{CC} = 4.5 V,	I_{OL} = 24 mA			0.35	0.5	
I_I	$\overline{OERB}$, C	V_{CC} = 5.5 V,	V_I = 7 V				0.1	mA
	D inputs	V_{CC} = 5.5 V,	V_I = 5.5 V				0.1	
I_{IH}	$\overline{OERB}$, C	V_{CC} = 5.5 V,	V_I = 2.7 V				20	μA
	D inputs‡						20	
I_{IL}	$\overline{OERB}$, C	V_{CC} = 5.5 V,	V_I = 0.4 V				−0.1	mA
	D inputs‡						−0.1	
I_O§		V_{CC} = 5.5 V,	V_O = 2.25 V		−30		−112	mA
I_{CC}	'ALS994	V_{CC} = 5.5 V, $\overline{OERB}$ high		Q outputs high		30	50	mA
				Q outputs low		52	82	
	'ALS995			$\overline{Q}$ outputs high		30	50	
				$\overline{Q}$ outputs low		55	85	

† All typical values are at V_{CC} = 5 V, T_A = 25°C.
‡ For I/O ports, the parameters I_{IH} and I_{IL} include the off-state output current.
§ The output conditions have been chosen to produce a current that closely approximates one-half the true short-circuit output current, I_{OS}.

2

LSI Devices

'ALS994 switching characteristics (see Figure 1)

PARAMETER	FROM (INPUT)	TO (OUTPUT)	V_{CC} = 5 V, C_L = 50 pF, T_A = 25°C			V_{CC} = 4.5 V to 5.5 V, C_L = 50 pF, T_A = 0°C to 70°C		UNIT
			MIN	TYP	MAX	MIN	MAX	
t_{PLH}	D	Q		7	10	3	14	ns
t_{PHL}				11	15	4	18	
t_{PLH}	C	Q		12	16	6	21	ns
t_{PHL}				16	21	8	27	
t_{en}	$\overline{OERB}$	D		11	17	4	21	ns
t_{dis}				9	13	2	16	

'ALS995 switching characteristics (see Figure 1)

PARAMETER	FROM (INPUT)	TO (OUTPUT)	V_{CC} = 5 V, C_L = 50 pF, T_A = 25°C			V_{CC} = 4.5 V to 5.5 V, C_L = 50 pF, T_A = 0°C to 70°C		UNIT
			MIN	TYP	MAX	MIN	MAX	
t_{PLH}	D	$\overline{Q}$		12	16	6	20	ns
t_{PHL}				9	12	4	15	
t_{PLH}	C	$\overline{Q}$		17	23	9	28	ns
t_{PHL}				14	19	7	22	
t_{en}	$\overline{OERB}$	D		12	18	4	21	ns
t_{dis}				8	12	2	15	

t_{en} = t_{PZH} or t_{PZL}
t_{dis} = t_{PHZ} or t_{PLZ}

TEXAS INSTRUMENTS
POST OFFICE BOX 225012 • DALLAS, TEXAS 75265

PARAMETER MEASUREMENT INFORMATION

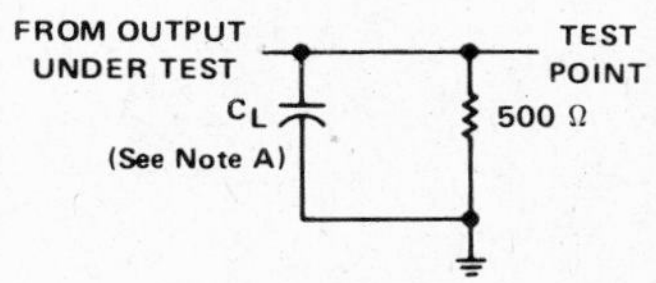
FROM OUTPUT
UNDER TEST
TEST
POINT
C_L
(See Note A)
500 Ω

LOAD CIRCUIT FOR
Q OR $\overline{Q}$ OUTPUTS

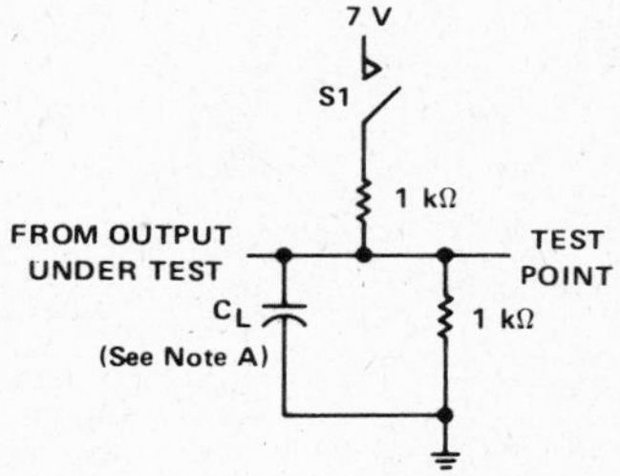
7 V
S1
1 kΩ
FROM OUTPUT
UNDER TEST
TEST
POINT
C_L
(See Note A)
1 kΩ

LOAD CIRCUIT FOR D OUTPUTS

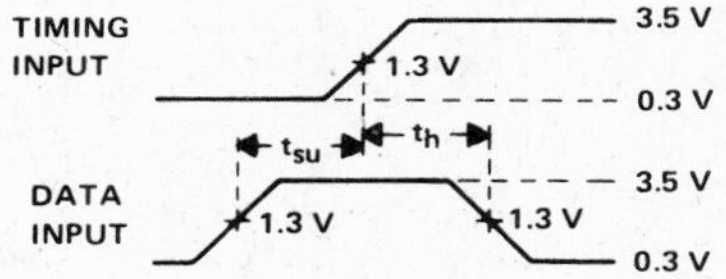
TIMING
INPUT
1.3 V
3.5 V
0.3 V
t_{su}
t_h
DATA
INPUT
1.3 V
1.3 V
3.5 V
0.3 V

VOLTAGE WAVEFORMS
SETUP AND HOLD TIMES

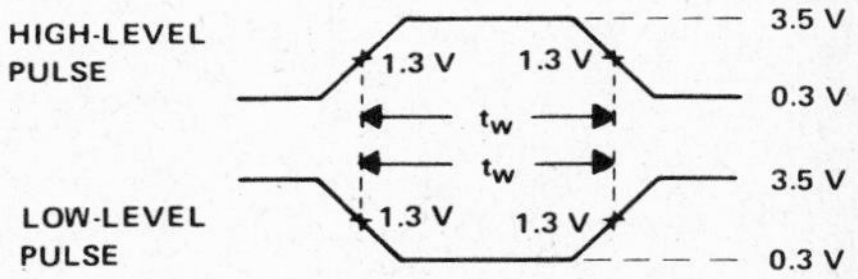
HIGH-LEVEL
PULSE
1.3 V
1.3 V
3.5 V
0.3 V
t_w
t_w
LOW-LEVEL
PULSE
1.3 V
1.3 V
3.5 V
0.3 V

VOLTAGE WAVEFORMS
PULSE WIDTHS

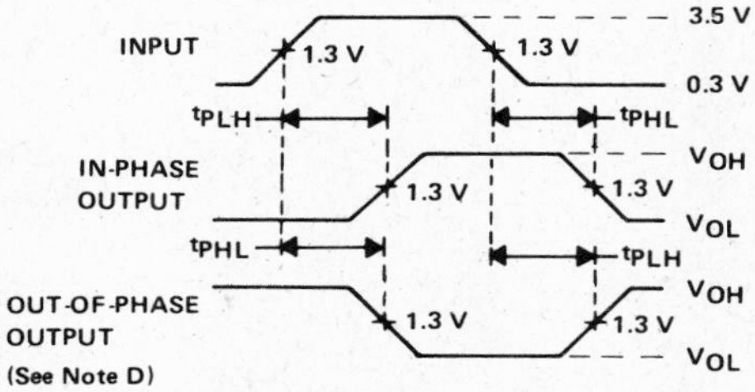
INPUT
1.3 V
1.3 V
3.5 V
0.3 V
t_{PLH}
t_{PHL}
IN-PHASE
OUTPUT
1.3 V
1.3 V
V_{OH}
V_{OL}
t_{PHL}
t_{PLH}
OUT-OF-PHASE
OUTPUT
(See Note D)
1.3 V
1.3 V
V_{OH}
V_{OL}

VOLTAGE WAVEFORMS
PROPAGATION DELAY TIMES

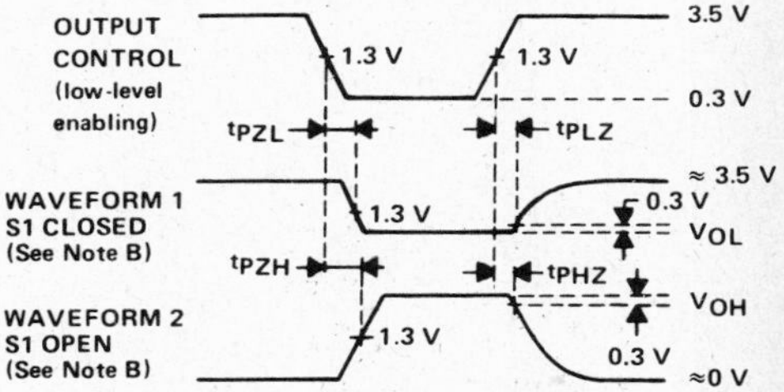
OUTPUT
CONTROL
(low-level
enabling)
1.3 V
1.3 V
3.5 V
0.3 V
t_{PZL}
t_{PLZ}
WAVEFORM 1
S1 CLOSED
(See Note B)
1.3 V
≈ 3.5 V
0.3 V
V_{OL}
t_{PZH}
t_{PHZ}
WAVEFORM 2
S1 OPEN
(See Note B)
1.3 V
V_{OH}
0.3 V
≈0 V

VOLTAGE WAVEFORMS
ENABLE AND DISABLE TIMES, THREE-STATE OUTPUTS

NOTES: A. C_L includes probe and jig capacitance.
B. Waveform 1 is for an output with internal conditions such that the output is low except when disabled by the output control. Waveform 2 is for an output with internal conditions such that the output is high except when disabled by the output control.
C. All input pulses have the following characteristics: PRR ≤ 1 MHz, $t_r = t_f = 2$ ns, duty cycle = 50%.
D. When measuring propagation delay times of 3-state outputs, switch S1 is open.

FIGURE 1

2
LSI Devices

SN74ALS996
8-BIT D-TYPE EDGE-TRIGGERED READ-BACK LATCHES

D2854, OCTOBER 1984—REVISED JANUARY 1986

- **3-State I/O-Type Read-Back Inputs**
- **Bus-Structured Pinout**
- **T/$\overline{C}$ Determines True or Complementary Data at Q Outputs**
- **Package Options Include Both Plastic and Ceramic Chip Carriers in Addition to Plastic and Ceramic DIPs**
- **Dependable Texas Instruments Quality and Reliability**

DW OR NT PACKAGE
(TOP VIEW)

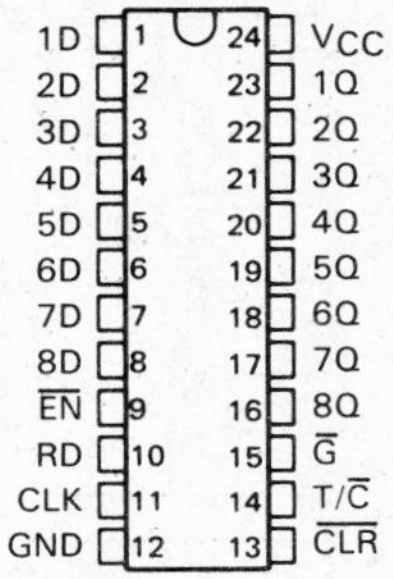
1D 1
2D 2
3D 3
4D 4
5D 5
6D 6
7D 7
8D 8
EN 9
RD 10
CLK 11
GND 12
24 VCC
23 1Q
22 2Q
21 3Q
20 4Q
19 5Q
18 6Q
17 7Q
16 8Q
15 G
14 T/C
13 CLR

FN PACKAGE
(TOP VIEW)

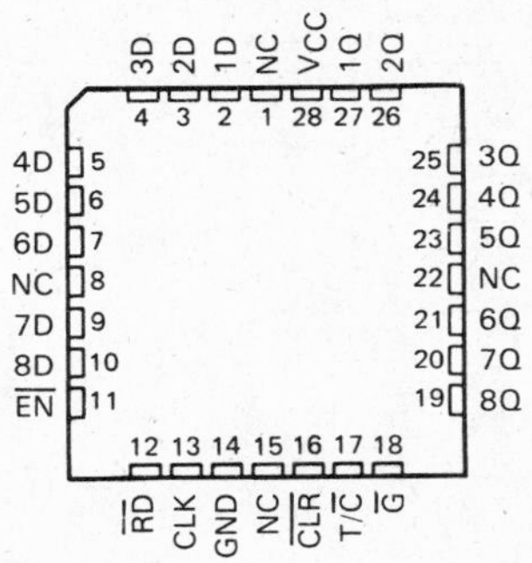
3D 2D 1D NC VCC 1Q 2Q
4 3 2 1 28 27 26
4D 5
5D 6
6D 7
NC 8
7D 9
8D 10
EN 11
25 3Q
24 4Q
23 5Q
22 NC
21 6Q
20 7Q
19 8Q
12 13 14 15 16 17 18
RD CLK GND NC CLR T/C G

NC—No internal connection.

description

These 8-bit registers are designed specifically for storing the contents of the input data bus plus providing the capability of reading-back the stored data onto that bus. The Q outputs are designed with bus-driving capability.

The edge-triggered flip-flops enter the data on the low-to-high transition of the clock (CLK) when enable ($\overline{EN}$) is low. Data can be read-back onto the data inputs by taking the read input ($\overline{RD}$) low, in addition to having $\overline{EN}$ low. Whenever $\overline{EN}$ is high, both the read-back and write modes are disabled. Transitions on $\overline{EN}$ should only be made with CLK high in order to prevent false clocking.

The polarity of the Q outputs can be controlled by the polarity input T/$\overline{C}$. When T/$\overline{C}$ is high, Q will be the same as is stored in the flip-flops. When T/$\overline{C}$ is low, the output data will be inverted. The Q outputs can be placed in a high-impedance state by taking the output control ($\overline{G}$) high. The output control $\overline{G}$ does not affect the internal operations of the register. Old data can be retained or new data can be entered while the outputs are off.

A low level at the clear input ($\overline{CLR}$) resets the internal registers low. The clear function is asynchronous and overrides all other register functions.

The -1 version of the SN74ALS996 is identical to the standard version except that the recommended maximum I_{OL} is increased to 48 milliamperes.

The SN74ALS996 is characterized for operation from 0°C to 70°C.

logic symbol†

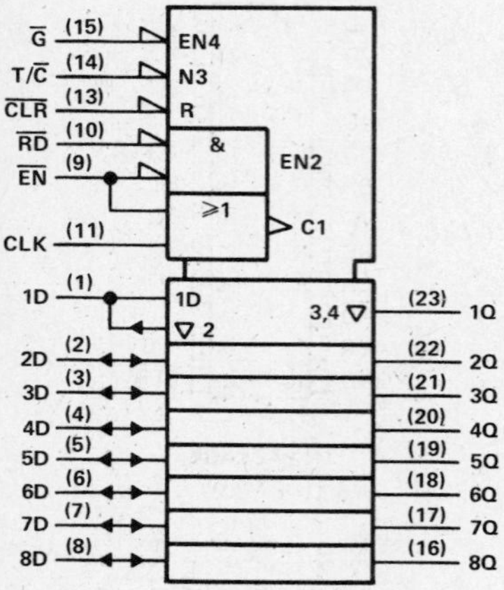
G̅ (15)
T/C̅ (14)
C̅L̅R̅ (13)
R̅D̅ (10)
E̅N̅ (9)
CLK (11)
EN4
N3
R
&
EN2
≥1
C1
1D (1)
1D
▽ 2
3,4 ▽
(23) 1Q
2D (2)
3D (3)
4D (4)
5D (5)
6D (6)
7D (7)
8D (8)
(22) 2Q
(21) 3Q
(20) 4Q
(19) 5Q
(18) 6Q
(17) 7Q
(16) 8Q

†This symbol is in accordance with ANSI/IEEE Std 91-1984 and IEC Publication 617-12.

logic diagram (positive logic)

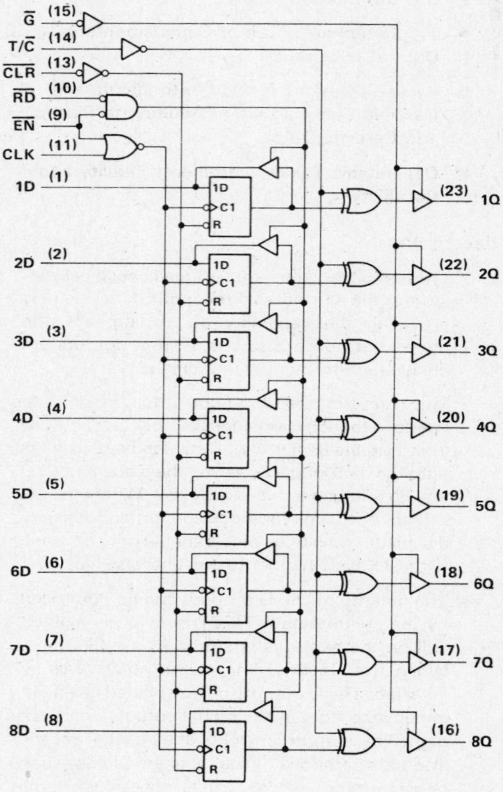
G̅ (15)
T/C̅ (14)
C̅L̅R̅ (13)
R̅D̅ (10)
E̅N̅ (9)
CLK (11)
1D (1)
2D (2)
3D (3)
4D (4)
5D (5)
6D (6)
7D (7)
8D (8)
1D
C1
R
(23) 1Q
(22) 2Q
(21) 3Q
(20) 4Q
(19) 5Q
(18) 6Q
(17) 7Q
(16) 8Q

Pin numbers shown are for DW and NT packages.

TEXAS INSTRUMENTS
POST OFFICE BOX 225012 • DALLAS, TEXAS 75265

timing diagram

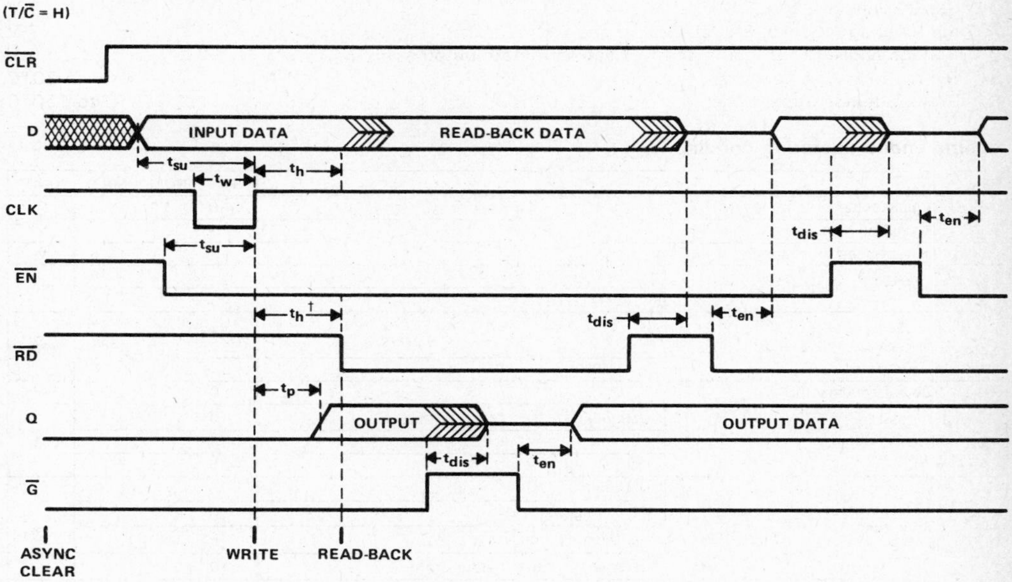
(T/C̄ = H)
CLR
D
INPUT DATA
READ-BACK DATA
t_{su}
t_w
t_h
CLK
t_{su}
EN
t_h†
RD
t_p
Q
OUTPUT
OUTPUT DATA
t_{dis}
t_{en}
G
t_{dis}
t_{en}
t_{dis}
t_{en}
ASYNC CLEAR
WRITE
READ-BACK

†This hold time ensures the readback circuit will not create a conflict on the input data bus.

absolute maximum ratings over operating free-air temperature range (unless otherwise noted)

Supply voltage, V_{CC} .... 7 V
Input voltage ($\overline{G}$, $\overline{RD}$, $\overline{EN}$, CLK, $\overline{CLR}$, and T/$\overline{C}$) .... 7 V
Voltage applied to D inputs and to disabled 3-state outputs .... 5.5 V
Operating free-air temperature range .... 0°C to 70°C
Storage temperature range .... −65°C to 150°C

recommended operating conditions

			MIN	NOM	MAX	UNIT
V_{CC}	Supply voltage		4.5	5	5.5	V
V_{IH}	High-level input voltage		2			V
V_{IL}	Low-level input voltage				0.8	V
I_{OH}	High-level output current	Q			2.6	mA
		D			−0.4	
I_{OL}	Low-level output current	Q			24	mA
					48†	
		D			8	
f_{clock}	Clock frequency		0		35	MHz
t_w	Pulse duration	$\overline{CLR}$ low	10			ns
		CLK low	14.5			
		CLK high	14.5			
t_{su}	Setup time	Data before CLK↑	15			ns
		$\overline{EN}$ low before CLK↑	10			
		CLK high before $\overline{EN}$↑ ‡	15			
		$\overline{CLR}$ high (inactive) before CLK↑	10			
t_h	Hold time	Data after CLK↑	0			ns
		$\overline{EN}$ low after CLK↑	5			
		$\overline{RD}$ high after CLK↑ §	5			
T_A	Operating free-air temperature		0		70	°C

† The 48-mA limit applies for the SN74ALS966-1 only and only if V_{CC} is maintained between 4.75 V and 5.25 V.
‡ This setup time guarantees that $\overline{EN}$ will not false clock the data register.
§ This hold time ensures there will be no conflict on the input data bus.

electrical characteristics over recommended operating free-air temperature range (unless otherwise noted)

PARAMETER		TEST CONDITIONS			MIN	TYP†	MAX	UNIT
V_{IK}		V_{CC} = 4.5 V,	I_I = −18 mA				−1.2	V
V_{OH}	All outputs	V_{CC} = 4.5 V to 5.5 V,	I_{OH} = −0.4 mA		V_{CC}−2			V
	Q	V_{CC} = 4.5 V,	I_{OH} = −2.6 mA		2.4	3.2		
V_{OL}	D	V_{CC} = 4.5 V,	I_{OL} = 4 mA			0.25	0.4	V
		V_{CC} = 4.5 V,	I_{OL} = 8 mA			0.35	0.5	
	Q	V_{CC} = 4.5 V,	I_{OL} = 12 mA			0.25	0.4	
		V_{CC} = 4.5 V, (I_{OL} = 48 mA for -1 versions)	I_{OL} = 24 mA			0.35	0.5	
I_{OZH}	Q	V_{CC} = 5.5 V,	V_I = 2.7 V				20	μA
I_{OZL}		V_{CC} = 5.5 V,	V_I = 0.4 V				−20	
I_I	D inputs	V_{CC} = 5.5 V,	V_I = 5.5 V				0.1	mA
	All others	V_{CC} = 5.5 V,	V_I = 7 V				0.1	
I_{IH}	D inputs‡	V_{CC} = 5.5 V,	V_I = 2.7 V				20	μA
	All others						20	
I_{IL}	D inputs‡	V_{CC} = 5.5 V,	V_I = 0.4 V				−0.1	mA
	All others						−0.1	
I_O§		V_{CC} = 5.5 V,	V_O = 2.25 V		−30		−112	mA
I_{CC}		V_{CC} = 5.5 V, $\overline{OERB}$ high		Q outputs high		35	55	mA
				Q outputs low		55	85	
				Q outputs disabled		42	65	

† All typical values are at V_{CC} = 5 V, T_A = 25°C.
‡ For I/O ports, the parameters I_{IH} and I_{IL} include the off-state output current.
§ The output conditions have been chosen to produce current that closely approximates one half of the true short-circuit output current, I_{OS}.

switching characteristics (see Figure 1)

PARAMETER	FROM (INPUT)	TO (OUTPUT)	V_{CC} = 5 V, C_L = 50 pF, T_A = 25°C			V_{CC} = 4.5 V to 5.5 V, C_L = 50 pF, T_A = 0°C to 70°C		UNIT
			MIN	TYP	MAX	MIN	MAX	
f_{max}				40		35		MHz
t_{PLH}	CLK (T/$\overline{C}$ = H or L)	Q		16	24	5	28	ns
t_{PHL}				16	24	5	28	
t_{PLH}	$\overline{CLR}$ (T/$\overline{C}$ = L)	Q		15	23	7	27	ns
t_{PHL}	$\overline{CLR}$ (T/$\overline{C}$ = H)			13	19	7	23	
t_{PLH}	T/$\overline{C}$	Q		13	20	5	23	ns
t_{PHL}				13	20	5	23	
t_{PHL}	$\overline{CLR}$	D		19	25	8	30	ns
t_{en}	$\overline{RD}$	D		9	15	3	16	ns
t_{dis}				10	16	3	19	
t_{en}	$\overline{EN}$	D		9	14	3	16	ns
t_{dis}				10	16	3	19	
t_{en}	$\overline{G}$	Q		8	13	4	15	ns
t_{dis}				4	8	1	10	

t_{en} = t_{PZH} or t_{PZL}
t_{dis} = t_{PHZ} or t_{PLZ}

2 LSI Devices

PARAMETER MEASUREMENT INFORMATION

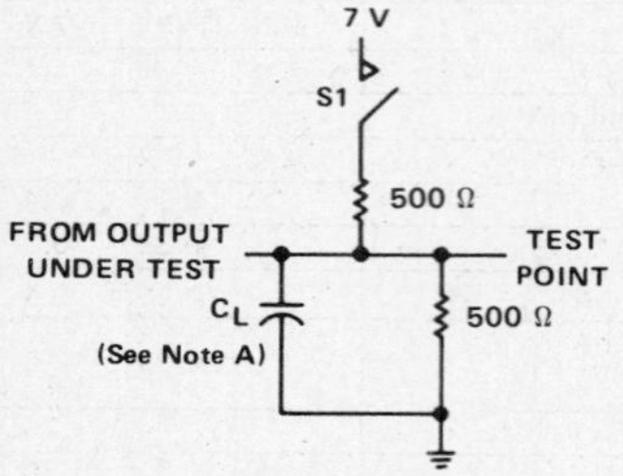
7 V
S1
500 Ω
FROM OUTPUT UNDER TEST
TEST POINT
C_L
(See Note A)
500 Ω

LOAD CIRCUIT FOR Q OUTPUTS

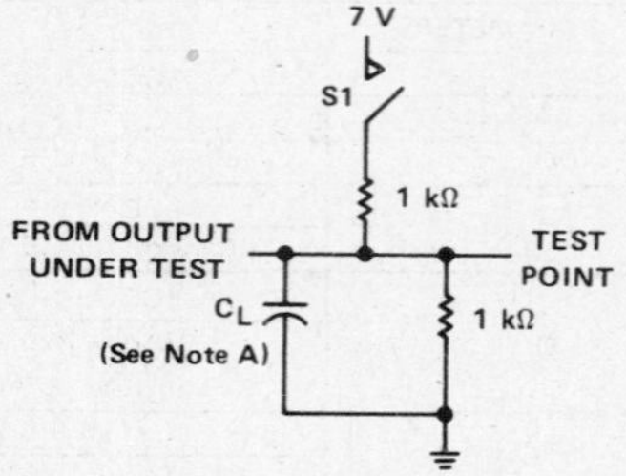
7 V
S1
1 kΩ
FROM OUTPUT UNDER TEST
TEST POINT
C_L
(See Note A)
1 kΩ

LOAD CIRCUIT FOR D OUTPUTS

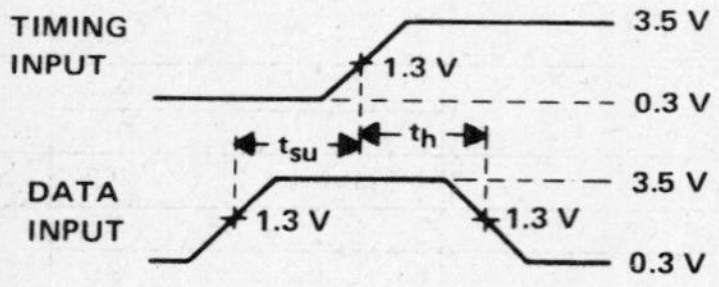
TIMING INPUT
3.5 V
1.3 V
0.3 V
t_{su}
t_h
DATA INPUT
3.5 V
1.3 V
1.3 V
0.3 V

VOLTAGE WAVEFORMS SETUP AND HOLD TIMES

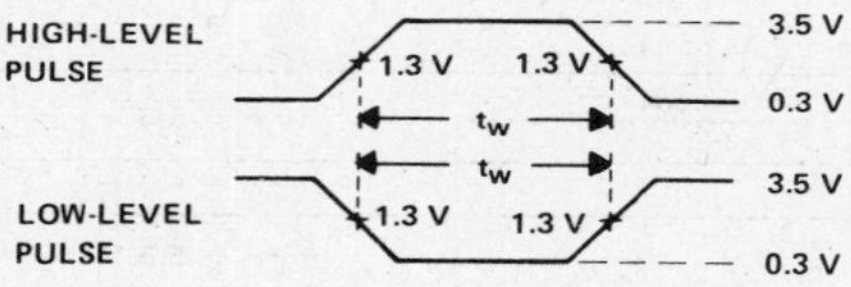
HIGH-LEVEL PULSE
3.5 V
1.3 V
1.3 V
0.3 V
t_w
t_w
LOW-LEVEL PULSE
3.5 V
1.3 V
1.3 V
0.3 V

VOLTAGE WAVEFORMS PULSE WIDTHS

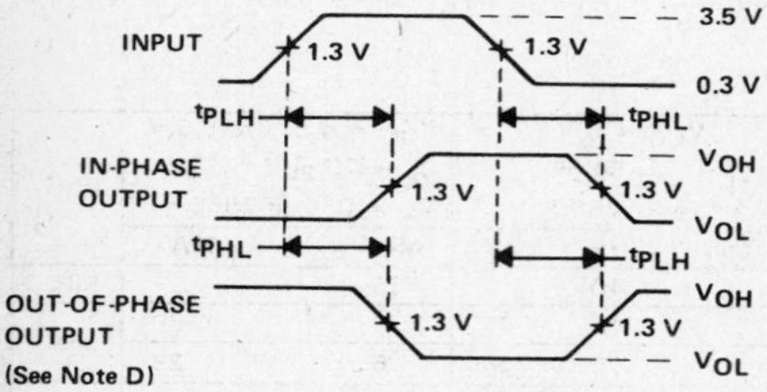
INPUT
1.3 V
1.3 V
3.5 V
0.3 V
t_{PLH}
t_{PHL}
IN-PHASE OUTPUT
1.3 V
1.3 V
V_{OH}
V_{OL}
t_{PHL}
t_{PLH}
OUT-OF-PHASE OUTPUT
(See Note D)
1.3 V
1.3 V
V_{OH}
V_{OL}

VOLTAGE WAVEFORMS PROPAGATION DELAY TIMES

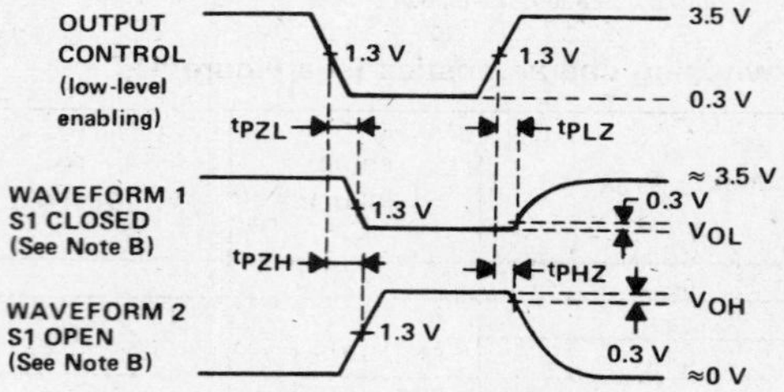
OUTPUT CONTROL (low-level enabling)
1.3 V
1.3 V
3.5 V
0.3 V
t_{PZL}
t_{PLZ}
WAVEFORM 1 S1 CLOSED (See Note B)
1.3 V
≈ 3.5 V
0.3 V
V_{OL}
t_{PZH}
t_{PHZ}
WAVEFORM 2 S1 OPEN (See Note B)
1.3 V
V_{OH}
0.3 V
≈0 V

VOLTAGE WAVEFORMS ENABLE AND DISABLE TIMES, THREE-STATE OUTPUTS

NOTES: A. C_L includes probe and jig capacitance.
B. Waveform 1 is for an output with internal conditions such that the output is low except when disabled by the output control. Waveform 2 is for an output with internal conditions such that the output is high except when disabled by the output control.
C. All input pulses have the following characteristics: PRR ≤ 1 MHz, $t_r = t_f = 2$ ns, duty cycle = 50%.
D. When measuring propagation delay times of 3-state outputs, switch S1 is open.

FIGURE 1

D1915, MAY 1985

- Package Options Include Compact 300-mil or Standard 600-mil DIPs and Both Plastic and Ceramic Chip Carriers
- Full Look-Ahead for High-Speed Operations on Long Words
- Arithmetic Operating Modes:
  - Addition
  - Subtraction
  - Shift Operand A One Position
  - Magnitude Comparison
  - Plus Twelve Other Arithmetic Operations
- Logic Function Modes
  - Exclusive-OR
  - Comparator
  - AND, NAND, OR, NOR
- Dependable Texas Instruments Quality and Reliability

SN54AS1181 . . . JT OR JW PACKAGE
SN74AS1181 . . . DW, NT, OR NW PACKAGE
(TOP VIEW)

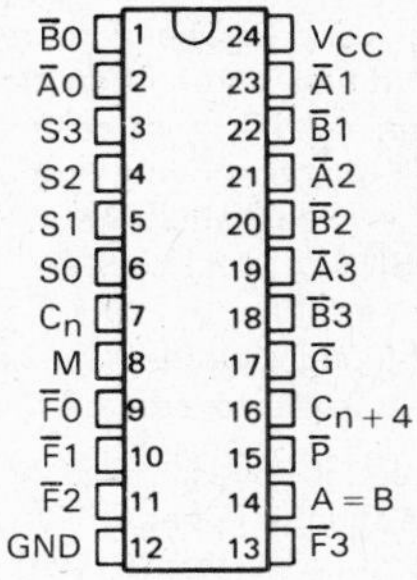
B̄0 1
Ā0 2
S3 3
S2 4
S1 5
S0 6
Cn 7
M 8
F̄0 9
F̄1 10
F̄2 11
GND 12
24 VCC
23 Ā1
22 B̄1
21 Ā2
20 B̄2
19 Ā3
18 B̄3
17 Ḡ
16 Cn+4
15 P̄
14 A=B
13 F̄3

SN54AS1181 . . . FK PACKAGE
SN74AS1181 . . . FN PACKAGE
(TOP VIEW)

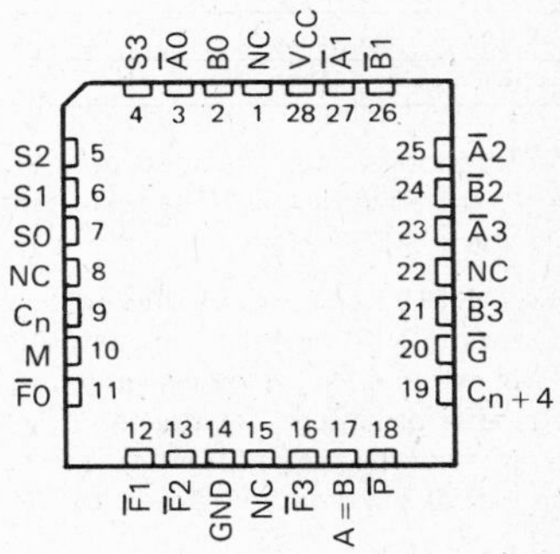
S3 Ā0 B0 NC VCC Ā1 B̄1
4 3 2 1 28 27 26
S2 5
S1 6
S0 7
NC 8
Cn 9
M 10
F̄0 11
25 Ā2
24 B̄2
23 Ā3
22 NC
21 B̄3
20 Ḡ
19 Cn+4
12 13 14 15 16 17 18
F̄1 F̄2 GND NC F̄3 A=B P̄

NC—No internal connection

logic symbol†

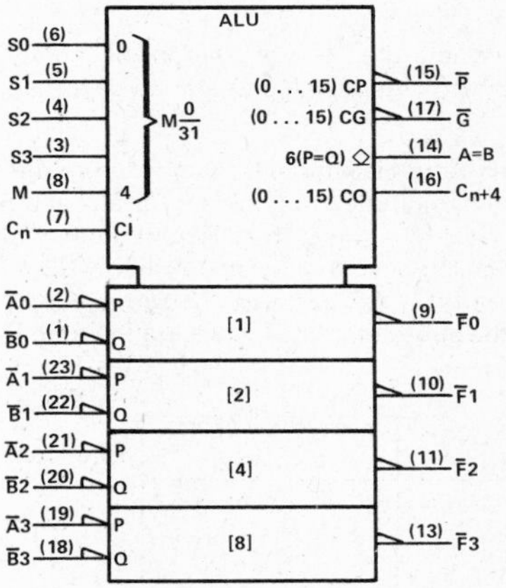
ALU
S0 (6) 0
S1 (5)
S2 (4)
S3 (3)
M (8) 4
M 0/31
Cn (7) CI
(0 . . . 15) CP (15) P̄
(0 . . . 15) CG (17) Ḡ
6(P=Q) (14) A=B
(0 . . . 15) CO (16) Cn+4
Ā0 (2) P
B̄0 (1) Q
[1]
(9) F̄0
Ā1 (23) P
B̄1 (22) Q
[2]
(10) F̄1
Ā2 (21) P
B̄2 (20) Q
[4]
(11) F̄2
Ā3 (19) P
B̄3 (18) Q
[8]
(13) F̄3

†This symbol is in accordance with ANSI/IEEE Std 91-1984 and IEC Publication 617-12.
Pin numbers shown are for DW, JT, JW, NT, and NW packages.

TYPICAL ADDITION TIMES (C_L = 15 pF, R_L = 280 Ω, T_A = 25°C

NUMBER OF BITS	ADDITION TIMES			PACKAGE COUNT		CARRY METHOD BETWEEN ALUs
	USING 'AS1181 AND'AS882	USING 'AS181A AND 'AS882	USING 'S181 AND 'S182	ARITHMETIC LOGIC UNITS	LOOK-AHEAD CARRY GENERATORS	
1 to 4	5 ns	5 ns	11 ns	1		NONE
5 to 8	10 ns	10 ns	18 ns	2		RIPPLE
9 to 16	14 ns	14 ns	19 ns	3 or 4	1	FULL LOOK-AHEAD
17 to 64	19 ns	19 ns	28 ns	5 to 16	2 to 5	FULL LOOK-AHEAD

TEXAS INSTRUMENTS
POST OFFICE BOX 225012 • DALLAS, TEXAS 75265

description

The 'AS1181 arithmetic logic units (ALU)/function generators have a complexity of 75 equivalent gates on a monolithic chip. These circuits perform 16 binary arithmetic operations on two 4-bit words as shown in Tables 1 and 2. These operations are selected by the four function-select lines (S0, S1, S2, S3) and include addition, subtraction, decrement, and straight transfer. When performing arithmetic manipulations, the internal carries must be enabled by applying a low-level voltage to the mode control input (M). A full carry look-ahead scheme is made available in these devices for fast, simultaneous carry generation by means of two cascade-outputs (pins 15 and 17) for the four bits in the package. When used in conjunction with the SN54AS882 or SN74AS882 full carry look-ahead circuits, high-speed arithmetic operations can be performed. The typical addition times shown previously illustrate the little additional time required for addition of longer words when full carry look-ahead is employed. The method of cascading 'AS882 circuits with these ALUs to provide multilevel full carry look-ahead is illustrated under signal designations.

If high speed is not of importance, a ripple-carry input (C_n) and a ripple-carry output (C_{n+4}) are available. However, the ripple-carry delay has also been minimized so that arithmetic manipulations for small word lengths can be performed without external circuitry.

The 'AS1181 will accommodate active-high or active-low data if the pin designations are interpreted as follows:

PIN NUMBER	2	1	23	22	21	20	19	18	9	10	11	13	7	16	15	17
Active-low data (Table 1)	$\overline{A0}$	$\overline{B0}$	$\overline{A1}$	$\overline{B1}$	$\overline{A2}$	$\overline{B2}$	$\overline{A3}$	$\overline{B3}$	$\overline{F0}$	$\overline{F1}$	$\overline{F2}$	$\overline{F3}$	C_n	C_{n+4}	$\overline{P}$	$\overline{G}$
Active-high data (Table 2)	A0	B0	A1	B1	A2	B2	A3	B3	F0	F1	F2	F3	$\overline{C}_n$	$\overline{C}_{n+4}$	X	Y

Subtraction is accomplished by 1's complement addition where the 1's complement of the subtrahend is generated internally. The resultant output is A − B − 1, which requires an end-around or forced carry to provide A − B.

The 'AS1181 can also be utilized as a comparator. The A = B output is internally decoded from the function outputs (F0, F1, F2, F3) so that when two words of equal magnitude are applied at the A and B inputs, it will assume a high level to indicate equality (A = B). The ALU must be in the subtract mode with $C_n = H$ when performing this comparison. The A = B output is open-collector so that it can be wired-AND connected to give a comparison for more than four bits. The carry output (C_{n+4}) can also be used to supply relative magnitude information. Again, the ALU must be placed in the subtract mode by placing the function select input S3, S2, S1, S0 at L, H, H, L, respectively.

INPUT C_n	OUTPUT C_{n+4}	ACTIVE-LOW DATA (FIGURE 1)	ACTIVE-HIGH DATA (FIGURE 2)
H	H	$A \geq B$	$A \leq B$
H	L	$A < B$	$A > B$
L	H	$A > B$	$A < B$
L	L	$A \leq B$	$A \geq B$

These circuits have been designed to not only incorporate all of the designer's requirements for arithmetic operations, but also to provide 16 possible functions of two Boolean variables without the use of external circuitry. These logic functions are selected by use of the four function-select inputs (S0, S1, S2, S3) with the mode-control input (M) at a high level to disable the internal carry. The 16 logic functions are detailed in Tables 1 and 2 and include exclusive-OR, NAND, AND, NOR, and OR functions.

TEXAS INSTRUMENTS
POST OFFICE BOX 225012 • DALLAS, TEXAS 75265

signal designations

In both Figures 1 and 2, the polarity indicators (⊳) indicate that the associated input or output is active-low with respect to the function shown inside the symbol and the symbols are the same in both figures. The signal designations in Figure 1 agree with the indicated internal functions based on active-low data, and are for use with the logic functions and arithmetic operations shown in Table 1. The signal designations have been changed in Figure 2 to accommodate the logic functions and arithmetic operations for the active-high data given in Table 2. The 'AS1181 together with 'AS882 and 'S182 can be used with the signal designation of either Figure 1 or Figure 2.

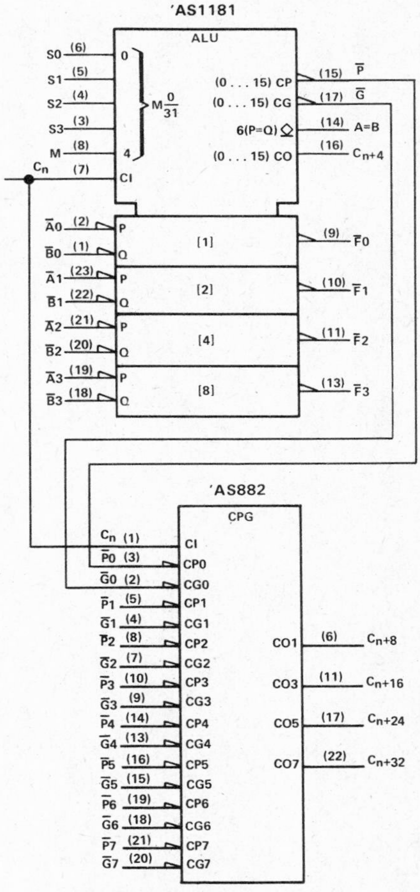
'AS1181
ALU
'AS882
CPG

FIGURE 1
(USE WITH TABLE 1)

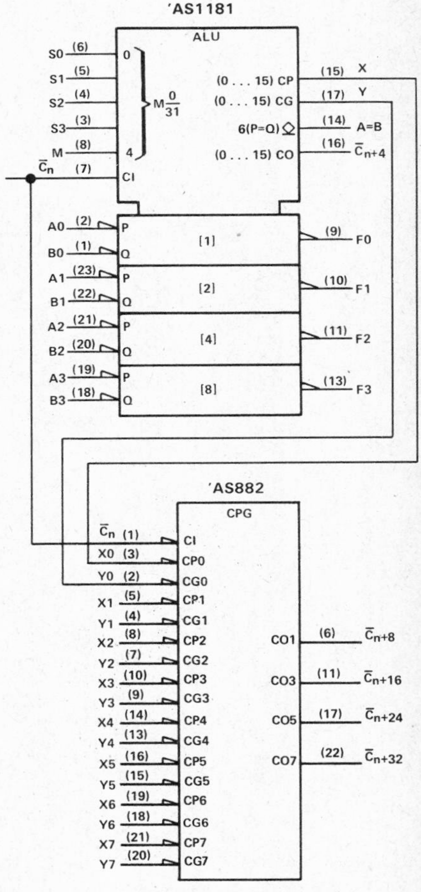
'AS1181
ALU
'AS882
CPG

FIGURE 2
(USE WITH TABLE 2)

Pin numbers shown for the 'AS1181 are for DW, JT, JW, NT, and NW packages.

TABLE 1

SELECTION				ACTIVE-LOW DATA		
				M = H LOGIC FUNCTIONS	M = L; ARITHMETIC OPERATIONS	
S3	S2	S1	S0		C_n = L (no carry)	C_n = H (with carry)
L	L	L	L	F = $\overline{A}$	F = A MINUS 1	F = A
L	L	L	H	F = $\overline{AB}$	F = AB MINUS 1	F = AB
L	L	H	L	F = $\overline{A}$ + B	F = A$\overline{B}$ MINUS 1	F = A$\overline{B}$
L	L	H	H	F = 1	F = MINUS 1 (2's COMP)	F = ZERO
L	H	L	L	F = $\overline{A + B}$	F = A PLUS (A + $\overline{B}$)	F = A PLUS (A + $\overline{B}$) PLUS 1
L	H	L	H	F = $\overline{B}$	F = AB PLUS (A + $\overline{B}$)	F = AB PLUS (A + $\overline{B}$) PLUS 1
L	H	H	L	F = $\overline{A \oplus B}$	F = A MINUS B MINUS 1	F = A MINUS B
L	H	H	H	F = A + $\overline{B}$	F = A + $\overline{B}$	F = (A + $\overline{B}$) PLUS 1
H	L	L	L	F = $\overline{A}$B	F = A PLUS (A + B)	F = A PLUS (A + B) PLUS 1
H	L	L	H	F = A $\oplus$ B	F = A PLUS B	F = A PLUS B PLUS 1
H	L	H	L	F = B	F = A$\overline{B}$ PLUS (A + B)	F = A$\overline{B}$ PLUS (A + B) PLUS 1
H	L	H	H	F = A + B	F = (A + B)	F = (A + B) PLUS 1
H	H	L	L	F = 0	F = A PLUS A †	F = A PLUS A PLUS 1
H	H	L	H	F = A$\overline{B}$	F = AB PLUS A	F = AB PLUS A PLUS 1
H	H	H	L	F = AB	F = A$\overline{B}$ PLUS A	F = A$\overline{B}$ PLUS A PLUS 1
H	H	H	H	F = A	F = A	F = A PLUS 1

TABLE 2

SELECTION				ACTIVE-HIGH DATA		
				M = H LOGIC FUNCTIONS	M = L; ARITHMETIC OPERATIONS	
S3	S2	S1	S0		$\overline{C}_n$ = H (no carry)	$\overline{C}_n$ = L (with carry)
L	L	L	L	F = $\overline{A}$	F = A	F = A PLUS 1
L	L	L	H	F = $\overline{A + B}$	F = A + B	F = (A + B) PLUS 1
L	L	H	L	F = $\overline{A}$B	F = A + $\overline{B}$	F = (A + $\overline{B}$) PLUS 1
L	L	H	H	F = 0	F = MINUS 1 (2's COMPL)	F = ZERO
L	H	L	L	F = $\overline{AB}$	F = A PLUS A$\overline{B}$	F = A PLUS A$\overline{B}$ PLUS 1
L	H	L	H	F = $\overline{B}$	F = (A + B) PLUS A$\overline{B}$	F = (A + B) PLUS A$\overline{B}$ PLUS 1
L	H	H	L	F = A $\oplus$ B	F = A MINUS B MINUS 1	F = A MINUS B
L	H	H	H	F = A$\overline{B}$	F = A$\overline{B}$ MINUS 1	F = A$\overline{B}$
H	L	L	L	F = $\overline{A}$ + B	F = A PLUS AB	F = A PLUS AB PLUS 1
H	L	L	H	F = $\overline{A \oplus B}$	F = A PLUS B	F = A PLUS B PLUS 1
H	L	H	L	F = B	F = (A + $\overline{B}$) PLUS AB	F = (A + $\overline{B}$) PLUS AB PLUS 1
H	L	H	H	F = AB	F = AB MINUS 1	F = AB
H	H	L	L	F = 1	F = A PLUS A †	F = A PLUS A PLUS 1
H	H	L	H	F = A + $\overline{B}$	F = (A + B) PLUS A	F = (A + B) PLUS A PLUS 1
H	H	H	L	F = A + B	F = (A + $\overline{B}$) PLUS A	F = (A + $\overline{B}$) PLUS A PLUS 1
H	H	H	H	F = A	F = A MINUS 1	F = A

†Each bit is shifted to the next more significant position.

TEXAS INSTRUMENTS
POST OFFICE BOX 225012 • DALLAS, TEXAS 75265

logic diagram (positive logic)

'AS1181

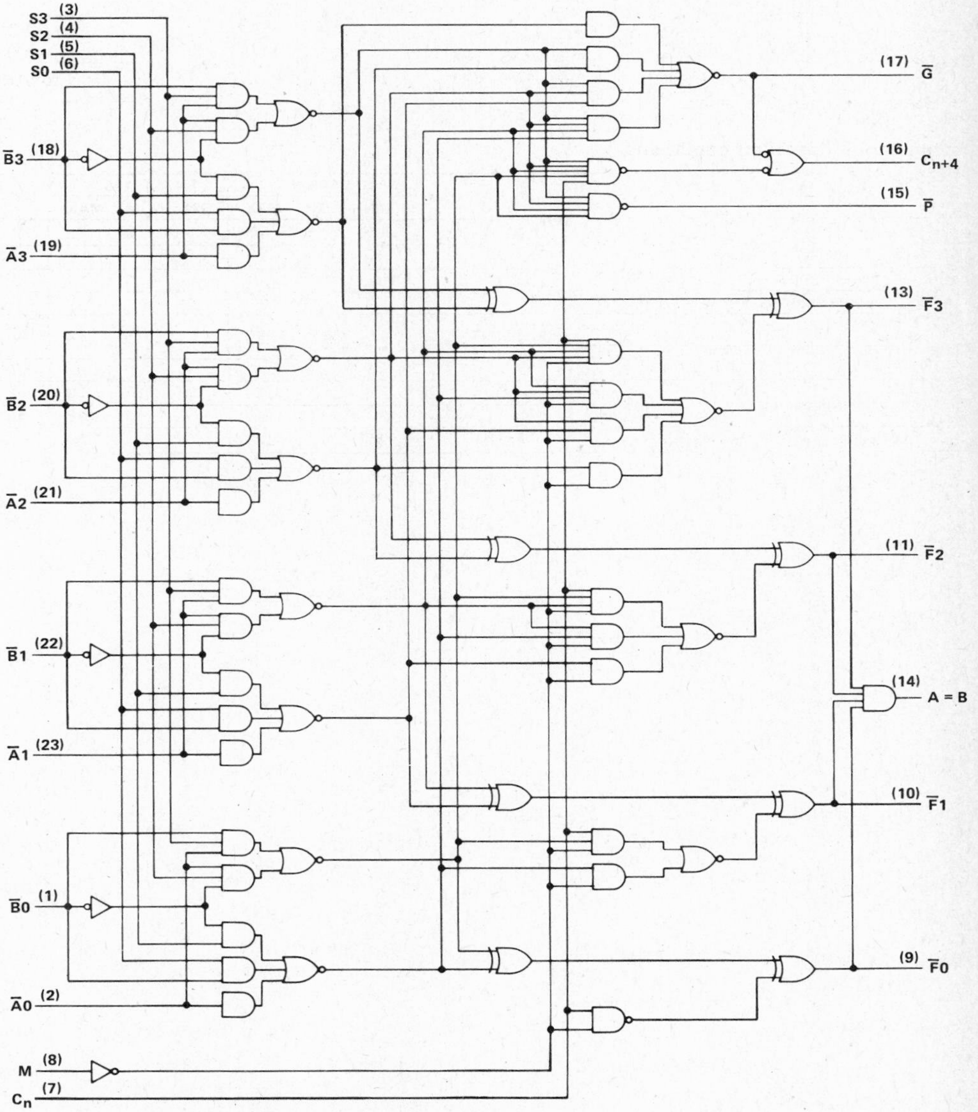
S3 (3)
S2 (4)
S1 (5)
S0 (6)
B̄3 (18)
Ā3 (19)
B̄2 (20)
Ā2 (21)
B̄1 (22)
Ā1 (23)
B̄0 (1)
Ā0 (2)
M (8)
Cn (7)
(17) Ḡ
(16) Cn+4
(15) P̄
(13) F̄3
(11) F̄2
(14) A = B
(10) F̄1
(9) F̄0

Pin numbers shown are for DW, JT, JW, NT, and NW packages.

absolute maximum ratings over operating free-air temperature range (unless otherwise noted)

Supply voltage, V_{CC} .... 7 V
Input voltage .... 7 V
Off-state output voltge (A = B output only) .... 7 V
Operating free-air temperature range: SN54AS1181 .... −55°C to 125°C
SN74AS1181 .... 0°C to 70°C
Storage temperature range .... −65°C to 150°C

recommended operating conditions

			SN54AS1181			SN74AS1181			UNIT
			MIN	NOM	MAX	MIN	NOM	MAX	
V_{CC}	Supply voltage		4.5	5	5.5	4.5	5	5.5	V
V_{IH}	High-level input voltage		2			2			V
V_{IL}	Low-level input voltage				0.8			0.8	V
V_{OH}	High-level output voltage	A = B output only			5.5			5.5	V
I_{OH}	High-level output current	All outputs except A = B and $\overline{G}$			−2			−2	mA
		$\overline{G}$ output			−3			−3	mA
I_{OL}	Low-level output current	All outputs except $\overline{G}$			20			20	mA
		$\overline{G}$ output			48			48	mA
T_A	Operating free-air temperature		−55		125	0		70	°C

electrical characteristics over recommended operating free-air temperature range (unless otherwise noted)

PARAMETER		TEST CONDITIONS		SN54AS1181 MIN	SN54AS1181 TYP†	SN54AS1181 MAX	SN74AS1181 MIN	SN74AS1181 TYP†	SN74AS1181 MAX	UNIT
V_{IK}		V_{CC} = 4.5 V,	I_I = −18 mA			−1.2			−1.2	V
V_{OH}	Any output except A = B	V_{CC} = 4.5 V to 5.5 V,	I_{OH} = −2 mA	$V_{CC}-2$			$V_{CC}-2$			V
	$\overline{G}$	V_{CC} = 4.5 V,	I_{OH} = −3 mA	2.4	3		2.4	3		V
I_{OH}	A = B	V_{CC} = 4.5 V,	V_{OH} = 5.5 V			0.1			0.1	mA
V_{OL}	Any output except $\overline{G}$	V_{CC} = 4.5 V,	I_{OL} = 20 mA		0.3	0.5		0.3	0.5	V
	$\overline{G}$	V_{CC} = 4.5 V,	I_{OL} = 48 mA		0.4	0.5		0.4	0.5	V
I_I	M input	V_{CC} = 5.5 V,	V_I = 7 V			0.1			0.1	mA
	Any A or B input					0.3			0.3	
	Any S input					0.4			0.4	
	Carry input					0.6			0.6	
I_{IH}	M input	V_{CC} = 5.5 V,	V_I = 2.7 V			20			20	μA
	Any A or B input					60			60	
	Any S input					80			80	
	Carry input					120			120	
I_{IL}	M input	V_{CC} = 5.5 V,	V_I = 0.4 V			−0.5			−0.5	mA
	Any A or B input					−1.5			−1.5	
	Any S input					−2			−2	
	Carry input					−3			−3	
I_O‡	All outputs except A = B and $\overline{G}$	V_{CC} = 5.5 V,	V_O = 2.25 V	−30		−112	−30		−112	mA
	$\overline{G}$			−30		−125	−30		−125	
I_{CC}		V_{CC} = 5.5 V			74	117		74	117	mA

†All typical values are at V_{CC} = 5 V, T_A = 25°C.
‡The output conditions have been chosen to produce a current that closely approximates one half of the true short-circuit output current, I_{OS}.

switching characteristics (see Note 1)

PARAMETER	FROM (INPUT)	TO (OUTPUT)	TEST CONDITIONS	V_{CC} = 4.5 V to 5.5 V, C_L = 50 pF, R_L = 500 Ω, T_A = MIN to MAX				UNIT
				SN54AS1181		SN74AS1181		
				MIN	MAX	MIN	MAX	
t_{PLH}	C_n	C_{n+4}		3	9	3	8.5	ns
t_{PHL}				2	7	2	6.5	
t_{PLH}	Any $\overline{A}$ or $\overline{B}$	C_{n+4}	M = 0 V, S1 = S2 = 0 V, S0 = S3 = 4.5 V ($\overline{SUM}$ mode)	3.5	13	5	12	ns
t_{PHL}				3.5	12.5	5	12	
t_{PLH}	Any $\overline{A}$ or $\overline{B}$	C_{n+4}	M = 0 V, S0 = S3 = 0 V, S1 = S2 = 4.5 V ($\overline{DIFF}$ mode)	5	14.5	5	13	ns
t_{PHL}				5	13.5	5	12.5	
t_{PLH}	C_n	Any $\overline{F}$	M = 0 V ($\overline{SUM}$ or $\overline{DIFF}$ mode)	3	10.5	3	9	ns
t_{PHL}				3	8	3	7.5	
t_{PLH}	Any $\overline{A}$ or $\overline{B}$	$\overline{G}$	M = 0 V, S1 = S2 = 0 V, S0 = S3 = 4.5 V ($\overline{SUM}$ mode)	3	8.5	3	8	ns
t_{PHL}				2	7	2	6	
t_{PLH}	Any $\overline{A}$ or $\overline{B}$	$\overline{G}$	M = 0 V, S0 = S3 = 0 V, S1 = S2 = 4.5 V ($\overline{DIFF}$ mode)	3	10.5	3	9.5	ns
t_{PHL}				2	9	2	7	
t_{PLH}	Any $\overline{A}$ or $\overline{B}$	$\overline{P}$	M = 0 V, S1 = S2 = 0 V, S0 = S3 = 4.5 V ($\overline{SUM}$ mode)	3	8.5	3	7.5	ns
t_{PHL}				2	7.5	2	6	
t_{PLH}	Any $\overline{A}$ or $\overline{B}$	$\overline{P}$	M = 0 V, S0 = S3 = 0 V, S1 = S2 = 4.5 V ($\overline{DIFF}$ mode)	3	10.5	3	9	ns
t_{PHL}				3	8.5	3	8	
t_{PLH}	$\overline{A}i$ or $\overline{B}i$	$\overline{F}i$	M = 0 V, S1 = S2 = 0 V, S0 = S3 = 4.5 V ($\overline{SUM}$ mode)	3	11	3	9.5	ns
t_{PHL}				3	9	3	7.5	
t_{PLH}	$\overline{A}i$ or $\overline{B}i$	$\overline{F}i$	M = 0 V, S0 = S3 = 0 V, S1 = S2 = 4.5 V ($\overline{DIFF}$ mode)	3	12	3	10.5	ns
t_{PHL}				3	11	3	9.5	
t_{PLH}	Any $\overline{A}$ or $\overline{B}$	Any $\overline{F}$	M = 0 V, S1 = S2 = 0 V, S0 = S3 = 4.5 V ($\overline{SUM}$ mode)	3	13.5	3	12	ns
t_{PHL}				3	13	3	11.5	
t_{PLH}	Any $\overline{A}$ or $\overline{B}$	Any $\overline{F}$	M = 0 V, S0 = S3 = 0 V, S1 = S2 = 4.5 V ($\overline{DIFF}$ mode)	3	16	3	14.5	ns
t_{PHL}				3	13	3	12.5	
t_{PLH}	$\overline{A}i$ or $\overline{B}i$	$\overline{F}i$	M = 4.5 V (LOGIC mode)	3	12.5	3	11	ns
t_{PHL}				3	10	3	9.5	
t_{PLH}	Any $\overline{A}$ or $\overline{B}$	A = B	M = 0 V, S0 = S3 = 0 V, S1 = S2 = 4.5 V ($\overline{DIFF}$ mode)	4	19	4	17	ns
t_{PHL}				5	18.5	5	15	
t_{PLH}	Any S	Any $\overline{F}$	M = 0 V ($\overline{ARITH}$ mode)	3	12.5	3	11	ns
t_{PHL}				3	11.5	3	11	
t_{PLH}	Any S	A = B	M = 0 V ($\overline{ARITH}$ mode)	5	20	5	18	ns
t_{PHL}				5	21	5	18	
t_{PLH}	Any S	C_{n+4}	M = 4.5 V (LOGIC mode)	2	16.5	4.5	15.5	ns
t_{PHL}				3	12.5	3	12	
t_{PLH}	Any S	$\overline{G}$	M = 0 V ($\overline{ARITH}$ mode)	3	9.5	3	9	ns
t_{PHL}				2	6.5	2	6	
t_{PLH}	Any S	$\overline{P}$	M = 4.5 V (LOGIC mode)	3	8.5	3	7.5	ns
t_{PHL}				2	6.5	2	6.5	
t_{PLH}	M	Any $\overline{F}$	S1 = S2 = 0 V, S0 = S3 = 4.5 V ($\overline{SUM}$ mode)	5	12	5	11.5	ns
t_{PHL}				5	12	5	11.5	
t_{PLH}	M	A = B	S1 = S2 = 0 V, S0 = S3 = 4.5 V ($\overline{SUM}$ mode)	7	19	7	17.5	ns
t_{PHL}				8	21	8	17.5	

NOTE 1: Load circuit and voltage waveforms are shown in Section 1.

PARAMETER MEASUREMENT INFORMATION

SUM MODE TEST TABLE

FUNCTION INPUTS: S0 = S3 = 4.5 V, S1 = S2 = M = 0 V

PARAMETER	INPUT UNDER TEST	OTHER INPUT SAME BIT		OTHER DATA INPUTS		OUTPUT UNDER TEST	OUTPUT WAVEFORM (SEE NOTE 1)
		APPLY 4.5 V	APPLY GND	APPLY 4.5 V	APPLY GND		
t_{PLH} t_{PHL}	$\overline{A}$i	$\overline{B}$i	None	Remaining $\overline{A}$ and $\overline{B}$	C_n	$\overline{F}$i	In-Phase
t_{PLH} t_{PHL}	$\overline{B}$i	$\overline{A}$i	None	Remaining $\overline{A}$ and $\overline{B}$	C_n	$\overline{F}$i	In-Phase
t_{PLH} t_{PHL}	$\overline{A}$i	$\overline{B}$i	None	None	Remaining $\overline{A}$ and $\overline{B}$, C_n	$\overline{P}$	In-Phase
t_{PLH} t_{PHL}	$\overline{B}$i	$\overline{A}$i	None	None	Remaining $\overline{A}$ and $\overline{B}$, C_n	$\overline{P}$	In-Phase
t_{PLH} t_{PHL}	$\overline{A}$i	None	$\overline{B}$i	Remaining $\overline{B}$	Remaining $\overline{A}$, C_n	$\overline{G}$	In-Phase
t_{PLH} t_{PHL}	$\overline{B}$i	None	$\overline{A}$i	Remaining $\overline{B}$	Remaining $\overline{A}$, C_n	$\overline{G}$	In-Phase
t_{PLH} t_{PHL}	C_n	None	None	All $\overline{A}$	All $\overline{B}$	Any $\overline{F}$ or C_{n+4}	In-Phase
t_{PLH} t_{PHL}	$\overline{A}$i	None	$\overline{B}$i	Remaining $\overline{B}$	Remaining $\overline{A}$, C_n	C_{n+4}	Out-of-Phase
t_{PLH} t_{PHL}	$\overline{B}$i	None	$\overline{A}$i	Remaining $\overline{B}$	Remaining $\overline{A}$, C_n	C_{n+4}	Out-of-Phase
t_{PLH} t_{PHL}	Any $\overline{A}$	None	$\overline{B}$i	Remaining $\overline{B}$, $\overline{A}3$	Remaining $\overline{A}$, C_n	Any $\overline{F}$	In-Phase
t_{PLH} t_{PHL}	Any $\overline{B}$	None	$\overline{A}$i	Remaining $\overline{A}$, $\overline{B}3$	Remaining $\overline{B}$, C_n	Any $\overline{F}$	In-Phase

NOTE 1: Load circuit and voltage waveforms are shown in Section 1.

2

LSI Devices

PARAMETER MEASUREMENT INFORMATION

$\overline{\text{DIFF}}$ MODE TEST TABLE

FUNCTION INPUTS: S1 = S2 = 4.5 V, S0 = S3 = M = 0 V

PARAMETER	INPUT UNDER TEST	OTHER INPUT SAME BIT		OTHER DATA INPUTS		OUTPUT UNDER TEST	OUTPUT WAVEFORM (SEE NOTE 1)
		APPLY 4.5 V	APPLY GND	APPLY 4.5 V	APPLY GND		
t_{PLH} t_{PHL}	$\overline{A}i$	None	$\overline{B}i$	Remaining $\overline{A}$	Remaining $\overline{B}$, C_n	$\overline{F}i$	In-Phase
t_{PLH} t_{PHL}	$\overline{B}i$	$\overline{A}i$	None	Remaining $\overline{A}$	Remaining $\overline{B}$, C_n	$\overline{F}i$	Out-of-Phase
t_{PLH} t_{PHL}	$\overline{A}i$	None	$\overline{B}i$	None	Remaining $\overline{A}$ and $\overline{B}$, C_n	$\overline{P}$	In-Phase
t_{PLH} t_{PHL}	$\overline{B}i$	$\overline{A}i$	None	None	Remaining $\overline{A}$ and $\overline{B}$, C_n	$\overline{P}$	Out-of-Phase
t_{PLH} t_{PHL}	$\overline{A}i$	$\overline{B}i$	None	None	Remaining $\overline{A}$ and $\overline{B}$, C_n	$\overline{G}$	In-Phase
t_{PLH} t_{PHL}	$\overline{B}i$	None	$\overline{A}i$	None	Remaining $\overline{A}$ and $\overline{B}$, C_n	$\overline{G}$	Out-of-Phase
t_{PLH} t_{PHL}	$\overline{A}i$	None	$\overline{B}i$	Remaining $\overline{A}$	Remaining $\overline{B}$, C_n	A = B	In-Phase
t_{PLH} t_{PHL}	$\overline{B}i$	$\overline{A}i$	None	Remaining $\overline{A}$	Remaining $\overline{B}$, C_n	A = B	Out-of-Phase
t_{PLH} t_{PHL}	C_n	None	None	All $\overline{A}$ and $\overline{B}$	None	C_{n+4} or any $\overline{F}$	In-Phase
t_{PLH} t_{PHL}	$\overline{A}i$	$\overline{B}i$	None	None	Remaining $\overline{A}$, $\overline{B}$, C_n	C_{n+4}	Out-of-Phase
t_{PLH} t_{PHL}	$\overline{B}i$	None	$\overline{A}i$	None	Remaining $\overline{A}$, $\overline{B}$, C_n	C_{n+4}	In-Phase
t_{PLH} t_{PHL}	Any $\overline{A}$	$\overline{B}i$	None	$\overline{A}3$	Remaining $\overline{A}$, $\overline{B}$, C_n	Any $\overline{F}$	In-Phase
t_{PLH} t_{PHL}	Any $\overline{B}$	None	$\overline{A}i$	$\overline{A}3$	Remaining $\overline{A}$, $\overline{B}$, C_n	Any $\overline{F}$	Out-of-Phase

NOTE 1: Load circuit and voltage waveforms are shown in Section 1.

TEXAS INSTRUMENTS
POST OFFICE BOX 225012 • DALLAS, TEXAS 75265

PARAMETER MEASUREMENT INFORMATION

LOGIC MODE TEST TABLE

FUNCTION INPUTS: S1 = S2 = M = 4.5 V, S0 = S3 = 0 V

PARAMETER	INPUT UNDER TEST	OTHER INPUT SAME BIT		OTHER DATA INPUTS		OUTPUT UNDER TEST	OUTPUT WAVEFORM (SEE NOTE 1)
		APPLY 4.5 V	APPLY GND	APPLY 4.5 V	APPLY GND		
t_{PLH} t_{PHL}	$\overline{A}i$	$\overline{B}$	None	None	Remaining $\overline{A}$ and $\overline{B}$, C_n	$\overline{F}i$	Out-of-Phase
t_{PLH} t_{PHL}	$\overline{B}i$	$\overline{A}i$	None	None	Remaining $\overline{A}$ and $\overline{B}$, C_n	$\overline{F}i$	Out-ot-Phase

INPUT BITS EQUAL/NOT EQUAL TEST TABLE

FUNCTION INPUTS: S0 = S3 = M = 4.5 V, S1 = S2 = 0 V

PARAMETER	INPUT UNDER TEST	OTHER INPUT SAME BIT		OTHER DATA INPUTS		OUTPUT UNDER TEST	OUTPUT WAVEFORM (SEE NOTE 1)
		APPLY 4.5 V	APPLY GND	APPLY 4.5 V	APPLY GND		
t_{PLH} t_{PHL}	$\overline{A}i$	$\overline{B}i$	None	Remaining $\overline{A}$ and $\overline{B}$, C_n	None	$\overline{P}$	Out-of-Phase
t_{PLH} t_{PHL}	$\overline{B}i$	$\overline{A}i$	None	Remaining $\overline{A}$ and $\overline{B}$, C_n	None	$\overline{P}$	Out-of-Phase
t_{PLH} t_{PHL}	$\overline{A}i$	None	$\overline{B}i$	Remaining $\overline{A}$ and $\overline{B}$, C_n	None	$\overline{P}$	In-Phase
t_{PLH} t_{PHL}	$\overline{B}i$	None	$\overline{A}i$	Remaining $\overline{A}$ and $\overline{B}$, C_n	None	$\overline{P}$	In-Phase
t_{PLH} t_{PHL}	$\overline{A}i$	$\overline{B}i$	None	Remaining $\overline{A}$ and $\overline{B}$, C_n	None	C_{n+4}	In-Phase
t_{PLH} t_{PHL}	$\overline{B}i$	$\overline{A}i$	None	Remaining $\overline{A}$ and $\overline{B}$, C_n	None	C_{n+4}	In-Phase
t_{PLH} t_{PHL}	$\overline{A}i$	None	$\overline{B}i$	Remaining $\overline{A}$ and $\overline{B}$, C_n	None	C_{n+4}	Out-of-Phase
t_{PLH} t_{PHL}	$\overline{B}i$	None	$\overline{A}i$	Remaining $\overline{A}$ and $\overline{B}$, C_n	None	C_{n+4}	Out-of-Phase

INPUT PAIRS HIGH/NOT HIGH TEST TABLE

FUNCTION INPUTS: S2 = M = 4.5 V, S0 = S1 = S3 = 0V

PARAMETER	INPUT UNDER TEST	OTHER INPUT SAME BIT		OTHER DATA INPUTS		OUTPUT UNDER TEST	OUTPUT WAVEFORM (SEE NOTE 1)
		APPLY 4.5 V	APPLY GND	APPLY 4.5V	APPLY GND		
t_{PLH} t_{PHL}	$\overline{A}i$	$\overline{B}i$	None	Remaining $\overline{A}$, C_n	Remaining $\overline{B}$	$\overline{P}$	In-Phase
t_{PLH} t_{PHL}	$\overline{B}i$	$\overline{A}i$	None	Remaining $\overline{B}$, C_n	Remaining $\overline{A}$	$\overline{P}$	In-Phase
t_{PLH} t_{PHL}	$\overline{A}i$	$\overline{B}i$	None	Remaining $\overline{A}$, C_n	Remaining $\overline{B}$	C_{n+4}	Out-of-Phase
t_{PLH} t_{PHL}	$\overline{B}i$	$\overline{A}i$	None	Remaining $\overline{B}$, C_n	Remaining $\overline{A}$	C_{n+4}	Out-of-Phase

NOTE 1: Load circuit and voltage waveforms are shown in Section 1.

PARAMETER MEASUREMENT INFORMATION

SELECT INPUT/LOGIC MODE TEST TABLE
FUNCTION INPUTS: M = 4.5 V

PARAMETER	INPUT UNDER TEST	OTHER INPUT SAME BIT		OTHER DATA INPUTS		OUTPUT UNDER TEST	OUTPUT WAVEFORM (SEE NOTE 1)
		APPLY 4.5 V	APPLY GND	APPLY 4.5 V	APPLY GND		
t_{PLH} t_{PHL}	Any S	—	—	Remaining $\overline{B}$	$\overline{A}$, $\overline{B0}$, C_n	C_{n+4}	Out-of-Phase
t_{PLH} t_{PHL}	Any S	—	—	$\overline{B}$, $\overline{A2}$	Remaining $\overline{A}$, C_n	$\overline{P}$	In-Phase

SELECT INPUT/ARITH MODE TEST TABLE
FUNCTION INPUTS: M = 0 V

PARAMETER	INPUT UNDER TEST	OTHER INPUT SAME BIT		OTHER DATA INPUTS		OUTPUT UNDER TEST	OUTPUT WAVEFORM (SEE NOTE 1)
		APPLY 4.5 V	APPLY GND	APPLY 4.5 V	APPLY GND		
t_{PLH} t_{PHL}	Any S	—	—	Remaining $\overline{A}$ and $\overline{B}$, C_n	$\overline{A0}$, $\overline{B0}$	Any $\overline{F}$	In-Phase
t_{PLH} t_{PHL}	Any S	—	—	Remaining $\overline{A}$ and $\overline{B}$, C_n	$\overline{A0}$, $\overline{B0}$	A = B	In-Phase
t_{PLH} t_{PHL}	Any S	—	—	Remaining $\overline{A}$ and $\overline{B}$, C_n	$\overline{A0}$, $\overline{B0}$	$\overline{G}$	In-Phase

MODE INPUT/$\overline{SUM}$ MODE TEST TABLE
FUNCTION INPUTS: S0 = S3 = 4.5 V, S1 = S2 = 0 V

PARAMETER	INPUT UNDER TEST	OTHER INPUT SAME BIT		OTHER DATA INPUTS		OUTPUT UNDER TEST	OUTPUT WAVEFORM (SEE NOTE 1)
		APPLY 4.5 V	APPLY GND	APPLY 4.5 V	APPLY GND		
t_{PLH} t_{PHL}	M	—	—	Remaining $\overline{A}$ and $\overline{B}$	$\overline{B2}$, $\overline{A2}$, C_n	Any $\overline{F}$	In-Phase
t_{PLH} t_{PHL}	M	—	—	Remaining $\overline{A}$ and $\overline{B}$	$\overline{B1}$, $\overline{A1}$, C_n	A = B	In-Phase

NOTE 1: Load circuit and voltage waveforms are shown in Section 1.

SN54ALS2967, SN74ALS2967, SN54ALS2968, SN74ALS2968 DYNAMIC MEMORY CONTROLLERS

D2900, JANUARY 1986

- Provides Control for 16K, 64K, and 256K Dynamic RAMs
- Highest-Order Two-Address Bits Select One of Four Banks of RAMs
- Supports Scrubbing Operations and Nibble-Mode Access
- Separate Output Enable for Multi-Channel Access to Memory
- 48-Pin Dual-In-Line Package
- 'ALS2968 is Designed to be Interchangeable with AMD AM2968

SN54ALS2967, SN54ALS2968 . . . JD PACKAGE
SN74ALS2967, SN74ALS2968 . . . JD OR N PACKAGE
(TOP VIEW)

Signal	Pin	Pin	Signal
$\overline{CS}$	1	48	$\overline{CASI}$ or CASI†
MSEL	2	47	$\overline{RAS0}$
A0	3	46	$\overline{CAS0}$
A9	4	45	$\overline{RAS1}$
A1	5	44	$\overline{CAS1}$
A10	6	43	Q0
A2	7	42	Q1
A11	8	41	Q2
A3	9	40	Q3
A12	10	39	Q4
A4	11	38	GND
A13	12	37	$\overline{OE}$
GND	13	36	V_{CC}
LE	14	35	Q5
A5	15	34	Q6
A14	16	33	Q7
A6	17	32	Q8
A15	18	31	$\overline{RAS2}$
A7	19	30	$\overline{CAS2}$
A16	20	29	$\overline{RAS3}$
A8	21	28	$\overline{CAS3}$
A17	22	27	$\overline{RASI}$ or RASI†
SEL0	23	26	MC0
SEL1	24	25	MC1

† 'ALS2967 has active-low inputs $\overline{CASI}$ and $\overline{RASI}$; 'ALS2968 has active-high inputs CASI and RASI.

description

The 'ALS2967 and 'ALS2968 dynamic memory controllers (DMCs) are designed for use in today's high-performance memory systems. The DMC acts as the address controller between any processor and dynamic memory array.

Two versions are provided that help simplify interfacing to the system dynamic timing controller. The 'ALS2967 offers active-low Row Address Strobe Input ($\overline{RASI}$) and Column Address Strobe Input ($\overline{CASI}$), while the 'ALS2968 offers active-high Row Address Strobe Input (RASI) and Column Address Strobe Input (CASI) inputs.

Using two 9-bit address latches, the DMC will hold the row and column addresses for any DRAM up to 256K. These latches and the two row/column refresh address counters feed into a 9-bit, 4-input MUX for output to the dynamic RAM address lines. A 2-bit bank select latch is provided to select one of the four $\overline{RAS}$ and $\overline{CAS}$ outputs. The two bits are normally obtained from the two highest-order address bits.

The 'ALS2967 and 'ALS2968 have two basic modes of operation, read/write and refresh. During normal read/write operations, the row and column addresses are multiplexed to the dynamic RAM, with the corresponding $\overline{RAS}$ and $\overline{CAS}$ signals activated to strobe the addresses into the RAM. In the refresh mode, the two counters cycle through the refresh addresses. If memory scrubbing is not being implemented, only the row counter is used. When memory scrubbing is being performed, both the row and column counters are used to perform read-modify-write cycles. In this mode all $\overline{RAS}$ outputs will be active (low) while only one $\overline{CAS}$ output is active at a time.

The SN54ALS2967 and SN54ALS2968 are characterized for operation over the full military temperature range of −55°C to 125°C. The SN74ALS2967 and SN74ALS2968 are characterized for operation from 0°C to 70°C.

logic symbols†

'ALS2967

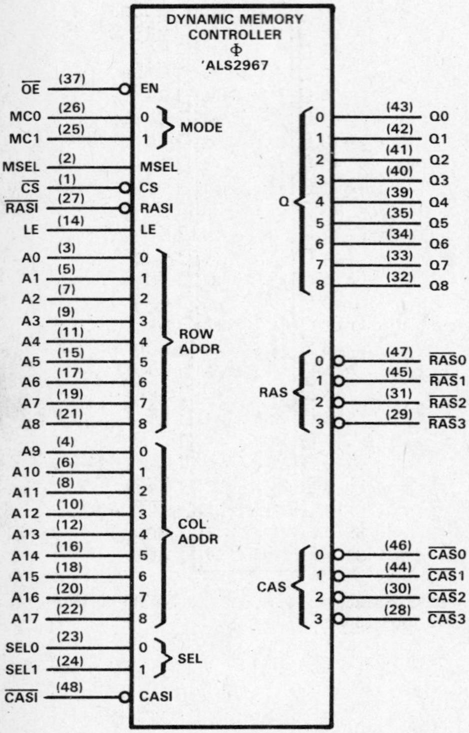
DYNAMIC MEMORY CONTROLLER
Φ
'ALS2967
OE (37) EN
MC0 (26) 0
MC1 (25) 1
MODE
MSEL (2) MSEL
CS (1) CS
RASI (27) RASI
LE (14) LE
A0 (3) 0
A1 (5) 1
A2 (7) 2
A3 (9) 3
A4 (11) 4
A5 (15) 5
A6 (17) 6
A7 (19) 7
A8 (21) 8
ROW ADDR
A9 (4) 0
A10 (6) 1
A11 (8) 2
A12 (10) 3
A13 (12) 4
A14 (16) 5
A15 (18) 6
A16 (20) 7
A17 (22) 8
COL ADDR
SEL0 (23) 0
SEL1 (24) 1
SEL
CASI (48) CASI
Q
0 (43) Q0
1 (42) Q1
2 (41) Q2
3 (40) Q3
4 (39) Q4
5 (35) Q5
6 (34) Q6
7 (33) Q7
8 (32) Q8
RAS
0 (47) RAS0
1 (45) RAS1
2 (31) RAS2
3 (29) RAS3
CAS
0 (46) CAS0
1 (44) CAS1
2 (30) CAS2
3 (28) CAS3

'ALS2968

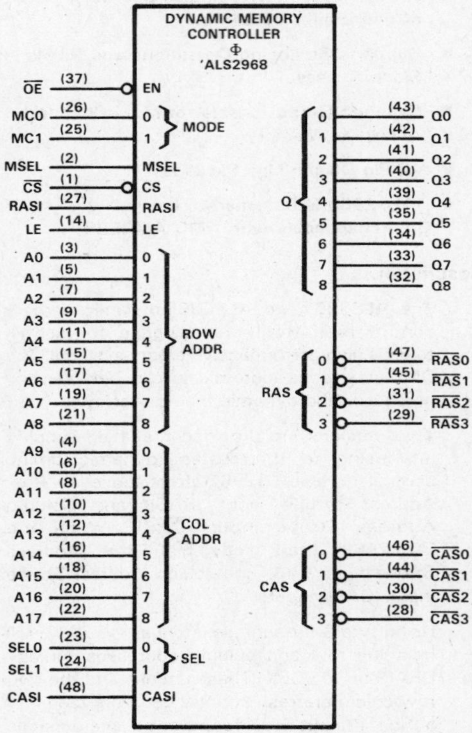
DYNAMIC MEMORY CONTROLLER
Φ
'ALS2968
OE (37) EN
MC0 (26) 0
MC1 (25) 1
MODE
MSEL (2) MSEL
CS (1) CS
RASI (27) RASI
LE (14) LE
A0 (3) 0
A1 (5) 1
A2 (7) 2
A3 (9) 3
A4 (11) 4
A5 (15) 5
A6 (17) 6
A7 (19) 7
A8 (21) 8
ROW ADDR
A9 (4) 0
A10 (6) 1
A11 (8) 2
A12 (10) 3
A13 (12) 4
A14 (16) 5
A15 (18) 6
A16 (20) 7
A17 (22) 8
COL ADDR
SEL0 (23) 0
SEL1 (24) 1
SEL
CASI (48) CASI
Q
0 (43) Q0
1 (42) Q1
2 (41) Q2
3 (40) Q3
4 (39) Q4
5 (35) Q5
6 (34) Q6
7 (33) Q7
8 (32) Q8
RAS
0 (47) RAS0
1 (45) RAS1
2 (31) RAS2
3 (29) RAS3
CAS
0 (46) CAS0
1 (44) CAS1
2 (30) CAS2
3 (28) CAS3

† These symbols are in accordance with ANSI/IEEE Std 91-1984 and IEC Publication 617-12.

TEXAS INSTRUMENTS
POST OFFICE BOX 225012 • DALLAS, TEXAS 75265

logic diagram (positive logic)

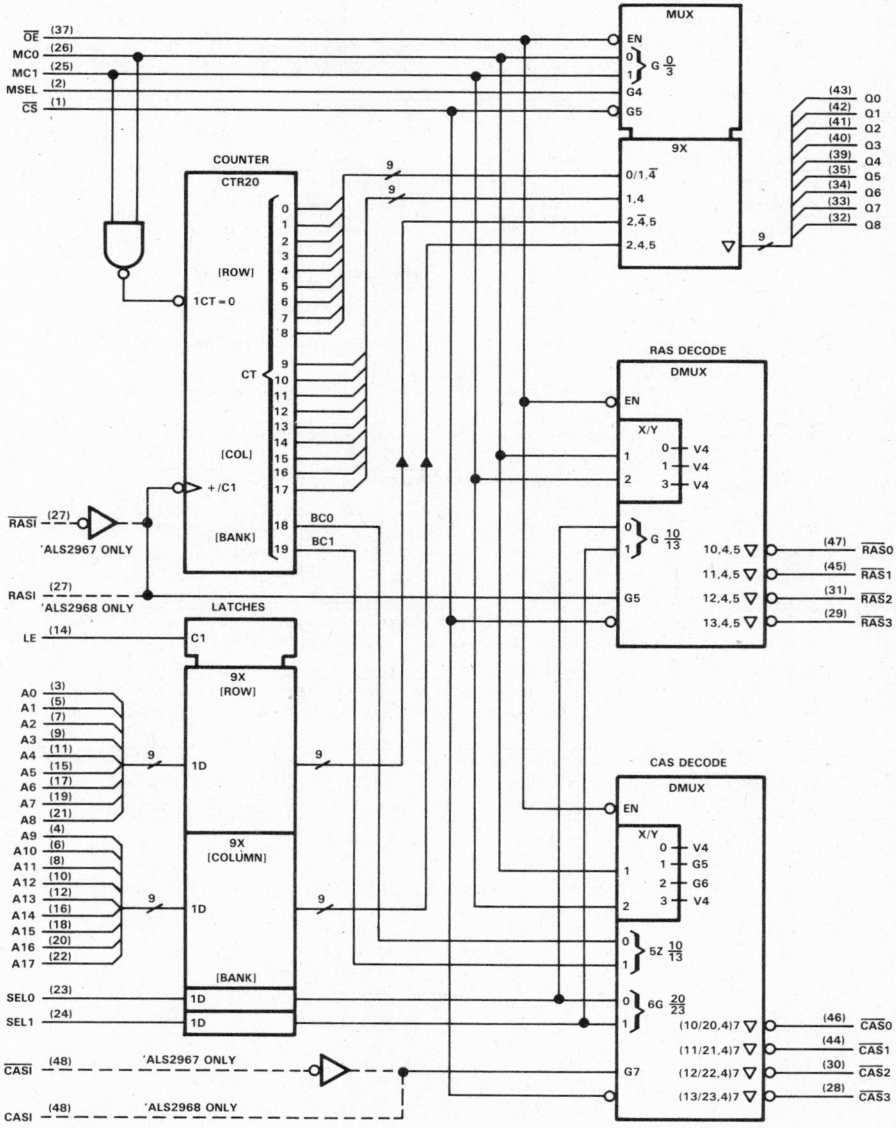
OE (37)
MC0 (26)
MC1 (25)
MSEL (2)
CS (1)
MUX
EN
G 0/3
G4
G5
9X
0/1,4̄
1,4
2,4̄,5
2,4,5
(43) Q0
(42) Q1
(41) Q2
(40) Q3
(39) Q4
(35) Q5
(34) Q6
(33) Q7
(32) Q8
COUNTER
CTR20
1CT=0
[ROW]
CT
[COL]
[BANK]
+/C1
BC0
BC1
RASI (27)
'ALS2967 ONLY
RASI (27)
'ALS2968 ONLY
RAS DECODE
DMUX
X/Y
V4
G 10/13
10,4,5
11,4,5
12,4,5
13,4,5
(47) RAS0
(45) RAS1
(31) RAS2
(29) RAS3
LATCHES
LE (14)
C1
9X
[ROW]
1D
A0 (3)
A1 (5)
A2 (7)
A3 (9)
A4 (11)
A5 (15)
A6 (17)
A7 (19)
A8 (21)
A9 (4)
A10 (6)
A11 (8)
A12 (10)
A13 (12)
A14 (16)
A15 (18)
A16 (20)
A17 (22)
9X
[COLUMN]
[BANK]
SEL0 (23)
SEL1 (24)
CAS DECODE
DMUX
G6
5Z 10/13
6G 20/23
G7
(10/20,4)7
(11/21,4)7
(12/22,4)7
(13/23,4)7
(46) CAS0
(44) CAS1
(30) CAS2
(28) CAS3
CASI (48) 'ALS2967 ONLY
CASI (48) 'ALS2968 ONLY

2
LSI Devices

TABLE 1. PIN FUNCTION

PIN NAME	DESCRIPTION
A0-A17	Address Inputs. A0-A8 are latched in as the nine-bit row address for the DRAM. These inputs drive Q0-Q8 when the DMC is in the read/write mode and MSEL is low. A9-A17 are latched in as the column address, and will drive Q0-Q8 when MSEL is high and the DMC is in the read/write mode. The addresses are latched when the Latch Enable (LE) input signal is low.
SEL0, SEL1	Bank Select. These two inputs are normally the two highest-order address bits and are used in the read/write mode to select which bank of memory will be receiving the $\overline{RAS}$ and $\overline{CAS}$ signals after $\overline{RASI}$ ('ALS2967) or RASI ('ALS2968) and $\overline{CASI}$ ('ALS2967) or CASI ('ALS2968) go active.
LE	Latch Enable. This active-high input causes the row, column, and bank select latches to become transparent, allowing the latches to accept new input data. A low input on LE latches the input data.
MSEL	Multiplexer Select. This input determines whether the row or column address will be sent to the memory address inputs. When MSEL is high, the column address is selected, while the row address is selected when MSEL is low. The address may come from either the address latch or refresh address counter depending on MC0 and MC1 (see Mode Control Function Table).
$\overline{CS}$	Chip Select. This active-low input is used to enable the DMC. When $\overline{CS}$ is active, the DMC operates normally in all four modes. When $\overline{CS}$ goes high, the device will not enter the read/write mode. This allows other devices to access the same memory that the DMC is controlling.
$\overline{OE}$	Output Enable. This active-low input enables/disables the output signals. When $\overline{OE}$ is high, the outputs of the DMC enter the high-impedance state.
MC0-MC1	Mode Controls. These inputs determine in which of the four modes the DMC operates. The description of each of the four operating modes is given in Table 2.
Q0-Q8	Address Outputs. These address outputs feed the DRAM address inputs and provide drive for memory systems having capacitance of up to 500 picofarads.
$\overline{RASI}$ or RASI	Row Address Strobe Input. During the normal memory cycles, the decoded $\overline{RAS}$n output ($\overline{RAS0}$, $\overline{RAS1}$, $\overline{RAS2}$, or $\overline{RAS3}$) is forced low after receipt of an active Row Address Strobe Input signal. In either Refresh mode, all four $\overline{RAS}$ outputs will be low while the Row Address Strobe Input signal is active. The $\overline{RASI}$ on the 'ALS2967 is an active-low input while on the 'ALS2968, RASI is an active-high input. (For more details see timing diagrams).
$\overline{RAS0}$-$\overline{RAS3}$	Row Address Strobe. Each of the Row Address Strobe outputs provides a $\overline{RAS}$ signal to one of the four banks of dynamic memory. Each $\overline{RAS}$n output will go low when selected by SEL0 and SEL1 after $\overline{RASI}$ ('ALS2967) or RASI ('ALS2968) goes active. All four go low in response to $\overline{RASI}$ ('ALS2967) or RASI ('ALS2968) while in the refresh mode.
$\overline{CASI}$ or CASI	Column Address Strobe Input. This input going active causes the selected $\overline{CAS}$ output to be forced low. The $\overline{CASI}$ input on the 'ALS2967 is active low input while on the 'ALS2968, CASI is active high input. (For more details see timing diagrams.)
$\overline{CAS0}$-$\overline{CAS3}$	Column Address Strobe. During normal Read/Write cycles the two selected bits (SEL0, SEL1) determine which $\overline{CAS}$ output will go active following $\overline{CASI}$ ('ALS2967) or CASI ('ALS2968) going active. When memory scrubbing is being performed, only the $\overline{CAS}$n signal selected will be active. For non-scrubbing cycles, all four $\overline{CAS}$ outputs will remain high.

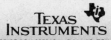

TEXAS INSTRUMENTS
POST OFFICE BOX 225012 • DALLAS, TEXAS 75265

TABLE 2. MODE-CONTROL FUNCTION TABLE

MC1	MC0	OPERATING MODE
L	L	Refresh Mode without Scrubbing. Refresh cycles are performed with only the row counter being used to generate the addresses. In this mode, all four $\overline{\text{RAS}}$ outputs are active while the four $\overline{\text{CAS}}$ outputs remain high.
L	H	Refresh with Scrubbing/Initialize. During this mode, refresh cycles are done with both the row and column counters generating the addresses. MSEL is used to select either the row or the column counter. All four $\overline{\text{RAS}}$ outputs go low in response to $\overline{\text{RASI}}$ ('ALS2967) or RASI ('ALS2968), while only one $\overline{\text{CAS}}$n output goes low in response to $\overline{\text{CASI}}$ ('ALS2967) or CASI ('ALS2968). The bank counter keeps track of which $\overline{\text{CAS}}$ output goes active. This mode can also be used during system power-up so that the memory can be written with a known data pattern.
H	L	Read/Write. This mode is used to perform read/write cycles. Both the Row and Column addresses are multiplexed to the address output lines using MSEL. SEL0 and SEL1 are decoded to determine which $\overline{\text{RAS}}$n and $\overline{\text{CAS}}$n outputs will be active.
H	H	Clear Refresh Counters. This mode clears the three refresh counters (row, column, and bank) on the inactive transition of $\overline{\text{RASI}}$ ('ALS2967) or RASI ('ALS2968), putting them at start of the refresh sequence (see timing diagrams for more detail). In this mode, all four $\overline{\text{RAS}}$ outputs are driven low after the active edge of $\overline{\text{RASI}}$ ('ALS2967) or RASI ('ALS2968) so that DRAM wake-up cycles may also be performed.

TABLE 3. ADDRESS OUTPUT FUNCTIONS

MODE	INPUTS				OUTPUTS Q0-Q8
	MC1	MC0	MSEL	$\overline{\text{CS}}$	
Refresh without scrubbing	L	L	X	X	Row counter address
Refresh with scrubbing	L	H	L	X	Row counter address
			H	X	Column counter address
Read/write	H	L	L	L	Row address†
			H	L	Column address†
			X	H	All L
Clear refresh counter‡	H	H	X	X	All L

TABLE 4. RAS OUTPUT FUNCTIONS

INPUTS							OUTPUTS			
'ALS2967 $\overline{\text{RASI}}$	'ALS2968 RASI	MC1	MC0	SEL1†	SEL0†	$\overline{\text{CS}}$	$\overline{\text{RAS0}}$	$\overline{\text{RAS1}}$	$\overline{\text{RAS2}}$	$\overline{\text{RAS3}}$
L	H	L	L	X	X	X	L	L	L	L
L	H	L	H	X	X	X	L	L	L	L
L	H	H	L	L	L	L	L	H	H	H
				L	H	L	H	L	H	H
				H	L	L	H	H	L	H
				H	H	L	H	H	H	L
				X	X	H	H	H	H	H
L	H	H	H	X	X	X	L	L	L	L
H	L	X	X	X	X	X	H	H	H	H

TABLE 5. CAS OUTPUT FUNCTIONS

INPUTS									OUTPUTS			
'ALS2967 $\overline{\text{CASI}}$	'ALS2968 CASI	MC1	MC0	SEL1†	SEL0†	INTERNAL BC1	INTERNAL BC0	CS	$\overline{\text{CAS0}}$	$\overline{\text{CAS1}}$	$\overline{\text{CAS2}}$	$\overline{\text{CAS3}}$
L	H	L	L	X	X	X	X	X	H	H	H	H
L	H	L	H	X	X	L	L	X	L	H	H	H
						L	H	X	H	L	H	H
						H	L	X	H	H	L	H
						H	H	X	H	H	H	L
L	H	H	L	L	L	X	X	L	L	H	H	H
				L	H	X	X	L	H	L	H	H
				H	L	X	X	L	H	H	L	H
				H	H	X	X	L	H	H	H	L
				X	X	X	X	H	H	H	H	H
L	H	H	H	X	X	X	X	X	H	H	H	H
H	L	X	X	X	X	X	X	X	H	H	H	H

† If LE is low, outputs will be the levels entered when LE was last high. If LE is high, outputs will follow address inputs as selected by MSEL.
‡ For 'ALS2967, clearing occurs on the low-to-high transition of $\overline{\text{RASI}}$; for 'ALS2968, clearing occurs on the high-to-low transition of RASI.

read/write operation details

During normal read/write operations, the row and column addresses are multiplexed to the dynamic RAM controlled by the MSEL input. The corresponding $\overline{RAS}$n and $\overline{CAS}$n output signals strobe the addresses into memory. The block diagram in Figure 1 shows a typical system interface for a one-megaword dynamic memory. The DMC is used to control the four banks of 256K memory.

For systems where addresses and data are multiplexed onto a single bus, the DMC uses latches, (row, column, and bank) to hold the address information. Figure 5 shows a typical timing diagram using the input latches. The twenty input latches are transparent when latch enable (LE) is high, and latch the input data whenever LE is taken low. For systems in which the processor has separate address and data buses, LE may be permanently high (see timing diagram in Figure 4).

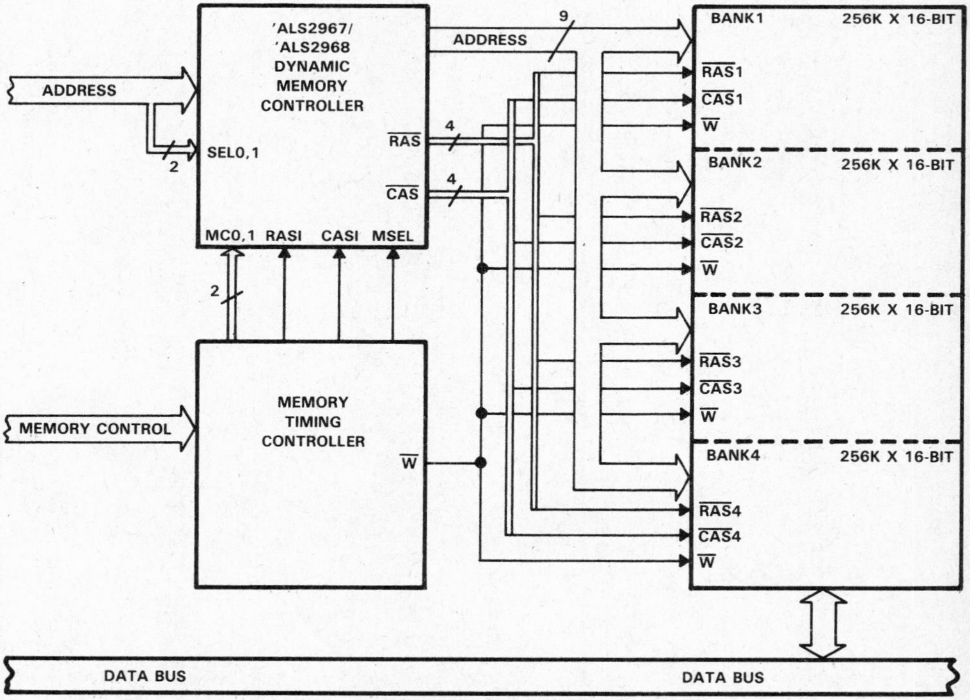
'ALS2967/
'ALS2968
DYNAMIC
MEMORY
CONTROLLER
ADDRESS
SEL0,1
2
RAS
CAS
4
4
9
ADDRESS
MC0,1 RASI CASI MSEL
2
MEMORY CONTROL
MEMORY
TIMING
CONTROLLER
W
BANK1 256K X 16-BIT
RAS1
CAS1
W
BANK2 256K X 16-BIT
RAS2
CAS2
W
BANK3 256K X 16-BIT
RAS3
CAS3
W
BANK4 256K X 16-BIT
RAS4
CAS4
W
DATA BUS
DATA BUS

FIGURE 1. 1-MEGAWORD X 16-BIT DYNAMIC MEMORY

read/write operations (continued)

The DMC is designed with heavy-duty outputs that are capable of driving four banks of 16-bit words, including six checkbits used for error detection and correction.

In addition to heavy-duty output drivers, the outputs are designed with balanced output impedances (25 Ω both high and low). This feature optimizes the drive low characteristics, based on safe undershoot, while providing symmetrical drive high characteristics. It also eliminates the external resistors required to pull the outputs up to the MOS V_{OH} level (V_{CC} − 1.5 V).

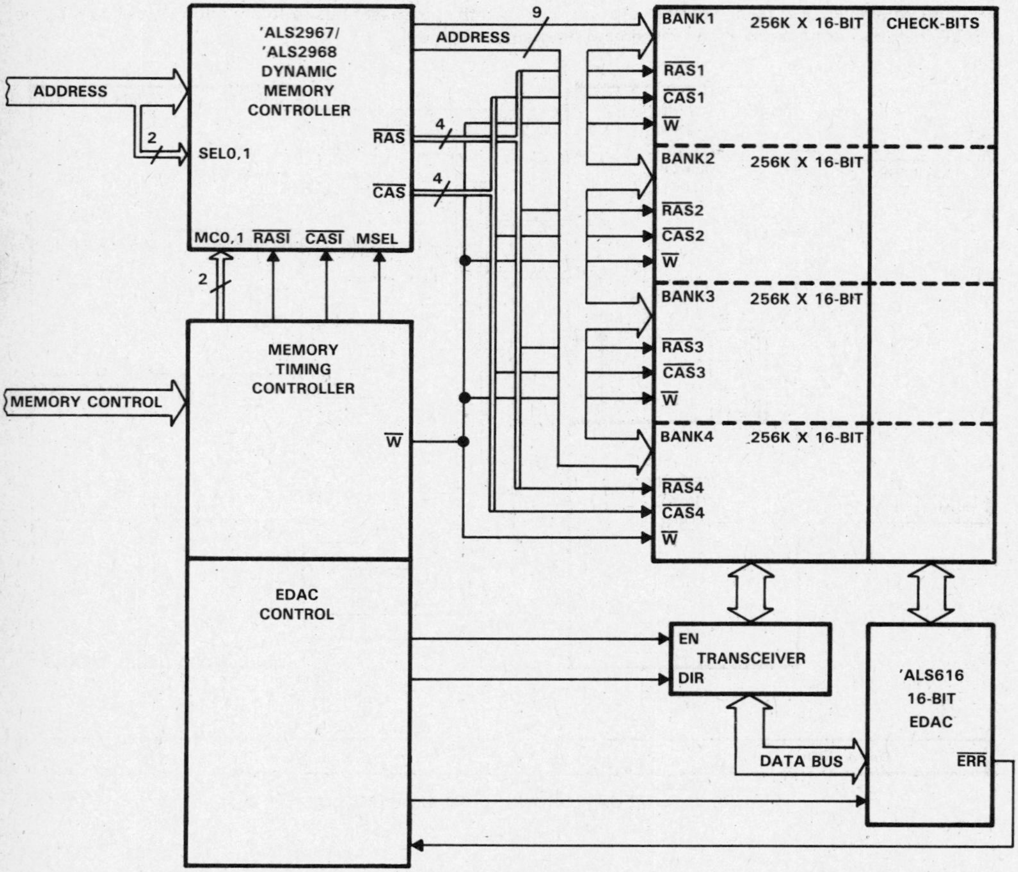
'ALS2967/
'ALS2968
DYNAMIC
MEMORY
CONTROLLER
ADDRESS
9
ADDRESS
2
SEL0,1
RAS
4
CAS
4
MC0,1 RASI CASI MSEL
2
MEMORY
TIMING
CONTROLLER
MEMORY CONTROL
W
EDAC
CONTROL
BANK1
256K X 16-BIT
CHECK-BITS
RAS1
CAS1
W
BANK2
256K X 16-BIT
RAS2
CAS2
W
BANK3
256K X 16-BIT
RAS3
CAS3
W
BANK4
256K X 16-BIT
RAS4
CAS4
W
EN
TRANSCEIVER
DIR
DATA BUS
'ALS616
16-BIT
EDAC
ERR

FIGURE 2. 1-MEGAWORD X 16-BIT DYNAMIC MEMORY WITH ERROR DETECTION AND CORRECTION

TEXAS INSTRUMENTS
POST OFFICE BOX 225012 • DALLAS, TEXAS 75265

memory expansion

With a 9-bit address path, the DMC can control up to one megaword when using 256K dynamic RAMs. If a larger memory size is desired, the DMC's chip select (CS) makes it easy to expand the memory size by using additional DMCs. A four-megaword memory system is shown in Figure 3.

To maintain maximum performance in 32-bit applications, it is recommended that individual bus drivers be used for each bank.

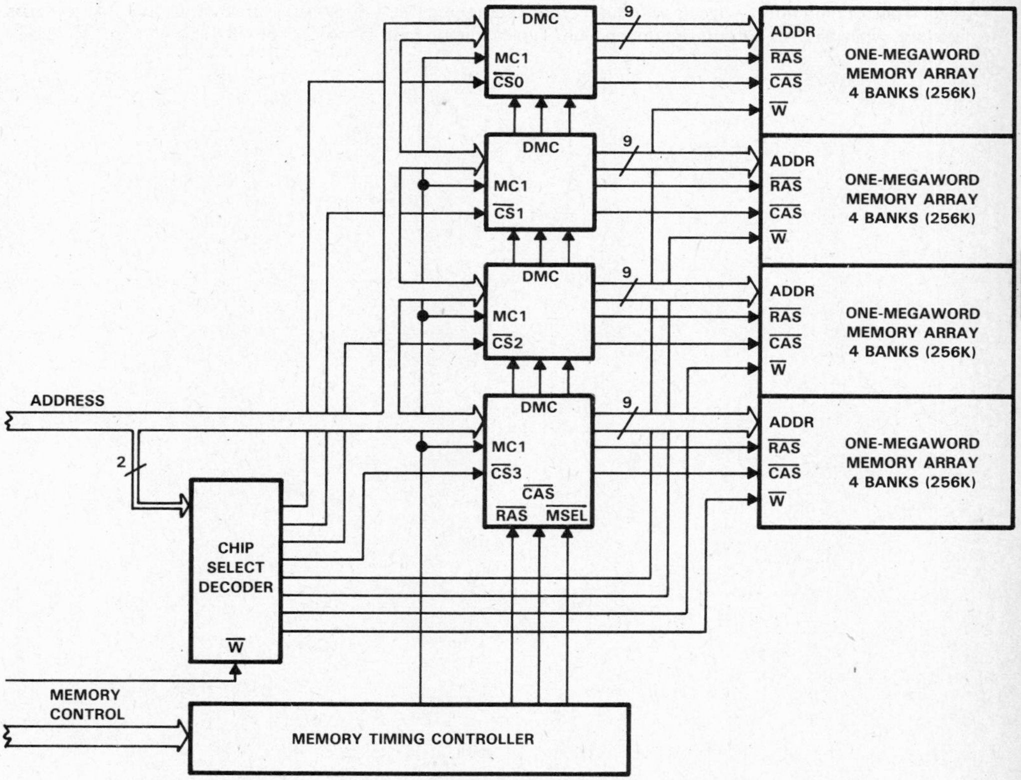
DMC
MC1
CS0
DMC
MC1
CS1
DMC
MC1
CS2
DMC
MC1
CS3
CAS
RAS
MSEL
9
9
9
9
ADDR
RAS
CAS
W
ONE-MEGAWORD MEMORY ARRAY 4 BANKS (256K)
ADDRESS
2
CHIP SELECT DECODER
W
MEMORY CONTROL
MEMORY TIMING CONTROLLER

FIGURE 3. 4-MEGAWORD X 16-BIT DYNAMIC MEMORY

refresh operations

The two 9-bit counters in the 'ALS2967 and 'ALS2968 support 128-, 256-, and 512-line refresh operations. Transparent, burst, synchronous, or asynchronous refresh modes are all possible. The refresh counters are advanced on the low-to-high transition of $\overline{\text{RASI}}$ on the 'ALS2967, and on the high-to-low transition of RASI on the 'ALS2968. The refresh counters are reset to zero on the low-to-high transition of $\overline{\text{RASI}}$ on the 'ALS2967, and on the high-to-low transition of RASI on the 'ALS2968, if MC1 and MC0 are at a low logic level. See Figure 8 for additional timing details.

When performing refresh cycles without memory scrubbing (MC1 and MC0 both low), all four $\overline{\text{RAS}}$ outputs go low, while all $\overline{\text{CAS}}$ outputs are driven high. Typical timing for this mode of operation is shown in Figure 6.

TEXAS INSTRUMENTS
POST OFFICE BOX 225012 • DALLAS, TEXAS 75265

absolute maximum ratings over operating free-air temperature range (unless otherwise noted)

Supply voltage, V_{CC}		7 V
Input voltage		7 V
Voltage applied to disabled 3-state output		5.5 V
Operating free-air temperature range:	SN54ALS2967, SN54ALS2968	−55°C to 125°C
	SN74ALS2967, SN74ALS2968	0°C to 70°C
Storage temperature range		−65°C to 150°C

recommended operating conditions

			SN54ALS2967 SN54ALS2968			SN74ALS2967 SN74ALS2968			UNIT
			MIN	NOM	MAX	MIN	NOM	MAX	
V_{CC}	Supply voltage		4.5	5	5.5	4.5	5	5.5	V
V_{IH}	High-level input voltage		2			2			V
V_{IL}	Low-level input voltage				0.8			0.8	V
I_{OH}	High-level output current				−1			−2.6	mA
I_{OL}	Low-level output current				12			12	mA
t_w	Pulse duration	(23) $\overline{RASI}$ low or RASI high	15			15			ns
		(24) $\overline{RASI}$ high or RASI low	15			15			
		(25) LE high	20			20			
t_{su}	Setup time	(26) An before LE↓	5			5			ns
		(27) SELn before LE↓	5			5			
		(28) MC0 or MC1 before $\overline{RASI}$↑ or RASI↓	25			25			
		(29) SELn before $\overline{RASI}$↓ or RASI↑	15			15			
t_h	Hold time	(30) An after LE↓	5			5			ns
		(31) SELn after LE↓	5			5			
T_A	Operating free-air temperature		−55		125	0		70	°C

electrical characteristics over recommended operating free-air temperature range (unless otherwise noted)

PARAMETER	TEST CONDITIONS		SN54ALS2967 SN54ALS2968			SN74ALS2967 SN74ALS2968			UNIT
			MIN	TYP†	MAX	MIN	TYP†	MAX	
V_{IK}	V_{CC} = 4.5 V,	I_I = −18 mA			−1.5			−1.5	V
V_{OH}	V_{CC} = 4.5 V,	I_{OH} = −1 mA	2.4	3.3					V
	V_{CC} = 4.5 V,	I_{OH} = −2.6 mA				2.4	3.2		
V_{OL}	V_{CC} = 4.5 V,	I_{OL} = 1 mA		0.15	0.5		0.15	0.5	V
	V_{CC} = 4.5 V,	I_{OL} = 12 mA		0.35	0.8		0.35	0.8	
I_{OL}‡	V_{CC} = 4.5 V,	V_O = 2 V	30			30			mA
I_{OZH}	V_{CC} = 5.5 V,	V_O = 2.7 V			20			20	μA
I_{OZL}	V_{CC} = 5.5 V,	V_O = 0.4 V			−20			−20	μA
I_I	V_{CC} = 5.5 V,	V_I = 7 V			0.1			0.1	mA
I_{IH}	V_{CC} = 5.5 V,	V_I = 2.7 V			20			20	μA
I_{IL}	V_{CC} = 5.5 V,	V_I = 0.4 V			−0.1			−0.1	mA
I_O§	V_{CC} = 5.5 V,	V_O = 2.25 V	−30		−112	−30		−112	mA
I_{CC}	V_{CC} = 5.5 V								mA

† All typical values are at V_{CC} = 5 V, T_A = 25°C.
‡ Not more than one output should be tested at a time, and duration should not exceed 1 second.
§ The output conditions have been chosen to produce a current that closely approximates one half the true short-circuit output current, I_{OS}.

2
LSI Devices

'ALS2967 switching characteristics, C_L = 50 pF

PARAMETER	FROM (INPUT)	TO (OUTPUT)	TEST CONDITIONS†	SN54ALS2967 MIN	SN54ALS2967 TYP‡	SN54ALS2967 MAX	SN74ALS2967 MIN	SN74ALS2967 TYP‡	SN74ALS2967 MAX	UNIT
$t_{pd(1)}$	$\overline{RASI}$	Any Q	V_{CC} = 4.5 V to 5.5 V, T_A = MIN to MAX		12			12		ns
$t_{pd(2)}$	$\overline{RASI}$	$\overline{RAS}$n			10			10		ns
$t_{pd(3)}$	$\overline{CASI}$	$\overline{CAS}$n			8			8		ns
$t_{pd(4)}$	Any A	Any Q			22			22		ns
$t_{pd(5)}$	MSEL	Any Q			14			14		ns
$t_{pd(6)}$	LE↑	Any Q			15			15		ns
$t_{pd(7)}$	LE↑	Any $\overline{RAS}$			15			15		ns
$t_{pd(8)}$	LE↑	Any $\overline{CAS}$			14			14		ns
$t_{pd(9)}$	MC0 or MC1	Any Q			15			15		ns
$t_{pd(10)}$	MC0 or MC1	Any $\overline{RAS}$			14			14		ns
$t_{pd(11)}$	MC0 or MC1	Any $\overline{CAS}$			12			12		ns
$t_{pd(12)}$	$\overline{CS}$	Any Q			16			16		ns
$t_{pd(13)}$	$\overline{CS}$	Any $\overline{RAS}$			12			12		ns
$t_{pd(14)}$	$\overline{CS}$	Any $\overline{CAS}$			11			11		ns
$t_{pd(15)}$	SEL0 or SEL1	Any $\overline{RAS}$			12			12		ns
$t_{pd(16)}$	SEL0 or SEL1	Any $\overline{CAS}$			11			11		ns
$t_{en(17)}$	$\overline{OE}$↓	Any Q			14			14		ns
$t_{en(18)}$	$\overline{OE}$↓	Any $\overline{RAS}$			13			13		ns
$t_{en(19)}$	$\overline{OE}$↓	Any $\overline{CAS}$			13			13		ns
$t_{dis(20)}$	$\overline{OE}$↑	Any Q			15			15		ns
$t_{dis(21)}$	$\overline{OE}$↑	Any $\overline{RAS}$			13			13		ns
$t_{dis(22)}$	$\overline{OE}$↑	Any $\overline{CAS}$			13			13		ns

'ALS2967 switching characteristics, C_L = 150 pF

PARAMETER	FROM (INPUT)	TO (OUTPUT)	TEST CONDITIONS†	SN54ALS2967 MIN	SN54ALS2967 TYP‡	SN54ALS2967 MAX	SN74ALS2967 MIN	SN74ALS2967 TYP‡	SN74ALS2967 MAX	UNIT
$t_{pd(1)}$	$\overline{RASI}$	Any Q	V_{CC} = 4.5 V to 5.5 V, T_A = MIN to MAX		17			17		ns
$t_{pd(2)}$	$\overline{RASI}$	$\overline{RAS}$n			15			15		ns
$t_{pd(3)}$	$\overline{CASI}$	$\overline{CAS}$n			14			14		ns
$t_{pd(4)}$	Any A	Any Q			27			27		ns
$t_{pd(5)}$	MSEL	Any Q			19			19		ns
$t_{pd(6)}$	LE↑	Any Q			20			20		ns
$t_{pd(7)}$	LE↑	Any $\overline{RAS}$			20			20		ns
$t_{pd(8)}$	LE↑	Any $\overline{CAS}$			19			19		ns
$t_{pd(9)}$	MC0 or MC1	Any Q			20			20		ns
$t_{pd(10)}$	MC0 or MC1	Any $\overline{RAS}$			19			19		ns
$t_{pd(11)}$	MC0 or MC1	Any $\overline{CAS}$			17			17		ns
$t_{pd(12)}$	$\overline{CS}$	Any Q			19			19		ns
$t_{pd(13)}$	$\overline{CS}$	Any $\overline{RAS}$			14			14		ns
$t_{pd(14)}$	$\overline{CS}$	Any $\overline{CAS}$			14			14		ns
$t_{pd(15)}$	SEL0 or SEL1	Any $\overline{RAS}$			15			15		ns
$t_{pd(16)}$	SEL0 or SEL1	Any $\overline{CAS}$			14			14		ns

† See Figures 10, 11, 12, and 13 for test circuit and switching waveforms.
‡ All typical values at V_{CC} = 5 V, T_A = 25°C.

'ALS2968 switching characteristics, C_L = 50 pF

PARAMETER	FROM (INPUT)	TO (OUTPUT)	TEST CONDITIONS†	SN54ALS2968			SN74ALS2968			UNIT
				MIN	TYP‡	MAX	MIN	TYP‡	MAX	
$t_{pd(1)}$	RASI	Any Q		5	12	20	5	12	20	ns
$t_{pd(2)}$	RASI	$\overline{\text{RAS}}$n		3	10	18	3	10	18	ns
$t_{pd(3)}$	CASI	$\overline{\text{CAS}}$n		3	8	17	3	8	17	ns
$t_{pd(4)}$	Any A	Any Q		5	22	30	5	22	30	ns
$t_{pd(5)}$	MSEL	Any Q		3	14	20	3	14	20	ns
$t_{pd(6)}$	LE↑	Any Q			15	25		15	25	ns
$t_{pd(7)}$	LE↑	Any $\overline{\text{RAS}}$			15	25		15	25	ns
$t_{pd(8)}$	LE↑	Any $\overline{\text{CAS}}$			14	24		14	24	ns
$t_{pd(9)}$	MC0 or MC1	Any Q		5	15	25	5	15	25	ns
$t_{pd(10)}$	MC0 or MC1	Any $\overline{\text{RAS}}$		3	14	21	3	14	21	ns
$t_{pd(11)}$	MC0 or MC1	Any $\overline{\text{CAS}}$	V_{CC} = 4.5 V to 5.5 V, T_A = MIN to MAX	3	12	19	3	12	19	ns
$t_{pd(12)}$	$\overline{\text{CS}}$	Any Q			16	23		16	23	ns
$t_{pd(13)}$	$\overline{\text{CS}}$	Any $\overline{\text{RAS}}$			12	20		12	20	ns
$t_{pd(14)}$	$\overline{\text{CS}}$	Any $\overline{\text{CAS}}$			11	19		11	19	ns
$t_{pd(15)}$	SEL0 or SEL1	Any $\overline{\text{RAS}}$			12	20		12	20	ns
$t_{pd(16)}$	SEL0 or SEL1	Any $\overline{\text{CAS}}$			11	18		11	18	ns
$t_{en(17)}$	$\overline{\text{OE}}$↓	Any Q			14	21		14	21	ns
$t_{en(18)}$	$\overline{\text{OE}}$↓	Any $\overline{\text{RAS}}$			13	19		13	19	ns
$t_{en(19)}$	$\overline{\text{OE}}$↓	Any $\overline{\text{CAS}}$			13	19		13	19	ns
$t_{dis(20)}$	$\overline{\text{OE}}$↑	Any Q			15	22		15	22	ns
$t_{dis(21)}$	$\overline{\text{OE}}$↑	Any $\overline{\text{RAS}}$			13	20		13	20	ns
$t_{dis(22)}$	$\overline{\text{OE}}$↑	Any $\overline{\text{CAS}}$			13	20		13	20	ns

'ALS2968 switching characteristics, C_L = 150 pF

PARAMETER	FROM (INPUT)	TO (OUTPUT)	TEST CONDITIONS†	SN54ALS2968			SN74ALS2968			UNIT
				MIN	TYP‡	MAX	MIN	TYP‡	MAX	
$t_{pd(1)}$	RASI	Any Q		12	17	30	12	17	30	ns
$t_{pd(2)}$	RASI	$\overline{\text{RAS}}$n		9	15	23	9	15	23	ns
$t_{pd(3)}$	CASI	$\overline{\text{CAS}}$n		9	14	22	9	14	22	ns
$t_{pd(4)}$	Any A	Any Q		10	27	35	10	27	35	ns
$t_{pd(5)}$	MSEL	Any Q		9	19	26	9	19	26	ns
$t_{pd(6)}$	LE↑	Any Q			20	28		20	28	ns
$t_{pd(7)}$	LE↑	Any $\overline{\text{RAS}}$			20	28		20	28	ns
$t_{pd(8)}$	LE↑	Any $\overline{\text{CAS}}$	V_{CC} = 4.5 V to 5.5 V, T_A = MIN to MAX		19	27		19	27	ns
$t_{pd(9)}$	MC0 or MC1	Any Q		10	20	27	10	20	27	ns
$t_{pd(10)}$	MC0 or MC1	Any $\overline{\text{RAS}}$		9	19	25	9	19	25	ns
$t_{pd(11)}$	MC0 or MC1	Any $\overline{\text{CAS}}$		9	17	23	9	17	23	ns
$t_{pd(12)}$	$\overline{\text{CS}}$	Any Q			19	27		19	27	ns
$t_{pd(13)}$	$\overline{\text{CS}}$	Any $\overline{\text{RAS}}$			14	22		14	22	ns
$t_{pd(14)}$	$\overline{\text{CS}}$	Any $\overline{\text{CAS}}$			14	22		14	22	ns
$t_{pd(15)}$	SEL0 or SEL1	Any $\overline{\text{RAS}}$			15	23		15	23	ns
$t_{pd(16)}$	SEL0 or SEL1	Any $\overline{\text{CAS}}$			14	22		14	22	ns

† See Figures 10, 11, 12, and 13 for test circuit and switching waveforms.
‡ All typical values at V_{CC} = 5 V, T_A = 25°C.

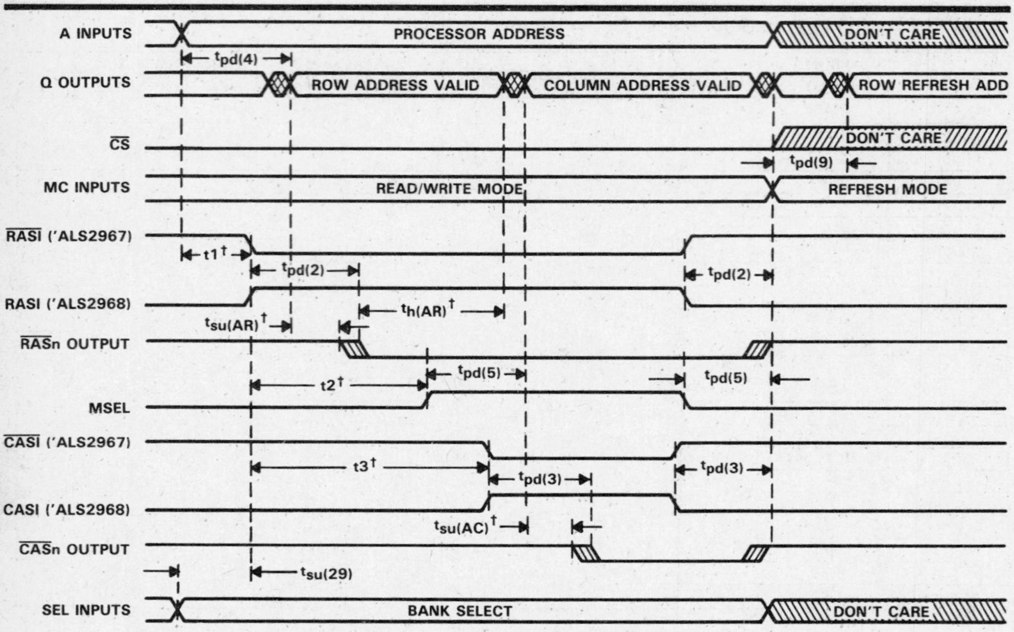
A INPUTS
PROCESSOR ADDRESS
DON'T CARE
tpd(4)
Q OUTPUTS
ROW ADDRESS VALID
COLUMN ADDRESS VALID
ROW REFRESH ADD
CS
DON'T CARE
tpd(9)
MC INPUTS
READ/WRITE MODE
REFRESH MODE
RASI ('ALS2967)
t1†
tpd(2)
tpd(2)
RASI ('ALS2968)
th(AR)†
tsu(AR)†
RASn OUTPUT
tpd(5)
t2†
tpd(5)
MSEL
CASI ('ALS2967)
t3†
tpd(3)
tpd(3)
CASI ('ALS2968)
tsu(AC)†
CASn OUTPUT
tsu(29)
SEL INPUTS
BANK SELECT
DON'T CARE

FIGURE 4. READ/WRITE CYCLE TIMING (MC1, MC0 = 1, 0), (LE = H)

† Parameters $t_{su(AR)}$, $t_{su(AC)}$, and $t_{h(AR)}$ are timing requirements of the dynamic RAM. Parameters t1, t2, and t3 represent the minimum timing requirements at the inputs to the DMC that guarantee DRAM timing specifications and maximum system performance. The minimum requirements for t1, t2, and t3 are as follows:

$t1(min) = t_{pd(4)}\ max + t_{su(AR)}\ min - t_{pd(2)}\ min$
$t2(min) = t_{pd(2)}\ max + t_{h(AR)}\ min - t_{pd(5)}\ min$
$t3(min) = t2\ min + t_{pd(5)}\ max + t_{su(AC)} - t_{pd(3)}\ min$

See the DRAM data sheet for applicable $t_{su(AR)}$, $t_{su(AR)}$, and $t_{h(AR)}$. In addition, note that propagation delay times given in the above equations are functions of capacitive loading. The values used in these equations must relate to actual system capacitive loading.

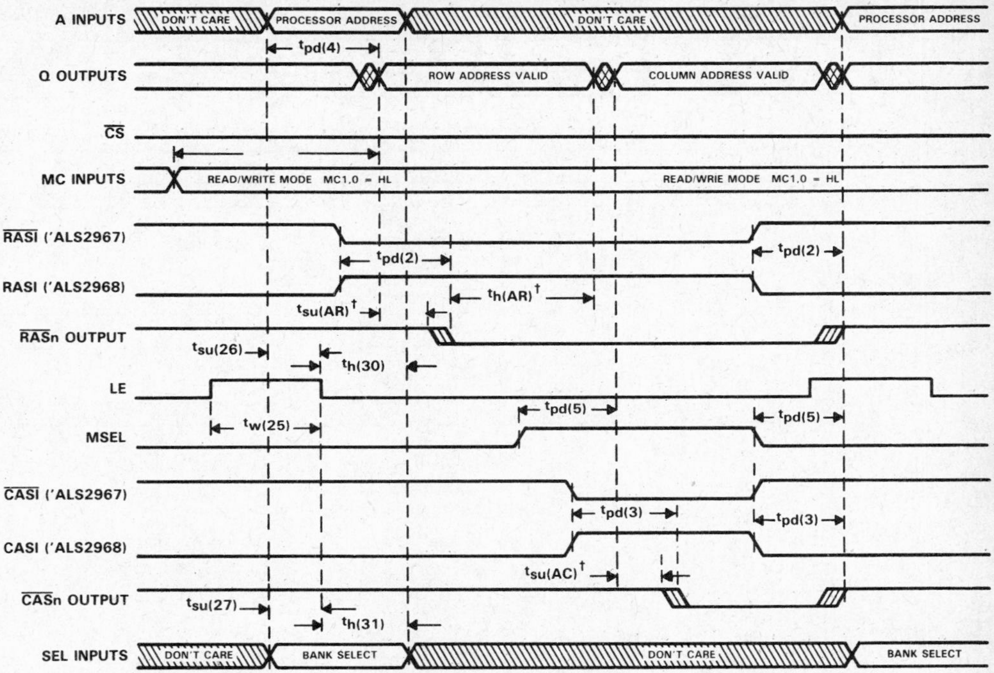
A INPUTS
DON'T CARE
PROCESSOR ADDRESS
DON'T CARE
PROCESSOR ADDRESS
tpd(4)
Q OUTPUTS
ROW ADDRESS VALID
COLUMN ADDRESS VALID
CS
MC INPUTS
READ/WRITE MODE MC1,0 = HL
READ/WRIE MODE MC1,0 = HL
RASI ('ALS2967)
tpd(2)
tpd(2)
RASI ('ALS2968)
th(AR)†
tsu(AR)†
RASn OUTPUT
tsu(26)
th(30)
LE
tpd(5)
tpd(5)
tw(25)
MSEL
CASI ('ALS2967)
tpd(3)
tpd(3)
CASI ('ALS2968)
tsu(AC)†
CASn OUTPUT
tsu(27)
th(31)
SEL INPUTS
DON'T CARE
BANK SELECT
DON'T CARE
BANK SELECT

FIGURE 5. READ/WRITE CYCLE TIMING USING INPUT LATCHES (MC1, MC0 = H, L)

† $t_{su(AR)}$, $t_{su(AC)}$, and $t_{h(AR)}$ are timing requirements of the dynamic RAM. See the DRAM data sheet for applicable specifications.

2 LSI Devices

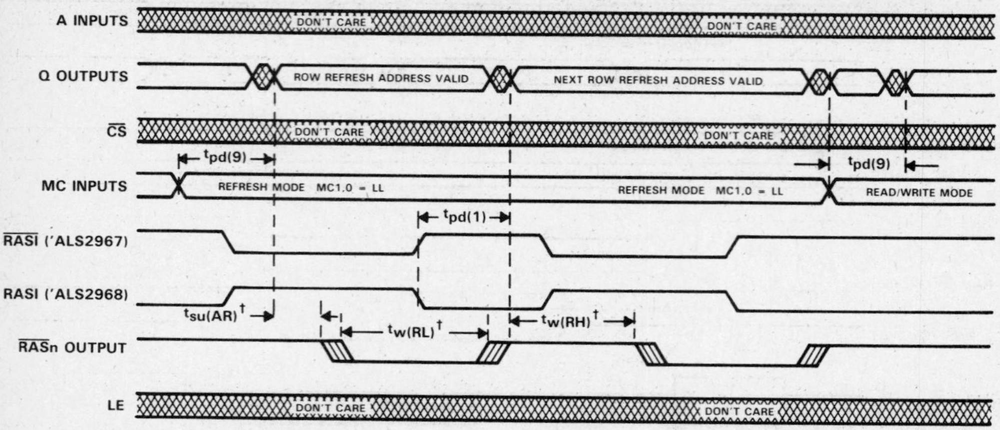
A INPUTS
DON'T CARE
DON'T CARE
Q OUTPUTS
ROW REFRESH ADDRESS VALID
NEXT ROW REFRESH ADDRESS VALID
CS
DON'T CARE
DON'T CARE
tpd(9)
tpd(9)
MC INPUTS
REFRESH MODE MC1,0 = LL
REFRESH MODE MC1,0 = LL
READ/WRITE MODE
tpd(1)
RASI ('ALS2967)
RASI ('ALS2968)
tsu(AR)†
tw(RL)†
tw(RH)†
RASn OUTPUT
LE
DON'T CARE
DON'T CARE

FIGURE 6. REFRESH CYCLE TIMING (MC1, MC0 = L, L) WITHOUT SCRUBBING

† $t_{su(AR)}$, $t_{w(RL)}$, and $t_{w(RH)}$ are timing requirements of the dynamic RAM. See DRAM data sheet for applicable specifications.

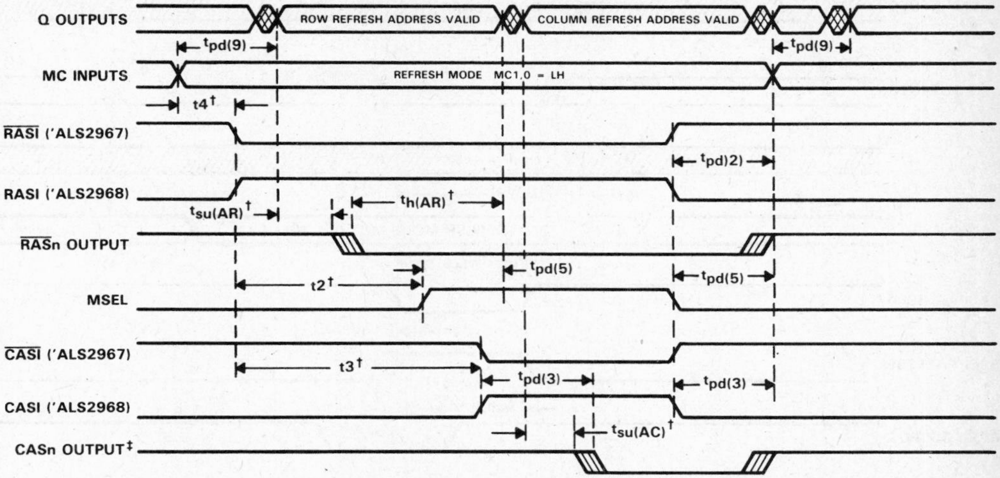
Q OUTPUTS
ROW REFRESH ADDRESS VALID
COLUMN REFRESH ADDRESS VALID
tpd(9)
tpd(9)
MC INPUTS
REFRESH MODE MC1,0 = LH
t4†
RASI ('ALS2967)
tpd)2)
RASI ('ALS2968)
tsu(AR)†
th(AR)†
RASn OUTPUT
tpd(5)
t2†
tpd(5)
MSEL
CASI ('ALS2967)
t3†
tpd(3)
tpd(3)
CASI ('ALS2968)
CASn OUTPUT‡
tsu(AC)†

FIGURE 7. REFRESH CYCLE TIMING (MC1, MC0 = L, H) WITH MEMORY SCRUBBING

† Parameters $t_{su(AR)}$, $t_{su(AC)}$, and $t_{h(AR)}$ are timing requirements of the dynamic RAM. Parameters t2, t3, and t4 represent the minimum timing requirements at the inputs to the DMC that guarantee DRAM timing specifications and maximum system performance. The minimum requirement for t2, t3, and t4 are as follows:

$t2(min) = t_{pd(2)}\ max + t_{h(AR)}\ min - t_{pd(5)}\ min$
$t3(min) = t2\ min + t_{pd(5)}\ max + t_{su(AC)} - t_{pd(3)}\ min$
$t4(min) = t_{pd(9)}\ max + t_{su(AR)}\ min - t_{pd(2)}\ min$

See the DRAM data sheet for applicable $t_{su(AR)}$, $t_{su(AC)}$, and $t_{h(AR)}$. In addition, note that propagation delay times given in the above equations are functions of capacitive loading. The values used in these equations must correspond to actual system capacitive loading.

‡ A $\overline{CAS}$n output is selected by the bank counter. All other $\overline{CAS}$n outputs will remain high.

2 LSI Devices

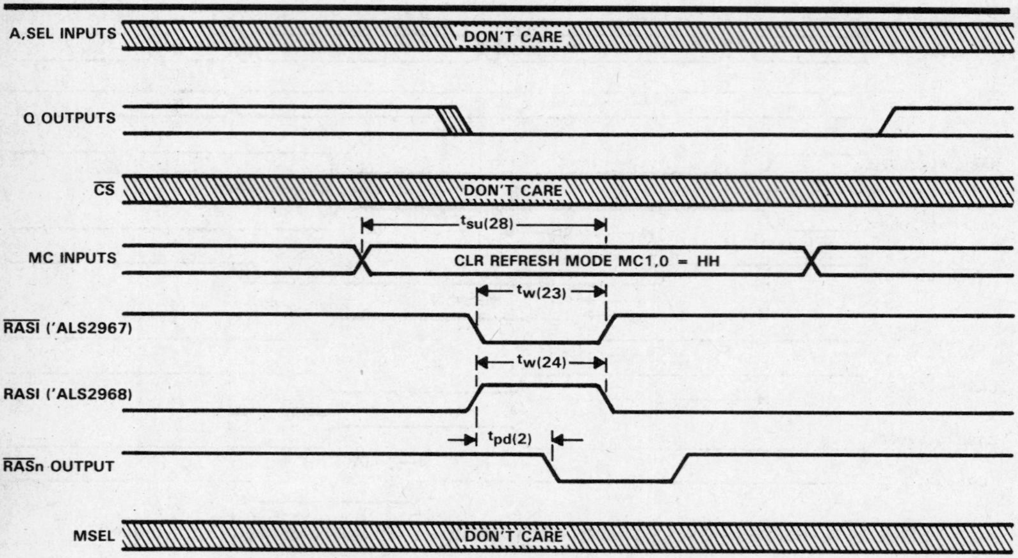
A,SEL INPUTS
DON'T CARE
Q OUTPUTS
CS
DON'T CARE
tsu(28)
MC INPUTS
CLR REFRESH MODE MC1,0 = HH
tw(23)
RASI ('ALS2967)
tw(24)
RASI ('ALS2968)
tpd(2)
RASn OUTPUT
MSEL
DON'T CARE

FIGURE 8. REFRESH COUNTER RESET (MC1, MC0 = H, H)

TEXAS INSTRUMENTS
POST OFFICE BOX 225012 • DALLAS, TEXAS 75265

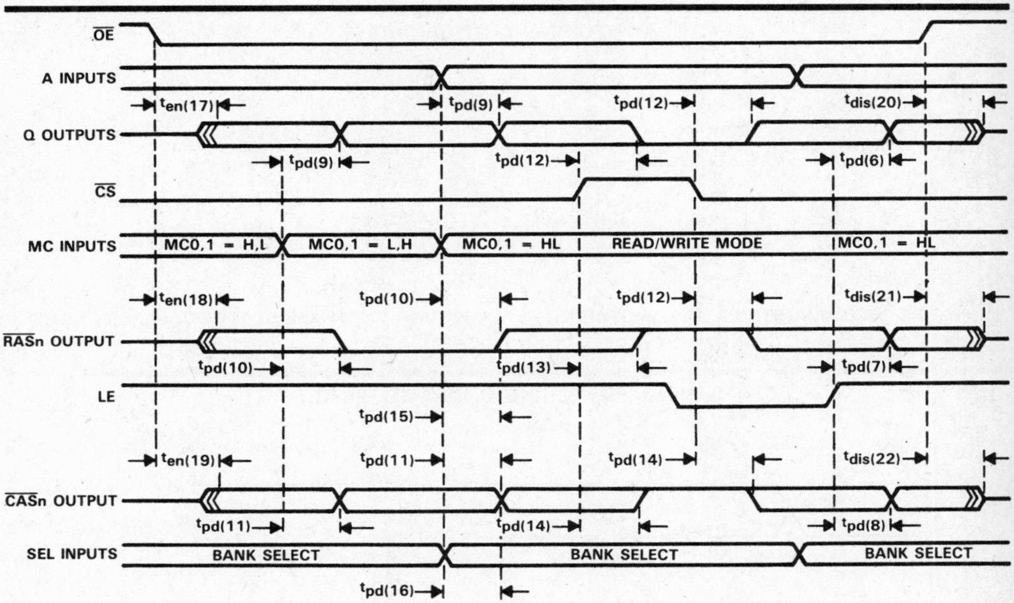
OE
A INPUTS
ten(17)
tpd(9)
tpd(12)
tdis(20)
Q OUTPUTS
tpd(9)
tpd(12)
tpd(6)
CS
MC INPUTS
MC0,1 = H,L
MC0,1 = L,H
MC0,1 = HL
READ/WRITE MODE
MC0,1 = HL
ten(18)
tpd(10)
tpd(12)
tdis(21)
RASn OUTPUT
tpd(10)
tpd(13)
tpd(7)
LE
tpd(15)
ten(19)
tpd(11)
tpd(14)
tdis(22)
CASn OUTPUT
tpd(11)
tpd(14)
tpd(8)
SEL INPUTS
BANK SELECT
BANK SELECT
BANK SELECT
tpd(16)

$\overline{RASI}$ ('ALS2967) = L, RASI ('ALS2968) = H, MSEL = H or L, $\overline{CASI}$ ('ALS2967) = L, CASI ('ALS2968) = H

FIGURE 9. MISCELLANEOUS TIMING

SWITCHING TEST CIRCUIT

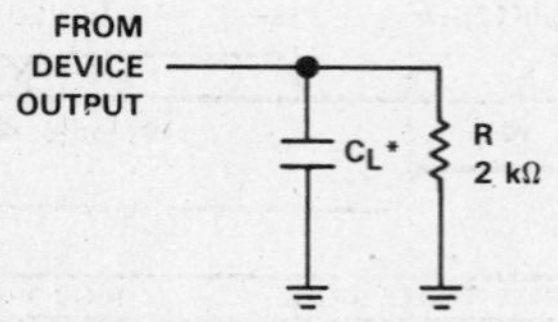
FROM
DEVICE
OUTPUT
C_L*
R
2 kΩ

* t_{pd} specified at C_L = 50, 150 pF

FIGURE 10. CAPACITIVE LOAD SWITCHING

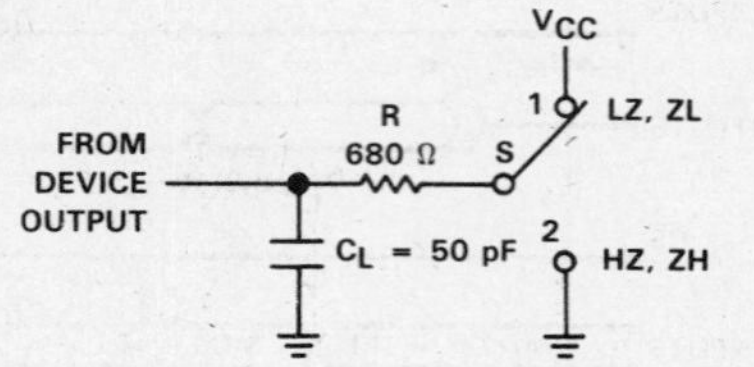
V_{CC}
1
LZ, ZL
R
680 Ω
S
FROM
DEVICE
OUTPUT
C_L = 50 pF
2
HZ, ZH

FIGURE 11. THREE-STATE ENABLE/DISABLE

TYPICAL SWITCHING CHARACTERISTICS

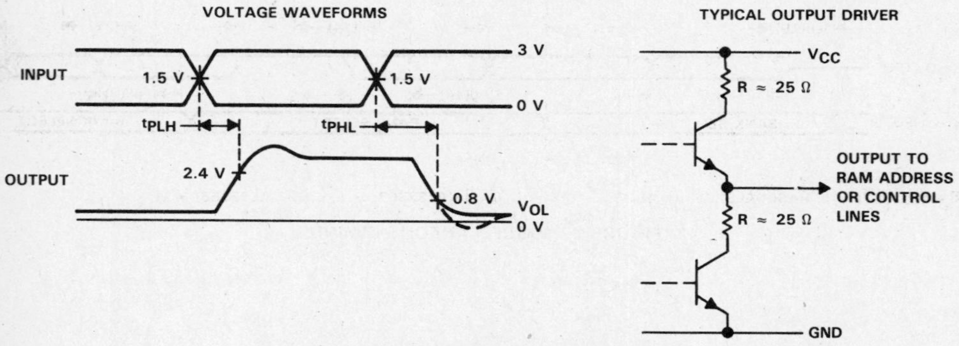
VOLTAGE WAVEFORMS
INPUT
1.5 V
1.5 V
3 V
0 V
t_{PLH}
t_{PHL}
OUTPUT
2.4 V
0.8 V
V_{OL}
0 V
TYPICAL OUTPUT DRIVER
V_{CC}
R ≈ 25 Ω
OUTPUT TO
RAM ADDRESS
OR CONTROL
LINES
R ≈ 25 Ω
GND

FIGURE 12. OUTPUT DRIVE LEVELS

THREE-STATE TIMING

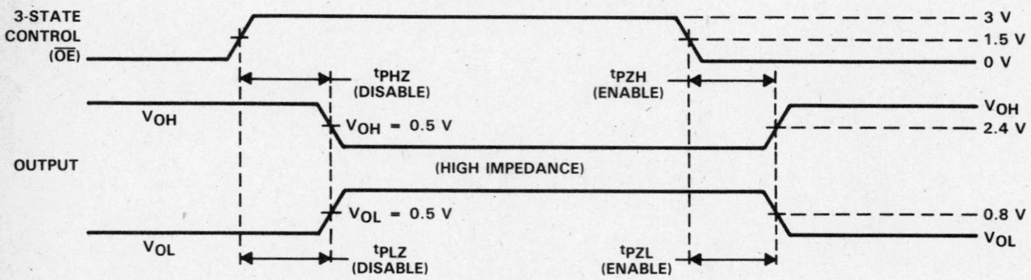
3-STATE
CONTROL
($\overline{OE}$)
3 V
1.5 V
0 V
t_{PHZ}
(DISABLE)
t_{PZH}
(ENABLE)
V_{OH}
V_{OH} − 0.5 V
V_{OH}
2.4 V
OUTPUT
(HIGH IMPEDANCE)
V_{OL} + 0.5 V
0.8 V
V_{OL}
V_{OL}
t_{PLZ}
(DISABLE)
t_{PZL}
(ENABLE)

NOTE: Decoupling is needed for all AC tests

FIGURE 13. THREE-STATE CONTROL LEVELS

SN54ALS6301, SN74ALS6301, SN54ALS6302, SN74ALS6302 DYNAMIC MEMORY CONTROLLERS

D2900, JANUARY 1986

- **Provides Control for 16K, 64K, 256K, and 1M Dynamic RAMs**
- **Highest-Order Two-Address Bits Select One of Four Banks of RAMs**
- **Supports Scrubbing Operations and Nibble-Mode Access**
- **Separate Output Enable for Multi-Channel Access to Memory**
- **52-Pin Dual-In-Line Package**

SN54ALS6301, SN54ALS6302 . . . JD PACKAGE
SN74ALS6301, SN74ALS6302 . . . JD OR N PACKAGE
(TOP VIEW)

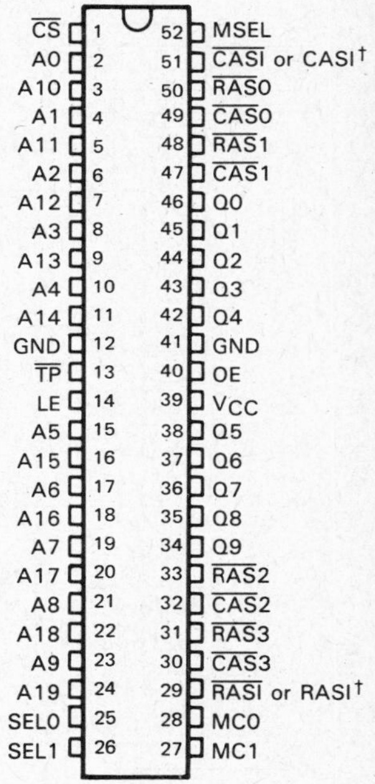
$\overline{CS}$ 1
A0 2
A10 3
A1 4
A11 5
A2 6
A12 7
A3 8
A13 9
A4 10
A14 11
GND 12
$\overline{TP}$ 13
LE 14
A5 15
A15 16
A6 17
A16 18
A7 19
A17 20
A8 21
A18 22
A9 23
A19 24
SEL0 25
SEL1 26
52 MSEL
51 $\overline{CASI}$ or CASI†
50 $\overline{RAS0}$
49 $\overline{CAS0}$
48 $\overline{RAS1}$
47 $\overline{CAS1}$
46 Q0
45 Q1
44 Q2
43 Q3
42 Q4
41 GND
40 OE
39 V_{CC}
38 Q5
37 Q6
36 Q7
35 Q8
34 Q9
33 $\overline{RAS2}$
32 $\overline{CAS2}$
31 $\overline{RAS3}$
30 $\overline{CAS3}$
29 $\overline{RASI}$ or RASI†
28 MC0
27 MC1

† 'ALS6301 has active-low inputs $\overline{CASI}$ and $\overline{RASI}$; 'ALS6302 has active-high inputs CASI and RASI.

description

The 'ALS6301 and 'ALS6302 dynamic memory controllers (DMCs) are designed for use in today's high-performance memory systems. The DMC acts as the address controller between any processor and dynamic memory array.

Two versions are provided that help simplify interfacing to the system dynamic timing controller. The 'ALS6301 offers active-low Row Address Strobe Input ($\overline{RASI}$) and Column Address Strobe Input ($\overline{CASI}$), while the 'ALS6302 offers active-high Row Address Strobe Input (RASI) and Column Address Strobe Input (CASI) inputs.

Using two 10-bit address latches, the DMC will hold the row and column addresses for any DRAM up to 1M. These latches and the two row/column refresh address counters feed into a 10-bit, 4-input MUX for output to the dynamic RAM address lines. A 2-bit bank select latch is provided to select one of the four $\overline{RAS}$ and $\overline{CAS}$ outputs. The two bits are normally obtained from the two highest-order address bits.

The 'ALS6301 and 'ALS6302 have two basic modes of operation, read/write and refresh. During normal read/write operations, the row and column addresses are multiplexed to the dynamic RAM, with the corresponding $\overline{RAS}$ and $\overline{CAS}$ signals activated to strobe the addresses into the RAM. In the refresh mode, the two counters cycle through the refresh addresses. If memory scrubbing is not being implemented, only the row counter is used. When memory scrubbing is being performed, both the row and column counters are used to perform read-modify-write cycles. In this mode all $\overline{RAS}$ outputs will be active (low) while only one $\overline{CAS}$ output is active at a time.

The SN54ALS6301 and SN54ALS6302 are characterized for operation over the full military temperature range of −55°C to 125°C. The SN74ALS6301 and SN74ALS6302 are characterized for operation from 0°C to 70°C.

logic diagram (positive logic)

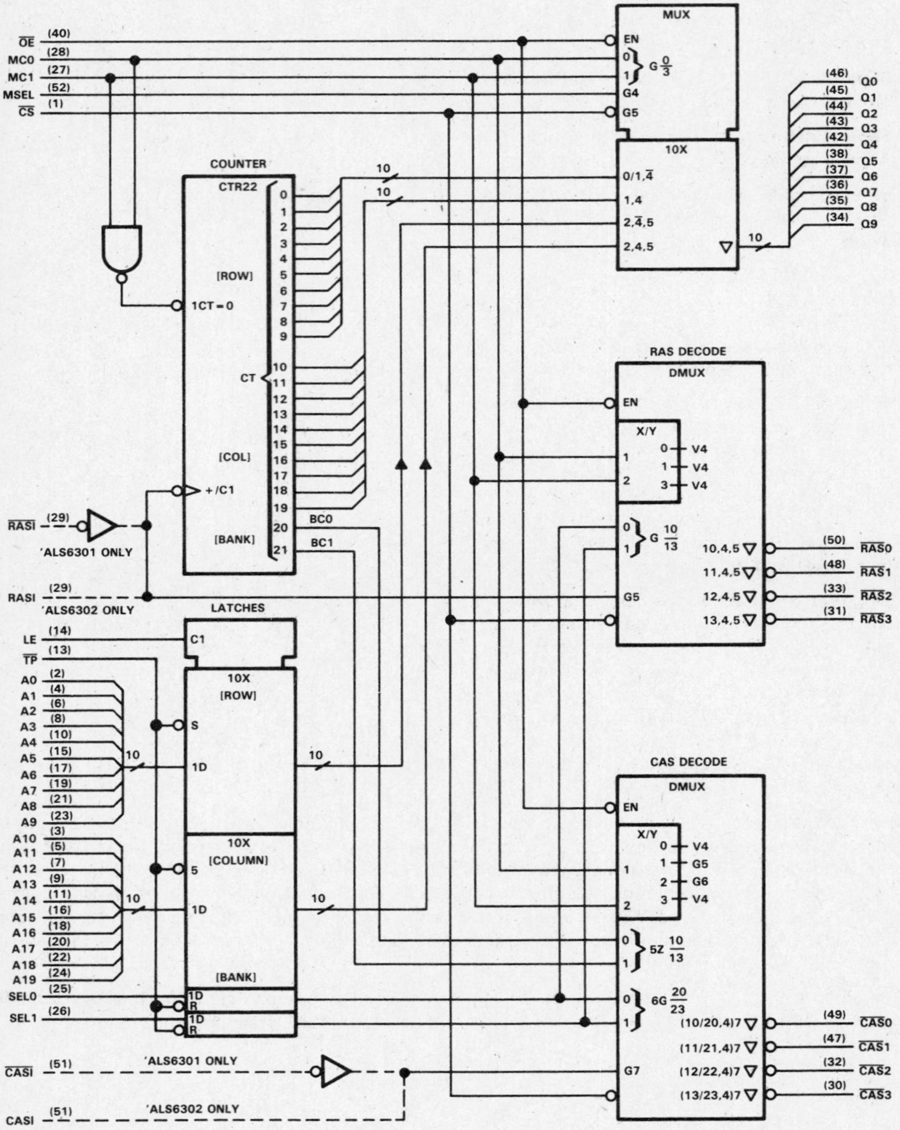
OE (40)
MC0 (28)
MC1 (27)
MSEL (52)
CS (1)
MUX
EN
G 0/3
G4
G5
10X
0/1,4
1,4
2,4,5
2,4,5
(46) Q0
(45) Q1
(44) Q2
(43) Q3
(42) Q4
(38) Q5
(37) Q6
(36) Q7
(35) Q8
(34) Q9
COUNTER
CTR22
[ROW]
1CT=0
CT
[COL]
+/C1
[BANK]
BC0
BC1
RASI (29)
'ALS6301 ONLY
RASI (29)
'ALS6302 ONLY
LATCHES
C1
LE (14)
TP (13)
10X
[ROW]
S
1D
10X
[COLUMN]
1D
[BANK]
SEL0 (25)
SEL1 (26)
A0 (2)
A1 (4)
A2 (6)
A3 (8)
A4 (10)
A5 (15)
A6 (17)
A7 (19)
A8 (21)
A9 (23)
A10 (3)
A11 (5)
A12 (7)
A13 (9)
A14 (11)
A15 (16)
A16 (18)
A17 (20)
A18 (22)
A19 (24)
RAS DECODE
DMUX
EN
X/Y
V4
G 10/13
G5
10,4,5
11,4,5
12,4,5
13,4,5
(50) RAS0
(48) RAS1
(33) RAS2
(31) RAS3
CAS DECODE
DMUX
X/Y
V4
G5
G6
5Z 10/13
6G 20/23
G7
(10/20,4)7
(11/21,4)7
(12/22,4)7
(13/23,4)7
(49) CAS0
(47) CAS1
(32) CAS2
(30) CAS3
CASI (51)
'ALS6301 ONLY
CASI (51)
'ALS6302 ONLY

TEXAS INSTRUMENTS
POST OFFICE BOX 225012 • DALLAS, TEXAS 75265

logic symbols†

'ALS6301

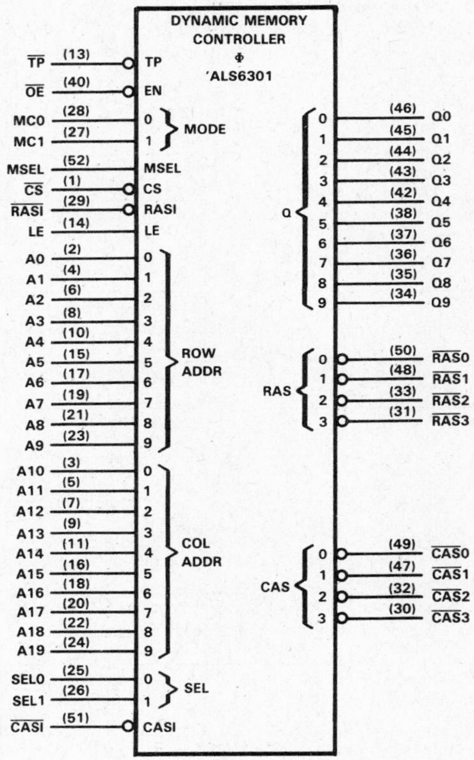
DYNAMIC MEMORY CONTROLLER
Φ
'ALS6301
TP
OE
MC0
MC1
MSEL
CS
RASI
LE
A0
A1
A2
A3
A4
A5
A6
A7
A8
A9
A10
A11
A12
A13
A14
A15
A16
A17
A18
A19
SEL0
SEL1
CASI
MODE
ROW ADDR
COL ADDR
SEL
Q
RAS
CAS
Q0
Q1
Q2
Q3
Q4
Q5
Q6
Q7
Q8
Q9
RAS0
RAS1
RAS2
RAS3
CAS0
CAS1
CAS2
CAS3

'ALS6302

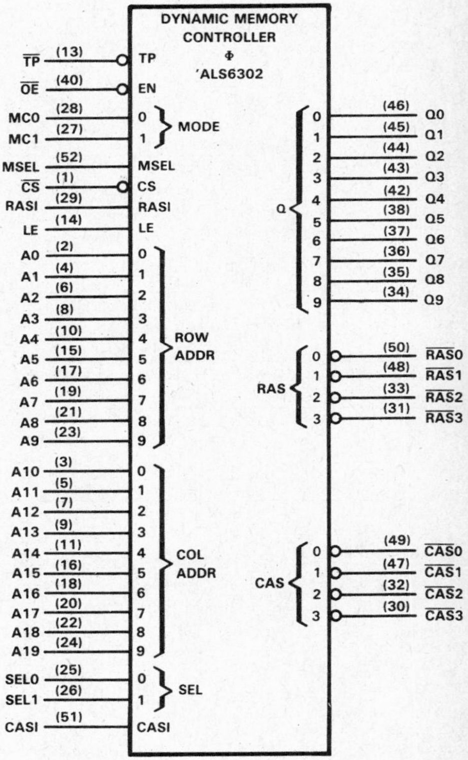
DYNAMIC MEMORY CONTROLLER
Φ
'ALS6302
TP
OE
MC0
MC1
MSEL
CS
RASI
LE
A0
A1
A2
A3
A4
A5
A6
A7
A8
A9
A10
A11
A12
A13
A14
A15
A16
A17
A18
A19
SEL0
SEL1
CASI
MODE
ROW ADDR
COL ADDR
SEL
Q
RAS
CAS
Q0
Q1
Q2
Q3
Q4
Q5
Q6
Q7
Q8
Q9
RAS0
RAS1
RAS2
RAS3
CAS0
CAS1
CAS2
CAS3

†These symbols are in accordance with ANSI/IEEE Std-91-1984 and IEC Publication 617-12.

TABLE 1. PIN FUNCTION

PIN NAME	DESCRIPTION
A0-A19	Address Inputs. A0-A9 are latched in as the nine-bit row address for the DRAM. These inputs drive Q0-Q9 when the DMC is in the read/write mode and MSEL is low. A10-A19 are latched in as the column address, and will drive Q0-Q8 when MSEL is high and the DMC is in the read/write mode. The addresses are latched when the Latch Enable (LE) input signal is low.
SEL0, SEL1	Bank Select. These two inputs are normally the two highest-order address bits and are used in the read/write mode to select which bank of memory will be receiving the $\overline{RAS}$ and $\overline{CAS}$ signals after $\overline{RASI}$ ('ALS6301) or RASI ('ALS6302) and $\overline{CASI}$ ('ALS6301) or CASI ('ALS6302) go active.
LE	Latch Enable. This active-high input causes the row, column, and bank select latches to become transparent, allowing the latches to accept new input data. A low input on LE latches the input data.
MSEL	Multiplexer Select. This input determines whether the row or column address will be sent to the memory address inputs. When MSEL is high, the column address is selected, while the row address is selected when MSEL is low. The address may come from either the address latch or refresh address counter depending on MC0 and MC1 (see Mode Control Function Table).
$\overline{CS}$	Chip Select. This active-low input is used to enable the DMC. When $\overline{CS}$ is active, the DMC operates normally in all four modes. When $\overline{CS}$ goes high, the device will not enter the read/write mode. This allows other devices to access the same memory that the DMC is controlling.
$\overline{OE}$	Output Enable. This active-low input enables/disables the output signals. When $\overline{OE}$ is high, the outputs of the DMC enter the high-impedance state.
MC0-MC1	Mode Controls. These inputs determine in which of the four modes the DMC operates. The description of each of the four operating modes is given in Table 2.
Q0-Q8	Address Outputs. These address outputs feed the DRAM address inputs and provide drive for memory systems having capacitance of up to 500 picofarads.
$\overline{RASI}$ or RASI	Row Address Strobe Input. During the normal memory cycles, the decoded $\overline{RAS}$n output ($\overline{RAS}$0, $\overline{RAS}$1, $\overline{RAS}$2, or $\overline{RAS}$3) is forced low after receipt of an active Row Address Strobe Input signal. In either Refresh mode, all four $\overline{RAS}$ outputs will be low while the Row Address Strobe Input signal is active. The $\overline{RASI}$ on the 'ALS6301 is an active-low input while on the 'ALS6302, RASI is an active-high input. (For more details see timing diagrams).
$\overline{RAS}$0-$\overline{RAS}$3	Row Address Strobe. Each of the Row Address Strobe outputs provides a $\overline{RAS}$ signal to one of the four banks of dynamic memory. Each $\overline{RAS}$n output will go low when selected by SEL0 and SEL1 after $\overline{RASI}$ ('ALS6301) or RASI ('ALS6302) goes active. All four go low in response to $\overline{RASI}$ ('ALS6301) or RASI ('ALS6302) while in the refresh mode.
$\overline{CASI}$ or CASI	Column Address Strobe Input. This input going active causes the selected $\overline{CAS}$ output to be forced low. The $\overline{CASI}$ input on the 'ALS6301 is active low input while on the 'ALS6302, CASI is active high input. (For more details see timing diagrams.)
$\overline{CAS}$0-$\overline{CAS}$3	Column Address Strobe. During normal Read/Write cycles the two selected bits (SEL0, SEL1) determine which $\overline{CAS}$ output will go active following $\overline{CASI}$ ('ALS6301) or CASI ('ALS6302) going active. When memory scrubbing is being performed, only the $\overline{CAS}$n signal selected will be active. For non-scrubbing cycles, all four $\overline{CAS}$ outputs will remain high.
$\overline{TP}$	This active-low test input asynchronously sets the row and column input latches high, while forcing the two bank select latches low. In normal operation, $\overline{TP}$ is tied high.

TABLE 2. MODE-CONTROL FUNCTION TABLE

MC1	MC0	OPERATING MODE
L	L	Refresh Mode without Scrubbing. Refresh cycles are performed with only the row counter being used to generate the addresses. In this mode, all four $\overline{\text{RAS}}$ outputs are active while the four $\overline{\text{CAS}}$ outputs remain high.
L	H	Refresh with Scrubbing/Initialize. During this mode, refresh cycles are done with both the row and column counters generating the addresses. MSEL is used to select either the row or the column counter. All four $\overline{\text{RAS}}$ outputs go low in response to $\overline{\text{RASI}}$ ('ALS6301) or RASI ('ALS6302), while only one $\overline{\text{CAS}}$n output goes low in response to $\overline{\text{CASI}}$ ('ALS6301) or CASI ('ALS6302). The bank counter keeps track of which $\overline{\text{CAS}}$ output goes active. This mode can also be used during system power-up so that the memory can be written with a known data pattern.
H	L	Read/Write. This mode is used to perform read/write cycles. Both the Row and Column addresses are multiplexed to the address output lines using MSEL. SEL0 and SEL1 are decoded to determine which $\overline{\text{RAS}}$n and $\overline{\text{CAS}}$n outputs will be active.
H	H	Clear Refresh Counters. This mode clears the three refresh counters (row, column, and bank) on the inactive transition of $\overline{\text{RASI}}$ ('ALS6301) or RASI ('ALS6302), putting them at start of the refresh sequence (see timing diagrams for more detail). In this mode, all four $\overline{\text{RAS}}$ outputs are driven low after the active edge of $\overline{\text{RASI}}$ ('ALS6301) or RASI ('ALS6302) so that DRAM wake-up cycles may also be performed.

SN74ALS8400
EXPANDABLE ERROR CHECKER AND CORRECTOR

D2921, APRIL 1986

- **Direct Replacement for National Semiconductor DP8400**
- **Fast Single- and Double-Error Detection**
- **Fast Single-Error Correction and Functionally Expandable to 100% Double-Error Correction Capability**
- **Double-Error Correction after Catastrophic Failure without Additional Check Bits or ICs**
- **Functionally Expandable Capability Up to Triple-Error Detection**
- **Expandable to and beyond 64 Bits with Additional 'ALS8400s**
- **Complete Error Recording**
- **Byte Parity Generating and Checking**
- **Separate Byte Controls for Data Output in Byte-Write Operation**
- **Syndrome I/O Port for Error Logging and Management**
- **Full Memory Check Diagnostic and Check Bits Simulation Diagnostics Capability**
- **Self-Test of 'ALS8400 on the Memory Card Under Processor Control**
- **Complete Memory Failure Detection**
- **Power-On Clears Data and Syndrome Latches**

JD
DUAL-IN-LINE PACKAGE
(TOP VIEW)

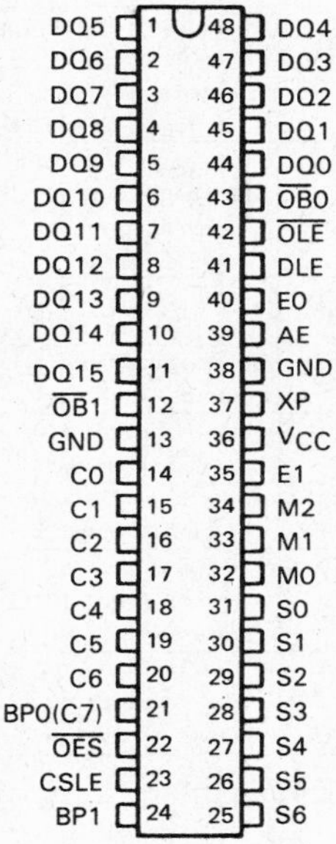
DQ5 1 48 DQ4
DQ6 2 47 DQ3
DQ7 3 46 DQ2
DQ8 4 45 DQ1
DQ9 5 44 DQ0
DQ10 6 43 $\overline{OB0}$
DQ11 7 42 $\overline{OLE}$
DQ12 8 41 DLE
DQ13 9 40 E0
DQ14 10 39 AE
DQ15 11 38 GND
$\overline{OB1}$ 12 37 XP
GND 13 36 V_{CC}
C0 14 35 E1
C1 15 34 M2
C2 16 33 M1
C3 17 32 M0
C4 18 31 S0
C5 19 30 S1
C6 20 29 S2
BP0(C7) 21 28 S3
$\overline{OES}$ 22 27 S4
CSLE 23 26 S5
BP1 24 25 S6

description

The 'ALS8400 is a monolithic Advanced Low-Power Schottky error checker and corrector (ECC) integrated circuit designed to aid in system reliability and integrity by detecting errors in memory data and correcting single- or double-bit errors. The ECC has a separate syndrome I/O bus, which can be used for error logging or error management. It can also be used in BYTE-WRITE applications (for up to 72 data bits) because it has separate byte controls for the data buffers. In 16- or 32-bit systems, the 'ALS8400 will generate and check system byte parity, if required, for integrity of the data supplied from or to the processor. There are three latch controls to enable latching of data in various modes and configurations.

The 'ALS8400 is easily expandable to other data configurations. For 32-bit data bus with seven check bits, two 'ALS8400s can be used in cascade with no other ICs. Three 'ALS8400s can be used for 48 bits, and four 'ALS8400s for 64 data bits, both using eight check bits. In all these configurations, single-error and double-error detection and single-error correction are easy to implement.

The 'ALS8400 is characterized for operation from °C to 70°C.

PIN NAMES	I/O	DESCRIPTION
AE	O	Any error output. In the normal read mode, when low, AE indicates no error and when high, indicates that an error has occurred. In any write mode, AE is permanently low.
BP0/C7	I/O	Byte parity 0/check bit 7. When XP is at 0 V, this pin is byte-0 parity I/O. In the normal write mode, BP0 receives system byte-0 parity, and in the normal read mode, outputs system byte-0 parity. When the XP pin is open or at V_{CC}, the BP0/C7 pin becomes the check bit C7 I/O, the eighth check bit for the memory check bits, for 48-bit expansion configuration and beyond.
BP1/S7	I/O	Byte parity 1/syndrome bit 7. When XP pin is at 0 V, this pin is byte 1 parity I/O. In the normal write mode, BP1 receives system byte-1 parity, and in the normal read mode outputs system byte-1 parity. When the XP pin is open or at V_{CC}, the BP1/S7 pin becomes the syndrome bit S7 I/O, the eighth syndrome bit, for 48-bit expansion configuration and beyond.
CSLE	I	Input check bit and syndrome latch enable. When high, the outputs of the check bit input latches follow input check bit and, if $\overline{OES}$ is low, the outputs of the syndrome input latches follow the syndrome bit bus.
C0-C6	I/O	Check-bit I/O port. A 7-bit bidirectional bus connected to the input of the check-bit input latches and the outputs of the check-bit output buffers. The check-bit output buffers are enabled whenever M2 pin is low.
DLE	I	Input data latch enable. When high, outputs of the data input latches follow the input data bus. When low, the data input latches store the input data.
DQ0-DQ15	I/O	Data I/O port. A 16-bit bidirectional data bus connected to the input of the data input latches and the outputs of the data output buffers, with DQ8-DQ15 also connected to the check-bit input latches.
E0	O	Error 0 output. In the normal read mode, E0 is high for a single-data error and low for other conditions. In the normal write mode, E0 becomes PE0 and is low if a parity error exists in byte-0 as transmitted from the processor.
E1	O	Error 1 output. In the normal read mode, E1 is high for a single-data error or a single check-bit error, and low for no error or a double error. In the normal write mode, E1 becomes PE1 and is low if a parity error exists in byte 1 as transmitted from the processor.
GND		System ground
M0-M2	I	Mode control inputs. These three controls define the eight major operational modes of the ECC. Table 1 describes the modes.
$\overline{OB}0$, $\overline{OB}1$	I	Output byte 0 and Output byte 1 enables. These inputs, when low, enable the outputs of the data output latches through the data output buffers onto the data bus. When $\overline{OB}0$ and $\overline{OB}1$ are high, the outputs of the data output buffers are placed in the high-impedance state.
$\overline{OES}$	I	Output enable syndromes. I/O control of the syndrome latches. When high, the outputs of the syndrome output buffers are placed in the high-impedance state and external syndromes pass through the syndrome input latches with CSLE high. When $\overline{OES}$ is low, the outputs of the syndrome output buffers are enabled and the generated syndromes appear on the syndrome bus, also CSLE is inhibited internally to the syndrome input latches.
$\overline{OLE}$	I	Output latch enable. When low, $\overline{OLE}$ enables the internally generated data to enter the data output latches, check bit output latches, and syndrome output latches. When $\overline{OLE}$ is high, the latches store the data.
S0-S6	I/O	Syndrome I/O port. A 7-bit bidirectional bus connected to the input of the syndrome input latches and the outputs of the syndrome output buffers.
V_{CC}	I	5-volt supply voltage input.
XP	I	Multiexpansion input to a three-level comparator. With XP at 0 V, only 6 or 7 check bits are available for expansion up to 40 bits, allowing byte parity capability. With XP open or at V_{CC}, expansion beyond 40 bits is possible, but byte-parity capability is no longer available. When XP is at V_{CC}, check-bit generator bits 6 and 7, the internally generated upper two check bits, are set low. When XP is open, check-bit generator bits 6 and 7 are set to word parity.

TEXAS INSTRUMENTS
POST OFFICE BOX 225012 • DALLAS, TEXAS 75265

functional description

The 'ALS8400, with its 16-bit bidirectional data bus connected to the memory data bus, monitors data between the processor and memory. It uses an encoding matrix to generate six check bits from the 16 bits of data. In a write cycle, the data word and the corresponding check bits are written into memory. When the same location of memory is subsequently read, the ECC generates six new check bits from the memory data and compares them with the six check bits read from memory to create six syndrome bits. If there is a difference (causing some syndrome bits to go high), then that memory location contains an error and the ECC indicates the type of error with three error flags. If the error is a single-bit error, the ECC will automatically correct it.

When the memory has more than one error, or better system integrity is preferred, double-error correction can be performed. One approach requires a further write-read cycle using complemented data and check bits from the ECC. If at least one of the two errors is a hard error, the ECC will correct both errors. This implementation requires no more memory check bits or ECCs than the single-error correct configuration.

functional block diagram (positive logic)

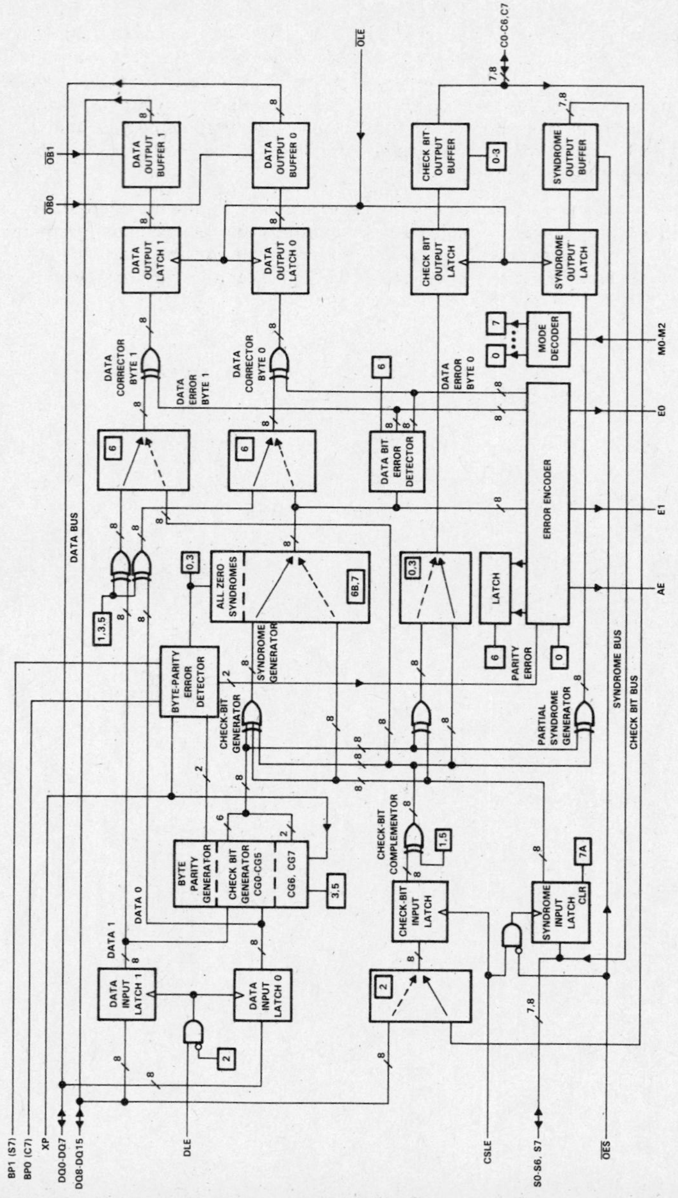
OLE
C0-C6, C7
OB1
OB0
DATA OUTPUT BUFFER 1
DATA OUTPUT BUFFER 0
DATA OUTPUT LATCH 1
DATA OUTPUT LATCH 0
CHECK BIT OUTPUT BUFFER
CHECK BIT OUTPUT LATCH
SYNDROME OUTPUT BUFFER
SYNDROME OUTPUT LATCH
MODE DECODER
M0-M2
DATA CORRECTOR BYTE 1
DATA ERROR BYTE 1
DATA CORRECTOR BYTE 0
DATA ERROR BYTE 0
DATA BIT ERROR DETECTOR
ERROR ENCODER
E0
E1
AE
LATCH
PARITY ERROR
DATA BUS
ALL ZERO SYNDROMES
SYNDROME GENERATOR
BYTE-PARITY ERROR DETECTOR
CHECK-BIT GENERATOR
PARTIAL SYNDROME GENERATOR
SYNDROME BUS
CHECK BIT BUS
BYTE PARITY GENERATOR
CHECK BIT GENERATOR CG0-CG5
CG6, CG7
CHECK-BIT COMPLEMENTOR
CHECK-BIT INPUT LATCH
SYNDROME INPUT LATCH CLR
DATA 1
DATA 0
DATA INPUT LATCH 1
DATA INPUT LATCH 0
BP1 (S7)
BP0 (C7)
XP
DQ0-DQ7
DQ8-DQ15
DLE
CSLE
S0-S6, S7
OES

D2936, NOVEMBER 1985—REVISED MARCH 1986

- Advanced Schottky IMPACT-X™ Process
- Three-Operand, 64-Word by 40-Bit Register File
- Supports 'AS888 and 'AS8832 Register File Expansion
- Four 10-Bit Input Ports with Individual Parity Checkers and Write Enables
- Four 10-Bit Output Ports with Individual Three-State Enables
- Two Write Address Ports
- Two Read Address Ports and Y Output Mux Permit LSH/MSH Swap Operations
- 156-Pin Package
- 8-mA Bus Drivers
- Texas Instruments Quality and Reliability

description

The SN54AS8834 and SN74AS8834 are high speed, three-operand, 64-word register files in a 156-pin ceramic pin grid array.

The register files are designed to support register file expansion for bit-slice systems using the'AS888 or 'AS8832. Internal parity checks and a 40-bit word width support I/O operations for graphics and 32-bit error detection and correction boards.

The SN54AS8834 is characterized for operation over the full military temperature range of −55°C to 125°C. The SN74AS8834 is characterized for operation from 0°C to 70°C.

logic symbol†

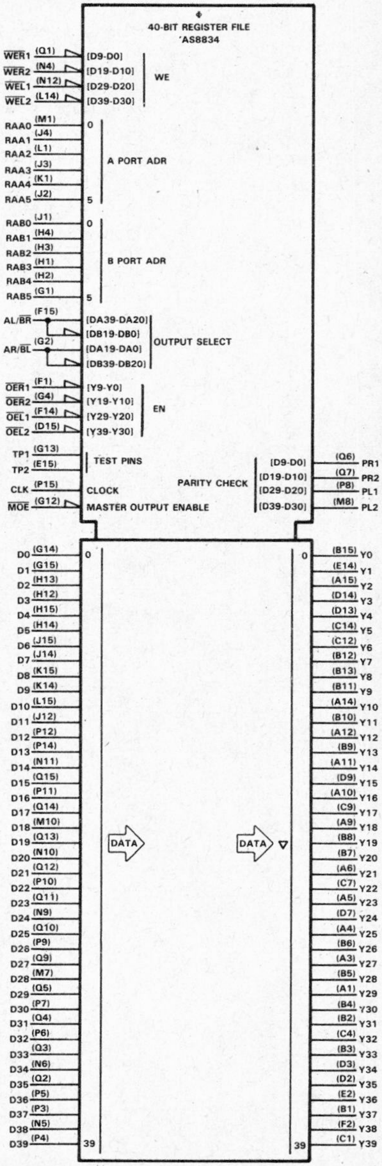
40-BIT REGISTER FILE
'AS8834
WER1 (Q1) [D9-D0]
WER2 (N4) [D19-D10]
WEL1 (N12) [D29-D20]
WEL2 (L14) [D39-D30]
WE
RAA0 (M1) 0
RAA1 (J4)
RAA2 (L1)
RAA3 (J3)
RAA4 (K1)
RAA5 (J2) 5
A PORT ADR
RAB0 (J1) 0
RAB1 (H4)
RAB2 (H3)
RAB3 (H1)
RAB4 (H2)
RAB5 (G1) 5
B PORT ADR
AL/BR (F15)
AR/BL (G2)
[DA39-DA20]
[DB19-DB0]
[DA19-DA0]
[DB39-DB20]
OUTPUT SELECT
OER1 (F1) [Y9-Y0]
OER2 (G4) [Y19-Y10]
OEL1 (F14) [Y29-Y20]
OEL2 (D15) [Y39-Y30]
EN
TP1 (G13)
TP2 (E15)
TEST PINS
CLK (P15) CLOCK
MOE (G12) MASTER OUTPUT ENABLE
PARITY CHECK
[D9-D0] (Q6) PR1
[D19-D10] (Q7) PR2
[D29-D20] (P8) PL1
[D39-D30] (M8) PL2
D0 (G14) D1 (G15) D2 (H13) D3 (H12) D4 (H15) D5 (H14) D6 (J15) D7 (J14) D8 (K15) D9 (K14)
D10 (L15) D11 (J12) D12 (P12) D13 (P14) D14 (N11) D15 (Q15) D16 (P11) D17 (Q14) D18 (M10) D19 (Q13)
D20 (N10) D21 (Q12) D22 (P10) D23 (Q11) D24 (N9) D25 (Q10) D26 (P9) D27 (Q9) D28 (M7) D29 (Q5)
D30 (P7) D31 (Q4) D32 (P6) D33 (Q3) D34 (N6) D35 (Q2) D36 (P5) D37 (P3) D38 (N5) D39 (P4)
DATA
DATA
0
39
0
39
(B15) Y0 (E14) Y1 (A15) Y2 (D14) Y3 (D13) Y4 (C14) Y5 (C12) Y6 (B12) Y7 (B13) Y8 (B11) Y9
(A14) Y10 (B10) Y11 (A12) Y12 (B9) Y13 (A11) Y14 (D9) Y15 (A10) Y16 (C9) Y17 (A9) Y18 (B8) Y19
(B7) Y20 (A6) Y21 (C7) Y22 (A5) Y23 (D7) Y24 (A4) Y25 (B6) Y26 (A3) Y27 (B5) Y28 (A1) Y29
(B4) Y30 (B2) Y31 (C4) Y32 (B3) Y33 (D3) Y34 (D2) Y35 (E2) Y36 (B1) Y37 (F2) Y38 (C1) Y39

IMPACT-X is a trademark of Texas Instruments

† This symbol is in accordance with ANSI/IEEE Std 91-1984.

SN54AS8834, SN74AS8834
GB PIN-GRID-ARRAY PACKAGE
(TOP VIEW)

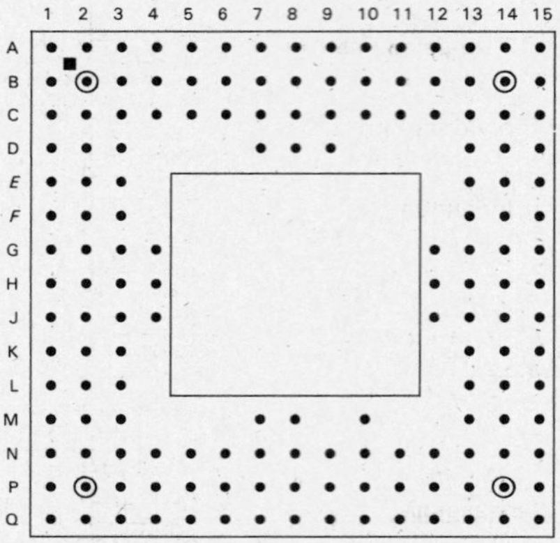
1 2 3 4 5 6 7 8 9 10 11 12 13 14 15
A B C D E F G H J K L M N P Q

PIN NO.	PIN NAME	PIN NO.	PIN NAME	PIN NO.	PIN NAME	PIN NO.	PIN NAME	PIN NO.	PIN NAME	PIN NO.	PIN NAME
A1	Y29	B12	Y7	D14	Y3	H12	D3	M3	WAR3	P5	D36
A2	NC	B13	Y8	D15	$\overline{OEL}2$	H13	D2	M7	D28	P6	D32
A3	Y27	B14	NC	E1	NC	H14	D5	M8	PL2	P7	D30
A4	Y25	B15	Y0	E2	Y36	H15	D4	M10	D18	P8	PL1
A5	Y23	C1	Y39	E3	GND1	J1	RAB0	M13	WAL3	P9	D26
A6	Y21	C2	NC	E13	GND1	J2	RAA5	M14	WAL2	P10	D22
A7	NC	C3	NC	E14	Y1	J3	RAA3	M15	NC	P11	D16
A8	NC	C4	Y32	E15	TP2	J4	RAA1	N1	NC	P12	D12
A9	Y18	C5	V_{CC1}	F1	$\overline{OER}1$	J12	D11	N2	WAR4	P13	WAL5
A10	Y16	C6	GND1	F2	Y38	J13	GND2	N3	WAR5	P14	D13
A11	Y14	C7	Y22	F3	GND2	J14	D7	N4	$\overline{WER}2$	P15	CLK
A12	Y12	C8	GND1	F13	GND2	J15	D6	N5	D38	Q1	$\overline{WER}1$
A13	NC	C9	Y17	F14	$\overline{OEL}1$	K1	RAA4	N6	D34	Q2	D35
A14	Y10	C10	GND1	F15	AL/$\overline{BR}$	K2	GND2	N7	V_{CC1}	Q3	D33
A15	Y2	C11	V_{CC1}	G1	RAB5	K3	GND2	N8	GND1	Q4	D31
B1	Y37	C12	Y6	G2	AR/$\overline{BL}$	K13	V_{CC2}	N9	D24	Q5	D29
B2	Y31	C13	NC	G3	V_{CC2}	K14	D9	N10	D20	Q6	PR1
B3	Y33	C14	Y5	G4	$\overline{OEB}2$	K15	D8	N11	D14	Q7	PR2
B4	Y30	C15	NC	G12	$\overline{MOE}$	L1	RAA2	N12	$\overline{WEL}1$	Q8	NC
B5	Y28	D1	NC	G13	TP1	L2	WAR0	N13	WAL4	Q9	D27
B6	Y26	D2	Y35	G14	D0	L3	V_{CC2}	N14	WAL0	Q10	D25
B7	Y20	D3	Y34	G15	D1	L13	WAL1	N15	NC	Q11	D23
B8	Y19	D7	Y24	H1	RAB3	L14	$\overline{WEL}2$	P1	NC	Q12	D21
B9	Y13	D8	V_{CC1}	H2	RAB4	L15	D10	P2	WAR1	Q13	D19
B10	Y11	D9	Y15	H3	RAB2	M1	RAA0	P3	D37	Q14	D17
B11	Y9	D13	Y4	H4	RAB1	M2	WAR2	P4	D39	Q15	D15

NC—No internal connection

PIN NAME	PIN NO.	I/O	DESCRIPTION
AL/$\overline{BR}$	F15	I	Output select for Y20-Y39 output data. High selects DA20-DA39; low selects DB0-DB19.
AR/$\overline{BL}$	G2	I	Output select for Y0-Y10 output data. High selects DA0-DA19; low selects DA20-DA39.
CLK	P15	I	Clocks data into register file on rising edge.
D0	G14	I	Input data bits 0 through 9
D1	G15		
D2	H13		
D3	H12		
D4	H15		
D5	H14		
D6	J15		
D7	J14		
D8	K15		
D9	K14		
D10	L15	I	Input data bits 10 through 19
D11	J12		
D12	P12		
D13	P14		
D14	N11		
D15	Q15		
D16	P11		
D17	Q14		
D18	M10		
D19	Q13		
D20	N10	I	Input data bits 20 through 29
D21	Q12		
D22	P10		
D23	Q11		
D24	N9		
D25	Q10		
D26	P9		
D27	Q9		
D28	M7		
D29	Q5		
D30	P7	I	Input data bits 30 through 39
D31	Q4		
D32	P6		
D33	Q3		
D34	N6		
D35	Q2		
D36	P5		
D37	P3		
D38	N5		
D39	P4		
GND1	E3		5-volt ground (All ground pins must be used.)
GND1	E13		
GND1	C6		
GND1	C8		
GND1	C10		
GND1	N8		

2

LSI Devices

PIN NAME	PIN NO.	I/O	DESCRIPTION
GND2	F3		
GND2	F13		
GND2	J13		2-volt ground (All ground pins must be used.)
GND2	K2		
GND2	D3		
M8	PL2	O	Parity check result. High indicates odd number of high inputs on D30-D39.
$\overline{\text{MOE}}$	G12	I	Master output enable, active low. Places Y0-Y39 and parity outputs in the high-impedance state when high.
NC	A2		
NC	A7		
NC	A8		
NC	A13		
NC	B14		
NC	C2		
NC	C3		
NC	C13		
NC	C15		No internal connection
NC	D1		
NC	E1		
NC	M15		
NC	N1		
NC	N15		
NC	P1		
NC	Q8		
$\overline{\text{OEL}}$1	F14		Y20-Y29 output enable, active low
$\overline{\text{OEL}}$2	D15	I	Y30-Y39 output enable, active low
$\overline{\text{OER}}$1	F1		Y0-Y9 output enable, active low
$\overline{\text{OER}}$2	G4		Y10-Y19 output enable, active low
PL1	P8		Parity check result. High indicates odd number of high inputs on D20-D29.
PL2	M8	O	Parity check result. High indicates odd number of high inputs on D30-D39.
PR1	Q6		Parity check result. High indicates odd number of high inputs on D0-D9.
PR2	Q7		Parity check result. High indicates odd number of high inputs on D10-D19.
RAA0	M1		
RAA1	J4		
RAA2	L1	I	Register file A port read address select (0 = LSB)
RAA3	J3		
RAA4	K1		
RAA5	J2		
RAB0	J1		
RAB1	H4		
RAB2	H3	I	Register file A port read address select (0 = LSB)
RAB3	H1		
RAB4	H2		
RAB5	G1		
TP1	G13	I	Functional testing input. During normal operation, should be maintained high or open.
TP2	E15		

TEXAS INSTRUMENTS
POST OFFICE BOX 225012 • DALLAS, TEXAS 75265

PIN NAME	PIN NO.	I/O	DESCRIPTION
V_{CC1}	C5		5-volt supply for TTL-compatible I/O
V_{CC1}	C11		
V_{CC1}	D8		
V_{CC1}	N7		
V_{CC2}	G3		2-volt supply for internal Schottky transistor logic
V_{CC2}	K13		
V_{CC2}	L3		
WAL0	N14	I	Write address for D20-D39 input data
WAL1	L13		
WAL2	M14		
WAL3	M13		
WAL4	N13		
WAL5	P13		
WAR0	L2	I	Write address for D0-D19 input data
WAR1	P2		
WAR2	M2		
WAR3	M3		
WAR4	N2		
WAR5	N3		
$\overline{WEL}1$	N12	I	D20-D29 write enable, active low
$\overline{WEL}2$	L14	I	D30-D39 write enable, active low
$\overline{WER}1$	Q1	I	D0-D9 write enable, active low
$\overline{WER}2$	N4	I	D10-D19 write enable, active low
Y0	B15	O	Output data bits 0 through 9
Y1	E14		
Y2	A15		
Y3	D14		
Y4	D13		
Y5	C14		
Y6	C12		
Y7	B12		
Y8	B13		
Y9	B11		
Y10	A14	O	Output data bits 10 through 19
Y11	B10		
Y12	A12		
Y13	B9		
Y14	A11		
Y15	D9		
Y16	A10		
Y17	C9		
Y18	A9		
Y19	B8		

PIN NAME	PIN NO.	I/O	DESCRIPTION
Y20	B7	O	Output data bits 20 through 29
Y21	A6		
Y22	C7		
Y23	A5		
Y24	D7		
Y25	A4		
Y26	B6		
Y27	A3		
Y28	B5		
Y29	A1		
Y30	B4	O	Output data bits 30 through 39
Y31	B2		
Y32	C4		
Y33	B3		
Y34	D3		
Y35	D2		
Y36	E2		
Y37	B1		
Y38	F2		
Y39	C1		

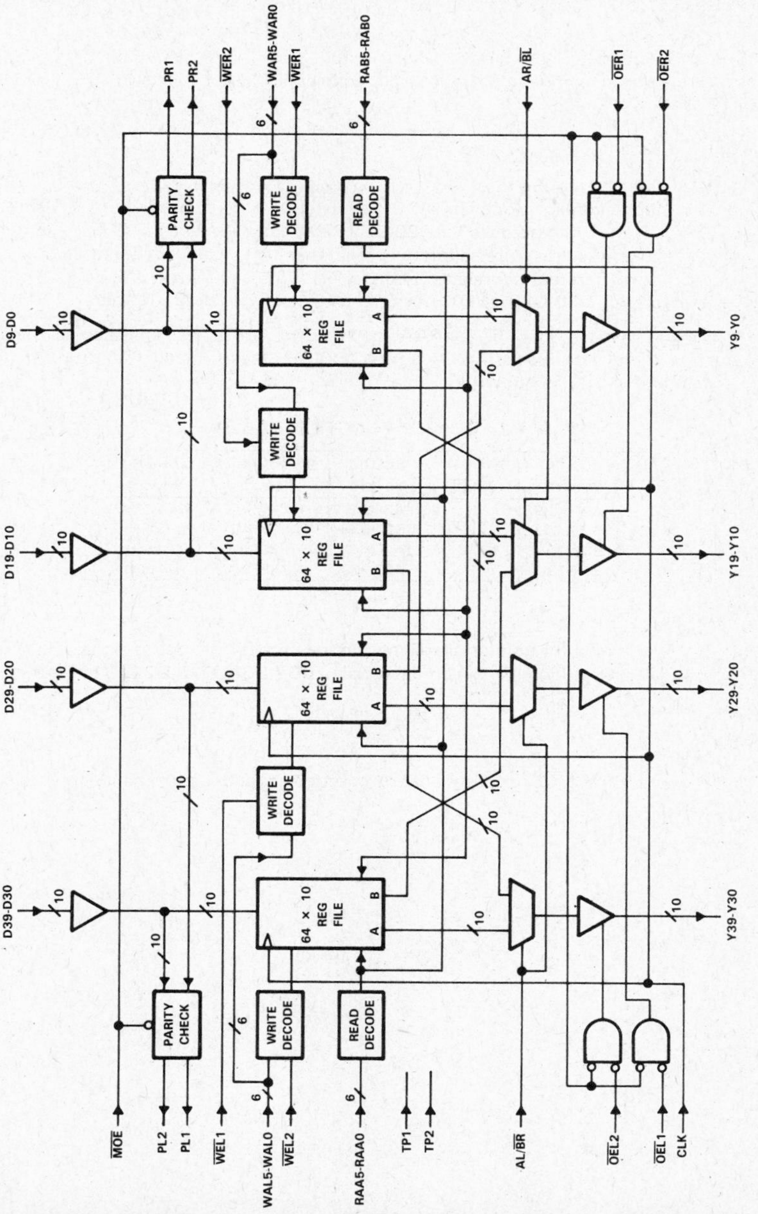
PR1
PR2
WER2
WAR5-WAR0
WER1
RAB5-RAB0
AR/BL
OER1
OER2
PARITY CHECK
WRITE DECODE
READ DECODE
D9-D0
D19-D10
D29-D20
D39-D30
64 × 10 REG FILE
A
B
Y9-Y0
Y19-Y10
Y29-Y20
Y39-Y30
MOE
PL2
PL1
WEL1
WAL5-WAL0
WEL2
RAA5-RAA0
TP1
TP2
AL/BR
OEL2
OEL1
CLK
10
6

ALS8834 REGISTER FILE

data input/output ports

Data is input to the 'AS8834 through four 10-bit data ports: D30-D39, D20-D29, D10-D19 and D0-D9. Data is output from the register file through four 10-bit output ports: Y30-Y39, Y20-Y29, Y10-Y19 and Y0-Y9. The Y ports are enabled by four active low output enables: $\overline{OEL}$2 for Y30-Y39, $\overline{OEL}$1 for Y20-Y29, $\overline{OER}$2 for Y10-Y19, and $\overline{OER}$1 for Y0-Y9.

register file addressing

Data is stored in the register file on the rising edge of the clock. Two write address ports and two read address ports operate independently to implement a 40-bit register file that supports MSH/LSH swap operations. WAL0-WAL5 is the write address for D20-D39 input data; WAR0-WAR5 is the write address for D0-D19 input data. These separate write addresses permit the most significant and the least significant half of a word to be stored at different addresses. Register file writes are enabled by four write enables: $\overline{WEL}$2 for D30-D39, $\overline{WEL}$1 for D20-D29, $\overline{WER}$2 for D10-D19, and $\overline{WER}$1 for D0-D9.

Two read address lines are also provided: RAA0-RAA5 and RAB0-RAB5. These lines control the selection of data to be output on internal data buses DA0-DA39 and DB0-DB39 respectively. Y-output data selection is controlled by AL/$\overline{BR}$ and AR/$\overline{BL}$ as shown in Table 1.

TABLE 1. OUTPUT FUNCTION TABLE

SIGNAL AL/$\overline{BR}$	RESULT Y20-Y39	SIGNAL AR/$\overline{BL}$	RESULT Y0-Y19	RESULT WHEN COMBINED Y20-Y39	RESULT WHEN COMBINED Y0-Y19
H	A20-A39	H	A0-A19	A (MSH)	A (LSH)
H	A20-A39	L	B20-B39	A (MSH)	B (MSH)
L	B0-B19	H	A0-A19	B (LSH)	A (LSH)
L	B0-B19	L	B20-B39	B (LSH)	B (MSH)

parity checkers

Two parity checkers are provided for data on the D input ports. A high on output signals PL2, PL1, PR2 or PR1 indicate an odd number of high signals on data inputs D30-D39, D20-D29, D10-D19 and D0-D9 respectively.

master output enable

When high, Master Output Enable, $\overline{MOE}$, places the four Y output ports and the four parity output ports in the high-impedance state.

absolute maximum ratings over operating temperature range (unless otherwise noted)

Supply voltage, V_{CC1} .... 7 V
Supply voltage, V_{CC2} .... 3 V
Input voltage .... 7 V
High-level voltage applied to 3-state outputs .... 5.5 V
Operating case temperature range: SN54AS8834 .... −55°C to 125°C
Operating free-air temperature range: SN74AS8834 .... 0°C to 70°C
Storage temperature range .... −65°C to 150°C

recommended operating conditions

PARAMETER		SN54AS8834			SN74AS8834			UNIT
		MIN	NOM	MAX	MIN	NOM	MAX	
V_{CC1}	I/O supply voltage	4.5	5	5.5	4.5	5	5.5	V
V_{CC2}	STL internal logic supply voltage	1.9	2	2.1	1.9	2	2.1	V
V_{IH}	High-level input voltage	2			2			V
V_{IL}	Low-level input voltage			0.8			0.8	V
I_{OH}	High-level output current			−1			2.6	mA
I_{OL}	Low-level output current			8			8	mA
T_C	Operating case temperature			125				°C
T_A	Operating free-air temperature	−55			0		70	°C

electrical characteristics over recommended operating temperature range (unless otherwise noted)

PARAMETER	TEST CONDITIONS		SN54AS8834			SN74AS8834			UNIT
			MIN	TYP†	MAX	MIN	TYP†	MAX	
V_{IK}	V_{CC1} = 4.5 V,	I_I = −18 mA			−1.2			−1.2	V
V_{OH}	V_{CC1} = 4.5 V,	I_{OH} = −1 mA	2.4						V
	V_{CC1} = 4.5 V,	I_{OH} = −2.6 mA				2.4			
V_{OL}	V_{CC1} = 4.5 V,	I_{OL} = 8 mA			0.5			0.5	V
I_{OZH}	V_{CC1} = 5.5 V,	V_O = 2.7 V						20	μA
I_{OZL}	V_{CC1} = 5.5 V,	V_O = 0.4 V						−0.4	mA
I_I	V_{CC1} = 5.5 V,	V_I = 7 V			0.1			0.1	mA
I_{IH}	V_{CC1} = 5.5 V,	V_I = 2.7 V			20			20	μA
I_{IL}	V_{CC1} = 5.5 V,	V_I = 0.5 V			−0.4			−0.4	mA
I_O‡	V_{CC1} = 5.5 V,	V_O = 2.25 V	−30		−112	−30		−112	mA
I_{CC1}	V_{CC1} = 5.5 V								mA
I_{CC2}	V_{CC2} = 2.1 V								mA

† All typical values are at V_{CC} = 5 V, T_A = 25°C.
‡ The output conditions have been chosen to produce a current that closely approximates one-half the true short-circuit current, I_{OS}.

2

LSI Devices

timing requirements

PARAMETER			SN54AS8834 MIN	SN54AS8834 MAX	SN74AS8834 MIN	SN74AS8834 MAX	UNIT
t_{su}	Setup time	$\overline{\text{WEL}}$1-$\overline{\text{WEL}}$2 before CLK↑					ns
		$\overline{\text{WER}}$1-$\overline{\text{WER}}$2 before CLK↑					
		WAL0-WAL5 before CLK↑					
		WAR0-WAR5 before CLK↑					
		D0-D39 before CLK↑					
t_h	Hold time	$\overline{\text{WEL}}$1-$\overline{\text{WEL}}$2 after CLK↑					ns
		$\overline{\text{WER}}$1-$\overline{\text{WER}}$2 after CLK↑					
		WAL0-WAL5 after CLK↑					
		WAR0-WAR5 after CLK↑					
		D0-D39 after CLK↑					

switching characteristics over recommended ranges of operating temperature and supply voltage (see Note 1)

PARAMETER	FROM (INPUT)	TO (OUTPUT)	SN54AS8834 MIN	SN54AS8834 MAX	SN74AS8834 MIN	SN74AS8834 MAX	UNIT
t_{pd}	D30-D39	PL2					ns
	D20-D29	PL1					
	D10-D19	PR2					
	D0-D9	PR1					
	RAA0-RAA5	Y0-Y39					
	RAB0-RAB5	Y0-Y39					
	AL/$\overline{\text{BR}}$	Y20-Y39					
	AR/$\overline{\text{BL}}$	Y0-Y19					
	CLK	Y0-Y39†					
t_{en}	$\overline{\text{MOE}}$	PL2-PL1 or PR2-PR1					ns
	$\overline{\text{MOE}}$	Y0-Y39					
	$\overline{\text{OEL}}$2	Y30-Y39					
	$\overline{\text{OEL}}$1	Y20-Y29					
	$\overline{\text{OER}}$2	Y10-Y19					
	$\overline{\text{OER}}$1	Y0-Y9					
t_{dis}	$\overline{\text{MOE}}$	PL2-PL1 or PR2-PR1					ns
	$\overline{\text{MOE}}$	Y0-Y39					
	$\overline{\text{OEL}}$2	Y30-Y39					
	$\overline{\text{OEL}}$1	Y20-Y29					
	$\overline{\text{OER}}$2	Y10-Y19					
	$\overline{\text{OER}}$1	Y0-Y9					

† When read and write address are already selected.

NOTE 1: Load circuit and voltage waveforms are shown in Section 1.

D2938, NOVEMBER 1985—REVISED MARCH 1986

- High-Speed ''Flash'' Shift Operations
- Shifts up to 32 Positions in Less than 25 ns
- Performs Logical, Circular, and Arithmetic Shifts
- 3-State Outputs Allow 32-Bit and 16-Bit Bus Interface
- 24-mA Bus Drivers
- 84-Pin Package
- Uses Less than 1.5 W (Max)
- Texas Instruments Quality and Reliability

description

The SN54AS8838 and SN74AS8838 are high-speed 32-bit barrel shifters in an 84-pin ceramic pin-grid array. The devices can shift up to 32 bits in a single instruction cycle of under 25 nanoseconds. Five basic shifts can be programmed: circular left and right, logical left and right, and arithmetic right.

Unlike conventional shift registers, whose shift operations are controlled by the number of input clock pulses applied, the number of positions to be shifted by the 'AS8838 is determined by an input decoder. This form of implementation does not require an input clock, thus, the shift operation is restricted only by internal propagation delays. The delay is the same regardless of the number of positions to be shifted, resulting in a high-speed ''flash'' shift.

Three-state output controls allow the devices to be interfaced with 32- or 16-bit data buses.

The SN54AS8838 is characterized for operation over the full military temperature range of −55°C to 125°C. The SN74AS8838 is characterized for operation from 0°C to 70°C.

SN54AS8838, SN74AS8838
GB PIN-GRID-ARRAY PACKAGE
(TOP VIEW)

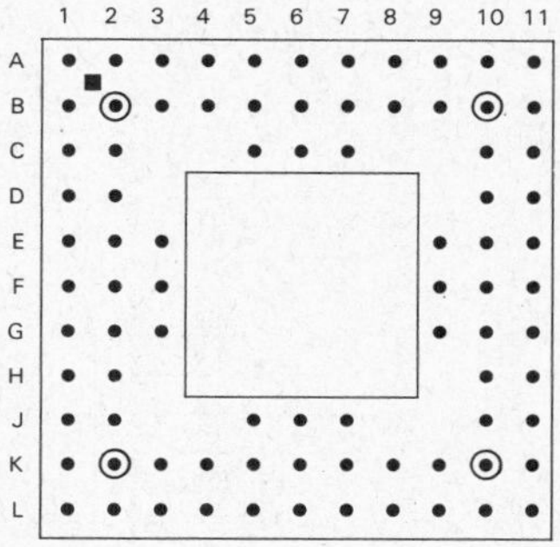
1 2 3 4 5 6 7 8 9 10 11
A
B
C
D
E
F
G
H
J
K
L

PIN NO.	PIN NAME	PIN NO.	PIN NAME
A1	GND	F9	$\overline{YOEL}$
A2	V_{CC2}	F10	Y7
A3	Y30	F11	Y6
A4	Y28	G1	D20
A5	Y25	G2	D19
A6	Y23	G3	D18
A7	GND	G9	Y4
A8	Y20	G10	Y5
A9	Y18	G11	GND
A10	Y16	H1	D17
A11	GND	H2	D16
B1	D31	H10	Y2
B2	GND	H11	Y3
B3	Y31	J1	D15
B4	Y29	J2	D14
B5	Y26	J5	D7
B6	Y24	J6	D2
B7	Y22	J7	MUX1
B8	Y19	J10	Y0
B9	Y17	J11	Y1
B10	V_{CC1}	K1	V_{CC1}
B11	Y15	K2	D13
C1	D29	K3	D11
C2	D30	K4	D9
C5	Y27	K5	D6
C6	$\overline{YOEM}$	K6	D3
C7	Y21	K7	D0
C10	Y14	K8	SFT4
C11	Y13	K9	GND
D1	D27	K10	SFT1
D2	D28	K11	SFT0
D10	Y12	L1	GND
D11	Y11	L2	D12
E1	D24	L3	D10
E2	D25	L4	D8
E3	D26	L5	D5
E9	Y10	L6	D4
E10	Y9	L7	D1
E11	Y8	L8	MUX0
F1	D23	L9	SFT3
F2	D22	L10	VCC2
F3	D21	L11	SFT2

This document contains information on products in more than one phase of development. The status of each device is indicated on the page(s) specifying its electrical characteristics.

TEXAS INSTRUMENTS
POST OFFICE BOX 225012 • DALLAS, TEXAS 75265

logic symbol†

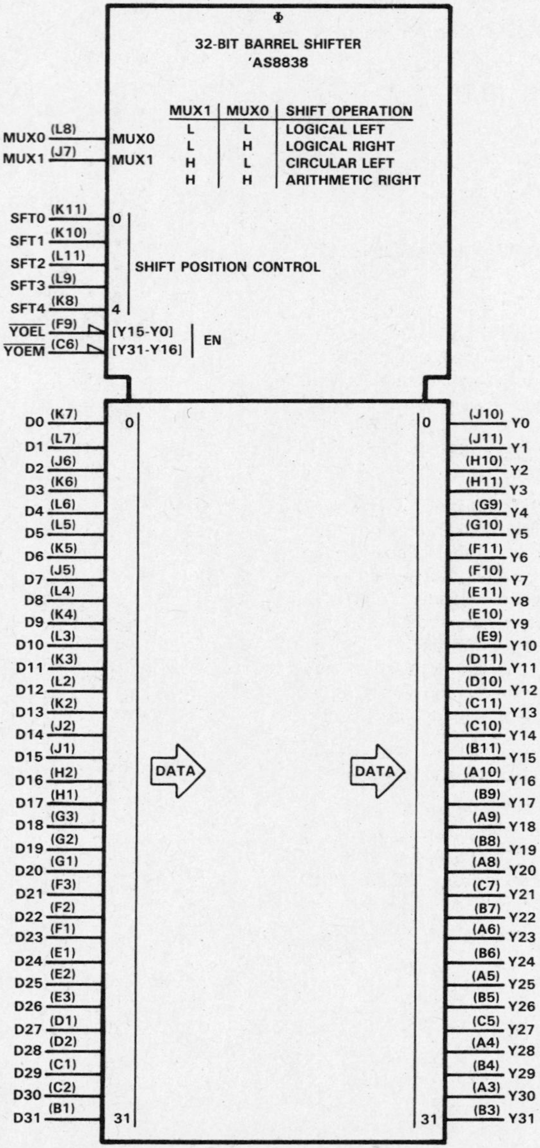
Φ
32-BIT BARREL SHIFTER
'AS8838
MUX1 | MUX0 | SHIFT OPERATION
L | L | LOGICAL LEFT
L | H | LOGICAL RIGHT
H | L | CIRCULAR LEFT
H | H | ARITHMETIC RIGHT
MUX0 (L8) MUX0
MUX1 (J7) MUX1
SFT0 (K11) 0
SFT1 (K10)
SFT2 (L11)
SFT3 (L9)
SFT4 (K8) 4
SHIFT POSITION CONTROL
YOEL (F9) [Y15-Y0]
YOEM (C6) [Y31-Y16]
EN
D0 (K7), D1 (L7), D2 (J6), D3 (K6), D4 (L6), D5 (L5), D6 (K5), D7 (J5), D8 (L4), D9 (K4), D10 (L3), D11 (K3), D12 (L2), D13 (K2), D14 (J2), D15 (J1), D16 (H2), D17 (H1), D18 (G3), D19 (G2), D20 (G1), D21 (F3), D22 (F2), D23 (F1), D24 (E1), D25 (E2), D26 (E3), D27 (D1), D28 (D2), D29 (C1), D30 (C2), D31 (B1)
0
31
DATA
DATA
0
31
(J10) Y0, (J11) Y1, (H10) Y2, (H11) Y3, (G9) Y4, (G10) Y5, (F11) Y6, (F10) Y7, (E11) Y8, (E10) Y9, (E9) Y10, (D11) Y11, (D10) Y12, (C11) Y13, (C10) Y14, (B11) Y15, (A10) Y16, (B9) Y17, (A9) Y18, (B8) Y19, (A8) Y20, (C7) Y21, (B7) Y22, (A6) Y23, (B6) Y24, (A5) Y25, (B5) Y26, (C5) Y27, (A4) Y28, (B4) Y29, (A3) Y30, (B3) Y31

†This symbol is in accordance with ANSI/IEEE Std 91-1984.

PIN NAME	PIN NO.	I/O	DESCRIPTION
D0	K7	I	Input data bits 0 through 31
D1	L7		
D2	J6		
D3	K6		
D4	L6		
D5	L5		
D6	K5		
D7	J5		
D8	L4		
D9	K4		
D10	L3		
D11	K3		
D12	L2		
D13	K2		
D14	J2		
D15	J1		
D16	H2		
D17	H1		
D18	G3		
D19	G2		
D20	G1		
D21	F3		
D22	F2		
D23	F1		
D24	E1		
D25	E2		
D26	E3		
D27	D1		
D28	D2		
D29	C1		
D30	C2		
D31	B1		
GND	A1		Ground (All ground pins must be used.)
GND	A7		
GND	A11		
GND	B2		
GND	G11		
GND	K9		
GND	L1		
MUX0	L8	I	Shift instruction control. Specifies the type of shift operation to be performed. See Table 1 for further information.
MUX1	J7		
SFT0	K11	I	Shift position control. Specifies the number of bit positions to shift. See Table 1 for further information.
SFT1	K10		
SFT2	L11		
SFT3	L9		
SFT4	K8		
V_{CC1}	B10		5-Volt supply for TTL-compatible I/O
V_{CC1}	K1		
V_{CC2}	A2		2-Volt supply for internal Schottky Transistor Logic (STL)
V_{CC2}	L10		

2

LSI Devices

PIN NAME	PIN NO.	I/O	DESCRIPTION
Y0	J10	O	Output data bits 0 through 10
Y1	J11		
Y2	H10		
Y3	H11		
Y4	G9		
Y5	G10		
Y6	F11		
Y7	F10		
Y8	E11		
Y9	E10		
Y10	E9		
Y11	D11	O	Output data bits 11 through 31
Y12	D10		
Y13	C11		
Y14	C10		
Y15	B11		
Y16	A10		
Y17	B9		
Y18	A9		
Y19	B8		
Y20	A8		
Y21	C7		
Y22	B7		
Y23	A6		
Y24	B6		
Y25	A5		
Y26	B5		
Y27	C5		
Y28	A4		
Y29	B4		
Y30	A3		
Y31	B3		
$\overline{\text{YOEL}}$	F9	I	Control input for the Y15-Y0 output port. When $\overline{\text{YOEL}}$ is low, Y15-Y0 is enabled.
$\overline{\text{YOEM}}$	C6	I	Control input for the Y31-Y16 output port. When $\overline{\text{YOEM}}$ is low, Y31-Y16 is enabled.

functional block diagram

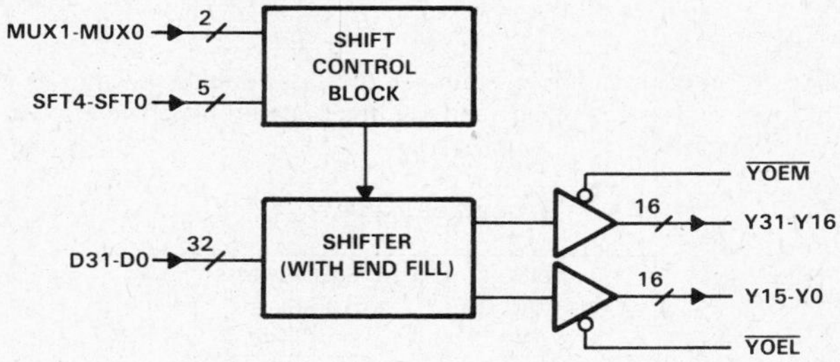
MUX1-MUX0
2
SFT4-SFT0
5
SHIFT
CONTROL
BLOCK
D31-D0
32
SHIFTER
(WITH END FILL)
YOEM
16
Y31-Y16
16
Y15-Y0
YOEL

data input/output

Data is input to the 'AS8838 through the D31-D0 data port and output through two 16-bit data ports, Y31-Y16 and Y15-Y0. Two 3-state output controls enable the Y data ports. The most significant half of the shift result is enabled when $\overline{\text{YOEM}}$ is low, the least significant half when $\overline{\text{YOEL}}$ is low.

shift control block

The shift control block decodes the MUX1-MUX0 instruction inputs and the SFT4-SFT0 shift position controls and transmits the resulting control signals to the shifter. MUX1-MUX0 control shift instruction selection as shown in Table 1. SFT4-SFT0 specify the number of bit positions to be shifted. For right shifts, the two's complement of the number of bit positions must be placed on SFT4-SFT0.

TABLE 1. INSTRUCTION SET

MUX1	MUX0	FUNCTION	OPERATION
L	L	Logical Left Shift	Shift left the number of bit positions defined by SFT4-SFT0. Fill vacated bit positions with zeros.
L	H	Logical Right Shift	Shift right the number of bit positions specified by the two's complement of SFT4-SFT0. Fill vacated bit positions with zeros. (A logical right shift with SFT4-SFT0 = 0 will fill all bits with zeros.)
H	L	Circular Left Shift	Circular left shift the number of bit positions defined by SFT4-SFT0. (A circular right shift can be performed by putting the two's complement of number of bits to be shifted on SFT4-SFT0.)
H	H	Arithmetic Right Shift	Shift right the number of bit positions defined by the two's complement of SFT4-SFT0. Fill vacated bit positions with the D31 input value (sign bit) (An arithmetic right shift with SFT4-SFT0 = 0 will fill all bits with the sign bit.).

2

LSI Devices

shift operation examples

logical shift left (M1 – M0 = LL)

In the shift left mode, SFT4-SFT0 define the number of bit positions to be shifted. The following example shifts a 32-bit word 8 positions to the left and fills the vacated bit positions with zeros.

CONTROL SIGNALS

SHIFT INSTRUCTION M2-M0	NUMBER OF BITS TO SHIFT SFT4-SFT0
00	01000

Assume D31-D0 is hex ABCD0123.

	D31-D0
Input Data	1010 1011 1100 1101 0000 0001 0010 0011

	Y31-Y0
Result	1100 1101 0000 0001 0010 0011 0000 0000

logical shift right (M1 – M0 = LH)

In the shift right mode, the two's complement of the number of bit positions to be shifted must be placed on SFT4-SFT0. The following example shifts a 32-bit word 8 positions to the right and fills the vacated bit positions with zeros.

CONTROL SIGNALS

SHIFT INSTRUCTION M2-M0	NUMBER OF BITS TO SHIFT SFT4-SFT0
01	11000

Assume D31-D0 is hex ABCD0123.

	D31-D0
Input Data	1010 1011 1100 1101 0000 0001 0010 0011

	Y31-Y0
Result	0000 0000 1010 1011 1100 1101 0000 0001

circular shift left (M1 – M0 = HL)

In the circular shift left mode, SFT4-SFT0 define the number of bit positions to be shifted. The following example circular shifts a 32-bit word 8 positions to the left.

CONTROL SIGNALS

SHIFT INSTRUCTION M2-M0	NUMBER OF BITS TO SHIFT SFT4-SFT0
10	01000

Assume D31-D0 is hex ABCD0123.

	D31-D0
Input Data	1010 1011 1100 1101 0000 0001 0010 0011

	Y31-Y0
Result	1100 1101 0000 0001 0010 0011 1010 1011

circular shift right (M1 – M0 = HL)

A circular right shift can be performed by placing the two's complement of the number of bit positions to be shifted on SFT4-SFT0 and using the circular left shift mode (M1 – M0 = HL). The following example circular shifts a 32-bit word 8 positions to the right.

CONTROL SIGNALS

SHIFT INSTRUCTION M2-M0	NUMBER OF BITS TO SHIFT SFT4-SFT0
10	11000

Assume D31-D0 is hex ABCD0123.

	D31-D0
Input Data	1010 1011 1100 1101 0000 0001 0010 0011

	Y31-Y0
Result	0010 0011 1010 1011 1100 1101 0000 0001

arithmetic shift right (M1 – M0 = HH)

In the arithmetic shift right mode, SFT4-SFT0 define the number of bit positions to be shifted. The following example shifts a 32-bit word 8 positions to the right and fills the vacated bit positions with the sign bit (D31 from the input data).

CONTROL SIGNALS

SHIFT INSTRUCTION M2-M0	NUMBER OF BITS TO SHIFT SFT4-SFT0
11	11000

Assume D31-D0 is hex ABCD0123.

	D31-D0
Input Data	1010 1011 1100 1101 0000 0001 0010 0011

	Y31-Y0
Result	1111 1111 1010 1011 1100 1101 0000 0001

absolute maximum ratings over operating temperature range (unless otherwise noted)

Supply voltage, V_{CC1} . . . . 7 V
Supply voltage, V_{CC2} . . . . 3 V
Input voltage . . . . 7 V
Operating case temperature range: SN54AS8838 . . . . −55°C to 125°C
Operating free-air temperature range: SN74AS8838 . . . . 0°C to 70°C
Storage temperature range . . . . −65°C to 150°C

recommended operating conditions

	PARAMETER	SN54AS8838			SN74AS8838			UNIT
		MIN	NOM	MAX	MIN	NOM	MAX	
V_{CC1}	I/O supply voltage	4.5	5	5.5	4.5	5	5.5	V
V_{CC2}	STL internal logic supply voltage	1.9	2	2.1	1.9	2	2.1	V
V_{IH}	High-level input voltage	2			2			V
V_{IL}	Low-level input voltage			0.8			0.8	V
I_{OH}	High-level output current			−1			2.6	mA
I_{OL}	Low-level output current			12			24	mA
T_A	Operating free-air temperature	−55			0		70	°C
T_C	Operating case temperature			125				°C

electrical characteristics over recommended operating temperature range (unless otherwise noted)

PARAMETER	TEST CONDITIONS		SN54AS8838 MIN	TYP†	MAX	UNIT
V_{IK}	V_{CC1} = 4.5 V,	I_I = −18 mA			−1.2	V
V_{OH}	V_{CC1} = 4.5 V to 5.5 V,	I_{OH} = −0.4 mA	$V_{CC}-2$			V
	V_{CC1} = 4.5 V,	I_{OH} = −1 mA	2.4			
V_{OL}	V_{CC1} = 4.5 V,	I_{OL} = 12 mA			0.4	V
	V_{CC1} = 4.5 V,	I_{OL} = 24 mA				
I_{OZH}	V_{CC1} = 5.5 V,	V_O = 2.7 V			20	μA
I_{OZL}	V_{CC1} = 5.5 V,	V_I = 0.4 V			−0.4	mA
I_I	V_{CC1} = 5.5 V,	V_I = 7 V			0.1	mA
I_{IH}	V_{CC1} = 5.5 V,	V_I = 2.7 V			20	μA
I_{IL}	V_{CC1} = 5.5 V,	V_I = 0.4 V			−0.4	mA
I_O‡	V_{CC1} = 5.5 V,	V_O = 2.25 V	−30		−112	mA
I_{CC1}	V_{CC1} = 5.5 V				150	mA
I_{CC2}	V_{CC2} = 2.1 V				145	mA

switching characteristics over recommended operating temperature range (see Note 1)

PARAMETER	FROM (INPUT)	TO (OUTPUT)	V_{CC} = 4.5 V to 5.5 V, C_L = 50 pF, R1 = 500 Ω, R2 = 500 Ω SN54AS8838 MIN	TYP†	MAX	UNIT
t_{pd}	MUX1-MUX0	Y31-Y0		22		ns
	SFT4-SFT0	Y31-Y0		22		
	D31-D0	Y31-Y0		22		
t_{en}	$\overline{\text{YOEL}}$	Y15-Y0		12		ns
	$\overline{\text{YOEM}}$	Y31-Y16		12		
t_{dis}	$\overline{\text{YOEL}}$	Y15-Y0		6		ns
	$\overline{\text{YOEM}}$	Y31-Y16		6		

† All typical values are at V_{CC1} = 5 V, T_A = 25°C.

‡ The output conditions have been chosen to produce a current that closely approximates one-half the true short-circuit current, I_{OS}.

NOTE 1: For load circuit and voltage waveforms, see pages 1-12 of *The TTL Data Book,* Volume 3, 1984.

electrical characteristics over recommended operating free-air temperature range (unless otherwise noted)

PARAMETER	TEST CONDITIONS		SN74AS8838 MIN	SN74AS8838 MAX	UNIT
V_{IK}	V_{CC1} = 4.5 V,	I_I = −18 mA		−1.2	V
V_{OH}	V_{CC1} = 4.5 V to 5.5 V,	I_{OH} = −0.4 mA	$V_{CC}-2$		V
	V_{CC1} = 4.5 V,	I_{OH} = −1 mA			
	V_{CC1} = 4.5 V,	I_{OH} = −2.6 mA	2.4		
V_{OL}	V_{CC1} = 4.5 V,	I_{OL} = 12 mA		0.4	V
	V_{CC1} = 4.5 V,	I_{OL} = 24 mA		0.5	
I_{OZH}	V_{CC1} = 5.5 V,	V_O = 2.7 V		20	μA
I_{OZL}	V_{CC1} = 5.5 V,	V_I = 0.4 V		−0.4	mA
I_I	V_{CC1} = 5.5 V,	V_I = 7 V		0.1	mA
I_{IH}	V_{CC1} = 5.5 V,	V_I = 2.7 V		20	μA
I_{IL}	V_{CC1} = 5.5 V,	V_I = 0.4 V		−0.4	mA
I_O‡	V_{CC1} = 5.5 V,	V_O = 2.25 V	−30	−112	mA
I_{CC1}	V_{CC1} = 5.5 V			150	mA
I_{CC2}	V_{CC2} = 2.1 V			145	mA

‡ The output conditions have been chosen to produce a current that closely approximates one-half the true short-circuit current, I_{OS}.

switching characteristics (see Note 1)

PARAMETER	FROM (INPUT)	TO (OUTPUT)	V_{CC} = 5 V, C_L = 50 pF, R1 = 500 Ω, R2 = 500 Ω, T_A = 25 °C SN74AS8838 MIN	TYP	MAX	V_{CC} = 4.5 V to 5.5 V, C_L = 50 pF, R1 = 500 Ω, R2 = 500 Ω, T_A = 0 °C to 70 °C SN74AS8838 MIN	MAX	UNIT
t_{pd}	MUX1-MUX0	Y31-Y0		22	26		29	ns
	SFT4-SFT0	Y31-Y0		20	22		25	
	D31-D0	Y31-Y0		22	26		29	
t_{en}	$\overline{YOEL}$	Y15-Y0		12	15		17	ns
	$\overline{YOEM}$	Y31-Y16		12	15		17	
t_{dis}	$\overline{YOEL}$	Y15-Y0		6	8		10	ns
	$\overline{YOEM}$	Y31-Y16		6	8		10	

NOTE 1: Load circuit and voltage waveforms are shown in Section 1.

TEXAS INSTRUMENTS
POST OFFICE BOX 225012 • DALLAS, TEXAS 75265

SN54ALS29818, SN54ALS29819
SN74ALS29818, SN74ALS29819
8-BIT DIAGNOSTICS/PIPELINE REGISTERS

D2298, JANUARY 1986

- **High-Speed 8-Bit Parallel Output Register**
- **Serial Shadow Register with Right-Shift Only**
- **'ALS29818 Performs Parallel-to-Serial and Serial-to-Parallel Conversion**
- **Designed Specifically for Use in Applications such as:**
  Write Control Store ('ALS29818)
  Serial Shadow-Register Diagnostics
- **'ALS29819 Provides Even-Parity Output**
- **Low Power Dissipation . . . 215 mW Typical**
- **'ALS29818 is Functionally Equivalent to AMD AM29818**
- **Package Options Include Both Plastic and Ceramic Chip Carriers in Addition to Plastic and Ceramic DIPs**
- **Dependable Texas Instruments Quality and Reliability**

description

The 'ALS29818 and 'ALS29819 are 8-bit output registers with on-chip shadow register for use in applications such as write control store and shadow register diagnostics.

The output registers of the 'ALS29818 and 'ALS29819 are loaded in parallel from either the I/O port (DQ0–DQ7) or the shadow register. The shadow register of the 'ALS29818 is loaded serially from either the I/O port (Y0–Y7) or the output register. The 'ALS29819 shadow register is loaded serially from the I/O port (DQ0–DQ7). In addition, the 'ALS29819 provides a Parity-Even (PE) output, which monitors parity of the output register. Operation of these devices is controlled by the Mode and SDI inputs as shown in the function table.

The SN54ALS29818 and SN54ALS29819 are characterized for operation over the full military temperature range of −55°C to 125°C. The SN74ALS29818 and SN74ALS29819 are characterized for operation from 0°C to 70°C.

SN54ALS29818 . . . JT PACKAGE
SN74ALS29818 . . . DW OR NT PACKAGE
(TOP VIEW)

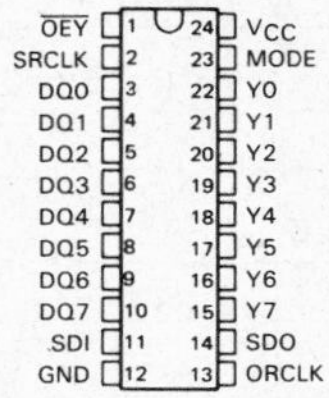
OEY 1 24 VCC
SRCLK 2 23 MODE
DQ0 3 22 Y0
DQ1 4 21 Y1
DQ2 5 20 Y2
DQ3 6 19 Y3
DQ4 7 18 Y4
DQ5 8 17 Y5
DQ6 9 16 Y6
DQ7 10 15 Y7
SDI 11 14 SDO
GND 12 13 ORCLK

SN54ALS29818 . . . FK PACKAGE
SN74ALS29818 . . . FN PACKAGE
(TOP VIEW)

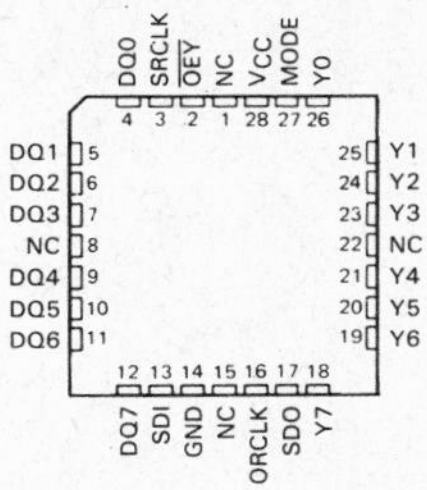
DQ0 SRCLK OEY NC VCC MODE Y0
4 3 2 1 28 27 26
DQ1 5 25 Y1
DQ2 6 24 Y2
DQ3 7 23 Y3
NC 8 22 NC
DQ4 9 21 Y4
DQ5 10 20 Y5
DQ6 11 19 Y6
12 13 14 15 16 17 18
DQ7 SDI GND NC ORCLK SDO Y7

SN54ALS29819 . . . JT PACKAGE
SN74ALS29819 . . . DW OR JT PACKAGE
(TOP VIEW)

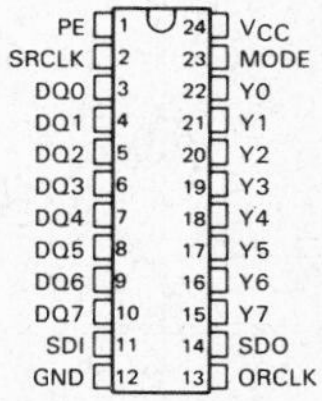
PE 1 24 VCC
SRCLK 2 23 MODE
DQ0 3 22 Y0
DQ1 4 21 Y1
DQ2 5 20 Y2
DQ3 6 19 Y3
DQ4 7 18 Y4
DQ5 8 17 Y5
DQ6 9 16 Y6
DQ7 10 15 Y7
SDI 11 14 SDO
GND 12 13 ORCLK

SN54ALS29819 . . . FK PACKAGE
SN74ALS29819 . . . FN PACKAGE
(TOP VIEW)

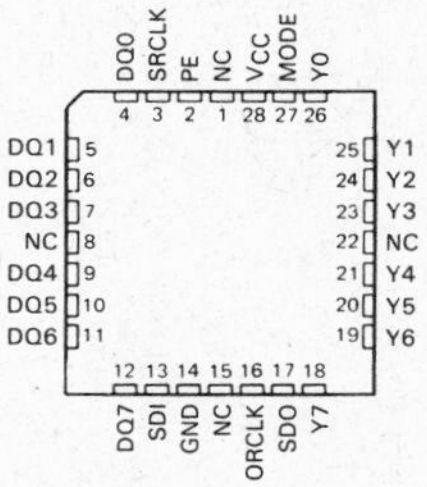
DQ0 SRCLK PE NC VCC MODE Y0
4 3 2 1 28 27 26
DQ1 5 25 Y1
DQ2 6 24 Y2
DQ3 7 23 Y3
NC 8 22 NC
DQ4 9 21 Y4
DQ5 10 20 Y5
DQ6 11 19 Y6
12 13 14 15 16 17 18
DQ7 SDI GND NC ORCLK SDO Y7

NC—No internal connection

PRODUCT PREVIEW documents contain information on products in the formative or design phase of development. Characteristic data and other specifications are design goals. Texas Instruments reserves the right to change or discontinue these products without notice.

'ALS29818 FUNCTION TABLE

INPUTS					OUTPUT AND I/O			OPERATION OR FUNCTION
MODE	$\overline{OEY}$	SDI	SRCLK	ORCLK	SDO	Y0–Y7	DQ0–DQ7	
L	X	X	↑	X	SR7	–	HI-Z	Serial input, shift right, disable DQ0–DQ7
H	H	L	↑	X	SDI	INPUT	HI-Z	Parallel load shadow register from Y0–Y7, disable DQ0–DQ7
H	L	L	↑	No ↑	SDI	OUTPUT	HI-Z	Parallel load shadow register from output register, disable DQ0–DQ7
L	X	X	X	↑	SR7	–	INPUT†	Load output register from DQ0–DQ7
L	X	X	↑	↑	SR7	–	INPUT†	Load output register from DQ0–DQ7 while shifting shadow register
H	X	X	No ↑	↑	SDI	–	–	Load output register from shadow register
H	X	X	X	X	SDI	–	–	Serial data in to serial data out
H	L	L	↑	↑	SDI	OUTPUT	HI-Z	Exchange data between registers, DQ0–DQ7 disabled
H	X	H	X	X	SDI	–	–	Hold shadow register, transitions on SRCLK do not effect shadow register
H	X	H	↑	X	SDI	–	OUTPUT	Enable DQ0–DQ7 for parallel shadow register output

†The DQ0–DQ7 outputs must be disabled before applying data to DQ0–DQ7.

'ALS29819 FUNCTION TABLE

INPUTS				OUTPUT AND I/O			OPERATION OR FUNCTION
MODE	SDI	SRCLK	ORCLK	SDO	Y0–Y7 PE	DQ0–DQ7	
L	X	↑	X	SR7	OUTPUT	HI-Z	Serial input, shift right
H	L	↑	X	SDI (L)	OUTPUT	INPUT	Parallel load shadow register from DQ0–DQ7
H	L	↑	↑	SDI (L)	OUTPUT	INPUT	Parallel load shadow register and output register from DQ0–DQ7
L X	X L	X X	↑ ↑	SR7	OUTPUT	INPUT	Load output register from DQ0–DQ7
L	X	↑	↑	SR7	OUTPUT	INPUT	Load output register from DQ0–DQ7 while shifting shadow register
H	H	No ↑	↑	SDI (H)	OUTPUT	OUTPUT	Load output register from shadow register
H	X	X	X	SDI	OUTPUT	–	Serial data in to serial data out
H	H	X	X	SDI (H)	OUTPUT	OUTPUT HOLD	Hold shadow register, enable DQ0–DQ7, transitions on SRCLK ignored
L X	X L	X X	X X	–	OUTPUT	HI-Z	Disable DQ0–DQ7 outputs

logic symbols†

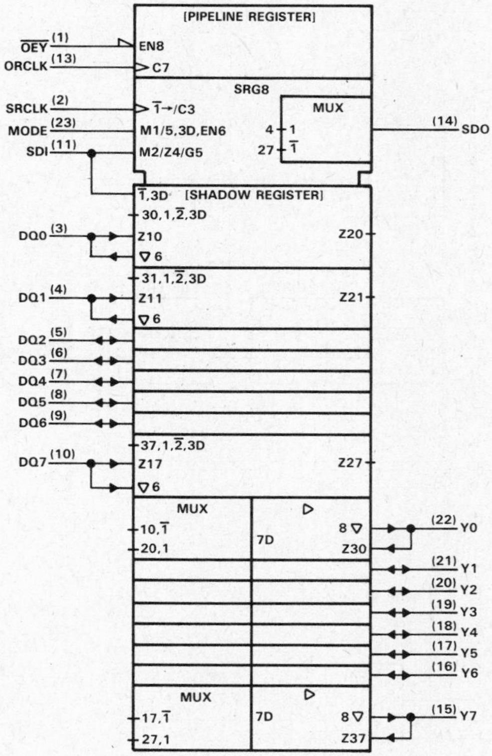
'ALS29818
[PIPELINE REGISTER]
OEY (1)
EN8
ORCLK (13)
C7
SRG8
SRCLK (2)
1→/C3
MODE (23)
M1/5,3D,EN6
SDI (11)
M2/Z4/G5
MUX
4 1
27 1
(14) SDO
1,3D [SHADOW REGISTER]
30,1,2,3D
DQ0 (3)
Z10
Z20
6
31,1,2,3D
DQ1 (4)
Z11
Z21
6
DQ2 (5)
DQ3 (6)
DQ4 (7)
DQ5 (8)
DQ6 (9)
37,1,2,3D
DQ7 (10)
Z17
Z27
6
MUX
10,1
20,1
7D
8
Z30
(22) Y0
(21) Y1
(20) Y2
(19) Y3
(18) Y4
(17) Y5
(16) Y6
MUX
17,1
27,1
7D
8
Z37
(15) Y7

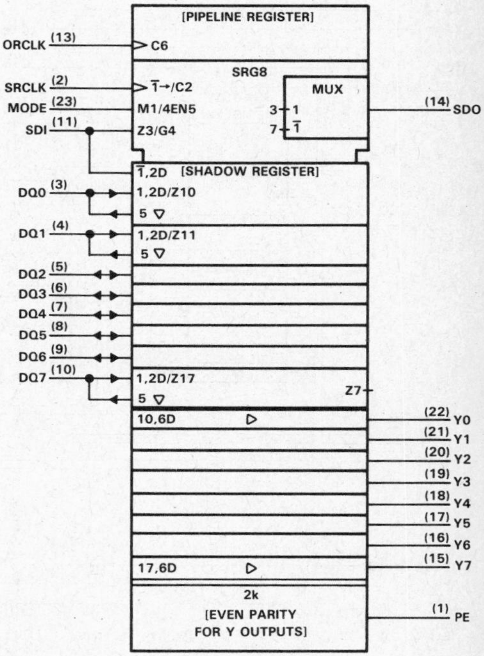
'ALS29819
[PIPELINE REGISTER]
ORCLK (13)
C6
SRG8
SRCLK (2)
1→/C2
MODE (23)
M1/4EN5
SDI (11)
Z3/G4
MUX
3 1
7 1
(14) SDO
1,2D [SHADOW REGISTER]
DQ0 (3)
1,2D/Z10
5
DQ1 (4)
1,2D/Z11
5
DQ2 (5)
DQ3 (6)
DQ4 (7)
DQ5 (8)
DQ6 (9)
DQ7 (10)
1,2D/Z17
5
Z7
10,6D
(22) Y0
(21) Y1
(20) Y2
(19) Y3
(18) Y4
(17) Y5
(16) Y6
17,6D
(15) Y7
2k
[EVEN PARITY
FOR Y OUTPUTS]
(1) PE

†These symbols are in accordance with ANSI/IEEE Std 91-1984 and IEC Publication 617-12.

logic diagrams (positive logic)

'ALS29818

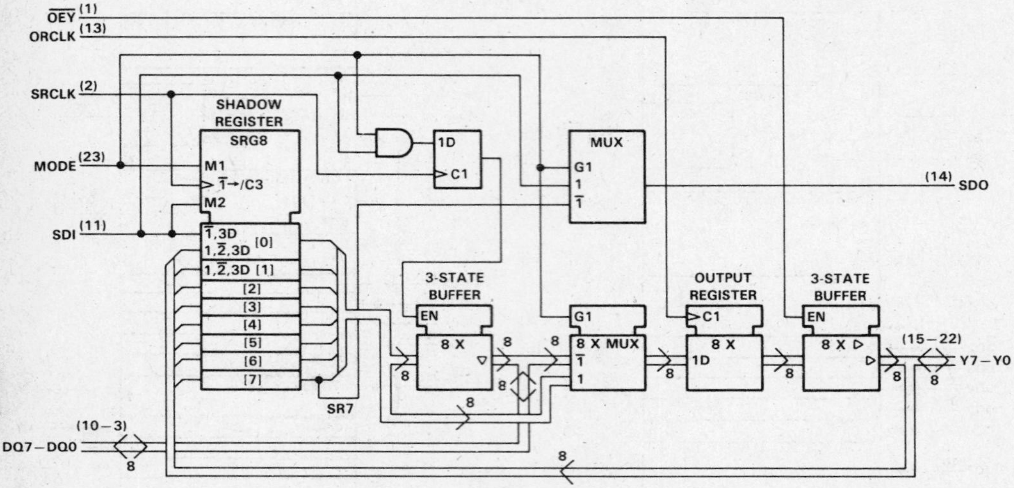
OEY (1)
ORCLK (13)
SRCLK (2)
MODE (23)
SDI (11)
SHADOW REGISTER
SRG8
M1
1→/C3
M2
1,3D
1,2,3D [0]
1,2,3D [1]
[2]
[3]
[4]
[5]
[6]
[7]
SR7
1D
C1
MUX
G1
1
1
(14) SDO
3-STATE BUFFER
EN
8 X
G1
8 X MUX
OUTPUT REGISTER
C1
8 X
1D
3-STATE BUFFER
EN
8 X
(15−22)
Y7−Y0
(10−3)
DQ7−DQ0
8

'ALS29819

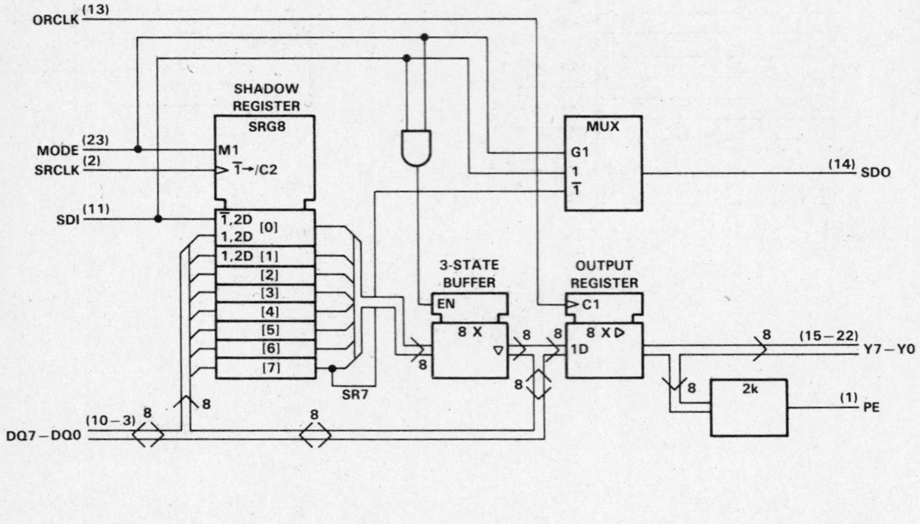
ORCLK (13)
SHADOW REGISTER
SRG8
MODE (23)
SRCLK (2)
M1
1→/C2
SDI (11)
1,2D
1,2D [0]
1,2D [1]
[2]
[3]
[4]
[5]
[6]
[7]
SR7
MUX
G1
1
1
(14) SDO
3-STATE BUFFER
EN
8 X
OUTPUT REGISTER
C1
8 X
1D
8
(15−22)
Y7−Y0
2k
(1) PE
(10−3)
DQ7−DQ0

TEXAS INSTRUMENTS
POST OFFICE BOX 225012 • DALLAS, TEXAS 75265

'ALS29818 gate-level logic diagram (positive logic)

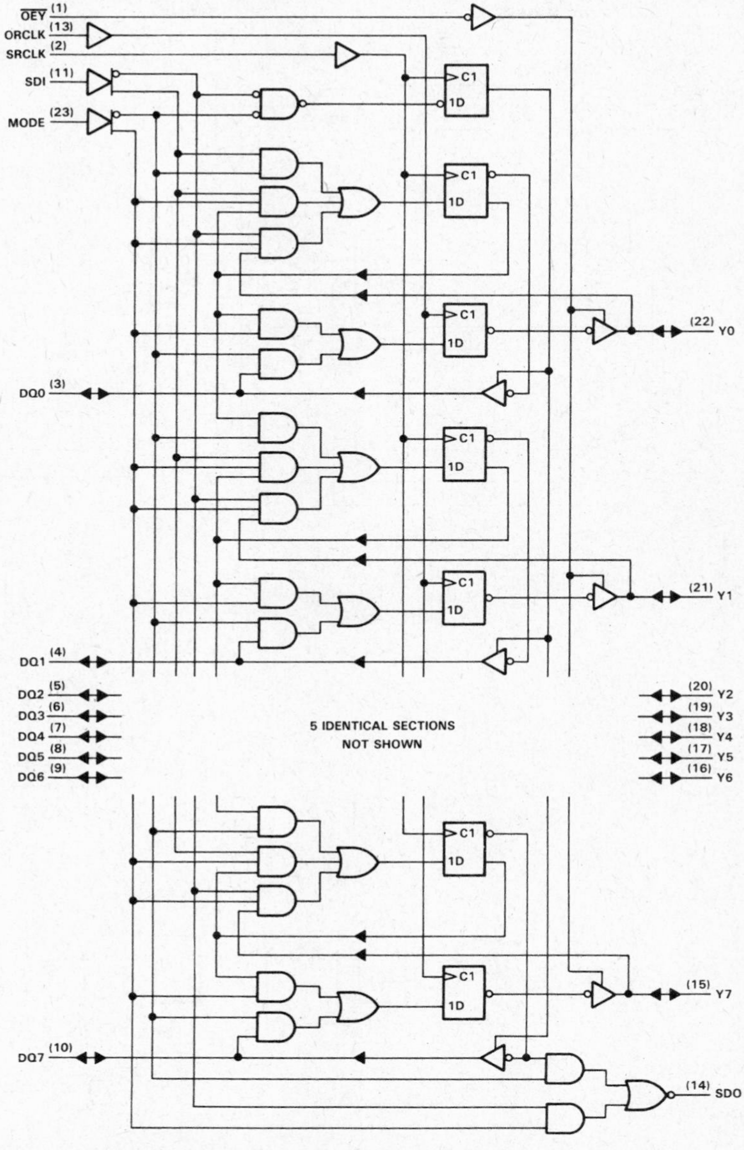
OEY (1)
ORCLK (13)
SRCLK (2)
SDI (11)
MODE (23)
C1
1D
DQ0 (3)
(22) Y0
DQ1 (4)
(21) Y1
DQ2 (5)
DQ3 (6)
DQ4 (7)
DQ5 (8)
DQ6 (9)
5 IDENTICAL SECTIONS
NOT SHOWN
(20) Y2
(19) Y3
(18) Y4
(17) Y5
(16) Y6
(15) Y7
DQ7 (10)
(14) SDO

Pin numbers shown are for DW, JT, and NT packages.

'ALS29819 gate-level logic diagram (positive logic)

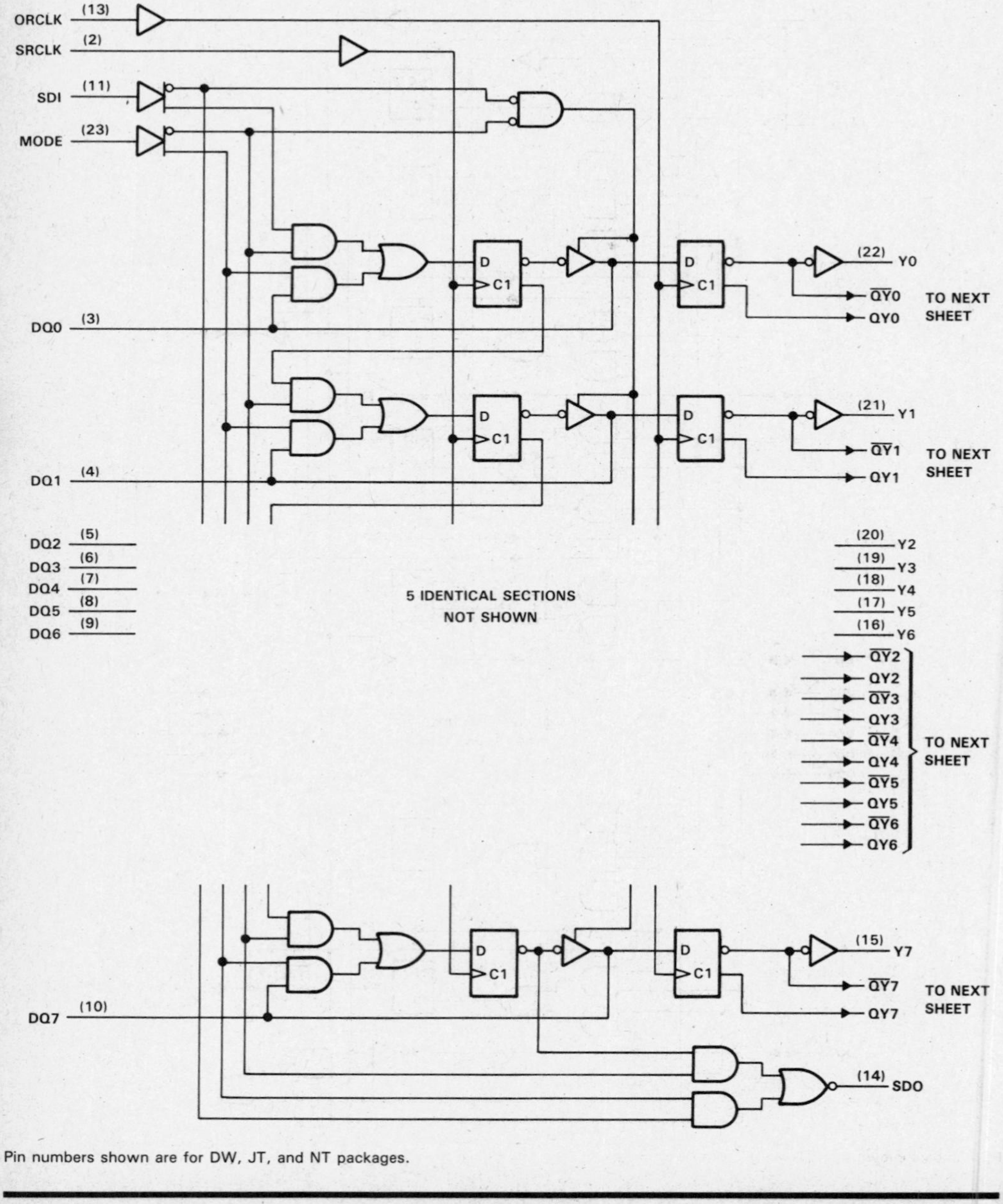
ORCLK (13)
SRCLK (2)
SDI (11)
MODE (23)
DQ0 (3)
DQ1 (4)
DQ2 (5)
DQ3 (6)
DQ4 (7)
DQ5 (8)
DQ6 (9)
DQ7 (10)
D
C1
(22) Y0
QY0
QY0
TO NEXT SHEET
(21) Y1
QY1
QY1
(20) Y2
(19) Y3
(18) Y4
(17) Y5
(16) Y6
QY2
QY2
QY3
QY3
QY4
QY4
QY5
QY5
QY6
QY6
5 IDENTICAL SECTIONS NOT SHOWN
(15) Y7
QY7
QY7
(14) SDO

Pin numbers shown are for DW, JT, and NT packages.

TEXAS INSTRUMENTS
POST OFFICE BOX 225012 • DALLAS, TEXAS 75265

'ALS29819 gate-level logic diagram (positive logic) (continued)

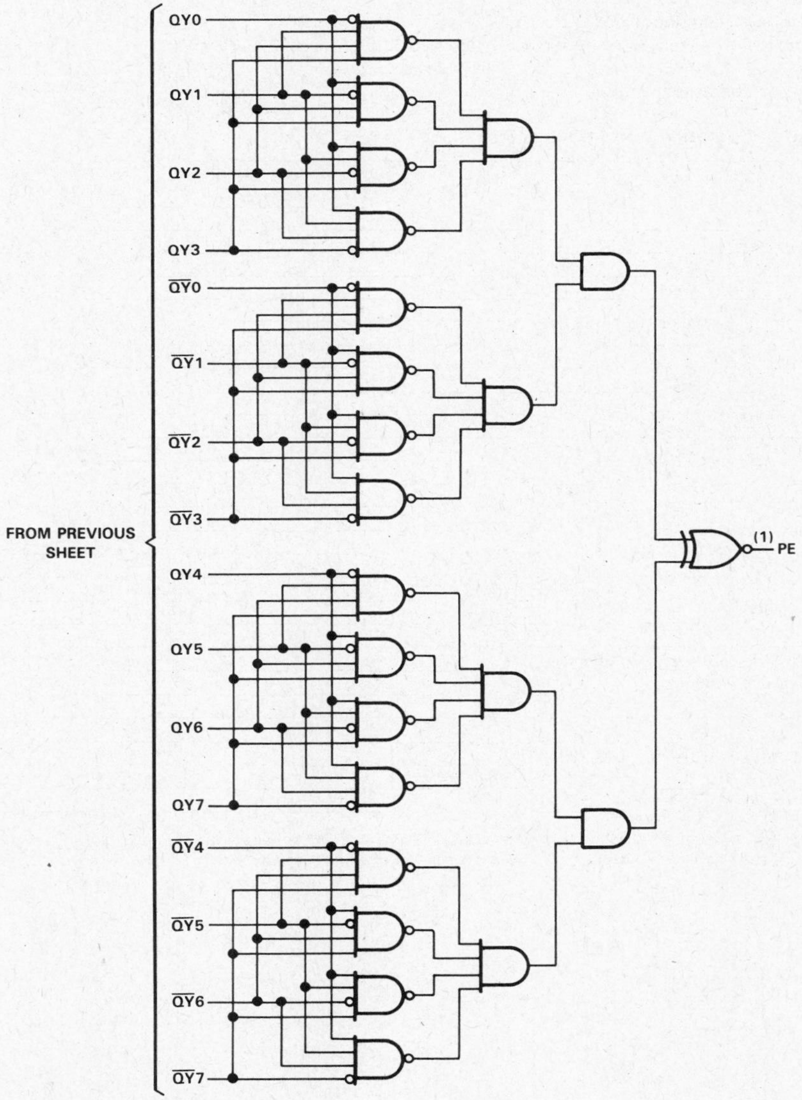
QY0
QY1
QY2
QY3
$\overline{QY0}$
$\overline{QY1}$
$\overline{QY2}$
$\overline{QY3}$
FROM PREVIOUS SHEET
QY4
QY5
QY6
QY7
$\overline{QY4}$
$\overline{QY5}$
$\overline{QY6}$
$\overline{QY7}$
(1)
PE

Pin numbers shown are for DW, JT, and NT packages.

absolute maximum ratings over operating free-air temperature range

Supply voltage, V_{CC} . . . . . 7 V
Input voltage, any input or I/O port . . . . . 5.5 V
Operating free-air temperature range: SN54ALS' . . . . . −55°C to 125°C
SN74ALS' . . . . . 0°C to 70°C
Storage temperature range . . . . . −65°C to 150°C

recommended operating conditions

			SN54ALS29818 SN54ALS29819			SN74ALS29818 SN74ALS29819			UNIT
			MIN	NOM	MAX	MIN	NOM	MAX	
V_{CC}	Supply voltage		4.5	5	5.5	4.75	5	5.25	V
V_{IH}	High-level input voltage		2			2			V
V_{IL}	Low-level input voltage				0.8			0.8	V
I_{OH}	High-level output current	Y0−Y7			−3			−3	mA
		All others			−1			−1	
I_{OL}	Low-level output current	Y0−Y7			16			24	mA
		All others			4			8	
f_{clock}	Clock frequency	SRCLK							MHz
		ORCLK							
t_w	Pulse duration	SRCLK high or low							ns
		ORCLK high or low							
t_{su}	Setup time before SRCLK↑	Y0−Y7							ns
		MODE							
		SDI							
		ORCLK ('ALS29818)†							
t_{su}	Setup time before ORCLK↑	DQ0−DQ7							ns
		MODE							
		SRCLK‡							
t_h	Hold time after SRCLK↑	Y0−Y7							ns
		MODE							
		SDI							
t_h	Hold time after ORCLK↑	DQ0−DQ7							ns
		MODE							
		SDI ('ALS29819)							
T_A	Operating free-air temperature		−55		125	0		70	°C

† This setup time ensures that the shadow register will see stable data from the output register.
‡ This setup time ensures that the output register will see stable data from the shadow register.

2

LSI Devices

electrical characteristics over recommended operating temperature range (unless otherwise noted)

PARAMETER		TEST CONDITIONS†		SN54ALS29818 SN54ALS29819			SN74ALS29818 SN74ALS29819			UNIT
				MIN	TYP‡	MAX	MIN	TYP‡	MAX	
V_{IK}		V_{CC} = MIN,	I_I = 18 mA			−1.2			−1.2	V
V_{OH}	All outputs	V_{CC} = MIN to MAX,	I_{OH} = −0.4 mA	$V_{CC}-2$			$V_{CC}-2$			V
	Y0−Y7	V_{CC} = MIN,	I_{OH} = −3 mA	2.4	3.2		2.4	3.2		
	All others	V_{CC} = MIN,	I_{OH} = −1 mA				2.4	3.2		
V_{OL}	All outputs	V_{CC} = MIN,	I_{OL} = 4 mA		0.25	0.5		0.25	0.5	V
		V_{CC} = MIN,	I_{OL} = 8 mA					0.35	0.5	
	Y0−Y7	V_{CC} = MIN,	I_{OL} = 16 mA		0.25	0.5		0.25	0.5	
		V_{CC} = MIN,	I_{OL} = 24 mA					0.35	0.5	
I_I	MODE	V_{CC} = MAX,	V_I = 5.5 V			0.4			0.4	mA
	SRCLK					0.3			0.3	
	SDI, $\overline{OEY}$					0.2			0.2	
	All others					0.1			0.1	
I_{IH}	MODE	V_{CC} = MAX,	V_I = 2.4 V			80			80	μA
	SRCLK					60			60	
	SDI, $\overline{OEY}$					40			40	
	All others§					20			20	
I_{IL}	MODE	V_{CC} = MAX,	V_I = 0.5 V			−0.4			−0.4	mA
	SRCLK					−0.3			−0.3	
	SDI, $\overline{OEY}$					−0.2			−0.2	
	All others§					−0.1			−0.1	
I_{OS}¶		V_{CC} = MAX,	V_O = 0	−75		−250	−75		−250	mA
I_{CC}		V_{CC} = MAX	(see Note 1)		43			43		mA

† For conditions shown as MIN or MAX, use appropriate value specified under recommended operating conditions.
‡ All typical values are at V_{CC} = 5 V, T_A = 25°C.
§ For I/O ports, the parameters I_{IH} and I_{IL} include the off-state output current.
¶ Not more than one output should be shorted at a time and duration of the short circuit should not exceed one second.
NOTE 1: I_{CC} is measured with all three-state outputs in the high-impedance state.

'ALS29818 switching characteristics (see Note 2)

PARAMETER		FROM (INPUT)	TO (OUTPUT)	TEST CONDITIONS See Figure 1	V_{CC} = 5 V, C_L = 50 pF, T_A = 25°C 'ALS29818			V_{CC} = MIN TO MAX,† C_L = 50 pF, T_A = MIN TO MAX† SN54ALS29818		SN74ALS29818		UNIT
					MIN	TYP	MAX	MIN	MAX	MIN	MAX	
f_{max}	SRCLK					37						MHz
	ORCLK					37						
t_{PLH}		MODE	SDO	R_L = 2 kΩ		8						ns
t_{PHL}						8						
t_{PLH}		SDI	SDO	R_L = 2 kΩ		8						ns
t_{PHL}						8						
t_{PLH}		ORCLK	Y0-Y7	R1 = 1 kΩ,		9						ns
t_{PHL}				R2 = 280 Ω		9						
t_{PLH}		SRCLK	SDO	R_L = 2 kΩ		13						ns
t_{PHL}						13						
t_{PLH}		SRCLK	DQ0-DQ7	R1 = 5 kΩ,								ns
t_{PHL}				R2 = 2 kΩ								
t_{PZH}		SRCLK	DQ0-DQ7	R1 = 5 kΩ,		16						ns
t_{PZL}				R2 = 2 kΩ		19						
t_{PHZ}		SRCLK	DQ0-DQ7	R1 = 5 kΩ,		16						ns
t_{PLZ}				R2 = 2 kΩ		19						
t_{PHZ}		$\overline{OEY}$	Y0-Y7	R1 = 1 kΩ,		7						ns
t_{PLZ}				R2 = 280 Ω		10						
t_{PZH}		$\overline{OEY}$	Y0-Y7	R1 = 1 kΩ,		6						ns
t_{PZL}				R2 = 280 Ω		9						

† For conditions shown as MIN or MAX, use the appropriate value specified under recommended operating conditions.

'ALS29819 switching characteristics (see Note 2)

PARAMETER		FROM (INPUT)	TO (OUTPUT)	TEST CONDITIONS See Figure 1	V_{CC} = 5 V, C_L = 50 pF, T_A = 25°C 'ALS29819 MIN	TYP	MAX	V_{CC} = MIN TO MAX,† C_L = 50 pF, T_A = MIN TO MAX† SN54ALS29819 MIN	MAX	SN74ALS29819 MIN	MAX	UNIT
f_{max}	SRCLK					37						MHz
	ORCLK					37						
t_{PLH}		MODE	SDO	R_L = 2 kΩ		8						ns
t_{PHL}						8						
t_{PLH}		SDI	SDO	R_L = 2 kΩ		8						ns
t_{PHL}						8						
t_{PLH}		ORCLK	Y0-Y7	R_L = 2 kΩ		9						ns
t_{PHL}						9						
t_{PLH}		ORCLK	PE	R_L = 2 kΩ		9						ns
t_{PHL}						5						
t_{PLH}		SRCLK	SDO	R_L = 2 kΩ		13						ns
t_{PHL}						13						
t_{PLH}		SRCLK	DQ0-DQ7	R1 = 5 kΩ, R2 = 2 kΩ		12						ns
t_{PHL}						12						
t_{PZH}		MODE or SDI	DQ0-DQ7	R1 = 5 kΩ, R2 = 2 kΩ		7						ns
t_{PZL}						9						
t_{PHZ}		MODE or SDI	DQ0-DQ7	R1 = 5 kΩ, R2 = 2 kΩ		7						ns
t_{PLZ}						9						

† For conditions shown as MIN or MAX, use the appropriate value specified under recommended operating conditions.

PARAMETER MEASUREMENT INFORMATION

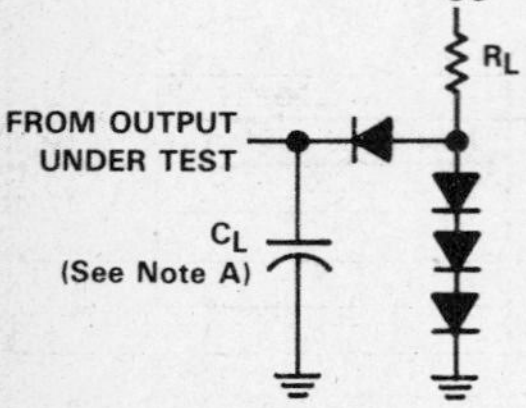
VCC
RL
FROM OUTPUT
UNDER TEST
CL
(See Note A)

LOAD CIRCUIT FOR
BI-STATE
TOTEM-POLE OUTPUTS

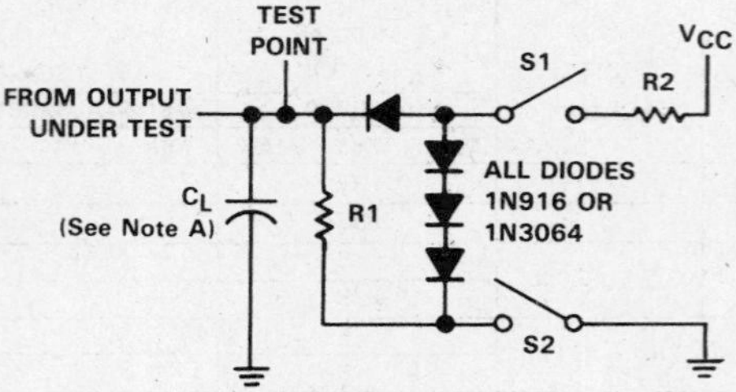
TEST
POINT
VCC
S1
R2
FROM OUTPUT
UNDER TEST
CL
(See Note A)
R1
ALL DIODES
1N916 OR
1N3064
S2

LOAD CIRCUIT FOR
THREE-STATE OUTPUTS

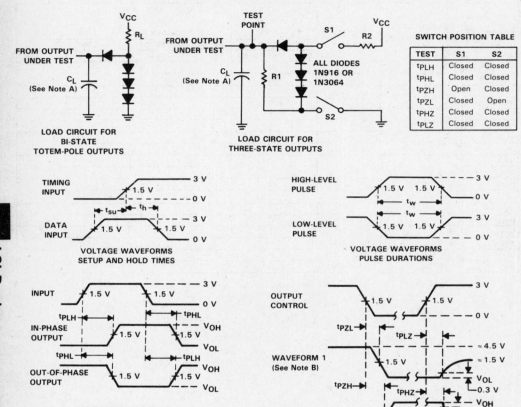

SWITCH POSITION TABLE

TEST	S1	S2
t_{PLH}	Closed	Closed
t_{PHL}	Closed	Closed
t_{PZH}	Open	Closed
t_{PZL}	Closed	Open
t_{PHZ}	Closed	Closed
t_{PLZ}	Closed	Closed

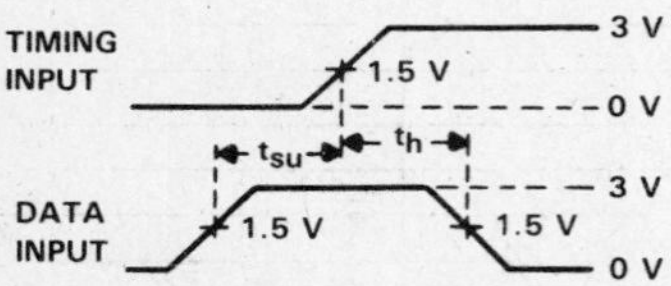
TIMING
INPUT
3 V
1.5 V
0 V
tsu
th
DATA
INPUT
3 V
1.5 V
1.5 V
0 V

VOLTAGE WAVEFORMS
SETUP AND HOLD TIMES

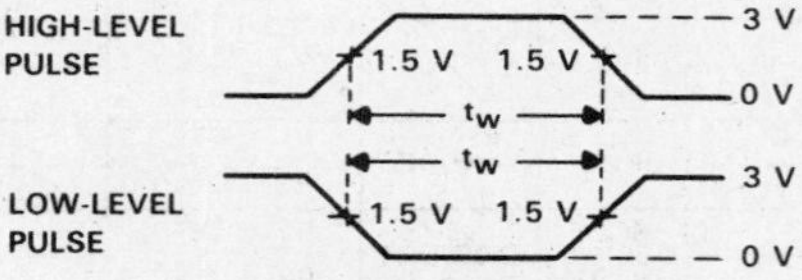
HIGH-LEVEL
PULSE
3 V
1.5 V
1.5 V
0 V
tw
tw
LOW-LEVEL
PULSE
3 V
1.5 V
1.5 V
0 V

VOLTAGE WAVEFORMS
PULSE DURATIONS

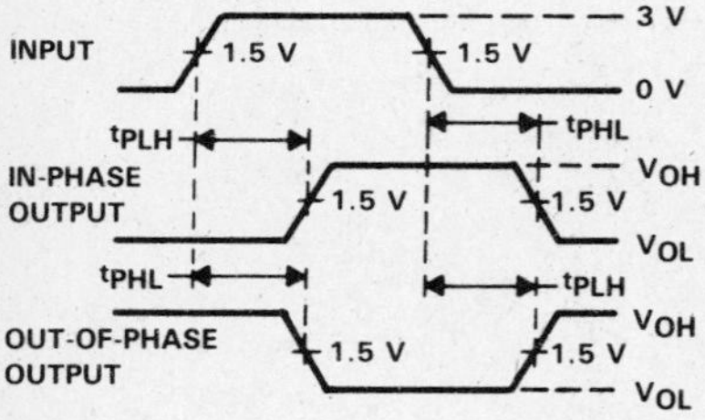
INPUT
3 V
1.5 V
1.5 V
0 V
tPLH
tPHL
IN-PHASE
OUTPUT
VOH
1.5 V
1.5 V
VOL
tPHL
tPLH
OUT-OF-PHASE
OUTPUT
VOH
1.5 V
1.5 V
VOL

VOLTAGE WAVEFORMS
PROPAGATION DELAY TIMES

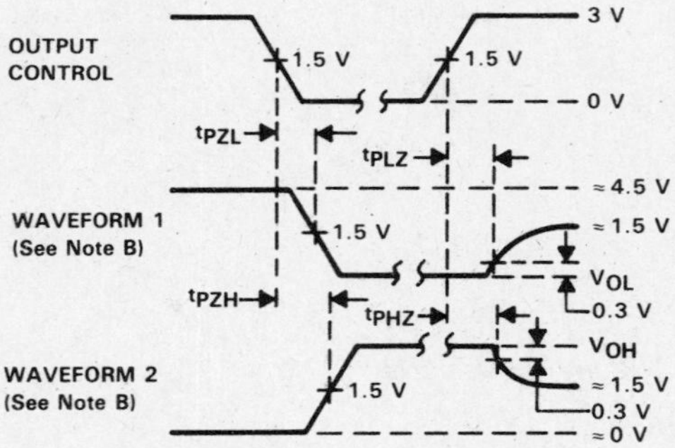
OUTPUT
CONTROL
3 V
1.5 V
1.5 V
0 V
tPZL
tPLZ
WAVEFORM 1
(See Note B)
≈4.5 V
1.5 V
≈1.5 V
VOL
0.3 V
tPZH
tPHZ
WAVEFORM 2
(See Note B)
VOH
1.5 V
≈1.5 V
0.3 V
≈0 V

VOLTAGE WAVEFORMS
ENABLE AND DISABLE TIMES, THREE-STATE OUTPUTS

NOTES: A. C_L includes probe and jig capacitance.

B. Waveform 1 is for an output with internal conditions such that the output is low except when disabled by the output control. Waveform 2 is for an output with internal conditions such that the output is high except when disabled by the output control.

C. All input pulses are supplied by generators having the following characteristics: PRR $\leq$ 10 MHz, Z_o = 50 Ω, $t_r \leq$ 2.5 ns, $t_f \leq$ 2.5 ns.

FIGURE 1

PRODUCT PREVIEW

SN54ALS29821, SN54ALS29822 SN74ALS29821, SN74ALS29822 10-BIT BUS INTERFACE FLIP-FLOPS WITH 3-STATE OUTPUTS

D2825, JANUARY 1986

- Functionally Equivalent to AMD's AM29821 and AM29822
- Provides Extra Data Width Necessary for Wider Address/Data Paths or Buses with Parity
- Outputs Have Undershoot Protection Circuitry
- Power-Up High-Impedance State
- Package Options Include Both Plastic and Ceramic Carriers in Addition to Plastic and Ceramic DIPs
- Buffered Control Inputs to Reduce DC Loading Effects
- Dependable Texas Instruments Quality and Reliability

SN54ALS29821 . . . JT PACKAGE
SN74ALS29821 . . . DW OR NT PACKAGE
(TOP VIEW)

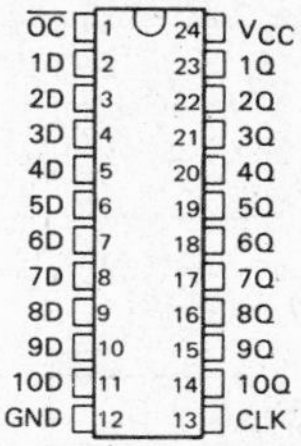
OC 1 24 VCC
1D 2 23 1Q
2D 3 22 2Q
3D 4 21 3Q
4D 5 20 4Q
5D 6 19 5Q
6D 7 18 6Q
7D 8 17 7Q
8D 9 16 8Q
9D 10 15 9Q
10D 11 14 10Q
GND 12 13 CLK

SN54ALS29821 . . . FK PACKAGE
SN74ALS29821 . . . FN PACKAGE
(TOP VIEW)

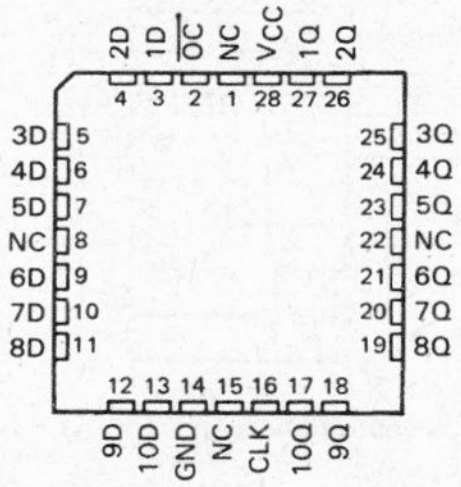
2D 1D OC NC VCC 1Q 2Q
4 3 2 1 28 27 26
3D 5
4D 6
5D 7
NC 8
6D 9
7D 10
8D 11
25 3Q
24 4Q
23 5Q
22 NC
21 6Q
20 7Q
19 8Q
12 13 14 15 16 17 18
9D 10D GND NC CLK 10Q 9Q

SN54ALS29822 . . . JT PACKAGE
SN74ALS29822 . . . DW OR NT PACKAGE
(TOP VIEW)

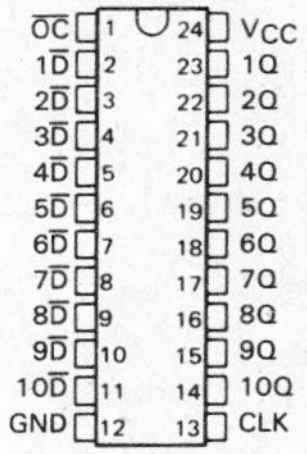
OC 1 24 VCC
1D 2 23 1Q
2D 3 22 2Q
3D 4 21 3Q
4D 5 20 4Q
5D 6 19 5Q
6D 7 18 6Q
7D 8 17 7Q
8D 9 16 8Q
9D 10 15 9Q
10D 11 14 10Q
GND 12 13 CLK

SN54ALS29822 . . . FK PACKAGE
SN74ALS29822 . . . FN PACKAGE
(TOP VIEW)

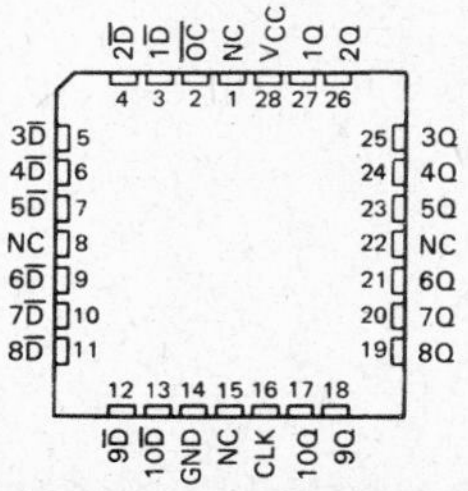
2D 1D OC NC VCC 1Q 2Q
4 3 2 1 28 27 26
3D 5
4D 6
5D 7
NC 8
6D 9
7D 10
8D 11
25 3Q
24 4Q
23 5Q
22 NC
21 6Q
20 7Q
19 8Q
12 13 14 15 16 17 18
9D 10D GND NC CLK 10Q 9Q

NC—No internal connection

description

These 10-bit flip-flops feature three-state outputs designed specifically for driving highly-capacitive or relatively low-impedance loads. They are particularly suitable for implementing wider buffer registers, I/O ports, bidirectional bus drivers with parity, and working registers.

The ten flip-flops are edge-triggered D-type flip-flops. On the positive transition of the clock the Q outputs on the 'ALS29821 will be true, and on the 'ALS29822 will be complementary to the data input.

A buffered output-control ($\overline{OC}$)input can be used to place the ten outputs in either a normal logic state (high or low levels) or a high-impedance state. In the high-impedance state the outputs neither load nor drive the bus lines significantly. The high-impedance state and increased drive provide the capability to drive the bus lines in a bus-organized system without need for interface or pull-up components. The output control does not affect the internal operation of the flip-flops. Old data can be retained or new data can be entered while the outputs are in the high-impedance state.

The SN54'family is characterized for operation over the full military temperature range of −55°C to 125°C. The SN74' family is characterized for operation from 0°C to 70°C.

TEXAS INSTRUMENTS
POST OFFICE BOX 225012 • DALLAS, TEXAS 75265

'ALS29821 FUNCTION TABLE (EACH FLIP-FLOP)

INPUTS			OUTPUT
$\overline{OC}$	CLK	D	Q
L	↑	H	H
L	↑	L	L
L	L	X	Q_0
H	X	X	Z

'ALS29821 logic symbol†

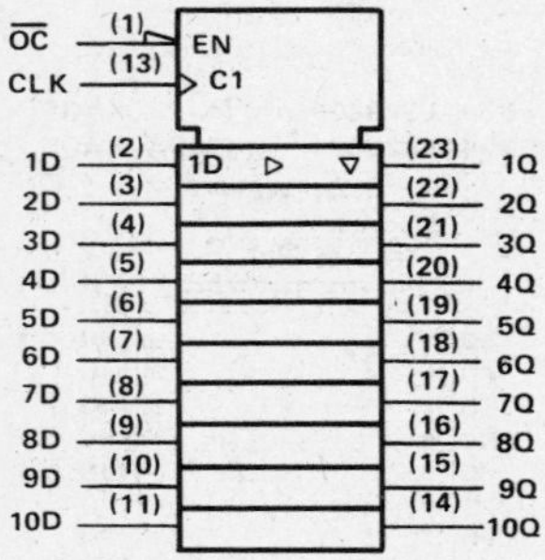
$\overline{OC}$
(1)
EN
(13)
CLK
C1
1D
2D
3D
4D
5D
6D
7D
8D
9D
10D
(2)
(3)
(4)
(5)
(6)
(7)
(8)
(9)
(10)
(11)
1D
(23)
(22)
(21)
(20)
(19)
(18)
(17)
(16)
(15)
(14)
1Q
2Q
3Q
4Q
5Q
6Q
7Q
8Q
9Q
10Q

†This symbol is in accordance with ANSI/IEEE Std 91-1984 and IEC Publication 617-12.

Pin numbers shown are for DW, JT, and NT packages.

'ALS29821 logic diagram (positive logic)

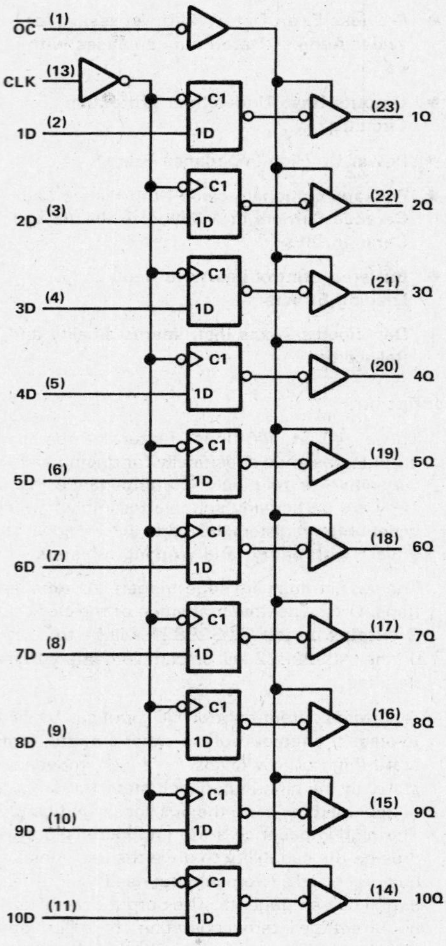
$\overline{OC}$ (1)
CLK (13)
1D (2)
2D (3)
3D (4)
4D (5)
5D (6)
6D (7)
7D (8)
8D (9)
9D (10)
10D (11)
C1
1D
(23) 1Q
(22) 2Q
(21) 3Q
(20) 4Q
(19) 5Q
(18) 6Q
(17) 7Q
(16) 8Q
(15) 9Q
(14) 10Q

Pin numbers shown are for DW, JT, and NT packages.

TEXAS INSTRUMENTS
POST OFFICE BOX 225012 • DALLAS, TEXAS 75265

2 LSI Devices

'ALS29822 FUNCTION TABLE (EACH FLIP-FLOP)

INPUTS			OUTPUT
$\overline{OC}$	CLK	$\overline{D}$	Q
L	↑	H	L
L	↑	L	H
L	L	X	Q_0
H	X	X	Z

'ALS29822 logic symbol†

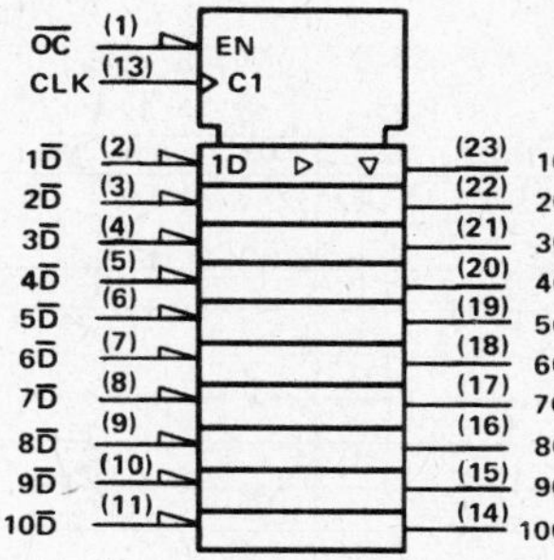
$\overline{OC}$ (1)
CLK (13)
EN
C1
1D
1$\overline{D}$ (2)
2$\overline{D}$ (3)
3$\overline{D}$ (4)
4$\overline{D}$ (5)
5$\overline{D}$ (6)
6$\overline{D}$ (7)
7$\overline{D}$ (8)
8$\overline{D}$ (9)
9$\overline{D}$ (10)
10$\overline{D}$ (11)
(23) 1Q
(22) 2Q
(21) 3Q
(20) 4Q
(19) 5Q
(18) 6Q
(17) 7Q
(16) 8Q
(15) 9Q
(14) 10Q

†This symbol is in accordance with ANSI/IEEE Std 91-1984 and IEC Publication 617-12.
Pin numbers shown are for DW, JT, and NT packages.

'ALS29822 logic diagram (positive logic)

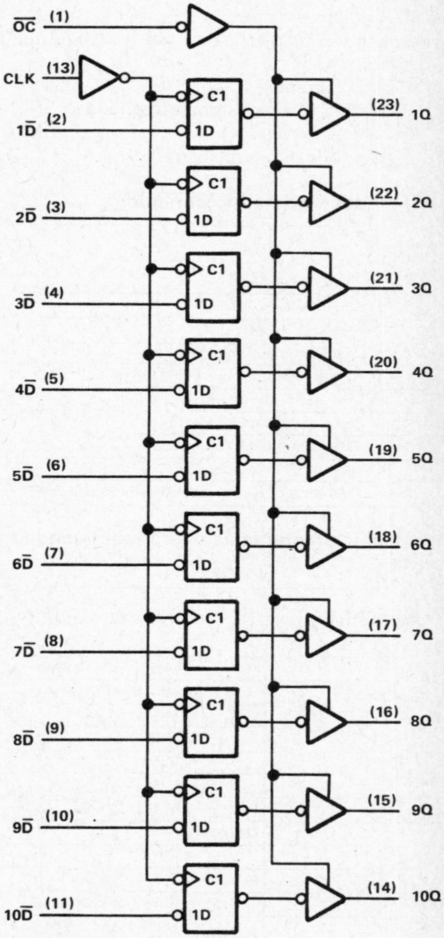
$\overline{OC}$ (1)
CLK (13)
C1
1D
1$\overline{D}$ (2)
2$\overline{D}$ (3)
3$\overline{D}$ (4)
4$\overline{D}$ (5)
5$\overline{D}$ (6)
6$\overline{D}$ (7)
7$\overline{D}$ (8)
8$\overline{D}$ (9)
9$\overline{D}$ (10)
10$\overline{D}$ (11)
(23) 1Q
(22) 2Q
(21) 3Q
(20) 4Q
(19) 5Q
(18) 6Q
(17) 7Q
(16) 8Q
(15) 9Q
(14) 10Q

Pin numbers shown are for DW, JT, and NT packages.

absolute maximum ratings over operating free-air temperature range (unless otherwise noted)

Supply voltage, V_{CC} . . . . 7 V
Input voltage . . . . 5.5 V
Voltage applied to a disabled 3-state output . . . . 5.5 V
Input current . . . . 100 mA
Output current . . . . −30 mA to 5 mA
Operating free-air temperature range: SN54ALS29821, SN54ALS29822 . . . . −55 °C to 125 °C
SN74ALS29821, SN74ALS29822 . . . . 0 °C to 70 °C
Storage temperature range . . . . −65 °C to 150 °C

recommended operating conditions

		SN54ALS29821 SN54ALS29822			SN74ALS29821 SN74ALS29822			UNIT
		MIN	NOM	MAX	MIN	NOM	MAX	
V_{CC}	Supply voltage	4.5	5	5.5	4.75	5	5.25	V
V_{IH}	High-level input voltage	2			2			V
V_{IL}	Low-level input voltage			0.8			0.8	V
I_{OH}	High-level output current			−15			−24	mA
I_{OL}	Low-level output currrent			32			48	mA
t_w	Pulse duration, CLK high or low							ns
t_{su}	Setup time, data before CLK↑							ns
t_h	Hold time, data after CLK↑							ns
T_A	Operating free-air temperature	−55		125	0		70	°C

electrical characteristics over recommended operating free-air temperature range (unless otherwise noted)

PARAMETER		TEST CONDITIONS†		SN54ALS29821 SN54ALS29822			SN74ALS29821 SN74ALS29822			UNIT
				MIN	TYP‡	MAX	MIN	TYP‡	MAX	
V_{IK}		V_{CC} = MIN,	I_I = −18 mA			−1.2			−1.2	V
V_{OH}		V_{CC} = MIN to MAX,	I_{OH} = −0.4 mA	V_{CC}−2			V_{CC}−2			V
		V_{CC} = MIN,	I_{OH} = −15 mA	2.4	3.3					
		V_{CC} = MIN,	I_{OH} = −24 mA				2.4	3.2		
V_{OL}		V_{CC} = MIN,	I_{OL} = 32 mA		0.25	0.4		0.25	0.4	V
		V_{CC} = MIN,	I_{OL} = 48 mA					0.35	0.5	
I_{OZH}		V_{CC} = MAX,	V_O = 2.4 V			20			20	μA
I_{OZL}		V_{CC} = MAX,	V_O = 0.4 V			−20			−20	μA
I_I		V_{CC} = MAX,	V_I = 5.5 V			0.1			0.1	mA
I_{IH}		V_{CC} = MAX,	V_I = 2.7 V			20			20	μA
I_{IL}		V_{CC} = MAX,	V_I = 0.4 V			−0.1			−0.1	mA
I_{OS}§		V_{CC} = MAX,	V_O = 0	−75		−250	−75		−250	mA
I_{CC}	'ALS29821	V_{CC} = MAX	Outputs high							mA
			Outputs low							
			Outputs disabled		48			48		
	'ALS29822		Outputs high							
			Outputs low							
			Outputs disabled		48			48		

† For conditions shown as MIN or MAX, use the appropriate value specified under recommended operating conditions.
‡ All typical values are at V_{CC} = 5 V, T_A = 25 °C.
§ Not more than one output should be shorted at a time and duration of the short circuit should not exceed one second.

Additional information on these products can be obtained from the factory as it becomes available.

switching characteristics

PARAMETER	FROM (INPUT)	TO (OUTPUT)	TEST CONDITIONS See Figure 1	V_{CC} = 5 V, T_A = 25°C 'ALS29821 'ALS29822			V_{CC} = MIN TO MAX,† T_A = MIN TO MAX† SN54ALS29821 SN54ALS29822		SN74ALS29821 SN74ALS29822		UNIT
				MIN	TYP	MAX	MIN	MAX	MIN	MAX	
t_{PLH}	CLK	Any Q	C_L = 300 pF								ns
t_{PHL}											
t_{PLH}			C_L = 50 pF		6						
t_{PHL}					7						
t_{PZH}	$\overline{OC}$	Any Q	C_L = 300 pF								ns
t_{PZL}											
t_{PZH}			C_L = 50 pF		12						
t_{PZL}					11						
t_{PHZ}	$\overline{OC}$	Any Q	C_L = 50 pF								ns
t_{PLZ}											
t_{PHZ}			C_L = 5 pF		5						
t_{PLZ}					6						

† For conditions shown as MIN or MAX, use the appropriate value specified under recommended operating conditions.

Additional information on these products can be obtained from the factory as it becomes available.

PARAMETER MEASUREMENT INFORMATION

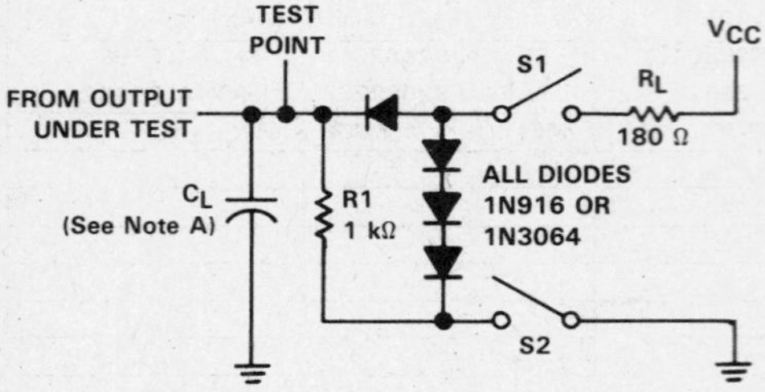
TEST POINT
FROM OUTPUT UNDER TEST
V_{CC}
S1
R_L
180 Ω
C_L (See Note A)
R1 1 kΩ
ALL DIODES 1N916 OR 1N3064
S2

LOAD CIRCUIT

SWITCH POSITION TABLE

TEST	S1	S2
t_{PLH}	Closed	Closed
t_{PHL}	Closed	Closed
t_{PZH}	Open	Closed
t_{PZL}	Closed	Open
t_{PHZ}	Closed	Closed
t_{PLZ}	Closed	Closed

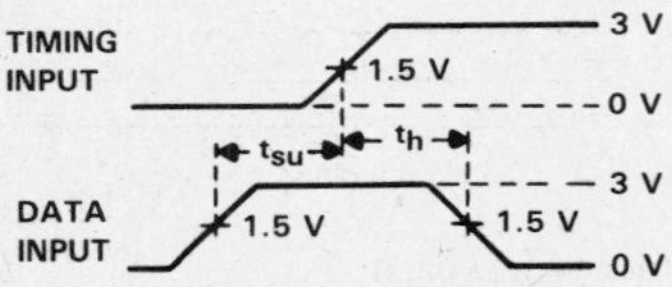
TIMING INPUT
3 V
1.5 V
0 V
t_{su}
t_h
DATA INPUT
1.5 V
1.5 V
3 V
0 V

VOLTAGE WAVEFORMS
SETUP AND HOLD TIMES

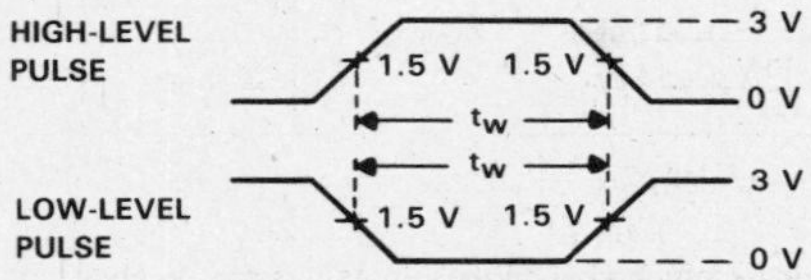
HIGH-LEVEL PULSE
1.5 V
1.5 V
3 V
0 V
t_w
t_w
LOW-LEVEL PULSE
1.5 V
1.5 V
3 V
0 V

VOLTAGE WAVEFORMS
PULSE DURATIONS

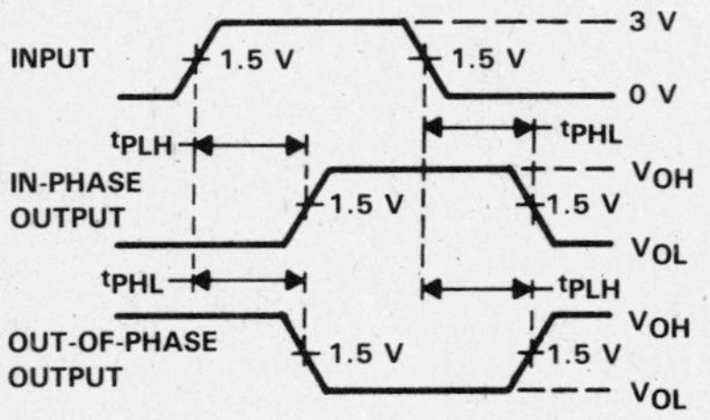
INPUT
1.5 V
1.5 V
3 V
0 V
t_{PLH}
t_{PHL}
IN-PHASE OUTPUT
1.5 V
1.5 V
V_{OH}
V_{OL}
t_{PHL}
t_{PLH}
OUT-OF-PHASE OUTPUT
1.5 V
1.5 V
V_{OH}
V_{OL}

VOLTAGE WAVEFORMS
PROPAGATION DELAY TIMES

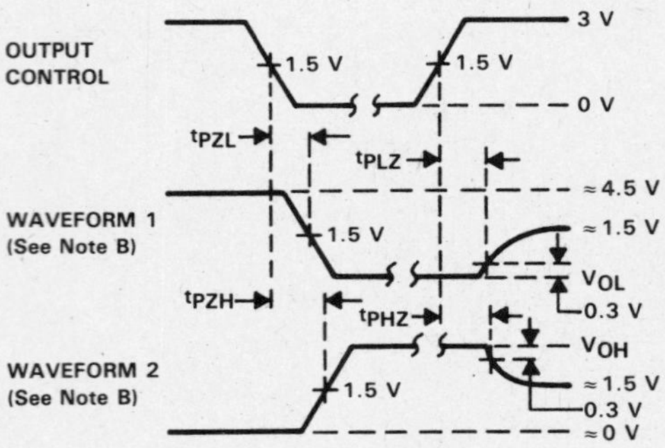
OUTPUT CONTROL
1.5 V
1.5 V
3 V
0 V
t_{PZL}
t_{PLZ}
≈4.5 V
WAVEFORM 1 (See Note B)
1.5 V
≈1.5 V
V_{OL}
0.3 V
t_{PZH}
t_{PHZ}
V_{OH}
WAVEFORM 2 (See Note B)
1.5 V
≈1.5 V
0.3 V
≈0 V

VOLTAGE WAVEFORMS
ENABLE AND DISABLE TIMES, THREE-STATE OUTPUTS

NOTES:
- A. C_L includes probe and jig capacitance.
- B. Waveform 1 is for an output with internal conditions such that the output is low except when disabled by the output control. Waveform 2 is for an output with internal conditions such that the output is high except when disabled by the output control.
- C. All input pulses are supplied by generators having the following characteristics: PRR $\leq$ 10 MHz, Z_o = 50 Ω, $t_r \leq 2.5$ ns, $t_f \leq 2.5$ ns.

FIGURE 1

TEXAS INSTRUMENTS
POST OFFICE BOX 225012 • DALLAS, TEXAS 75265

SN54ALS29823, SN54ALS29824
SN74ALS29823, SN74ALS29824
9-BIT BUS INTERFACE FLIP-FLOPS WITH 3-STATE OUTPUTS

D2825, JANUARY 1986

- **Functionally Equivalent to AMD's AM29823 and AM29824**
- **Provides Extra Data Width Necessary for Wider Address/Data Paths or Buses with Parity**
- **Outputs Have Undershoot Protection Circuitry**
- **Power-Up High-Impedance State**
- **Buffered Control Inputs to Reduce DC Loading Effects**
- **Package Options Include both Plastic and Ceramic Carriers in Addition to Plastic and Ceramic DIPs**
- **Dependable Texas Instruments Quality and Reliability**

description

These 9-bit flip-flops feature three-state outputs designed specifically for driving highly capacitive or relatively low-impedance loads. They are particularly suitable for implementing wider buffer registers, I/O ports, bidirectional bus drivers, parity bus interfacing and working registers.

With the clock enable ($\overline{CLKEN}$) low, the nine D-type edge-triggered flip-flops enter data on the low-to-high transitions of the clock. Taking $\overline{CLKEN}$ high will disable the clock buffer, thus latching the outputs. The 'ALS29823 has noninverting D inputs and the 'ALS29824 has inverting D inputs. Taking the $\overline{CLR}$ input low causes the nine Q outputs to go low independently of the clock.

A buffered output-control input ($\overline{OC}$)can be used to place the nine outputs in either normal logic state (high or low level) or a high-impedance state. In the high-impedance state the outputs neither load nor drive the bus lines significantly. The high-impedance state and increased drive provide the capability to drive the bus lines in a bus-organized system without need for interface or pull-up components. The output control does not affect the internal operation of the flip-flops. Old data can be retained or new data can be entered while the outputs are in the high-impedance state.

SN54ALS29823 . . . JT PACKAGE
SN74ALS29823 . . . DW OR NT PACKAGE
(TOP VIEW)

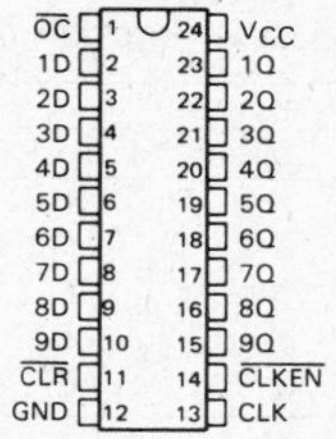
$\overline{OC}$ 1 24 VCC
1D 2 23 1Q
2D 3 22 2Q
3D 4 21 3Q
4D 5 20 4Q
5D 6 19 5Q
6D 7 18 6Q
7D 8 17 7Q
8D 9 16 8Q
9D 10 15 9Q
$\overline{CLR}$ 11 14 $\overline{CLKEN}$
GND 12 13 CLK

SN54ALS29823 . . . FK PACKAGE
SN74ALS29823 . . . FN PACKAGE
(TOP VIEW)

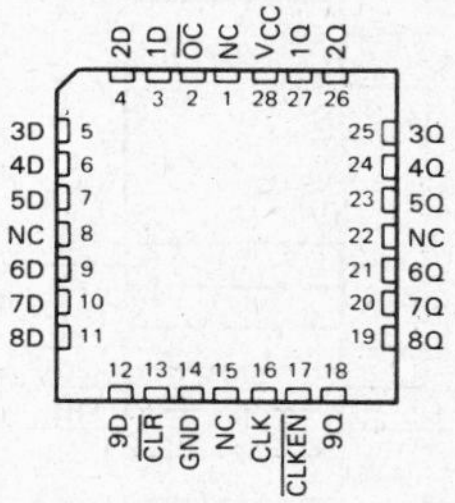
2D 1D $\overline{OC}$ NC VCC 1Q 2Q
4 3 2 1 28 27 26
3D 5 25 3Q
4D 6 24 4Q
5D 7 23 5Q
NC 8 22 NC
6D 9 21 6Q
7D 10 20 7Q
8D 11 19 8Q
12 13 14 15 16 17 18
9D $\overline{CLR}$ GND NC CLK $\overline{CLKEN}$ 9Q

SN54ALS29824 . . . JT PACKAGE
SN74ALS29824 . . . DW OR NT PACKAGE
(TOP VIEW)

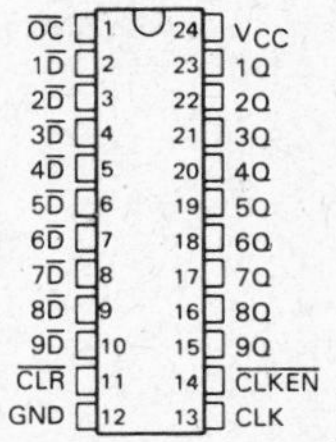
$\overline{OC}$ 1 24 VCC
$\overline{1D}$ 2 23 1Q
$\overline{2D}$ 3 22 2Q
$\overline{3D}$ 4 21 3Q
$\overline{4D}$ 5 20 4Q
$\overline{5D}$ 6 19 5Q
$\overline{6D}$ 7 18 6Q
$\overline{7D}$ 8 17 7Q
$\overline{8D}$ 9 16 8Q
$\overline{9D}$ 10 15 9Q
$\overline{CLR}$ 11 14 $\overline{CLKEN}$
GND 12 13 CLK

SN54ALS29824 . . . FK PACKAGE
SN74ALS29824 . . . FN PACKAGE
(TOP VIEW)

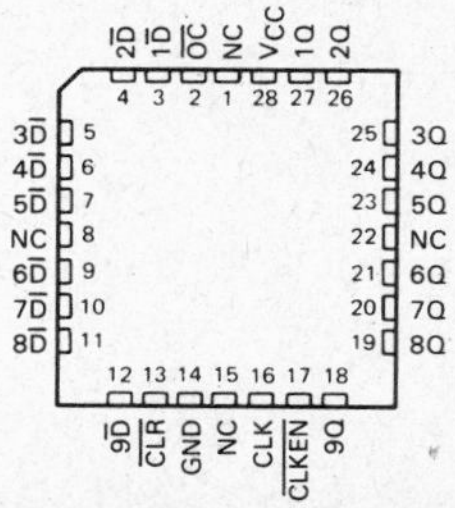
$\overline{2D}$ $\overline{1D}$ $\overline{OC}$ NC VCC 1Q 2Q
4 3 2 1 28 27 26
$\overline{3D}$ 5 25 3Q
$\overline{4D}$ 6 24 4Q
$\overline{5D}$ 7 23 5Q
NC 8 22 NC
$\overline{6D}$ 9 21 6Q
$\overline{7D}$ 10 20 7Q
$\overline{8D}$ 11 19 8Q
12 13 14 15 16 17 18
$\overline{9D}$ $\overline{CLR}$ GND NC CLK $\overline{CLKEN}$ 9Q

The SN54AS' family is characterized for operation over the full military temperature range of −55°C to 125°C. The SN74AS' family is characterized for operation from 0°C to 70°C.

'ALS29823 FUNCTION TABLE

INPUTS					OUTPUT
$\overline{OC}$	$\overline{CLR}$	$\overline{CLKEN}$	CLK	D	Q
L	L	X	X	X	L
L	H	L	↑	H	H
L	H	L	↑	L	L
L	H	H	X	X	Q_0
H	X	X	X	X	Z

'ALS29823 logic symbol†

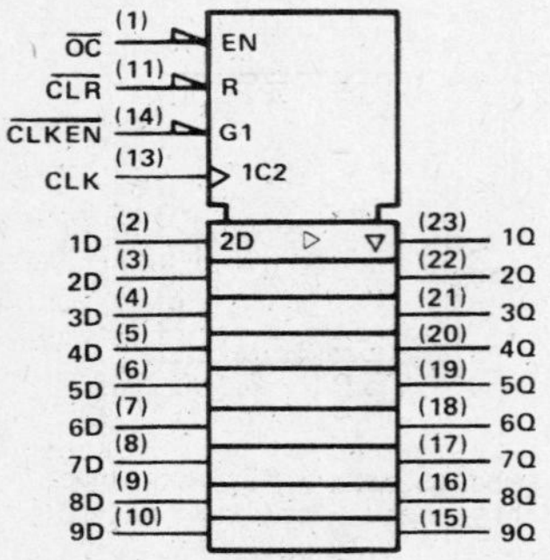
OC
CLR
CLKEN
CLK
EN
R
G1
1C2
2D
1D
2D
3D
4D
5D
6D
7D
8D
9D
1Q
2Q
3Q
4Q
5Q
6Q
7Q
8Q
9Q

† This symbol is in accordance with ANSI/IEEE Std 91-1984 and IEC Publication 617-12

'ALS29823 logic diagram (positive logic)

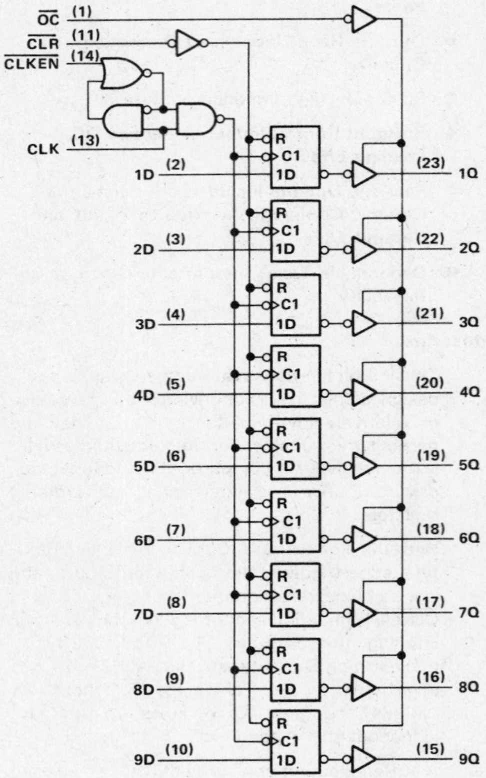
OC
CLR
CLKEN
CLK
R
C1
1D
1D
2D
3D
4D
5D
6D
7D
8D
9D
1Q
2Q
3Q
4Q
5Q
6Q
7Q
8Q
9Q

Pin numbers shown are for DW, JT, and NT packages.

TEXAS INSTRUMENTS
POST OFFICE BOX 225012 • DALLAS, TEXAS 75265

'ALS29824 FUNCTION TABLE

INPUTS					OUTPUT
$\overline{OC}$	$\overline{CLR}$	$\overline{CLKEN}$	CLK	$\overline{D}$	Q
L	L	X	X	X	L
L	H	L	↑	H	L
L	H	L	↑	L	H
L	H	H	X	X	Q_0
H	X	X	X	X	Z

'ALS29824 logic symbol†

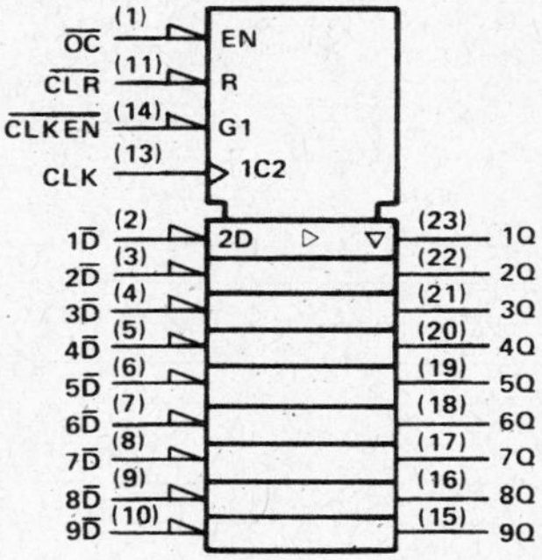
(1) OC EN
(11) CLR R
(14) CLKEN G1
(13) CLK 1C2
(2) 1D 2D (23) 1Q
(3) 2D (22) 2Q
(4) 3D (21) 3Q
(5) 4D (20) 4Q
(6) 5D (19) 5Q
(7) 6D (18) 6Q
(8) 7D (17) 7Q
(9) 8D (16) 8Q
(10) 9D (15) 9Q

† This symbol is in accordance with ANSI/IEEE Std 91-1984 and IEC Publication 617-12.

'ALS29824 logic diagram (positive logic)

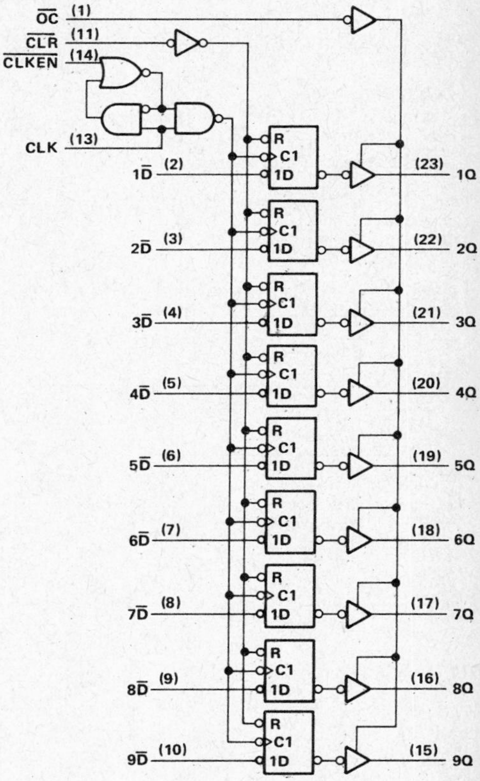
OC (1)
CLR (11)
CLKEN (14)
CLK (13)
R
C1
1D
1D (2) (23) 1Q
2D (3) (22) 2Q
3D (4) (21) 3Q
4D (5) (20) 4Q
5D (6) (19) 5Q
6D (7) (18) 6Q
7D (8) (17) 7Q
8D (9) (16) 8Q
9D (10) (15) 9Q

Pin numbers shown are for DW, JT, and NT packages.

absolute maximum ratings over operating free-air temperature range (unless otherwise noted)

Supply voltage, V_{CC} . . . . 7 V
Input voltage . . . . 5.5 V
Voltage applied to a disabled 3-state output . . . . 5.5 V
Input current . . . . 100 mA
Output current . . . . −30 mA to 5 mA
Operating free-air temperature range: SN54ALS29823, SN54ALS29824 . . . . −55°C to 125°C
SN74ALS29823, SN74ALS29824 . . . . 0°C to 70°C
Storage temperature range . . . . −65°C to 150°C

recommended operating conditions

			SN54ALS29823 SN54ALS29824			SN74ALS29823 SN74ALS29824			UNIT
			MIN	NOM	MAX	MIN	NOM	MAX	
V_{CC}	Supply voltage		4.5	5	5.5	4.75	5	5.25	V
V_{IH}	High-level input voltage		2			2			V
V_{IL}	Low-level input voltage				0.8			0.8	V
I_{OH}	High-level output current				−15			−24	mA
I_{OL}	Low-level output current				32			48	mA
t_w	Pulse duration	$\overline{\text{CLR}}$ low							ns
		CLK high or low							
t_{su}	Setup time before CLK↑	$\overline{\text{CLR}}$ inactive							ns
		Data							
		$\overline{\text{CLKEN}}$ high or low							
t_h	Hold time, $\overline{\text{CLKEN}}$ or data after CLK↑								ns
T_A	Operating free-air temperature		−55		125	0		70	°C

2

LSI Devices

electrical characteristics over recommended operating free-air temperature range (unless otherwise noted)

PARAMETER		TEST CONDITIONS†		SN54ALS29823 SN54ALS29824			SN74ALS29823 SN74ALS29824			UNIT
				MIN	TYP‡	MAX	MIN	TYP‡	MAX	
V_{IK}		V_{CC} = MIN	I_I = −18 mA			−1.2			−1.2	V
V_{OH}		V_{CC} = MIN to MAX,	I_{OH} = −0.4 mA	$V_{CC}-2$			$V_{CC}-2$			V
		V_{CC} = MIN,	I_{OH} = −15 mA	2.4	3.3					
		V_{CC} = MIN,	I_{OH} = −24 mA				2.4	3.2		
V_{OL}		V_{CC} = MIN,	I_{OL} = 32 mA		0.25	0.4		0.25	0.4	V
		V_{CC} = MIN,	I_{OL} = 48 mA					0.35	0.5	
I_{OZH}		V_{CC} = MAX,	V_O = 2.4 V			20			20	μA
I_{OZL}		V_{CC} = MAX,	V_O = 0.4 V			−20			−20	μA
I_I		V_{CC} = MAX,	V_I = 5.5 V			0.1			0.1	mA
I_{IH}		V_{CC} = MAX,	V_I = 2.7 V			20			20	μA
I_{IL}		V_{CC} = MAX,	V_I = 0.4 V			−0.1			−0.1	mA
I_{OS}§		V_{CC} = MAX,	V_O = 0	−75		−250	−75		−250	mA
I_{CC}	'ALS29823	V_{CC} = MAX	Outputs high							mA
			Outputs low							
			Outputs disabled		48			48		
	'ALS29824		Outputs high							
			Outputs low							
			Outputs disabled		48			48		

† For conditions shown as MIN or MAX, use appropriate value specificed under recommended operating conditions.
‡ All typical values are at V_{CC} = 5 V, T_A = 25°C.
§ Not more than one output should be shorted at a time and duration of the short circuit should not exceed one second.

Additional Information on these products can be obtained from the factory as it becomes available.

switching characteristics

PARAMETER	FROM (INPUT)	TO (OUTPUT)	TEST CONDITIONS See Figure 1	V_{CC} = 5 V, T_A = 25°C 'ALS29823 'ALS29824			V_{CC} = MIN TO MAX,† T_A = MIN TO MAX† SN54ALS29823 SN54ALS29824		SN74ALS29823 SN74ALS29824		UNIT
				MIN	TYP	MAX	MIN	MAX	MIN	MAX	
t_{PLH}	CLK	Any Q	C_L = 300 pF								ns
t_{PHL}											
t_{PLH}			C_L = 50 pF		5.5						
t_{PHL}					6.5						
t_{PHL}	$\overline{CLR}$	Any Q	C_L = 50 pF		13						ns
t_{PZH}	$\overline{OC}$	Any Q	C_L = 300 pF								ns
t_{PZL}											
t_{PZH}			C_L = 50 pF		12						
t_{PZL}					11						
t_{PHZ}	$\overline{OC}$	Any Q	C_L = 50 pF								ns
t_{PLZ}											
t_{PHZ}			C_L = 5 pF		5						
t_{PLZ}					5.5						

† For conditions shown as MIN or MAX, use the appropriate value specified under recommended operating conditions.

Additional information on these products can be obtained from the factory as it becomes available.

D flip-flop signal conventions

It is normal TI practice to name the outputs and other inputs of a D-type flip-flop and to draw its logic symbol based on the assumption of true data (D) inputs. Then outputs that produce data in phase with the data inputs are called Q and those producing complementary data are called Q. An input that causes a Q output to go high or a Q output to go low is called Preset; an input that causes a Q output to go high or a Q output to go low is called Clear. Bars are used over these pin names (PRE and CLR) if they are active-low.

The devices on this data sheet are second-source designs and the pin-name convention used by the original manufacturer has been retained. That makes it necessary to designate the inputs and outputs of the inverting circuit D and Q. In some applications it may be advantageous to redesignate the inputs and outputs as D and Q. In that case, outputs should be renamed as shown below. Also shown are corresponding changes in the graphical symbol. Arbitrary pin numbers are shown in parentheses.

Notice that Q and Q exchange names, which causes Preset and Clear to do likewise. Also notice that the polarity indicators (⊿) on PRE and CLR remain since these inputs are still active-low, but that the presence or absence of the polarity changes at D, Q, and Q. Of course pin 5 (Q) is still in phase with the data input D, but now both are considered active high.

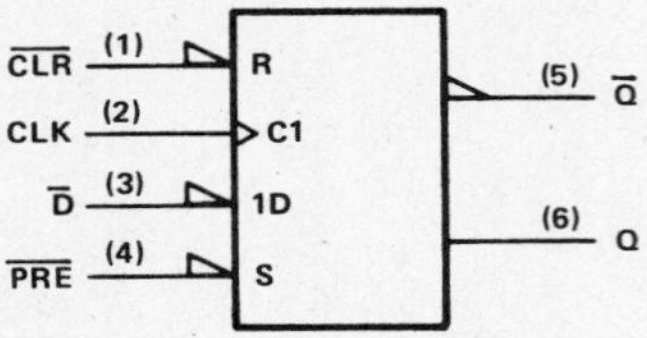
$\overline{CLR}$ (1) R
CLK (2) C1
$\overline{D}$ (3) 1D
$\overline{PRE}$ (4) S
(5) $\overline{Q}$
(6) Q

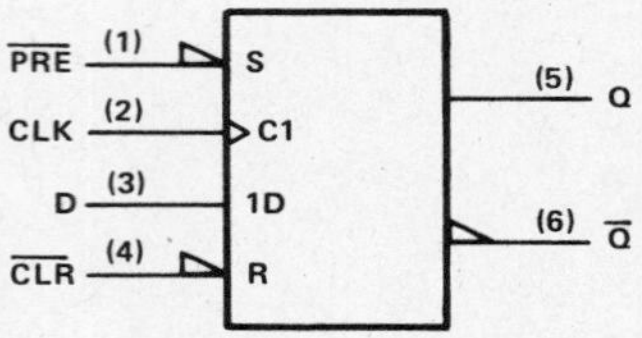
$\overline{PRE}$ (1) S
CLK (2) C1
D (3) 1D
$\overline{CLR}$ (4) R
(5) Q
(6) $\overline{Q}$

TEXAS INSTRUMENTS
POST OFFICE BOX 225012 • DALLAS, TEXAS 75265

PARAMETER MEASUREMENT INFORMATION

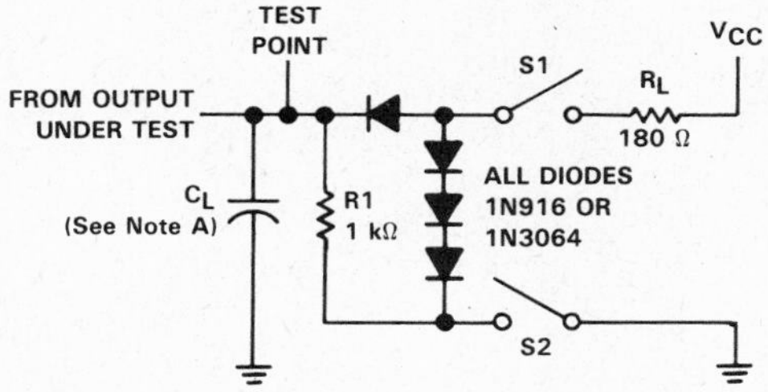
TEST POINT
FROM OUTPUT UNDER TEST
S1
R_L
180 Ω
V_{CC}
C_L (See Note A)
R1 1 kΩ
ALL DIODES 1N916 OR 1N3064
S2

LOAD CIRCUIT

SWITCH POSITION TABLE

TEST	S1	S2
t_{PLH}	Closed	Closed
t_{PHL}	Closed	Closed
t_{PZH}	Open	Closed
t_{PZL}	Closed	Open
t_{PHZ}	Closed	Closed
t_{PLZ}	Closed	Closed

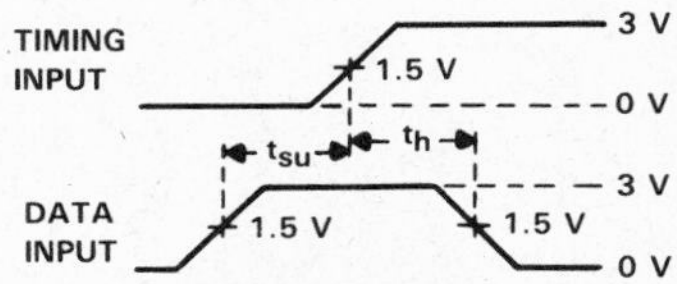
TIMING INPUT
3 V
1.5 V
0 V
t_{su}
t_h
DATA INPUT
1.5 V
1.5 V
3 V
0 V

VOLTAGE WAVEFORMS
SETUP AND HOLD TIMES

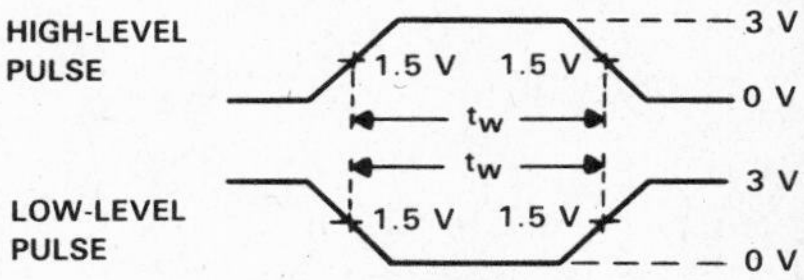
HIGH-LEVEL PULSE
1.5 V
1.5 V
3 V
0 V
t_w
LOW-LEVEL PULSE
t_w
1.5 V
1.5 V
3 V
0 V

VOLTAGE WAVEFORMS
PULSE DURATIONS

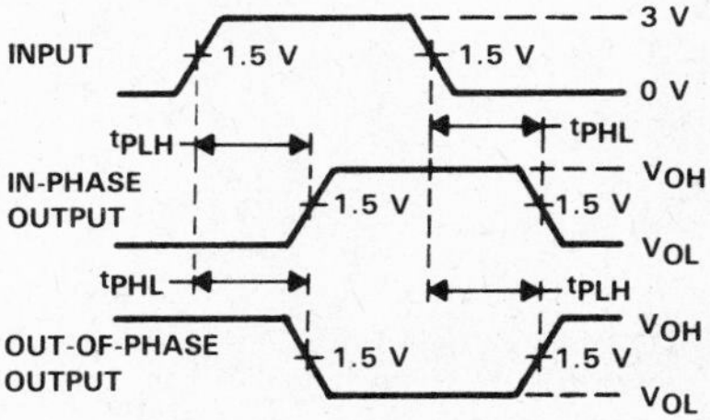
INPUT
1.5 V
1.5 V
3 V
0 V
t_{PLH}
t_{PHL}
IN-PHASE OUTPUT
1.5 V
1.5 V
V_{OH}
V_{OL}
t_{PHL}
t_{PLH}
OUT-OF-PHASE OUTPUT
1.5 V
1.5 V
V_{OH}
V_{OL}

VOLTAGE WAVEFORMS
PROPAGATION DELAY TIMES

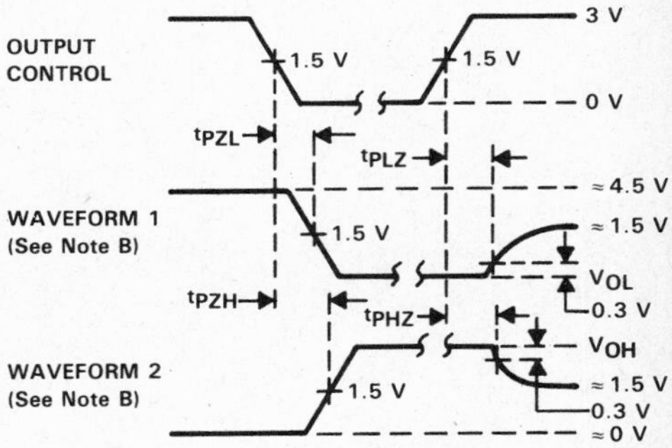
OUTPUT CONTROL
1.5 V
1.5 V
3 V
0 V
t_{PZL}
t_{PLZ}
≈4.5 V
WAVEFORM 1 (See Note B)
1.5 V
≈1.5 V
V_{OL}
0.3 V
t_{PZH}
t_{PHZ}
V_{OH}
WAVEFORM 2 (See Note B)
1.5 V
≈1.5 V
0.3 V
≈0 V

VOLTAGE WAVEFORMS
ENABLE AND DISABLE TIMES, THREE-STATE OUTPUTS

NOTES: A. C_L includes probe and jig capacitance.
B. Waveform 1 is for an output with internal conditions such that the output is low except when disabled by the output control. Waveform 2 is for an output with internal conditions such that the output is high except when disabled by the output control.
C. All input pulses are supplied by generators having the following characteristics: PRR ≤ 10 MHz, Z_O = 50 Ω, t_r ≤ 2.5 ns, t_f ≤ 2.5 ns.

FIGURE 1

2 LSI Devices

SN54ALS29825, SN54ALS29826 SN74ALS29825, SN74ALS29826 8-BIT BUS INTERFACE FLIP-FLOPS WITH 3-STATE OUTPUTS

D2829, JANUARY 1986

- Functionally Equivalent to AMD's AM29825 and AM29826
- Improved I_{OH} Specifications
- Multiple Output Enables Allow Multiuser Control of the Interface
- Outputs Have Undershoot Protection Circuitry
- Power-Up High-Impedance State
- Package Options Include Both Plastic and Ceramic Chip Carriers in Addition to Plastic and Ceramic DIPs
- Buffered Control Inputs to Reduce DC Loading Effect
- Dependable Texas Instruments Quality and Reliability

SN54ALS29825 . . . JT PACKAGE
SN74ALS29825 . . . DW OR NT PACKAGE
(TOP VIEW)

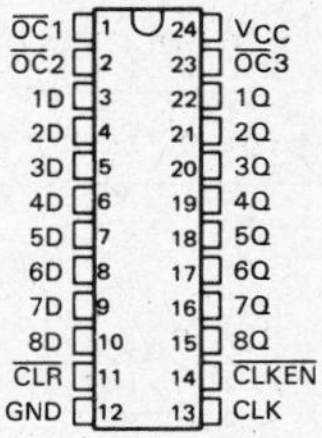
OC1 1 24 VCC
OC2 2 23 OC3
1D 3 22 1Q
2D 4 21 2Q
3D 5 20 3Q
4D 6 19 4Q
5D 7 18 5Q
6D 8 17 6Q
7D 9 16 7Q
8D 10 15 8Q
CLR 11 14 CLKEN
GND 12 13 CLK

SN54ALS29825 . . . FK PACKAGE
SN74ALS29825 . . . FN PACKAGE
(TOP VIEW)

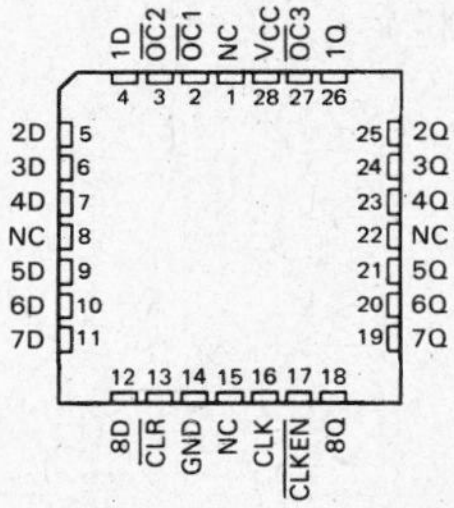
1D OC2 OC1 NC VCC OC3 1Q
4 3 2 1 28 27 26
2D 5 25 2Q
3D 6 24 3Q
4D 7 23 4Q
NC 8 22 NC
5D 9 21 5Q
6D 10 20 6Q
7D 11 19 7Q
12 13 14 15 16 17 18
8D CLR GND NC CLK CLKEN 8Q

description

These 8-bit flip-flops feature three-state outputs designed specifically for driving highly capacitive or relatively low-impedance loads. They are particularly suitable for implementing multiuser registers, I/O ports, bidirectional bus drivers, and working registers.

With the clock enable ($\overline{\text{CLKEN}}$) low, the eight D-type edge-triggered flip-flops enter data on the low-to-high transitions of the clock. Taking $\overline{\text{CLKEN}}$ high will disable the clock buffer, thus latching the outputs. The 'ALS29825 has non-inverting D inputs and the 'ALS29826 has inverting $\overline{\text{D}}$ inputs. Taking the $\overline{\text{CLR}}$ input low causes the eight Q outputs to go low independently of the clock.

Multiuser buffered output-control inputs ($\overline{\text{OC}}$1, $\overline{\text{OC}}$2, and $\overline{\text{OC}}$3) can be used to place the eight outputs in either a normal logic state (high or low level) or a high-impedance state. In the high-impedance state the outputs neither load nor drive the bus lines significantly. The high-impedance state and increased drive provide the capability to drive the bus lines in a bus-organized system without need for interface or pull-up components. The output controls do not affect the internal operation of the flip-flops. Old data can be retained or new data can be entered while the outputs are in the high-impedance state.

SN54ALS29826 . . . JT PACKAGE
SN74ALS29826 . . . DW OR NT PACKAGE
(TOP VIEW)

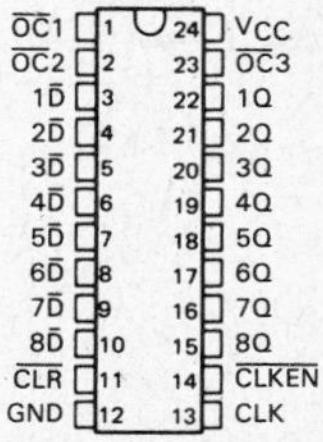
OC1 1 24 VCC
OC2 2 23 OC3
1D 3 22 1Q
2D 4 21 2Q
3D 5 20 3Q
4D 6 19 4Q
5D 7 18 5Q
6D 8 17 6Q
7D 9 16 7Q
8D 10 15 8Q
CLR 11 14 CLKEN
GND 12 13 CLK

SN54ALS29826 . . . FK PACKAGE
SN74ALS29826 . . . FN PACKAGE
(TOP VIEW)

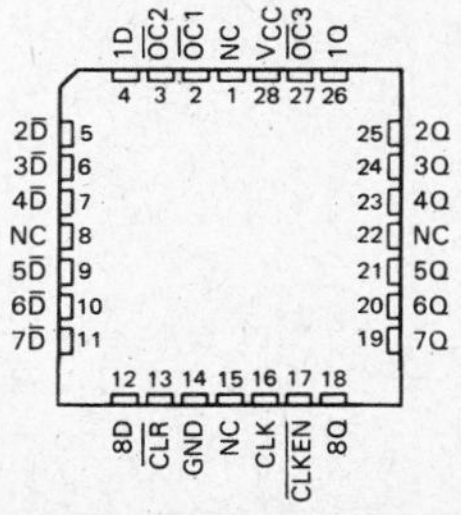
1D OC2 OC1 NC VCC OC3 1Q
4 3 2 1 28 27 26
2D 5 25 2Q
3D 6 24 3Q
4D 7 23 4Q
NC 8 22 NC
5D 9 21 5Q
6D 10 20 6Q
7D 11 19 7Q
12 13 14 15 16 17 18
8D CLR GND NC CLK CLKEN 8Q

NC—No internal connection

TEXAS INSTRUMENTS
POST OFFICE BOX 225012 • DALLAS, TEXAS 75265

The SN54' family is characterized for operation over the full military temperature range of −55°C to 125°C. The SN74' family is characterized for operation from 0°C to 70°C.

'ALS29825 FUNCTION TABLE

INPUTS					OUTPUT
$\overline{OC}$*	$\overline{CLR}$	$\overline{CLKEN}$	CLK	D	Q
L	L	X	X	X	L
L	H	L	↑	H	H
L	H	L	↑	L	L
L	H	H	X	X	Q_0
H	X	X	X	X	Z

$\overline{OC}$* = H if any of $\overline{OC}$1, $\overline{OC}$2, or $\overline{OC}$3 is high.
$\overline{OC}$* = L if all of $\overline{OC}$1, $\overline{OC}$2, and $\overline{OC}$3 are low.

'ALS29825 logic symbol†

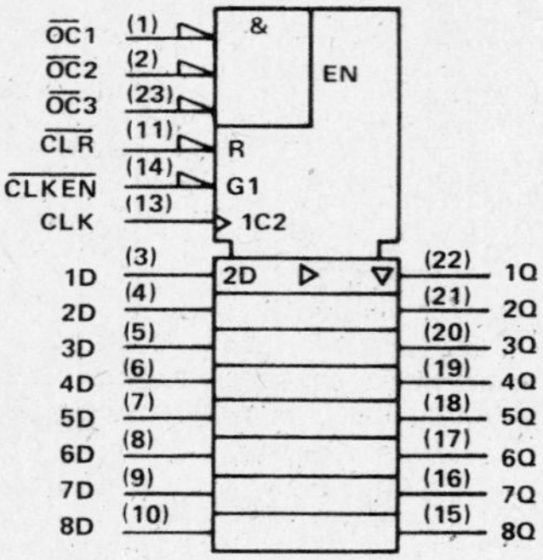
$\overline{OC1}$ (1)
$\overline{OC2}$ (2)
$\overline{OC3}$ (23)
$\overline{CLR}$ (11)
$\overline{CLKEN}$ (14)
CLK (13)
&
EN
R
G1
1C2
2D
1D (3)
2D (4)
3D (5)
4D (6)
5D (7)
6D (8)
7D (9)
8D (10)
(22) 1Q
(21) 2Q
(20) 3Q
(19) 4Q
(18) 5Q
(17) 6Q
(16) 7Q
(15) 8Q

† This symbol is in accordance with ANSI/IEEE Std 91-1984 and IEC Publication 617-12
Pin numbers shown are for DW, JT, and NT packages.

'ALS29825 logic diagram (positive logic)

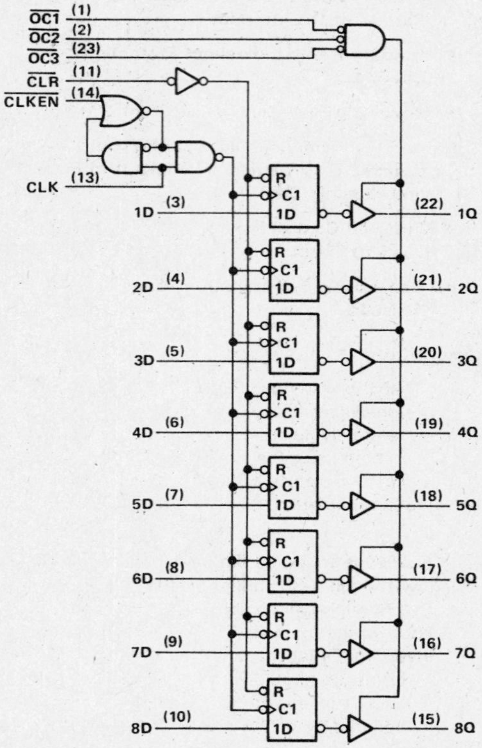
$\overline{OC1}$ (1)
$\overline{OC2}$ (2)
$\overline{OC3}$ (23)
$\overline{CLR}$ (11)
$\overline{CLKEN}$ (14)
CLK (13)
R
C1
1D
1D (3)
2D (4)
3D (5)
4D (6)
5D (7)
6D (8)
7D (9)
8D (10)
(22) 1Q
(21) 2Q
(20) 3Q
(19) 4Q
(18) 5Q
(17) 6Q
(16) 7Q
(15) 8Q

Pin numbers are for DW, JT, and NT packages.

'ALS29826 FUNCTION TABLE

INPUTS					OUTPUT
$\overline{OC}$*	$\overline{CLR}$	$\overline{CLKEN}$	CLK	$\overline{D}$	Q
L	L	X	X	X	L
L	H	L	↑	H	L
L	H	L	↑	L	H
L	H	H	X	X	Q_0
H	X	X	X	X	Z

$\overline{OC}$* = H if any of $\overline{OC}$1, $\overline{OC}$2, or $\overline{OC}$3 is high.
$\overline{OC}$* = L if all of $\overline{OC}$1, $\overline{OC}$2, and $\overline{OC}$3 are low.

'ALS29826 logic symbol†

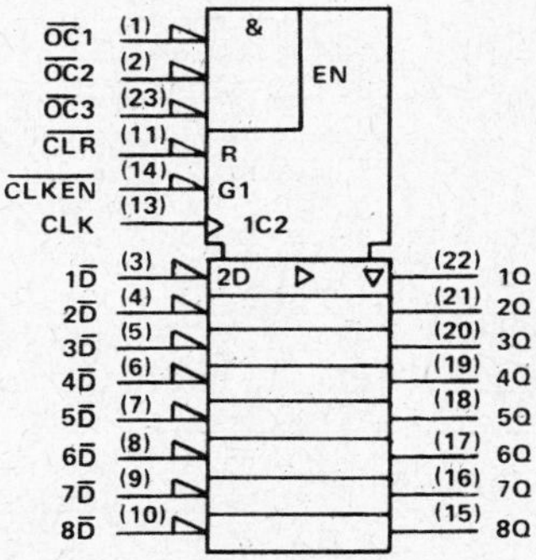
OC1 (1)
OC2 (2)
OC3 (23)
CLR (11)
CLKEN (14)
CLK (13)
&
EN
R
G1
1C2
2D
1D (3)
2D (4)
3D (5)
4D (6)
5D (7)
6D (8)
7D (9)
8D (10)
(22) 1Q
(21) 2Q
(20) 3Q
(19) 4Q
(18) 5Q
(17) 6Q
(16) 7Q
(15) 8Q

† This symbol is in accordance with ANSI/IEEE Std 91-1984 and IEC Publication 617-12.
Pin numbers are for DW, JT, and NT packages.

'ALS29826 logic diagram (positive logic)

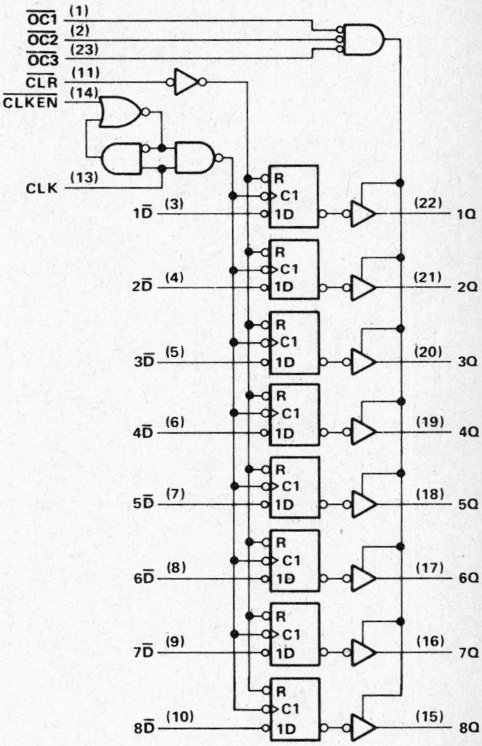
OC1 (1)
OC2 (2)
OC3 (23)
CLR (11)
CLKEN (14)
CLK (13)
R
C1
1D
1D (3)
2D (4)
3D (5)
4D (6)
5D (7)
6D (8)
7D (9)
8D (10)
(22) 1Q
(21) 2Q
(20) 3Q
(19) 4Q
(18) 5Q
(17) 6Q
(16) 7Q
(15) 8Q

Pin numbers shown are for DW, JT, and NT packages.

absolute maximum ratings over operating free-air temperature range (unless otherwise noted)

Supply voltage, V_{CC} . . . . 7 V
Input voltage . . . . 7 V
Voltage applied to a disabled 3-state output . . . . 5.5 V
Input current . . . . 100 mA
Output current . . . . −30 mA to 5 mA
Operating free-air temperature range:
SN54ALS29825, SN54ALS29826 . . . . −55°C to 125°C
SN74ALS29825, SN74ALS29826 . . . . 0°C to 70°C
Storage temperature range . . . . −65 to 150°C

recommended operating conditions

			SN54ALS29825 SN54ALS29826			SN74ALS29825 SN74ALS29826			UNIT
			MIN	NOM	MAX	MIN	NOM	MAX	
V_{CC}	Supply voltage		4.5	5	5.5	4.75	5	5.25	V
V_{IH}	High-level input voltage		2			2			V
V_{IL}	Low-level input voltage				0.8			0.8	V
I_{OH}	High-level output current				−15			−24	mA
I_{OL}	Low-level output current				32			48	mA
t_w	Pulse duration	$\overline{CLR}$ low							ns
		CLK high							
		CLK low							
t_{su}	Setup time before CLK↑	$\overline{CLR}$ inactive							ns
		Data							
		$\overline{CLKEN}$ high or low							
t_h	Hold time, data after CLK↑	Data							ns
		$\overline{CLKEN}$							
T_A	Operating free-air temperature		−55		125	0		70	°C

electrical characteristics over recommended operating free-air temperature range (unless otherwise noted)

PARAMETER		TEST CONDITIONS†		SN54ALS29825 SN54ALS29826			SN74ALS29825 SN74ALS29826			UNIT
				MIN	TYP‡	MAX	MIN	TYP‡	MAX	
V_{IK}		V_{CC} = MIN,	I_I = −18 mA			−1.2			−1.2	V
V_{OH}		V_{CC} = MIN to MAX,	I_{OH} = −0.4 mA	V_{CC}−2			V_{CC}−2			V
		V_{CC} = MIN,	I_{OH} = −15 mA	2.4	3.3					
		V_{CC} = MIN,	I_{OH} = −24 mA				2.4	3.2		
V_{OL}		V_{CC} = MIN,	I_{OL} = 32 mA		0.25	0.4		0.25	0.4	V
		V_{CC} = MIN,	I_{OL} = 48 mA					0.35	0.5	
I_{OZH}		V_{CC} = MAX,	V_O = 2.4 V			20			20	μA
I_{OZL}		V_{CC} = MAX,	V_O = 0.4 V			−20			−20	μA
I_I		V_{CC} = MAX,	V_I = 5.5 V			0.1			0.1	mA
I_{IH}		V_{CC} = MAX,	V_I = 2.7 V			20			20	μA
I_{IL}		V_{CC} = MAX,	V_I = 0.4 V			−0.1			−0.1	mA
I_{OS}§		V_{CC} = MAX,	V_O = 0	−75		−250	−75		−250	mA
I_{CC}	'ALS29825	V_{CC} = MAX	Outputs high							mA
			Outputs low							
			Outputs disabled		48			48		
	'ALS29826		Outputs high							
			Outputs low							
			Outputs disabled		48			48		

† For conditions shown as MIN or MAX, use the appropriate value specified under recommended operating conditions.
‡ All typical values are at V_{CC} = 5 V, T_A = 25°C.
§ Not more than one output should be shorted at a time and duration of the short circuit should not exceed one second.

Additional information on these products can be obtained from the factory as it becomes available.

switching characteristics

PARAMETER	FROM (INPUT)	TO (OUTPUT)	TEST CONDITIONS See Figure 1	V_{CC} = 5 V, T_A = 25°C 'ALS29825 'ALS29826			V_{CC} = MIN TO MAX,† T_A = MIN TO MAX† SN54ALS29825 SN54ALS29826		SN74ALS29825 SN74ALS29826		UNIT
				MIN	TYP	MAX	MIN	MAX	MIN	MAX	
t_{PLH}	CLK	Any Q	C_L = 300 pF								ns
t_{PHL}											
t_{PLH}			C_L = 50 pF		6						
t_{PHL}					7						
t_{PHL}	$\overline{CLR}$	Any Q	C_L = 50 pF		13						ns
t_{PZH}	$\overline{OC}$	Any Q	C_L = 300 pF								ns
t_{PZL}											
t_{PZH}			C_L = 50 pF		12						
t_{PZL}					11						
t_{PHZ}	$\overline{OC}$	Any Q	C_L = 50 pF								ns
t_{PLZ}											
t_{PHZ}			C_L = 5 pF		5						
t_{PLZ}					6						

† For conditions shown as MIN or MAX, use the appropriate value specified under recommended operating conditions.

Additional information on these products can be obtained from the factory as it becomes available.

D flip-flop signal conventions

It is normal TI practice to name the outputs and other inputs of a D-type flip-flop and to draw its logic symbol based on the assumption of true data (D) inputs. Then outputs that produce data in phase with the data inputs are called Q and those producing complementary data are called $\overline{Q}$. An input that causes a Q output to go high or a $\overline{Q}$ output to go low is called Preset; an input that causes a $\overline{Q}$ output to go high or a Q output to go low is called Clear. Bars are used over these pin names ($\overline{PRE}$ and $\overline{CLR}$) if they are active-low.

The devices on this data sheet are second-source designs and the pin-name convention used by the original manufacturer has been retained. That makes it necessary to designate the inputs and outputs of the inverting circuit $\overline{D}$ and Q. In some applications it may be advantageous to redesignate the inputs and outputs as D and $\overline{Q}$. In that case, outputs should be renamed as shown below. Also shown are corresponding changes in the graphical symbol. Arbitrary pin numbers are shown in parentheses.

Notice that Q and $\overline{Q}$ exchange names, which causes Preset and Clear to do likewise. Also notice that the polarity indicators (◺) on $\overline{PRE}$ and $\overline{CLR}$ remain since these inputs are still active-low, but that the presence or absence of the polarity changes at $\overline{D}$, Q, and $\overline{Q}$. Of course pins 5 (Q) is still in phase with the data input D, but now both are considered active high.

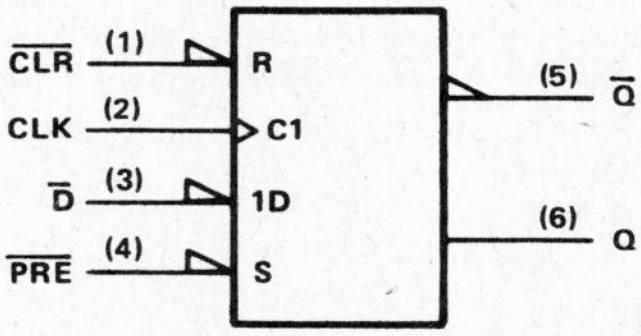
CLR
(1)
R
CLK
(2)
C1
D
(3)
1D
PRE
(4)
S
(5)
Q
(6)
Q

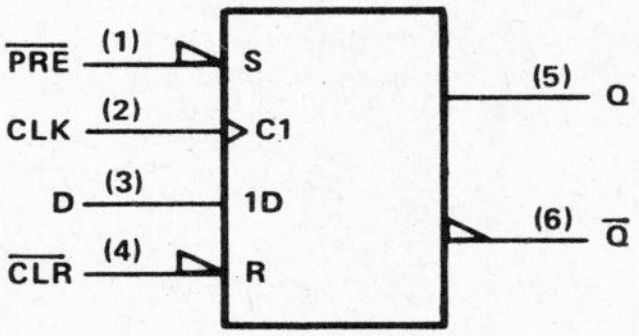
PRE
(1)
S
CLK
(2)
C1
D
(3)
1D
CLR
(4)
R
(5)
Q
(6)
Q

PARAMETER MEASUREMENT INFORMATION

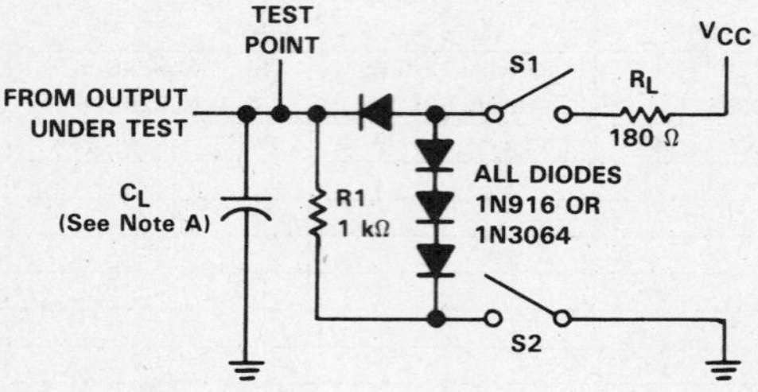
TEST POINT
FROM OUTPUT UNDER TEST
C_L (See Note A)
R1 1 kΩ
S1
R_L
180 Ω
V_{CC}
ALL DIODES 1N916 OR 1N3064
S2

LOAD CIRCUIT

SWITCH POSITION TABLE

TEST	S1	S2
t_{PLH}	Closed	Closed
t_{PHL}	Closed	Closed
t_{PZH}	Open	Closed
t_{PZL}	Closed	Open
t_{PHZ}	Closed	Closed
t_{PLZ}	Closed	Closed

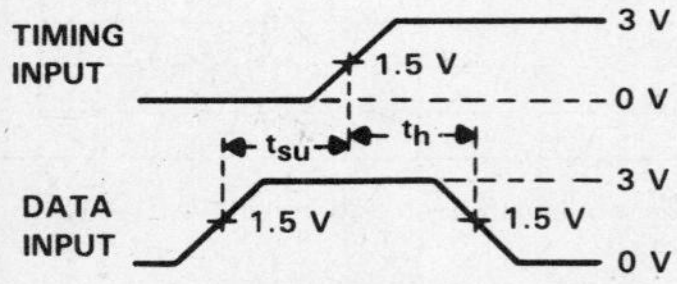
TIMING INPUT
DATA INPUT
3 V
0 V
1.5 V
t_{su}
t_h

VOLTAGE WAVEFORMS
SETUP AND HOLD TIMES

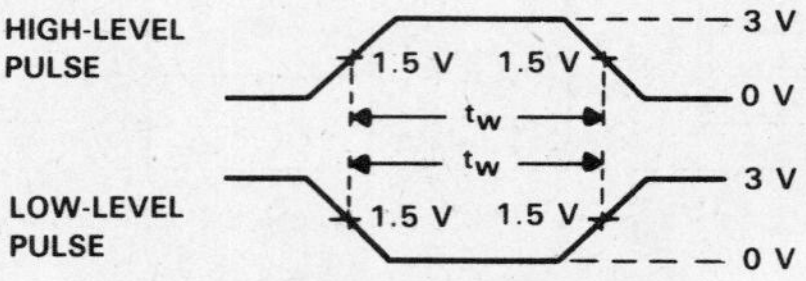
HIGH-LEVEL PULSE
LOW-LEVEL PULSE
1.5 V
t_w
3 V
0 V

VOLTAGE WAVEFORMS
PULSE DURATIONS

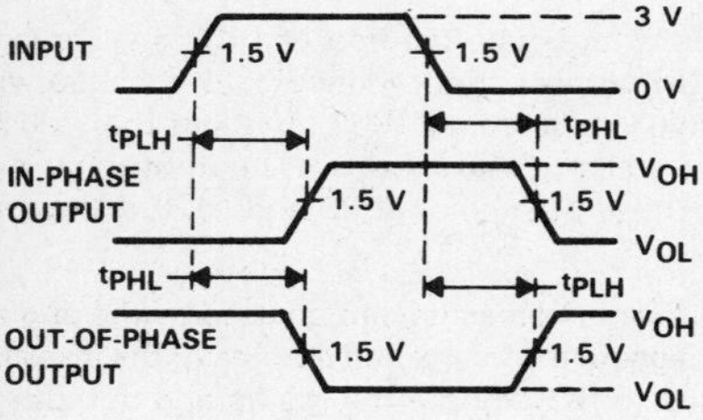
INPUT
IN-PHASE OUTPUT
OUT-OF-PHASE OUTPUT
1.5 V
3 V
0 V
t_{PLH}
t_{PHL}
V_{OH}
V_{OL}

VOLTAGE WAVEFORMS
PROPAGATION DELAY TIMES

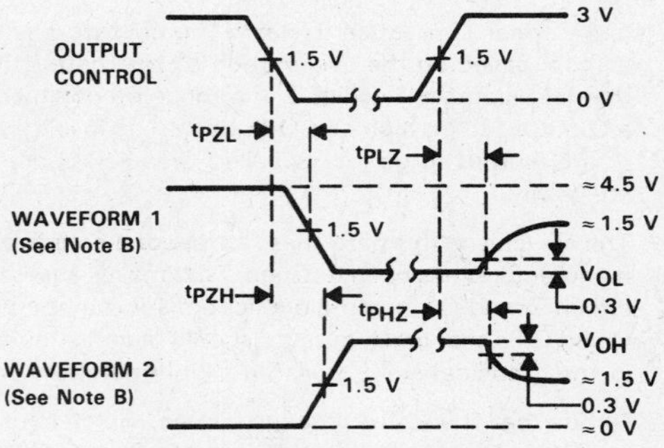
OUTPUT CONTROL
WAVEFORM 1 (See Note B)
WAVEFORM 2 (See Note B)
1.5 V
3 V
0 V
t_{PZL}
t_{PLZ}
t_{PZH}
t_{PHZ}
≈ 4.5 V
≈ 1.5 V
V_{OL}
0.3 V
V_{OH}
≈ 0 V

VOLTAGE WAVEFORMS
ENABLE AND DISABLE TIMES, THREE-STATE OUTPUTS

NOTES: A. C_L includes probe and jig capacitance.
B. Waveform 1 is for an output with internal conditions such that the output is low except when disabled by the output control. Waveform 2 is for an output with internal conditions such that the output is high except when disabled by the output control.
C. All input pulses are supplied by generators having the following characteristics: PRR ≤ 10 MHz, Z_O = 50 Ω, t_r ≤ 2.5 ns, t_f ≤ 2.5 ns.

FIGURE 1

TEXAS INSTRUMENTS
POST OFFICE BOX 225012 • DALLAS, TEXAS 75265

SN54ALS29827, SN54ALS29828
SN74ALS29827, SN74ALS29828
10-BIT BUFFERS AND BUS DRIVERS WITH 3-STATE OUTPUTS

D2912, JANUARY 1986

- **Functionally Equivalent to AM29827 and AM29828**
- **3-State Outputs Drive Bus Lines or Buffer Memory Address Registers**
- **P-N-P Inputs Reduce D-C Loading**
- **Data Flow-Thru Pinout (All Inputs on Opposite Side from Outputs)**
- **Power-Up High-Impedance State**
- **Package Options Include Both Plastic and Ceramic Chip Carriers in Addition to Plastic and Ceramic DIPs**
- **Dependable Texas Instruments Quality and Reliability**

SN54ALS' . . . JT PACKAGE
SN74ALS' . . . DW OR NT PACKAGE
(TOP VIEW)

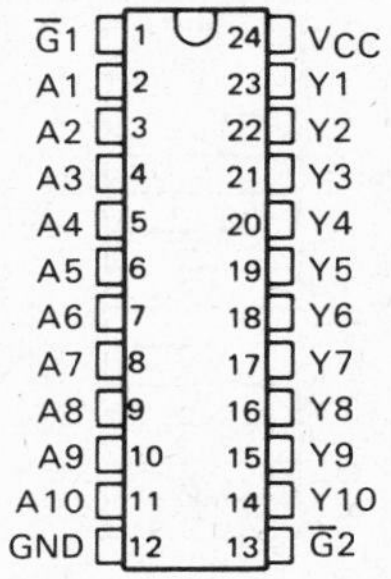
$\overline{G1}$ 1
A1 2
A2 3
A3 4
A4 5
A5 6
A6 7
A7 8
A8 9
A9 10
A10 11
GND 12
24 V_{CC}
23 Y1
22 Y2
21 Y3
20 Y4
19 Y5
18 Y6
17 Y7
16 Y8
15 Y9
14 Y10
13 $\overline{G2}$

SN54ALS' . . . FK PACKAGE
SN74ALS' . . . FN PACKAGE
(TOP VIEW)

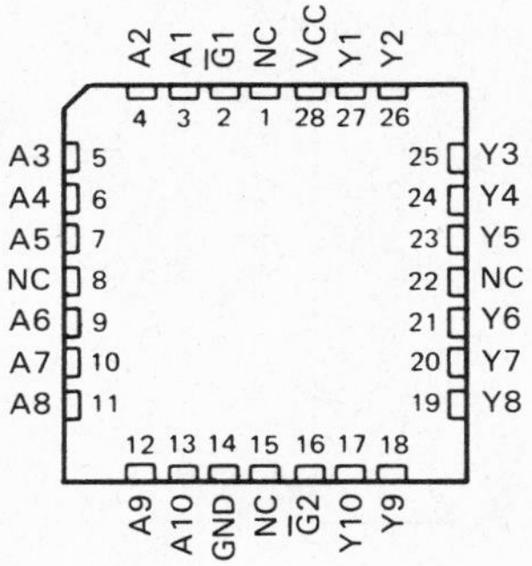
A2 A1 $\overline{G1}$ NC V_{CC} Y1 Y2
4 3 2 1 28 27 26
A3 5
A4 6
A5 7
NC 8
A6 9
A7 10
A8 11
25 Y3
24 Y4
23 Y5
22 NC
21 Y6
20 Y7
19 Y8
12 13 14 15 16 17 18
A9 A10 GND NC $\overline{G2}$ Y10 Y9

description

These 10-bit buffers and bus drivers provide high-performance bus interface for wide data paths or busses carrying parity.

The three-state control gate is a 2-input NOR such that if either $\overline{G1}$ or $\overline{G2}$ is high, all ten outputs are in the high-impedance state.

The 'ALS29827 provides true data and the 'ALS29828 provides inverted data at the outputs.

The SN54' family is characterized for operation over the full military temperature range of −55°C to 125°C. The SN74' family is characterized for operation from 0°C to 70°C.

logic symbols†

'ALS29827

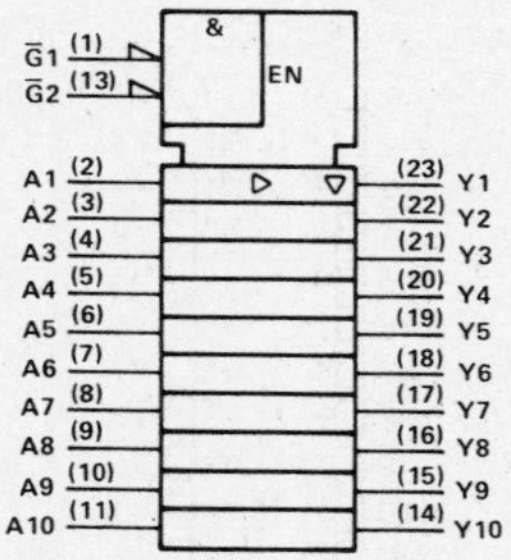
&
EN
G̅1 (1)
G̅2 (13)
A1 (2)
A2 (3)
A3 (4)
A4 (5)
A5 (6)
A6 (7)
A7 (8)
A8 (9)
A9 (10)
A10 (11)
(23) Y1
(22) Y2
(21) Y3
(20) Y4
(19) Y5
(18) Y6
(17) Y7
(16) Y8
(15) Y9
(14) Y10

'ALS29828

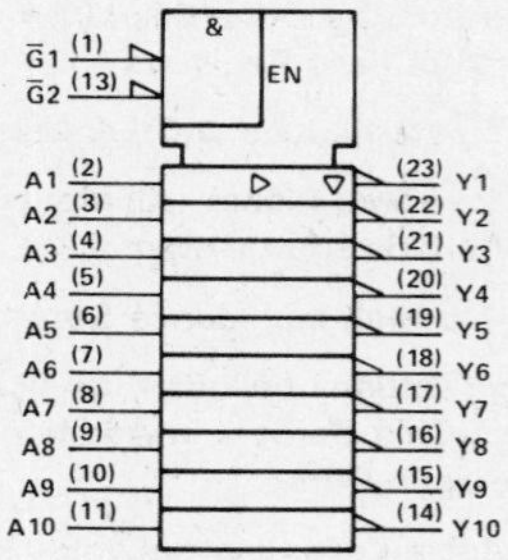
&
EN
G̅1 (1)
G̅2 (13)
A1 (2)
A2 (3)
A3 (4)
A4 (5)
A5 (6)
A6 (7)
A7 (8)
A8 (9)
A9 (10)
A10 (11)
(23) Y1
(22) Y2
(21) Y3
(20) Y4
(19) Y5
(18) Y6
(17) Y7
(16) Y8
(15) Y9
(14) Y10

†These symbols are in accordance with ANSI/IEEE Std 91-1984 and IEC Publication 617-12.

logic diagrams (positive logic)

'ALS29827

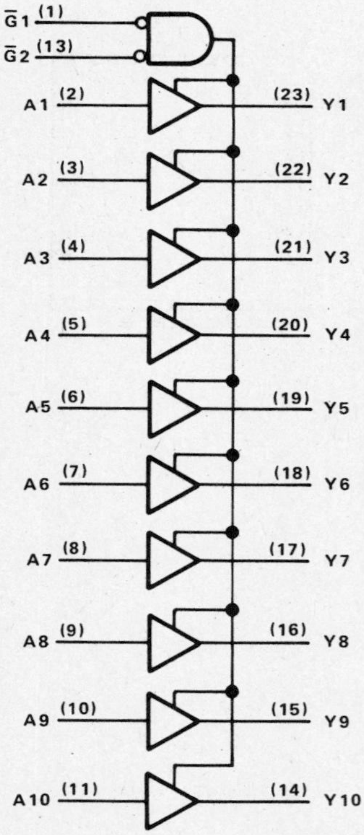
G̅1 (1)
G̅2 (13)
A1 (2)
A2 (3)
A3 (4)
A4 (5)
A5 (6)
A6 (7)
A7 (8)
A8 (9)
A9 (10)
A10 (11)
(23) Y1
(22) Y2
(21) Y3
(20) Y4
(19) Y5
(18) Y6
(17) Y7
(16) Y8
(15) Y9
(14) Y10

'ALS29828

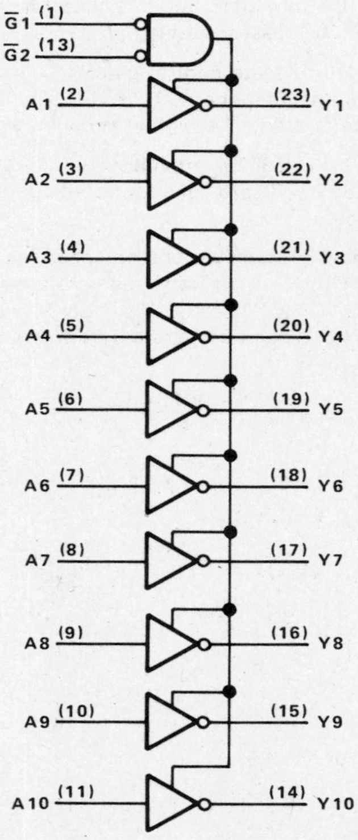
G̅1 (1)
G̅2 (13)
A1 (2)
A2 (3)
A3 (4)
A4 (5)
A5 (6)
A6 (7)
A7 (8)
A8 (9)
A9 (10)
A10 (11)
(23) Y1
(22) Y2
(21) Y3
(20) Y4
(19) Y5
(18) Y6
(17) Y7
(16) Y8
(15) Y9
(14) Y10

Pin numbers shown are DW, JT, and NT packages.

2

LSI Devices

TEXAS INSTRUMENTS
POST OFFICE BOX 225012 • DALLAS, TEXAS 75265

absolute maximum ratings over operating free-air temperature range (unless otherwise noted)

Supply voltage, V_{CC} . . . . 7 V
Input voltage . . . . 5.5 V
Voltage applied to a disabled 3-state output . . . . 5.5 V
Operating free-air temperature range: SN54ALS29827, SN54ALS29828 . . . . . . −55°C to 125°C
SN74ALS29827, SN74ALS29828 . . . . 0°C to 70°C
Storage temperature range . . . . −65°C to 150°C

recommended operating conditions

		SN54ALS29827 SN54ALS29828			SN74ALS29827 SN74ALS29828			UNIT
		MIN	NOM	MAX	MIN	NOM	MAX	
V_{CC}	Supply voltage	4.5	5	5.5	4.75	5	5.25	V
V_{IH}	High-level input voltage	2			2			V
V_{IL}	Low-level input voltage			0.8			0.8	V
I_{OH}	High-level output current			−15			−24	mA
I_{OL}	Low-level output current			32			48	mA
T_A	Operating free-air temperature	−55		125	0		70	°C

electrical characteristics over recommended operating free-air temperature range (unless otherwise noted)

PARAMETER		TEST CONDITIONS†		SN54ALS29827 SN54ALS29828			SN74ALS29827 SN74ALS29828			UNIT
				MIN	TYP‡	MAX	MIN	TYP‡	MAX	
V_{IK}		V_{CC} = MIN,	I_I = −18 mA			−1.2			−1.2	V
V_{OH}		V_{CC} = MIN to MAX,	I_{OH} = −0.4 mA	V_{CC}−2			V_{CC}−2			V
		V_{CC} = MIN,	I_{OH} = −15 mA	2						
		V_{CC} = MIN,	I_{OH} = −24 mA				2			
V_{OL}		V_{CC} = MIN,	I_{OL} = 32 mA		0.25	0.4		0.25	0.4	V
		V_{CC} = MIN,	I_{OL} = 48 mA					0.35	0.5	
I_{OZH}		V_{CC} = MAX,	V_O = 2.4 V			20			20	μA
I_{OZL}		V_{CC} = MAX,	V_O = 0.4 V			−20			−20	μA
I_I		V_{CC} = MAX,	V_I = 5.5 V			0.1			0.1	mA
I_{IH}		V_{CC} = MAX,	V_I = 2.7 V			20			20	μA
I_{IL}		V_{CC} = MAX,	V_I = 0.4 V			−0.1			−0.1	mA
I_{OS}§		V_{CC} = MAX,	V_O = 0	−75		−250	−75		−250	mA
I_{CC}	'ALS29827	V_{CC} = MAX	Outputs high		16			16		mA
			Outputs low		20			20		
			Outputs disabled		19			19		
	'ALS29828	V_{CC} = MAX	Outputs high		12			12		mA
			Outputs low		16			16		
			Outputs disabled		14			14		

† For conditions shown as MIN or MAX, use the appropriate value specified under recommended operating conditions.
‡ All typical values are at V_{CC} = 5 V, T_A = 25°C.
§ Not more than one output should be shorted at a time and duration of the short circuit should not exceed one second.

Additional information on these products can be obtained from the factory as it becomes available.

2 LSI Devices

switching characteristics

PARAMETER	FROM (INPUT)	TO (OUTPUT)	TEST CONDITIONS See Figure 1	V_{CC} = 5 V, T_A = 25°C 'ALS29827 'ALS29828			V_{CC} = MIN TO MAX,† T_A = MIN TO MAX† SN54ALS29827 SN54ALS29828		SN74ALS29827 SN74ALS29828		UNIT
				MIN	TYP	MAX	MIN	MAX	MIN	MAX	
t_{PLH}	A	Y	C_L = 300 pF		8						ns
t_{PHL}					11						
t_{PLH}			C_L = 50 pF		5						
t_{PHL}					5						
t_{PZH}	$\overline{G}$	Y	C_L = 300 pF		11						ns
t_{PZL}					18						
t_{PZH}			C_L = 50 pF		7						
t_{PZL}					10						
t_{PHZ}	$\overline{G}$	Y	C_L = 50 pF		11						ns
t_{PLZ}					5						
t_{PHZ}			C_L = 5 pF		4						
t_{PLZ}					4						

† For conditions shown as MIN or MAX, use the appropriate value specified under recommended operating conditions.

Additional information on these products can be obtained from the factory as it becomes available.

TEXAS INSTRUMENTS
POST OFFICE BOX 225012 • DALLAS, TEXAS 75265

PARAMETER MEASUREMENT INFORMATION

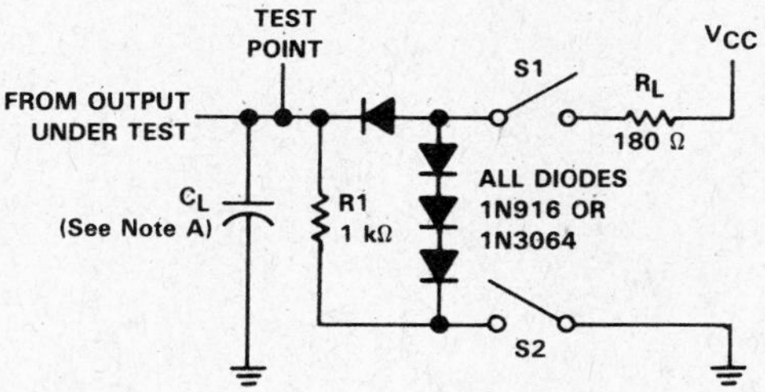
TEST POINT
VCC
S1
RL
FROM OUTPUT UNDER TEST
180 Ω
CL (See Note A)
R1 1 kΩ
ALL DIODES 1N916 OR 1N3064
S2

LOAD CIRCUIT

SWITCH POSITION TABLE

TEST	S1	S2
t_{PLH}	Closed	Closed
t_{PHL}	Closed	Closed
t_{PZH}	Open	Closed
t_{PZL}	Closed	Open
t_{PHZ}	Closed	Closed
t_{PLZ}	Closed	Closed

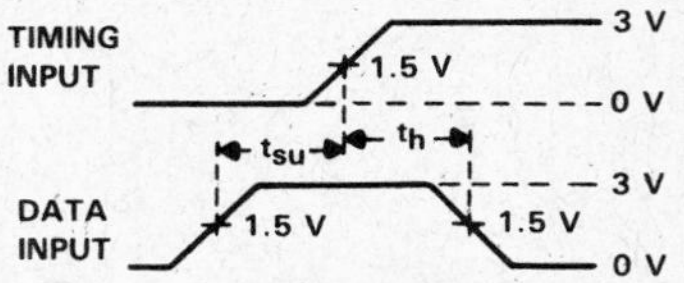
TIMING INPUT
3 V
1.5 V
0 V
tsu
th
DATA INPUT
3 V
1.5 V
1.5 V
0 V

VOLTAGE WAVEFORMS
SETUP AND HOLD TIMES

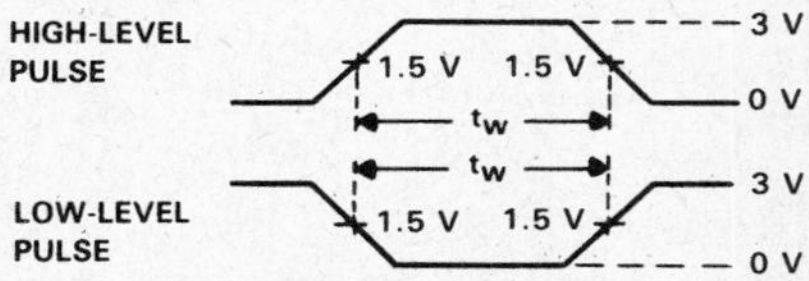
HIGH-LEVEL PULSE
3 V
1.5 V
1.5 V
0 V
tw
tw
LOW-LEVEL PULSE
3 V
1.5 V
1.5 V
0 V

VOLTAGE WAVEFORMS
PULSE DURATIONS

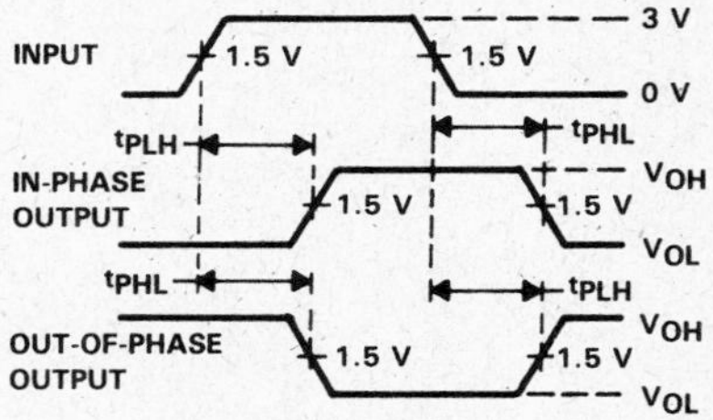
INPUT
1.5 V
1.5 V
3 V
0 V
tPLH
tPHL
IN-PHASE OUTPUT
1.5 V
1.5 V
VOH
VOL
tPHL
tPLH
OUT-OF-PHASE OUTPUT
1.5 V
1.5 V
VOH
VOL

VOLTAGE WAVEFORMS
PROPAGATION DELAY TIMES

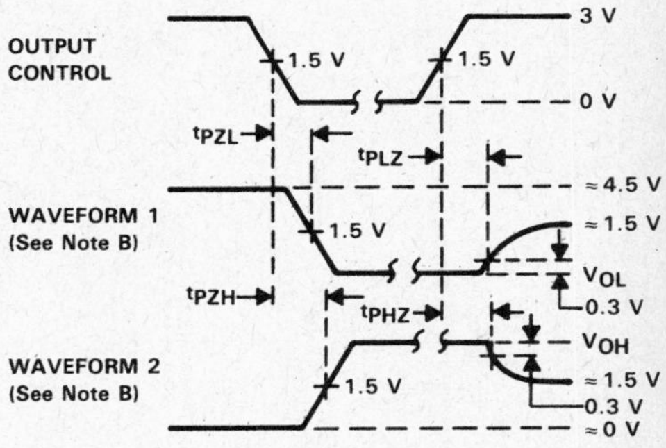
OUTPUT CONTROL
1.5 V
1.5 V
3 V
0 V
tPZL
tPLZ
≈4.5 V
WAVEFORM 1 (See Note B)
1.5 V
≈1.5 V
VOL
0.3 V
tPZH
tPHZ
VOH
WAVEFORM 2 (See Note B)
1.5 V
≈1.5 V
0.3 V
≈0 V

VOLTAGE WAVEFORMS
ENABLE AND DISABLE TIMES, THREE-STATE OUTPUTS

NOTES: A. C_L includes probe and jig capacitance.
B. Waveform 1 is for an output with internal conditions such that the output is low except when disabled by the output control. Waveform 2 is for an output with internal conditions such that the output is high except when disabled by the output control.
C. All input pulses are supplied by generators having the following characteristics: PRR ≤ 10 MHz, Z_O = 50 Ω, t_r ≤ 2.5 ns, t_f ≤ 2.5 ns.

FIGURE 1

PRODUCT PREVIEW

SN54ALS29861, SN54ALS29862
SN74ALS29861, SN74ALS29862
10-BIT BUS TRANSCEIVERS WITH 3-STATE OUTPUTS

D2915, JANUARY 1986

- Functionally Equivalent to AM29861 and AM29862
- Choice of True or Inverting Logic
- Power-Up High-Impedance State
- Package Options Include Both Plastic and Ceramic Chip Carriers in Addition to Plastic and Ceramic DIPs
- Dependable Texas Instruments Quality and Reliability

SN54ALS' . . . JT PACKAGE
SN74ALS' . . . DW OR NT PACKAGE
(TOP VIEW)

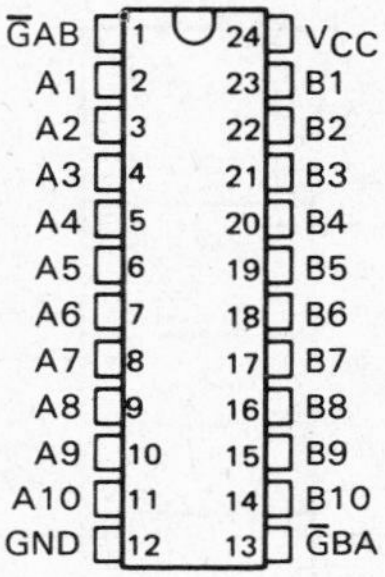

$\overline{GAB}$ 1 24 VCC
A1 2 23 B1
A2 3 22 B2
A3 4 21 B3
A4 5 20 B4
A5 6 19 B5
A6 7 18 B6
A7 8 17 B7
A8 9 16 B8
A9 10 15 B9
A10 11 14 B10
GND 12 13 $\overline{GBA}$

SN54ALS' . . . FK PACKAGE
SN74ALS' . . . FN PACKAGE
(TOP VIEW)

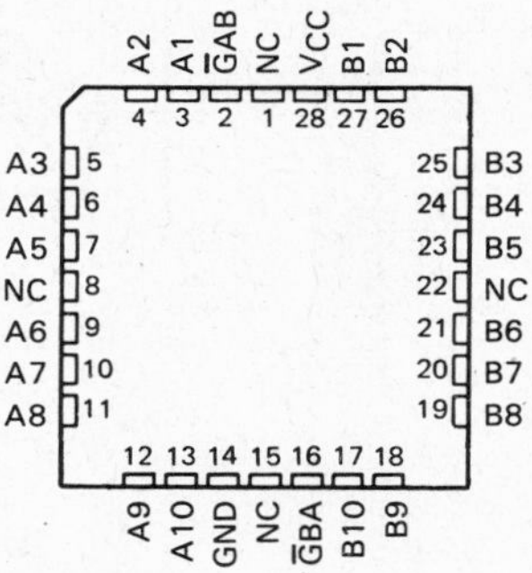

A2 A1 $\overline{GAB}$ NC VCC B1 B2
4 3 2 1 28 27 26
A3 5
A4 6
A5 7
NC 8
A6 9
A7 10
A8 11
25 B3
24 B4
23 B5
22 NC
21 B6
20 B7
19 B8
12 13 14 15 16 17 18
A9 A10 GND NC $\overline{GBA}$ B10 B9

NC—No internal connection

description

These 10-bit bus transceivers are designed for asynchronous two-way communication between data buses. The control function implementation allows for maximum flexibility in timing.

These devices allow data transmission from the A bus to the B bus or from the B bus to the A bus depending upon the logic levels at the enable inputs ($\overline{GBA}$ and $\overline{GAB}$).

The enable inputs can be used to disable the device so that the buses are effectively isolated.

The SN54' family is characterized for operation over the full military temperature range of −55°C to 125°C. The SN74' family is characterized for operation from 0°C to 70°C.

FUNCTION TABLE

INPUTS		OPERATION	
$\overline{GAB}$	$\overline{GBA}$	ALS29861	ALS29862
L	H	A to B	$\overline{A}$ to B
H	L	B to A	$\overline{B}$ to A
H	H	Isolation	Isolation
L	L	Latch A and B (A = B)	Latch A and B (A = $\overline{B}$)

PRODUCT PREVIEW documents contain information on products in the formative or design phase of development. Characteristic data and other specifications are design goals. Texas Instruments reserves the right to change or discontinue these products without notice.

logic symbols†

'ALS29861

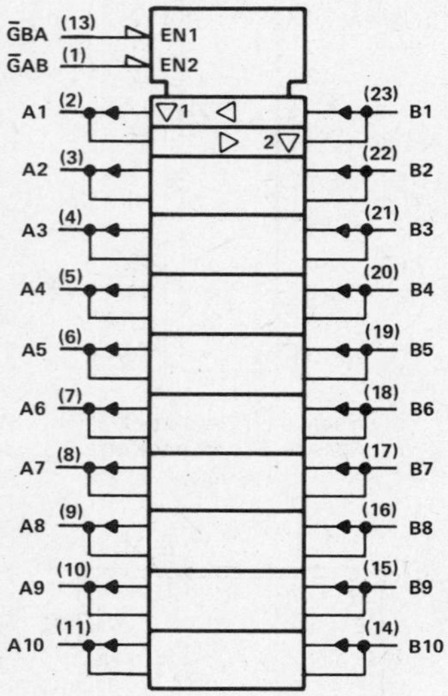
GBA
(13)
EN1
GAB
(1)
EN2
A1
(2)
▽1
2▽
B1
(23)
A2
(3)
(22)
B2
A3
(4)
(21)
B3
A4
(5)
(20)
B4
A5
(6)
(19)
B5
A6
(7)
(18)
B6
A7
(8)
(17)
B7
A8
(9)
(16)
B8
A9
(10)
(15)
B9
A10
(11)
(14)
B10

'ALS29862

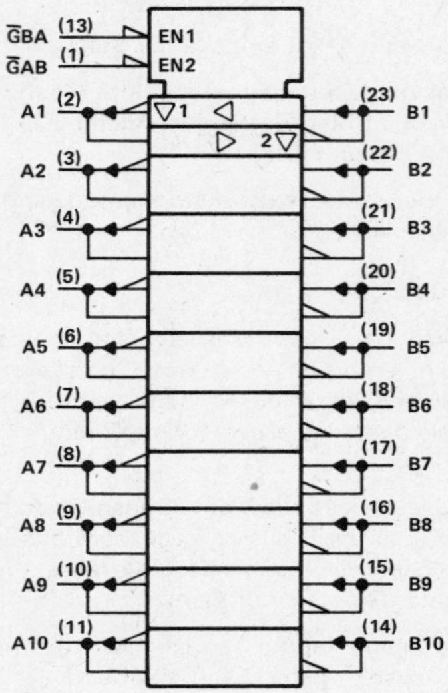
GBA
(13)
EN1
GAB
(1)
EN2
A1
(2)
▽1
2▽
B1
(23)
A2
(3)
(22)
B2
A3
(4)
(21)
B3
A4
(5)
(20)
B4
A5
(6)
(19)
B5
A6
(7)
(18)
B6
A7
(8)
(17)
B7
A8
(9)
(16)
B8
A9
(10)
(15)
B9
A10
(11)
(14)
B10

† These symbols are in accordance with ANSI/IEEE Std 91-1984 and IEC Publication 617-12.
Pin numbers shown are for DW, JT, and NT packages.

2

LSI Devices

logic diagrams

'ALS29861

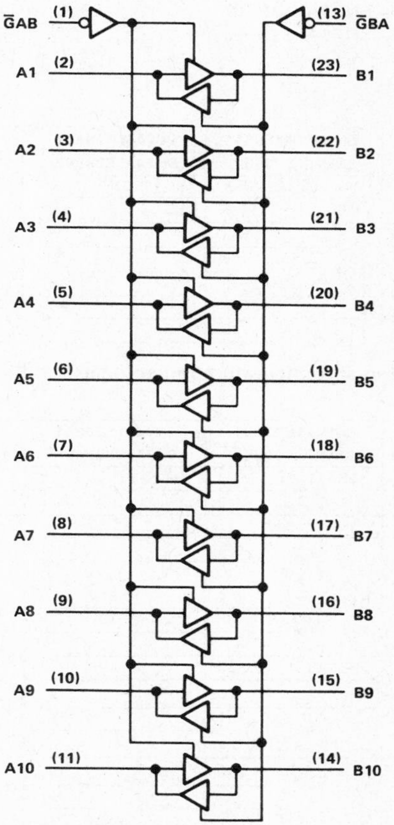
$\overline{G}$AB
(1)
(13)
$\overline{G}$BA
A1 (2) (23) B1
A2 (3) (22) B2
A3 (4) (21) B3
A4 (5) (20) B4
A5 (6) (19) B5
A6 (7) (18) B6
A7 (8) (17) B7
A8 (9) (16) B8
A9 (10) (15) B9
A10 (11) (14) B10

'ALS29862

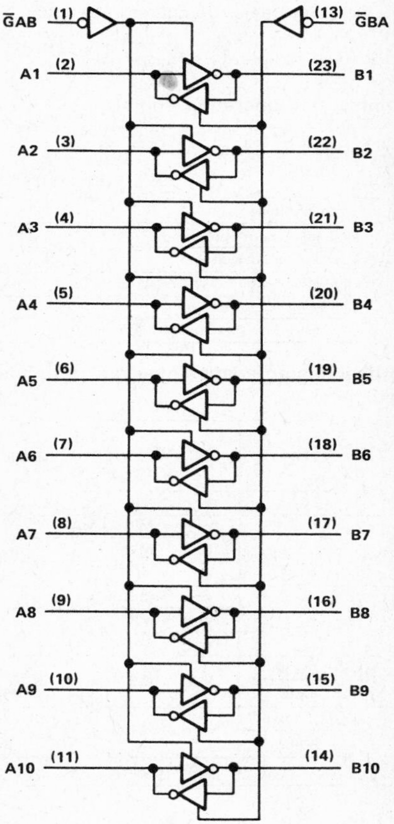
$\overline{G}$AB
(1)
(13)
$\overline{G}$BA
A1 (2) (23) B1
A2 (3) (22) B2
A3 (4) (21) B3
A4 (5) (20) B4
A5 (6) (19) B5
A6 (7) (18) B6
A7 (8) (17) B7
A8 (9) (16) B8
A9 (10) (15) B9
A10 (11) (14) B10

Pin numbers shown are for DW, JT, and NT packages.

absolute maximum ratings over operating free-air temperature range (unless otherwise noted)

Supply voltage, V_{CC} . . . . 7 V
Input voltage: All inputs and I/O ports . . . . 5.5 V
Operating free-air temperature range: SN54ALS29861, SN54ALS29862 . . . . . . −55 °C to 125 °C
SN74ALS29861, SN74ALS29862 . . . . 0 °C to 70 °C
Storage temperature range . . . . −65 °C to 150 °C

recommended operating conditions

		SN54ALS29861 SN54ALS29862			SN74ALS29861 SN74ALS29862			UNIT
		MIN	NOM	MAX	MIN	NOM	MAX	
V_{CC}	Supply voltage	4.5	5	5.5	4.5	5	5.5	V
V_{IH}	High-level input voltage	2			2			V
V_{IL}	Low-level input voltage			0.8			0.8	V
I_{OH}	High-level output current			−15			−24	mA
I_{OL}	Low-level output current			32			48	mA
T_A	Operating free-air temperature	−55		125	0		70	°C

electrical characteristics over recommended operating free-air temperature range (unless otherwise noted)

PARAMETER		TEST CONDITIONS†		SN54ALS29861 SN54ALS29862			SN74ALS29861 SN74ALS29862			UNIT
				MIN	TYP‡	MAX	MIN	TYP‡	MAX	
V_{IK}		V_{CC} = MIN,	I_I = −18 mA			−1.2			−1.2	V
V_{OH}		V_{CC} = MIN to MAX,	I_{OH} = −0.4 mA	V_{CC}−2			V_{CC}−2			V
		V_{CC} = MIN,	I_{OH} = −15 mA	2						
		V_{CC} = MIN,	I_{OH} = −24 mA				2			
V_{OL}		V_{CC} = MIN,	I_{OL} = 32 mA		0.25	0.4		0.25	0.4	V
		V_{CC} = MIN,	I_{OL} = 48 mA					0.35	0.5	
I_I		V_{CC} = MAX,	V_I = 5.5 V							mA
I_{IH}	Control inputs	V_{CC} = MAX,	V_I = 2.7 V			20			20	μA
	A or B ports§					20			20	
I_{IL}	Control inputs	V_{CC} = MAX,	V_I = 0.4 V			−0.1			−0.1	mA
	A or B ports§					−0.1			−0.1	
I_{OS}¶		V_{CC} = MAX,	V_O = 0	−75		−250	−75		−250	mA
I_{CC}	'ALS29861	V_{CC} = MAX	Outputs high		28			28		mA
			Outputs low		38			38		
			Outputs disabled		36			36		
	'ALS29862		Outputs high		22			22		
			Outputs low		30			30		
			Outputs disabled		28			28		

† For conditions shown as MIN or MAX, use appropriate value specified under recommended operating conditions.
‡ All typical values are at V_{CC} = 5 V, T_A = 25 °C.
§ For I/O ports, the parameters I_{IH} and I_{IL} include the off-state output current.
¶ Not more than one output should be shorted at a time and duration of the short circuit should not exceed one second.

'ALS29861 switching characteristics

PARAMETER	FROM (INPUT)	TO (OUTPUT)	TEST CONDITIONS See Figure 1	V_{CC} = 5 V, T_A = 25°C 'ALS29861			V_{CC} = MIN TO MAX,† T_A = MIN TO MAX† SN54ALS29861		SN74ALS29861		UNIT
				MIN	TYP	MAX	MIN	MAX	MIN	MAX	
t_{PLH}	A or B	B or A	C_L = 300 pF		8						ns
t_{PHL}					11						
t_{PLH}			C_L = 50 pF		5						
t_{PHL}					5						
t_{PZH}	$\overline{G}$AB or $\overline{G}$BA	A or B	C_L = 300 pF		11						ns
t_{PZL}					17						
t_{PZH}			C_L = 50 pF		7						
t_{PZL}					10						
t_{PHZ}	$\overline{G}$AB or $\overline{G}$BA	A or B	C_L = 50 pF		11						ns
t_{PLZ}					5						
t_{PHZ}			C_L = 5 pF		4						
t_{PLZ}					4						

'ALS29862 switching characteristics

PARAMETER	FROM (INPUT)	TO (OUTPUT)	TEST CONDITIONS See Figure 1	V_{CC} = 5 V, T_A = 25°C 'ALS29862			V_{CC} = MIN TO MAX,† T_A = MIN TO MAX† SN54ALS29862		SN74ALS29862		UNIT
				MIN	TYP	MAX	MIN	MAX	MIN	MAX	
t_{PLH}	A or B	B or A	C_L = 300 pF		7						ns
t_{PHL}					11						
t_{PLH}			C_L = 50 pF		4						
t_{PHL}					5						
t_{PZH}	$\overline{G}$AB or $\overline{G}$BA	A or B	C_L = 300 pF		11						ns
t_{PZL}					17						
t_{PZH}			C_L = 50 pF		7						
t_{PZL}					10						
t_{PHZ}	$\overline{G}$AB or $\overline{G}$BA	A or B	C_L = 50 pF		11						ns
t_{PLZ}					5						
t_{PHZ}			C_L = 5 pF		4						
t_{PLZ}					4						

† For conditions shown as MIN or MAX, use the appropriate value specified under recommended operating conditions.

Additional information on these products can be obtained from the factory as it becomes available.

PARAMETER MEASUREMENT INFORMATION

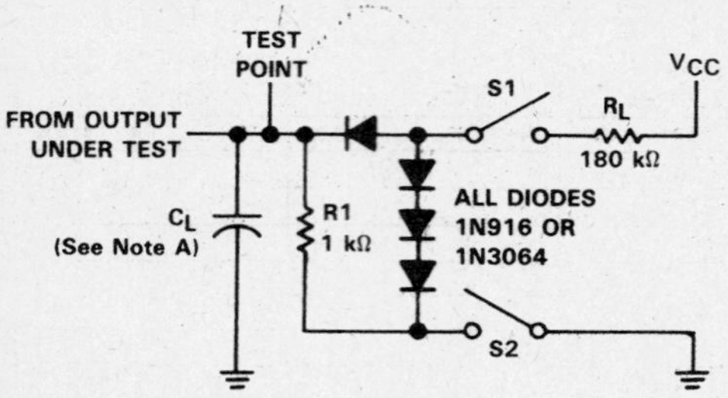
TEST
POINT
FROM OUTPUT
UNDER TEST
S1
VCC
RL
180 kΩ
CL
(See Note A)
R1
1 kΩ
ALL DIODES
1N916 OR
1N3064
S2

LOAD CIRCUIT

SWITCH POSITION TABLE

TEST	S1	S2
t_{PLH}	Closed	Closed
t_{PHL}	Closed	Closed
t_{PZH}	Open	Closed
t_{PZL}	Closed	Open
t_{PHZ}	Closed	Closed
t_{PLZ}	Closed	Closed

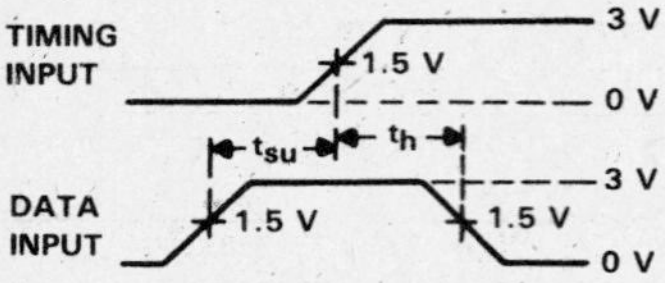
TIMING
INPUT
3 V
1.5 V
0 V
tsu
th
DATA
INPUT
3 V
1.5 V
1.5 V
0 V

VOLTAGE WAVEFORMS
SETUP AND HOLD TIMES

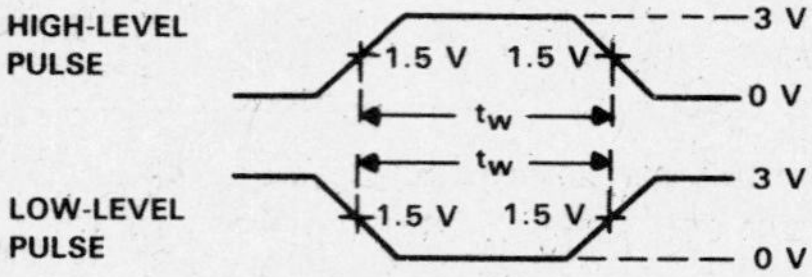
HIGH-LEVEL
PULSE
1.5 V
1.5 V
3 V
0 V
tw
tw
LOW-LEVEL
PULSE
1.5 V
1.5 V
3 V
0 V

VOLTAGE WAVEFORMS
PULSE DURATIONS

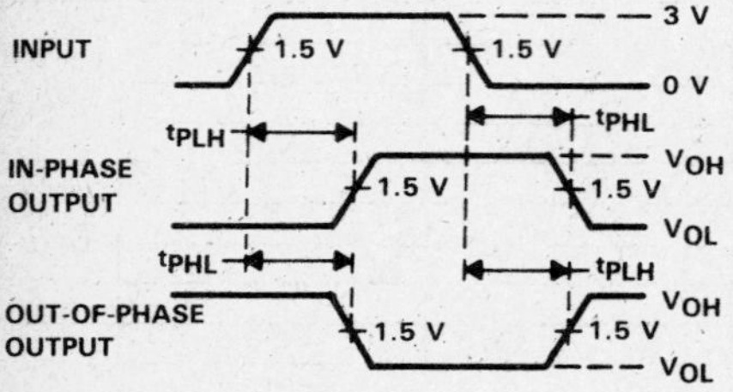
INPUT
1.5 V
1.5 V
3 V
0 V
tPLH
tPHL
IN-PHASE
OUTPUT
1.5 V
1.5 V
VOH
VOL
tPHL
tPLH
OUT-OF-PHASE
OUTPUT
1.5 V
1.5 V
VOH
VOL

VOLTAGE WAVEFORMS
PROPAGATION DELAY TIMES

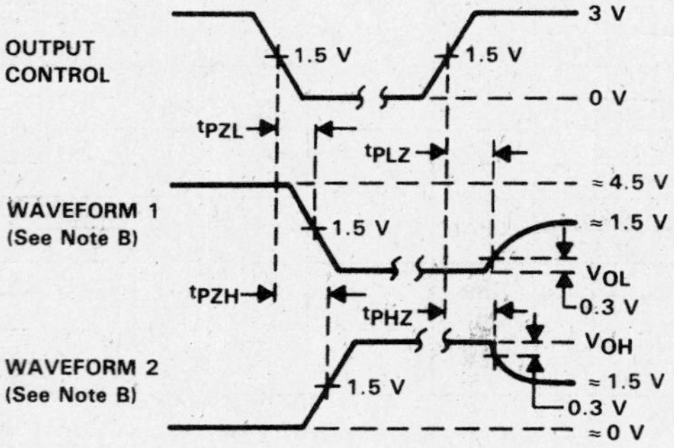
OUTPUT
CONTROL
1.5 V
1.5 V
3 V
0 V
tPZL
tPLZ
≈ 4.5 V
WAVEFORM 1
(See Note B)
1.5 V
≈ 1.5 V
VOL
0.3 V
tPZH
tPHZ
VOH
WAVEFORM 2
(See Note B)
1.5 V
≈ 1.5 V
0.3 V
≈ 0 V

VOLTAGE WAVEFORMS
ENABLE AND DISABLE TIMES, THREE-STATE OUTPUTS

NOTES: A. C_L includes probe and jig capacitance.

B. Waveform 1 is for an output with internal conditions such that the output is low except when disabled by the output control. Waveform 2 is for an output with internal conditions such that the output is high except when disabled by the output control.

C. All input pulses are supplied by generators having the following characteristics: PRR ≤ 10 MHz, Z_O = 50 Ω, t_r ≤ 2.5 ns, t_f ≤ 2.5 ns.

FIGURE 1

SN54ALS29863, SN54ALS29864
SN74ALS29863, SN74ALS29864
9-BIT BUS TRANSCEIVERS WITH 3-STATE OUTPUTS

D2915, JANUARY 1986

- **Functionally Equivalent to AM29863 and AM29864**
- **Choice of True or Inverting Logic**
- **Power-Up High-Impedance State**
- **Package Options Include Both Plastic and Ceramic Chip Carriers in Addition to Plastic and Ceramic DIPs**
- **Dependable Texas Instruments Quality and Reliability**

SN54ALS' . . . JT PACKAGE
SN74ALS' . . . DW OR NT PACKAGE
(TOP VIEW)

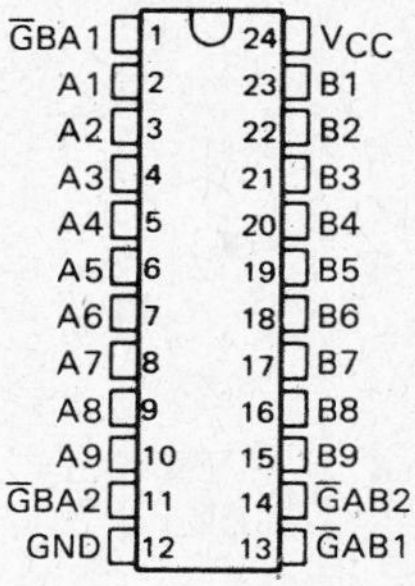

$\overline{\mathrm{GBA}}$1 1
A1 2
A2 3
A3 4
A4 5
A5 6
A6 7
A7 8
A8 9
A9 10
$\overline{\mathrm{GBA}}$2 11
GND 12
24 V_{CC}
23 B1
22 B2
21 B3
20 B4
19 B5
18 B6
17 B7
16 B8
15 B9
14 $\overline{\mathrm{GAB}}$2
13 $\overline{\mathrm{GAB}}$1

SN54ALS' . . . FK PACKAGE
SN74ALS' . . . FN PACKAGE
(TOP VIEW)

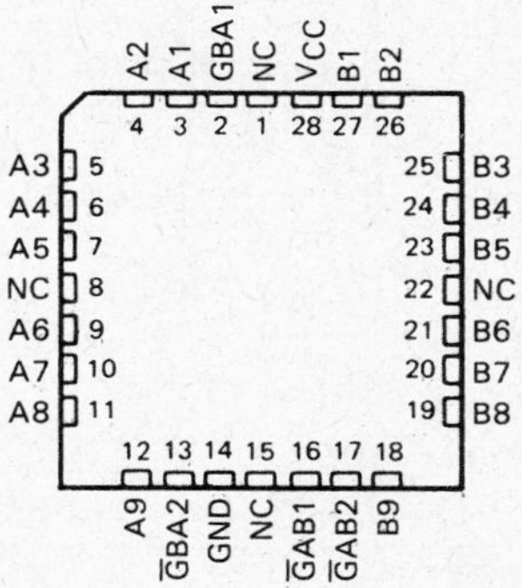

A2 A1 $\overline{\mathrm{GBA}}$1 NC V_{CC} B1 B2
4 3 2 1 28 27 26
A3 5
A4 6
A5 7
NC 8
A6 9
A7 10
A8 11
25 B3
24 B4
23 B5
22 NC
21 B6
20 B7
19 B8
12 13 14 15 16 17 18
A9 $\overline{\mathrm{GBA}}$2 GND NC $\overline{\mathrm{GAB}}$1 $\overline{\mathrm{GAB}}$2 B9

NC – No internal connection

description

These 9-bit bus transceivers are designed for asynchronous two-way communication between data buses. The control function implementation allows for maximum flexibility in timing.

These devices allow data transmission from the A bus to the B bus or from the B bus to the A bus depending upon the logic levels at the enable inputs ($\overline{\mathrm{GBA}}$1, $\overline{\mathrm{GBA}}$2, $\overline{\mathrm{GAB}}$1, and $\overline{\mathrm{GAB}}$2).

The SN54' family is characterized for operation over the full military temperature range of −55°C to 125°C. The SN74' family is characterized for operation from 0°C to 70°C.

FUNCTION TABLE

ENABLE INPUTS				OPERATION	
$\overline{\mathrm{GAB}}$1	$\overline{\mathrm{GAB}}$2	$\overline{\mathrm{GBA}}$1	$\overline{\mathrm{GBA}}$2	'ALS29863	'ALS29864
L	L	L	L	Latch A and B	Latch A and B
L	L	H	X	A to B	A to $\overline{\mathrm{B}}$
L	L	X	H		
H	X	L	L	B to A	B to $\overline{\mathrm{A}}$
X	H	L	L		
H	X	H	X	Isolation	Isolation
H	X	X	H		
X	H	X	H		
X	H	H	X		

PRODUCT PREVIEW documents contain information on products in the formative or design phase of development. Characteristic data and other specifications are design goals. Texas Instruments reserves the right to change or discontinue these products without notice.

TEXAS INSTRUMENTS
POST OFFICE BOX 225012 • DALLAS, TEXAS 75265

logic symbols†

'ALS29863

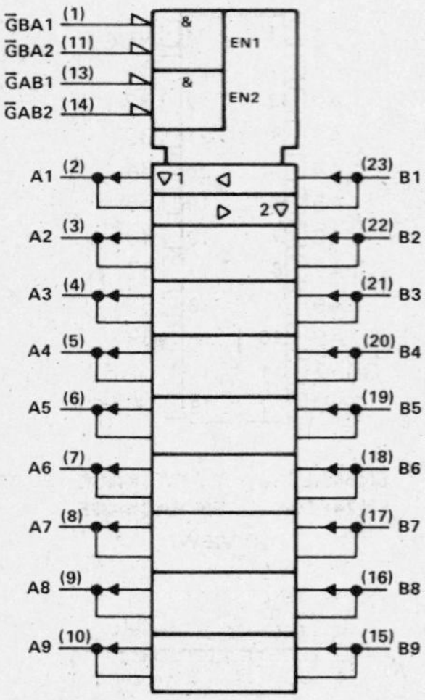
$\overline{G}$BA1 (1)
$\overline{G}$BA2 (11)
$\overline{G}$AB1 (13)
$\overline{G}$AB2 (14)
&
EN1
&
EN2
1
2
A1 (2)
A2 (3)
A3 (4)
A4 (5)
A5 (6)
A6 (7)
A7 (8)
A8 (9)
A9 (10)
(23) B1
(22) B2
(21) B3
(20) B4
(19) B5
(18) B6
(17) B7
(16) B8
(15) B9

'ALS29864

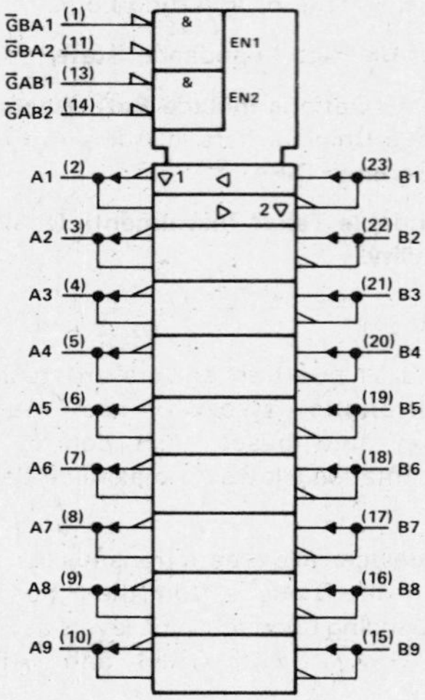
$\overline{G}$BA1 (1)
$\overline{G}$BA2 (11)
$\overline{G}$AB1 (13)
$\overline{G}$AB2 (14)
&
EN1
&
EN2
1
2
A1 (2)
A2 (3)
A3 (4)
A4 (5)
A5 (6)
A6 (7)
A7 (8)
A8 (9)
A9 (10)
(23) B1
(22) B2
(21) B3
(20) B4
(19) B5
(18) B6
(17) B7
(16) B8
(15) B9

†These symbols are in accordance with ANSI/IEEE Std 91-1984 and IEC Publication 617-12.

logic diagrams

'ALS29863

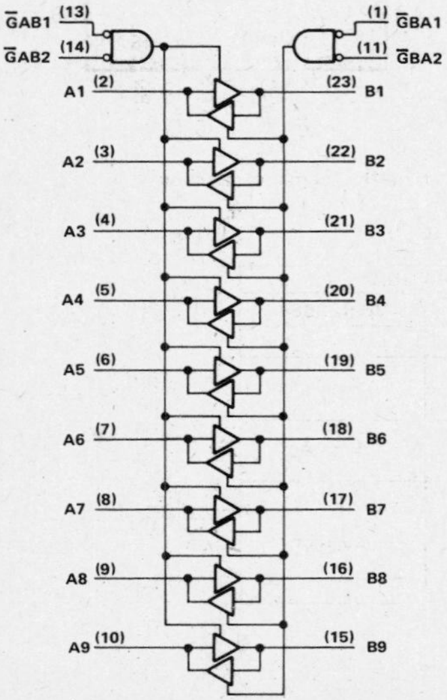
$\overline{G}$AB1 (13)
$\overline{G}$AB2 (14)
(1) $\overline{G}$BA1
(11) $\overline{G}$BA2
A1 (2)
A2 (3)
A3 (4)
A4 (5)
A5 (6)
A6 (7)
A7 (8)
A8 (9)
A9 (10)
(23) B1
(22) B2
(21) B3
(20) B4
(19) B5
(18) B6
(17) B7
(16) B8
(15) B9

'ALS29864

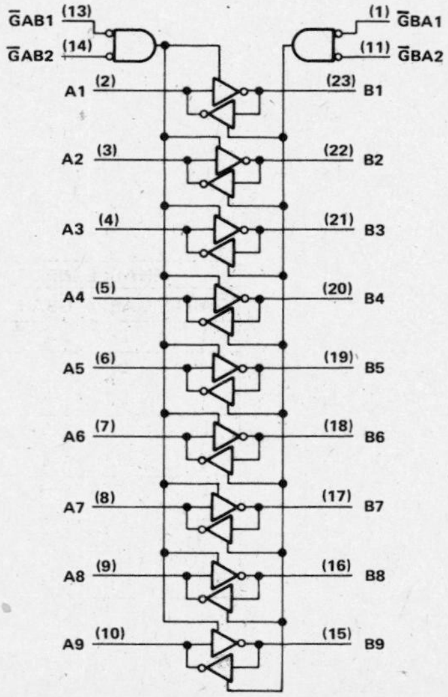
$\overline{G}$AB1 (13)
$\overline{G}$AB2 (14)
(1) $\overline{G}$BA1
(11) $\overline{G}$BA2
A1 (2)
A2 (3)
A3 (4)
A4 (5)
A5 (6)
A6 (7)
A7 (8)
A8 (9)
A9 (10)
(23) B1
(22) B2
(21) B3
(20) B4
(19) B5
(18) B6
(17) B7
(16) B8
(15) B9

Pin numbers shown are for DW, JT, and NT packages.

TEXAS INSTRUMENTS
POST OFFICE BOX 225012 • DALLAS, TEXAS 75265

absolute maximum ratings over operating free-air temperature range (unless otherwise noted)

Supply voltage, V_{CC} . . . . 7 V
Input voltage: All inputs and I/O ports . . . . 5.5 V
Operating free-air temperature range: SN54ALS29863, SN54ALS29864 . . . . −55°C to 125°C
SN74ALS29863, SN74ALS29864 . . . . 0°C to 70°C
Storage temperature range . . . . −65°C to 150°C

recommended operating conditions

		SN54ALS29863 SN54ALS29864			SN74ALS29863 SN74ALS29864			UNIT
		MIN	NOM	MAX	MIN	NOM	MAX	
V_{CC}	Supply voltage	4.5	5	5.5	4.5	5	5.5	V
V_{IH}	High-level input voltage	2			2			V
V_{IL}	Low-level input voltage			0.8			0.8	V
I_{OH}	High-level output current			−15			−24	mA
I_{OL}	Low-level output current			32			48	mA
T_A	Operating free-air temperature	−55		125	0		70	°C

electrical characteristics over recommended operating free-air temperature range (unless otherwise noted)

PARAMETER		TEST CONDITIONS†		SN54ALS29863 SN54ALS29864			SN74ALS29863 SN74ALS29864			UNIT
				MIN	TYP‡	MAX	MIN	TYP‡	MAX	
V_{IK}		V_{CC} = MIN,	I_I = −18 mA			−1.2			−1.2	V
V_{OH}		V_{CC} = MIN to MAX,	I_{OH} = −0.4 mA	$V_{CC}-2$			$V_{CC}-2$			V
		V_{CC} = MIN,	I_{OH} = −15 mA	2						
		V_{CC} = MIN,	I_{OH} = −24 mA				2			
V_{OL}		V_{CC} = MIN,	I_{OH} = −32 mA		0.25	0.4		0.25	0.4	V
		V_{CC} = MIN,	I_{OL} = 48 mA					0.35	0.5	
I_I		V_{CC} = MAX,	V_I = 5.5 V							mA
I_{IH}	Control inputs	V_{CC} = MAX,	V_I = 2.7 V			20			20	μA
	A or B ports§					20			20	
I_{IL}	Control inputs	V_{CC} = MAX,	V_I = 0.4 V			−0.1			−0.1	mA
	A or B ports§					−0.1			−0.1	
I_{OS}¶		V_{CC} = MAX,	V_O = 0	−75		−250	−75		−250	mA
I_{CC}	'ALS29863	V_{CC} = MAX	Outputs high		26			26		mA
			Outputs low		35			35		
			Outputs disabled		34			34		
	'ALS29864		Outputs high		20			20		
			Outputs low		27			27		
			Outputs disabled		26			26		

† For conditions shown as MIN or MAX, use appropriate value specified under recommended operating conditions.
‡ All typical values are at V_{CC} = 5 V, T_A = 25°C.
§ For I/O ports, the parameters I_{IH} and I_{IL} include the off-state output current.
¶ Not more than one output should be shorted at a time and duration of the short circuit should not exceed one second.

'ALS29863 switching characteristics

PARAMETER	FROM (INPUT)	TO (OUTPUT)	TEST CONDITIONS See Figure 1	V_{CC} = 5 V, T_A = 25°C 'ALS29863			V_{CC} = MIN TO MAX,† T_A = MIN TO MAX † SN54ALS29863		SN74ALS29863		UNIT
				MIN	TYP	MAX	MIN	MAX	MIN	MAX	
t_{PLH}	A or B	B or A	C_L = 300 pF		8						ns
t_{PHL}					11						
t_{PLH}			C_L = 50 pF		5						
t_{PHL}					5						
t_{PZH}	$\overline{\mathrm{G}}$AB or $\overline{\mathrm{G}}$BA	A or B	C_L = 300 pF		11						ns
t_{PZL}					17						
t_{PZH}			C_L = 50 pF		7						
t_{PZL}					10						
t_{PHZ}	$\overline{\mathrm{G}}$AB or $\overline{\mathrm{G}}$BA	A or B	C_L = 50 pF		11						ns
t_{PLZ}					5						
t_{PHZ}			C_L = 5 pF		4						
t_{PLZ}					4						

'ALS29864 switching characteristics

PARAMETER	FROM (INPUT)	TO (OUTPUT)	TEST CONDITIONS See Figure 1	V_{CC} = 5 V, T_A = 25°C 'ALS29864			V_{CC} = MIN TO MAX,† T_A = MIN TO MAX † SN54ALS29864		SN74ALS29864		UNIT
				MIN	TYP	MAX	MIN	MAX	MIN	MAX	
t_{PLH}	A or B	B or A	C_L = 300 pF		7						ns
t_{PHL}					11						
t_{PLH}			C_L = 50 pF		4						
t_{PHL}					5						
t_{PZH}	$\overline{\mathrm{G}}$AB or $\overline{\mathrm{G}}$BA	A or B	C_L = 300 pF		11						ns
t_{PZL}					17						
t_{PZH}			C_L = 50 pF		7						
t_{PZL}					10						
t_{PHZ}	$\overline{\mathrm{G}}$AB or $\overline{\mathrm{G}}$BA	A or B	C_L = 50 pF		11						ns
t_{PLZ}					5						
t_{PHZ}			C_L = 5 pF		4						
t_{PLZ}					4						

† For conditions shown as MIN or MAX, use the appropriate value specified under recommended operating conditions.

Additional information on these products can be obtained from the factory as it becomes available.

TEXAS INSTRUMENTS
POST OFFICE BOX 225012 • DALLAS, TEXAS 75265

PARAMETER MEASUREMENT INFORMATION

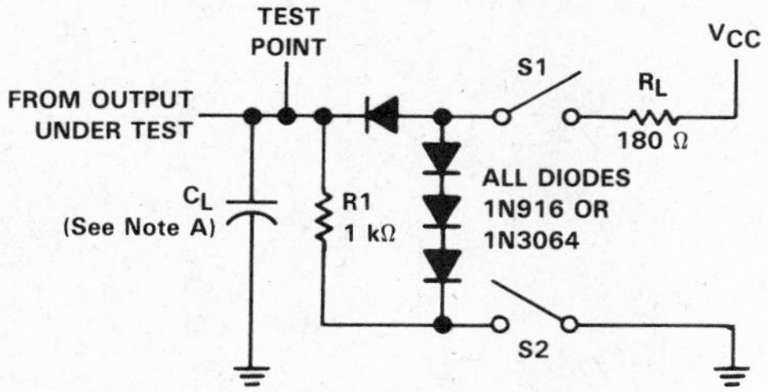
TEST POINT
FROM OUTPUT UNDER TEST
V_{CC}
S1
R_L
180 Ω
C_L (See Note A)
R1 1 kΩ
ALL DIODES 1N916 OR 1N3064
S2

LOAD CIRCUIT

SWITCH POSITION TABLE

TEST	S1	S2
t_{PLH}	Closed	Closed
t_{PHL}	Closed	Closed
t_{PZH}	Open	Closed
t_{PZL}	Closed	Open
t_{PHZ}	Closed	Closed
t_{PLZ}	Closed	Closed

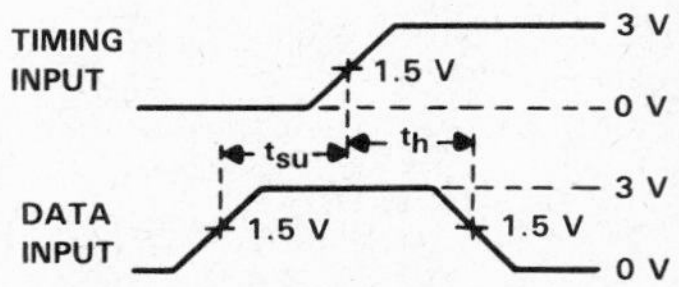
TIMING INPUT
DATA INPUT
1.5 V
3 V
0 V
t_{su}
t_h

VOLTAGE WAVEFORMS
SETUP AND HOLD TIMES

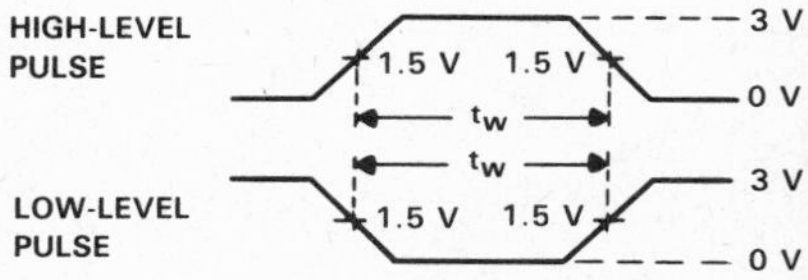
HIGH-LEVEL PULSE
LOW-LEVEL PULSE
1.5 V
3 V
0 V
t_w

VOLTAGE WAVEFORMS
PULSE DURATIONS

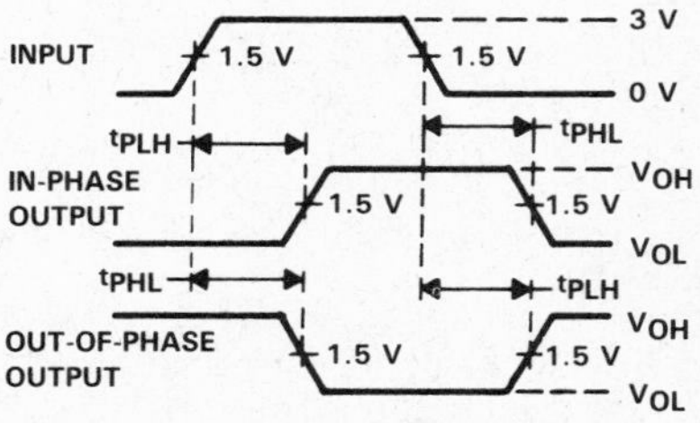
INPUT
IN-PHASE OUTPUT
OUT-OF-PHASE OUTPUT
1.5 V
3 V
0 V
t_{PLH}
t_{PHL}
V_{OH}
V_{OL}

VOLTAGE WAVEFORMS
PROPAGATION DELAY TIMES

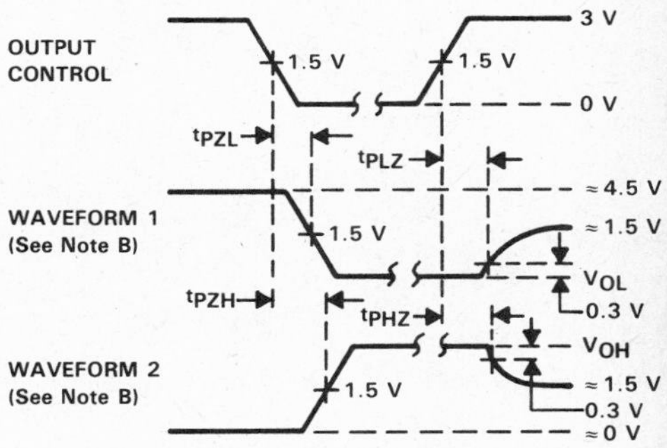
OUTPUT CONTROL
WAVEFORM 1 (See Note B)
WAVEFORM 2 (See Note B)
3 V
0 V
1.5 V
t_{PZL}
t_{PLZ}
t_{PZH}
t_{PHZ}
≈ 4.5 V
≈ 1.5 V
V_{OL}
0.3 V
V_{OH}
≈ 0 V

VOLTAGE WAVEFORMS
ENABLE AND DISABLE TIMES, THREE-STATE OUTPUTS

NOTES: A. C_L includes probe and jig capacitance.

B. Waveform 1 is for an output with internal conditions such that the output is low except when disabled by the output control. Waveform 2 is for an output with internal conditions such that the output is high except when disabled by the output control.

C. All input pulses are supplied by generators having the following characteristics: PRR ≤ 10 MHz, Z_O = 50 Ω, t_r ≤ 2.5 ns, t_f ≤ 2.5 ns.

FIGURE 1

D2834, SEPTEMBER 1984—REVISED SEPTEMBER 1985

- **16-Bit by 16-Bit Parallel Multiplication/Accumulation**
- **35-Bit-Wide Accumulator**
- **Inputs are TTL-Voltage Compatible**
- **Outputs Capable of Driving up to 10 LSTTL Loads**
- **Single 5-V Power Supply**
- **Low Power Dissipation . . . 150 mW Typical**
- **Pin-for-Pin Compatible with TRW TDC1010J (DIP only) and AM29510 (DIP only)**
- **High-Speed Twin-Well CMOS Process**
- **Package Options Include Ceramic and Plastic Chip Carriers and DIPs**
- **Dependable Texas Instruments Quality and Reliability**

JD OR N DUAL-IN-LINE PACKAGE

(TOP VIEW)

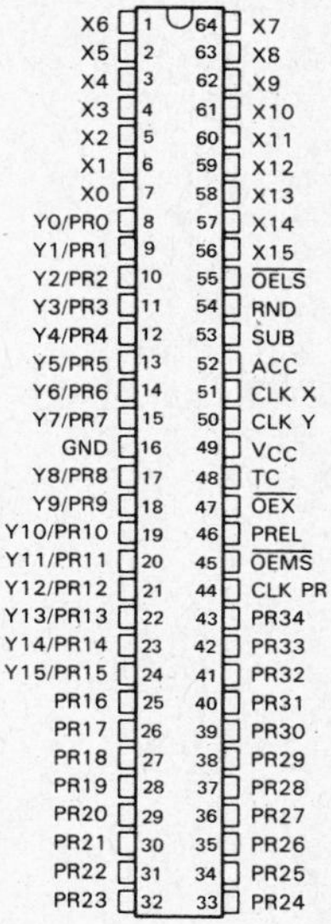
X6 1 64 X7
X5 2 63 X8
X4 3 62 X9
X3 4 61 X10
X2 5 60 X11
X1 6 59 X12
X0 7 58 X13
Y0/PR0 8 57 X14
Y1/PR1 9 56 X15
Y2/PR2 10 55 OELS
Y3/PR3 11 54 RND
Y4/PR4 12 53 SUB
Y5/PR5 13 52 ACC
Y6/PR6 14 51 CLK X
Y7/PR7 15 50 CLK Y
GND 16 49 VCC
Y8/PR8 17 48 TC
Y9/PR9 18 47 OEX
Y10/PR10 19 46 PREL
Y11/PR11 20 45 OEMS
Y12/PR12 21 44 CLK PR
Y13/PR13 22 43 PR34
Y14/PR14 23 42 PR33
Y15/PR15 24 41 PR32
PR16 25 40 PR31
PR17 26 39 PR30
PR18 27 38 PR29
PR19 28 37 PR28
PR20 29 36 PR27
PR21 30 35 PR26
PR22 31 34 PR25
PR23 32 33 PR24

description

The THCT1010 is a TTL-voltage-compatible, low-power, high-speed 16-bit by 16-bit multiplier/accumulator for digital signal processing, digital filters, fast Fourier transformations, array processing, and microprocessor throughput enhancement. These devices are pin-for-pin equivalent to the TRW TDC1010J but dissipate 20 times less power. The lower power dissipation causes the differences between junction and ambient temperatures to be minimized and, therefore, eliminates the heat-sink requirements and increases reliability. High speed is achieved by using a modified Booth algorithm, a feed-forward carry circuit, and a conditional sum adder that enhances the final adder stage of the multiplier.

The THCT1010 inputs consist of three registers, a 16-bit X input, a 16-bit Y input, and an input control register. The 35-bit output product register consists of a 16-bit most-significant-product (MSP) bus, a 16-bit least-significant-product (LSP) bus that is shared with the 16-bit Y input bus, and a 3-bit extended-product (XTP) bus (PR32 through PR34); see the functional block diagram. The input registers are

FK OR FN CHIP-CARRIER PACKAGE

(TOP VIEW)

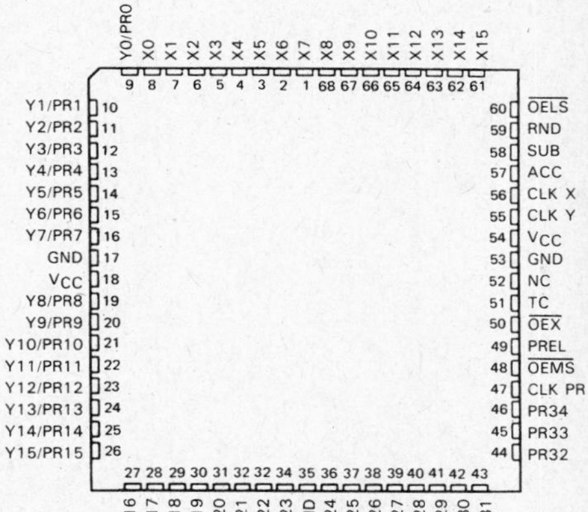
Y0/PR0 X0 X1 X2 X3 X4 X5 X6 X7 X8 X9 X10 X11 X12 X13 X14 X15
9 8 7 6 5 4 3 2 1 68 67 66 65 64 63 62 61
Y1/PR1 10
Y2/PR2 11
Y3/PR3 12
Y4/PR4 13
Y5/PR5 14
Y6/PR6 15
Y7/PR7 16
GND 17
VCC 18
Y8/PR8 19
Y9/PR9 20
Y10/PR10 21
Y11/PR11 22
Y12/PR12 23
Y13/PR13 24
Y14/PR14 25
Y15/PR15 26
60 OELS
59 RND
58 SUB
57 ACC
56 CLK X
55 CLK Y
54 VCC
53 GND
52 NC
51 TC
50 OEX
49 PREL
48 OEMS
47 CLK PR
46 PR34
45 PR33
44 PR32
27 28 29 30 31 32 32 34 35 36 37 38 39 40 41 42 43
PR16 PR17 PR18 PR19 PR20 PR21 PR22 PR23 GND PR24 PR25 PR26 PR27 PR28 PR29 PR30 PR31

NC—No internal connection

Caution. These devices have limited built-in gate protection. The leads should be shorted together or the device placed in conductive foam during storage or handling to prevent electrostatic damage to the MOS gates.

independently controlled by CLK X and CLK Y, and the product registers are D-type positive-edge-triggered flip-flops. Separate three-state output enables are provided for each output product register. These, in combination with the independent input clocks, allow operation on a microprocessor bus.

The THCT1010 has a round control (RND) that rounds the product to the 19 most significant bits. The preload control (PREL) is used in conjunction with the output enables to initialize the contents of the output registers. The THCT1010 will perform multiplication and addition, multiplication and subtraction, or straight multiplication depending upon the states of the accumulate control (ACC) and subtractor control (SUB). The TC control provides the capability of formatting the input data to be either two's complement or unsigned magnitude.

The THCT1010-160M is characterized for operation over the full military temperature range of −55°C to 125°C. The THCT1010-140E is characterized for operation from −40°C to 85°C. The THCT1010-100 is characterized for operation from 0°C to 70°C.

PIN NO.	PIN NAME	DESCRIPTION
56–64, 1–7	X15 thru X0	X data inputs, X15 is the most-significant bit. The data is loaded into the X register on the rising edge of CLKX.
8–15, 17–24	Y0/PR0 thru Y15/PR15	I/O ports for least significant product (LSP) bits of output product register, input ports for Y data. Y0/PR0 is the least significant bit. The mode is controlled by the PREL and $\overline{\text{OEMS}}$ pins.
25–43	PR16 thru PR34	I/O ports for output product register bits. PR16 through PR31 are the most-significant product (MSP) bits. PR32 through PR34 are the extended product (XTP) bits. The mode is controlled by PREL, $\overline{\text{OELS}}$, $\overline{\text{OEX}}$.
44	CLK PR	Product clock input. On the low-to-high transition, latches the LSP, MSP, and XTP into the output product register.
45	OEMS	Active-low output enable for MSP output product register. When high, causes the PR31 through PR16 outputs to be in the high-impedance state.
46	PREL	Preload control. When high, the output product register's outputs are disabled. When an output enable ($\overline{\text{OELS}}$, $\overline{\text{OEMS}}$, $\overline{\text{OEX}}$) is high, preload data can be entered into the output product register from the PR I/O lines on the rising edge of CLK PR.
47	$\overline{\text{OEX}}$	Active-low output enable for XTP output product register. When high, causes the PR32 through PR34 outputs to be in the high-impedance state.
48	TC	Two's complement control. When TC is high, the input data is in two's complement format. When TC is low, the input data is in unsigned magnitude format. The TC signal is loaded into the control register on the rising edge of CLK X or CLK Y.
50	CLK Y	Y clock input. On the low-to-high transition, clocks data in from the Y inputs.
51	CLK X	X clock input. On the low-to-high transition, clocks data in from the X inputs.
52	ACC	Accumulator control. When ACC is high and SUB is low, the content of the output product register is added to the next product generated. The sum is then placed in the output product register on the rising edge of CLK PR. When ACC is low, the product is stored directly into the output register on the rising edge of CLK PR. The ACC signal is loaded into the control register at the rising edge of CLK X or CLK Y.
53	SUB	Subtraction control. When SUB and ACC are high, the content of the output product register is subtracted from the next product generated. The result is then placed in the output product register on the rising edge of CLK PR. When SUB is low and ACC is high, the addition operation is performed instead of subtraction. When ACC is low, SUB is a "Don't Care". The SUB signal is loaded into the control register on the rising edge of CLK X or CLK Y.
54	RND	Round control. When high, causes the product of the X and Y inputs to be rounded to the 19 most significant bits by adding a 1 to the MSB of the LSP. The RND signal is loaded into the control register on the rising edge of CLK X or CLK Y.
55	$\overline{\text{OELS}}$	Active-low output enable for LSP output product register. When high, causes the PR0 through PR15 outputs to be in the high-impedance state.

Pin numbers shown are for the JD and N packages.

PRELOAD FUNCTION TABLE

PREL	$\overline{OEX}$	$\overline{OEMS}$	$\overline{OELS}$	XTP	MSP	LSP
L	L	L	L	(PR32–PR34)	(PR16–PR31)	(PR0–PR15)
L	L	L	H	(PR32–PR34)	(PR16–PR31)	Z
L	L	H	L	(PR32–PR34)	Z	(PR0–PR15)
L	L	H	H	(PR32–PR34)	Z	Z
L	H	L	L	Z	(PR16–PR31)	(PR0–PR15)
L	H	L	H	Z	(PR16–PR31)	Z
L	H	H	L	Z	Z	(PR0–PR15)
L	H	H	H	Z	Z	Z
H	L	L	L	Z	Z	Z
H	L	L	H	Z	Z	PL
H	L	H	L	Z	PL	Z
H	L	H	H	Z	PL	PL
H	H	L	L	PL	Z	Z
H	H	L	H	PL	Z	PL
H	H	H	L	PL	PL	Z
H	H	H	H	PL	PL	PL

PL = Output buffers at high impedance or output disabled. Preload data supplied externally at output pins will be loaded into the output register on the rising edge of CLK PR.

logic symbol

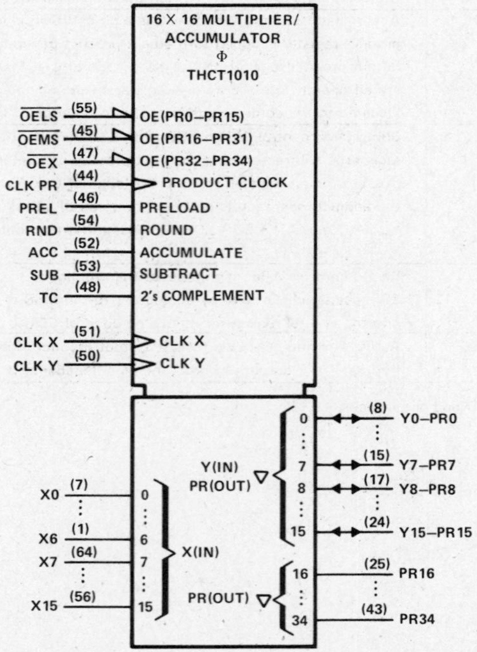
16 X 16 MULTIPLIER/
ACCUMULATOR
Φ
THCT1010
OELS (55) OE(PR0–PR15)
OEMS (45) OE(PR16–PR31)
OEX (47) OE(PR32–PR34)
CLK PR (44) PRODUCT CLOCK
PREL (46) PRELOAD
RND (54) ROUND
ACC (52) ACCUMULATE
SUB (53) SUBTRACT
TC (48) 2's COMPLEMENT
CLK X (51) CLK X
CLK Y (50) CLK Y
X0 (7) 0
X6 (1) 6
X7 (64) 7
X15 (56) 15
X(IN)
Y(IN)
PR(OUT)
0 (8) Y0–PR0
7 (15) Y7–PR7
8 (17) Y8–PR8
15 (24) Y15–PR15
PR(OUT)
16 (25) PR16
34 (43) PR34

Pin numbers shown are for the JD and N packages.

TEXAS INSTRUMENTS
POST OFFICE BOX 225012 • DALLAS, TEXAS 75265

logic diagram (positive logic)

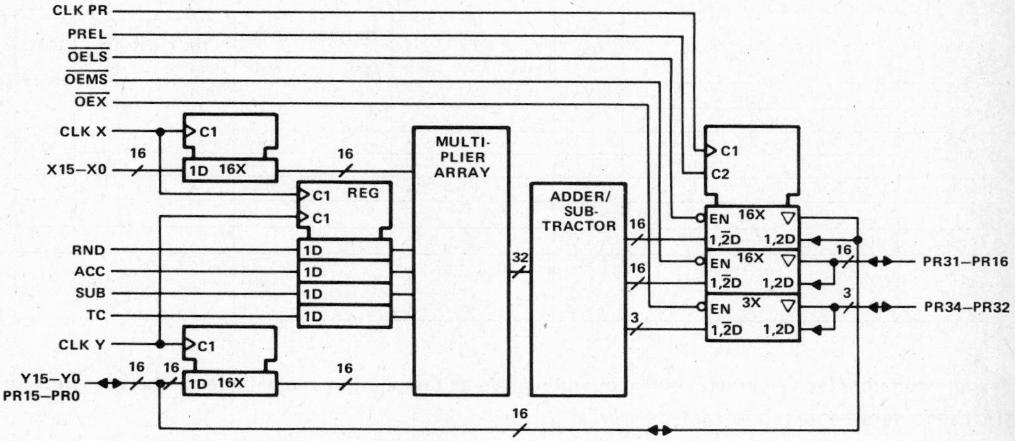
CLK PR
PREL
OELS
OEMS
OEX
CLK X
X15–X0
RND
ACC
SUB
TC
CLK Y
Y15–Y0
PR15–PR0
C1
1D 16X
C1 REG
1D
MULTI-
PLIER
ARRAY
ADDER/
SUB-
TRACTOR
32
16
3
C2
EN 16X
1,2D
EN 3X
PR31–PR16
PR34–PR32

Pin numbers shown are for the JD and N packages.

absolute maximum ratings over operating free-air temperature range†

Supply voltage range, V_{CC}	−0.5 V to 7 V
Input diode current, I_{IK} ($V_I < 0$ or $V_I > V_{CC}$)	±20 mA
Output diode current, I_{OK} ($V_O < 0$ or $V_O > V_{CC}$)	±20 mA
Continuous output current, I_O ($V_O = 0$ to V_{CC})	±25 mA
Continuous current through V_{CC} or GND pins	±50 mA
Lead temperature 1,6 mm (1/16 inch) from case for 60 seconds	300°C
Storage temperature range	−65°C to 150°C

†Stresses beyond those listed under "absolute maximum ratings" may cause permanent damage to the device. These are stress ratings only and functional operation of the device at these or any other conditions beyond those indicated under "recommended operating conditions" is not implied. Exposure to absolute-maximum-rated conditions for extended periods may affect device reliability.

recommended operating conditions

			THCT1010-160M			THCT1010-140E			THCT1010-100			UNIT
			MIN	NOM	MAX	MIN	NOM	MAX	MIN	NOM	MAX	
V_{CC}	Supply voltage		4.5	5	5.5	4.5	5	5.5	4.5	5	5.5	V
V_{IH}	High-level input voltage	V_{CC} = 4.5 V to 5.5 V	2			2			2			V
V_{IL}	Low-level input voltage	V_{CC} = 4.5 V to 5.5 V	0		0.8	0		0.8	0		0.8	V
V_I	Input voltage		0		V_{CC}	0		V_{CC}	0		V_{CC}	V
V_O	Output voltage		0		V_{CC}	0		V_{CC}	0		V_{CC}	V
t_t	Input transition (rise and fall) times		0		500	0		500	0		500	ns
T_A	Operating free-air temperature		−55		125	−40		85	0		70	°C

2

LSI Devices

electrical characteristics over recommended operating free-air temperature range (unless otherwise noted)

PARAMETER	TEST CONDITIONS	V_{CC}	T_A = 25°C MIN	T_A = 25°C TYP	T_A = 25°C MAX	THCT1010-160M MIN	THCT1010-160M MAX	THCT1010-140E THCT1010-100 MIN	THCT1010-140E THCT1010-100 MAX	UNIT
V_{OH}	$V_I = V_{IH}$ or V_{IL}, $I_{OH} = -20\ \mu A$	4.5 V	4.4			4.4		4.4		V
	$V_I = V_{IH}$ or V_{IL}, $I_{OH} = -4$ mA	4.5 V	3.86			3.7		3.76		
V_{OL}	$V_I = V_{IH}$ or V_{IL}, $I_{OL} = 20\ \mu A$	4.5 V			0.1		0.1		0.1	V
	$V_I = V_{IH}$ or V_{IL}, $I_{OL} = 4$ mA	4.5 V			0.32		0.4		0.37	
I_I	$V_I = 0$ to V_{CC}	5.5 V		±5	±100		±1000		±1000	nA
I_{OZ}	$V_O = V_{CC}$ or 0, $V_I = V_{IH}$ or V_{IL}	5.5 V		±0.01	±0.5		±10		±5	µA
I_{CC}†	$V_I = V_{CC}$ or 0, $I_O = 0$	5.5 V			0.75		2		1	mA
C_i		4.5 V to 5.5 V		3	10		10		10	pF

†See Figure 4.

timing requirements over recommended operating free-air temperature range (unless otherwise noted)

THCT1010-160M, THCT1010-140E

		V_{CC}	T_A = 25°C MIN	T_A = 25°C MAX	THCT1010-160M MIN	THCT1010-160M MAX	THCT1010-140E MIN	THCT1010-140E MAX	UNIT
t_w	Pulse duration, clocks X and Y high or low	4.5 V	20		30		25		ns
		5.5 V	20		30		25		
t_{su}	Setup time, X input before CLK X↑ or Y input before CLK Y↑	4.5 V	10		30		25		ns
		5.5 V	10		30		25		
t_h	Hold time, X input after CLK X↑	4.5 V	6		12		10		ns
		5.5 V	6		12		10		
t_h	Hold time, Y input after CLK Y↑ or preload data after CLK PR↑	4.5 V	1		7		5		ns
		5.5 V	1		7		5		

THCT1010-100

			V_{CC}	T_A = 25°C MIN	T_A = 25°C MAX	THCT1010-100 MIN	THCT1010-100 MAX	UNIT
t_w	Pulse duration, clocks X and Y high or low		4.75 V	20		25		ns
t_{su}	Setup time, X input before CLK X↑ or Y input before CLK Y↑		4.75 V	10		20		ns
t_h	Hold time	X input after CLK X↑	4.75 V	6		10		ns
		Y input after CLK Y↑ or preload data after CLK PR↑	4.75 V	1		5		ns

switching characteristics over recommended operating free-air temperature range (unless otherwise noted), C_L = 50 pF (see Figure 3)

THCT1010-160M, THCT1010-140E

PARAMETER		V_{CC}	T_A = 25°C MIN	T_A = 25°C TYP†	T_A = 25°C MAX	THCT1010-160M MIN	THCT1010-160M MAX	THCT1010-140E MIN	THCT1010-140E MAX	UNIT
t_{pd}	Propagation delay time	4.5 V		45			65		55	ns
		5.5 V					60		50	
t_{en}	Enable time	4.5 V		35			65		45	ns
		5.5 V					60		40	
t_{dis}	Disable time	4.5 V		35			60		45	ns
		5.5 V					55		40	
t_{macc}	Multiply/accumulate time	4.5 V		100			160		140	ns
		5.5 V					140		120	

C_{pd}	Power dissipation capacitance	No load, T_A = 25°C	750 pF typ

THCT1010-100

PARAMETER		V_{CC}	T_A = 25°C MIN	T_A = 25°C TYP†	T_A = 25°C MAX	THCT1010-100 MIN	THCT1010-100 MAX	UNIT
t_{pd}	Propagation delay time	4.75 V		35			45	ns
t_{en}	Enable time	4.75 V		30			40	ns
t_{dis}	Disable time	4.75 V		30			40	ns
t_{macc}	Multiply/accumulate time	4.75 V		90			100	ns

†Typical values are at V_{CC} = 5 V.

PARAMETER MEASUREMENT INFORMATION

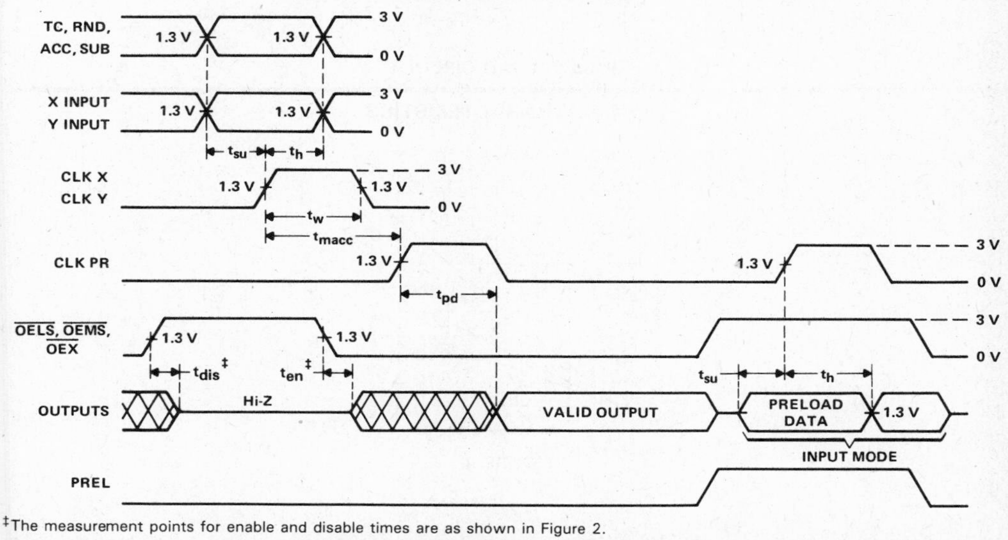
TC, RND, ACC, SUB
X INPUT
Y INPUT
CLK X
CLK Y
CLK PR
OELS, OEMS, OEX
OUTPUTS
PREL
1.3 V
3 V
0 V
tsu
th
tw
tmacc
tpd
tdis‡
ten‡
Hi-Z
VALID OUTPUT
PRELOAD DATA
INPUT MODE

‡The measurement points for enable and disable times are as shown in Figure 2.

FIGURE 1. VOLTAGE WAVEFORMS

PARAMETER MEASUREMENT INFORMATION

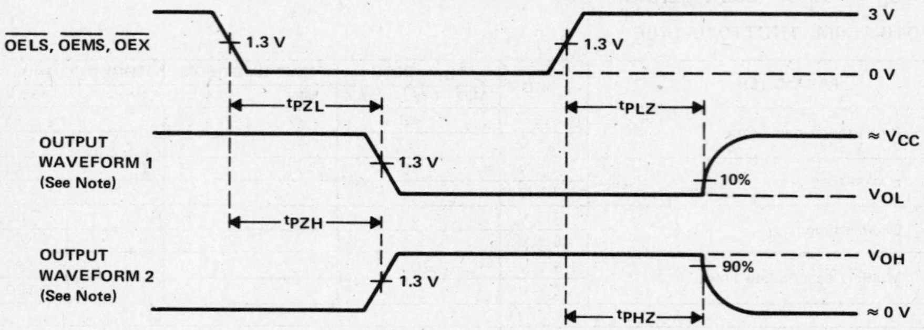
OELS, OEMS, OEX
1.3 V
1.3 V
3 V
0 V
tPZL
tPLZ
OUTPUT
WAVEFORM 1
(See Note)
1.3 V
≈ VCC
10%
VOL
tPZH
OUTPUT
WAVEFORM 2
(See Note)
1.3 V
90%
VOH
≈ 0 V
tPHZ

NOTE: Waveform 1 is for an output with internal conditions such that the output is low except when disabled by the output control. Waveform 2 is for an output with internal conditons such that the output is high except when disabled by the output control.

FIGURE 2. DETAILED VOLTAGE WAVEFORMS FOR ENABLE AND DISABLE TIMES

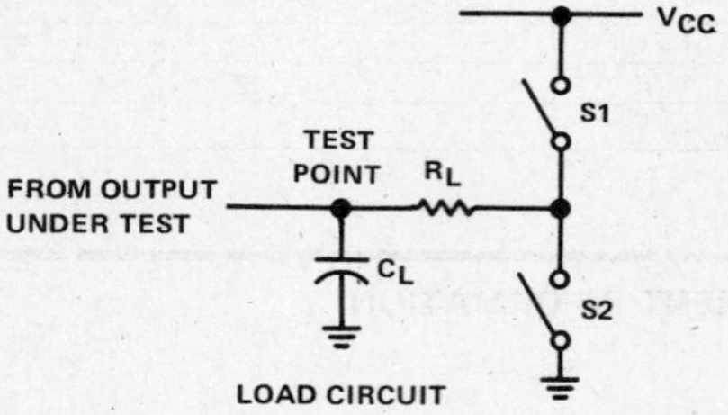
VCC
S1
TEST
POINT
RL
FROM OUTPUT
UNDER TEST
CL
S2
LOAD CIRCUIT

PARAMETER		R_L	C_L†	S_1	S_2
t_{en}	t_{PZH}	1 kΩ	50 pF	OPEN	CLOSED
	t_{PZL}			CLOSED	OPEN
t_{dis}	t_{PHZ}	1 kΩ	50 pF	OPEN	CLOSED
	t_{PLZ}			CLOSED	OPEN
t_{pd} or t_t		—	50 pF	OPEN	OPEN

†C_L includes probe and test fixture capacitance

FIGURE 3. LOAD CIRCUITS

TYPICAL CHARACTERISTICS

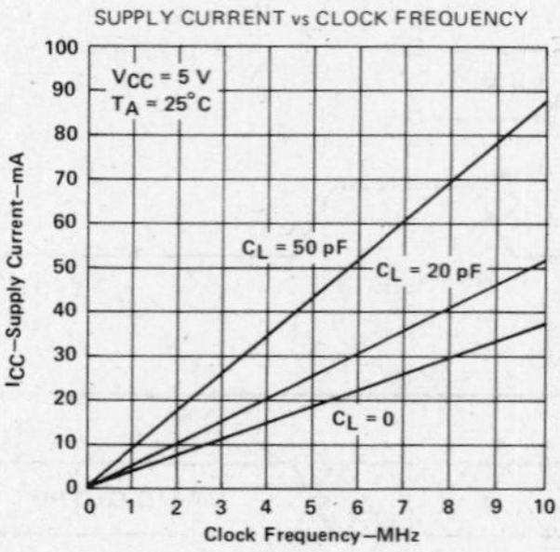
SUPPLY CURRENT vs CLOCK FREQUENCY
VCC = 5 V
TA = 25°C
ICC–Supply Current–mA
CL = 50 pF
CL = 20 pF
CL = 0
Clock Frequency–MHz
0
10
20
30
40
50
60
70
80
90
100
0 1 2 3 4 5 6 7 8 9 10

FIGURE 4

TEXAS INSTRUMENTS
POST OFFICE BOX 225012 • DALLAS, TEXAS 75265

THERMAL INFORMATION

THERMAL RESISTANCE

PACKAGE	PINS	JUNCTION-TO-CASE THERMAL RESISTANCE, $R_{\theta JC}$ (°C/W)	JUNCTION-TO-FREE-AIR THERMAL RESISTANCE, $R_{\theta JA}$ (°C/W)
FK	68	8	36
FN	68		
JD	64	9	32
N	64		

ORDERING INSTRUCTIONS

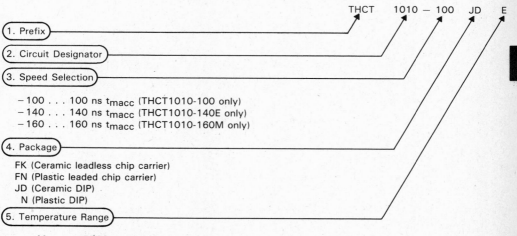

THCT 1010 — 100 JD E

1. Prefix
2. Circuit Designator
3. Speed Selection

   −100 . . . 100 ns t_{macc} (THCT1010-100 only)
   −140 . . . 140 ns t_{macc} (THCT1010-140E only)
   −160 . . . 160 ns t_{macc} (THCT1010-160M only)

4. Package

   FK (Ceramic leadless chip carrier)
   FN (Plastic leaded chip carrier)
   JD (Ceramic DIP)
   N (Plastic DIP)

5. Temperature Range

   M . . . −55°C to 125°C
   E . . . −40°C to 85°C
   (Blank) . . . 0°C to 70°C

THCT2000M, THCT2000E DIRECTION DISCRIMINATORS

D2889, NOVEMBER 1985

- Inputs are TTL- and CMOS-Voltage Compatible
- Interfaces Mechanical Devices to Data Bus
- Identifies and Measures Forward or Backward Rotation or Direction
- Measures Pulse Duration and Frequency
- Cascadable 16-Bit Up/Down Counter
- 8-Bit Parallel 3-State Bus with Each Output Capable of Driving up to 15 LSTTL Loads
- Dependable Texas Instruments Quality and Reliability

THCT2000M . . . JD PACKAGE
THCT2000E . . . JD OR N PACKAGE
(TOP VIEW)

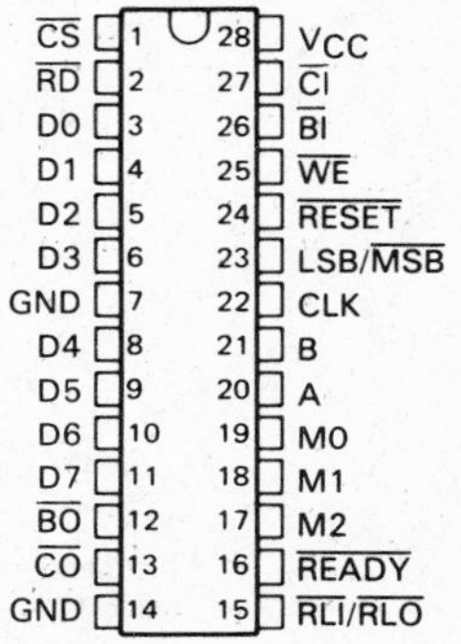
CS 1
RD 2
D0 3
D1 4
D2 5
D3 6
GND 7
D4 8
D5 9
D6 10
D7 11
BO 12
CO 13
GND 14
28 VCC
27 CI
26 BI
25 WE
24 RESET
23 LSB/MSB
22 CLK
21 B
20 A
19 M0
18 M1
17 M2
16 READY
15 RLI/RLO

THCT2000M . . . FK PACKAGE
THCT2000E . . . FN PACKAGE
(TOP VIEW)

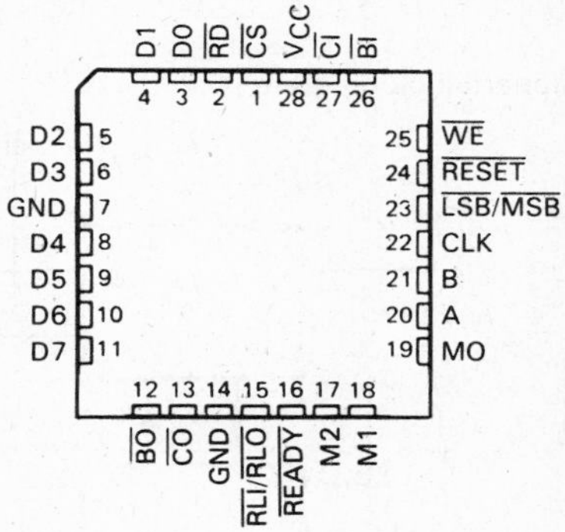
D1 D0 RD CS VCC CI BI
4 3 2 1 28 27 26
D2 5
D3 6
GND 7
D4 8
D5 9
D6 10
D7 11
25 WE
24 RESET
23 LSB/MSB
22 CLK
21 B
20 A
19 MO
12 13 14 15 16 17 18
BO CO GND RLI/RLO READY M2 M1

description

The THCT2000 direction discriminator can determine the direction and displacement of a mechanical device based on input signals from two transducers in quadrature. It can also measure a pulse duration using a known clock rate, or a frequency over a known time interval. It includes a 16-bit counter, which can be used separately. Several of these devices may be cascaded to provide accuracy greater than 16-bits.

The device may be used in many diverse applications, and is specifically designed for use in many types of microprocessor-based systems. Some of the possibilities include motor controls, robotics, tracker balls (mice), lathe or tooling machines, automobiles, and conveyer belts or other transport mechanisms.

The THCT2000M is characterized for operation over the full military temperature range of −55°C to 125°C. The THCT2000E is characterized for operation from −40°C to 85°C.

logic symbol†

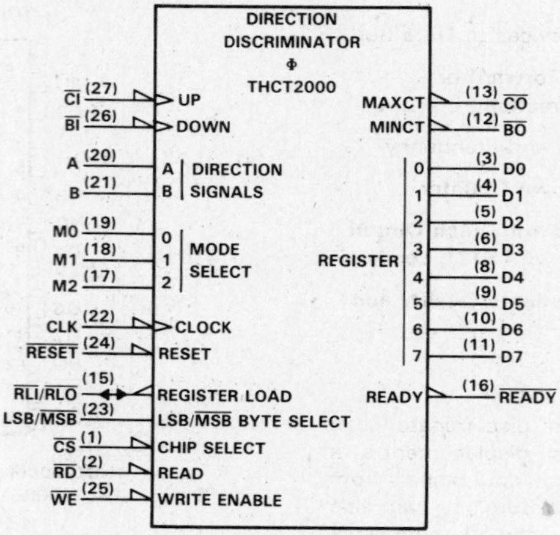
DIRECTION
DISCRIMINATOR
Φ
THCT2000
CI (27) UP
BI (26) DOWN
A (20) A
B (21) B
DIRECTION
SIGNALS
M0 (19) 0
M1 (18) 1
M2 (17) 2
MODE
SELECT
CLK (22) CLOCK
RESET (24) RESET
RLI/RLO (15) REGISTER LOAD
LSB/MSB (23) LSB/MSB BYTE SELECT
CS (1) CHIP SELECT
RD (2) READ
WE (25) WRITE ENABLE
MAXCT (13) CO
MINCT (12) BO
REGISTER
0 (3) D0
1 (4) D1
2 (5) D2
3 (6) D3
4 (8) D4
5 (9) D5
6 (10) D6
7 (11) D7
READY (16) READY

† This symbol is in accordance with ANSI/IEEE Std 91-1984.

functional block diagram

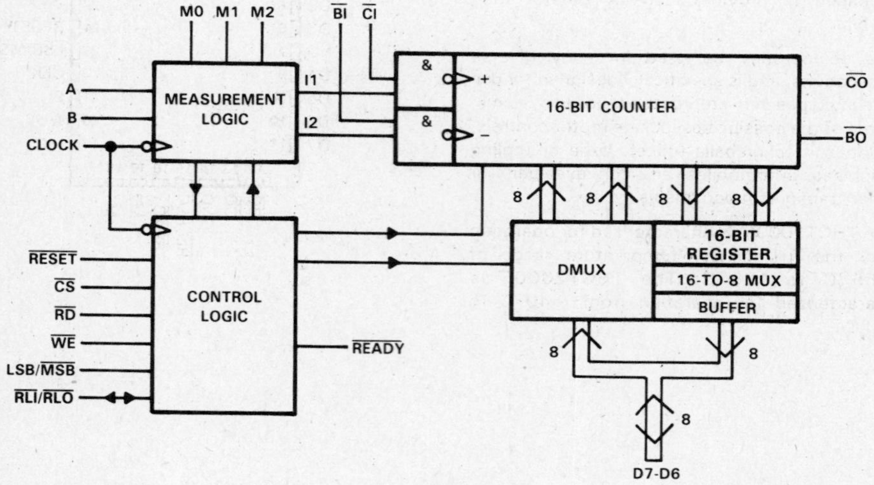
M0 M1 M2
BI CI
A
B
CLOCK
MEASUREMENT
LOGIC
I1
I2
&
&
+
−
16-BIT COUNTER
CO
BO
8
8
8
8
RESET
CS
RD
WE
LSB/MSB
RLI/RLO
CONTROL
LOGIC
READY
DMUX
16-BIT
REGISTER
16-TO-8 MUX
BUFFER
8
8
8
D7-D6

PIN NAME	PIN NUMBER	DESCRIPTION
A, B	20, 21	Signal measurement inputs.
$\overline{BI}$	26	Cascade input for counting down. In mode 0, $\overline{BI}$ is used as the clock input for counting down. Triggering occurs on the high-to-low transition.
$\overline{BO}$	12	Counter output underflow signal. Active (low) for a duration equal to the low level of the input clock.
$\overline{CI}$	27	Cascade input for counting up. In mode 0, $\overline{CI}$ is used as the clock input for counting up. Triggering occurs on the high-to-low transition.
CLK	22	Clock input. Used for internal synchronization and control timing.
$\overline{CO}$	13	Counter output overflow signal. Active (low) for a duration equal to the low level of the input clock.
$\overline{CS}$	1	Chip select input. This active-low input is used to enable read and write functions. For additional details, see read and write timing diagrams.
D0-D7	3, 4, 5, 6, 8, 9, 10, 11	Counter load inputs/register output data lines.
GND	7, 14	Pins 7 and 14 are both internally connected to the ground rail of the integrated circuit but both should be connected to the system ground for proper operation.
LSB/$\overline{MSB}$	23	Byte select input. During read operations, a high level selects the least significant byte, while a low level selects the most significant byte. For write operations, this input directs the data on the bus into the least significant or most significant byte position of the counter. See write timing diagrams for additional details.
M0, M1, M2	19, 18, 17	Mode select inputs.
$\overline{RD}$	2	Read input. When active (low) in conjunction with $\overline{CS}$ low, the data stored in the output register will be present on the data bus as selected by the LSB/$\overline{MSB}$ input. See read timing diagrams for additional details.
$\overline{READY}$	16	Ready output. When active (low), this output indicates to the processor that it may complete the read or write operation. $\overline{READY}$ is synchronous with the negative-going edge of CLK. This output requires a pullup resistor (1 kΩ nominal).
$\overline{RESET}$	24	Counter and control logic reset. When active (low), the counter is asynchronously reset to zero while the control logic is asynchronously initialized to the proper state as determined by the mode control inputs. The output register is not affected by $\overline{RESET}$.
$\overline{RLI}/\overline{RLO}$	15	Register load input/register load output (open drain). This pin can be used as an input to directly load the output register, or it can be used as an output to detect whenever the output register has been loaded. When used as an output, a pullup resistor (1 kΩ nominal) is required. See read timing diagrams for additional details.
V_{CC}	28	Power supply voltage.
$\overline{WE}$	25	Write enable input. When active (low) in conjunction with $\overline{CS}$ low, the data present on D0-D7 will be asynchronously loaded into the counter as selected by LSB/$\overline{MSB}$. See write timing diagrams for additional details.

D2905, OCTOBER 1985

- Inputs are TTL- and CMOS-Voltage Compatible
- Controls Operation of 64K and 256K Dynamic RAMs
- Creates Static RAM Appearance
- One Package Contains Address Multiplexer, Refresh Control, and Timing Control
- Directly Addresses and Drives Up to 2 Megabytes of Memory Without External Drivers
- Operates from Microprocessor Clock
  - No Crystals, Delay Lines, or RC Networks
  - Eliminates Arbitration Delays
- Refresh May Be Internally or Externally Initiated
- Versatile
  - Strap-Selected Refresh Rate
  - Synchronous, Predictable Refresh
  - Selection of Distributed, Transparent, and Cycle-Steal Refresh Modes
  - Interfaces Easily to Popular Microprocessors
  - Asynchronous $\overline{\text{RESET}}$ Function Provided in FK and FN Packages
- High-Performance Si-Gate CMOS Technology
- Strap-Selected Wait State Generation for Microprocessor/Memory Speed Matching
- Ability to Synchronize or Interleave Controller with the Microprocessor System (Including Multiple Controllers)
- 3-State Outputs Allow Multiport Memory Configuration
- Performance Range:
  125 ns ALE low to $\overline{\text{CAS}}$ low
- Compatible with TMS4500A/B and with VTI VL4500A and VL4502
- Available in Plastic and Ceramic Chip Carriers in Addition to Plastic and Ceramic DIPs
- Dependable Texas Instruments Quality and Reliability

THCT4502 . . . JD OR N PACKAGE
(TOP VIEW)

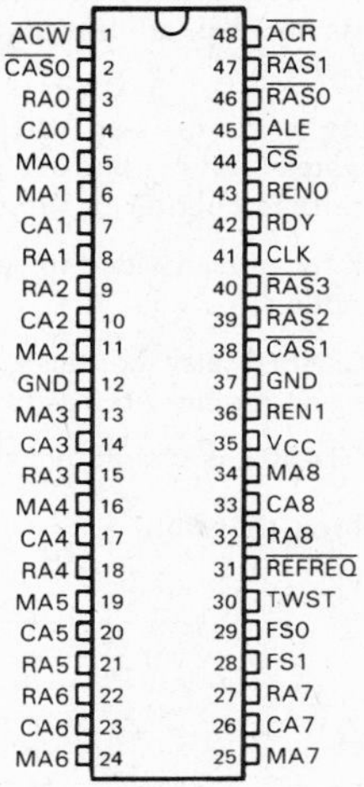
ACW 1
CAS0 2
RA0 3
CA0 4
MA0 5
MA1 6
CA1 7
RA1 8
RA2 9
CA2 10
MA2 11
GND 12
MA3 13
CA3 14
RA3 15
MA4 16
CA4 17
RA4 18
MA5 19
CA5 20
RA5 21
RA6 22
CA6 23
MA6 24
48 ACR
47 RAS1
46 RAS0
45 ALE
44 CS
43 REN0
42 RDY
41 CLK
40 RAS3
39 RAS2
38 CAS1
37 GND
36 REN1
35 VCC
34 MA8
33 CA8
32 RA8
31 REFREQ
30 TWST
29 FS0
28 FS1
27 RA7
26 CA7
25 MA7

THCT4502 . . . FK OR FN PACKAGE
(TOP VIEW)

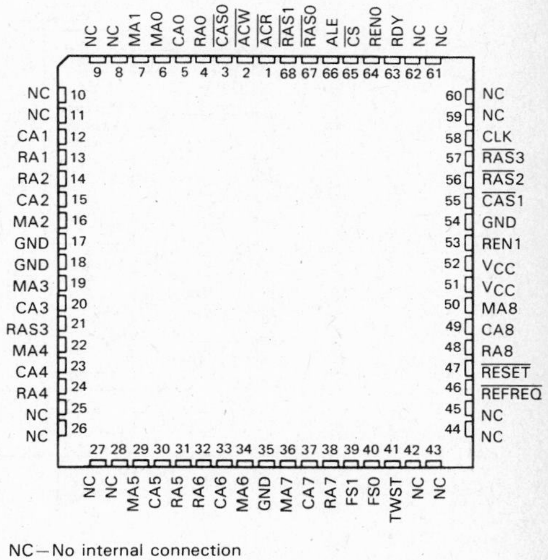
NC 9
NC 8
MA1 7
MA0 6
CA0 5
RA0 4
CAS0 3
ACW 2
ACR 1
RAS1 68
RAS0 67
ALE 66
CS 65
REN0 64
RDY 63
NC 62
NC 61
NC 10
NC 11
CA1 12
RA1 13
RA2 14
CA2 15
MA2 16
GND 17
GND 18
MA3 19
CA3 20
RAS3 21
MA4 22
CA4 23
RA4 24
NC 25
NC 26
60 NC
59 NC
58 CLK
57 RAS3
56 RAS2
55 CAS1
54 GND
53 REN1
52 VCC
51 VCC
50 MA8
49 CA8
48 RA8
47 RESET
46 REFREQ
45 NC
44 NC
NC 27
NC 28
MA5 29
CA5 30
RA5 31
RA6 32
CA6 33
MA6 34
GND 35
MA7 36
CA7 37
RA7 38
FS1 39
FS0 40
TWST 41
NC 42
NC 43

NC—No internal connection

2

LSI Devices

TEXAS INSTRUMENTS
POST OFFICE BOX 225012 • DALLAS, TEXAS 75265

description

The THCT4502 is a monolithic DRAM system controller providing address multiplexing, timing, control and refresh/access arbitration functions to simplify the interface of dynamic RAMs to microprocessor systems.

The controller contains an 18-bit multiplexer that generates the address lines for the memory device from the 18 system address bits and provides the strobe signals required by the memory to decode the address. A 9-bit refresh counter generates up to 512 row addresses required to refresh.

A refresh timer is provided to generate the necessary timing to refresh the dynamic memories and ensure data retention.

The THCT4502 also contains refresh/access arbitration circuitry to resolve conflicts between access requests and memory-refresh cycles.

The THCT4502 is characterized for operation from 0°C to 70°C.

functional block diagram

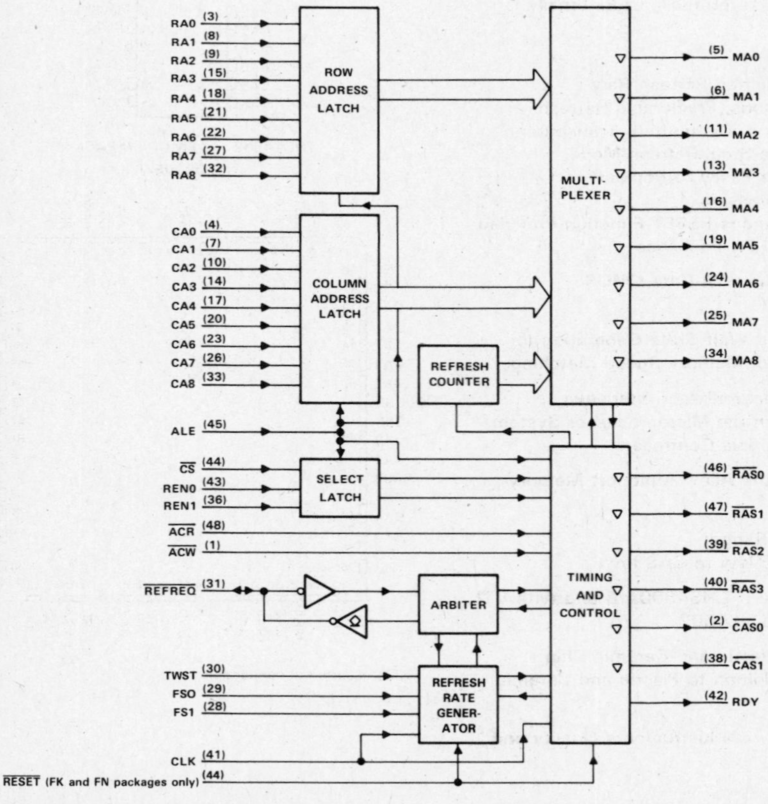
RA0 (3)
RA1 (8)
RA2 (9)
RA3 (15)
RA4 (18)
RA5 (21)
RA6 (22)
RA7 (27)
RA8 (32)
ROW ADDRESS LATCH
CA0 (4)
CA1 (7)
CA2 (10)
CA3 (14)
CA4 (17)
CA5 (20)
CA6 (23)
CA7 (26)
CA8 (33)
COLUMN ADDRESS LATCH
REFRESH COUNTER
MULTI-PLEXER
(5) MA0
(6) MA1
(11) MA2
(13) MA3
(16) MA4
(19) MA5
(24) MA6
(25) MA7
(34) MA8
ALE (45)
CS (44)
REN0 (43)
REN1 (36)
SELECT LATCH
ACR (48)
ACW (1)
REFREQ (31)
ARBITER
TIMING AND CONTROL
(46) RAS0
(47) RAS1
(39) RAS2
(40) RAS3
(2) CAS0
(38) CAS1
(42) RDY
TWST (30)
FS0 (29)
FS1 (28)
REFRESH RATE GENER-ATOR
CLK (41)
RESET (FK and FN packages only) (44)

Pin numbers shown are for JD and N packages.

TEXAS INSTRUMENTS
POST OFFICE BOX 225012 • DALLAS, TEXAS 75265

pin descriptions

RA0-RA8	Input	Row Address — These address inputs are used to generate the row address for the multiplexer.
CA0-CA8	Input	Column Address — These address inputs are used to generate the column address for the multiplexer.
MA0-MA8	Output	Memory Address — These three-state outputs are designed to drive the addresses of the dynamic RAM array.
ALE	Input	Address Latch Enable — This input is used to latch the 18 address inputs, $\overline{\text{CS}}$, REN0, and REN1. This also initiates an access cycle if $\overline{\text{CS}}$ is low. The rising edge (low level to high level) of ALE returns all $\overline{\text{RAS}}$ outputs to the high level.
$\overline{\text{CS}}$	Input	Chip Select — A low on this input enables an access cycle. The trailing edge of ALE latches the chip select input.
REN0, REN1	Inputs	$\overline{\text{RAS}}$ Enable 0 and 1 — These inputs are used to select one of four banks of RAM when $\overline{\text{CS}}$ is low. When REN1 is low, the lower banks are enabled via $\overline{\text{CAS0}}$, $\overline{\text{RAS0}}$, and $\overline{\text{RAS1}}$. When REN1 is high, the higher banks are enabled via $\overline{\text{CAS1}}$, $\overline{\text{RAS2}}$ and $\overline{\text{RAS3}}$. REN0 selects $\overline{\text{RAS0}}$ and $\overline{\text{RAS2}}$ when low, or $\overline{\text{RAS1}}$ and $\overline{\text{RAS3}}$ when high. (see Table 2).
$\overline{\text{ACR}}$, $\overline{\text{ACW}}$	Input	Access Control, Read; Access Control, Write — A low on either of these inputs causes the column address to appear on MA0-MA8 and a low-going pulse from $\overline{\text{CAS}}$. The rising edge of $\overline{\text{ACR}}$ or $\overline{\text{ACW}}$ terminates the cycle by forcing $\overline{\text{RAS}}$ and $\overline{\text{CAS}}$ high. When $\overline{\text{ACR}}$ and $\overline{\text{ACW}}$ are both low, MA0-MA8, $\overline{\text{RAS0}}$, $\overline{\text{RAS1}}$, $\overline{\text{RAS2}}$, $\overline{\text{RAS3}}$, $\overline{\text{CAS0}}$ and $\overline{\text{CAS1}}$ go into a high-impedance (floating) state.
CLK	Input	System Clock — This input provides the master timing to generate refresh cycle timings and refresh rate. Refresh rate is determined by the TWST, FS1, and FS0 inputs.
$\overline{\text{REFREQ}}$	Input	Refresh Request — This input should be driven by an open-collector or open-drain output. On input, a low-going edge initiates a refresh cycle and will cause the internal refresh timer to be reset on the next falling edge of the CLK. As an output, a low-going edge signals an internal refresh request and that the refresh timer will be reset on the next low-going edge of CLK. $\overline{\text{REFREQ}}$ will remain low until the refresh cycle is in progress and the current refresh address is present on MA0-MA8. (Note: $\overline{\text{REFREQ}}$ contains an internal active pullup with a nominal resistance of 10 kΩ, which is disabled when $\overline{\text{REFREQ}}$ is low).
$\overline{\text{RAS0}}$, $\overline{\text{RAS1}}$ $\overline{\text{RAS2}}$, $\overline{\text{RAS3}}$	Output	Row Address Strobe — These three-state outputs are used to latch the row address into the bank of DRAMs selected by REN0 and REN1. On refresh, all $\overline{\text{RAS}}$ signals are active.
$\overline{\text{CAS0}}$, $\overline{\text{CAS1}}$	Output	Column Address Strobe — These three-state outputs are used to latch the column address into the DRAM array.
RDY	Output	Ready — This totem-pole output synchronizes memories that are too slow to guarantee microprocessor access time requirements. This output is also used to inhibit access cycles during refresh when in cycle-steal mode.

pin descriptions (continued)

TWST	Input	Timing/Wait Strap — A high on this input indicates a wait state should be added to each memory cycle. In addition it is used in conjunction with FS0 and FS1 to determine refresh rate and timing or initialize the controller.
FS0, FS1	Inputs	Frequency Select 0; Frequency Select 1 — These are strap inputs to select Mode and Frequency of operation as shown in Table 1.
$\overline{\text{RESET}}$†	Input	$\overline{\text{RESET}}$ — Active-low input to initialize the controller asynchronously. Refresh Address is set to IFF_{16}, internal refresh requests, synchronizer, and frequency divider are cleared. (Note: $\overline{\text{RESET}}$ contains an internal pullup resistor with a nominal resistance of 100 kΩ, which allows this pin to be left open.)

†This function is available only in the FK and FN packages.

TABLE 1. STRAP CONFIGURATION

STRAP INPUT MODES			WAIT STATES FOR MEMORY ACCESS	REFRESH RATE	MINIMUM CLOCK FREQUENCY (MHz)	REFRESH FREQUENCY (kHz)	CLOCK CYCLES FOR EACH REFRESH
TWST	FS1	FS0					
L	L	L†	0	EXTERNAL	–	REFREQ	4
L	L	H	0	EXTERNAL	–	REFREQ	3
L	H	L	0	CLK ÷ 61	3.904	64-95‡	3
L	H	H	0	CLK ÷ 91	5.824	64-88§	4
H	L	L	1	CLK ÷ 61	3.904	64-95‡	3
H	L	H	1	CLK ÷ 91	5.824	64-75‡	4
H	H	L	1	CLK ÷ 106	6.784	64-73‡	4
H	H	H	1	CLK ÷ 121	7.744	64-83¶	4

† This strap configuration resets the Refresh Timer Circuitry.
‡ Upper figure in refresh frequency is the frequency that is produced if the minimum clock frequency of the next select state is used.
§ Refresh frequency if clock frequency is 8 MHz.
¶ Refresh frequency if clock frequency is 10 MHz.

TABLE 2. OUTPUT STROBE SELECTION

CONTROL INPUT		SELECTED OUTPUT					
REN1	REN0	$\overline{\text{RAS0}}$	$\overline{\text{RAS1}}$	$\overline{\text{RAS2}}$	$\overline{\text{RAS3}}$	$\overline{\text{CAS0}}$	$\overline{\text{CAS1}}$
L	L	X				X	
L	H		X			X	
H	L			X			X
H	H				X		X

NOTE: Changing the logic value of REN1 after a low-to-high transition of ALE and before $\overline{\text{ACX}}$ rises causes the other $\overline{\text{CAS}}$ to fall. Both $\overline{\text{CAS}}$ signals remain low until $\overline{\text{ACX}}$ rises.

functional description

The THCT4502 consists of six basic blocks: address and select latches, refresh rate generator, refresh counter, the multiplexer, the arbiter, and the timing and control block.

address and select latches

The address and select latches allow the DRAM controller to be used in systems that multiplex address and data on the same lines without external latches. The row address latches are transparent, meaning that while ALE is high, the output at MA0-MA8 follows the inputs RA0-RA8.

refresh rate generator

The refresh rate generator is a counter that indicates to the arbiter that it is time for a refresh cycle. The counter divides the clock frequency according to the configuration straps as shown in Table 1. The counter is reset when a refresh cycle is requested or when TWST, FS1, and FS0 are low. The configuration straps allow the matching of memories to the system access time. Upon power-up it is necessary to provide a reset signal by driving all three straps to the controller (or $\overline{\text{RESET}}$ for devices in the FK and FN packages only) low. A systems power-on reset ($\overline{\text{RESET}}$) can be used to do this by connecting it to those straps that are desired high during operation. During this reset period, at least four clock cycles should occur.

refresh counter

The refresh counter contains the address of the row to be refreshed. The counter is decremented after each refresh cycle. A low-to-high transition on TWST sets the refresh counter to $1FF_{16}$ (511_{10}).

multiplexer

The multiplexer provides the DRAM array with row, column, and refresh addresses at the proper times. Its inputs are the address latches and the refresh counter. The outputs provide up to 18 multiplexed addresses on nine lines.

arbiter

The arbiter provides two operational cycles: access and refresh. The arbiter resolves conflicts between cycle requests and cycles in execution, and schedules the inhibited cycle when used in cycle-steal mode.

timing and control block

The timing and control block executes the operational cycle at the request of the arbiter. It provides the DRAM array with $\overline{\text{RAS}}$ and $\overline{\text{CAS}}$ signals. It provides the CPU with a RDY signal. It controls the multiplexer during all cycles. It resets the refresh rate generator and decrements the refresh counter during refresh cycles.

absolute maximum ratings over operating free-air temperature range (unless otherwise noted)†

Supply voltage range, V_{CC} (See Note 1)	−1.5 V to 7 V
Input diode current, I_{IK} ($V_I < 0$, $V_I > V_{CC}$)	±20 mA
Output diode current, I_{OK} ($V_O < 0$, $V_O > V_{CC}$)	±20 mA
Continuous output current, I_O (V_O = 0 to V_{CC})	±35 mA
Continuous current through V_{CC} or GND pins	±70 mA
Operating free-air temperature range	0°C to 70°C
Storage temperature range	−65°C to 150°C
Lead temperature 1,6 mm (1/16 inch) from case for 60 seconds: FK or JD package	300°C
Lead temperature 1,6 mm (1/16 inch) from case for 10 seconds: FN or N package	260°C

† Stresses beyond those listed under "Absolute Maximum Ratings" may cause permanent damage to the device. This is stress rating only, and functional operation of the device at these or any other conditions beyond those indicated in the "Recommended Operating Conditions" section of this specification is not implied. Exposure to absolute-maximum-rated conditions for extended periods may affect device reliability.

NOTE 1: Voltage values are with respect to network ground.

recommended operating conditions

		MIN	NOM	MAX	UNIT
V_{CC}	Supply voltage	4.5	5	5.5	V
V_{IH}	High-level input voltage	2		$V_{CC}+0.5$	V
V_{IL}	Low-level input voltage	-0.5[†]		0.8	V
V_O	Output voltage	-0.5		$V_{CC}+0.5$	V
t_t	Input transition (rise and fall) time	0		500	ns
T_A	Operating free-air temperature	0		70	°C

† The algebraic convention, where the more negative (less positive) limit is designated as minimum, is used in this data sheet for logic voltage levels only.

electrical characteristics over recommended operating free-air temperature range (unless otherwise noted)

PARAMETER			TEST CONDITIONS	V_{CC}	$T_A = 25°C$					UNIT
					MIN	TYP	MAX	MIN	MAX	
V_{OH}	High-level output voltage	MA0–MA8, $\overline{\text{RAS0}}$–$\overline{\text{RAS3}}$, $\overline{\text{CAS0}}$–$\overline{\text{CAS1}}$	$I_{OH} = -20\ \mu A$	4.5 V	4.4			4.4		V
			$I_{OH} = -6$ mA	4.5 V	3.86			3.76		
		RDY	$I_{OH} = -20\ \mu A$	4.5 V	4.4			4.4		
			$I_{OH} = -4$ mA	4.5 V	3.86			3.76		
		$\overline{\text{REFREQ}}$	$I_{OH} = -20\ \mu A$	4.5 V	4			3.8		
V_{OL}	Low-level output voltage	RDY, $\overline{\text{REFREQ}}$	$I_{OL} = 20\ \mu A$	4.5 V			0.1		0.1	V
			$I_{OL} = 4$ mA	4.5 V			0.32		0.37	
		MA0–MA8, $\overline{\text{RAS0}}$–$\overline{\text{RAS3}}$, $\overline{\text{CAS0}}$, $\overline{\text{CAS1}}$	$I_{OL} = 20\ \mu A$	4.5 V			0.1		0.1	
			$I_{OL} = 6$ mA	4.5 V			0.32		0.37	
I_{IH}	High-level input current except $\overline{\text{REFREQ}}$		$V_I = 5.5$ V	5.5 V			0.1		1	μA
I_{IL}	Low-level input current	$\overline{\text{REFREQ}}$	$V_I = 0$	5.5 V			-5		-50	μA
		$\overline{\text{RESET}}$					-100		-250	
		All others					-0.1		-1	
I_{OZ}[‡]	Off-state output current (3-state outputs only)		$V_O = 0$ to 5.5 V	5.5 V			± 5		± 50	μA
I_{CC}	Supply current		$V_I = V_{CC}$ or 0, $I_O = 0$	5.5 V			5		15	mA
ΔI_{CC}[§]	Supply current change		One input at 0.5 V or 2.4 V, Other inputs at 0 V or V_{CC}	5.5 V		1.4	2.4		3	mA
C_i	Input capacitance		$V_I = 0$, f = 1 MHz	5.5 V		5	10		10	pF

‡ This parameter, I_{OZ}, the high impedance-state output current, applies only for three-state outputs and transceiver I/O pins.
§ This is the increase in supply current for each input that is at one of the specified TTL voltage levels rather than 0 V or V_{CC}.

timing requirements over recommended ranges of supply voltage and operating free-air temperature (unless otherwise noted)

PARAMETER		THCT4502-125 MIN	THCT4502-125 MAX	UNIT
$t_{c(C)}$	CLK cycle time	100		ns
$t_{w(CH)}$	CLK high pulse duration	45		ns
$t_{w(CL)}$	CLK low pulse duration	45		ns
t_{AEL-CL}	Time delay, ALE low to CLK starting low (see Note 1)	25		ns
t_{CL-AEL}	Time delay, CLK low to ALE starting low (see Note 1)	15		ns
t_{CL-AEH}	Time delay, CLK low to ALE	15		ns
$t_{w(AEH)}$	Pulse width ALE high	45		ns
t_{AV-AEL}	Time delay, address REN1, $\overline{CS}$ valid to ALE low	10		ns
t_{AEL-AX}	Time delay, ALE low to address not valid	15		ns
$t_{AEL-ACL}$	Time delay, ALE low to $\overline{ACX}$ low (see Notes 3, 4, 5, and 6)	$t_{h(RA)}+30$		ns
t_{ACH-CL}	Time delay, $\overline{ACX}$ high to CLK low (see Notes 3 and 7)	30		ns
t_{ACL-CH}	Time delay, $\overline{ACX}$ low to CLK starting high (to remove RDY)	30		ns
t_{RQL-CL}	Time delay, $\overline{REFREQ}$ low to CLK starting low (see Note 8)	35		ns
$t_{w(RQL)}$	Pulse width $\overline{REFREQ}$ low	30		ns
$t_{w(ACL)}$	$\overline{ACX}$ low width (see Note 9)	120		ns
t_{reset}	Power-up reset	$4t_{cCLK}$		ns

NOTES: 1. Coincidence of the trailing edge of CLK and the trailing edge of ALE should be avoided as the refresh/access occurs on the trailing CLK edge.

2. If ALE rises before $\overline{ACX}$ and a refresh request is present, the falling edge of CLK after t_{CL-AEH} will output the refresh address to MA0-MA7 and initiate a refresh cycle.

3. These specifications relate to system timing and do not directly reflect device performance.

4. On the access grant cycle following refresh, the occurrence of $\overline{CAS}$ low depends on the relative occurrence of ALE low to $\overline{ACX}$ low. If $\overline{ACX}$ occurs prior to or coincident with ALE, then $\overline{CAS}$ is timed from the CLK high transition that causes $\overline{RAS}$ low. If $\overline{ACX}$ occurs 20 ns or more after ALE, then $\overline{CAS}$ is timed from the CLK low transition following the CLK high transition causing $\overline{RAS}$ low.

5. For maximum speed access (internal delays on both access and access grant cycles), $\overline{ACX}$ should occur prior to or coincident with ALE.

6. $t_{h(RA)}$ is the dynamic memory row address hold time. $\overline{ACX}$ should follow ALE by $t_{AEL-CEL}$ in systems where the required $t_{h(RA)}$ is greater than $t_{REL-MAX}$ minimum.

7. The minimum of 20 ns is specified to ensure arbitration will occur on falling CLK edge, t_{ACH-CL} also affects precharge time such that the minimum t_{ACH-CL} should be equal or greater than: $t_{w(RH)} - t_{w(CL)} + 30$ ns (for a cycle where $\overline{ACX}$ high occurs prior to ALE high) where $t_{w(RH)}$ is the DRAM $\overline{RAS}$ precharge time.

8. This parameter is necessary only if refresh arbitration is to occur on this low-going CLK edge (in systems where refresh is synchronized to external events).

9. The specification $t_{w(ACL)}$ is designed to allow a $\overline{CAS}$ pulse. This assures normal operation of the device in testing and system operation.

switching characteristics over recommended supply voltage range and operating free-air temperature range (see Figure 1)

PARAMETER		TEST CONDITIONS	THCT4502-125		UNIT
			MIN	MAX	
$t_{AEL-REL}$	Time delay, ALE low to $\overline{RAS}$ starting low	C_L = 180 pF		45	ns
$t_{RAV-MAV}$	Time delay, row address valid to memory address valid	C_L = 360 pF		50	ns
$t_{AEH-MAV}$	Time delay, ALE high to valid memory address	C_L = 360 pF		90	ns
$t_{AEL-RYL}$	Time delay, ALE to RDY starting low (TWST = 1 or refresh in progress)	C_L = 40 pF		40	ns
$t_{AEL-CEL}$	Time delay, ALE low to $\overline{CAS}$ starting low (see Note 10)	C_L = 360 pF	50	125	ns
$t_{AEH-REH}$	Time delay, ALE high to $\overline{RAS}$ starting high	C_L = 180 pF		50	ns
$t_{ACL-MAX}$	Row address valid after $\overline{ACX}$	C_L = 360 pF	15		ns
$t_{MAV-CEL}$	Time delay, memory address valid to $\overline{CAS}$ starting low	C_L = 360 pF	0		ns
$t_{ACL-CEL}$	Time delay, $\overline{ACX}$ low to $\overline{CAS}$ starting low (see Note 10)	C_L = 360 pF	40	100	ns
$t_{ACH-REH}$	Time delay, $\overline{ACX}$ to $\overline{RAS}$ starting high	C_L = 180 pF		55	ns
$t_{ACH-CEH}$	Time delay, $\overline{ACX}$ high to $\overline{CAS}$ starting high	C_L = 360 pF	5	45	ns
$t_{ACH-MAX}$	Column address valid after $\overline{ACX}$ high	C_L = 360 pF	10		ns
t_{CH-RYH}	Time delay, CLK high to RDY starting high (after $\overline{ACX}$ low) (see Note 11)	C_L = 40 pF		60	ns
$t_{RFL-RFL}$	Time delay, $\overline{REFREQ}$ external till supported by $\overline{REFREQ}$ internal	C_L = 40 pF		35	ns
t_{CH-RFL}	Time delay, CLK high till $\overline{REFREQ}$ internal starting low	C_L = 40 pF		50	ns
t_{CL-MAV}	Time delay, CLK low till refrefresh address valid	C_L = 360 pF		100	ns
t_{CH-RRL}	Time delay, CLK high till refresh $\overline{RAS}$ starting low	C_L = 180 pF	10	60	ns
$t_{MAV-RRL}$	Time delay, refresh address valid till refresh $\overline{RAS}$ low	C_L = 180 pF	5		ns
t_{CL-RFH}	Time delay, CLK low to $\overline{REFREQ}$ starting high (3 cycle refresh)	C_L = 40 pF		70	ns
t_{CH-RFH}	Time delay, CLK high to $\overline{REFREQ}$ starting high (4 cycle refresh)	C_L = 40 pF		70	ns
t_{CH-RRH}	Time delay, CLK high to refresh $\overline{RAS}$ starting high	C_L = 160 pF	5	60	ns
t_{CH-MAX}	Refresh address valid after CLK high	C_L = 360 pF	10		ns

NOTES: 10. The falling edge of $\overline{CAS}$ occurs when both ALE low to $\overline{CAS}$ low time delay ($t_{AEL-CEL}$) and $\overline{ACX}$ low to $\overline{CAS}$ low time delay ($t_{ACL-CEL}$) have elapsed, i.e., if $\overline{ACX}$ goes low prior to ($t_{AEL-CEL} - t_{ACL-CEL}$) after the falling edge of ALE, the falling edge of $\overline{CAS}$ is measured from the falling edge of ALE ($t_{AEL-CEL}$). Otherwise, the access time increases and the falling edge of $\overline{CAS}$ is measured from the falling edge of $\overline{ACX}$ ($t_{ACL-CEL}$).

11. RDY returns high on the rising edge of CLK. If TWST = 0, then on an access grant cycle RDY goes high on the same edge that causes access $\overline{RAS}$ low. If TWST = 1, then RDY goes to the high level on the first rising CLK edge after $\overline{ACX}$ goes low on access cycles and on the next rising edge after the edge that causes access $\overline{RAS}$ low on access grant cycles (assuming $\overline{ACX}$ low).

TEXAS INSTRUMENTS
POST OFFICE BOX 225012 • DALLAS, TEXAS 75265

switching characteristics over recommended supply voltage range and operating free-air temperature range (see Figure 1) (continued)

PARAMETER		TEST CONDITIONS	THCT4502-125		UNIT
			MIN	MAX	
$t_{CH\text{-}REL}$	Time delay, CLK high till access $\overline{RAS}$ starting low	C_L = 180 pF		60	ns
$t_{CL\text{-}CEL}$	Time delay, CLK low to access $\overline{CAS}$ starting low (see Note 12)	C_L = 360 pF		100	ns
$t_{CL\text{-}MAX}$	Row address valid after CLK low	C_L = 360 pF	25		ns
$t_{REL\text{-}MAX}$	Row address valid after $\overline{RAS}$ low	C_L = 360 pF	25		ns
$t_{AEH\text{-}MAX}$	Column address valid after ALE high	C_L = 360 pF	10		ns
t_{dis}	Output disable time (3-state outputs)	C_L = 360 pF		125	ns
t_{en}	Output enable time (3-state outputs)	C_L = 360 pF		75	ns
$t_{CAV\text{-}CEL}$	Time delay, column address valid to $\overline{CAS}$ starting low after refresh (see Note 12)	C_L = 360 pF	0		ns
$t_{CH\text{-}CEL}$	Time delay, CLK high to access $\overline{CAS}$ starting low (see Note 13)	C_L = 360 pF		180	ns
$t_{t(CEL)}$	$\overline{CAS}$ fall time	C_L = 360 pF		20	ns
$t_{t(CEH)}$	$\overline{CAS}$ rise time	C_L = 360 pF		50	ns
$t_{t(REL)}$	$\overline{RAS}$ fall time	C_L = 180 pF		30	ns
$t_{t(REH)}$	$\overline{RAS}$ rise time	C_L = 180 pF		40	ns
$t_{t(MAV)}$	Address transition time	C_L = 180 pF		40	ns
$t_{t(RYL)}$	RDY fall time	C_L = 40 pF		20	ns
$t_{t(RYH)}$	RDY rise time	C_L = 40 pF		50	ns

NOTES: 12. The occurrence of $\overline{CAS}$ low is guaranteed not to occur until the column address is valid on MAX.

13. On the access grant cycle following refresh, the occurrence of $\overline{CAS}$ low depends on the relative occurrence of ALE low to $\overline{ACX}$ low. If $\overline{ACX}$ occurs prior to or coincident with ALE then $\overline{CAS}$ is timed from the CLK high transition that causes $\overline{RAS}$ low. If $\overline{ACX}$ occurs 20 ns or more after ALE then $\overline{CAS}$ is timed from the CLK low transition following the CLK high transition causing $\overline{RAS}$ low. (See Refresh Cycle Timing Diagram)

PARAMETER MEASUREMENT INFORMATION

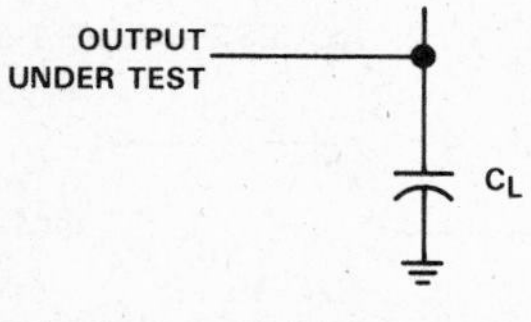
OUTPUT
UNDER TEST
C_L

FIGURE 1. LOAD CIRCUIT

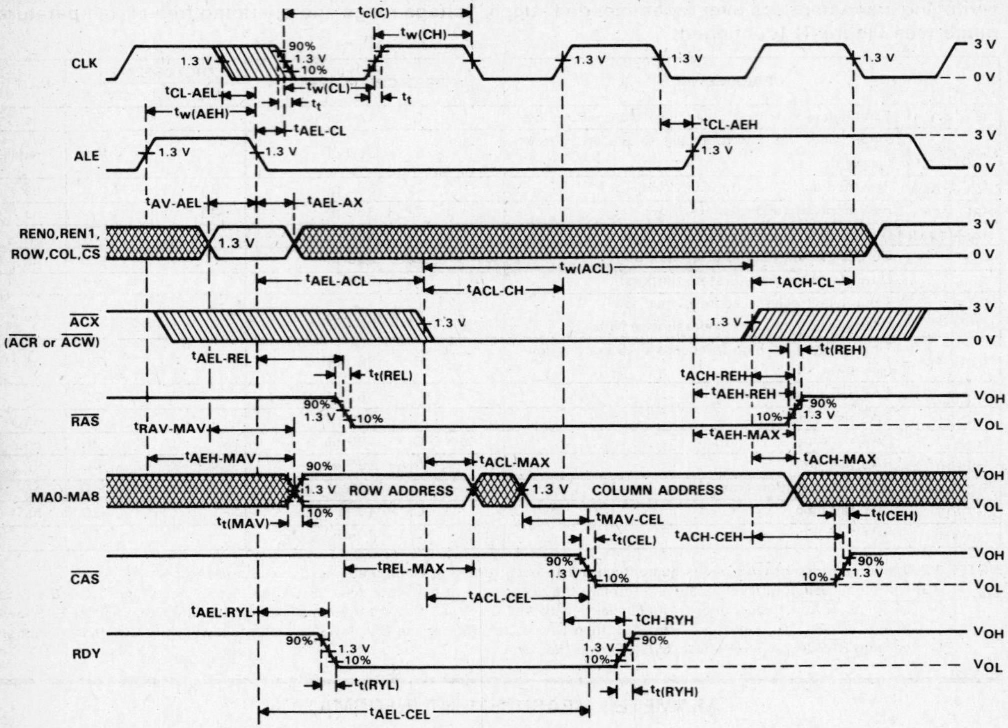
CLK
ALE
REN0,REN1,
ROW,COL,$\overline{CS}$
$\overline{ACX}$
($\overline{ACR}$ or $\overline{ACW}$)
$\overline{RAS}$
MA0-MA8
$\overline{CAS}$
RDY
ROW ADDRESS
COLUMN ADDRESS
$t_{c(C)}$
$t_{w(CH)}$
$t_{w(CL)}$
$t_{CL\text{-}AEL}$
$t_{w(AEH)}$
$t_{AEL\text{-}CL}$
$t_{CL\text{-}AEH}$
$t_{AV\text{-}AEL}$
$t_{AEL\text{-}AX}$
$t_{w(ACL)}$
$t_{AEL\text{-}ACL}$
$t_{ACL\text{-}CH}$
$t_{ACH\text{-}CL}$
$t_{t(REH)}$
$t_{AEL\text{-}REL}$
$t_{t(REL)}$
$t_{ACH\text{-}REH}$
$t_{AEH\text{-}REH}$
$t_{RAV\text{-}MAV}$
$t_{AEH\text{-}MAX}$
$t_{AEH\text{-}MAV}$
$t_{ACL\text{-}MAX}$
$t_{ACH\text{-}MAX}$
$t_{t(MAV)}$
$t_{MAV\text{-}CEL}$
$t_{t(CEL)}$
$t_{ACH\text{-}CEH}$
$t_{t(CEH)}$
$t_{REL\text{-}MAX}$
$t_{ACL\text{-}CEL}$
$t_{AEL\text{-}RYL}$
$t_{CH\text{-}RYH}$
$t_{t(RYL)}$
$t_{t(RYH)}$
$t_{AEL\text{-}CEL}$
t_t
1.3 V
90%
10%
3 V
0 V
V_{OH}
V_{OL}

NOTE 14: All transition times (t_t) are measured between 10% and 90% points.

FIGURE 2. ACCESS CYCLE TIMING

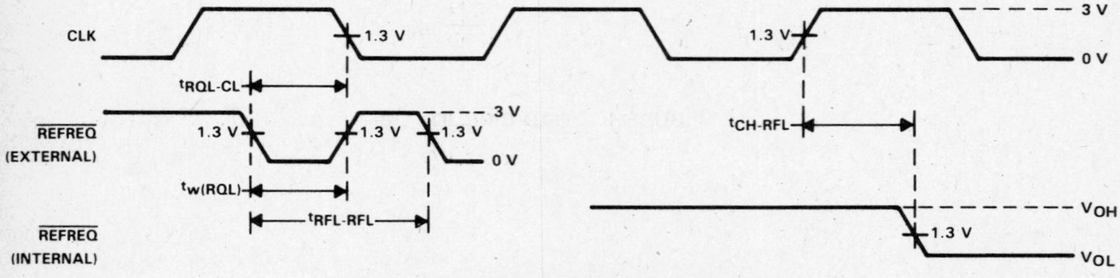
CLK
$\overline{REFREQ}$
(EXTERNAL)
$\overline{REFREQ}$
(INTERNAL)
$t_{RQL\text{-}CL}$
$t_{w(RQL)}$
$t_{RFL\text{-}RFL}$
$t_{CH\text{-}RFL}$
1.3 V
3 V
0 V
V_{OH}
V_{OL}

FIGURE 3. REFRESH REQUEST TIMING

NOTE 15: All input pulses are supplied by generators having the following characteristics: PRR $\leq$ 1 MHz, $Z_{out} = 50\ \Omega$, t_r = 6 ns, t_f = 6 ns.

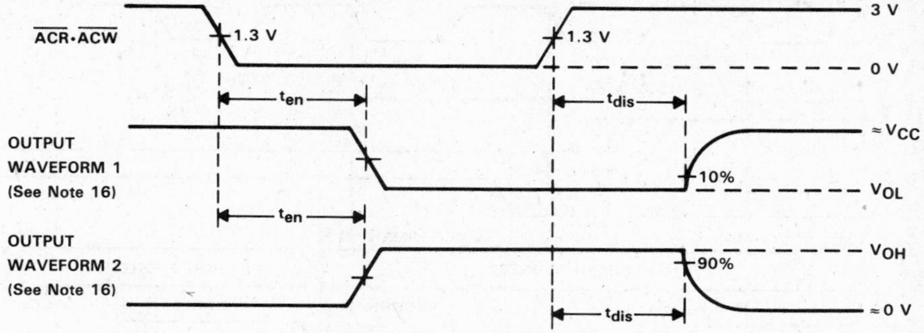
ACR•ACW
1.3 V
1.3 V
3 V
0 V
ten
tdis
OUTPUT
WAVEFORM 1
(See Note 16)
≈VCC
10%
VOL
ten
OUTPUT
WAVEFORM 2
(See Note 16)
VOH
90%
≈0 V
tdis

VOLTAGE WAVEFORMS

NOTE 16: Waveform 1 is for an output with internal conditions such that the output is low except when disabled by the access controls. Waveform 2 is for an output with internal conditions such that the output is high except when disabled by the access controls.

FIGURE 4. ENABLE AND DISABLE TIMES FOR 3-STATE OUTPUTS

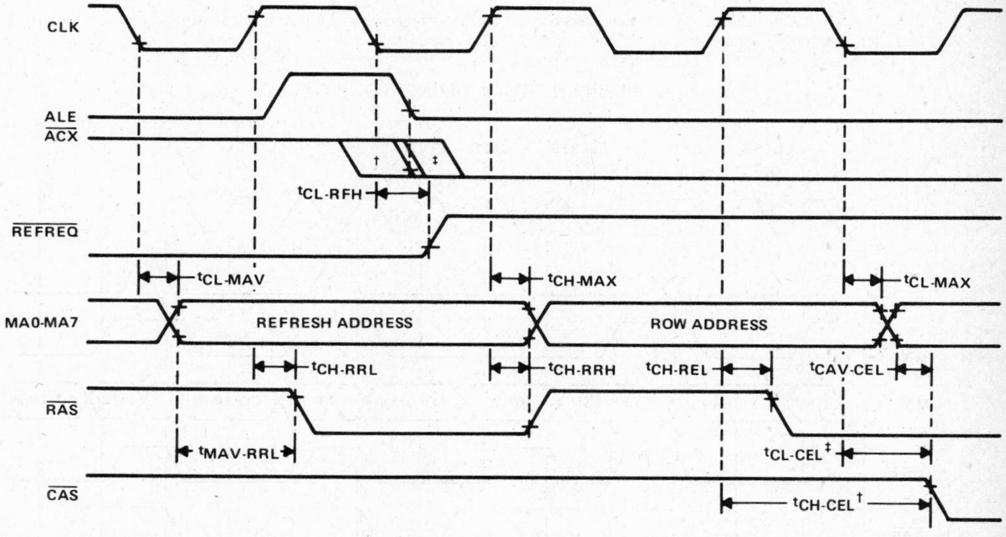
CLK
ALE
ACX
†
‡
tCL-RFH
REFREQ
tCL-MAV
tCH-MAX
tCL-MAX
MA0-MA7
REFRESH ADDRESS
ROW ADDRESS
tCH-RRL
tCH-RRH
tCH-REL
tCAV-CEL
RAS
tMAV-RRL
tCL-CEL‡
CAS
tCH-CEL†

† On access grant cycle following refresh, $\overline{CAS}$ low and address multiplexing are timed from CLK high transition ($t_{CH\text{-}CEL}$) if $\overline{ACX}$ low occurs prior to or coincident with the falling edge of ALE.

‡ On access grant cycle following refresh, $\overline{CAS}$ low and address multiplexing are timed from CLK low transition ($t_{CL\text{-}CEL}$) if $\overline{ACX}$ low occurs 20 ns or more after the falling edge of ALE.

NOTE 15: All input pulses are supplied by generators having the following characteristics: PRR ≤ 1 MHz, Z_{out} = 50 Ω, t_r = 6 ns, t_f = 6 ns.

FIGURE 5. REFRESH CYCLE TIMING (THREE CYCLE)

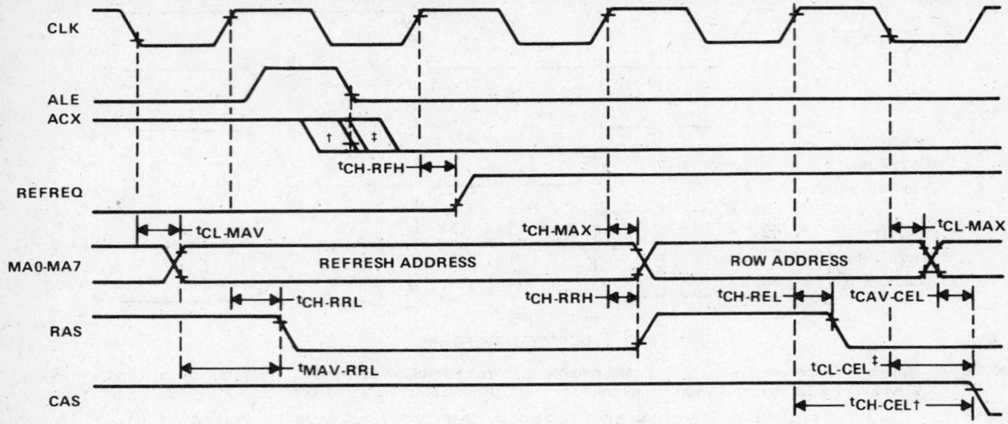
CLK
ALE
ACX
†
‡
tCH-RFH
REFREQ
tCL-MAV
tCH-MAX
tCL-MAX
MA0-MA7
REFRESH ADDRESS
ROW ADDRESS
tCH-RRL
tCH-RRH
tCH-REL
tCAV-CEL
RAS
tMAV-RRL
tCL-CEL‡
CAS
tCH-CEL†

† On access grant cycle following refresh, $\overline{CAS}$ low and address multiplexing are timed from CLK high transition (t_{CH-CEL}) if $\overline{ACX}$ low occurs prior to or coincident with the falling edge of ALE.

‡ On access grant cycle following refresh, $\overline{CAS}$ low and address multiplexing are timed from CLK low transition (t_{CL-CEL}) if $\overline{ACX}$ low occurs 20 ns or more after the falling edge of ALE.

NOTE 15: All input pulses are supplied by generators having the following characteristics: PRR ≤ 1 MHz, Z_{out} = 50 Ω, t_r = 6 ns, t_f = 6 ns.

FIGURE 6. REFRESH CYCLE TIMING (FOUR CYCLE)

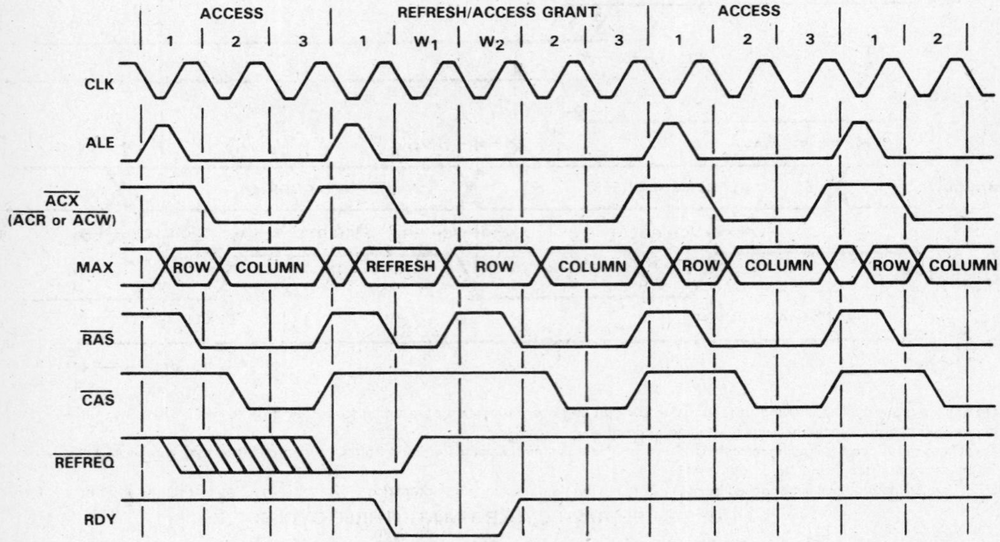
ACCESS
REFRESH/ACCESS GRANT
ACCESS
1
2
3
1
W1
W2
2
3
1
2
3
1
2
CLK
ALE
ACX
(ACR or ACW)
MAX
ROW
COLUMN
REFRESH
ROW
COLUMN
ROW
COLUMN
ROW
COLUMN
RAS
CAS
REFREQ
RDY

FIGURE 7. TYPICAL ACCESS/REFRESH/ACCESS CYCLE (THREE-CYCLE, TWST IS LOW)

TEXAS INSTRUMENTS
POST OFFICE BOX 225012 • DALLAS, TEXAS 75265

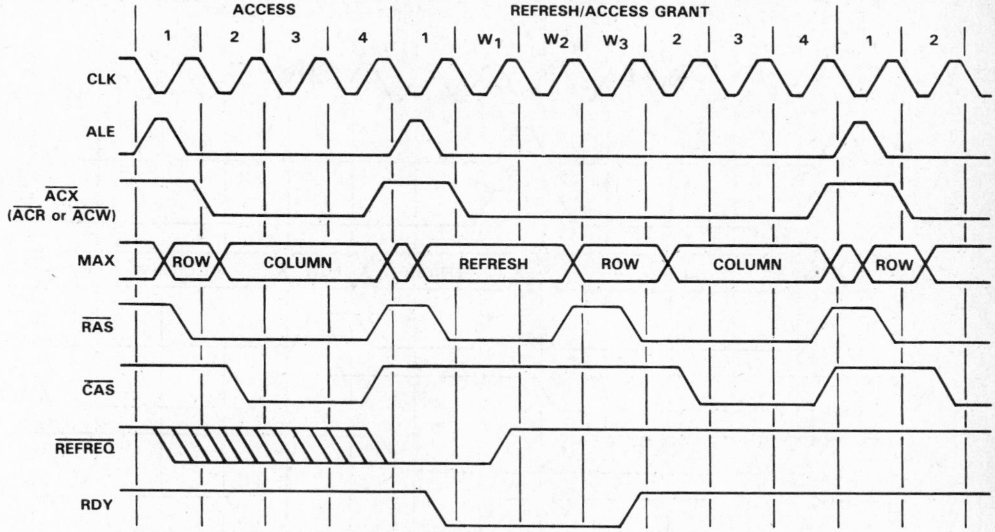
ACCESS
REFRESH/ACCESS GRANT
1 2 3 4 1 W1 W2 W3 2 3 4 1 2
CLK
ALE
ACX
(ACR or ACW)
MAX
ROW
COLUMN
REFRESH
ROW
COLUMN
ROW
RAS
CAS
REFREQ
RDY

FIGURE 8. TYPICAL ACCESS/REFRESH/ACCESS CYCLE (FOUR-CYCLE, TWST IS LOW)

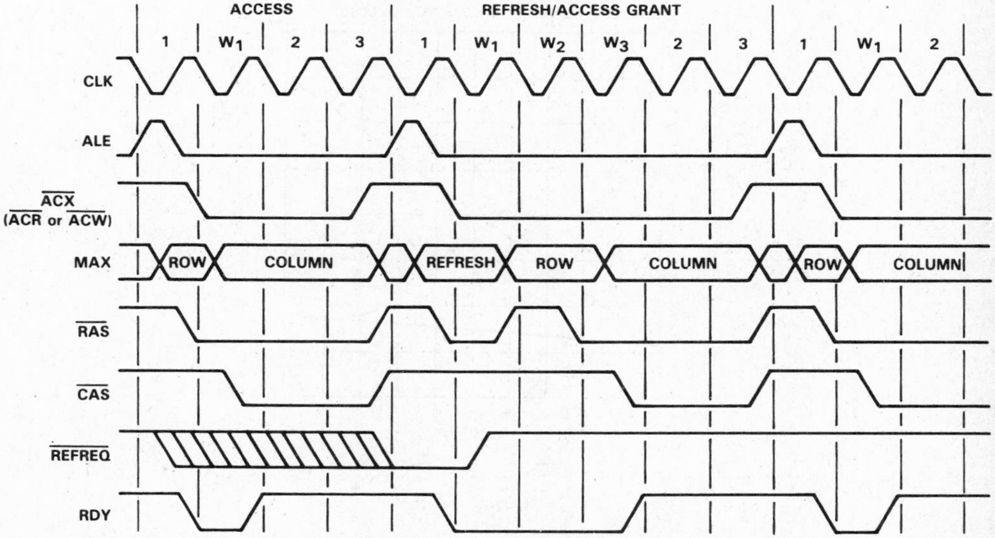
ACCESS
REFRESH/ACCESS GRANT
1 W1 2 3 1 W1 W2 W3 2 3 1 W1 2
CLK
ALE
ACX
(ACR or ACW)
MAX
ROW
COLUMN
REFRESH
ROW
COLUMN
ROW
COLUMN
RAS
CAS
REFREQ
RDY

FIGURE 9. TYPICAL ACCESS/REFRESH/ACCESS CYCLE (THREE-CYCLE, TWST IS HIGH)

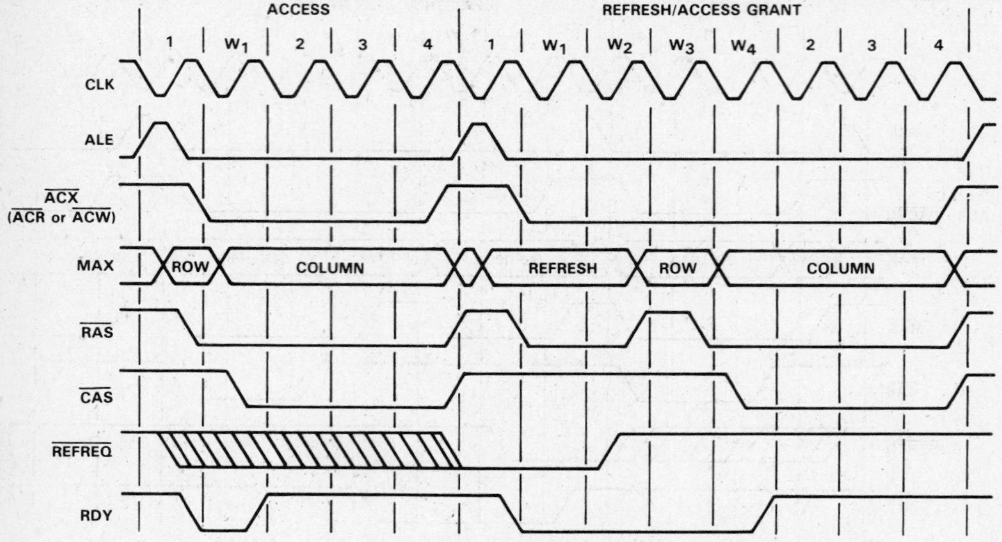
ACCESS
REFRESH/ACCESS GRANT
1
W_1
2
3
4
1
W_1
W_2
W_3
W_4
2
3
4
CLK
ALE
$\overline{ACX}$
($\overline{ACR}$ or $\overline{ACW}$)
MAX
ROW
COLUMN
REFRESH
ROW
COLUMN
$\overline{RAS}$
$\overline{CAS}$
$\overline{REFREQ}$
RDY

FIGURE 10. TYPICAL ACCESS/REFRESH/ACCESS CYCLE (FOUR-CYCLE, TWST IS HIGH)

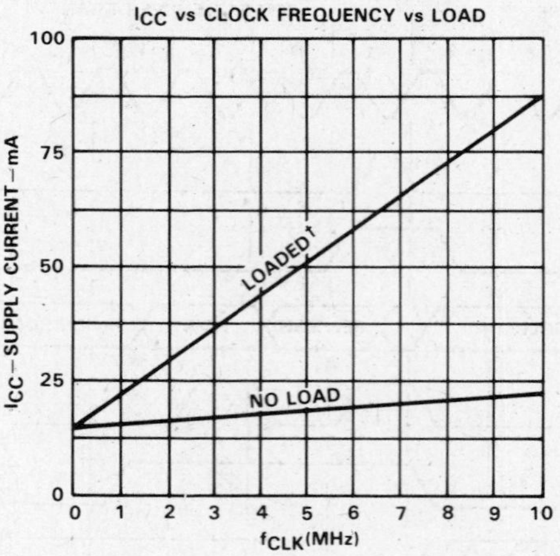
I_{CC} vs CLOCK FREQUENCY vs LOAD
I_{CC}—SUPPLY CURRENT—mA
100
75
50
25
0
LOADED†
NO LOAD
0
1
2
3
4
5
6
7
8
9
10
f_{CLK}(MHz)

†Load is 360 pF for $\overline{CAS}$ and MA outputs, 180 pF for all $\overline{RAS}$ outputs.

FIGURE 11.

TEXAS INSTRUMENTS
POST OFFICE BOX 225012 • DALLAS, TEXAS 75265

ORDERING INSTRUCTIONS

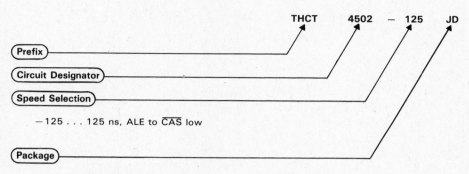

THCT 4502 — 125 JD

Prefix → THCT

Circuit Designator → 4502

Speed Selection → 125

—125 . . . 125 ns, ALE to $\overline{\text{CAS}}$ low

Package → JD

N, JD (Dual in-line packages)
FK, FN (Chip carrier packages)

PRODUCT PREVIEW

THCT29520, THCT29521 MULTILEVEL PIPELINE REGISTERS

D2925, NOVEMBER 1985—REVISED APRIL 1986

- Four 8-Bit Registers
- Dual 2-Level or Single 4-Level Pipeline Registers
- Any One of Four Registers Selectable for Output
- High-Speed Low-Power CMOS Logic
- Fully TTL Compatible
- Dependable Texas Instruments Quality and Reliability

NT OR DW PACKAGE
(TOP VIEW)

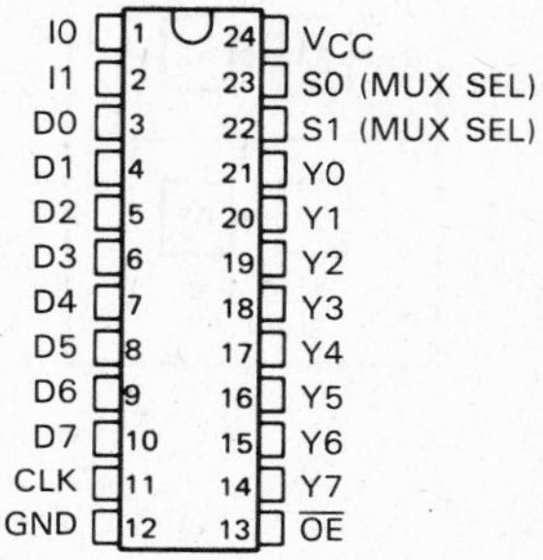
I0 1
I1 2
D0 3
D1 4
D2 5
D3 6
D4 7
D5 8
D6 9
D7 10
CLK 11
GND 12
24 VCC
23 S0 (MUX SEL)
22 S1 (MUX SEL)
21 Y0
20 Y1
19 Y2
18 Y3
17 Y4
16 Y5
15 Y6
14 Y7
13 OE

description

The THCT29520 and THCT29521 are high-speed CMOS multilevel pipeline registers. They are interchangeable with the Advanced Micro Device bipolar AM29520 and AM29521 but dissipate a fraction of the power.

The THCT29520 and THCT29521 contain four 8-bit positive-edge-triggered registers. The registers can operate as one set of 4-level pipeline registers or two sets of 2-level pipeline registers. The output can be selected from any one of the four registers.

The THCT29520 and THCT29521 differ in the way data is transferred in the dual 2-level register modes (I = 01 or 10). For the THCT29520, new data is written into the first-level register while the old data in the first-level register is shifted into the second-level register. For the THCT29521, new data is written over the old data in the first-level register. The data in the second-level register remains unchanged.

The THCT29520 and THCT29521 are characterized for operation from 0°C to 70°C. The THCT29520E and THCT29521E are characterized for operation from −40°C to 85°C.

THCT29520 MODES

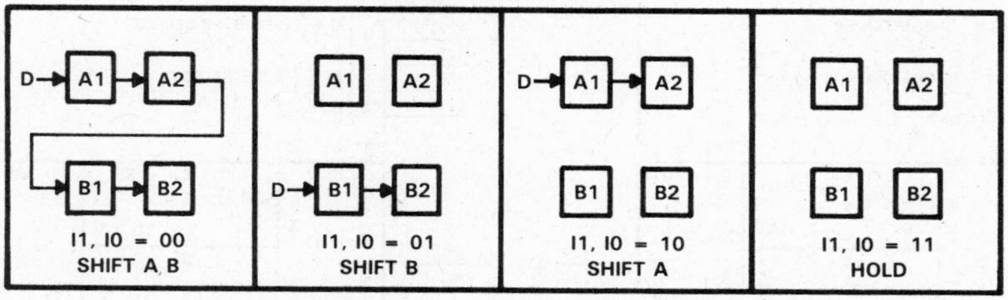
D A1 A2
B1 B2
I1, I0 = 00
SHIFT A B
A1 A2
D B1 B2
I1, I0 = 01
SHIFT B
D A1 A2
B1 B2
I1, I0 = 10
SHIFT A
A1 A2
B1 B2
I1, I0 = 11
HOLD

I1	I0	OPERATION	A1	A2	B1	B2
L	L	SHIFT A B	D	$A1_0$	$A2_0$	$B1_0$
L	H	SHIFT B	$A1_0$	$A2_0$	D	$B1_0$
H	L	SHIFT A	D	$A1_0$	$B1_0$	$B2_0$
H	H	HOLD	$A1_0$	$A2_0$	$B1_0$	$B2_0$

TEXAS INSTRUMENTS
POST OFFICE BOX 225012 • DALLAS, TEXAS 75265

THCT29521 MODES

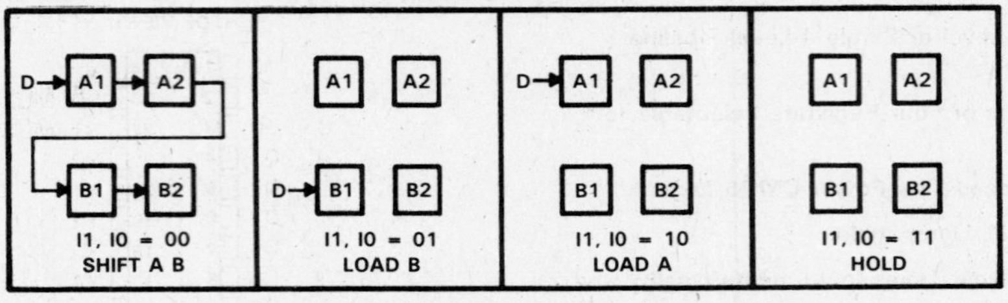
D
A1
A2
B1
B2
I1, I0 = 00
SHIFT A B
A1
A2
D
B1
B2
I1, I0 = 01
LOAD B
D
A1
A2
B1
B2
I1, I0 = 10
LOAD A
A1
A2
B1
B2
I1, I0 = 11
HOLD

I1	I0	OPERATION	A1	A2	B1	B2
L	L	SHIFT A B	D	$A1_0$	$A2_0$	$B1_0$
L	H	LOAD B	$A1_0$	$A2_0$	D	$B2_0$
H	L	LOAD A	D	$A2_0$	$B1_0$	$B2_0$
H	H	HOLD	$A1_0$	$A2_0$	$B1_0$	$B2_0$

OUTPUT FUNCTION TABLE

INPUTS			OUTPUT
$\overline{OE}$	S1	S0	Y
L	L	L	B2
L	L	H	B1
L	H	L	A2
L	H	H	A1
H	X	X	Z

logic symbols†

THCT29520

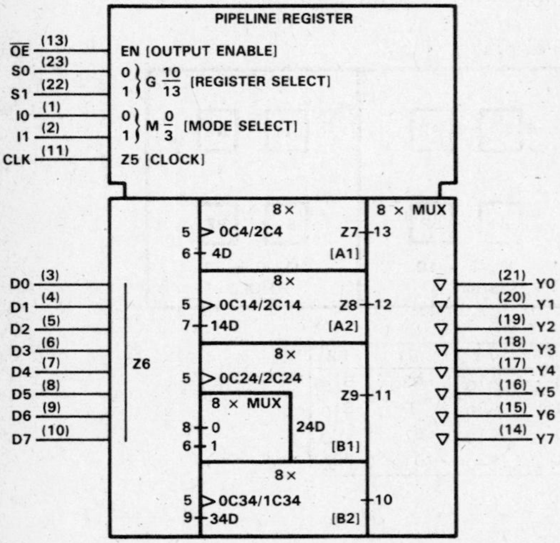
PIPELINE REGISTER
$\overline{OE}$ (13) EN [OUTPUT ENABLE]
S0 (23)
S1 (22)
0 1 } G 10/13 [REGISTER SELECT]
I0 (1)
I1 (2)
0 1 } M 0/3 [MODE SELECT]
CLK (11) Z5 [CLOCK]
8×
5 >0C4/2C4
6 4D
Z7 13
[A1]
8 × MUX
8×
5 >0C14/2C14
7 14D
Z8 12
[A2]
8×
5 >0C24/2C24
8 × MUX
8 0
6 1
24D
Z9 11
[B1]
8×
5 >0C34/1C34
9 34D
10
[B2]
Z6
D0 (3)
D1 (4)
D2 (5)
D3 (6)
D4 (7)
D5 (8)
D6 (9)
D7 (10)
(21) Y0
(20) Y1
(19) Y2
(18) Y3
(17) Y4
(16) Y5
(15) Y6
(14) Y7

THCT29521

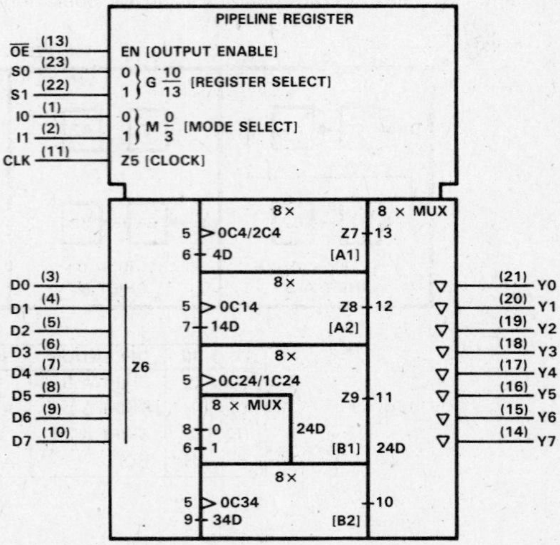
PIPELINE REGISTER
$\overline{OE}$ (13) EN [OUTPUT ENABLE]
S0 (23)
S1 (22)
0 1 } G 10/13 [REGISTER SELECT]
I0 (1)
I1 (2)
0 1 } M 0/3 [MODE SELECT]
CLK (11) Z5 [CLOCK]
8×
5 >0C4/2C4
6 4D
Z7 13
[A1]
8 × MUX
8×
5 >0C14
7 14D
Z8 12
[A2]
8×
5 >0C24/1C24
8 × MUX
8 0
6 1
24D
Z9 11
[B1]
24D
8×
5 >0C34
9 34D
10
[B2]
Z6
D0 (3)
D1 (4)
D2 (5)
D3 (6)
D4 (7)
D5 (8)
D6 (9)
D7 (10)
(21) Y0
(20) Y1
(19) Y2
(18) Y3
(17) Y4
(16) Y5
(15) Y6
(14) Y7

†These symbols are in accordance with ANSI/IEEE Std 91-1984 and IEC Publication 617-12.

TEXAS INSTRUMENTS
POST OFFICE BOX 225012 • DALLAS, TEXAS 75265

logic diagram (positive logic)

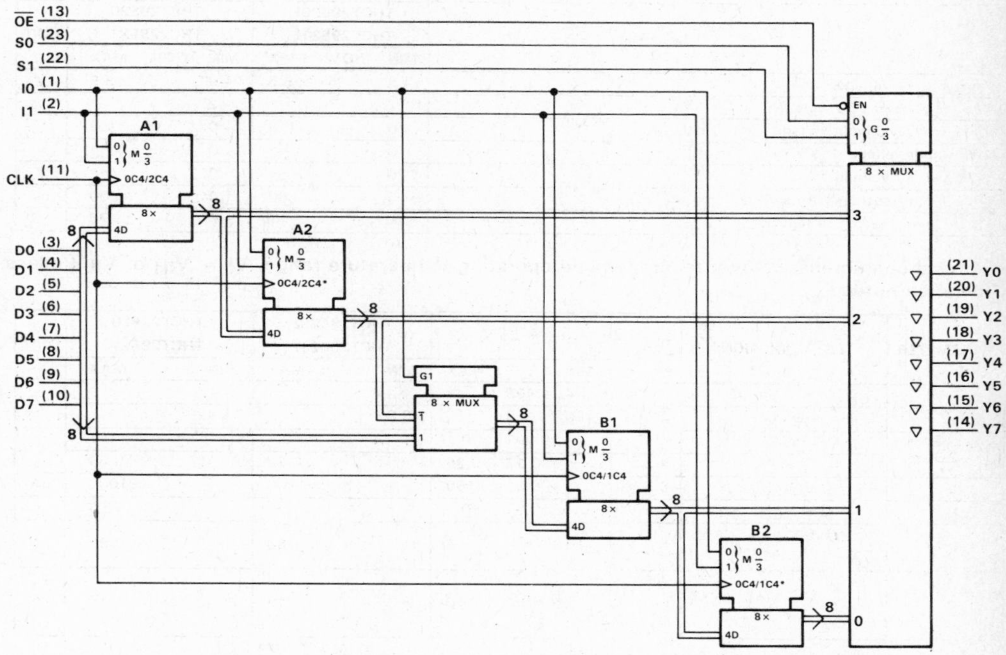
OE (13)
S0 (23)
S1 (22)
I0 (1)
I1 (2)
CLK (11)
D0 (3)
D1 (4)
D2 (5)
D3 (6)
D4 (7)
D5 (8)
D6 (9)
D7 (10)
A1
0 } M 0/3
1
0C4/2C4
8×
4D
A2
0C4/2C4*
B1
0C4/1C4
B2
0C4/1C4*
G1
8 × MUX
EN
G 0/3
8
3
2
1
0
(21) Y0
(20) Y1
(19) Y2
(18) Y3
(17) Y4
(16) Y5
(15) Y6
(14) Y7

* The label ''0C4/2C4'' means that the clock in register A2 affects the eight data inputs of that register, collectively labeled ''4D'', only in modes 0 and 2 (I1, I0 = L L and H L, respectively). This logic diagram applies specifically for the THCT29520. For the THCT29521, the labels marked with the asterisks in registers A2 and B2 would both be reduced to ''0C4'' indicating that these clocks have effect only in mode 0 in that device. Otherwise this diagram applies to both devices.

absolute maximum rating over operating free-air temperature range (see Note 1)

Supply voltage, V_{CC}	−0.5 V to 7 V
Input diode current, I_{IK} ($V_I < 0$ or $V_I > V_{CC}$)	±20 mA
Output diode current, I_{OK} ($V_O < 0$ or $V_O > V_{CC}$)	±20 mA
Continuous output current, I_O ($V_O = 0$ to V_{CC})	±35 mA
Continuous current through V_{CC} or GND	±70 mA
Lead temperature 1,6 mm (1/16 inch) from case for 60 seconds	300 °C
Storage temperature range	−65 °C to 150 °C

NOTE 1: Stress beyond those listed under ''absolute maximum ratings'' may cause permanent damage to the device. These are stress ratings only and functional operation of the device at these or any other conditions beyond those indicated in the ''recommended operating conditions'' section of this specification is not implied. Exposure to absolute-maximum-rated conditions for extended periods may affect device reliability.

recommended operating conditions

		THCT29520E THCT29521E			THCT29520 THCT29521			UNIT
		MIN	NOM	MAX	MIN	NOM	MAX	
V_{CC}	Supply voltage	4.5	5	5.5	4.5	5	5.5	V
V_{IH}	High-level input voltage	2			2			V
V_{IL}	Low-level input voltage	0		0.8	0		0.8	V
V_I	Input voltage	0		V_{CC}	0		V_{CC}	V
V_O	Output voltage	0		V_{CC}	0		V_{CC}	V
t_t	Input transition (rise and fall) time	0		500	0		500	ns
T_A	Operating free-air temperature	−40		85	−0		70	°C

electrical characteristics over recommended operating temperature range, $V_I = V_{IH}$ or V_{IL} (unless otherwise noted)

PARAMETER	TEST CONDITIONS	V_{CC}	$T_A = 25°C$			THCT29520E THCT29521E		THCT29520 THCT29521		UNIT
			MIN	TYP	MAX	MIN	MAX	MIN	MAX	
V_{OH}	$I_{OH} = -20\ \mu A$	4.5 V	4.4	4.499		4.4		4.4		V
	$I_{OH} = -8$ mA	4.5 V	3.9	4.3		3.8		3.8		
V_{OL}	$I_{OL} = 20\ \mu A$	4.5 V		0.001	0.1		0.1		0.1	V
	$I_{OL} = 8$ mA	4.5 V		0.17	0.26		0.33		0.33	
I_I	$V_I = 0$ to V_{CC}	5.5 V		±0.1	+100		±1000		±1000	nA
I_{OZ}	$V_I = 0$ or V_{CC}	5.5 V		±0.01	±0.5		±5		±5	μA
I_{CC}	$V_I < 0.5$ V or > 2.4 V, $I_O = 0$	4.5 V			8		80		80	μA
C_i		4.5 V to 5.5 V		3	10		10		10	pF

timing requirements over recommended operating free-air temperature range

PARAMETER		V_{CC}	$T_A = 25°C$			THCT29520E THCT29521E		THCT29520 THCT29521		UNIT
			MIN	TYP	MAX	MIN	MAX	MIN	MAX	
t_w	Pulse duration, CLK high or low	4.5 V		6		12		12		ns
		5.5 V		5		10		10		
t_{su}	Setup time before CLK↑	4.5 V		10		15		15		ns
		5.5 V		8		13		13		
t_h	Hold time after CLK↑	4.5 V		0		0		0		ns
		5.5 V		0		0		0		

TEXAS INSTRUMENTS
POST OFFICE BOX 225012 • DALLAS, TEXAS 75265

switching characteristics over recommended free-air temperature range, C_L = 50 pF (unless otherwise noted) See Note 2

PARAMETER	FROM	TO	V_{CC}	T_A = 25°C			THCT29520E THCT29521E		THCT29520 THCT29521		UNIT
				MIN	TYP	MAX	MIN	MAX	MIN	MAX	
t_{pd}	CLK ↑	Y	4.5 V		18			27		26	ns
			5.5 V		16			25		24	
t_{pd}	S0, S1	Y	4.5 V		17			27		26	ns
			5.5 V		15			25		24	
t_{en}	$\overline{OE}$ ↓	Y	4.5 V		10			16		15	ns
			5.5 V		7			15		14	
t_{dis}	$\overline{OE}$ ↑	Y	4.5 V		14			20		20	ns
			5.5 V		13			20		20	
t_t		Y	4.5 V		7			12		12	ns
			5.5 V		7			12		12	

C_{pd}	Power dissipation capacitance†	No load, T_A = 25°C	110 pF typ

†No load dynamic power dissipation, $P_d = C_{pd} V_{CC}^2 f + I_{CC} V_{CC}$

NOTE 2: For load circuit and voltage waveforms, see page 1-14 of the *High-Speed CMOS Logic Data Book*, 1984.

D2911, MARCH 1982—REVISED SEPTEMBER 1985

- **Fast Address to Match Valid Delay — Three Speed Ranges: 35 ns, 45 ns, 55 ns**
- **512 × 9 Internal RAM**
- **300-Mil 24-Pin Ceramic Side-Brazed or Plastic Dual-In-Line or Small Outline Packages**
- **Max Power Dissipation: 660 mW**
- **On-Chip Parity Generation and Checking**
- **Parity Error Output/Force Parity Error Input**
- **On-Chip Address/Data Comparator**
- **Asynchronous, Single-Cycle Reset**
- **Easily Expandable**
- **Fully Static**
- **Reliable SMOS (Scaled NMOS) Technology**
- **TTL- and CMOS-Compatible Inputs and Outputs**

DW, JD, OR NT PACKAGE
(TOP VIEW)

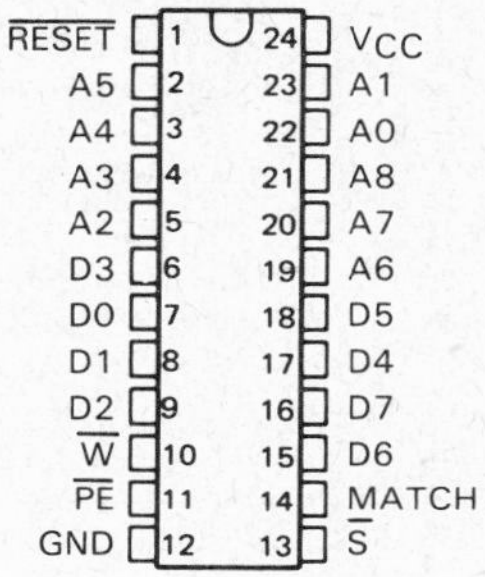
$\overline{RESET}$ 1
A5 2
A4 3
A3 4
A2 5
D3 6
D0 7
D1 8
D2 9
$\overline{W}$ 10
$\overline{PE}$ 11
GND 12
24 V_{CC}
23 A1
22 A0
21 A8
20 A7
19 A6
18 D5
17 D4
16 D7
15 D6
14 MATCH
13 $\overline{S}$

description

This 8-bit-slice cache address comparator consists of a high-speed 512 × 9 static RAM array, parity generator, parity checker, and 9-bit high-speed comparator. It is fabricated using N-channel silicon gate technology for high speed and simple interface with MOS and bipolar TTL circuits. The cache address comparator is easily cascadable for wider tag addresses or deeper tag memories. Significant reductions in cache memory component count, board area, and power dissipation can be achieved with this device.

When $\overline{S}$ is low and $\overline{W}$ is high, the cache address comparator compares the contents of the memory location addressed by A0-A8 with the data on D0-D7 plus generated parity. An equality is indicated by a high level on the MATCH output. A low-level output from $\overline{PE}$ signifies a parity error in the internal RAM data. $\overline{PE}$ is an N-channel open-drain output for easy OR-tying. During a write cycle ($\overline{S}$ and $\overline{W}$ low), data on D0-D7 plus generated even parity are written in the 9-bit memory location addressed by A0-A8. Also during write, a parity error may be forced by holding $\overline{PE}$ low.

A $\overline{RESET}$ input is provided for initialization. When $\overline{RESET}$ goes low, all 512 × 9 RAM locations are cleared and the MATCH output is forced high.

The cache address comparator operates from a single +5 V supply and is offered in a 24-pin 300-mil ceramic side brazed or plastic dual-in-line packages. The device is fully TTL compatible and is characterized for operation from 0°C to 70°C.

MATCH OUTPUT DESCRIPTION

MATCH = V_{OH} if: [A0-A8] = D0-D7 + parity,
or: $\overline{RESET}$ = V_{IL},
or: $\overline{S}$ = V_{IH},
or: $\overline{W}$ = V_{IL}

MATCH = V_{OL} if: [A0-A8] ≠ D0-D7 + parity,
with $\overline{RESET}$ = V_{IH},
$\overline{S}$ = V_{IL}, and $\overline{W}$ = V_{IH}

FUNCTION TABLE

OUTPUT		FUNCTION
MATCH	$\overline{PE}$	DESCRIPTION
L	L	Parity Error
L	H	Not Equal
H	L	Undefined Error
H	H	Equal

Where S = V_{IL}, W = V_{IH}, RESET = V_{IH}

functional block diagram (positive logic)

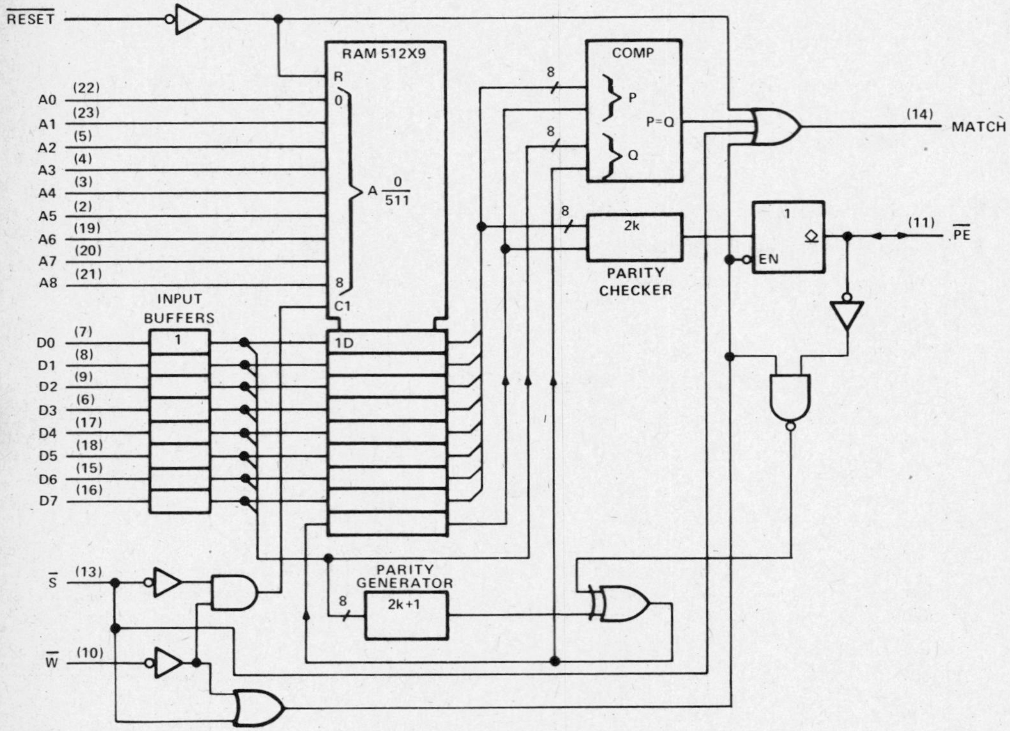
RESET
A0
A1
A2
A3
A4
A5
A6
A7
A8
(22)
(23)
(5)
(4)
(3)
(2)
(19)
(20)
(21)
RAM 512X9
R
0
A 0/511
8
C1
1D
INPUT BUFFERS
1
D0
D1
D2
D3
D4
D5
D6
D7
(7)
(8)
(9)
(6)
(17)
(18)
(15)
(16)
COMP
P
Q
P=Q
8
(14)
MATCH
2k
PARITY CHECKER
1
EN
(11)
PE
PARITY GENERATOR
2k+1
S
(13)
W
(10)

This diagram has been changed to correct errors in previous versions. No functional change has been made in the chip.

TEXAS INSTRUMENTS
POST OFFICE BOX 225012 • DALLAS, TEXAS 75265

PIN FUNCTIONAL DESCRIPTION

PIN NAME	PIN NO.	DESCRIPTION
$\overline{RESET}$	1	$\overline{RESET}$ input. Asynchronously clears entire RAM array and forces MATCH high when $\overline{RESET}$ is at V_{IL} and $\overline{W}$ is at V_{IH}.
A0	22	Address inputs. Address 1 of 512-by-9-bit random-access memory locations. Must be stable for the duration of the write cycle.
A1	23	
A2	5	
A3	4	
A4	3	
A5	2	
A6	19	
A7	20	
A8	21	
D0	7	Data inputs. Compared with memory location addressed by A0-A8 when $\overline{W}$ is at V_{IH} and $\overline{S}$ is at V_{IL}. Provide input data to RAM when $\overline{W}$ is at V_{IL} and $\overline{S}$ is at V_{IL}.
D1	8	
D2	9	
D3	6	
D4	17	
D5	18	
D6	15	
D7	16	
$\overline{W}$	10	Write control input. Writes D0 through D7 and generated parity into RAM and forces MATCH high when $\overline{W}$ is at V_{IL} and $\overline{S}$ is at V_{IL}. Places selected device in compare mode if $\overline{W}$ is at V_{IH}.
$\overline{PE}$	11	Parity error input/output. During write cycles, $\overline{PE}$ can force a parity error into the 9-bit location specified by A0 through A8 when $\overline{PE}$ is at V_{IL}. For compare cycles, $\overline{PE}$ at V_{OL} indicates a parity error in the stored data. $\overline{PE}$ is an open-drain output so an external pull-up resistor is required.
GND	12	Ground
$\overline{S}$	13	Chip select input. Enables device when $\overline{S}$ is at V_{IL}. Deselects device and forces MATCH high when $\overline{S}$ is at V_{IH}.
MATCH	14	When MATCH output is at V_{OH} during a compare cycle, D0 through D7 plus parity equal the contents of the 9-bit memory location addressed by A0 through A8.
V_{CC}	24	5-V supply voltage

absolute maximum ratings over operating free-air temperature range (unless otherwise specified)

Supply voltage range, V_{CC} (see Note 1) . . . . −1.5 to 7 V
Input voltage range, any input . . . . −1.5 to 7 V
Continuous power dissipation . . . . 1 W
Operating free-air temperature range . . . . 0°C to 70°C
Storage temperature range . . . . −65°C to 150°C

NOTE 1: All voltage values are with respect to GND.

recommended operating conditions

PARAMETER	MIN	NOM	MAX	UNIT
Supply voltage, V_{CC}	4.5	5	5.5	V
High-level input voltage, V_{IH}	2		6	V
Low-level input voltage, V_{IL} (See Note 2)	−1		0.8	V
Operating free-air temperature, T_A	0		70	°C

NOTE 2: The algebraic convention, where the more negative (less positive) limit is designated as minimum, is used in this data sheet for logic voltage levels only.

electrical characteristics over recommended operating free-air temperature range (unless otherwise noted)

PARAMETER		TEST CONDITIONS	TMS2150-3			TMS2150-4 TMS2150-5			UNIT
			MIN	TYP	MAX	MIN	TYP	MAX	
$V_{OH(M)}$	MATCH high-level output voltage	I_{OH} = −2 mA, V_{CC} = 4.5 V	2.4			2.4			V
		I_{OH} = −20 μA, V_{CC} = 4.5 V	3.5			3.5			
$V_{OL(M)}$	MATCH low-level output voltage	I_{OL} = 4 mA, V_{CC} = 4.5 V			0.4			0.4	V
$V_{OL(PE)}$	$\overline{PE}$ low-level output voltage	I_{OL} = 12 mA, V_{CC} = 4.5 V			0.4			0.4	V
I_I	Input current	V_I = 0 V to 5.5 V			10			10	μA
$I_{OL(PE)}$	$\overline{PE}$ output sink current	V_{OL} = 0.4 V, V_{CC} = 4.5 V	12			12			mA
I_{OS}	Short-circuit MATCH output current	V_O = GND, V_{CC} = 5.5 V			−150			−150	mA
I_{CC1}	Supply current (operative)	$\overline{RESET}$ = V_{IH}			145			135	mA
I_{CC2}	Suply current (reset)	$\overline{RESET}$ = V_{IL}			155			145	mA
C_i	Input capacitance	V_I = 0 V, f = 1 MHz			5			5	pF
C_o	Output capacitance	V_O = 0 V, f = 1 MHz			6			6	pF

switching characteristics over recommended ranges of supply voltage and operating free-air temperature

PARAMETER		TMS2150-3		TMS2150-4		TMS2150-5		UNIT
		MIN	MAX	MIN	MAX	MIN	MAX	
$t_{a(A)}$	Access time from address to MATCH		35		45		55	ns
$t_{a(A-P)}$	Access time from address to $\overline{PE}$		45		55		65	ns
$t_{a(S)}$	Access time from $\overline{S}$ to MATCH		20		25		35	ns
$t_{p(D)}$	Propagation time, data inputs to MATCH		20		35		45	ns
$t_{p(R-MH)}$	Propagation time, $\overline{RESET}$ low to MATCH high		30		30		40	ns
$t_{p(S-MH)}$	Propagation time, $\overline{S}$ high to MATCH high		20		25		35	ns
$t_{p(W-MH)}$	Propagation time, $\overline{W}$ low to MATCH high		20		25		35	ns
$t_{p(W-PH)}$	Propagation time, $\overline{W}$ low to $\overline{PE}$ high		20		25		35	ns
$t_{v(A)}$	MATCH valid time after change of address	5		5		5		ns
$t_{v(A-P)}$	$\overline{PE}$ valid time after change of address	15		15		15		ns

timing requirements over recommended ranges of supply voltage and operating free-air temperature

PARAMETER		TMS2150-3		TMS2150-4		TMS2150-5		UNIT
		MIN	MAX	MIN	MAX	MIN	MAX	
$t_{c(W)}$	Write cycle time, without writing $\overline{PE}$	30		40		50		ns
$t_{cPE(W)}$	Write cycle time, writing $\overline{PE}$ (see Note 3)	35		40		50		ns
$t_{c(rd)}$	Read cycle time	35		45		55		ns
$t_{w(RL)}$	Pulse duration, $\overline{RESET}$ low	35		35		45		ns
$t_{w(WL)}$	Pulse duration, $\overline{W}$ low, without writing $\overline{PE}$	20		25		30		ns
$t_{wPE(WL)}$	Pulse duration, $\overline{W}$ low, writing $\overline{PE}$ (see Note 3)	35		40		45		ns
$t_{su(A)}$	Address setup time before $\overline{W}$ low	0		0		0		ns
$t_{su(D)}$	Data setup time before $\overline{W}$ high	20		25		30		ns
$t_{su(P)}$	$\overline{PE}$ setup time before $\overline{W}$ high (see Note 3)	20		25		30		ns
$t_{su(S)}$	Chip select setup time before $\overline{W}$ high	20		25		30		ns
$t_{su(RH)}$	$\overline{RESET}$ inactive setup time before first tag cycle	0		0		0		ns
$t_{h(A)}$	Address hold time after $\overline{W}$ high	0		0		5		ns
$t_{h(D)}$	Data hold time after $\overline{W}$ high	5		5		10		ns
$t_{h(P)}$	$\overline{PE}$ hold time after $\overline{W}$ high	0		0		5		ns
$t_{h(S)}$	Chip select hold time after $\overline{W}$ high	0		0		0		ns
t_{AVWH}	Address valid to write enable high	30		40		50		ns

NOTE 3: Parameters $t_{wPE(WL)}$ and $t_{su(P)}$ apply only during the write cycle time when writing a parity error, $t_{cPE(W)}$.

ac test conditions

Input pulse levels . . . . GND to 3 V
Input rise and fall times . . . . 5 ns
Input timing reference levels . . . . 1.5 V
Output timing reference level . . . . 1.5 V
Output loading . . . . See Figures 1 and 2

PARAMETER MEASUREMENT INFORMATION

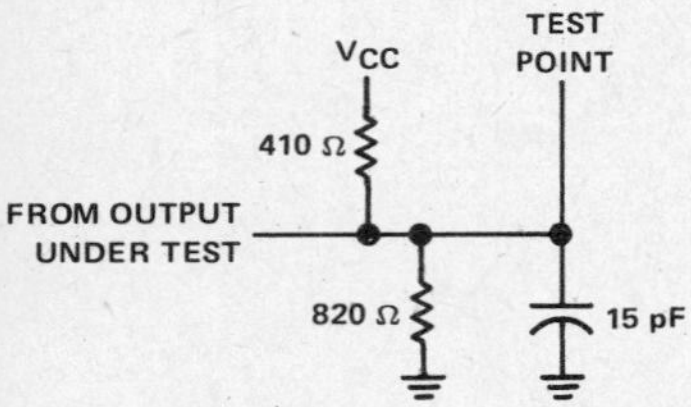
VCC
TEST POINT
410 Ω
FROM OUTPUT UNDER TEST
820 Ω
15 pF

FIGURE 1. $\overline{PE}$ OUTPUT LOAD CIRCUIT

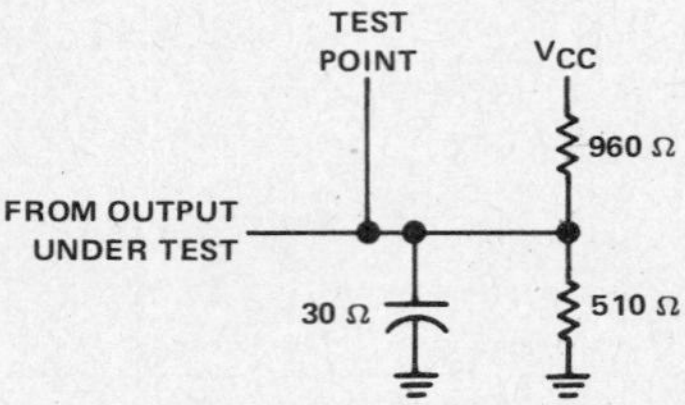
TEST POINT
VCC
960 Ω
FROM OUTPUT UNDER TEST
30 Ω
510 Ω

FIGURE 2. MATCH OUTPUT LOAD CIRCUIT

compare cycle timing (see Note 4)

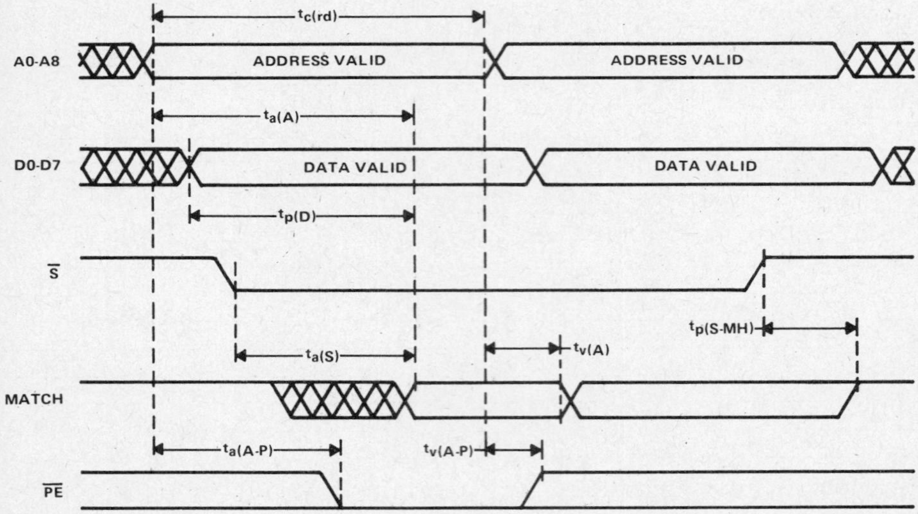
tc(rd)
A0-A8
ADDRESS VALID
ADDRESS VALID
ta(A)
D0-D7
DATA VALID
DATA VALID
tp(D)
S
tp(S-MH)
tv(A)
ta(S)
MATCH
ta(A-P)
tv(A-P)
PE

NOTE 4: Input pulse levels are 0 V and 3 V, with rise and fall times of 5 ns. The timing reference levels on the input pulses are 0.8 V and 2.0 V. The timing reference level for output pulses is 1.5 V. See Figures 1 and 2 for output loading.

TEXAS INSTRUMENTS
POST OFFICE BOX 225012 • DALLAS, TEXAS 75265

PARAMETER MEASUREMENT INFORMATION

write cycle timing (see Note 4)

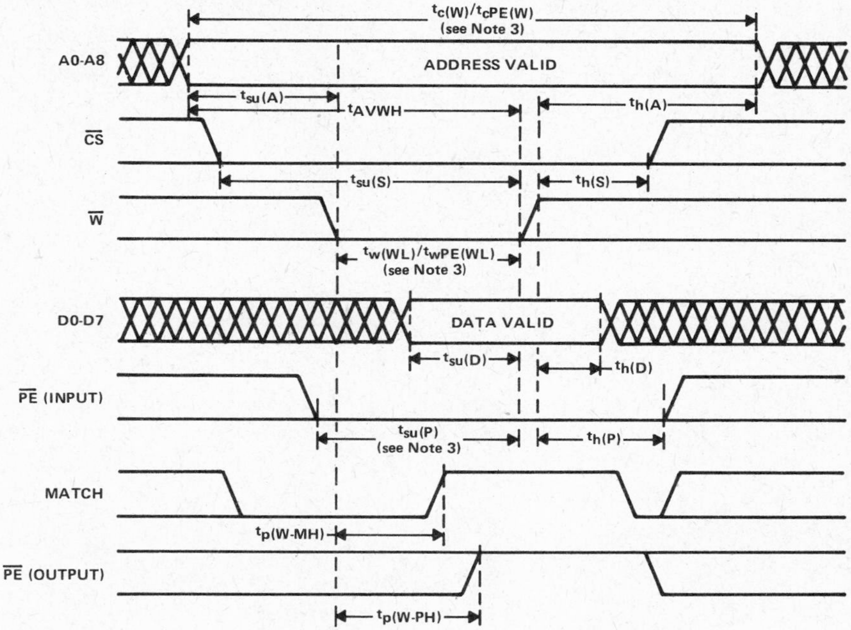

$t_{c(W)}/t_{cPE(W)}$
(see Note 3)
A0-A8
ADDRESS VALID
$t_{su(A)}$
t_{AVWH}
$t_{h(A)}$
$\overline{CS}$
$t_{su(S)}$
$t_{h(S)}$
$\overline{W}$
$t_{w(WL)}/t_{wPE(WL)}$
(see Note 3)
D0-D7
DATA VALID
$t_{su(D)}$
$t_{h(D)}$
$\overline{PE}$ (INPUT)
$t_{su(P)}$
(see Note 3)
$t_{h(P)}$
MATCH
$t_{p(W\text{-}MH)}$
$\overline{PE}$ (OUTPUT)
$t_{p(W\text{-}PH)}$

reset cycle timing (see Note 4)

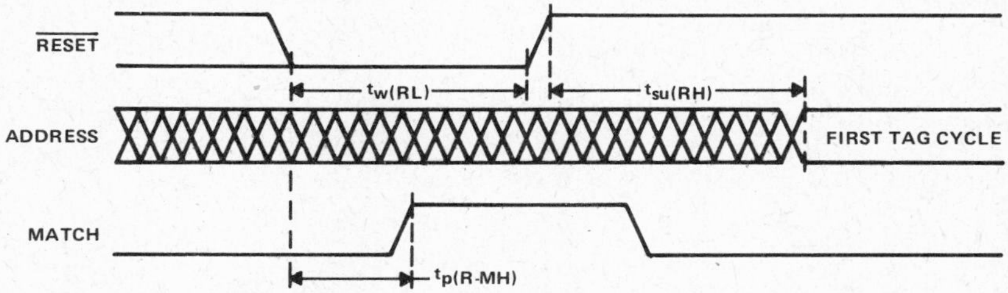

$\overline{RESET}$
$t_{w(RL)}$
$t_{su(RH)}$
ADDRESS
FIRST TAG CYCLE
MATCH
$t_{p(R\text{-}MH)}$

NOTES: 3. Parameters $t_{wPE(WL)}$ and $t_{su(P)}$ apply only during the write cycle time when writing a parity error, $t_{cPE(W)}$.
4. Input pulse levels are 0 V and 3 V, with rise and fall times of 5 ns. The timing reference levels on the input pulses are 0.8 V and 2.0 V. The timing reference level for output pulses is 1.5 V. See Figures 1 and 2 for output loading.

2
LSI Devices

D2674, JANUARY 1982—REVISED AUGUST 1985

- Controls Operation of 8K, 16K, 32K, and 64K Dynamic RAMs
- Creates Static RAM Appearance
- One Package Contains Address Multiplexer, Refresh Control, and Timing Control
- Directly Addresses and Drives Up to 256K Bytes of Memory Without External Drivers
- Operates from Microprocessor Clock
  — No Crystals, Delay Lines, or RC Networks
  — Eliminates Arbitration Delays
- Refresh May Be Internally or Externally Initiated
- Versatile
  — Strap-Selected Refresh Rate
  — Synchronous, Predictable Refresh
  — Selection of Distributed, Transparent, and Cycle-Steal Refresh Modes
  — Interfaces Easily to Popular Microprocessors
- Strap-Selected Wait-State Generation for Microprocessor/Memory Speed Matching
- Ability to Synchronize or Interleave Controller with the Microprocessor System (including Multiple Controllers)
- 3-State Outputs Allow Multiport Memory Configuration
- Performance Ranges of 150 ns, 200 ns, or 250 ns

TMS4500A . . . NL PACKAGE
(TOP VIEW)

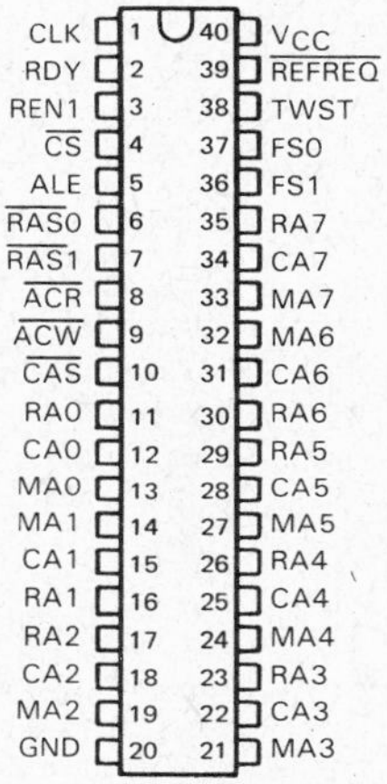
CLK 1 40 VCC
RDY 2 39 REFREQ
REN1 3 38 TWST
CS 4 37 FS0
ALE 5 36 FS1
RAS0 6 35 RA7
RAS1 7 34 CA7
ACR 8 33 MA7
ACW 9 32 MA6
CAS 10 31 CA6
RA0 11 30 RA6
CA0 12 29 RA5
MA0 13 28 CA5
MA1 14 27 MA5
CA1 15 26 RA4
RA1 16 25 CA4
RA2 17 24 MA4
CA2 18 23 RA3
MA2 19 22 CA3
GND 20 21 MA3

TMS4500A . . . FN PACKAGE
(TOP VIEW)

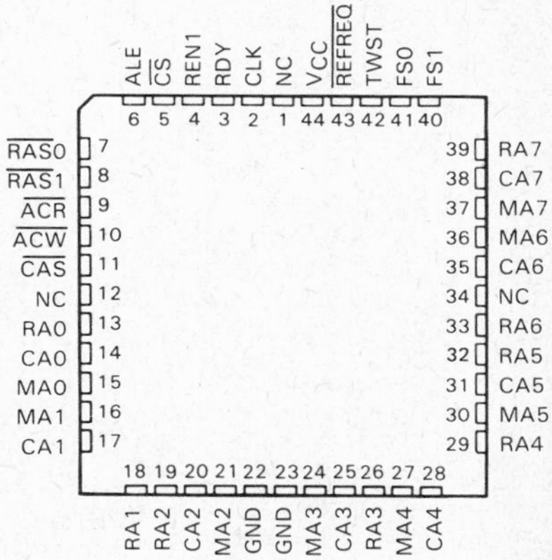
ALE CS REN1 RDY CLK NC VCC REFREQ TWST FS0 FS1
6 5 4 3 2 1 44 43 42 41 40
RAS0 7
RAS1 8
ACR 9
ACW 10
CAS 11
NC 12
RA0 13
CA0 14
MA0 15
MA1 16
CA1 17
39 RA7
38 CA7
37 MA7
36 MA6
35 CA6
34 NC
33 RA6
32 RA5
31 CA5
30 MA5
29 RA4
18 19 20 21 22 23 24 25 26 27 28
RA1 RA2 CA2 MA2 GND GND MA3 CA3 RA3 MA4 CA4

description

The TMS4500A is a monolithic DRAM system controller designed to provide address multiplexing, timing, control and refresh/access arbitration functions to simplify the interface of dynamic RAMs to microprocessor systems.

The controller contains a 16-bit multiplexer that generates the address lines for the memory device from the 16 system address bits and provides the strobe signals required by the memory to decode the address. An 8-bit refresh counter generates the 256-row addresses required for refresh.

A refresh timer is provided that generates the necessary timing to refresh the dynamic memories and assure data retention.

The TMS4500A also contains refresh/access arbitration circuitry to resolve conflicts between memory access requests and memory refresh cycles. The TMS4500A is offered in a 40-pin, 600-mil dual-in-line plastic package and 44-pin, 650-mil square plastic chip carrier package. It is characterized for operation from 0°C to 70°C.

BLOCK DIAGRAM

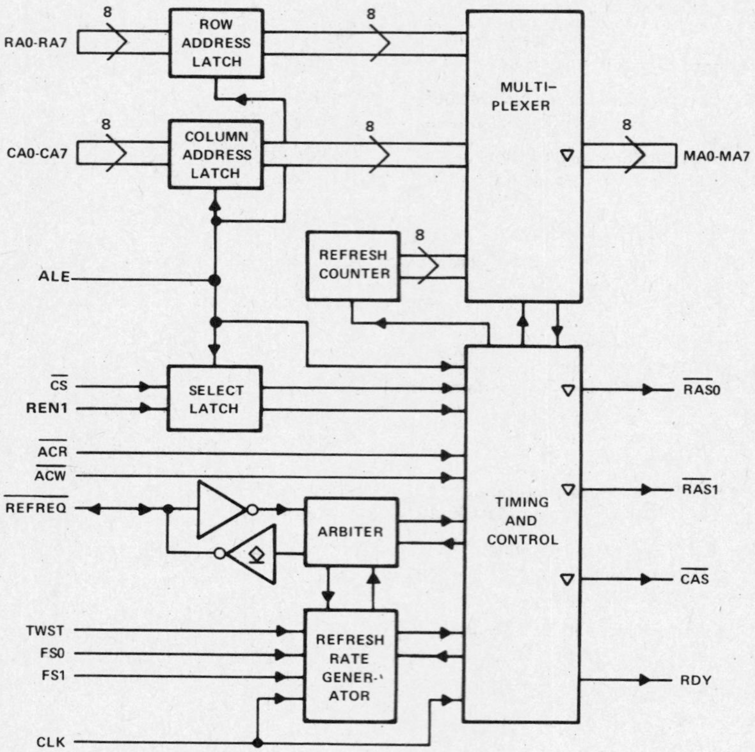
RA0-RA7
8
ROW ADDRESS LATCH
8
MULTI-PLEXER
CA0-CA7
8
COLUMN ADDRESS LATCH
8
8
MA0-MA7
8
REFRESH COUNTER
ALE
CS
REN1
SELECT LATCH
RAS0
ACR
ACW
RAS1
REFREQ
ARBITER
TIMING AND CONTROL
CAS
TWST
FS0
FS1
REFRESH RATE GENER-ATOR
RDY
CLK

pin descriptions

RA0—RA7	Input	Row Address — These address inputs are used to generate the row address for the multiplexer.
CA0—CA7	Input	Column Address — These address inputs are used to generate the column address for the multiplexer.
MA0—MA7	Output	Memory Address — These three-state outputs are designed to drive the addresses of the dynamic RAM array.
ALE	Input	Address Latch Enable — This input is used to latch the 16 address inputs, $\overline{CS}$ and REN1. This also initiates an access cycle if chip select is valid. The rising edge (low level to high level) of ALE returns $\overline{RAS}$ to the high level.
$\overline{CS}$	Input	Chip Select — A low on this input enables an access cycle. The trailing edge of ALE latches the chip select input.

TEXAS INSTRUMENTS
POST OFFICE BOX 225012 • DALLAS, TEXAS 75265

pin descriptions (continued)

REN1	Input	RAS Enable 1 — This input is used to select one of two banks of RAM via the $\overline{\text{RAS0}}$ and $\overline{\text{RAS1}}$ outputs when chip select is present. When it is low, $\overline{\text{RAS0}}$ is selected; when it is high, $\overline{\text{RAS1}}$ is selected.
$\overline{\text{ACR}}$, ACW	Input	Access Control, Read; Access Control, Write — A low on either of these inputs causes the column address to appear on MA0—MA7 and the column address strobe. The rising edge of $\overline{\text{ACR}}$ or $\overline{\text{ACW}}$ terminates the cycle by ending $\overline{\text{RAS}}$ and $\overline{\text{CAS}}$ strobes. When $\overline{\text{ACR}}$ and $\overline{\text{ACW}}$ are both low, MA0—MA7, $\overline{\text{RAS0}}$, $\overline{\text{RAS1}}$, and $\overline{\text{CAS}}$ go into a high-impedance (floating) state.
CLK	Input	System Clock — This input provides the master timing to generate refresh cycle timings and refresh rate. Refresh rate is determined by the TWST, FS1, FS0 inputs.
$\overline{\text{REFREQ}}$	Input/Output	Refresh Request — (This input should be driven by an open-collector output.) On input, a low-going edge initiates a refresh cycle and will cause the internal refresh timer to be reset on the next falling edge of the CLK. As an output, a low-going edge signals an internal refresh request and that the refresh timer will be reset on the next low-going edge of CLK. $\overline{\text{REFREQ}}$ will remain low until the refresh cycle in progress and the current refresh address is present on MA0—MA7. (Note: $\overline{\text{REFREQ}}$ contains an internal pull-up resistor with a nominal resistance of 10 kilohms.)
$\overline{\text{RAS0}}$, $\overline{\text{RAS1}}$	Output	Row Address Strobe — These three-state outputs are used to latch the row address into the bank of DRAMs selected by REN1. On refresh both signals are driven.
$\overline{\text{CAS}}$	Output	Column Address Strobe — This three-state output is used to latch the column address into the DRAM array.
RDY	Output	Ready — This totem-pole output synchronizes memories that are too slow to guarantee microprocessor access time requirements. This output is also used to inhibit access cycles during refresh when in cycle-steal mode.
TWST	Input	Timing/Wait Strap — A high on this input indicates a wait state should be added to each memory cycle. In addition it is used in conjunction with FS0 and FS1 to determine refresh rate and timing.
FS0, FS1	Input	Frequency Select 0; Frequency Select 1 — These are strap inputs to select Mode and Frequency of operation as shown in Table 1.

TABLE 1. STRAP CONFIGURATION

STRAP INPUT MODES			WAIT STATES FOR MEMORY ACCESS	REFRESH RATE	MINIMUM CLK FREQ. (MHz)	REFRESH FREQ. (kHz)	CLOCK FOR EACH FOR EACH REFRESH
TWST	FS1	FS0					
L	L	L†	0	EXTERNAL	—	REFREQ	4
L	L	H	0	CLK ÷ 31	1,984	64-95‡	3
L	H	L	0	CLK ÷ 46	2,944	64-85‡	3
L	H	H	0	CLK ÷ 61	3,904	64-82§	4
H	L	L	1	CLK ÷ 46	2,944	64-85‡	3
H	L	H	1	CLK ÷ 61	3,904	64-80‡	4
H	H	L	1	CLK ÷ 76	4,864	64-77‡	4
H	H	H	1	CLK ÷ 91	5,824	64-88¶	4

† This strap configuration resets the Refresh Timer circuitry.

‡ The highest frequency in the refresh frequency column is the frequency that is produced if the minimum CLK frequency of the next select state is used.

§ The highest frequency in the refresh column is the refresh frequency if the CLK frequency is 5 MHz.

¶ The highest frequency in the refresh column is the refresh frequency if the CLK frequency is 8 MHz.

functional description

TMS4500A consists of six basic blocks; address and select latches, refresh rate generator, refresh counter, the multiplexer, the arbiter, and timing and control block.

address and select latches

The address and select latches allow the DRAM controller to be used in systems that multiplex address and data on the same lines without external latches. The row address latches are transparent, meaning that while ALE is high, the output at MA0—MA7 follows the inputs RA0—RA7.

refresh rate generator

The refresh rate generator is a counter that indicates to the arbiter that it is time for a refresh cycle. The counter divides the clock frequency according to the configuration straps as shown in Table 1. The counter is reset when a refresh cycle is requested or when TWST, FS1 and FS0 are low. The configuration straps allow the matching of memories to the system access time.

Upon Power-Up it is necessary to provide a reset signal by driving all three straps to the controller low to initialize internal counters. A system's low-active, power-on reset ($\overline{\text{RESET}}$) can be used to accomplish this by connecting it to those straps that are desired high during operation. During this reset period, at least four clock cycles should occur.

refresh counter

The refresh counter contains the address of the row to be refreshed. The counter is decremented after each refresh cycle. [A low-to-high transition on TWST sets the refresh counter to FF_{16} (255_{10}).]

multiplexer

The multiplexer provides the DRAM array with row, column, and refresh addresses at the proper times. Its inputs are the address latches and the refresh counter. The outputs provide up to 16 multiplexed addresses on eight lines.

arbiter

The arbiter provides two operational cycles: access and refresh. The arbiter resolves conflicts between cycle requests and cycles in execution, and schedules the inhibited cycle when used in cycle-steal mode.

timing and control block

The timing and control block executes the operational cycle at the request of the arbiter. It provides the DRAM array with $\overline{\text{RAS}}$ and $\overline{\text{CAS}}$ signals. It provides the CPU with a RDY signal. It controls the multiplexer during all cycles. It resets the refresh rate generator and decrements the refresh counter during refresh cycles.

absolute maximum ratings over operating free-air temperature range (unless otherwise noted)†

Supply voltage range, V_{CC} (see Note 1) . . . . −1.5 V to 7 V
Input voltage range (any input) . . . . −1.5 V to 7 V
Continuous power dissipation . . . . 1.2 W
Operating free-air temperature range . . . . 0 °C to 70 °C
Storage temperature range . . . . −65 °C to 150 °C

† Stresses beyond those listed under "Absolute Maximum Ratings" may cause permanent damage to the device. These are stress ratings only and functional operation of the device at these or any other conditions beyond those indicated in the "Recommended Operating Conditions" section of this specification is not implied. Exposure to absolute maximum-rated conditions for extended periods may affect device reliability.

NOTE 1: Voltage values are with respect to the ground terminal.

recommended operating conditions

PARAMETER	MIN	NOM	MAX	UNIT
Supply voltage, V_{CC}	4.5	5	5.5	V
High-level input voltage, V_{IH}	2.4		6	V
Low-level input voltage, V_{IL}	−1‡		0.8	V
High-level output current, I_{OH}			−1	mA
Low-level output current, I_{OL}			4	mA
Short-circuit output current, I_{OS}§			−50	mA
Operating free-air temperature, T_A	0		70	°C

‡ The algebraic convention, where the less positive (more negative) limit is designated as minimum, is used in this data sheet for logic voltage levels only.

§ Not more than one output should be shorted at a time.

electrical characteristics over recommended operating free-air temperature range (unless otherwise noted)

PARAMETER			TEST CONDITIONS	MIN	TYP¶	MAX	UNIT
V_{OH}	High-level output voltage	MA0-MA7, RDY	V_{CC} = 4.5 V, I_{OH} = −1 mA	2.4			V
		$\overline{\text{RAS0}}$, $\overline{\text{RAS1}}$, $\overline{\text{CAS}}$		2.7			
		$\overline{\text{REFREQ}}$	V_{CC} = 4.5 V, I_{OH} = −100 μA	2.4			
V_{OL}	Low-level output voltage		V_{CC} = 4.5 V, I_{OL} = 4 mA			0.4	V
I_{IH}	High-level input current except $\overline{\text{REFREQ}}$		V_I = 5.5 V			10	μA
I_{IL}	Low-level input current	$\overline{\text{REFREQ}}$	V_I = 0			−1.25	mA
		All others				−10	μA
I_{OZ}	Off-state output current		V_{CC} = 5.5 V, V_O = 0 to 4.5 V			±50	μA
I_{CC}	Operating supply current		T_A = 0 °C		100	140	mA
C_i	Input capacitance		V_I = 0, f = 1 MHz		5		pF
C_o	Output capacitance		V_O = 0, f = 1 MHz		6		pF

¶ All typical values are at V_{CC} = 5 V, T_A = 25 °C.

timing requirements over recommended supply voltage range and operating free-air temperature (unless otherwise noted)

PARAMETER		TMS4500A-15		TMS4500A-20		TMS4500A-25		UNIT
		MIN	MAX	MIN	MAX	MIN	MAX	
$t_{c(C)}$	CLK cycle time	100		120		140		
$t_{w(CH)}$	CLK high pulse duration	40		40		40		
$t_{w(CL)}$	CLK low pulse duration	40		45		45		
t_t	Transition time, all inputs		50		50		50	
$t_{AEL\text{-}CL}$	Time delay, ALE low to CLK starting low (see Note 1)	10		10		15		
$t_{CL\text{-}AEL}$	Time delay, CLK low to ALE starting low (see Note 1)	10		10		15		
$t_{CL\text{-}AEH}$	Time delay, CLK low to ALE starting high (see Note 2)	15		20		20		
$t_{w(AEH)}$	Pulse duration, ALE high	50		60		60		
$t_{AV\text{-}AEL}$	Time delay, address REN1, $\overline{CS}$ valid to ALE low	5		10		15		ns
$t_{AEL\text{-}AX}$	Time delay, ALE low to address not valid	10		10		10		
$t_{AEL\text{-}ACL}$	Time delay, ALE low to $\overline{ACX}$ low (see Notes 3, 4, 5, and 6)	$t_{h(RA)}+30$		$t_{h(RA)}+40$		$t_{h(RA)}+50$		
$t_{ACH\text{-}CL}$	Time delay, $\overline{ACX}$ high to CLK low (see Notes 3 and 7)	20		20		20		
$t_{ACL\text{-}CH}$	Time delay, $\overline{ACX}$ low to CLK starting high (to remove RDY)	30		30		30		
$t_{RQL\text{-}CL}$	Time delay, $\overline{REFREQ}$ low to CLK starting low (see Note 8)	20		20		20		
$t_{w(RQL)}$	Pulse duration, $\overline{REFREQ}$ low	20		20		20		
$t_{w(ACL)}$	$\overline{ACX}$ low duration (see Note 9)	110		140		175		

NOTES:
1. Coincidence of the trailing edge of CLK and the trailing edge of ALE should be avoided as the refresh/access occurs on the trailing CLK edge. A trailing edge of CLK should occur during the interval from $\overline{ACX}$ high to ALE low.
2. If ALE rises before $\overline{ACX}$ and a refresh request is present, the falling edge of CLK after $t_{CL\text{-}AEH}$ will output the refresh address to MA0-MA7 and initiate a refresh cycle.
3. These specifications relate to system timing and do not directly reflect device performance.
4. On the access grant cycle following refresh, the occurrence of $\overline{CAS}$ low depends on the relative occurrence of ALE low to $\overline{ACX}$ low. If $\overline{ACX}$ occurs prior to or coincident with ALE then $\overline{CAS}$ is timed from the CLK high transition that causes $\overline{RAS}$ low. If $\overline{ACX}$ occurs 20 ns or more after ALE then $\overline{CAS}$ is timed from the CLK low transition following the CLK high transition causing $\overline{RAS}$ low.
5. For maximum speed access (internal delays on both access and access grant cycles), $\overline{ACX}$ should occur prior to or coincident with ALE.
6. $t_{h(RA)}$ is the dynamic memory row address hold time. $\overline{ACX}$ should follow ALE by $t_{AEL\text{-}CEL}$ in systems where the required $t_{h(RA)}$ is greater than $t_{REL\text{-}MAX}$ minimum.
7. The minimum of 20 ns is specified to ensure arbitration will occur on falling CLK edge, $t_{ACH\text{-}CL}$ also affects precharge time such that the minimum $t_{ACH\text{-}CL}$ should be equal or greater than: $t_{w(RH)} - t_{w(CL)} + 30$ ns (for a cycle where $\overline{ACX}$ high occurs prior to ALE high) where $t_{w(RH)}$ is the DRAM $\overline{RAS}$ precharge time.
8. This parameter is necessary only if refresh arbitration is to occur on this low-going CLK edge (in systems where refresh is synchronized to external events).
9. The specification $t_{w(ACL)}$ is designed to allow a $\overline{CAS}$ pulse. This assures normal operation of the device in testing and system operation.

TEXAS INSTRUMENTS
POST OFFICE BOX 225012 • DALLAS, TEXAS 75265

switching characteristics over recommended supply voltage range and operating free-air temperature range (see Figure 1)

PARAMETER		TEST CONDITIONS	TMS4500A-15		TMS4500A-20		TMS4500A-25		UNIT
			MIN	MAX	MIN	MAX	MIN	MAX	
$t_{AEL-REL}$	Time delay, ALE low to $\overline{RAS}$ starting low	C_L = 160 pF		35		40		50	ns
$t_{RAV-MAV}$	Time delay, row address valid to memory address valid	C_L = 160 pF		45		50		60	ns
$t_{AEH-MAV}$	Time delay, ALE high to valid memory address	C_L = 160 pF		65		75		90	ns
$t_{AEL-RYL}$	Time delay, ALE to RDY starting low (TWST = 1 or refresh in progress)	C_L = 40 pF		40		40		40	ns
$t_{AEL-CEL}$	Time delay, ALE low to $\overline{CAS}$ starting low (see Note 10)	C_L = 160 pF	60	150	70	200	80	250	ns
$t_{AEH-REH}$	Time delay, ALE high to $\overline{RAS}$ starting high	C_L = 160 pF		30		30		40	ns
$t_{ACL-MAX}$	Row address valid after $\overline{ACX}$ low	C_L = 160 pF	15		20		25		ns
$t_{MAV-CEL}$	Time delay, memory address valid to $\overline{CAS}$ starting low	C_L = 160 pF	0		0		0		ns
$t_{ACL-CEL}$	Time delay, $\overline{ACX}$ low to $\overline{CAS}$ starting low (see Note 10)	C_L = 160 pF	40	100	45	130	50	165	ns
$t_{ACH-REH}$	Time delay, $\overline{ACX}$ to $\overline{RAS}$ starting high	C_L = 160 pF		30		40		50	ns
$t_{ACH-CEH}$	Time delay, $\overline{ACX}$ high to $\overline{CAS}$ starting high	C_L = 160 pF	5	30	10	40	15	50	ns
$t_{ACH-MAX}$	Column address valid after $\overline{ACX}$ high	C_L = 160 pF	10		15		15		ns
t_{CH-RYH}	Time delay, CLK high to RDY starting high (after $\overline{ACX}$ low) (see Note 11)	C_L = 40 pF		40		45		60	ns
$t_{RFL-RFL}$	Time delay, $\overline{REFREQ}$ external till supported by $\overline{REFREQ}$ internal	C_L = 40 pF		30		35		35	ns
t_{CH-RFL}	Time delay, CLK high till $\overline{REFREQ}$ internal starting low	C_L = 40 pF		30		35		45	ns
t_{CL-MAV}	Time delay, CLK low till refresh address valid	C_L = 160 pF		75		100		125	ns
t_{CH-RRL}	Time delay, CLK high till refresh $\overline{RAS}$ starting low	C_L = 160 pF	10	50	15	60	20	80	ns
$t_{MAV-RRL}$	Time delay, refresh address valid till refresh $\overline{RAS}$ low	C_L = 160 pF	5		5		5		ns
t_{CL-RFH}	Time delay, CLK low to $\overline{REFREQ}$ starting high (3 cycle refresh)	C_L = 160 pF		50		55		75	ns
t_{CH-RFH}	Time delay, CLK high to $\overline{REFREQ}$ starting high (4 cycle refresh)	C_L = 160 pF		50		55		75	ns
t_{CH-RRH}	Time delay, CLK high to refresh $\overline{RAS}$ starting high	C_L = 160 pF	5	35	10	45	10	60	ns
t_{CH-MAX}	Refresh address valid after CLK high	C_L = 160 pF	15		20		25		ns

NOTES: 10. The falling edge of $\overline{CAS}$ occurs when both ALE low to $\overline{CAS}$ low time delay ($t_{AEL-CEL}$) and $\overline{ACX}$ low to $\overline{CAS}$ low time delay ($t_{ACL-CEL}$) have elapsed, i.e., if $\overline{ACX}$ goes low prior to ($t_{AEL-CEL}$ − $t_{ACL-CEL}$) after the falling edge of ALE, the falling edge of $\overline{CAS}$ is measured from the falling edge of ALE ($t_{AEL-CEL}$). Otherwise, the access time increases and the falling edge of $\overline{CAS}$ is measured from the falling edge of $\overline{ACX}$ ($t_{ACL-CEL}$).

11. RDY returns high on the rising edge of CLK. If TWST = 0, then on an access grant cycle RDY goes high on the same edge that causes access $\overline{RAS}$ low. If TWST = 1, then RDY goes to the high level on the first rising CLK edge after $\overline{ACX}$ goes low on access cycles and on the next rising edge after the edge that causes access $\overline{RAS}$ low on access grant cycles (assuming $\overline{ACX}$ low).

switching characteristics over recommended supply voltage range and operating free-air temperature range (see Figure 1) (continued)

PARAMETER		TEST CONDITIONS	TMS4500A-15		TMS4500A-20		TMS4500A-25		UNIT
			MIN	MAX	MIN	MAX	MIN	MAX	
t_{CH-REL}	Time delay, CLK high till access $\overline{RAS}$ starting low			60		70		95	ns
t_{CL-CEL}	Time delay, CLK low to access $\overline{CAS}$ starting low (see Note 12)	C_L = 160 pF		125		140		185	
t_{CL-MAX}	Row address valid after CLK low		25		30		40		
$t_{REL-MAX}$	Row address valid after $\overline{RAS}$ low		25		30		35		
$t_{AEH-MAX}$	Column address valid after ALE high		10		15		20		
t_{dis}	Output disable time (3-state outputs)			100		125		165	
t_{en}	Output enable time (3-state outputs)			75		80		105	
$t_{CAV-CEL}$	Time delay, column address valid to $\overline{CAS}$ starting low after refresh	C_L = 160 pF	0		0		0		
t_{CH-CEL}	Time delay, CLK high to access $\overline{CAS}$ starting low (see Note 12)			180		200		235	
t_{ACL-CL}	$\overline{ACX}$ low to CLK starting low	C_L = 40 pF	25		35		45		
$t_{ACL-RYH}$	$\overline{ACX}$ low to RDY starting high	C_L = 40 pF		40		50		60	
t_{CL-ACL}	CLK low to $\overline{ACX}$ starting low	C_L = 40 pF	0		0		0		
$t_{t(CEL)}$	$\overline{CAS}$ fall time	C_L = 320 pF		15		20		25	
$t_{t(CEH)}$	$\overline{CAS}$ rise time			30		35		45	
$t_{t(REL)}$	$\overline{RAS}$ fall time			15		20		25	
$t_{t(REH)}$	$\overline{RAS}$ rise time	C_L = 160 pF		15		20		25	
$t_{t(MAV)}$	Address transition time			20		20		25	
$t_{t(RYL)}$	RDY fall time	C_L = 40 pF		10		15		20	
$t_{t(RYH)}$	RDY rise time			20		25		35	

NOTE 12: On the access grant cycle following refresh, the occurrence of $\overline{CAS}$ low depends on the relative occurrence of ALE low to $\overline{ACX}$ low. If $\overline{ACX}$ occurs prior to or coincident with ALE then $\overline{CAS}$ is timed from the CLK high transition that causes $\overline{RAS}$ low. If $\overline{ACX}$ occurs 20 ns or more after ALE then $\overline{CAS}$ is timed from the CLK low transition following the CLK high transition causing $\overline{RAS}$ low. (See Refresh Cycle Timing Diagram)

PARAMETER MEASUREMENT INFORMATION

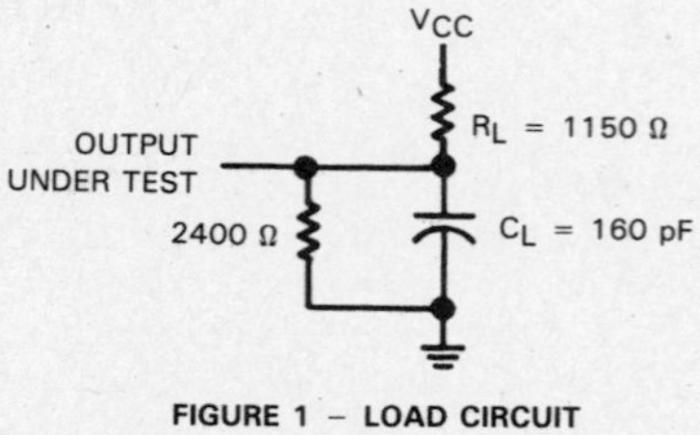
VCC
RL = 1150 Ω
OUTPUT
UNDER TEST
2400 Ω
CL = 160 pF

FIGURE 1 – LOAD CIRCUIT

2 LSI Devices

access cycle timing

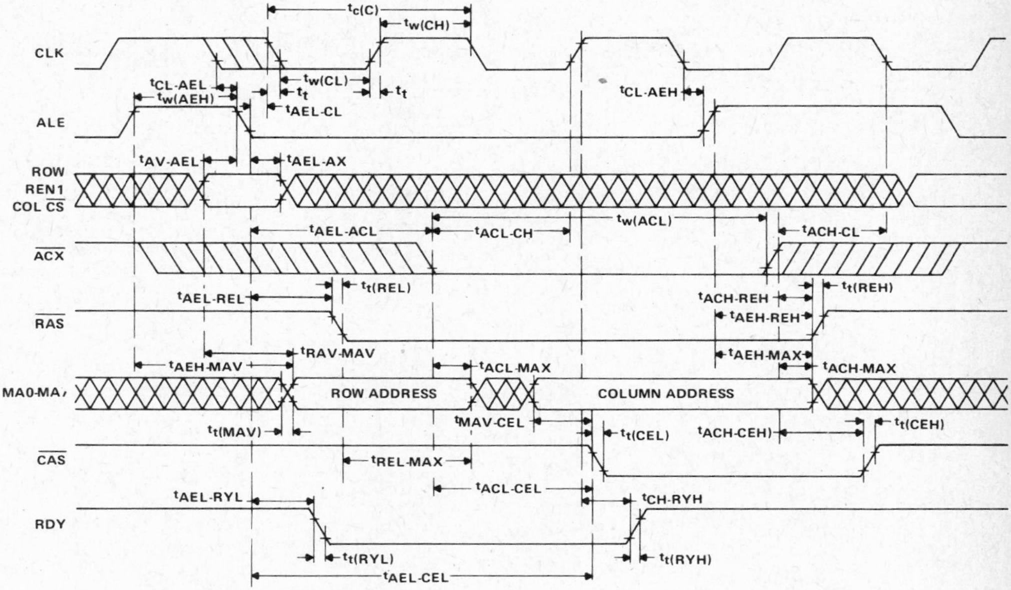
CLK
ALE
ROW
REN1
COL CS
ACX
RAS
MA0-MA7
CAS
RDY
ROW ADDRESS
COLUMN ADDRESS
tc(C)
tw(CH)
tw(CL)
tCL-AEL
tw(AEH)
tt
tAEL-CL
tCL-AEH
tAV-AEL
tAEL-AX
tAEL-ACL
tACL-CH
tw(ACL)
tACH-CL
tt(REL)
tAEL-REL
tACH-REH
tt(REH)
tAEH-REH
tRAV-MAV
tAEH-MAX
tAEH-MAV
tACL-MAX
tACH-MAX
tMAV-CEL
tt(MAV)
tt(CEL)
tACH-CEH
tt(CEH)
tREL-MAX
tACL-CEL
tAEL-RYL
tCH-RYH
tt(RYL)
tt(RYH)
tAEL-CEL

refresh request timing

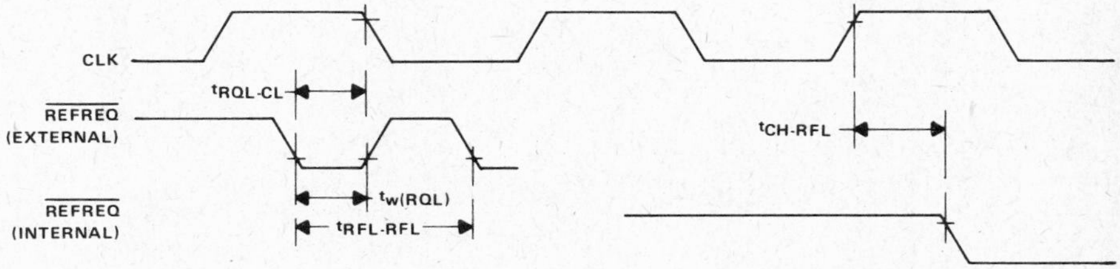
CLK
REFREQ
(EXTERNAL)
REFREQ
(INTERNAL)
tRQL-CL
tw(RQL)
tRFL-RFL
tCH-RFL

ready timing (ACX during CLK high) (see notes 13 thru 16)

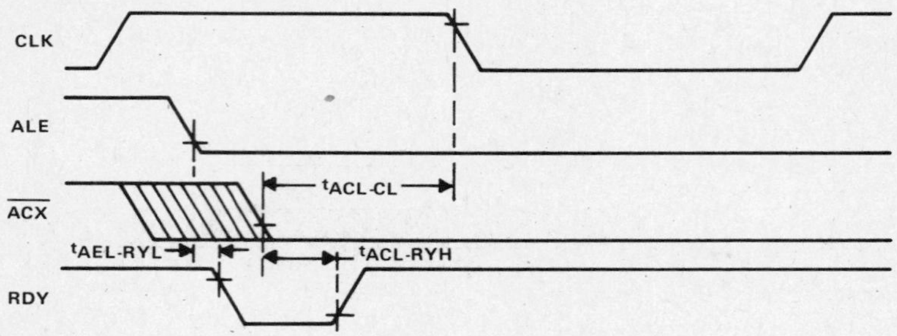
CLK
ALE
$\overline{ACX}$
RDY
$t_{ACL\text{-}CL}$
$t_{AEL\text{-}RYL}$
$t_{ACL\text{-}RYH}$

RDY starting high is timed from $\overline{ACX}$ low ($t_{ACL\text{-}RYH}$) for the condition $\overline{ACX}$ going low while CLK high.

ready timing (ACX during CLK low) (see notes 13 thru 16)

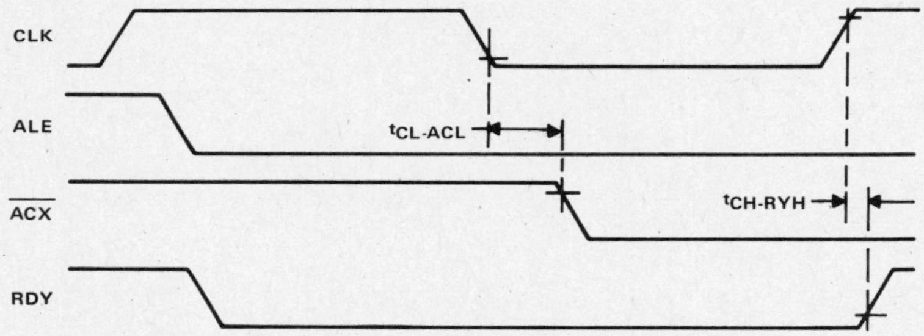
CLK
ALE
$\overline{ACX}$
RDY
$t_{CL\text{-}ACL}$
$t_{CH\text{-}RYH}$

RDY starting high is timed from CLK high ($t_{CH\text{-}RYH}$) for the condition ACX going low while CLK low.

NOTES:
13. For RDY high transition (during normal access) to be timed from the rising edge of CLK, $\overline{ACX}$ must occur $t_{CL\text{-}ACL}$ after the falling edge of CLK.
14. For $\overline{ACX}$ prior to the falling edge of CLK by $t_{ACL\text{-}CL}$, the RDY high transition will be $t_{ACL\text{-}RYH}$.
15. $t_{ACL\text{-}CL}$ is a limiting parameter for control of RDY to be dependent upon $\overline{ACX}$ low.
16. During the interval for $t_{ACL\text{-}CL}$ < MINIMUM to $t_{CL\text{-}ACL}$ > MINIMUM, the control of RDY may vary between the rising clock edge or falling edge of $\overline{ACX}$.

output 3-state timing

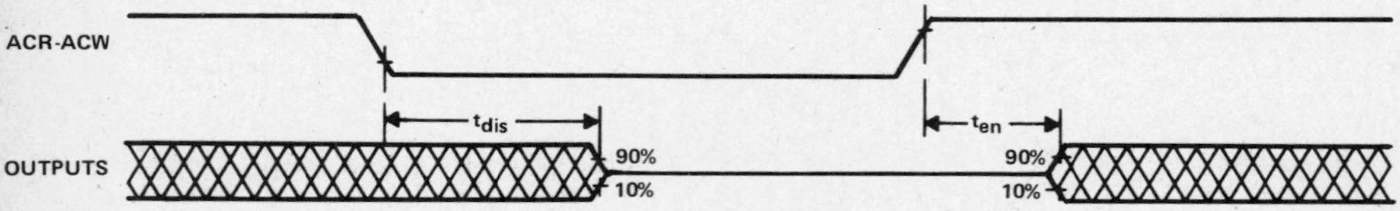
ACR-ACW
OUTPUTS
t_{dis}
t_{en}
90%
10%
90%
10%

TEXAS INSTRUMENTS
POST OFFICE BOX 225012 • DALLAS, TEXAS 75265

refresh cycle timing (three-cycle)

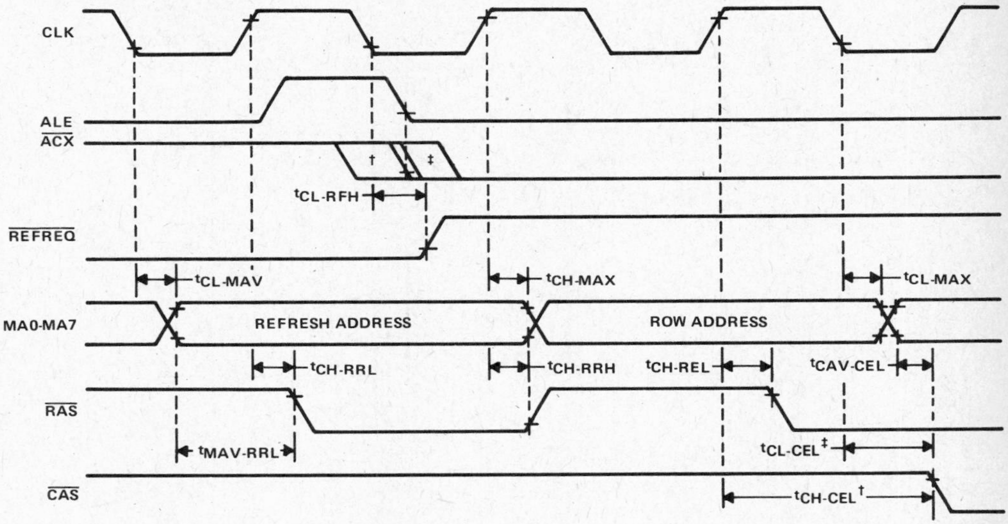
CLK
ALE
$\overline{ACX}$
†
‡
t_{CL-RFH}
$\overline{REFREQ}$
t_{CL-MAV}
t_{CH-MAX}
t_{CL-MAX}
MA0-MA7
REFRESH ADDRESS
ROW ADDRESS
t_{CH-RRL}
t_{CH-RRH}
t_{CH-REL}
$t_{CAV-CEL}$
$\overline{RAS}$
$t_{MAV-RRL}$
t_{CL-CEL}‡
$\overline{CAS}$
t_{CH-CEL}†

refresh cycle timing (four-cycle)

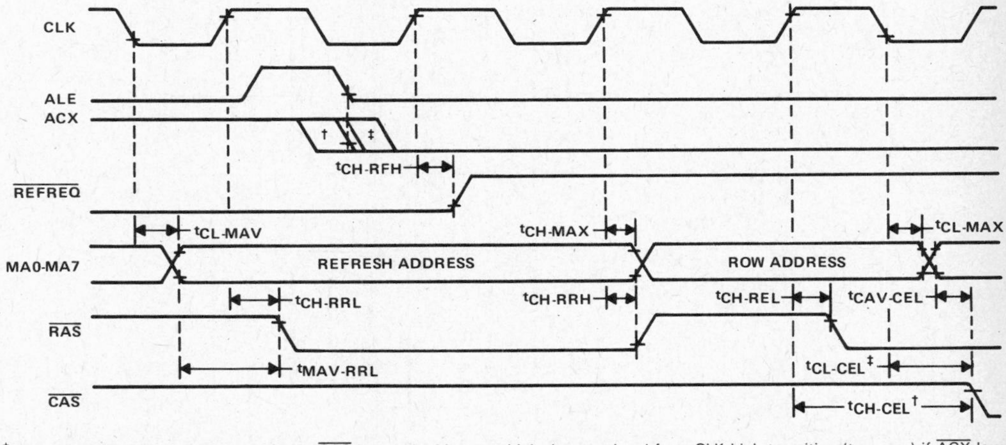
CLK
ALE
ACX
†
‡
t_{CH-RFH}
$\overline{REFREQ}$
t_{CL-MAV}
t_{CH-MAX}
t_{CL-MAX}
MA0-MA7
REFRESH ADDRESS
ROW ADDRESS
t_{CH-RRL}
t_{CH-RRH}
t_{CH-REL}
$t_{CAV-CEL}$
$\overline{RAS}$
$t_{MAV-RRL}$
t_{CL-CEL}‡
$\overline{CAS}$
t_{CH-CEL}†

† On access grant cycle following refresh, $\overline{CAS}$ low and address multiplexing are timed from CLK high transition (t_{CH-CEL}) if $\overline{ACX}$ low occurs prior to or coincident with the falling edge of ALE.

‡ On access grant cycle following refresh, $\overline{CAS}$ low and address multiplexing are timed from CLK low transition (t_{CL-CEL}) if $\overline{ACX}$ low occurs 20 ns or more after the falling edge of ALE.

typical access/refresh/access cycle
(three-cycle, TWST is low)

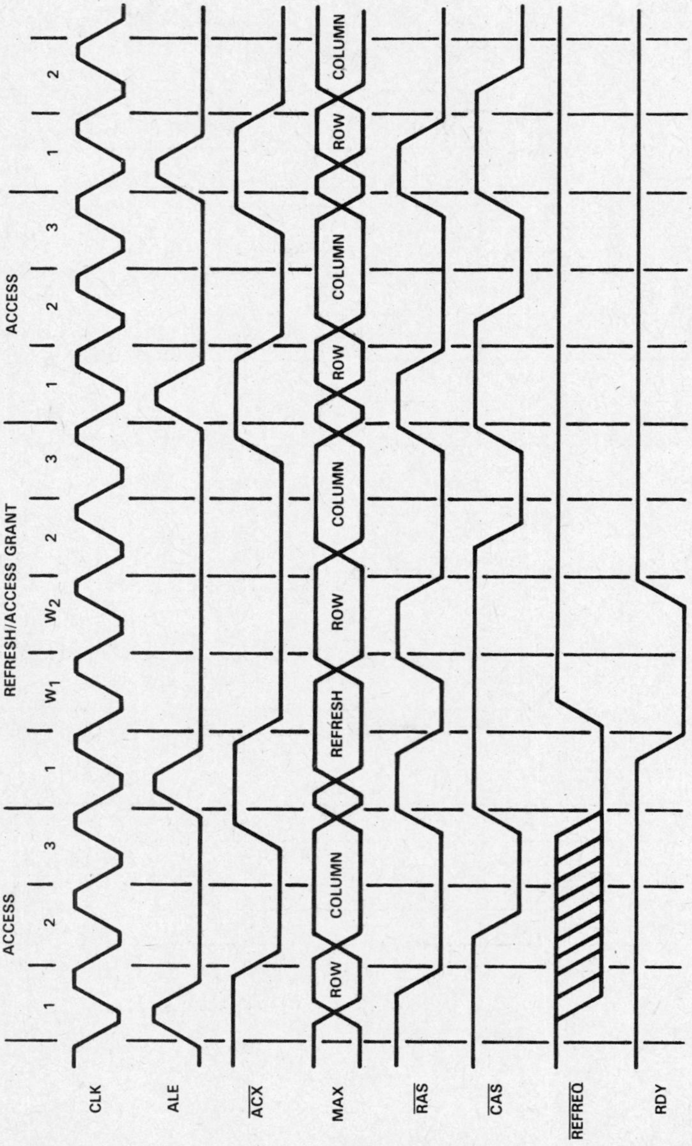
ACCESS
REFRESH/ACCESS GRANT
ACCESS
1
2
3
1
W_1
W_2
2
3
1
2
3
1
2
ROW
COLUMN
REFRESH
ROW
COLUMN
ROW
COLUMN
ROW
COLUMN
CLK
ALE
$\overline{ACX}$
MAX
$\overline{RAS}$
$\overline{CAS}$
$\overline{REFREQ}$
RDY

typical access/refresh/access cycle
(four-cycle, TWST is low)

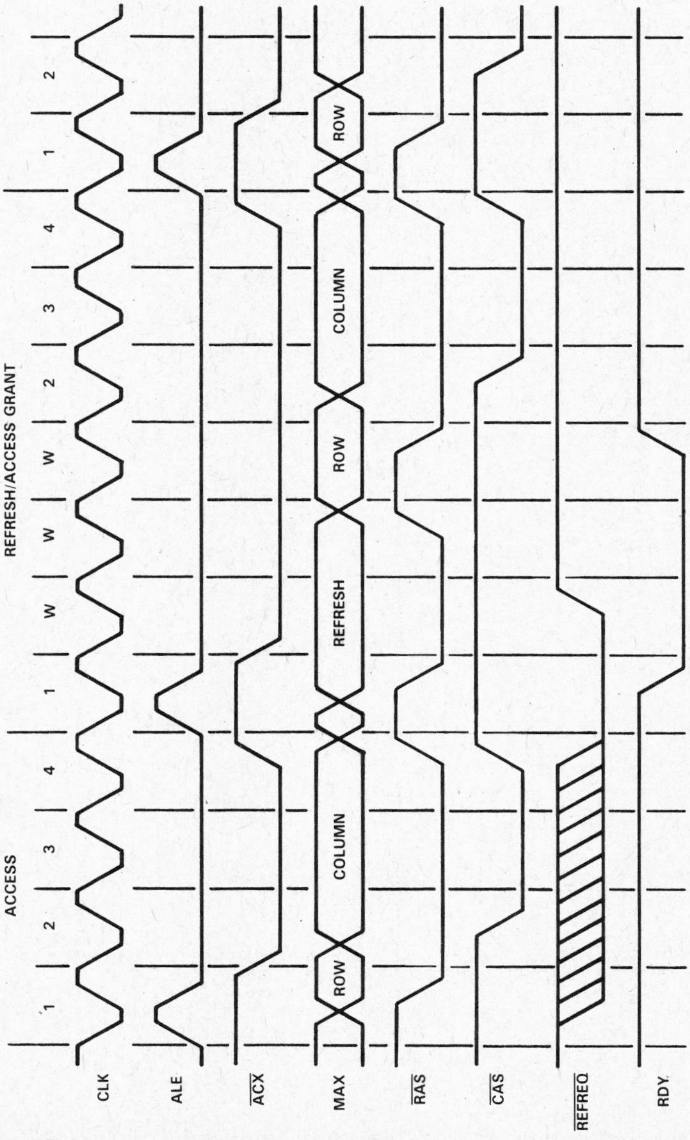
ACCESS
REFRESH/ACCESS GRANT
1
2
3
4
1
W
W
W
2
3
4
1
2
ROW
COLUMN
REFRESH
ROW
COLUMN
ROW
CLK
ALE
ACX
MAX
RAS
CAS
REFREQ
RDY

typical access/refresh/access cycle (three-cycle, TWST is high)

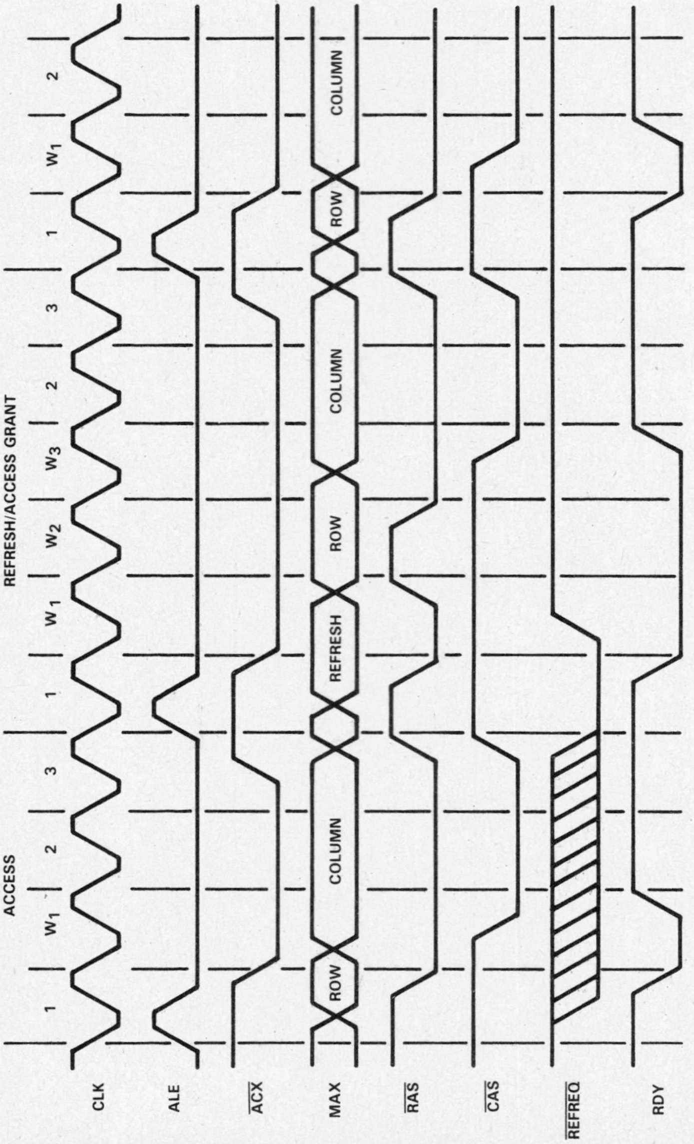
ACCESS
REFRESH/ACCESS GRANT
1
W_1
2
3
1
W_1
W_2
W_3
2
3
1
W_1
2
ROW
COLUMN
REFRESH
ROW
COLUMN
ROW
COLUMN
CLK
ALE
$\overline{ACX}$
MAX
$\overline{RAS}$
$\overline{CAS}$
$\overline{REFREQ}$
RDY

TEXAS INSTRUMENTS
POST OFFICE BOX 225012 • DALLAS, TEXAS 75265

typical access/refresh/access cycle
(four-cycle, TWST is high)

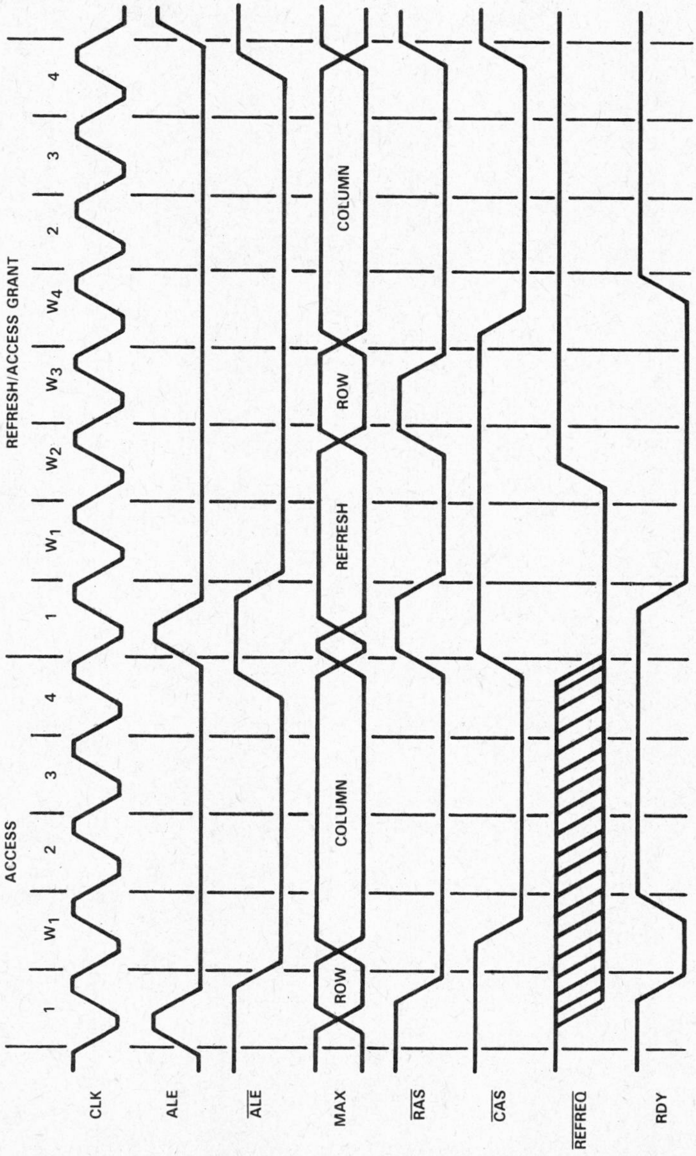
ACCESS
REFRESH/ACCESS GRANT
1
W1
2
3
4
W2
W3
W4
CLK
ALE
ALE
MAX
RAS
CAS
REFREQ
RDY
ROW
COLUMN
REFRESH

Advanced Schottky Family

TEXAS INSTRUMENTS

IMPORTANT NOTICE

Advanced Schottky Family (ALS/AS) Application

Contents

List of Illustrations

List of Illustrations (Continued)

List of Tables

INTRODUCTION

The purpose of this Application Report is to assist the designers of high-performance digital logic systems in the use of the new series of Advanced Schottky-clamped* TTL integrated circuits.

Detailed electrical characteristics of these devices are provided and, if available, tables have been included that compare specific parameters of the devices with those of other logic families. In addition, interfamily information is provided to allow system designers to mix logic families in the same circuit. This allows the designer to use the relative merits of each logic family in high preformance state-of-the-art designs.

The major subject areas covered in this Application Report are as follows:

- Advanced Schottky process
- Fanouts
- Transfer characteristics
- Input and output parameters
- Speed and power information
- Noise margins
- Power supply considerations
- Noise sources and their abatement
- Back panel and printed circuit wiring guidelines
- Line driving and receiving

INTRODUCTION TO ADVANCED SCHOTTKY-CLAMPED TTL

Series 54/74 transistor-transistor logic (TTL) has, since its introduction in 1965, become the most popular digital integrated circuit logic family ever offered. Its popularity has allowed the development of high-volume production techniques which have made it the most economical approach to the implementation of major portions of medium-to-high performance digital logic systems. These systems range from simple decision making to highly complex real-time computer installations that handle worldwide data processing.

The proliferation of and economical impact of these digital logic systems has created a demand for constant improvement in efficiency. In response to demand, Texas Instruments examined the advantages gained by Schottky clamping. An increase in speed and performance was discovered in the use of Schottky barrier-diode clamping. The process was patented in the United States and the Schottky series 54S/74S catalog parts were made available in the early 1970s. A series 54LS/74LS was introduced later. The series 54LS/74LS was slower that the 54S/74S series but had a much lower power consumption.

*Integrated Schottky-Barrier-diode-clamped transistor is patented by Texas Instruments Incorporated, U.S. Patent Number 3,463,975.

Recent innovations in integrated circuit design have made it possible to develop two new families: the Advanced Schottky (54AS/74AS) series and the Advanced Low-Power Schottky (54ALS/74ALS) series. The 'ALS and 'AS series provide considerable higher speeds than the 'LS and 'S series, respectively. The 'ALS series offers a substantial reduction in power consumption over the 'LS series, and the 'AS series offers a substantial reduction in power consumption over the 'S series. The 'ALS/'AS series is pin-to-pin compatible with the 'LS/'S series.

SPEED-POWER SLOTS FILLED BY 'ALS AND 'AS TTL

Digital integrated circuits have historically been characterized for both speed and power. The series 54S/74S devices contain 19 mW NAND gates and 125-MHz flip-flops and the series 54LS/74LS devices contain 2-mW NAND gates and 45-MHz flip-flops. Either of these logic families could be used to design a 2-MHz system, therefore categorization strictly on the basis of power and speed is inconclusive with respect to system efficiency. To provide a means of measuring the overall circuit efficiency and performance, a speed-power product efficiency index for integrated circuits was developed. The rating of an integrated circuit is obtained by multiplying the gate propagation delay by the gate power dissipation.

Table 1 provides propagation delay times, power dissipation, and speed-power product for the Texas Instruments TTL series. In addition, it provides flip-flop frequency for each family as an indicator of system performance. The speed-power product rating system (measured in picojoules) is divided into circuits where speed is the prime factor and circuits where low-power is the prime factor. The 'ALS series speed-power product is approximately 4 times less than that of the 'LS series and the 'AS series speed-power product is approximately 4 times less than the 'S series. Figure 1 is a graphic analysis of the speed-power points for the various TTL families.

ADDITIONAL ADVANTAGES OFFERED BY 'ALS AND 'AS DEVICES

The 'ALS and 'AS devices offer the following additional advantages:

1. TTL compatible with 54/74, 54S/74S, 54L/74L, 54LS/74LS, and 54H/74H series gates for selectively upgrading existing systems
2. Suppresses the effects of line ringing and significantly reduces undershoot
3. Higher thresholds (noise immunity) and better stability across operating free-air temperature range
4. Input current requirement reduced by up to 50%

Table 1. Typical Performance Characteristics by TTL Series

CIRCUIT TECHNOLOGY	MINIMIZING POWER					MINIMIZING DELAY TIME				
	FAMILY	PROP DELAY (ns)	PWR DISS (mW)	SPD/PWR PRODUCT (pJ)	MAXIMUM FLIP-FLOP FREQ (MHz)	FAMILY	PROP DELAY (ns)	PWR DISS (mW)	SPD/PWR PRODUCT (pJ)	MAXIMUM FLIP-FLOP FREQ (MHz)
Gold Doped	TTL	10	10	100	35	TTL	10	10	100	35
	L TTL	33	1	33	3	H TTL	6	22	132	50
Schottky Clamped	LS TTL	9	2	18	45	S TTL	3	19	57	125
	'ALS	4	1.2	4.8	70	'AS	1.7	8	13.6	200

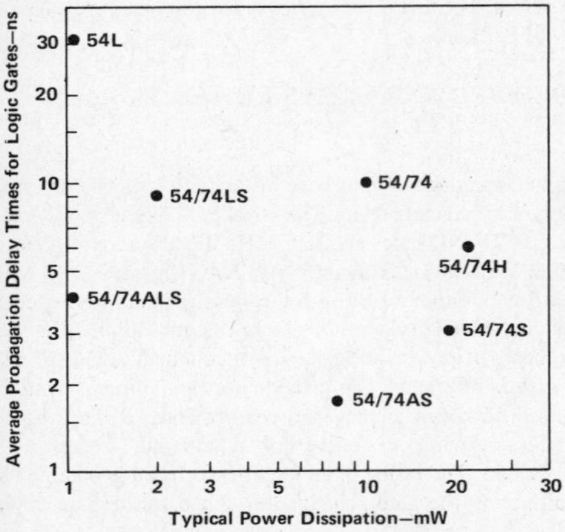
Average Propagation Delay Times for Logic Gates—ns
30
20
10
5
3
2
1
54L
54/74LS
54/74
54/74H
54/74ALS
54/74S
54/74AS
1
2
3
5
10
20
30
Typical Power Dissipation—mW

Figure 1. Speed-Power Relationships of Digital Integrated Circuits

5. Fanout is doubled
6. Terminated lines or controlled impedance circuit boards are normally not required.
7. The 'AS series offers shorter propagation delays and higher clock frequencies with relatively low power consumption.
8. The maximum flip-flop frequency has been increased to 200 MHz.

CONCEPTS OF DEFINING SERIES 'AS AND 'ALS

Both the 'ALS and 'AS series are electrically and pinout compatible with existing TTL series. The 'ALS series is suitable for replacing all TTL families except in the very highest frequency applications. Replacement with 'ALS will result in lower power consumption, smaller power supply current spikes, and, in some cases, better noise immunity than the other families. In those cases where a very high operating frequency is required, the 'AS series can be used. The 'AS devices require less than one-half of the supply current of the 'S series and has approximately twice the clocking frequency. The 'ALS devices are ideal for improving effeciency at the lower speeds. The 'AS devices are ideal for replacement of high-speed logic families including ECL 10K series.

Compatibility With Other TTL Families

To ensure complete electrical compatibility in systems using or intending to use a mixture of existing TTL families and the new 'ALS/'AS families, specific guidelines have been implemented. These guidelines ensure the continuation of desirable characteristics and incorporate newer techniques to improve performance and/or simplify the use of TTL families. Figure 2 illustrates the comparison of essential parameters of each family and shows that complete compatibility is maintained throughout the 54/74 families.

Fanout

The compatible ratings for fanout simplify the implementation of logic and provide a freedom of choice in the use of any of the seven performance ranges to design a digital logic system. Any of the Texas Instruments TTL series gates can be used to drive any other gate without the use of an interface or level-shifting circuit. The use of totem-pole-(push-pull) type output stages provides a low output impedance and the capability for both sourcing and sinking current. The output is easily adapted for driving MOS and CMOS circuits as well as the interface circuits between the output and the devices it controls. Figure 3 illustrates fanout capability.

USING THE SCHOTTKY BARRIER DIODE

The Advanced Schottky Family has been developed from two earlier concepts: the Baker Clamp and the Schottky Barrier-Diode (SBD). The use of the Baker Clamp and SBD concepts resulted in the Schottky Clamped Transistor. The Schottky clamped transistor produced the increased switching speed associated with the S series integrated circuits. The additional advances that have led to the development of 'ALS and 'AS gates and the actual gates are discussed later.

Analysis of the Schottky Clamped Transistor

The use of the Baker Clamp, shown in Figure 4, is a method of avoiding saturation of a discrete transistor. The diode forward voltage is 0.3 V to 0.4 V as compared to 0.7 V for the base-emitter junction diode. When the transistor is turned on, base current drives the transistor toward

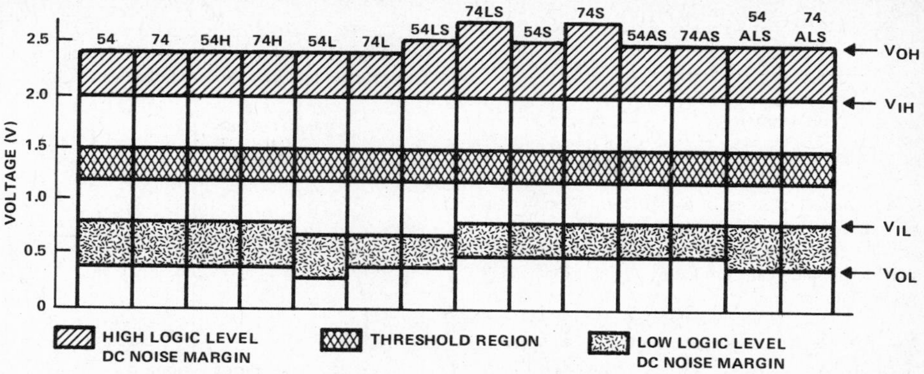

VOLTAGE (V)
2.5
2.0
1.5
1.0
0.5
0
54
74
54H
74H
54L
74L
54LS
74LS
54S
74S
54AS
74AS
54 ALS
74 ALS
VOH
VIH
VIL
VOL
HIGH LOGIC LEVEL DC NOISE MARGIN
THRESHOLD REGION
LOW LOGIC LEVEL DC NOISE MARGIN

Figure 2. Series 54/74 TTL Family Compatible Levels Showing DC Noise Margins

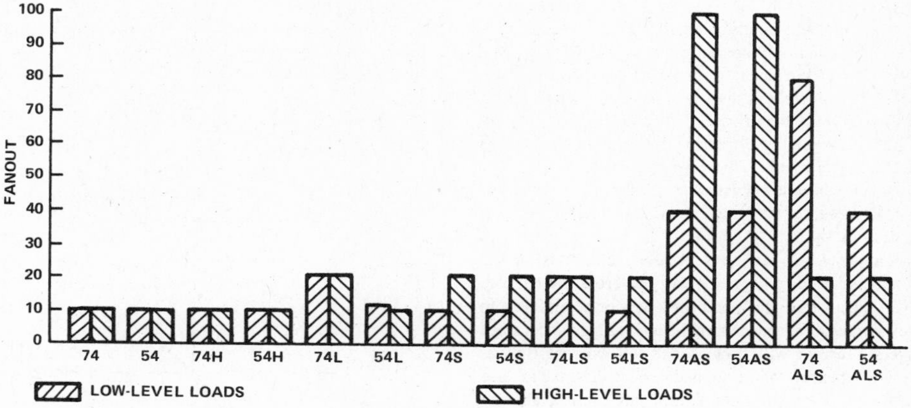

FANOUT
100
90
80
70
60
50
40
30
20
10
0
74
54
74H
54H
74L
54L
74S
54S
74LS
54LS
74AS
54AS
74 ALS
54 ALS
LOW-LEVEL LOADS
HIGH-LEVEL LOADS

Figure 3. Fanout Capability

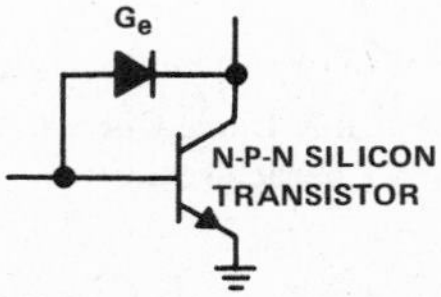

Ge
N-P-N SILICON TRANSISTOR

Figure 4. Baker Clamp

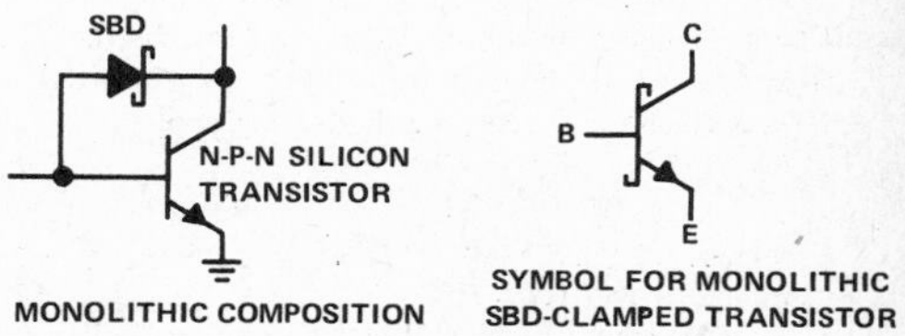

SBD
N-P-N SILICON TRANSISTOR
C
B
E
MONOLITHIC COMPOSITION
SYMBOL FOR MONOLITHIC SBD-CLAMPED TRANSISTOR

Figure 5. The Schottky-Clamped Transistor

saturation. The collector voltage drops, the germanium diode begins to conduct forward current, and excess base drive is diverted from the base-collector junction of the transistor. This causes the transistor to be held out of deep saturation, the excess base charge to not be stored, and the turn-off time to be dramatically reduced.

A germanium diode cannot be incorporated into a monolithic silicon integrated circuit. Therefore, the germanium diode must be replaced with a silicon diode which has a lower forward voltage drop than the base-collector junction of the transistor. A normal p-n diode will not meet this requirement. The SBD illustrated in Figure 5 can be used to meet the requirement.

The SBD illustrated in Figure 6 is a rectifying metal-semiconductor contact formed between a metal and a highly doped N semiconductor.

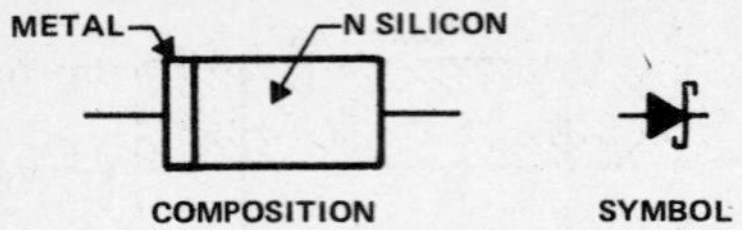
METAL
N SILICON
COMPOSITION
SYMBOL

Figure 6. Schottky Barrier-Diode

The qualitative physics of an SBD is illustrated in Figure 7. The valence and conduction bands in a metal overlap make available a large number of free-energy states. The free-energy states can be filled by any electrons which are injected into the conduction band. A finite number of electrons exist in the conduction band of a semiconductor. The number of electrons depends mainly upon the thermal energy and the level of impurity atoms in the material. When a metal-semiconductor junction is formed, free electrons flow across the junction from the semiconductor, via the conduction band, and fill the free-energy states in the metal. This flow of electrons builds a depletion potential across the barrier. This depletion potential opposes the electron flow and, eventually, is sufficient to sustain a balance where there is no net electron flow across the barrier.

Under forward bias (metal positive), there are many electrons with enough thermal energy to cross the barrier potential into the metal. This forward bias is called "hot injection." Because the barrier width is decreased as forward bias V_F increases, forward current will increase rapidly with an increase in V_F.

When the SBD is reverse biased, electrons in the semiconductor require greater energy to cross the barrier. However, electrons in the metal see a barrier potential from the side essentially independent of the bias voltage and a small net reverse current will flow. Since this current flow is relatively independent of the applied reverse bias, the reverse current flow will not increase significantly until avalanche breakdown occurs.

A simple metal-n semiconductor collector contact is an ohmic contact while the SBD contact is a rectifying contact. The difference is controlled by the level of doping in the semiconductor material. As the doping is increased, the contact becomes more ohmic. Figure 8 illustrates the current-voltage characteristics according the doping applied.

Current in the SBD is carried by majority carriers. Current in the p-n junction is carried by minority carriers. The resultant minority carrier storage causes the switching

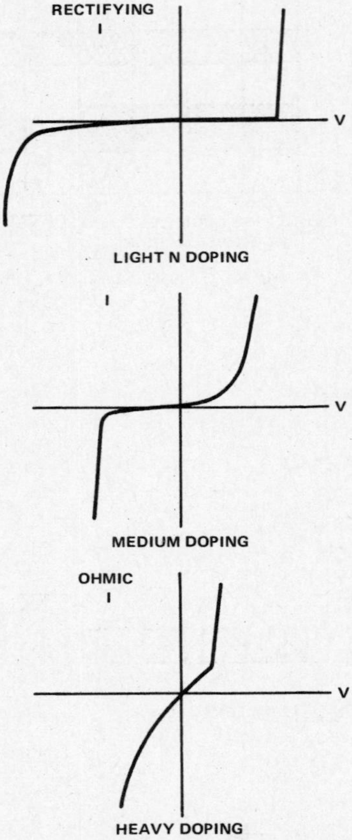
RECTIFYING
I
V
LIGHT N DOPING
I
V
MEDIUM DOPING
OHMIC
I
V
HEAVY DOPING

Figure 8. Metal-N Diode Current-Voltage Characteristics

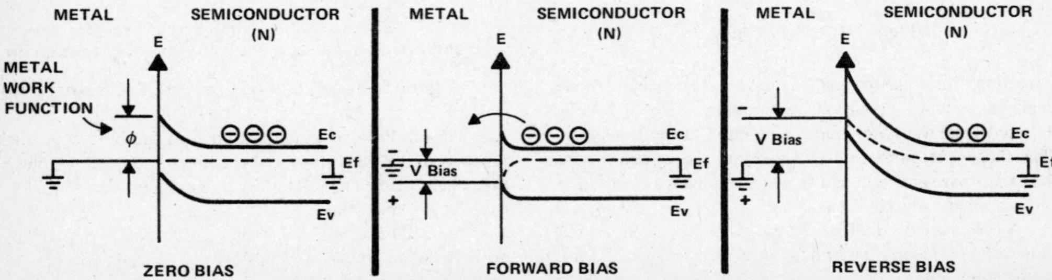
METAL
SEMICONDUCTOR (N)
E
METAL WORK FUNCTION
φ
Ec
Ef
Ev
ZERO BIAS
METAL
SEMICONDUCTOR (N)
E
V Bias
Ec
Ef
Ev
FORWARD BIAS
METAL
SEMICONDUCTOR (N)
E
V Bias
Ec
Ef
Ev
REVERSE BIAS

Figure 7. Schottky Barrier-Diode Energy Diagrams

time of a p-n junction to be limited when switched from forward bias to reverse bias. A p-n junction is inherently slower than an SBD even when doped with gold.

Another major difference between the SBD and p-n junction is the forward voltage drop. For diodes of the same surface area, the SBD will have a larger forward current at the same forward bias regardless of the type of metal used. The SBD forward voltage drop is lower at a given current than a p-n junction. Figure 9 illustrates the current carriers and forward current-voltage characteristics differences between the SBD and p-n junction. The SBD meets the requirements of a silicon diode which will clamp a silicon n-p-n transistor out of saturation.

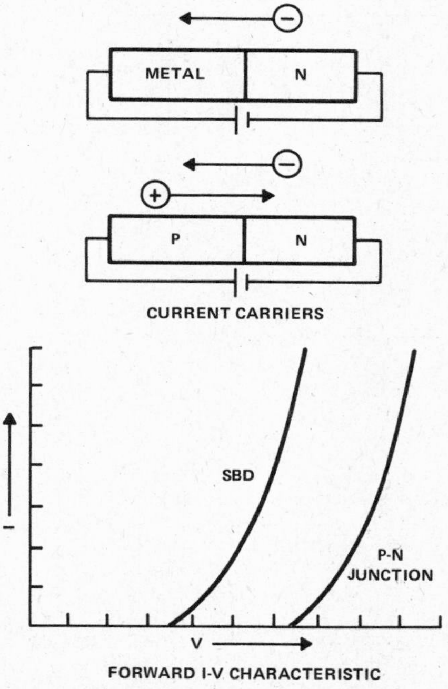
METAL
N
P
N
CURRENT CARRIERS
SBD
P-N
JUNCTION
V
I
FORWARD I-V CHARACTERISTIC

Figure 9. Differences Between P-N and Schottky Barrier-Diodes

The Advanced Schottky process differs from the Schottky process in that it uses ion implantation of impurities instead of diffusion. Ion implantation gives greater control on the depth of doping and resolution. Because of a thinner epitaxial layer and smaller all around geometries, smaller parasitic capacitances are encountered. The performance of the SBD is also enhanced by the use of oxide isolation of the transistors. This reduces the collector-substrate capacitance. Figure 10 illustrates the 'LS/'S process which consists of conventional masks, junction isolation, and a standard metal system and Figure 11 illustrates the 'ALS/'AS process which consists of composed masks, ion implantation, oxide isolation, and a standard metal system.

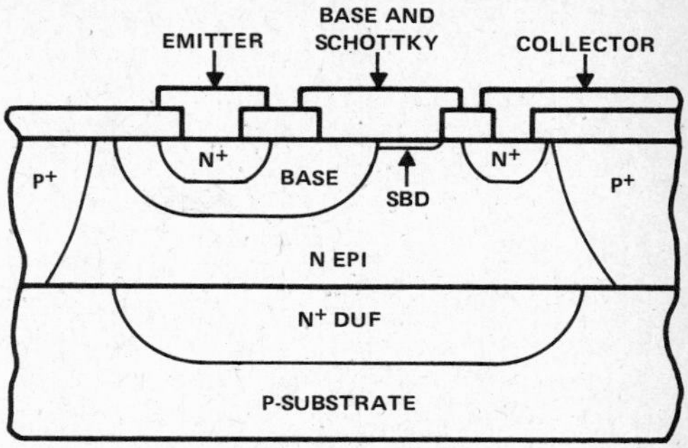
EMITTER
BASE AND
SCHOTTKY
COLLECTOR
N+
BASE
SBD
N+
P+
P+
N EPI
N+ DUF
P-SUBSTRATE

Figure 10. Standard Process ('LS/'S)

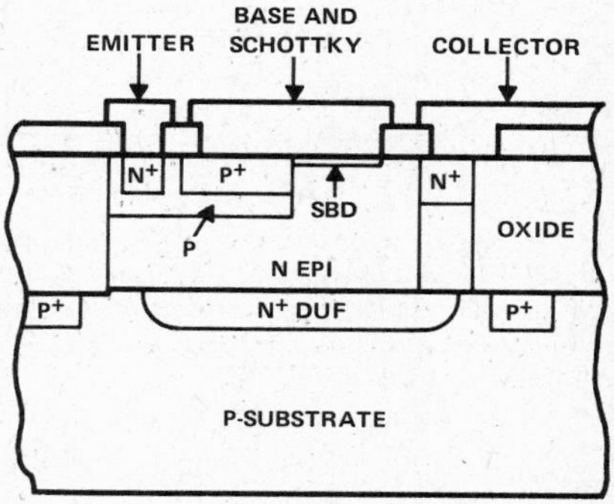
EMITTER
BASE AND
SCHOTTKY
COLLECTOR
N+
P+
SBD
N+
OXIDE
P
N EPI
P+
N+ DUF
P+
P-SUBSTRATE

Figure 11. Advanced Process ('ALS/'AS)

Analysis of 'ALS and 'AS NAND Gates

The 'ALS and 'AS NAND gates in Figures 12 and 13 combine the desirable features of improved TTL circuits with the technological advantages of full Schottky clamping, ion implantation, and oxide isolation to achieve very fast switching times at a reduced speed-power product. The improvements and advantages are as follows:

1. Full Schottky clamping of all saturating transistors virtually eliminates storing excessive base charge and significantly enhances turn-off time of the transistors.
2. Elimination of transistor storage time provides stable switching times across the temperature range.
3. An active turn-off is added to square up the transfer characteristic and provide an improved high-level noise immunity.

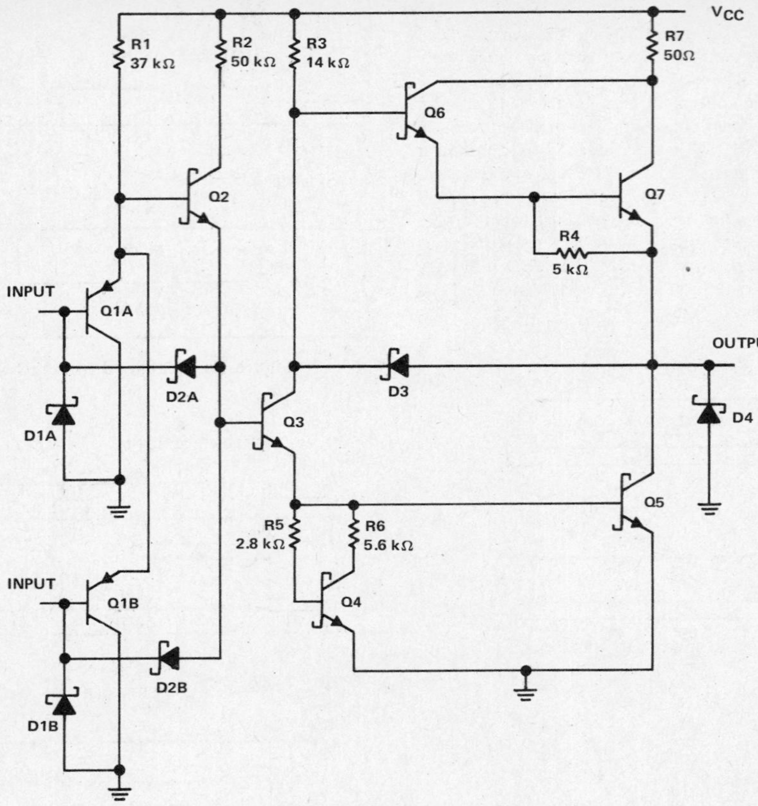
VCC
R1
37 kΩ
R2
50 kΩ
R3
14 kΩ
R7
50Ω
Q6
Q2
Q7
R4
5 kΩ
INPUT
Q1A
OUTPUT
D2A
D3
D1A
Q3
D4
Q5
R5
2.8 kΩ
R6
5.6 kΩ
INPUT
Q1B
Q4
D2B
D1B

Figure 12. 'ALS00A NAND Gate Schematic

4. Input and output clamping is implemented with Schottky diodes to reduce negative-going excursions on the inputs and outputs. Because of its lower forward voltage drop and fast recovery time, the Schottky input diode provides improved clamping action over a conventional p-n junction diode.
5. The ion implantation process allows small geometries giving less parasitic capacitances so that switching times are decreased.
6. The reduction of the epi-substrate capacitance using oxide isolation also decreases switching times.

A key feature of the 'ALS and 'AS families is the improvement in typical input-threshold voltage. Figure 12 is a schematic diagram of the 'ALS00A NAND gate. Figure 13 is a schematic diagram of the 'AS00 NAND gate. The input threshold voltage of the devices is determined by the equation:

$$VT = V_{BE} \text{ of Q2} + V_{BE} \text{ of Q3} + V_{BE} \text{ of Q5} - V_{BE} \text{ of Q1A (or } V_{BE} \text{ of Q1B)} \quad (1)$$

From Eq. (1) it can be determined that the input threshold voltage is two times V_{BE} or approximately 1.4 V. Low-level input current I_{IL} is reduced in the 'ALS00A/'AS00 gates because of the improved input circuits. Buffering by transistors Q1A (or Q1B) and Q2 causes a significant reduction in low-level input current. Low-level input current is determined by the equation:

$$I_{IL} = V_{CC} - V_{BE} \text{ of Q1A} - V_I/[R(h_{FE} \text{ of Q1A} + 1)] \quad (2)$$

By using Eq. (2) low-level input current is reduced by at least the factor of h_{FE} of Q1A + 1 and is typically $-10\ \mu A$ for the 'ALS00A and $-50\ \mu A$ for the 'AS00. High-level output voltage V_{OH} is determined primarily by V_{CC},

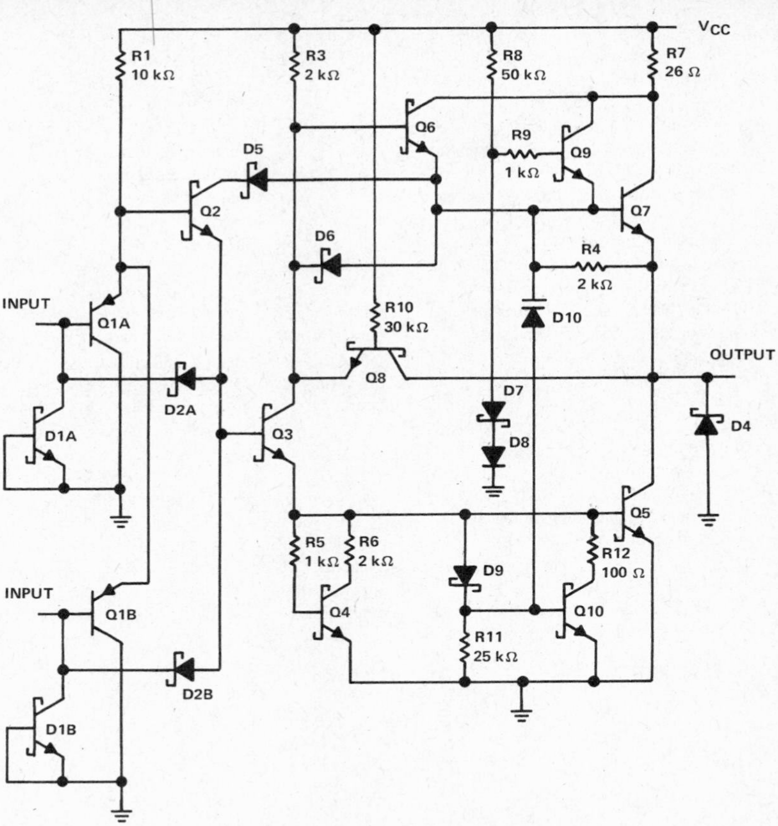
VCC
R1
10 kΩ
R3
2 kΩ
R8
50 kΩ
R7
26 Ω
Q6
R9
1 kΩ
Q9
D5
Q2
Q7
D6
R4
2 kΩ
INPUT
Q1A
R10
30 kΩ
D10
OUTPUT
Q8
D7
D2A
D4
D1A
Q3
D8
Q5
R5
1 kΩ
R6
2 kΩ
R12
100 Ω
D9
INPUT
Q1B
Q4
Q10
R11
25 kΩ
D2B
D1B

Figure 13. 'AS00 NAND Gate Schematic

resistors R4 and R7, and transistors Q6 and Q7. With no load, the high-level output voltage is approximately equal to $V_{CC} - V_{BE}$ of Q6 because the voltage across resistor R4 is 0 V. For medium-level currents, the high-level output voltage is equal to $V_{CC} - V_{BE}$ of Q6 $- V_{BE}$ of Q7 because of the Darlington gain of transistors Q6 and Q7. The current through resistor R3 is typically less than 1 μA and, therefore, the voltage drop is negligible. As conduction through transistors Q6 and Q7 is increased, the voltage drop across limiting resistor R7 will increase until the Schottky clamping diode of transistor Q6 starts to become forward biased. At this point, the current through resistor R3 (and the voltage drop) is no longer negligible and the high-level output voltage is determined by:

$$V_{OH} = V_{CC} - I_{OH \text{ through R7}} \times R7 - V_{CE} \text{ of Q6} - V_{BE} \text{ of Q7} \quad (3)$$

Low-level output voltage V_{OL} is determined by the turning on of transistor Q5. When the input is high and transistor Q2 is turned on, high-current transistor Q5 is turned on by a current path through transistor Q3 and resistor R3. Sufficient base drive is supplied to keep transistor Q5 fully turned on at an apparent output resistance of 14 Ω for 'ALS and 6Ω for 'AS.

The fanout is up to 40 for a '54ALS device that is driving a '54ALS device and up to 80 for a '74ALS device, that is driving a '74ALS device and provides a guaranteed low-level output current of 4 mA and 8 mA, respectively.

The increase in speed-power product of '54ALS/'74ALS devices, a factor four times better than '54LS/'74LS devices, is due to the design consideration of the quiescent and switching operations of the circuit. In the quiescent state, transistor Q2 allows the use of a reduced low-level input current. This reduces the fanout and reduces the overall quiescent current requirements.

The design of diodes D2 and D3 (or transistor Q8) and transistor Q4 enhances the speed-power product of the device. Transistor Q4 reduces the turn-off time and consequently the current transients caused by conduction overlap of transistor Q5. The same principle is used by diodes D2 and D3 and transistor Q3 in turning off transistor Q7. In addition, the active turn-off design produces a square transfer characteristic.

The 'AS00 gate has additional circuits not on the 'ALS00A gate. The circuits are added to enhance the throughput of the 'AS Family.

Transistor Q10 has been added as a discharge path for the base-collector capacitance of transistor Q5. Without transistor Q10, rising voltages at the collector of transistor Q5 would force current, via the base-collector capacitance, into the base of transistor Q5 causing it to turn on. However, diode D10 causes transistor Q10 to turn on (during rising voltage) and keeps transistor Q5 turned off. Diodes D6 and D9 serve as a discharge path for capacitor-diode D10.

CIRCUIT PARAMETERS

Worst-case testing of 'ALS/'AS devices provides a margin of safety. [All dc limits shown on the data sheet are guaranteed over the entire temperature range (−55 °C to 125 °C) for series 54ALS/54AS and 0 °C to 70 °C for series 74ALS/74AS)]. In addition, the dc limits are guaranteed over the entire supply voltage range (4.5 V to 5.5 V).

Transfer Characteristics

Since the most common application for a logic gate is to drive a similar logic gate, the input and output logic levels must be compatible. The input and output logic levels for 'ALS/'AS devices are as follows:

V_{IL} — The voltage value required for a low-level input voltage that guarantees operation

V_{IH} — The voltage value required for a high-level input voltage that guarantees operation

V_{OL} — The guaranteed maximum low-level output voltage of a gate

V_{OH} — The guaranteed minimum high-level output voltage of a gate.

With the exception of high-level ouput voltage (which is a direct function of supply voltage), these values remain virtually unchanged over the temperature range and under normal operating conditions of the device.

Analysis of the input and output response characteristics of 'ALS/'AS TTL gates is necessary to understand the operation of these devices in most system applications. The dc response characteristics can best be depicted by an input voltage V_I versus output voltage V_O transfer plot.

Figure 14 plots the 'ALS/'AS characteristics as compared with members of other TTL logic families.

As shown in Figure 14, the 'ALS and 'AS devices exhibit a much better output savings when compared with standard TTL devices. The better high-level output voltage is primarily because of the active turn off of the low-level output transistor. The diode voltage drop in the normal output is replaced by a low-current V_{BE} voltage drop. This provides

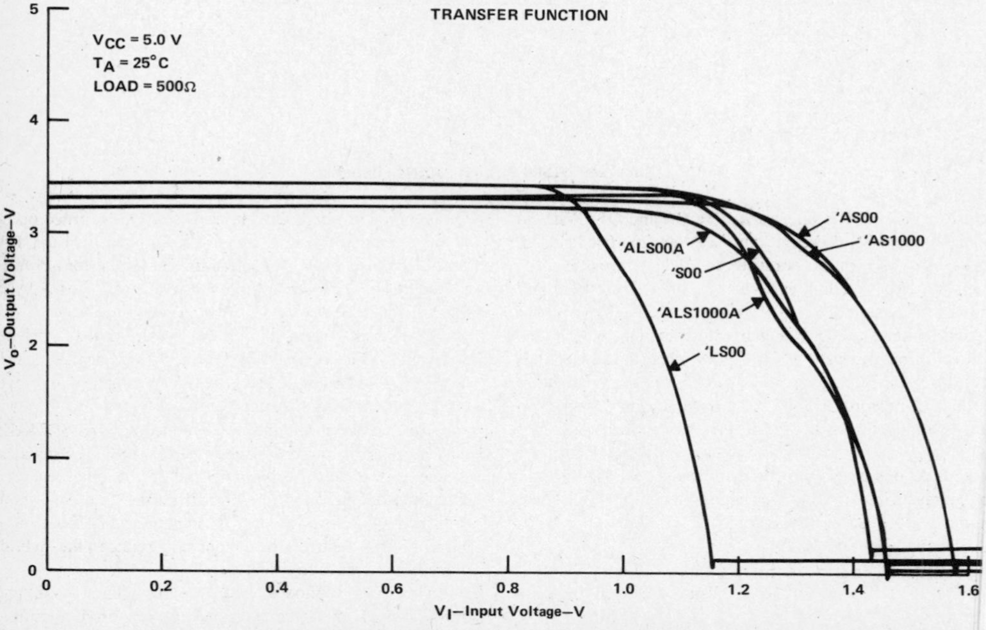

TRANSFER FUNCTION
VCC = 5.0 V
TA = 25°C
LOAD = 500Ω
'AS00
'AS1000
'ALS00A
'S00
'ALS1000A
'LS00
VO—Output Voltage—V
VI—Input Voltage—V
0
0.2
0.4
0.6
0.8
1.0
1.2
1.4
1.6
1
2
3
4
5

Figure 14. Input Voltage vs Output Voltage of 'ALS/'AS

3 Application Reports

a better high-level noise immunity in 'ALS and and 'AS over standard TTL devices.

Input Characteristics

To use 'ALS/'AS devices fully, a knowledge of the input and output characteristics is required. This is particularly true when a device interfaces with a device not in the same TTL series. In addition, knowledge of voltage and current relationships for all elements is important for proper design.

Figure 15 illustrates a typical plot for input current I_I versus input voltage, V_I, characteristics for 'ALS/'AS gate inputs during normal operation. A typical series 54/74 characteristic plot is also shown for reference. Any device used to drive a TTL gate must source and sink current. Conventionally, current flowing toward a device input terminal is designated as positive and current flowing out of a device input terminal is designated as negative. Low-level input current is negative current because it flows out of the input terminal. High-level input current is a positive current because it flows into the input terminal.

For transmission line conditions, a more accurate plot of the reverse bias section of these curves is required. These curves, Figure 16, are characteristic of the input clamping diode.

Low-Level Input Current

Figure 17 illustrates the dc equivalent of a standard 'ALS/'AS input circuit and shows the input current paths during a low-level input state. The low-level input current is primarily determined by resistor R1. However, low-level input current is also a function of the supply voltage, the ambient temperature, and the low-level input voltage. To

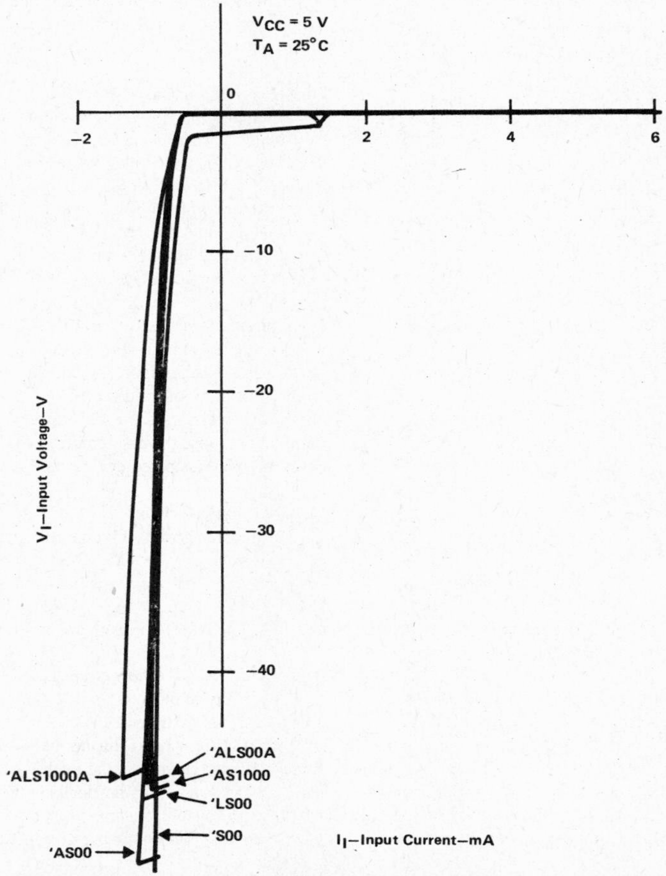

VCC = 5 V
TA = 25°C
0
−2
2
4
6
−10
−20
−30
−40
VI—Input Voltage—V
'ALS00A
'ALS1000A
'AS1000
'LS00
'S00
'AS00
II—Input Current—mA

Figure 15. Input Current vs Input Voltage for TTL Families

3 Application Reports

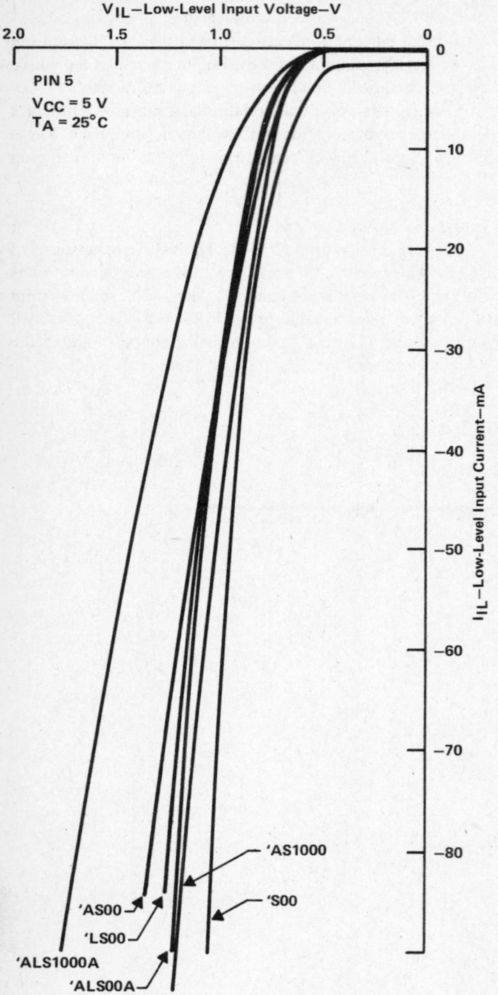
V_{IL}—Low-Level Input Voltage—V
2.0
1.5
1.0
0.5
0
PIN 5
V_{CC} = 5 V
T_A = 25°C
0
−10
−20
−30
−40
−50
−60
−70
−80
I_{IL}—Low-Level Input Current—mA
'AS1000
'S00
'AS00
'LS00
'ALS1000A
'ALS00A

Figure 16. Low-Level Input Current vs High-Level Input Voltage for TTL Families

assure desired device operation under all possible conditions, the worst-case test is performed on all devices. Supply voltage is taken to the highest allowable value to cause the low-level input current to be at a maximum. With the exception of the input under test, all unused inputs are taken to a high level. This enhances any contribution of these inputs to the low-level input current of the emitter under test.

Input Clamping Diode Test

The quality of the input clamping SBD (D2 in Figure 17) is tested by ensuring that the forward voltage drop is not

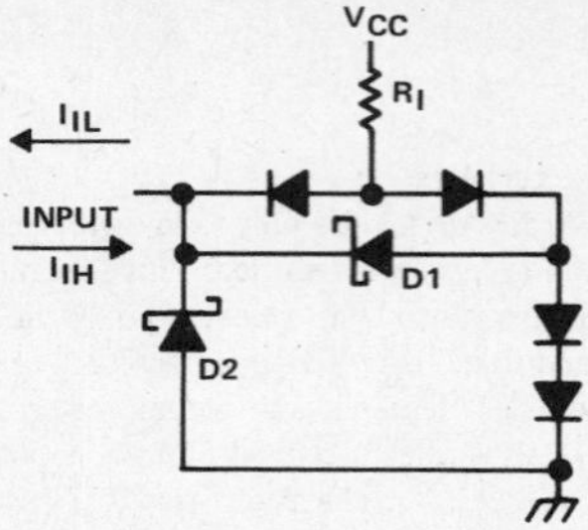
V_{CC}
R_I
I_{IL}
INPUT
I_{IH}
D1
D2

Figure 17. DC Equivalent Input Circuit for Series 'ALS Gate

greater than −1.2 V for 'AS and −1.5 V for 'ALS with a forward current of 18 mA. These values are guaranteed at minimum supply voltage and are valid across the operating temperature range. The characteristic of the input diode is illustrated in Figure 16.

High-Level Input Current

Another input parameter that must be measured and controlled is high-level input current. To ensure desired device operation under all possible conditions, the worst-case test is performed with all unused inputs grounded and supply voltage at its maximum value. This provides the highest value of low-level input current. Those devices with a high-level input current of sufficient magnitude to cause a degradation of high-level output voltage at an output must be screened out.

Input Breakdown Test

An additional high-level input current test is performed to check for base-emitter breakdown under the application of the full range of input voltages. This test is performed under the worst-case supply voltage conditions and is important because the base-emitter junction is small and can easily be overdissipated during the breakdown conditions.

Output Characteristics

The most versatile TTL output configuration is the push-pull (totem-pole) type. The totem-pole output has a low output impedance drive capability at both high and low logic levels. Both 'ALS and 'AS families use this configuration and have fanouts of 40 in both the high- and low-level states.

High-Level Output Characteristics

The ability of the totem-pole output to supply high-level output current is parametrically tested by applying a high-level input current value during measurement of high-level output voltage. However, the quality of the output stage is best indicated by parametrically measuring its current sourcing I_{OS} capability when connected to ground. Figure 18 shows the equivalent output circuit under high-level output conditions.

Figure 19 illustrates typical high-level characteristics. When measuring worst-case high-level output voltage, minimum supply voltage is used. A worst-case low-level input voltage is applied to an input and all unused inputs are tied to supply voltage.

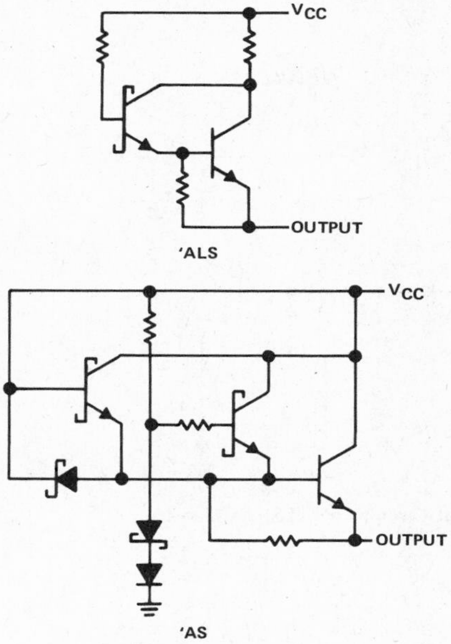

VCC
OUTPUT
'ALS
VCC
OUTPUT
'AS

Figure 18. Equivalent Output Circuit for 'ALS/'AS Gates

Low-Level Output Characteristics

Figure 20 shows that section of the output drive circuit which produces a low-level output voltage V_{OL}. This characteristic is also tested at minimum supply voltage. Figure 21 illustrates the typical curve.

Switching Speed

Two switching-speed parameters are guaranteed on Series 'ALS and 'AS gates: propagation delay time for a high-level to a low-level at the output t_{PHL}, and a low-level to high-level transition time t_{PLH}. Both parameters are specified with respect to the input pulse using standard test conditions as follows:

V_{CC} = 4.5 V to 5.5 V
C_L = 50 pF
R_L = 500
T_A = MIN to MAX

Under these conditions, times in the order of 4 ns for 'ALS and 1.7 ns for 'AS are typical. Figures 22 and 23 illustrate how the propagation delay time for 'ALS and 'AS devices vary with load capacitance.

Most current in the output stage is drawn when both output transistors are on (i.e., during output transitions, the average power dissipation of a gate with a totem-pole output increases with operating frequency). This is caused by more high-current transitions per second at the output as the frequency increases. Figure 24 illustrates the effect for both 'ALS and 'AS devices.

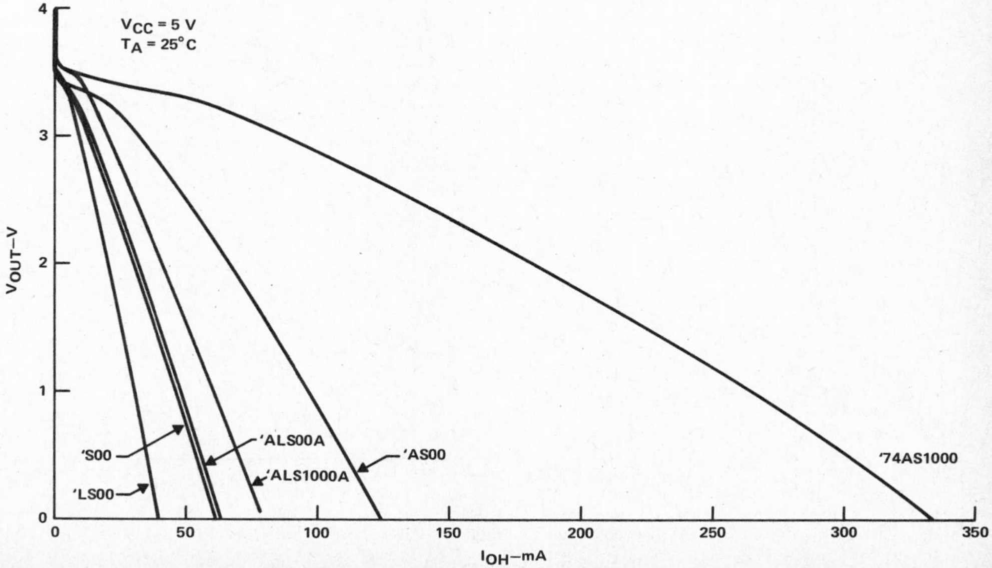

VCC = 5 V
TA = 25°C
VOUT–V
4
3
2
1
0
'S00
'LS00
'ALS00A
'ALS1000A
'AS00
'74AS1000
0
50
100
150
200
250
300
350
IOH–mA

Figure 19. High-Level Output Voltage vs High-Level Output Current

DC Noise Margins

Noise margin is a voltage specification which guarantees the static dc immunity of a circuit to adverse operating conditions. Noise margin is defined as the difference between the worst-case input logic level (V_{IH} minimum or V_{IL} maximum) and the guaranteed worst-case output (V_{OH} minimum or V_{OL} maximum) specified to drive the inputs. Table 2 lists the worst-case output limits for the 'AS and 'ALS families.

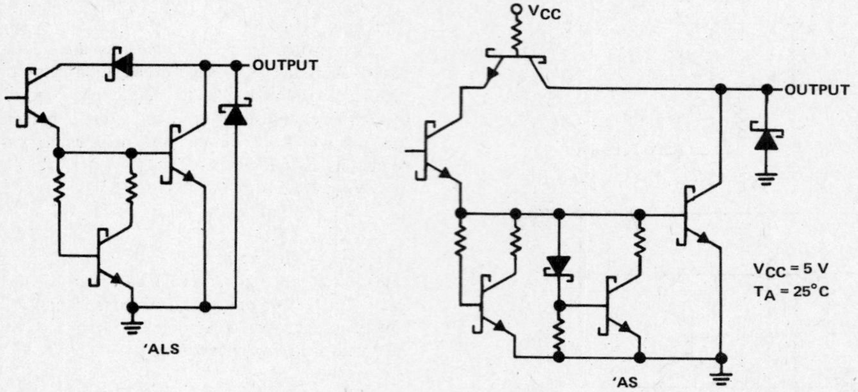

OUTPUT
'ALS
VCC
OUTPUT
VCC = 5 V
TA = 25°C
'AS

Figure 20. Low-Level Output Circuit for 'ALS/'AS Gates

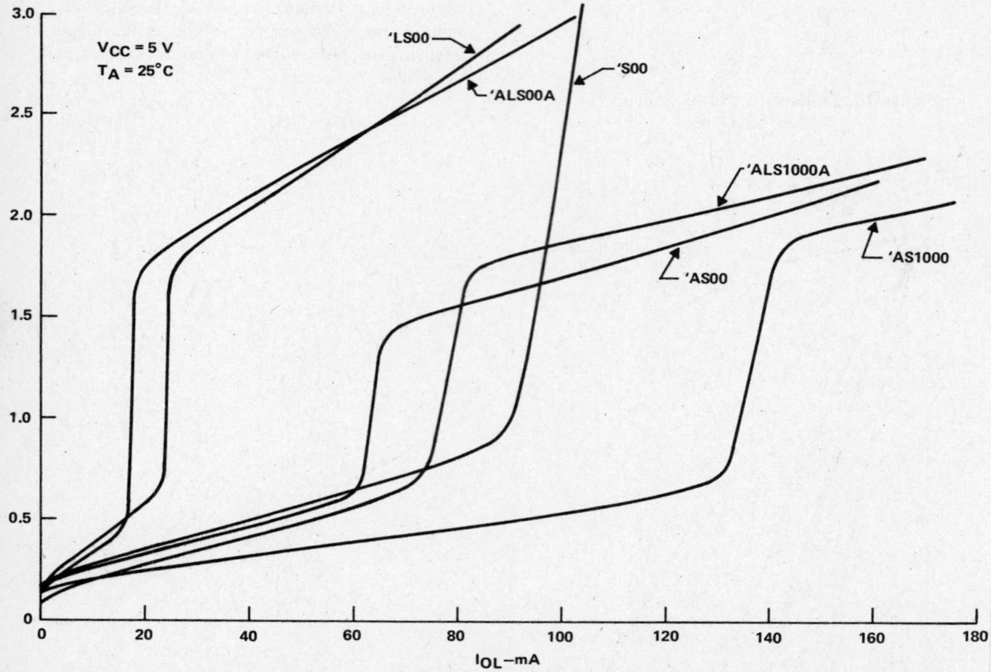

3.0
2.5
2.0
1.5
1.0
0.5
0
VOL–V
VCC = 5 V
TA = 25°C
'LS00
'ALS00A
'S00
'ALS1000A
'AS00
'AS1000
0
20
40
60
80
100
120
140
160
180
IOL–mA

Figure 21. Low-Level Output Voltage vs Low-Level Output Current

3 Application Reports

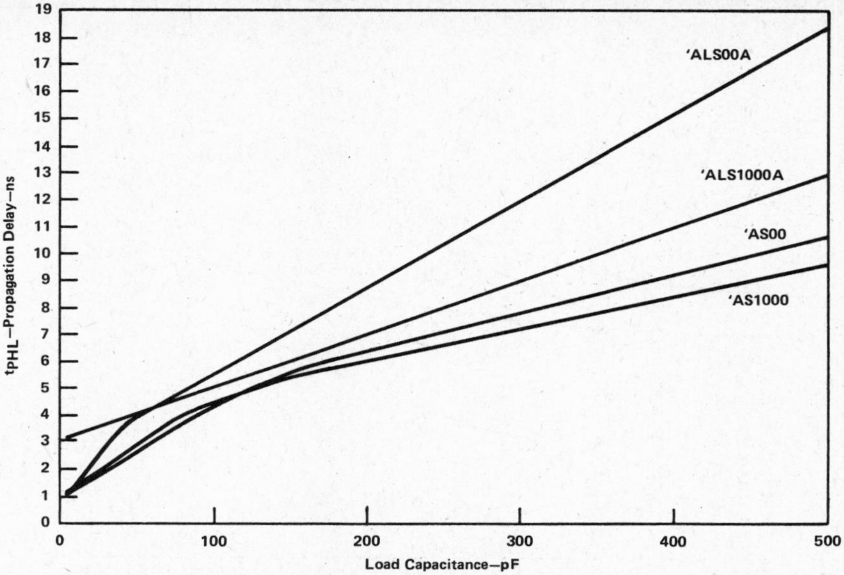

tPHL—Propagation Delay—ns
0
1
2
3
4
5
6
7
8
9
10
11
12
13
14
15
16
17
18
19
0
100
200
300
400
500
Load Capacitance—pF
'ALS00A
'ALS1000A
'AS00
'AS1000

Figure 22. High- to Low-Level Propagation Delay vs Load Capacitance

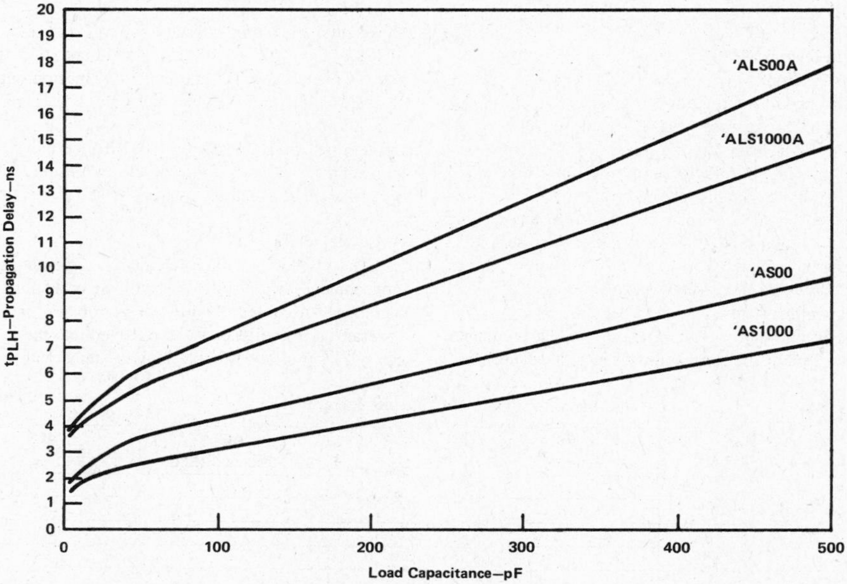

tPLH—Propagation Delay—ns
0
1
2
3
4
5
6
7
8
9
10
11
12
13
14
15
16
17
18
19
20
0
100
200
300
400
500
Load Capacitance—pF
'ALS00A
'ALS1000A
'AS00
'AS1000

Figure 23. Low- to High-Level Propagation Delay vs Load Capacitance

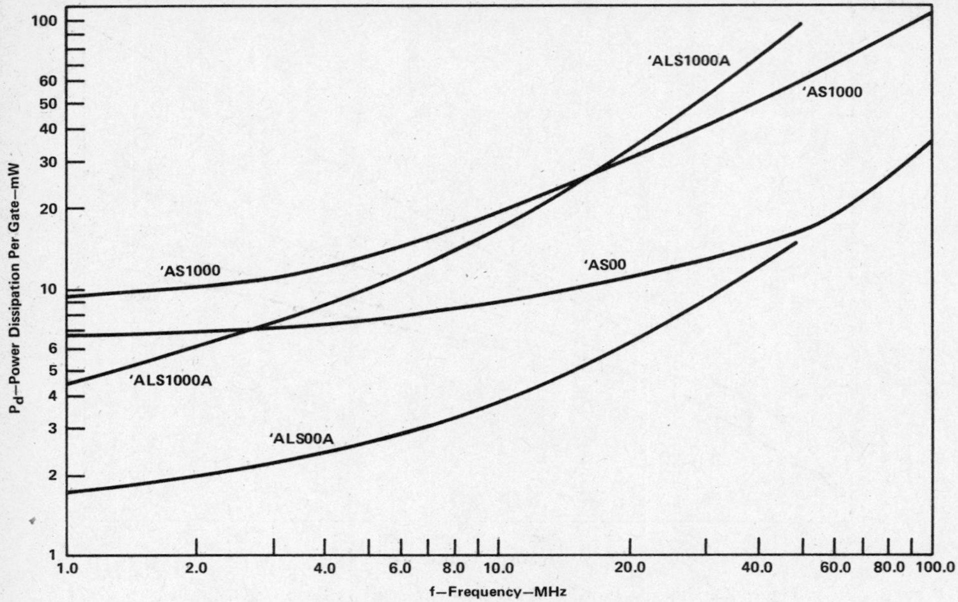

100
60
50
40
30
20
10
6
5
4
3
2
1
Pd—Power Dissipation Per Gate—mW
'ALS1000A
'AS1000
'AS1000
'AS00
'ALS1000A
'ALS00A
1.0
2.0
4.0
6.0
8.0
10.0
20.0
40.0
60.0
80.0
100.0
f—Frequency—MHz

Figure 24. Power Dissipation per Gate vs Frequency

Specified Logic Levels and Thresholds

The high-level noise margin is obtained by subtracting V_{OH} minimum from V_{IH} minimum. The low-level noise margin is obtained by subtracting V_{IL} maximum from V_{OL} maximum. The worst-case high-level noise margin is guaranteed to be at least 500 mV for both 'AS and 'ALS devices and at least 300 mV for low-level noise immunity across the operating free-air temperature ranges.

The usefulness of noise margins at the system design level is the ability of a device to be impervious to noise spikes at the input. The input voltage falls into one of three categories: low-logic state (between ground and 0.8 V), threshold region (between 0.8 V and 2 V), or high-logic state (between 2 V and V_{CC}). If an input voltage remains exclusively in the low-logic or high-logic state, it can undergo any excursions within that state. A level change from 5.5 V to 2 V or from ground to 0.8 V should not affect the output state of the device. To guarantee an expected output level change, the appropriate input has to undergo a change from one input state to the other input state (i.e., a transition through the threshold region). If a device will not remain in the correct state when voltage excursions on the input are occurring, it is violating its truth table.

Noise Rejection

The ability of a logic element to operate in a noise environment involves more than the dc or ac noise margins previously discussed. To present a problem, an externally generated noise pulse must be received into the system and cause a malfunction. Stable logic systems with no storage

Table 2. Worst Case Output Parameters

PARAMETER (V)	'AS (0°C to 70°C)	'ALS (0°C to 70°C)	'AS (−55°C to 125°C)	'ALS (−55°C to 125°C)
V_{IH}(MIN)	2	2	2	2
V_{IL}(MAX)	0.8	0.8	0.8	0.8
V_{OH}(MIN) @ CC = 4.5 V*	2.5	2.5	2.5	2.5
V_{OL}(MAX)	0.5	0.5	0.5	0.4
High Level Noise Margin ($V_{OH}-V_{IH}$)	0.5	0.5	0.5	0.5
Low Level Noise Margin ($V_{IL}-V_{OL}$)	0.3	0.3	0.3	0.4

*Actual specification for $V_{OH(min)}$ is V_{CC} − 2 V.

elements are practically impervious to ac noise. However, large dc voltages could cause noise problems. Systems with triggerable storage elements or those operating fast enough for the noise to appear as a signal are much more susceptible to noise.

The noise voltage must be radiated or coupled into the circuit. The amount of noise required to develop a given voltage is a function of the circuit impedance. Because of the low output impedance of TTL circuits, noise immunity is improved. Noise is transferred from the source (with some arbitrary impedance) through a coupling impedance to the impedance of the circuit under consideration.

Figure 25 shows a circuit where the coupling impedance is stray capacitance and the load impedance is provided by the gates. The relatively tight coupling of this circuit and the loading effect on the driving source is significant enough

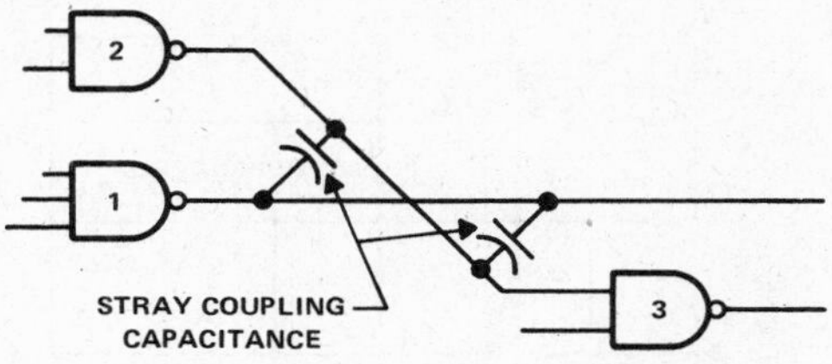
2
1
3
STRAY COUPLING
CAPACITANCE

Figure 25. Stray Coupling Capacitance

to be considered. However, since the source effect is difficult to assess and is in a direction to improve rather than degrade the noise rejection, its effects are ignored. This results in a worst-case type of response indication. In the case of radiated noise, the source resistance is a definite factor in noise coupling and essentially replaces the reactive coupling impedance.

By ignoring the driving source impedance to make conditions more nearly standard, it is possible to determine a set of curves relating the developed noise pulse to the noise source amplitude, the noise rise or fall time, the coupling impedance, and the load impedance. Curves have been developed[1] for several different input waveforms. Since the 'ALS waveform is essentially a ramp with a dv/vt of 1 V/ns (approximately 2.5 V/ns for 'AS), the most applicable curve is that for a ramp input.

Figure 26(a) shows the equivalent circuit from which the ramp response plot in Figure 26(b) was developed. The input pulse shown in Figure 26(c) is a ramp input.

$$e_i(t) = \frac{E_i}{T}\, t$$

where

E_i = Maximum input voltage and
T = Total rise time of input voltage

The output pulse is represented analytically by

$$e_0(t) = \frac{E_i}{T}\, RC\left(1 - e^{-\frac{t/T}{RC/T}}\right)$$

$$e_0(i) = E_i\, \tau\left(1 - e^{-i/\tau}\right)$$

where

$$\tau = \frac{RC}{T}$$

$$\theta(i) = \tau\left(1 - e^{-i/\tau}\right)$$

$$\theta(i) = \frac{e_0(i)}{E_i}$$

with holding for unit time. This is followed by an exponentially decaying voltage with a time constant τ. Values of τ and i on the figure are normalized by the value of the total rise time of the stimulated noise pulse e_i. Using Figure 26(b), the pulse width and amplitude of the coupled noise pulse can be estimated.

As an example, using the circuit shown in Figure 25, apply a noise pulse of 3 V in amplitude and rising at 1 V/ns

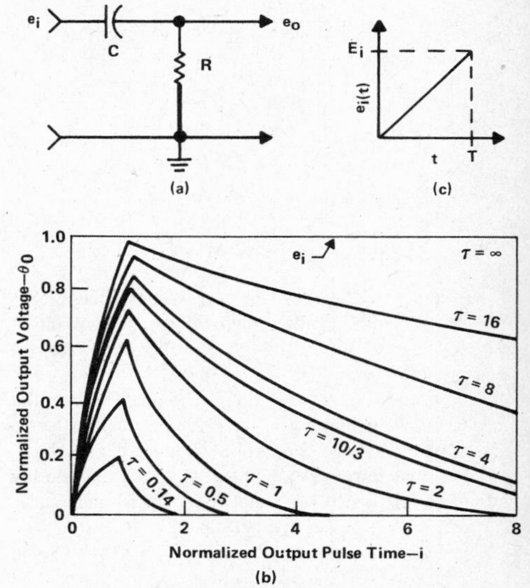
e$_i$
C
R
e$_o$
(a)
E$_i$
e$_i$(t)
t
T
(c)
1.0
0.8
0.6
0.4
0.2
0
Normalized Output Voltage—θo
e$_i$
τ = ∞
τ = 16
τ = 8
τ = 10/3
τ = 4
τ = 2
τ = 1
τ = 0.5
τ = 0.14
0
2
4
6
8
Normalized Output Pulse Time—i
(b)

Figure 26. Evaluations of Gate Response to Fast Input Pulses

with gate 2 at a high-logic state. Assume a nominal output impedance of 58 Ω (30 Ω for 'AS) and coupling capacitance of 10 pF. Use the following formula:

$$\text{Total rise time T} = \frac{3\ \text{V}}{1\ \text{V/ns}^{**}} = 3\ \text{ns}^{\dagger}$$

$$\tau = \frac{\text{RC}}{\text{T}} = \frac{(10 \times 10^{-12})(58)}{3}$$

$$= \frac{0.58 \times 10^{-9}}{3} = 0.19\ \text{ns}$$

**2.5 V/ns for 'AS

†1.2 ns for 'AS

To convert the normalized values of τ and i in Figure 26(b) to actual values, multiply by 3 ns. The output voltage scale will be multiplied by 3 V. Using the $\tau = 0.19$ curve gives a peak e_0 of 0.57 V (0.19 × 3) and a pulse width of 3 ns at the 50% points. To determine whether this pulse will cause interference, enter these values (0.57 V and 3 ns) on the graph shown in Figure 27. Since the gates have approximately 1.8 V of noise immunity at this point, they should not be affected.

If an open-collector gate is used with a passive 1 kΩ pull-up resistor, the situation would change. Use the following formula:

$$\text{Total rise time} = \frac{3\ \text{V}}{1\ \text{V/ns}^{**}} = 3\ \text{ns}^{\dagger}$$

$$\tau = \frac{(10 \times 10^{-12})(1 \times 10^{3})}{3}$$

$$= \frac{10 \times 10^{-9}}{3} = \frac{10}{3}\ \text{ns}$$

**2.5 V/ns for 'AS

†1.2 ns for 'AS

Now the amplitude (from the curves) approaches 2.58 V (0.86 × 3) and the pulse width at the 50% points is approximately 8.52 ns (2.84 × 3). The next gate will propagate this pulse.

This example is an oversimplification. The coupling impedances are complex (but resolvable into RLC series coupling elements) and the gate output impedance changes with load. Our purpose is to show why and how the low impedance of the active TTL output rejects noise and to make a comparison with a passive pull-up.

The ability to operate in a noisy environment is an interaction of the built-in operating margins, the time required for the device to react, and the ease with which a noise voltage is developed. In all cases, except the ability to react to short noise pulses, the TTL design has emhasized noise rejection.

Nothing has been discussed concerning noise in devices other than gate circuits. Many MSI devices are complex gate networks and, because of their small size, are more superior in a noisy environment operation than their discrete gate equivalents. Noise tolerance of latching devices is implied in the setup times, hold times, clock pulse width, data pulse widths, and similar parameters. Output impedances and input noise margins are quite similar to those of the gates and may be treated in a similar manner. If a latching device does become noise triggered, the effective error is stored and does not disappear with the noise.

Parameter measurement information is shown in Figure 28.

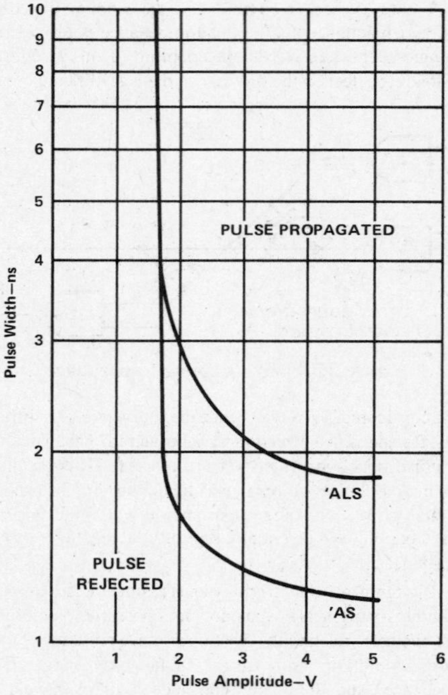

10
9
8
7
6
5
4
3
2
1
Pulse Width—ns
PULSE PROPAGATED
'ALS
PULSE
REJECTED
'AS
1
2
3
4
5
6
Pulse Amplitude—V

Figure 27. Theoretical Required Pulse Width vs Pulse Amplitude for 'AS and 'ALS Inputs

GUIDELINES FOR SERIES 'ALS/'AS TTL SYSTEM DESIGN

System layout and design requirements for Advanced Schottky TTL circuits are essentially the same as those guidelines which have previously been established and are applicable for all high-performance digital systems. Tables 3 through 6 provide a brief summary of the solutions to most design decisions needed to implement systems using Advanced Schottky TTL. Supplementary data which may be useful for developing specific answers to unique problems is provided later.

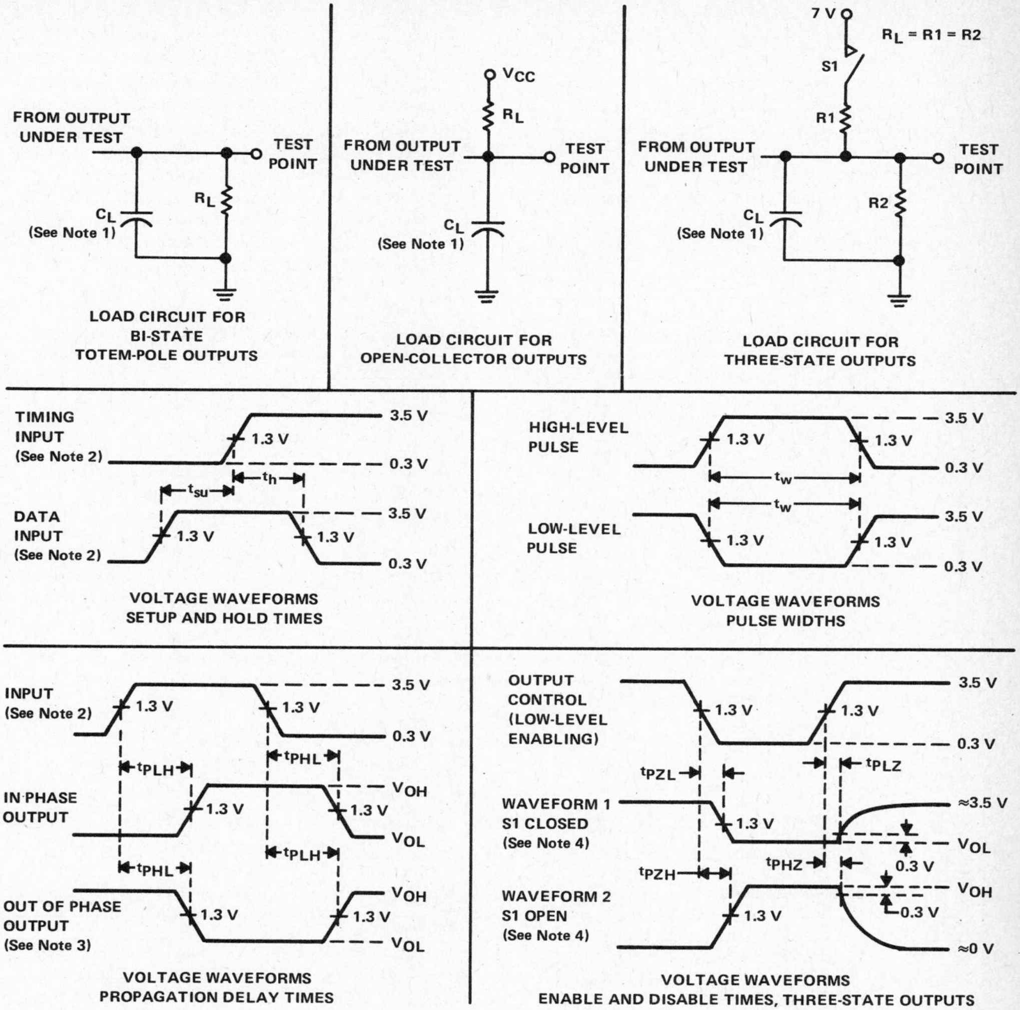

FROM OUTPUT UNDER TEST
TEST POINT
R_L
C_L (See Note 1)
LOAD CIRCUIT FOR BI-STATE TOTEM-POLE OUTPUTS
V_{CC}
R_L
FROM OUTPUT UNDER TEST
TEST POINT
C_L (See Note 1)
LOAD CIRCUIT FOR OPEN-COLLECTOR OUTPUTS
7 V
R_L = R1 = R2
S1
R1
FROM OUTPUT UNDER TEST
TEST POINT
R2
C_L (See Note 1)
LOAD CIRCUIT FOR THREE-STATE OUTPUTS
TIMING INPUT (See Note 2)
3.5 V
1.3 V
0.3 V
t_h
t_{su}
DATA INPUT (See Note 2)
3.5 V
1.3 V
1.3 V
0.3 V
VOLTAGE WAVEFORMS SETUP AND HOLD TIMES
HIGH-LEVEL PULSE
3.5 V
1.3 V
1.3 V
0.3 V
t_w
t_w
LOW-LEVEL PULSE
3.5 V
1.3 V
1.3 V
0.3 V
VOLTAGE WAVEFORMS PULSE WIDTHS
INPUT (See Note 2)
3.5 V
1.3 V
1.3 V
0.3 V
t_{PLH}
t_{PHL}
IN PHASE OUTPUT
V_{OH}
1.3 V
1.3 V
V_{OL}
t_{PHL}
t_{PLH}
OUT OF PHASE OUTPUT (See Note 3)
V_{OH}
1.3 V
1.3 V
V_{OL}
VOLTAGE WAVEFORMS PROPAGATION DELAY TIMES
OUTPUT CONTROL (LOW-LEVEL ENABLING)
3.5 V
1.3 V
1.3 V
0.3 V
t_{PZL}
t_{PLZ}
WAVEFORM 1 S1 CLOSED (See Note 4)
≈3.5 V
1.3 V
V_{OL}
t_{PHZ}
0.3 V
t_{PZH}
WAVEFORM 2 S1 OPEN (See Note 4)
V_{OH}
1.3 V
0.3 V
≈0 V
VOLTAGE WAVEFORMS ENABLE AND DISABLE TIMES, THREE-STATE OUTPUTS

NOTES: 1. C_L includes probe and jig capacitance.
2. All input pulses have the following characteristics PRR ≤ 1 MHz, $t_r = t_f = 2$ ns, duty cycle = 50%.
3. When measuring propagation delay times of 3-state outputs, switch S1 is open.
4. Waveform 1 is for an output with internal conditions such that the output is low except when disabled by the output control. Waveform 2 is for an output with internal conditions such that the output is high except when disabled by the output control.

Figure 28. Parameter Measurement Information

POWER SUPPLY REGULATION

Power supply regulation cannot be treated as if it is an independent characteristic of the device involved. Power supply regulation, along with temperature range, affects noise margins, fanout, switching-speed, and several other parameters. The characteristics most affected are noise margin and fanout. When these two parameters are within the specified limits, the power-supply regulation will normally be within specified limits. However, on a device where auxiliary parameters are more critically specified, a more restrictive power-supply regulation is normally required. When power-supply regulation is slightly outside the specified limits for TTL devices, the device may still operate satisfactorily. However, if high ambient-noise levels and extreme temperatures are encountered, failures may occur.

Application of a supply voltage above 7 V (absolute maximum rating) will result in damage to the circuit.

Since power dissipation in the package is directly related to supply voltage, the maximum recommended supply voltage for TTL devices is specified at 5.5 V. This provides an adequate margin to ensure that functional capability and long-term reliability are not jeopardized.

High-level output voltage is almost directly proportional to supply voltage (i.e., a drop in supply voltage causes a drop in high-level output voltage and an increase in supply voltage results in an increase in high-level output voltage). Because of this relationship, high-level output voltage for 'ALS/'AS devices is specified as supply voltage −2 V (V_{CC} −2 V).

Since high-level output voltage is directly related to supply voltage, the output current of the device is also directly related. The output current value is established by choosing output conditions to produce a current that is approximately one-half of the true short-circuit current.

It is advantageous to regulate or clamp the maximum supply voltage at 5.5 V including noise ripple and spikes. When this conditions exists, unused AND and NAND gates can be connected directly to the supply voltage.

Table 3. Guidelines for Systems Design for Advanced Schottky TTL

ITEM	GUIDELINE
Single wire connections	Wire lengths up to approximately 12 inches may be used. A form of ground plane is desirable. Use point-to-point routing rather than parallel. If the wire is longer than 12 inches, use either a dense ground plane with the wire routed as close to it as possible, or use a twisted-pair cable.
Coaxial and twisted-pair cables	Design around approximately 80 Ω to 100 Ω of characteristic impedance. Cross talk increases at higher impedances. Use a coaxial cable of 93 Ω impedance (e.g., Microdot 293−3913). For twisted-pair cable, use number 26 or number 28 wire with the insulation twisted at the rate of 30 turns per foot.
Transmission-line-ground	Ensure that transmission-line ground returns are carried through at both transmitting and receiving ends. V_{CC} decoupling ground, device ground, and transmission-line ground should have a common tie point.
Cross talk	Use point-to-point back-panel wiring to minimize noise pickup between lines. Avoid long unshielded parallel runs. However, if they must be used, they should carry signals that propagate in the same direction.
Reflections	Reflections occur when data interconnects become long enough that 2-line propagation delays are pulse transition times. For series TTL, reflections are normally of no importance for lines shorter than 12 inches.
Resistive pull-up	If fanout of driving output permits, use approximately 300 Ω of resistive pull-up at the receiving end of long cables. This provides added noise margin and more rapid rise times.

Table 4. Guidelines for Printed Circuit Board Layout for Advanced Schottky TTL

ITEM	GUIDELINE
Signal connections	Whenever possible, distribute loads along direct connections. Signal leads should be kept as short as possible. However, lead lengths of up to 15 inches will perform satisfactorily. This is especially for large boards that use a ground plane, ground, and/or V_{CC} plane. In addition, it will perform satisfactorily for small boards using ground mesh or grid. In high-frequency applications, avoid radial fanouts and stubs. If they must be used to drive some loads, reduce lead length proportionally and avoid sharp bends. Normal on-board fanouts and interconnections do not require terminations. Response of lines driving large numbers or highly capacitive loads can be improved with terminations of 300 Ω to V_{CC} and 600 Ω to ground in parallel with the last load if fanout of the driving output permits.
Conductor widths	Signal-line widths down to 0.015 inch are adequate for most signal leads.
Signal-line spacing	Signal-lead spacing on any layer down to 0.015 inch can be used especially if care is taken to avoid adjacent use of maximum length and minimum spacing. Increase spacing wherever layout permits. Pay particular attention to clock and/or other sensitive signals.
Insulator material	Thickness of insulation material used for a multilayer board is not critical. If ground and V_{CC} planes or meshes are used, their capacitive proximity can be used to reduce the number of decoupling capacitors needed and this also supplements the supply bypass capacitor.

Table 5. Guidelines for General Usage of Advanced Schottky TTL

ITEM	GUIDELINE
Power supply	For RF bypass supply primary, maintain ripple and regulation at less than or equal to 10%.
V_{CC} decoupling	Decouple every 2 to 5 packages with RF capacitors of 0.01 to 0.1 μF. Capacitors should be located as near as possible to the decoupled devices. Decouple line driving or receiving devices separately with 0.1 μF capacitors between V_{CC} and the ground pins.
On-board grounding	A ground plane is essential when the PCB is relatively large (over 12 inches). Smaller boards will work with ground and/or V_{CC} mesh or grid.
System grounding	Try to simulate bus bars with a width to thickness ratio greater than or equal to 4. This can be accomplished by multiple parallel wires or by using flat braid. Performance will be enhanced when a copper or silver-copper bus is used. The width to thickness ratio required will vary between systems, but greater than or equal to 4 will satisfy most systems.

Table 6. Guidelines for Gates and Flip-Flops Using Advanced Schottky TTL

ITEM	GUIDELINE
Data input rise and fall times	Reduce input rise and fall times as driver output impedance increases. Rise and fall times should be equal to or less than 15 ns/V and essentially free of noise ripple.
Unused input of AND and NAND gates and unused preset and clear inputs of flip-flops	Tie the unused input of AND and NAND gates and the unused preset and/or clear inputs of flip-flops as follows: 1. Directly to V_{CC}, if the input voltage rating of 5.5 V maximum is not exceeded. 2. Through a resistor equal to or greater than 1 kΩ to V_{CC}. Several inputs can be tied to one resistor. 3. Directly to a used input of the same gate, if maximum fanout of driving device will not be exceeded. Only the high-level loading of the driver is increased. 4. Directly to an unused gate output, if the gate is wired to provide a constant high-level output. Input voltage should not exceed 5.5 V.
Unused input of NOR gates	Tie unused input to used input of same gate, if maximum fanout of driving device will not be exceeded or tie unused input to ground.
Unused gates	Tie input of unused NAND and NOR gates to ground for lowest power drain. Tie inputs of unused AND gates high and use output for driving unused AND or NAND gate inputs.
Increasing gate/buffer fanout	Connect gates of same package in parallel.
Clock pulse of flip-flops	Drive clock inputs with a TTL output. If not available, rise and fall times should be less than 50 ns/V and free of ripple noise spikes.

SUPPLY VOLTAGE RIPPLE

Ripple in the supply voltage is generally considered a part of the supply voltage regulation. However, when combined with other effects (e.g., slow rise times), ripple voltage is more significant.

The effect of ripple voltage V_R can appear on either the supply voltage V_{CC} or the ground supply GND. When ripple appears on the supply voltage, it causes modulation of the input signal. The extent of the effect depends upon circuit parameters and source impedance.

The turning on of transistor Q5, shown in Figures 12 and 13, is controlled by the voltage at the base of transistor Q2 with respect to ground in accordance with the formula:

$$V_B = V_{BE} \text{ of Q2} + V_{BE} \text{ of Q3} + V_{BE} \text{ of Q5}$$

When ripple voltage is modulated onto the input voltage, the amplitude depends on the source impedance (Figure 29). The amplitude can be determined by the following equation:

$$\Delta V_R = V_R\left(\frac{R1/\beta}{R1/\beta + R2}\right)$$

$$= V_R\left(\frac{R1}{R1 + \beta R2}\right)$$

where R1 = source impedance

β = gain of transistor Q1.

Ripple voltage has the effect of adding extra pulses to the input signal (Figure 30). When ripple voltage appears in the ground supply, the threshold voltage is modulated and extra pulses occur (Figure 31).

Although decreasing the source impedance will reduce the effects of ripple voltage, it cannot be eliminated entirely because the emitter-base junction has an apparent resistance of approximately 30 Ω. Because of cancellation between the driving gate and the driven gate, low-frequency ripple is not a problem.

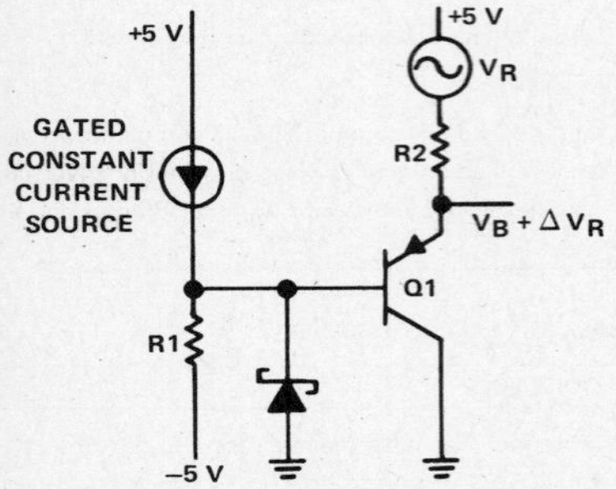
+5 V
+5 V
VR
GATED
CONSTANT
CURRENT
SOURCE
R2
VB + ΔVR
Q1
R1
−5 V

Figure 29. Effect of Source Impedance on Input Noise

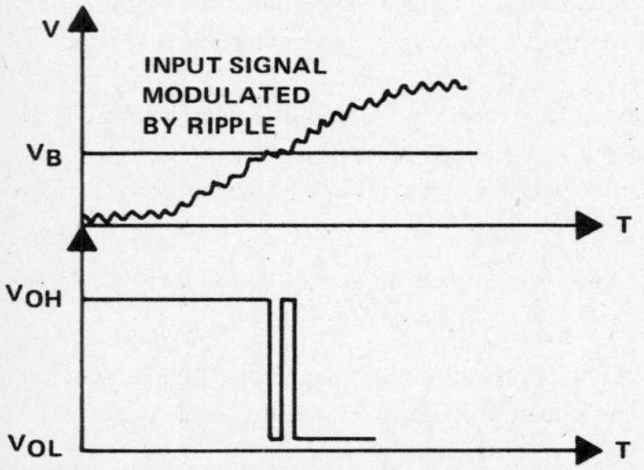
V
INPUT SIGNAL
MODULATED
BY RIPPLE
VB
T
VOH
VOL
T

Figure 30. Spurious Output Produced by Supply Voltage Ripple

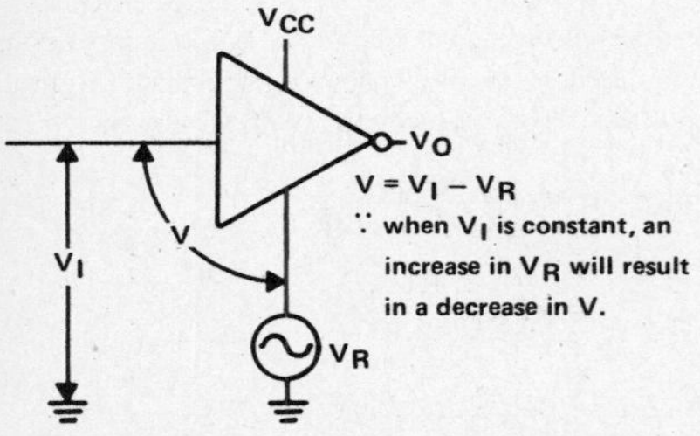
VCC
VO
V = VI − VR
∵ when VI is constant, an
increase in VR will result
in a decrease in V.
V
VI
VR

Figure 31. Effect of Ground Noise on Noise Margin

NOISE CONSIDERATIONS

Extraneous voltages and currents (called noise) introduced into a digital logic circuit are discussed in the following paragraphs. Figure 32(a) is a typical digital logic circuit consisting of a NAND gate and a J-K flip-flop. When a small noise pulse is coupled onto the clock input [(Figure 32(b)], the flip-flop does not respond and the Q output is correct. However, when a large noise pulse is coupled onto the clock input [(Figure 32(c)], the flip-flop sees the pulse as a clock transition and an erroneous Q output occurs. Therefore, it is essential to protect digital logic circuits from noise.

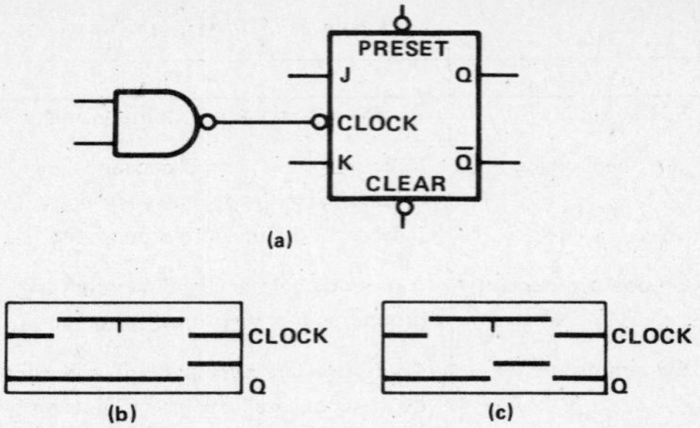
PRESET
J
Q
CLOCK
K
Q̄
CLEAR
(a)
CLOCK
Q
(b)
CLOCK
Q
(c)

Figure 32. Typical Logic Circuit with Noisy Input

Noise Types and Control Methods

The noise types encountered in digital logic systems, their source, and the method of controlling them are as follows:

1. External noise — External noises radiated into the system. The sources include circuit breakers, motor brushes, arcing relay contacts, and magnetic-field-generating. The methods of controlled to be considered are shielding, grounding, or decoupling.
2. Power-line noise — Noise coupled through the ac or dc power distribution system. The initial sources and controlling methods are the same as for external noise.
3. Cross talk — Noise induced into signal lines from adjacent signal lines. Controlling methods to consider are shielding, grounding, decoupling, and, where possible, increasing the distance between the signal lines.
4. Signal-current noise — Noise generated in stray impedances throughout the circuit. The controlling methods to consider are shielding, grounding, decoupling, and, where possible, reduction of stray capacitance in the circuit.
5. Transmission-line reflections — Noise from unterminated transmission lines that cause ringing and overshoot. The method of control is to use, where possible, terminated transmission lines.
6. Supply-current spikes — Noise caused by switching several digital loads simultaneously. The controlling method is to design, where possible, the system so that digital loads are not switched simultaneously.

Shielding

In addition to its own internally generated noise, electrical equipment must operate in an extremely noisy environment. Noise pulses, which may come from a number of sources, consist of an electrostatic field, and electromagnetic field, or both. The noise waveform must be prevented from entering the equipment. This is accomplished by shielding. Since the noise fields are usually changing at a rapid rate, the shield required to exclude them may be very small. For effective exclusion, the sensitive circuits must be completely shielded.

Aluminum or similar materials are effective in stopping electrostatic noise. However, only a ferrous metal can successfully protect equipment against magnetic fields. While it is helpful to connect the system to earth ground, the shield system must be complete and must be grounded to the system ground to prevent the shield from coupling noise into the system.

External noise may be conducted into the system by the power lines. Decoupling and filtering of these lines should be standard design procedure.

Grounding and Decoupling

The total propagation delay is of secondary importance in generation of internal noise. The actual transition time determines the amplitude and frequency spectrum of the generated signal at the higher harmonics. Application of the Fourier integral to series 'ALS/'AS waveforms shows frequency components of significant amplitude that exceed 100 MHz. Because of the frequency spectrum generated when an 'ALS/'AS device switches, a system using these devices must consider problems caused by radio frequency (RF) even though the repetition rates may be only a few megahertz. The transient currents generated by charging capacitors, changes in the levels of dc, line driving, etc., must be considered. In Figure 33 for example, a gate driving a transmission line is represented by a voltage source E, having an output impedance Z_S connected to an impedance Z_O, and loaded with a resistance R_L.

Until after a reflected pulse returns from the termination of the transmitting device, line termination is not a factor in drive current. In a practical TTL circuit, the line termination must be high relative to the line impedance. For explanation purposes, assume that the source voltage is 5 V in amplitude, the output impedance of the source is 50 Ω and the line impedance is 50 Ω. When the source voltage makes the transition from 0 V to 5 V, the voltage across the input of the line V_I is determined by the following equation:

$$V_I = E \frac{Z_O}{Z_S + Z_O} = 2.5 \text{ V}$$

where E = source voltage
Z_O = line impedance
Z_S = source impedance

For the 50 Ω line to become charged, the current that must flow onto the line is determined by the following equation:

$$I_{line} \frac{V_{in}}{Z_O} = \frac{2.5}{50} = 50 \text{ mA}$$

In addition, this current flows in the ground return, which, in this case, is the transmission-line ground. If the line and return are originated and terminated close to the driving and receiving devices, there is no discontinuity in the line. Where the ground is poorly returned, the current flow sees the discontinuity in the cable as a high impedance and a noise spike is generated (i.e., the ground current sees a low impedance and a current cancellation if the ground is properly carried through and, if not, it sees a high impedance). Figure 34 presents a specific example. Assume that the gate driving the line is switched from the high to low state. Current flow is indicated by the arrow marked with an I. Since the line is improperly returned to the driver, a pulse is developed across the impedance. A possible consequence is the false output of gate 3 (G3).

If the ground return is properly connected, the proper results are obtained. The impedance discontinuity is eliminated and current cancellation occurs at the ground point. Undesirable voltage spikes are then eliminated. Two empirical rules to reduce transmission-line currents have been established and have been found to be effective (Figure 35).

1. Carry all returns, including twisted pair and coaxial cables, to a good ground termination. Ground line returns close to the driving and receiving devices.

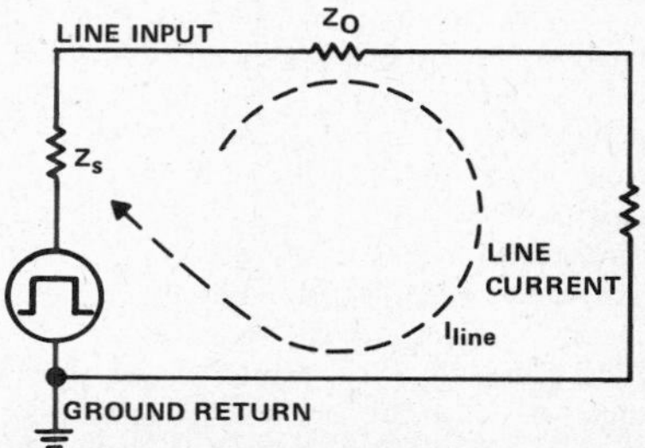

LINE INPUT
Zo
Zs
R
LINE
CURRENT
Iline
GROUND RETURN

Figure 33. Diagram Representing a Gate Driving a Transmission Line

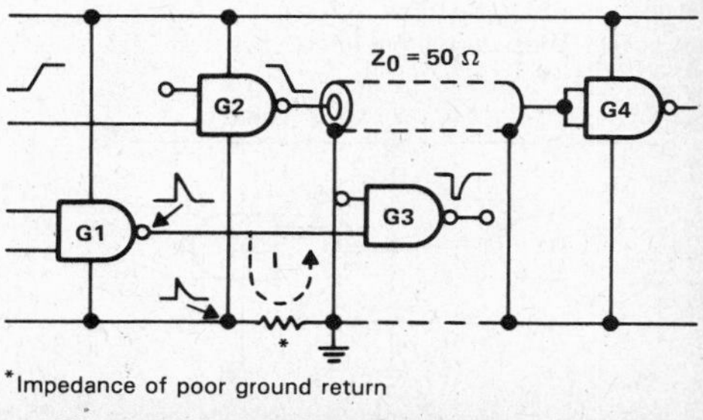

Zo = 50 Ω
G1
G2
G3
G4
*Impedance of poor ground return

Figure 34. Noise Generation Caused by Poor Transmission-Line Return

2. Decouple the supply voltage of line-driving and line-receiving gates with a 0.1-μF disk ceramic capacitor.

As the devices change state, current levels change because of the different device currents required in each state, the external loading, the transients caused by charging and discharging capacitive loads, and the conduction overlap in the totem-pole output stage. When a gate changes states, its internal supply current changes from high to low (these values are stated on the data sheet for each device). In addition, any capacitance, stray or otherwise, must be charged or discharged for a logic state change. The capacitance must be charged by a current determined by

$$I = C \frac{dv}{dt} \tag{4}$$

If the total stray capacitance on a gate output, the logic-level voltage excursion, and the associated rise or fall times are known, then the ideal-case instantaneous current during the transition can be calculated.

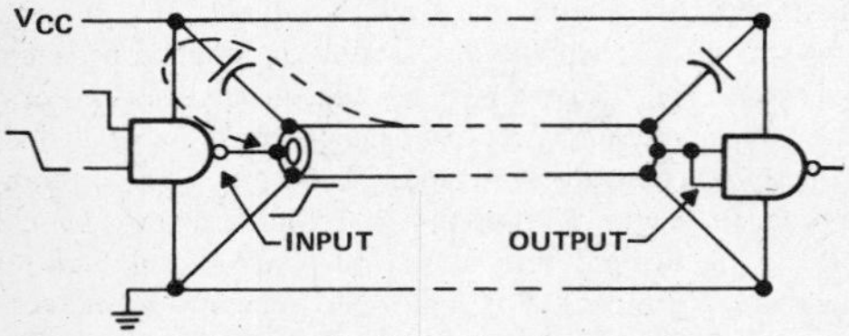

VCC
INPUT
OUTPUT

Broken arrow shows path of line-charging current

Figure 35. Ideal Transmission-Line Current Handling

From Eq. (4) it can be determined that the current transient for charging load capacitance will increase with higher speed TTL circuits. Therefore, the Series 54ALS/74ALS devices will have lower transient current than the Series 54AS/74AS devices. Another parameter that should be considered is the value of R7 (shown in Figures 12 and 13). Resistor R7 acts as a limit on the charging current.

The current required for charging load capacitance C_L (Figure 36) is supplied by the supply voltage when the transition is from logic low to logic high at the output of gate 1 (G1). When the output of G1 goes from high to low, the load capacitance is shorted to ground by transistor Q5 (shown in Figures 12 and 13) and has no effect on supply current.

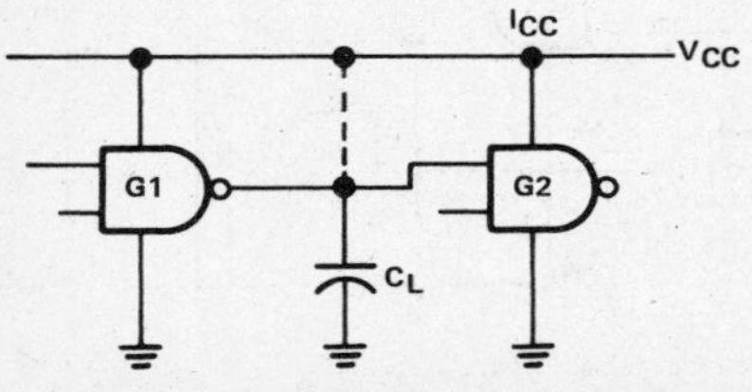

ICC
VCC
G1
G2
CL

C_L includes all capacitance: stray, device, etc.

Figure 36. Circuit with Effective Capacitive Loading

A characteristic common to all TTL totem-pole output stages contributes an additional current transient when the output changes from a logic low to a logic high. This transient, or spike, is caused by the overlap in conduction of the output transistors Q7 and Q5 (shown in Figures 12 and 13). The situation arises because transistor Q7 can turn on faster than transistor Q5 can turn off. This places a direct circuit consisting of transistors Q7 and Q5 and resistor R4 between supply voltage and ground. For all series 'ALS TTL circuits, the maximum possible peak current can be determined by

$$I_{CC}max = \frac{V_{CC} - V_{CEQ6} - V_{BEQ7} - V_{CEQ5}}{R7}$$

However, due to the active turnoff circuit (consisting of R5, R6, and Q4), Q5 will be only slightly in the linear region and the current spike will be less.

The total supply-current switching transient is then a combination of three major effects: the difference in high-level and low-level supply current, the charging of load capacitance, and the conduction overlap. Tests were performed to demonstrate these effects. The results are shown in Figure 37. Six types of series TTL devices were tested with no load (i.e., the oscilloscope was connected to the output only when measuring V_O and the photographs were double exposed). This was to approximate the effects of conduction overlap isolated from the transient caused by charging load capacitance. Different vertical scales were used on some of the photographs.

The results are almost as predicted. The low-power devices have the lower transients. Since it is the fastest circuit, the SN74AS00 device should be highest. However, a decrease is shown, and the reason for the decrease is explained (Figure 39). The additional circuits to reduce conduction overlap of the output transistors result in a smaller transient even though the typical switching time is 1.7 ns compared to 9 ns for the Series 54/74LS.

The second series of tests shown in Figure 37 cover a capacitive load of 50 pF. For this test, all of the supply current transient peaks increase in amplitude and width.

Because of the larger transient currents, voltage spikes on the supply voltage measured at the IC package are also increased.

From these tests, it can be concluded that the condition to be avoided (the only one that can be avoided) is unnecessary stray capacitance in circuit wiring. The charging of load capacitance, in most cases, overshadows the other two effects with respect to noise produced on the supply voltage line by switching current transients.

The flow paths of these currents have been investigated to determine the grounding and decoupling necessary to counteract their effects. Supply voltage decoupling may be accomplished by one of two methods. Maintaining low impedance from the individual circuit supply voltage to

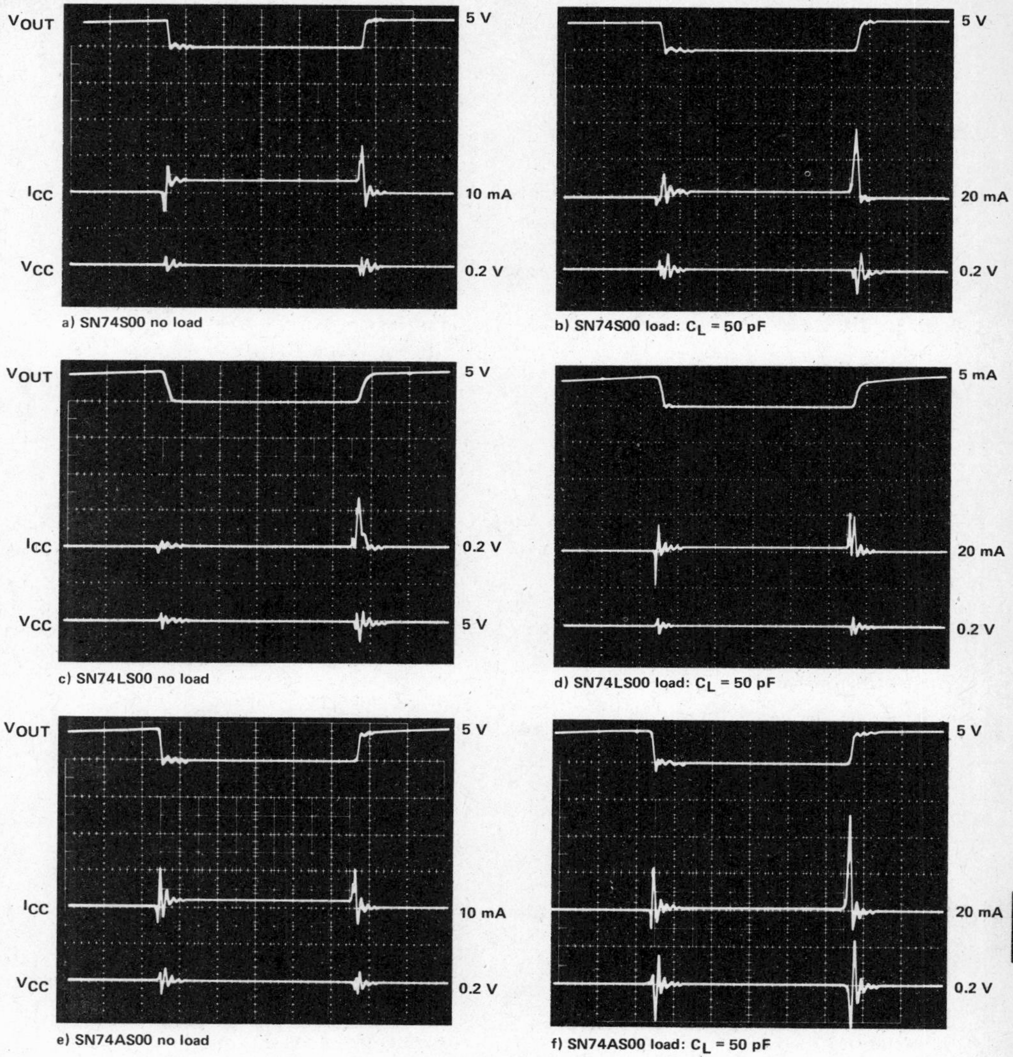

V_{OUT}
5 V
I_{CC}
10 mA
V_{CC}
0.2 V
a) SN74S00 no load
V_{OUT}
5 V
I_{CC}
20 mA
V_{CC}
0.2 V
b) SN74S00 load: C_L = 50 pF
V_{OUT}
5 V
I_{CC}
0.2 V
V_{CC}
5 V
c) SN74LS00 no load
5 mA
20 mA
0.2 V
d) SN74LS00 load: C_L = 50 pF
V_{OUT}
5 V
I_{CC}
10 mA
V_{CC}
0.2 V
e) SN74AS00 no load
5 V
20 mA
0.2 V
f) SN74AS00 load: C_L = 50 pF

NOTES: 1. V_{CC} = 5 V
2. Sweep is 50 ns/division
3. Rise and fall times of input pulse are 1 ns
4. Vertical scales are in units shown per division

Figure 37(a). Supply-Current Transient Comparisons

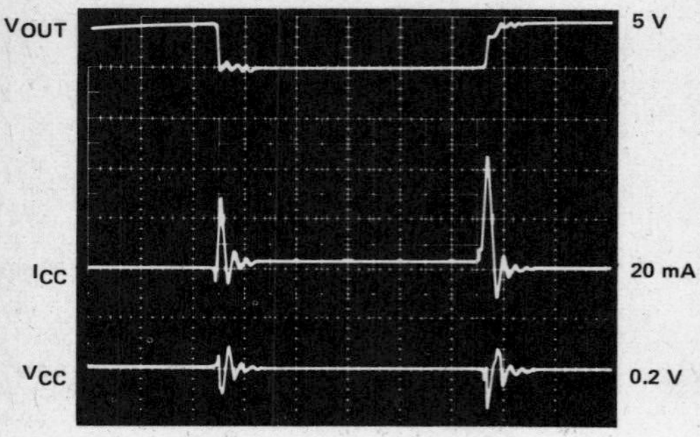

V_{OUT}
I_{CC}
V_{CC}
5 V
20 mA
0.2 V

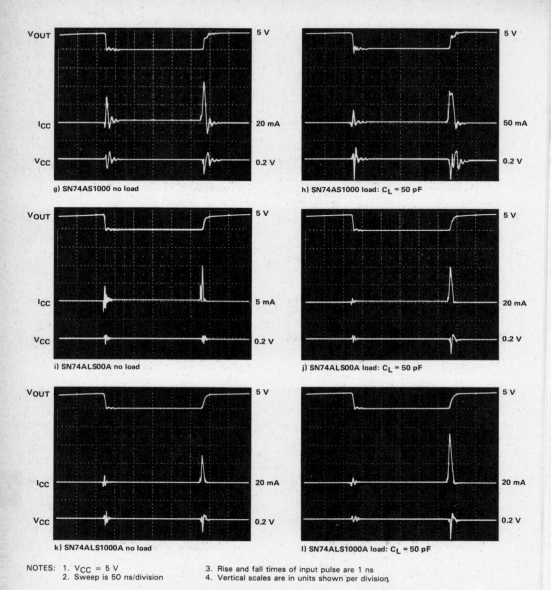

g) SN74AS1000 no load

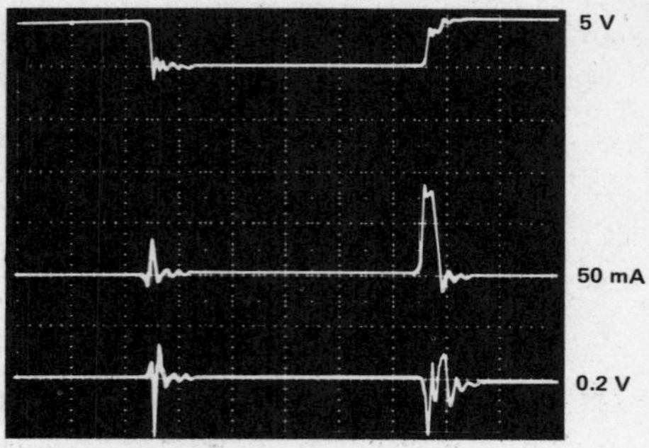

5 V
50 mA
0.2 V

h) SN74AS1000 load: C_L = 50 pF

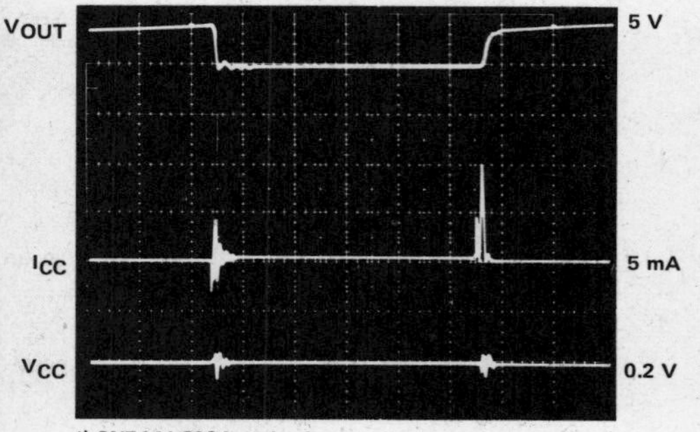

V_{OUT}
I_{CC}
V_{CC}
5 V
5 mA
0.2 V

i) SN74ALS00A no load

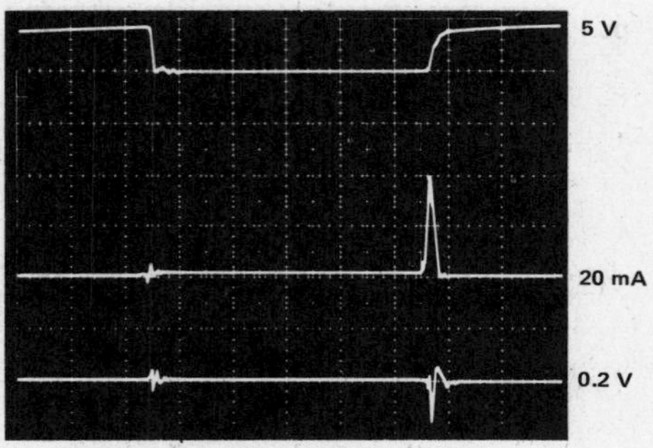

5 V
20 mA
0.2 V

j) SN74ALS00A load: C_L = 50 pF

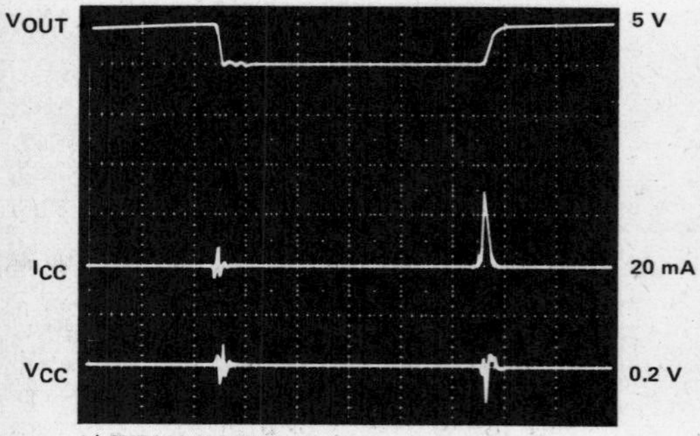

V_{OUT}
I_{CC}
V_{CC}
5 V
20 mA
0.2 V

k) SN74ALS1000A no load

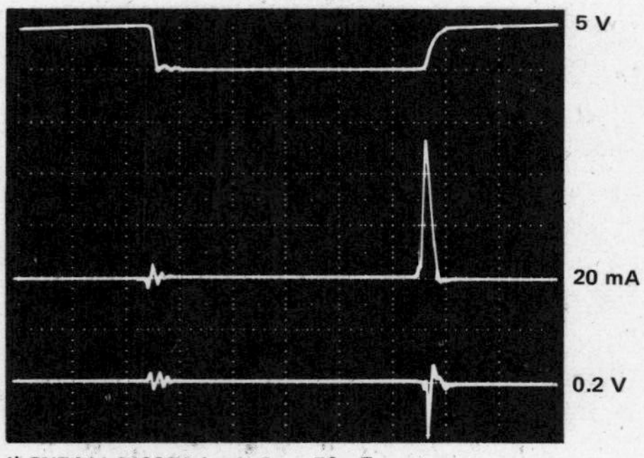

5 V
20 mA
0.2 V

l) SN74ALS1000A load: C_L = 50 pF

NOTES:
1. V_{CC} = 5 V
2. Sweep is 50 ns/division
3. Rise and fall times of input pulse are 1 ns
4. Vertical scales are in units shown per division

Figure 37(b). Supply-Current Transient Comparisons

ground is common to both methods. In the first method, the supply voltage line may be considered as a transmission line back to a low impedance supply. The positive bus can be laminated with a ground bus to form a strip transmission line of extremely low impedance. This line can be electrically approximated with lumped capacitances as shown in Figure 38. The inductances are usually a distributed component which must be minimized to lower the line impedance.

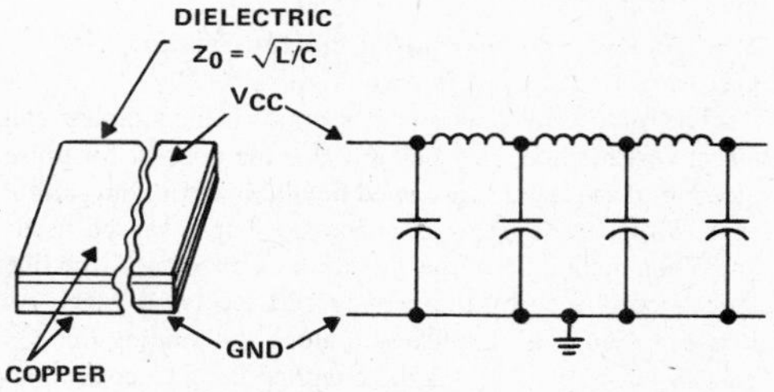

DIELECTRIC
Z0 = √L/C
VCC
GND
COPPER

Figure 38. Transmission-Line Power Buses

The second method is to consider the supply voltage bus as a dc connecting element only and to provide a low-impedance path near the devices for the transient currents to be grounded (Figure 39).

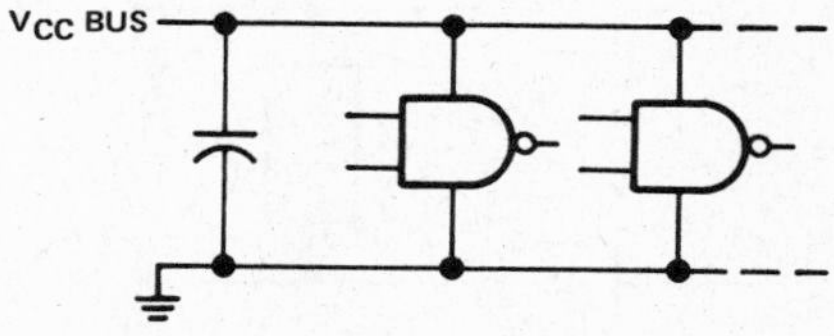

VCC BUS

Figure 39. Capacitive Storage Supply Voltage System

For effective filtering and decoupling, the capacitors must be able to supply the change in current for a period of time greater than the pulse width of this current. Since the problem is essentially one of dc changes due to logic state coupled with high-frequency transients associated with the changes, two different values of time constant must be considered. Capacitors combining the high capacitance required for long periods with the low series reactance required for fast transients are prohibitive in cost and size. A good compromise is the arrangement shown in Figure 40.

The typical component values may be found for the RF capacitor C1 by assuming that the parameters have common values as follows:

$$\Delta I_{CC} = 50 \text{ mA}$$
$$\Delta V = 0.1 \text{ V}$$
$$\Delta T = 20 \text{ ns}$$

Then the equation is as follows:

$$C1 = \frac{\Delta I_{CC}}{\Delta V/\Delta T} = \frac{(50)(20) \times 10^{-12}}{0.1/(20 \times 10^{-9})}$$

$$= \frac{50 \times 10^{-3}}{0.1} = 10{,}000 \times 10^{-12}$$

$$= 0.01\ \mu F$$

The same method may be used for the low-frequency capacitor C2. However, the factor ΔT, which was a worst-case transient time for calculating C2, now becomes a bit ambiguous. An analysis of the current cycling on a statistical basis is the best method in all but the simplest systems. The recommended procedure is to decouple using 10 μF to 50 μF capacitors.

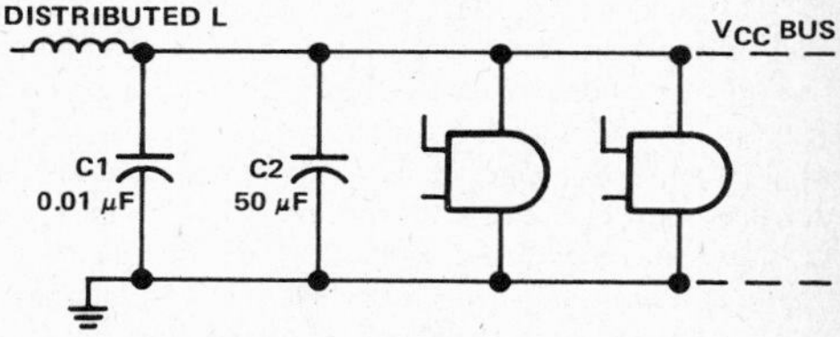

DISTRIBUTED L
VCC BUS
C1
0.01 μF
C2
50 μF

Figure 40. Commonly Used Power Distribution and Decoupling System

A discrete inductance of 2 μH to 10 μH is sometimes used for additional decoupling. However, its benefits are questionable and its usefulness should be evaluated for the individual system. The low-pass filter formed must be capable of keeping the transients confined and off the distribution bus. The possibility of resonance in the inductor or LC combination must be considered.

Noise spikes on the supply voltage line that do not force the gate output below the threshold level do not present a serious problem. Downward spikes as large as 3 V can be tolerated on the supply voltage line without propagating through the logic system. The system designer can be confident that supply voltage noise can be handled even with minimal consideration.

Ground noise, however, cannot be treated lightly. Pulses on a high-impedance ground line can easily exceed the noise threshold. Only if a good ground system is maintained can this problem be overcome. If proper attention is paid to the ground system, noise problems can be minimized.

The concept of a common-ground-plane structure as used in RF and high-speed digital systems is quite different from the concept of the common-ground point as used in low-frequency circuits. The more closely the chassis and ground can approach to being an integral unit, the better the noise suppression characteristics of the system. Consequently, all parts of the chassis and ground bus system must be bound tightly together both electrically and mechanically. Floating or poorly grounded sections not only break the integrity of the ground system, but may actually act as a noise distribution system.

For grounds and decoupling on printed circuit boards, the most desirable arrangement is a double-clad or multilayer board with a solid ground plane or a mesh. Where component density prohibits this, the ideal should be relaxed only as far as necessary. Cross talk and ground noise can be reduced on large boards with a ground plane. Some suggestions for board grounds where a plane is not practical are as follows:

1. Use as wide a ground strap as possible.
2. Form a complete loop around the board by bringing both sides of the board through separate pins to the system ground.

The supply voltage line can provide part of the ground mesh on the board, provided it is properly decoupled. For a TTL system, a good guideline is 0.01 μF per synchronously driven gate and at least 0.1 μF for each 20 gates, regardless of synchronization. This capacitance may be lumped, but is more effective if distributed over the board. A good rule is to permit no more than 5 inches of wire between any two package supply-voltage points. Radio-frequency-type capacitors must be used for decoupling. Disk ceramics are best. It is sometimes a good practice to decouple the board from the external supply-voltage line with a 2.2 μF capacitor. However, this is optional and the RF capacitors are still required. In addition, it is recommended that gates driving long lines have the supply voltage decoupled at the gate supply voltage terminal and that the capacitor ground, device ground, and transmission-line ground be connected to a common point.

Cross Talk

When currents and voltages are impressed on a connecting line in a system, it is impossible for adjacent lines to remain unaffected. Static and magnetic fields interact and opposing ground currents flow, creating linking magnetic fields. These cross-coupling effects are lumped together and called cross talk.

Back-Panel Interconnections

Interconnecting signal lines can be grouped into three broad categories: coaxial lines, twisted-pair lines, and straight wire lines. Because of the low impedance and shielding characteristics of coaxial cable, its cross talk is minimal and is not a problem with TTL.

Figure 41 illustrates a practical type of signal transmission line. The mutual reactances L_m and C_m which form the noise coupling paths and the line parameters L_s and C_g which govern the line impedance, will vary with the type of line used. Since cross talk is a function of the ratio of the mutual impedances to the line characteristic impedances, the selection of transmission-line type must be at least partially a factor in cross-talk considerations.

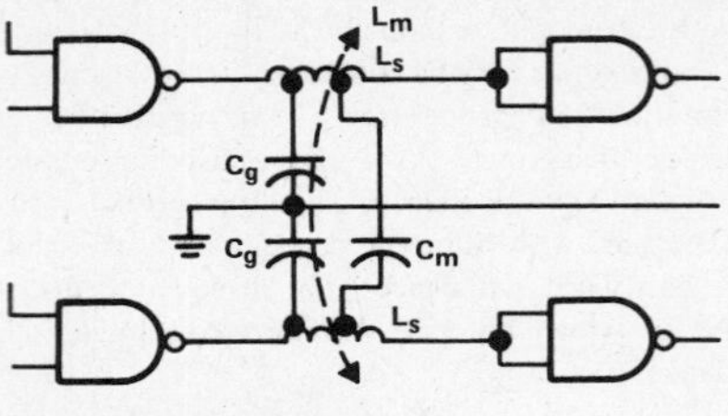
Lm
Ls
Cg
Cg
Cm
Ls

ALL GATES SN74ALS00

Figure 41. Equivalent Circuit for Sending Line

The use of direct-wired connections is the simplest and lowest cost method, but they are also the poorest for noise rejection. If the lead is not cabled tightly together with similar leads, direct leads up to 12 inches in length can be used.

When the length of the signal line is increased, the line impedance is seen by the driving and receiving gates. As shown in Figure 42, a pulse sent along the sending line G3 and G4 will be coupled via the coupling impedance Z_C onto the receiving line G1 and G2, which can be in either of the two logic states. The extent to which cross talk will occur depends on the type of lines used and their relationship to each other.

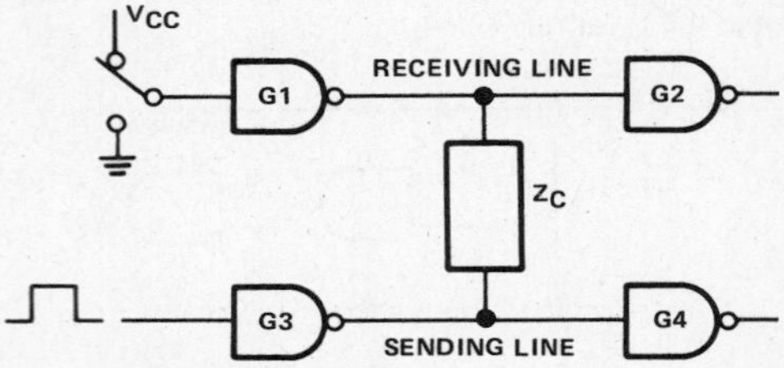
VCC
RECEIVING LINE
G1
G2
ZC
G3
G4
SENDING LINE

(Z_C) – COUPLING IMPEDANCE

Figure 42. Equivalent Circuit for Cross Talk

The voltage impressed on the sending line by gate G3 is determined by the equation:

$$V_{SL} = \frac{V_{G3} Z_0}{R_{S3} + Z_0} \tag{5}$$

where

V_{G3} = open-circuit logic voltage swing generated by gate G3
R_{S3} = output impedance of gate G3
Z_0 = line impedance
V_{SL} = voltage impressed on the sending line.

The relationship for the equation is illustrated in Figures 43 and 44.

The coupling from the sending line to the receiving line can be represented by taking coupling impedance Z_c into

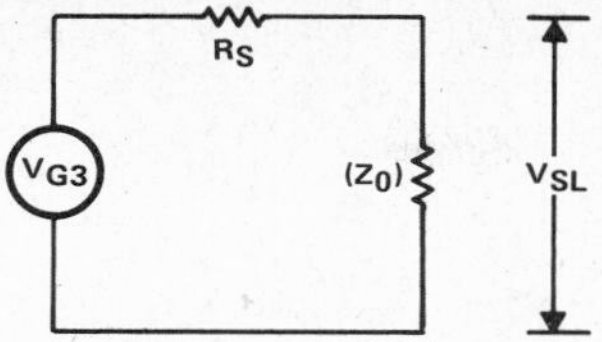

RS
VG3
(Z0)
VSL

Figure 43. Capacitive Cross Talk Between Two Signal Lines

account. An equivalent circuit to represent the coupling from the sending line to the receiving line is shown in Figure 44.

As the voltage impressed on the sending line propagates farther along the line, it can be represented as voltage source V_{SL} with a source impedance of Z_{01} (Figure 45). V_{SL} is then coupled to the receiving line via the coupling capacitance, where the impedance looking into the line is line impedance in both directions. Therefore the equation becomes

$$V_{RL} = V_{SL} \frac{\frac{Z_0}{2}}{(1.5\ Z_0 + Z_c)}$$

The voltage impressed on the receiving line (V_{RL}) then propagates along the receiving line to gate G2 which can be considered as an open circuit and voltage doubling occurs. Therefore:

$$V_{in(2)} = 2\ V_{RL} = V_{G3}\left(\frac{1}{1.5 + \frac{Z_c}{Z_0}}\right)\left(\frac{Z_0}{RS3 + Z_0}\right)$$

In the switching period, the transistor has a very low output impedance. Then $R_{S3} \ll Z_0$ and $V_{in(2)}$ can be simplified to the following:

$$V_{in(2)} = V_{G3}\left(\frac{1}{1.5 + \frac{Z_c}{Z_0}}\right)$$

The term $V_{in(2)}/V_{G3}$ can be defined as the cross-talk coupling constant.

The worst-case for signal line cross talk occurs when sending and receiving lines are close together but widely separated from a ground return path. The lines then have a high characteristic impedance and a low coupling impedance.

For example, if we assume a coupling impedance of 50 pF at 150 MHz with a line impedance of approximately 200 Ω then:

$$\frac{V_{in(2)}}{V_{G3}} = 0.62$$

This level is unsatisfactory because none of the very high-speed logic circuits has a guaranteed noise margin greater than one-third of the logic swing. Such potential cross talk can be avoided by not using the close spacing of conductors.

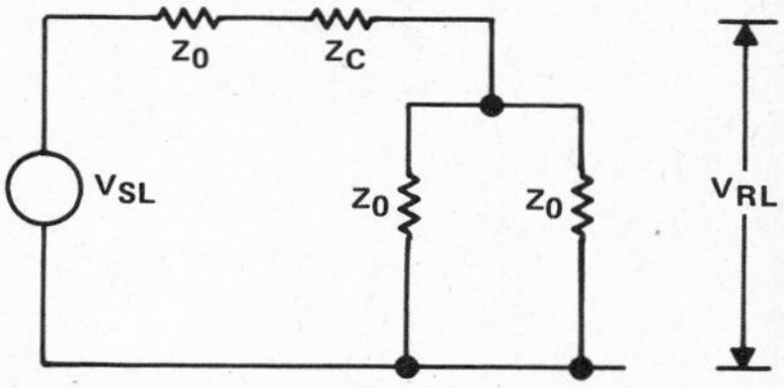

Z0
Zc
VSL
Z0
Z0
VRL

Figure 45. Equivalent Cross-Talk Network

Mutual coupling can be reduced by using coaxial cable or shielded twisted pairs. When mutual inductance and capacitance are decreased, line capacitance is increased and imposes restrictions on the driver. Coaxial cable combines very high mutual impedance with low characteristic impedance and shielding. It effectively eliminates cross talk, but is necessary in only the noisiest environments. Twisted pairs are adequate for most applications and are typically less expensive and easier to use.

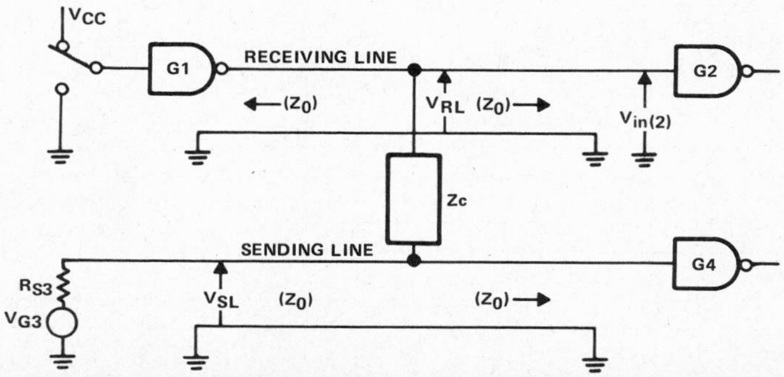

VCC
G1
RECEIVING LINE
←(Z0)
VRL (Z0)→
Vin(2)
G2
Zc
SENDING LINE
G4
RS3
VG3
VSL
(Z0)
(Z0)→

Figure 44. Coupling Impedances Involved in Cross Talk

Printed Circuit Card Conductors

Signal interconnections on a two-sided or multilayer printed circuit card can be grouped into two general categories: microstrip lines and strip lines. The microstrip line (Figure 46) consists of a signal conductor separated from a ground plane by a dielectric insulating material. A strip line (Figure 47) consists of a signal conductor within a dielectric insulating material and the conductor being centered between two parallel conductor planes. The important features of these type of printed circuit conductors are that the impedances are highly predictable, can be closely controlled, and the process is relatively inexpensive because standard printed circuit board manufacturing techniques are used. Typical impedances of these types of conductors with respect to their physical size and relative spacings are shown in Tables 7 and 8.

Table 7. Typical Impedance of Microstrip Lines

Dimensions		Line Impedance	Capacitance
H (mils)	W (mils)	Z_O (Ω)	per Foot (pF)
6	20	35	40
6	15	40	35
15	20	56	30
15	15	66	26
30	20	80	20
30	15	89	18
60	20	105	16
60	15	114	14
100	20	124	13
100	15	132	12

Relative dielectric constant ≈5

Table 8. Typical Impedance of Strip Lines

Dimensions		Line Impedance	Capacitance
H'a = H'b = (mils)	W (mils)	Z_O (Ω)	per Foot (pF)
6	20	27	80
6	15	32	70
10	20	34	67
10	15	40	56
12	20	37	57
12	15	43	48
20	20	44	48
20	15	51	42
30	20	55	39
30	15	61	35

Relative dielectric constant ≈5, and H'a = H'b

Cross talk on a printed circuit board is also a function of the mutual reactances and the line parameters which govern the line impedance. A microstrip line and a strip line are, by definition, conductors placed relatively close to a ground plane. Therefore, they have at least one inherent property which tends to reduce cross talk. In addition, the thickness (H) of the dielectric and the spacing (S) of the conductors can be implemented selectively to reduce the amount of possible cross talk. The effects of these two dimensions on cross talk have been evaluated and are shown graphically in Figure 48. The data shown can be used to estimate the maximum crosstalk which will be encountered under the most unfavorable conditions.

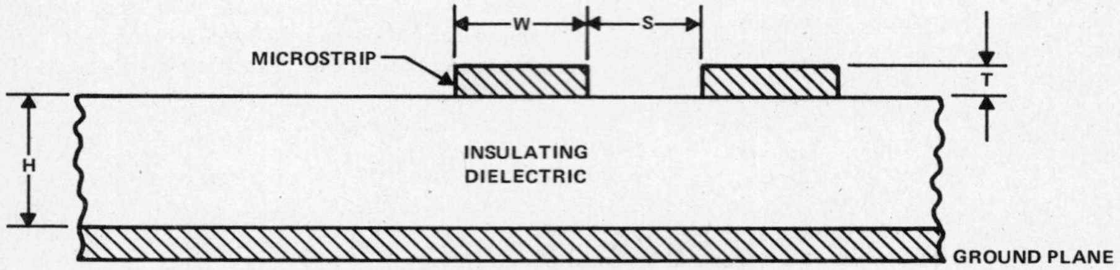
W
S
MICROSTRIP
T
H
INSULATING
DIELECTRIC
GROUND PLANE

Figure 46. Microstrip Line

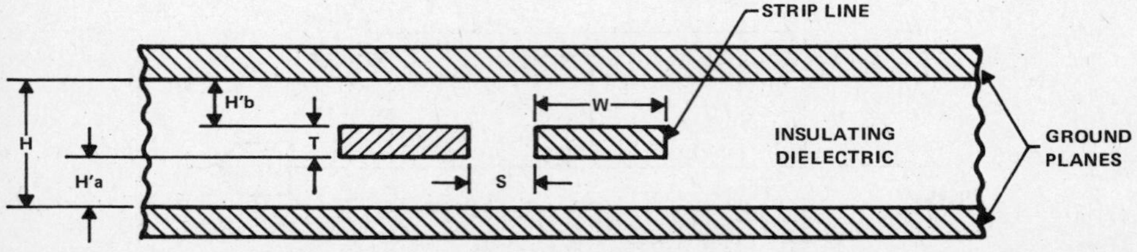
STRIP LINE
H'b
W
H
T
H'a
S
INSULATING
DIELECTRIC
GROUND
PLANES

Figure 47. Strip Line

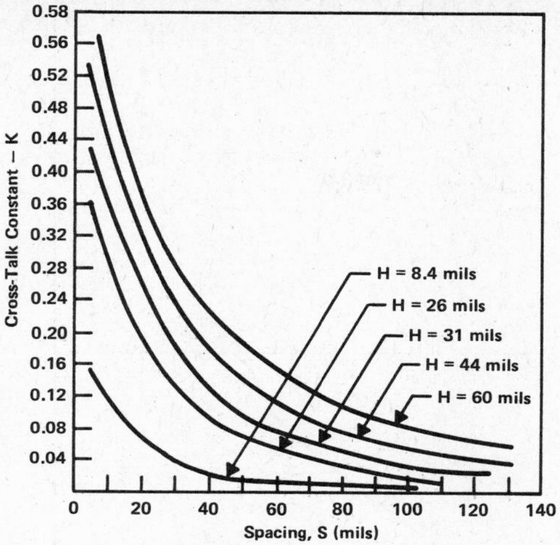
Cross-Talk Constant – K
0.58
0.56
0.52
0.48
0.44
0.40
0.36
0.32
0.28
0.24
0.20
0.16
0.12
0.08
0.04
0
20
40
60
80
100
120
140
Spacing, S (mils)
H = 8.4 mils
H = 26 mils
H = 31 mils
H = 44 mils
H = 60 mils

Figure 48. Line Spacing Versus Cross-Talk Constant

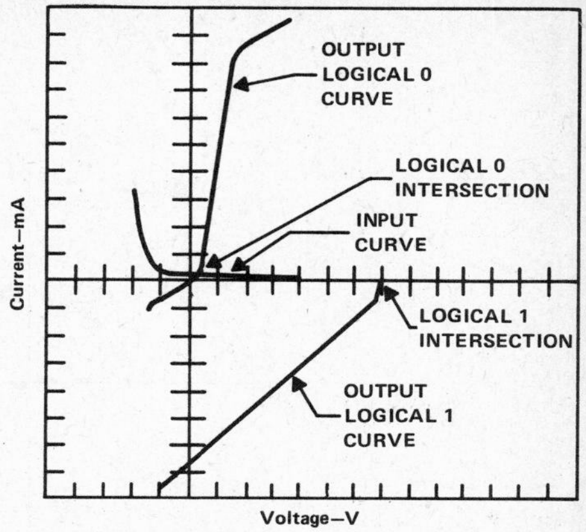
OUTPUT
LOGICAL 0
CURVE
LOGICAL 0
INTERSECTION
INPUT
CURVE
LOGICAL 1
INTERSECTION
OUTPUT
LOGICAL 1
CURVE
Current–mA
Voltage–V

Figure 49. TTL Bergeron Diagram

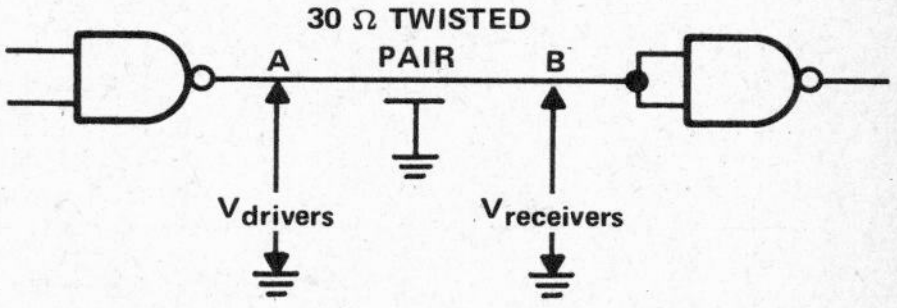
30 Ω TWISTED
PAIR
A
B
Vdrivers
Vreceivers

Figure 50. 'ALS/'AS Driving Twisted Pair

Transmission-Line Driving Reflections

When the interconnections used to transfer digital information become long enough so that line propagation delay is equal to or greater than the pulse transition times, the effects of reflections must be considered. These reflections are created because most TTL interconnections are not terminated in their characteristic impedance. Reflections lead to reduced noise margins, excessive delays, ringing, and overshoot. Some method must be used to analyze these reflections. Because neither the gate input nor output impedance is linear, basic transmission-line equations are applicable but unwieldy. Transmission-line characteristics of TTL interconnections can be analyzed by using a simple graphic technique.

Figure 49 shows piecewise linear plots of a gate input and both (logic-high and logic-low) states of the output for a typical TTL device. The output curves are plotted with positive slopes. The input is inverted because it is at the receiving end of a transmission line. The logic-high and logic-low intersections are indicated on the plot. These points are the steady-state values which will be observed on a lossless transmission line (Figure 50).

Figure 50 shows a typical TTL interconnection using a twisted-pair cable which, in this example, has a characteristic impedance of approximately 30 Ω. To evaluate a logic-high to logic-low 'AS transition see Figures 51 and 52. The equation $-1/Z_0$ ($Z_0 = 30\ \Omega$), which represents the transmission line, is superimposed on the output characteristic curves in the Bergeron plot. Since evaluation of a logic-high to logic-low transition is desired, the $-1/Z_0$ line starts at the point of intersection of the impedance curves of the input and output for a logic-high state. The slope $-1/Z_0$ then proceeds toward the logic-low output curve. At time t_0, the driver output voltage is determined by the intersection of $-1/Z_0$ and the logic-low output curve (1.2 V). The transmission-line slope now becomes $1/Z_0$ and is drawn toward the input curve. At time t_1 [$t_{(n+1)} - t_n$ = time delay of line], the receiving gate sees −0.7 V. Now the line slope changes back to $-1/Z_0$ and the output curve for a logic low is approached. This action continues until the logic-low intersection is reached. Figure 52 plots driver and receiver voltages versus time for this example.

A logic-low to logic-high transition is treated in approximately the same manner (Figure 53). The Bergeron line $-1/Z_0$ starts at the intersection for a logic low. At time t_0, the driver output rises to 2.2 V and, at time t_1, the receiving gate input goes to approximately 4.35 V. Both output and input voltages are plotted in Figure 54.

Figures 55 through 58 illustrate 'ALS transitions and are treated in the same manner as the 'AS.

The scope photographs in Figures 59 through 66 show the effectiveness of the graphic techniques. In most cases, the calculated and experimental values of voltage steps agree within reason. The ringing that appears for the open wire is not immediately obvious. This is because the input and output curves in this region lie practically along the positive horizontal axis. At the scale used for graphic analysis, it is difficult to go much beyond the first few reflections. The graphic analysis is idealized and stray capacitance and inductance are not considered.

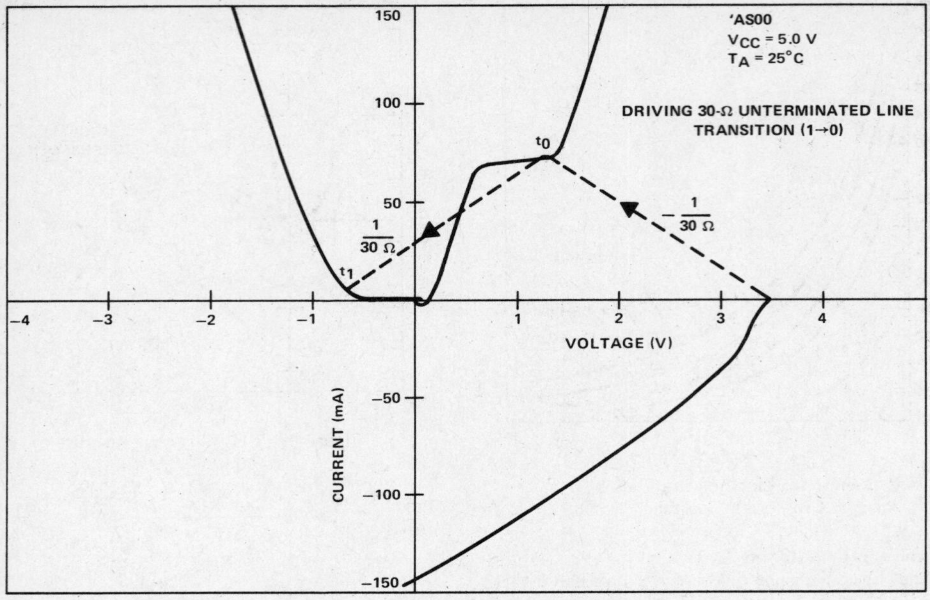
'AS00
V_{CC} = 5.0 V
T_A = 25°C
DRIVING 30-Ω UNTERMINATED LINE
TRANSITION (1→0)
150
100
50
−50
−100
−150
t_0
t_1
1/30 Ω
−1/30 Ω
−4
−3
−2
−1
1
2
3
4
VOLTAGE (V)
CURRENT (mA)

Figure 51. 'AS −ve Transition Bergeron Diagram

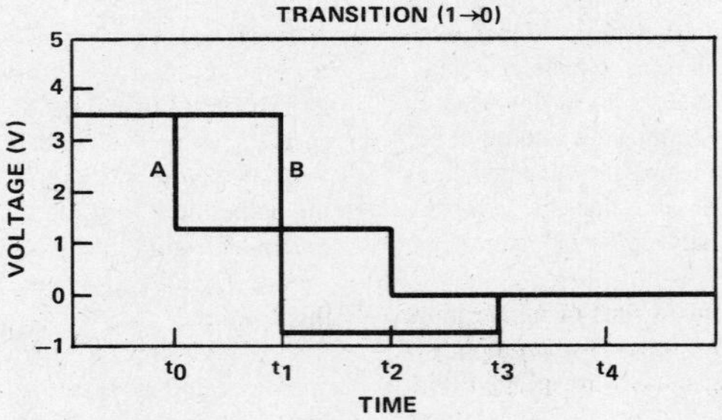
TRANSITION (1→0)
5
4
3
2
1
0
−1
A
B
VOLTAGE (V)
t_0
t_1
t_2
t_3
t_4
TIME

Figure 52. 'AS −ve Voltage/Time Plot

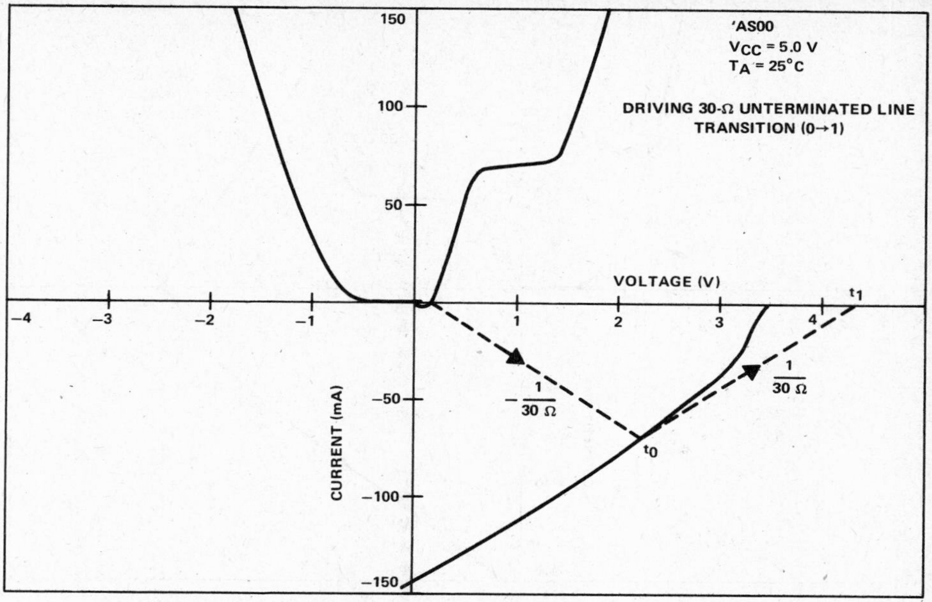

'AS00
V_{CC} = 5.0 V
T_A = 25°C
DRIVING 30-Ω UNTERMINATED LINE
TRANSITION (0→1)
VOLTAGE (V)
CURRENT (mA)
150
100
50
−50
−100
−150
−4
−3
−2
−1
1
2
3
4
$-\frac{1}{30\ \Omega}$
$\frac{1}{30\ \Omega}$
t_0
t_1

Figure 53. 'AS +ve Transition Bergeron Diagram

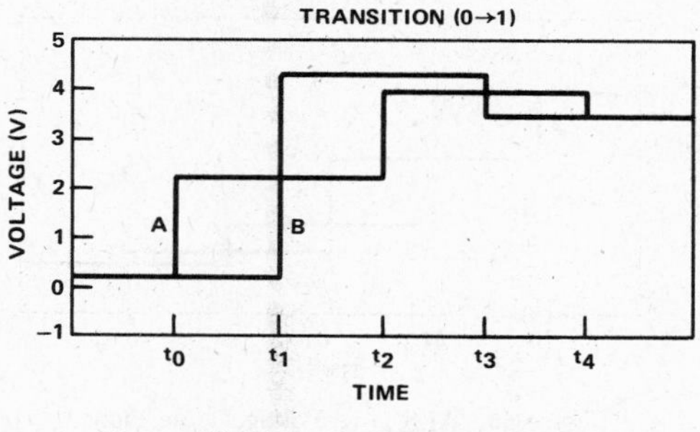

TRANSITION (0→1)
VOLTAGE (V)
TIME
5
4
3
2
1
0
−1
A
B
t_0
t_1
t_2
t_3
t_4

Figure 54. 'AS +ve Voltage/Time Plot

3

Application Reports

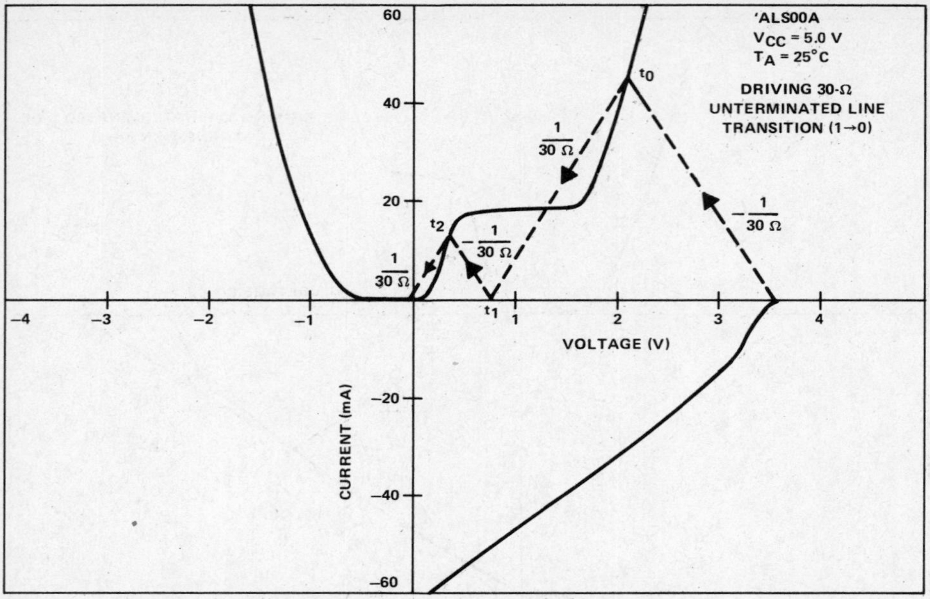
'ALS00A
V_{CC} = 5.0 V
T_A = 25°C
DRIVING 30-Ω
UNTERMINATED LINE
TRANSITION (1→0)
VOLTAGE (V)
CURRENT (mA)
t0
t1
t2
1/30 Ω
−1/30 Ω

Figure 55. 'ALS – ve Transition Bergeron Diagram

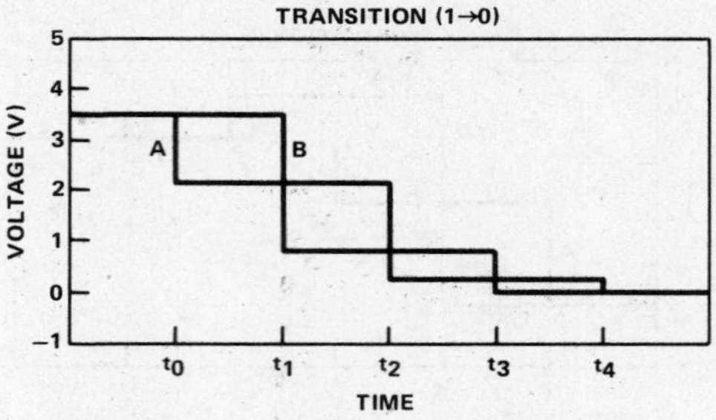
TRANSITION (1→0)
VOLTAGE (V)
A
B
t0
t1
t2
t3
t4
TIME

Figure 56. 'ALS – ve Voltage/Time Plot

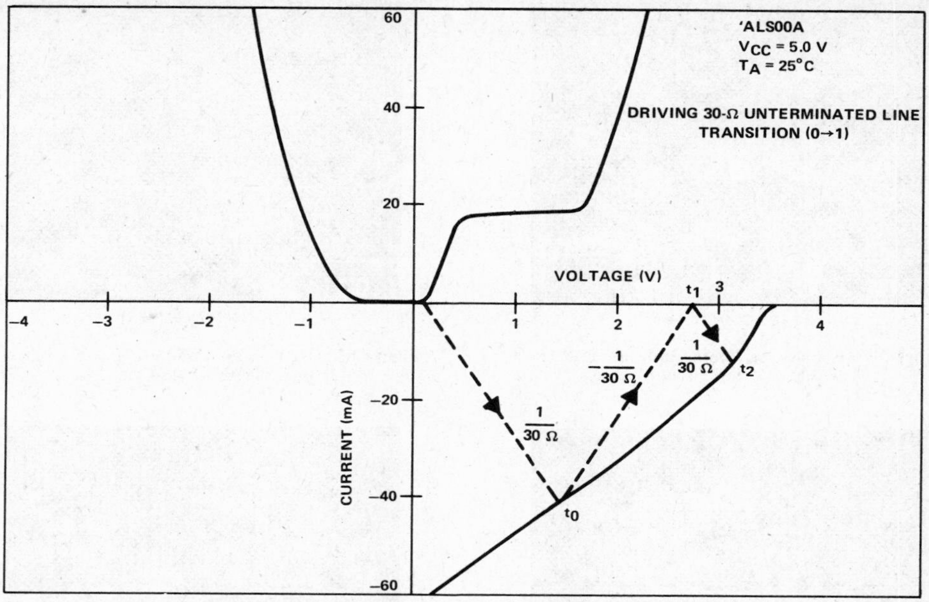
'ALS00A
VCC = 5.0 V
TA = 25°C
DRIVING 30-Ω UNTERMINATED LINE
TRANSITION (0→1)
VOLTAGE (V)
CURRENT (mA)
60
40
20
−20
−40
−60
−4
−3
−2
−1
1
2
3
4
t1
t2
t0
1/30 Ω
−1/30 Ω
1/30 Ω

Figure 57. 'ALS +ve Transition Bergeron Diagram

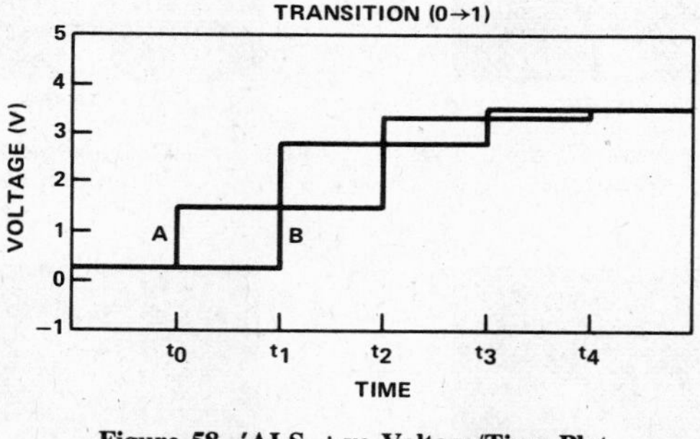
TRANSITION (0→1)
VOLTAGE (V)
5
4
3
2
1
0
−1
A
B
t0
t1
t2
t3
t4
TIME

Figure 58. 'ALS +ve Voltage/Time Plot

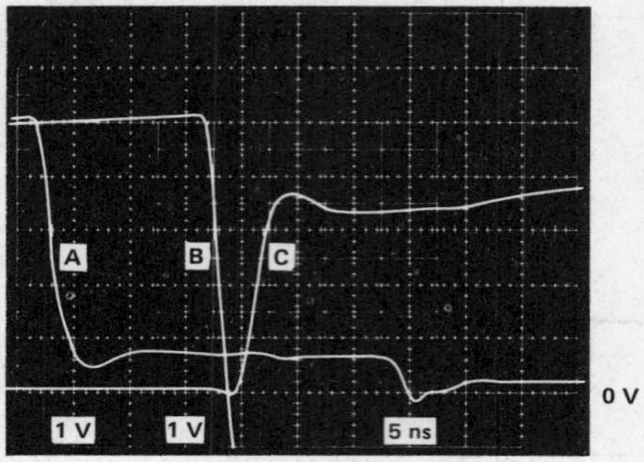
A
B
C
0 V
1 V
1 V
5 ns

TRANSITION (1 → 0)

Figure 59. Oscilloscope Photograph of 'AS001 −ve Transition Using 50-Ohm Line

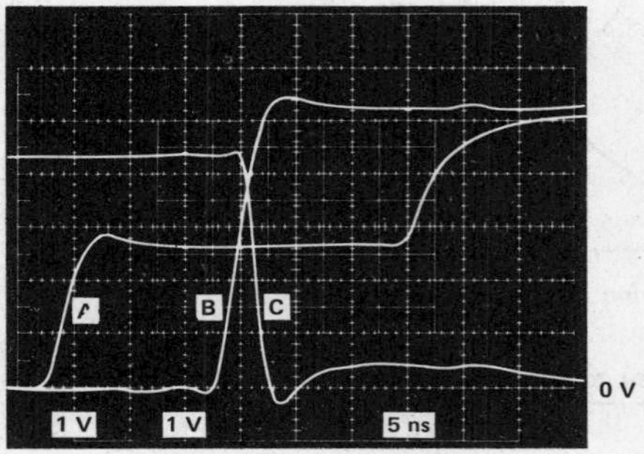
B
C
0 V
1 V
1 V
5 ns

TRANSITION (0 → 1)

Figure 60. Oscilloscope Photograph of 'AS00 +ve Transition Using 50-Ohm Line

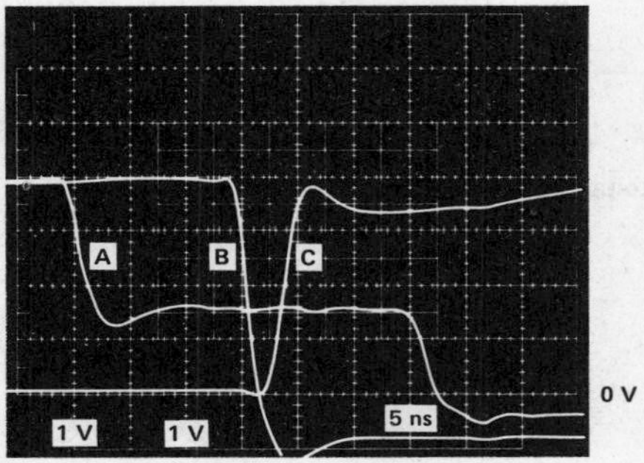
A
B
C
0 V
1 V
1 V
5 ns

TRANSITION (1 → 0)

Figure 61. Oscilloscope Photograph of 'AS00 −ve Transition Using 25-Ohm Line

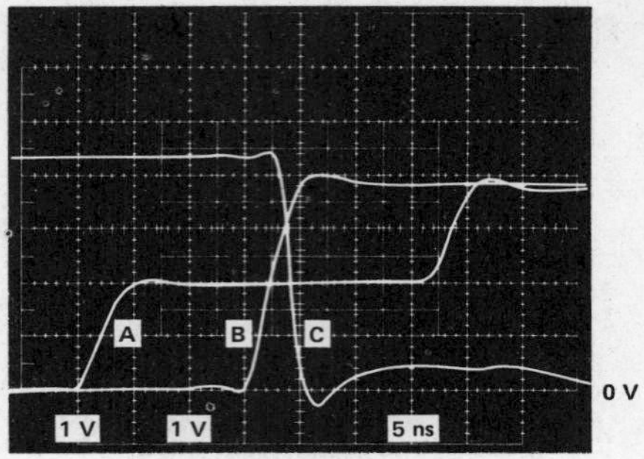
A
B
C
0 V
1 V
1 V
5 ns

TRANSITION (0 → 1)

Figure 62. Oscilloscope Photograph of 'AS00 +ve Transition Using 25-Ohm Line

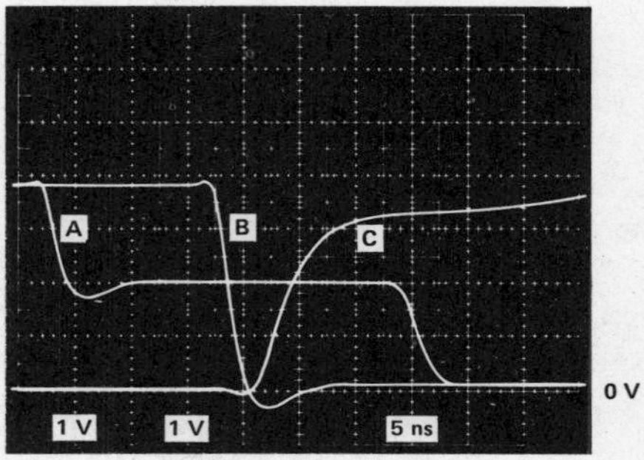
A
B
C
0 V
1 V
1 V
5 ns

TRANSITION (1 → 0)

Figure 63. Oscilloscope Photograph of 'ALS00A −ve Transition Using 50-Ohm Line

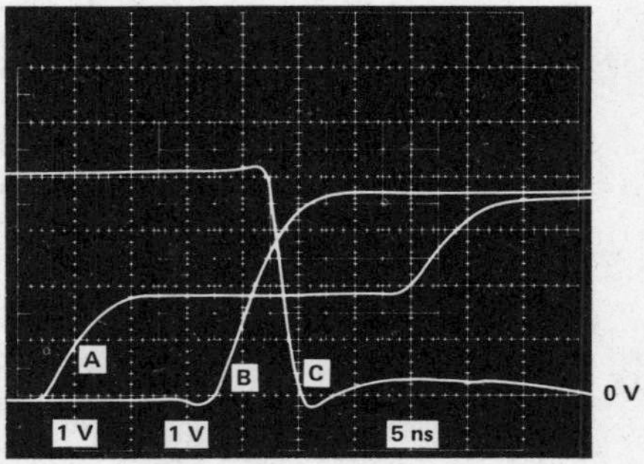
A
B
C
0 V
1 V
1 V
5 ns

TRANSITION (0 → 1)

Figure 64. Oscilloscope Photograph of 'ALS00A +ve Transition Using 50-Ohm Line

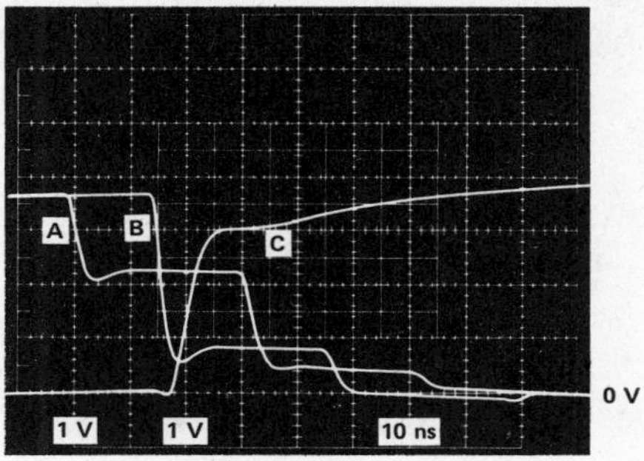

A
B
C
0 V
1 V
1 V
10 ns

TRANSITION (1 → 0)

Figure 65. Oscilloscope Photograph of 'ALS00A −ve Transition Using 25-Ohm Line

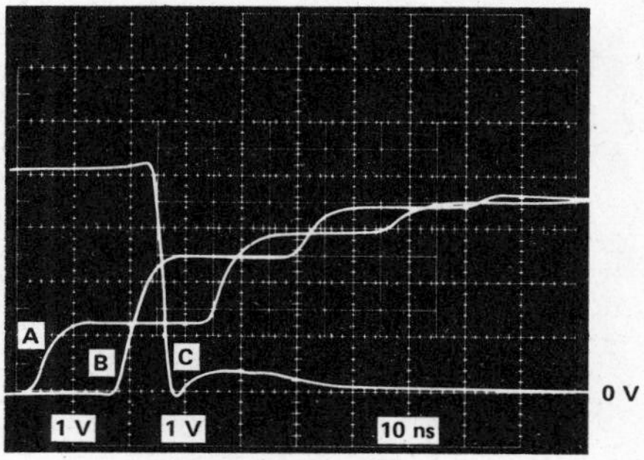

A
B
C
0 V
1 V
1 V
10 ns

TRANSITION (0 → 1)

Figure 66. Oscilloscope Photograph of 'ALS00A +ve Transition Using 25-Ohm Line

References

1. W.C. Elmore and M. Sands, *Electronics Experimental Techniques,* McGraw-Hill Book Co., New York, 30ff. (1949).
2. M. Williams and S. Miller, *Series 54ALS/74ALS Schottky TTL Applications B215*, Texas Instruments Limited, Bedford, England, August 1982.

Acknowledgment

This application report is an updated version of Reference 2 with significant contributions by the technical engineering staff at Texas Instruments and particularly by Rock Cozad, Rich Moore, and Bob Strong.

Appendix A
Normalized Load Factors

Normalizing output drive capability and input current requirements can be very useful to designers of systems using two or more of the TI TTL series of devices. It provides a set of load factors (input cuurent requirements in Table A-1), which can be summed and compared directly to the fanout capability (see Table A-2) of the output being considered. The load factor values shown are valid for any input rated at one unit load.

The loading of these type of outputs can be checked from any column. However, most designs use one of the series as the basic building block and, since the tables cover each series individually, the designer has the choice of working from the column containing the normalized fanout. As an example, the designers of a system using series 'AS as the basic circuit will probably find that the use of the 'AS00 and 'AS1000 columns will suit best because both fanout and load factors are expressed for these series of devices.

The use of these simple and easy-to-remember numbers was developed within each series to make the verification of output loading a matter of counting the number of inputs connected to a particular output. When mixtures of series are used, a common denominator (normalized factor) becomes useful.

USE OF TABLES A-1 AND A-2

Every possible combination of the seven 54/74 TTL families is included in these tables. If, for example, the existing system used 74S series logic and it is desired that some of it be replaced by series 74ALS logic, a quick check should be made on whether the 'ALS can be supplied with sufficient input current. By taking the 74S row and 'ALS, column figures of 2.5 and 20 are obtained for high- and low-level loads, respectively (see Table A-1). This indicates that, for high logic levels, two and one-half 'ALS gates can be driven for each 'S series gate removed. However, if more 74S series gates are being driven by this 'ALS device, the fanout between 'ALS and 'S series gate is required, you can now use Table A-2.

The 'ALS row and the 'S column are chosen. The figures are 8 for the high-logic level and 4 for the low-logic level. In this case the lowest figure is taken so that the interconnection is reliable for both logic states. So each 'ALS gate inserted will drive 4 'S series gates.

Table A-1. Normalized Input Currents

SERIES	I/O	INPUT CURRENT (mA)	INPUT CURRENT NORMALIZED								
			'00	'H00	'L00	'LS00	'S00	'AS00	'ALS00A	'AS1000	'ALS1000A
54/7400	HI	0.04	1	0.8	4	2	0.8	2	2	2	2
54/7400	LO	1.6	1	0.8	8.89	4	0.8	3.2	16	3.2	16
54H/74H00	HI	0.05	1.25	1	5	2.5	1	2.5	2.5	2.5	2.5
54H/74H00	LO	2	1.25	1	11.11	5	1	4	20	4	20
54/74L00	HI	0.01	0.25	0.2	1	0.5	0.2	0.5	0.5	0.5	0.5
54/74L00	LO	0.18	0.11	0.09	1	0.45	0.09	0.36	1.8	0.36	1.8
54LS/74LS00	HI	0.02	0.5	0.4	2	1	0.4	1	1	1	1
54LS/74LS00	LO	0.4	0.25	0.2	2.22	1	0.2	0.8	4	0.8	4
54S/74S00	HI	0.05	1.25	1	5	2.5	1	2.5	2.5	2.5	2.5
54S/74S00	LO	2	1.25	1	11.11	5	1	4	20	4	20
54AS/74AS00	HI	0.02	0.5	0.4	2	1	0.4	1	1	1	1
54AS/74AS00	LO	0.5	0.31	0.25	2.78	1.25	0.25	1	5	1	5
54ALS/74ALS00A	HI	0.02	0.5	0.4	2	1	0.4	1	1	1	1
54ALS/74ALS00A	LO	0.1	0.06	0.05	0.56	0.25	0.05	0.2	1	0.2	1
54AS1000	HI	0.02	0.5	0.4	2	1	0.4	1	1	1	1
54AS1000	LO	0.5	0.31	0.25	2.78	1.25	0.25	1	5	1	5
54ALS1000A	HI	0.02	0.5	0.4	2	1	0.4	1	1	1	1
54ALS1000A	LO	0.1	0.06	0.05	0.56	0.25	0.05	0.2	1	0.2	1

Table A-1 is normally used (in combination with Table A-2) when replacing one logic family with another in an existing system.

Table A-2 is normally used when originally designing a system which employs several TTL families to optimize performance.

Table A-2. Fanout Capability (Output Currents Normalized to Input Currents)

SERIES	I/O	OUTPUT CURRENT (mA)		OUTPUT DRIVE NORMALIZED								
				'00	'H00	'L00	'LS00	'S00	'AS00	'ALS00A	'AS1000	'ALS1000A
			*HI	0.04	0.05	0.01	0.02	0.05	0.02	0.02	0.02	0.02
			†LO	1.6	2	0.18	0.4	2	0.5	0.1	0.5	0.1
54/7400	HI	0.4		10	8	40	20	8	20	20	20	20
54/7400	LO	16		10	8	88.89	40	8	32	160	32	160
54H/74H00	HI	0.5		12.5	10	50	25	10	25	25	25	25
54H/74H00	LO	20		12.5	10	111.11	50	10	40	200	40	200
54L00	HI	0.1		2.5	2	10	5	2	5	5	5	5
54L00	LO	2		1.25	1	11.11	5	1	4	20	4	20
74L00	HI	0.2		5	4	20	10	4	10	10	10	10
74L00	LO	3.6		2.25	1.8	20	9	1.8	7.2	36	7.2	36
54LS/74LS00	HI	0.4		10	8	40	20	8	20	20	20	20
54LS00	LO	4		2.5	2	22.22	10	2	8	40	8	40
74LS00	LO	8		5	4	44.44	20	4	16	80	16	80
54S/74S00	HI	1		25	20	100	50	20	50	50	50	50
54S/74S00	LO	20		12.5	10	111.11	50	10	40	200	40	200
54AS/74AS00	HI	2		50	40	200	100	40	100	100	100	100
54AS/74AS00	LO	20		12.5	10	111.11	50	10	40	200	40	200
54ALS/74ALS00A	HI	0.4		10	8	40	20	8	20	20	20	20
54ALS00A	LO	4		2.5	2	22.22	10	2	8	40	8	40
74ALS00A	LO	8		5	4	44.44	20	4	16	80	16	80
54AS1000	HI	40		1000	800	4000	2000	800	2000	2000	2000	2000
54AS1000	LO	40		25	20	222.22	100	20	80	400	80	400
74AS1000	HI	48		1200	960	4800	2400	960	2400	2400	2400	2400
74AS1000	LO	48		30	24	266.67	120	24	96	480	96	480
54ALS1000A	HI	1		25	20	100	50	20	50	50	50	50
54ALS1000A	LO	12		7.5	6	66.67	30	6	24	120	24	120
74ALS1000A	HI	2		65	52	260	130	52	130	130	130	130
74ALS1000A	LO	24		15	12	133.33	60	12	48	240	48	240

*Input Current HI

†Input Curent LO

Appendix B

Letter Symbols, Terms, and Definitions

These symbols, terms, and definitions are in accordance with those currently agreed upon by the JEDEC Council of the Electronics Industries Association (EIA) for use in the USA and by the International Electrotechnical Commission (IEC) for international use. The definitions are grouped into sections applying to voltages, currents, switching characteristics, and classification of circuit complexity.

VOLTAGES

V_{IH} **High-level input voltage**
An input voltage level within the more positive (less negative) of the two ranges of values used to represent the binary variables. A minimum value is specified which is the least-positive (most-negative) value of high-level input voltage for which operation of the logic element within specification limits is guaranteed.

V_{IL} **Low-level input voltage**
An input voltage level within the less positive (more negative) of the two ranges of values used to represent the binary variables. A maximum value is specified which is the most-positive (least-negative) value of low-level input voltage for which operation of the logic element within specification limits is guaranteed.

V_{T+} **Positive-going threshold voltage**
The voltage level at a transition-operated input that causes operation of the logic element according to specification as the input voltage rises from a level below the negative-going threshold voltage, V_{T-}.

V_{T-} **Negative-going threshold voltage**
The voltage level at a transition-operated input that causes operation of the logic element according to specification as the input voltage falls from a level above the positive-going threshold voltage, V_{T+}.

V_{OH} **High-level output voltage**
The voltage at an output terminal for a specified output current I_{OH} with input conditions applied that according to the product specification will establish a high level at the output.

V_{OL} **Low-level output voltage**
The voltage at an output terminal for a specified output current I_{OL} with input conditions applied that according to the product specification will establish a low level at the output.

$V_{O(on)}$ **On-state output voltage**
The voltage at an output terminal for a specified output current with input conditions applied that according to the product specification will cause the output switching element to be in the on state.

Note: This characteristic is usually specified only for outputs not having internal pull-up elements.

$V_{O(off)}$ **Off-state output voltage**
The voltage at an output terminal for a specified output current with input conditions applied that according to the specification will cause the output switching element to be in the off state.

Note: This characteristic is usually specified only for outputs not having internal pull-up elements.

CURRENT

I_{IH} **High-level input current**
The current flowing into* an input when a specified high-level voltage is applied to that input.

I_{IL} **Low-level input current**
The current flowing into* an input when a specified low-level voltage is applied to that input.

*Current flowing out of a terminal is a negative value.

I_{OH} **High-level output current**
The current flowing into* the output with a specified high-level output voltage V_{OH} applied.

Note: This parameter is usually specified for open-collector outputs intended to drive other logic circuits.

$I_{O(off)}$ **Off-state output current**
The current flowing into* an output with a specified output voltage applied and input conditions applied that according to the product specification will cause the output switching element to be in the off state.

Note: This parameter is usually specified for open-collector outputs intended to drive devices other than logic circuits or for three-state outputs.

I_{OS} **Short-circuit output current**
The current flowing into* an output when that output is short-circuited to ground (or other specified potential) with input conditions applied to establish the output logic level farthest from ground potential (or other specified potential).

I_{CCH} **Supply current, output(s) high**
The current flowing into* the V_{CC} supply terminal of a circuit when the reference output(s) is (are) at a high-level voltage.

I_{CCL} **Supply current, output(s) low**
The current flowing into* the V_{CC} supply terminal of a circuit when the reference output(s) is (are) at a low-level voltage.

DYNAMIC CHARACTERISTICS

f_{max} **Maximum clock frequency**
The highest rate at which the clock input of a bistable circuit can be driven through its required sequence while maintaining stable transitions of logic level at the output with input conditions established that should cause a change of output state with each clock pulse.

t_{HZ} **Output disable time (of a three-state output) from high level**
The time between the specified reference points on the input and output voltage waveforms with the three-state output changing from the defined high level to a high-impedance (off) state.

t_{LZ} **Output disable time (of a three-state output) from low level**
The time between the specified reference points on the input and output voltage waveforms with the three-state output changing from the defined low level to a high-impedance (off) state.

t_{PLH} **Propagation delay time, low-to-high-level output**
The time between the specified reference points on the input and output voltage waveforms with the output changing from the defined low level to the defined high level.

t_{PHL} **Propagation delay time, high-to-low-level output**
The time between the specified reference points on the input and output voltage waveforms with the output changing from the defined high level to the defined low level.

t_{TLH} **Transition time, low-to-high-level output**
The time between a specified low-level voltage and a specified high-level voltage on a waveform that is changing from the defined low level to the defined high level.

t_{THL} **Transition time, high-to-low-level output**
The time between a specified high-level voltage and a specified low-level voltage on a waveform that is changing from the defined high level to the defined low level.

t_w **Average pulse width**
The time between 50% amplitude points (or other specified reference points) on the leading and trailing edges of a pulse.

*Current flowing out of a terminal is a negative value.

t_h **Hold time**
The time interval for which a signal or pulse is retained at a specified input terminal after an active transition occurs at another specified input terminal.

$t_{release}$ **Release time**
The time interval between the release from a specified input terminal of data intended to be recognized and the occurrence of an active transition at another specified input terminal.

Note: When specified, the interval designated ''release time'' falls within the setup interval and constitutes, in effect, a negative hold time.

t_{su} **Setup time**
The time interval for which a signal is applied and maintained at a specified input terminal before an active transition occurs at another specified input terminal.

t_{ZH} **Output enable time (of a three-state output) to high level**
The time between the specified reference points on the input and output voltage waveforms with the three-state output changing from a high-impedance (off) state to the defined high level.

t_{ZL} **Output enable time (of a three-state output) to low level**
The time between the specified reference points on the input and output voltage waveforms with the three-state output changing from a high-impedance (off) state to the defined low level.

CLASSIFICATION OF CIRCUIT COMPLEXITY

Gate equivalent circuit
A basic unit-of-measure of relative digital-circuit complexity. The number of gate equivalent circuits is that number of individual logic gates that would have to be interconnected to perform the same function.

LSI **Large-scale integration**
A concept whereby a complete major subsystem or system function is fabricated as a single microcircuit. In this context a major subsystem or system, whether logical or linear, is considered to be one that contains 100 or more equivalent gates or circuitry of similar complexity.

MSI **Medium-scale integration**
A concept whereby a complete subsystem or system function is fabricated as a single microcircuit. The subsystem or system is smaller than for LSI, but whether digital or linear, is considered to be one that contains 12 or more equivalent gates or circuitry of similar complexity.

SSI **Small-scale integration**
Integrated circuits of less complexity than medium-scale integration (MSI).

*Current flowing out of a terminal is a negative value.

Error Detection and Correction
Using SN54/74ALS632A, SN54/74ALS633 through SN54/74ALS635

Robert Breuninger

Contributors
W.T. Greer, Jr., David Mondeel, Jay Maxey

TEXAS INSTRUMENTS

IMPORTANT NOTICE

Texas Instruments (TI) reserves the right to make changes in the devices or the device specifications identified in this publication without notice. TI advises its customers to obtain the latest version of device specifications to verify, before placing orders, that the information being relied upon by the customer is current.

TI warrants performance of its semiconductor products, including SNJ and SMJ devices, to current specifications in accordance with TI's standard warranty. Testing and other quality control techniques are utilized to the extent TI deems such testing necessary to support this warranty. Unless mandated by government requirements, specific testing of all parameters of each device is not necessarily performed.

In the absence of written agreement to the contrary, TI assumes no liability for TI applications assistance, customer's product design, or infringement of patents or copyrights of third parties by or arising from use of semiconductor devices described herein. Nor does TI warrant or represent that any license, either express or implied, is granted under any patent right, copyright, or other intellectual property right of TI covering or relating to any combination, machine, or process in which such semiconductor devices might be or are used.

INTRODUCTION

NEED FOR ERROR CORRECTION

With memory systems continuing to expand and the expectation of 256K DRAMs in the near future, it has become increasingly important that system designers consider error detection and correction. Generally, the larger the chip density, the greater the probability for device errors. It is easy to recognize this probability when one considers that a 32-bit × 64K memory, using 64K DRAMs, equates to approximately 2.1 million bits of information. This expands to 8.4 million bits of information when using 256K DRAMs. For memory sizes larger than 1/2 million bits, it is generally considered that error detection and correction is required to guarantee high reliability.

The SN54/74ALS632A, SN54/74ALS633 through SN54/74ALS635 provide a simple solution to these requirements in 32-bit machines. In addition, the 'ALS632A and ALS633 provide the necessary hardware to perform byte-write operations which are typically used in the more advanced systems. To ensure the integrity of the error detection and correction circuit itself, diagnostic capabilities have been provided in all four devices.

The 'ALS632A series devices are not limited to only 32-bit systems. They can easily be implemented in 16- or 24-bit systems. In the case of 16-bit systems, the additional memory needed for holding the check bits can be reduced when compared to conventional 16-bit EDAC's.

The pin function table and mechanical data for the 'ALS632A, ALS633 through 'ALS635 are shown respectively as Table 1 and Figure 1.

OPERATIONAL DESCRIPTION

WRITE MODE

During a memory write cycle, the EDAC is required to generate a 7-bit check word to accompany the 32-bit data word before being written into memory. To place the 'ALS632A, 'ALS633 through 'ALS635 in the write mode, simply take S1 and S0 low. Output enable controls $\overline{\text{OEB}}$0 through $\overline{\text{OEB}}$3 for the 'ALS632A, 'ALS633, or $\overline{\text{OEDB}}$ for the 'ALS634, 'ALS635, must be taken high before the data word can be applied. Output enable control $\overline{\text{OECS}}$ must be taken low to pass the check word to the external bus.

The check word will be generated in not more than 48 ns* after the data word has been applied. The 'ALS632A series EDACs can be made to appear transparent to memory, during the write mode, because typical write times of most DRAMs are much larger than the propagation delay of data to check word.

READ-FLAG-CORRECT OPERATION

During a memory read cycle, the function of the 'ALS632A series EDACs is to compare the 32-bit data word against the 7-bit check word previously stored in memory. It will then flag and correct any single-bit error which may have occurred. Single bit errors will be detected through the $\overline{\text{ERR}}$ flag and double bit errors will be detected through the $\overline{\text{MERR}}$ flag. Figure 2 shows a typical timing diagram of the read-flag-correct operation.

When S0 is taken high, the EDAC will internally begin the correction process, although it should be noted that the error flags are enabled while in the read mode. For many applications, the simplest operation can be obtained by always executing the correction cycle, regardless if a single-bit error has occurred.

IMPORTANT TIMING CONSIDERATIONS FOR READ-FLAG-CORRECT MODE

The most frequently asked question for an EDAC is how fast can a correction cycle be executed. Before S0 can be taken high, the data and check word must be set up at least 10 ns*. In addition, the data and check word must be held for at least 15 ns* after S0 goes high. This ensures the data and check word is saved in the EDAC's input latches. After the hold time has been satisfied, the source which is driving the data bus can be placed in high impedance and the EDAC's output drivers can be enabled. This is accomplished by taking $\overline{\text{OEB}}$0 through $\overline{\text{OEB}}$3 ('ALS632A, 'ALS633) or $\overline{\text{OEDB}}$ ('ALS634, 'ALS635) low.

If the minimum data set up time is used as a reference, and the output drivers are enabled after the minimum data hold time, then correction will be accomplished in not more than 58 ns*.

READ MODIFY-WRITE OPERATIONS

The'ALS632A and 'ALS633 contain the necessary hardware to perform byte-write operations. The 'ALS634 and 'ALS635 are not capable of byte-write operations because they do not contain an output data latch or individual byte controls. When performing a read-modify-write function, typically the user would first want to perform the read-flag-correct cycle as discussed before, and shown in Figure 2. This ensures that corrected data is used at the start of the modity-write operation.

The corrected data is then latched into the output data latch by taking $\overline{\text{LEDBO}}$ from low to high. Upon completing this, modifying any byte or bytes is easily accomplished by taking the appropriate byte control $\overline{\text{OEB}}$0 through $\overline{\text{OEB}}$3 high. This allows the user to place the modified byte or bytes back onto the data bus while retaining the other byte or bytes. An example of a read-

*These times are based on SN74ALS632A data.

ceramic packages – side-braze (JD suffix)

This is a hermetically sealed ceramic package with a metal cap and side-brazed tin-plated leads.

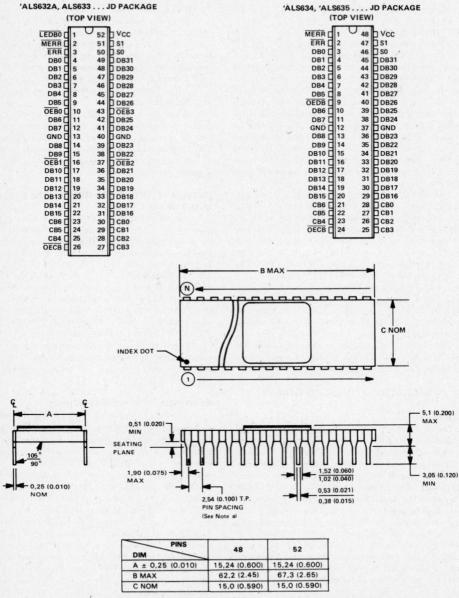

'ALS632A, ALS633 . . . JD PACKAGE
(TOP VIEW)

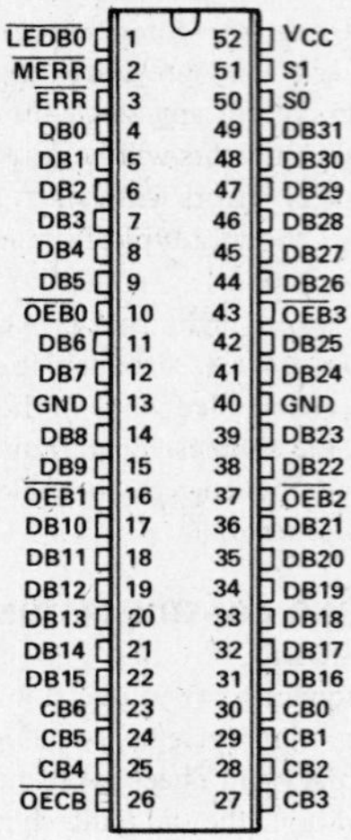

LEDB0 1 52 VCC
MERR 2 51 S1
ERR 3 50 S0
DB0 4 49 DB31
DB1 5 48 DB30
DB2 6 47 DB29
DB3 7 46 DB28
DB4 8 45 DB27
DB5 9 44 DB26
OEB0 10 43 OEB3
DB6 11 42 DB25
DB7 12 41 DB24
GND 13 40 GND
DB8 14 39 DB23
DB9 15 38 DB22
OEB1 16 37 OEB2
DB10 17 36 DB21
DB11 18 35 DB20
DB12 19 34 DB19
DB13 20 33 DB18
DB14 21 32 DB17
DB15 22 31 DB16
CB6 23 30 CB0
CB5 24 29 CB1
CB4 25 28 CB2
OECB 26 27 CB3

'ALS634, 'ALS635 . . . . JD PACKAGE
(TOP VIEW)

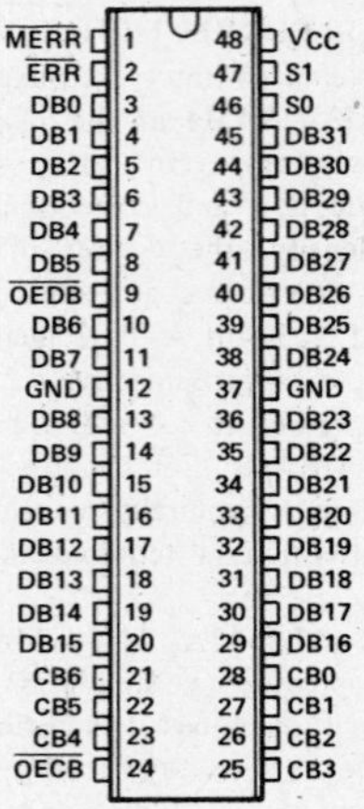

MERR 1 48 VCC
ERR 2 47 S1
DB0 3 46 S0
DB1 4 45 DB31
DB2 5 44 DB30
DB3 6 43 DB29
DB4 7 42 DB28
DB5 8 41 DB27
OEDB 9 40 DB26
DB6 10 39 DB25
DB7 11 38 DB24
GND 12 37 GND
DB8 13 36 DB23
DB9 14 35 DB22
DB10 15 34 DB21
DB11 16 33 DB20
DB12 17 32 DB19
DB13 18 31 DB18
DB14 19 30 DB17
DB15 20 29 DB16
CB6 21 28 CB0
CB5 22 27 CB1
CB4 23 26 CB2
OECB 24 25 CB3

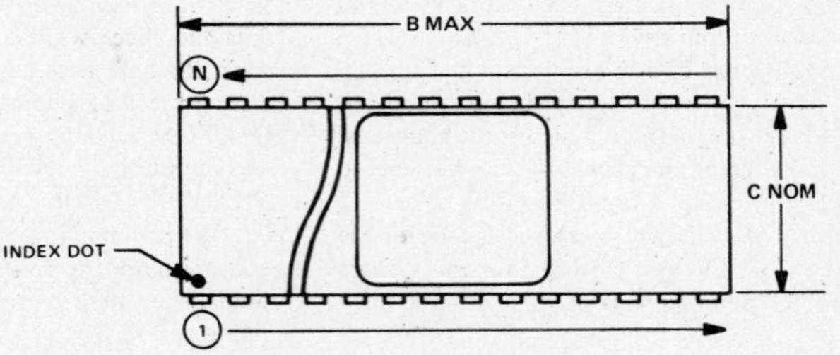

B MAX
N
C NOM
INDEX DOT
1

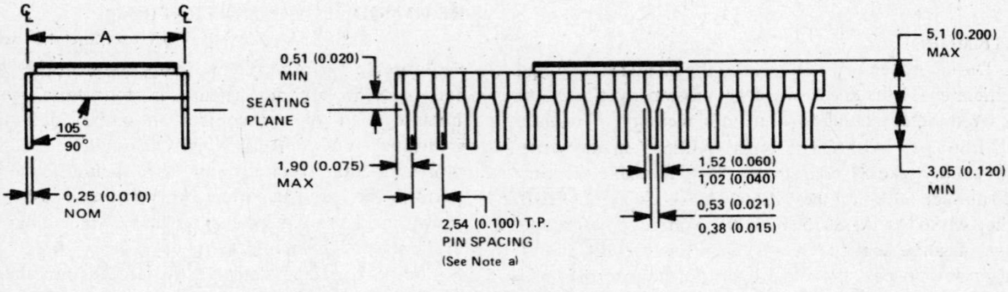

A
105°
90°
0,25 (0.010)
NOM
0,51 (0.020)
MIN
SEATING
PLANE
1,90 (0.075)
MAX
2,54 (0.100) T.P.
PIN SPACING
(See Note a)
1,52 (0.060)
1,02 (0.040)
0,53 (0.021)
0,38 (0.015)
5,1 (0.200)
MAX
3,05 (0.120)
MIN

DIM \ PINS	48	52
A ± 0,25 (0.010)	15,24 (0.600)	15,24 (0.600)
B MAX	62,2 (2.45)	67,3 (2.65)
C NOM	15,0 (0.590)	15,0 (0.590)

ALL DIMENSIONS ARE IN MILLIMETERS AND PARENTHETICALLY IN INCHES

NOTE: a. Each pin centerline is located within 0,25 (0.010) of its true longitudinal position.

Figure 1. Mechanical Data for 'ALS632A, 'ALS633 through 'ALS635

Table I. Pin Function for 'ALS632A, 'ALS633 through 'ALS635

PIN NAME	DESCRIPTION
S1, S0	Selects the operating mode of the EDAC S1 S0 MODE OPERATION L L WRITE Input dataword and output checkword H L READ & FLAG Input dataword and output error flags H H CORRECT Latched input data and checkword/output corrected Data and error syndrome code L H DIAGNOSTIC Input various datawords against latched checkword/output valid error flags
DB0 through DB31	I/O port for entering or outputing data
$\overline{\text{OEB0}}$ through $\overline{\text{OEB3}}$ (ALS632A, 'ALS633)	Three state control for the data I/O port. A high allows data to be entered, and low outputs the data. Each pin controls 8 data I/O ports (or one byte). $\overline{\text{OEB0}}$ controls DB0 through DB7, $\overline{\text{OEB1}}$ controls DB8 through DB15, $\overline{\text{OEB2}}$ controls DB16 through DB23, and $\overline{\text{OEB3}}$ controls DB24 through DB31.
$\overline{\text{OEDB}}$ (ALS634, ALS635)	Three state control for the data 1/O port. When low allows data to outputed and a high allows data to be entered.
$\overline{\text{LEDB0}}$	Controls the dataword output latch. When low, the data output latch is transparent. When high, the latch stores whatever data was setup at its inputs when the last low to high transistion occured on the pin.
CS0 through CS6	I/O Port for entering or outputing the checkword. It is also used to output the syndrome error code during the error correction mode.
$\overline{\text{OECS}}$	Three state control for the checkword I/O port. A high allows data to be entered and a low allows either the checkword or syndrome code (depending on EDAC mode) to be outputed.
$\overline{\text{ERR}}$	Single error output flag, a low indicates at least a single bit error.
$\overline{\text{MERR}}$	Multiple error output flag, when low indicates two or more errors present

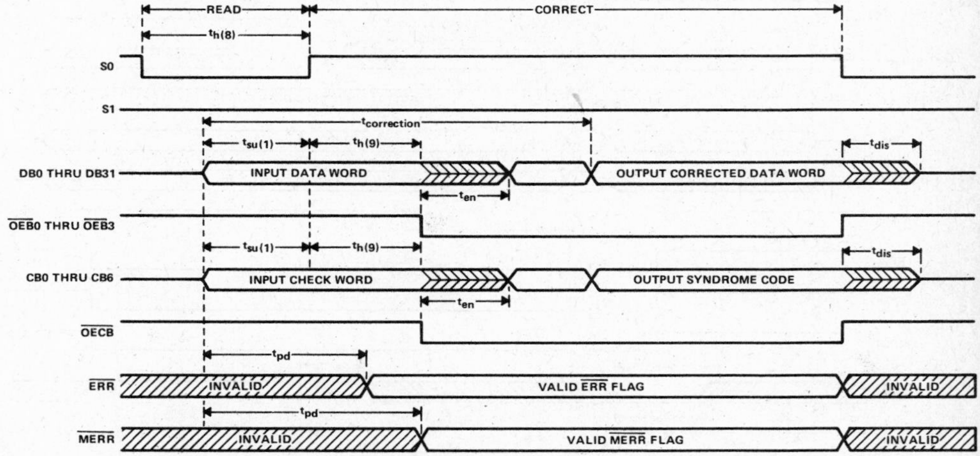
READ
CORRECT
th(8)
S0
S1
tcorrection
tsu(1)
th(9)
tdis
DB0 THRU DB31
INPUT DATA WORD
OUTPUT CORRECTED DATA WORD
ten
OEB0 THRU OEB3
CB0 THRU CB6
INPUT CHECK WORD
OUTPUT SYNDROME CODE
OECB
tpd
ERR
INVALID
VALID ERR FLAG
MERR
VALID MERR FLAG

Figure 2. Read-Flag-Correct Timing Diagram

modify-write for byte 0 is shown in Figure 3. Since the check word is no longer valid for the modified data word, a new one is easily generated by taking S0 and S1 low. After the appropriate propagation delay, the new check word will be available.

IMPORTANT TIMING CONSIDERATIONS FOR READ-MODIFY WRITE OPERATIONS

$\overline{\text{LEDB0}}$ should not be brought from low to high until 45 ns* after S0 goes high. This will ensure that corrected data is latched into the data output latches. On the other hand, $\overline{\text{LEDB0}}$ should be brought high no later than 0 ns* before S0 and S1 goes low. Again, this is to ensure that the corrected data is stored into the data output latches. Also of importance is the new check word will be available no later than 48 ns* after S0 and S1 goes low.

DIAGNOSTIC MODE OPERATION

The purpose of the diagnostic mode is to provide the user with the capability of easily detecting when the EDAC or memory is failing. There are several possibilities as to how a user might employ this feature, but Figure 4 shows a typical timing diagram of some diagnostics which can be performed with these devices. Generally, the user would first place the EDAC in the read mode (S0 = L, S1 = H), then apply a valid check word and data word. A valid check word is one in which the user knows what the associated data word . The user would next place the EDAC into the diagnostic mode by taking S0 high, and S1 low. This latches the valid check word into its input latches but leaves the data input latches transparent. To verify that the valid check word was latched properly, $\overline{\text{OECS}}$ can be taken low causing the valid check word to be placed back onto the bus. Since the data input latches remain transparent, this allows the user to apply various diagnostic data words against the valid check word. A diagnostic data word is one in which either a single or double bit error exists. In either case, the error flags should respond. The output data latch can be verified by taking $\overline{\text{LEDBO}}$ high and confirming the stored diagnostic data word is the same. This is made possible because error correction is disabled while in the diagnostic mode (S0 = H, S1 = L). Taking S1 high and $\overline{\text{LEDBO}}$ low will verify that the EDAC will correct the data word. Also, the error syndrome code can be verified by taking $\overline{\text{OECS}}$ low. It should be noted that only the 'ALS632A and 'ALS633 are capable of this pass through verification of the diagnostic data word. The 'ALS634 and 'ALS635 do not have the output data latch required to perform this function.

16-BIT SYSTEMS USING THE ALS632A SERIES EDACs

The 'ALS632A series EDACs can reduce the memory size required in 16-bit systems where conventional 16-bit EDACs (6 check bits, 16 data bits) are presently used. Figure 5 shows the typical system architecture for the 16-bit EDAC. In this system, 88 devices would be required for the 22-bit × 256K memory array, assuming 64K DRAMs are used. It is easy to see that 27.3%, or 24 devices, are

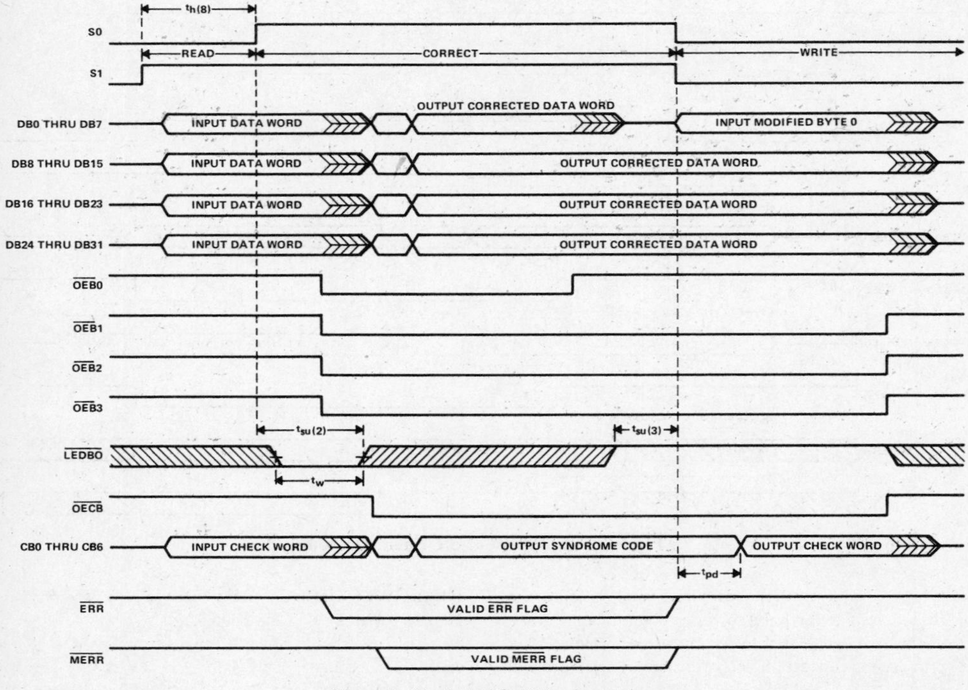

S0
S1
READ
CORRECT
WRITE
DB0 THRU DB7
DB8 THRU DB15
DB16 THRU DB23
DB24 THRU DB31
INPUT DATA WORD
OUTPUT CORRECTED DATA WORD
INPUT MODIFIED BYTE 0
OEB0
OEB1
OEB2
OEB3
LEDBO
OECB
CB0 THRU CB6
INPUT CHECK WORD
OUTPUT SYNDROME CODE
OUTPUT CHECK WORD
ERR
VALID ERR FLAG
MERR
VALID MERR FLAG

Figure 3. Read-Modify-Write Operation

required for storing the check bits. When using the 'ALS632A series EDACs, the memory required for the check bits can be reduced to 17.9%, or only 14 devices. This reduces the total number of DRAMs required by 10 devices. Figure 6 shows the architecture when using the 32-bit EDAC. The four 'LS646s are used to group two 16-bit data words into one 32-bit data word. In addition, this type of system can be used in byte-write operations where the other system cannot.

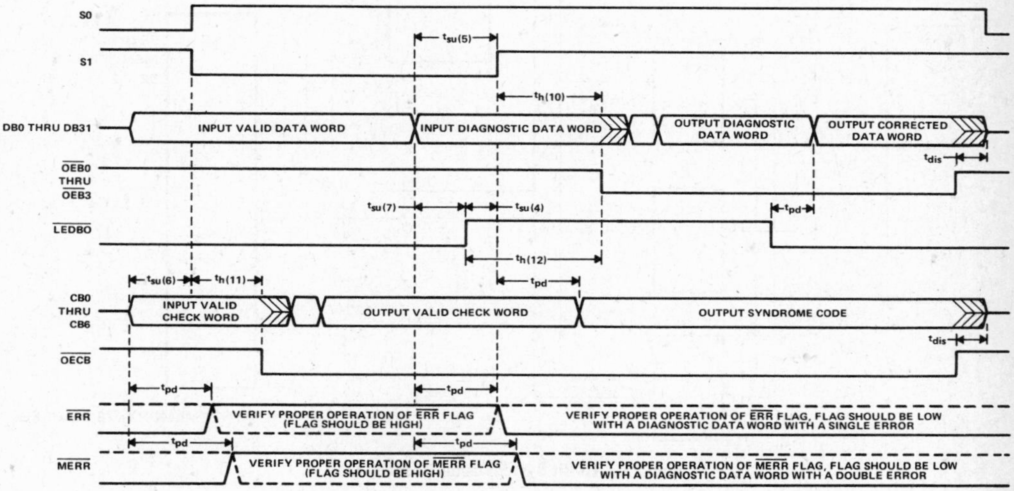

S0
S1
DB0 THRU DB31
INPUT VALID DATA WORD
INPUT DIAGNOSTIC DATA WORD
OUTPUT DIAGNOSTIC DATA WORD
OUTPUT CORRECTED DATA WORD
OEB0 THRU OEB3
LEDBO
CB0 THRU CB6
INPUT VALID CHECK WORD
OUTPUT VALID CHECK WORD
OUTPUT SYNDROME CODE
OECB
ERR
VERIFY PROPER OPERATION OF ERR FLAG (FLAG SHOULD BE HIGH)
VERIFY PROPER OPERATION OF ERR FLAG, FLAG SHOULD BE LOW WITH A DIAGNOSTIC DATA WORD WITH A SINGLE ERROR
MERR
VERIFY PROPER OPERATION OF MERR FLAG (FLAG SHOULD BE HIGH)
VERIFY PROPER OPERATION OF MERR FLAG, FLAG SHOULD BE LOW WITH A DIAGNOSTIC DATA WORD WITH A DOUBLE ERROR

Figure 4. Diagnostic Mode Timing Diagram

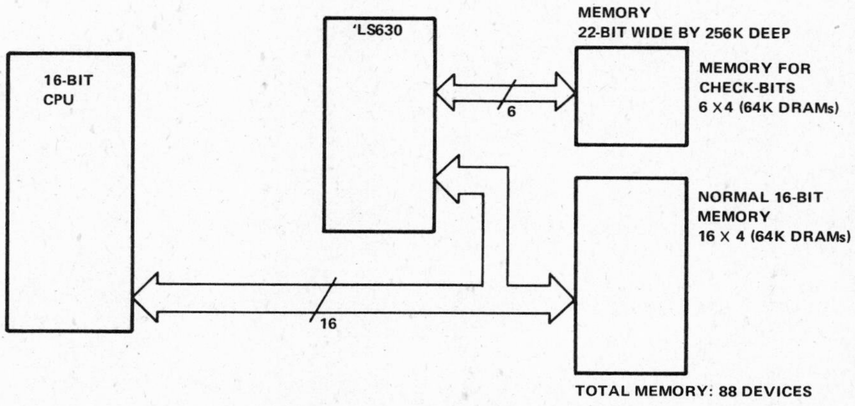

16-BIT CPU
'LS630
MEMORY
22-BIT WIDE BY 256K DEEP
MEMORY FOR CHECK-BITS
6 X4 (64K DRAMs)
6
NORMAL 16-BIT MEMORY
16 X 4 (64K DRAMs)
16
TOTAL MEMORY: 88 DEVICES

Figure 5. 16-Bit System using Conventional 16-Bit EDAC

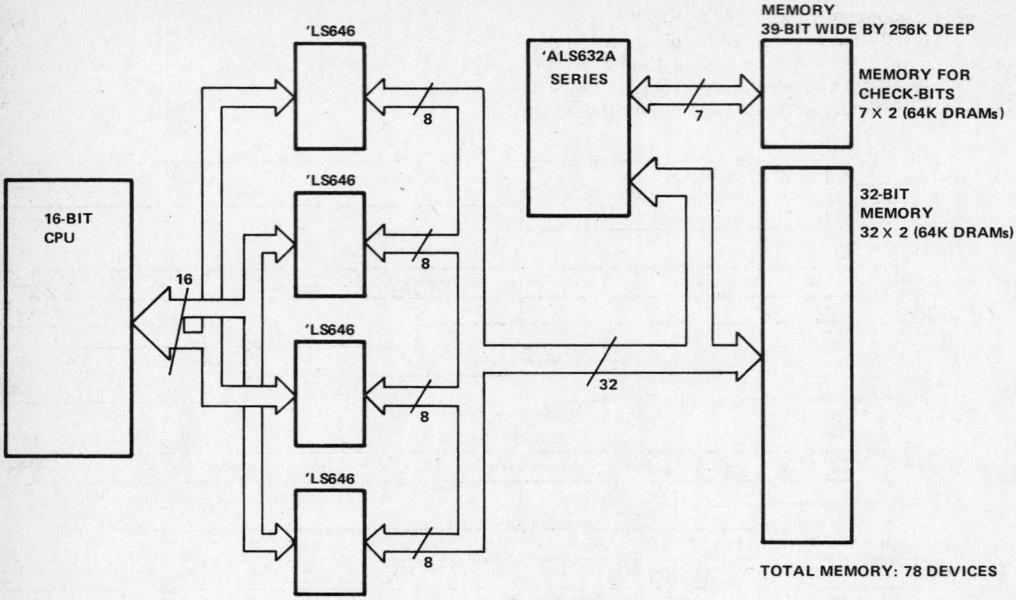
MEMORY
39-BIT WIDE BY 256K DEEP
'LS646
'ALS632A
SERIES
MEMORY FOR
CHECK-BITS
7 X 2 (64K DRAMs)
'LS646
16-BIT
CPU
32-BIT
MEMORY
32 X 2 (64K DRAMs)
16
'LS646
32
'LS646
8
7
TOTAL MEMORY: 78 DEVICES

Figure 6. 16-Bit System using 32-Bit EDAC

MEMORY MAPPING USING SN54/74LS610 THRU SN54/74LS613

Author
Thomas J. Tyson

Contributors
Deene Ogden, Jim Gallia and Dennis Frailey
Low Power Schottky Applications Group

INTRODUCTION

Microprocessors, due to the advent of high density semiconductor memories (i.e., 64K or larger), are being used more and more in systems featuring memory structures larger than 64K bytes. The majority of the microprocessors in use or available today have a 16-bit address bus, with a maximum addressing capability of 64K words. Due to this limitation, some sort of memory mapping is necessary to adapt these microprocessors to applications where large memory structures are required.

The memory mappers (SN54/74LS610 through SN54/74LS613) from TI were designed to alleviate this addressing limitation. These devices employ a paged memory mapping technique in expanding the system memory address bus by 8 bits, thus effectively increasing the system addressing capability by a factor of 2^8 or 256. For microprocessors with a 16-bit address bus (such as the Z-80, the 8085 and the 6800), this results in an increase in the maximum addressing capability from 64K bytes to 16M bytes and for the TMS9900 (which has a 15-bit address bus), the result is an increase from 32K words to 8M words (word = 2 bytes).

In the mapping operation, the four MSBs of the microprocessor address word are used to access one of the sixteen 12-bit registers of the memory mapper's 16 × 12-bit RAM array. Each mapper register is capable of holding a 12-bit address which will be termed the page address and will be used as the 12 MSBs of the memory address bus. The remaining 12 bits (11 in the case of the TMS9900) of the microprocessor address bus will be transferred directly to memory from the microprocessor and will be used to address the memory locations within each page. (See Figure 1)

The memory will be organized into 2^x pages (where x equals the number of bits of the page address) with 2^{n-4} words or bytes (where n is the bit length of the microprocessor address bus) per page. Once loaded, the mapper can access only 16 pages or 64K bytes (32K words in the TMS9900 case). In order to access more pages, the memory mapper RAM array must be reloaded with 16 new page addresses. This is done by the microprocessor via the data bus with the mapper in the WRITE mode. (A more detailed description of the modes of operation will be given later in this report.)

FUNCTIONAL DESCRIPTION

A functional block diagram of the SN54/74LS610 memory mapper, which consists mainly of: a 4-bit 2-to-1 multiplexer, a 16 × 12-bit RAM array, a 12-bit 2-to-1 multiplexer, 24 3-state buffers, control logic and in the case of 'LS610 and 'LS611, a 12-bit transparent latch, as shown in Figure 2. Table I lists the functional differences between the 'LS610, 'LS611, 'LS612, and 'LS613. Table II lists the function of each pin.

Depending on the state of the input control signals (i.e., $\overline{CS}$, R/$\overline{W}$, $\overline{STROBE}$, $\overline{MM}$, and $\overline{ME}$), the mapper can be operated in three basic modes of operation, I/O (READ or WRITE), MAP and PASS. An explanation of each mode and the control signals necessary to achieve that mode of operation is given below: (Refer to Table III)

Input/Output Mode

In this mode a page address can be loaded either into a mapper register or can be read from a memory mapper register depending on the state of the R/$\overline{W}$ (READ/WRITE) input. This input signal controls either the READ or WRITE function of the I/O Mode.

WRITE Mode

One of the sixteen 12-bit registers is loaded with a page address via the D0-D11 I/O ports from the microprocessor. The address of the selected register is inputted via the RS0-RS3 inputs and is usually the four LSBs of the microprocessor address word. The chip select ($\overline{CS}$), the strobe ($\overline{STROBE}$) and R/$\overline{W}$ controls should all be low.

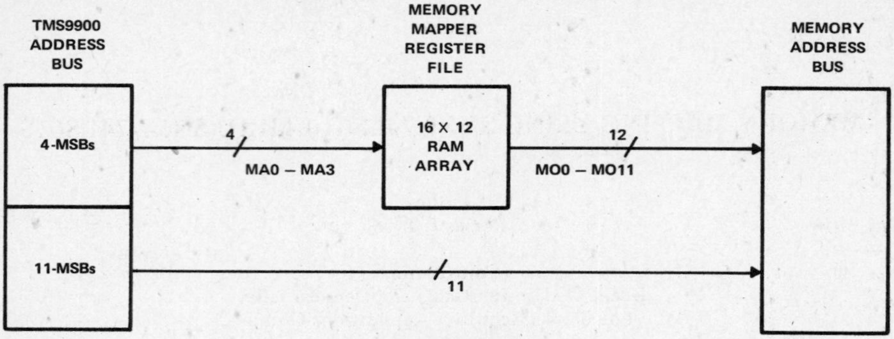
TMS9900
ADDRESS
BUS
4-MSBs
11-MSBs
4
MA0 – MA3
MEMORY
MAPPER
REGISTER
FILE
16 X 12
RAM
ARRAY
12
MO0 – MO11
11
MEMORY
ADDRESS
BUS

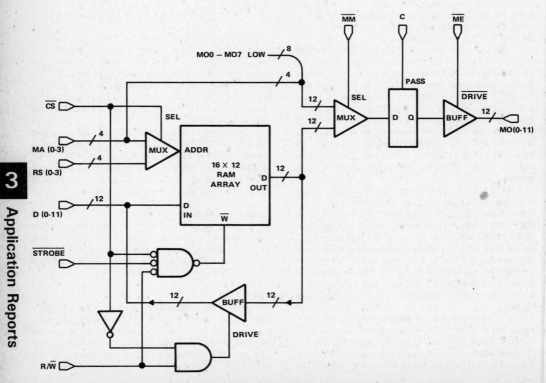

Figure 1. Mapping Operation

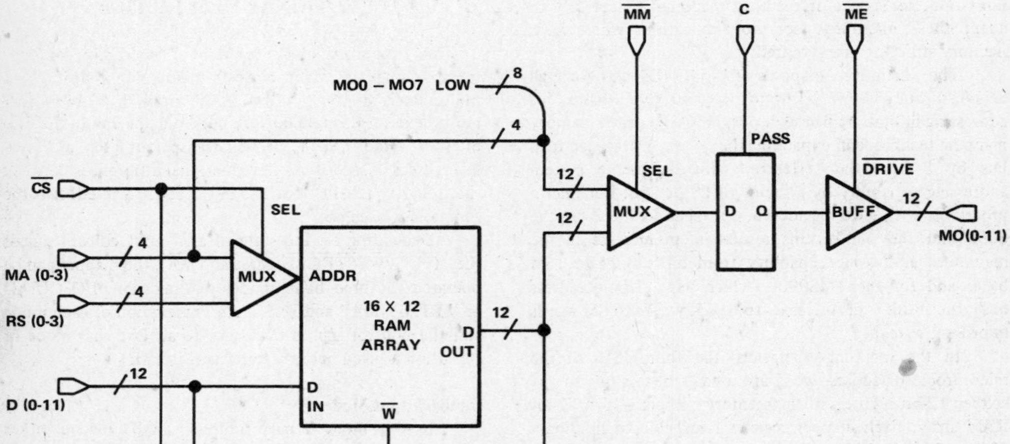
MM
C
ME
MO0 – MO7 LOW
8
4
PASS
SEL
DRIVE
CS
SEL
12
MUX
D Q
BUFF
12
MO(0-11)
4
MA (0-3)
MUX
ADDR
4
RS (0-3)
16 X 12
RAM
ARRAY
12
D
OUT
12
D (0-11)
D
IN
W
STROBE
12
12
BUFF
DRIVE
R/W

Figure 2. Logic Diagram of the Memory Mapper 'LS610

Table I. Device Comparison

Device	Map Outputs Latched	Map Output Type
SN54/74LS610	Yes	3-State
SN54/74LS611	Yes	Open-collector
SN54/74LS612	No	3-State
SN54/74LS613	No	Open-collector

READ Mode

The contents of one of the sixteen 12-bit registers is read from the mapper via the D0-D11 I/O ports. As in the WRITE mode, the mapper register is selected by the address on the RS0-RS3 inputs. Again chip select ($\overline{CS}$) should be low, while the R/$\overline{W}$ should be kept high.

MAP Mode

The contents of one of the sixteen 12-bit memory mapper registers is outputted to the system address bus via the MO0-MO11 outputs. The address on MA0-MA3 selects the mapper register and is usually the four MSBs of the microprocessor address word. The chip select ($\overline{CS}$) must be inactive (high), the map mode ($\overline{MM}$) control and the map enable ($\overline{ME}$) must both be active (low). The n–4 LSBs, where n equals the microprocessor address bit length, of the microprocessor address bus will be transferred directly to memory from the microprocessor, while the remaining 12 MSBs of the system address bus will be driven onto the bus by the memory mapper.

Table II. Pin Functions

Pin	Pin Name	Functional Description
7-12 29-34	D0 thru D11	I/O connections to data and control bus used for reading from and writing to the map register selected by RS0-RS3 when $\overline{CS}$ is low. Mode controlled by R/$\overline{W}$. (D0 corresponds to MO0 and is the most significant bit.)
36, 38, 1, 3	RS0 thru RS3	Register select inputs for I/O operations. (RS3 is the least significant bit.)
6	R/$\overline{W}$	Read or write control used in I/O operations to select the condition of the data bus. When high, the data bus outputs are active for reading the map register. When low, the data bus is used to write into the register.
5	$\overline{STROBE}$	Strobe input used to enter data into the selected map register during I/O operations.
4	$\overline{CS}$	Chip select input. A low input level selects the memory mapper (assuming more than one used) for an I/O operation.
35, 37, 39, 2	MA0 thru MA3	Map address inputs to select one of 16 map registers when in map mode ($\overline{MM}$ low and $\overline{CS}$ high). (MA3 is the least significant bit.)
14-19 22-27	MO0 thru MO11	Map outputs. Present the map register contents to the system memory address bus in the map mode. In the pass mode, these outputs provide the map address data on MO8-MO11 and low levels on MO0-MO7. (MO11 is the least significant bit.)
13	$\overline{MM}$	Map mode input. When low, 12 bits of data are transferred from the selected map register to the map outputs. When high (pass mode), the four bits present on the map address inputs are passed to the map outputs.
21	$\overline{ME}$	Map enable for the map outputs. A low level allows the outputs to be active while a high input level puts the outputs at high impedance.
28	C	Latch enable input for the 'LS610 and 'LS611 (no internal connection for 'LS612 and 'LS613). A high level will transparently pass data to the map outputs. A low level will latch the outputs.
40, 20	V_{CC}, GND	Power supply (5 V) and network ground (substrate) pins.

Table III. Modes of Operation

MAPPER INPUTS	I/O		MAP	PASS
	WRITE (LOAD)	READ (VERIFY)		
$\overline{CS}$	Active (Low)	Active (Low)	Inactive (High)	Inactive (High)
$\overline{STROBE}$	Active (Low)	Don't Care	Don't Care	Don't Care
R/$\overline{W}$	Low	High	Don't Care	Don't Care
$\overline{MM}$	Don't Care	Don't Care	Active (Low)	Inactive (High)
$\overline{ME}$	Inactive (High)	Inactive (High)	Active	Active
RS0-RS3	Address of Selected Register	Address of Selected Register	Don't Care	Don't Care
MA0-MA3	Don't Care	Don't Care	Address of Selected Register	Address of Selected Register
MO0-MO11	High Impedance	High Impedance	Valid Address	Valid Address
D0-D11	Register contents to be loaded (input)	Register contents to be read (output)	Input Mode	Input Mode

PASS Mode

The four LSBs (MO8-MO11) of the memory mapper address bus (MO0-MO11) will be the same as the address on the MA0-MA3 input bus, while the remaining eight MSBs of the memory mapper address bus will all be low. The chip select ($\overline{CS}$) and the map mode ($\overline{MM}$) should both the inactive (high); map enable ($\overline{ME}$) should be active. In other words, the address on the system address bus will be the same as the address outputted by the microprocessor, and the memory mapper becomes transparent to the system.

SYSTEMS INTEGRATION

The flexibility of the memory mapper is such that it can be used with microprocessors that have either an 8-bit or a 16-bit data bus. In order to use the memory mapper to its fullest potential (i.e., expand the address bus by eight bits) with an 8-bit microprocessor, the 12-bit page address must be multiplexed into the mapper via the 8-bit data bus. This means that the time it normally takes to load or read the memory mapper will be at least doubled and extra external circuitry will be necessary. If the requirement of the system is such that the address bus needs to be increased by only four bits, then there is no need for multiplexing in the page address. Of course this means that the address bus is expanded to only 20 bits resulting in a 1-megabyte addressing capability. Next in this report, we will look at two 8-bit systems utilizing the 'LS612 memory mapper.

TMS9995-Based System

Figure 3 shows a TMS9995-based system using the 'LS612 to expand the address bus by four bits. The TMS9995 is an 8-bit microprocessor with a 16-bit address bus. This system employs the Programmable System Interface (TMS9901) to control the operation of the mapper. The control of the mapper is software programmable via the I/O ports of the TMS9901. Since the mapper registers are viewed as part of the logical memory space, an address decode (AD0) of the 12 MSBs is gated with a CRU bit to select the mapper for a READ or WRITE operation. The specific mapper register is then selected by the four LSBs of the microprocessor address bus (A15-A12) via the RS0-RS3 inputs of the mapper. Table IV shows the state of the three control signals P0, P1 and AD0 and the corresponding mode of operation of the mapper. When placed in the I/O mode, the READ or WRITE operation is then controlled by memory signals from the microprocessor (i.e., $\overline{WE}$/$\overline{CRUCLK}$, $\overline{MEMEN}$, and $\overline{DB\ IN}$). On POWER-UP and RESET, the I/O ports of the '9901 are put into the input mode. The pull-up resistors R1 and R2 will ensure the mapper is placed in the pass mode during POWER-UP and RESET. The resultant address bus is 20 bits wide, and SA19 is the LSB.

Z-80-Based System

Figure 4 shows another 8-bit (Z-80-based) system using the TI memory mapper. In this case, the control of the mapper is implemented by two flip-flops feeding $\overline{MM}$ and $\overline{CS}$. These flip-flops are programmed by the Z-80 and are addressed by the data bus, D0-D1. Table V shows the necessary states of D0 and D1 to set the mapper in its proper mode of operation. Again during POWER-UP or RESET, the flip-flops are both cleared by $\overline{RST}$, which is supplied by the system and which puts the mapper in the pass mode.

Table IV. TMS9900/'LS610 Control Signals

MEMORY MAPPER MODE OF OPERATION	CONTROL SIGNALS		
	P1	P0	AD0
MAP	L	H	L
PASS	H	H	L
I/O	H	L	L

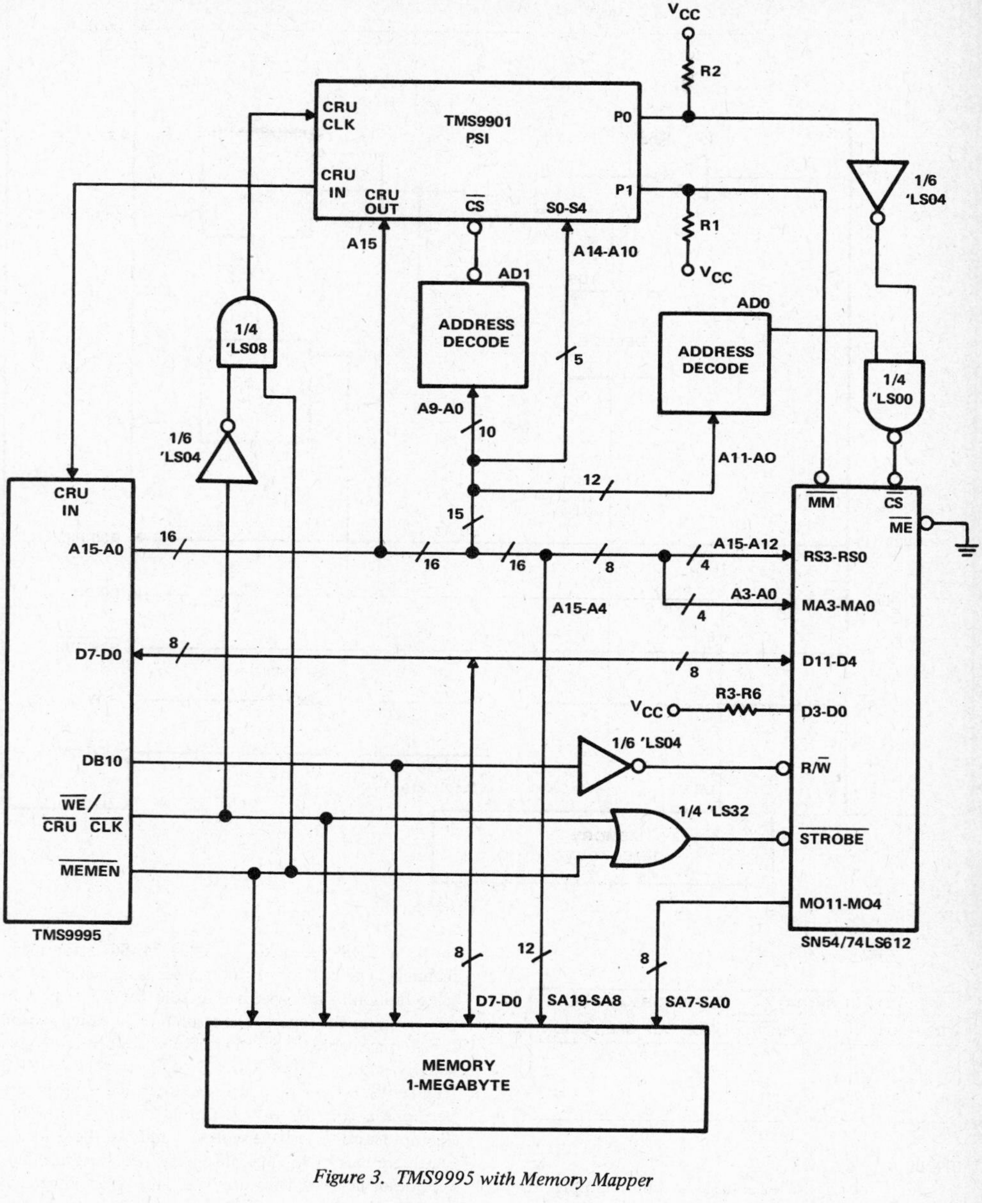

VCC
R2
CRU CLK
TMS9901 PSI
P0
CRU IN
CRU OUT
CS
S0-S4
P1
1/6 'LS04
A15
A14-A10
R1
VCC
AD1
ADDRESS DECODE
AD0
ADDRESS DECODE
1/4 'LS08
5
1/4 'LS00
A9-A0
10
1/6 'LS04
A11-AO
CRU IN
12
MM
CS
15
ME
A15-A0
16
16
16
8
A15-A12
4
RS3-RS0
A3-A0
MA3-MA0
A15-A4
4
D7-D0
8
8
D11-D4
R3-R6
VCC
D3-D0
1/6 'LS04
DB10
R/W
WE/
CRU CLK
1/4 'LS32
STROBE
MEMEN
MO11-MO4
TMS9995
SN54/74LS612
8
12
8
D7-D0
SA19-SA8
SA7-SA0
MEMORY
1-MEGABYTE

Figure 3. TMS9995 with Memory Mapper

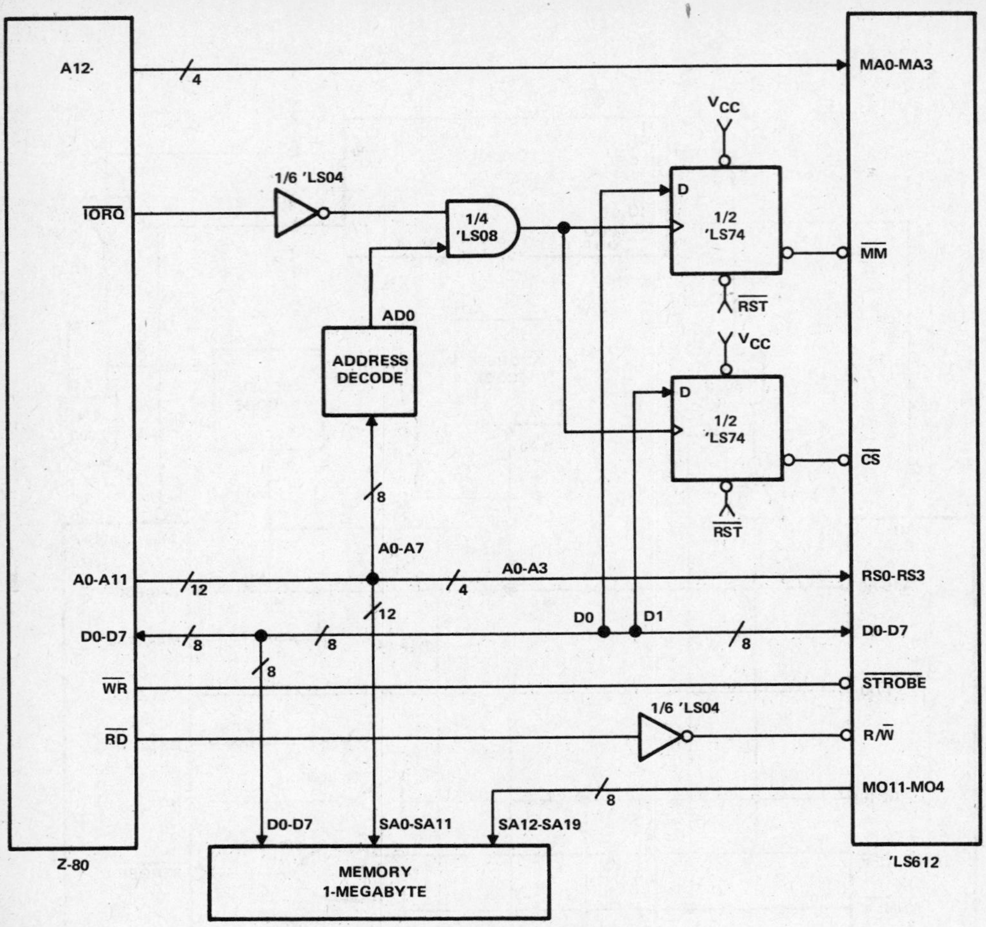

A12-
4
MA0-MA3
VCC
1/6 'LS04
IORQ
1/4
'LS08
D
1/2
'LS74
MM
RST
AD0
ADDRESS
DECODE
VCC
D
1/2
'LS74
CS
RST
8
A0-A7
A0-A3
A0-A11
12
4
RS0-RS3
12
D0
D1
D0-D7
8
8
8
D0-D7
8
WR
STROBE
1/6 'LS04
RD
R/W
MO11-MO4
8
D0-D7
SA0-SA11
SA12-SA19
Z-80
MEMORY
1-MEGABYTE
'LS612

Figure 4. Z-80 with Memory Mapper

Table V. Z-80/LS'610 Control Signals

CONTROL SIGNALS			MEMORY MAPPER
D0	D1	(AD0) $\overline{\text{IORQ}}$	MODE OF OPERATION
L	L	↑	PASS
H	L	↑	MAP
L	H	↑	I/O

TMS9900-Based System

One of the limitations of using an 8-bit microprocessor with the memory mapper, without multiplexing the page address, is that the address bus can only be expanded four bits. In a 16-bit system, one based on a 16-bit microprocessor like the TMS9900, no extra circuitry is necessary to load the mapper with the full 12-bit address. Figure 5 shows a TMS9900 with an SN54/74LS612 for memory mapping. The control of the mapper is implemented in the same fashion as the system using the TMS9995 mentioned previously in the report. The resultant addressing capability is eight megawords. These TI microprocessors have set aside address space for RESET, XOP and INTERRUPT VECTORS, which are addressed when the microprocessor performs a context switch. During a context switch, the microprocessor must be able to address these locations which are part of the logical address (i.e., locations that are capable of being addressed by the microprocessor independently). One method, besides placing the mapper into the pass mode, is to load the memory mapper register whose 4-bit address is 0_H with the address of the first page of physical memory. This, like the pass mode, will effectively make the memory mapper appear to be transparent.

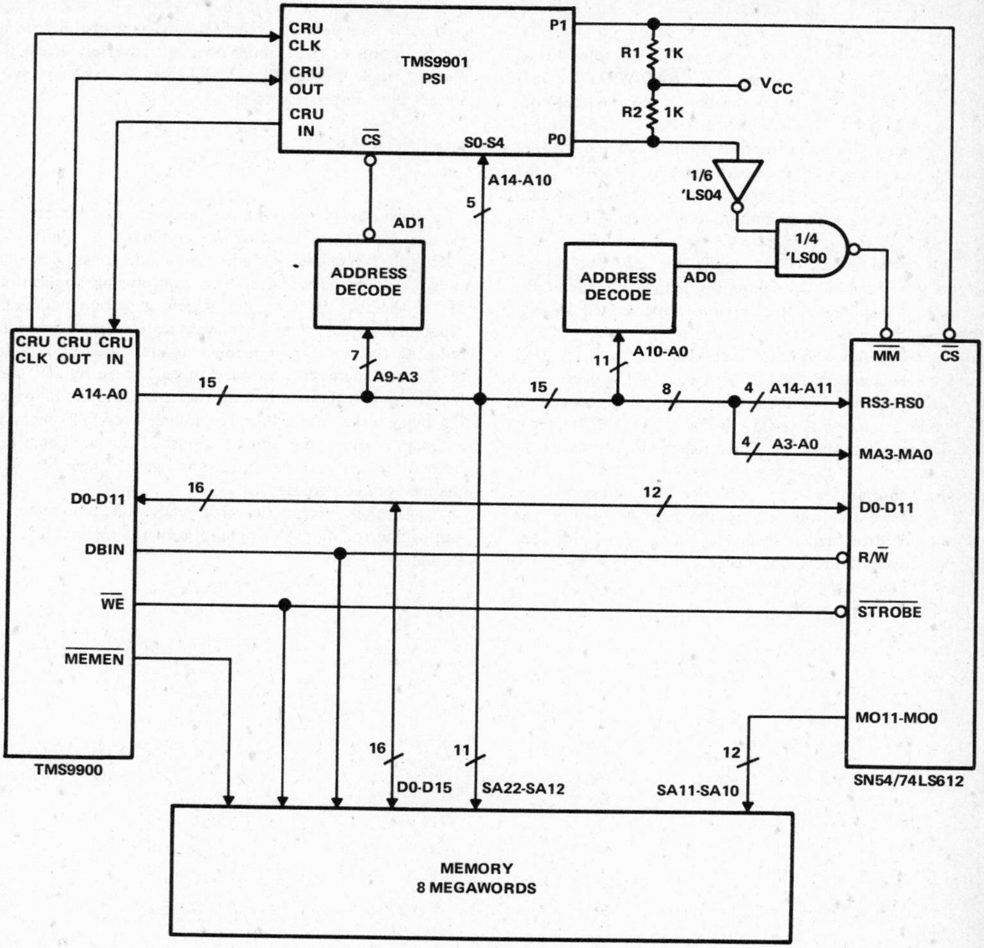
CRU
CLK
CRU
OUT
CRU
IN
TMS9901
PSI
P1
CS
S0-S4
P0
R1
1K
R2
1K
V_{CC}
1/6
'LS04
1/4
'LS00
A14-A10
5
AD1
ADDRESS
DECODE
ADDRESS
DECODE
AD0
7
A9-A3
11
A10-A0
CRU CRU CRU
CLK OUT IN
A14-A0
15
15
8
4
A14-A11
4
A3-A0
MM
CS
RS3-RS0
MA3-MA0
D0-D11
16
12
D0-D11
DBIN
R/W
WE
STROBE
MEMEN
MO11-MO0
16
11
12
TMS9900
D0-D15
SA22-SA12
SA11-SA10
SN54/74LS612
MEMORY
8 MEGAWORDS

Figure 5. TMS9900 with Memory Mapper

Another point worth noting is that in all three of the previously mentioned systems, the $\overline{ME}$ input was always connected to ground. This caused the mapper address buffers to be enabled during all modes of operation of the mapper. This is only a problem during the I/O mode where, when loading the mapper register, other memory locations are also being written into. The method used to avoid destroying data already in memory was to put the mapper into the pass mode during the I/O operation. This was accomplished simply by pulling $\overline{MM}$ input high, thus making the system address equal to the microprocessor address.

Multimapper Systems

In a system employing a single memory mapper, the maximum active addressing capability is only 16 pages, if increased addressing capabilities are needed, the mapper must be reloaded. To avoid this procedure, another mapper may be added to the system. This will not increase the overall addressing capability of the system, but it will double the amount of active pages and will also afford twice the active addressing capability. Even though the control of two mappers is a little more detailed than the control of one, the same basic methods employed in the systems with one mapper can be used here.

TIMING

The subject of how the mapper affects the critical timing parameters of the memory READ/WRITE cycles and what changes, if any, are needed to accommodate the mapper, have not been discussed in this report. First, looking at the I/O mode of operation where the mapper registers are either loaded or read from, it is seen that the mapper registers can be regarded as standard common I/O, static RAMs, with maximum access times (RS to valid MO, $T_A = 25°C$, $C_L = 50$ pF, $V_{CC} = 5$ V) of 75 ns. Once the I/O mode is set ($\overline{CS}$ = low), the only two signals necessary to read or write into the mapper are $\overline{STROBE}$ and R/$\overline{W}$. As shown in the previously mentioned system, these signals were supplied directly from the microprocessor with no wait states necessary to perform either function. This will be the case with most microprocessors.

In the MAP and PASS mode, the main concern is the maximum access time (MA to MO). This access time is specified at a maximum of 70 ns, which, depending on the timing of the microprocessor and the memory used, may or may not cause any problems. In the Z-80-based system, no wait states were introduced by the mapper because the memory control signals become active 95 ns after the microprocessor address bus became valid. This gives the address bus sufficient time to settle down.

In conclusion, it can be said that for most microprocessors and memory available at the time of this writing, the operation of the mapper does not adversely affect the memory cycle timing and is flexible enough to be used with almost all microprocessors.

SUMMARY

The possible uses of the memory mapper and the various techniques that can be employed to control its operation are numerous and only some examples were shown in this report. Some of the other possible applications of the mapper include: (1) achieving system addressing capability greater than 16 megabytes is accomplished by reducing the number of mapper registers used by a factor of 2, thus increasing the size of each page by the same factor of 2 without affecting the total amount of pages; (2) being used in systems employing DMA; (3) memory protection which can be accomplished by sacrificing one or two bits of the page address, and gating these bits with the memory control signals.

Another technique that may be employed in controlling the modes of operation of the mapper is to use PROMs.

Bit-Slice Processor Applications
8-Bit Family

Frank Laczko, Bob Myers, Richard Nawrocki,
Rick Noblitt, and Sally Towlen

VLSI Systems Engineering
214/995-4720

TEXAS
INSTRUMENTS

Contents

Title *Page*

Section 1
Introduction

Section 2
2910 Microprogram Controller Emulation Using the 'AS890 Microsequencer

Section 3
Minimum Cycle Time Delay Calculations for a 16-Bit System

Section 4
32-Bit CPU Design with the 'AS888/'AS890

Section 5
An Adaptive Clock Generator to Increase 'AS888 System Speed

Section 6
Floating-Point System Design Using the 'AS888/'AS890

List of Illustrations

List of Programs

List of Tables

Section 1

Introduction

Bit-slice technology has gained widespread acceptance among CPU designers over the past several years as a means of increasing system speed and reducing the discrete logic needed for CPU construction. TI's recent entries on the market, the SN74AS888 8-bit processor slice and its companion microsequencer, the SN74AS890, increase processing throughput per unit area to an extent never before realized in bit-slice systems, making them well suited to the construction of high-speed systems with flexible instruction sets.

This is the first in a series of application books addressed to users of TI's bit-slice products. It discusses ways to take advantage of the 'AS888/'AS890's increased speed in the areas of CPU design and floating point processing, compares their performance with similar products, and presents a means of achieving optimum speed by adding an adaptive clock circuit to an 'AS888/'AS890 system. Also included is a 2910 emulator, which allows users to take advantage of the 'AS890's increased speed and greatly expanded addressing range, while still retaining existing 2910 software. Brief abstracts of the papers in this volume are given below.

Section 2, "2910 Microprogram Controller Emulation using the 'AS890 Microsequencer," converts the 16 instructions of the 2910 into 'AS890 commands, using programmable array logic (PALs) for fast emulation. By using the emulator, accessible microcode store can be quadrupled from 4,096 to 16,384 memory locations, and advantage can be taken of the 'AS890's deeper stack.

Section 3, "Minimum Cycle Time Delay Calculations for a 16-Bit System," examines some timings for systems using TI's 'AS888-1/'AS890-1, AMD's Am2901C/2910A, and AMD's Am2903A/2910A. Four cases are considered: addition, addition followed by a shift of the result, unsigned integer multiplication and unsigned integer division.

Section 4, "32-Bit CPU Design with the 'AS888/'AS890," takes a look at constructing a central processing unit by cascading four 'AS888s to form a 32-bit ALU and the 'AS890 sequencer to address a control store containing the system microcode. Microcode and assembly code are given for an instruction fetch routine and for unsigned multiplications.

Section 5, "An Adaptive Clock Generator to Increase 'AS888 System Speed," uses an adaptive circuit to generate clock pulses for an 'AS888-based system. The clock cycle length is optimally matched to the propagation delay of the 'AS888 for each individual instruction, further increasing the speed of the system. The circuit is linked to the 'AS888 with a PROM that decodes 888 instructions into cycle lengths. A BASIC program calculates instruction lengths and generates a file that can be transmitted to a Data I/O PROM programmer.

Section 6, "Floating Point Design using the 'AS888/'AS890," provides a model for floating point system design, illustrating the step by step development of a utility to compute sin(x). By developing a sin(x) algorithm, a microprogram is generated and hardware requirements are identified in an interactive manner.

The application notes in this volume were prepared by the following members of VLSI Systems Engineering:

Bob Myers (Sections 3 and 4)
Richard Nawrocki (Section 2)
Rick Noblitt (Sections 5 and 6)

Please contact the authors at 214/995-4720 if you need additional information.

Section 2

2910 Microprogram Controller Emulation using the 'AS890 Microsequencer

The 'AS890 microsequencer, with its powerful instruction set, can be microprogrammed to emulate the popular 2910 microprogram controller. By converting the 16 instructions of the 2910 into the appropriate 'AS890 commands, 2910 users can both quadruple accessible microcode store from 4,096 to 16,384 memory locations and take advantage of the 'AS890's deeper stack, while retaining existing microprograms and preserving prior investments in software without loss of system performance. Programmable Read Only Memory (PROM) can be used to implement the system, or TI's Programmable Array Logic PAL® can be selected for faster emulation.

EMULATOR CONFIGURATION

The DRB inputs of the 'AS890 are used as the 2910 emulator's D (direct data) inputs. JSRP and JRP (2910 instructions 5 and 7) conditionally select the counter/register, requiring the counter/register contents to be available through the Y-output multiplexer. The 'AS890 does not directly support this function, but it can be accomplished by enabling either the DRA or DRB ports as an output and selecting the appropriate path through the Y-multiplexer.

JSRP and JRP also require that direct data input and existing register/counter contents be available at the Y-multiplexer concurrently. The emulator uses direct data port DRA and register/counter A for this purpose. Two '74AS244 buffers are used to isolate DRA from DRB so that register/counter A can be loaded from the Direct Data input and DRA can be used to send the register/counter's contents to the Y-multiplexer.

Figure 2-1 shows the configuration of the 2910 emulator. To provide fast propagation delays, two TIBPAL16L8-15s, with a maximum propagation delay of 15 ns, are used for the control PALs. Because the TIBPAL16L8-15 will only accommodate seven product terms and eight were required for the condition code input to the 'AS890, it is driven by two outputs of the control PAL. These outputs are selectively enabled using the $\overline{\text{CCEN}}$ input (see Programs 2-1 and 2-5 for detailed PAL equations).

Typical switching delays for the 2910 emulator are summarized in Table 2-1.

MICROINSTRUCTION CONVERSION

Table 2-2 lists Y-multiplexer, stack and register control encodings that can be used to convert the 2910 instruction set into 'AS890 microinstructions. The effect of these encodings on the Y-multiplexer, stack and register controls is shown in Table 2-3. Data from Table 2-2 was used as input to a universal program logic compiler to produce the emulator's two control PALs. Files generated for each PAL by the compiler include:

1. a logic description file
2. a listing of expanded product terms and fuse map
3. simulation results
4. a JEDEC file.

These are reproduced at the end of this application note. The CUPL™ software used to develop the PALs is available from Texas Instruments or from Assisted Technology, Inc., San Jose, CA.

2910 EMULATION DIFFERENCES

The architecture of the 'AS890 does not lend itself to a complete emulation of the 2910 controller. Differences are noted below.

Loop Counts

The 2910 register/counter is tested for a zero value prior to decrementing and branching on conditional loops. The counter is usually loaded with a value that is one less

Table 2-1. Typical Switching Characteristics

SET-UP AND HOLD TIMES			COMBINATIONAL DELAYS			
			FROM	TO		
INPUT	Ts	Th		Y	PL,MAP VECT	FULL
D → R (Inst. = 5,7)	15	0	D0-D13 (Inst. = 5,7)	15		
D → R (Inst. ≠ 5,7)	8	0	D0-D13 (Inst. ≠ 5,7)	8		
D → Pc (Inst. = 5,7)	28	0	I0-I3 (Inst. = 5,7,9)	27	10	
D → Pc (Inst. ≠ 5,7)	20	0	I0-I3 (Inst. ≠ 5,7,9)	22	10	
I3-I0	36	0	$\overline{\text{CC}}$	22		
$\overline{\text{CC}}$	36	0	$\overline{\text{CCEN}}$	22		
$\overline{\text{CCEN}}$	36	0	CP	18		25
CI	12	0	CP (I = 8,9,F & CNTR = 2)	24		25
RLD	36	0	OE	8		

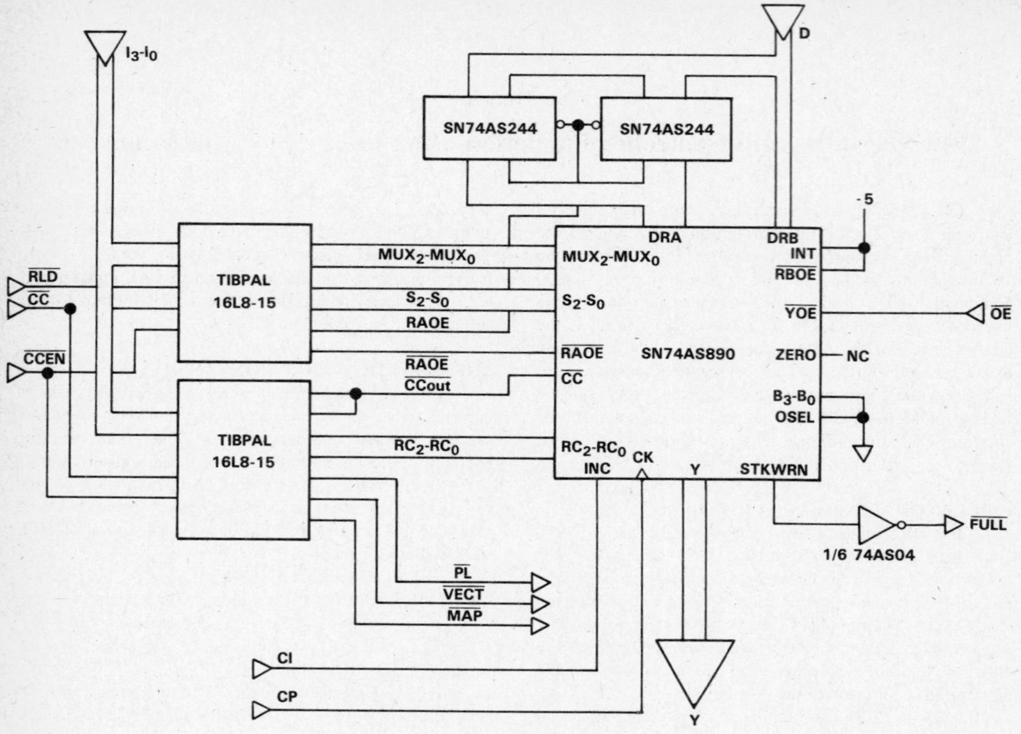

I_3-I_0
D
SN74AS244
SN74AS244
-5
TIBPAL
16L8-15
MUX$_2$-MUX$_0$
$\overline{RLD}$
$\overline{CC}$
S$_2$-S$_0$
RAOE
$\overline{CCEN}$
$\overline{RAOE}$
CCout
TIBPAL
16L8-15
RC$_2$-RC$_0$
DRA
DRB
MUX$_2$-MUX$_0$
INT
$\overline{RBOE}$
S$_2$-S$_0$
$\overline{YOE}$
$\overline{OE}$
$\overline{RAOE}$
SN74AS890
ZERO
NC
$\overline{CC}$
B$_3$-B$_0$
OSEL
RC$_2$-RC$_0$
CK
INC
Y
STKWRN
$\overline{FULL}$
1/6 74AS04
$\overline{PL}$
$\overline{VECT}$
$\overline{MAP}$
CI
CP
Y

Figure 2-1. 2910 Emulator Block Diagram

than the desired loop count. The 'AS890 tests for a one prior to decrementing. Therefore, the 2910 emulator requires that the actual loop count, rather than loop count minus one, be loaded into the register/counter.

Three of the 2910 instructions (RFCT, RPCT, and TWB) execute once and terminate the counter decrement when a zero is found in the register/counter. The emulator requires a one in the register/counter to execute these instructions and terminate the counter decrement. Loading a zero into the register/counter before decrementing will cause the emulator to loop 16,384 times.

Register Loading

Using the 2910's register load (RLD) input during a JSRP or JRP instruction allows external data to be input to the register/counter while the current value in the register/counter is output on the Y-bus. This is not the case with the 'AS890, where an external value placed on DRA for input to the register/counter will also be sent to the Y-multiplexer outputs. A register load using the emulator must therefore be implemented independently of the JSRP or JRP instructions.

Stack Full Indication

The 'AS890 stack is nine levels deep, compared to the 2910's five-level stack. The 2910 signals that all five levels of the stack are used by setting FULL low. The emulator's FULL signal is set to zero when its eighth stack location is used, indicating that only one location remains available. A low value will also appear at the FULL output when a stack POP is to be executed and the stack is empty.

Data Path Widths

Because the 'AS890 supports 14-bit data paths instead of the 2910's 12-bit paths, the number of address locations that can be accessed by the emulator can be expanded from 4,096 to 16,634 locations.

Table 2-2. 'AS890 Encodings for Am2910 Instructions

I3-I0	MNEMONIC	NAME	$\overline{\text{CCEN}}$ = LOW and $\overline{\text{CC}}$ = HIGH				$\overline{\text{CCEN}}$ = HIGH or $\overline{\text{CC}}$ = LOW				ENABLE
			$\overline{\text{CCOUT}}$	RC	S	MUX	CCOUT	RC	S	MUX	
0	JZ	JUMP ZERO	H	LLL	LLL	HHH	H	LLL	LLL	HHH	PL
1	CJS	COND JSB PL	H	LLL	HLH	HHH	L	LLL	HLH	HHH	PL
2	JMAP	JUMP MAP	H	LLL	HHH	HLL	H	LLL	HHH	HLL	MAP
3	CJP	COND JUMP PL	H	LLL	HHH	HHH	L	LLL	HHH	HHH	PL
4	PUSH	PUSH/COND LD CNTR	H	LLL	HHL	HHH	H	LHL	HHL	HHH	PL
5	JSRP	COND JSB R/PL	L	LLL	HHL	HLL	H	LLL	HHL	HLL	PL
6	CJV	COND JUMP VECTOR	H	LLL	HHH	HHH	L	LLL	HHH	HHH	VECT
7	JRP	COND JUMP R/PL	L	LLL	HHH	HLL	H	LLL	HHH	HLL	PL
8	RFCT	RPT LOOP, CNTR ≠ 0	L	LLH	LHL	LLH	L	LLH	LHL	LLH	PL
9	RPCT	RPT LOOP, CNTR ≠ 0	L	LLH	HHH	HLL	L	LLH	HHH	HLL	PL
A	CRTN	COND RTN	H	LLL	LHH	LHH	L	LLL	LHH	LHH	PL
B	CJPP	COND JUMP PL & POP	H	LLL	LHH	HHH	L	LLL	LHH	HHH	PL
C	LDCT	LD CNTR 7 CONTINUE	H	LHL	HHH	HHH	H	LHL	HHH	HHH	PL
D	LOOP	TEST END LOOP	L	LLL	LHL	LHH	H	LLL	LHL	LHH	PL
E	CONT	CONTINUE	H	LLL	HHH	HHH	H	LLL	HHH	HHH	PL
F	TWB	THREE-WAY BRANCH	L	LLH	LHL	LHH	H	LLH	LHL	LHH	PL

Table 2-3. Effect of Table 2-2 Encodings on 'AS890 Control Signals

I3-I0	MNEMONIC	NAME	ZERO	$\overline{\text{CCEN}}$ = LOW and $\overline{\text{CC}}$ = HIGH				$\overline{\text{CCEN}}$ = HIGH or $\overline{\text{CC}}$ = LOW				ENABLE
				$\overline{\text{CCOUT}}$	RC	S	MUX	CCOUT	RC	S	MUX	
0	JZ	JUMP ZERO		H	Hold	Reset	0	H	Hold	Reset	0	PL
1	CJS	COND JSB PL		H	Hold	Hold	MPC	L	Hold	Push	DRB	PL
2	JMAP	JUMP MAP		H	Hold	Hold	DRB	H	Hold	Hold	DRB	MAP
3	CJP	COND JUMP PL		H	Hold	Hold	MPC	L	Hold	Hold	DRB	PL
4	PUSH	PUSH/COND LD CNTR		H	Hold	Push	MPC	H	LoadA	Push	MPC	PL
5	JSRP	COND JSB R/PL		L	Hold	Push	DRA	H	Hold	Push	DRB	PL
6	CJV	COND JUMP VECTOR		H	Hold	Hold	MPC	L	Hold	Hold	DRB	VECT
7	JRP	COND JUMP R/PL		L	Hold	Hold	DRA	H	Hold	Hold	DRB	PL
8	RFCT	RPT LOOP, CNTR ≠ 0	L	L	DecA	Hold	STK	L	DecA	Hold	STK	PL
			H	L	DecA	Pop	MPC	L	DecA	Pop	MPC	PL
9	RPCT	RPT LOOP, CNTR ≠ 0	L	L	DecA	Hold	DRA	L	DecA	Hold	DRA	PL
			H	L	DecA	Hold	MPC	L	DecA	Hold	MPC	PL
A	CRTN	COND RTN		H	Hold	Hold	MPC	L	Hold	Pop	STK	PL
B	CJPP	COND JUMP PL & POP		H	Hold	Hold	MPC	L	Hold	Pop	DRB	PL
C	LDCT	LD CNTR 7 CONTINUE		H	LoadA	Hold	MPC	H	LoadA	Hold	MPC	PL
D	LOOP	TEST END LOOP		L	Hold	Hold	STK	H	Hold	Pop	MPC	PL
E	CONT	CONTINUE		H	Hold	Hold	MPC	H	Hold	Hold	MPC	PL
F	TWB	THREE-WAY BRANCH	L	L	DecA	Hold	STK	H	DecA	Pop	MPC	PL
			H	L	DecA	Pop	DRB	H	Hold	Pop	MPC	PL

Program 2-1. Logic Equations Used to Generate Emulator PAL 1

```
CUPL VERSION 2.02A COPYRIGHT (c) 1983,84,85 ASSISTED TECHNOLOGY, INC. -- LISTING

SOURCE FILE: B:2910EM          DEVICE: p16L8


                PARTNO    2910EM ;
                NAME      '74AS890/2910 EMULATOR PAL 1 ;
                DATE      04/04/85 ;
                REV       01 ;
                DESIGNER  RICHARD D. NAWROCKI ;
                COMPANY   TEXAS INSTRUMENTS ;
                ASSEMBLY  00001 ;
                LOCATION  U100 ;

/*******************************************************************/
/*                                                                 */
/*   THIS DEVICE GENERATES CONTROL SIGNALS FOR THE '74AS890        */
/*   EMULATION OF THE 2910 MICROPROGRAM CONTROLLER.                */
/*                                                                 */
/*   ALLOWABLE TARGET DEVICE TYPES: PAL16L8A                       */
/*******************************************************************/

/**  INPUTS  **/

PIN  [1..4] = [I0..3]   ;      /* 2910 INSTRUCTION CODE           */
PIN   5     =  RLD      ;      /* 2910 REGISTER LOAD              */

/**  OUTPUTS  **/

PIN  19       =  RAOE    ;     /*  74AS890 DRA OUTPUT ENABLE      */
PIN  [18..16] = [MUX0..2];     /*  74AS890 MUX_Y CONTROL          */
PIN  [15..13] = [S0..2]  ;     /*  74AS890 STACK CONTROL          */
PIN  12       = EN_244   ;     /*  74AS244 OUTPUT ENABLES         */

/** DECLARATIONS AND INTERMEDIATE VARIABLE DEFINITIONS **/

 FIELD INSTRUCTION = [I3..0]   ;
 FIELD STACK       = [S2..0]   ;
 FIELD Y_MUX       = [MUX2..0] ;


/**  LOGIC EQUATIONS  **/

 !RAOE   = INSTRUCTION:[5,7] & RLD ;

 !EN_244 = INSTRUCTION:[0..4,6,8..F] # (INSTRUCTION:[5,7] & !RLD) ;

 STACK   = INSTRUCTION:1 & 'H'5
         # INSTRUCTION:[2,3,6,7,9,C,E] & 'H'7
         # INSTRUCTION:[4,5] & 'H'6
         # INSTRUCTION:[8,D,F] & 'H'2
         # INSTRUCTION:[A,B] & 'H'3 ;

  Y_MUX  = INSTRUCTION:[0,1,3,4,6,B,C,E] & 'H'7
         # INSTRUCTION:[2,5,7,9] & 'H'4
         # INSTRUCTION:8 & 'H'1
         # INSTRUCTION:[A,D,F] & 'H'3 ;




JEDEC FUSE CHECKSUM        (7103)
JEDEC TRANSMIT CHECKSUM          (259E)
```

Program 2-2. Expanded Product Terms, Symbol Table and Fuse Plot for Emulator PAL 1

```
CUPL            2.02A
DEVICE          P16L8  DLIB-C-18-5
PARTNO          2910EM
NAME            '74AS890/2910 EMULATOR PAL 1
REVISION        01
DATE            04/04/85
DESIGNER        RICHARD D. NAWROCKI
COMPANY         TEXAS INSTRUMENTS
ASSEMBLY        00001
LOCATION        U100

===============================================================================
                            EXPANDED PRODUCT TERMS
===============================================================================

EN_244  ->
     I3
   # !I2  & !I3
   # !I0  & I2  & !I3
   # I0  & I2  & !I3  & !RLD

INSTRUCTION  ->
     I3  , I2  , I1  , I0

MUX0  ->
     I0  & I2  & !I3
   # !I0  & I1  & !I2  & !I3
   # I0  & !I1  & !I2  & I3

MUX1  ->
     I0  & I2  & !I3
   # !I1  & !I2  & I3
   # !I0  & I1  & !I2  & !I3

MUX2  ->
     !I0  & !I2  & I3
   # I0  & I2  & I3

RAOE  ->
     I0  & I2  & !I3  & RLD

S0  ->
     I0  & !I1  & I2
   # !I0  & !I1  & !I3
   # I0  & I2  & I3
   # !I0  & !I1  & !I2

S1  ->
     !I1  & !I2  & !I3

S2  ->
     I1  & !I2  & I3
   # !I0  & !I1  & !I2
   # I0  & I2  & I3

STACK  ->
     S2  , S1  , S0

Y_MUX  ->
     MUX2  , MUX1  , MUX0

EN_244.OE  ->
     1

MUX0.OE  ->
     1

MUX1.OE  ->
     1

MUX2.OE  ->
     1

RAOE.OE  ->
     1

S0.OE  ->
     1

S1.OE  ->
     1

S2.OE  ->
     1
```

3 Application Reports

Program 2-2. Expanded Product Terms, Symbol Table and Fuse Plot for Emulator PAL 1 (Continued)

```
================================================================================
                                  SYMBOL TABLE
================================================================================

POL    NAME            EXT    PIN    TYPE    USED    MAX
---    ----            ---    ---    ----    ----    ---

       EN_244                 12     V       4       7
       I0                     1      V       -       -
       I1                     2      V       -       -
       I2                     3      V       -       -
       I3                     4      V       -       -
       INSTRUCTION            0      F       -       -
       MUX0                   18     V       3       7
       MUX1                   17     V       3       7
       MUX2                   16     V       2       7
       RAOE                   19     V       1       7
       RLD                    5      V       -       -
       S0                     15     V       4       7
       S1                     14     V       1       7
       S2                     13     V       3       7
       STACK                  0      F       -       -
       Y_MUX                  0      F       -       -
       EN_244          OE     12     D       1       1
       MUX0            OE     18     D       1       1
       MUX1            OE     17     D       1       1
       MUX2            OE     16     D       1       1
       RAOE            OE     19     D       1       1
       S0              OE     15     D       1       1
       S1              OE     14     D       1       1
       S2              OE     13     D       1       1

LEGEND    D : DEFAULT VAR    F : FIELD          I : INTERMEDIATE VAR
          U : UNDEFINED      V : VAR            X : EXTENDED VAR
          N : NODE           M : EXTENDED NODE


================================================================================
                                   FUSE PLOT
================================================================================

PIN #19                                   PIN #17
 0000 --------------------------------     0512 --------------------------------
 0032 --x-x----x--x-------------------     0544 --x-x----x----------------------
 0064 xxxxxxxxxxxxxxxxxxxxxxxxxxxxxxxx     0576 -x---x--x-----------------------
 0096 xxxxxxxxxxxxxxxxxxxxxxxxxxxxxxxx     0608 x--x-x---x----------------------
 0128 xxxxxxxxxxxxxxxxxxxxxxxxxxxxxxxx     0640 xxxxxxxxxxxxxxxxxxxxxxxxxxxxxxxx
 0160 xxxxxxxxxxxxxxxxxxxxxxxxxxxxxxxx     0672 xxxxxxxxxxxxxxxxxxxxxxxxxxxxxxxx
 0192 xxxxxxxxxxxxxxxxxxxxxxxxxxxxxxxx     0704 xxxxxxxxxxxxxxxxxxxxxxxxxxxxxxxx
 0224 xxxxxxxxxxxxxxxxxxxxxxxxxxxxxxxx     0736 xxxxxxxxxxxxxxxxxxxxxxxxxxxxxxxx
PIN #18                                   PIN #16
 0256 --------------------------------     0768 --------------------------------
 0288 --x-x----x----------------------     0800 ---x-x--x-----------------------
 0320 x--x-x---x----------------------     0832 --x-x---x-----------------------
 0352 -xx--x--x-----------------------     0864 xxxxxxxxxxxxxxxxxxxxxxxxxxxxxxxx
 0384 xxxxxxxxxxxxxxxxxxxxxxxxxxxxxxxx     0896 xxxxxxxxxxxxxxxxxxxxxxxxxxxxxxxx
 0416 xxxxxxxxxxxxxxxxxxxxxxxxxxxxxxxx     0928 xxxxxxxxxxxxxxxxxxxxxxxxxxxxxxxx
 0448 xxxxxxxxxxxxxxxxxxxxxxxxxxxxxxxx     0960 xxxxxxxxxxxxxxxxxxxxxxxxxxxxxxxx
 0480 xxxxxxxxxxxxxxxxxxxxxxxxxxxxxxxx     0992 xxxxxxxxxxxxxxxxxxxxxxxxxxxxxxxx
```

Program 2-2. Expanded Product Terms, Symbol Table and Fuse Plot for Emulator PAL 1 (Continued)

```
PIN #15
 1024 --------------------------------
 1056 -xx-x---------------------------
 1088 -x-x-----x----------------------
 1120 --x-x---x-----------------------
 1152 -x-x-x--------------------------
 1184 xxxxxxxxxxxxxxxxxxxxxxxxxxxxxxxx
 1216 xxxxxxxxxxxxxxxxxxxxxxxxxxxxxxxx
 1248 xxxxxxxxxxxxxxxxxxxxxxxxxxxxxxxx
PIN #14
 1280 --------------------------------
 1312 -x---x---x----------------------
 1344 xxxxxxxxxxxxxxxxxxxxxxxxxxxxxxxx
 1376 xxxxxxxxxxxxxxxxxxxxxxxxxxxxxxxx
 1408 xxxxxxxxxxxxxxxxxxxxxxxxxxxxxxxx
 1440 xxxxxxxxxxxxxxxxxxxxxxxxxxxxxxxx
 1472 xxxxxxxxxxxxxxxxxxxxxxxxxxxxxxxx
 1504 xxxxxxxxxxxxxxxxxxxxxxxxxxxxxxxx
PIN #13
 1536 --------------------------------
 1568 x----x--x-----------------------
 1600 -x-x-x--------------------------
 1632 --x-x---x-----------------------
 1664 xxxxxxxxxxxxxxxxxxxxxxxxxxxxxxxx
 1696 xxxxxxxxxxxxxxxxxxxxxxxxxxxxxxxx
 1728 xxxxxxxxxxxxxxxxxxxxxxxxxxxxxxxx
 1760 xxxxxxxxxxxxxxxxxxxxxxxxxxxxxxxx
PIN #12
 1792 --------------------------------
 1824 --------x-----------------------
 1856 -----x---x----------------------
 1888 ---xx----x----------------------
 1920 --x-x----x---x------------------
 1952 xxxxxxxxxxxxxxxxxxxxxxxxxxxxxxxx
 1984 xxxxxxxxxxxxxxxxxxxxxxxxxxxxxxxx
 2016 xxxxxxxxxxxxxxxxxxxxxxxxxxxxxxxx

LEGEND     X : FUSE NOT BLOWN
           - : FUSE BLOWN
```

3 Application Reports

Program 2-3. Simulation Results for Emulator PAL 1

```
                 NAME      '74AS890/2910 EMULATOR PAL 1;
                 DATE      04/04/85;
                 REV       01 ;
                 DESIGNER  RICHARD D. NAWROCKI ;
                 COMPANY   TEXAS INSTRUMENTS ;
                 ASSEMBLY  00001 ;
                 LOCATION  U100 ;

/************************************************************/
/*   THIS DEVICE GENERATES CONTROL SIGNALS FOR THE          */
/*   '74AS890 EMULATOR OF THE 2910 MICROPROGRAM SEQUENCER. */
/************************************************************/

ORDER:
   I3, %2, I2, %2, I1, %2, I0, %2,
         RLD, %2, RAOE, %2, EN_244, %2,
         MUX2, %2, MUX1, %2, MUX0, %2,
         S2, %2, S1, %2, S0 ;

```

SIMULATION RESULTS

	I3	I2	I1	I0	RLD	RAOE	EN_244	MUX2	MUX1	MUX0	SS2	SS1	SS0
INSTRUCTION 0													
0001:	0	0	0	0	1	H	L	H	H	H	L	L	L
0002:	0	0	0	0	0	H	L	H	H	H	L	L	L
INSTRUCTION 1													
0003:	0	0	0	1	1	H	L	H	H	H	H	L	H
0004:	0	0	0	1	0	H	L	H	H	H	H	L	H
INSTRUCTION 2													
0005:	0	0	1	0	1	H	L	H	L	L	H	H	H
0006:	0	0	1	0	0	H	L	H	L	L	H	H	H
INSTRUCTION 3													
0007:	0	0	1	1	1	H	L	H	H	H	H	H	H
0008:	0	0	1	1	0	H	L	H	H	H	H	H	H
INSTRUCTION 4													
0009:	0	1	0	0	1	H	L	H	H	H	H	H	L
0010:	0	1	0	0	0	H	L	H	H	H	H	H	L
INSTRUCTION 5													
0011:	0	1	0	1	1	L	H	H	L	L	H	H	L
0012:	0	1	0	1	0	H	L	H	L	L	H	H	L
INSTRUCTION 6													
0013:	0	1	1	0	1	H	L	H	H	H	H	H	H
0014:	0	1	1	0	0	H	L	H	H	H	H	H	H
INSTRUCTION 7													
0015:	0	1	1	1	1	L	H	H	L	L	H	H	H
0016:	0	1	1	1	0	H	L	H	L	L	H	H	H
INSTRUCTION 8													
0017:	1	0	0	0	1	H	L	L	L	H	L	H	L
0018:	1	0	0	0	0	H	L	L	L	H	L	H	L
INSTRUCTION 9													
0019:	1	0	0	1	1	H	L	H	L	L	H	H	H
0020:	1	0	0	1	0	H	L	H	L	L	H	H	H
INSTRUCTION A													
0021:	1	0	1	0	1	H	L	L	H	H	L	H	H
0022:	1	0	1	0	0	H	L	L	H	H	L	H	H
INSTRUCTION B													
0023:	1	0	1	1	1	H	L	H	H	H	L	H	H
0024:	1	0	1	1	0	H	L	H	H	H	L	H	H
INSTRUCTION C													
0025:	1	1	0	0	1	H	L	H	H	H	H	H	H
0026:	1	1	0	0	0	H	L	H	H	H	H	H	H
INSTRUCTION D													
0027:	1	1	0	1	1	H	L	L	H	H	L	H	L
0028:	1	1	0	1	0	H	L	L	H	H	L	H	L
INSTRUCTION E													
0029:	1	1	1	0	1	H	L	H	H	H	H	H	H
0030:	1	1	1	0	0	H	L	H	H	H	H	H	H
INSTRUCTION F													
0031:	1	1	1	1	1	H	L	L	H	H	L	H	L
0032:	1	1	1	1	0	H	L	L	H	H	L	H	L

Program 2-4. JEDEC Printout for Emulator PAL 1

```
CUPL            2.02A
DEVICE          p16L8  DLIB-c-18-5
PARTNO          2910EM
NAME            '74AS890/2910 EMULATOR PAL 1
REVISION        01
DATE            04/04/85
DESIGNER        RICHARD D. NAWROCKI
COMPANY         TEXAS INSTRUMENTS
ASSEMBLY        00001
LOCATION        U100
*QP20
*QF2048
*G0
*F0
*L0000 11111111111111111111111111111111
*L0032 11010111101101111111111111111111
*L0256 11111111111111111111111111111111
*L0288 11010111101111111111111111111111
*L0320 01101011101111111111111111111111
*L0352 10011011011111111111111111111111
*L0512 11111111111111111111111111111111
*L0544 11010111101111111111111111111111
*L0576 10111011011111111111111111111111
*L0608 01101011101111111111111111111111
*L0768 11111111111111111111111111111111
*L0800 11101011011111111111111111111111
*L0832 11010111011111111111111111111111
*L1024 11111111111111111111111111111111
*L1056 10010111111111111111111111111111
*L1088 10101111101111111111111111111111
*L1120 11010111011111111111111111111111
*L1152 10101011111111111111111111111111
*L1280 11111111111111111111111111111111
*L1312 10111011101111111111111111111111
*L1536 11111111111111111111111111111111
*L1568 01111011011111111111111111111111
*L1600 10101011111111111111111111111111
*L1632 11010111011111111111111111111111
*L1792 11111111111111111111111111111111
*L1824 11111111011111111111111111111111
*L1856 11111011101111111111111111111111
*L1888 11100111101111111111111111111111
*L1920 11010111101110111111111111111111
*C7103
*V0001 00001XXXXNXLLLLHHHHN
*V0002 00000XXXXNXLLLLHHHHN
*V0003 10001XXXXNXLHLHHHHHN
*V0004 10000XXXXNXLHLHHHHHN
*V0005 01001XXXXNXLHHHHLLHN
*V0006 01000XXXXNXLHHHHLLHN
*V0007 11001XXXXNXLHHHHHHHN
*V0008 11000XXXXNXLHHHHHHHN
*V0009 00101XXXXNXLHHLHHHHN
*V0010 00100XXXXNXLHHLHHHHN
*V0011 10101XXXXNXHHHLHLLLN
*V0012 10100XXXXNXLHHLHLLHN
*V0013 01101XXXXNXLHHHHHHHN
*V0014 01100XXXXNXLHHHHHHHN
*V0015 11101XXXXNXHHHHHLLLN
*V0016 11100XXXXNXLHHHHLLHN
*V0017 00011XXXXNXLLHLLLHHN
*V0018 00010XXXXNXLLHLLLHHN
*V0019 10011XXXXNXLHHHHLLHN
*V0020 10010XXXXNXLHHHHLLHN
*V0021 01011XXXXNXLLHHLHHHN
*V0022 01010XXXXNXLLHHLHHHN
*V0023 11011XXXXNXLLHHHHHHN
*V0024 11010XXXXNXLLHHHHHHN
*V0025 00111XXXXNXLHHHHHHHN
*V0026 00110XXXXNXLHHHHHHHN
*V0027 10111XXXXNXLLHLLHHHN
*V0028 10110XXXXNXLLHLLHHHN
*V0029 01111XXXXNXLHHHHHHHN
*V0030 01110XXXXNXLHHHHHHHN
*V0031 11111XXXXNXLLHLLHHHN
*V0032 11110XXXXNXLLHLLHHHN
*0757
```

3

Application Reports

Program 2-5. Logic Equations Used to Generate Emulator PAL 2

```
CUPL VERSION 2.02A COPYRIGHT (c) 1983,84,85 ASSISTED TECHNOLOGY, INC. -- LISTING

SOURCE FILE: B:2910EM1          DEVICE: p16L8

                 PARTNO    2910EM1 ;
                 NAME      '74AS890/2910 EMULATOR PAL 2 ;
                 DATE      04/04/85 ;
                 REV       01 ;
                 DESIGNER  RICHARD D. NAWROCKI ;
                 COMPANY   TEXAS INSTRUMENTS ;
                 ASSEMBLY  00001 ;
                 LOCATION   U101 ;

/*****************************************************************/
/*   THIS DEVICE GENERATES CONTROL SIGNALS FOR THE '74AS890      */
/*   EMULATION OF THE 2910 MICROPROGRAM CONTROLLER.              */
/*                                                               */
/*   ALLOWABLE TARGET DEVICE TYPES:  PAL16L8                     */
/*****************************************************************/

/**  INPUTS  **/

PIN  [1..4]  =  [I0..3]  ;      /*  2910 INSTRUCTION CODE          */
PIN  5       =   RLD     ;      /*  2910 REGISTER LOAD             */
PIN  6       =   CC      ;      /* 2910 CONDITION CODE             */
PIN  7       =   CCEN    ;      /* 2910 CONDITION CODE ENABLE      */

/**  OUTPUTS  **/

PIN  19      = CC_OUT0   ;      /* 74AS890 CONDITION CODE (1 OF 2) */
PIN  18      = CC_OUT1   ;      /* 74AS890 CONDITION CODE (2 OF 2) */
PIN [17..15] = [RC2..0]  ;      /* 74AS890 REGISTER/COUNTER CONTROL*/
PIN 14       = PL        ;      /* 2910 PIPELINE MAP OUTPUT        */
PIN  13      = MAP       ;      /* 2910 PROM MAP OUTPUT.           */
PIN  12      = VECT      ;      /* 2910 VECTOR MAP OUTPUT          */

/** DECLARATIONS AND INTERMEDIATE VARIABLE DEFINITIONS **/

 FIELD INSTRUCTION = [I3..0]  ;
 FIELD COUNTER     = [RC2..0] ;

/**  LOGIC EQUATIONS  **/

 !PL   = INSTRUCTION:[0,1,3..5,7..F] ;

 !MAP  = INSTRUCTION:2 ;

 !VECT = INSTRUCTION:6 ;

 COUNTER = 'H'2 & INSTRUCTION:C
         # ('H'2 & INSTRUCTION:4 & (CCEN # !CC))
         # 'H'2 & !RLD
         # 'H'1 & RLD & INSTRUCTION:[8,9,F] ;

  CC_OUT0.OE = CCEN ;

  CC_OUT1.OE = !CCEN ;

 !CC_OUT0 = INSTRUCTION:[1,3,6,8..B] ;

 !CC_OUT1 = INSTRUCTION:[1,3,6,8..B] & !CC
          # INSTRUCTION:[5,7,D,F] & CC
          # INSTRUCTION:[8,9] ;


JEDEC FUSE CHECKSUM        (791A)
JEDEC TRANSMIT CHECKSUM          (3521)
```

Program 2-6. Expanded Product Terms, Symbol Table and Fuse Plot for Emulator PAL 2

```
CUPL            2.02A
DEVICE          p16L8  DLIB-c-18-5
PARTNO          2910EM1
NAME            '74AS890/2910 EMULATOR PAL 2
REVISION        01
DATE            04/04/85
DESIGNER        RICHARD D. NAWROCKI
COMPANY         TEXAS INSTRUMENTS
ASSEMBLY        00001
LOCATION        U101

==================================================================================
                          EXPANDED PRODUCT TERMS
==================================================================================
CC_OUT0  ->
    !I2  & I3
  # I0  & !I2  & !I3
  # !I0  & I1  & I2  & !I3

CC_OUT0.oe  ->
    CCEN

CC_OUT1  ->
    !CC  & !I2  & I3
  # !I1  & !I2  & I3
  # CC  & I0  & I2
  # !CC  & I0  & !I2  & !I3
  # !CC  & !I0  & I1  & I2  & !I3

CC_OUT1.oe  ->
    !CCEN

COUNTER  ->
    RC2  , RC1  , RC0

INSTRUCTION  ->
    I3  , I2  , I1  , I0

MAP  ->
    !I0  & I1  & !I2  & !I3

PL  ->
    I3
  # !I1  & !I3
  # I0  & I1  & !I3

RC0  ->
    !I0  & I1
  # !I1  & I2
  # I1  & !I2
  # !I3
  # !RLD

RC1  ->
    I0  & RLD
  # !I2  & RLD
  # I1  & RLD
  # !CCEN  & CC  & !I3  & RLD

RC2  ->
    1

VECT  ->
    !I0  & I1  & I2  & !I3

MAP.oe  ->
    1

PL.oe  ->
    1

RC0.oe  ->
    1

RC1.oe  ->
    1

RC2.oe  ->
    1

VECT.oe  ->
    1
```

3

Application Reports

Program 2-6. Expanded Product Terms, Symbol Table and Fuse Plot for Emulator PAL 2 (Continued)

```
==============================================================================
                                 SYMBOL TABLE
==============================================================================

POL    NAME             EXT     PIN     TYPE     USED     MAX
---    ----             ---     ---     ----     ----     ---

       CCEN                     7       V        -        -
       CC                       6       V        -        -
       CC_OUT0                  19      V        3        7
       CC_OUT0          OE      19      X        1        1
       CC_OUT1                  18      V        5        7
       CC_OUT1          OE      18      X        1        1
       COUNTER                  0       F        -        -
       I0                       1       V        -        -
       I1                       2       V        -        -
       I2                       3       V        -        -
       I3                       4       V        -        -
       INSTRUCTION              0       F        -        -
       MAP                      13      V        1        7
       PL                       14      V        3        7
       RC0                      15      V        5        7
       RC1                      16      V        4        7
       RC2                      17      V        1        7
       RLD                      5       V        -        -
       VECT                     12      V        1        7
       MAP              OE      13      D        1        1
       PL               OE      14      D        1        1
       RC0              OE      15      D        1        1
       RC1              OE      16      D        1        1
       RC2              OE      17      D        1        1
       VECT             OE      12      D        1        1

LEGEND    D : DEFAULT VAR     F : FIELD      I : INTERMEDIATE VAR
          U : UNDEFINED       V : VAR        X : EXTENDED VAR
          N : NODE            M : EXTENDED NODE


==============================================================================
                                  FUSE PLOT
==============================================================================

PIN #19                                   PIN #16
 0000 --------------------x-----------     0768 --------------------------------
 0032 -----x--x-----------------------     0800 --x---------x-------------------
 0064 --x--x---x----------------------     0832 -----x------x-------------------
 0096 x--xx----x----------------------     0864 x-----------x-------------------
 0128 xxxxxxxxxxxxxxxxxxxxxxxxxxxxxxxx     0896 ---------x--x---x----x----------
 0160 xxxxxxxxxxxxxxxxxxxxxxxxxxxxxxxx     0928 xxxxxxxxxxxxxxxxxxxxxxxxxxxxxxxx
 0192 xxxxxxxxxxxxxxxxxxxxxxxxxxxxxxxx     0960 xxxxxxxxxxxxxxxxxxxxxxxxxxxxxxxx
 0224 xxxxxxxxxxxxxxxxxxxxxxxxxxxxxxxx     0992 xxxxxxxxxxxxxxxxxxxxxxxxxxxxxxxx
PIN #18                                   PIN #15
 0256 ---------------------x----------     1024 --------------------------------
 0288 -----x--x--------x--------------     1056 x--x----------------------------
 0320 -x---x--x-----------------------     1088 -x--x---------------------------
 0352 --x-x-----------x---------------     1120 x----x--------------------------
 0384 --x--x---x-------x--------------     1152 ---------x----------------------
 0416 x--xx----x-------x--------------     1184 -------------x------------------
 0448 xxxxxxxxxxxxxxxxxxxxxxxxxxxxxxxx     1216 xxxxxxxxxxxxxxxxxxxxxxxxxxxxxxxx
 0480 xxxxxxxxxxxxxxxxxxxxxxxxxxxxxxxx     1248 xxxxxxxxxxxxxxxxxxxxxxxxxxxxxxxx
PIN #17                                   PIN #14
 0512 --------------------------------     1280 --------------------------------
 0544 --------------------------------     1312 --------x-----------------------
 0576 xxxxxxxxxxxxxxxxxxxxxxxxxxxxxxxx     1344 -x-------x----------------------
 0608 xxxxxxxxxxxxxxxxxxxxxxxxxxxxxxxx     1376 x-x------x----------------------
 0640 xxxxxxxxxxxxxxxxxxxxxxxxxxxxxxxx     1408 xxxxxxxxxxxxxxxxxxxxxxxxxxxxxxxx
 0672 xxxxxxxxxxxxxxxxxxxxxxxxxxxxxxxx     1440 xxxxxxxxxxxxxxxxxxxxxxxxxxxxxxxx
 0704 xxxxxxxxxxxxxxxxxxxxxxxxxxxxxxxx     1472 xxxxxxxxxxxxxxxxxxxxxxxxxxxxxxxx
 0736 xxxxxxxxxxxxxxxxxxxxxxxxxxxxxxxx     1504 xxxxxxxxxxxxxxxxxxxxxxxxxxxxxxxx
```

Program 2-6. Expanded Product Terms, Symbol Table and Fuse Plot for Emulator PAL 2 (Continued)

```
PIN #13
 1536 --------------------------------
 1568 x--x-x---x----------------------
 1600 xxxxxxxxxxxxxxxxxxxxxxxxxxxxxxxx
 1632 xxxxxxxxxxxxxxxxxxxxxxxxxxxxxxxx
 1664 xxxxxxxxxxxxxxxxxxxxxxxxxxxxxxxx
 1696 xxxxxxxxxxxxxxxxxxxxxxxxxxxxxxxx
 1728 xxxxxxxxxxxxxxxxxxxxxxxxxxxxxxxx
 1760 xxxxxxxxxxxxxxxxxxxxxxxxxxxxxxxx
PIN #12
 1792 --------------------------------
 1824 x--xx----x----------------------
 1856 xxxxxxxxxxxxxxxxxxxxxxxxxxxxxxxx
 1888 xxxxxxxxxxxxxxxxxxxxxxxxxxxxxxxx
 1920 xxxxxxxxxxxxxxxxxxxxxxxxxxxxxxxx
 1952 xxxxxxxxxxxxxxxxxxxxxxxxxxxxxxxx
 1984 xxxxxxxxxxxxxxxxxxxxxxxxxxxxxxxx
 2016 xxxxxxxxxxxxxxxxxxxxxxxxxxxxxxxx

LEGEND     x : FUSE NOT BLOWN
           - : FUSE BLOWN
```

Program 2-7. Simulation Results for Emulator PAL 2

```
NAME       '74AS890/2910 EMULATOR PAL 2 ;
DATE       04/04/85 ;
REV        01 ;
DESIGNER   RICHARD D. NAWROCKI ;
COMPANY    TEXAS INSTRUMENTS ;
ASSEMBLY   00001 ;
LOCATION   U101 ;

/*************************************************************/
/*   THIS DEVICE GENERATES CONTROL SIGNALS FOR THE           */
/*   '74AS890 EMULATOR OF THE 2910 MICROPROGRAM SEQUENCER.   */
/*************************************************************/

ORDER:
   I3, %2, I2, %2, I1, %2, I0, %2,
        CC, %2, CCEN, %2, RLD, %2,
        PL, %2, MAP, %2, VECT, %2,
        CC_OUT1, %2, CC_OUT0, %2,
        RC2, %2, RC1, %2, RC0  ;

=====================================================================
                        SIMULATION RESULTS
=====================================================================
                                          C  C
                                          C  C
                                          _  _
                       C           V  O  O
                       C  R     M  E  U  U  R  R  R
         I  I  I  I  C  E  L  P  A  C  T  T  C  C  C
         3  2  1  0  C  N  D  L  P  T  1  0  2  1  0
        _____________________  ____________________________
       INSTRUCTION 0
0001:  0  0  0  0  1  0  1  L  H  H  H  Z  L  L  L
0002:  0  0  0  0  1  0  0  L  H  H  H  Z  L  H  L
0003:  0  0  0  0  0  0  1  L  H  H  H  Z  L  L  L
0004:  0  0  0  0  0  0  0  L  H  H  H  Z  L  H  L
0005:  0  0  0  0  1  1  1  L  H  H  Z  H  L  L  L
0006:  0  0  0  0  1  1  0  L  H  H  Z  H  L  H  L
0007:  0  0  0  0  0  1  1  L  H  H  Z  H  L  L  L
0008:  0  0  0  0  0  1  0  L  H  H  Z  H  L  H  L
       INSTRUCTION 1
0009:  0  0  0  1  1  0  1  L  H  H  H  Z  L  L  L
0010:  0  0  0  1  1  0  0  L  H  H  H  Z  L  H  L
0011:  0  0  0  1  0  0  1  L  H  H  L  Z  L  L  L
0012:  0  0  0  1  0  0  0  L  H  H  L  Z  L  H  L
0013:  0  0  0  1  1  1  1  L  H  H  Z  L  L  L  L
0014:  0  0  0  1  1  1  0  L  H  H  Z  L  L  H  L
0015:  0  0  0  1  0  1  1  L  H  H  Z  L  L  L  L
0016:  0  0  0  1  0  1  0  L  H  H  Z  L  L  H  L
       INSTRUCTION 2
0017:  0  0  1  0  1  0  1  H  L  H  H  Z  L  L  L
0018:  0  0  1  0  1  0  0  H  L  H  H  Z  L  H  L
0019:  0  0  1  0  0  0  1  H  L  H  H  Z  L  L  L
0020:  0  0  1  0  0  0  0  H  L  H  H  Z  L  H  L
0021:  0  0  1  0  1  1  1  H  L  H  Z  H  L  L  L
0022:  0  0  1  0  1  1  0  H  L  H  Z  H  L  H  L
0023:  0  0  1  0  0  1  1  H  L  H  Z  H  L  L  L
0024:  0  0  1  0  0  1  0  H  L  H  Z  H  L  H  L
       INSTRUCTION 3
0025:  0  0  1  1  1  0  1  L  H  H  H  Z  L  L  L
0026:  0  0  1  1  1  0  0  L  H  H  H  Z  L  H  L
0027:  0  0  1  1  0  0  1  L  H  H  L  Z  L  L  L
0028:  0  0  1  1  0  0  0  L  H  H  L  Z  L  H  L
0029:  0  0  1  1  1  1  1  L  H  H  Z  L  L  L  L
0030:  0  0  1  1  1  1  0  L  H  H  Z  L  L  H  L
0031:  0  0  1  1  0  1  1  L  H  H  Z  L  L  L  L
0032:  0  0  1  1  0  1  0  L  H  H  Z  L  L  H  L
```

Program 2-7. Simulation Results for Emulator PAL 2 (Continued)

```
                                         C   C
                                         C   C
                                         -   -
                       C             V   O   O
                       C   R     M   E   U   U   R   R   R
    I   I   I   I   C  E   L  P  A   C   T   T   C   C   C
    3   2   1   0   C  N   D  L  P   T   1   0   2   1   0
    _____________________________  ________________________
    INSTRUCTION 4
0033: 0 1 0 0 1 0 1  L  H  H  H  Z  L  L  L
0034: 0 1 0 0 1 0 0  L  H  H  H  Z  L  H  L
0035: 0 1 0 0 0 0 1  L  H  H  H  Z  L  H  L
0036: 0 1 0 0 0 0 0  L  H  H  H  Z  L  H  L
0037: 0 1 0 0 1 1 1  L  H  H  Z  H  L  H  L
0038: 0 1 0 0 1 1 0  L  H  H  Z  H  L  H  L
0039: 0 1 0 0 0 1 1  L  H  H  Z  H  L  H  L
0040: 0 1 0 0 0 1 0  L  H  H  Z  H  L  H  L
    INSTRUCTION 5
0041: 0 1 0 1 1 0 1  L  H  H  L  Z  L  L  L
0042: 0 1 0 1 1 0 0  L  H  H  L  Z  L  H  L
0043: 0 1 0 1 0 0 1  L  H  H  H  Z  L  L  L
0044: 0 1 0 1 0 0 0  L  H  H  H  Z  L  H  L
0045: 0 1 0 1 1 1 1  L  H  H  Z  H  L  L  L
0046: 0 1 0 1 1 1 0  L  H  H  Z  H  L  H  L
0047: 0 1 0 1 0 1 1  L  H  H  Z  H  L  L  L
0048: 0 1 0 1 0 1 0  L  H  H  Z  H  L  H  L
    INSTRUCTION 6
0049: 0 1 1 0 1 0 1  H  H  L  H  Z  L  L  L
0050: 0 1 1 0 1 0 0  H  H  L  H  Z  L  H  L
0051: 0 1 1 0 0 0 1  H  H  L  L  Z  L  L  L
0052: 0 1 1 0 0 0 0  H  H  L  L  Z  L  H  L
0053: 0 1 1 0 1 1 1  H  H  L  Z  L  L  L  L
0054: 0 1 1 0 1 1 0  H  H  L  Z  L  L  H  L
0055: 0 1 1 0 0 1 1  H  H  L  Z  L  L  L  L
0056: 0 1 1 0 0 1 0  H  H  L  Z  L  L  H  L
    INSTRUCTION 7
0057: 0 1 1 1 1 0 1  L  H  H  L  Z  L  L  L
0058: 0 1 1 1 1 0 0  L  H  H  L  Z  L  H  L
0059: 0 1 1 1 0 0 1  L  H  H  H  Z  L  L  L
0060: 0 1 1 1 0 0 0  L  H  H  H  Z  L  H  L
0061: 0 1 1 1 1 1 1  L  H  H  Z  H  L  L  L
0062: 0 1 1 1 1 1 0  L  H  H  Z  H  L  H  L
0063: 0 1 1 1 0 1 1  L  H  H  Z  H  L  L  L
0064: 0 1 1 1 0 1 0  L  H  H  Z  H  L  H  L
    INSTRUCTION 8
0065: 1 0 0 0 1 0 1  L  H  H  L  Z  L  L  H
0066: 1 0 0 0 1 0 0  L  H  H  L  Z  L  H  L
0067: 1 0 0 0 0 0 1  L  H  H  L  Z  L  L  H
0068: 1 0 0 0 0 0 0  L  H  H  L  Z  L  H  L
0069: 1 0 0 0 1 1 1  L  H  H  Z  L  L  L  H
0070: 1 0 0 0 1 1 0  L  H  H  Z  L  L  H  L
0071: 1 0 0 0 0 1 1  L  H  H  Z  L  L  L  H
0072: 1 0 0 0 0 1 0  L  H  H  Z  L  L  H  L
    INSTRUCTION 9
0073: 1 0 0 1 1 0 1  L  H  H  L  Z  L  L  H
0074: 1 0 0 1 1 0 0  L  H  H  L  Z  L  H  L
0075: 1 0 0 1 0 0 1  L  H  H  L  Z  L  L  H
0076: 1 0 0 1 0 0 0  L  H  H  L  Z  L  H  L
0077: 1 0 0 1 1 1 1  L  H  H  Z  L  L  L  H
0078: 1 0 0 1 1 1 0  L  H  H  Z  L  L  H  L
0079: 1 0 0 1 0 1 1  L  H  H  Z  L  L  L  H
0080: 1 0 0 1 0 1 0  L  H  H  Z  L  L  H  L
    INSTRUCTION A
0081: 1 0 1 0 1 0 1  L  H  H  H  Z  L  L  L
0082: 1 0 1 0 1 0 0  L  H  H  H  Z  L  H  L
0083: 1 0 1 0 0 0 1  L  H  H  L  Z  L  L  L
0084: 1 0 1 0 0 0 0  L  H  H  L  Z  L  H  L
0085: 1 0 1 0 1 1 1  L  H  H  Z  L  L  L  L
0086: 1 0 1 0 1 1 0  L  H  H  Z  L  L  H  L
0087: 1 0 1 0 0 1 1  L  H  H  Z  L  L  L  L
0088: 1 0 1 0 0 1 0  L  H  H  Z  L  L  H  L
```

Program 2-7. Simulation Results for Emulator PAL 2 (Continued)

```
                                     C   C
                                     C   C
                                     -   -
                   C           V     O   O
                   C   R     M E     U   U   R   R   R
    I  I  I  I  C  E   L   P A C     T   T   C   C   C
    3  2  1  0  C  N   D   L P T     1   0   2   1   0
   ____________________    _____________________________
    INSTRUCTION B
0089: 1  0  1  1  1  0  1   L  H  H  H  Z  L  L  L
0090: 1  0  1  1  1  0  0   L  H  H  H  Z  L  H  L
0091: 1  0  1  1  0  0  1   L  H  H  L  Z  L  L  L
0092: 1  0  1  1  0  0  0   L  H  H  L  Z  L  H  L
0093: 1  0  1  1  1  1  1   L  H  H  Z  L  L  L  L
0094: 1  0  1  1  1  1  0   L  H  H  Z  L  L  H  L
0095: 1  0  1  1  0  1  1   L  H  H  Z  L  L  L  L
0096: 1  0  1  1  0  1  0   L  H  H  Z  L  L  H  L
    INSTRUCTION C
0097: 1  1  0  0  1  0  1   L  H  H  H  Z  L  H  L
0098: 1  1  0  0  1  0  0   L  H  H  H  Z  L  H  L
0099: 1  1  0  0  0  0  1   L  H  H  H  Z  L  H  L
0100: 1  1  0  0  0  0  0   L  H  H  H  Z  L  H  L
0101: 1  1  0  0  1  1  1   L  H  H  Z  H  L  H  L
0102: 1  1  0  0  1  1  0   L  H  H  Z  H  L  H  L
0103: 1  1  0  0  0  1  1   L  H  H  Z  H  L  H  L
0104: 1  1  0  0  0  1  0   L  H  H  Z  H  L  H  L
    INSTRUCTION D
0105: 1  1  0  1  1  0  1   L  H  H  L  Z  L  L  L
0106: 1  1  0  1  1  0  0   L  H  H  L  Z  L  H  L
0107: 1  1  0  1  0  0  1   L  H  H  H  Z  L  L  L
0108: 1  1  0  1  0  0  0   L  H  H  H  Z  L  H  L
0109: 1  1  0  1  1  1  1   L  H  H  Z  H  L  L  L
0110: 1  1  0  1  1  1  0   L  H  H  Z  H  L  H  L
0111: 1  1  0  1  0  1  1   L  H  H  Z  H  L  L  L
0112: 1  1  0  1  0  1  0   L  H  H  Z  H  L  H  L
    INSTRUCTION E
0113: 1  1  1  0  1  0  1   L  H  H  H  Z  L  L  L
0114: 1  1  1  0  1  0  0   L  H  H  H  Z  L  H  L
0115: 1  1  1  0  0  0  1   L  H  H  H  Z  L  L  L
0116: 1  1  1  0  0  0  0   L  H  H  H  Z  L  H  L
0117: 1  1  1  0  1  1  1   L  H  H  Z  H  L  L  L
0118: 1  1  1  0  1  1  0   L  H  H  Z  H  L  H  L
0119: 1  1  1  0  0  1  1   L  H  H  Z  H  L  L  L
0120: 1  1  1  0  0  1  0   L  H  H  Z  H  L  H  L
    INSTRUCTION F
0121: 1  1  1  1  1  0  1   L  H  H  L  Z  L  L  H
0122: 1  1  1  1  1  0  0   L  H  H  L  Z  L  H  L
0123: 1  1  1  1  0  0  1   L  H  H  H  Z  L  L  H
0124: 1  1  1  1  0  0  0   L  H  H  H  Z  L  H  L
0125: 1  1  1  1  1  1  1   L  H  H  Z  H  L  L  H
0126: 1  1  1  1  1  1  0   L  H  H  Z  H  L  H  L
0127: 1  1  1  1  0  1  1   L  H  H  Z  H  L  L  H
0128: 1  1  1  1  0  1  0   L  H  H  Z  H  L  H  L
```

Program 2-8. JEDEC Printout for Emulator PAL 2

```
CUPL            2.02A
DEVICE          P16L8  DLIB-c-18-5
PARTNO          2910EM1
NAME            '74AS890/2910 EMULATOR PAL 2
REVISION        01
DATE            04/04/85
DESIGNER        RICHARD D. NAWROCKI
COMPANY         TEXAS INSTRUMENTS
ASSEMBLY        00001
LOCATION        U101
*QP20
*QF2048
*G0
*F0
*L0000 11111111111111111111011111111111
*L0032 11111011011111111111111111111111
*L0064 11011011101111111111111111111111
*L0096 01100111101111111111111111111111
*L0256 11111111111111111111101111111111
*L0288 11111011011111111011111111111111
*L0320 10111011011111111111111111111111
*L0352 11010111111111110111111111111111
*L0384 11011011101111111011111111111111
*L0416 01100111101111111011111111111111
*L0512 11111111111111111111111111111111
*L0544 11111111111111111111111111111111
*L0768 11111111111111111111111111111111
*L0800 11011111111101111111111111111111
*L0832 11111011111101111111111111111111
*L0864 01111111111101111111111111111111
*L0896 11111111101101110111101111111111
*L1024 11111111111111111111111111111111
*L1056 01101111111111111111111111111111
*L1088 10110111111111111111111111111111
*L1120 01111011111111111111111111111111
*L1152 11111111101111111111111111111111
*L1184 11111111111110111111111111111111
*L1280 11111111111111111111111111111111
*L1312 11111111011111111111111111111111
*L1344 10111111101111111111111111111111
*L1376 01011111101111111111111111111111
*L1536 11111111111111111111111111111111
*L1568 01101011101111111111111111111111
*L1792 11111111111111111111111111111111
*L1824 01100111101111111111111111111111
*C791A
*V0001 0000110XXNXHHLLLLHZN
*V0002 0000010XXNXHHLLHLHZN
*V0003 0000100XXNXHHLLLLHZN
*V0004 0000000XXNXHHLLHLHZN
*V0005 0000111XXNXHHLLLLZHN
*V0006 0000011XXNXHHLLHLZHN
*V0007 0000101XXNXHHLLLLZHN
*V0008 0000001XXNXHHLLHLZHN
*V0009 1000110XXNXHHLLLLHZN
*V0010 1000010XXNXHHLLHLHZN
*V0011 1000100XXNXHHLLLLLZN
*V0012 1000000XXNXHHLLHLLZN
*V0013 1000111XXNXHHLLLLZLN
*V0014 1000011XXNXHHLLHLZLN
*V0015 1000101XXNXHHLLLLZLN
*V0016 1000001XXNXHHLLHLZLN
*V0017 0100110XXNXHLHLLLHZN
*V0018 0100010XXNXHLHLHLHZN
*V0019 0100100XXNXHLHLLLHZN
*V0020 0100000XXNXHLHLHLHZN
*V0021 0100111XXNXHLHLLLZHN
*V0022 0100011XXNXHLHLHLZHN
*V0023 0100101XXNXHLHLLLZHN
*V0024 0100001XXNXHLHLHLZHN
*V0025 1100110XXNXHHLLLLHZN
*V0026 1100010XXNXHHLLHLHZN
*V0027 1100100XXNXHHLLLLLZN
```

3 Application Reports

Program 2-8. JEDEC Printout for Emulator PAL 2 (Continued)

```
*V0028 1100000XXNXHHLLHLLZN
*V0029 1100111XXNXHHLLLLZLN
*V0030 1100011XXNXHHLLHLZLN
*V0031 1100101XXNXHHLLLLZLN
*V0032 1100001XXNXHHLLHLZLN
*V0033 0010110XXNXHHLLLLHZN
*V0034 0010010XXNXHHLLHLHZN
*V0035 0010100XXNXHHLLHLHZN
*V0036 0010000XXNXHHLLHLHZN
*V0037 0010111XXNXHHLLHLZHN
*V0038 0010011XXNXHHLLHLZHN
*V0039 0010101XXNXHHLLHLZHN
*V0040 0010001XXNXHHLLHLZHN
*V0041 1010110XXNXHHLLLLLZN
*V0042 1010010XXNXHHLLHLLZN
*V0043 1010100XXNXHHLLLLHZN
*V0044 1010000XXNXHHLLHLHZN
*V0045 1010111XXNXHHLLLLZHN
*V0046 1010011XXNXHHLLHLZHN
*V0047 1010101XXNXHHLLLLZHN
*V0048 1010001XXNXHHLLHLZHN
*V0049 0110110XXNXLHHLLLHZN
*V0050 0110010XXNXLHHLHLHZN
*V0051 0110100XXNXLHHLLLLZN
*V0052 0110000XXNXLHHLHLLZN
*V0053 0110111XXNXLHHLLLZLN
*V0054 0110011XXNXLHHLHLZLN
*V0055 0110101XXNXLHHLLLZLN
*V0056 0110001XXNXLHHLHLZLN
*V0057 1110110XXNXHHLLLLLZN
*V0058 1110010XXNXHHLLHLLZN
*V0059 1110100XXNXHHLLLLHZN
*V0060 1110000XXNXHHLLHLHZN
*V0061 1110111XXNXHHLLLLZHN
*V0062 1110011XXNXHHLLHLZHN
*V0063 1110101XXNXHHLLLLZHN
*V0064 1110001XXNXHHLLHLZHN
*V0065 0001110XXNXHHLHLLLZN
*V0066 0001010XXNXHHLLHLLZN
*V0067 0001100XXNXHHLHLLLZN
*V0068 0001000XXNXHHLLHLLZN
*V0069 0001111XXNXHHLHLLZLN
*V0070 0001011XXNXHHLLHLZLN
*V0071 0001101XXNXHHLHLLZLN
*V0072 0001001XXNXHHLLHLZLN
*V0073 1001110XXNXHHLHLLLZN
*V0074 1001010XXNXHHLLHLLZN
*V0075 1001100XXNXHHLHLLLZN
*V0076 1001000XXNXHHLLHLLZN
*V0077 1001111XXNXHHLHLLZLN
*V0078 1001011XXNXHHLLHLZLN
*V0079 1001101XXNXHHLHLLZLN
*V0080 1001001XXNXHHLLHLZLN
*V0081 0101110XXNXHHLLLLHZN
*V0082 0101010XXNXHHLLHLHZN
*V0083 0101100XXNXHHLLLLLZN
*V0084 0101000XXNXHHLLHLLZN
*V0085 0101111XXNXHHLLLLZLN
*V0086 0101011XXNXHHLLHLZLN
*V0087 0101101XXNXHHLLLLZLN
*V0088 0101001XXNXHHLLHLZLN
*V0089 1101110XXNXHHLLLLHZN
*V0090 1101010XXNXHHLLHLHZN
*V0091 1101100XXNXHHLLLLLZN
*V0092 1101000XXNXHHLLHLLZN
*V0093 1101111XXNXHHLLLLZLN
*V0094 1101011XXNXHHLLHLZLN
*V0095 1101101XXNXHHLLLLZLN
*V0096 1101001XXNXHHLLHLZLN
*V0097 0011110XXNXHHLLHLHZN
*V0098 0011010XXNXHHLLHLHZN
*V0099 0011100XXNXHHLLHLHZN
*V0100 0011000XXNXHHLLHLHZN
*V0101 0011111XXNXHHLLHLZHN
*V0102 0011011XXNXHHLLHLZHN
*V0103 0011101XXNXHHLLHLZHN
*V0104 0011001XXNXHHLLHLZHN
*V0105 1011110XXNXHHLLLLLZN
*V0106 1011010XXNXHHLLHLLZN
*V0107 1011100XXNXHHLLLLHZN
*V0108 1011000XXNXHHLLHLHZN
*V0109 1011111XXNXHHLLLLZHN
*V0110 1011011XXNXHHLLHLZHN
*V0111 1011101XXNXHHLLLLZHN
*V0112 1011001XXNXHHLLHLZHN
*V0113 0111110XXNXHHLLLLHZN
*V0114 0111010XXNXHHLLHLHZN
*V0115 0111100XXNXHHLLLLHZN
*V0116 0111000XXNXHHLLHLHZN
*V0117 0111111XXNXHHLLLLZHN
*V0118 0111011XXNXHHLLHLZHN
*V0119 0111101XXNXHHLLLLZHN
*V0120 0111001XXNXHHLLHLZHN
*V0121 1111110XXNXHHLHLLLZN
*V0122 1111010XXNXHHLLHLLZN
*V0123 1111100XXNXHHLHLLHZN
*V0124 1111000XXNXHHLLHLHZN
*V0125 1111111XXNXHHLHLLZHN
*V0126 1111011XXNXHHLLHLZHN
*V0127 1111101XXNXHHLHLLZHN
*V0128 1111001XXNXHHLLHLZHN
*A128
```

3 Application Reports

Section 3
Minimum Cycle Time Delay Calculations for a 16-Bit System

This article examines some timings for a typical 16-bit computer system using a bit-slice processor and microsequencer. Comparative data for systems using TI's 'AS888-1/'AS890-1, AMD's Am2901C/2910A, and AMD's Am2903A/2910A are presented. Timing calculations are based on data from TI SN74AS888/890 family data sheets and from the *AMD2900 Family Bipolar Microprocessor Logic and Interface 1985 Data Book.*

16-BIT COMPUTER SYSTEM DESIGN

Figure 3-1 shows a basic design for a 16-bit computer system. The computer control unit (CCU), shown on the left side of the dotted line, executes microcode from the microprogram memory (also known as the control store). A one-level pipeline design is used to speed data processing, allowing the address and contents of the next instruction to be fetched while the current instruction is being executed. The arithmetic logic unit, consisting of the bit-slice processor chips and any other logic needed to process the data, is shown on the right side of the figure.

This section compares the time required to perform the following functions, using TI's SN74AS888-1/890-1, AMD's Am2901C/2910A and AMD's Am2903A/2910A bit-slice products:

1. addition
2. addition with a shift
3. unsigned integer multiplication
4. unsigned integer division.

Cases 3 and 4 are not included in the Am2901C/Am2910A discussion, since the Am2901C does not incorporate internal multiplication or division algorithms.

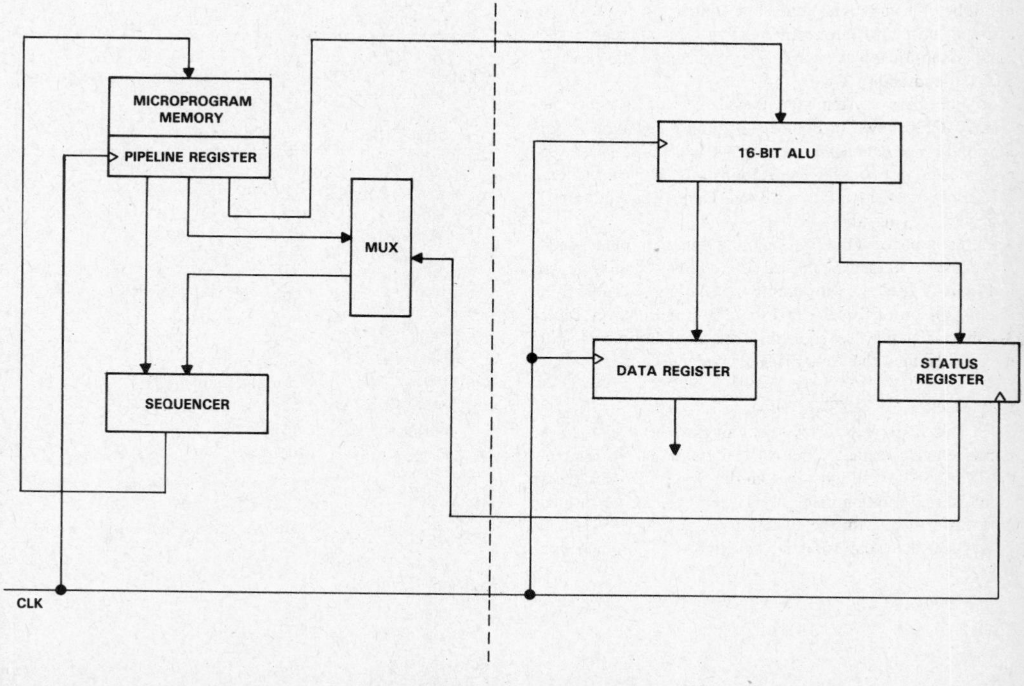

MICROPROGRAM MEMORY
PIPELINE REGISTER
MUX
SEQUENCER
16-BIT ALU
DATA REGISTER
STATUS REGISTER
CLK

Figure 3-1. 16-Bit Computer System

Benchmark I: Comparison of Am2903A/2910A with 'AS888-1/'AS890-1

Design of a 16-bit system that is Am2903A-based is presented in Figure 3-2. The same system implemented with the 'AS888-1 and 'AS890-1 is shown in Figure 3-3. These systems are used to calculate timings for the four cases discussed in this section. Timings for the control path are given in the first test case and remain constant for the remaining three cases.

Tables 3-1 and 3-2 contain timing results for addition using the two chip sets; Tables 3-3 and 3-4 analyze the add with shift combination. It can be seen that the TI system runs 36% faster for addition and 32% faster for addition followed by a shift of the result.

Figures 3-4 and 3-5 show the ALU data paths used for multiplication and division by the two systems. Tables 3-5, 3-6 and 3-7 display timings for the critical path calculations for these operations. Increases in speed using the TI parts are even more significant here, where multiplication is faster by 42% and division faster by 37%.

Benchmark II: Comparison of Am2901C/2910A with 'AS888-1/'AS890-1

The same 16-bit system can be constructed with Am2901C slices. Since the Am2901C has a smaller instruction set than the Am2903A or the 'AS888-1, multiplication and division must be emulated using external add with shift hardware and bit testing. For this reason, the comparison for this benchmark is restricted to the cases of addition and addition with shift.

The basic system for these two cases using the Am2901C is shown in Figure 3-6; timing calculations for the control and data paths are listed in Table 3-8. These can be compared directly with the 'AS888 design and calculations shown previously in Figure 3-3 and Table 3-2. Addition is 13% faster using the AS888-1.

To implement the shift function, two multiplexers and an exclusive-OR gate are needed. A modified design is shown in Figure 3-7, along with timing calculations in Table 3-9. A comparison of these with Figure 3-3 and data in Table 3-4 shows that the TI system performs an addition with shift 25% faster than the Am2901C equivalent.

SUMMARY OF RESULTS

Table 3-10 summarizes the timings of the various cases implemented with the TI and AMD parts. It can be seen that the TI 'AS888-1/'AS890-1 system runs faster than the others in all cases. Addition using the TI parts can be performed 26% faster than with the system using the Am2901C and 36% faster than that using the Am2903A. Addition with a shift is 25% faster on the TI system than the Am2901C system and 32% faster than the Am2903C. An even wider variance occurs with the more complicated algorithms: multiplication is 42% faster using the TI chip; division is 37% faster.

Table 3-1. Am2903A/Am2910A Timings for Addition

COMPONENT	DATA PATH	TIME (NS)
Data Loop		
Pipeline register	Clock to output	9
Am2903A	A, B to $\overline{G}$, $\overline{P}$	52
Am2902A	$\overline{G0}$, $\overline{P0}$ to C_{n+z}	7
Am2903A	C_n to C_{n+4}, OVR, Z, Y	35
Am2903A	Setup time	5
	Total for data loop	108
Control Loop		
Pipeline register	Clock to output	9
MUX	Select to output	13
Am2910A	$\overline{CC}$ to output	30
PROM	Access time	20
Pipeline register	Setup time	2
	Total for control loop	74
	Critical path for Am2903 addition	108

Table 3-2. 'AS888-1/'AS890-1 Timings for Addition

COMPONENT	DATA PATH	TIME (NS)
Data Loop		
Pipeline register	Clock to output	9
'AS888-1	A, B to C_{n+8}	30
'AS888-1	C_n to C_{n+8}, OVR, Z, Y	27
Register	Setup time	2
	Total for data loop	68
Control Loop		
Pipeline register	Clock to output	9
MUX	Select to output	13
'AS890-1	$\overline{CC}$ to output	25
PROM	Access time	20
Pipeline register	Setup time	2
	Total Control Loop	69
	Critical path for 'AS888 addition	69

Table 3-3. Am2903A/Am2910A Timings for Addition with Shift

COMPONENT	DATA PATH	TIME (NS)
Data Loop		
Pipeline register	Clock to output	9
Am2903A	A, B to $\overline{G}$, $\overline{P}$	52
Am2902A	$\overline{G0}$, $\overline{P0}$ to C_{n+z}	7
Am2903A	C_n to C_{n+4}, $\overline{SIO0}$	23
Am2903A	$\overline{SIO(n)}$ shift to Y	23
Am2903A	RAM setup	5
	Total for data loop	119
Control Loop		
Pipeline register	Clock to output	9
MUX	Select to output	13
Am2910A	$\overline{CC}$ to output	30
PROM	Access time	20
Pipeline register	Setup time	2
	Total for control loop	74
Critical path for AM2903 addition with shift		119

Table 3-4. 'AS888-1/'AS890-1 Timings for Addition with Shift

COMPONENT	DATA PATH	TIME (NS)
Data Loop		
Pipeline register	Clock to output	9
'AS888-1	A, B to C_{n+8}	30
'AS888-1	C_n to C_{n+8}, $\overline{SIO0}$	25
'AS888-1	$\overline{SIO(n)}$ shift to Y	14
'AS888-1	Register file setup time	2
	Total for data loop	80
Control Loop		
Pipeline register	Clock to output	9
MUX	Select to output	13
'AS890-1	$\overline{CC}$ to output	25
PROM	Access time	20
Pipeline register	Setup time	2
	Total for control loop	69
Critical path for 'AS888 addition with shift		80

Table 3-5. Am2903A/Am2910A Timings for Multiplication

COMPONENT	DATA PATH	TIME (NS)
Data Loop		
Am2918	Clock to output	27
Am2903A	I8-I0 to $\overline{G}$, $\overline{P}$	71
Am2902A	$\overline{G0}$, $\overline{P0}$ to C_{n+z}	7
Am2903A	C_n to C_{n+4}, $\overline{SIO0}$	23
Am2903A	$\overline{SIO(n)}$ shift to Y	23
	Total for data loop	151
Control Loop		
Pipeline register	Clock to output	9
MUX	Select to output	13
Am2910A	$\overline{CC}$ to output	30
PROM	Access time	20
Pipeline register	Setup time	2
	Total for control loop	74
Critical path for Am2903 multiplication		151

Table 3-6. Am2903A/Am2910A Timings for Division

COMPONENT	DATA PATH	TIME (NS)
Data Loop		
Am2918	Clock to output	27
Am2903A	I8-I0 to $\overline{G}$, $\overline{P}$	50
Am2902A	$\overline{G0}$, $\overline{P0}$ to C_{n+z}	7
Am2903A	C_n to C_{n+4}, $\overline{SIO0}$	32
Am2903A	$\overline{SIO(n)}$ shift to Y	23
	Total for data loop	139
Control Loop		
Pipeline register	Clock to output	9
MUX	Select to output	13
Am2910A	$\overline{CC}$ to output	30
PROM	Access time	20
Pipeline register	Setup time	2
	Total for control loop	74
Critical path for Am2903 division		139

Table 3-7. 'AS888-1/'AS890-1 Timings for Multiplication and Division

COMPONENT	DATA PATH	TIME (NS)
Data Loop		
'AS888-1	Clock to C_{n+8}	46
'AS888-1	C_n to $\overline{SIO}$	25
'AS888-1	$\overline{SIO(n)}$ shift to Y	14
'AS888-1	Register file setup time	2
	Total for data loop	87
Control Loop		
Pipeline register	Clock to output	9
MUX	Select to output	13
'AS890-1	$\overline{CC}$ to output	25
PROM	Access time	20
Pipeline register	Setup time	2
	Total Control Loop	69
Critical path for 'AS888 multiplication or division		87

Table 3-8. Am2901C/Am2910A Timings for Addition

COMPONENT	DATA PATH	TIME (NS)
Data Loop		
Pipeline register	Clock to output	9
Am2901C	A, B to $\overline{G}$, $\overline{P}$	37
Am2902A	$\overline{G0}$, $\overline{P0}$ to C_{n+z}	7
Am2901C	C_n to C_{n+4}, OVR, F3, F = 0, Y	25
Register	Setup time	2
	Total for data loop	80
Control Loop		
Pipeline register	Clock to output	9
MUX	Select to output	13
Am2910A	$\overline{CC}$ to output	30
PROM	Access time	20
Pipeline register	Setup time	2
	Total for control loop	74
Critical path for Am2901C addition		80

Table 3-9. Am2901C/Am2910A Timings for Addition with Shift

COMPONENT	DATA PATH	TIME (NS)
Data Loop		
Pipeline register	Clock to output	9
Am2901C	A, B to $\overline{G}$, $\overline{P}$	37
Am2902A	$\overline{G0}$, $\overline{P0}$ to C_{n+z}	7
Am2901C	C_n to F3, OVR	22
XOR and MUX		21
Am2901C	RAM3 setup	12
	Total for data loop	108
Control Loop		
Pipeline register	Clock to output	9
MUX	Select to output	13
Am2910A	$\overline{CC}$ to output	30
PROM	Access time	20
Pipeline register	Setup time	2
	Total for control loop	74
Critical path for Am2903 addition with shift		108

Table 3-10. Summary of Results

	CALCULATED TIMINGS								
	DATA PATHS			CONTROL PATHS			SYSTEM CLOCK		
Operation	Am2901C	Am2903A	'AS888-1	Am2901C	Am2903A	'AS888-1	Am2901C	Am2903A	'AS888-1
Addition	80	108	68	74	74	69	80	108	69
Addition with Shift	108	119	80	74	74	69	108	119	80
Multiplication	—	151	87	—	74	69	—	151	87
Division	—	139	87	—	74	69	—	139	87

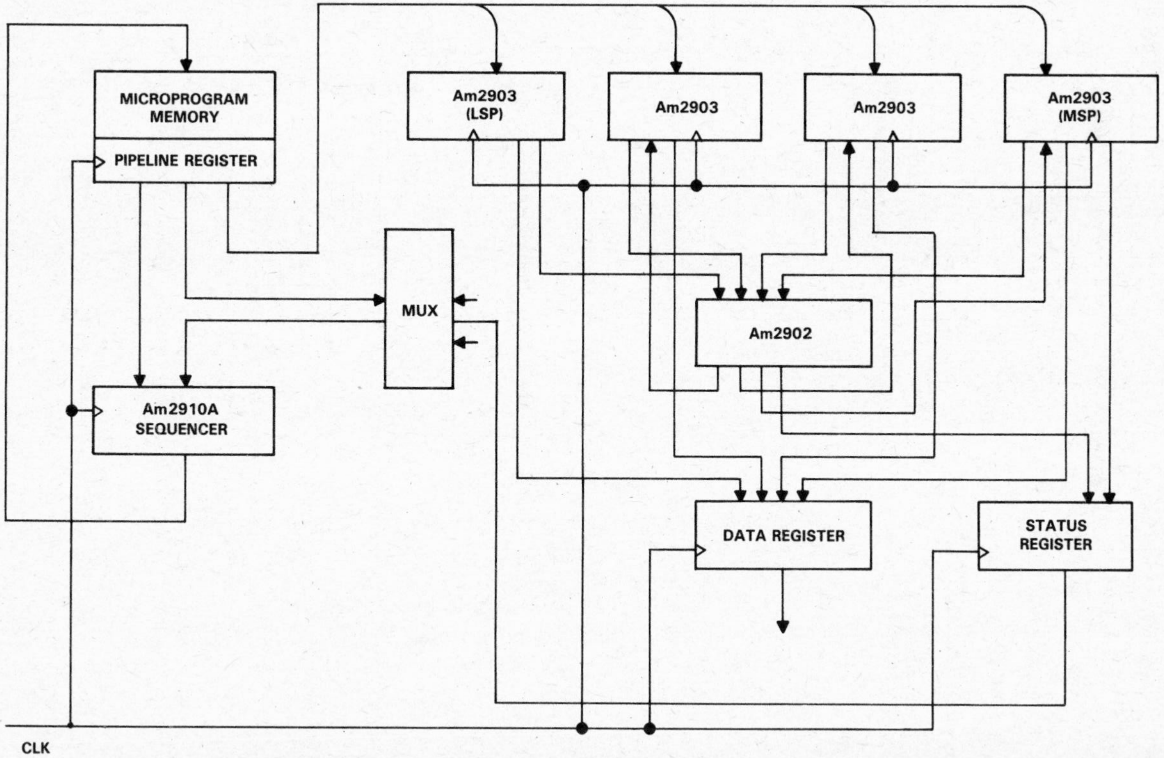
MICROPROGRAM MEMORY
PIPELINE REGISTER
Am2910A SEQUENCER
MUX
Am2903 (LSP)
Am2903
Am2903
Am2903 (MSP)
Am2902
DATA REGISTER
STATUS REGISTER
CLK

Figure 3-2. Am2903-Based 16-Bit Computer System

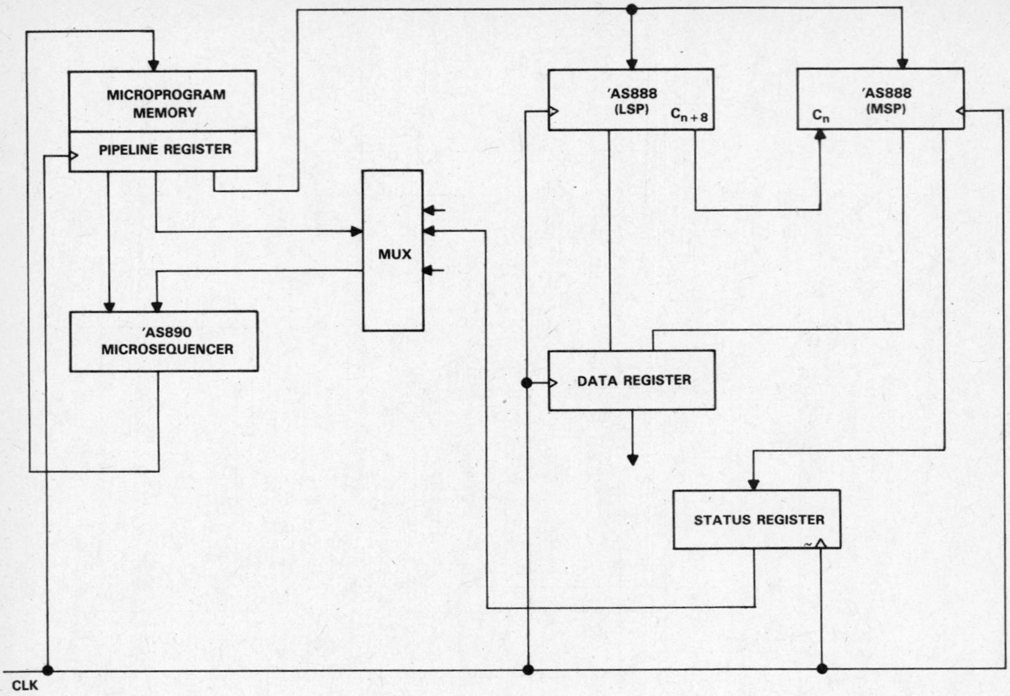
MICROPROGRAM MEMORY
PIPELINE REGISTER
'AS890 MICROSEQUENCER
MUX
'AS888 (LSP)
C_{n+8}
'AS888 (MSP)
C_n
DATA REGISTER
STATUS REGISTER
CLK

Figure 3-3. 'AS888-Based 16-Bit Computer System

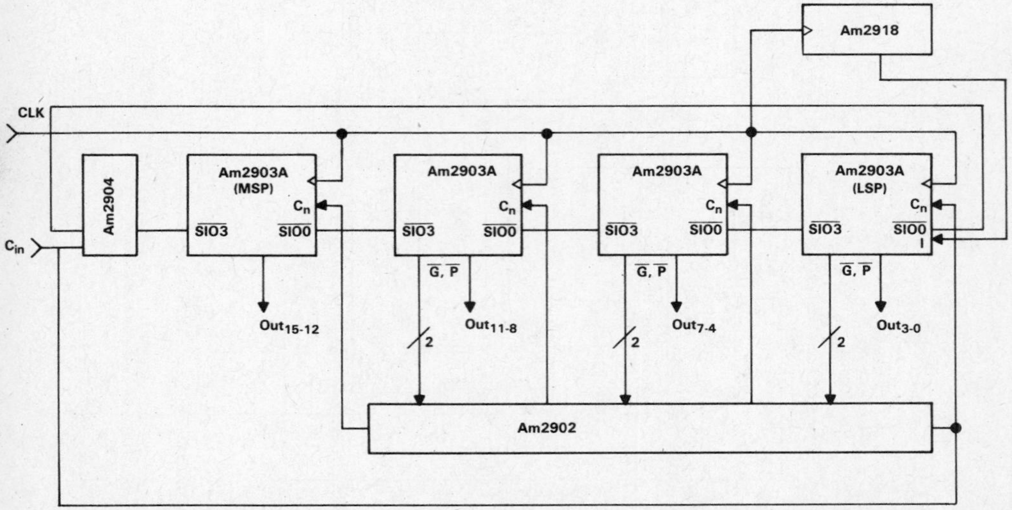
Am2918
CLK
C_{in}
Am2904
Am2903A (MSP)
Am2903A
Am2903A
Am2903A (LSP)
C_n
$\overline{SIO3}$
$\overline{SIO0}$
I
$\overline{G}, \overline{P}$
Out_{15-12}
Out_{11-8}
Out_{7-4}
Out_{3-0}
2
Am2902

Figure 3-4. ALU Path for Multiplication and Division in the Am2903A System

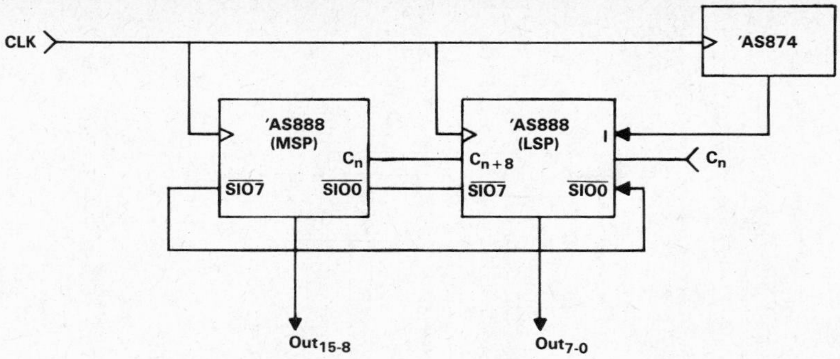
CLK
'AS874
'AS888
(MSP)
Cn
SIO7
SIO0
'AS888
(LSP)
Cn+8
SIO7
SIO0
I
Cn
Out15-8
Out7-0

Figure 3-5. ALU Path for Multiplication and Division in the 'AS888 System

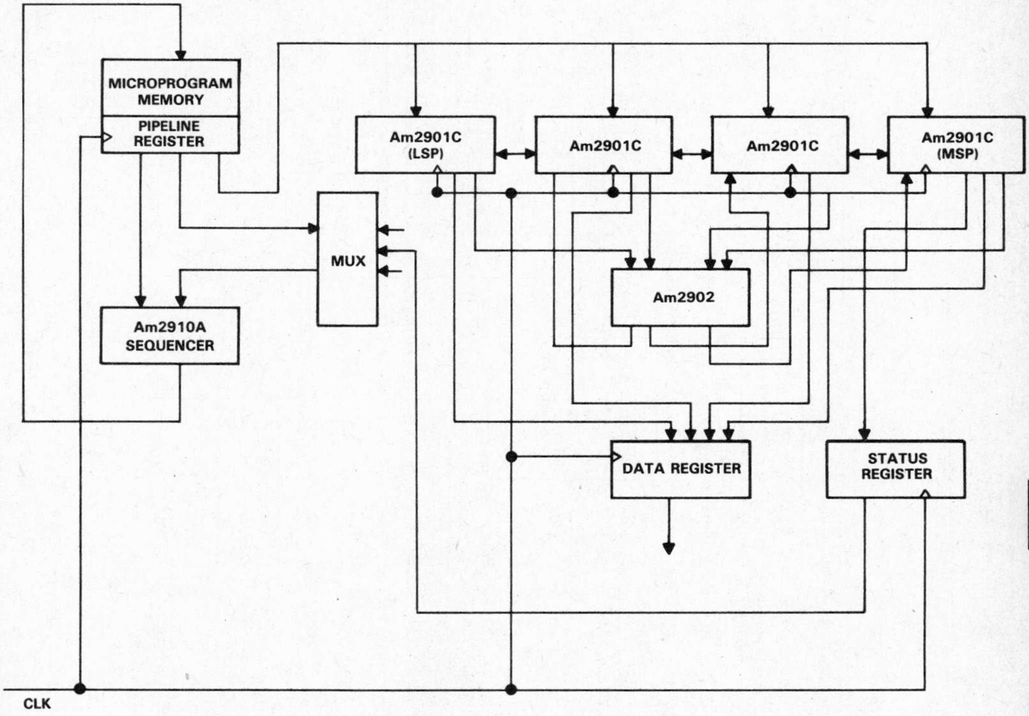
MICROPROGRAM
MEMORY
PIPELINE
REGISTER
Am2901C
(LSP)
Am2901C
Am2901C
Am2901C
(MSP)
MUX
Am2902
Am2910A
SEQUENCER
DATA REGISTER
STATUS
REGISTER
CLK

Figure 3-6. Am2901C-Based 16-Bit Computer System

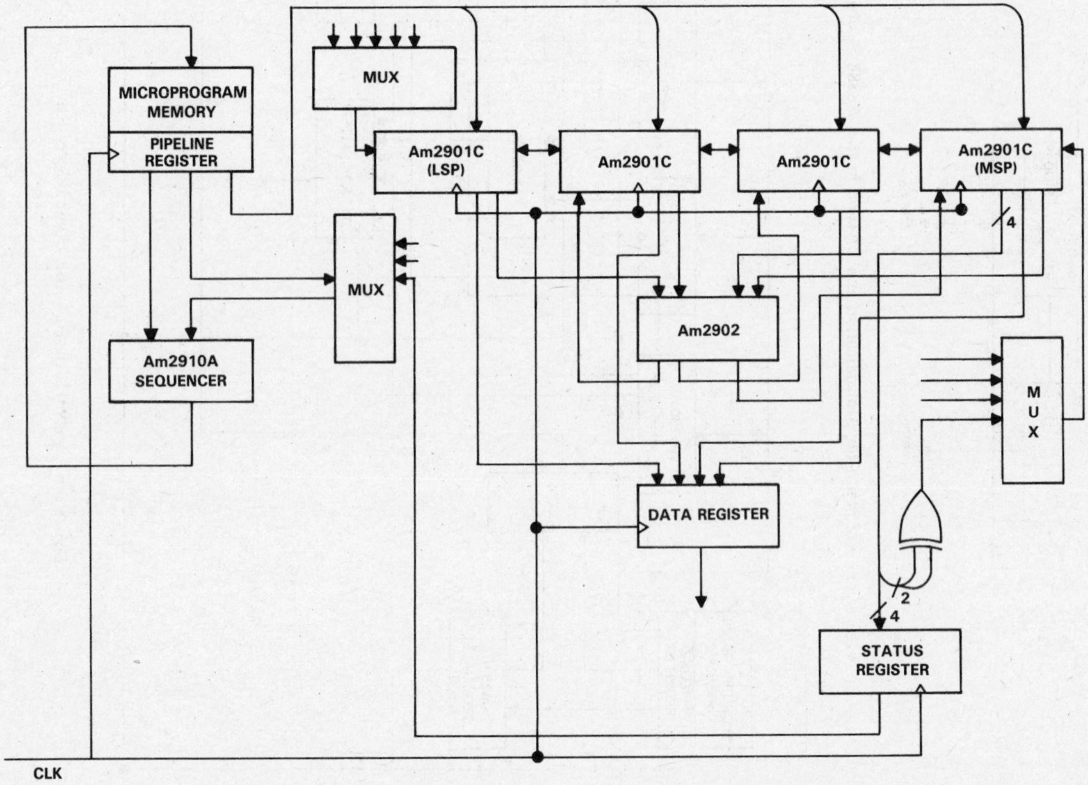
MICROPROGRAM MEMORY
PIPELINE REGISTER
Am2910A SEQUENCER
MUX
MUX
Am2901C (LSP)
Am2901C
Am2901C
Am2901C (MSP)
Am2902
DATA REGISTER
M U X
STATUS REGISTER
4
2
4
CLK

Figure 3-7. Modified Design of Am2901C-Based System

Section 4
32-Bit CPU Design With the 'AS888/'AS890

Microprogramming and bit slice technology have made possible the development of powerful systems using flexible instructions sets and wide address/data buses to access more than one gigaword of physical main memory. This section discusses one design approach to such a system, using 'AS888 bit slice and 'AS890 microsequencer components.

A structured approach to system design, such as that illustrated in Figure 4-1, is recommended in developing custom bit-slice designs. The product specification gives a starting point or basis for the project. In this example, four 'AS888 bit slices are used to implement the 32-bit arithmetic portion of the CPU, and an 'AS890 microsequencer is used for ALU and system control. A group of PROMs stores the microinstructions; a writable control store could also be implemented using additional control logic and components to load and modify the microprogram memory. The system is designed to access more than one gigaword of memory.

Since speed is a concern, carry look-ahead rather than ripple-through logic is recommended. If ripple-through logic were used, the system clock would need to be slowed down to allow the propagation of the carry bits through the various 'AS888 stages. By using carry look-ahead, the amount of time needed for the data to stabilize is greatly reduced by anticipating the carry across the 'AS888 packages.

So that the scratchpad area can be used for address calculations and mathematical computations, the 'AS888's internal register file is dedicated for system functions. To provide the system user with a macrolevel equivalent of register locations, a 16-word external register file is also included. Access to the external register file is under microprogram control, allowing address selection to come from the microcode itself or from one of the three operand fields of the instruction register.

PROMs eliminate the use of main memory as a source for constants used in initialization or table look-up functions. Accessing main memory for table values would require time and slow system throughput; by placing fixed values in fast PROMs, access time is kept to a minimum and system throughput is not altered.

Control, data and address buses shared by the system are accessed by three-state registers. The control register supplies the non-CPU part of a computer system with control signals. The data bus allows the ALU to supply data for the rest of the system and can also be a source of data for the ALU; this is accomplished by using three-state registers to drive the bidirectional data bus, along with registers to sample the bus. The address bus uses one of the external register file locations to maintain a program counter, thus allowing a 32-bit address bus capable of addressing about 4 gigawords

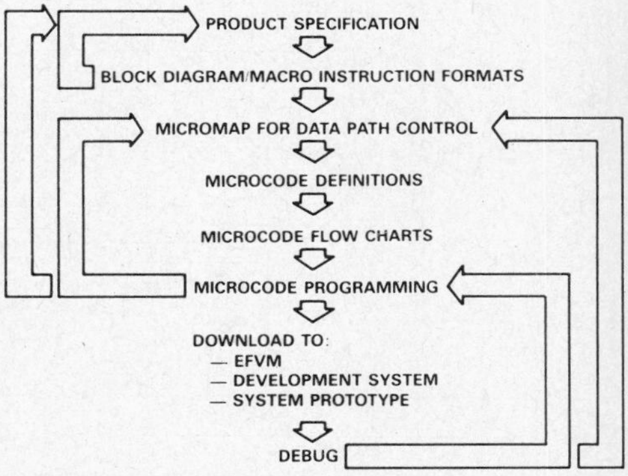
PRODUCT SPECIFICATION
BLOCK DIAGRAM/MACRO INSTRUCTION FORMATS
MICROMAP FOR DATA PATH CONTROL
MICROCODE DEFINITIONS
MICROCODE FLOW CHARTS
MICROCODE PROGRAMMING
DOWNLOAD TO:
— EFVM
— DEVELOPMENT SYSTEM
— SYSTEM PROTOTYPE
DEBUG

Figure 4-1. System Design Approach

of main memory. Using three-state drivers for this bus enables other subsystems to take control of the system buses.

A pipeline register supplies the microsequencer and the ALU with both data and instructions. To get macrocode into the system, an instruction register and a mapping PROM are used to convert the opcode to a microprogram routine address. The condition code signal, used for testing various conditions, is supplied by a register-input-based PAL. PAL inputs can be fixed values or combinations of the status signals coming from the ALU. The read address select pins for the 'AS888's internal B register can be sourced from the microword itself or from three nibbles of the macroword, to provide offsets for the N-way branches to various microcode routines.

DESIGNING A 32-BIT SYSTEM

A typical 32-bit system block diagram using the 'AS888 Bit-Slice and 'AS890 Microsequencer is shown in Figures 4-2 and 4-3. It can be broken down into two sections, the ALU (arithmetic logic unit) and the CCU (computer control unit). The ALU section performs all manipulation of data both to and from main memory, such as arithmetic and logical operations. The CCU section controls instruction (macro-code) flow and any miscellaneous control operations, such as fetching instructions or supplying addresses for main memory access.

Construction of the ALU

To cascade the four 'AS888s to obtain the 32-bit arithmetic unit shown in Figure 4-4, the shift multiplex $\overline{\text{SIO0}}$

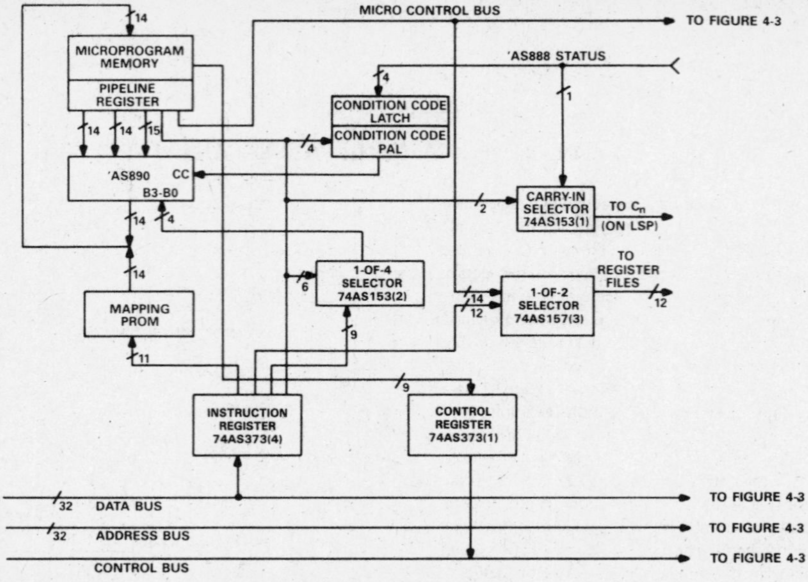
MICRO CONTROL BUS
TO FIGURE 4-3
'AS888 STATUS
MICROPROGRAM MEMORY
PIPELINE REGISTER
CONDITION CODE LATCH
CONDITION CODE PAL
'AS890
CC
B3-B0
CARRY-IN SELECTOR 74AS153(1)
TO C_n (ON LSP)
TO REGISTER FILES
1-OF-4 SELECTOR 74AS153(2)
1-OF-2 SELECTOR 74AS157(3)
MAPPING PROM
INSTRUCTION REGISTER 74AS373(4)
CONTROL REGISTER 74AS373(1)
DATA BUS
ADDRESS BUS
CONTROL BUS
TO FIGURE 4-3
TO FIGURE 4-3
TO FIGURE 4-3

Figure 4-2. CCU Block Diagram

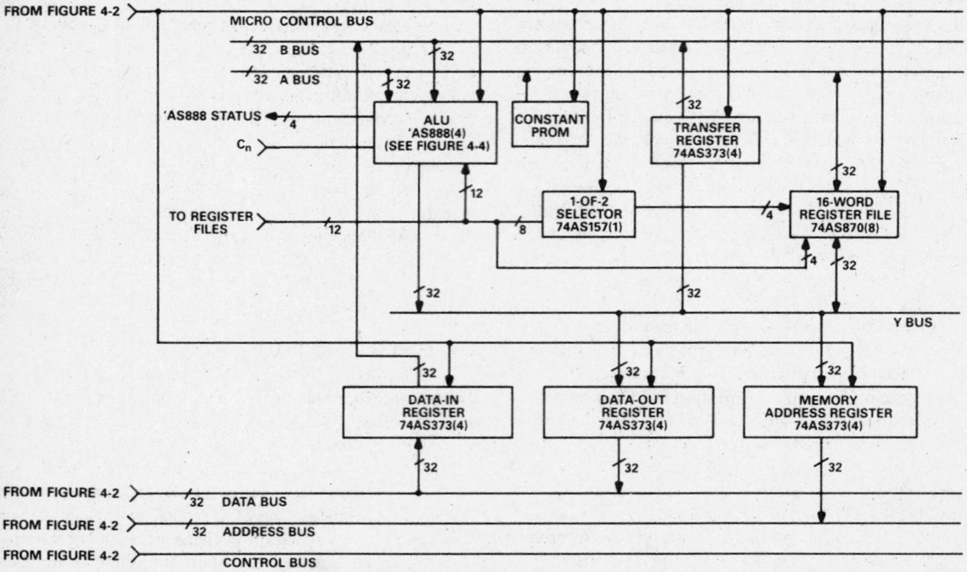
FROM FIGURE 4-2
MICRO CONTROL BUS
B BUS
A BUS
'AS888 STATUS
C_n
ALU 'AS888(4) (SEE FIGURE 4-4)
CONSTANT PROM
TRANSFER REGISTER 74AS373(4)
TO REGISTER FILES
1-OF-2 SELECTOR 74AS157(1)
16-WORD REGISTER FILE 74AS870(8)
Y BUS
DATA-IN REGISTER 74AS373(4)
DATA-OUT REGISTER 74AS373(4)
MEMORY ADDRESS REGISTER 74AS373(4)
FROM FIGURE 4-2
DATA BUS
FROM FIGURE 4-2
ADDRESS BUS
FROM FIGURE 4-2
CONTROL BUS

Figure 4-3. ALU Block Diagram

3 Application Reports

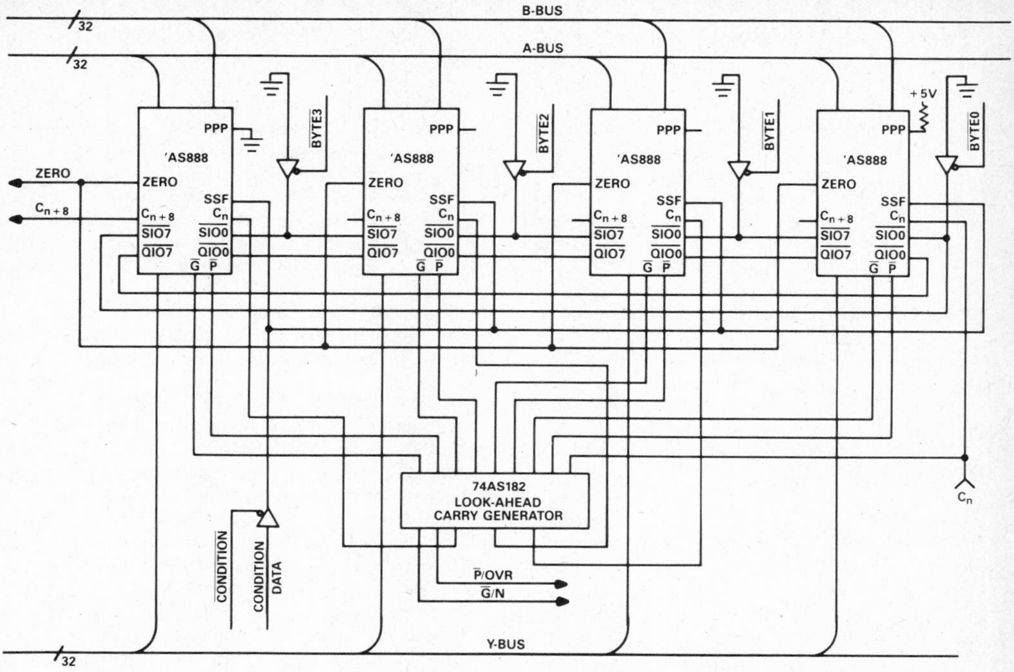
B-BUS
A-BUS
32
32
'AS888
'AS888
'AS888
'AS888
PPP
ZERO
Cn+8
ZERO
SSF
Cn+8
Cn
SIO7
SIO0
QIO7
QIO0
G P
BYTE3
BYTE2
BYTE1
BYTE0
+5V
74AS182
LOOK-AHEAD
CARRY GENERATOR
Cn
CONDITION
CONDITION DATA
P/OVR
G/N
Y-BUS
32

Figure 4-4. Cascaded 'AS888 Packages

and $\overline{\text{QIO0}}$ terminals are connected to the $\overline{\text{SIO7}}$ and $\overline{\text{QIO7}}$ terminals of adjacent packages, and the least significant package's signals are connected to the most-significant package's. Optionally, the SN74ALS240 inverting gates can be connected to the $\overline{\text{SIO0}}$-$\overline{\text{SIO7}}$ terminals and the byte inputs to implement byte and bit control. Another chip, the SN74AS182 look-ahead carry generator, provides a ripple-carry function, to help system throughput.

The design includes a 16-word register file, the SN74AS870 (see Figure 4-3). This allows the user to access 16 working areas for temporary data storage or address calculations such as indexing. In this design example, the 'AS888's internal register file is not accessible directly by the user; it is reserved for microcode operations, such as address computation and temporary storage for arithmetic operations. Addressing the register files is permitted through the microprogram or from the macrocode instruction register under microcode control. The transfer register connected to the 'AS888's Y and DB buses allows for feedback into the 'AS888 under microprogram control. Since the constant PROMs and the external register file share the A bus, they cannot be accessed at the same time. The transfer register enables data from the external register file to be transmitted to the B bus, making possible the addition of operands from the constant PROMs and the external register file, for example.

Constant PROMs are also included to simplify the programming and operation of the ALU by supplying fixed data for various operations, such as:

1. Clearing the system register files for initialization. This brings the system up to a known state.
2. Supplying a correction value to the offset in a branch instruction,i.e., converting a 16-bit offset to a true 32-bit address.
3. Table look-up for fixed mathematical operations, such as computing sines and cosines.

Construction of the CCU

Sequencing and branching operations at speeds compatible with the 'AS888 are supplied by the 'AS890, a microprogrammed controller working as a powerful microsequencer. Features of the 'AS890 include:

1. Stack capability. The 9-word stack can be accessed by using a stack pointer or a read pointer; the latter is designed for nondestructive dumping of the stack contents.
2. Register/counter facility. Two registers, DRA and DRB, can be used for latching data from the external data buses or as counters for loops.

A ZERO signal is generated when the decremented counter reaches a zero value.

3. Interrupt control. A register for temporarily holding the return address is supplied; upon entering the interrupt routine, the contents of the return register must be pushed onto the stack for later use.
4. Next address generation. The Y output multiplexer offers a selection of same or incremented address, address from DRA or DRB buses, address from stack, or a concatenation of DRA13-DRA4 and B3-B0.

A microprogram memory/pipeline register supplies the microsequencer and the rest of the system with instructions (see Figure 4-2). The memory might consist of ROMs, or it could be a writable-control store with support logic to allow loading or updating of the control store. For a general purpose machine with a fixed instruction set, ROMs would be more economic.

Some 'AS890 instructions are influenced by the $\overline{\text{CC}}$ input. Many are variations of branch and jump instructions. To form and supply $\overline{\text{CC}}$, a register can be used to latch the state of the 'AS888 and supply inputs to a PAL for decoding, based upon the microcode's needs. Combinatorial logic in the PAL allows multiple or single events to be selected or provides a fixed value of "1" or "0" for forced conditions.

To supply the microsequencer with the proper address of the microcode-equivalent version of the macrocode instruction, an instruction register and mapping PROM are needed. Under microprogram control, the instruction register samples the data bus to get the macrocode instruction. The opcode portion is passed to the mapping PROM to form an address to the microcode routine. When the microcode is ready to jump to the routine, it turns off the Y bus output of the 'AS890 and enables the output of the mapping PROM. An optional means of altering the address uses B3-B0 inputs of the 'AS890 to implement an N-way branch routine. In this method, the ten most significant address bits of DRA or DRA are concatenated with the B3-B0 bits to supply an address.

Control information is supplied to the rest of the system via the control register and bus. By setting various bits within the control register, information can be passed to other subsystems, such as memory and I/O peripherals. Bit 0 could represent the read/write control line while bit 1 could select memory or I/O for the read/write. Bit 2 might function to enable interrupts and bit 3 to indicate when the system should enter a "wait" state for slow memory. The remaining control bits can be programmed by the system designer to indicate additional condition states of the "macrosystem'.

Addressing of the register files, both 'AS888 internal and 'AS870 external, is done through the use of two 1-of-2 selector banks. The first bank selects address source; this design offers a choice for operand processing of fixed values from the microcode or values from the macroinstruction latched in the instruction register. The second bank selects the first or second operand as an address source for port 0 of the external register file; port 1 uses the third operand as an address source. It should be noted that the design presented in Figure 4-2 is a one-level pipeline that is instruction-data based. The address and contents of the next instruction are being fetched while the current instruction is being executed. Tracing through the data flow, the following can be observed:

1. The pipeline register contains the current instruction being executed
2. The ALU has just executed its instruction, and has the current status ready at its output pins
3. The status register that is attached to the ALU contains the previous instruction's resulting status
4. The contents of the next microprogram word are being fetched at the same time that the current instruction is being executed.

TRACING THROUGH A 32-BIT COMPUTER

With the 'AS888 and 'AS890 as foundation chips, the typical 32-bit supermini of Figures 4-2 and 4-3 can now be functionally traced. First, note that the data of the main program is handled separately from that of the microcode—each on its own bus. The system is initialized by setting the "clear" signal high—this causes a forced jump to the beginning of the microcode memory. Instructions carried out by the microcode at this point might run system diagnostics, clear all registers throughout the 'AS888-based system, and set up the initial macrocode program address. In this design, the first program address to fetch an instruction from main memory comes from a fixed value in the microcode memory; it is possible to allow the address to be retrieved from a permanent location in main memory or from either a front panel or console, by modifying the microcode program slightly.

Table 4-1 illustrates the microcode format for this design. Note that it contains control signals for all chips involved in the design. Some of these, such as $\overline{\text{TRANSLATCH}}$ and $\overline{\text{MARLATCH}}$, are used with the system clock to provide controlled loading of the various holding registers. Others supply necessary addressing information, directing input from either the main data bus or from the microcode word itself.

The FETCH routine is shown in functional, assembler and microcoded forms in Tables 4-2, 4-3 and 4-4. First, the program counter is read from the external register file and stored into the memory address register. After the program counter is placed on the address bus, the program counter is updated and stored while the data from memory is allowed to settle down to a stable condition. The data is then latched in both the instruction register and data-in register.

The opcode field of the instruction register is passed through the mapping PROM to convert the opcode to an equivalent microcode routine address. When $\overline{\text{YOE}}$ is forced high by the microcode, the 'AS890 is three-stated from the Y bus and the mapping PROM's output is taken out of the three-state mode to supply an address to the control store (microprogram memory); a forced jump is made to the microcode routine to perform the instruction.

Table 4-1. Microcode Definition

MICROCODE FIELD	PIN NAME	INPUT TO	FUNCTION
0–13	DRA13–DRA0	'AS890	Used for next-address branches
14–27	DRB13–DRB0	'AS890	Used for loading counter
28–30	RC2–RC0	'AS890	Register/counter controls
31–33	S2–S0	'AS890	Stack control
34–36	MUX2–MUX0	'AS890	MUX control of Y output bus
37	$\overline{\text{INT}}$	'AS890	Interrupt control
38	$\overline{\text{RAOE}}$	'AS890	Enables DRA output
39	$\overline{\text{RBOE}}$	'AS890	Enables DRB output
40	OSEL	'AS890	Mux control for DRA source
41	INC	'AS890	Incrementer control
42	$\overline{\text{YOE}}$	'AS890	Enables Y output bus
43–50	I7-I0	'AS888	Instruction inputs
51	$\overline{\text{OEA}}$	'AS888	DA bus enable
52	$\overline{\text{EA}}$	'AS888	ALU input operand select
53	$\overline{\text{OEB}}$	'AS888	DB bus enable
54	OEY	'AS888	Y bus output enable
55	SELY	'AS888	Y bus select
56–57	EB1–EB0	'AS888	ALU input operand selects
58	$\overline{\text{WE}}$	'AS888	Register file write enable
59	$\overline{\text{MAP}}$	PROM	Enables mapping PROM to 'AS890 Y bus
60	$\overline{\text{IR}}$	Latch	Latches data bus to instruction register
61	$\overline{\text{CR}}$	Latch	Latches control data to bus
62–69	CTRL7–CTRL0	Latch	Data for control latch
70–71	BSEL1–BSEL0	Multiplexer	Selects data for 'AS890
72–75	B3–B0	Multiplexer	Microcode data to switch
76	$\overline{\text{CONDCD}}$	Latch	Controls latch of 'AS888 status
77–80	SELC3–SELC0	PAL	Selects combination of 'AS888 status
81	$\overline{\text{DTALATCHI}}$	Latch	Controls latching of data-in
82	$\overline{\text{DTAIN}}$	Latch	Enables data-in output to bus
83	$\overline{\text{DTALATCHO}}$	Latch	Controls latching of data-out
84	$\overline{\text{DTAOUT}}$	Latch	Enables data-out output to DB bus
85	$\overline{\text{MARLATCH}}$	Latch	Controls latching of address
86	$\overline{\text{MAR}}$	Latch	Enables MAR output to address bus
87	$\overline{\text{CONSTPROM}}$	PROM	Enables PROM to DA bus
88–99	A11–A0	PROM	Address of constant in PROM
100	SWITCH2	Multiplexer	Selects microcode or Instruction Register data
101	SWITCH1	Multiplexer	Selects microcode or Instruction Register data
102–105	A3–A0	Multiplexer	Register file address ('AS888)
106–109	B3–B0	Multiplexer	Register file address ('AS888)
110–113	C3–C0	Multiplexer	Register file address ('AS888)
114	$\overline{\text{REGUWR}}$	Register File	Port 0 write enable
115	$\overline{\text{REGLWR}}$	Register File	Port 1 write enable
116	$\overline{\text{REGU}}$	Register File	Chip enable on port 0
117	$\overline{\text{REGL}}$	Register File	Chip enable on port 1
118	$\overline{\text{TRANSLATCH}}$	Latch	Controls latch between Y and DB bus
119	$\overline{\text{TRANS}}$	Latch	Enables output to DB bus
120	SELCN2	Multiplexer	Supplies carry input to 'AS888
121	SELCN1	Multiplexer	Supplies carry input to 'AS888
122	REGUB	Multiplexer	Selects address for external register file
123–126	$\overline{\text{BYTE3}}$ – $\overline{\text{BYTE0}}$	Three-state	Enables data for byte/bit operations

Table 4-2. Functional Listing of Fetch

FETCH:	MAR = PC, Enable MAR output
	PC = PC + 1
	IR = DIR = data bus, Disable 'AS890 Y bus, Enable mapping PROM to Y bus

Table 4-3. Assembler Listing of Fetch

FETCH: OP890 ,,,111,10;INC;	Set 'AS890 for continue
OP888 NOP,GROUP5,10,,,1111;	Perform NOP and read external register 15
OEY;SELY;	Enable Y bus output
CR;CTRL 00000011;	Generate external control bus signals
SELC 01;	Select fixed CC value to 'AS890
MARLATCH;MAR;	Latch value on Y bus and enable output
SWITCH 00;REGL;	Select address source and enable port
TRANSLATCH	Latch Y bus for transfer to B bus
OP890 ,,,111,10;INC;	Set 'AS890 for continue
OP888 PASS,INCS,00,,,1111;	Increment program counter
OEB;OEY;	Enable Y bus output
SELC 01;	Select fixed CC value to 'AS890
MAR;	Output address to address bus
REGLWR;REGL;	Update program counter in register file
TRANS;	Enable transfer latch output to B bus
SELCN 01	Select carry input to LSP to be "1"
OP890 ,,,111,10;	Set 'AS890 for continue
OP888 NOP,GROUP5,10;	Perform NOP
MAP;	Enable mapping PROM to 'AS890 Y bus
IR;	Latch data bus to get macrolevel code
SELC 01	Select fixed CC value to 'AS890
DTALATCHI;	Put data bus also in data register
MAR	Output address to address bus

Key to Table 4-3

OP888 a,b,c,d,e,f
where:

a	=	upper bits of instruction, 17-14	d	=	A address of register files
b	=	lower bits of instruction, 13-10	e	=	B address of register files
c	=	value of EB1–EB0	f	=	C address of register files

OP890 v,w,x,y,z
where:

v	=	DRA value, 14-bits	y	=	S2–S0
w	=	DRB value, 14-bits	z	=	MUX2–MUX0
x	=	RC2–RC0			

After the routine is complete, a jump is made back to the FETCH routine by using the next-address supplied by the microprogram. It is up to the system designer/programmer to make sure that all system housekeeping is performed, so that nothing causes a fatal endless loop.

DEFINING THE MACROCODE INSTRUCTION FORMAT

Since this is a 32-bit design, a variety of instruction formats are available. The size of the opcode along with the types of addressing used, will affect both system size and performance. The formats shown in Table 4-5 will be used for discussion.

All Table 4-5 formats have an opcode field of 11 bits and source/destination fields of 7 bits; the first three bits of the latter designate the address type, and the remaining four bits are used for register access. The opcode length allows 2,048 macrocoded instructions to be mapped to equivalent microcoded routines. The address fields can specify any of the following modes: register, relative, autoincrement/autodecrement, indexed, absolute, and deferred. The offset used in the Type 0 instruction can be used for branch-based instructions, for an offset range of ± 32727.

TRACING A MACROCODE INSTRUCTION

Microcode for a Type 3 multiplication instruction is shown in Table 4-6, using the following assumptions:

1. Code for retrieving the operands will not be shown. Jumps will be made to routines that will place the temporary operands into internal register locations 2 and 3 of the 'AS888, after being fetched from main memory.

Table 4-4. Microcode Listing of Fetch

DRA13-DRA0	DRB13-DRB0	RC2-RC0	S2-S0	MUX2-MUX0	INT RAOE RBOE OSEL INC YOE	I7-I0	OEA EA OEB OEY SELY EB1 EB0 WE	MAP IR CR
0 0 0 0 0 0 0 0 0 0 0 0 0 0	0 0 0 0 0 0 0 0 0 0 0 0 0 0	0 0 0	1 1 1	0 1 0	1 1 1 0 1 0	1 1 1 1 1 1 1 1	1 1 1 0 1 1 0 1	1 1 0
0 0 0 0 0 0 0 0 0 0 0 0 0 0	0 0 0 0 0 0 0 0 0 0 0 0 0 0	0 0 0	1 1 1	0 1 0	1 1 1 0 1 0	1 1 1 1 0 1 0 0	1 1 0 0 0 0 0 1	1 1 1
0 0 0 0 0 0 0 0 0 0 0 0 0 0	0 0 0 0 0 0 0 0 0 0 0 0 0 0	0 0 0	1 1 1	0 1 0	1 1 1 0 0 1	1 1 1 1 1 1 1 1	0 1 1 1 1 1 0 1	0 0 1

Table 4-4. Microcode Listing of Fetch (Continued)

CTRL7-CTRL0	BSEL1-BSEL0	B3-B0	CONDCO	SELC3-SELC0	DTALATCHI DTAIN DTALATCHO DTAOUT MARLATCH MAR CONSTPRROM	A11-A0	SWITCH2-SWITCH1	A3-A0	B3-B0	C3-C0	REGUWR REGLWR REGU REGL TRANSLATCH TRANS SELCN2 SELCN1 REGUB	BYTE3-BYTE0
0 0 0 0 0 0 1 1	0 0	0 0 0 0	1	0 0 0 1	1 1 1 1 0 0 1	0 0 0 0 0 0 0 0 0 0 0 0	0 0	0 0 0 0	0 0 0 0	1 1 1 1	1 1 1 0 0 1 0 0 0	1 1 1 1
0 0 0 0 0 0 0 0	0 0	0 0 0 0	1	0 0 0 1	1 1 1 1 1 0 1	0 0 0 0 0 0 0 0 0 0 0 0	0 0	0 0 0 0	0 0 0 0	1 1 1 1	1 0 1 0 1 0 0 1 0	1 1 1 1
0 0 0 0 0 0 0 0	0 0	0 0 0 0	1	0 0 0 1	0 1 1 1 1 0 1	0 0 0 0 0 0 0 0 0 0 0 0	0 0	0 0 0 0	0 0 0 0	0 0 0 0	1 1 1 1 1 1 0 0 0	1 1 1 1

Table 4-5. Possible Instruction Formats

TYPE 0 — OPCODE + 16-BIT OFFSET

0 — 10	11 — 15	16 — 31
Opcode	Not Used	Offset

TYPE 1 — OPCODE + DESTINATION

0 — 10	11 — 24	25 — 31
Opcode	Not used	Destination

TYPE 2 — OPCODE + SOURCE + DESTINATION

0 — 10	11 — 17	18 — 24	25 — 31
Opcode	Not used	Source	Destination

TYPE 3 — OPCODE + SOURCE1 + SOURCE2 + DESTINATION

0 — 10	11 — 17	18 — 24	25 — 31
Opcode	Source	Source	Destination

Table 4-6. Functional Listing of Multiply

```
UMULI3:
  JUMPSUB SOURCE1                 Get first operand
  JUMPSUB SOURCE2,                Get second operand
    BCOUNT=32                     Load DB counter register
  REG 9=0                         Clear temporary accumulator
  MQ=REG 2                        Load multiplier
LOOP:
  UMULI WITH REG 3                Issue the multiply
    DECREMENT BCOUNT,             Decrement the DB counter
    BRANCH TO LOOP IF NOT ZERO,   Loop back until done
    LATCH 'AS888 STATUS,          Store 'AS888 flags
    REG 9=ALU                     Store intermediate result
  REG 8=MQ                        Store intermediate result
  JUMPSUB STORPSW                 Update macro program status
  JUMPSUB MDEST                   Store result at destination
  JUMP FETCH                      Get next instruction
```

3 Application Reports

Table 4-7. Assembler Code of Multiply

UMULI3:	
OP890 SOURCE1,,,110,110;	Perform a subroutine branch
INC;YOE;	Increment address and enable Y bus
OP888 NOP;GROUP5;	Tell 'AS888 to do nothing during jump
SELC 0001;	Set CC to "1" to set up 'AS890 continue
MAR	Maintain address on main address buss
OP890 SOURCE2,0000000100000,110,110,110;	Perform subroutine branch and load B counter
INC;YOE;	Increment microaddress and enable Y bus
OP888 NOP,GROUP5;	Tell 'AS888 to do nothing during jump
SELC 0001;	Set CC to "1" to set up 'AS890 continue
MAR	Maintain address on main address bus
OP890 ,,,111,110;	Perform a continue instruction
INC;YOE;	Increment microaddress and enable Y bus
OP888 CLEAR,GROUP5,,,,1001;	Zero out register file accumulator
WE;	Enable writing to register file
SELC 0001;	Set CC to "1" to set up 'AS890 continue
MAR	Maintain address on main address buss
OP890 LOOP,,,111,110;	Perform a continue instruction
INC;YOE;	Increment microaddress and enable Y bus
OP888 LOADMQ,INCS,,,0010;	Load MQ register with S + Cn, from external register file
MAR	Maintain address on main address bus
LOOP:	
OP890 LOOP,,101,111,100;	Decrement B and loop til ZERO = 1
INC;YOE;	Increment microaddress and enable Y bus
OP888 UMULI,GROUP4,01,0011,,1001;	Perform unsigned multiply on accumulator
WE;	Update register file accumulator
MAR	Maintain address on main address bus
OP890 ,,,111,110;	Perform a continue instruction
INC;YOE;	Increment microaddress and enable Y bus
OP888 PASS,INCS,,,,1000;	Put S + Cn in temporary register file
WE;	Allow updating of register file
MAR	Maintain address on main address bus
OP890 STORPSW,,,110,110;	Perform a subroutine branch
INC;YOE;	Increment microaddress and enable Y bus
OP888 NOP,GROUP5;	Tell 'AS888 to do nothing during jump
SELC 0001;	Set CC to "1" for set up 'AS890 continue
MAR	Maintain address on main address bus
OP890 FETCH,,,111;	Perform a branch to FETCH routine
INC;YOE;	Increment microaddress and enable Y bus
OP888 NOP,GROUP5;	Tell 'AS888 to do nothing during jump
SELC 0001	Set CC to "1" for 'AS890 continue

Key to Table 4-7.

OP888 a,b,c,d,e,f
where:
- a = upper bits of instruction, 17-14
- b = lower bits of instruction, 13-10
- c = value of EB1-EB0
- d = A address of register files
- e = B address of register files
- f = C address of register files

OP890 v,w,x,y,z
where:
- v = DRA value, 14-bits
- w = DRB value, 14-bits
- x = RC2-RC0
- y = S2-S0
- z = MUX2-MUX0

Table 4-8. Microcode Listing of Multiply

DRA13-DRA0	DRB13-DRB0	RC2-RC0	S2-S0	MUX2-MUX0	INT RAOE RBOE OSEL INC YOE	I7-I0	OEA EA OEB OEY SELY EB1 EB0 WE	MAP IR CR
0 0 0 0 0 0 0 0 0 0 1 1 0 0	0 0 0 0 0 0 0 0 0 0 0 0 0 0	0 0 0	1 1 0	1 1 0	1 1 1 0 1 0	1 1 1 1 1 1 1 1	1 1 1 1 0 0 0 1	1 1 1
0 0 0 0 0 0 0 0 0 1 0 0 0 0	0 0 0 0 0 0 0 0 1 0 0 0 0 0	1 1 0	1 1 0	1 1 0	1 1 1 0 1 0	1 1 1 1 1 1 1 1	1 1 1 1 0 0 0 1	1 1 1
0 0 0 0 0 0 0 0 0 0 0 0 0 0	0 0 0 0 0 0 0 0 0 0 0 0 0 0	0 0 0	1 1 1	1 1 0	1 1 1 0 1 0	1 1 1 1 0 0 0 0	1 1 1 0 0 0 0 0	1 1 1
0 0 0 0 1 0 0 0 0 0 1 0 0 0	0 0 0 0 0 0 0 0 0 0 0 0 0 0	0 0 0	1 1 1	1 1 0	1 1 1 0 1 0	1 1 1 0 0 1 0 0	1 1 1 0 0 0 0 1	1 1 1
0 0 0 0 1 0 0 0 0 0 1 0 0 0	0 0 0 0 0 0 0 0 0 0 0 0 0 0	1 0 1	1 1 1	1 0 0	1 1 1 0 1 0	1 1 0 1 0 0 0 0	1 1 1 0 0 0 1 0	1 1 1
0 0 0 0 0 0 0 0 0 0 0 0 0 0	0 0 0 0 0 0 0 0 0 0 0 0 0 0	0 0 0	1 1 1	1 0 1	1 1 1 0 1 0	1 1 1 1 1 1 1 1	1 1 1 0 0 0 1 0	1 1 1
0 0 0 0 0 0 0 0 0 1 0 1 0 0	0 0 0 0 0 0 0 0 0 0 0 0 0 0	0 0 0	1 1 0	1 1 0	1 1 1 0 1 0	1 1 1 1 1 1 1 1	1 1 1 1 0 0 0 1	1 1 1
0 0 0 0 0 0 0 0 0 1 1 0 0 0	0 0 0 0 0 0 0 0 0 0 0 0 0 0	0 0 0	1 1 0	1 1 0	1 1 1 0 1 0	1 1 1 1 1 1 1 1	1 1 1 1 0 0 0 1	1 1 1
0 0 0 0 0 0 0 0 0 0 0 0 1 1	0 0 0 0 0 0 0 0 0 0 0 0 0 0	0 0 0	1 1 1	0 0 0	1 1 1 0 1 0	1 1 1 1 1 1 1 1	1 1 1 1 0 0 0 1	1 1 1

Table 4-8. Microcode Listing of Multiply (Continued)

CTRL7-CTRL0	BSEL1-BSEL0	B3-B0	CONDCO	SELC3-SELC0	DTALATCHI DTAIN DTALATCHO DTAOUT MARLATCH MAR CONSTPRROM	A11-A0	SWITCH2-SWITCH1	A3-A0	B3-B0	C3-C0	REGUWR REGLWR REGU REGL TRANSLATCH TRANS SELCN2 SELCN1 REGUB	BYTE3-BYTE0
0 0 0 0 0 0 0 0	0 0	0 0 0 0	1	0 0 0 1	1 1 1 1 1 0 1	0 0 0 0 0 0 0 0 0 0 0 0	0 0	0 0 0 0	0 0 0 0	0 0 0 0	1 1 1 1 1 1 0 0 0	1 1 1 1
0 0 0 0 0 0 0 0	0 0	0 0 0 0	1	0 0 0 1	1 1 1 1 1 0 1	0 0 0 0 0 0 0 0 0 0 0 0	0 0	0 0 0 0	0 0 0 0	0 0 0 0	1 1 1 1 1 1 0 0 0	1 1 1 1
0 0 0 0 0 0 0 0	0 0	0 0 0 0	1	0 0 0 1	1 1 1 1 1 0 1	0 0 0 0 0 0 0 0 0 0 0 0	0 0	0 0 0 0	0 0 0 0	1 0 0 1	1 1 1 1 1 1 0 0 0	1 1 1 1
0 0 0 0 0 0 0 0	0 0	0 0 0 0	0	0 0 0 1	1 1 1 1 1 0 1	0 0 0 0 0 0 0 0 0 0 0 0	0 0	0 0 0 0	0 0 1 0	0 0 0 0	1 1 0 1 1 1 0 0 0	1 1 1 1
0 0 0 0 0 0 0 0	0 0	0 0 0 0	0	0 0 0 1	1 1 1 1 1 0 1	0 0 0 0 0 0 0 0 0 0 0 0	0 0	0 0 1 1	0 0 0 0	1 0 0 1	1 0 1 0 1 1 0 0 0	1 1 1 1
0 0 0 0 0 0 0 0	0 0	0 0 0 0	0	0 0 0 1	1 1 1 1 1 0 1	0 0 0 0 0 0 0 0 0 0 0 0	0 0	0 0 0 0	0 0 0 0	1 0 0 0	1 0 1 0 1 1 0 0 0	1 1 1 1
0 0 0 0 0 0 0 0	0 0	0 0 0 0	0	0 0 0 1	1 1 1 1 1 0 1	0 0 0 0 0 0 0 0 0 0 0 0	0 0	0 0 0 0	0 0 0 0	0 0 0 0	1 1 1 1 1 1 0 0 0	1 1 1 1
0 0 0 0 0 0 0 0	0 0	0 0 0 0	1	0 0 0 1	1 1 1 1 1 0 1	0 0 0 0 0 0 0 0 0 0 0 0	0 0	0 0 0 0	0 0 0 0	0 0 0 0	1 1 1 1 1 1 0 0 0	1 1 1 1
0 0 0 0 0 0 0 0	0 0	0 0 0 0	1	0 0 0 1	1 1 1 1 1 1 1	0 0 0 0 0 0 0 0 0 0 0 0	0 0	0 0 0 0	0 0 0 0	0 0 0 0	1 1 1 1 1 1 0 0 0	1 1 1 1

2. A jump to a routine to store the product in the destination will be handled similarly.
3. Multiplication will be unsigned; the result will be placed in two temporary locations of the 'AS888.
4. An update to the program status word, which the user can access at the macrocode level, must also be performed but is not shown.

Assembler code is shown in Table 4-7; a microcode listing is given in Table 4-8. The first two lines of microcode are subroutine jumps to opcode fetching routines, which store the operands in register files 2 and 3 in the 'AS888. The next two instructions load up the 'AS890 with a counter constant for the multiply loop, load the MQ register of the 'AS888 with the multiplier and clear the register that is temporarily used for the accumulator.

A loop is then entered to perform the multiply instruction 32 times to form the product, with the multiplicand coming from the internal register file of the 'AS888. Upon exiting the loop, the MQ register is stored in a temporary register location in the 'AS888. The MQ register now contains the least significant bits of the result and the temporary accumulator the most significant bits. A subroutine jump is made to the program status word update routine; this will take the status flags of the last multiplication iteration and change the macrolevel status word. The next subroutine jump is to a destination routine, which is followed by a branch to the FETCH routine to get the next macroinstruction to be executed.

SYSTEM ENHANCEMENTS

The above example provides a broad overview of 32-bit system design using the 'AS888 and 'AS890. Certain additional options may enhance system performance. These include:

1. Status latching. The design does not take into account changes that need to be examined at the microlevel while retaining macrolevel status information. One solution would be to include another register in parallel to the status latch

and provide control to choose between the two to form the condition code value.

2. Interrupts. To efficiently use a computer system, interrupts are used to alter program flow in the case of I/O programming and real-time applications (involving hardware timers). To include this capability, external hardware must be included and the microcode modified accordingly.
3. Control store. One way of implementing microprogram memory is to use a ROM-based design. It is becoming more common to design a writable control store, a completely RAM-based or part RAM, part ROM storage system, that can be altered by system operation, such as initialization from a floppy disk subsystem, or by the user to optimize or implement new macrolevel instructions. The cost of implementation must be weighed with the risks involved in changing instructions which may not be supported by other sites.
4. Instruction word definitions. Changing the instruction word definitions will have an effect on both system design and performance. Removing Type 3 instructions from the design, for example, will have an effect on both hardware and software: the external register file addressing must be changed and the 1-of-2 selector removed. Likewise, changing the opcode length may restrict the instruction address capability and also cause either an increase or decrease in the microcode size.
5. Dynamic memory access (DMA). The above system does not support dynamic memory access. To include this function requires a change in the address output control, along with support circuitry for the type of DMA selected. Some error detection and correction logic for main memory might also be included.
6. Computer control unit. The design presented here shows a one-level pipeline architecture that is instruction-data based. System throughput may be increased by converting to a pipeline of greater depth, or using another variety of one-level pipeline, such as instruction-address based or address-data based. Care must be taken when increasing the size of the pipeline, especially when handling branch/jump situations. The reader is advised to carefully research this area before implementing any design.

Table 4-9. Critical Delay Path Analysis

CONTROL LOOP			DATA LOOP		
COMPONENT	DATA PATH	TIME (NS)	COMPONENT	DATA PATH	TIME (NS)
Pipeline register	Clock to output	9	'AS888-1	Clock to C_n	46
MUX	Select to output	13	'AS182	C_n to C_{n+z}	5
'AS890-1	$\overline{CC}$ to output	25	'AS888-1	C_n to $\overline{SIO}$	25
PROM	Access time	20	'AS888-1	$\overline{SIO}$ to Y	14
Pipeline register	Setup time	2			
		69			90

Table 4-10. Fetch Timing Comparison

FETCH	'AS888 32-BIT	Z8001	8086-1	80286	68000L
Data width	32	16	16	16	16
No. of cycles	4	3	4	4	4
Clock rate	11.11 MHz	4 MHz	10 MHz	10 MHz	8 MHz
Total time	360 ns	750 ns	400 ns	400 ns	600 ns

Table 4-11. Multiply Timing Comparison

MULTIPLY	'AS888 32-BIT	'AS888 16-BIT	Z8001	8086-1	80286	68000L
Size	32 × 32	16 × 16	16 × 16	16 × 16	16 × 16	16 × 16
No. of cycles	35	19	70	128	21	≤74
Clock rate	11.11 MHz	10.98 MHz	4 MHz	10 MHz	10 MHz	8 MHz
Total time	3.150 μs	1.729 μs	17.5 μs	12.8 μs	2.1 μs	≤9.25 μs

TIMING AND SYSTEM THROUGHPUT

A critical path analysis was undertaken to determine the maximum clock rate for the proposed system. The longest delay path is the multiplication data path, which involves the internal register file and the shift function of the 'AS888. Table 4-9 contains the critical delay calculations for both the ALU and CCU. Since both portions of the system must be satisfied, a clock rate of 90 ns was selected for the following comparisons.

FETCH ANALYSIS

Most microprocessors perform an instruction fetch in a pipeline mode; the next instruction is fetched while the current instruction is executing. The fetch code shown earlier requires a minimum of four cycles: three to issue the code and one to break the pipeline for processing the batch. This results in a total time of 360 ns, based on a 90 ns cycle time. Fetch times for the representative microprocessors have been estimated from data books and are shown in Table 4-10; wait states for slow memory are not included. As can be seen from the table, the 'AS888 design example is estimated to run from 1.1 to 2.1 times faster than the 16-bit microprocessors.

MULTIPLICATION ANALYSIS

This analysis assumes that multiplication is unsigned integer and register to register based. No account is taken of time needed for instruction fetch or operand fetch or store.

The basic loop for the multiply takes 35 cycles: 2 for accumulator and multiplier setup, 32 for actual multiply loop and 1 to store the least significant bits in an internal register file. Given a cycle time of 90 ns, a 32 by 32 bit multiplication can be implemented in 2.275 microseconds. A 16-bit multiply requires 16 iterations of the inner loop; both timings are included in Table 4-11 for comparison. Values for the 16-bit multiplies of the representative microprocessors have been estimated from data books.

As shown in Table 4-11, the 16 by 16 multiply can be performed with the 'AS888 at a faster rate than the 16-bit microprocessors. Even comparing the 32 by 32 multiply of the application design, one can see that the 'AS888 based system has a better macroinstruction execution speed. Using the 'AS888 and 'AS890 in a system design will allow high throughput and a flexible architecture.

Section 5

An Adaptive Clock Generator To Increase 'AS888 System Speed

'AS888-1 instructions execute within 50 to 90 ns; over half execute in less than 60 ns. It is therefore possible to enhance the speed of an 'AS888 system using an adaptive clock generator that spaces clock pulses according to the time required to complete each operation. The advantage of using this circuit is that the system can process each instruction in almost exactly the time it takes the desired results to reach steady-state. The alternative is to use a periodic 90 ns clock and waste use of 'AS888 "idle time." Just how fast the system will run with the adaptive clock is a function of the statistical distribution of microinstructions within any given microprogram.

The time required for an 'AS888 instruction depends on whether shift, carry, register file read, ZERO status test and/or N status test are used. These operations require varying lengths of time to execute, depending on the number of 'AS888 internal delays involved. Whether shift and/or carry are used is determined by the 'AS888 instruction field. ALU source operands can originate from the register file or the DA and DB buses; this is determined by the state of the $\overline{\text{EA}}$ and EB1-EB0 inputs. Whether or not ZERO or N status are tested depends on other system signals, such as a status select field in the microinstruction to select ALU status during conditional branching. Depending on the system architecture, the pipelining scheme used and the flexibility of the microprogram, the designer may wish to ensure that test ZERO and test N signals be made available during the cycle in which ZERO or N are generated in order to better match clock pulse spacing to processing delay. By also providing a register file read signal, the clock spacing will be optimally matched to the processing delay.

CIRCUIT DESCRIPTION

A diagram of the adaptive clock circuit is given in Figure 5-1. The circuit consists of a PROM decoder and a programmable oscillator. The PROM contains a table of cycle length codes as a function of the 'AS888 instruction field, register file read (RFRD), ZERO test (ZTST) and N test (NTST). These signals are connected to the PROM address inputs from the control store outputs as shown. If the RFRD, ZTST and NTST signals are not available, these inputs can be tied high, or a smaller PROM can be used.

The cycle length codes residing in PROM are used to select one of nine delays in the programmable delay line oscillator. The selected delay provides the phase shift required for oscillation. Two progammable delay lines (Data Delay Devices PDU-1613-5) are needed; they must be alternately switched into the feedback loop so that each has time to empty. The programmable delay lines establish the timing from leading edge to leading edge of the clock for an overall error of only ± 3.5 ns. The delays for various fixed-length delay lines are indicated by the numbers in the numbered boxes in Figure 5-1.

Timing for this circuit is shown in Figure 5-2. RST initializes the circuit. When RST releases, the open collector output of U4a provides an initial rising edge from which all successive rising edges are regenerated. Toggle flip-flop U3a switches between the two halves of the oscillator. Latches U6a and U6b are alternately enabled by the Q and $\overline{\text{Q}}$ outputs of U3b. In this manner only one delay line at a time is selected to receive a pulse. U3a generates $\overline{\text{OE1}}$ and $\overline{\text{OE2}}$ which select the available delay line for output. The pulse width regulation is also initiated by U3a. TQ and $\overline{\text{TQ}}$ serve as references for edge detectors U5a-U5d. The fixed delay lines shape $\overline{\text{OC1}}$, CLR1, $\overline{\text{OC2}}$, and CLR2. The output control $\overline{\text{OC1}}$ (or $\overline{\text{OC2}}$) on U6a (or U6b) turns off several nanoseconds after a rising transition in TQ (or $\overline{\text{TQ}}$) has occurred thereby holding Q1 (or Q2) high. This stretches the on-time of the pulse to nearly 50 ns. U6a (or U6b) is cleared 10 ns later. After another 10 ns the output control turns on again, allowing the Q which was just cleared to establish the falling edge of the stretched pulse. This stretched pulse then enters the selected delay line, U7 (or U8), exiting at a time established by the cycle length code. The delay line output enable, $\overline{\text{OE1}}$ (or $\overline{\text{OE2}}$) switches in the delay line before its pulse is ready to exit. In this manner, the width of the previous pulse is regulated to within 20 to 30 ns.

PROM PROGRAM

The cycle lengths are defined by analyzing the propagation delays from the 'AS888 data sheet given in Table 5-1. Variations in cycle lengths depend on whether shift, carry, register file read, ZERO test or N test are used. The algorithm for determining cycle length is flowcharted in Figures 5-3—5-6. Total cycle length is found by adding up all the contributing delays for each possible case. Sums less than 50 ns must be adjusted to 50 ns since this is the minimum clock cycle length specified in the data sheet. Seven nanoseconds is used as the propagation time for $\overline{\text{G}}$/P to Cn; this assumes an 'AS182 lookahead carry generator is used with the 'AS888. Each total delay is rounded up to the nearest integer multiple of 5 ns, which gives nine possible outcomes.

Use of the shifters or carry is inherent in each instruction as shown in Table 5-2. Cycle length codes can be generated by looking up Table 5-2 for each instruction, performing the algorithm in Figures 5-3—5-6, and encoding

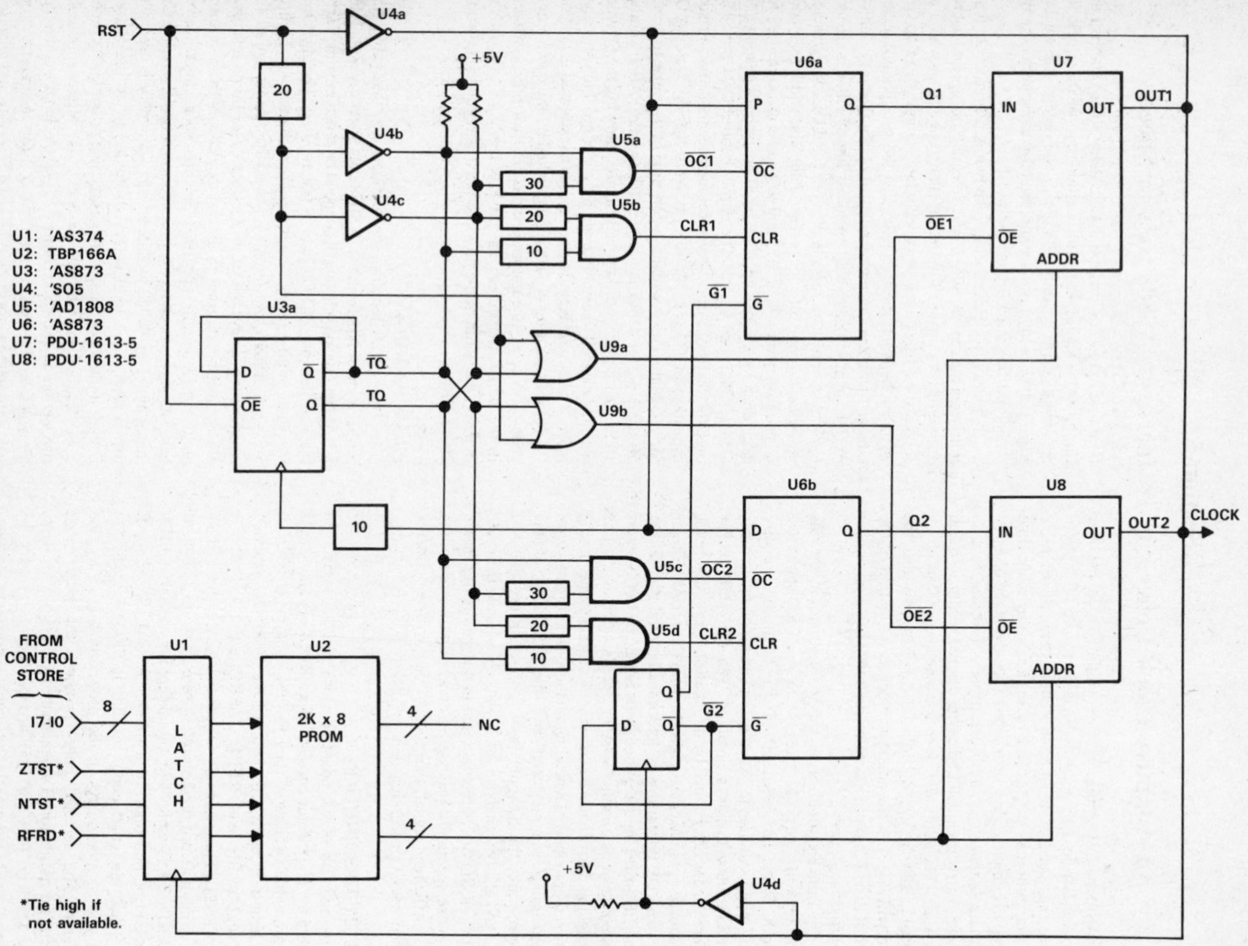
RST
U4a
20
+5V
U4b
U4c
U5a
U5b
30
20
10
OC1
CLR1
G1
U6a
P
Q
OC
CLR
G
Q1
U7
IN
OUT
OE
ADDR
OUT1
OE1
U1: 'AS374
U2: TBP166A
U3: 'AS873
U4: 'SO5
U5: 'AD1808
U6: 'AS873
U7: PDU-1613-5
U8: PDU-1613-5
U3a
D
Q
OE
TQ
U9a
U9b
10
U6b
D
Q
OC
CLR
G
Q2
U8
IN
OUT
OE
ADDR
OUT2
CLOCK
U5c
U5d
OC2
CLR2
OE2
G2
FROM
CONTROL
STORE
I7-I0
8
ZTST*
NTST*
RFRD*
U1
LATCH
U2
2K x 8
PROM
4
NC
+5V
U4d
*Tie high if
not available.

Figure 5-1. Adaptive Clock Generator Circuit

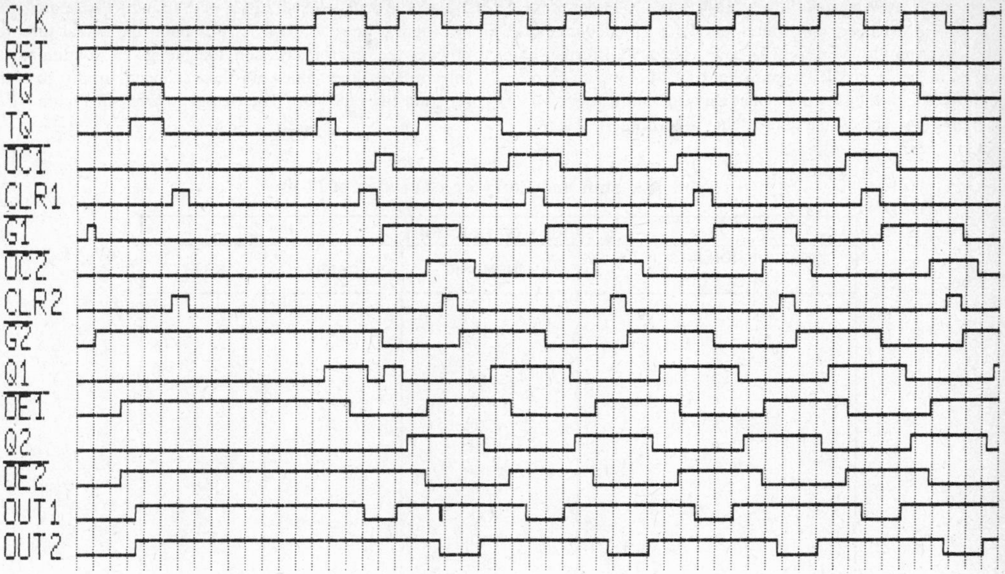
CLK
RST
TQ
TQ
OC1
CLR1
G1
OC2
CLR2
G2
Q1
OE1
Q2
OE2
OUT1
OUT2

Figure 5-2. Adaptive Clock Generator Timing Diagram

Table 5-1. 'AS888-1 Timing Characteristics

PARAMETER	FROM (INPUT)	TO (OUTPUT)										UNIT
		Y	C_{n+8}	$\overline{G}, \overline{P}$	Z*	N	OVR	DA	DB	$\overline{QIO}$	$\overline{SIO}$	
t_{pd}	A3-A0, B3-B0	44	30	36	50	44	44	17	17	48	48	ns
	DA7-DA0, DB7-DB0	36	24	24	46	41	32	—	—	40	40	
	C_n	22	8	—	27	21	16	—	—	25	25	
	$\overline{EA}$	40	25	25	49	41	41	—	—	44	44	
	$\overline{EB}$	40	25	25	49	41	41	—	—	44	44	
	I7-I0	46	27	27	50	42	35	—	—	45	45	
	$\overline{OEB}$	—	—	—	—	—	—	—	12	—	—	
	$\overline{OEY}$	12	—	—	—	—	—	—	—	—	—	
	$\overline{QIO}$ (n) Shift	14	—	—	20	—	—	—	—	—	—	
	$\overline{SIO}$ (n) Shift	14	—	—	20	18	—	—	—	—	—	
	CK	50	46	46	50	50	50	30	30	50	50	
	$\overline{OEA}$	—	—	—	—	—	—	12	—	—	—	
	SSF**	—	—	—	—	—	9	—	—	—	—	

*Load resistor R1 = 100

**For byte instructions only.

NOTE 1: For load circuit and voltage waveforms, see page 1-12 of *The TTL Data Book*, Volume 3, 1984.

each of the nine possible time delays with a number from 0 to 8. A BASIC program which follows this procedure and generates the PROM data in Data I/O hex-ASCII format is shown in Program 5-1. Program lines 147-149 look up carry and shift for each instruction. Once carry and shift are known, the program solves the total delay algorithm in Figures 5-3—5-6 for all cases of ZTST, NTST, and RFRD as shown in program lines 163-184. At this point the actual time to process the microinstruction for the given conditions is solved. The time values are then encoded from 0 to 8 in program lines 188-195. The output is listed in Figure 5-7.

Table 5-2. Shift and Carry as a Function of I7-I0

GROUP 1 INSTRUCTIONS			
INSTRUCTION BITS (I3-I0) HEX CODE	**MNEMONIC**	**CARRY**	**SHIFT**
0			
1	ADD	✓	
2	SUBR	✓	
3	SUBS	✓	
4	INCS	✓	
5	INCNS	✓	
6	INCR	✓	
7	INCNR	✓	
8			
9	XOR		
A	AND		
B	OR		
C	NAND		
D	NOR		
E	ANDNR		
F			
GROUP 2 INSTRUCTIONS			
INSTRUCTION BITS (I7-I4) HEX CODE	**MNEMONIC**	**CARRY**	**SHIFT**
0	SRA		✓
1	SRAD		✓
2	SRL		✓
3	SRLD		✓
4	SLA		✓
5	SLAD		✓
6	SLC		✓
7	SLCD		✓
8	SRC		✓
9	SRCD		✓
A	MQSRA		✓
B	MQSRL		✓
C	MQSLL		✓
D	MQSLC		✓
E	LOADMQ		
F	PASS		

Table 5-2. Shift and Carry as a Function of I7-I0 (Continued)

INSTRUCTION BITS (I7-I0) HEX CODE	MNEMONIC	CARRY	SHIFT
GROUP 3 INSTRUCTIONS			
08	SET1	✓	
18	SET0		
28	TB1		
38	TB0		
48	ABS	✓	
58	SMTC	✓	
68	ADDI	✓	
78	SUBI	✓	
88	BADD	✓	
98	BSUBS	✓	
A8	BSUBR	✓	
B8	BINCS	✓	
C8	BINCNS	✓	
D8	BXOR		
E8	BAND		
F8	BOR		
GROUP 4 INSTRUCTIONS			
00	CRC		✓
10	SEL	✓	
20	SNORM	✓	✓
30	DNORM		✓
40	DIVRF	✓	
50	SDIVQF	✓	
60	SMULI	✓	✓
70	SMULT	✓	✓
80	SDIVIN		✓
90	SDIVIS	✓	✓
A0	SDIVI	✓	✓
B0	UDIVIS	✓	✓
C0	UDIVI	✓	✓
D0	UMULI	✓	✓
E0	SDIVIT	✓	✓
F0	UDIVIT	✓	✓
GROUP 5 INSTRUCTIONS			
0F	CLR		
1F	CLR		
2F	CLR		
3F	CLR		
4F	CLR		
5F	CLR		
6F	CLR		
7F	BCDBIN	✓	✓
8F	EX3BC	✓	
9F	EX3C	✓	
AF	SDIVO	✓	
BF	CLR		
CF	CLR		
DF	BINEX3	✓	✓
EF	CLR		
FF	NOP		

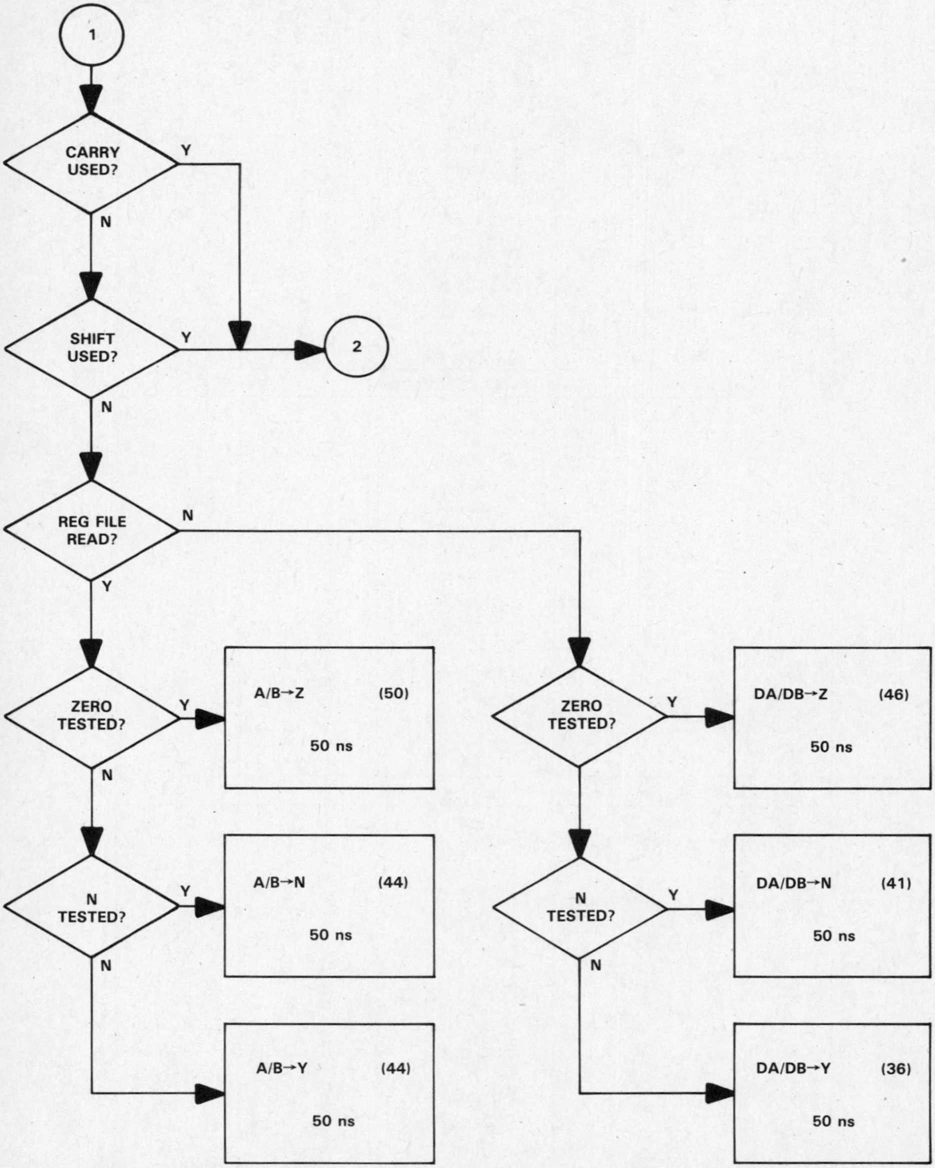
1
CARRY USED?
Y
N
SHIFT USED?
Y
2
N
REG FILE READ?
N
Y
ZERO TESTED?
Y
A/B→Z (50)
50 ns
N
N TESTED?
Y
A/B→N (44)
50 ns
N
A/B→Y (44)
50 ns
ZERO TESTED?
Y
DA/DB→Z (46)
50 ns
N TESTED?
Y
DA/DB→N (41)
50 ns
N
DA/DB→Y (36)
50 ns

Figure 5-3. Propagation Delay Without Carry and Without Shift

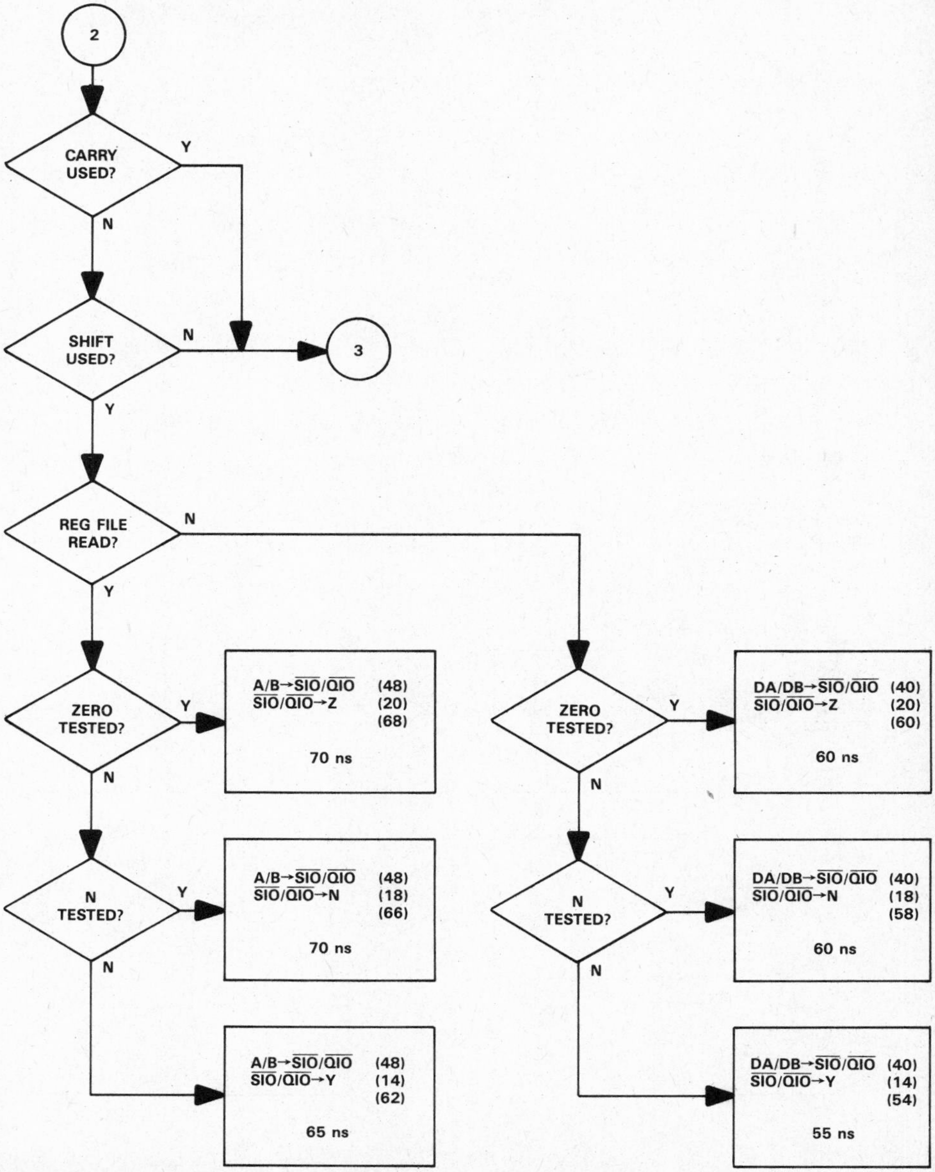
2
CARRY USED?
Y
N
SHIFT USED?
N
3
Y
REG FILE READ?
N
Y
ZERO TESTED?
Y
A/B→$\overline{SIO}/\overline{QIO}$ (48)
$\overline{SIO}/\overline{QIO}$→Z (20)
(68)
70 ns
N
N TESTED?
Y
A/B→$\overline{SIO}/\overline{QIO}$ (48)
$\overline{SIO}/\overline{QIO}$→N (18)
(66)
70 ns
N
A/B→$\overline{SIO}/\overline{QIO}$ (48)
$\overline{SIO}/\overline{QIO}$→Y (14)
(62)
65 ns
ZERO TESTED?
Y
DA/DB→$\overline{SIO}/\overline{QIO}$ (40)
$\overline{SIO}/\overline{QIO}$→Z (20)
(60)
60 ns
N
N TESTED?
Y
DA/DB→$\overline{SIO}/\overline{QIO}$ (40)
$\overline{SIO}/\overline{QIO}$→N (18)
(58)
60 ns
N
DA/DB→$\overline{SIO}/\overline{QIO}$ (40)
$\overline{SIO}/\overline{QIO}$→Y (14)
(54)
55 ns

Figure 5-4. Propagation Delay Without Carry and With Shift

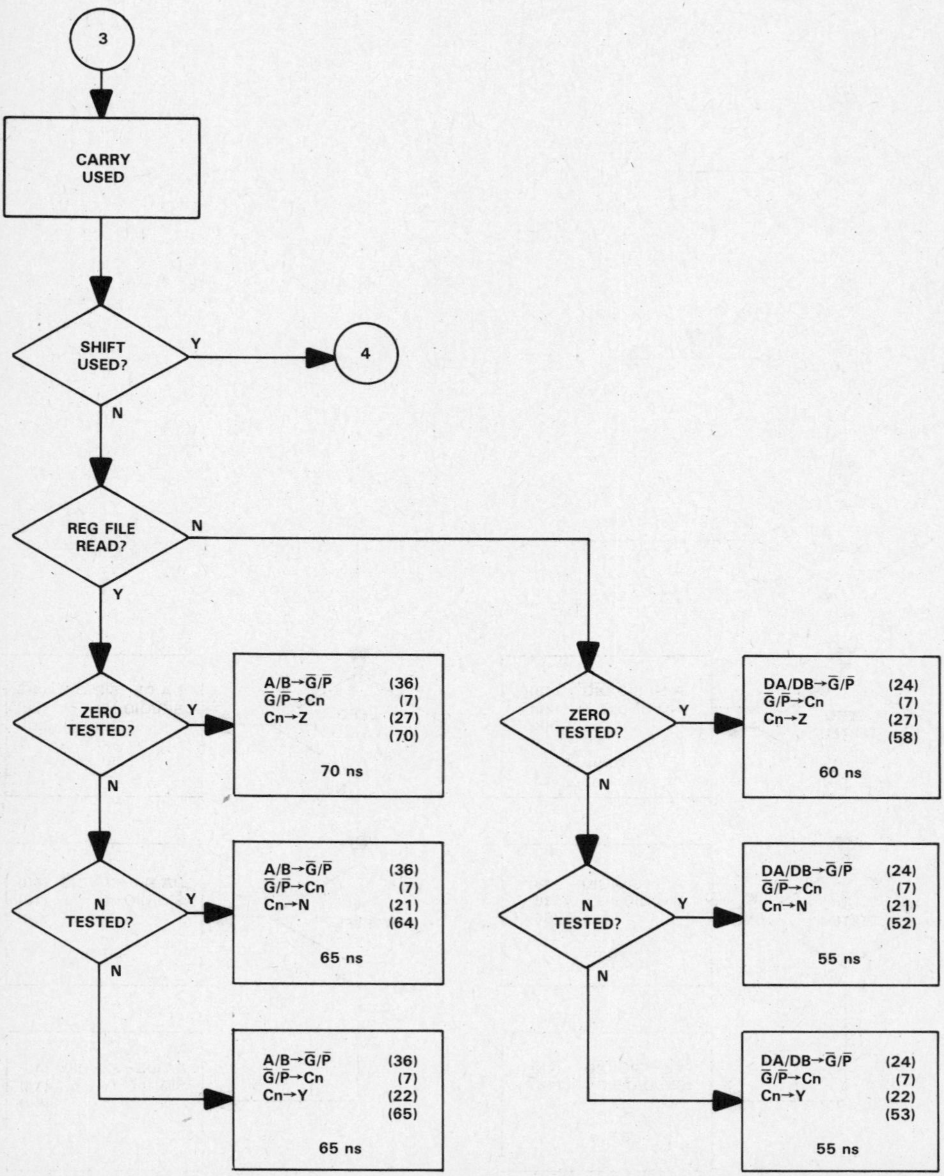
3
CARRY USED
SHIFT USED?
Y
4
N
REG FILE READ?
N
Y
ZERO TESTED?
Y
A/B→G̅/P̅ (36)
G̅/P̅→Cn (7)
Cn→Z (27)
(70)
70 ns
N
N TESTED?
Y
A/B→G̅/P̅ (36)
G̅/P̅→Cn (7)
Cn→N (21)
(64)
65 ns
N
A/B→G̅/P̅ (36)
G̅/P̅→Cn (7)
Cn→Y (22)
(65)
65 ns
ZERO TESTED?
Y
DA/DB→G̅/P̅ (24)
G̅/P̅→Cn (7)
Cn→Z (27)
(58)
60 ns
N
N TESTED?
Y
DA/DB→G̅/P̅ (24)
G̅/P̅→Cn (7)
Cn→N (21)
(52)
55 ns
N
DA/DB→G̅/P̅ (24)
G̅/P̅→Cn (7)
Cn→Y (22)
(53)
55 ns

Figure 5-5. Propagation Delay With Carry and Without Shift

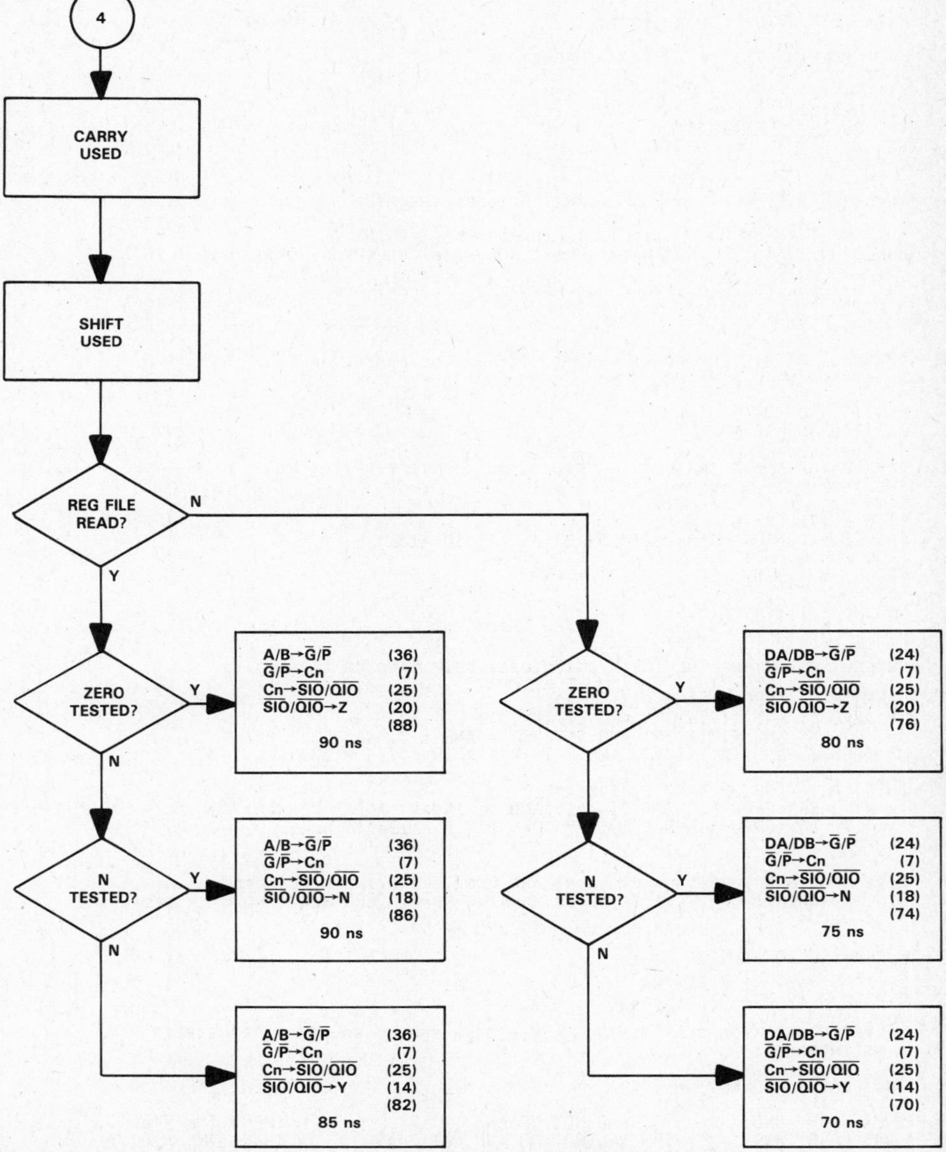

4
CARRY USED
SHIFT USED
REG FILE READ?
N
Y
ZERO TESTED?
Y
N
A/B→$\overline{G}$/$\overline{P}$ (36)
$\overline{G}$/$\overline{P}$→Cn (7)
Cn→$\overline{SIO}$/$\overline{QIO}$ (25)
$\overline{SIO}$/$\overline{QIO}$→Z (20)
(88)
90 ns
N TESTED?
Y
N
A/B→$\overline{G}$/$\overline{P}$ (36)
$\overline{G}$/$\overline{P}$→Cn (7)
Cn→$\overline{SIO}$/$\overline{QIO}$ (25)
$\overline{SIO}$/$\overline{QIO}$→N (18)
(86)
90 ns
A/B→$\overline{G}$/$\overline{P}$ (36)
$\overline{G}$/$\overline{P}$→Cn (7)
Cn→$\overline{SIO}$/$\overline{QIO}$ (25)
$\overline{SIO}$/$\overline{QIO}$→Y (14)
(82)
85 ns
ZERO TESTED?
Y
DA/DB→$\overline{G}$/$\overline{P}$ (24)
$\overline{G}$/$\overline{P}$→Cn (7)
Cn→$\overline{SIO}$/$\overline{QIO}$ (25)
$\overline{SIO}$/$\overline{QIO}$→Z (20)
(76)
80 ns
N TESTED?
Y
N
DA/DB→$\overline{G}$/$\overline{P}$ (24)
$\overline{G}$/$\overline{P}$→Cn (7)
Cn→$\overline{SIO}$/$\overline{QIO}$ (25)
$\overline{SIO}$/$\overline{QIO}$→N (18)
(74)
75 ns
DA/DB→$\overline{G}$/$\overline{P}$ (24)
$\overline{G}$/$\overline{P}$→Cn (7)
Cn→$\overline{SIO}$/$\overline{QIO}$ (25)
$\overline{SIO}$/$\overline{QIO}$→Y (14)
(70)
70 ns

Figure 5-6. Propagation Delay With Carry and With Shift

```
100 '************************************************************************
101    CLS                                                                   :'*
102    PRINT "             'AS888-1 ADAPTIVE CLOCK GENERATOR                 ":'*
103    PRINT "              PROM DATA GENERATION PROGRAM                     ":'*
104    PRINT "                      MAY 24, 1985                             ":'*
105 '                                                                        :'*
106 '************************************************************************
107 '
108 DEFINT A-Z
109 DIM TABLE(4096)
110 '
111 ' DEFINE TRANSMISSION CONTROL CHARACTERS
112 '
113 STX$=CHR$(2)
114 ETX$=CHR$(3)
115 CR$=CHR$(13)+CHR$(10)
116 TX$=STX$
117 BS$=CHR$(8)
118 '
119 ' INPUT USER'S PROM DATA FILE NAME AND OPEN THE FILE
120 '
121 PRINT:INPUT "PROM DATA OUTPUT FILE NAME";OF$ : PRINT
122 OPEN "O",#1,OF$ : PRINT "WRITING CYCLE LENGTH CODES TO ";OF$;"..." : PRINT
123 '
124 ' SET UP DATA I/O PROGRAMMER FOR HEX-ASCII (COMMA) FORMAT
125 '
126 PRINT #1,"53A"
127 '
128 ' FOR EACH 'AS888 INSTRUCTION (BITS I7-I0), DETERMINE IF
129 ' SHIFT AND/OR CARRY ARE USED
130 '
131 FOR I7I4 = 0 TO 15
132  FOR I3I0 = 0 TO 15
133 '
134 ' DEFINE THE 8-BIT INSTRUCTION FIELD AND IDENTIFY WHICH GROUP(S)
135 ' THE INSTRUCTION BELONGS TO
136 '
137   I7I0 = I7I4 * 16 + I3I0
138   GROUP1 = (I3I0<>0) AND (I3I0<>8) AND (I3I0<>15)
139   GROUP2 = GROUP1
140   GROUP3 = (I3I0 = 8)
141   GROUP4 = (I3I0 = 0)
142   GROUP5 = (I3I0 = 15)
143 '
144 '
145 ' DETERMINE WHETHER THE INSTRUCTION USES SHIFT AND/OR CARRY
146 '
147   CARRY =    (GROUP1 AND (I7I4<8))
      OR (GROUP3 AND (I7I4>3)  AND (I7I4<13))
      OR (GROUP4 AND (I7I4<>0) AND (I7I4<>3) AND (I7I4<>8))
      OR (GROUP5 AND ( (I7I4>7) AND  (I7I4<11) OR (I7I4 = 13)))
148 '
149   SHIFT =     (GROUP2 AND (I7I4<14))
              OR (GROUP4 AND (I7I4<>1) AND (I7I4<>4) AND (I7I4<>5))
              OR (GROUP5 AND ((I7I4=7) OR  (I7I4 = 13)))
150 '
151 '
152 ' GIVEN WHETHER SHIFT AND/OR CARRY ARE USED, FIND THE WORST CASE DELAY
153 ' (IN INCREMENTS OF 5 NS) IF REGISTER FILE READ, ZERO TEST AND/OR N TEST
154 ' ALSO OCCUR
155 '
156 FOR RF =  0 TO -1 STEP -1
157 FOR Z =  0 TO  -1 STEP -1
158 FOR N =  0 TO  -1 STEP -1
159 '
160 ' SOLVE PROPAGATION DELAY USING 'AS888 DATA SHEET; ROUND UP TO NEAREST
161 ' 5 NS INCREMENT
162 '
163 IF NOT CARRY AND NOT SHIFT                                    THEN TIME = 50
164 '
165 IF NOT CARRY AND     SHIFT AND NOT RF AND     Z               THEN TIME = 60
166 IF NOT CARRY AND     SHIFT AND NOT RF AND NOT Z AND         N THEN TIME = 60
```

Program 5-1. BASIC Program to Generate PROM Data

```
167 IF NOT CARRY AND     SHIFT AND NOT RF AND NOT Z AND NOT N THEN TIME = 55
168 IF NOT CARRY AND     SHIFT AND     RF AND     Z           THEN TIME = 70
169 IF NOT CARRY AND     SHIFT AND     RF AND NOT Z AND     N THEN TIME = 70
170 IF NOT CARRY AND     SHIFT AND     RF AND NOT Z AND NOT N THEN TIME = 65
171 '
172 IF     CARRY AND NOT SHIFT AND     RF AND     Z           THEN TIME = 60
173 IF     CARRY AND NOT SHIFT AND     RF AND NOT Z AND     N THEN TIME = 55
174 IF     CARRY AND NOT SHIFT AND     RF AND NOT Z AND NOT N THEN TIME = 55
175 IF     CARRY AND NOT SHIFT AND NOT RF AND     Z           THEN TIME = 70
176 IF     CARRY AND NOT SHIFT AND NOT RF AND NOT Z AND     N THEN TIME = 65
177 IF     CARRY AND NOT SHIFT AND NOT RF AND NOT Z AND NOT N THEN TIME = 65
178 '
179 IF     CARRY AND     SHIFT AND     RF AND     Z           THEN TIME = 80
180 IF     CARRY AND     SHIFT AND     RF AND NOT Z AND     N THEN TIME = 75
181 IF     CARRY AND     SHIFT AND     RF AND NOT Z AND NOT N THEN TIME = 70
182 IF     CARRY AND     SHIFT AND NOT RF AND     Z           THEN TIME = 90
183 IF     CARRY AND     SHIFT AND NOT RF AND NOT Z AND     N THEN TIME = 90
184 IF     CARRY AND     SHIFT AND NOT RF AND NOT Z AND NOT N THEN TIME = 85
185 '
186 ' ENCODE THE TIME DELAYS AS FOLLOWS
187 '
188 IF TIME = 50 THEN CODE = 0
189 IF TIME = 55 THEN CODE = 1
190 IF TIME = 60 THEN CODE = 2
191 IF TIME = 65 THEN CODE = 3
192 IF TIME = 70 THEN CODE = 4
193 IF TIME = 75 THEN CODE = 5
194 IF TIME = 80 THEN CODE = 6
195 IF TIME = 85 THEN CODE = 7
196 IF TIME = 90 THEN CODE = 8
197 '
198 ' WRITE THE SELECT CODE TO THE OUTPUT FILE
199 ' IN DATA I/O HEX ASCII (COMMA) FORMAT
200 '
201 IF ADDR=4095 THEN TX$=ETX$
202 IF ADDR/16=INT(ADDR/16) THEN PRINT #1,TX$;"$A";RIGHT$("000"+HEX$(ADDR),4);".
"; ELSE PRINT #1,",";
203 PRINT #1,"0";RIGHT$(STR$(CODE),1);
204 ADDR=ADDR+1
205 TX$=ETX$+CR$+STX$
206 NEXT:NEXT:NEXT
207 PRINT STRING$(14,8);INT(100*ADDR/4096);"%";TAB(6);" COMPLETE";
208 NEXT:NEXT
209 CLOSE 1:PRINT"PROM DATA FILE ";OF$;" IS READY.":SYSTEM
210 '
211 ' END
212 '
```

Program 5-1. BASIC Program to Generate PROM Data (Continued)

```
53A
$A0000.01,02,02,02,03,04,04,04,07,08,08,08,04,05,06,06
$A0010.07,08,08,08,04,05,06,06,07,08,08,08,04,05,06,06
$A0020.07,08,08,08,04,05,06,06,07,08,08,08,04,05,06,06
$A0030.07,08,08,08,04,05,06,06,07,08,08,08,04,05,06,06
$A0040.00,00,00,00,00,00,00,00,07,08,08,08,04,05,06,06
$A0050.07,08,08,08,04,05,06,06,07,08,08,08,04,05,06,06
$A0060.07,08,08,08,04,05,06,06,07,08,08,08,04,05,06,06
$A0070.07,08,08,08,04,05,06,06,00,00,00,00,00,00,00,00
$A0080.03,03,04,04,01,01,02,02,07,08,08,08,04,05,06,06
$A0090.07,08,08,08,04,05,06,06,07,08,08,08,04,05,06,06
$A00A0.07,08,08,08,04,05,06,06,07,08,08,08,04,05,06,06
$A00B0.07,08,08,08,04,05,06,06,07,08,08,08,04,05,06,06
$A00C0.00,00,00,00,00,00,00,00,07,08,08,08,04,05,06,06
$A00D0.07,08,08,08,04,05,06,06,07,08,08,08,04,05,06,06
$A00E0.07,08,08,08,04,05,06,06,07,08,08,08,04,05,06,06
$A00F0.07,08,08,08,04,05,06,06,00,00,00,00,00,00,00,00
$A0100.07,08,08,08,04,05,06,06,07,08,08,08,04,05,06,06
$A0110.07,08,08,08,04,05,06,06,07,08,08,08,04,05,06,06
$A0120.07,08,08,08,04,05,06,06,07,08,08,08,04,05,06,06
$A0130.07,08,08,08,04,05,06,06,07,08,08,08,04,05,06,06
$A0140.00,00,00,00,00,00,00,07,08,08,08,04,05,06,06
$A0150.07,08,08,08,04,05,06,06,07,08,08,08,04,05,06,06
$A0160.07,08,08,08,04,05,06,06,07,08,08,08,04,05,06,06
$A0170.07,08,08,08,04,05,06,06,00,00,00,00,00,00,00,00
$A0180.01,02,02,02,03,04,04,04,07,08,08,08,04,05,06,06
$A0190.07,08,08,08,04,05,06,06,07,08,08,08,04,05,06,06
$A01A0.07,08,08,08,04,05,06,06,07,08,08,08,04,05,06,06
$A01B0.07,08,08,08,04,05,06,06,07,08,08,08,04,05,06,06
$A01C0.00,00,00,00,00,00,00,07,08,08,08,04,05,06,06
$A01D0.07,08,08,08,04,05,06,06,07,08,08,08,04,05,06,06
$A01E0.07,08,08,08,04,05,06,06,07,08,08,08,04,05,06,06
$A01F0.07,08,08,08,04,05,06,06,00,00,00,00,00,00,00,00
$A0200.03,03,04,04,01,01,02,02,07,08,08,08,04,05,06,06
$A0210.07,08,08,08,04,05,06,06,07,08,08,08,04,05,06,06
$A0220.07,08,08,08,04,05,06,06,07,08,08,08,04,05,06,06
$A0230.07,08,08,08,04,05,06,06,07,08,08,08,04,05,06,06
$A0240.03,03,04,04,01,01,02,02,07,08,08,08,04,05,06,06
$A0250.07,08,08,08,04,05,06,06,07,08,08,08,04,05,06,06
$A0260.07,08,08,08,04,05,06,06,07,08,08,08,04,05,06,06
$A0270.07,08,08,08,04,05,06,06,00,00,00,00,00,00,00,00
$A0280.03,03,04,04,01,01,02,02,07,08,08,08,04,05,06,06
$A0290.07,08,08,08,04,05,06,06,07,08,08,08,04,05,06,06
$A02A0.07,08,08,08,04,05,06,06,07,08,08,08,04,05,06,06
$A02B0.07,08,08,08,04,05,06,06,07,08,08,08,04,05,06,06
$A02C0.03,03,04,04,01,01,02,02,07,08,08,08,04,05,06,06
$A02D0.07,08,08,08,04,05,06,06,07,08,08,08,04,05,06,06
$A02E0.07,08,08,08,04,05,06,06,07,08,08,08,04,05,06,06
$A02F0.07,08,08,08,04,05,06,06,00,00,00,00,00,00,00,00
$A0300.07,08,08,08,04,05,06,06,07,08,08,08,04,05,06,06
$A0310.07,08,08,08,04,05,06,06,07,08,08,08,04,05,06,06
$A0320.07,08,08,08,04,05,06,06,07,08,08,08,04,05,06,06
$A0330.07,08,08,08,04,05,06,06,07,08,08,08,04,05,06,06
$A0340.03,03,04,04,01,01,02,02,07,08,08,08,04,05,06,06
$A0350.07,08,08,08,04,05,06,06,07,08,08,08,04,05,06,06
$A0360.07,08,08,08,04,05,06,06,07,08,08,08,04,05,06,06
$A0370.07,08,08,08,04,05,06,06,00,00,00,00,00,00,00,00
$A0380.07,08,08,08,04,05,06,06,07,08,08,08,04,05,06,06
$A0390.07,08,08,08,04,05,06,06,07,08,08,08,04,05,06,06
$A03A0.07,08,08,08,04,05,06,06,07,08,08,08,04,05,06,06
$A03B0.07,08,08,08,04,05,06,06,07,08,08,08,04,05,06,06
$A03C0.03,03,04,04,01,01,02,02,07,08,08,08,04,05,06,06
$A03D0.07,08,08,08,04,05,06,06,07,08,08,08,04,05,06,06
$A03E0.07,08,08,08,04,05,06,06,07,08,08,08,04,05,06,06
$A03F0.07,08,08,08,04,05,06,06,01,02,02,02,03,04,04,04
$A0400.01,02,02,02,03,04,04,04,01,02,02,02,03,04,04,04
$A0410.01,02,02,02,03,04,04,04,01,02,02,02,03,04,04,04
$A0420.01,02,02,02,03,04,04,04,01,02,02,02,03,04,04,04
$A0430.01,02,02,02,03,04,04,04,01,02,02,02,03,04,04,04
$A0440.03,03,04,04,01,01,02,02,01,02,02,02,03,04,04,04
$A0450.01,02,02,02,03,04,04,04,01,02,02,02,03,04,04,04
$A0460.01,02,02,02,03,04,04,04,01,02,02,02,03,04,04,04
$A0470.01,02,02,02,03,04,04,04,03,03,04,04,01,01,02,02
$A0480.07,08,08,08,04,05,06,06,01,02,02,02,03,04,04,04
$A0490.01,02,02,02,03,04,04,04,01,02,02,02,03,04,04,04
$A04A0.01,02,02,02,03,04,04,04,01,02,02,02,03,04,04,04
$A04B0.01,02,02,02,03,04,04,04,01,02,02,02,03,04,04,04
$A04C0.03,03,04,04,01,01,02,02,01,02,02,02,03,04,04,04
$A04D0.01,02,02,02,03,04,04,04,01,02,02,02,03,04,04,04
$A04E0.01,02,02,02,03,04,04,04,01,02,02,02,03,04,04,04
$A04F0.01,02,02,02,03,04,04,04,03,03,04,04,01,01,02,02
$A0500.07,08,08,08,04,05,06,06,01,02,02,02,03,04,04,04
$A0510.01,02,02,02,03,04,04,04,01,02,02,02,03,04,04,04
$A0520.01,02,02,02,03,04,04,04,01,02,02,02,03,04,04,04
$A0530.01,02,02,02,03,04,04,04,01,02,02,02,03,04,04,04
$A0540.03,03,04,04,01,01,02,02,01,02,02,02,03,04,04,04
$A0550.01,02,02,02,03,04,04,04,01,02,02,02,03,04,04,04
$A0560.01,02,02,02,03,04,04,04,01,02,02,02,03,04,04,04
$A0570.01,02,02,02,03,04,04,04,03,03,04,04,01,01,02,02
$A0580.07,08,08,08,04,05,06,06,01,02,02,02,03,04,04,04
$A0590.01,02,02,02,03,04,04,04,01,02,02,02,03,04,04,04
$A05A0.01,02,02,02,03,04,04,04,01,02,02,02,03,04,04,04
$A05B0.01,02,02,02,03,04,04,04,01,02,02,02,03,04,04,04
$A05C0.03,03,04,04,01,01,02,02,01,02,02,02,03,04,04,04
$A05D0.01,02,02,02,03,04,04,04,01,02,02,02,03,04,04,04
$A05E0.01,02,02,02,03,04,04,04,01,02,02,02,03,04,04,04
$A05F0.01,02,02,02,03,04,04,04,00,00,00,00,00,00,00,00
$A0600.07,08,08,08,04,05,06,06,01,02,02,02,03,04,04,04
$A0610.01,02,02,02,03,04,04,04,01,02,02,02,03,04,04,04
$A0620.01,02,02,02,03,04,04,04,01,02,02,02,03,04,04,04
$A0630.01,02,02,02,03,04,04,04,01,02,02,02,03,04,04,04
$A0640.03,03,04,04,01,01,02,02,01,02,02,02,03,04,04,04
$A0650.01,02,02,02,03,04,04,04,01,02,02,02,03,04,04,04
$A0660.01,02,02,02,03,04,04,04,01,02,02,02,03,04,04,04
$A0670.01,02,02,02,03,04,04,04,00,00,00,00,00,00,00,00
$A0680.07,08,08,08,04,05,06,06,01,02,02,02,03,04,04,04
$A0690.01,02,02,02,03,04,04,04,01,02,02,02,03,04,04,04
$A06A0.01,02,02,02,03,04,04,04,01,02,02,02,03,04,04,04
$A06B0.01,02,02,02,03,04,04,04,01,02,02,02,03,04,04,04
$A06C0.00,00,00,00,00,00,00,00,01,02,02,02,03,04,04,04
$A06D0.01,02,02,02,03,04,04,04,01,02,02,02,03,04,04,04
$A06E0.01,02,02,02,03,04,04,04,01,02,02,02,03,04,04,04
$A06F0.01,02,02,02,03,04,04,04,07,08,08,08,04,05,06,06
$A0700.07,08,08,08,04,05,06,06,00,00,00,00,00,00,00,00
$A0710.00,00,00,00,00,00,00,00,00,00,00,00,00,00,00,00
$A0720.00,00,00,00,00,00,00,00,00,00,00,00,00,00,00,00
$A0730.00,00,00,00,00,00,00,00,00,00,00,00,00,00,00,00
$A0740.00,00,00,00,00,00,00,00,00,00,00,00,00,00,00,00
$A0750.00,00,00,00,00,00,00,00,00,00,00,00,00,00,00,00
$A0760.00,00,00,00,00,00,00,00,00,00,00,00,00,00,00,00
$A0770.00,00,00,00,00,00,00,00,00,00,00,00,00,00,00,00
$A0780.07,08,08,08,04,05,06,06,00,00,00,00,00,00,00,00
$A0790.00,00,00,00,00,00,00,00,00,00,00,00,00,00,00,00
$A07A0.00,00,00,00,00,00,00,00,00,00,00,00,00,00,00,00
$A07B0.00,00,00,00,00,00,00,00,00,00,00,00,00,00,00,00
$A07C0.00,00,00,00,00,00,00,00,00,00,00,00,00,00,00,00
$A07D0.00,00,00,00,00,00,00,00,00,00,00,00,00,00,00,00
$A07E0.00,00,00,00,00,00,00,00,00,00,00,00,00,00,00,00
$A07F0.00,00,00,00,00,00,00,00,00,00,00,00,00,00,00,00
```

Figure 5-7. PROM Data

Section 6

Floating-Point System Design Using the 'AS888/'AS890

Bit-slice processor architecture addresses the problem of optimizing system performance while allowing the user to balance hardware complexity against software flexibility. Bit-slice systems usually operate at or near the speed of the most primitive of programmable processors, the PROM state sequencer. Of course, bit-slice architecture incorporates circuitry dedicated not only to sequencing, but also data processing (ALU) operations. In keeping with the trend of these programmable devices to track the speed of fast discrete hardware, the 'AS888 8-bit slice ALU and 'AS890 microsequencer have been produced in Advanced Schottky bipolar technology. In addition to sheer speed, the components feature greater density (2 micron geometry) for greater functionality (more special purpose circuitry on board). The impact will be faster, more powerful systems in applications which previously pushed the limits of bit-slice processors.

Consider an application in which bit-slice architecture has dominated for years: CPU design. The micro-programmed CPU itself spans a spectrum of uses ranging from general purpose minicomputers to compact airborne computers. A specific example which illustrates various facets of design using the 'AS888 and 'AS890 is a CPU with a floating-point utility to compute sin(x).

The design process can be subject to many influences, including personal preference, available development tools, peculiarities of the application, and constraints from the user, customer or manufacturing environment. No hard and fast design rules could be applied universally, but most designers will start with a specific plan in mind.

The goal of this example is to produce the hardware and microprogram which will implement the sin(x) function in floating-point arithmetic. Before the microprogram can be assembled, the hardware must be defined since the fields of the microinstruction are dedicated to specific hardware once the microinstruction register is hardwired to the devices it controls. Since the final architecture chosen depends on trade-offs between implementing certain operations in hardware or software, critical applications will require that a cursory analysis of the software be made before the hardware is cast in concrete. Attempting to develop microcode for a tentative architecture will force the issue on which operations are better suited for hardware. Before the architecture or the microprogram requirements can be known, the algorithms which describe the application processes must be defined. Once an algorithm is formulated it can be broken down into operations involving variable and constant quantities. The variables can be assigned to registers and then the algorithm can be translated into a microprogram. The following steps illustrate the plan for this CPU design example incorporating a floating-point sin(x) utility:

- Step 1: Choose a floating-point number system
- Step 2: Choose an algorithm for approximating sin(x)
- Step 3: Make 'AS888 register assignments
- Step 4: Substitute registers for variables in the algorithm
- Step 5: Decompose steps of the algorithm into simple operations
- Step 6: Translate into 'AS888/890 operations; identify subroutines
- Step 7: Expand subroutines into 'AS888/890 operations
- Step 8: Evaluate trade-offs and block diagram the hardware
- Step 9: Define microinstruction fields during detailed hardware design
- Step 10: Assemble the microprogram

STEP 1: CHOOSE A FLOATING-POINT NUMBER SYSTEM

An IEEE floating-point format will be chosen for this example for portability of data and software. It is important to note that the IEEE defines many standards in arithmetic processing, but for simplicity this example will encompass only number format. Furthermore, while several formats are IEEE compatible, only the basic single-precision format will be considered.

The IEEE basic single-precision format is defined as a 32-bit representation in which the component fields are a 1-bit sign *s*, an 8-bit biased exponent *e* and a 23-bit fraction *f* which are assembled in the following order:

s	*e*	*f*
31		0

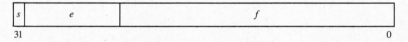

The quantity is evaluated as $(-1)^s 2^{e-127} (1.f)$. Not-a-number, zero and infinity have special representations. The one preceding the binary point is implied and is called the implicit one or implicit bit. It coincides with the fact that the digits are normalized (left justified).

STEP 2: CHOOSE AN ALGORITHM FOR Sin(x)

Many algorithms are discussed in the literature for approximating useful quantities like sin(x). Literature research is a good place to start to familiarize oneself with various algorithms and trade-offs for a particular application. Computer simulation is also useful to compare algorithms for speed and accuracy. R.F. Ruckdeschel in *BASIC Scientific Subroutines*, Vol. 1 (BYTE, McGraw-Hill Publications Co., New York, N.Y., 1981, pp. 159—191) discusses trade-offs and provides a simulation in BASIC for a sin(x) algorithm. An adaptation of this material has been chosen for this example:

A) Reduce angle range to first quadrant. ($0 \leq x \leq \pi/2$)

B) Compute $\sin(x) \simeq \sum_{n=0}^{6} A_n x^{2n-1}$. The coefficients are:

Coefficient	Decimal	IEEE hex
A_0	1.000000	3F80 0000
A_1	−0.1666667	BE2A AAAD
A_2	0.008333333	3C08 8888
A_3	−0.0001984127	B950 0D01
A_4	0.000002755760	3638 EF99
A_5	−0.00000002507060	B2D7 5AD5
A_6	0.0000000001641060	2F34 6FBC

The algorithm can be implemented in the following steps:

A) Reduce angle range to first quadrant. ($0 \leq x \leq \pi/2$)

1) SIGN = SGN(x)
2) ABSX = ‖x‖
3) XNEW = ABSX − 2π × INT(ABSX/2π)
4) If XNEW > π then SIGN = −SIGN and XNEW = XNEW − π
5) If XNEW > π/2 then XNEW = π − XNEW

where

$$\mathrm{SGN}(x) = \begin{cases} +1 & \text{if } x \geq 0 \\ -1 & \text{if } x < 0 \end{cases}$$

INT(x) = integer function

B) Compute $\sin(x) \simeq \sum_{n=0}^{6} A_n\, x^{2n-1}$.

1) Let XSQR = XNEW^2; INITIALIZE SINX = 0
2) Do i = 6 to 1 step −1
   SINX = XSQR × SINX + A(i)
   Enddo
3) SINX = SIGN × XNEW × SINX

Step B-2 computes the summation in a geometric series for economy. The major difference between steps A and B is that A requires more diverse ALU operations while B uses only multiplication and addition recursively.

STEP 3: MAKE 'AS888 REGISTER ASSIGNMENTS

Just as in assembly language programming, registers must be allocated for variables. Using Rn to denote the 'AS888 register whose address is n, where $0 \leq n \leq F$ (hex), the following register assignments can be made:

R0 = X
R1 = SIGN
R2 = ABSX
R3 = XNEW
R4 = XSQR
R5 = SINX

The following constants can also be defined:

Constant	Decimal	IEEE hex
PI = π	3.141593	4059 0FDB
PIOVR2 = $\pi/2$	1.570797	3FC9 0FDB
2PI = 2π	6.283185	40C9 0FDB
1OVR2PI = $1/2\pi$	0.159155	3E22 F981

STEP 4: SUBSTITUTE REGISTERS FOR VARIABLES IN THE ALGORITHM

Now the algorithm can be rewritten with registers replacing variables:

A) Reduce angle range to first quadrant ($0 \leq x \leq \pi/2$).
   1) R1 = SGN(R0)
   2) R2 = ‖R0‖
   3) R3 = R2 − 2π × INT(R2/2π)
   4) If R3 > π then R1 = −R1; R3 = R3 − π
   5) If R3 > $\pi/2$ then R3 = π − R3

B) Compute $\sin(x) \simeq \sum_{n=0}^{6} A_n x^{2n-1}$.
   1) Let R4 = R0^2; INITIALIZE R5 = 0
   2) Do i=6 to 1 step −1
         R5 = R4 × R5 + A(i)
      Enddo
   3) R5 = R1 × R0 × R5

Since various references to constants are made, it is probably best to load constants as needed rather than attempt to allocate registers for them. Constants can be loaded from a constant field in the microinstruction or from ROM. The trade-off is 32 bits by 16K of micromemory versus 32 bits by the number of constants (typically less than 16K). For this example, it will be assumed that a constant field in the microinstruction is acceptable.

STEP 5: DECOMPOSE STEPS IN THE ALGORITHM INTO SIMPLE OPERATIONS

The sin(x) function can be microprogrammed as a subroutine; let FSIN be its entry address. R0 would be loaded with x before FSIN was called. Upon return, R5 would contain sin(x). Now decompose the steps in the algorithm into simple arithmetic and logical operations. Other operations can be left as functions to be defined later.

```
FSIN: SUBROUTINE

; A) Reduce angle range to first quadrant. (0 ≤ x ≤ π/2)

    R1 = SGN(R0)                       ;  1) Let R1 = Sign of R0

    R2 = ABS(R0)                       ;  2) R2 = ‖R0‖

    R3 = R2 * 1OVR2PI                  ;  3) R3 = R2 − 2π * INT(R2/2π)
    R3 = INT(R3)                       ;
    R3 = R3 * 2PI                      ;
    R3 = R2 − R3                       ;

    Y = R3 − PI                        ;  4) If R3 > π,
    Jump if Negative to Step A-5       ;
    R1 = −R1                           ;     then R1 = −R1;
    R3 = R3 − PI                       ;     R3 = R3 − π

    Y = PIOVR2 − R3                    ;
    Jump if Negative to Step B-1       ;  5) If R3 > π/2
    R3 = PI − R3                       ;     then R3 = π − R3
```

; B) Compute $\sin(x) \simeq \sum_{n=0}^{6} A_n x^{2n-1}$

```
R4 = R0 * R0                    ;  1) Let R4 = R0^2. Let R5 = 0
R5 = 0                          ;

R5 = R4 * R5                    ;  2) Do i=6 to 1 step -1
R5 = R5 + A6                    ;     R5 = R4 × R5 + A(i)
R5 = R4 * R5                    ;     Enddo
R5 = R5 + A5                    ;
R5 = R4 * R5                    ;     (To implement a loop,
R5 = R5 + A4                    ;     use an 'AS890 counter
R5 = R4 * R5                    ;     to index a memory containing
R5 = R5 + A3                    ;     the constants.)
R5 = R4 * R5                    ;
R5 = R5 + A2                    ;
R5 = R4 * R5                    ;
R5 = R5 + A1                    ;
R5 = R4 * R5                    ;
R5 = R5 + A0                    ;

R5 = R0 * R5                    ;  3) R5 = R1 × R0 × R5
R5 = R5 * R1 : RETURN           ;

END SUBROUTINE
```

STEP 6: TRANSLATE INTO 'AS888/890 INSTRUCTIONS; IDENTIFY SUBROUTINES

The simplified steps of the algorithm can be represented fairly easily as 'AS888/890 instructions. Necessary functions (and suggested names) can be identified by inspection as:

1) FMUL — Floating-point multiplication
2) FADD — Floating-point addition
3) FINT — Floating-point integer conversion
4) FINV — Floating-point additive inverse (to subtract using FADD)
5) FABS — Floating-point absolute value
6) FSGN — Floating-point sign test
7) FCHS — Floating-point change of sign (to multiply by SIGN)

"Function" in this context refers to a special operation regardless of how it is coded. In fact, FMUL and FADD are fairly complex and require detailed explanation. FINV, FABS, FSGN and FCHS are single instruction operations that mask or mask and test. FINT requires several inline instructions or a subroutine and will be left to the interested reader as an exercise. Now the steps of the algorithm can be translated into 'AS888/890 operations which include references to these functions.

```
FSIN: SUBROUTINE

; A) Reduce angle range to first quadrant. (0 ≤ x ≤ π/2)

     R1 = FSGN(R0)                   ; Get sign bit (MSB)
     R2 = FABS(R0)                   ; Take absolute value (clear MSB)
     R3 = FMUL(R2,1OVR2PI)           ; Multiply register and constant
     R3 = FINT(R3)                   ; Floating-point integer conversion
     R3 = FMUL(R3,2PI)               ; Multiply register and constant
     R3 = FADD(R2,INV(R3))           ; Subtract registers by adding inverse
     Y = FADD(R3,NEGPI) : TEST NEG   ; Subtract by adding negative constant
     JT SIN1                         ; Jump if true (jump if negative)
     R1 = FINV(R1)                   ; Complement sign of R1
     R3 = FADD(R3,NEGPI)             ; Subtract by adding negative constant
SIN1:Y = PIOVR2 - R3 : TEST NEG      ; Subtract to compare (don't store)
     JT SIN2                         ; Jump if true (jump if negative)
     R3 = FADD(PI,FINV(R3))          ; Subtract by adding negative register
```

; B) Compute $\sin(x) \simeq \sum_{n=0}^{6} A_n X^{2n-1}$

```
SIN2: R4 = FMUL(R0,R0)                  ; Square by multiplying
      R5 = A6                           ; Initialize series
      R5 = FMUL(R4,R5)                  ; Multiply registers
      R5 = FADD(R5,A5)                  ; Add coefficient
      R5 = FMUL(R4,R5)                  ; Multiply registers
      R5 = FADD(R5,A4)                  ; Add coefficient
      R5 = FMUL(R4,R5)                  ; Multiply registers
      R5 = FADD(R5,A3)                  ; Add coefficient
      R5 = FMUL(R4,R5)                  ; Multiply registers
      R5 = FADD(R5,A2)                  ; Add coefficient
      R5 = FMUL(R4,R5)                  ; Multiply registers
      R5 = FADD(R5,A1)                  ; Add coefficient
      R5 = FMUL(R4,R5)                  ; Multiply registers
      R5 = FADD(R5,A0)                  ; Add coefficient
      R5 = FMUL(R0,R5)                  ; Multiply registers
      R5 = FCHS(R5,R1) : RETURN         ; Change MSB of R5 to MSB of R1

END SUBROUTINE
```

This contrived language has a syntax which may be suitable for a source program. For the sake of illustration, it can be assumed that the microassembler recognizes this particular syntax. The series was computed inline instead of using a loop since it is relatively short. If a loop were used, a means of indexing the constants would be required.

STEP 7: EXPAND SUBROUTINES INTO 'AS888/890 OPERATIONS

FMUL and FADD algorithms can now be expanded. Since they are called extensively from FSIN, they are more critical to the efficiency of the final design. Wherever possible, it is desirable to reduce the execution time of both in order to maintain efficiency.

Floating-Point Multiplication

Let M1 be the multiplier and M2 be the multiplicand whose product is P. Let the sign, exponent and fraction fields of their IEEE representation be:

```
M1 : |S1|E1|F1|
M2 : |S2|E2|F2|
 P : |S3|E3|F3|
```

P is found by multiplying mantissas (fraction plus implicit one) and adding exponents. Since M1 and M2 are normalized, the range of $1.F1 \times 1.F2$ is

$$1.00\ldots0 \leq 1.F1 \times 1.F2 \leq 11.1\ldots10$$

The implicit bit may "overflow" into bit position 24. This type of overflow must be detected so that the result can be normalized. Normalization requires right shifting the result of $1.F1 \times 1.F2$ and incrementing E3. The implicit bit is then cleared when S3, E3 and M3 are packed to form P. The floating-point multiplication algorithm may then be defined as follows:

1) Unpack M1 into signed fraction (SF1) and exponent (E1)
2) Set the implicit bit in SF1
3) Unpack M2 into signed fraction (SF2) and exponent (E2)
4) Set the implicit bit in SF2
5) Perform SF3 = SF1 × SF2 using signed integer multiplication
6) Perform E3 = E1 + E2
7) Test SF3 for overflow into bit 24
8) If true, then increment E3 and right shift SF3
9) Clear the implicit bit in SF3
10) Pack E3 and SF3 to get P

3

Application Reports

As before, the steps of this algorithm can be broken down into simpler operations:

1) Unpack M1 into signed fraction (SF1) and exponent (E1)
   E1 = FEXP(M1)
   SF1 = FRAC(M1)

2) Set the implicit bit in SF1
   SF1 = SF1 OR BIT23

3) Unpack M2 into signed fraction (SF2) and exponent (E2)
   E2 = FEXP (M2)
   SF2 = FRAC (M2)

4) Set the implicit bit in SF2
   SF2 = SF2 OR BIT23

5) Perform SF3 = SF1 × SF2 using signed integer multiplication
   SF3 = IMUL (SF1, SF2)

6) Perform E3 = E1 + E2
   E3 = E1 + E2

7) Test SF3 for overflow into bit 24
   TEST (SF3 AND BIT24)
   JUMP IF FALSE to step 9

8) If true, then increment E3 and right shift SF3
   INC E3
   SF3 = RSHFT (SF3)

9) Clear the implicit bit in SF3.
   SF3 = SF3 AND NOT_BIT23

10) Pack E3 and SF3 to get P
   P = SF3 OR E3

FEXP, FRAC, testing bit 24 and setting/clearing bit 23 are all mask operations that translate into single 'AS888 instructions. The integer multiplication (IMUL) is simply the multiplication algorithm supported by the 'AS888 instruction set. No significant hardware features are required to do floating-point multiplication, nor are any subroutines required to support it.

Register assignments can now be made as before. Since FSIN uses registers in the lower half of the register file, it might be preferable to restrict FMUL to the upper registers. For example:

RF = P
RE = M1, F1, SF1
RD = M2, F2, SF2
RC = E1
RB = E2

RE and RD can share variables that need not be preserved. Using this assignment, FMUL computes RF = FMUL(RE,RD). RE and RD must be loaded prior to calling FMUL and RF must be stored upon return. By substituting registers for variables and reorganizing operations in the FMUL algorithm to better fit 'AS888/890 operations the following source program may be created:

```
FMUL: SUBROUTINE

        RC = FEXP(RE)           ; Unpack M1 into exponent
        RE = FRAC(RE)           ;  and fraction
        RE = RE OR BIT23        ; Set implicit bit
        MQ = SMTC(RE)           ; Prepare to multiply

        RB = FEXP(RD)           ; Unpack M2 into exponent
        RD = FMAG(RD)           ;  and fraction
        RD = RD OR BIT23        ; Set implicit bit
        RD = SMTC(RD)           ; Prepare to multiply
```

3 Application Reports

```
          RE = 0 : RCA = #22d                  ; Initialize to multiply
          RE = SMULI RD : LOOP RCA             ; Integer multiplication iteration
          RE = SMULT RD                        ; Final step in signed multiply
          Y= TB0(RE,BIT1):BYTE= #0100b:TEST Z ; Test ''overflow''
          JF FMUL1                             ; Jump if false (exponent ok)

          INEX(RC)                             ; Increment exponent: add 00800000
          RE = SRA(RE)                         ; Shift fraction to normalize

FMUL1:RC = RC + RB : TEST CARRY                ; Add exponents and test carry
          JT ERROR                             ; Jump if carry true to handler

          RE = SMTC(RE)                        ; Get sign magnitude fraction
          RE = RE AND #807F_FFFFh              ; Clear implicit bit
          RF = RE OR RC : RETURN               ; Pack fraction and exponent
```

Floating-Point Addition

The floating-point addition algorithm (FADD) is slightly more complex than FMUL, since the two addends will usually not have the same exponent. Therefore the smaller (absolute value) addend must first be chosen by comparing exponents. Then it must be denormalized to align its digits with the digits of the larger addend. In other words, the two addends must have the same exponent before their fractions can be added. This process can be described by the following algorithm:

```
 1) Unpack A1 to get SF1 and E1
 2) Set implicit bit in SF1
 3) Unpack A2 to get SF2 and E2
 4) Set implicit bit in SF2
 5) If E2 > E1 then go to step 9
    (‖A1‖ ≤ ‖A2‖)
 6) Let DIFF = E1 - E2
 7) Do i = 1 to DIFF
      SF2 = RSHFT(SF2) (Arithmetic right shift)
    Enddo
 8) Let E3 = E1 , go to step 12
    (‖A2‖ > ‖A1‖)
 9) Let DIFF = E2 - E1
10) Do i = 1 to DIFF
      SF1 = RSHFT(SF1) (Arithmetic right shift)
      Enddo

11) Let E3 = E2
12) SF3 = SF1 + SF2
13) Test ''overflow'' into bit 24
14) Jump if false to step 17
15) Increment exponent E3
16) Normalize signed fraction with right arithmetic shift
17) Clear implicit bit
18) Pack: SUM = SF3 or E3
19) Return
```

Register assignments for variables must now be made. Since FSIN uses registers in the lower half of the 'AS888 register file, it is necessary to use the upper registers:

```
RF = SUM
RE = A1, F1, SF1
RD = A2, F2, SF2
RC = E1
RB = E2
```

By slightly reorganizing the sequence to better fit 'AS888/890 operations, the following microprogram to perform FADD can be created:

```
FADD: SUBROUTINE

; 1)  Unpack A1 to get SF1 and E1
         RC = FEXP(RE)                       ; Get exponent (E1)
         RE = FRAC(RE)                       ; Get signed fraction (SF1)

; 2)  Set implicit bit in SF1
         MQ = RE OR BIT23                    ; Set implicit bit
         RE = SMTC(RE)                       ; Convert to two's complement

; 3)  Unpack A2 to get SF2 and A2
         RB = FEXP(RD)                       ; Get exponent (E2)
         RD = FRAC(RD)                       ; Get signed fraction (SF2)

; 4)  Set implicit bit in SF2
         RD = RD OR BIT23                    ; Set implicit bit
         RD = SMTC(RD)                       ; Convert to two's complement

; 5)  If E2 > E1 then go to step 9
         RF = RC - RB : TEST NEGATIVE        ; Compare A2 from A1
         JT FADD1 : RCA = #8                 ; Jump if E2 > E1; set up loop count

; 6)  Let DIFF = E1 - E2.
         Y/RF = SLC(RF) : LOOP RCA           ; Rotate 8 times to get difference
         RCA = Y/RF                          ; Load difference in loop counter

; 7)  Do i = 1 to DIFF
;           SF2 = RSHFT(SF2)
;        Enddo
         RD = SRA(RD) : LOOP RCA             ; Orient digits of smaller addend

; 8)  Let E3 = E1, go to step 12
         RB = RC : JUMP FADD2                ; Swap registers and branch

; 9)  Let DIFF = E2 - E1

FADD1: RF = NOT(RF)                          ; Complement result of E1 - E2
         Y/RF = SLC(RF) : LOOP RCA           ; Shift 8 times to get DIFF
         RCA = Y/RF                          ; Load DIFF in loop counter

;10)  Do i = 1 TO DIFF
;           SF1 = RSHFT(SF1)
;        Enddo
         RE = SRA(RE) : LOOP RCA             ; Align SF1 with SF2

;11)  Let E3 = E2 (no instruction required — RB already has E2 in it)

;12)  SF3 = SF1 + SF2

FADD2: RF = RD + RE                          ; Add
         RF = SMTC(RF)                       ; Convert to sign-magnitude

;13)  Test "overflow" into bit 24
         RF = TB0 (RF, BIT24)                ; Check for normalization

;14)  Jump if false to step 17
         JF FADD3                            ; If so, finish and exit

;15)  Else increment exponent
         INC RB : TEST NEG                   ; Test for exponent overflow

;16)  Normalize signed fraction
         RF = SRA(RF) : JT ERROR             ; Jump to error handler if overflow
```

```
;17) Clear implicit bit

FADD3: RF = SET0 (RF, BIT23)                 ; Reset bit 23 of RF

;18) Pack: SUM = SF3 OR E3
         RF = RF OR RB : RETURN               ; OR signed fraction and exponent
```

There is an important consequence of FADD which impacts the hardware. Since the number of shifts required to denormalize the small addend is data dependent (computed in the ALU), it is necessary to provide a path between the ALU Y bus and the 'AS890 DRA bus. All the other operations are simple 'AS888/890 instructions, including the FRAC and FEXP mask operations discussed during the development of FMUL. ERROR is a floating-point overflow error handler.

STEP 8: EVALUATE TRADE-OFFS AND BLOCK DIAGRAM THE HARDWARE

A rough estimate of the FSIN worst case execution time can be arrived at by making the following observations about FSIN, FMUL and FADD:

FMUL
  integer recursion ≃ 22 cycles
  other instructions ≃ 18 cycles
  total ≃ 40 cycles

FADD
  denormalization ≃ 23 cycles
  other instructions ≃ 25 cycles
  total ≃ 50 cycles

FSIN
  number of calls to FMUL = 12
  number of calls to FADD = 11
  number of other cycles ≃ 10

Approximate worst case total = 10 + (12 × 40) + (11 × 50) = 1040 cycles. At 50 nanoseconds per cycle, this requires approximately 52 microseconds. There are few improvements that could be made in hardware to speed this time, except perhaps the addition of a flash multiplier which would reduce the integer computation by about 20 cycles (an overall reduction of about two percent). A barrel shifter could have the same benefit during floating-point addition for a total reduction of about 4 percent. For the sake of simplicity, it will be assumed that 52 microseconds is acceptable for the sin(x) computation.

Another issue which must be considered is the problem of loading the 'AS888 and 'AS890 with constants. A slight materials cost reduction might be realized by storing constants in table PROMs rather than in control store memory. An interesting use of the DRA and DRB ports on the 'AS890 would be to use the output of RCA or RCB to index data in the constant PROM. This would allow long series to be implemented in loop form rather than the inline method used in FSIN. Once again, the constant PROM will not be implemented for the sake of simplicity.

Now the architecture can be designed to meet the requirements identified throughout this analysis:

1) A path between the 'AS888 Y bus and the 'AS890 DRA bus.
2) A path between the microinstruction register and the 'AS890 DRA bus for loading loop counts and branch addresses.
3) A path between the microinstruction register and the 'AS888 Y bus for loading constants.
4) Independent control of $\overline{\text{SIO0}}$ in each 'AS888 slice to allow bit/byte instructions.
5) A status register to store 'AS888 status for testing.
6) A status mux to test the 'AS888 status, bit 23 of the 'AS888 Y bus, bit 24 of the 'AS888 Y bus and hardwired 0 and 1.

A system having these features is illustrated in Figure 6-1.

STEP 9: DEFINE MICROINSTRUCTION FIELDS DURING DETAILED HARDWARE DESIGN

The detailed hardware design will produce a wiring diagram that fixes the position within the microinstruction of each of the various control signals that are connected from the microinstruction register to the 'AS888, 'AS890, status mux and any other special hardware. Once this design is complete it is possible for the assembler to sort the control bits of each instruction properly so that they will be properly oriented when the microprogram is installed in the target system.

STEP 10: ASSEMBLE THE MICROPROGRAM

TI is currently developing an 'AS888/890 microassembler. Several microassemblers are commercially available, and many users prefer to write their own. The microprogram shown in Table 6-1 was hand-assembled, but has a syntax that is suitable for interpretation by a user-written assembler.

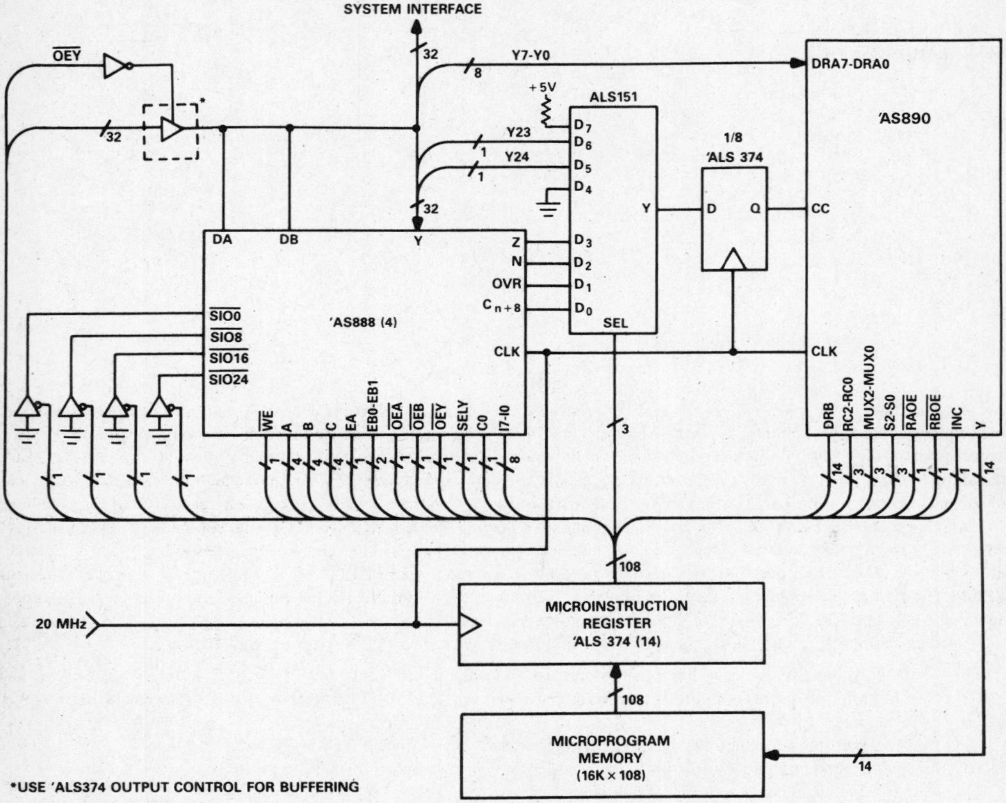
SYSTEM INTERFACE
OEY
Y7-Y0
DRA7-DRA0
'AS890
+5V
ALS151
Y23
Y24
1/8
'ALS 374
D
Q
CC
DA
DB
Y
Z
N
OVR
Cn+8
SIO0
SIO8
SIO16
SIO24
'AS888 (4)
CLK
SEL
WE A B C EA EB0-EB1 OEA OEB OEY SELY C0 I7-I0
DRB RC2-RC0 MUX2-MUX0 S2-S0 RAOE RBOE INC Y
MICROINSTRUCTION
REGISTER
'ALS 374 (14)
20 MHz
MICROPROGRAM
MEMORY
(16K × 108)
*USE 'ALS374 OUTPUT CONTROL FOR BUFFERING

Figure 6-1. Block Diagram of Floating-Point Processor

Table 6.1. Floating Point Sin(x) Microprogram

Address	Label	Source	$\overline{WE}$	A3-A0	B3-B0	C3-C0	$\overline{EA}$	EB1-EB0	$\overline{OEA}$	$\overline{OEB}$	OEY	SELY	Cn	I7-I0	32-bit Constant	$\overline{SIO0}$	$\overline{SIO8}$	$\overline{SIO16}$	$\overline{SIO24}$	RC2-RC0	MUX2-MUX0	S2-S0	DRB13-DRB0	$\overline{RAOE}$	$\overline{RBOE}$	$\overline{INC}$	SEL
		* R1 = FSGN(R0)																									
0000	SIN:	R1 = R0 AND #8000 0000h	0	0	X	1	0	2	1	1	1	0	0	FA	80000000	1	1	1	1	0	2	7	XXXX	1	1	1	7
		* R2 = FABS(R0)																									
0001		R2 = R0	0	0	X	2	0	X	1	1	1	0	0	F6	XXXXXXXX	1	1	1	1	0	2	7	XXXX	1	1	1	7
0002		R2 = R0 SET0 #80h : BYTE = #1000b	0	0	2	8	0	0	1	1	1	0	0	18	XXXXXXXX	1	1	1	0	0	2	7	XXXX	1	1	1	7
		* R3 = FMUL(R2,1OVR2PI)																									
0003		RE = R2	0	2	X	E	0	X	1	1	1	0	0	F6	XXXXXXXX	1	1	1	1	0	2	7	XXXX	1	1	1	7
0004		RD = #3EA2 F984h	0	X	X	D	X	X	1	1	1	1	X	FF	3EA2F984	1	1	1	1	0	2	7	XXXX	1	1	1	7
0005		JSR FMUL	1	X	X	X	X	X	1	1	1	X	X	FF	XXXXXXXX	1	1	1	1	0	1	4	0060	1	1	1	7
0006		R3 = RF	0	F	X	3	0	X	1	1	1	0	0	F6	XXXXXXXX	1	1	1	1	0	2	7	XXXX	1	1	1	7
		* R3 = FINT(R3)																									
0007		RF = R3	0	3	X	F	0	X	1	1	1	0	0	F6	XXXXXXXX	1	1	1	1	0	2	7	XXXX	1	1	1	7
0008		JSR FINT [EXERCISE FOR READER]	1	X	X	X	X	X	1	1	1	X	X	FF	XXXXXXXX	1	1	1	1	0	1	4	. . . .	1	1	1	7
0009		R3 = RF	0	F	X	3	0	X	1	1	1	0	0	F6	XXXXXXXX	1	1	1	1	0	2	7	XXXX	1	1	1	7
		* R3 = FMUL(R3,2PI)																									
000A		RE = R3	0	3	X	E	0	X	1	1	1	0	0	F6	XXXXXXXX	1	1	1	1	0	2	7	XXXX	1	1	1	7
000B		RD = #40C9 0FDBh	0	X	X	D	X	X	1	1	1	0	X	FF	40C90FDB	1	1	1	1	0	2	7	XXXX	1	1	1	7
000C		JSR FMUL	1	X	X	X	X	X	1	1	1	X	X	FF	XXXXXXXX	1	1	1	1	0	1	4	0060	1	1	1	7
000D		R3 = RF	0	F	X	3	0	X	1	1	1	0	0	F6	XXXXXXXX	1	1	1	1	0	2	7	XXXX	1	1	1	7
		* R3 = FADD(R2,INV(R3))																									
000E		RE = R2	0	2	X	E	0	X	1	1	1	0	0	F6	XXXXXXXX	1	1	1	1	0	2	7	XXXX	1	1	1	7
000F		RD = R5 XOR #8000 0000h	0	5	X	D	0	2	1	1	1	0	0	F9	80000000	1	1	1	1	0	2	7	XXXX	1	1	1	7
0010		JSR FADD	1	X	X	X	X	X	1	1	1	X	X	FF	XXXXXXXX	1	1	1	1	0	1	4	0074	1	1	1	7
0011		R3 = RF	0	F	X	3	0	X	1	1	1	0	0	F6	XXXXXXXX	1	1	1	1	0	2	7	XXXX	1	1	1	7
		* Y = FADD(R2,NEGPI)																									
0012		RE = R2	0	2	X	E	0	X	1	1	1	0	0	F6	XXXXXXXX	1	1	1	1	0	2	7	XXXX	1	1	1	7
0013		RD = #C059 0FDBh	0	X	X	D	X	X	1	1	1	0	X	FF	C0590FDB	1	1	1	1	0	2	7	XXXX	1	1	1	7
0014		JSR FADD	1	X	X	X	X	X	1	1	1	X	X	FF	XXXXXXXX	1	1	1	1	0	1	4	0074	1	1	1	7
0015		Y = RF : TEST NEG	1	F	X	X	0	X	1	1	0	0	0	F6	XXXXXXXX	1	1	1	1	0	2	7	XXXX	1	1	1	2
0016		JT SIN1	1	X	X	X	X	X	1	1	1	X	X	FF	XXXXXXXX	1	1	1	1	0	1	7	0000	1	1	1	7
		* R1 = FINV(R1)																									
0017		R1 = R1 XOR #8000 0000h	0	1	X	1	0	2	1	1	1	0	0	F9	80000000	1	1	1	1	0	2	7	XXXX	1	1	1	7
		* R3 = FADD(R3,NEGPI)																									
0018		RE = R3	0	3	X	E	0	X	1	1	1	0	0	F6	XXXXXXXX	1	1	1	1	0	2	7	XXXX	1	1	1	7
0019		RD = #C059 0FDBh	0	3	X	D	X	X	1	1	1	1	X	FF	C0590FDB	1	1	1	1	0	2	7	XXXX	1	1	1	7
001A		JSR FADD	1	X	X	X	X	X	1	1	1	X	X	FF	XXXXXXXX	1	1	1	1	0	1	4	0074	1	1	1	7
001B		R3 = RF	0	F	X	3	0	X	1	1	1	0	0	F6	XXXXXXXX	1	1	1	1	0	2	7	XXXX	1	1	1	7
	* SIN1:	Y = FADD (PIOVR2,INV(R3)) : TEST NEG																									
001C	SIN1:	RE = #3FC9 0FDBh	0	X	X	E	X	X	1	1	1	1	0	F6	35C90FDB	1	1	1	1	0	2	7	XXXX	1	1	1	7
001D		RD = R3 XOR #8000 0000h	0	3	X	D	0	2	1	1	1	0	0	F9	80000000	1	1	1	1	0	2	7	XXXX	1	1	1	7
001E		JSR FADD	1	X	X	X	X	X	1	1	1	X	X	FF	XXXXXXXX	1	1	1	1	0	1	4	0074	1	1	1	7
001F		Y = RF : TEST NEG	1	F	X	X	0	X	1	1	0	0	0	F6	XXXXXXXX	1	1	1	1	0	2	7	XXXX	1	1	1	2
0020		JT SIN2	1	X	X	X	X	X	1	1	1	X	X	FF	XXXXXXXX	1	1	1	1	0	1	7	0000	1	1	1	7
		* R3 = FADD(PI,FINV(R3))																									
0021		RE = #4059 0FDBh	0	X	X	E	X	X	1	1	1	1	0	F6	40590FDB	1	1	1	1	0	2	7	XXXX	1	1	1	7
0022		RD = R3 XOR #8000 0000h	0	3	X	D	0	2	1	1	1	0	0	F9	80000000	1	1	1	1	0	2	7	XXXX	1	1	1	7
0023		JSR FADD	1	X	X	X	X	X	1	1	1	X	X	FF	XXXXXXXX	1	1	1	1	0	1	4	0074	1	1	1	7
0024		R3 = RF	0	F	X	3	0	X	1	1	1	0	0	F6	XXXXXXXX	1	1	1	1	0	2	7	XXXX	1	1	1	7
	* SIN2:	R4 = FMUL(R0,R0)																									
0025	SIN2:	RE = R0	0	0	X	E	0	X	1	1	1	0	0	F6	XXXXXXXX	1	1	1	1	0	2	7	XXXX	1	1	1	7
0026		RD = R0	0	0	X	D	0	X	1	1	1	0	0	F6	XXXXXXXX	1	1	1	1	0	2	7	XXXX	1	1	1	7
0027		JSR FMUL	1	X	X	X	X	X	1	1	1	X	X	FF	XXXXXXXX	1	1	1	1	0	1	4	0060	1	1	1	7
0028		R4 = RF	0	F	X	4	0	X	1	1	1	0	0	F6	XXXXXXXX	1	1	1	1	0	2	7	XXXX	1	1	1	7

Table 6.1. Floating Point Sin(x) Microprogram (Continued)

Address	Instruction	WE	A3-A0	B3-B0	C3-C0	EA	EB1-EB0	OEA	OEB	OEY	SELY	Cn	I7-I0	32-bit Constant	SIO0	SIO8	SIO16	SIO24	RC2-RC0	MUX2-MUX0	S2-S0	DRB13-DRB0	RAOE	RBOE	INC	SEL
	* R5 = A6																									
0029	R5 = #2F34 6FBCh	0	X	X	5	0	X	1	1	1	1	0	F 6	2 F 3 4 6 F B C	1	1	1	1	0	2	7	X X X X	1	1	1	7
	* R5 = FMUL(R4,R5)																									
002A	RE = R4	0	4	X	E	0	X	1	1	1	0	0	F 6	X X X X X X X X	1	1	1	1	0	2	7	X X X X	1	1	1	7
002B	RD = R5	0	5	X	D	0	X	1	1	1	0	0	F 6	X X X X X X X X	1	1	1	1	0	2	7	X X X X	1	1	1	7
002C	JSR FMUL	1	X	X	X	X	X	1	1	1	X	X	F F	X X X X X X X X	1	1	1	1	0	1	4	0 0 6 0	1	1	1	7
002D	R5 = RF	0	F	X	5	0	X	1	1	1	0	0	F 6	X X X X X X X X	1	1	1	1	0	2	7	X X X X	1	1	1	7
	* R5 = FADD(R5,A5)																									
002E	RE = R5	0	5	X	E	0	X	1	1	1	0	0	F 6	X X X X X X X X	1	1	1	1	0	2	7	X X X X	1	1	1	7
002F	RD = #B2D7 5AD5h	0	X	X	D	X	X	1	1	1	1	X	F F	B 2 D 7 5 A D 5	1	1	1	1	0	2	7	X X X X	1	1	1	7
0030	JSR FADD	1	X	X	X	X	X	1	1	1	X	X	F F	X X X X X X X X	1	1	1	1	0	1	4	0 0 7 4	1	1	1	7
0031	R5 = RF	0	F	X	5	0	X	1	1	1	0	0	F 6	X X X X X X X X	1	1	1	1	0	2	7	X X X X	1	1	1	7
	* R5 = FMUL(R4,R5)																									
0032	RE = R4	0	4	X	E	0	X	1	1	1	0	0	F 6	X X X X X X X X	1	1	1	1	0	2	7	X X X X	1	1	1	7
0033	RD = R5	0	5	X	D	0	X	1	1	1	0	0	F 6	X X X X X X X X	1	1	1	1	0	2	7	X X X X	1	1	1	7
0034	JSR FMUL	1	X	X	X	X	X	1	1	1	X	X	F F	X X X X X X X X	1	1	1	1	0	1	4	0 0 6 0	1	1	1	7
0035	R5 = RF	0	F	X	5	0	X	1	1	1	0	0	F 6	X X X X X X X X	1	1	1	1	0	2	7	X X X X	1	1	1	7
	* R5 = FADD(R5,A4)																									
0036	RE = R5	0	5	X	E	0	X	1	1	1	0	0	F 6	X X X X X X X X	1	1	1	1	0	2	7	X X X X	1	1	1	7
0037	RD = #3638 EF99h	0	X	X	D	X	X	1	1	1	1	X	F F	3 6 3 8 E F 9 9	1	1	1	1	0	2	7	X X X X	1	1	1	7
0038	JSR FADD	1	X	X	X	X	X	1	1	1	X	X	F F	X X X X X X X X	1	1	1	1	0	1	4	0 0 7 4	1	1	1	7
0039	R5 = RF	0	F	X	5	0	X	1	1	1	0	0	F 6	X X X X X X X X	1	1	1	1	0	2	7	X X X X	1	1	1	7
	* R5 = FMUL(R4,R5)																									
003A	RE = R4	0	4	X	E	0	X	1	1	1	0	0	F 6	X X X X X X X X	1	1	1	1	0	2	7	X X X X	1	1	1	7
003B	RD = R5	0	5	X	D	0	X	1	1	1	0	0	F 6	X X X X X X X X	1	1	1	1	0	2	7	X X X X	1	1	1	7
003C	JSR FMUL	1	X	X	X	X	X	1	1	1	X	X	F F	X X X X X X X X	1	1	1	1	0	1	4	0 0 6 0	1	1	1	7
003D	R5 = RF	0	F	X	5	0	X	1	1	1	0	0	F 6	X X X X X X X X	1	1	1	1	0	2	7	X X X X	1	1	1	7
	* R5 = FADD(R5,A3)																									
003E	RE = R5	0	5	X	E	0	X	1	1	1	0	0	F 6	X X X X X X X X	1	1	1	1	0	2	7	X X X X	1	1	1	7
003F	RD = #B950 0D01h	0	X	X	D	X	X	1	1	1	1	X	F F	B 9 5 0 0 D 0 1	1	1	1	1	0	2	7	X X X X	1	1	1	7
0040	JSR FADD	1	X	X	X	X	X	1	1	1	X	X	F F	X X X X X X X X	1	1	1	1	0	1	4	0 0 7 4	1	1	1	7
0041	R5 = RF	0	F	X	5	0	X	1	1	1	0	0	F 6	X X X X X X X X	1	1	1	1	0	2	7	X X X X	1	1	1	7
	* R5 = FMUL(R4,R5)																									
0042	RE = R4	0	4	X	E	0	X	1	1	1	0	0	F 6	X X X X X X X X	1	1	1	1	0	2	7	X X X X	1	1	1	7
0043	RD = R5	0	5	X	D	0	X	1	1	1	0	0	F 6	X X X X X X X X	1	1	1	1	0	2	7	X X X X	1	1	1	7
0044	JSR FMUL	1	X	X	X	X	X	1	1	1	X	X	F F	X X X X X X X X	1	1	1	1	0	1	4	0 0 6 0	1	1	1	7
0045	R5 = RF	0	F	X	5	0	X	1	1	1	0	0	F 6	X X X X X X X X	1	1	1	1	0	2	7	X X X X	1	1	1	7
	* R5 = FADD(R5,A2)																									
0046	RE = R5	0	5	X	E	0	X	1	1	1	0	0	F 6	X X X X X X X X	1	1	1	1	0	2	7	X X X X	1	1	1	7
0047	RD = #3C08 8888h	0	X	X	D	X	X	1	1	1	1	X	F F	3 C 0 8 8 8 8 8	1	1	1	1	0	2	7	X X X X	1	1	1	7
0048	JSR FADD	1	X	X	X	X	X	1	1	1	X	X	F F	X X X X X X X X	1	1	1	1	0	1	4	0 0 7 4	1	1	1	7
0049	R5 = RF	0	F	X	5	0	X	1	1	1	0	0	F 6	X X X X X X X X	1	1	1	1	0	2	7	X X X X	1	1	1	7
	* R5 = FMUL(R4,R5)																									
004A	RE = R4	0	4	X	E	0	X	1	1	1	0	0	F 6	X X X X X X X X	1	1	1	1	0	2	7	X X X X	1	1	1	7
004B	RD = R5	0	5	X	D	0	X	1	1	1	0	0	F 6	X X X X X X X X	1	1	1	1	0	2	7	X X X X	1	1	1	7
004C	JSR FMUL	1	X	X	X	X	X	1	1	1	X	X	F F	X X X X X X X X	1	1	1	1	0	1	4	0 0 6 0	1	1	1	7
004D	R5 = RF	0	F	X	5	0	X	1	1	1	0	0	F 6	X X X X X X X X	1	1	1	1	0	2	7	X X X X	1	1	1	7
	* R5 = FADD(R5,A1)																									
004E	RE = R5	0	5	X	E	0	X	1	1	1	0	0	F 6	X X X X X X X X	1	1	1	1	0	2	7	X X X X	1	1	1	7
004F	RD = #BE2A AAADh	0	X	X	D	X	X	1	1	1	1	1	F F	B E 2 A A A A D	1	1	1	1	0	2	7	X X X X	1	1	1	7
0050	JSR FADD	1	X	X	X	X	X	1	1	1	X	X	F F	X X X X X X X X	1	1	1	1	0	1	4	0 0 7 4	1	1	1	7
0051	R5 = RF	0	F	X	5	0	X	1	1	1	0	0	F 6	X X X X X X X X	1	1	1	1	0	2	7	X X X X	1	1	1	7
	* R5 = FMUL(R4,R5)																									
0052	RE = R4	0	4	X	E	0	X	1	1	1	0	0	F 6	X X X X X X X X	1	1	1	1	0	2	7	X X X X	1	1	1	7
0053	RD = R5	0	5	X	D	0	X	1	1	1	0	0	F 6	X X X X X X X X	1	1	1	1	0	2	7	X X X X	1	1	1	7
0054	JSR FMUL	1	X	X	X	X	X	1	1	1	X	X	F F	X X X X X X X X	1	1	1	1	0	1	4	0 0 6 0	1	1	1	7
0055	R5 = RF	0	F	X	5	0	X	1	1	1	0	0	F 6	X X X X X X X X	1	1	1	1	0	2	7	X X X X	1	1	1	7

Table 6.1. Floating Point Sin(x) Microprogram (Continued)

			$\overline{WE}$ A3-A0 B3-B0 C3-C0 $\overline{EA}$ EB1-EB0 $\overline{OEA}$ $\overline{OEB}$ OEY SELY Cn I7-I0	32-bit Constant	$\overline{SIO0}$ $\overline{SIO8}$ $\overline{SIO16}$ $\overline{SIO24}$	RC2-RC0 MUX2-MUX0 S2-S0 DRB13-DRB0 $\overline{RAOE}$ $\overline{RBOE}$ $\overline{INC}$	SEL
		* R5 = FADD(R5,A0)					
0056		RE = R5	0 5 X E 0 X 1 1 1 0 0 F 6	X X X X X X X X	1 1 1 1	0 2 7 X X X X 1 1 1	7
0057		RD = #3F80 0000h	0 X X D X X 1 1 1 1 X F F	3 F 8 0 0 0 0 0	1 1 1 1	0 2 7 X X X X 1 1 1	7
0058		JSR FADD	1 X X X X X 1 1 1 X X F F	X X X X X X X X	1 1 1 1	0 1 4 0 0 7 4 1 1 1	7
0059		R5 = RF	0 F X 5 0 X 1 1 1 0 0 F 6	X X X X X X X X	1 1 1 1	0 2 7 X X X X 1 1 1	7
		* R5 = FMUL(R0,R5)					
005A		RE = R0	0 0 X E 0 X 1 1 1 0 0 F 6	X X X X X X X X	1 1 1 1	0 2 7 X X X X 1 1 1	7
005B		RD = R5	0 5 X D 0 X 1 1 1 0 0 F 6	X X X X X X X X	1 1 1 1	0 2 7 X X X X 1 1 1	7
005C		JSR FMUL	1 X X X X X 1 1 1 X X F F	X X X X X X X X	1 1 1 1	0 1 4 0 0 6 0 1 1 1	7
005D		R5 = RF	0 F X 5 0 X 1 1 1 0 0 F 6	X X X X X X X X	1 1 1 1	0 2 7 X X X X 1 1 1	7
		* R5 = FCHS(R5,R1) : RETURN					
005E		R1 = R1 OR #7FFF FFFFh	0 1 X 1 0 2 1 1 1 0 0 F B	B 7 F F F F F F	1 1 1 1	0 2 7 X X X X 1 1 1	7
005F		R5 = R5 XOR R1 : RETURN	0 5 1 5 0 0 1 1 1 0 0 F 0	X X X X X X X X	1 1 1 1	0 2 2 X X X X 1 1 1	7
		* RC = FEXP(RE)					
0060	FMUL:	RC = RE AND #7F80 0000h	0 E X C 0 2 1 1 1 0 0 F A	7 F 8 0 0 0 0 0	1 1 1 1	0 2 7 X X X X 1 1 1	7
		* RE = FRAC(RE)					
0061		RE = RE AND #807F FFFFh	0 E X E 0 2 1 1 1 0 0 F A	8 0 7 F F F F F	1 1 1 1	0 2 7 X X X X 1 1 1	7
		* RE = RE OR bit23					
0062		RE = RE OR #0080 0000h	0 E X F 0 2 1 1 1 0 0 F B	0 0 8 0 0 0 0 0	1 1 1 1	0 2 7 X X X X 1 1 1	7
		* MQ = SMTC(RE)					
0063		RE = SMTC(RE)	0 X E E X 0 1 1 1 1 0 5 8	X X X X X X X X	1 1 1 1	0 2 7 X X X X 1 1 1	7
0064		LOADMQ : PASS	1 E X X 0 X 1 1 1 1 0 E 6	X X X X X X X X	1 1 1 1	0 2 7 X X X X 1 1 1	7
		* RB = FEXP(RD)					
0065		RB = RD AND #7F80 0000h	0 D X B 0 2 1 1 1 0 0 F A	7 F 8 0 0 0 0 0	1 1 1 1	0 2 7 X X X X 1 1 1	7
		* RD = FRAC(RD)					
0066		RD = RD AND #807F FFFFh	0 D X D 0 2 1 1 1 0 0 F A	8 0 7 F F F F F	1 1 1 1	0 2 7 X X X X 1 1 1	7
0067		RD = RD OR bit23	0 D X D 0 2 1 1 1 0 0 F B	0 0 8 0 0 0 0 0	1 1 1 1	0 2 7 X X X X 1 1 1	7
0068		RD = SMTC(RD)	0 X D D X 0 1 1 1 1 D 5 8	X X X X X X X X	1 1 1 1	0 2 7 X X X X 1 1 1	7
0069		RE = 0 : RCB = #22D	0 E E E 0 0 1 1 1 1 0 F 9	0 0 0 0 0 0 1 6	1 1 1 1	6 1 7 X X X X 1 1 1	4
006A		RE = SMULI RD : LOOP RCB	0 D E E 0 0 1 1 1 1 0 6 0	X X X X X X X X	1 1 1 1	5 6 7 0 0 6 A 1 1 1	4
006B		RE = SMULT RD	0 D E E 0 0 1 1 1 0 0 7 0	X X X X X X X X	1 1 1 1	0 6 7 X X X X 1 1 1	7
006C		TB0(RE,bit1) : BYTE = #0100b : TEST Z	0 0 F 0 0 0 1 1 1 1 0 3 8	X X X X X X X X	1 0 1 1	0 2 7 X X X X 1 1 1	4
006D		JT FMUL1	1 X X X X X X 1 1 1 X F F	X X X X X X X X	1 1 1 1	0 1 7 X X X X 1 1 1	7
		* INEX RC					
006E		RC = RC ADD #0080 0000h	0 C X C 0 2 1 1 1 0 0 F 1	0 0 8 0 0 0 0 0	1 1 1 1	0 2 7 X X X X 1 1 1	7
006F		RE = SRA(RE)	0 E X E 0 X 1 1 1 0 0 0 6	X X X X X X X X	1 1 1 1	0 2 7 X X X X 1 1 1	7
0070	FMUL1:	RC = RC ADD RB : TEST CARRY	0 C B C 0 0 1 1 1 0 0 F 1	X X X X X X X X	1 1 1 1	0 2 7 X X X X 1 1 1	0
0071		JT ERROR	1 X X X X X 1 1 1 X X F F	X X X X X X X X	1 1 1 1	0 1 7 X X X X 1 1 1	7
0072		RE = SMTC(RE)	0 X E E X 0 1 1 1 1 0 5 8	X X X X X X X X	1 1 1 1	0 2 7 X X X X 1 1 1	7
0073		RE = RE AND #807F FFFFh	0 E X E 0 2 1 1 1 0 0 F A	8 0 7 F F F F F	1 1 1 1	0 2 7 X X X X 1 1 1	7
	* FADD:	RC = FEXP(RE)					
0074	FADD:	RC = RC AND #7F80 0000	0 C X C 0 2 1 1 1 0 0 F A	7 F 8 0 0 0 0 0	1 1 1 1	0 2 7 X X X X 1 1 1	7
		* RE = FRAC(RE)					
0075		RE = RE AND #807F FFFFh	0 E X E 0 2 1 1 1 0 0 F A	8 0 7 F F F F F	1 1 1 1	0 2 7 X X X X 1 1 1	7
0076		MQ = RE OR bit23	1 E X X 0 1 1 1 1 0 0 E B	0 0 8 0 0 0 0 0	1 1 1 1	0 2 7 X X X X 1 1 1	7
0077		RE = SMTC(RE)	0 E X E 0 2 1 1 1 0 0 F A	8 0 7 F F F F F	1 1 1 1	0 2 7 X X X X 1 1 1	7
		* RB = FEXP(RD)					
0078		RB = RD AND #7F80 0000	0 D X B 0 2 1 1 1 0 0 F A	7 F 8 0 0 0 0 0	1 1 1 1	0 2 7 X X X X 1 1 1	7

Table 6.1. Floating Point Sin(x) Microprogram (Continued)

Address	Instruction	$\overline{\text{WE}}$	A3-A0	B3-B0	C3-C0	$\overline{\text{EA}}$	EB1-EB0	$\overline{\text{OEA}}$	$\overline{\text{OEB}}$	OEY	SELY	Cn	I7-I0	32-bit Constant	$\overline{\text{SIO0}}$	$\overline{\text{SIO8}}$	$\overline{\text{SIO16}}$	$\overline{\text{SIO24}}$	RC2-RC0	MUX2-MUX0	S2-S0	DRB13-DRB0	$\overline{\text{RAOE}}$	$\overline{\text{RBOE}}$	$\overline{\text{INC}}$	SEL
	* RD = FRAC(RD)																									
0079	RE = RE AND #807F FFFFh	0	E	X	E	0	2	1	1	1	0	0	F A	8 0 7 F F F F F	1	1	1	1	0	2	7	X X X X	1	1	1	7
007A	RD = RD OR bit23	0	D	X	D	0	2	1	1	1	0	0	F B	0 0 8 0 0 0 0 0	1	1	1	1	0	2	7	X X X X	1	1	1	7
007B	RD = SMTC(RD)	0	X	D	D	X	0	1	1	1	1	0	5 8	X X X X X X X X	1	1	1	1	0	2	7	X X X X	1	1	1	7
007C	RF = RC − RB : C0=0: TEST NEG	0	C	B	F	0	0	1	1	1	0	0	F 3	X X X X X X X X	1	1	1	1	0	2	7	X X X X	1	1	1	2
007D	JT FADD1 : RCB = #8	1	X	X	X	X	X	1	1	1	X	X	F F	X X X X X X X 8	1	1	1	1	6	1	7	X X X X	1	1	1	4
007E	Y/RF = SLC(RF) : LOOP RCB	0	F	X	F	0	X	1	1	0	X	0	6 6	X X X X X X X X	1	1	1	1	5	6	7	0 0 7 E	1	1	1	4
007F	Y = RF : RCA = Y	1	X	X	X	X	X	1	1	0	0	X	F F	X X X X X X X X	1	1	1	1	2	7	7	0 0 8 0	1	1	1	7
0080	RD = SRA(RD) : LOOP RCA	0	D	X	D	0	X	1	1	1	0	0	0 6	X X X X X X X X	1	1	1	1	1	6	7	0 0 7 E	1	1	1	4
0081	RB = RC : JUMP FADD2	0	C	X	B	0	X	1	1	1	0	X	F F	X X X X X X X X	1	1	1	1	0	2	7	X X X X	1	1	1	7
0082 FADD1:	RF = NOT RF	0	F	X	F	0	X	1	1	1	0	0	F 7	X X X X X X X X	1	1	1	1	0	2	7	X X X X	1	1	1	7
0083	Y/RF = SLC(RF) : LOOP RCB	0	F	X	F	0	X	1	1	0	0	0	6 6	X X X X X X X X	1	1	1	1	6	1	7	X X X X	1	1	1	4
0084	Y = RF : RCA = Y	1	X	X	X	X	X	1	1	0	0	X	F F	X X X X X X X X	1	1	1	1	5	6	7	0 0 8 4	1	1	1	4
0085	RE = SRA(RE) : LOOP RCA	0	E	X	E	0	X	1	1	1	0	0	0 6	X X X X X X X X	1	1	1	1	2	7	7	0 0 8 6	1	1	1	7
0086 FADD2:	RF = RD + RE	0	D	E	F	0	0	1	1	1	0	0	F 1	X X X X X X X X	1	1	1	1	0	2	7	X X X X	1	1	1	7
0087	RF = SMTC(RF)	0	X	F	F	X	0	1	1	1	1	0	5 8	X X X X X X X X	1	1	1	1	0	2	7	X X X X	1	1	1	7
0088	RF = TB0 (RF, bit24) : TEST Z	0	0	F	0	0	0	1	1	1	1	0	3 8	X X X X X X X X	0	1	1	1	0	2	7	X X X X	1	1	1	4
0089	JF FADD3	1	X	X	X	X	X	1	1	1	X	X	F F	X X X X X X X X	1	1	1	1	0	4	7	X X X X	1	1	1	7
008A	INC RB : TEST NEG	0	B	X	B	0	X	1	1	1	1	1	F 6	X X X X X X X X	1	1	1	1	0	2	7	X X X X	1	1	1	3
008B	RF = SRA(RF) : JT ERROR	0	F	7	F	0	X	1	1	1	0	0	0 6	X X X X X X X X	1	1	1	1	0	1	7	X X X X	1	1	1	7
008C FADD3:	RF = SET0 (RF, bit23)	0	7	F	0	0	0	1	1	1	1	0	1 8	X X X X X X X X	1	0	1	1	0	2	7	X X X X	1	1	1	7
008D	RF = RF OR RB : RETURN	0	F	B	F	0	0	1	1	1	0	0	F B	X X X X X X X X	1	1	1	1	0	2	2	X X X X	1	1	1	7

3

Application Reports

Excerpt from
SN74AS888, SN74AS890 Bit-Slice Processor User's Guide

TEXAS INSTRUMENTS

IMPORTANT NOTICE

4. 32-Bit CPU Design Methodology

Microprogramming and bit-slice technology have made possible the development of powerful systems using flexible instructions sets and wide address/data buses to access more than one Gigaword of physical main memory. This section discusses one design approach to such a system, using 'AS888 bit-slice and 'AS890 microsequencer components.

A structured approach to system design, such as that illustrated in Figure 4-1, is recommended in developing custom bit-slice designs. The product specification gives a starting point or basis for the project. In this example, four 'AS888 bit slices are used to implement the 32-bit arithmetic portion of the CPU, and an 'AS890 microsequencer is used for ALU and system control. A group of PROMs stores the microinstructions; a writable control store could also be implemented using additional control logic and components to load and modify the microprogram memory. The system is designed to access more than one Gigaword of memory.

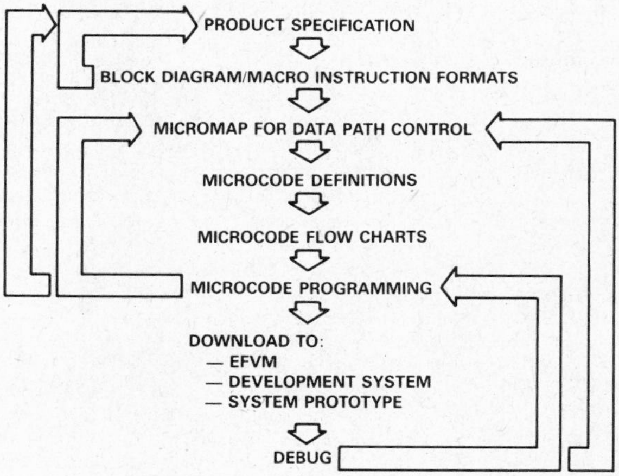

PRODUCT SPECIFICATION
BLOCK DIAGRAM/MACRO INSTRUCTION FORMATS
MICROMAP FOR DATA PATH CONTROL
MICROCODE DEFINITIONS
MICROCODE FLOW CHARTS
MICROCODE PROGRAMMING
DOWNLOAD TO:
— EFVM
— DEVELOPMENT SYSTEM
— SYSTEM PROTOTYPE
DEBUG

Figure 4-1. System Design Approach

Since speed is a concern, carry look-ahead rather than ripple-through logic is recommended. If ripple-through logic were used, the system clock would need to be slowed down to allow the propagation of the carry bits through the various 'AS888 stages. By using carry look-ahead, the amount of time needed for the data to stabilize is greatly reduced by anticipating the carry across the 'AS888 packages.

So that the scratchpad area can be used for address calculations and mathematical computations, the 'AS888's internal register file is dedicated for system functions. To provide the system user with a macrolevel equivalent of register locations, a 16-word external register file is also included. Access to the external register file will be under microprogram control, allowing address selection to come from the microcode itself or from one of the three operand fields of the instruction register.

PROMs eliminate the use of main memory as a source for constants used in initialization or table look-up functions. Accessing main memory for table values would require time and slow system throughput; by placing fixed values in fast PROMs, access time is kept to a minimum and system throughput is not altered.

Control, data and address buses shared by the system are accessed by three-state registers. The control register, as explained in section 4.1.2, supplies the non-CPU part of a computer system with control signals. The data bus allows the ALU to supply data for the rest of the system and can also be a source of data for the ALU; this is accomplished by using three-state registers to drive the bi-directional data bus, along with registers to sample the bus. The address bus uses one of the external register file locations to maintain a program counter, thus allowing a 32-bit address bus capable of addressing about four Gigawords of main memory. Using three-state drivers for this bus enables other subsystems to take control of the system buses.

A pipeline register supplies the microsequencer and the ALU with both data and instructions. To get macrocode into the system, an instruction register and a mapping PROM are used to convert the opcode to a microprogram routine address. The condition code signal, used for testing various conditions, is supplied by a register-input based PAL. PAL inputs can be fixed values or combinations of the status signals coming from the ALU. The read address select pins for the 'AS888's internal B register can be sourced from the microword itself or from three nibbles of the macroword, to provide offsets for the N-way branches to various microcode routines.

4.1 Designing a 32-Bit System

A typical 32-bit system block diagram using the 'AS888 bit-slice and 'AS890 microsequencer is shown in Figures 4-2 and 4-3. It can be broken down into two sections, the ALU (arithmetic logic unit) and the CCU (computer control unit). The ALU section performs all manipulation of data both to and from main memory, such as arithmetic and logical operations. The CCU section controls instruction (macrocode) flow and any miscellaneous control operations, such as fetching instructions or supplying addresses for main memory access.

4.1.1 Construction of the ALU

To cascade the four 'AS888s to obtain the 32-bit arithmetic unit shown in Figure 4-4, the shift multiplex $\overline{SIO0}$ and $\overline{QIO0}$ terminals are connected to the $\overline{SIO7}$ and $\overline{QIO7}$ terminals of adjacent packages, and the least significant package's signals are connected to the most-significant package's. Optionally, SN74ALS240 inverting gates can be connected to the $\overline{SIO0}$-$\overline{SIO7}$ terminals and the byte inputs to implement byte and bit control. Another chip, the SN74AS182 look-ahead carry generator, provides a ripple-carry function, to help system throughput.

The design includes a 16-word register file, the SN74AS870 (see Figure 4-3). This allows the user to access 16 working areas for temporary data storage or address calculations such as indexing. In this design example, the 'AS888's internal register file is not accessible directly by the user; it is reserved for microcode operations, such as address computation and temporary storage for arithmetic operations. Addressing the register files is permitted through the microprogram or from the macrocode instruction register under microcode control.

The transfer register connected to the 'AS888's Y and DB buses allows for feedback into the 'AS888 under microprogram control. Since the constant PROMs and the external register file share the A bus, they cannot be accessed at the same time. The transfer register enables data from the external register file to be transmitted to the B bus, making possible the addition of operands from the constant PROMs and the external register file, for example.

Constant PROMs are also included to simplify the programming and operation of the ALU by supplying fixed data for various operations, such as:

1) Clearing the system register files for initialization. This will bring the system up to a known state.
2) Supplying a correction value to the offset in a branch instruction, i.e., converting a 16-bit offset to a true 32-bit address.
3) Table look-up for fixed mathematical operations, such as computing sines and cosines.

4.1.2 Construction of the CCU

Sequencing and branching operations at speeds compatible with the 'AS888 are supplied by the 'AS890, a microprogrammed controller working as a powerful microsequencer (see Figure 3-1). Features of the 'AS890 include:

1) Stack capability. The 9-word stack can be accessed by using a stack pointer or a read pointer; the latter is designed for non-destructive dumping of the stack contents.
2) Register/counter facility. Two registers, DRA and DRB, can be used for latching data from the external data buses or as counters for loops. A ZERO signal is generated when the decremented counter reaches a zero value.
3) Interrupt control. A register for temporarily holding the return address is supplied; upon entering the interrupt routine, the contents of the return register must be pushed onto the stack for later use.
4) Next address generation. The Y output multiplexer offers a selection of same or incremented address, address from DRA or DRB buses, address from stack, or a concatenation of DRA13-DRA4 and B3-B0.

A microprogram memory/pipeline register supplies the microsequencer and the rest of the system with instructions (see Figure 4-2). The memory might consist of ROMs, or it could be a writable-control store with support logic to allow loading or updating of the control store. For a general purpose machine with a fixed instruction set, ROMs would be more economic.

Some 'AS890 instructions are influenced by the $\overline{CC}$ input. Many are variations of branch and jump instructions. To form and supply $\overline{CC}$, a register can be used to latch the state of the 'AS888 and supply inputs to a PAL for decoding, based upon the microcode's needs. Combinatorial logic in the PAL allows multiple or single events to be selected or provides a fixed value of "1" or "0" for forced conditions.

To supply the microsequencer with the proper address of the microcode-equivalent version of the macrocode instruction, an instruction register and mapping PROM are needed. Under microprogram control, the instruction register samples the data bus to get the macrocode instruction. The opcode portion is passed to the mapping PROM to form an address to the microcode routine. When the microcode is ready to jump to the routine, it turns off the Y bus output of the 'AS890 and enables the output of the mapping PROM. An optional means of altering the address uses B3-B0 inputs of the 'AS890 to implement a N-way branch routine. In this method, the ten most significant address bits of DRA or DRA are concatenated with the B3-B0 bits to supply an address.

Control information is supplied to the rest of the system via the control register and bus. By setting various bits within the control register, information can be passed to other subsystems, such as memory and I/O peripherals. Bit 0 could represent the read/write control line while bit 1 could select memory or I/O for the read/write. Bit 2 might function to enable interrupts and bit 3 to indicate when the system should enter a "wait" state for slow memory. The remaining control bits can be programmed by the system designer to indicate additional condition states of the "macrosystem".

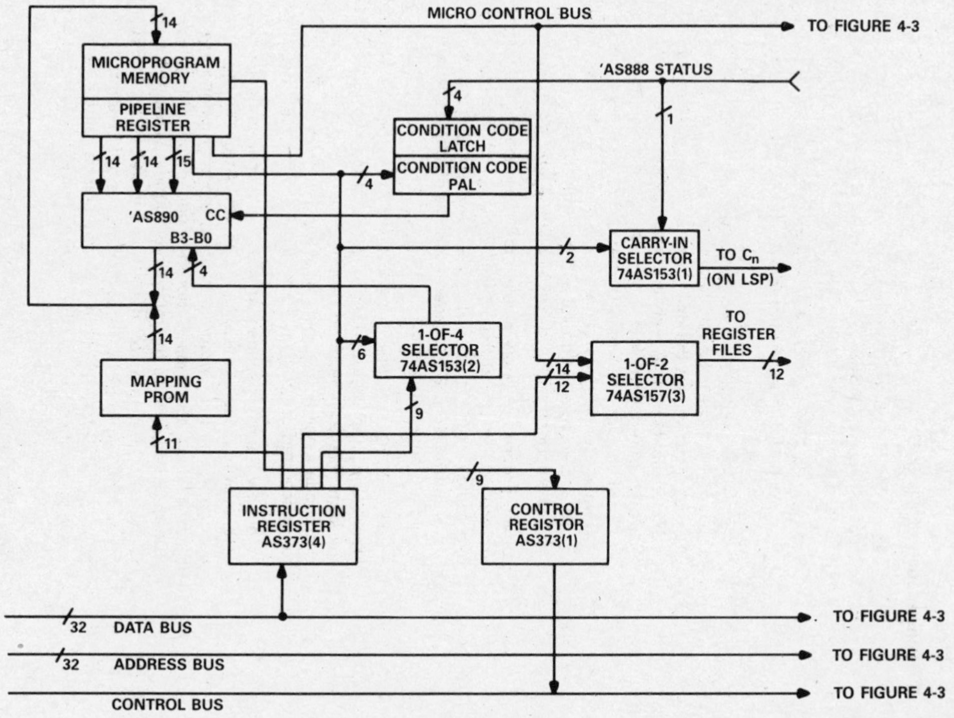
MICRO CONTROL BUS
TO FIGURE 4-3
'AS888 STATUS
MICROPROGRAM MEMORY
PIPELINE REGISTER
CONDITION CODE LATCH
CONDITION CODE PAL
'AS890
CC
B3-B0
CARRY-IN SELECTOR 74AS153(1)
TO C_n (ON LSP)
TO REGISTER FILES
1-OF-4 SELECTOR 74AS153(2)
1-OF-2 SELECTOR 74AS157(3)
MAPPING PROM
INSTRUCTION REGISTER AS373(4)
CONTROL REGISTOR AS373(1)
DATA BUS
ADDRESS BUS
CONTROL BUS
TO FIGURE 4-3
TO FIGURE 4-3
TO FIGURE 4-3
14
14
14
15
4
4
1
2
14
4
14
6
14
12
12
9
11
9
32
32

Figure 4-2. CCU Block Diagram

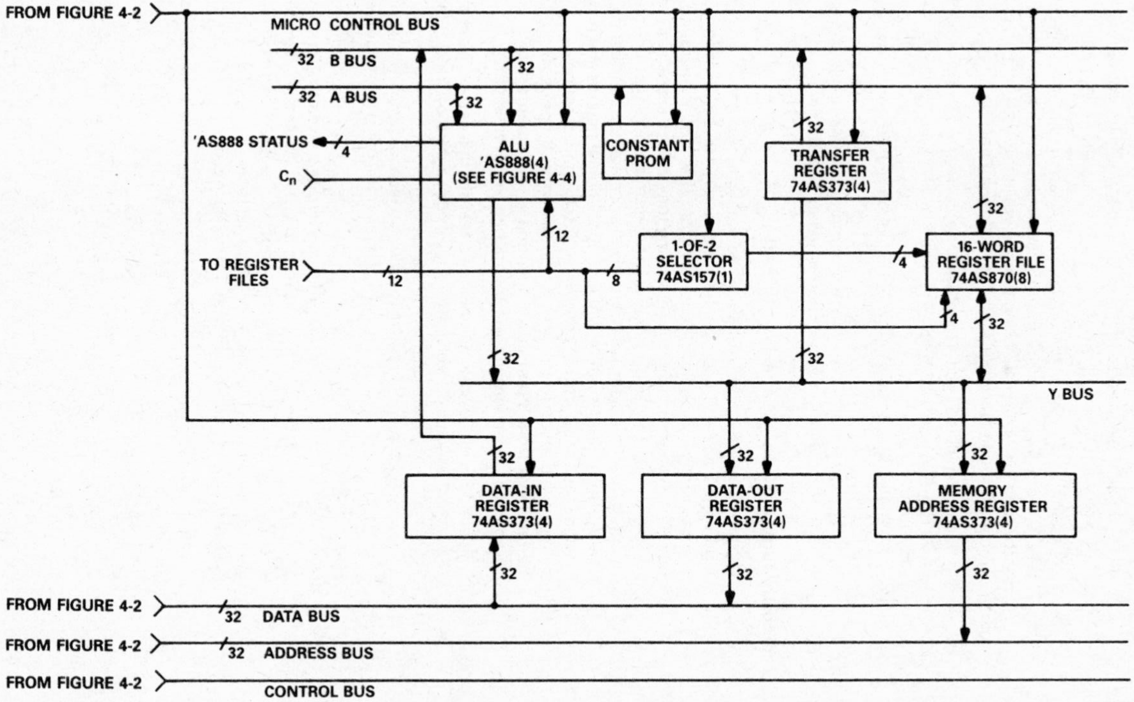

FROM FIGURE 4-2
MICRO CONTROL BUS
32 B BUS
32 A BUS
'AS888 STATUS
4
Cn
TO REGISTER FILES
12
ALU
'AS888(4)
(SEE FIGURE 4-4)
CONSTANT PROM
TRANSFER REGISTER 74AS373(4)
1-OF-2 SELECTOR 74AS157(1)
16-WORD REGISTER FILE 74AS870(8)
8
32
Y BUS
DATA-IN REGISTER 74AS373(4)
DATA-OUT REGISTER 74AS373(4)
MEMORY ADDRESS REGISTER 74AS373(4)
FROM FIGURE 4-2
32 DATA BUS
FROM FIGURE 4-2
32 ADDRESS BUS
FROM FIGURE 4-2
CONTROL BUS

Figure 4-3. ALU Block Diagram

Addressing of the register files, both the 'AS888 internal and the 'AS870 external, is done through the use of two 1-of-2 selector banks. The first bank selects address source; this design offers a choice for operand processing of fixed values from the microcode or values from the macroinstruction latched in the instruction register. The second bank selects the first or second operand as an address source for port 0 of the external register file; port 1 uses the third operand as an address source.

It should be noted that the design presented in Figure 4-2 for the computer control unit is a one-level pipeline that is instruction-data based.The address and contents of the next instruction are being fetched while the current instruction is being executed. Tracing through the data flow, the following can be observed:

1) The pipeline register contains the current instruction being executed;
2) The ALU has just executed its instruction, and has the current status ready at its output pins;
3) The status register that is attached to the ALU contains the previous instruction's resulting status;
4) The contents of the next microprogram word are being fetched at the same time that the current instruction is being executed.

4.2 Tracing through a 32-Bit Computer

With the 'AS888 and 'AS890 as foundation chips, the typical 32-bit supermini of Figures 4-2 and 4-3 can now be functionally traced. First, note that the data of the main program is handled separately from that of the microcode — each on its own bus. The system is initialized by setting the ''clear'' signal high — this causes a forced jump to the beginning of the microcode memory. Instructions carried out by the microcode at this point might run system diagnostics, clear all registers throughout the 'AS888-based system, and set up the initial macrocode program address. In this design, the first program address to fetch an instruction from main memory comes from a fixed value in the microcode memory; it is possible to allow the address to be retrieved from a permanent location in main memory or from either a front panel or console, by modifying the microcode program slightly.

Table 4-1 illustrates the microcode format for this design. Note that it contains control signals for all chips involved in the design. Some of these, such as $\overline{\text{TRANSLATCH}}$ and $\overline{\text{MARLATCH}}$, are used with the system clock to provide controlled loading of the various holding registers. Others supply necessary addressing information, directing input from either the main data bus or from the microcode word itself.

The FETCH routine is shown in functional, assembler and microcoded forms in Tables 4-2, 4-3 and 4-4. First, the program counter is read from the external register file and stored into the memory address register. After the program counter is placed on the address bus, the program counter is updated and stored while the data from memory is allowed to settle down to a stable condition. The data is then latched in both the instruction register and data-in register.

The opcode field of the instruction register is passed through the mapping PROM to convert the opcode to an equivalent microcode routine address. When $\overline{\text{YOE}}$ is forced high by the microcode, the 'AS890 is tri-stated from the Y bus, and the mapping PROM's output is taken out of the tri-state mode to supply an address to the control store (microprogram memory); a forced jump is made to the microcode routine to perform the instruction.

After the routine is complete, a jump is made back to the FETCH routine using the next-address supplied by the microprogram. It is up to the system designer/programmer to make sure that all system housekeeping is performed so that nothing causes a fatal endless loop.

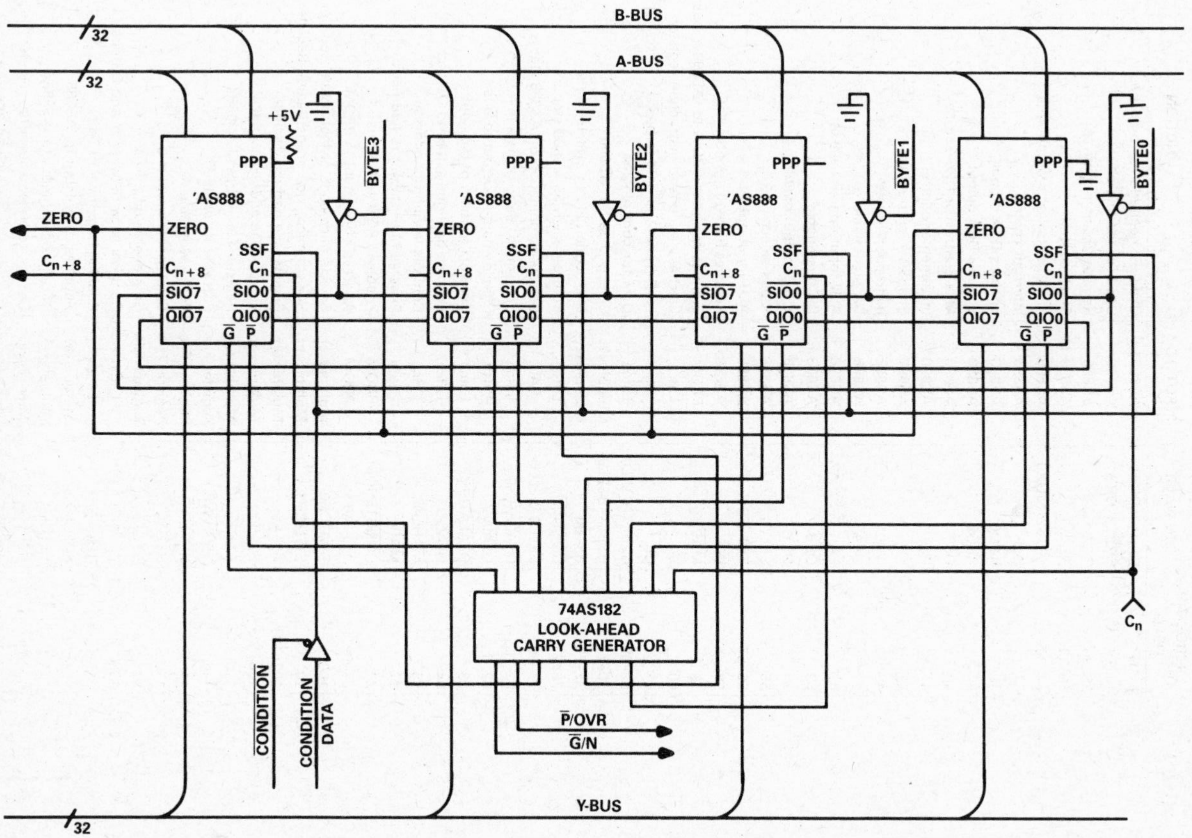
B-BUS
A-BUS
Y-BUS
32
'AS888
PPP
SSF
ZERO
Cn+8
Cn
SIO7
QIO7
SIO0
QIO0
G
P
BYTE0
BYTE1
BYTE2
BYTE3
+5V
74AS182
LOOK-AHEAD
CARRY GENERATOR
P/OVR
G/N
CONDITION
CONDITION DATA

Figure 4-4. Cascaded 'AS888 Packages

Table 4-1. Microcode Definition

MICROCODE FIELD	PIN NAME	INPUT TO	FUNCTION
0–13	DRA13–DRA0	'AS890	Used for next-address branches
14–27	DRB13–DRB0	'AS890	Used for loading counter
28–30	RC2–RC0	'AS890	Register/counter controls
31–33	S2–S0	'AS890	Stack control
34–36	MUX2–MUX0	'AS890	MUX control of Y output bus
37	$\overline{\text{INT}}$	'AS890	Interrupt control
38	$\overline{\text{RAOE}}$	'AS890	Enables DRA output
39	$\overline{\text{RBOE}}$	'AS890	Enables DRB output
40	OSEL	'AS890	Mux control for DRA source
41	INC	'AS890	Incrementer control
42	$\overline{\text{YOE}}$	'AS890	Enables Y output bus
43–50	I7-I0	'AS888	Instruction inputs
51	$\overline{\text{OEA}}$	'AS888	DA bus enable
52	$\overline{\text{EA}}$	'AS888	ALU input operand select
53	$\overline{\text{OEB}}$	'AS888	DB bus enable
54	OEY	'AS888	Y bus output enable
55	SELY	'AS888	Y bus select
56–57	EB1–EB0	'AS888	ALU input operand selects
58	$\overline{\text{WE}}$	'AS888	Register file write enable
59	$\overline{\text{MAP}}$	PROM	Enables mapping PROM to 'AS890 Y bus
60	$\overline{\text{IR}}$	Latch	Latches data bus to instruction register
61	$\overline{\text{CR}}$	Latch	Latches control data to bus
62–69	CTRL7–CTRL0	Latch	Data for control latch
70–71	BSEL1–BSEL0	Multiplexer	Selects data for 'AS890
72–75	B3–B0	Multiplexer	Microcode data to switch
76	$\overline{\text{CONDCD}}$	Latch	Controls latch of 'AS888 status
77–80	SELC3–SELC0	PAL	Selects combination of 'AS888 status
81	$\overline{\text{DTALATCHI}}$	Latch	Controls latching of data-in
82	$\overline{\text{DTAIN}}$	Latch	Enables data-in output to bus
83	$\overline{\text{DTALATCHO}}$	Latch	Controls latching of data-out
84	$\overline{\text{DTAOUT}}$	Latch	Enables data-out output to DB bus
85	$\overline{\text{MARLATCH}}$	Latch	Controls latching of address
86	$\overline{\text{MAR}}$	Latch	Enables MAR output to address bus
87	$\overline{\text{CONSTPROM}}$	PROM	Enables PROM to DA bus
88–99	A11–A0	PROM	Address of constant in PROM
100	SWITCH2	Multiplexer	Selects microcode or Instruction Register data
101	SWITCH1	Multiplexer	Selects microcode or Instruction Register data
102–105	A3–A0	Multiplexer	Register file address ('AS888)
106–109	B3–B0	Multiplexer	Register file address ('AS888)
110–113	C3–C0	Multiplexer	Register file address ('AS888)
114	$\overline{\text{REGUWR}}$	Register File	Port 0 write enable
115	$\overline{\text{REGLWR}}$	Register File	Port 1 write enable
116	$\overline{\text{REGU}}$	Register File	Chip enable on port 0
117	$\overline{\text{REGL}}$	Register File	Chip enable on port 1
118	$\overline{\text{TRANSLATCH}}$	Latch	Controls latch between Y and DB bus
119	$\overline{\text{TRANS}}$	Latch	Enables output to DB bus
120	SELCN2	Multiplexer	Supplies carry input to 'AS888
121	SELCN1	Multiplexer	Supplies carry input to 'AS888
122	REGUB	Multiplexer	Selects address for external register file
123–126	$\overline{\text{BYTE3}}$ – $\overline{\text{BYTE0}}$	Three-state	Enables data for byte/bit operations

Table 4-2. Functional Listing of Fetch

FETCH:	MAR = PC, Enable MAR output
	PC = PC + 1
	IR = DIR = data bus, Disable 'AS890 Y bus, Enable mapping PROM to Y bus

Table 4-3. Assembler Listing of Fetch

FETCH: OP890 ,,,111,10;INC;	Set 'AS890 for continue
OP888 NOP,GROUP5,10,,,1111;	Perform NOP and read external register 15
OEY;SELY;	Enable Y bus output
CR;CTRL 00000011;	Generate external control bus signals
SELC 01;	Select fixed CC value to 'AS890
MARLATCH;MAR;	Latch value on Y bus and enable output
SWITCH 00;REGL;	Select address source and enable port
TRANSLATCH	Latch Y bus for transfer to B bus
OP890 ,,,111,10;INC;	Set 'AS890 for continue
OP888 PASS,INCS,00,,,1111;	Increment program counter
OEB;OEY;	Enable Y bus output
SELC 01;	Select fixed CC value to 'AS890
MAR;	Output address to address bus
REGLWR;REGL;	Update program counter in register file
TRANS;	Enable transfer latch output to B bus
SELCN 01	Select carry input to LSP to be "1"
OP890 ,,,111,10;	Set 'AS890 for continue
OP888 NOP,GROUP5,10;	Perform NOP
MAP;	Enable mapping PROM to 'AS890 Y bus
IR;	Latch data bus to get macrolevel code
SELC 01	Select fixed CC value to 'AS890
DTALATCHI;	Put data bus also in data register
MAR	Output address to address bus

Key to Table 4-3

OP888 a,b,c,d,e,f

where:

- a = upper bits of instruction, 17-14
- b = lower bits of instruction, 13-10
- c = value of EB1–EB0
- d = A address of register files
- e = B address of register files
- f = C address of register files

OP890 v,w,x,y,z

where:

- v = DRA value, 14-bits
- w = DRB value, 14-bits
- x = RC2–RC0
- y = S2–S0
- z = MUX2–MUX0

Table 4-4. Microcode Listing of Fetch

DRA13-DRA0	DRB13-DRB0	RC2-RC0	S2-S0	MUX2-MUX0	INT RAOE RBOE OSEL INC YOE	I7-I0	OEA EA OEB OEY SELY EB1 EB0 WE	MAP IR CR
0 0 0 0 0 0 0 0 0 0 0 0 0 0	0 0 0 0 0 0 0 0 0 0 0 0 0 0	0 0 0	1 1 1	0 1 0	1 1 1 0 1 0	1 1 1 1 1 1 1 1	1 1 1 0 1 1 0 1	1 1 0
0 0 0 0 0 0 0 0 0 0 0 0 0 0	0 0 0 0 0 0 0 0 0 0 0 0 0 0	0 0 0	1 1 1	0 1 0	1 1 1 0 1 0	1 1 1 1 0 1 0 0	1 1 0 0 0 0 0 1	1 1 1
0 0 0 0 0 0 0 0 0 0 0 0 0 0	0 0 0 0 0 0 0 0 0 0 0 0 0 0	0 0 0	1 1 1	0 1 0	1 1 1 0 0 1	1 1 1 1 1 1 1 1	0 1 1 1 1 1 0 1	0 0 1

Table 4-4. Microcode Listing of Fetch (continued)

CTRL7-CTRL0	BSEL1-BSEL0	B3-B0	CONDCO	SELC3-SELC0	DTALATCHI DTAIN DTALATCHO DTAOUT MARLATCH MAR CONSTPRROM	A11-A0	SWITCH2-SWITCH1	A3-A0	B3-B0	C3-C0	REGUWR REGLWR REGU REGL TRANSLATCH TRANS SELCN2 SELCN1 REGUB	BYTE3-BYTE0
0 0 0 0 0 0 1 1	0 0	0 0 0 0	1	0 0 0 1	1 1 1 1 0 0 1	0 0 0 0 0 0 0 0 0 0 0 0	0 0	0 0 0 0	0 0 0 0	1 1 1 1	1 1 1 0 0 1 0 0 0	1 1 1 1
0 0 0 0 0 0 0 0	0 0	0 0 0 0	1	0 0 0 1	1 1 1 1 1 0 1	0 0 0 0 0 0 0 0 0 0 0 0	0 0	0 0 0 0	0 0 0 0	1 1 1 1	1 0 1 0 1 0 0 1 0	1 1 1 1
0 0 0 0 0 0 0 0	0 0	0 0 0 0	1	0 0 0 1	0 1 1 1 1 0 1	0 0 0 0 0 0 0 0 0 0 0 0	0 0	0 0 0 0	0 0 0 0	0 0 0 0	1 1 1 1 1 1 0 0 0	1 1 1 1

4.3 Defining the Macrocode Instruction Format

Since this is a 32-bit design, a variety of instruction formats are available. The size of the opcode, along with the types of addressing used, will affect both system size and performance. The formats shown in Table 4-5 will be used for discussion.

All Table 4-5 formats have an opcode field of 11 bits and source/destination fields of 7 bits; the first three bits of the latter designate the address type, and the remaining four bits are used for register access. The opcode length allows 2,048 macrocoded instructions to be mapped to equivalent microcoded routines. The address fields can specify any of the following modes: register, relative, autoincrement/autodecrement, indexed, absolute, and deferred. The offset used in the Type 0 instruction can be used for branch-based instructions, for an offset range of ±32727.

Table 4-5. Possible Instruction Formats

TYPE 0 — OPCODE + 16-BIT OFFSET

0 — 10	11 — 15	16 — 31
Opcode	Not Used	Offset

TYPE 1 — OPCODE + DESTINATION

0 — 10	11 — 24	25 — 31
Opcode	Not used	Destination

TYPE 2 — OPCODE + SOURCE + DESTINATION

0 — 10	11 — 17	18 — 24	25 — 31
Opcode	Not used	Source	Destination

TYPE 3 — OPCODE + SOURCE1 + SOURCE2 + DESTINATION

0 — 10	11 — 17	18 — 24	25 — 31
Opcode	Source	Source	Destination

4.4 Tracing a Macrocode Instruction

Microcode for a Type 3 multiplication instruction is shown in Table 4-6, using the following assumptions:

1) Code for retrieving the operands will not be shown. Jumps will be made to routines that will place the temporary operands into internal register locations 2 and 3 of the 'AS888, after being fetched from main memory.
2) A jump to a routine to store the product in the destination will be handled similarly.
3) Multiplication will be unsigned; the result will be placed in two temporary locations of the 'AS888.
4) An update to the program status word, which the user can access at the macrocode level must also be performed, but is not shown.

Assembler code is shown in Table 4-7; a microcode listing is given in Table 4-8. The first two lines of microcode are subroutine jumps to opcode fetching routines, which store the operands in register files 2 and 3 in the 'AS888. The next two instructions load up the 'AS890 with a counter constant for performing the multiply loop, load the MQ register of the 'AS888 with the multiplier and clear the register that is temporarily used for the accumulator.

Table 4-6. Functional Listing of Multiply

UMULI3:	
JUMPSUB SOURCE1	Get first operand
JUMPSUB SOURCE2,	Get second operand
BCOUNT=32	Load DB counter register
REG 9=0	Clear temporary accumulator
MQ=REG 2	Load multiplier
LOOP:	
UMULI WITH REG 3	Issue the multiply
DECREMENT BCOUNT,	Decrement the DB counter
BRANCH TO LOOP IF NOT ZERO,	Loop back until done
LATCH 'AS888 STATUS,	Store 'AS888 flags
REG 9=ALU	Store intermediate result
REG 8=MQ	Store intermediate result
JUMPSUB STORPSW	Update macro program status
JUMPSUB MDEST	Store result at destination
JUMP FETCH	Get next instruction

A loop is then entered to perform the multiply instruction 32 times to form the product, with the multiplicand coming from the internal register file of the 'AS888. Upon exiting the loop, the MQ register is stored in a temporary register location in the 'AS888. The MQ register now contains the least-significant bits of the result and the temporary accumulator the most significant bits. A subroutine jump is made to the program status word update routine; this will take the status flags of the last multiplication iteration and change the macrolevel status word. The next subroutine jump is to a destination routine, which is followed by a branch to the FETCH routine to get the next macro instruction to be executed.

4.5 System Enhancements

The above example provides a broad overview of 32-bit system design using the 'AS888 and 'AS890. Certain additional options may enhance system performance. These include:

1) Status latching. The design does not take into account changes that need to be examined at the microlevel while retaining macrolevel status information. One solution would be to include another register in parallel to the status latch and provide control to choose between the two to form the condition code value.
2) Interrupts. To efficiently use a computer system, interrupts are used to alter program flow in the case of I/O programming and real-time applications (involving hardware timers). To include this capability, external hardware must be included and the microcode modified accordingly. Information on interrupt implementation is given in section 3.
3) Control store. One way of implementing microprogram memory is to use a ROM-based design. It is becoming more common to design a writable control store, a completely RAM-based or part RAM, part ROM storage system, that can be altered by system operation, such as initialization from a floppy disk subsystem, or by the user to optimize or implement new macrolevel instructions. The cost of implementation must be weighed with the risks involved in changing instructions which may not be supported by other sites.
4) Instruction word definitions. Changing the instruction word definitions will have an effect on both system design and performance. Removing Type 3 instructions from the design, for example, will have an effect on both hardware and software: the external register file addressing must be changed and the 1-of-2 selector

Table 4-7. Assembler Code of Multiply

UMULI3:	
OP890 SOURCE1,,,110,110;	Perform a subroutine branch
INC;YOE;	Increment address and enable Y bus
OP888 NOP;GROUP5;	Tell 'AS888 to do nothing during jump
SELC 0001;	Set CC to "1" to set up 'AS890 continue
MAR	Maintain address on main address buss
OP890 SOURCE2,0000000100000,110,110,110;	Perform subroutine branch and load B counter
INC;YOE;	Increment microaddress and enable Y bus
OP888 NOP,GROUP5;	Tell 'AS888 to do nothing during jump
SELC 0001;	Set CC to "1" to set up 'AS890 continue
MAR	Maintain address on main address bus
OP890 ,,,111,110;	Perform a continue instruction
INC;YOE;	Increment microaddress and enable Y bus
OP888 CLEAR,GROUP5,,,,1001;	Zero out register file accumulator
WE;	Enable writing to register file
SELC 0001;	Set CC to "1" to set up 'AS890 continue
MAR	Maintain address on main address buss
OP890 LOOP,,,111,110;	Perform a continue instruction
INC;YOE;	Increment microaddress and enable Y bus
OP888 LOADMQ,INCS,,,0010;	Load MQ register with S + Cn, from external register file
MAR	Maintain address on main address bus
LOOP:	
OP890 LOOP,,101,111,100;	Decrement B and loop til ZERO = 1
INC;YOE;	Increment microaddress and enable Y bus
OP888 UMULI,GROUP4,01,0011,,1001;	Perform unsigned multiply on accumulator
WE;	Update register file accumulator
MAR	Maintain address on main address bus
OP890 ,,,111,110;	Perform a continue instruction
INC;YOE;	Increment microaddress and enable Y bus
OP888 PASS,INCS,,,,1000;	Put S + Cn in temporary register file
WE;	Allow updating of register file
MAR	Maintain address on main address bus
OP890 STORPSW,,,110,110;	Perform a subroutine branch
INC;YOE;	Increment microaddress and enable Y bus
OP888 NOP,GROUP5;	Tell 'AS888 to do nothing during jump
SELC 0001;	Set CC to "1" for set up 'AS890 continue
MAR	Maintain address on main address bus
OP890 FETCH,,,111;	Perform a branch to FETCH routine
INC;YOE;	Increment microaddress and enable Y bus
OP888 NOP,GROUP5;	Tell 'AS888 to do nothing during jump
SELC 0001	Set CC to "1" for 'AS890 continue

Key to Table 4-7.

OP888 a,b,c,d,e,f
where:
- a = upper bits of instruction, 17-14
- b = lower bits of instruction, 13-10
- c = value of EB1-EB0
- d = A address of register files
- e = B address of register files
- f = C address of register files

OP890 v,w,x,y,z
where:
- v = DRA value, 14-bits
- w = DRB value, 14-bits
- x = RC2-RC0
- y = S2-S0
- z = MUX2-MUX0

removed. Likewise, changing the opcode length may restrict the instruction address capability and also cause either an increase or decrease in the microcode size.

5) Dynamic memory access (DMA). The above system does not support dynamic memory access. To include this function requires a change in the address output control, along with support circuitry for the type of DMA selected. Some error detection and correction logic for main memory might also be included.

6) Computer control unit. The design presented here shows a one-level pipeline architecture that is instruction-data based. System throughput may be increased by converting to a pipeline of greater depth, or using another variety of one-level pipeline, such as instruction-address based or address-data based. Care must be taken when increasing the size of the pipeline, especially when handling branch/jump situations. The reader is advised to carefully research this area before implementing any design.

4.6 Timing and System Throughput

A critical path analysis was undertaken to determine the maximum clock rate for the proposed system. The longest delay path is the multiplication data path, which involves the internal register file and the shift function of the 'AS888. Table 4-9 contains the critical delay calculations for both the ALU and CCU. Since both portions of the system must be satisfied, a clock rate of 90 ns was selected for the following comparisons.

4.6.1 Fetch Analysis

Most microprocessors perform an instruction fetch in a pipeline mode; the next instruction is fetched while the current instruction is executing. The fetch code shown earlier requires a minimum of four cycles: three to issue the code and one to break the pipeline for processing the branch. This results in a total time of 360 ns, based on a 90 ns cycle time. Fetch times for the representative microprocessors have been estimated from data books and are shown in Table 4-10; wait states for slow memory are not included. As can be seen from the table, the 'AS888 design example is estimated to run from 1.1 to 2.1 times faster than the 16-bit microprocessors.

4.6.2 Multiplication Analysis

This analysis assumes that multiplication is unsigned integer and register to register based. No account is taken of time needed for instruction fetch or operand fetch or store.

The basic loop for the multiply takes 35 cycles: 2 for accumulator and multiplier set up, 32 for actual multiply loop and 1 to store the least-significant bits in an internal register file. Given a cycle time of 90 ns, a 32 by 32 bit multiplication can be implemented in 2.275 microseconds. A 16-bit multiply requires 16 iterations of the inner loop; both timings are included in Table 4-11 for comparison. Values for the 16-bit multiplies of the representative microprocessors have been estimated from data books.

As shown in Table 4-11, the 16 by 16 multiply can be performed with the 'AS888 at a faster rate than the 16-bit microprocessors. Even comparing the 32 by 32 multiply of the application design, one can see that the 'AS888 based system has a better macroinstruction execution speed. Using the 'AS888 and 'AS890 in a system design will allow high throughput and permit a flexible architecture.

Table 4-8. Microcode Listing of Multiply

DRA13-DRA0	DRB13-DRB0	RC2-RC0	S2-S0	MUX2-MUX0	INT RAOE RBOE OSEL INC YOE	I7-I0	OEA EA OEB OEY SELY EB1 EB0 WE	MAP IR CR
0 0 0 0 0 0 0 0 0 0 1 1 0 0	0 0 0 0 0 0 0 0 0 0 0 0 0 0	0 0 0	1 1 0	1 1 0	1 1 1 0 1 0	1 1 1 1 1 1 1 1	1 1 1 1 0 0 0 1	1 1 1
0 0 0 0 0 0 0 0 0 1 0 0 0 0	0 0 0 0 0 0 0 0 1 0 0 0 0 0	1 1 0	1 1 0	1 1 0	1 1 1 0 1 0	1 1 1 1 1 1 1 1	1 1 1 1 0 0 0 1	1 1 1
0 0 0 0 0 0 0 0 0 0 0 0 0 0	0 0 0 0 0 0 0 0 0 0 0 0 0 0	0 0 0	1 1 1	1 1 0	1 1 1 0 1 0	1 1 1 1 0 0 0 0	1 1 1 0 0 0 0 0	1 1 1
0 0 0 0 1 0 0 0 0 0 1 0 0 0	0 0 0 0 0 0 0 0 0 0 0 0 0 0	0 0 0	1 1 1	1 1 0	1 1 1 0 1 0	1 1 1 0 0 1 0 0	1 1 1 0 0 0 0 1	1 1 1
0 0 0 0 1 0 0 0 0 0 1 0 0 0	0 0 0 0 0 0 0 0 0 0 0 0 0 0	1 0 1	1 1 1	1 0 0	1 1 1 0 1 0	1 1 0 1 0 0 0 0	1 1 1 0 0 0 1 0	1 1 1
0 0 0 0 0 0 0 0 0 0 0 0 0 0	0 0 0 0 0 0 0 0 0 0 0 0 0 0	0 0 0	1 1 1	1 0 1	1 1 1 0 1 0	1 1 1 1 1 1 1 1	1 1 1 0 0 0 1 0	1 1 1
0 0 0 0 0 0 0 0 0 1 0 1 0 0	0 0 0 0 0 0 0 0 0 0 0 0 0 0	0 0 0	1 1 0	1 1 0	1 1 1 0 1 0	1 1 1 1 1 1 1 1	1 1 1 1 0 0 0 1	1 1 1
0 0 0 0 0 0 0 0 0 1 1 0 0 0	0 0 0 0 0 0 0 0 0 0 0 0 0 0	0 0 0	1 1 0	1 1 0	1 1 1 0 1 0	1 1 1 1 1 1 1 1	1 1 1 1 0 0 0 1	1 1 1
0 0 0 0 0 0 0 0 0 0 0 0 1 1	0 0 0 0 0 0 0 0 0 0 0 0 0 0	0 0 0	1 1 1	0 0 0	1 1 1 0 1 0	1 1 1 1 1 1 1 1	1 1 1 1 0 0 0 1	1 1 1

Table 4-8. Microcode Listing of Multiply (continued)

CTRL7-CTRL0	BSEL1-BSEL0	B3-B0	CONDCO	SELC3-SELC0	DTALATCHI DTAIN DTALATCHO DTAOUT MARLATCH MAR CONSTPRROM	A11-A0	SWITCH2-SWITCH1	A3-A0	B3-B0	C3-C0	REGUWR REGLWR REGU REGL TRANSLATCH TRANS SELCN2 SELCN1 REGUB	BYTE3-BYTE0
0 0 0 0 0 0 0 0	0 0	0 0 0 0	1	0 0 0 1	1 1 1 1 1 0 1	0 0 0 0 0 0 0 0 0 0 0 0	0 0	0 0 0 0	0 0 0 0	0 0 0 0	1 1 1 1 1 1 0 0 0	1 1 1 1
0 0 0 0 0 0 0 0	0 0	0 0 0 0	1	0 0 0 1	1 1 1 1 1 0 1	0 0 0 0 0 0 0 0 0 0 0 0	0 0	0 0 0 0	0 0 0 0	0 0 0 0	1 1 1 1 1 1 0 0 0	1 1 1 1
0 0 0 0 0 0 0 0	0 0	0 0 0 0	1	0 0 0 1	1 1 1 1 1 0 1	0 0 0 0 0 0 0 0 0 0 0 0	0 0	0 0 0 0	0 0 0 0	1 0 0 1	1 1 1 1 1 1 0 0 0	1 1 1 1
0 0 0 0 0 0 0 0	0 0	0 0 0 0	0	0 0 0 1	1 1 1 1 1 0 1	0 0 0 0 0 0 0 0 0 0 0 0	0 0	0 0 0 0	0 0 1 0	0 0 0 0	1 1 0 1 1 1 0 0 0	1 1 1 1
0 0 0 0 0 0 0 0	0 0	0 0 0 0	0	0 0 0 1	1 1 1 1 1 0 1	0 0 0 0 0 0 0 0 0 0 0 0	0 0	0 0 1 1	0 0 0 0	1 0 0 1	1 0 1 0 1 1 0 0 0	1 1 1 1
0 0 0 0 0 0 0 0	0 0	0 0 0 0	0	0 0 0 1	1 1 1 1 1 0 1	0 0 0 0 0 0 0 0 0 0 0 0	0 0	0 0 0 0	0 0 0 0	1 0 0 0	1 0 1 0 1 1 0 0 0	1 1 1 1
0 0 0 0 0 0 0 0	0 0	0 0 0 0	0	0 0 0 1	1 1 1 1 1 0 1	0 0 0 0 0 0 0 0 0 0 0 0	0 0	0 0 0 0	0 0 0 0	0 0 0 0	1 1 1 1 1 1 0 0 0	1 1 1 1
0 0 0 0 0 0 0 0	0 0	0 0 0 0	1	0 0 0 1	1 1 1 1 1 0 1	0 0 0 0 0 0 0 0 0 0 0 0	0 0	0 0 0 0	0 0 0 0	0 0 0 0	1 1 1 1 1 1 0 0 0	1 1 1 1
0 0 0 0 0 0 0 0	0 0	0 0 0 0	1	0 0 0 1	1 1 1 1 1 1 1	0 0 0 0 0 0 0 0 0 0 0 0	0 0	0 0 0 0	0 0 0 0	0 0 0 0	1 1 1 1 1 1 0 0 0	1 1 1 1

Table 4-9. Critical Delay Path Analysis

CONTROL PATH			DATA PATH		
Pipeline Reg.	Clock to Output	9	'AS888-1	Clock to C_n	46
MUX	Select to Output	13	'AS182	C_n to C_{n+z}	5
'AS890-1	CC to Output	25	'AS888-1	C_n to SIO	25
PROM	Access Time	20	'AS888-1	SIO to Y	14
Pipeline Reg.	Setup Time	2			90 ns
		69 ns			

Table 4-10. Fetch Timing Comparison

FETCH	'AS888 32-BIT	Z8001	8086-1	80286	68000L
Data width	32	16	16	16	16
No. of cycles	4	3	4	4	4
Clock rate	11.11 MHz	4 MHz	10 MHz	10 MHz	8 MHz
Total time	360 ns	750 ns	400 ns	400 ns	600 ns

Table 4-11. Multiply Timing Comparison

MULTIPLY	'AS888 32-BIT	'AS888 16-BIT	Z8001	8086-1	80286	68000L
Size	32 × 32	16 × 16	16 × 16	16 × 16	16 × 16	16 × 16
No. of cycles	35	19	70	128	21	≤74
Clock rate	11.11 MHz	10.98 MHz	4 MHz	10 MHz	10 MHz	8 MHz
Total time	3.150 μs	1.729 μs	17.5 μs	12.8 μs	2.1 μs	≤9.25 μs

5. Floating-Point System Design

Bit-slice processor architecture addresses the problem of optimizing system performance while allowing the user to balance hardware complexity against software flexibility. Bit-slice systems usually operate at or near the speed of the most primitive of programmable processors, the PROM state sequencer. Of course, bit-slice architecture incorporates circuitry dedicated not only to sequencing, but also data processing (ALU) operations. In keeping with the trend of these programmable devices to track the speed of fast discrete hardware, the 'AS888 8-bit slice ALU and 'AS890 microsequencer have been produced in Advanced Schottky bipolar technology. In addition to sheer speed, the components feature greater density (2 micron geometry) for greater functionality (more special purpose circuitry on board). The impact will be faster, more powerful systems in applications which previously pushed the limits of bit-slice processors.

Consider an application in which bit-slice architecture has dominated for years: CPU design. The microprogrammed CPU itself spans a spectrum of uses ranging from general purpose minicomputers to compact airborne computers. A specific example which illustrates various facets of design using the 'AS888 and 'AS890 is a CPU with a floating-point utility to compute sin(x).

The design process can be subject to many influences, including personal preference, available development tools, peculiarities of the application, and constraints from the user, customer or manufacturing environment. No hard and fast design rules could be applied universally, but most designers will start with a specific plan in mind.

The goal of this example is to produce the hardware and microprogram which will implement the sin(x) function in floating-point arithmetic. Before the microprogram can be assembled, the hardware must be defined since the fields of the microinstruction are dedicated to specific hardware once the microinstruction register is hardwired to the devices it controls. Since the final architecture chosen depends on tradeoffs between implementing certain operations in hardware or software, critical applications will require that a cursory analysis of the software be made before the hardware is cast in concrete. Attempting to develop microcode for a tentative architecture will force the issue on which operations are better suited for hardware. Before the architecture or the microprogram requirements can be known, the algorithms which describe the application processes must be defined. Once an algorithm is formulated it can be broken down into operations involving variable and constant quantities. The variables can be assigned to registers and then the algorithm can be translated into a microprogram. The following steps illustrate the plan for this CPU design example incorporating a floating-point sin(x) utility:

Step 1: Choose a floating-point number system
Step 2: Choose an algorithm for approximating sin(x)
Step 3: Make 'AS888 register assignments
Step 4: Substitute registers for variables in the algorithm
Step 5: Decompose steps of the algorithm into simple operations
Step 6: Translate into 'AS888/890 operations; identify subroutines
Step 7: Translate subroutines into 'AS888/890 operations
Step 8: Evaluate tradeoffs and block diagram the hardware
Step 9: Define microinstruction fields during detailed hardware design
Step 10: Assemble the microprogram

5.1 Choose a Floating-Point Number System

An IEEE floating-point format will be chosen for this example for portability of data and software. It is important to note that the IEEE defines many standards in arithmetic processing, but for simplicity this example will encompass only number format. Furthermore, while several formats are IEEE compatible, only the basic single-precision format will be considered.

The IEEE basic single-precision format is defined as a 32-bit representation in which the component fields are a 1-bit sign *s*, an 8-bit biased exponent *e* and a 23-bit fraction *f* which are assembled in the following order:

s	*e*	*f*
31		0

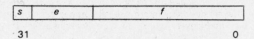

The quantity is evaluated as $(-1)^s\, 2^{e-127}\, (1.f)$. Not-a-number, zero and infinity have special representations. The one preceding the binary point is implied and is called the implicit one or implicit bit. It coincides with the fact that the digits are normalized (left justified).

5.2 Choose an Algorithm for Sin(x)

Many algorithms are discussed in the literature for approximating useful quantities like sin(x). Literature research is a good place to start to familiarize oneself with various algorithms and tradeoffs for a particlar application. Computer simulation is also useful to compare algorithms for speed and accuracy. R.F. Ruckdeschel in *BASIC Scientific Subroutines*, Vol. 1 (BYTE, McGraw-Hill Publications Co. New York, N.Y., 1981, pp. 159–191 discusses tradeoffs and provides a simulation in BASIC for a sin(x) algorithm. An adaptation of this material has been chosen for this example:

A) Reduce angle range to first quadrant. $(0 \le x \le \pi/2)$

B) Compute $\sin(x) \simeq \sum_{n=0}^{6} A_n x^{2n-1}$. The coefficients are:

Coefficient	Decimal	IEEE hex
A_0	1.000000	3F80 0000
A_1	−0.1666667	BE2A AAAD
A_2	0.008333333	3C08 8888
A_3	−0.0001984127	B950 0D01
A_4	0.000002755760	3638 EF99
A_5	−0.00000002507060	B2D7 5AD5
A_6	0.0000000001641060	2F34 6FBC

The algorithm can be implemented in the following steps:

A) Reduce angle range to first quadrant. ($0 \le x \le \pi/2$)

1) SIGN = SGN(x)
2) ABSX = $\|x\|$
3) XNEW = ABSX − 2π × INT(ABSX/2π)
4) If XNEW > π then SIGN = −SIGN and XNEW = XNEW − π
5) If XNEW > $\pi/2$ then XNEW = π − XNEW

where

$$\mathrm{SGN}(x) = \begin{cases} +1 \text{ if } x \ge 0 \\ -1 \text{ if } x < 0 \end{cases}$$

INT(x) = integer function

B) Compute $\sin(x) \simeq \sum_{n=0}^{6} A_n x^{2n-1}$.

1) Let XSQR = XNEW^2; INITIALIZE SINX = 0
2) Do i = 6 to 1 step −1
   SINX = XSQR × SINX + A(i)
   Enddo
3) SINX = SIGN × XNEW × SINX

Step B-2 computes the summation in a geometric series for economy. The major difference between steps A and B is that A requires more diverse ALU operations while B uses only multiplication and addition recursively.

5.3 Make 'AS888 Register Assignments

Just as in assembly language programming, registers must be allocated for variables. Using Rn to denote the 'AS888 register whose address is n, where $0 \le n \le F$ (hex), the following register assignments can be made:

R0 = X
R1 = SIGN
R2 = ABSX
R3 = XNEW
R4 = XSQR
R5 = SINX

The following constants can also be defined:

Constant	Decimal	IEEE hex
PI = π	3.141593	4059 0FDB
PIOVR2 = $\pi/2$	1.570797	3FC9 0FDB
2PI = 2π	6.283185	40C9 0FDB
1OVR2PI = $1/2\pi$	0.159155	3E22 F981

3

Application Reports

5.4 Substitute Registers for Variables in the Algorithm

Now the algorithm can be rewritten with registers replacing variables:

A) Reduce angle range to first quadrant ($0 \leq x \leq \pi/2$).

1) R1 = SGN(RO)
2) R2 = ‖RO‖
3) R3 = R2 − 2π × INT(R2/2π)
4) If R3> π then R1 = −R1; R3 = R3 − π
5) If R3 > π/2 then R3 = π − R3

B) Compute $\sin(x) \simeq \sum_{n=0}^{6} A_n x^{2n-1}$.

1) Let R4 = RO²; INITIALIZE R5 = 0
2) Do i=6 to 1 step −1
   R5 = R4 × R5 + A(i)
   Enddo
3) R5 = R1 × RO × R5

Since various references to constants are made, it is probably best to load constants as needed rather than attempt to allocate registers for them. Constants can be loaded from a constant field in the microinstruction or from ROM. The tradeoff is 32 bits by 16K of micromemory versus 32 bits by the number of constants (typically less than 16K). For this example, it will be assumed that a constant field in the microinstruction is acceptable.

5.5 Decompose Steps in the Algorithm into Simple Operations

The sin(x) function can be microprogrammed as a subroutine; let FSIN be its entry address. RO would be loaded with x before FSIN were called. Upon return, R5 would contain sin(x). Now decompose the steps in the algorithm into simple arithmetic and logical operations. Other operations can be left as functions to be defined later.

```
FSIN: SUBROUTINE

; A) Reduce angle range to first quadrant. (0 ≤ x ≤ π/2)

    R1 = SGN(RO)                     ;  1) Let R1 = Sign of RO

    R2 = ABS(RO)                     ;  2) R2 = ‖RO‖

    R3 = R2 * 1OVR2PI                ;  3) R3 = R2 − 2π * INT(R2/2π)
    R3 = INT(R3)                     ;
    R3 = R3 * 2PI                    ;
    R3 = R2 − R3                     ;

    Y = R3 − PI                      ;  4) If R3 > π,
    Jump if Negative to Step A-5     ;
    R1 = −R1                         ;     then R1 = −R1;
    R3 = R3 − PI                     ;     R3 = R3 − π

    Y = PIOVR2 − R3                  ;
    Jump if Negative to Step B-1     ;  5) If R3 > π/2
    R3 = PI − R3                     ;     then R3 = π − R3
```

; B) Compute $\sin(x) \simeq \sum_{n=0}^{6} A_n x^{2n-1}$

```
    R4 = R0 * R0                  ;  1) Let R4 = R0². Let R5 = 0
    R5 = 0                        ;

    R5 = R4 * R5                  ;  2) Do i=6 to 1 step -1
    R5 = R5 + A6                  ;       R5 = R4 × R5 + A(i)
    R5 = R4 * R5                  ;     Enddo
    R5 = R5 + A5                  ;
    R5 = R4 * R5                  ;     (To implement a loop,
    R5 = R5 + A4                  ;     use an 'AS890 counter
    R5 = R4 * R5                  ;     to index a memory containing
    R5 = R5 + A3                  ;     the constants.)
    R5 = R4 * R5                  ;
    R5 = R5 + A2                  ;
    R5 = R4 * R5                  ;
    R5 = R5 + A1                  ;
    R5 = R4 * R5                  ;
    R5 = R5 + A0                  ;

    R5 = R0 * R5                  ;  3) R5 = R1 × R0 × R5
    R5 = R5 * R1 : RETURN         ;

END SUBROUTINE
```

5.6 Translate into 'AS888/890 Instructions; Identify Subroutines

The simplified steps of the algorithm can be represented fairly easily as 'AS888/890 instructions. Necessary functions (and suggested names) can be identified by inspection as:

1) FMUL — Floating-point multiplication
2) FADD — Floating-point addition
3) FINT — Floating-point integer conversion
4) FINV — Floating-point additive inverse (to subtract using FADD)
5) FABS — Floating-point absolute value
6) FSGN — Floating-point sign test
7) FCHS — Floating-point change of sign (to multiply by SIGN)

"Function" in this context refers to a special operation regardless of how it is coded. In fact, FMUL and FADD are fairly complex and require detailed explanation. FINV, FABS, FSGN and FCHS are single instruction operations that mask or mask and test. FINT requires several inline instructions or a subroutine and will be left to the interested reader as an exercise. Now the steps of the algorithm can be translated into 'AS888/890 operations which include references to these functions.

```
FSIN: SUBROUTINE

;  A) Reduce angle range to first quadrant. (0 ≤ x ≤ π/2)

         R1 = FSGN(R0)                     ; Get sign bit (MSB)
         R2 = FABS(R0)                     ; Take absolute value (clear MSB)
         R3 = FMUL(R2,1OVR2PI)             ; Multiply register and constant
         R3 = FINT(R3)                     ; Floating-point integer conversion
         R3 = FMUL(R3,2PI)                 ; Multiply register and constant
         R3 = FADD(R2,INV(R3))             ; Subtract registers by adding inverse
         Y = FADD(R3,NEGPI) : TEST NEG     ; Subtract by adding negative constant
         JT SIN1                           ; Jump if true (jump if negative)
         R1 = FINV(R1)                     ; Complement sign of R1
         R3 = FADD(R3,NEGPI)               ; Subtract by adding negative constant
SIN1:    Y = PIOVR2 - R3 : TEST NEG        ; Subtract to compare (don't store)
         JT SIN2                           ; Jump if true (jump if negative)
         R3 = FADD(PI,FINV(R3))            ; Subtract by adding negative register
```

; B) Compute $\sin(x) \simeq \sum_{n=0}^{6} A_n X^{2n-1}$

```
SIN2:    R4 = FMUL(R0,R0)                  ; Square by multiplying
         R5 = A6                           ; Initialize series
         R5 = FMUL(R4,R5)                  ; Multiply registers
         R5 = FADD(R5,A5)                  ; Add coefficient
         R5 = FMUL(R4,R5)                  ; Multiply registers
         R5 = FADD(R5,A4)                  ; Add coefficient
         R5 = FMUL(R4,R5)                  ; Multiply registers
         R5 = FADD(R5,A3)                  ; Add coefficient
         R5 = FMUL(R4,R5)                  ; Multiply registers
         R5 = FADD(R5,A2)                  ; Add coefficient
         R5 = FMUL(R4,R5)                  ; Multiply registers
         R5 = FADD(R5,A1)                  ; Add coefficient
         R5 = FMUL(R4,R5)                  ; Multiply registers
         R5 = FADD(R5,A0)                  ; Add coefficient
         R5 = FMUL(R0,R5)                  ; Multiply registers
         R5 = FCHS(R5,R1) : RETURN         ; Change MSB of R5 to MSB of R1

END SUBROUTINE
```

This contrived language has a syntax which may be suitable for a source program. For the sake of illustration, it can be assumed that the microassembler recognizes this particular syntax. The series was computed inline instead of using a loop since it is relatively short. If a loop were used, a means of indexing the constants would be required.

5.7 Expand Subroutines into 'AS888/890 Operations

FMUL and FADD algorithms can now be expanded. Since they are called extensively from FSIN, they are more critical to the efficiency of the final design. Wherever possible, it is desirable to reduce the execution time of both in order to maintain efficiency.

5.7.1 Floating-Point Multiplication

Let M1 be the multiplier and M2 be the multiplicand whose product is P. Let the sign, exponent and fraction fields of their IEEE representation be:

M1 : |S1|E1|F1|
M2 : |S2|E2|F2|
P : |S3|E3|F3|

P is found by multiplying mantissas (fraction plus implicit one) and adding exponents. Since M1 and M2 are normalized, the range of $1.F1 \times 1.F2$ is

$$1.00...0 \leq 1.F1 \times 1.F2 \leq 11.1...10$$

The implicit bit may "overflow" into bit position 24. This type of overflow must be detected so that the result can be normalized. Normalization requires right shifting the result of $1.F1 \times 1.F2$ and incrementing E3. The implicit bit is then cleared when S3, E3 and M3 are packed to form P. The floating-point multiplication algorithm may then be defined as follows:

1) Unpack M1 into signed fraction (SF1) and exponent (E1)
2) Set the implicit bit in SF1
3) Unpack M2 into signed fraction (SF2) and exponent (E2)
4) Set the implicit bit in SF2
5) Perform SF3 = SF1 × SF2 using signed integer multiplication
6) Perform E3 = E1 + E2
7) Test SF3 for overflow into bit 24
8) If true, then increment E3 and right shift SF3
9) Clear the implicit bit in SF3
10) Pack E3 and SF3 to get P

As before, the steps of this algorithm can be broken down into simpler operations:

1) Unpack M1 into signed fraction (SF1) and exponent (E1)
   E1 = FEXP(M1)
   SF1 = FRAC(M1)

2) Set the implicit bit in SF1
   SF1 = SF1 OR BIT23

3) Unpack M2 into signed fraction (SF2) and exponent (E2)
   E2 = FEXP (M2)
   SF2 = FRAC (M2)

4) Set the implicit bit in SF2
   SF2 = SF2 OR BIT23

5) Perform SF3 = SF1 × SF2 using signed integer multiplication
   SF3 = IMUL (SF1, SF2)

6) Perform E3 = E1 + E2
   E3 = E1 + E2

7) Test SF3 for overflow into bit 24
   TEST (SF3 AND BIT24)
   JUMP IF FALSE to step 9

8) If true, then increment E3 and right shift SF3
   INC E3
   SF3 = RSHFT (SF3)

9) Clear the implicit bit in SF3.
   SF3 = SF3 AND NOT_BIT23

10) Pack E3 and SF3 to get P
   P = SF3 OR E3

FEXP, FRAC, testing bit 24 and setting/clearing bit 23 are all mask operations that translate into single 'AS888 instructions. The integer multiplication (IMUL) is simply the multiplication algorithm supported by the 'AS888 instruction set. No significant hardware features are required to do floating-point multiplication, nor are any subroutines required to support it.

Register assignments can now be made as before. Since FSIN uses registers in the lower half of the register file, it might be preferable to restrict FMUL to the upper registers. For example:

```
RF = P
RE = M1, F1, SF1
RD = M2, F2, SF2
RC = E1
RB = E2
```

RE and RD can share variables that need not be preserved. Using this assignment, FMUL computes RF = FMUL(RE,RD). RE and RD must be loaded prior to calling FMUL and RF must be stored upon return. By substituting registers for variables and reorganizing operations in the FMUL algorithm to better fit 'AS888/890 operations the following source program may be created:

```
FMUL:  SUBROUTINE

       RC = FEXP(RE)                       ; Unpack M1 into exponent
       RE = FRAC(RE)                       ;   and fraction
       RE = RE OR BIT23                    ; Set implicit bit
       MQ = SMTC(RE)                       ; Prepare to multiply

       RB = FEXP(RD)                       ; Unpack M2 into exponent
       RD = FMAG(RD)                       ;   and fraction
       RD = RD OR BIT23                    ; Set implicit bit
       RD = SMTC(RD)                       ; Prepare to multiply

       RE = 0 : RCA = #22d                 ; Initialize to multiply
       RE = SMULI RD : LOOP RCA            ; Integer multiplication iteration
       RE = SMULT RD                       ; Final step in signed multiply
       Y= TBO(RE,BIT1):BYTE= #0100b:TEST Z ; Test ''overflow''
       JF FMUL1                            ; Jump if false (exponent ok)

       INEX(RC)                            ; Increment exponent: add 00800000
       RE = SRA(RE)                        ; Shift fraction to normalize

FMUL1:RC = RC + RB : TEST CARRY            ; Add exponents and test carry
       JT ERROR                            ; Jump if carry true to handler

       RE = SMTC(RE)                       ; Get sign magnitude fraction
       RE = RE AND #807F_FFFFh             ; Clear implicit bit
       RF = RE OR RC : RETURN              ; Pack fraction and exponent
```

5.7.2 Floating-Point Addition

The floating-point addition algorithm (FADD) is slightly more complex than FMUL, since the two addends will usually not have the same exponent. Therefore the smaller (absolute value) addend must first be chosen by comparing exponents. Then it must be denormalized to align its digits with the digits of the larger addend. In other words, the two addends must have the same exponent before their fractions can be added. This process can be described by the following algorithm:

```
 1) Unpack A1 to get SF1 and E1
 2) Set implicit bit in SF1
 3) Unpack A2 to get SF2 and E2
 4) Set implicit bit in SF2
 5) If E2 > E1 then go to step 9
    (‖A1‖ ≤ ‖A2‖)
 6) Let DIFF = E1 - E2
 7) Do i = 1 to DIFF
      SF2 = RSHFT(SF2)  (Arithmetic right shift)
    Enddo
 8) Let E3 = E1 , go to step 12
    (‖A2‖ > ‖A1‖)
 9) Let DIFF = E2 - E1
10) Do i = 1 to DIFF
      SF1 = RSHFT(SF1)  (Arithmetic right shift)
    Enddo
11) Let E3 = E2
12) SF3 = SF1 + SF2
13) Test "overflow" into bit 24
14) Jump if false to step 17
15) Increment exponent E3
16) Normalize signed fraction with right arithmetic shift
17) Clear implicit bit
18) Pack: SUM = SF3 or E3
19) Return
```

Register assignments for variables must now be made. Since FSIN uses registers in the lower half of the 'AS888 register file, it is necessary to use the upper registers:

```
RF = SUM
RE = A1, F1, SF1
RD = A2, F2, SF2
RC = E1
RB = E2
```

By slightly reorganizing the sequence to better fit 'AS888/890 operations, the following microprogram to perform FADD can be created:

```
FADD: SUBROUTINE

; 1) Unpack A1 to get SF1 and E1
      RC = FEXP(RE)                   ; Get exponent (E1)
      RE = FRAC(RE)                   ; Get signed fraction (SF1)

; 2) Set implicit bit in SF1
      MQ = RE OR BIT23                ; Set implicit bit
      RE = SMTC(RE)                   ; Convert to two's complement
```

```
; 3) Unpack A2 to get SF2 and A2
       RB = FEXP(RD)                        ; Get exponent (E2)
       RD = FRAC(RD)                        ; Get signed fraction (SF2)

; 4) Set implicit bit in SF2
       RD = RD OR BIT23                     ; Set implicit bit
       RD = SMTC(RD)                        ; Convert to two's complement

; 5) If E2 > E1 then go to step 9
       RF = RC - RB : TEST NEGATIVE         ; Compare A2 from A1
       JT FADD1 : RCA = #8                  ; Jump if E2 > E1; set up loop count

; 6) Let DIFF = E1 - E2.
       Y/RF = SLC(RF) : LOOP RCA            ; Rotate 8 times to get difference
       RCA = Y/RF                           ; Load difference in loop counter

; 7) Do i = 1 to DIFF
       SF2 = RSHFT(SF2)
    Enddo
       RD = SRA(RD) : LOOP RCA              ; Orient digits of smaller addend

; 8) Let E3 = E1, go to step 12
       RB = RC : JUMP FADD2                 ; Swap registers and branch

; 9) Let DIFF = E2 - E1

FADD1: RF = NOT(RF)                         ; Complement result of E1 - E2
       Y/RF = SLC(RF) : LOOP RCA            ; Shift 8 times to get DIFF
       RCA = Y/RF                           ; Load DIFF in loop counter

;10) Do i = 1 TO DIFF
       SF1 = RSHFT(SF1)
    Enddo
       RE = SRA(RE) : LOOP RCA              ; Align SF1 with SF2

;11) Let E3 = E2 (no instruction required — RB already has E2 in it)

;12) SF3 = SF1 + SF2

FADD2: RF = RD + RE                         ; Add
       RF = SMTC(RF)                        ; Convert to sign-magnitude

;13) Test "overflow" into bit 24
       RF = TBO (RF, BIT24)                 ; Check for normalization

;14) Jump if false to step 17
       JF FADD3                             ; If so, finish and exit

;15) Else increment exponent
       INC RB : TEST NEG                    ; Test for exponent overflow

;16) Normalize signed fraction
       RF = SRA(RF) : JT ERROR              ; Jump to error handler if overflow

;17) Clear implicit bit

FADD3: RF = SETO (RF, BIT23)                ; Reset bit 23 of RF

;18) Pack: SUM = SF3 OR E3
       RF = RF OR RB : RETURN               ; Or signed fraction and exponent
```

There is an important consequence of FADD which impacts the hardware. Since the number of shifts required to denormalize the small addend is data dependent (computed in the ALU) it is necessary to provide a path between the ALU Y bus and the 'AS890 DRA bus. All the other operations are simple 'AS888/890 instructions, including the FRAC and FEXP mask operations discussed during the development of FMUL. ERROR is a floating-point overflow error handler.

5.8 Evaluate Tradeoffs and Block Diagram the Hardware

A rough estimate of the FSIN worst case execution time can be arrived at by making the following observations about FSIN, FMUL and FADD:

FMUL
- integer recursion ≃ 22 cycles
- other instructions ≃ 18 cycles
- total ≃ 40 cycles

FADD
- denormalization ≃ 23 cycles
- other instructions ≃ 25 cycles
- total ≃ 50 cycles

FSIN
- number of calls to FMUL = 12
- number of calls to FADD = 11
- number of other cycles ≃ 10

Approximate worst case total = 10 + (12 × 40) + (11 × 50) = 1040 cycles. At 50 nanoseconds per cycle, this requires approximately 52 microseconds. There are few improvements that could be made in hardware to speed this time, except perhaps the addition of a flash multiplier which would reduce the integer computation by about 20 cycles (an overall reduction of about two percent). A barrel shifter could have the same benefit during floating-point addition for a total reduction of about 4 percent. For the sake of simplicity, it will be assumed that 52 microseconds is acceptable for the sin(x) computation.

Another issue which must be considered is the problem of loading the 'AS888 and 'AS890 with constants. A slight materials cost reduction might be realized by storing constants in table PROMs rather than in control store memory. An interesting use of the DRA and DRB ports on the 'AS890 would be to use the output of RCA or RCB to index data in the constant PROM. This would allow long series to be implemented in loop form rather than the inline method used in FSIN. Once again, the constant PROM will not be implemented for the sake of simplicity.

Now the architecture can be designed to meet the requirements identified throughout this analysis:

1) A path between the 'AS888 Y bus and the 'AS890 DRA bus.
2) A path between the microinstruction register and the 'AS890 DRA bus for loading loop counts and branch addresses.
3) A path between the microinstruction register and the 'AS888 Y bus for loading constants.
4) Independent control of $\overline{\text{SIO0}}$ in each 'AS888 slice to allow bit/byte instructions.
5) A status register to store 'AS888 status for testing.
6) A status mux to test the 'AS888 status, bit 23 of the 'AS888 Y bus, bit 24 of the 'AS888 Y bus and hardwired 0 and 1.

A system having these features is illustrated in Figure 5.1.

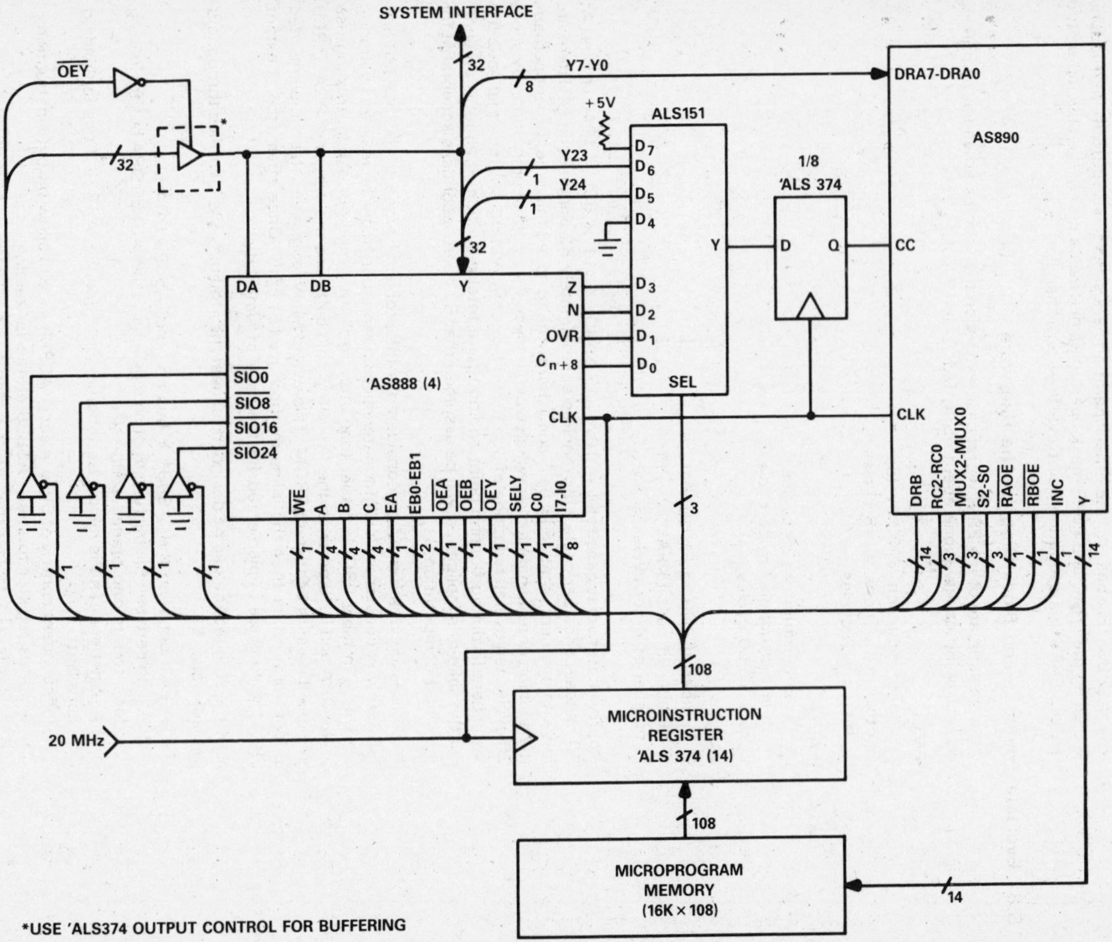
SYSTEM INTERFACE
32
Y7-Y0
8
OEY
*
32
+5V
ALS151
D7
D6
D5
D4
D3
D2
D1
D0
SEL
Y
Y23
Y24
1
1
32
1/8
'ALS 374
D
Q
CC
AS890
DRA7-DRA0
CLK
DRB
RC2-RC0
MUX2-MUX0
S2-S0
RAOE
RBOE
INC
Y
14
3
3
3
1
1
1
14
DA
DB
Y
Z
N
OVR
Cn+8
CLK
'AS888 (4)
SIO0
SIO8
SIO16
SIO24
WE
A
B
C
EA
EB0-EB1
OEA
OEB
OEY
SELY
C0
I7-I0
1
4
4
4
1
2
1
1
1
1
1
8
1
1
1
1
3
108
20 MHz
MICROINSTRUCTION
REGISTER
'ALS 374 (14)
108
MICROPROGRAM
MEMORY
(16K × 108)
14

*USE 'ALS374 OUTPUT CONTROL FOR BUFFERING

Figure 5-1. Block Diagram of Floating-Point Processor

5.9 Define Microinstruction Fields During Detailed Hardware Design

The detailed hardware design will produce a wiring diagram that fixes the position within the microinstruction of each of the various control signals that are connected from the microinstruction register to the 'AS888, 'AS890, status mux and any other special hardware. Once this design is complete it is possible for the assembler to sort the control bits of each instruction so that they will be properly oriented when the microprogram is installed in the target system.

5.10 Assemble the Microprogram

TI is currently developing an 'AS888/890 microassembler. Several microassemblers are commercially available, and many users prefer to write their own. The microprogram shown in Table 5-1 was hand-assembled, but has a syntax that is suitable for interpretation by a user-written assembler.

Table 5.1. Floating Point Sin(x) Microprogram

Address	Microcode	WE	A3-A0	B3-B0	C3-C0	EA	EB1-EB0	OEA	OEB	OEY	SELY	Cn	I7-I0	32-bit Constant	SIO0	SIO8	SIO16	SIO24	RC2-RC0	MUX2-MUX0	S2-S0	DRB13-DRB0	RAOE	RBOE	INC	SEL
	* R1 = FSGN(R0)																									
0000 SIN:	R1 = R0 AND #8000 0000h	0	0	X	1	0	2	1	1	1	0	0	F A	8 0 0 0 0 0 0 0	1	1	1	1	0	2	7	X X X X	1	1	1	7
	* R2 = FABS(R0)																									
0001	R2 = R0	0	0	X	2	0	X	1	1	1	0	0	F 6	X X X X X X X X	1	1	1	1	0	2	7	X X X X	1	1	1	7
0002	R2 = R0 SET0 #80h : BYTE = #1000b	0	0	2	8	0	0	1	1	1	0	0	1 8	X X X X X X X X	1	1	1	0	0	2	7	X X X X	1	1	1	7
	* R3 = FMUL(R2,1OVR2PI)																									
0003	RE = R2	0	2	X	E	0	X	1	1	1	0	0	F 6	X X X X X X X X	1	1	1	1	0	2	7	X X X X	1	1	1	7
0004	RD = #3EA2 F984h	0	X	X	D	X	X	1	1	1	1	X	F F	3 E A 2 F 9 8 4	1	1	1	1	0	2	7	X X X X	1	1	1	7
0005	JSR FMUL	1	X	X	X	X	X	1	1	1	X	X	F F	X X X X X X X X	1	1	1	1	0	1	4	0 0 6 0	1	1	1	7
0006	R3 = RF	0	F	X	3	0	X	1	1	1	0	0	F 6	X X X X X X X X	1	1	1	1	0	2	7	X X X X	1	1	1	7
	* R3 = FINT(R3)																									
0007	RF = R3	0	3	X	F	0	X	1	1	1	0	0	F 6	X X X X X X X X	1	1	1	1	0	2	7	X X X X	1	1	1	7
0008	JSR FINT [EXERCISE FOR READER]	1	X	X	X	X	X	1	1	1	X	X	F F	X X X X X X X X	1	1	1	1	0	1	4	. . . .	1	1	1	7
0009	R3 = RF	0	F	X	3	0	X	1	1	1	0	0	F 6	X X X X X X X X	1	1	1	1	0	2	7	X X X X	1	1	1	7
	* R3 = FMUL(R3,2PI)																									
000A	RE = R3	0	3	X	E	0	X	1	1	1	0	0	F 6	X X X X X X X X	1	1	1	1	0	2	7	X X X X	1	1	1	7
000B	RD = #40C9 0FDBh	0	X	X	D	X	X	1	1	1	0	X	F F	4 0 C 9 0 F D B	1	1	1	1	0	2	7	X X X X	1	1	1	7
000C	JSR FMUL	1	X	X	X	X	X	1	1	1	X	X	F F	X X X X X X X X	1	1	1	1	0	1	4	0 0 6 0	1	1	1	7
000D	R3 = RF	0	F	X	3	0	X	1	1	1	0	0	F 6	X X X X X X X X	1	1	1	1	0	2	7	X X X X	1	1	1	7
	* R3 = FADD(R2,INV(R3))																									
000E	RE = R2	0	2	X	E	0	X	1	1	1	0	0	F 6	X X X X X X X X	1	1	1	1	0	2	7	X X X X	1	1	1	7
000F	RD = R5 XOR #8000 0000h	0	5	X	D	0	2	1	1	1	0	0	F 9	8 0 0 0 0 0 0 0	1	1	1	1	0	2	7	X X X X	1	1	1	7
0010	JSR FADD	1	X	X	X	X	X	1	1	1	X	X	F F	X X X X X X X X	1	1	1	1	0	1	4	0 0 7 4	1	1	1	7
0011	R3 = RF	0	F	X	3	0	X	1	1	1	0	0	F 6	X X X X X X X X	1	1	1	1	0	2	7	X X X X	1	1	1	7

Table 5.1. Floating Point Sin(x) Microprogram (continued)

Address	Label	Instruction	WE	A3-A0	B3-B0	C3-C0	EA	EB1-EB0	OEA	OEB	OEY	SELY	Cn	I7-I0	32-bit Constant	SIO0	SIO8	SIO16	SIO24	RC2-RC0	MUX2-MUX0	S2-S0	DRB13-DRB0	RAOE	RBOE	INC	SEL
		* Y = FADD(R2,NEGPI)																									
0012		RE = R2	0	2	X	E	0	X	1	1	1	0	0	F 6	X X X X X X X X	1	1	1	1	0	2	7	X X X X	1	1	1	7
0013		RD = #C059 0FDBh	0	X	X	D	X	X	1	1	1	0	X	F F	C 0 5 9 0 F D B	1	1	1	1	0	2	7	X X X X	1	1	1	7
0014		JSR FADD	1	X	X	X	X	X	1	1	1	X	X	F F	X X X X X X X X	1	1	1	1	0	1	4	0 0 7 4	1	1	1	7
0015		Y = RF : TEST NEG	1	F	X	X	0	X	1	1	0	0	0	F 6	X X X X X X X X	1	1	1	1	0	2	7	X X X X	1	1	1	2
0016		JT SIN1	1	X	X	X	X	X	1	1	1	X	X	F F	X X X X X X X X	1	1	1	1	0	1	7	0 0 0 0	1	1	1	7
		* R1 = FINV(R1)																									
0017		R1 = R1 XOR #8000 0000h	0	1	X	1	0	2	1	1	1	0	0	F 9	8 0 0 0 0 0 0 0	1	1	1	1	0	2	7	X X X X	1	1	1	7
		* R3 = FADD(R3,NEGPI)																									
0018		RE = R3	0	3	X	E	0	X	1	1	1	0	0	F 6	X X X X X X X X	1	1	1	1	0	2	7	X X X X	1	1	1	7
0019		RD = #C059 0FDBh	0	3	X	D	X	X	1	1	1	1	X	F F	C 0 5 9 0 F D B	1	1	1	1	0	2	7	X X X X	1	1	1	7
001A		JSR FADD	1	X	X	X	X	X	1	1	1	X	X	F F	X X X X X X X X	1	1	1	1	0	1	4	0 0 7 4	1	1	1	7
001B		R3 = RF	0	F	X	3	0	X	1	1	1	0	0	F 6	X X X X X X X X	1	1	1	1	0	2	7	X X X X	1	1	1	7
	* SIN1:	Y = FADD (PIOVR2,INV(R3)) : TEST NEG																									
001C	SIN1:	RE = #3FC9 0FDBh	0	X	X	E	X	X	1	1	1	1	0	F 6	3 5 C 9 0 F D B	1	1	1	1	0	2	7	X X X X	1	1	1	7
001D		RD = R3 XOR #8000 0000h	0	3	X	D	0	2	1	1	1	0	0	F 9	8 0 0 0 0 0 0 0	1	1	1	1	0	2	7	X X X X	1	1	1	7
001E		JSR FADD	1	X	X	X	X	X	1	1	1	X	X	F F	X X X X X X X X	1	1	1	1	0	1	4	0 0 7 4	1	1	1	7
001F		Y = RF : TEST NEG	1	F	X	X	0	X	1	1	0	0	0	F 6	X X X X X X X X	1	1	1	1	0	2	7	X X X X	1	1	1	2
0020		JT SIN2	1	X	X	X	X	X	1	1	1	X	X	F F	X X X X X X X X	1	1	1	1	0	1	7	0 0 0 0	1	1	1	7
		* R3 = FADD(PI,FINV(R3))																									
0021		RE = #4059 0FDBh	0	X	X	E	X	X	1	1	1	1	0	F 6	4 0 5 9 0 F D B	1	1	1	1	0	2	7	X X X X	1	1	1	7
0022		RD = R3 XOR #8000 0000h	0	3	X	D	0	2	1	1	1	0	0	F 9	8 0 0 0 0 0 0 0	1	1	1	1	0	2	7	X X X X	1	1	1	7
0023		JSR FADD	1	X	X	X	X	X	1	1	1	X	X	F F	X X X X X X X X	1	1	1	1	0	1	4	0 0 7 4	1	1	1	7
0024		R3 = RF	0	F	X	3	0	X	1	1	1	0	0	F 6	X X X X X X X X	1	1	1	1	0	2	7	X X X X	1	1	1	7
	* SIN2:	R4 = FMUL(R0,R0)																									
0025	SIN2:	RE = R0	0	0	X	E	0	X	1	1	1	0	0	F 6	X X X X X X X X	1	1	1	1	0	2	7	X X X X	1	1	1	7
0026		RD = R0	0	0	X	D	0	X	1	1	1	0	0	F 6	X X X X X X X X	1	1	1	1	0	2	7	X X X X	1	1	1	7
0027		JSR FMUL	1	X	X	X	X	X	1	1	1	X	X	F F	X X X X X X X X	1	1	1	1	0	1	4	0 0 6 0	1	1	1	7
0028		R4 = RF	0	F	X	4	0	X	1	1	1	0	0	F 6	X X X X X X X X	1	1	1	1	0	2	7	X X X X	1	1	1	7

Table 5.1. Floating Point Sin(x) Microprogram (continued)

Address	Source	WE	A3-A0	B3-B0	C3-C0	EA	EB1-EB0	OEA	OEB	OEY	SELY	Cn	I7-I0	32-bit Constant	SIO0	SIO8	SIO16	SIO24	RC2-RC0	MUX2-MUX0	S2-S0	DRB13-DRB0	RAOE	RBOE	INC	SEL
	* R5 = A6																									
0029	R5 = #2F34 6FBCh	0	X	X	5	0	X	1	1	1	1	0	F6	2F346FBC	1	1	1	1	0	2	7	XXXX	1	1	1	7
	* R5 = FMUL(R4,R5)																									
002A	RE = R4	0	4	X	E	0	X	1	1	1	0	0	F6	XXXXXXXX	1	1	1	1	0	2	7	XXXX	1	1	1	7
002B	RD = R5	0	5	X	D	0	X	1	1	1	0	0	F6	XXXXXXXX	1	1	1	1	0	2	7	XXXX	1	1	1	7
002C	JSR FMUL	1	X	X	X	X	X	1	1	1	X	X	FF	XXXXXXXX	1	1	1	1	0	1	4	0060	1	1	1	7
002D	R5 = RF	0	F	X	5	0	X	1	1	1	0	0	F6	XXXXXXXX	1	1	1	1	0	2	7	XXXX	1	1	1	7
	* R5 = FADD(R5,A5)																									
002E	RE = R5	0	5	X	E	0	X	1	1	1	0	0	F6	XXXXXXXX	1	1	1	1	0	2	7	XXXX	1	1	1	7
002F	RD = #B2D7 5AD5h	0	X	X	D	X	X	1	1	1	1	X	FF	B2D75AD5	1	1	1	1	0	2	7	XXXX	1	1	1	7
0030	JSR FADD	1	X	X	X	X	X	1	1	1	X	X	FF	XXXXXXXX	1	1	1	1	0	1	4	0074	1	1	1	7
0031	R5 = RF	0	F	X	5	0	X	1	1	1	0	0	F6	XXXXXXXX	1	1	1	1	0	2	7	XXXX	1	1	1	7
	* R5 = FMUL(R4,R5)																									
0032	RE = R4	0	4	X	E	0	X	1	1	1	0	0	F6	XXXXXXXX	1	1	1	1	0	2	7	XXXX	1	1	1	7
0033	RD = R5	0	5	X	D	0	X	1	1	1	0	0	F6	XXXXXXXX	1	1	1	1	0	2	7	XXXX	1	1	1	7
0034	JSR FMUL	1	X	X	X	X	X	1	1	1	X	X	FF	XXXXXXXX	1	1	1	1	0	1	4	0060	1	1	1	7
0035	R5 = RF	0	F	X	5	0	X	1	1	1	0	0	F6	XXXXXXXX	1	1	1	1	0	2	7	XXXX	1	1	1	7
	* R5 = FADD(R5,A4)																									
0036	RE = R5	0	5	X	E	0	X	1	1	1	0	0	F6	XXXXXXXX	1	1	1	1	0	2	7	XXXX	1	1	1	7
0037	RD = #3638 EF99h	0	X	X	D	X	X	1	1	1	1	X	FF	3638EF99	1	1	1	1	0	2	7	XXXX	1	1	1	7
0038	JSR FADD	1	X	X	X	X	X	1	1	1	X	X	FF	XXXXXXXX	1	1	1	1	0	1	4	0074	1	1	1	7
0039	R5 = RF	0	F	X	5	0	X	1	1	1	0	0	F6	XXXXXXXX	1	1	1	1	0	2	7	XXXX	1	1	1	7
	* R5 = FMUL(R4,R5)																									
003A	RE = R4	0	4	X	E	0	X	1	1	1	0	0	F6	XXXXXXXX	1	1	1	1	0	2	7	XXXX	1	1	1	7
003B	RD = R5	0	5	X	D	0	X	1	1	1	0	0	F6	XXXXXXXX	1	1	1	1	0	2	7	XXXX	1	1	1	7
003C	JSR FMUL	1	X	X	X	X	X	1	1	1	X	X	FF	XXXXXXXX	1	1	1	1	0	1	4	0060	1	1	1	7
003D	R5 = RF	0	F	X	5	0	X	1	1	1	0	0	F6	XXXXXXXX	1	1	1	1	0	2	7	XXXX	1	1	1	7

Table 5.1. Floating Point Sin(x) Microprogram (continued)

Address	Instruction	WE	A3-A0	B3-B0	C3-C0	EA	EB1-EB0	OEA	OEB	OEY	SELY	Cn	I7-I0	32-bit Constant	SIO0	SIO8	SIO16	SIO24	RC2-RC0	MUX2-MUX0	S2-S0	DRB13-DRB0	RAOE	RBOE	INC	SEL
	* R5 = FADD(R5,A3)																									
003E	RE = R5	0	5	X	E	0	X	1	1	1	0	0	F 6	X X X X X X X X	1	1	1	1	0	2	7	X X X X	1	1	1	7
003F	RD = #B950 0D01h	0	X	X	D	X	X	1	1	1	1	X	F F	B 9 5 0 0 D 0 1	1	1	1	1	0	2	7	X X X X	1	1	1	7
0040	JSR FADD	1	X	X	X	X	X	1	1	1	X	X	F F	X X X X X X X X	1	1	1	1	0	1	4	0 0 7 4	1	1	1	7
0041	R5 = RF	0	F	X	5	0	X	1	1	1	0	0	F 6	X X X X X X X X	1	1	1	1	0	2	7	X X X X	1	1	1	7
	* R5 = FMUL(R4,R5)																									
0042	RE = R4	0	4	X	E	0	X	1	1	1	0	0	F 6	X X X X X X X X	1	1	1	1	0	2	7	X X X X	1	1	1	7
0043	RD = R5	0	5	X	D	0	X	1	1	1	0	0	F 6	X X X X X X X X	1	1	1	1	0	2	7	X X X X	1	1	1	7
0044	JSR FMUL	1	X	X	X	X	X	1	1	1	X	X	F F	X X X X X X X X	1	1	1	1	0	1	4	0 0 6 0	1	1	1	7
0045	R5 = RF	0	F	X	5	0	X	1	1	1	0	0	F 6	X X X X X X X X	1	1	1	1	0	2	7	X X X X	1	1	1	7
	* R5 = FADD(R5,A2)																									
0046	RE = R5	0	5	X	E	0	X	1	1	1	0	0	F 6	X X X X X X X X	1	1	1	1	0	2	7	X X X X	1	1	1	7
0047	RD = #3C08 8888h	0	X	X	D	X	X	1	1	1	1	X	F F	3 C 0 8 8 8 8 8	1	1	1	1	0	2	7	X X X X	1	1	1	7
0048	JSR FADD	1	X	X	X	X	X	1	1	1	X	X	F F	X X X X X X X X	1	1	1	1	0	1	4	0 0 7 4	1	1	1	7
0049	R5 = RF	0	F	X	5	0	X	1	1	1	0	0	F 6	X X X X X X X X	1	1	1	1	0	2	7	X X X X	1	1	1	7
	* R5 = FMUL(R4,R5)																									
004A	RE = R4	0	4	X	E	0	X	1	1	1	0	0	F 6	X X X X X X X X	1	1	1	1	0	2	7	X X X X	1	1	1	7
004B	RD = R5	0	5	X	D	0	X	1	1	1	0	0	F 6	X X X X X X X X	1	1	1	1	0	2	7	X X X X	1	1	1	7
004C	JSR FMUL	1	X	X	X	X	X	1	1	1	X	X	F F	X X X X X X X X	1	1	1	1	0	1	4	0 0 6 0	1	1	1	7
004D	R5 = RF	0	F	X	5	0	X	1	1	1	0	0	F 6	X X X X X X X X	1	1	1	1	0	2	7	X X X X	1	1	1	7
	* R5 = FADD(R5,A1)																									
004E	RE = R5	0	5	X	E	0	X	1	1	1	0	0	F 6	X X X X X X X X	1	1	1	1	0	2	7	X X X X	1	1	1	7
004F	RD = #BE2A AAADh	0	X	X	D	X	X	1	1	1	1	1	F F	B E 2 A A A A D	1	1	1	1	0	2	7	X X X X	1	1	1	7
0050	JSR FADD	1	X	X	X	X	X	1	1	1	X	X	F F	X X X X X X X X	1	1	1	1	0	1	4	0 0 7 4	1	1	1	7
0051	R5 = RF	0	F	X	5	0	X	1	1	1	0	0	F 6	X X X X X X X X	1	1	1	1	0	2	7	X X X X	1	1	1	7
	* R5 = FMUL(R4,R5)																									
0052	RE = R4	0	4	X	E	0	X	1	1	1	0	0	F 6	X X X X X X X X	1	1	1	1	0	2	7	X X X X	1	1	1	7
0053	RD = R5	0	5	X	D	0	X	1	1	1	0	0	F 6	X X X X X X X X	1	1	1	1	0	2	7	X X X X	1	1	1	7
0054	JSR FMUL	1	X	X	X	X	X	1	1	1	X	X	F F	X X X X X X X X	1	1	1	1	0	1	4	0 0 6 0	1	1	1	7
0055	R5 = RF	0	F	X	5	0	X	1	1	1	0	0	F 6	X X X X X X X X	1	1	1	1	0	2	7	X X X X	1	1	1	7

Table 5.1. Floating Point Sin(x) Microprogram (continued)

Address	Source	WE	A3-A0	B3-B0	C3-C0	EA	EB1-EB0	OEA	OEB	OEY	SELY	Cn	I7-I0	32-bit Constant	SIO0	SIO8	SIO16	SIO24	RC2-RC0	MUX2-MUX0	S2-S0	DRB13-DRB0	RAOE	RBOE	INC	SEL
	* R5 = FADD(R5,A0)																									
0056	RE = R5	0	5	X	E	0	X	1	1	1	0	0	F 6	X X X X X X X X	1	1	1	1	0	2	7	X X X X	1	1	1	7
0057	RD = #3F80 0000h	0	X	X	D	X	X	1	1	1	1	X	F F	3 F 8 0 0 0 0 0	1	1	1	1	0	2	7	X X X X	1	1	1	7
0058	JSR FADD	1	X	X	X	X	X	1	1	1	X	X	F F	X X X X X X X X	1	1	1	1	0	1	4	0 0 7 4	1	1	1	7
0059	R5 = RF	0	F	X	5	0	X	1	1	1	0	0	F 6	X X X X X X X X	1	1	1	1	0	2	7	X X X X	1	1	1	7
	* R5 = FMUL(R0,R5)																									
005A	RE = R0	0	0	X	E	0	X	1	1	1	0	0	F 6	X X X X X X X X	1	1	1	1	0	2	7	X X X X	1	1	1	7
005B	RD = R5	0	5	X	D	0	X	1	1	1	0	0	F 6	X X X X X X X X	1	1	1	1	0	2	7	X X X X	1	1	1	7
005C	JSR FMUL	1	X	X	X	X	X	1	1	1	X	X	F F	X X X X X X X X	1	1	1	1	0	1	4	0 0 6 0	1	1	1	7
005D	R5 = RF	0	F	X	5	0	X	1	1	1	0	0	F 6	X X X X X X X X	1	1	1	1	0	2	7	X X X X	1	1	1	7
	* R5 = FCHS(R5,R1) : RETURN																									
005E	R1 = R1 OR #7FFF FFFFh	0	1	X	1	0	2	1	1	1	0	0	F B	B 7 F F F F F F	1	1	1	1	0	2	7	X X X X	1	1	1	7
005F	R5 = R5 XOR R1 : RETURN	0	5	1	5	0	0	1	1	1	0	0	F 0	X X X X X X X X	1	1	1	1	0	2	2	X X X X	1	1	1	7
	* RC = FEXP(RE)																									
0060 FMUL:	RC = RE AND #7F80 0000h	0	E	X	C	0	2	1	1	1	0	0	F A	7 F 8 0 0 0 0 0	1	1	1	1	0	2	7	X X X X	1	1	1	7
	* RE = FRAC(RE)																									
0061	RE = RE AND #807F FFFFh	0	E	X	E	0	2	1	1	1	0	0	F A	8 0 7 F F F F F	1	1	1	1	0	2	7	X X X X	1	1	1	7
	* RE = RE OR bit23																									
0062	RE = RE OR #0080 0000h	0	E	X	F	0	2	1	1	1	0	0	F B	0 0 8 0 0 0 0 0	1	1	1	1	0	2	7	X X X X	1	1	1	7
	* MQ = SMTC(RE)																									
0063	RE = SMTC(RE)	0	X	E	E	X	0	1	1	1	1	0	5 8	X X X X X X X X	1	1	1	1	0	2	7	X X X X	1	1	1	7
0064	LOADMQ : PASS	1	E	X	X	0	X	1	1	1	1	0	E 6	X X X X X X X X	1	1	1	1	0	2	7	X X X X	1	1	1	7
	* RB = FEXP(RD)																									
0065	RB = RD AND #7F80 0000h	0	D	X	B	0	2	1	1	1	0	0	F A	7 F 8 0 0 0 0 0	1	1	1	1	0	2	7	X X X X	1	1	1	7

Table 5.1. Floating Point Sin(x) Microprogram (continued)

Address	Label	Statement	WE A3-A0 B3-B0 C3-C0 EA EB1-EB0 OEA OEB OEY SELY Cn I7-I0	32-bit Constant	SIO0 SIO8 SIO16 SIO24	RC2-RC0 MUX2-MUX0 S2-S0 DRB13-DRB0 RAOE RBOE INC	SEL
	*	RD = FRAC(RD)					
0066		RD = RD AND #807F FFFFh	0 D X D 0 2 1 1 1 0 0 F A	8 0 7 F F F F F	1 1 1 1	0 2 7 X X X X 1 1 1	7
0067		RD = RD OR bit23	0 D X D 0 2 1 1 1 0 0 F B	0 0 8 0 0 0 0 0	1 1 1 1	0 2 7 X X X X 1 1 1	7
0068		RD = SMTC(RD)	0 X D D X 0 1 1 1 1 D 5 8	X X X X X X X X	1 1 1 1	0 2 7 X X X X 1 1 1	7
0069		RE = 0 : RCB = #22D	0 E E E 0 0 1 1 1 1 0 F 9	0 0 0 0 0 0 1 6	1 1 1 1	6 1 7 X X X X 1 1 1	4
006A		RE = SMULI RD : LOOP RCB	0 D E E 0 0 1 1 1 1 0 6 0	X X X X X X X X	1 1 1 1	5 6 7 0 0 6 A 1 1 1	4
006B		RE = SMULT RD	0 D E E 0 0 1 1 1 0 0 7 0	X X X X X X X X	1 1 1 1	0 6 7 X X X X 1 1 1	7
006C		TB0(RE,bit1) : BYTE = #0100b : TEST Z	0 0 F 0 0 0 1 1 1 1 0 3 8	X X X X X X X X	1 0 1 1	0 2 7 X X X X 1 1 1	4
006D		JT FMUL1	1 X X X X X X 1 1 1 X F F	X X X X X X X X	1 1 1 1	0 1 7 X X X X 1 1 1	7
	*	INEX RC					
006E		RC = RC ADD #0080 0000h	0 C X C 0 2 1 1 1 0 0 F 1	0 0 8 0 0 0 0 0	1 1 1 1	0 2 7 X X X X 1 1 1	7
006F		RE = SRA(RE)	0 E X E 0 X 1 1 1 0 0 0 6	X X X X X X X X	1 1 1 1	0 2 7 X X X X 1 1 1	7
0070	FMUL1:	RC = RC ADD RB : TEST CARRY	0 C B C 0 0 1 1 1 0 0 F 1	X X X X X X X X	1 1 1 1	0 2 7 X X X X 1 1 1	0
0071		JT ERROR	1 X X X X X X 1 1 1 X X F F	X X X X X X X X	1 1 1 1	0 1 7 X X X X 1 1 1	7
0072		RE = SMTC(RE)	0 X E E X 0 1 1 1 1 0 5 8	X X X X X X X X	1 1 1 1	0 2 7 X X X X 1 1 1	7
0073		RE = RE AND #807F FFFFh	0 E X E 0 2 1 1 1 0 0 F A	8 0 7 F F F F F	1 1 1 1	0 2 7 X X X X 1 1 1	7
	* FADD:	RC = FEXP(RE)					
0074	FADD:	RC = RC AND #7F80 0000	0 C X C 0 2 1 1 1 0 0 F A	7 F 8 0 0 0 0 0	1 1 1 1	0 2 7 X X X X 1 1 1	7
	*	RE = FRAC(RE)					
0075		RE = RE AND #807F FFFFh	0 E X E 0 2 1 1 1 0 0 F A	8 0 7 F F F F F	1 1 1 1	0 2 7 X X X X 1 1 1	7
0076		MQ = RE OR bit23	1 E X X 0 1 1 1 1 0 0 E B	0 0 8 0 0 0 0 0	1 1 1 1	0 2 7 X X X X 1 1 1	7
0077		RE = SMTC(RE)	0 E X E 0 2 1 1 1 0 0 F A	8 0 7 F F F F F	1 1 1 1	0 2 7 X X X X 1 1 1	7
	*	RB = FEXP(RD)					
0078		RB = RD AND #7F80 0000	0 D X B 0 2 1 1 1 0 0 F A	7 F 8 0 0 0 0 0	1 1 1 1	0 2 7 X X X X 1 1 1	7

Table 5.1. Floating Point Sin(x) Microprogram (continued)

Address	Instruction	WE A3-A0 B3-B0 C3-C0 EA EB1-EB0 OEA OEB OEY SELY Cn I7-I0	32-bit Constant	SIO0 SIO8 SIO16 SIO24	RC2-RC0 MUX2-MUX0 S2-S0 DRB13-DRB0	RAOE RBOE INC	SEL
	* RD = FRAC(RD)						
0079	RE = RE AND #807F FFFFh	0 E X E 0 2 1 1 1 0 0 F A	8 0 7 F F F F F	1 1 1 1	0 2 7 X X X X	1 1 1	7
007A	RD = RD OR bit23	0 D X D 0 2 1 1 1 0 0 F B	0 0 8 0 0 0 0 0	1 1 1 1	0 2 7 X X X X	1 1 1	7
007B	RD = SMTC(RD)	0 X D D X 0 1 1 1 1 0 5 8	X X X X X X X X	1 1 1 1	0 2 7 X X X X	1 1 1	7
007C	RF = RC − RB : C0=0: TEST NEG	0 C B F 0 0 1 1 1 0 0 F 3	X X X X X X X X	1 1 1 1	0 2 7 X X X X	1 1 1	2
007D	JT FADD1 : RCB = #8	1 X X X X X 1 1 1 X X F F	X X X X X X X 8	1 1 1 1	6 1 7 X X X X	1 1 1	4
007E	Y/RF = SLC(RF) : LOOP RCB	0 F X F 0 X 1 1 0 X 0 6 6	X X X X X X X X	1 1 1 1	5 6 7 0 0 7 E	1 1 1	4
007F	Y = RF : RCA = Y	1 X X X X X 1 1 0 0 X F F	X X X X X X X X	1 1 1 1	2 7 7 0 0 8 0	1 1 1	7
0080	RD = SRA(RD) : LOOP RCA	0 D X D 0 X 1 1 1 0 0 0 6	X X X X X X X X	1 1 1 1	1 6 7 0 0 7 E	1 1 1	4
0081	RB = RC : JUMP FADD2	0 C X B 0 X 1 1 1 0 X F F	X X X X X X X X	1 1 1 1	0 2 7 X X X X	1 1 1	7
0082 FADD1:	RF = NOT RF	0 F X F 0 X 1 1 1 0 0 F 7	X X X X X X X X	1 1 1 1	0 2 7 X X X X	1 1 1	7
0083	Y/RF = SLC(RF) : LOOP RCB	0 F X F 0 X 1 1 0 0 0 6 6	X X X X X X X X	1 1 1 1	6 1 7 X X X X	1 1 1	4
0084	Y = RF : RCA = Y	1 X X X X X 1 1 0 0 X F F	X X X X X X X X	1 1 1 1	5 6 7 0 0 8 4	1 1 1	4
0085	RE = SRA(RE) : LOOP RCA	0 E X E 0 X 1 1 1 0 0 0 6	X X X X X X X X	1 1 1 1	2 7 7 0 0 8 6	1 1 1	7
0086 FADD2:	RF = RD + RE	0 D E F 0 0 1 1 1 0 0 F 1	X X X X X X X X	1 1 1 1	0 2 7 X X X X	1 1 1	7
0087	RF = SMTC(RF)	0 X F F X 0 1 1 1 1 0 5 8	X X X X X X X X	1 1 1 1	0 2 7 X X X X	1 1 1	7
0088	RF = TB0 (RF, bit24) : TEST Z	0 0 F 0 0 0 1 1 1 1 0 3 8	X X X X X X X X	0 1 1 1	0 2 7 X X X X	1 1 1	4
0089	JF FADD3	1 X X X X X 1 1 1 X X F F	X X X X X X X X	1 1 1 1	0 4 7 X X X X	1 1 1	7
008A	INC RB : TEST NEG	0 B X B 0 X 1 1 1 1 1 F 6	X X X X X X X X	1 1 1 1	0 2 7 X X X X	1 1 1	3
008B	RF = SRA(RF) : JT ERROR	0 F 7 F 0 X 1 1 1 0 0 0 6	X X X X X X X X	1 1 1 1	0 1 7 X X X X	1 1 1	7
008C FADD3:	RF = SET0 (RF, bit23)	0 7 F 0 0 0 1 1 1 1 0 1 8	X X X X X X X X	1 0 1 1	0 2 7 X X X X	1 1 1	7
008D	RF = RF OR RB : RETURN	0 F B F 0 0 1 1 1 0 0 F B	X X X X X X X X	1 1 1 1	0 2 2 X X X X	1 1 1	7

ORDERING INSTRUCTIONS

Electrical characteristics presented in this data book, unless otherwise noted, apply for circuit type(s) listed in the page heading regardless of package. The availability of a circuit function in a particular package is denoted by an alphabetical reference above the pin-connection diagram(s). These alphabetical references refer to mechanical outline drawings shown in this section.

Factory orders for circuits described in this catalog should include a four-part type number as explained in the following example.

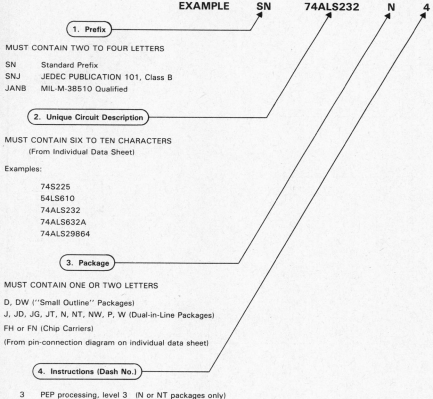

EXAMPLE SN 74ALS232 N 4

1. Prefix

MUST CONTAIN TWO TO FOUR LETTERS

SN	Standard Prefix
SNJ	JEDEC PUBLICATION 101, Class B
JANB	MIL-M-38510 Qualified

2. Unique Circuit Description

MUST CONTAIN SIX TO TEN CHARACTERS
(From Individual Data Sheet)

Examples:

74S225
54LS610
74ALS232
74ALS632A
74ALS29864

3. Package

MUST CONTAIN ONE OR TWO LETTERS

D, DW (''Small Outline'' Packages)

J, JD, JG, JT, N, NT, NW, P, W (Dual-in-Line Packages)

FH or FN (Chip Carriers)

(From pin-connection diagram on individual data sheet)

4. Instructions (Dash No.)

3 PEP processing, level 3 (N or NT packages only)

†These circuits in dual-in-line and ''small outline'' packages are shipped in one of the carriers shown below. Unless a specific method of shipment is specified by the customer (with possible additional costs), circuits will be shipped in the most practical carrier. Please contact your TI sales representative for the method that will best suit your particular needs.

''Small Outline'' (D, DW)
Dual-in-Line (J, JD, JG, JT, N, NT, NW, P, W)

— A-Channel Plastic Tubing

— Tape and Reel

— Barnes Carrier (W only)

D plastic "small outline" packages

Each of these "small outline" packages consists of a circuit mounted on a lead frame and encapsulated within a plastic compound. The compound will withstand soldering temperature with no deformation, and circuit performance characteristics will remain stable when operated in high-humidity conditions. Leads require no additional cleaning or processing when used in soldered assembly.

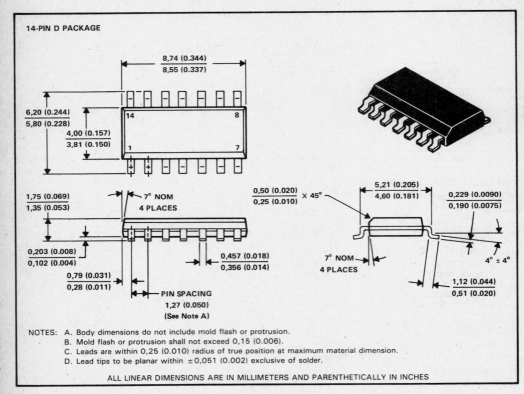

14-PIN D PACKAGE

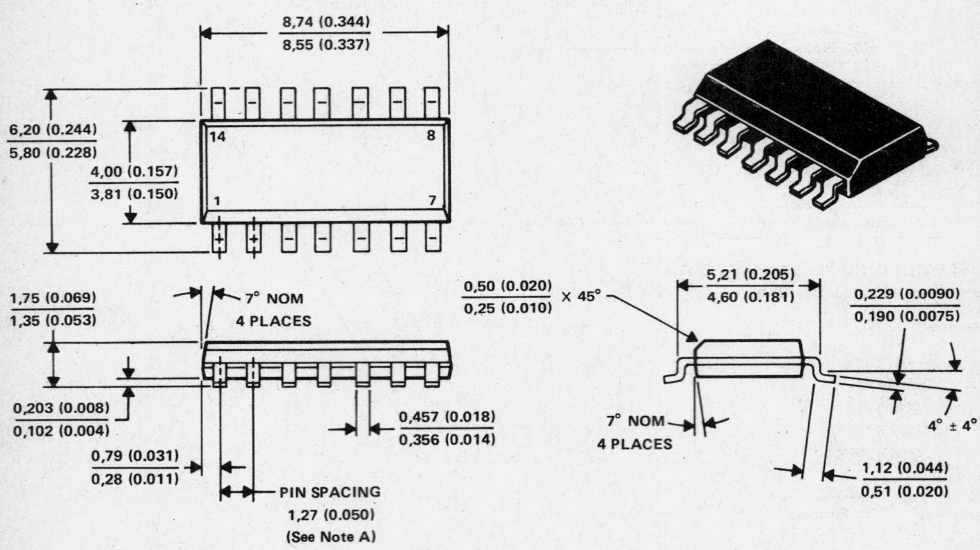

8,74 (0.344)
8,55 (0.337)
6,20 (0.244)
5,80 (0.228)
4,00 (0.157)
3,81 (0.150)
14
8
1
7
1,75 (0.069)
1,35 (0.053)
7° NOM
4 PLACES
0,203 (0.008)
0,102 (0.004)
0,457 (0.018)
0,356 (0.014)
0,79 (0.031)
0,28 (0.011)
PIN SPACING
1,27 (0.050)
(See Note A)
0,50 (0.020)
0,25 (0.010)
X 45°
5,21 (0.205)
4,60 (0.181)
0,229 (0.0090)
0,190 (0.0075)
7° NOM
4 PLACES
4° ± 4°
1,12 (0.044)
0,51 (0.020)

NOTES: A. Body dimensions do not include mold flash or protrusion.
B. Mold flash or protrusion shall not exceed 0,15 (0.006).
C. Leads are within 0,25 (0.010) radius of true position at maximum material dimension.
D. Lead tips to be planar within ±0,051 (0.002) exclusive of solder.

ALL LINEAR DIMENSIONS ARE IN MILLIMETERS AND PARENTHETICALLY IN INCHES

D plastic "small outline" packages

Each of these "small outline" packages consists of a circuit mounted on a lead frame and encapsulated within a plastic compound. The compound will withstand soldering temperature with no deformation, and circuit performance characteristics will remain stable when operated in high-humidity conditions. Leads require no additional cleaning or processing when used in soldered assembly.

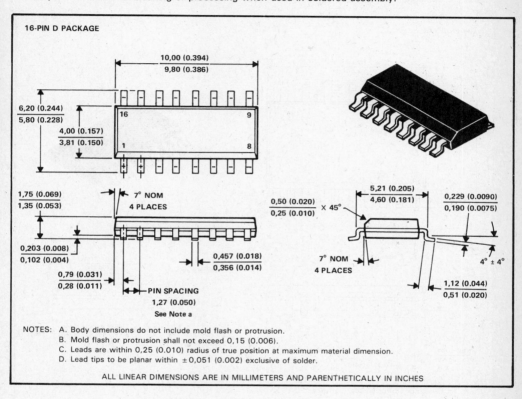

16-PIN D PACKAGE

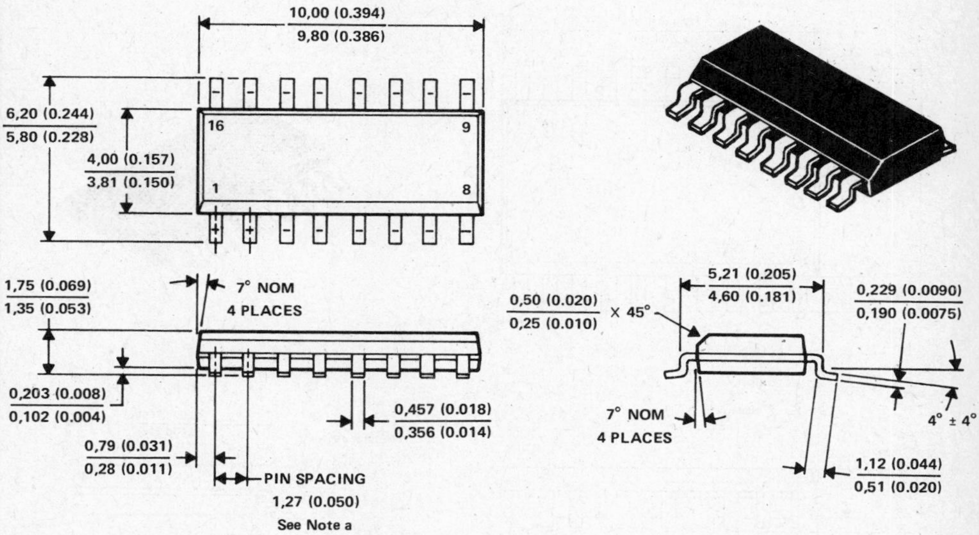
10,00 (0.394)
9,80 (0.386)
6,20 (0.244)
5,80 (0.228)
4,00 (0.157)
3,81 (0.150)
16
9
1
8
1,75 (0.069)
1,35 (0.053)
7° NOM
4 PLACES
0,203 (0.008)
0,102 (0.004)
0,457 (0.018)
0,356 (0.014)
0,79 (0.031)
0,28 (0.011)
PIN SPACING
1,27 (0.050)
See Note a
5,21 (0.205)
4,60 (0.181)
0,50 (0.020)
0,25 (0.010)
X 45°
0,229 (0.0090)
0,190 (0.0075)
7° NOM
4 PLACES
4° ± 4°
1,12 (0.044)
0,51 (0.020)

NOTES: A. Body dimensions do not include mold flash or protrusion.
B. Mold flash or protrusion shall not exceed 0,15 (0.006).
C. Leads are within 0,25 (0.010) radius of true position at maximum material dimension.
D. Lead tips to be planar within ±0,051 (0.002) exclusive of solder.

ALL LINEAR DIMENSIONS ARE IN MILLIMETERS AND PARENTHETICALLY IN INCHES

DW plastic "small outline" packages

Each of these "small outline" packages consists of a circuit mounted on a lead frame and encapsulated within a plastic compound. The compound will withstand soldering temperature with no deformation, and circuit performance characteristics will remain stable when operated in high-humidity conditions. Leads require no additional cleaning or processing when used in soldered assembly.

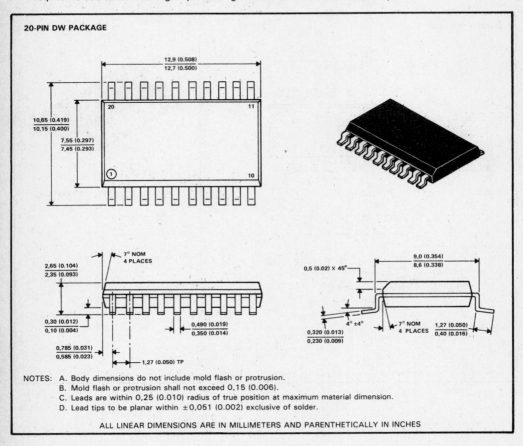

20-PIN DW PACKAGE

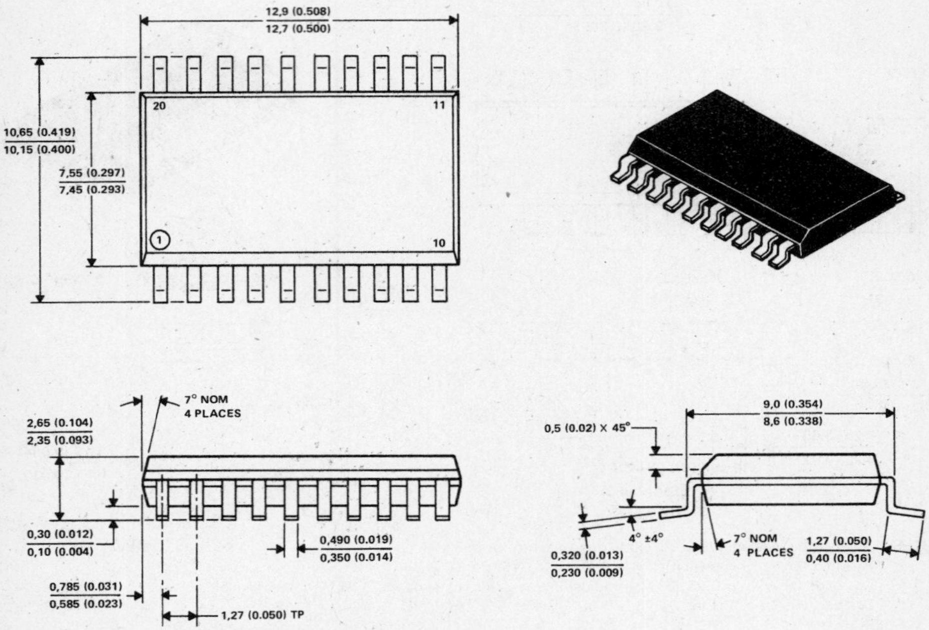

12,9 (0.508)
12,7 (0.500)
20
11
10,65 (0.419)
10,15 (0.400)
7,55 (0.297)
7,45 (0.293)
1
10
7° NOM
4 PLACES
2,65 (0.104)
2,35 (0.093)
0,30 (0.012)
0,10 (0.004)
0,490 (0.019)
0,350 (0.014)
0,785 (0.031)
0,585 (0.023)
1,27 (0.050) TP
9,0 (0.354)
8,6 (0.338)
0,5 (0.02) X 45°
4° ±4°
7° NOM
4 PLACES
1,27 (0.050)
0,40 (0.016)
0,320 (0.013)
0,230 (0.009)

NOTES: A. Body dimensions do not include mold flash or protrusion.
B. Mold flash or protrusion shall not exceed 0,15 (0.006).
C. Leads are within 0,25 (0.010) radius of true position at maximum material dimension.
D. Lead tips to be planar within ±0,051 (0.002) exclusive of solder.

ALL LINEAR DIMENSIONS ARE IN MILLIMETERS AND PARENTHETICALLY IN INCHES

TEXAS INSTRUMENTS
POST OFFICE BOX 225012 • DALLAS, TEXAS 75265

DW plastic ''small outline'' packages

Each of these ''small outline'' packages consists of a circuit mounted on a lead frame and encapsulated within a plastic compound. The compound will withstand soldering temperature with no deformation, and circuit performance characteristics will remain stable when operated in high-humidity conditions. Leads require no additional cleaning or processing when used in soldered assembly.

24-PIN DW PACKAGE

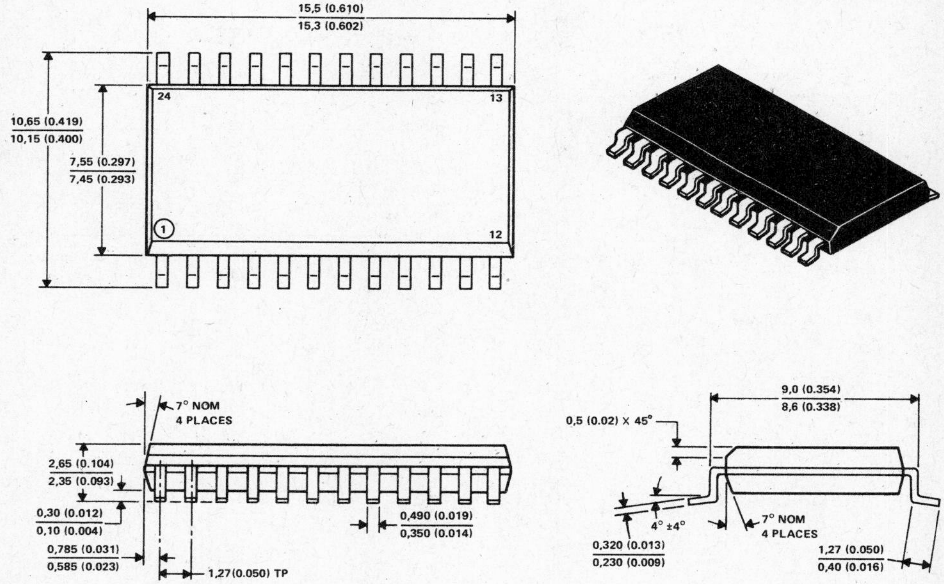
15,5 (0.610)
15,3 (0.602)
24
13
1
12
10,65 (0.419)
10,15 (0.400)
7,55 (0.297)
7,45 (0.293)
7° NOM
4 PLACES
2,65 (0.104)
2,35 (0.093)
0,30 (0.012)
0,10 (0.004)
0,785 (0.031)
0,585 (0.023)
1,27(0.050) TP
0,490 (0.019)
0,350 (0.014)
9,0 (0.354)
8,6 (0.338)
0,5 (0.02) X 45°
4° ±4°
0,320 (0.013)
0,230 (0.009)
7° NOM
4 PLACES
1,27 (0.050)
0,40 (0.016)

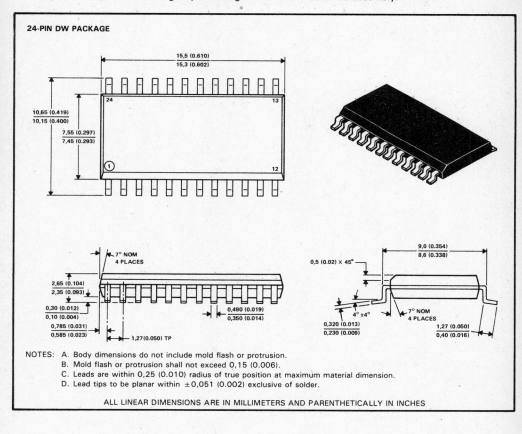

NOTES: A. Body dimensions do not include mold flash or protrusion.
B. Mold flash or protrusion shall not exceed 0,15 (0.006).
C. Leads are within 0,25 (0.010) radius of true position at maximum material dimension.
D. Lead tips to be planar within ±0,051 (0.002) exclusive of solder.

ALL LINEAR DIMENSIONS ARE IN MILLIMETERS AND PARENTHETICALLY IN INCHES

FK ceramic chip carrier packages

Each of these hermetically sealed chip carrier packages has a three-layer ceramic base with a metal lid and braze seal. The packages are intended for surface mounting on solder lands on 1,27 (0.050-inch) centers. terminals require no additional cleaning or processing when used in soldered assembly.

FK package terminal assignments conform to JEDEC Standards 1 and 2.

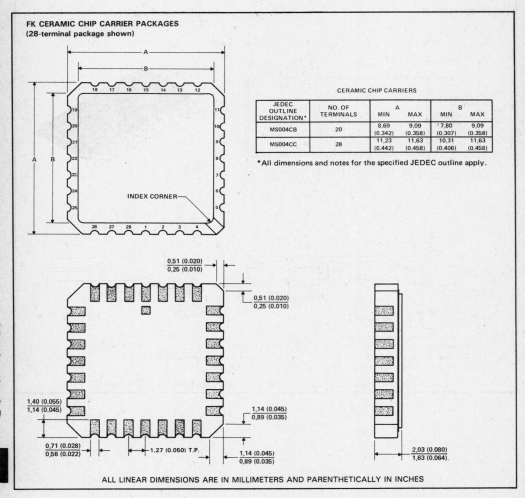

FK CERAMIC CHIP CARRIER PACKAGES
(28-terminal package shown)

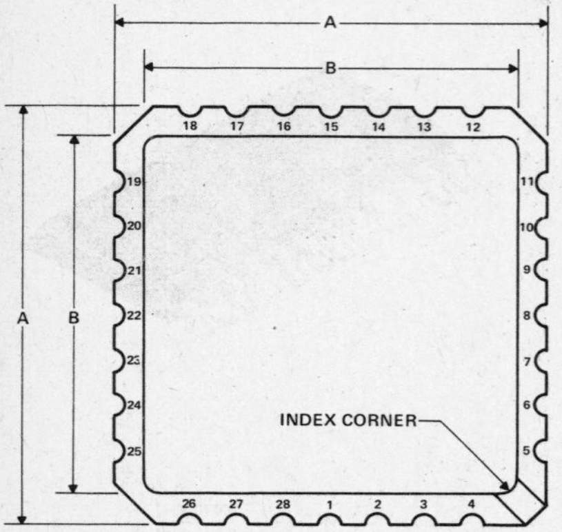
A
B
18 17 16 15 14 13 12
19 20 21 22 23 24 25
11 10 9 8 7 6 5
26 27 28 1 2 3 4
INDEX CORNER

CERAMIC CHIP CARRIERS

JEDEC OUTLINE DESIGNATION*	NO. OF TERMINALS	A MIN	A MAX	B MIN	B MAX
MS004CB	20	8,69 (0.342)	9,09 (0.358)	7,80 (0.307)	9,09 (0.358)
MS004CC	28	11,23 (0.442)	11,63 (0.458)	10,31 (0.406)	11,63 (0.458)

*All dimensions and notes for the specified JEDEC outline apply.

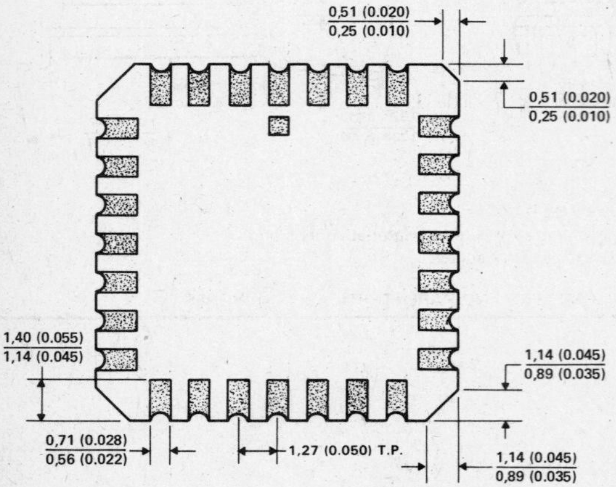
0,51 (0.020)
0,25 (0.010)
0,51 (0.020)
0,25 (0.010)
1,40 (0.055)
1,14 (0.045)
1,14 (0.045)
0,89 (0.035)
0,71 (0.028)
0,56 (0.022)
1,27 (0.050) T.P.
1,14 (0.045)
0,89 (0.035)

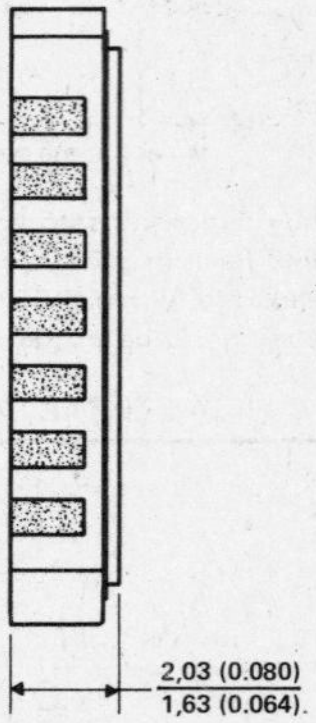
2,03 (0.080)
1,63 (0.064)

ALL LINEAR DIMENSIONS ARE IN MILLIMETERS AND PARENTHETICALLY IN INCHES

TEXAS INSTRUMENTS
POST OFFICE BOX 225012 • DALLAS, TEXAS 75265

FN plastic chip carrier package

Each of these chip carrier packages consists of a circuit mounted on a lead frame and encapsulated within an electrically nonconductive plastic compound. The compound withstands soldering temperatures with no deformation, and circuit performance characteristics remain stable when the devices are operated in high-humidity conditions. The packages are intended for surface mounting on solder lands on 1,27 (0.050) centers. Leads require no additional cleaning or processing when used in soldered assembly.

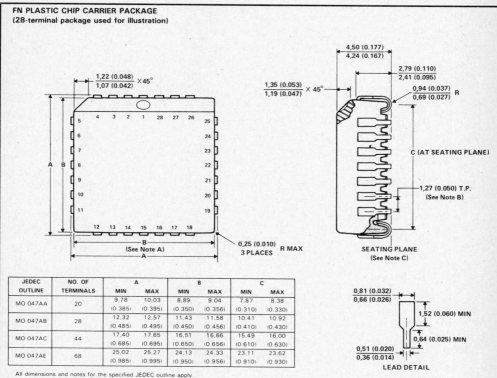

FN PLASTIC CHIP CARRIER PACKAGE
(28-terminal package used for illustration)

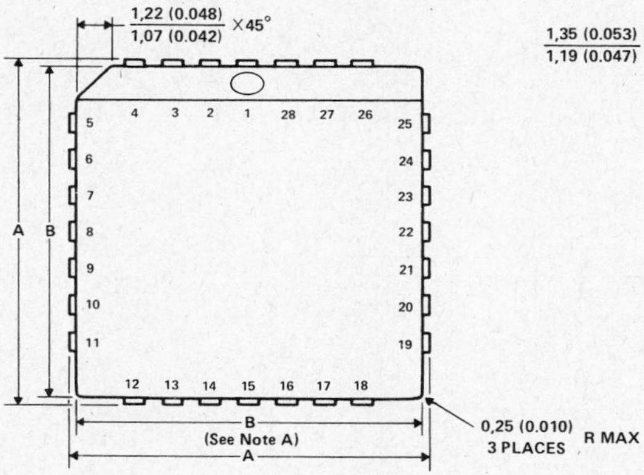
1,22 (0.048)
1,07 (0.042)
X45°
4 3 2 1 28 27 26
5 6 7 8 9 10 11
25 24 23 22 21 20 19
12 13 14 15 16 17 18
A
B
B
(See Note A)
A
0,25 (0.010)
3 PLACES
R MAX

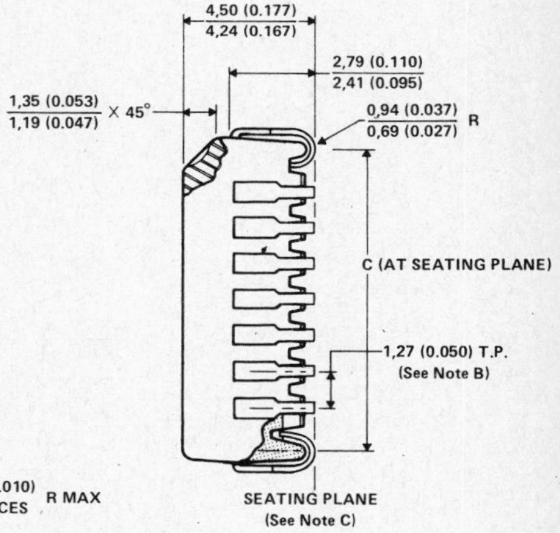
4,50 (0.177)
4,24 (0.167)
2,79 (0.110)
2,41 (0.095)
1,35 (0.053)
1,19 (0.047)
X 45°
0,94 (0.037)
0,69 (0.027)
R
C (AT SEATING PLANE)
1,27 (0.050) T.P.
(See Note B)
SEATING PLANE
(See Note C)

JEDEC OUTLINE	NO. OF TERMINALS	A		B		C	
		MIN	MAX	MIN	MAX	MIN	MAX
MO 047AA	20	9.78 (0.385)	10.03 (0.395)	8.89 (0.350)	9.04 (0.356)	7.87 (0.310)	8.38 (0.330)
MO 047AB	28	12.32 (0.485)	12.57 (0.495)	11.43 (0.450)	11.58 (0.456)	10.41 (0.410)	10.92 (0.430)
MO 047AC	44	17.40 (0.685)	17.65 (0.695)	16.51 (0.650)	16.66 (0.656)	15.49 (0.610)	16.00 (0.630)
MO 047AE	68	25.02 (0.985)	25.27 (0.995)	24.13 (0.950)	24.33 (0.956)	23.11 (0.910)	23.62 (0.930)

All dimensions and notes for the specified JEDEC outline apply.

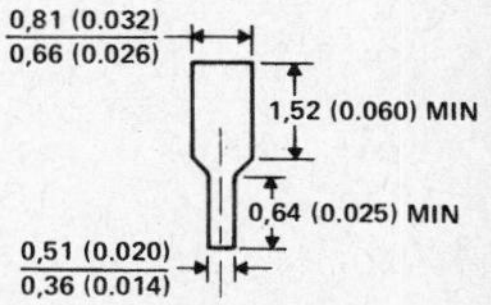
0,81 (0.032)
0,66 (0.026)
1,52 (0.060) MIN
0,64 (0.025) MIN
0,51 (0.020)
0,36 (0.014)

LEAD DETAIL

NOTES: A. Centerline of center pin each side is within 0,10 (0.004) of package centerline as determined by dimension B.
B. Location of each pin is within 0,127 (0.005) of true position with respect to center pin on each side.
C. The lead contact points are planar within 0,10 (0.004).

ALL LINEAR DIMENSIONS ARE IN MILLIMETERS AND PARENTHETICALLY IN INCHES

68-pin GB pin grid array ceramic package

This is a hermetically sealed ceramic package with metal cap and gold-plated pins.

68-PIN GB PACKAGE

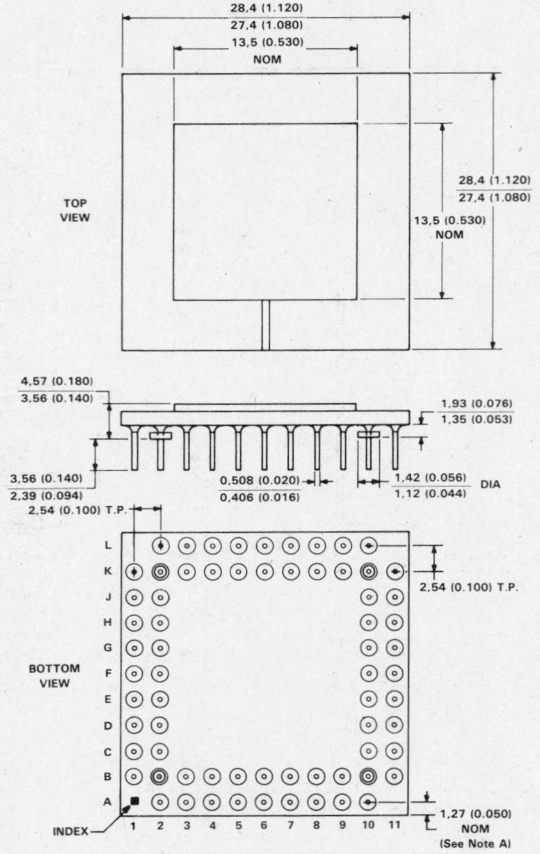
28,4 (1.120)
27,4 (1.080)
13,5 (0.530) NOM
TOP VIEW
28,4 (1.120)
27,4 (1.080)
13,5 (0.530) NOM
4,57 (0.180)
3,56 (0.140)
1,93 (0.076)
1,35 (0.053)
3,56 (0.140)
2,39 (0.094)
0,508 (0.020)
0,406 (0.016)
1,42 (0.056)
1,12 (0.044)
DIA
2,54 (0.100) T.P.
L
K
J
H
G
F
E
D
C
B
A
2,54 (0.100) T.P.
BOTTOM VIEW
INDEX
1 2 3 4 5 6 7 8 9 10 11
1,27 (0.050) NOM (See Note A)

NOTE A: Pins are located within 0,127 (0.005) radius of true position relative to each other at maximum material condition and within 0,254 (0.010) radius relative to the center of the ceramic.

ALL LINEAR DIMENSIONS ARE IN MILLIMETERS AND PARENTHETICALLY IN INCHES

TEXAS INSTRUMENTS
POST OFFICE BOX 225012 • DALLAS, TEXAS 75265

J ceramic packages (including JD, JT, and JW dual-in-line packages)

Each of these hermetically sealed dual-in-line packages consists of a ceramic base, ceramic cap, and a lead frame. Hermetic sealing is accomplished with glass. The packages are intended for insertion in mounting-hole rows on 7,62 (0.300) or 15,24 (0.600) centers. Once the leads are compressed and inserted sufficient tension is provided to secure the package in the board during soldering. Tin-plated ("bright-dipped") leads require no additional cleaning or processing when used in soldered assembly.

NOTE: For the 14-, 16-, and 20-pin packages, the letter J is used by itself since these packages are available only in the 7,62 (0.300) row spacing. For the 24-pin packages, if no second letter or row spacing is specified, the package is assumed to have 15,24 (0.600) row spacing.

14-PIN J CERAMIC

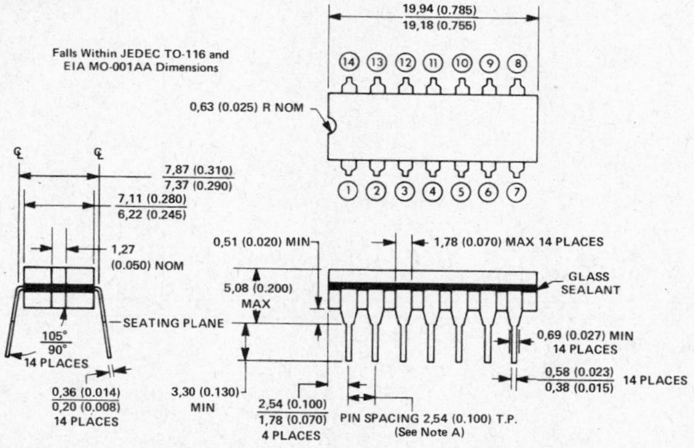
19,94 (0.785)
19,18 (0.755)
Falls Within JEDEC TO-116 and EIA MO-001AA Dimensions
0,63 (0.025) R NOM
7,87 (0.310)
7,37 (0.290)
7,11 (0.280)
6,22 (0.245)
1,27 (0.050) NOM
0,51 (0.020) MIN
1,78 (0.070) MAX 14 PLACES
GLASS SEALANT
5,08 (0.200) MAX
SEATING PLANE
105°
90°
14 PLACES
0,69 (0.027) MIN 14 PLACES
0,58 (0.023)
0,38 (0.015) 14 PLACES
0,36 (0.014)
0,20 (0.008)
14 PLACES
3,30 (0.130) MIN
2,54 (0.100)
1,78 (0.070)
4 PLACES
PIN SPACING 2,54 (0.100) T.P.
(See Note A)

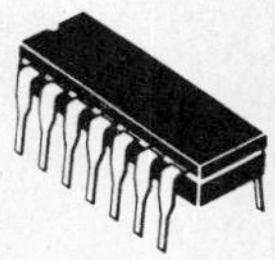

ALL LINEAR DIMENSIONS ARE IN MILLIMETERS AND PARENTHETICALLY IN INCHES

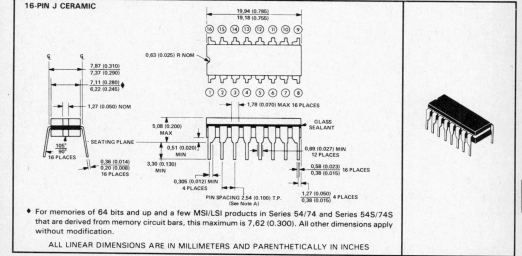

16-PIN J CERAMIC

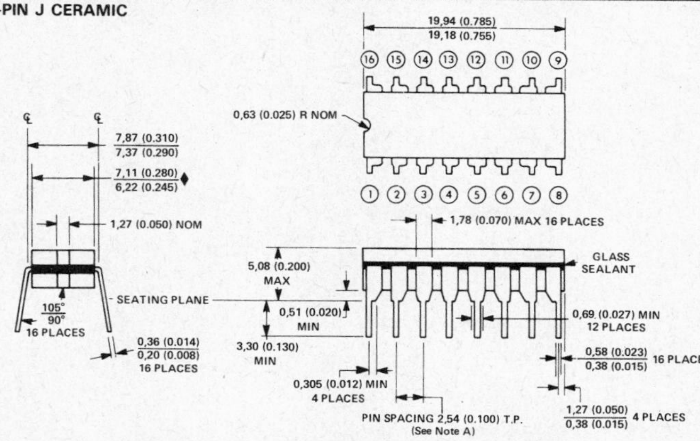
19,94 (0.785)
19,18 (0.755)
0,63 (0.025) R NOM
7,87 (0.310)
7,37 (0.290)
7,11 (0.280)
6,22 (0.245)
1,27 (0.050) NOM
1,78 (0.070) MAX 16 PLACES
5,08 (0.200) MAX
GLASS SEALANT
SEATING PLANE
105°
90°
16 PLACES
0,51 (0.020) MIN
0,69 (0.027) MIN 12 PLACES
0,36 (0.014)
0,20 (0.008)
16 PLACES
3,30 (0.130) MIN
0,58 (0.023)
0,38 (0.015) 16 PLACES
0,305 (0.012) MIN 4 PLACES
PIN SPACING 2,54 (0.100) T.P.
(See Note A)
1,27 (0.050)
0,38 (0.015) 4 PLACES

♦ For memories of 64 bits and up and a few MSI/LSI products in Series 54/74 and Series 54S/74S that are derived from memory circuit bars, this maximum is 7,62 (0.300). All other dimensions apply without modification.

ALL LINEAR DIMENSIONS ARE IN MILLIMETERS AND PARENTHETICALLY IN INCHES

NOTE A: Each pin centerline is located within 0,25 (0.010) of its true longitudinal position.

J ceramic dual-in-line packages (continued)

20-PIN J CERAMIC

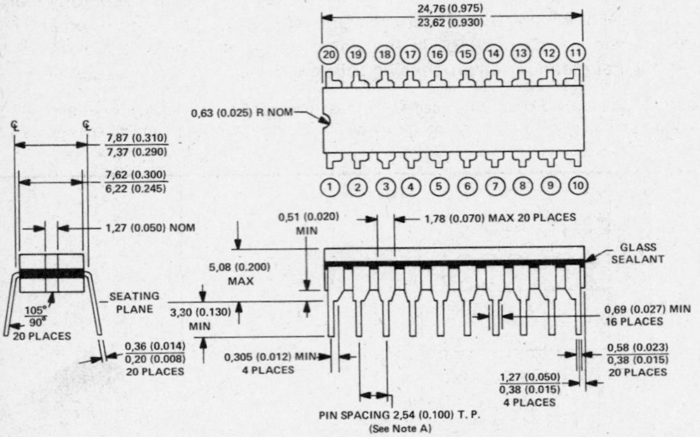
24,76 (0.975)
23,62 (0.930)
20 19 18 17 16 15 14 13 12 11
0,63 (0.025) R NOM
1 2 3 4 5 6 7 8 9 10
7,87 (0.310)
7,37 (0.290)
7,62 (0.300)
6,22 (0.245)
1,27 (0.050) NOM
0,51 (0.020) MIN
1,78 (0.070) MAX 20 PLACES
GLASS SEALANT
5,08 (0.200) MAX
SEATING PLANE
105°
90°
20 PLACES
3,30 (0.130) MIN
0,69 (0.027) MIN
16 PLACES
0,36 (0.014)
0,20 (0.008)
20 PLACES
0,305 (0.012) MIN
4 PLACES
0,58 (0.023)
0,38 (0.015)
20 PLACES
1,27 (0.050)
0,38 (0.015)
4 PLACES
PIN SPACING 2,54 (0.100) T. P.
(See Note A)

ALL LINEAR DIMENSIONS ARE IN MILLIMETERS AND PARENTHETICALLY IN INCHES

24-PIN JT CERAMIC, 0.300-INCH ROW SPACING

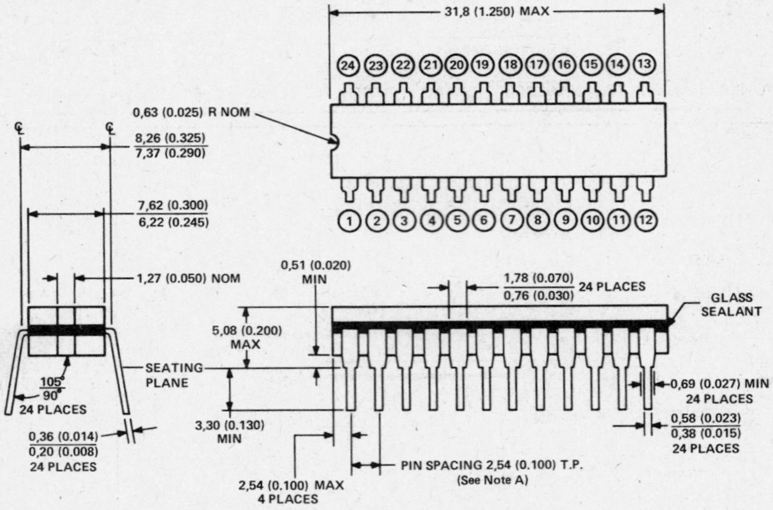
31,8 (1.250) MAX
24 23 22 21 20 19 18 17 16 15 14 13
0,63 (0.025) R NOM
8,26 (0.325)
7,37 (0.290)
7,62 (0.300)
6,22 (0.245)
1 2 3 4 5 6 7 8 9 10 11 12
1,27 (0.050) NOM
0,51 (0.020) MIN
1,78 (0.070)
0,76 (0.030)
24 PLACES
GLASS SEALANT
5,08 (0.200) MAX
SEATING PLANE
105°
90°
24 PLACES
0,69 (0.027) MIN
24 PLACES
3,30 (0.130) MIN
0,36 (0.014)
0,20 (0.008)
24 PLACES
0,58 (0.023)
0,38 (0.015)
24 PLACES
PIN SPACING 2,54 (0.100) T.P.
(See Note A)
2,54 (0.100) MAX
4 PLACES

ALL LINEAR DIMENSIONS ARE IN MILLIMETERS AND PARENTHETICALLY IN INCHES

NOTE A: Each pin centerline is located within 0,25 (0.010) of its true longitudinal position.

TEXAS INSTRUMENTS
POST OFFICE BOX 225012 • DALLAS, TEXAS 75265

J ceramic dual-in-line packages (continued)

24-PIN JW CERAMIC

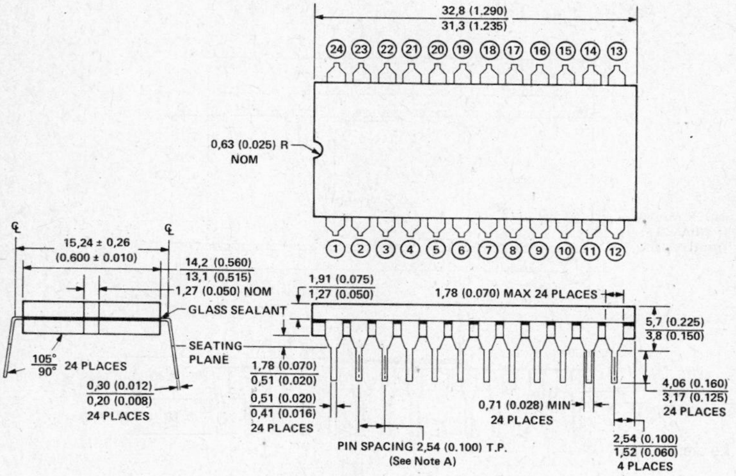
32,8 (1.290)
31,3 (1.235)
24 23 22 21 20 19 18 17 16 15 14 13
0,63 (0.025) R
NOM
1 2 3 4 5 6 7 8 9 10 11 12
15,24 ± 0,26
(0.600 ± 0.010)
14,2 (0.560)
13,1 (0.515)
1,27 (0.050) NOM
GLASS SEALANT
SEATING
PLANE
105°
90°
24 PLACES
0,30 (0.012)
0,20 (0.008)
24 PLACES
1,91 (0.075)
1,27 (0.050)
1,78 (0.070) MAX 24 PLACES
5,7 (0.225)
3,8 (0.150)
1,78 (0.070)
0,51 (0.020)
0,51 (0.020)
0,41 (0.016)
24 PLACES
0,71 (0.028) MIN
24 PLACES
4,06 (0.160)
3,17 (0.125)
24 PLACES
PIN SPACING 2,54 (0.100) T.P.
(See Note A)
2,54 (0.100)
1,52 (0.060)
4 PLACES

Falls within JEDEC MO-015AA dimensions

ALL LINEAR DIMENSIONS ARE IN MILLIMETERS AND PARENTHETICALLY IN INCHES

NOTE A: Each pin centerline is located within 0,25 (0.010) of its true longitudinal position.

J ceramic dual-in-line packages (continued)

This is a hermetically sealed ceramic package with a metal cap and side-brazed tin-plated leads.

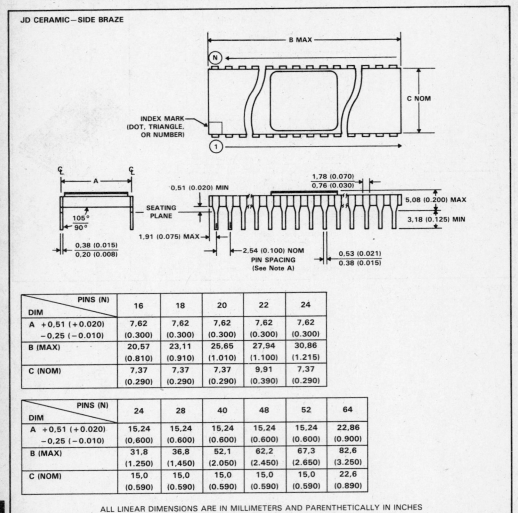

JD CERAMIC—SIDE BRAZE

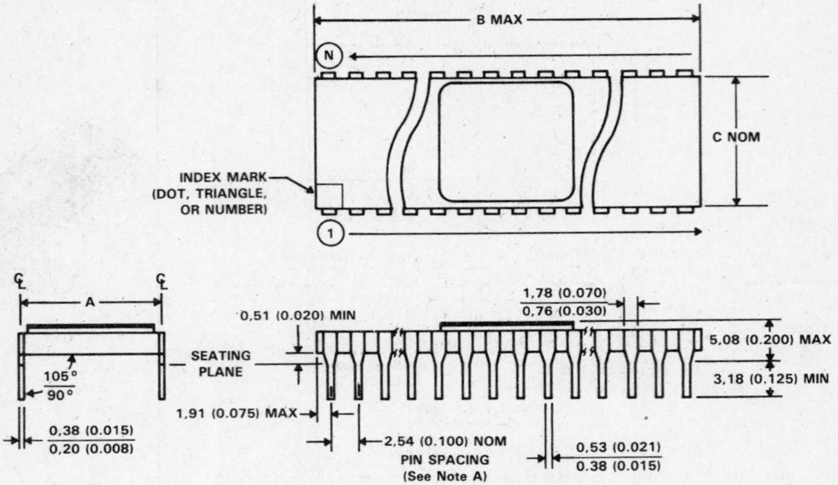

B MAX
N
C NOM
INDEX MARK
(DOT, TRIANGLE,
OR NUMBER)
1
℄
℄
A
0,51 (0.020) MIN
1,78 (0.070)
0,76 (0.030)
5,08 (0.200) MAX
SEATING
PLANE
3,18 (0.125) MIN
105°
90°
1,91 (0.075) MAX
0,38 (0.015)
0,20 (0.008)
2,54 (0.100) NOM
PIN SPACING
(See Note A)
0,53 (0.021)
0.38 (0.015)

DIM \ PINS (N)	16	18	20	22	24
A +0,51 (+0.020) −0,25 (−0.010)	7,62 (0.300)	7,62 (0.300)	7,62 (0.300)	7,62 (0.300)	7,62 (0.300)
B (MAX)	20,57 (0.810)	23,11 (0.910)	25,65 (1.010)	27,94 (1.100)	30,86 (1.215)
C (NOM)	7,37 (0.290)	7,37 (0.290)	7,37 (0.290)	9,91 (0.390)	7,37 (0.290)

DIM \ PINS (N)	24	28	40	48	52	64
A +0,51 (+0.020) −0,25 (−0.010)	15,24 (0,600)	15,24 (0.600)	15,24 (0.600)	15,24 (0.600)	15,24 (0.600)	22,86 (0.900)
B (MAX)	31,8 (1.250)	36,8 (1,450)	52,1 (2.050)	62,2 (2.450)	67,3 (2.650)	82,6 (3.250)
C (NOM)	15,0 (0.590)	15,0 (0.590)	15,0 (0.590)	15,0 (0.590)	15,0 (0.590)	22,6 (0.890)

ALL LINEAR DIMENSIONS ARE IN MILLIMETERS AND PARENTHETICALLY IN INCHES

NOTE A: Each pin centerline is located within 0,25 (0.010) of its true longitudinal position.

TEXAS INSTRUMENTS
POST OFFICE BOX 225012 • DALLAS, TEXAS 75265

N plastic packages (including NT and NW dual-in-line packages)

Each of these dual-in-line packages consists of a circuit mounted on a lead frame and encapsulated within an electrically nonconductive plastic compound. The compound will withstand soldering temperature with no deformation, and circuit performance characteristics will remain stable when operated in high-humidity conditions. The packages are intended for insertion in mounting-hole rows on 7,62 (0.300), 15,24 (0.600), or 22,86 (0.900) centers. Once the leads are compressed and inserted, sufficient tension is provided to secure the package in the board during soldering. Leads require no additional cleaning or processing when used in soldered assembly.

NOTE: For all except 24-pin packages, the letter N is used by itself since only the 24-pin package is available in more than one row-spacing. For the 24-pin package, the 7,62 (0.300) version is designated NT; the 15,24 (0.600) version is designated NW. If no second letter or row-spacing is specified, the package is assumed to have 15,24 (0.600) row-spacing.

14-PIN N PLASTIC

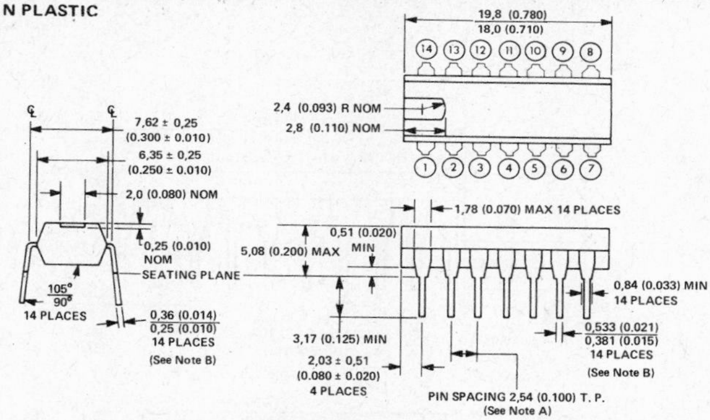
19,8 (0.780)
18,0 (0.710)
2,4 (0.093) R NOM
2,8 (0.110) NOM
7,62 ± 0,25
(0.300 ± 0.010)
6,35 ± 0,25
(0.250 ± 0.010)
2,0 (0.080) NOM
1,78 (0.070) MAX 14 PLACES
0,51 (0.020) MIN
0,25 (0.010) NOM
5,08 (0.200) MAX
SEATING PLANE
105°
90°
14 PLACES
0,84 (0.033) MIN
14 PLACES
0,36 (0.014)
0,25 (0.010)
14 PLACES
(See Note B)
3,17 (0.125) MIN
0,533 (0.021)
0,381 (0.015)
14 PLACES
(See Note B)
2,03 ± 0,51
(0.080 ± 0.020)
4 PLACES
PIN SPACING 2,54 (0.100) T. P.
(See Note A)

Falls Within JEDEC TO-116 and EIA MO-001AA Dimensions

ALL LINEAR DIMENSIONS ARE IN MILLIMETERS AND PARENTHETICALLY IN INCHES

16-PIN N PLASTIC

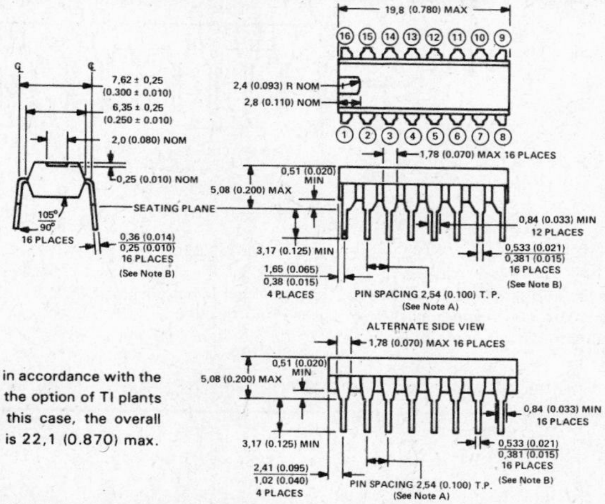
19,8 (0.780) MAX
2,4 (0.093) R NOM
2,8 (0.110) NOM
7,62 ± 0,25
(0.300 ± 0.010)
6,35 ± 0,25
(0.250 ± 0.010)
2,0 (0.080) NOM
1,78 (0.070) MAX 16 PLACES
0,51 (0.020) MIN
0,25 (0.010) NOM
5,08 (0.200) MAX
SEATING PLANE
105°
90°
16 PLACES
0,36 (0.014)
0,25 (0.010)
16 PLACES
(See Note B)
0,84 (0.033) MIN
12 PLACES
3,17 (0.125) MIN
0,533 (0.021)
0,381 (0.015)
16 PLACES
(See Note B)
1,65 (0.065)
0,38 (0.015)
4 PLACES
PIN SPACING 2,54 (0.100) T. P.
(See Note A)
ALTERNATE SIDE VIEW
1,78 (0.070) MAX 16 PLACES
0,51 (0.020) MIN
5,08 (0.200) MAX
0,84 (0.033) MIN
16 PLACES
3,17 (0.125) MIN
0,533 (0.021)
0,381 (0.015)
16 PLACES
(See Note B)
2,41 (0.095)
1,02 (0.040)
4 PLACES
PIN SPACING 2,54 (0.100) T.P.
(See Note A)

Parts may be supplied in accordance with the alternate side view at the option of TI plants located in Europe. In this case, the overall length of the package is 22,1 (0.870) max.

ALL LINEAR DIMENSIONS ARE IN MILLIMETERS AND PARENTHETICALLY IN INCHES

NOTES: A. Each pin centerline is located within 0,25 (0.010) of its true longitudinal position.

B. For solder-dipped leads, this dimension applies from the lead tip to the standoff.

N plastic dual-in-line packages (continued)

20-PIN N PACKAGE

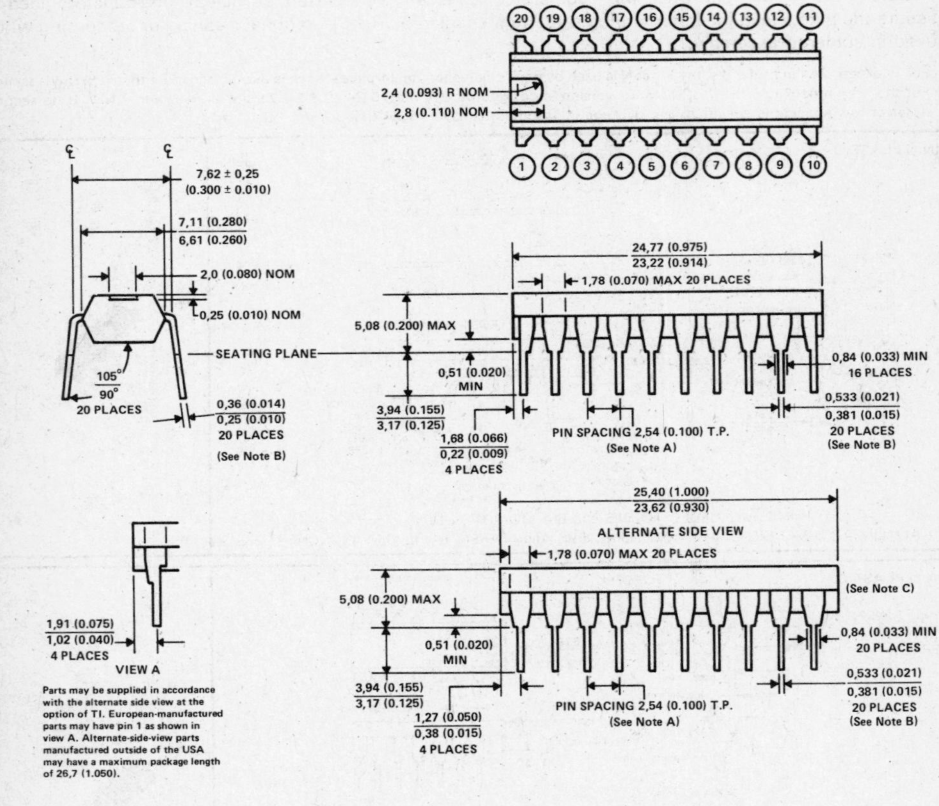
20 19 18 17 16 15 14 13 12 11
2,4 (0.093) R NOM
2,8 (0.110) NOM
1 2 3 4 5 6 7 8 9 10
7,62 ± 0,25
(0.300 ± 0.010)
7,11 (0.280)
6,61 (0.260)
2,0 (0.080) NOM
0,25 (0.010) NOM
SEATING PLANE
105°
90°
20 PLACES
0,36 (0.014)
0,25 (0.010)
20 PLACES
(See Note B)
24,77 (0.975)
23,22 (0.914)
1,78 (0.070) MAX 20 PLACES
5,08 (0.200) MAX
0,51 (0.020)
MIN
3,94 (0.155)
3,17 (0.125)
1,68 (0.066)
0,22 (0.009)
4 PLACES
PIN SPACING 2,54 (0.100) T.P.
(See Note A)
0,84 (0.033) MIN
16 PLACES
0,533 (0.021)
0,381 (0.015)
20 PLACES
(See Note B)
25,40 (1.000)
23,62 (0.930)
ALTERNATE SIDE VIEW
1,78 (0.070) MAX 20 PLACES
(See Note C)
5,08 (0.200) MAX
0,51 (0.020)
MIN
3,94 (0.155)
3,17 (0.125)
1,27 (0.050)
0,38 (0.015)
4 PLACES
PIN SPACING 2,54 (0.100) T.P.
(See Note A)
0,84 (0.033) MIN
20 PLACES
0,533 (0.021)
0,381 (0.015)
20 PLACES
(See Note B)
1,91 (0.075)
1,02 (0.040)
4 PLACES
VIEW A
Parts may be supplied in accordance with the alternate side view at the option of TI. European-manufactured parts may have pin 1 as shown in view A. Alternate-side-view parts manufactured outside of the USA may have a maximum package length of 26,7 (1.050).

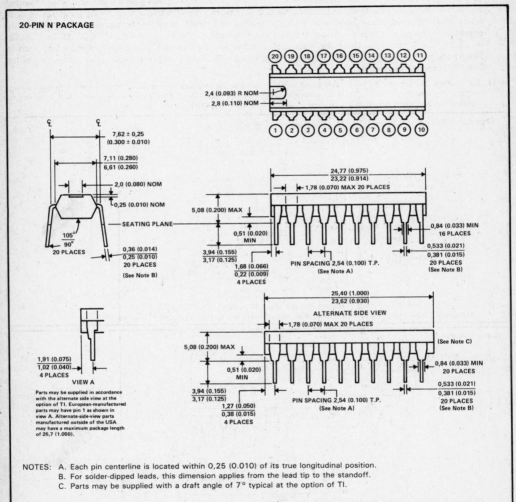

NOTES: A. Each pin centerline is located within 0,25 (0.010) of its true longitudinal position.
B. For solder-dipped leads, this dimension applies from the lead tip to the standoff.
C. Parts may be supplied with a draft angle of 7° typical at the option of TI.

ALL LINEAR DIMENSIONS ARE IN MILLIMETERS AND PARENTHETICALLY IN INCHES

TEXAS INSTRUMENTS
POST OFFICE BOX 225012 • DALLAS, TEXAS 75265

N plastic dual-in-line packages (continued)

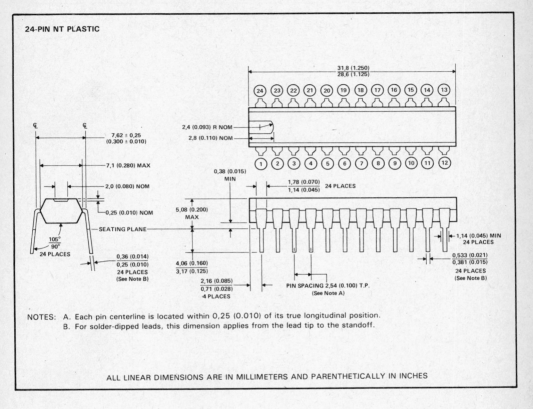

24-PIN NT PLASTIC

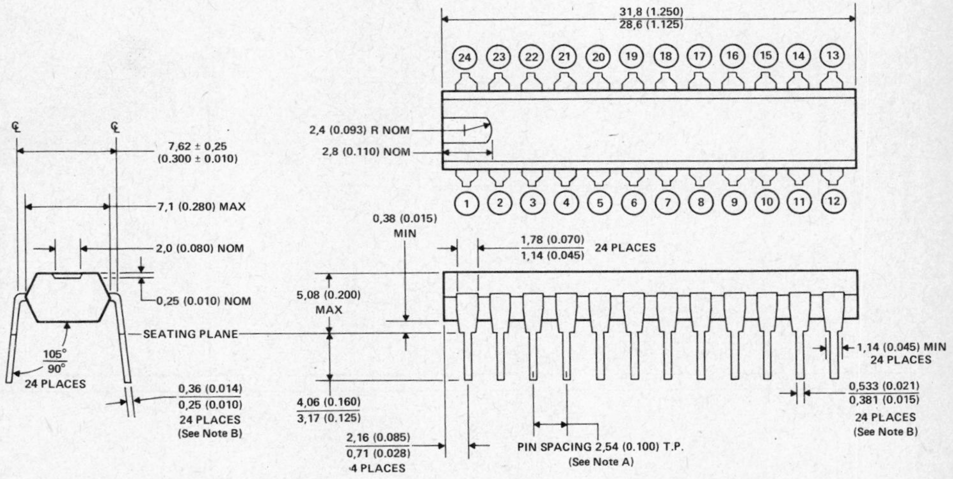
31,8 (1.250)
28,6 (1.125)
24 23 22 21 20 19 18 17 16 15 14 13
1 2 3 4 5 6 7 8 9 10 11 12
2,4 (0.093) R NOM
2,8 (0.110) NOM
7,62 ± 0,25
(0.300 ± 0.010)
7,1 (0.280) MAX
2,0 (0.080) NOM
0,25 (0.010) NOM
SEATING PLANE
105°
90°
24 PLACES
0,36 (0.014)
0,25 (0.010)
24 PLACES
(See Note B)
0,38 (0.015)
MIN
5,08 (0.200)
MAX
4,06 (0.160)
3,17 (0.125)
2,16 (0.085)
0,71 (0.028)
4 PLACES
1,78 (0.070)
1,14 (0.045)
24 PLACES
PIN SPACING 2,54 (0.100) T.P.
(See Note A)
1,14 (0.045) MIN
24 PLACES
0,533 (0.021)
0,381 (0.015)
24 PLACES
(See Note B)

NOTES: A. Each pin centerline is located within 0,25 (0.010) of its true longitudinal position.
B. For solder-dipped leads, this dimension applies from the lead tip to the standoff.

ALL LINEAR DIMENSIONS ARE IN MILLIMETERS AND PARENTHETICALLY IN INCHES

Mechanical Data 4

N plastic dual-in-line packages (continued)

24-PIN NW PLASTIC

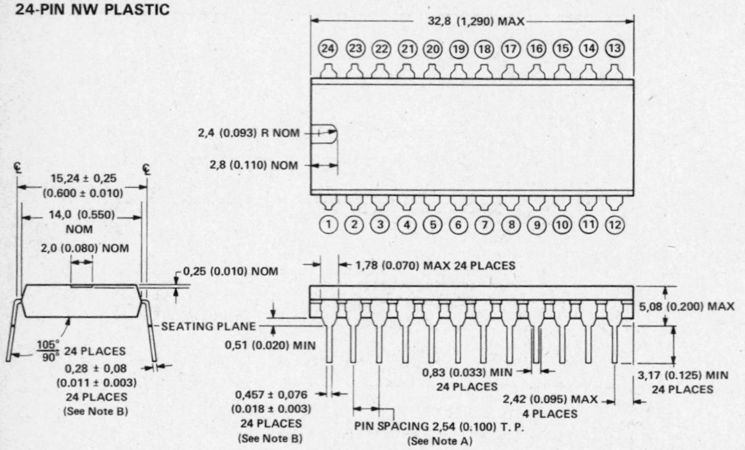
32,8 (1,290) MAX
24 23 22 21 20 19 18 17 16 15 14 13
2,4 (0.093) R NOM
2,8 (0.110) NOM
1 2 3 4 5 6 7 8 9 10 11 12
15,24 ± 0,25
(0.600 ± 0.010)
14,0 (0.550)
NOM
2,0 (0.080) NOM
0,25 (0.010) NOM
1,78 (0.070) MAX 24 PLACES
5,08 (0.200) MAX
SEATING PLANE
0,51 (0.020) MIN
105°
90°
24 PLACES
0,28 ± 0,08
(0.011 ± 0.003)
24 PLACES
(See Note B)
0,83 (0.033) MIN
24 PLACES
3,17 (0.125) MIN
24 PLACES
0,457 ± 0,076
(0.018 ± 0.003)
24 PLACES
(See Note B)
2,42 (0.095) MAX
4 PLACES
PIN SPACING 2,54 (0.100) T. P.
(See Note A)

ALL LINEAR DIMENSIONS ARE IN MILLIMETERS AND PARENTHETICALLY IN INCHES

28-PIN N PLASTIC

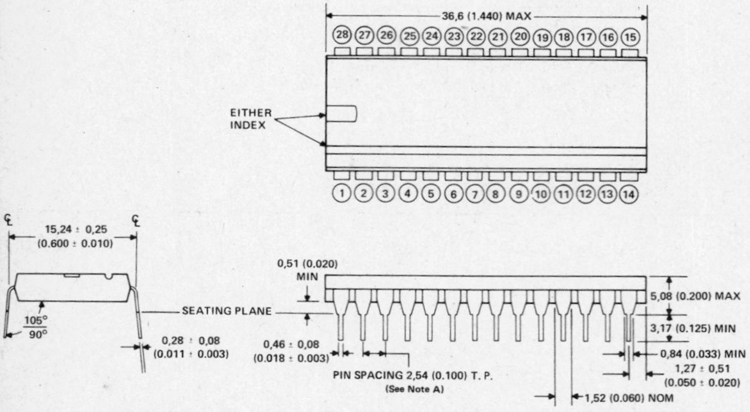
36,6 (1.440) MAX
28 27 26 25 24 23 22 21 20 19 18 17 16 15
EITHER
INDEX
1 2 3 4 5 6 7 8 9 10 11 12 13 14
15,24 ± 0,25
(0.600 ± 0.010)
0,51 (0.020)
MIN
5,08 (0.200) MAX
SEATING PLANE
3,17 (0.125) MIN
105°
90°
0,28 ± 0,08
(0.011 ± 0.003)
0,46 ± 0,08
(0.018 ± 0.003)
0,84 (0.033) MIN
1,27 ± 0,51
(0.050 ± 0.020)
PIN SPACING 2,54 (0.100) T. P.
(See Note A)
1,52 (0.060) NOM

ALL LINEAR DIMENSIONS ARE IN MILLIMETERS AND PARENTHETICALLY IN INCHES

NOTES: A. Each pin centerline is located within 0,25 (0.010) of its true longitudinal position.
B. For solder-dipped leads, this dimension applies from the lead tip to the standoff.

N plastic dual-in-line packages (continued)

40-PIN N PLASTIC

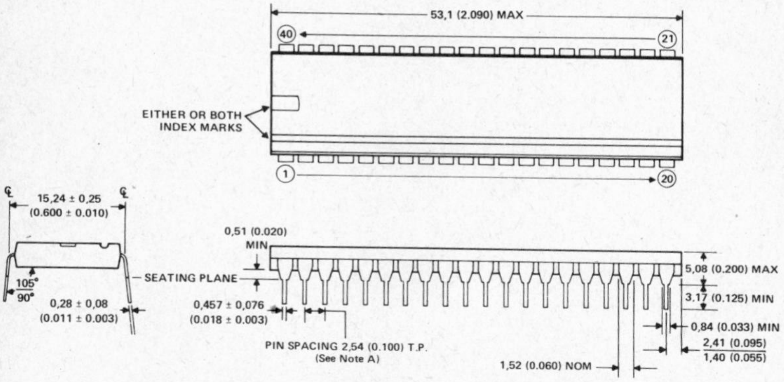
53,1 (2.090) MAX
40
21
EITHER OR BOTH INDEX MARKS
1
20
15,24 ± 0,25 (0.600 ± 0.010)
0,51 (0.020) MIN
SEATING PLANE
105°
90°
0,28 ± 0,08 (0.011 ± 0.003)
0,457 ± 0,076 (0.018 ± 0.003)
PIN SPACING 2,54 (0.100) T.P. (See Note A)
1,52 (0.060) NOM
5,08 (0.200) MAX
3.17 (0.125) MIN
0,84 (0.033) MIN
2,41 (0.095)
1,40 (0.055)

ALL LINEAR DIMENSIONS ARE IN MILLIMETERS AND PARENTHETICALLY IN INCHES

48-PIN, 52-PIN, AND 64-PIN N PLASTIC

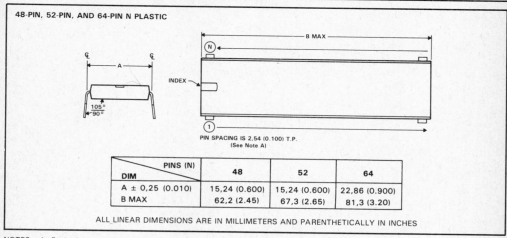

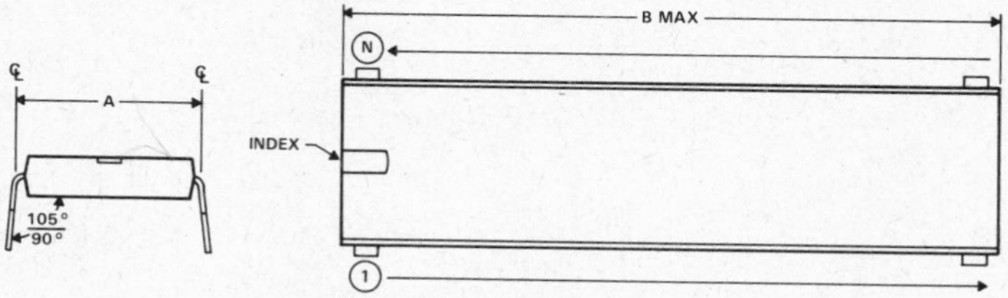
A
105°
90°
B MAX
N
INDEX
1
PIN SPACING IS 2,54 (0.100) T.P. (See Note A)

DIM \ PINS (N)	48	52	64
A ± 0,25 (0.010)	15,24 (0.600)	15,24 (0.600)	22,86 (0.900)
B MAX	62,2 (2.45)	67,3 (2.65)	81,3 (3.20)

ALL LINEAR DIMENSIONS ARE IN MILLIMETERS AND PARENTHETICALLY IN INCHES

NOTES: A. Each pin centerline is located within 0,25 (0.010) of its true longitudinal position.

Mechanical Data

4

TI Sales Offices

ALABAMA: Huntsville (205) 837-7530.

ARIZONA: Phoenix (602) 995-1007;
Tucson (602) 624-3276.

CALIFORNIA: Irvine (714) 660-8187;
Sacramento (916) 929-1521;
San Diego (619) 278-9601;
Santa Clara (408) 980-9000;
Torrance (213) 217-7010;
Woodland Hills (818) 704-7759.

COLORADO: Aurora (303) 368-8000.

CONNECTICUT: Wallingford (203) 269-0074.

FLORIDA: Ft. Lauderdale (305) 973-8502;
Maitland (305) 660-4600; **Tampa** (813) 870-6420.

GEORGIA: Norcross (404) 662-7900.

ILLINOIS: Arlington Heights (312) 640-2925.

INDIANA: Ft. Wayne (219) 424-5174;
Indianapolis (317) 248-8555.

IOWA: Cedar Rapids (319) 395-9550.

MARYLAND: Baltimore (301) 944-8600.

MASSACHUSETTS: Waltham (617) 895-9100.

MICHIGAN: Farmington Hills (313) 553 1500;
Grand Rapids (616) 957-4200.

MINNESOTA: Eden Prairie (612) 828-9300.

MISSOURI: Kansas City (816) 523-2500;
St. Louis (314) 569-7600.

NEW JERSEY: Iselin (201) 750-1050.

NEW MEXICO: Albuquerque (505) 345-2555.

NEW YORK: East Syracuse (315) 463-9291;
Endicott (607) 754-3900; **Melville** (516) 454-6600;
Pittsford (716) 385-6770;
Poughkeepsie (914) 473-2900.

NORTH CAROLINA: Charlotte (704) 527-0930;
Raleigh (919) 876-2725.

OHIO: Beachwood (216) 464-6100;
Dayton (513) 258-3877.

OREGON: Beaverton (503) 643-6758.

PENNSYLVANIA: Ft. Washington (215) 643-6450;
Coraopolis (412) 771-8550.

PUERTO RICO: Hato Rey (809) 753-8700

TEXAS: Austin (512) 250-7655;
Houston (713) 778-6592; **Richardson** (214) 680-5082;
San Antonio (512) 496-1779.

UTAH: Murray (801) 266-8972.

VIRGINIA: Fairfax (703) 849-1400.

WASHINGTON: Redmond (206) 881-3080.

WISCONSIN: Brookfield (414) 785-7140.

CANADA: Nepean, Ontario (613) 726-1970;
Richmond Hill, Ontario (416) 884-9181;
St. Laurent, Quebec (514) 335-8392.

TI Regional Technology Centers

CALIFORNIA: Irvine (714) 660-8140,
Santa Clara (408) 748-2220.

GEORGIA: Norcross (404) 662-7945.

ILLINOIS: Arlington Heights (312) 640-2909.

MASSACHUSETTS: Waltham (617) 895-9197.

TEXAS: Richardson (214) 680-5066.

CANADA: Nepean, Ontario (613) 726-1970

Customer Response Center

TOLL FREE: (800) 232-3200

OUTSIDE USA: (214) 995-6611
(8:00 a.m. — 5:00 p.m. CST)

TI Distributors

TI AUTHORIZED DISTRIBUTORS IN USA

Arrow Electronics
Diplomat Electronics
General Radio Supply Company
Graham Electronics
Kierulff Electronics
Marshall Industries
Milgray Electronics
Newark Electronics
Time Electronics
R.V. Weatherford Co.
Wyle Laboratories
Zeus Component, Inc. (Military)

TI AUTHORIZED DISTRIBUTORS IN CANADA

Arrow Electronics Canada
Future Electronics

TI AUTHORIZED DISTRIBUTORS IN USA

—OBSOLETE PRODUCT ONLY—
Rochester Electronics, Inc.
Newburyport, Massachusetts
(617) 462-9332

ALABAMA: Arrow (205) 837-6955;
Kierulff (205) 883-6070; Marshall (205) 881-9235.

ARIZONA: Arrow (602) 968-4800;
Kierulff (602) 437-0750; Marshall (602) 968-6181;
Wyle (602) 866-2888.

CALIFORNIA: Los Angeles/Orange County:
Arrow (818) 701-7500, (714) 838-5422;
Kierulff (213) 725-0325, (714) 731-5711, (714) 220-6300;
Marshall (818) 999-5001, (818) 442-7204,
(714) 660-0951; R.V. Weatherford (714) 966-1447,
(213) 849-3451, Wyle (213) 322-8100, (818) 880-9001,
(714) 863-9953; Zeus (714) 632-6880;
Sacramento: Arrow (916) 925-7456;
Marshall (916) 635-9700; Wyle (916) 638-5282;
San Diego: Arrow (619) 565-4800;
Kierulff (619) 278-2112; Marshall (619) 578-9600;
Wyle (619) 565-9171;
San Francisco Bay Area: Arrow (408) 745-6600;
(415) 487-4600; Kierulff (408) 971-2600;
Marshall (408) 943-4600; Wyle (408) 727-2500;
Zeus (408) 998-5121.

COLORADO: Arrow (303) 696-1111;
Kierulff (303) 790-4444; Wyle (303) 457-9953.

CONNECTICUT: Arrow (203) 265-7741;
Diplomat (203) 797-9674; Kierulff (203) 265-1115;
Marshall (203) 265-3822; Milgray (203) 795-0714.

FLORIDA: Ft. Lauderdale: Arrow (305) 429-8200;
Diplomat (305) 974-8700; Kierulff (305) 486-4004;
Orlando: Arrow (305) 725-1480;
Marshall (305) 841-1878; Milgray (305) 647-5747;
Zeus (305) 365-3000; **Tampa:** Arrow (813) 576-8995;
Diplomat (813) 443-4514; Kierulff (813) 576-1966.

TEXAS INSTRUMENTS

Creating useful products
and services for you.

GEORGIA: Arrow (404) 449-8252;
Kierulff (404) 447-5252; Marshall (404) 923-5750.

ILLINOIS: Arrow (312) 397-3440;
Diplomat (312) 595-1000; Kierulff (312) 250-0500;
Marshall (312) 490-0155; Newark (312) 784-5100.

INDIANA: Indianapolis: Arrow (317) 243-9353;
Graham (317) 634-8202; Marshall (317) 297-0483;
Ft. Wayne: Graham (219) 423-3422.

IOWA: Arrow (319) 395-7230.

KANSAS: Kansas City: Arrow (913) 642-0592;
Marshall (913) 492-3121.

MARYLAND: Arrow (301) 995-0003;
Diplomat (301) 995-1226; Kierulff (301) 636-5800;
Milgray (301) 995-6169; Marshall (301) 840-9450;
Zeus (301) 997-1118.

MASSACHUSETTS: Arrow (617) 933-8130;
Diplomat (617) 935-6611; Kierulff (617) 667-8331;
Marshall (617) 272-8200; Time (617) 532-6200;
Zeus (617) 863-8800.

MICHIGAN: Detroit: Arrow (313) 971-8220;
Marshall (313) 525-5850; Newark (313) 967-0600;
Grand Rapids: Arrow (616) 243-0912.

MINNESOTA: Arrow (612) 830-1800;
Kierulff (612) 941-7500; Marshall (612) 559-2211.

MISSOURI: St. Louis: Arrow (314) 567-6888;
Kierulff (314) 739-0855.

NEW HAMPSHIRE: Arrow (603) 668-6968.

NEW JERSEY: Arrow (201) 575-5300, (609) 596-8000;
Diplomat (201) 785-1830;
General Radio (609) 964-8560; Kierulff (201) 575-6750;
(609) 235-1444; Marshall (201) 882-0320,
(609) 234-9100; Milgray (609) 983-5010.

NEW MEXICO: Arrow (505) 243-4566.

NEW YORK: Long Island: Arrow (516) 231-1000;
Diplomat (516) 454-6400; Marshall (516) 273-2053;
Milgray (516) 420-9800; Zeus (914) 937-7400;
Rochester: Arrow (716) 427-0300;
Marshall (716) 235-7620;
Syracuse: Arrow (315) 652-1000;
Diplomat (315) 652-5000; Marshall (607) 798-1611.

NORTH CAROLINA: Arrow (919) 876-3132,
(919) 725-8711; Kierulff (919) 872-8410;
Marshall (919) 878-9882.

OHIO: Cleveland: Arrow (216) 248-3990;
Kierulff (216) 587-6558; Marshall (216) 248-1788.
Columbus: Arrow (614) 885-8362;
Dayton: Arrow (513) 435-5563; Graham (513) 435-8660;
Kierulff (513) 439-0045; Marshall (513) 236-8088.

OKLAHOMA: Arrow (918) 665-7700;
Kierulff (918) 252-7537.

OREGON: Arrow (503) 684-1690;
Kierulff (503) 641-9153; Wyle (503) 640-6000;
Marshall (503) 644-5050.

PENNSYLVANIA: Arrow (412) 856-7000,
(215) 928-1800; General Radio (215) 922-7037.

RHODE ISLAND: Arrow (401) 431-0980

TEXAS: Austin: Arrow (512) 835-4180;
Kierulff (512) 835-2090; Marshall (512) 837-1991;
Wyle (512) 834-9957; **Dallas:** Arrow (214) 380-6464;
Kierulff (214) 343-2400; Marshall (214) 233-5200;
Wyle (214) 235-9953; Zeus (214) 783-7010;
Houston: Arrow (713) 530-4700;
Marshall (713) 789-6600;
Kierulff (713) 530-7030; Wyle (713) 879-9953.

UTAH: Diplomat (801) 486-4134;
Kierulff (801) 973-6913; Wyle (801) 974-9953.

WASHINGTON: Arrow (206) 643-4800;
Kierulff (206) 575-4420; Wyle (206) 453-8300;
Marshall (206) 747-9100.

WISCONSIN: Arrow (414) 792-0150; Kierulff
(414) 784-8160; Marshall (414) 797-8400.

CANADA: Calgary: Future (403) 235-5325;
Edmonton: Future (403) 438-2858;
Montreal: Arrow Canada (514) 735-5511;
Future (514) 694-7710;
Ottawa: Arrow Canada (613) 226-6903;
Future (613) 820-8313;
Quebec City: Arrow Canada (418) 687-4231;
Toronto: Arrow Canada (416) 661-0220;
Future (416) 638-4771;
Vancouver: Future (604) 294-1166.

BP

TI Worldwide Sales Offices

ALABAMA: Huntsville: 500 Wynn Drive, Suite 514, Huntsville, AL 35805, (205) 837-7530.

ARIZONA: Phoenix: 8825 N. 23rd Ave., Phoenix, AZ 85021, (602) 995-1007.

CALIFORNIA: Irvine: 17891 Cartwright Rd., Irvine, CA 92714, (714) 660-8187; **Sacramento:** 1900 Point West Way, Suite 171, Sacramento, CA 95815, (916) 929-1521; **San Diego:** 4333 View Ridge Ave., Suite B., San Diego, CA 92123, (619) 278-9601; **Santa Clara:** 5353 Betsy Ross Dr., Santa Clara, CA 95054, (408) 980-9000; **Torrance:** 690 Knox St., Torrance, CA 90502, (213) 217-7010; **Woodland Hills:** 21220 Erwin St., Woodland Hills, CA 91367, (818) 704-7759.

COLORADO: Aurora: 1400 S. Potomac Ave., Suite 101, Aurora, CO 80012, (303) 368-8000.

CONNECTICUT: Wallingford: 9 Barnes Industrial Park Rd., Barnes Industrial Park, Wallingford, CT 06492, (203) 269-0074.

FLORIDA: Ft. Lauderdale: 2765 N.W. 62nd St., Ft. Lauderdale, FL 33309, (305) 973-8502; **Maitland:** 2601 Maitland Center Parkway, Maitland, FL 32751, (305) 660-4600; **Tampa:** 5010 W. Kennedy Blvd., Suite 101, Tampa, FL 33609, (813) 870-6420.

GEORGIA: Norcross: 5515 Spalding Drive, Norcross, GA 30092, (404) 662-7900

ILLINOIS: Arlington Heights: 515 W. Algonquin, Arlington Heights, IL 60005, (312) 640-2925.

INDIANA: Ft. Wayne: 2020 Inwood Dr., Ft. Wayne, IN 46815, (219) 424-5174; **Indianapolis:** 2346 S. Lynhurst, Suite J-400, Indianapolis, IN 46241, (317) 248-8555.

IOWA: Cedar Rapids: 373 Collins Rd. NE, Suite 200, Cedar Rapids, IA 52402, (319) 395-9550.

MARYLAND: Baltimore: 1 Rutherford Pl., 7133 Rutherford Rd., Baltimore, MD 21207, (301) 944-8600.

MASSACHUSETTS: Waltham: 504 Totten Pond Rd., Waltham, MA 02154, (617) 895-9100.

MICHIGAN: Farmington Hills: 33737 W. 12 Mile Rd., Farmington Hills, MI 48018, (313) 553-1500.

MINNESOTA: Eden Prairie: 11000 W. 78th St., Eden Prairie, MN 55344 (612) 828-9300.

MISSOURI: Kansas City: 8080 Ward Pkwy., Kansas City, MO 64114, (816) 523-2500; **St. Louis:** 11816 Borman Drive, St. Louis, MO 63146, (314) 569-7600.

NEW JERSEY: Iselin: 485E U.S. Route 1 South, Parkway Towers, Iselin, NJ 08830 (201) 750-1050

NEW MEXICO: Albuquerque: 2820-D Broadbent Pkwy NE, Albuquerque, NM 87107, (505) 345-2555.

NEW YORK: East Syracuse: 6365 Collamer Dr., East Syracuse, NY 13057, (315) 463-9291; **Endicott:** 112 Nanticoke Ave., P.O. Box 618, Endicott, NY 13760, (607) 754-3900; **Melville:** 1 Huntington Quadrangle, Suite 3C10, P.O. Box 2936, Melville, NY 11747, (516) 454-6600; **Pittsford:** 2851 Clover St., Pittsford, NY 14534, (716) 385-6770; **Poughkeepsie:** 385 South Rd., Poughkeepsie, NY 12601, (914) 473-2900.

NORTH CAROLINA: Charlotte: 8 Woodlawn Green, Woodlawn Rd., Charlotte, NC 28210, (704) 527-0930; **Raleigh:** 2809 Highwoods Blvd., Suite 100, Raleigh, NC 27625, (919) 876-2725.

OHIO: Beachwood: 23408 Commerce Park Rd., Beachwood, OH 44122, (216) 464-6100; **Dayton:** Kingsley Bldg., 4124 Linden Ave., Dayton, OH 45432, (513) 258-3877.

OREGON: Beaverton: 6700 SW 105th St., Suite 110, Beaverton, OR 97005, (503) 643-6758.

PENNSYLVANIA: Ft. Washington: 260 New York Dr., Ft. Washington, PA 19034, (215) 643-6450; **Coraopolis:** 420 Rouser Rd., 3 Airport Office Park, Coraopolis, PA 15108, (412) 771-8550.

PUERTO RICO: Hato Rey: Mercantil Plaza Bldg., Suite 505, Hato Rey, PR 00919, (809) 753-8700.

TEXAS: Austin: P.O. Box 2909, Austin, TX 78769, (512) 250-7655; **Richardson:** 1001 E. Campbell Rd., Richardson, TX 75080, (214) 680-5082; **Houston:** 9100 Southwest Frwy., Suite 237, Houston, TX 77036, (713) 778-6592; **San Antonio:** 1000 Central Parkway South, San Antonio, TX 78232, (512) 496-1779.

UTAH: Murray: 5201 South Green SE, Suite 200, Murray, UT 84107, (801) 266-8972.

VIRGINIA: Fairfax: 2750 Prosperity, Fairfax, VA 22031, (703) 849-1400.

WASHINGTON: Redmond: 5010 148th NE, Bldg B, Suite 107, Redmond, WA 98052, (206) 881-3080.

WISCONSIN: Brookfield: 450 N. Sunny Slope, Suite 150, Brookfield, WI 53005, (414) 785-7140.

CANADA: Nepean: 301 Moodie Drive, Mallorn Center, Nepean, Ontario, Canada, K2H9C4, (613) 726-1970. **Richmond Hill:** 280 Centre St. E., Richmond Hill L4C1B1, Ontario, Canada (416) 884-9181; **St. Laurent:** Ville St. Laurent Quebec, 9460 Trans Canada Hwy., St. Laurent, Quebec, Canada H4S1R7, (514) 335-8392.

ARGENTINA: Texas Instruments Argentina S.A.I.C.F.: Esmeralda 130, 15th Floor, 1035 Buenos Aires, Argentina, 1+394-3008.

AUSTRALIA (& NEW ZEALAND): Texas Instruments Australia Ltd.: 6-10 Talavera Rd., North Ryde (Sydney), New South Wales, Australia 2113, 2 + 887-1122; 5th Floor, 418 St. Kilda Road, Melbourne, Victoria, Australia 3004, 3 + 267-4677; 171 Philip Highway, Elizabeth, South Australia 5112, 8 + 255-2066.

AUSTRIA: Texas Instruments Ges.m.b.H.: Industriestrabe B/16, A-2345 Brunn/Gebirge, 2236-846210.

BELGIUM: Texas Instruments N.V. Belgium S.A.: Mercure Centre, Raketstraat 100, Rue de la Fusee, 1130 Brussels, Belgium, 2/720.80.00.

BRAZIL: Texas Instruments Electronicos do Brasil Ltda.: Rua Paes Leme, 524-7 Andar Pinheiros, 05424 Sao Paulo, Brazil, 0815-6166.

DENMARK: Texas Instruments A/S, Mairelundvej 46E, DK-2730 Herlev, Denmark, 2 - 91 74 00.

FINLAND: Texas Instruments Finland OY: Teollisuuskatu 19D 00511 Helsinki 51, Finland, (90) 701-3133.

FRANCE: Texas Instruments France: Headquarters and Prod. Plant, BP 05, 06270 Villeneuve-Loubet, (93) 20-01-01; Paris Office, BP 67 8-10 Avenue Morane-Saulnier, 78141 Velizy-Villacoublay, (3) 946-97-12; Lyon Sales Office, L'Oree D'Ecully, Batiment B, Chemin de la Forestiere, 69130 Ecully, (7) 833-04-40; Strasbourg Sales Office, Le Sebastopol 3, Quai Kleber, 67055 Strasbourg Cedex, (88) 22-12-66; Rennes, 23-25 Rue du Puits Mauger, 35100 Rennes, (99) 31-54-86; Toulouse Sales Office, Le Peripole—2, Chemin du Pigeonnier de la Cepiere, 31100 Toulouse, (61) 44-18-19; Marseille Sales Office, Noilly Paradis—146 Rue Paradis, 13006 Marseille, (91) 37-25-30.

TEXAS INSTRUMENTS

Creating useful products
and services for you

GERMANY (Fed. Republic of Germany): Texas Instruments Deutschland GmbH: Haggertystrasse 1, D-8050 Freising, 8161+80-4591; Kurfuerstendamm 195/196, D-1000 Berlin 15, 30+882-7365; III, Hagen 43/Kibbelstrasse, .19, D-4300 Essen, 201-24250; Frankfurter Allee 6-8, D-6236 Eschborm 1, 06196+8070; Hamburgerstrasse 11, D-2000 Hamburg 76, 040+220-1154, Kirchhorsterstrasse 2, D-3000 Hannover 51, 511+648021; Maybachstrabe 11, D-7302 Ostfildern 2-Nelingen, 711+547001; Mixikoring 19, D-2000 Hamburg 60, 40+637+0061; Postfach 1309, Roonstrasse 16, D-5400 Koblenz, 261+35044.

HONG KONG (+ PEOPLES REPUBLIC OF CHINA): Texas Instruments Asia Ltd., 8th Floor, World Shipping Ctr., Harbour City, 7 Canton Rd., Kowloon, Hong Kong, 3 + 722-1223.

IRELAND: Texas Instruments (Ireland) Limited: Brewery Rd., Stillorgan, County Dublin, Eire, 1 831311.

ITALY: Texas Instruments Semiconduttori Italia Spa: Viale Delle Scienze, 1, 02015 Cittaducale (Rieti), Italy, 746 694.1; Via Salaria KM 24 (Palazzo Cosma), Monterotondo Scalo (Rome), Italy, 6+9003241; Viale Europa, 38-44, 20093 Cologno Monzese (Milano), 2 2532541; Corso Svizzera, 185, 10100 Torino, Italy, 11 774545; Via J. Barozzi 6, 40100 Bologna, Italy, 51 355851.

JAPAN: Texas Instruments Asia Ltd.: 4F Aoyama Fuji Bldg., 6-12, Kita Aoyama 3-Chome, Minato-ku, Tokyo, Japan 107, 3-498-2111; Osaka Branch, 5F, Nissho Iwai Bldg., 30 Imabashi 3- Chome, Higashi-ku, Osaka, Japan 541, 06-204-1881; Nagoya Branch, 7F Daini Toyota West Bldg., 10-27, Meieki 4-Chome, Nakamura-ku Nagoya, Japan 450, 52-583-8691.

KOREA: Texas Instruments Supply Co.: 3rd Floor, Samon Bldg., Yuksam-Dong, Gangnam-ku, 135 Seoul, Korea, 2+462-8001.

MEXICO: Texas Instruments de Mexico S.A.: Mexico City, AV Reforma No. 450 — 10th Floor, Mexico, D.F., 06600, 5+514-3003.

MIDDLE EAST: Texas Instruments: No. 13, 1st Floor Mannai Bldg., Diplomatic Area, P.O. Box 26335, Manama Bahrain, Arabian Gulf, 973+274681.

NETHERLANDS: Texas Instruments Holland B.V., P.O. Box 12995, (Bullewijk) 1100 CB Amsterdam, Zuid-Oost, Holland 20+5602911.

NORWAY: Texas Instruments Norway A/S: PB106, Refstad 131, Oslo 1, Norway, (2) 155090.

PHILIPPINES: Texas Instruments Asia Ltd.: 14th Floor, Ba- Lepanto Bldg., 8747 Paseo de Roxas, Makati, Metro Manila, Philippines, 2+8188987.

PORTUGAL: Texas Instruments Equipamento Electronico (Portugal), Lda.: Rua Eng. Frederico Ulrich, 2650 Moreira Da Maia, 4470 Maia, Portugal, 2-948-1003.

SINGAPORE (+ INDIA, INDONESIA, MALAYSIA, THAILAND): Texas Instruments Asia Ltd.: 12 Lorong Bakar Batu, Unit 01-02, Kolam Ayer Industrial Estate, Republic of Singapore, 747-2255.

SPAIN: Texas Instruments Espana, S.A.: C/Jose Lazaro Galdiano No. 6, Madrid 16, 1/458.14.58.

SWEDEN: Texas Instruments International Trade Corporation (Sverigefilialen): Box 39103, 10054 Stockholm, Sweden, 8 - 235480.

SWITZERLAND: Texas Instruments, Inc., Reidstrasse 6, CH-8953 Dietikon (Zuerich) Switzerland, 1-740 2220.

TAIWAN: Texas Instruments Supply Co.: Room 903, 205 Tun Hwan Rd., 71 Sung-Kiang Road, Taipei, Taiwan, Republic of China, 2 + 521-9321.

UNITED KINGDOM: Texas Instruments Limited: Manton Lane, Bedford, MK41 7PA, England, 0234 67466; St. James House, Wellington Road North, Stockport, SK4 2RT, England, 61+442-7162.

BM

Please send me the following Texas Instruments Bit-Slice Processor User's Guide(s):

DB01 ☐ SN74AS888/890, 8-Bit-Slice Processor User's Guide
DB02 ☐ SN74AS897, 16-Bit Barrel Shifter User's Guide
DB03 ☐ 74AS-EVM-8, Bit-Slice Evaluation Module User's Guide

NAME
TITLE
COMPANY
ADDRESS
M/S
CITY STATE ZIP
PHONE ( ) EXT.

SDV01IDV600R Expires 5/87

Please send me the following Texas Instruments Bit-Slice Processor User's Guide(s):

DB01 ☐ SN74AS888/890, 8-Bit-Slice Processor User's Guide
DB02 ☐ SN74AS897, 16-Bit Barrel Shifter User's Guide
DB03 ☐ 74AS-EVM-8, Bit-Slice Evaluation Module User's Guide

NAME
TITLE
COMPANY
ADDRESS
M/S
CITY STATE ZIP
PHONE ( ) EXT.

SDV01IDV600R Expires 5/87

PLACE
STAMP
HERE

Texas Instruments
Literature Response Center
P.O. Box 809066
Dallas, Texas 75380-9066

PLACE
STAMP
HERE

Texas Instruments
Literature Response Center
P.O. Box 809066
Dallas, Texas 75380-9066